MANAGERIAL ACCOUNTING

MANAGERIAL ACCOUNTING

Henry R. Anderson
Ph.D., C.P.A., C.M.A.
Professor of Accounting
Director, School of Accounting
University of Central Florida

Belverd E. Needles, Jr.
Ph.D., C.P.A., C.M.A.
Arthur Andersen & Co. Alumni
Distinguished Professor of Accounting
DePaul University

James C. Caldwell
Ph.D., C.P.A.
Partner, Educational Consulting Services
Arthur Andersen & Co.
Dallas / Fort Worth

HOUGHTON MIFFLIN COMPANY   BOSTON
Dallas   Geneva, Illinois   Palo Alto   Princeton, New Jersey

To **Professor Joseph A. Silvoso**
University of Missouri, Columbia
Professor Vernon K. Zimmerman
University of Illinois, Campaign-Urbana
Professor Robert B. Sweeney
Memphis State University (formerly of the
University of Alabama)

For instilling in us the desire to work toward improving the education and practice of accountancy.

Cover photograph by Ralph Mercer.

Materials from the Certified Management Accountant Examinations, copyright © 1973, 1974, 1982, 1983, 1984, by the National Association of Accountants, are reprinted and/or adapted with permission.

Problem adapted from material published by American Institute of Certified Public Accountants. Used by permission.

Pages 413–418: Adapted from Gerald R. Crowningshield, *Cost Accounting,* 3 ed. (Boston: Houghton Mifflin, 1973), pp. 303–308. Used by permission.

Printed in the U.S.A.

Library of Congress Catalog Card Number: 88-81318

ISBN: 0-395-32458-0

CDEFGHIJ-RMT-9543

CONTENTS

PREFACE

Managerial Accounting is a comprehensive text for students who have no previous training in management accounting concepts and techniques. Designed for both accounting and nonaccounting majors, *Managerial Accounting* is normally intended for use following a one-semester course in financial accounting. For a quarter-system curriculum in introductory accounting, this book should be adopted in the middle of the second quarter and used throughout the third quarter. This textbook can also be used independent of a financial accounting course, but in this case some supplemental information may be necessary. *Managerial Accounting* is part of a well-integrated package of materials, including both manual and computer ancillaries, for students and instructors. Special emphasis is on the changes in management accounting caused by the new automated manufacturing environment.

Objectives of This Textbook

The field of management accounting is experiencing many changes. Automation and the just-in-time operating philosophy are creating new challenges for the management accountant. Yet most concepts and practices taught in traditional managerial accounting courses are still applicable to a majority of businesses today. Managerial accounting relates to the internal operations of a company and is useful to profit-oriented enterprises in service, merchandising, and manufacturing industries as well as government and other not-for-profit organizations. The traditional body of knowledge associated with the study of management accounting remains relevant to many of these organizations.

The first fourteen chapters of *Managerial Accounting* concentrate on traditional management accounting topics. Part One introduces the field of management accounting and focuses on examples of nonfinancial data analysis. Special terminology and the statement of cost of goods manufactured conclude Part One. In Part Two, product costing is the focal point. A thorough exposure to both job order costing and process costing enables students to compute the unit cost of a product or service.

Part Three looks at the budgetary control function of an organization and the management accounting tools often used in this area. Discussions about cost behavior, cost-volume-profit relationships, and responsibility accounting precede the study of budgeting, standard costing, and variance analysis. Part Four is devoted mainly to decision support analysis. The four chapters in Part Four focus on pricing decisions, government contract pricing, short-term operating decisions, capital expenditure decisions, and special decisions associated with decentralized organizations, including transfer pricing approaches. Upon mastering the learning objectives in Chapters 1 through 14, students will have a knowledge base comparable to that gained from study in a traditional introductory managerial accounting course.

But within the business community, significant operating changes have had far-reaching effects on the theory and practice of management accounting. Companies are adopting the just-in-time operating philosophy and shifting from labor-intensive processes to partially or fully automated facilities. These changes have been occurring for more than a decade, yet the teaching and *practice* of management accounting have stayed virtually the same. Beginning in 1987, *Management Accounting* and other accounting and business periodicals began publishing articles illustrating how many existing management accounting practices and concepts are counterproductive to the new manufacturing environment. An entirely revised set of management accounting policies and procedures is evolving to fit the informational needs of managers in this new environment.

To date, no managerial accounting textbook had addressed this new dynamic area of practice in a meaningful and realistic manner. Our objectives in writing this textbook were:

1. Provide traditional coverage of the topics relevant to the study and practice of management accounting.
2. Cover these topics at a level suitable for freshmen and sophomores as well as first-year M.B.A. students.
3. Create two new chapters dedicated to the new management accounting concepts and practices necessary in a JIT operating environment.

Coverage of Relevant Management Accounting Topics

This text contains eighteen chapters; the first fourteen are devoted to the traditional topics covered in a managerial accounting course. Chapters 15 and 16 introduce the just-in-time philosophy, automated production facilities, and management accounting theory and practices related to this new manufacturing environment. Sometimes considered financial accounting topics, the statement of cash flows and financial statement analysis, Chapters 17 and 18, respectively, may be taught at any point in the course.

Two Unique Chapters on Automation and the Just-in-Time Operating Philosophy

Chapter 15 introduces the JIT philosophy. This innovative approach to manufacturing requires reorganization of the factory layout and a continuous flow of products through the process. Chapter 15 defines the JIT philosophy, discusses the concept of computer-integrated manufacturing, compares a traditional (functional) factory layout with one designed for a JIT environment, identifies the elements supporting the JIT philosophy, examines product costing in a JIT environment, demonstrates the use of the Raw-in-Process Inventory account, and illustrates the use of process costing techniques in a JIT situation.

Chapter 16 analyzes the management accounting issues in product costing, performance measures, capital investments, and reporting. Unique product costing problems connected with the move to automated systems and the JIT environment are discussed and illustrated. The need for nonfinancial performance measures are described and examples provided. The concept of *full cost profit margin* is explained and compared with the traditional contribution margin. Capital expenditure decision differences are highlighted. Finally, guidelines for effective management reporting within the new manufacturing environment are provided. The contents of these two unique chapters give the student a thorough introduction to JIT, automation, and related management accounting issues.

Features of This Textbook

In writing *Managerial Accounting* we included the same features that made our previous textbooks among those most widely used in accounting education. These features include:

1. Readability and a clear presentation
2. Learning objectives integrated throughout the package
3. Authoritative, practical, and contemporary content
4. Emphasis on decision making
5. Strict quality control
6. Most complete and flexible learning package

Readability and a Clear Presentation

The intended audience of this book influenced the design and organization in several ways. First, the timing of concepts and techniques has been carefully planned to facilitate learning. This is a very important concern in a managerial accounting course because the material is usually covered rapidly. Students must grasp and retain fundamental concepts quickly so that enough time can be spent on the topics covered later in the course. Second, management accounting concepts and practices are introduced in a simple but realistic way. Terminology and product costing, fundamental to a managerial accounting course, are covered first to provide the proper background for the remainder of the book. Students are then ready to tackle the more difficult topics in Parts Three, Four, Five and Six. Third, management accounting is presented as the primary source of information for management. Emphasis is on relevancy and timely reporting. Fourth, the focus throughout is on understanding rather than memorization and on interpretation and decision making rather than mere mechanics.

We judiciously chose the topics to be covered so that they can be presented with the same readability, pacing of topics, clarity of presentation, and balance of concepts and practices that appear in an optimally organized principles-level textbook. For maximum flexibility, we also included a series of five appendixes of optional topics.

Learning by Objectives

We followed a definite pedagogical approach when writing *Managerial Accounting*. We extensively used integrated learning objectives and learning theory. Learning objectives are integrated throughout the text and package, from the preview and presentation of the chapters to the assignment material, chapter reviews, study aids, and testing and evaluation materials.

Authoritative, Practical, and Contemporary Content

This book presents accounting as it is practiced, but the concepts underlying each accounting practice are also carefully explained. Accounting terms and concepts are defined according to current pronouncements of the CASB, NAA, AICPA, and FASB. In addition, we took steps to ensure that, to the extent possible within the framework of introductory accounting, the practical material is realistic in terms of how accounting is practiced today.

Emphasis on Decision Making

Another objective is to present the contemporary business world and the real-life complexities of accounting in a clear, concise, easy-to-understand manner. Accounting is treated as an information system that helps management make economic decisions. In addition to other questions, exercises, and problems, each chapter's assignments include two decision-oriented features: an exercise in "Interpreting Accounting Information" and a "Management Decision Case." In each situation students are required to extract quantitative information from the exercise or case and make an interpretation or a decision.

Strict Quality Control

We developed, together with our publisher, a system of quality control applied to all parts of the package to ensure the most technically and conceptually accurate textbook and package possible. Among many other steps, this system involves thorough reviews by users, authors' visits to and discussion with users, extensive in-house editorial review and accuracy checking, and class testing.

Complete and Flexible Learning Package

Finally, we believe that *Managerial Accounting* is the most complete and flexible package for a first-year management accounting course in the market today. All parts of the text fit within the pedagogical system of learning by objectives that we established. This comprehensive approach to learning is described in the following sections.

Pedagogical Features

Learning Objectives. Action-oriented objectives at the beginning of each chapter indicate in precise terms what students should be able to do when they complete the chapter. The objectives are stated again in the margins beside pertinent text discussion. The end-of-chapter review clearly relates each objective to the content of the chapter. The end-of-chapter assignments are also keyed to specific learning objectives.

Real-World Applications. Many chapters include graphs or tables illustrating the practice of actual businesses in relation to the chapter's topics. In addition, most of the exercises in Interpreting Accounting Information are based on experiences similar to those of real companies.

Key Terms and Glossary. Throughout the book, key accounting terms are emphasized in bold color type and clearly defined in context. These terms are also summarized in the review section of each chapter as well as assembled in a comprehensive glossary for easy reference.

Chapter Review. A unique feature of each chapter is a special review section comprising (1) a Review of Learning Objectives that summarizes the main points of the chapter in relation to the objectives, (2) a review of key concepts and terms, and (3) a Review Problem with complete solution to demonstrate the chapter's major procedures before students tackle the exercises and problems.

Questions. Discussion questions at the end of each chapter focus, for the most part, on major concepts and terms.

Classroom Exercises. Classroom Exercises provide practice in applying concepts taught in the chapter and are very effective in illustrating lecture points. Each exercise is keyed to the learning objectives. In addition, transparencies are available for all exercise solutions.

Interpreting Accounting Information. This feature asks the student to interpret internal management reports and information. Each exercise requires students to demonstrate their ability to interpret information by extracting data from what they read and by making a computation and interpretation.

A and B Problems. We included two sets of problems to provide maximum flexibility in homework assignments. In general, the problems are arranged in order of difficulty, with Problems A-1 or B-1 for each chapter being the simplest and the last in the series the most comprehensive. A and B problems have been matched by topic so that A-1 and B-1, for example, are equivalent in content and level of difficulty. In addition, all problems are keyed to the learning objectives. Difficulty ratings, time estimates, and solutions are available to the instructor. Transparencies of all solutions are also available.

Management Decision Cases. Each chapter contains a case that emphasizes the usefulness of accounting information in making decisions. The business background and information for each case are presented in a decision context. The decision maker may be a manager, an outside analyst, or a consultant. In the role of decision makers students are asked to extract the relevant data from the case, perform computations as necessary, and make a decision.

Appendixes. To provide maximum flexibility, we included five appendixes at the end of the book on optional topics that may be inserted as desired by the school or faculty. Each appendix is in minichapter format, with questions, exercises, and problems. The topics of these appendixes are:

Appendix A   Accounting for Government and Not-for-Profit Organizations

Appendix B   Quantitative Tools for Analysis

Appendix C   The Use of Future Value and Present Value in Accounting

Appendix D   Future Value and Present Value Tables

Appendix E   International Accounting

Supplementary Learning Materials

Study Guide with Selected Readings

This learning aid is a chapter-by-chapter guide to help students understand the main points of the chapter. Each chapter begins with a summary, organized by learning objective, of the major concepts and applications in the chapter. Next, to test students' basic knowledge of the chapter content, there are matching, completion, true-false, and multiple-choice exercises. Finally, students are asked to apply their knowledge in short exercises. All answers are provided at the end of the Study Guide.

The Study Guide also contains readings selected from professional journals and the popular press to provide broader understanding of the topics in the chapters. There is also a summary of management accounting theory.

Working Papers

Working Papers are designed to accompany all the Exercises, Interpreting Accounting Information Cases, A and B Problems, and Management Decision Cases in the text. Forms are provided for each problem, with column headings and certain information preprinted for easy identification.

Practice Set

The Windham Company. This practice set is really two sets in one. The first (used after Chapter 3) requires students to prepare the worksheet and financial statements for a manufacturer using a periodic inventory system. The second (used after Chapter 4) covers the same tasks for a manufacturing firm using a perpetual inventory system. The practice set has been formatted in such a way that it can be easily solved using the LOTUS® 1-2-3 spreadsheet. This practice set is available in workbook format, requiring about 10 hours.

Management Decision Cases

McHenry Hotels, Inc. This case involves the systematic analysis of the Dallas branch of McHenry Hotels, Inc., a chain of luxury hotels. Students are required to evaluate all major aspects of the hotel's operations, including its accounting system, past and future profitability, and budget, and prepare a comprehensive report for the Board of Directors. (This case may be started after Chapter 8.)

Callson Industries, Inc. This managerial accounting decision case concerns a company that has converted its manufacturing facilities to a JIT environment but has not yet changed its management accounting approach to include new procedures and reports that give managers relevant and timely information about operations. The required analyses of the case provide a step-by-step conversion process for this fastener manufacturer. Students deal firsthand with the development of an internal accounting and reporting system involving the new manufacturing environment. (This case may be worked during or following completion of Chapters 15 and 16.)

LOTUS® Problems for
Accounting Software and Workbook

This disk-based program, when used with the LOTUS® spreadsheet software, allows students to select preprogrammed worksheets and use them to solve problems from the text. The workbook contains instructions for using the program. A guide to the templates is available.

LOTUS® Problems for Managerial Accounting

Using the power of LOTUS® 1-2-3 software, students solve problems and explore what-if scenarios. The workbook and accompanying software teach students how to use the computer, the spreadsheet software, and prepared templates to work managerial accounting problems.

Instructor's Resource Materials

Instructor's Handbook with Achievement Tests. The Instructor's Handbook provides for each chapter a list of the topic headings in the text; a learning objectives chart for the end-of-chapter assignments; an analysis of the time and difficulty involved to solve each problem; lecture resource materials that provide, for each learning objective, a summary statement, a list of new words, terms, and related text illustrations, and a suggested lecture outline.

Instructor's Solutions Manual. The Instructor's Solutions Manual contains solutions to all questions, exercises, and problems in the text. Each problem is rated by level of difficulty (easy, medium, or difficult) and time needed to solve it. Charts indicate the learning objectives covered by each question, exercise, and problem.

Check List of Key Figures. This item is available in quantity to instructors.

Test Bank. The Test Bank contains approximately 1,800 items, with about 30 true-false questions, 55 multiple-choice questions, 10 exercises, and 5 problems per chapter. Every question is carefully matched to a specific learning objective in the text and classified according to one of four levels of student mastery: recall, comprehension and understanding, applications, and analysis.

Microtest and Call-in Testing Service. This item is a computer version of the Test Bank.

Boxed Solutions Transparencies and Lecture Outlines. More than 600 flexible mylar transparencies (printed in oversize, clear, 11-point bold type) provide instructors with solutions to every exercise and problem in the text. A nine- to ten-page lecture outline for each chapter is included.

Teaching Transparencies. About 50 two-color teaching transparencies are supplied for instructors' use.

Grade Performance Analyzer. This computerized gradebook program for microcomputers facilitates orderly record keeping, calculating, and posting of student grades.

Acknowledgments

An introductory managerial accounting text is a long and demanding project that cannot succeed without the help of colleagues. We are grateful to many professors and other professional colleagues as well as students for constructive comments that led to improvements in the text. Unfortunately, space does not permit us to mention all those who contributed to this volume.

Some of those who were supportive and who had an impact on the text are:

Professor John Aheto
Pace University

Professor Joseph Aubert
Bemidji State University

Professor D. Dale Bandy
University of Central Florida

Professor Anne C. Baucom
*University of North Carolina—
Charlotte*

Professor Wilfred Beaupre
San Juan College

Professor Linda Benz
Jefferson Community College

Professor Gregory Bischoff
Houston Community College

Deanna O. Burgess
University of Central Florida

Professor Martin J. Canavan
Skidmore College

Professor Kenneth L. Coffey
*Johnson County Community
College*

Professor William Costello
Harcum Junior College

Professor Richard Cross
Bentley College

Professor Jarvis Dean
*Chattanooga State Technical
Community College*

Professor Frank Falcetta
Middlesex Community College

Professor Thomas Forsythe
Brown University

Professor Esther Grant
Hillsborough Community College

Professor Raymond Green
Texas Tech University

Margaret Griffith

Professor Judy Hansen
*Waukesha County Technical
Institute*

Professor Michael Haselkorn
Bentley College

Professor Roger Hehman
*Raymond Walters College of
University of Cincinnati*

Professor Arthur Hirchfield
Bronx Community College

Professor George Holdren
University of Nebraska—Lincoln

Professor Bonnie Jack-Givens
Avila College

Professor Alice James
Meridian Junior College

Professor Mark Kiel
*North Carolina Agricultural and
Technical State University*

Professor Rhonda Kodjayan
Mundelein College

Donna Randall Lacey

Professor Robert Landry
Massasoit Community College

Professor Nancy Magrone
*Delaware Technical and
Community College*

Professor Greg Merrill
University of San Diego

Professor Juan Rivera
University of Notre Dame

Professor Harold L. Royer
Miami-Dade Community College

Professor John H. Salter
University of Central Florida

Professor Marilyn P. Salter
University of Central Florida

Professor Joseph Schliep
Normandale Community College

Professor Nathan Schmukler
Long Island University

Professor Donald L. Seat
Valdosta State College

Professor S. Murray Simons
Northeastern University

Professor David A. Skougstad
Metropolitan State College

Professor John R. Stewart
University of Northern Colorado

Dr. DuWayne Wacker
University of North Dakota

Professor Loren K. Waldman
Franklin University

Dr. Richard B. Watson
*University of California—
Santa Barbara*

Professor Robert Wennagel
College of the Mainland

Professor Kenneth Winter
*University of Wisconsin—
Whitewater*

Professor Gilroy J. Zuckerman
North Carolina State University

New Manufacturing
Environment:

William Branier
Arthur Andersen & Co. Chicago

Professor Robert E. Bennett
Northern Illinois University

John Caspari
Grand Valley State University

Michelle L. Guard

Professor Robert A. Howell
New York University
Howell Management Corporation

Alfred M. King
National Association of Accountants

Kim Lazar
Coopers & Lybrand, Orlando

Professor C. J. McNair
University of Rhode Island

Stephen R. Soucy
Howell Management Corporation

Sandra A. VanTrease
Price Waterhouse, St. Louis

Permission has been received from the Institute of Certified Management
Accountants of the National Association of Accountants to use questions
and/or unofficial answers from past CMA examinations.

H.R.A.　　B.E.N.　　J.C.C.

MANAGERIAL ACCOUNTING

PART ONE

Basic Concepts of Management Accounting

Management accounting practices differ from those studied in a financial accounting course. Financial accounting concepts and procedures are designed to handle the measurement and reporting of problems pertaining to the general accounting system of an organization. The preparation of general-purpose financial statements used by people outside the business entity, such as bankers and stockholders, is also an important aspect of financial accounting. Management accounting practices and procedures are used to support the actions of internal management.

Part One introduces the student to the basic concepts, terminology, and practices underlying management accounting. Specific types of information are needed by managers to support day-to-day and long-term decisions. The management accountant provides these data.

Chapter 1 describes the field of management accounting, compares management accounting with financial accounting, and focuses on the analysis of nonfinancial data, which is common in the work of the management accountant.

Chapter 2 discusses the basic terminology used in accounting for internal operations. Reporting of manufacturing costs is also highlighted and illustrated.

1. Describe the field
   of management
   accounting.
2. Distinguish be-
   tween manage-
   ment accounting
   and financial
   accounting.
3. Compare the
   information needs
   of a manager of:
   (a) a manufacturing
   company; (b) a
   bank; and (c) a
   department store.
4. Identify the
   important questions
   a manager must
   consider before
   preparing a
   managerial report.
5. Prepare analyses of
   nonfinancial data.
6. State the differences
   between accounting
   for a manufacturing
   and a merchandising
   company.
7. Describe a Certified
   Management
   Accountant (CMA)
   and state the
   requirements one
   must satisfy to attain
   this designation.

CHAPTER 1

Introduction to Management Accounting

Managerial accounting is an important body of knowledge for everyone planning a career in the business world. The significance of the discipline is that the language of managerial or management accounting represents the basic communications system *within* any business enterprise. Planning (budgeting) and control (measuring performance) are vital to the success of both profit-oriented and not-for-profit organizations. Every business must manage its financial and human resources, and the field of management accounting provides the necessary mechanism.

The first course in accounting usually centers on Financial Accounting issues and practices. Although financial accounting and management accounting have much in common and are interrelated, there are fundamental differences between the two disciplines. This chapter begins by defining management accounting. The two disciplines of financial accounting and management accounting are then compared and contrasted. This chapter also discusses the information needs of managers and the important questions that must be answered before a report or analysis can be prepared. Since much of a management accountant's work deals with nonfinancial data, several cases are used to illustrate these important types of reports.

The chapter concludes by comparing accounting for manufacturing and merchandising companies and by looking at the requirements for becoming a Certified Management Accountant (CMA). After studying this chapter, you should be able to meet the learning objectives listed on the left.

Financial Accounting Versus Management Accounting: Making the Transition

Management accounting, which is an extension of financial accounting, applies primarily to a company's internal operations and the decisions managers must make to carry out a company's mission. Different rules are applicable for accounting information created and prepared for management's use than for information reported to the general public. It is important that you understand the significance of these rules.

To help you make the transition from financial accounting to management accounting, think for a moment about your own life. You exist in an environment and a society composed of hundreds of rules and regulations. Some are social conduct rules, and others are legal, moral, ethical, and religious rules. Collectively, they determine your environment. Now, reflect on your home life as you were growing up. Remember all of those special rules laid down as law by your parents? Keep your room clean. Do your chores and your homework before going out. Dinner is served at 6:30 P.M., no later! Be on your best behavior when your grandparents arrive. When you entered your home, did you leave your external rules at the doorstep and assume an entirely new set when you went inside? Of course not. You simply added a new set of rules to those standards and created your own environment within your home.

When looking at the world of accounting, consider financial accounting as comprising all rules governing the accounting for and reporting of financial information that must be disclosed to people outside the company. Special rules apply to the gathering of this information, putting it into a workable accounting system, and combining it into a meaningful set of financial statements at year end. All this is done primarily for people outside the company, such as stockholders, bankers, creditors, and brokers.

The rules applicable to management accounting are similar to special rules in the home. Management accounting exists primarily for the benefit of people inside the company. Usually there is a lot more information available to managers than to people outside the company. And what you can do with that information to make it more meaningful to those managers is limited only by your imagination, not a set of rigid rules. Your overall guideline is that the report or analysis must be meaningful and answer the question or issue under review.

There are many accounting procedures and policies from financial accounting that carry over into management accounting, so you should not put what you have learned thus far on the shelf. Many of these concepts, such as depreciation techniques, cash collection and disbursement procedures, inventory valuation methods, and the recognition of what is an asset or a liability, will be needed in your study of management accounting. A new set of rules for generating information for internal managers will be described in this book.

One important, additional point needs mentioning. A knowledge of management accounting is just as important to your career as a knowledge of financial accounting. If you plan to become a CPA, you will need your management accounting background when auditing a manufacturing company or service organization. If you become an accountant for a company or government organization, management accounting principles will be part of your daily life. And if you are destined for a position in marketing, finance, or management, you will have to deal with management accountants to obtain information to run your department or business. In other words, no matter what you do in the business world, you must rely on management accounting in one way or another.

Management Accounting

OBJECTIVE 1
Describe the field
of management
accounting

The field of management accounting consists of specific types of information gathering and reporting functions and related accounting techniques and procedures. When collectively applied to a company's financial and production data, management accounting procedures will satisfy management's information needs.

All business managers require accurate, timely information for pricing, planning, and decision-making purposes. Managers of production, merchandising, government, and service-oriented enterprises all depend on management accounting information. Management accounting is often associated with large multidivisional corporations with many segments engaged in manufacturing and assembly. These large corporations need more complex accounting and reporting systems than do small, one-owner businesses such as a neighborhood grocery store or a shoe store. Even though large corporations need large *amounts* of information, small- and medium-size businesses need certain *types* of financial information just as much as large corporations. The types of data needed to ensure efficient operating conditions do not depend entirely on an organization's size.

The National Association of Accountants, in *Statement No. 1A* of its series of *Statements on Management Accounting*, defined **management accounting** as:

. . . the process of identification, measurement, accumulation, analysis, preparation, interpretation, and communication of financial information used by management to plan, evaluate, and control within the organization and to assure appropriate use and accountability for its resources.[1]

Three types of financial information are needed to manage a company effectively: (1) manufacturing and service-oriented companies need product costing information; (2) all companies need data to plan and control operations; and (3) managers need special reports and analyses to support their decisions.

Product costing is the first type of information. It uses cost accounting techniques to gather production information, assign specific costs to product batches, and calculate product unit costs. Product costing techniques are discussed in Chapters 3 and 4.

Data for planning and control are organized in ways that help management plan production and its related costs. As production goes on and expected costs are incurred, formal control procedures are used to compare planned and actual costs so that the effectiveness of operations and management can be measured. Chapters 5 through 10 focus on these planning and control functions of management accounting.

Special reports and analyses help management in decision making. All management decisions should be supported by analyses of alternative courses of action. The accountant is expected to supply information for these decisions. Several approaches used by accountants are discussed in Chapters 11 through 14.

1. National Association of Accountants, *Statement No. 1A* (New York, 1982).

Comparing Management Accounting with Financial Accounting

OBJECTIVE 2
Distinguish between management accounting and financial accounting

Students often have problems coping with management accounting concepts and procedures because they have been trained in the procedures and rules governing financial accounting. Management accounting has rules, too, but it is much more open and places fewer restrictions on the accountant's day-to-day efforts. Fewer restrictions mean somewhat less defined methods for doing things. In this section we will take a closer look at the differences between management accounting and financial accounting. The comparison focuses primarily on (1) primary users of information; (2) types of accounting systems; (3) restrictive guidelines; (4) units of measurement; (5) focal point for analysis; (6) frequency of reporting; and (7) degree of reliability in the information generated. These areas of comparison are summarized in Table 1-1.

Table 1-1. Comparison of Financial and Management Accounting

Areas of Comparison	Financial Accounting	Management Accounting
1. Primary users of information	Persons and organizations outside the business entity	Various levels of internal management
2. Types of accounting systems	Double-entry systems	Not restricted to double-entry system; any useful system
3. Restrictive guidelines	Adherence to generally accepted accounting principles	No guides or restrictions: only criterion is usefulness
4. Units of measurement	Historical dollar	Any useful monetary or physical measurement, such as labor hour or machine hour; if dollars are used, may be historical or future dollars
5. Focal point for analysis	Business entity as a whole	Various segments of the business entity
6. Frequency of reporting	Periodically on regular basis	Whenever needed; may not be on a regular basis
7. Degree of reliability	Demands objectivity; historical in nature	Heavily subjective for planning purposes, but objective data are used when relevant; futuristic in nature

Primary Users of Information

The users of traditional financial statements are external to the company preparing the report. Internal management is responsible for preparing a company's annual financial statements, but this information is disclosed primarily for external users.

In comparison, internal reports and analyses prepared by the management accountant are used by every member of management. The content of the reports varies, depending on the level of management being served, the department or segment being analyzed, and the purpose underlying each report. Emphasis is placed on supplying relevant information to people responsible for particular activities. Examples of different types and uses of internally generated information include: unit cost analyses for product costing purposes, budgets for planning future operations, control reports by responsibility unit for measuring performance, relevant cost reports for short-run decision making, and capital budgeting analyses for corporate long-run planning.

Types of Accounting Systems

Financial statements prepared for external use are made up of dollar totals that reflect the balances of all accounts included in a company's general ledger. Before financial data are entered into the general ledger, the amounts must be coded, adjusted, and translated into a form suitable for a double-entry accounting system. Special journals, ledgers, and other analyses used to process financial accounting information are based on the double-entry system.

The analyses and flow of accounting data inside a company need not depend on the double-entry format. Data may be gathered for small segments or large divisions and may be expressed in units of measurement other than historical dollars. The information need not flow into and through general ledger accounts as in financial accounting. Special reports may be prepared for a particular manager's use with the process ending there. Under these conditions the information storage and retrieval system must have greater capabilities than those required for financial accounting. The major criterion in designing internal accounting systems is that the generated reports and analyses must be *useful* for meeting the information needs of management.

Restrictive Guidelines

Financial accounting is concerned with analyzing, classifying, recording, and reporting a company's financial activities. Since financial statements are prepared primarily for people external to the company, accountants must adhere to generally accepted accounting standards and principles that govern the recording, measuring, and reporting of financial information. Although necessary for protective and credibility purposes, generally accepted accounting principles confine accountants to a finite number of accounting practices. Examples of such restrictions include principles that involve matching revenues with expenses, stating inventories at lower of cost or market, reporting fixed assets at acquisition costs, realizing revenue in appropriate periods, and reporting on a consistent basis.

Management accounting has only one restrictive guideline: the accounting practice or technique used must produce *useful* information. Before tackling a problem, the management accountant must decide what information will be useful to the recipient of the report. He or she must then choose the appropriate concepts, procedures, and techniques to solve the problem. To illustrate, suppose management at Erin Company is deciding whether to purchase a piece of equipment. Return on investment information is relevant to the decision. Before return on investment can be computed, however, the financial effect of the new machine on company operations must be determined. This analysis requires estimates of increases in product sales, changes in variable and fixed manufacturing and selling costs, and changes in administrative costs. Once these amounts have been estimated, the management accountant must select an appropriate method for determining the machine's return on investment. Several approaches are available, and the method selected should be the most accurate one for the circumstances. Since the information is only for internal use, there is no need to stay within the restrictive guidelines for recording and reporting information to people outside the company.

Units of Measurement

The fourth area of comparison between financial and management accounting is the units of measurement used as a basis for reports and analyses. Financial accounting serves a stewardship or accountability function by providing financial information about a company's past events. All information is presented in dollar amounts. The common unit of measurement associated with financial accounting is the historical dollar. Transactions that are summarized in the financial statements have already occurred, and the financial effects are objectively measurable.

Management accountants are not restricted to using the historical dollar and can employ any measurement unit *useful* in a situation. Historical dollars may be used in the short run for cost control analyses and for measuring trends for routine planning tasks. However, most management decisions are based on analyses using expected future dollars. Most decisions require forecasts and projections of operating data and must be based on estimates of future dollar flows. In addition to monetary units, the management accountant uses such measures as machine hours, labor hours, and product or service units as bases for analysis. The common denominator underlying all measurement, reporting, and analysis in management accounting is usefulness to a situation.

Focal Point for Analysis

Typically, financial accounting records and reports information on the assets, equities, and net income of a *company as a whole*. Financial statements summarize the transactions of an organization. Management accounting, on the other hand, usually involves analyses of *various segments* of a business, such as cost centers, profit centers, divisions, or departments, or some specific aspect of its operations. Reports can range from analyzing revenues and expenses of an entire division to investigating materials used by one department or operating cell.

Frequency of Reporting

Financial statements developed for external use are usually prepared on a regular basis: monthly, quarterly, and/or annually. Periodic reporting at regular intervals is a basic concept of financial accounting. Management accounting reports may be prepared monthly, quarterly, and/or annually on a regular basis, or they may be requested daily or on an irregular basis. The key issues are that each report generated must be useful to its recipient and be prepared whenever needed.

Degree of Reliability

Financial information included in financial statements prepared for external use is past data, summarized as of a particular date for the user. This information results from transactions that already have happened. For this reason the information is determined *objectively* and is verifiable. Management accounting is concerned primarily with planning and control of internal operations. Planning and managerial decision making are activities that are more future related. Past expense and revenue transactions, although useful for establishing trends, are not usually relevant to planning activities and must be replaced by *subjective* estimates of future events.

These seven areas of comparison should help you make the transition from financial accounting to management accounting. A management accountant is typically involved with analyses dealing with units of output, machine hours, or direct labor hours in addition to reports centering on dollar amounts. Budgeted data are important to the management accountant, and the analysis of management's plans is a continual concern.

In many cases reports generated by the management accountant have a direct bearing on the company's profitability and are considered confidential to management. Leaks of such information could give the competition an unfair advantage in the marketplace. So, whereas financial accounting's main emphasis is on full and accurate accounting for and disclosure of a company's operating results, management accounting's thrust is on helping management accomplish its objectives.

Information Needs of Management

When talking about accounting for management, one includes the information needs of management in all types of businesses. Although it is customary to discuss manufacturing operations when addressing the topic of management accounting, you must remember that any manager in any business, from a conglomerate to a family grocery store, relies daily on management accounting information. Service organizations, such as banks, hotels, public accounting firms, insurance companies, and attor-

OBJECTIVE 3
Compare the
information
needs of a man-
ager of: (a) a
manufacturing
company; (b) a
bank; and (c) a
department store

neys' offices, need internal accounting information to determine the costs of providing their services and the prices to charge. Retail organizations, such as Sears Roebuck & Co. and Neiman-Marcus, use management accounting reports to manage operations and maximize profits. Not-for-profit and government units and agencies use internal accounting information to develop budgets and performance reports during normal operations (see Appendix A).

Understanding the importance and significance of management accounting reports and analyses is critical to your study of business. Management accounting principles and procedures are not just for accountants. Management personnel, financial analysts, real estate brokers, insurance agents, bankers, marketing research people, economists, hotel managers, and salespeople are just a few of the managers making decisions from information supplied by the management accountant. Every person employed in a management-related job must help develop and rely on management accounting information.

To illustrate how widely management accounting information is used, we will now examine three types of business enterprise: a manufacturing company, a bank, and a department store. The reports and analyses needed by each management team will be identified. After a brief discussion of each type of business, information needs will be charted and compared.

The Manufacturing Company

One of the most important aspects of management accounting for a manufacturing company is to provide product costing information. This is understandable, since a manufacturer's primary purpose is to take raw materials, such as wood, steel, and rubber, and transform them into finished products, such as furniture, automobiles, and tires. Product costing information is used to identify weak production areas, control costs, support pricing decisions, and set inventory values. Budgets are also an integral part of the flow of management information. Such documents are used as both planning and control tools. Managers in a manufacturing company also require continuous information about production planning and scheduling, product-line management and development, cash management, capital expenditure decision analysis, and selling and distribution expense analysis. Information is also needed for reporting purposes and for computing state and federal taxes.

Information used to make operating decisions is extremely important to manufacturing managers. Special orders may be received, and the manager must be able to respond prudently. When several products are involved, constant monitoring of the sales mix is important. Having to decide whether it is more economical to make a part or purchase it from an outside vendor is common in the manufacturing environment. Often, two or more products emerge from a common raw material, such as gasoline and motor oil from crude oil. Such a situation often requires information to support a decision either to (1) sell the product when it can be first identified or (2) process it further to make a more salable and profitable product. These are but a few of the information needs of managers in a manufacturing company.

The Bank

If a manufacturing company is in business to make a product, what is the primary purpose of a bank? No, not to make money! At least not to physically make the green stuff. The United States Mint prints and distributes this country's money. Of course, the bank is in business to make a profit, but so is the manufacturer. The bank provides its customers with various services for a fee. Loans are available, and interest is assessed as payment for the service. Checking accounts usually have either a monthly fee or a minimum balance requirement so that the bank can lend the money and earn interest income. A small charge is assessed for certified checks, and fees are charged for safe deposit boxes. Although the list of services is longer for larger banks, the idea of providing financial services for a fee describes the banking business.

Bank managers require many types of internally generated reports. The key to managing a bank's resources rests with its accounting information system. Balancing and monitoring cash reserves is critical. Managers are responsible for customers' savings accounts and federal deposit reserves required by the Federal Reserve Board and other government agencies. Federal auditors and independent auditors are required to make surprise visits to check on how banks manage their funds.

In addition to using the cash balancing and monitoring system, bank managers use budgets and service-line analysis reports extensively. Cash management for internal use is also important. Bank managers make capital expenditure decisions in much the same way as managers in manufacturing. Although normal operating decisions differ in many ways, the bank manager must continually analyze the services provided and the optimal service mix of the bank, just as the manufacturing manager must analyze the products manufactured and the optimal product mix to be produced. Loan activities require an effective system for credit verification with related reporting. Monitoring of loan payments and delinquent loans is very important.

Recently, banks have started adopting product costing procedures. Since a bank's products are its services, it needs information to determine if its services operate efficiently and are cost effective. Therefore, information on cost per loan, cost per savings transaction, and cost per checking account maintenance has become increasingly important to bank managers.

The Department Store

Instead of being a customer, imagine yourself as a store manager. You have just stepped inside the local J.C. Penney department store. What is the most important thing you should be concerned about here? Product costing information? Cost of maintaining a checking account? Traffic in the parking lot? No, none of these things. But there are three correct answers: customers, personnel, and merchandise. The most important asset of a department store is its merchandise. It is the manager who is responsible for: (1) ordering proper items in economical quantities; (2) safely storing merchandise once it is received; (3) displaying items so customers will be attracted to them; (4) marketing merchandise through the local media; and (5) distributing items to customers.

To manage these areas of responsibility, a manager needs a complete accounting information system made up of reports, requisitions, controls, and analyses. Market surveys and other types of market research often support purchase decisions made by a company's buyer. Also, knowing the most economical quantity to order helps keep costs down. And inventory records are critical once the merchandise has been received. These documents supply the manager with information on merchandise quality, deterioration, obsolescence, losses caused by theft, quantity on hand, reorder point, and current demand data.

As you can see, a store manager needs internal accounting information to control merchandise. But store managers are involved in other areas as well, including: (1) budgeting; (2) cash management; (3) product sales-line analyses; (4) capital expenditure analyses; (5) product selling cost analyses; (6) report preparation for all levels of management and taxing authorities; and (7) operating decisions concerning sales mix, special orders, and personnel placement. All these reports and analyses involve management accounting assistance.

Comparison of Information Needs of Managers

In Table 1-2 the information needs of the managers in a manufacturing company, a bank, and a department store are compared. Each manager has his or her special needs, depending on the type of business activity involved. A banker, for example, has different concerns and interests than does a department store manager. Yet, despite the differences, managers have many similar needs. Budgets are found in any successful business. Cash management is always important. Special operating decisions and capital expenditure decisions are usually required. Preparing reports and reporting information on taxes is part of any profitable enterprise. In short, many types of management accounting information are important to all managers.

How to Prepare a Management Accounting Report or Analysis

OBJECTIVE 4
Identify the important questions a manager must consider before preparing a managerial report

Are you ready to begin your study of management accounting? You have already seen how important this discipline is to your future, whether you become a management accountant or another type of business manager. Regardless of your future business position, you will be required to prepare and interpret reports and analyses. Such preparation does not depend on formats memorized while you were a student in an accounting class. Of course, you may want to refer to your old textbook for help and assistance, but report formats and structures are decided by the person developing the report and by the time constraints of the project.

Table 1-2. Comparison of Information Needs of Management

Reports and Analyses	Manufacturing Company	Bank	Department Store
Product/service costing			
For cost control	X	X	X
For pricing decisions	X	X	
For inventory valuation	X		
Budget preparation	X	X	X
Cash management system			
Normal operating funds	X	X	X
Funds held/managed for others		X	
Production planning	X		
Product-line management	X		
Service-line management		X	
Merchandise-line management			X
Capital expenditure analysis	X	X	X
Distribution/selling			
Expense analysis	X		X
Special reporting activities	X	X	X
Inventory control systems			
Materials	X		
Work in process	X		
Finished goods	X		
Merchandise			X
Funds on deposit		X	
Operating decisions			
Special orders	X		X
Sales mix	X		X
Service mix		X	
Make or buy	X		
Sell or process further	X		
Preparation of tax reports	X	X	X

In each of the following chapters, you will find report formats that help convey each chapter's contents.   Most are formats that have been used in business, and they provide useful information.

As a manager, however, you should think of a report in the same way that an athlete thinks of an athletic record.   Every record will someday be broken and a new record set.   Every report can be improved on, and a manager should strive to create new and more informative ones.   When a specific information need arises, your textbook will probably be un-available as a reference. What you will need instead are a few simple guidelines for preparing new reports or improving old ones.

Report preparation depends on the four W's: Why? What? Who? and When?

Why? Answering the question, "Why are you going to prepare this report?" serves to establish the report's characteristics and is instrumental in answering the other three questions. Therefore, the manager should write down the purpose of a report before creating it. Many reports prepared by circumventing this step are unfocused and do not fulfill the intended need.

What? Once the purpose of a report is stated, its maker must decide what information the report should contain to satisfy that purpose. In addition, the presentation method should be established. The information should be relevant to the decision and easy to read and understand. Cluttered reports do not communicate information. A report should address the purpose directly.

Who? The "who" question can take several forms: For whom are you preparing the report? To whom should the report be distributed? Who will read it? All three answers will dictate the report's format. If the report is prepared for only one manager, it may be less structured than one being distributed to a dozen managers or sent to stockholders. Widely distributed reports normally contain concise, summarized infor-mation, whereas reports prepared for a company's president are more detailed.

When? When is the report due? Timing is the key to effective reporting. A report is useful only when its information is timely. Preparation time is often limited by a report's urgency. Quick reports often lack accuracy. This tradeoff between accuracy and urgency is a normal constraint, and it is one the report maker must become accustomed to and master.

Illustrative Cases:
Analysis of Nonfinancial Data

OBJECTIVE 5
Prepare analyses of nonfinancial data

In making the transition from financial accounting to management ac-counting, you must become accustomed to dealing with units of meas-urement other than a typical historical dollar. Most people connect accounting with the analysis of money. However, this chapter will begin your study of management accounting with a different perspective. Although management accountants do prepare analyses expressed in dollars, they also confront problems requiring solutions formulated around such items as machine hours, labor hours, units of output, number of employees, and number of requests for a service.

The purpose of this section is to illustrate three decision support situations, all requiring nonfinancial data. Since the information needs of a manufacturing company, a bank, and a department store have already been compared, the nonfinancial cases will also center on these types of businesses.

Case One: Granville Manufacturing Company. The Granville Manufacturing Company in Hough, Mississippi, produces a special product called "Form-fit Ski Boots." Shoe moldings are cast in the Molding Department. This department employs seven people: three direct labor employees who run the molding machines and four helpers. Data on hours worked in February are summarized below.

Granville Manufacturing Company
Summary of Labor Hours—Molding Department
For February 19x8

	Hours Worked							
	Week 1		Week 2		Week 3		Week 4	
Employee	Direct Labor	Helper Labor	Direct Labor	Helper Labor	Direct Labor	Helper Labor	Direct Labor	Helper Labor
T. Brown	44		40		46		37	
L. Erickson	48		36		40		44	
K. Golden		40		36		36		40
C. Hune	40		40		44		48	
P. Hugstad		42		44		44		40
R. Miyaki		32		48		32		48
L. Mulhulland		48		48		46		48

Management has determined that twelve pairs of boots should be produced for each hour of direct labor worked. Actual production for February is shown below.

Week 1	1,428 pairs	Week 3	1,348 pairs
Week 2	1,227 pairs	Week 4	1,302 pairs

Required

Analyze production activity for February. Should management be concerned about productivity in the Molding Department? What information supports your answer?

Solution to Case One

The schedule in Exhibit 1-1 analyzes labor hours worked by the Molding Department and production output in relation to target units of output. As you can see, the department is consistently under the set target. Causing even more concern, the percentage under target increases by

Exhibit 1-1. Analysis of Nonfinancial Data—Manufacturing Company

Granville Manufacturing Company
Analysis of Labor Hours—Molding Department
For February 19x8

Summary of Labor Hours Worked:

	Hours Worked									
	Week 1		Week 2		Week 3		Week 4		Totals	
Employee	Direct Labor	Helper Labor	Direct Labor	Helper Labor	Direct Labor	Helper Labor	Direct Labor	Helper Labor	Direct Labor	Helper Labor
T. Brown	44		40		46		37		167	
L. Erickson	48		36		40		44		168	
K. Golden		40		36		36		40		152
C. Hune	40		40		44		48		172	
P. Hugstad		42		44		44		40		170
R. Miyaki		32		48		32		48		160
L. Mulhulland		48		48		46		48		190
	132	162	116	176	130	158	129	176	507	672

Analysis of Production:

	Week 1	Week 2	Week 3	Week 4	Totals
Units* that should have been produced: (12 × direct labor hours)	1,584	1,392	1,560	1,548	6,084
Units produced	1,428	1,227	1,348	1,302	5,305
Units under target	156	165	212	246	779
Percent under target	9.85%	11.85%	13.59%	15.89%	12.80%

* Unit equals one pair of boots.

almost 2 percent each week. This is a bad sign, and the productivity of machine operators should be investigated. Remember, this does not say the employees are at fault. The cause could be bad materials or inefficient machines. The analysis simply says that something is wrong, and it must be analyzed and corrected.

Case Two: Winter Springs National Bank. Candice Hall supervises tellers at Winter Springs National Bank. The bank has six drive-up windows, each requiring a full-time teller. Historically, each teller has serviced an average of thirty customers per hour. However, on November 1 management imposed a new check-scanning procedure that has decreased the number of customers serviced per hour.

Data on the number of customers serviced for the three-month period ending December 31, 19x9, are shown in Part A of Exhibit 1-2. Each teller works an average of 170 hours per month. Based on a history of rush and slack periods, window #1 has traditionally been the busiest.

Exhibit 1-2. Analysis of Nonfinancial Data—Bank

Winter Springs National Bank
Summary of Number of Customers Serviced
For the Quarter Ended December 31, 19x9

Part A	Number of Customers Serviced			
Window	October	November	December	Quarter Totals
#1	5,428	5,186	5,162	15,776
#2	5,220	4,980	4,920	15,120
#3	5,280	4,820	4,960	15,060
#4	5,120	4,840	4,880	14,840
#5	5,100	4,700	4,840	14,640
#6	4,452	4,494	4,380	13,326
Totals	30,600	29,020	29,142	88,762

Part B	Number of Customers Serviced Per Hour			
Window	October	November	December	Quarter Totals
#1	31.93	30.51	30.36	30.93
#2	30.71	29.29	28.94	29.65
#3	31.06	28.35	29.18	29.53
#4	30.12	28.47	28.71	29.10
#5	30.00	27.65	28.47	28.71
#6	26.19	26.44	25.76	26.13
Totals	180.01	170.71	171.42	174.05
Average per hour per window	30.00*	28.45	28.57	29.01*

* Difference due to rounding.

Each window thereafter receives progressively less business. The average of 30 customers per hour is an average of all six windows.

Ms. Hall is preparing a report for management on the effects of the new procedure. To assist her, you have been asked to calculate a new average for customers serviced per hour for both November and December.

Solution to Case Two

Part B of Exhibit 1-2 shows an analysis of the number of customers serviced over the three months by each teller window. Using the 170-hour monthly average per teller, you can compute the number of customers

| Exhibit 1-3. Analysis of Nonfinancial Data—Department Store |

Halfacre Dry Goods Store
Analysis of Deliveries
For the Four Weeks Ending January 28, 19x8

Weekly Average, Previous Year	Truck	Number of Deliveries				
		First Week	Second Week	Third Week	Fourth Week	Total Deliveries
400	#1	360	380	440	460	1,640
450	#2	480	460	500	540	1,980
400	#3	390	410	420	480	1,700
500	#4	520	480	560	600	2,160
1,750		1,750	1,730	1,920	2,080	7,480

serviced per hour by dividing the number of customers serviced by 170. By averaging the customer service rates for six tellers, you get 28.45 and 28.57 for November and December respectively. As you can see, the service rate has decreased. But December's average is higher than November's, so the tellers are becoming more accustomed to the new procedure.

Case Three: Halfacre Dry Goods Store. Halfacre Dry Goods Store, a high-volume establishment, features home delivery to attract customers. Located in Newport Beach, California, the company uses four delivery trucks to handle its home-delivery business. Recently, demand for home delivery has increased significantly. The controller, Mr. Marion, has developed two alternatives for solving the store's delivery-demand problem. The first alternative is to purchase a fifth truck and hire a fifth driver. The second alternative is to hire someone to schedule deliveries more efficiently, thereby saving time and increasing the number of deliveries per truck. Before committing to the truck-purchase alternative, Mr. Marion has decided to try the scheduling idea.

Delivery data for the most recent four-week period are shown in Exhibit 1-3. The scheduler began her duties at the beginning of week three. She immediately divided the territory into four delivery regions. Actual deliveries were scheduled by location within each region to cut down mileage and backtracking. Mr. Marion's goal was to increase deliveries by 10 percent. Did the scheduler work out, or should Mr. Marion purchase a fifth truck?

Solution to Case Three

Total deliveries per week were

First week	1,750	Third week	1,920
Second week	1,730	Fourth week	2,080

To achieve Mr. Marion's goal, there must be at least 1,925 weekly deliveries (1,750 × 110%). From the information given, the scheduler seems to be meeting the target set by Mr. Marion.

Merchandising Versus Manufacturing Operations

OBJECTIVE 6
State the differences between accounting for a manufacturing and a merchandising company

Much of your accounting education has centered on the merchandising organization. Thus, it is important here to explain the differences in accounting for manufacturing firms and merchandising firms. Many types of businesses gather information on costs, but doing so is especially important in manufacturing. Figures 1-1 and 1-2 show how the computation of cost of goods sold differs between manufacturing and merchandising companies.

A merchandising company normally buys a product ready for resale when it is received. Nothing needs to be done to the product to make it salable except possibly to prepare a special package or display. As

Figure 1-1. Cost of Goods Sold: A Merchandising Company

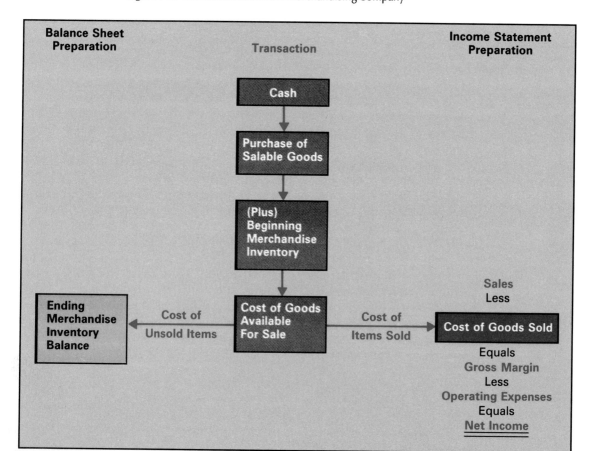

shown in Figure 1-1, total beginning merchandise inventory plus purchases is the basis for computing both the cost of goods sold and ending
merchandise inventory balances. Costs assigned to unsold items make
up the ending inventory balance. The difference between the cost of
goods available for sale and the ending inventory amount is the cost of
goods sold during the period. The following example shows this
computation:

Beginning merchandise inventory	$ 2,000
Plus total purchases of salable goods	8,000
Cost of goods available for sale	$10,000
Less ending merchandise inventory	(2,700)
Cost of goods sold	$ 7,300

This example and Figure 1-1 show how easy it is to compute the cost of
goods sold for a merchandising company. The only expenditure occurs
when salable goods are purchased. Any items unsold at year end make
up the ending inventory balance. The remainder of the purchase costs

Figure 1-2. Cost of Goods Sold: A Manufacturing Company

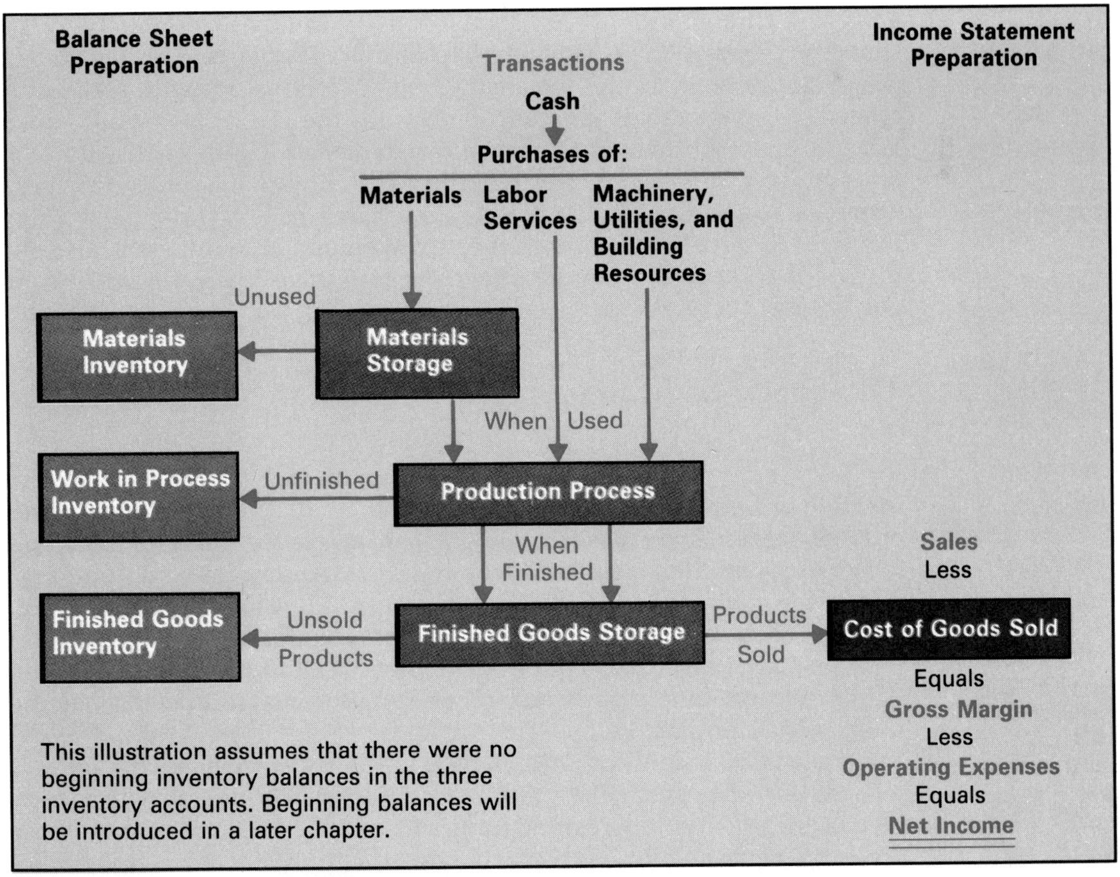

(plus any balance in beginning merchandise inventory) are reported as Cost of Goods Sold.

Computing the cost of goods sold for a manufacturing company is more complex. As shown in Figure 1-2, instead of one inventory account, a manufacturer maintains three inventory accounts: Materials Inventory, Work in Process Inventory, and Finished Goods Inventory.

Purchased materials unused during the production process make up the year-end Materials Inventory balance. The cost of materials used plus the costs of labor services and factory overhead are transferred to the Work in Process Inventory account when the materials, labor services, and overhead items are used in the production process. (Factory overhead includes such items as utility costs, depreciation of factory machinery and building, and supplies.)

The three types of costs discussed above are often called simply materials, labor, and overhead (abbreviated M, L, and OH). These costs are accumulated in the Work in Process Inventory account during an accounting period. When a batch or order is completed, all manufacturing costs assigned to the completed units are moved to the Finished Goods Inventory account. Costs remaining in the Work in Process Inventory account belong to partly completed units. These costs make up the ending balance in the Work in Process Inventory account.

The Finished Goods Inventory account is set up in much the same way as the Merchandise Inventory account in Figure 1-1. Costs of completed goods are entered into the Finished Goods Inventory account. Then, as shown in Figure 1-2, costs attached to unsold items at year end make up the ending balance in the Finished Goods Inventory account. All costs related to units sold are transferred to the Cost of Goods Sold account and reported on the income statement. To make this flow of costs clearer, the next chapter will discuss the three manufacturing cost elements: direct materials, direct labor, and factory (manufacturing) overhead. The three manufacturing inventory accounts will also be discussed. They will then be integrated into the computation of cost of goods sold.

The Certified Management Accountant (CMA)

OBJECTIVE 7
Describe a Certified Management Accountant (CMA) and state the requirements one must satisfy to attain this designation

In 1972, the National Association of Accountants (NAA) created the Institute of Certified Management Accountants (ICMA), a separate wing of NAA responsible for establishing and maintaining a program leading to the Certified Management Accountant (CMA) designation. The program was developed because of the need to recognize professional competence in the field of management accounting. This program parallels the CPA certificate program of the American Institute of Certified Public Accountants, which recognizes professional competence in the public accounting field.

Management accounting has come a long way since its inception as a recognized accounting discipline. As a result of these developments, management accounting can no longer be considered a minor part of the accounting profession. The management accountant has a right to be recognized, and the CMA program has been designed for this purpose. The objectives of the program clearly state this intent and are as follows:

1. To foster higher educational standards in the field of management accounting.
2. To establish management accounting as a recognized profession by identifying the role of the management accountant, the underlying body of knowledge, and by outlining a course of study by which such knowledge can be acquired.
3. To assist employers, educators, and students by establishing an objective measure of an individual's knowledge and competence in the profession of management accounting.[2]

Management Accounting and the CMA

To appreciate fully the body of knowledge demanded of the CMA, one has to take a panoramic view of the field of management accounting. Within our free enterprise environment, a corporation's destiny is a function of its actions. Each action is the result of a decision. Every decision is based on relevant information and/or management intuition (reliance on intuition tends to diminish as the business environment becomes more complex). Information supplied to management on a relevant, timely basis, then, is the key to a corporation's success. Supplying this information is usually the responsibility of the management accountant.

CMA Examination Coverage

To become a CMA, one must exhibit specific levels of proficiency in the following areas: (1) economics and business finance; (2) organization and behavior, including ethical considerations; (3) public reporting standards, auditing and taxes; (4) internal reporting and analysis; and (5) decision analysis, including modeling and information systems.

Part 1, "Economics and Business Finance," focuses on the environment within which the management accounting cycle operates. Decisions based on information supplied by the accountant may have corporate, national, and even international economic repercussions. Knowledge of our free enterprise system, the economics of the firm (microeconomics), and corporate capital management and capital markets is required in varying degrees in all decisions made by management. It stands to reason, then, that the supplier of the information upon which these decisions are based must be familiar with these concepts and be able to incorporate them into data-gathering and utilization techniques.

Part 2, "Organization and Behavior, Including Ethical Considerations," centers on the organizational functions and hierarchy of management and the behavioral ramifications of accounting reports. To achieve its objectives, management must rely on the people in the organization. The goals and the steps leading to their attainment must be clearly communicated to the individuals responsible for each action. Performance

---

2. "Certificate in Management Accounting Established by NAA," *Management Accounting* (March 1972), p. 13.

reports generated by the management accountant should be relevant to the responsibilities of the individual, stated in explicit terms, and motivational in nature (showing successful areas as well as problem situations). Budgets and performance standards should be developed using criteria that are realistic and controllable by the people responsible for them. Using a responsibility accounting format as the basis for the flow of timely, relevant information, the management accountant should consider the recipients' receptiveness to the contents of each report as well as its quantitative accuracy.

Financial accounting cannot be ignored by the management accountant. Operational information generated for internal purposes also provides information for external reporting of the results of operations. Knowledge of current reporting standards is essential for the management accountant. For this reason, Part 3 of the CMA examination covers "Public Reporting Standards, Auditing and Taxes." Knowledge of the purposes and approaches to both internal and external auditing is the key to an efficient, controlled accounting system. Tax accounting is included in this area not only because of the need to compute the annual tax liability but also because the management accountant must be aware of the tax consequences inherent in management's operational decisions.

Parts 4 and 5 of the CMA examination zero in on the traditional areas of management accounting. Part 4, "Internal Reporting and Analysis," deals with information theory, preparation of financial statements, profit planning and budgetary controls, standard costs for manufacturing and service industries, and analysis of accounts. Part 5, "Decision Analysis, Including Modeling and Information Systems," is the quantitative section of the exam. It includes such topics as fundamentals of decision processes, decision analysis, model building, and planning and control of information systems.

Overall, the CMA examination coverage is well conceived and pertinent to the interests and responsibilities of management accountants. Some topics deal specifically with the duties and responsibilities of the management accountant. Others deal in general terms with environmental conditions within which management accountants must function. Taken together, the examination topics cover the entire field of management accounting.

Admission Requirements

Admission to the CMA program requires an applicant to satisfy one of the following conditions:

1. Hold a baccalaureate degree—in any major—from an accredited college or university, or
2. Achieve a score satisfactory to the Credentials Committee of the ICMA on either the Graduate Record Examination (GRE) or the Graduate Management Admission Test (GMAT), or
3. Be a Certified Public Accountant or hold a comparable professional qualification outside the United States that is approved by the Credentials Committee.

Those who are interested in learning more about the CMA program or who wish to apply for the examination should write to:

> Institute of Certified Management Accountants
> 10 Paragon Drive
> P.O. Box 405
> Montvale, New Jersey 07645–0405

Chapter Review

Review of Learning Objectives

1. **Describe the field of management accounting.**
   Management accounting is the process of identifying, measuring, accumulating, analyzing, preparing, and communicating information used by management. This information is used to plan, evaluate, and control the organization and to ensure that its resources are appropriately used and accounted for. The field of management accounting is made up of appropriate accounting techniques and procedures for information gathering and reporting. When applied to a company's financial and production data, management accounting procedures will satisfy management's information needs. The information needed includes: (a) product costing information; (b) data for planning and control of operations; and (c) special reports and analyses to support management decisions.

2. **Distinguish between management accounting and financial accounting.**
   Management accounting and financial accounting can be contrasted in seven areas. People and organizations outside the business unit are the primary users of financial accounting information, whereas various levels of internal management use management accounting information. There is no restriction on the types of accounting systems one can use in management accounting, but financial accounting centers on the double-entry system. Restrictive guidelines for financial accounting are composed of all generally accepted accounting standards, whereas management accounting's only restriction is that the information be useful to the recipient. Although the historical dollar is the main unit of measurement in financial accounting, any useful unit of measurement may be used in management accounting. The business unit as a whole is the focal point of any analysis in financial accounting, but a management accounting analysis may focus on a division, a department, or even a machine. Frequency of reporting is on a regular, periodic basis in financial accounting; in management accounting, on an as-needed basis. Financial accounting deals with things that have happened, and so its degree of reliability demands objectivity; whereas management accounting often focuses on the future and can be heavily subjective.

3. **Compare the information needs of a manager of: (a) a manufacturing company; (b) a bank; and (c) a department store.**
   The information needs of a manager of a manufacturing company, a bank, or a department store vary, depending on the type of business activity involved. The manufacturer needs product costing information and is involved with various types of inventory. The banker requires special analyses for fund

management and control. A department store manager needs merchandise control information. But despite these differences, each of these managers requires many types of similar information, such as budgets, tax reports, operating decision analyses, cash management data, and capital expenditure data.

4. **Identify the important questions a manager must consider before preparing a managerial report.**
   Report preparation depends on the four "W" questions: Why? What? Who? and When? The why question is answered by stating the purpose of the report. Once that has been stated, the report maker must determine what information the report should contain to satisfy that purpose. The who question can take several forms: For whom are you preparing the report? To whom should the report be distributed? Who will read it? Finally, there is the question of when. When is the report due?

5. **Prepare analyses of nonfinancial data.**
   Most people connect the discipline of accounting with the analysis of money. Management accountants do prepare analyses expressed in dollars, but they also confront problems requiring solutions formulated around labor hours, machine hours, units of output, number of employees, and number of requests for service.

6. **State the differences between accounting for a manufacturing and a merchandising company.**
   Accounting methods used by a manufacturing company differ in important ways from those used by a merchandising company. Management accountants at a manufacturing company must maintain an internal accounting system for classifying and assigning production and production-related costs to the products manufactured. A manufacturing accounting system uses three inventory accounts: Materials Inventory, Work in Process Inventory, and Finished Goods Inventory. Manufacturing costs must flow through all three inventory accounts. This flow results in a more complex internal accounting system.
   Merchandise accounting concentrates on the business that purchases a product ready for resale when it is received. Only one account, Merchandise Inventory, is used to record and account for items in inventory. Because the items in merchandise inventory are purchased in salable condition, the cost flow from time of purchase to time of sale involves a maximum of four of the following accounts, depending on whether the periodic or perpetual system is used: Cash or Accounts Payable, Purchases or Merchandise Inventory, Freight In, and Cost of Goods Sold.

7. **Describe a Certified Management Accountant (CMA) and state the requirements one must satisfy to attain this designation.**
   A Certified Management Accountant is a person competent in the management accounting discipline who has acquired the necessary background and has passed a two and one-half day examination. The examination consists of five parts: (1) economics and business finance; (2) organization and behavior, including ethical considerations; (3) public reporting standards, auditing, and taxes; (4) internal reporting and analysis; and (5) decision analysis, including modeling and information systems.

Review of Concepts and Terminology

The following important concept was introduced in this chapter:

(L.O.1) **Management accounting** The process of identification, measurement, accumulation, analysis, preparation, interpretation, and communication of financial information used by management to plan, evaluate, and control within the organization and to assure appropriate use and accountability for its resources.

Review Problem

Nonfinancial Data

Ken Becker Surfaces, Inc., is a house painting company located in Rock Island, Illinois. The company employs twelve painters. Mr. Becker manages the operation and does all of the estimating and billing work. Two painters specialize in interior painting, three painters are exterior trim specialists, and the remaining seven are semi-skilled, all-purpose painters. Mr. Becker prepared the following projection of work hours for the month of June:

	Projected Hours to Be Worked				
	Week #1	Week #2	Week #3	Week #4	Totals
Mason Apartments:					
Interior	60	60	48	32	200
Exterior trim	100	60	48	24	232
General painting	180	160	120	60	520
Gantry Building:					
Interior	20	20	32	48	120
Exterior trim	20	60	72	96	248
General painting	100	120	160	220	600
Totals	480	480	480	480	1,920

On July 2, Mr. Becker assembled the actual hour data that is shown on the following page.

Mr. Becker is concerned about the excess labor hours worked during June. The July forecast needs to be developed, but he needs further analysis of June's data before proceeding.

	Actual Hours Worked				
	Week #1	Week #2	Week #3	Week #4	Totals
Mason Apartments:					
Interior	72	76	68	52	268
Exterior trim	88	56	44	20	208
General painting	220	180	144	76	620
Gantry Building:					
Interior	24	32	48	64	168
Exterior trim	16	52	64	88	220
General painting	116	136	184	260	696
Totals	536	532	552	560	2,180

Required

1. Prepare an analysis that shows the number of hours over or under projected hours for each job assignment in June.
2. From your analysis in part **1**, what trouble areas would you point out to Mr. Becker? Suggest some solutions.

Answer to Review Problem

1.	Hours Worked (Over) or Under Projected Hours				
	Week #1	Week #2	Week #3	Week #4	Totals
Mason Apartments:					
Interior	(12)	(16)	(20)	(20)	(68)
Exterior trim	12	4	4	4	24
General painting	(40)	(20)	(24)	(16)	(100)
Gantry Building:					
Interior	(4)	(12)	(16)	(16)	(48)
Exterior trim	4	8	8	8	28
General painting	(16)	(16)	(24)	(40)	(96)
Totals	(56)	(52)	(72)	(80)	(260)

2. Both the interior and semi-skilled painters are taking more time to complete the jobs than was anticipated by Mr. Becker. Either his estimates were wrong, the quality of the painting materials was poor, or some of the painters need to be reprimanded or dismissed.

Chapter Assignments

Questions

1. Describe the field of management accounting, including the three areas in which management needs information.
2. Identify how the primary users of information, types of accounting systems, and restrictive guidelines differ between management accounting and financial accounting.
3. Compare management accounting and financial accounting. Include units of measurement, focal point of analysis, frequency of reporting, and degree of reliability in your comparison.
4. Does the size of a business dictate the type or amount of financial information needed by management? Explain your answer.
5. What types of information are important to a manager in a manufacturing company?
6. How do the information needs of a bank manager differ from those of a manager in a department store? What needs are similar?
7. Why should a person specializing in marketing, finance, or management be familiar with management accounting?
8. What are the four "W" questions related to report preparation? Explain the importance of each question.
9. An analysis of nonfinancial data is important to the management accountant. Why?
10. What is the difference between a merchandising company and a manufacturing company? Include a description of inventory cost flows for each type of company in your answer.
11. List the five parts of the CMA examination.

Classroom Exercises

Exercise 1-1.
Definitions of
Management
Accounting
(L.O. 1)

There are many definitions and descriptions of management accounting. The National Association of Accountants, in *Statement No. 1A* in its series *Statements on Management Accounting*, defined management accounting as:

. . . the process of identification, measurement, accumulation, analysis, preparation, and communication of financial information used by management to plan, evaluate, and control within the organization and to assure appropriate use and accountability for its resources. Management accounting also comprises the preparation of financial reports for nonmanagement groups such as shareholders, creditors, regulatory agencies, and tax authorities.[3]

In *The Modern Accountant's Handbook*, management (managerial) accounting is described as follows:

"Managerial accounting, although generally anchored to the financial accounting framework, involves a broader information-processing system. It deals in many units of measure and produces a variety of reports designed for specific purposes. Its scope encompasses the past, the present, and the future. Its purposes include short- and long-range planning, cost determination, control of activities, assessment of objectives and program performance, and provision of basic information for decision making.[4]

3. National Association of Accountants, *Statement No. 1A* (New York, 1982).
4. Edwards and Black, *The Modern Accountant's Handbook* (Homewood, IL: Dow Jones-Irwin, 1976), p. 830.

1. Compare these two statements on management accounting.
2. "It is impossible to distinguish the point at which financial accounting ends and management accounting begins."   Explain this statement.

Exercise 1-2.
Types of
Accounting
Systems
(L.O.2)

Many management accounting analyses are not limited by the double-entry accounting system.   Two such analyses are shown below.

a. Budgeted materials purchases for March

Aluminum ingots	$ 80,000
Copper ingots	140,000
Silver ingots	500,000
Total estimated materials costs	$720,000

b. Determining an appropriate selling price for a new product

Estimated manufacturing costs per unit	$51.00
Operating expenses (40% of manufacturing costs)	20.40
Profit factor (25% of manufacturing & operating costs)	17.85
Projected selling price	$89.25

1. Do the above analyses require a journal entry to become effective?
2. When will the above information enter the general ledger?

Exercise 1-3.
Management
Information Needs
(L.O.3)

The following statement was overheard by Linda Hutcheson, the newly appointed senior budget analyst for the LaRue Corporation.   The statement was made by the vice president of sales in a conversation with the controller.

Budgets are made up of guesswork and do not apply to sales people.   Budgets tend to restrict our movement and thereby inhibit sales efforts and hold down sales. Budgets should be applicable only to production people who need to keep their costs down and concentrate on efficient operating plans and procedures.

Do you agree with the vice president?   Defend your answer, basing your arguments on the information needs of managers.

Exercise 1-4.
Management
Structure and
Information Needs
(L.O.4)

The F. D. Fowler Corporation employs executives in the following positions:

Production manager, Division 1
Management accountant, Division 2
Sales manager, Division 1
Sales manager, Division 2
Vice president, Engineering
Chief engineer, Division 2
Corporate controller
Chairman of the board
Vice president, Sales
Production manager, Division 2

Management accountant, Division 1
Corporate secretary/treasurer
Chief engineer, Division 1
Production vice president
President
Corporate legal counsel

1. Prepare a diagram or chart, showing the organizational hierarchy of this management team. **Hint:** Start at the top with the chairman of the board and work down. Show positions with seemingly similar power and stature on the same horizontal level.
2. What types of information would the corporate controller request from the management accountant of Division 2 before designing a reporting system for the sales area?

Exercise 1-5.
Nonfinancial Data
Analysis
(L.O. 5)

Sachdev Landscapes, Inc., specializes in lawn installations requiring Kentucky bluegrass sod. The sod comes in 1-yard squares. The company uses the guideline of 250 square yards per person per hour to evaluate the performance of its sod layers.

During the first week of March, the following actual data were collected:

Employee	Hours Worked	Square Yards of Sod Planted
R. Elam	38	9,120
G. W. Krull	45	11,250
J. B. Boatsman	40	9,800
E. E. Milam	42	8,820
H. P. Schaefer	44	11,440
F. L. Neumann	45	11,250

Evaluate the performance of the six employees.

Exercise 1-6.
Manufacturer
Versus
Merchandiser
(L.O. 6)

Tahoe Corporation has two divisions, the Incline Division and the Keys Division, that operate as autonomous units. Incline manufactures powerboats. Keys, as a marine supplies merchandiser, is responsible for sales and service of Incline's products.

1. Explain the flow of operating costs through the records of each division, and describe each type of cost.
2. What will be the differences in each division's financial statements?

Exercise 1-7.
Balance Sheet
Interpretation
(L.O. 6)

Gist Corporation is located in Houston, Texas. The corporation's balance sheet on July 31 is shown on the next page.

1. Is Gist Corporation a merchandising firm or a manufacturing company?
2. Identify at least five reasons for your answer to **1** above.

Gist Corporation
Balance Sheet
July 31, 19x8

Assets

Current Assets
  Cash | | $ 16,400
  Accounts Receivable | | 290,000

Current Assets			
Cash		$ 16,400	
Accounts Receivable		290,000	
Materials Inventory		18,700	
Work in Process Inventory		50,600	
Finished Goods Inventory		40,400	
Prepaid Factory Insurance		23,100	
Small Tools		24,000	
Total Current Assets			$ 463,200
Machinery and Equipment			
Factory Machinery	$720,000		
Less Accumulated Depreciation	132,000	$588,000	
Office Equipment	$ 94,000		
Less Accumulated Depreciation	47,000	47,000	
Total Machinery and Equipment			635,000
Total Assets			$1,098,200

Liabilities and Stockholders' Equity

Liabilities			
Current Liabilities			
Accounts Payable		$ 22,500	
Income Taxes Withheld		30,000	
FICA Taxes Payable		12,000	
United States Government Bonds Payable		2,000	
Union Dues Payable		3,500	
Federal Income Taxes Payable		32,600	
Total Liabilities			$ 102,600
Stockholders' Equity			
Common Stock		$750,000	
Retained Earnings, July 1, 19x8	$205,600		
Net Income, July 19x8	40,000		
Retained Earnings, July 31, 19x8		245,600	
Total Stockholders' Equity			995,600
Total Liabilities and Stockholders' Equity			$1,098,200

Interpreting Accounting Information

Financial Statement Users: Otto Enterprises (L.O.2)

Otto Enterprises is a corporation. It produces and distributes household cleaning products nationally. Common and preferred stocks of the company are traded on a regional stock exchange. There are four divisions in the firm, and each is headed by a vice president. The following condensed financial statements appeared in Otto's annual report for 19x7:

Otto Enterprises
Balance Sheet
December 31, 19x7

Assets		Liabilities and Stockholders' Equity		
Current Assets		Liabilities		
Cash	$ 20,000	Current Liabilities		
Receivables (net)	10,000	Accounts Payable	$20,000	
Inventories	30,000	Accrued Liabilities	5,000	
Prepaid Expenses	5,000	Total Current Liabilities		$ 25,000
Total Current Assets	$ 65,000	Bonds Payable		40,000
		Total Liabilities		$ 65,000
Buildings and Equipment (net)	75,000	Stockholders' Equity		
Total Assets	$140,000	Preferred Stock	$20,000	
		Common Stock	40,000	
		Retained Earnings	15,000	
		Total Stockholders' Equity		75,000
		Total Liabilities and Stockholders' Equity		$140,000

Otto Enterprises
Income Statement
For the Year 19x7

Net Sales	$200,000
Cost of Goods Sold	95,000
Gross Margin on Sales	$105,000
Selling and Administrative Expenses	80,000
Operating Income	$ 25,000
Interest Expenses	5,000
Income Before Taxes	$ 20,000
Income Taxes	5,000
Net Income ($.30 per share)	$ 15,000

Required

Discuss the usefulness of the annual report's information in decisions and evaluations normally made by the following people:

a. Holders of Otto common stock
b. Holders of Otto preferred stock
c. Potential stockholders in Otto securities
d. Company president and board of directors
e. Company bondholders
f. Vice presidents of each division
g. Plant superintendents
h. District sales managers
i. Cost center supervisors in each plant
j. Salaried employees who are nonsupervisory

Problem Set A

Problem 1A-1.
Approach to Report
Preparation
(L.O. 3, 4)

Lanzilloti Industries, Inc., is deciding whether to expand its "Jeans by Louis" line of men's clothing. Sales in units of this product were 22,500, 28,900, and 36,200 in 19x6, 19x7, and 19x8 respectively. The product has been very profitable, averaging 35 percent profit (above cost) over the three-year period. Lanzilloti has ten sales representatives covering seven states in the Northeast. Present production capacity is about 40,000 jeans per year. There is adequate plant space for additional equipment, and the labor needed can be easily hired and trained.

The company's management is made up of four vice presidents: vice president of marketing, vice president of production, vice president of finance, and vice president of data processing. Each of these people is directly responsible to the president, Louis Lanzilloti.

Required

1. What types of information will Mr. Lanzilloti need before he can decide whether to expand the "Jeans by Louis" product line?
2. Assume one of the reports needed to support Mr. Lanzilloti's decision is an analysis of sales over the past three years. This analysis should be broken down by sales representative. Answer the four "W" questions as they pertain to this report.
3. Design a format for the report in **2** above.

Problem 1A-2.
Nonfinancial Data
Analysis:
Manufacturing
(L.O. 5)

St. Patrick Surfboards, Inc., manufactures state-of-the-art surfboards and related equipment. Charles Reilly is manager of the New England branch. The production process is made up of the following departments and tasks: (1) Molding Department, where the board's base is molded; (2) Sanding Department, where the base is sanded after being taken out of the mold; (3) Fiber-Ap Department, where a fiber glass coating is applied; and (4) Finishing Department, where a finishing coat of fiber glass is applied and the board is inspected. After the molding process, all functions are performed by hand.

Mr. Reilly is concerned about the labor hours being worked by his employees. The New England branch utilizes a two-shift labor force. The actual hours worked for the past four weeks are summarized below.

	Actual Hours Worked—First Shift				
Department	**Week #1**	**Week #2**	**Week #3**	**Week #4**	**Totals**
Molding	420	432	476	494	1,822
Sanding	60	81	70	91	302
Fiber-Ap	504	540	588	572	2,204
Finishing	768	891	952	832	3,443

	Actual Hours Worked—Second Shift				
Department	**Week #1**	**Week #2**	**Week #3**	**Week #4**	**Totals**
Molding	360	357	437	462	1,616
Sanding	60	84	69	99	312
Fiber-Ap	440	462	529	506	1,937
Finishing	670	714	782	726	2,892

Expected labor hours per product for each operation are: Molding, 3.4 hours; Sanding, .5 hour; Fiber-Ap, 4.0 hours; and Finishing, 6.5 hours. Actual units completed were as follows:

Week	First Shift	Second Shift
1	120	100
2	135	105
3	140	115
4	130	110

Required

1. Prepare an analysis to determine the average actual labor hours worked per board for each phase of the production process and for each shift.
2. Using the information from **1** above and the expected labor hours per board for each department, prepare an analysis showing the differences in each phase of each shift. Identify reasons for the differences.

Problem 1A-3.
Nonfinancial Data
Analysis: Bank
(L.O. 5)

Torrington State Bank was formed in 1869. It has had a record of slow, steady growth since inception. Management has always kept the processing of information as current as technology allows. Belinda Kessing, manager of the SUNY branch, is upgrading the check-sorting equipment in her office. There are eight check-sorting machines in operation. Information on the number of checks sorted by machine for the past eight weeks is summarized below.

					Weeks			
Machine	**One**	**Two**	**Three**	**Four**	**Five**	**Six**	**Seven**	**Eight**
AA	89,260	89,439	89,394	90,288	90,739	90,658	90,676	90,630
AB	91,420	91,237	91,602	91,969	91,950	92,502	92,446	92,816
AC	94,830	95,020	94,972	95,922	96,401	96,315	96,334	96,286
AD	91,970	91,786	92,153	92,522	92,503	93,058	93,002	93,375
AE	87,270	87,445	87,401	88,275	88,716	88,636	88,654	88,610
BA	92,450	92,265	92,634	93,005	92,986	93,544	93,488	93,862
BB	91,910	92,094	92,048	92,968	93,433	93,349	93,368	93,321
BC	90,040	89,860	90,219	90,580	90,562	91,105	91,051	91,415
BD	87,110	87,190	87,210	130,815	132,320	133,560	134,290	135,770
BE	94,330	94,519	94,471	95,416	95,893	95,807	95,826	95,778

The SUNY branch has increased its checking business significantly over the past two years. Ms. Kessing must decide whether to purchase additional check-sorting machines or attachments for the existing machines to increase productivity. Five weeks ago the Green Company convinced her to experiment with one such attachment, and it was placed on Machine BD. Ms. Kessing is impressed with the attachment but has yet to decide between the two courses of action.

Required (show computations to support your answers)

1. If the Green Company attachment costs about the same as a new check-sorting machine, which alternative should Ms. Kessing choose?
2. Would you change your recommendation if two attachments could be purchased for the price of one check-sorting machine?
3. If three attachments could be purchased for the price of one check-sorting machine, what action would you recommend?

Problem 1A-4.
Manufacturing
Company Balance
Sheet
(L.O. 6)

The analysis at the top of the following page represents the balance sheet accounts at Cassagio Manufacturing Company after closing entries were made. Net income for the year is still identified for the purposes of report preparation.

Required

Using the information in the analysis and proper form, prepare a balance sheet for the Cassagio Manufacturing Company as of December 31, 19x9. **Hint:** Production Supplies and Tools are a current asset. Patents are classified as "Other Assets."

Ledger Accounts	Debit	Credit
Cash	$ 16,000	
Accounts Receivable	30,000	
Materials Inventory, 12/31/x9	42,000	
Work in Process Inventory, 12/31/x9	17,400	
Finished Goods Inventory, 12/31/x9	52,700	
Production Supplies and Tools	8,600	
Land	200,000	
Factory Building	400,000	
Factory Equipment	250,000	
Sales Warehouse	148,000	
Accumulated Depreciation, Building		$ 110,000
Accumulated Depreciation, Equipment		72,000
Accumulated Depreciation, Warehouse		35,000
Patents	27,300	
Accounts Payable		19,800
Accrued Property Taxes		12,000
Income Taxes Payable		50,000
Mortgage Payable, due in one year		20,000
Mortgage Payable		380,000
Common Stock		260,000
Retained Earnings, 1/1/x9		100,000
Net Income for 19x9		133,200
	$1,192,000	$1,192,000

Problem Set B

Problem 1B-1.
Approach to Report
Preparation
(L.O.3,4)

Debbie Most recently purchased Lawn & Garden Supplies, Inc., a wholesale distributor of lawn- and garden-care equipment and supplies. The company, headquartered in Baltimore, Maryland, has four distribution centers: Boston, Massachusetts; Rye, New York; Reston, Virginia; and Lawrenceville, New Jersey. These distribution centers service fourteen eastern states. Company profits were $125,400, $237,980, and $467,200 for 19x7, 19x8, and 19x9 respectively.

Shortly after purchasing the company, Ms. Most appointed people to fill the following positions: vice president, marketing; vice president, distribution; corporate controller; and vice president, research and development. Ms. Most has called a meeting of her management group. She would like to create a deluxe retail lawn and garden center that would include a large, fully landscaped plant and tree nursery. The purposes of the retail center would be (1) to test equipment and supplies before selecting them for sales and distribution and (2) to showcase the effects of using the company's products. The retail center must also make a profit on sales.

Required

1. What types of information will Ms. Most need before deciding whether to create the retail lawn and garden center?
2. Assume one of the reports needed to support Ms. Most's decision analyzes locations for the new retail center. The report came from the vice president of research and development. Respond to the four "W" questions as they pertain to this report.
3. Design a format for the report in **2** above.

Problem 1B-2.
Nonfinancial Data
Analysis:
Manufacturing
(L.O. 5)

Flagstaff Enterprises makes sports shoes for every major sports activity. The "Awesome Shoe" is one of the company's leading products. This shoe is lightweight, long wearing, and inexpensive. Production of the Awesome Shoe is composed of five operations and tasks: (1) Cutting/Lining Department, where cloth tops are cut and lined; (2) Molding Department, where the shoe's rubber base is formed; (3) Bonding Department, where the cloth top is bonded to the rubber base; (4) Soling Department, where the sole is attached to the rubber base; and (5) Finishing Department, where the shoe is trimmed, stitched, and laced.

Recently, manufacturing costs have been increasing for the Awesome Shoe. Controller Ron Pitt has been investigating the production process to determine the problems. Everything points to the labor hours required to make the shoe. Actual labor hours worked in a recent week are shown below.

Actual Hours Worked						
Operation	Monday	Tuesday	Wednesday	Thursday	Friday	Total
Cutting/lining	300	310	305	300	246	1,461
Molding	144	186	183	200	246	959
Bonding	456	434	488	450	492	2,320
Soling	408	434	366	400	492	2,100
Finishing	600	620	549	625	615	3,009

The company has estimated that the following labor hours for each department should be needed to complete a pair of Awesome Shoes: Cutting/lining, .2 hour; Molding, .1 hour; Bonding, .4 hour; Soling, .3 hour; and Finishing, .5 hour. During the week under review, the number of actual pairs of Awesome Shoes produced were: 1,200 pairs on Monday; 1,240 pairs on Tuesday; 1,220 pairs on Wednesday; 1,250 pairs on Thursday; and 1,230 pairs on Friday.

Required

1. Prepare an analysis to determine the average actual labor hours worked per day per pair of shoes for each operation in the production process.
2. Comparing the average actual labor hours worked from **1** above and the expected labor hours per pair of shoes per department, prepare an analysis showing differences in each operation for each day. Identify reasons for those differences.

Problem 1B-3.
Nonfinancial Data
Analysis: Airport
(L.O. 5)

The Medford County Airport at Long Plains, Nebraska, has experienced increased air traffic over the past year. How passenger traffic flow is handled is important to airport management. Because of the requirement that all passengers must be checked for possible weapons, passenger flow has slowed significantly. Medford County Airport uses eight metal detector devices to screen passengers. The airport is open from 6:00 a.m. to 10:00 p.m. daily, and present machinery allows a maximum of 45,000 passengers to be checked each day.

Four of the metal detector machines have been selected for special analysis to determine if additional equipment is needed or if a passenger traffic director could solve the problem. The passenger traffic director would be responsible for guiding people to different machines and instructing them on the detection process. This solution would be less expensive than acquiring new machines, and so a suitable person will be assigned to this function on a trial basis. Management hopes this procedure will quicken passenger traffic flow by at least 10 percent. Makers of the machinery have stated that each machine can handle an average of 400 passengers per hour. Data on passenger traffic through the four machines for the past ten days is shown below.

		Passengers Checked by Metal Detector Machines			
Date	Machine I	Machine II	Machine III	Machine IV	Totals
March 6	5,620	5,490	5,436	5,268	21,814
March 7	5,524	5,534	5,442	5,290	21,790
March 8	5,490	5,548	5,489	5,348	21,875
March 9	5,436	5,592	5,536	5,410	21,974
March 10	5,404	5,631	5,568	5,456	22,059
March 11	5,386	5,667	5,594	5,496	22,143
March 12	5,364	5,690	5,638	5,542	22,234
March 13	5,678	6,248	6,180	6,090	24,196
March 14	5,720	6,272	6,232	6,212	24,436
March 15	5,736	6,324	6,372	6,278	24,710

In the past, passenger traffic flow has favored Machine I because of its location. Overflow traffic goes to Machines II, III, and IV in that order.

The passenger traffic director began her duties on March 13. If this choice of alternatives results in at least a 10 percent increase in passengers handled, management will employ a second traffic director for the remaining four machines. It will then scrap the idea of purchasing additional metal detectors.

Required (show computations to support your answers)

1. Did the passenger traffic director pass the minimum test set up by management, or should airport officials purchase additional metal detector machines?
2. Is there anything unusual in the analysis that management should have looked into regarding the rate of passenger traffic flow?

**Problem 1B-4.
Manufacturing
Company Balance
Sheet
(L.O. 6)**

Espey Industries, Inc., manufactures racing hubs for sports car enthusiasts. Balances in balance sheet accounts at year end are shown below. Closing entries have been made, but net income has been separated so that year-end financial statements can be prepared.

Required

Using the information given and the proper form, prepare a balance sheet for Espey Industries, Inc., as of December 31, 19x8. **Hint:** Production Supplies and Small Tools are current assets. Patents are classified as "Other Assets."

Ledger Accounts	Debit	Credit
Cash	$ 24,000	
Accounts Receivable	47,000	
Materials Inventory, 12/31/x8	51,000	
Work in Process Inventory, 12/31/x8	37,900	
Finished Goods Inventory, 12/31/x8	64,800	
Production Supplies	5,700	
Small Tools	9,330	
Land	160,000	
Factory Building	575,000	
Factory Equipment	310,000	
Accumulated Depreciation, Building		$ 219,000
Accumulated Depreciation, Factory Equipment		117,000
Patents	33,500	
Accounts Payable		36,900
Accrued Insurance		6,700
Income Taxes Payable		61,500
Mortgage Payable, due in one year		18,000
Mortgage Payable		325,000
Common Stock		200,000
Retained Earnings, 1/1/x8		196,000
Net Income for 19x8		138,130
	$1,318,230	$1,318,230

Management Decision Case

**McCartney
Manufacturing
Company:
Nonfinancial Data
Analysis
(L.O. 4, 5)**

As a subcontractor in the jet aircraft industry, McCartney Manufacturing Company specializes in the production of housings for landing gear on jet airplanes. The company, located in Selden, New York, employs approximately 150 people. Two shifts, a day shift and a night shift, normally work forty-hour weeks. Production begins on Machine #1, where the housing material is cut from huge sheets of metal into pieces weighing 1,800 pounds each. Machine #2 bends the pieces into cylinder-shaped products and trims off the rough edges. On Machine #3 the seam of the cylinder is welded, and the entire piece is pushed into a large die to mold the housing into its final shape.

Scrap is a costly problem for the company. Management has asked the controller, Chuck Heck, to prepare an analysis of scrap for the past four-week period.

The analysis performed by Mr. Heck is summarized in the following tables:

		Units of Production—Day Shift			
Machine	**Week #1**	**Week #2**	**Week #3**	**Week #4**	**Totals**
1A*	1,020	1,008	996	990	4,014
1B*	1,024	1,020	1,026	1,032	4,102
2	2,020	2,006	2,018	2,012	8,056
3	1,998	2,004	2,014	2,012	8,028

		Units of Production—Night Shift			
Machine	**Week #1**	**Week #2**	**Week #3**	**Week #4**	**Totals**
1A*	1,010	1,014	1,018	1,024	4,066
1B*	1,026	1,012	996	990	4,024
2	1,996	1,992	1,990	1,984	7,962
3	1,988	1,986	1,986	1,980	7,940

* It takes output of two Machine #1's to supply inputs for a single Machine #2.

Note that the total number of units being worked on decreases as production moves from Machine #1 to Machine #2 and from Machine #2 to Machine #3. Assume that this decrease represents units that are scrapped because of poor workmanship or faulty equipment.

Actual scrap generation is summarized in the following tables:

		Pounds of Scrap Generation—Day Shift			
Machine	**Week #1**	**Week #2**	**Week #3**	**Week #4**	**Totals**
1A	36,720	54,288	71,856	82,440	245,304
1B	36,864	36,720	36,936	37,152	147,672
2	43,200	39,600	7,200	18,000	108,000
3	39,600	3,600	7,200	0	50,400

	Pounds of Scrap Generation—Night Shift				
Machine	Week #1	Week #2	Week #3	Week #4	Totals
1A	36,360	36,504	36,648	36,864	146,376
1B	36,936	58,032	75,456	78,840	249,264
2	72,000	61,200	43,200	54,000	230,400
3	14,400	10,800	7,200	7,200	39,600

Company officials expect the following production quotas and amounts of scrap:

Machine #1: Cuts 25 pieces per hour; scrap from trimmings and spoilage equals 2 percent of output weight.

Machine #2: Bends 50 pieces per hour; spoilage occurs at a rate of one per two hundred pieces attempted.

Machine #3: Welds and forms 50 pieces per hour; one out of every 400 pieces is found to be defective at the end of the process. These pieces cannot be reworked and are scrapped.

Required

1. Using actual production data, prepare an analysis of pounds of scrap generation expected for an average day shift and night shift.
2. Using the data computed in **1** above and the actual information on scrap generation, analyze the differences between actual and expected scrap poundage.
3. What areas of the production process should Mr. Heck investigate further? Why?
4. Do you suspect machine failure or human inefficiency to be the root of the problem? Defend your answer.

Operating Costs: Terms, Classifications, and Reporting

Management accounting includes three interrelated functions that comprise a company's internal accounting system: (1) determining product or service costs for inventory valuation and cost control purposes; (2) providing information for the planning and control phases of internal operations; and (3) aiding top management in decision-making activities. All three functions require cost information from past, current, or future operations.

In this chapter we acquaint you with the various kinds of manufacturing costs and their classification and reporting possibilities. Emphasis is placed on the manufacturing environment, primarily because these cost classifications and reporting techniques are used extensively by companies involved in manufacturing. As stated earlier, however, management accounting is also important to companies in service-related industries. Thus, following the discussion of accounting for manufacturing costs, this chapter concludes by briefly covering some of these concepts and their application to a service business.

Your study of management accounting continues with an analysis of the three manufacturing cost elements: direct materials costs, direct labor costs, and factory overhead costs. Computing a product's unit cost sums up that discussion and leads into an analysis of the three manufacturing inventory accounts: Materials Inventory, Work in Process Inventory, and Finished Goods Inventory. Studying manufacturing cost flow within the accounting system is an appropriate way to introduce reporting in a manufacturing setting. The statement of cost of goods manufactured is a prerequisite to preparing an income statement for a production-oriented company. After studying this chapter, you should be able to meet the learning objectives listed on the left. A work sheet analysis for a manufacturing company, based on perpetual and periodic inventories, is covered in a special analysis in The Windham Company Practice Case.

Manufacturing Cost Elements

Manufacturing costs can be classified in many ways. Some costs can be traced directly to one product or batch of products. Other costs cannot be traced directly to products. In gathering information for business decisions, a particular cost may be important

OBJECTIVE 1
State the differences between the three manufacturing cost elements: (a) direct materials costs; (b) direct labor costs; and (c) factory overhead costs

to one type of decision analysis and ignored in another. When changing from an external financial reporting approach to an internal or management accounting approach, some costs take on different characteristics. In fact, manufacturing costs can be reclassified in different ways, depending on the goal of the cost analysis.

The most common classification scheme, as mentioned before, is to group manufacturing costs into one of three classes: (1) direct materials costs; (2) direct labor costs; and (3) indirect manufacturing costs. This last class of costs is often referred to as factory overhead. **Direct costs** can be traced to specific products. **Indirect costs** must be assigned to products by some general plan for allocation.

Direct Materials Costs

All manufactured products are made from basic direct materials. The basic material may be iron ore for steel, sheet steel for automobiles, or flour for bread. These examples show the link between a basic raw material and a final product.

The way a company buys, stores, and uses materials is important. Timely purchasing is important because if the company runs out of materials, the manufacturing process will be forced to shut down. Shutting down production results in no products, unhappy customers, and loss of sales and profits. Buying too many direct materials, on the other hand, can lead to high storage costs.

Proper storage of materials will avoid waste and spoilage. Large enough storage space and orderly storage procedures are essential. Materials must be handled and stored properly to guarantee their satisfactory use in production. Proper records make it possible to find goods easily. Such records reduce problems caused by lost or misplaced items.

Direct materials are materials that become part of the finished product and can be conveniently and economically traced to specific product units. The costs of these materials are direct costs. In some cases, even though a material becomes part of a finished product, the expense of actually tracing the cost of a specific material is too great. Examples include nails in furniture, bolts in automobiles, and rivets in airplanes. These minor materials and other production supplies that cannot be conveniently or economically traced to specific products are accounted for as **indirect materials**. Indirect materials costs are part of factory overhead costs, which are discussed later in this chapter.

OBJECTIVE 2
Identify the source documents used to collect information on manufacturing cost accumulation

Direct Materials Purchases. Direct materials are a sizable expenditure each year, so special care must be taken in purchasing them. A company must be careful to buy proper amounts and to ensure it receives quality goods. An efficient purchasing system uses several important documents to account for direct materials purchases. The **purchase requisition** (or **purchase request**), which starts in the production department, is used to begin the materials purchasing process. The requisition describes the items to be purchased and the quantities needed. It must be approved by a qualified manager or supervisor.

From the information on the purchase requisition, the purchasing department prepares a formal purchase order. Some copies of the purchase order are sent to the vendor or supplier; the remaining copies are kept for internal use. When the ordered goods are received, a receiving report is prepared. It is matched against the descriptions and quantities listed on the purchase order. Usually, the materials are inspected for inferior quality or damage as soon as they arrive. The purchasing process is complete when the company gets an invoice from the vendor and approves it for payment.

Direct Materials Usage. Controlling direct materials costs does not end with the receipt and inspection of purchased goods. The materials must be stored in a safe place. They must be counted at regular intervals. And they should be issued into production only with the approval of a production supervisor. It is important to keep the materials storage areas clean and orderly and to lock up valuable items. Regular physical counts are necessary to see how many units are on hand and to test the inventory accounting system. Materials should be issued to production only when an approved materials requisition form is presented to the storeroom clerk. The materials requisition form, shown in Figure 2-1, is essential for controlling direct materials. Besides providing the supervisor's approval signature, the materials requisition describes the types and quantities of goods needed and received.

Direct Labor Costs

Labor services are, in essence, purchased from employees working in the factory. In addition, other types of labor are purchased from people and organizations outside the company. However, the labor cost usually associated with manufacturing is that of factory personnel. These personnel include machine operators; maintenance workers; managers and supervisors; support personnel; and people who handle, inspect, and store materials. Because these people are all connected in some way with the production process, their wages and salaries must be accounted for as production costs and, finally, as costs of products. However, it is difficult to trace many of these costs directly to individual products.

To help overcome this problem, the wages of machine operators and other workers involved in actually shaping the product are classified as direct labor costs. Direct labor costs include all labor costs for specific work performed on products that can be conveniently and economically traced to end products. Labor costs for production-related activities that cannot be connected with or conveniently or economically traced to end products are called indirect labor costs. These costs include the wages and salaries of such workers as machine helpers, supervisors, and other support personnel. Like indirect materials costs, indirect labor costs are accounted for as factory overhead costs.

Labor Documentation. Labor time-records are important to both the employee and the company. The employee wants to be paid at the

Figure 2-1. The Materials Requisition Form

Benton Publishing Company Boston, Massachusetts				Materials Requisition	
				No. 49621	

Charge to Job No. _14 - 629_

Requested by _Jim Roberts_   Date _4/27/x9_

Department _Binding_

Part Number	Description	Quantity Requested	Quantity Issued	Unit Cost	Total Cost
16 T	Glue	140 gallons	60 gallons	$12.40	$744.00

Issued by _L. Sanchez_   Date Received _5/1/x9_

Approved by _A. Schroeder_

Received by _J. Roberts_

correct rate for all hours worked. The company does not want to underpay or overpay its employees. In addition, company management wants a record kept of hours worked on products or batches of products made during the period. For these reasons accounting for wages and salaries requires careful attention.

The basic time-record is called an employee timecard. On each employee's timecard either the supervisor or a time clock records the employee's daily starting and finishing times. Normally, a company uses another set of labor cards to help verify the time recorded on the timecards and to keep track of labor costs per job or batch of goods produced. These documents, called job cards, record the time spent by an employee on a certain job. Each eight-hour period recorded on a timecard may be supported by several job cards. Special job cards also record machine downtime, which may stem from machine repair or product design changes. Job cards verify the time worked by each employee and help control labor time per job.

Gross Versus Net Payroll. Accounting for direct and indirect labor costs often causes misunderstanding. People sometimes confuse gross payroll with net payroll. For internal accounting purposes, gross wages and salaries are used. Net payroll is the amount paid to the employee after all payroll deductions have been subtracted from gross wages. Payroll deductions, such as those for federal income taxes and social security taxes, are paid by the employee. The employer just withholds them and pays them to the government and other organizations for the employee. Gross payroll is a measure of the total wages and salaries earned by employees, including payroll deductions. It is used to compute total manufacturing costs. The following example shows the difference between gross and net payroll:

Gross wages earned:		
40 hours at $10/hour		$400.00
Less deductions		
Federal income taxes withheld	$82.50	
FICA taxes withheld	26.00	
U.S. government savings bond	37.50	
Union dues	12.50	
Insurance premiums	21.00	
Total deductions		179.50
Net wages paid (amount of check)		$220.50

The employee receives net wages of only $220.50, even though the company pays $400.00 in wages and deductions. The amounts withheld from the employee's gross wages are paid by the company to the taxing agencies, savings plan, union, and insurance companies. Gross payroll in this case is $400.00, and it is the gross payroll that must be accounted for as a cost of production and assigned to products or jobs. Net payroll is primarily important to the employee.

Labor-related Costs. Other labor-related manufacturing costs fall into two categories: employee benefits and employer payroll taxes. Employee benefits are considered part of an employee's compensation package. They may include paid vacations, holiday and sick pay, and an employee pension plan. Other benefits might be life and medical insurance, performance bonuses, profit sharing, and recreation facilities. Most of these costs vary in direct proportion to labor costs.

Besides the payroll taxes paid by the employee, there are payroll-related taxes paid by the employer. For every dollar of social security (FICA) tax withheld from the paycheck, the employer usually pays an equal amount. The company must also pay state and federal unemployment compensation taxes. Agreements between management and labor as well as government regulations are sources of some labor-related costs. Company management may spend other money on a voluntary basis for the benefit of its employees.

Most labor-related costs are incurred in direct proportion to wages and salaries earned by the employees. As much as possible, labor-related costs dependent on direct labor costs and conveniently traceable to them should be accounted for as part of direct labor. All other labor-related costs should be classified as factory overhead. However, because of the size and complexity of payroll systems, most labor-related costs are not traced to individual employees. Such costs are normally calculated from wages and salaries by means of a predetermined rate based on past experience. For instance, a company may incur twelve cents of labor-related costs for every dollar of wages and salaries earned by employees. In this case labor-related costs average 12 percent of labor costs. Therefore, if direct labor totaled $6,000 for a period of time, total direct labor cost would be $6,720 ($6,000 plus 12 percent, or $720, in labor-related costs). Total indirect labor cost would be computed in the same manner, as shown in the next section.

Factory Overhead

The third manufacturing cost element is a catchall for manufacturing costs that cannot be classified as direct materials or direct labor costs. Factory overhead costs are a varied collection of production-related costs that cannot be practically or conveniently traced to end products. This collection of costs is also called manufacturing overhead, factory burden, and indirect manufacturing costs. Examples of the major classifications of factory overhead costs are listed below.

Indirect materials and supplies: nails, rivets, lubricants, and small tools

Indirect labor costs: lift-truck driver's wages, maintenance and inspection labor, engineering labor, machine helpers, and supervisors

Other indirect factory costs: building maintenance, machinery and tool maintenance, property taxes, property insurance, pension costs, depreciation on plant and equipment, rent expense, and utility expense

Although this list is incomplete, it includes many common overhead costs and shows how varied they are.

Overhead Cost Behavior. Cost behavior is an important concept in management accounting. Manufacturing costs tend either to rise and fall with the volume of production or to stay the same within certain ranges of output. Variable manufacturing costs increase or decrease in direct proportion to the number of units produced. Examples include: direct materials costs; direct labor costs; indirect materials and supply costs; most indirect labor costs; and small-tool costs.

Production costs that stay fairly constant during the accounting period are called fixed manufacturing costs. Even with changes in productive output, these costs tend to stay the same. Examples of fixed manufacturing costs are fire insurance premiums, factory rent, supervisors' salaries, and depreciation on machinery. Some costs are called semivariable because part of the cost is fixed and part varies with usage. Telephone charges (basic charge plus long-distance charges) and utility bills are generally semivariable.

Cost behavior will be explored further in Chapter 5. In accounting for factory overhead costs, cost behavior analysis helps assign these indirect costs to units of output.

Overhead Cost Allocation. A cost is classified as a factory overhead cost when it cannot be directly traced to an end product. Yet a product's total cost obviously includes factory overhead costs. Somehow factory overhead costs must be identified with and assigned to specific products or jobs. Because direct materials and direct labor costs are traceable to products, assigning their costs to units of output is relatively easy. Factory overhead costs, however, must be assigned to products by some cost allocation method. Cost allocation methods are explained in Chapters 3 and 5.

Unit Cost Determination

OBJECTIVE 3
Compute a product's unit cost

Direct materials, direct labor, and factory overhead costs constitute total manufacturing costs for a period of time or a batch of products. Product unit cost for each job completed is computed by dividing the total cost of materials, labor, and factory overhead for that job by the total units produced. For example, assume that Roland Products, Inc., produced 3,000 units of output for Job 12K. Costs for Job 12K included the following: direct materials, $3,000; direct labor, $5,400; and factory overhead, $2,700. The company's unit cost for Job 12K would be computed as follows:

Direct materials: $3,000 ÷ 3,000 units	$1.00
Direct labor: $5,400 ÷ 3,000 units	1.80
Factory overhead: $2,700 ÷ 3,000 units	.90
Total unit cost: $11,100 ÷ 3,000 units	$3.70

The unit cost described above was computed when the job ended and when all information was known. What about situations needing this information a month before the job is started? Unit cost figures must then be estimated. Assume that accounting personnel developed the following estimates for another product: $2.50 per unit for direct materials, $4.50 per unit for direct labor, and 50 percent of direct labor cost for factory overhead. The unit cost would then be as follows:

Direct materials	$2.50
Direct labor	4.50
Factory overhead (50% × $4.50)	2.25
Total unit cost	$9.25

This $9.25 unit cost is based on estimates. Still, it is useful for job costing and as a starting point for product pricing.

Product and Period Costs

OBJECTIVE 4
Distinguish between product costs and period costs

Product costs and *period costs* are two terms commonly used in analyzing costs. Product costs consist of the three manufacturing cost elements: direct materials, direct labor, and factory overhead. They are incurred in making products and are inventoriable. That is, product costs are associated with the materials, work in process, and finished goods inventories. They provide values for the ending balances of these inventories on year-end financial statements. Product costs are also considered unexpired costs because, as inventory balances, they are company assets. Assets, as you may recall, are economic resources expected to benefit future operations.

Period costs (expenses) are costs that cannot be inventoried. Examples include selling and administrative expenses, since selling and administrative resources are used up in the same period in which they originate. Period costs are linked to services consumed during the current period and would never be used to determine a product's unit cost or to establish ending inventory balances.

Periodic Versus Perpetual Inventory Methods in Manufacturing Accounting

Cost flow in accounting for manufacturing costs depends on how a company chooses to handle its inventories. The periodic and perpetual inventory methods were discussed in your financial accounting course. Because these methods are related to management accounting systems, we also include a brief discussion here. A company using the periodic inventory method records materials purchases in a separate purchases account and assigns manufacturing costs to individual labor accounts and various factory overhead cost accounts in the general ledger. Beginning inventory balances in the general ledger remain unchanged during the period. No costs flow through the Materials, Work in Process, and Finished Goods Inventory accounts during the accounting period. Year-end inventory values are found by counting the items on hand and placing a cost on these goods. Inventory accounts are then adjusted to reflect the cost of the ending inventories.

If a company uses the perpetual inventory method, manufacturing costs flow through inventory accounts as goods and services are bought and used in the production process. Inventory account balances are updated perpetually. In this way it is possible to know these account balances at any point in time. Materials purchased are debited to the Materials Inventory account. The cost of materials used, direct labor, and factory overhead items are entered into the Work in Process Inventory account. The cost of completed units is debited directly to the Finished Goods Inventory account.

The perpetual inventory method is in common use. Greater accuracy and better inventory control are the major benefits of this approach.

However, a perpetual inventory system is expensive to install and maintain. For this reason, many small companies still use a periodic inventory approach.

Manufacturing Inventory Accounts

Most manufacturing companies use the perpetual inventory approach. In the remaining sections of this book, you are to assume that a company uses the perpetual inventory method unless otherwise indicated. Accounting for inventories is the more difficult part of manufacturing accounting when compared with merchandising accounting. Instead of dealing with one account—Merchandise Inventory—*three* accounts must be used: Materials Inventory, Work in Process Inventory, and Finished Goods Inventory.

Materials Inventory

The Materials Inventory account, also called the Stores and Materials Inventory Control account, is made up of the balances of materials and supplies on hand. This account is maintained in much the same way as the Merchandise Inventory account. The main difference is in the way that the costs of items in inventory are assigned. For the merchandising company, goods taken out of inventory are items that have been sold. When a sale is made, an entry is needed to debit Cost of Goods Sold and to credit Merchandise Inventory for the cost of the item. Materials, on the other hand, are usually not purchased for resale but for use in manufacturing a product. Therefore, an item taken out of Materials Inventory and requisitioned into production is transferred to the Work in Process Inventory account (not Cost of Goods Sold). Figure 2-2 compares the accounting treatment of merchandise inventory with that of materials inventory.

Work in Process Inventory

All manufacturing costs incurred and assigned to products being produced are classified as Work in Process Inventory costs. This inventory account has no counterpart in merchandise accounting. A thorough understanding of the concept of Work in Process Inventory is vital in manufacturing accounting. Figure 2-3 on page 51 shows the various costs that become part of Work in Process Inventory and the way costs are transferred out of the account.

The requisitioning of materials into production, shown initially in Figure 2-2, begins the production process. These materials must be cut, molded, assembled, or in some other way changed into a finished product. To make this change, people, machines, and other factory resources (buildings, electricity, supplies, and so on) must be used. All of these costs are manufacturing cost elements, and all of them enter into accounting for Work in Process Inventory.

Direct labor dollars earned by factory employees are also product costs. Since these people work on specific products, their labor costs are assigned to those products by including the labor dollars earned as part of the Work in Process Inventory account. (Specific product costing is the topic of the next two chapters. At this point you should assume that all direct labor costs will be included in the Work in Process Inventory account.)

Figure 2-2. Merchandise Inventory Versus Materials Inventory Accounting (Perpetual)

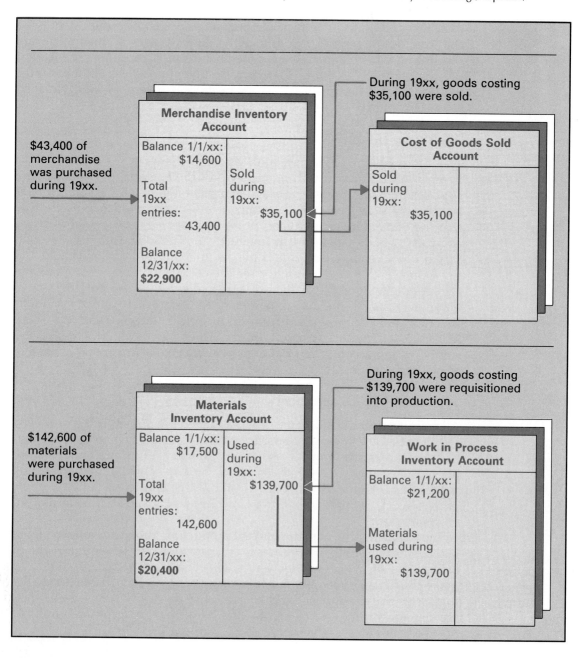

Overhead costs are product costs and must be assigned to specific products. Thus they, too, are included in the Work in Process Inventory account. As discussed earlier, there are too many overhead costs to account for on an individual basis. To reduce the amount of work needed to assign these costs to products, they are accumulated and accounted for under one account title: Factory Overhead Control. These costs are then assigned to products by using an overhead rate. Using this rate, called a predetermined overhead rate, costs are transferred from the Factory Overhead account to the Work in Process Inventory account. In the example in Figure 2-3, factory overhead costs of $156,200 were charged to the Work in Process Inventory account. The predetermined overhead rate will be discussed in Chapter 3.

As products are completed, they are put into the finished goods storage area. These products now have materials, direct labor, and factory overhead costs assigned to them. When products are completed, their costs no longer belong to work (products) in process. Therefore, when the completed products are sent to the storage area, their costs are transferred from the Work in Process Inventory account to the Finished Goods Inventory account. The balance remaining in the Work in Process

Figure 2-3. The Work in Process Inventory Account (Perpetual)

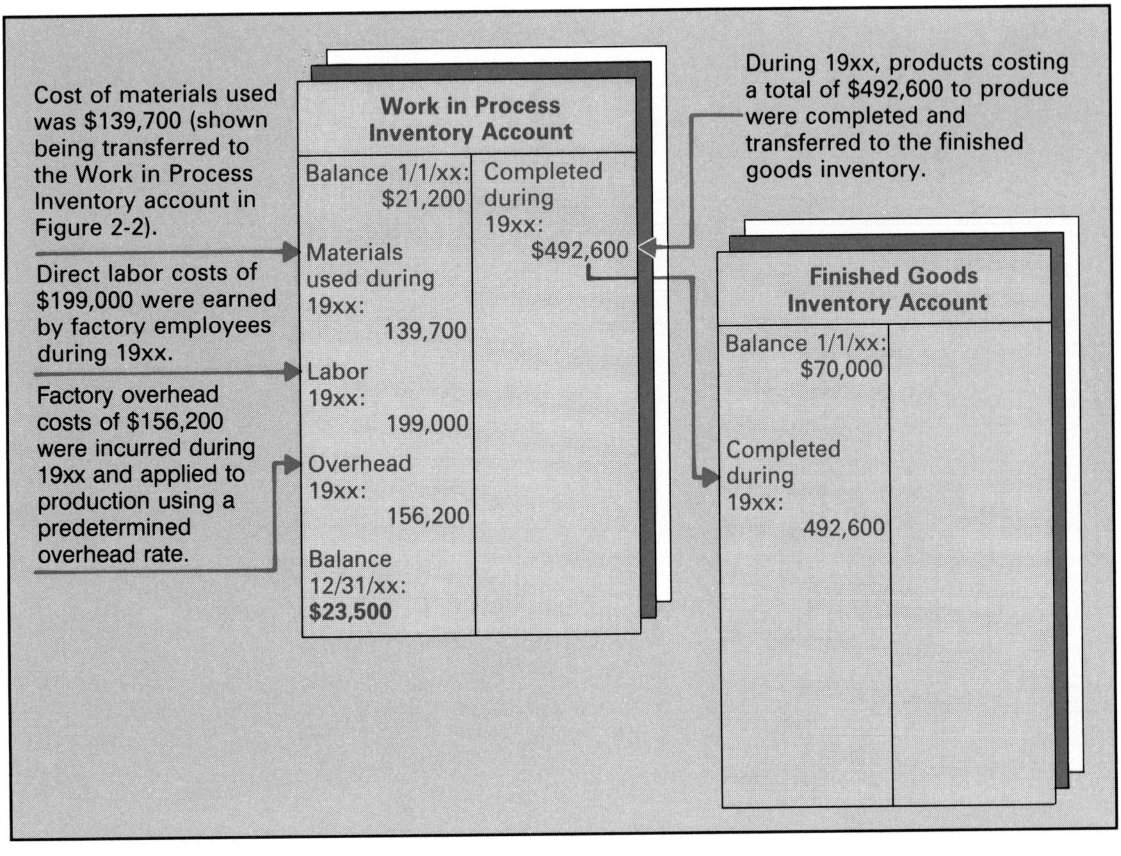

Cost of materials used was $139,700 (shown being transferred to the Work in Process Inventory account in Figure 2-2).

Direct labor costs of $199,000 were earned by factory employees during 19xx.

Factory overhead costs of $156,200 were incurred during 19xx and applied to production using a predetermined overhead rate.

Work in Process Inventory Account

Balance 1/1/xx: $21,200	Completed during 19xx: $492,600
Materials used during 19xx: 139,700	
Labor 19xx: 199,000	
Overhead 19xx: 156,200	
Balance 12/31/xx: **$23,500**	

During 19xx, products costing a total of $492,600 to produce were completed and transferred to the finished goods inventory.

Finished Goods Inventory Account

| Balance 1/1/xx: $70,000 | |
| Completed during 19xx: 492,600 | |

Inventory account ($23,500 in Figure 2-3) represents the costs that were assigned to products partly completed and still in process at the end of the period.

Finished Goods Inventory

The **Finished Goods Inventory** account, like Materials Inventory, has some characteristics of the Merchandise Inventory account. You have already seen how costs are moved from the Work in Process Inventory account to the Finished Goods Inventory account. At this point Finished Goods Inventory takes on the characteristics of Merchandise Inventory. If you compare the Merchandise Inventory account analysis in Figure 2-2 with the accounting for Finished Goods Inventory in Figure 2-4, you will see that the credit side of both accounts is handled in the same way. Both examples show that when goods or products are sold, the costs of those goods are moved from the Finished Goods Inventory account to the Cost of Goods Sold account. However, the accounting procedures affecting the debit side of the Finished Goods Inventory account differ from those for the Merchandise Inventory account. In a manufacturing firm salable products are produced rather than purchased. All costs debited to Finished Goods Inventory represent transfers from the Work in Process Inventory account. At the end of an accounting period, the

Figure 2-4. Accounting for Finished Goods Inventory (Perpetual)

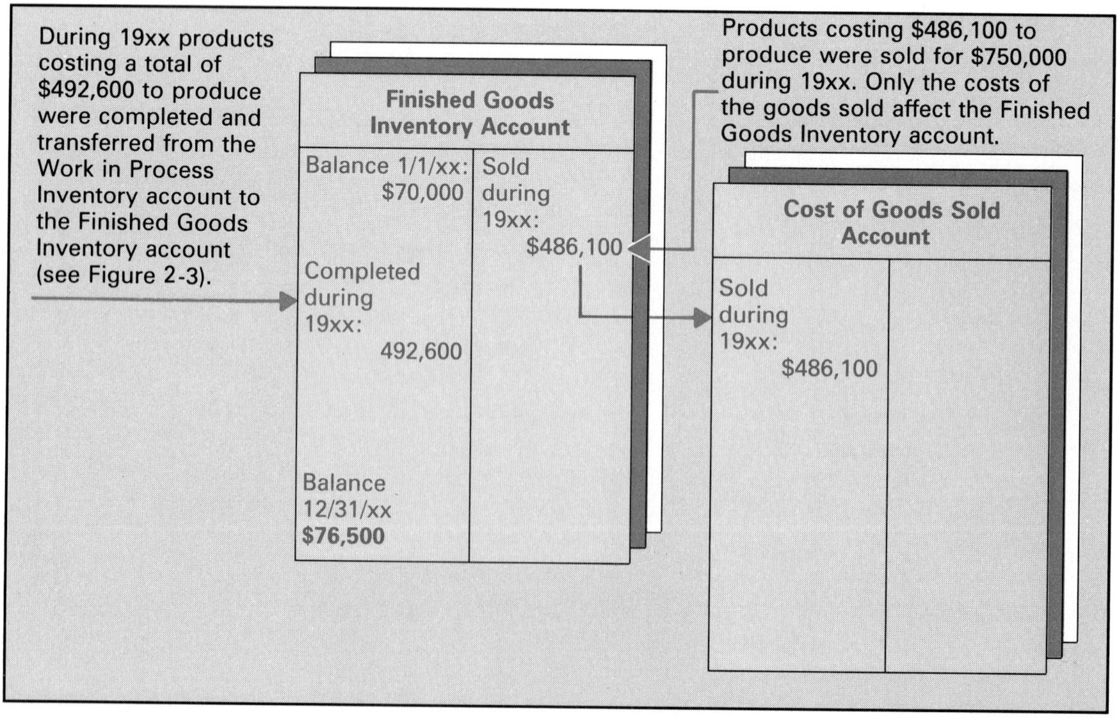

During 19xx products costing a total of $492,600 to produce were completed and transferred from the Work in Process Inventory account to the Finished Goods Inventory account (see Figure 2-3).

Products costing $486,100 to produce were sold for $750,000 during 19xx. Only the costs of the goods sold affect the Finished Goods Inventory account.

Finished Goods Inventory Account

Balance 1/1/xx: $70,000	Sold during 19xx: $486,100
Completed during 19xx: 492,600	
Balance 12/31/xx $76,500	

Cost of Goods Sold Account

Sold during 19xx: $486,100	

balance in the Finished Goods Inventory account is made up of the costs of products completed but unsold as of that date.

Manufacturing Cost Flow

Product costing, inventory valuation, and financial reporting depend on a defined, structured flow of manufacturing costs. This **manufacturing cost flow** was outlined in the discussion of the three manufacturing inventory accounts. Figure 2-5 sums up the entire cost-flow process as it relates to accounts in the general ledger. At this point do not worry about the actual journal entries needed to make this cost flow operational. These entries will be illustrated in Chapter 3.

Here we will concentrate on the general pattern of manufacturing cost flow, as shown in Figure 2-6 on page 55. The cost flow begins with costs being incurred. Manufacturing costs start in many ways. They may be cash payments, incurred liabilities, fixed asset depreciation, or expired prepaid expenses. Once these costs have been incurred, they are recorded as either direct materials, direct labor, or factory overhead costs. As the resources are used up, the company transfers its costs to the Work in Process Inventory account. When production is completed, costs assigned to finished units are transferred to the Finished Goods Inventory account. In much the same way, costs attached to units sold are transferred to the Cost of Goods Sold account. Before going on, compare the cost flow as it moves through the general ledger accounts in Figure 2-5 with the general pattern shown in Figure 2-6. Both figures show the same type of cost flow.

The Manufacturing Statement

Financial statements of manufacturing companies differ little from those of merchandising companies. Depending on the industry, the account titles found on the balance sheet (statement of financial position) are the same in most corporations. (Examples include Cash, Accounts Receivable, Buildings, Machinery, Accounts Payable, and Capital Stock.) Even the income statements for a merchandiser and a manufacturer are similar. However, a closer look shows that the heading Cost of Goods Manufactured is used in place of the Purchases account. Also, the Merchandise Inventory account is replaced by Finished Goods Inventory. Note these differences on the income statement of the Windham Company (Exhibit 2-1 on page 56).

The key to preparing an income statement for a manufacturing company is to determine the cost of goods manufactured. This dollar amount is the end result of a special manufacturing statement, the statement of cost of goods manufactured, which is prepared to support the figure on the income statement.

Figure 2-5. Manufacturing Cost Flow: An Example

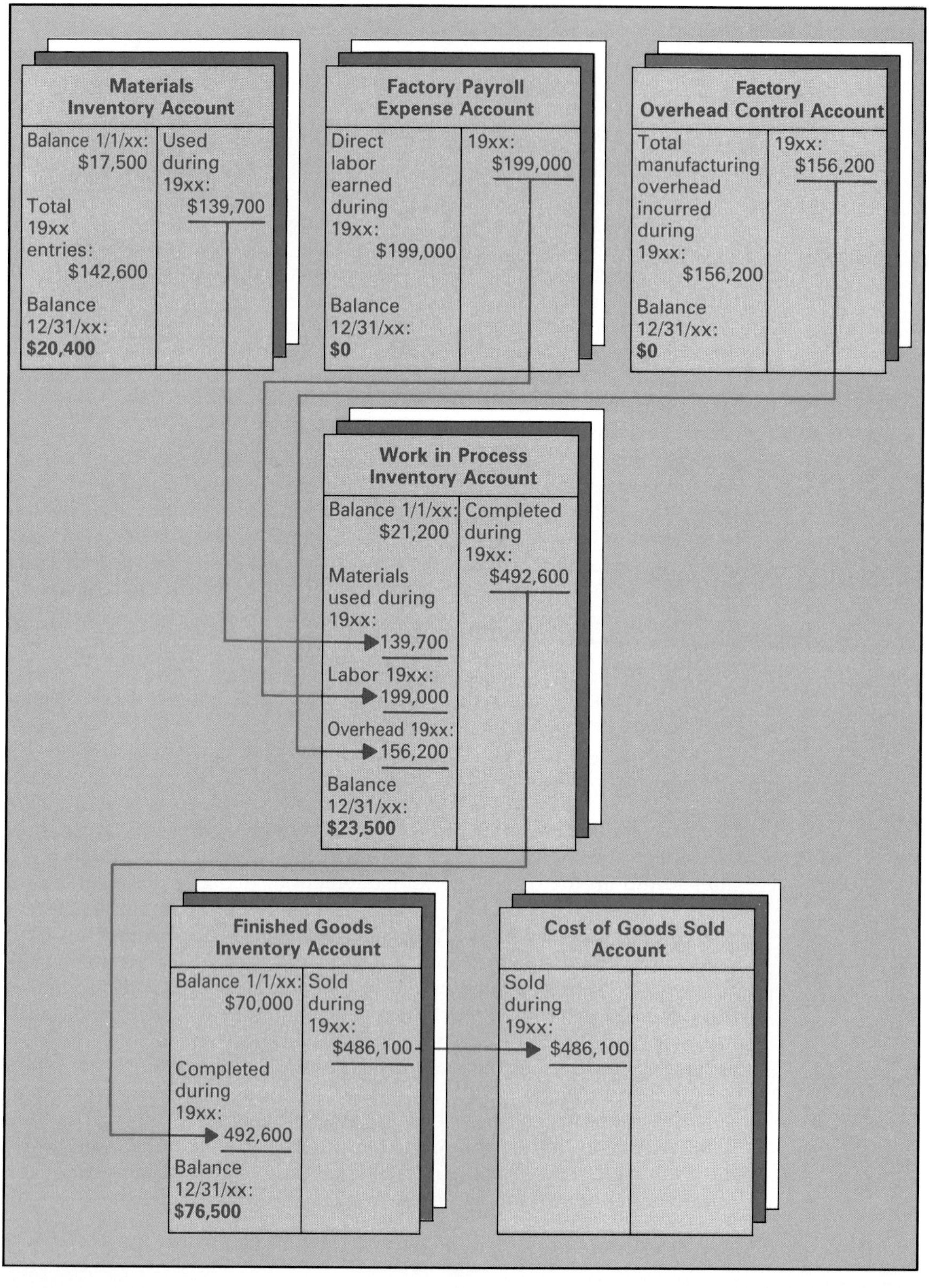

Materials Inventory Account	
Balance 1/1/xx: $17,500	Used during 19xx: $139,700
Total 19xx entries: $142,600	
Balance 12/31/xx: **$20,400**	

Factory Payroll Expense Account	
Direct labor earned during 19xx: $199,000	19xx: $199,000
Balance 12/31/xx: **$0**	

Factory Overhead Control Account	
Total manufacturing overhead incurred during 19xx: $156,200	19xx: $156,200
Balance 12/31/xx: **$0**	

Work in Process Inventory Account	
Balance 1/1/xx: $21,200	Completed during 19xx: $492,600
Materials used during 19xx: 139,700	
Labor 19xx: 199,000	
Overhead 19xx: 156,200	
Balance 12/31/xx: **$23,500**	

Finished Goods Inventory Account	
Balance 1/1/xx: $70,000	Sold during 19xx: $486,100
Completed during 19xx: 492,600	
Balance 12/31/xx: **$76,500**	

Cost of Goods Sold Account	
Sold during 19xx: $486,100	

Figure 2-6. Manufacturing Cost Flow: Basic Concepts

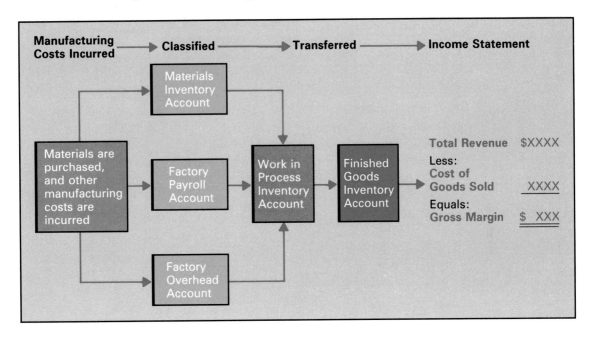

Statement of Cost of Goods Manufactured

OBJECTIVE 6

Prepare a statement of cost of goods manufactured

The flow of manufacturing costs, shown in Figures 2-2 through 2-6, provides the basis for accounting for manufacturing costs. In this process all manufacturing costs incurred are considered product costs. They are used to compute ending inventory balances and cost of goods sold. The costs flowing from one account to another during the year have been combined into one number in the illustrations to help show the basic idea. In fact, hundreds of transactions occur during a year, and each transaction affects part of the cost flow process. At the end of the year, the flow of all manufacturing costs incurred during the year is summarized in the **statement of cost of goods manufactured**. This statement gives the dollar amount of costs for products completed and moved to Finished Goods Inventory during the year. The amount for cost of goods manufactured should be the same as the amount transferred from the Work in Process Inventory account to the Finished Goods Inventory account during the year.

The statement of cost of goods manufactured is shown in Exhibit 2-2 on page 57. Even though this statement is rather complex, it can be pieced together in three steps. The *first step* is to compute the cost of materials used. Add the materials purchases for the period to the beginning balance in the Materials Inventory account. This subtotal represents the cost of materials available for use during the year. Then subtract the balance of the ending Materials Inventory from the cost of materials available for use. The difference is the cost of materials used during the accounting period.

Exhibit 2-1. Income Statement for a Manufacturing Company		

Windham Company
Income Statement
For the Year Ended December 31, 19xx

Net Sales		$750,000
Cost of Goods Sold		
Finished Goods Inventory, Jan. 1, 19xx	$ 70,000	
Cost of Goods Manufactured (Exhibit 2-2)	492,600	
Total Cost of Finished Goods Available for Sale	562,600	
Less Finished Goods Inventory, Dec. 31, 19xx	76,500	
Cost of Goods Sold		486,100
Gross Margin from Sales		263,900
Operating Expenses		
Selling Expenses		
Salaries and Commissions	$46,500	
Advertising	19,500	
Other Selling Expenses	7,400	
Total Selling Expenses		73,400
General and Administrative Expenses		
Administrative Salaries	$65,000	
Franchise and Property Taxes	72,000	
Other General and Administrative Expenses	11,300	
Total General and Administrative Expenses	148,300	
Total Operating Expenses		221,700
Income from Operations		42,200
Less Interest Expense		4,600
Net Income Before Taxes		37,600
Income Taxes Expense		11,548
Net Income		$ 26,052

Computation of Cost of Materials Used

Beginning Balance: Materials Inventory	$ 17,500
Plus Materials Purchases (net)	142,600
Cost of Materials Available for Use	$160,100
Less Ending Balance: Materials Inventory	20,400
Cost of Materials Used	$139,700

Exhibit 2-2. Statement of Cost of Goods Manufactured

Windham Company
Statement of Cost of Goods Manufactured
For the Year Ended December 31, 19xx

	Materials Used		
	Materials Inventory, Jan. 1, 19xx	$ 17,500	
	Materials Purchases (net)	142,600	
Step	Cost of Materials Available for		
One	Use	$160,100	
	Less Materials Inventory,		
	December 31, 19xx	20,400	
	Cost of Materials Used		$139,700
	Direct Labor		199,000
	Factory Overhead Costs		
	Indirect Labor	$ 46,400	
	Power	25,200	
Step	Depreciation Expense, Machinery		
Two	and Equipment	14,800	
	Depreciation Expense,		
	Factory Building	16,200	
	Small Tools Expense	2,700	
	Factory Insurance Expense	1,600	
	Supervision Expense	37,900	
	Other Factory Costs	11,400	
	Total Factory Overhead Costs		156,200
	Total Manufacturing Costs		$494,900
	Add Work in Process Inventory,		
	January 1, 19xx		21,200
Step	Total Cost of Work in Process During		
Three	the Year		$516,100
	Less Work in Process Inventory,		
	December 31, 19xx		23,500
	Cost of Goods Manufactured		$492,600

Before going to the next step, trace these numbers back to the Materials Inventory account in Figure 2-2 to see how that account is related to the statement of cost of goods manufactured.

Calculating total manufacturing costs for the year is the *second step*. As shown in Figure 2-3, the costs of materials used and direct labor are added to total factory overhead costs incurred during the year. This step is shown on the following page as well as in Exhibit 2-2.

Computation of Total Manufacturing Costs

Cost of Materials Used	$139,700
Plus Direct Labor Costs	199,000
Plus Total Factory Overhead Costs	156,200
Total Manufacturing Costs	$494,900

The *third step* shown in Exhibit 2-2 changes total manufacturing costs into total cost of goods manufactured for the year. Add the beginning Work in Process Inventory balance to total manufacturing costs for the period to arrive at the total cost of work in process during the year. From this amount subtract the ending Work in Process Inventory balance for the year to get the cost of goods manufactured.

Computation of Cost of Goods Manufactured

Total Manufacturing Costs	$494,900
Plus Beginning Balance: Work in Process Inventory	21,200
Total Cost of Work in Process During the Year	$516,100
Less Ending Balance: Work in Process Inventory	23,500
Cost of Goods Manufactured	$492,600

The term *total manufacturing costs* must not be confused with the cost of goods manufactured. **Total manufacturing costs** are the total costs for materials used, direct labor, and factory overhead incurred and charged to production during an accounting period. **Cost of goods manufactured** consists of the total manufacturing costs attached to units of a product *completed* during an accounting period. To understand the difference between these two dollar amounts, review the computation just shown. Total manufacturing costs of $494,900 incurred during the current year are added to the beginning balance in Work in Process Inventory. Costs of $21,200 in the beginning balance, by definition, are costs from an earlier period. The costs of two accounting periods are now being mixed to arrive at the total cost of work in process during the year, or $516,100. The costs of ending products still in process ($23,500) are then subtracted from the total cost of work in process during the year. The remainder, $492,600, is the cost of goods manufactured (completed) during the year. It is assumed that the items in beginning inventory were completed first. Costs attached to the ending Work in Process Inventory are part of the current period's total manufacturing costs. But they will not become part of the cost of goods manufactured until the next accounting period when the products are completed.

Cost of Goods Sold and the Income Statement

Exhibits 2-1 and 2-2 demonstrate the relationship between the statement of cost of goods manufactured and the income statement. The total amount of cost of goods manufactured during the period is carried over to the income statement. There it is used to compute cost of goods sold.

OBJECTIVE 7
*Prepare an
income
statement for a
manufacturing
company*

The cost of goods manufactured is added to the beginning balance of Finished Goods Inventory to get the total cost of finished goods available for sale during the period. The cost of goods sold is then computed by subtracting the ending balance in Finished Goods Inventory (cost of goods completed but unsold) from the total cost of finished goods available for sale. Cost of goods sold is considered an expense for the period in which the related products were sold.

Computation of Cost of Goods Sold

Beginning Balance: Finished Goods Inventory	$ 70,000
Plus Cost of Goods Manufactured	492,600
Total Cost of Finished Goods Available for Sale	$562,600
Less Ending Balance: Finished Goods Inventory	76,500
Cost of Goods Sold	$486,100

Note that the above computation is similar to the computation of cost of goods sold in the income statement in Exhibit 2-1. The other parts of the income statement in Exhibit 2-1 should be familiar from discussions in your financial accounting course.

Product Costs in a Service-oriented Business

OBJECTIVE 8
*Apply cost
classification
concepts to a
service-oriented
business*

Costs are classified as product or period costs for many reasons, including: (1) to determine the unit manufacturing costs so that inventories can be valued and selling prices created and verified; (2) to report production costs on the income statement; and (3) to analyze costs for control purposes. When someone shifts from a manufacturing environment to a service-oriented environment, the only major difference is that he or she is no longer dealing with a physical product that can be assembled, stored, and valued. Services are rendered and cannot be stored up or placed in a vault.

So how does this affect the types of cost classifications? Only one cost classification is affected, *the materials costs*. No longer is something being made from a type of material. Rendering a loan service, representing someone in a court of law, selling an insurance policy, or computing a person's taxes are typical services performed by professionals. If you were asked to compute the unit cost of one of these services, what types of costs would you be dealing with?

The most important cost would be the professional labor involved, and the same definition is applicable; that is, the direct labor cost must be traceable to the service rendered. In addition to the labor cost, any type of business, whether it is manufacturing, service, or not-for-profit, will incur various overhead costs. In a service business those overhead costs associated with and incurred for the purpose of offering a service are classified as service overhead (like factory overhead) and, along with professional labor costs, are considered service costs (like product costs) rather than period costs.

As an example, assume that the Loan Department at the Orange Bank of Commerce wants to determine the total costs incurred in processing a typical loan application. Its policy for the past five years has been to charge a $150 fee for processing a home-loan application. Ms. Kim Lazar, chief loan officer, thinks the fee is far too low. Considering the way operating costs have soared in the past five years, she proposes that the fee be doubled. You have been asked to compute the cost of processing a typical home-loan application.

The following information concerning the processing of a loan application has been given to you:

Direct Professional Labor:
  Loan Processor's Monthly Salary:

4 people at $3,000 each	$12,000

Indirect Monthly Loan Department Overhead Costs:

Chief Loan Officer's Salary	$ 4,500
Telephone Expense	750
Depreciation, Building	2,800
Depreciation, Equipment	1,750
Depreciation, Automobiles	1,200
Legal Advice	2,460
Legal Forms/Supplies	320
Customer Relations	640
Credit Check Function	1,980
Advertising	440
Internal Audit Function	2,400
Utilities Expense	1,690
Clerical Personnel	3,880
Miscellaneous	290
Total Overhead Costs	$25,100

In addition, you discover that all appraisal and title search activities are performed by people outside the bank, and their fees are treated as separate loan costs. One hundred home-loan applications are usually processed each month.

The Loan Department performs several functions in addition to home-loan application tasks. Roughly one-half of the department is involved in loan collection activities. After determining how many of the processed loans were not home loans, you conclude that only 25 percent of the overhead costs of the Loan Department were applicable to the processing of home-loan applications. A computation for the cost of processing one home-loan application is given below.

Direct Professional Labor Cost:

$12,000 ÷ 100	$120.00

Service Overhead Cost:

$25,100 × 25% ÷ 100	62.75
Total Processing Cost Per Loan	$182.75

Finally, you conclude that the loan officer was correct; the present fee does not cover the current costs of processing a typical home-loan application. However, doubling the loan fee seems inappropriate. To allow for a profit margin, the loan fee could be raised to $225 or $250.

Chapter Review

Review of Learning Objectives

1. **State the differences between the three manufacturing cost elements: (a) direct materials costs; (b) direct labor costs; and (c) factory overhead costs.**
   Direct materials are materials and parts that become part of the finished product and can be conveniently and economically traced to specific product units. Direct labor costs include all labor costs for specific work performed on products that can be conveniently and economically traced to end products. All other production-related costs are classified and accounted for as factory overhead costs. These costs cannot be practically or conveniently traced to end products, so they must be assigned to the products by some cost allocation method. The classifying of manufacturing costs into the three elements described above is important for product costing, inventory valuation, and product pricing.

2. **Identify the source documents used to collect information on manufacturing cost accumulation.**
   Purchase requisitions list the items or materials needed by the production departments. The purchasing department then uses the purchase order to order the items. When the items or materials come in from vendors, the receiving report is used to identify the items and to match them against purchase orders to ensure that the correct items were received. The materials requisition is used to request items and to prove that items or materials were issued into the production process. Timecards record each employee's daily starting and finishing times. Job cards record time spent by each employee on each job. Job cards are matched against timecards to verify the time worked by each employee and to control labor time per job.

3. **Compute a product's unit cost.**
   The unit cost of a product is made up of the costs of materials, labor, and factory overhead. These three cost components are accumulated for a batch of products as they are produced. When the batch has been completed, the number of units produced is divided into the total costs incurred to determine product unit cost.

4. **Distinguish between product costs and period costs.**
   Product costs consist of the three manufacturing cost elements: direct materials, direct labor, and factory overhead. Such costs are incurred in making products and can be inventoried. Period costs are costs that cannot be inventoried and are linked to services consumed during the period, such as selling and administrative expenses.

5. **Describe the nature, contents, and flow of costs through the Materials, Work in Process, and Finished Goods inventory accounts.**
The flow of costs through inventory accounts begins when costs are incurred for materials, direct labor, and factory overhead. Materials costs flow first into the Materials Inventory account. This account is used to record the costs of materials when they are received and again when they are issued for use in a company's production process. All manufacturing-related costs—materials, direct labor, and factory overhead—are recorded in the Work in Process Inventory account as they enter the production process. When products are completed, their costs are transferred from the Work in Process Inventory account to the Finished Goods Inventory account. Costs remain in the Finished Goods Inventory account until the products are sold. At that time their costs are transferred to the Cost of Goods Sold account.

6. **Prepare a statement of cost of goods manufactured.**
Preparing a statement of cost of goods manufactured involves three steps. The first is to compute the cost of materials used. Total materials purchases are added to the beginning balance of Materials Inventory to arrive at the cost of materials available for use. From this amount the ending Materials Inventory balance is subtracted to get the cost of materials used. The second step is to compute the total manufacturing costs for the period. Costs of direct labor and factory overhead are added to the cost of materials used to arrive at this amount. The third step is to compute the cost of goods manufactured. Total manufacturing costs and the beginning balance in the Work in Process Inventory account are added. Their sum is called total cost of work in process during the year. By subtracting the ending Work in Process Inventory balance from total cost of work in process, you get the cost of goods manufactured.

7. **Prepare an income statement for a manufacturing company.**
The major change to make in preparing an income statement for a manufacturing company is the requirement that the cost of goods manufactured be determined before the cost of goods sold is computed. Cost of goods manufactured is added to the beginning balance of Finished Goods Inventory to arrive at the total cost of finished goods available for sale. When the ending balance of Finished Goods Inventory (cost of unsold goods) is subtracted from the total cost of goods available for sale, the difference represents the costs attached to the goods sold.

8. **Apply cost classification concepts to a service-oriented business.**
Most types of costs incurred by a manufacturer and called product costs are also incurred by a service-oriented company. The only major difference is that you are no longer dealing with a physical product that can be assembled, stored, and valued. Services are rendered and cannot be stored up or placed in a vault. Only the materials cost classification is affected when applying the various cost classifications to service companies. To determine the cost of performing a particular service, professional labor and service-related overhead costs are included in the analysis.

Review of Concepts and Terminology

The following important concepts were introduced in this chapter:

(L.O. 1)   **Direct costs:** Manufacturing costs that are traceable to specific products.

(L.O. 1)   **Indirect costs:** Manufacturing costs that are not traceable to specific products.

(L.O.1)   **Direct materials:**   Materials that become part of the finished product and can be conveniently and economically traced to specific product units.

(L.O.1)   **Indirect materials:**   Minor materials and other production supplies that cannot be conveniently or economically traced to specific products.

(L.O.2)   **Direct labor:**   Labor costs for specific work performed on products that can be conveniently and economically traced to end products.

(L.O.2)   **Indirect labor:**   Labor costs for production-related activities that cannot be connected with or conveniently and economically traced to end products.

(L.O.2)   **Net payroll:**   The amount paid to the employee after all payroll deductions have been subtracted from gross wages.

(L.O.2)   **Gross payroll:**   A measure of the total wages and salaries earned by employees, including payroll deductions.

(L.O.2)   **Factory overhead:**   A varied collection of production-related costs that cannot be practically or conveniently traced to end products.

(L.O.2)   **Variable manufacturing costs:**   Costs that increase or decrease in direct proportion to the number of units produced.

(L.O.2)   **Fixed manufacturing costs:**   Production costs that stay fairly constant during the accounting period.

(L.O.4)   **Product costs:**   Costs consisting of three manufacturing cost elements—direct materials, direct labor, and factory overhead.

(L.O.4)   **Period costs (expenses):**   Costs that cannot be inventoried.

(L.O.5)   **Materials Inventory:**   An account, also called the Stores and Materials Inventory Control account, made up of the balances of materials and supplies on hand.

(L.O.5)   **Work in Process Inventory:**   All manufacturing costs incurred and assigned to products being produced.

(L.O.5)   **Finished Goods Inventory:**   An inventory account unique to the manufacturing or production area to which the costs assigned to all completed products are transferred.

(L.O.5)   **Manufacturing cost flow:**   The defined or structured flow of direct materials, direct labor, and manufacturing overhead costs from their incurrence through the inventory accounts and finally to the Cost of Goods Sold account.

(L.O.6)   **Statement of cost of goods manufactured:**   Formal statement summarizing the flow of all manufacturing costs incurred during a period.

(L.O.6)   **Total manufacturing costs:**   The total costs for materials used, direct labor, and factory overhead incurred and charged to production during an accounting period.

(L.O.6)   **Cost of goods manufactured:**   The total manufacturing costs attached to units of a product completed during an accounting period.

Other important terms introduced in this chapter are:

job cards (p. 44)
materials requisition (p. 43)
purchase order (p. 43)
purchase requisition or purchase request (p. 42)
receiving report (p. 43)
timecard (p. 44)

Review Problem
Cost of Goods Manufactured—Three Fundamental Steps

The management of the Augustana Company requires the controller to prepare a statement of cost of goods manufactured in addition to the year-end balance sheet and income statement. During 19x8, $405,625 of materials were purchased. Operating data and inventory account balances for 19x8 follow:

Account	Balance
Direct Labor: 31,420 hours at $8.50/hour	$267,070
Plant Supervision	52,500
Indirect Labor: 62,280 hours at $5.25/hour	326,970
Factory Insurance	8,100
Utilities	29,220
Depreciation, Factory Building	46,200
Depreciation, Equipment	42,800
Manufacturing Supplies	9,460
Repairs and Maintenance	14,980
Selling and Administrative Expenses	96,480
Materials Inventory, Jan. 1, 19x8	94,210
Work in Process Inventory, Jan. 1, 19x8	101,640
Finished Goods Inventory, Jan. 1, 19x8	148,290
Materials Inventory, Dec. 31, 19x8	96,174
Work in Process Inventory, Dec. 31, 19x8	100,400
Finished Goods Inventory, Dec. 31, 19x8	141,100

Required

To review the three basic steps for computing cost of goods manufactured, do the following:

1. Prepare a schedule showing the calculation of the cost of materials used during the year.
2. Given the cost of materials used, develop an analysis to find total manufacturing costs for the year.
3. Given total manufacturing costs for the year, prepare an analysis to find the cost of goods manufactured during the year.

Answer to Review Problem

1. Computation of cost of materials used:

Beginning Balance: Materials Inventory	$ 94,210
Plus Materials Purchases	405,625
Cost of Materials Available for Use	$ 499,835
Less Ending Balance: Materials Inventory	96,174
Cost of Materials Used	$ 403,661

2. Computation of total manufacturing costs:

Cost of Materials Used		$ 403,661
Plus Direct Labor		267,070
Plus Factory Overhead Cost:		
Plant Supervision	$ 52,500	
Indirect Labor	326,970	
Factory Insurance	8,100	
Utilities	29,220	
Depreciation, Factory Building	46,200	
Depreciation, Equipment	42,800	
Manufacturing Supplies	9,460	
Repairs and Maintenance	14,980	
Total Factory Overhead Costs		530,230
Total Manufacturing Costs		$1,200,961

3. Computation of cost of goods manufactured:

Total Manufacturing Costs	$1,200,961
Plus Beginning Balance: Work in Process Inventory	101,640
Total Cost of Work in Process During the Year	$1,302,601
Less Ending Balance: Work in Process Inventory	100,400
Cost of Goods Manufactured	$1,202,201

Chapter Assignments

Questions

1. What are the three kinds of costs included in a product's cost?
2. What is the difference between a period cost and a product cost?
3. Define a direct cost. How is it different from an indirect cost?
4. Define direct materials.
5. Describe the following: purchase requisition (request), purchase order, and receiving report.
6. How is direct labor different from indirect labor?
7. What are the two kinds of labor-related costs? Discuss each one.
8. What characteristics identify a cost as being part of factory overhead?
9. What is meant by cost behavior?
10. How does the periodic inventory method differ from the perpetual inventory method?
11. Identify and describe the three inventory accounts used by a manufacturing company.
12. What is meant by manufacturing cost flow?
13. Describe how to compute the cost of materials used.
14. How do total manufacturing costs differ from the cost of goods manufactured?

15. How is the cost of goods manufactured used in computing the cost of goods sold?
16. "The concept of product costs is not applicable to service-oriented companies." Is this statement correct? Defend your answer.
17. Since service-oriented companies do not maintain Work in Process and Finished Goods inventories, what use do they have for unit cost information?
18. Identify two types of service companies, state their primary services, and discuss a method that could control the costs of these services.

Classroom Exercises

Exercise 2-1.
Manufacturing Cost Flow
(L.O. 1, 2, 5)

Using the ideas illustrated in Figures 2-5 and 2-6 and discussed in this chapter, describe in detail the flow of materials costs through the recording process of a cost accounting system. Include in your answer all general ledger accounts affected and all recording documents used. Prepare your answer in proper order.

Exercise 2-2.
Documentation
(L.O. 2)

Rolla Company manufactures a complete line of music boxes. Seventy percent of its products are standard items produced in long production runs. The remaining thirty percent are special orders, involving requests for specific tunes. These special-order boxes cost from three to six times more than the standard product because additional materials and labor are used.

Shawna Lynne, controller, recently received a complaint memorandum from Mr. Heinrichshaus, production supervisor, about the new network of source documents being added to the cost accounting system. These new documents include a materials purchase requisition, a purchase order form, a materials receiving report, and a materials use requisition. Mr. Heinrichshaus claims these forms create extra "busy work" and interrupt the normal flow of production.

Prepare a written response from Ms. Lynne, fully explaining the purpose of each document.

Exercise 2-3.
Cost Classification
(L.O. 4)

The following is a list of typical costs incurred by a garment maker: (a) gasoline and oil for salesperson's automobile; (b) telephone charges; (c) dyes for yardage; (d) seamstresses' regular hourly labor; (e) thread; (f) president's subscription to *The Wall Street Journal*; (g) sales commissions; (h) business forms used in the office; (i) buttons and zippers; (j) depreciation of sewing machines; (k) property taxes on the factory; (l) advertising; (m) brand labels; (n) administrative salaries; (o) interest on business loans; (p) starch and fabric conditioners; (q) patterns; (r) hourly workers' vacation pay; (s) roof repair to office; (t) packaging.

1. At the time these costs are incurred, which ones will be classified as period costs? Which ones will be treated as product costs?
2. Of the costs identified as product costs, which are direct costs? Which are indirect costs?

Exercise 2-4.
Unit Cost Determination
(L.O. 3)

The Reis Winery is one of the finest and oldest wineries in the country. One of its most famous products is an exquisite red table wine called Leon Millot. This wine is made from Leon Millot grapes grown in Missouri's Ozark region. Recently, management has become concerned about the increasing cost of making

Leon Millot and needs to find out if the current $9 per bottle selling price is adequate. The following information is given to you for analysis:

Batch size:	10,550 bottles

Costs:	
Materials:	
Leon Millot Grapes	$16,880
Chancellor Grapes	4,220
Bottles	5,275
Labor:	
Pickers/Loaders	2,110
Crusher	422
Processors	9,495
Bottler	633
Storage and Racking	11,605
Production overhead:	
Depreciation, Equipment	2,743
Depreciation, Building	5,275
Utilities	1,055
Indirect Labor	6,330
Supervision	9,495
Supplies	3,165
Storage Fixtures	2,532
Chemicals	2,110
Repairs	1,477
Miscellaneous	633
Total production costs	$85,455

1. Compute the unit cost per bottle for materials, labor, and production overhead.
2. What would you advise company management regarding the price per bottle of Leon Millot wine? Defend your answer.

Exercise 2-5.
Concept of Three Types of Inventories
(L.O. 5)

"For manufacturing companies the concept of inventories must be expanded to include three types: Materials Inventory, Work in Process Inventory, and Finished Goods Inventory."

Briefly explain how the three inventory accounts function and how they relate to each other.

Exercise 2-6.
Cost of Materials Used
(L.O. 6)

Data for the cost of materials for the month that ended July 31, 19xx, are as follows: Materials Inventory on July 1, 19xx, was $34,200, and Materials Inventory on July 31, 19xx, totaled $41,910. During July the company purchased $120,600 in materials on account from Angels Company and $42,200 in materials for cash from Mets Company. In addition, $60,000 was paid on the Angels account balance.

Compute the cost of materials used during July 19xx.

Exercise 2-7.
Periodic Versus
Perpetual
Inventory Methods
(L.O. 5)

1. In as much detail as possible, discuss the differences between the periodic and the perpetual inventory methods. Be sure to describe the kinds of businesses that might use each method.
2. Would the periodic or perpetual inventory method be more suitable for each business listed below? Be able to defend your answers.

a. Home appliance retailer
b. Grocery store
c. Computer hardware company
d. Retailer of fine jewelry
e. Sporting goods store
f. Grain elevator
g. Discount department store
h. Auto parts store
i. Pool supplies store
j. Paper manufacturer
k. Fertilizer manufacturer
l. Tire manufacturer
m. Cosmetics outlet for exclusive distributorship
n. Car dealer
o. Office supplies store

Exercise 2-8.
Computing
Total Manu-
facturing Costs
(L.O. 6)

The partial trial balance of Waring Millinery, Inc., is shown below. Inventory accounts still reflect balances at the beginning of the period. Period-end balances are $57,000, $85,800, and $36,200 for Materials Inventory, Work in Process Inventory, and Finished Goods Inventory respectively.

	Debit	Credit
Accounts Receivable	$157,420	
Materials Inventory	68,400	
Work in Process Inventory	74,400	
Finished Goods Inventory	41,400	
Accounts Payable		$ 89,250
Sales		911,940
Purchases	301,600	
Direct Labor	191,200	
Operating Supplies Expense, Factory	21,700	
Depreciation Expense, Machinery	54,100	
Fire Loss	82,000	
Insurance Expense, Factory	9,700	
Indirect Labor Expense	56,900	
Supervisory Salaries, Factory	32,700	
President's Salary	39,900	
Property Tax Expense, Factory	9,400	
Other Indirect Manufacturing Expenses	26,500	

From the above information, prepare a schedule (in good form) for computing total manufacturing costs for the period ending May 31, 19xx.

Exercise 2-9.
Statement of Cost
of Goods
Manufactured
(L.O. 6)

Information on the manufacturing costs incurred by the Ferrigno Company for the month ended August 31, 19xx, is as follows:

Purchases of materials during August were $49,000.
Direct labor was 10,400 hours at $5.75 per hour.

These factory overhead costs were incurred: Utilities, $2,870; Supervision, $18,600; Indirect Supplies, $6,000; Depreciation, $5,200; Insurance, $830; and Miscellaneous, $700.

Inventories on August 1 were as follows: Materials, $58,600; Work in Process, $53,250; Finished Goods, $40,500.

Inventories on August 31 were as follows: Materials, $60,100; Work in Process, $47,400; Finished Goods, $42,450.

From the information given, prepare a statement of cost of goods manufactured.

Exercise 2-10.
Computing Cost of
Goods Sold
(L.O. 6, 7)

Rosati Distilleries, Inc., produces a deluxe line of wines and beverages. During 19xx, the company operated at record levels with sales totaling $965,000. The accounting department has already determined that total manufacturing costs for the period were $455,500. Operating expenses for the year were $199,740. Inventory balances were as follows:

	Jan. 1, 19xx	Dec. 31, 19xx
Materials Inventory	$35,490	$28,810
Work in Process Inventory	67,400	51,980
Finished Goods Inventory	94,820	79,320

Assuming a 34 percent tax rate, prepare an income statement for the year ended December 31, 19xx.

Exercise 2-11.
Cost Accounting
for a Service-
oriented Business
(L.O. 8)

Preparing appraisals of both residential and commercial real estate is the main function of Abbey Appraisers, Inc. Most of its procedures are similar in time and nature for each class of property appraised. Dana Abbey, president of the company, is concerned about increased costs and the apparent need to increase appraisal fees. For the current year the company charges $450 for a residential appraisal and $900 for a commercial appraisal.

The following information pertains to the month of August 19x9, which has just ended:

Professional Labor			Depreciation,	
Appraisers			Office Equipment	470
Two at 160 hours			Automobile Expenses	282
at $24/hour	$7,680		Supervision	1,880
Apprentices			Library Maintenance	
Three at 180 hours			and Update	564
at $10/hour	5,400		Telephone Expense	376
Appraisal Overhead			Valuation Service	1,128
Clerical Staff	1,551		Equipment Repairs	517
Forms and Supplies	282		Liability Insurance	1,316
Utilities	423		Outside Consultants	658
Depreciation, Automobile	752		Miscellaneous	235
Depreciation, Building	329			

During August, 34 residential and 30 commercial appraisals were completed. Expected hours are as follows:

	Residential	Commercial
Appraisers	3.5 hours	7.0 hours
Apprentices	5.0 hours	10.0 hours

Overhead is normally apportioned to residential and commercial jobs on a one-third to two-thirds basis respectively.

1. Determine if Abbey Appraisers, Inc., made a profit during August.
2. Should the appraisal fees be increased? If so, by how much?

Interpreting Accounting Information

**Gregor
Manufacturing
Company**
(L.O. 6, 7)

Gregor Manufacturing Company manufactures sheet-metal products for heating and air conditioning installations. For the past several years its income has declined, and this past year, 19x9, was particularly bad. The company's statements of cost of goods manufactured and its income statements for 19x8 and 19x9 are shown below and on the next page. You have been asked to comment on the company's profit situation and to give reasons for its deterioration.

Gregor Manufacturing Company Statement of Cost of Goods Manufactured For the Years Ended December 31, 19x9 and 19x8				
	19x9		**19x8**	
Materials Used				
Materials Inventory, January 1	$ 89,660		$ 92,460	
Materials Purchases	789,640		760,040	
Cost of Materials Available for Use	$879,300		$852,500	
Less Materials Inventory, December 31	94,930		89,660	
Cost of Materials Used		$ 784,370		$ 762,840
Direct Labor		871,410		879,720
Factory Overhead Costs				
Indirect Labor	$ 82,660		$ 71,980	
Power Expense	34,990		32,550	
Insurance Expense	22,430		18,530	
Supervision	125,330		120,050	
Depreciation Expense	75,730		72,720	
Other Factory Expenses	41,740		36,280	
Total Factory Overhead Costs		382,880		352,110
Total Manufacturing Costs		$2,038,660		$1,994,670
Add Work in Process Inventory, January 1		148,875		152,275
Total Cost of Work in Process During the Year		$2,187,535		$2,146,945
Less Work in Process Inventory, December 31		146,750		148,875
Cost of Goods Manufactured		$2,040,785		$1,998,070

Gregor Manufacturing Company Income Statement For the Years Ended December 31, 19x9 and 19x8				
		19x9		19x8
Net Sales		$3,442,960		$3,496,220
Cost of Goods Sold				
Finished Goods Inventory, January 1	$ 192,640		$ 184,820	
Cost of Goods Manufactured	2,040,785		1,998,070	
Total Cost of Finished Goods Available for Sale	$2,233,425		$2,182,890	
Less Finished Goods Inventory, December 31	186,630		192,640	
Cost of Goods Sold		2,046,795		1,990,250
Gross Margin from Sales		$1,396,165		$1,505,970
Operating Expenses				
Sales Salaries and Commissions Expense	$ 494,840		$ 429,480	
Advertising Expense	216,110		194,290	
Other Selling Expenses	82,680		72,930	
Administrative Expenses	342,600		295,530	
Total Operating Expenses		1,136,230		992,230
Income from Operations		$ 259,935		$ 513,740
Other Revenues and Expenses				
Interest Expense		54,160		56,815
Net Income Before Taxes		$ 205,775		$ 456,925
Income Taxes Expense (34 percent)		69,964		155,355
Net Income		$ 135,811		$ 301,570

Required

1. In preparing your comments, compute the following ratios for each year:
   a. Ratios of cost of materials used to total manufacturing costs, direct labor to total manufacturing costs, and total factory overhead to total manufacturing costs.
   b. Ratios of gross margin from sales to sales, operating expenses to sales, and net income to sales.
2. From your evaluation of ratios computed in **1**, state the probable causes of the decline in net income.
3. What other factors or ratios do you believe should be considered?

Problem Set A

Problem 2A-1.
Unit Cost
Computation
(L.O. 3)

ERV Industries, Inc., manufactures videodiscs for several leading recording studios in the United States and Europe. Department 1401 is responsible for the electronic circuitry in each disc. Some parts are purchased from outside vendors; others are produced internally. Department 1211 applies the plastic-like surface to the discs and packages them for shipment.

A recent order for 2,000 discs from the SAM Company was produced during July. Parts other than the direct materials used in the production and assembly processes were purchased for this job from UMSL Corporation. Those parts cost $3,960. Also, department 1401 incurred the following costs for this job: direct materials used, $1,300; direct labor, $1,680; and factory overhead, $1,460. Costs incurred by Department 1211 included: $1,120 in direct materials used; $420 in direct labor; and $600 in factory overhead. All 2,000 units were completed and shipped during the month.

Required

1. Compute the unit cost for each of the two departments.
2. Compute the total unit cost for the SAM Company order.
3. The selling price for this order was $5.30 per unit. Was the selling price adequate? List the assumptions and/or computations on which you based your answer. What suggestions would you make to ERV Industries' management concerning the pricing of future orders?

Problem 2A-2.
Factory Overhead:
Cost Flow
(L.O. 1, 2)

A working knowledge of the make-up of the cost category called factory overhead is essential to understanding the elements, purpose, and operation of a cost accounting system.

Required

1. Identify the characteristics of factory overhead.
2. Are factory overhead costs always indirect costs? Why?
3. List three examples of a factory overhead cost.
4. Diagram the flow of factory overhead costs in a manufacturing environment. List the documents used to record these costs, and link the documents to specific parts of the cost flow diagram.
5. Merlot Industries in Grapevine, California, produces oak wine barrels. The oak wood is purchased in large slabs and milled to size. Metal barrel-rings are purchased from an outside vendor. The following factory overhead costs were incurred in June: indirect mill labor, $21,420; indirect assembly labor, $18,210; administrative salaries, $8,100; depreciation expense for equipment, $2,800; factory rent, $3,400; utilities expense, $1,800; and small tools expense, $1,410.   Identify each of the above costs as either a variable cost or a fixed cost. Give reasons for your answers.

Problem 2A-3.
Cost of Goods
Manufactured:
Three Fundamental
Steps
(L.O. 6)

England Company manufactures a line of aquatic equipment, including a new gill-like device that produces oxygen from water and replaces large, cumbersome pressurized air tanks. Management requires a quarterly statement of cost of goods manufactured as well as an income statement.   As the company's accountant, you have determined the following account balances for the quarter ended October 31, 19xx:

Purchases of Materials During Quarter	$360,000
Small Tools Expense	8,240
Factory Insurance Expense	2,690
Factory Utilities Expense	7,410
Depreciation Expense, Building	16,240
Depreciation Expense, Equipment	12,990
Selling Expenses	32,600
Plant Supervisor's Salary	16,250

Direct Labor	214,700
Indirect Labor	81,400
Repairs and Maintenance, Factory	21,200
Miscellaneous Factory Overhead	14,120
Indirect Materials and Supplies, Factory	39,400
Materials Inventory, August 1, 19xx	51,600
Materials Inventory, October 31, 19xx	56,240
Work in Process Inventory, August 1, 19xx	34,020
Work in Process Inventory, October 31, 19xx	41,900
Finished Goods Inventory, August 1, 19xx	39,200
Finished Goods Inventory, October 31, 19xx	40,200

Required

Highlight the three basic steps used in preparing the statement of cost of goods manufactured by doing the following:

1. Prepare an analysis in which you calculate the cost of materials used during the quarter.
2. Using the figure calculated in **1**, prepare a schedule showing the total manufacturing costs for the quarter.
3. From the amount computed in **2**, prepare a final schedule in which you can derive the cost of goods manufactured for the quarter.

Problem 2A-4.
Statement of Cost
of Goods
Manufactured
(L.O. 6)

Wasa Manufacturing Company produces replicas of Viking ships. These models are sold at Scandinavian gift shops throughout the world. Financial records of the company show the following inventory balances on May 1, 19x7: Materials, $110,400; Work in Process, $96,250; and Finished Goods, $42,810. On April 30, 19x8, inventory balances were: Materials, $116,250; Work in Process, $87,900; and Finished Goods, $51,620.

During the 19x7–x8 fiscal year, $494,630 in materials were purchased, and payroll records indicate that direct labor costs totaled $315,970. Overhead costs for the period included: indirect materials and supplies, $27,640; indirect labor, $92,710; depreciation expense, building, $19,900; depreciation expense, equipment, $14,240; heating expense, $9,810; electricity, $8,770; repairs and maintenance expense, $5,110; liability and fire insurance expense, $2,980; property taxes, building, $3,830; design and rework expense, $16,770; and supervision expense, $95,290. Other costs for the period included shipping costs, $41,720, and administrative salaries, $102,750.

Required

Using the information provided above, prepare a statement of cost of goods manufactured for the fiscal year ended April 30, 19x8.

Problem 2A-5.
Statement
Preparation:
Manufacturing
Company
(L.O. 6, 7)

The Peach River Company produces lighting fixtures. All parts are purchased, and the primary function of the company is to assemble the fixtures. Information for the quarter ended December 31, 19x7, is shown on the following page.

During the three-month period, the company purchased $72,480 in fixtures; $21,660 in shades; $32,780 in electrical parts; and $9,460 in wire. Direct labor for the period was 16,000 hours at an average wage rate of $7.50 per hour. Factory overhead costs for the period were: indirect labor, $38,870; assembly supplies, $3,930; factory rent, $3,000; insurance expense, $940; repairs and maintenance, $3,880; and depreciation of equipment, $2,600. Total sales for the three months were $601,770, and general, selling, and administrative expenses totaled $196,820. Assume an income tax rate of 34 percent.

	October 1	December 31
Inventories:		
Materials		
Fixtures	$ 46,810	$ 52,020
Shades	16,660	15,940
Electrical parts	29,890	30,470
Wire	11,250	10,840
Work in Process	87,910	90,130
Finished Goods	106,520	101,260

Required

1. Compute the cost of each of the four materials used during the quarter.
2. Using good form, prepare a statement of cost of goods manufactured for the quarter ended December 31, 19x7.
3. Using your answer in **2,** prepare an income statement for the same period.

Problem Set B

**Problem 2B-1.
Unit Cost
Computation**
(L.O.3)

Hugo Industries has recently finished production on Job HA-32. The corporation's cost accountant is ready to calculate the unit cost for this order. Relevant information for the month ended March 31, 19xx, follows. The number of units produced was 38,480. Cost information for Department F-14 included 3,210 liters at $3.00 per liter for direct materials used, 168 hours at $8.50 per hour for direct labor incurred, and $2,514 in factory overhead. Cost data for Department G-12 included 900 liters at $5.57 per liter for direct materials used, 400 hours at $7.80 per hour for direct labor incurred, and $6,570 in factory overhead. Cost data for Department H-15 included 2,005 liters at $5.00 per liter for direct materials used, 420 hours at $8.00 per hour for direct labor incurred, and $4,711 in factory overhead. Each unit produced was processed through three departments, F-14, G-12, and H-15, in that order. There was no ending Work in Process Inventory as of March 31, 19xx.

Required

1. Compute the unit cost for each of the three departments. Carry to one-tenth of a cent.
2. Compute the total unit cost.
3. Order HA-32 was specially made for the Jessie Company. The selling price was $53,325. Determine whether the selling price was appropriate. List the assumptions or computations on which you base your answer. What advice, if any, would you offer to the management of Hugo Industries on the pricing of future orders?

**Problem 2B-2.
Direct Materials:
Cost Flow**
(L.O.1,2)

A solid working knowledge of direct materials cost is important for understanding the elements, purpose, and operation of a cost accounting system.

Required

1. Name the characteristics of direct materials and indirect materials.
2. Give at least two examples for each of the two cost categories listed in **1.**
3. Prepare a diagram showing the flow of all materials costs for a manufacturing concern. Show which documents are used to record materials costs, and relate these documents to specific parts in the cost flow diagram.
4. If a direct materials invoice for $600 is dated September 2, with terms 2/10 and n/30, how much should be paid on September 8? On September 29?

Problem 2B-3.
Cost of Goods
Manufactured:
Three Fundamental
Steps
(L.O. 6)

McGillicuddy Metallurgists, Inc., is a large manufacturing firm that prepares financial statements on a quarterly basis. Assume that you are working in the firm's accounting department. Preparing a statement of the cost of goods manufactured is one of your regular, quarterly duties. Account balances are as follows for the quarter ended March 31, 19xx:

Office Supplies Expense	$ 2,870	Small Tools Expense	$	900
Depreciation Expense, Plant and Equipment	15,230	Materials Inventory, Jan. 1, 19xx		597,950
President's Salary	26,000	Materials Inventory, Mar. 31, 19xx		615,030
Property Taxes, Office	950	Work in Process Inventory, Jan. 1, 19xx		729,840
Equipment Repairs Expense, Factory	2,290	Work in Process Inventory, Mar. 31, 19xx		715,560
Plant Supervisors' Salaries	19,750	Finished Goods Inventory, Jan. 1, 19xx		575,010
Insurance Expense, Plant and Equipment	2,040			
Direct Labor	148,310	Finished Goods Inventory, Mar. 31, 19xx		602,840
Utility Expenses, Plant	4,420	Purchases of Materials During the Quarter		1,425,330
Indirect Labor	16,000			
Manufacturing Supplies Expense	4,760			

Required

Highlight the three basic steps in preparing the statement of cost of goods manufactured by doing the following:

1. Prepare an analysis to calculate the cost of materials used during the quarter.
2. Using the figure calculated in **1,** prepare a schedule, showing the total manufacturing costs for the quarter.
3. From the figure derived in **2,** prepare a final schedule, showing cost of goods manufactured for the quarter.

Problem 2B-4.
Statement of Cost
of Goods
Manufactured
(L.O. 6)

Winemakers Andor and Tizson operate a large vineyard in California that produces a full and varied line of wines. The company, whose fiscal year begins on November 1, has just completed a record-breaking year, which ended October 31, 19x7. Production figures for this period are as follows:

Account	Nov. 1, 19x6	Oct. 31, 19x7
Materials Inventory	$ 3,956,200	$ 4,203,800
Work in Process Inventory	7,371,000	6,764,500
Finished Goods Inventory	10,596,400	10,883,200

Materials purchased during the year amounted to $3,750,000. Direct labor hours totaled 242,500, at an average labor rate of $5.20 per hour. The following factory overhead costs were incurred during the year: depreciation expense, plant and equipment, $885,600; operating supplies expense, $507,300; property tax expense, plant and equipment, $214,200; material handlers' labor expense, $1,013,700; small tools expense, $72,400; utilities expense, $1,936,500; and employee benefits expense, $746,100.

Required

Using proper form, prepare a statement of cost of goods manufactured from the information provided.

Problem 2B-5.
Statement
Preparation:
Manufacturing
Company
(L.O. 6, 7)

The Spencer Pharmaceuticals Corporation manufactures various drugs, which are marketed internationally. Inventory information for April 19x8 was as follows:

	April 1	April 30
Materials:		
Natural Minerals	$ 88,700	$ 70,600
Basic Organic Compounds	124,300	111,400
Catalysts	40,500	28,900
Suspension Agents	32,900	42,200
Total Materials	$286,400	$253,100
Work in Process	$108,800	$ 97,200
Finished Goods	$211,700	$214,100

Purchases of materials for April were: natural minerals, $24,610; basic organic compounds, $50,980; catalysts, $42,670; and suspension agents, $24,340. Direct labor costs were computed on the basis of 30,000 hours at $6 per hour. Actual factory overhead costs incurred in April were: operating supplies, $5,700; janitorial and material-handling labor, $29,100; employee benefits, $110,800; heat, light, and power, $54,000; depreciation, factory, $14,400; property taxes, $8,000; and expired portions of insurance premiums, $12,000. Net sales for April were $1,188,400. General and administrative expenses were $162,000. Income is taxed at a rate of 34 percent.

Required

1. Compute the cost of each of the four materials used during April.
2. Using good form, prepare a statement of cost of goods manufactured for the month ended April 30.
3. Using your answer in **2**, prepare an income statement for the same period.

Management Decision Case

St. James
Municipal Hospital
(L.O. 1, 2, 3, 8)

Hospitals are run in a competitive environment, and they rely heavily on cost data to keep their pricing structures in line with those of competitors. St. James Municipal Hospital is such a case. Located in a large city, the hospital offers three broad types of service. *General services* (dietary, housekeeping, maintenance, patient-care coordination, and general and administrative services) are the first type of service. *Ancillary services* (anesthesiology, blood bank, central and sterile supply, electrodiagnosis, laboratory, operating and recovery room, pharmacy, radiology, and respiratory therapy) are the second type. *Nursing care services* (acute or intensive care units, intermediate care units, neonatal (newborn) nursery, and nursing administration) are the third type.

The hospital's controller is Donnie Kristof. She is reviewing the billing procedure for patients using the thirty intensive care units (ICUs) in the facility. Each unit contains a regular hospital bed and a great deal of special equipment. Special suction equipment, oxygen flow meters at bedside, endotracheal tubes to assist breathing, a portable respirator, back-up suction machinery, and multiple IVs (intravenous feeding lines) with automatic drip counters are among the equipment in each unit. An H.P. Swan Ganz machine has a cardiac catheter tube that, when inserted into the heart, constantly monitors the pressure inside the heart chambers. One of the most important pieces of equipment at each bedside in the ICU is the cardiac monitor that displays the patient's heartbeat. A set of central monitors at the nurses' station helps nurses watch for instances of tachycardia (excessively rapid heartbeat), arrhythmia (irregular heartbeat), or bradycardia (abnormally slow heartbeat). An alarm system attached to the monitor warns the nurses when the patient's heartbeat is over or under acceptable limits. To equip an ICU today costs about $85,000 per room. Use of the equipment is billed to the patient at a rate of $150 per day. This charge includes a 25 percent markup to cover hospital overhead and profit.

Other ICU patient costs include the following:

Doctors' Care	2 hours per day @ $160 per hour (actual)
Special Nursing Care	8 hours per day @ $35 per hour (actual)
Regular Nursing Care	24 hours per day @ $18 per hour (average)
Medicines	$37 per day (average)
Medical Supplies	$34 per day (average)
Room Rental	$50 per day (average)
Food and Service	$40 per day (average)

For billing purposes, as with equipment charges, the hospital adds 25 percent to all costs to cover its operating costs and profit.

Required

1. From the costs listed, identify the direct costs used in determining the "cost per patient day" for an ICU.
2. Compute the cost per patient day.
3. Compute the billing per patient day, using the hospital's markup rate, which covers operating expenses and profit.
4. Many hospitals use separate markup rates for each cost when preparing billing statements. Industry averages revealed the following markup rates:

Doctors' Care	30%	Medical Supplies	50%
Special Nursing Care	40%	Room Rental	20%
Regular Nursing Care	50%	Food and Service	25%
Medicines	50%	Equipment	30%

Using these rates, recompute the billing per patient day for an ICU.
5. Using the information in **3** and **4**, which billing procedure would you recommend to the hospital's director? Why?

Product Costing Systems

Management accounting has three primary functions: (1) supplying management with product or service cost information, (2) assisting management in the planning and operating control areas, and (3) providing data that is used to support management decisions. Part Two focuses on the first function—the development of the unit cost of a product or service. There are many techniques used for product costing and every company adds its unique procedures. However, two primary product costing methods serve as a basis for developing special practices tailored to a particular business environment. These two methods are Job Order Costing and Process Costing.

Chapter 3 defines absorption costing, describes the development and use of predetermined overhead rates, and then focuses on product costing within a job order cost system.

Chapter 4 illustrates cost flow through the work-in-process inventory account, introduces the concept of equivalent production, and then analyzes product costing in a process cost environment.

Product Costing: The Job Order System

Determining a product's unit cost is one of the basic functions of a cost accounting system. Business success depends on product costing information in several ways. First, unit costs are an important element in determining an adequate, fair, and competitive selling price. Second, product costing information often forms the basis for forecasting and controlling operations and costs. Finally, product unit costs are needed to arrive at ending inventory balances.

One important reason for having a cost accounting system is to figure out the cost of manufacturing an individual product or batch of products. Such cost accounting systems vary from one company to another. But each system is designed to give information that company management thinks is important. In this chapter the basic information on manufacturing accounting, discussed in Chapter 2, is applied to a traditional product costing system: the job order costing system. A job order is a customer order for a specific number of specially designed, made-to-order products. Thus, you will learn to compute product costs in job order situations. Then you will link these costs to units completed and transferred to Finished Goods Inventory.

However, before discussing a specific product cost accounting system, more background information is needed. In the first part of this chapter, the two most common product costing systems—job order costing and process costing—are compared. Next, the concept of absorption costing is explained. Then, predetermined overhead rates and their application to specific jobs or products are discussed. The primary emphasis is then placed on describing and illustrating the job order cost accounting system. After studying this chapter, you should be able to meet the learning objectives listed on the left. A work sheet analysis based on perpetual inventories for a manufacturing company is covered in a special analysis in The Windham Company Practice Case.

Job Order Versus Process Costing

Job order costing and process costing are the two traditional, basic approaches to product cost accounting systems. Actual cost accounting systems may differ widely. However, all are based on one of these two product costing concepts. The systems are then adjusted to fit a particular industry, company, or operating department. The objective of the two systems is the same. Both are meant to provide product unit cost information for product pricing, cost control, inventory valuation, and income statement preparation. End-of-period values for the Cost of Goods Sold, the Work in Process Inventory, and the Finished Goods Inventory accounts are computed by using product unit cost data.

Characteristics of Job Order Costing

A job order cost accounting system is a product costing system used by companies making one-of-a-kind or special-order products. In such a system direct materials, direct labor, and factory overhead costs are assigned to specific job orders or batches of products. In computing unit costs, the total manufacturing costs for each job order are divided by the number of good units produced for that order. Industries that use a job order cost accounting system include those that make ships, airplanes, large machines, and other types of special orders.

The primary characteristics of a job order cost system are as follows: (1) It collects all manufacturing costs and assigns them to specific jobs or batches of product. (2) It measures costs for each completed job rather than for set time periods. (3) It uses just one Work in Process Inventory account in the general ledger. This account is supported by a subsidiary ledger of job order cost sheets for each job still in process at period end.

Characteristics of Process Costing

A process cost accounting system is a product costing system used by companies that make many similar products or that have a continuous production flow. Production processes based on the just-in-time operating concept also utilize a process costing system. In these cases, it is more economical to account for product-related costs for a period of time (a week or a month) than to try to assign them to specific products or job orders. Unit costs are computed by dividing total manufacturing costs assigned to a department or work center during a week or month by the number of good units produced during that time period. If a product is routed through four departments, four unit cost amounts are added together to find the product's total unit cost. Companies producing paint, oil and gas, automobiles, bricks, or soft drinks use some type of process costing system.

The main characteristics of a process cost accounting system are as follows: (1) Manufacturing costs are grouped by department or work center, with little concern for specific job orders. (2) The system emphasizes a weekly or monthly time period rather than the time it takes to complete a specific order. (3) The system uses several Work in Process Inventory accounts—one for each department or work center in the manufacturing process. Process costing will be discussed in detail in Chapter 4.

The Concept of Absorption Costing

OBJECTIVE 2
Describe the
concept of
absorption
costing

Product costing is possible only when the accounting system can define the types of manufacturing costs to be included in the analysis. For instance, should all factory overhead costs be considered costs of making the product, or only the variable factory overhead costs? Usually, it is assumed that product costing is governed by the concept of absorption costing. **Absorption costing** is an approach to product costing that assigns *all* types of manufacturing costs to individual products. The costs of direct materials, direct labor, variable factory overhead, and fixed factory overhead are all assigned to products. The product costing systems discussed in both this chapter and Chapter 4 apply the absorption costing concept.

Direct materials and direct labor costs are not difficult to handle in product costing because they can be conveniently and economically traced to products. Factory overhead costs, on the other hand, are not so easy to trace directly to products. For example, for a company making lawn and garden equipment, how much machine depreciation should be assigned to a single lawnmower? How about the costs of electrical power and indirect labor? One solution would be to wait until the end of the accounting period. All variable and fixed factory overhead costs incurred could then be added up. This amount could next be divided by the number of units produced during the period. This procedure would be an acceptable method of computing unit cost if the following two conditions exist: (1) All products are alike and require the same manufacturing operations. (2) Computation of product unit costs can wait until the end of the period. Such a situation is seldom found in industry. A company usually makes many different products, and it needs product costing information to set prices for goods before they are produced. Therefore, under absorption costing a predetermined overhead rate must be used to allocate factory overhead costs to products.

Predetermined Overhead Rates

OBJECTIVE 3
Compute a pre-
determined over-
head rate, and
use this rate to
apply overhead
costs to produc-
tion

Factory overhead costs are a problem for the management accountant. Actual overhead costs fluctuate from month to month because of the timing of fixed overhead costs. Therefore, some method must be used to allocate overhead costs to products. How can these costs be estimated and assigned to certain products or jobs before the end of the accounting period? The most common way is to use a **predetermined overhead rate** for each department or other operating unit. This rate can be defined as an overhead cost factor used to assign factory overhead costs to specific products or jobs. It is based on *estimated* overhead costs and production levels for the period. The rate is computed by following the three steps explained on the next page.

1. **Estimate factory overhead costs.** Using cost behavior analysis, estimate all factory overhead costs. Do so for each production department in the coming accounting period. (Cost behavior analysis is useful in this procedure and will be discussed in Chapter 5.) Add the totals for all the production departments. For example, suppose the total costs of rent, utilities, insurance, and all other factory overhead costs for the coming year are expected to be $450,000.

2. **Select a basis for allocating costs, and estimate its amount.** A way must be found to connect overhead costs to the products produced by using some measure of production activity. Common measures of production activity are labor hours, dollars of direct labor cost, machine hours, or units of output. The basis chosen should link the overhead cost to the product produced in a meaningful way. For instance, if an operation is more labor-hour than machine-hour intensive (as in the typical assembly line), then labor hours would be a good basis to use in overhead allocation. In the example suppose that overhead per hour of direct labor is the most useful measure. Management believes that 25,000 hours of direct labor will be used during the year.

3. **Divide the total overhead costs estimated for the period by the total estimated basis (hours, dollars, or units).** The result is the predetermined overhead rate. The computation for this example is as follows:

$$\text{Predetermined overhead rate per direct labor hour} = \frac{\text{total estimated overhead costs}}{\text{total estimated direct labor hours}}$$

$$= \frac{\$450,000}{25,000 \text{ hours}}$$

$$= \$18 \text{ of overhead per direct labor hour}$$

Overhead costs are then applied to each product, using this rate. Now, assume it takes one-half hour of direct labor to produce one unit. The overhead rate is $18 per direct labor hour. That unit is therefore assigned a factory overhead cost of $9. This amount is then added to the direct materials and direct labor costs already assigned to the product. The sum is the total unit cost.

Importance of Good Estimates

The whole process of overhead cost allocation depends on two factors for its success. One is a careful estimate of the total amount of overhead. The other is a good forecast of the production activity that will be used as the allocation basis.

Estimating total overhead costs is critical. If this estimate is wrong, the overhead rate will be wrong. The result will be that either too much or too little overhead cost will be assigned to the products produced. Therefore, in developing this estimate, the management accountant must be careful to include all factory overhead items and make accurate forecasts of their costs.

Overhead costs are generally estimated in the normal budgeting process. Expected overhead costs are gathered from all departments involved either directly or indirectly in the production process. The accounting department receives and totals each department's schedules of estimated costs. Costs of supporting service departments, such as maintenance and electrical departments, have only an indirect connection with products. Therefore, these costs must be distributed among the production departments. They can then be included as part of total factory overhead when computing the predetermined overhead rate for the period.

Forecasting production activity is also critical to the success of overhead cost allocation. First, a decision must be made as to which activity base is most appropriate—labor hours, labor dollars, machine hours, or units of output. The basis chosen should be one that relates to the overhead cost in a causal or beneficial way. For example, a greater number of machine hours would cause higher electricity costs and depreciation charges. Therefore, departments that are equipment intensive, such as those in which one person runs twenty-five or thirty machines by remote control, would use machine hours as the allocation basis. The object is to pick the one activity base that varies most with total overhead costs. Selecting an inappropriate activity base will mean that overhead costs assigned to individual jobs or products will not be closely related to actual overhead costs.

Exhibit 3-1 sums up the whole process of overhead cost allocation. In the first phase the predetermined overhead rate is computed. This is done by estimating total overhead costs and total production activity. In the second phase the predetermined overhead rate is used to compute the amount of overhead costs to be applied to products or jobs during the period.

Underapplied or Overapplied Overhead

OBJECTIVE 4
Dispose of underapplied or overapplied overhead

Much time and effort can go into estimating and allocating factory overhead costs. Still, actual overhead costs and actual production activities seldom agree with these estimates. Changes in anticipated costs or increases/decreases in the activity base cause differences (or variances) to occur. Differences in either area cause factory overhead to be **underapplied** or **overapplied**. That is, the amount of overhead costs assigned to products is less or more than the actual amount of overhead costs incurred. These actual overhead costs must be accounted for by making a quarterly or annual adjustment. Monthly differences between actual overhead incurred and overhead costs applied are normally not adjusted. In many cases monthly differences tend to offset one another, leaving only a small adjustment to be made at year end.

An example will illustrate the accounting problems of using predetermined overhead rates. Assume that the accounting records of the West Company show the overhead transactions below. Also assume that all overhead costs are debited to one general ledger controlling account—the Factory Overhead Control account—instead of to individual overhead accounts.

Exhibit 3-1. Overhead Cost Allocation

Phase I: Computing the Predetermined Overhead Rate

Develop Overhead Cost Estimates
Estimate overhead costs for each production
department.

Develop Allocation (Activity) Basis Estimates
1. Select an allocation basis for each production
   department that has a causal or beneficial
   relationship to the costs being assigned to the
   end product or job.
2. Carefully estimate the activity level of each
   department for the coming period.

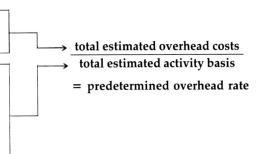

Phase II: Using the Rate to Assign Overhead Costs

**predetermined overhead rate × amount of activity
per job order = overhead cost assigned to that
particular job order or batch of products**

May 25 Paid utility bill for three months, $1,420.
     27 Recorded usage of indirect materials and supplies, $940.
June 21 Paid indirect labor wages, $2,190.
Aug. 12 Paid property taxes on factory building, $620.
Sept. 9 Recorded expiration of prepaid insurance premium, $560.
Nov. 27 Recorded depreciation of machinery and equipment for the year, $1,210.

These transactions resulted in the following entries:

May 25	Factory Overhead Control*	1,420	
	Cash		1,420
	To record payment of 3-month utility bill		
May 27	Factory Overhead Control*	940	
	Materials (or Supplies) Inventory		940
	To record usage of indirect materials and supplies		
June 21	Factory Overhead Control*	2,190	
	Factory Payroll		2,190
	To distribute indirect labor from factory payroll		
Aug. 12	Factory Overhead Control*	620	
	Cash		620
	To record payment of property taxes on factory building		

Sept. 9	Factory Overhead Control*	560	
	Prepaid Insurance		560
	To record expiration of		
	insurance premiums		
Nov. 27	Factory Overhead Control*	1,210	
	Accumulated Depreciation,		
	Machinery and Equipment		1,210
	To record depreciation		
	for the year		

*When the Factory Overhead Control account is used, all types of factory overhead costs are debited when incurred to the Factory Overhead Control account. A subsidiary ledger containing each individual overhead account is maintained. This procedure is illustrated later in the chapter.

The previous entries record actual overhead expenses. However, they do not help in assigning these costs to products. Nor do they help in transferring costs to the Work in Process Inventory account. Such a transfer must occur before product unit costs can be computed.

Here, the predetermined overhead rate is useful. Assume that the predetermined overhead rate for the period was $2.50 per direct labor hour. The following list of jobs completed during the period shows the number of direct labor hours for each job. It also shows the overhead cost applied to each one.

Job	Direct Labor Hours	×	Rate	=	Overhead Applied
16-2	520		$2.50		$1,300
19-4	718		2.50		1,795
17-3	622		2.50		1,555
18-6	416		2.50		1,040
21-5	384		2.50		960
	2,660				$6,650

A journal entry like the one below was used to record the application of predetermined overhead costs to each job worked on during the period. This entry charges Work in Process Inventory with a prorated share of estimated overhead costs and records the amount applied to Job 16-2. Normally, this entry is made when payroll is recorded, since overhead costs can be applied only after the number of labor hours is known. But in this example weekly and monthly labor data are unavailable. Thus, estimated overhead is applied to the completed job.

June 1	Work in Process Inventory	1,300	
	Factory Overhead Applied		1,300
	To record application of		
	overhead costs to Job 16-2		

Similar entries would be prepared for each job worked on during the accounting period.

After posting all actual overhead transactions discussed earlier, overhead costs applied and actual overhead costs can be compared. The resulting general ledger account entries and balances are as follows:

Factory Overhead Control (Incurred)			Factory Overhead Applied	
5/25	1,420		Job 16-2	1,300
5/27	940		Job 19-4	1,795
6/21	2,190		Job 17-3	1,555
8/12	620		Job 18-6	1,040
9/9	560		Job 21-5	960
11/27	1,210		**Bal.**	**6,650**
Bal.	**6,940**			

At year end these records of the West Company show that overhead has been *under*applied by $290 ($6,940 − $6,650). More actual overhead costs were incurred than were applied to products. The predetermined overhead rate was a little low. That is, it did not apply all overhead costs incurred to products produced. The $290 must now be added to the production costs of the period.

Two courses of action are available. First, if the $290 difference is considered small, or if most of the items worked on during the year have been sold, the entire amount can be charged to Cost of Goods Sold. This approach is the most common one because it is easy to apply. The adjusting entry would be as follows:

Factory Overhead Applied	6,650	
Cost of Goods Sold	290	
Factory Overhead Control		6,940
To close out overhead accounts and		
to charge underapplied overhead		
to the Cost of Goods Sold account		

Another method is used if the amount of the adjustment is large or if many of the products worked on during the year are unsold at year end. When this approach is used, underapplied or overapplied overhead is divided at year end among the Work in Process Inventory, Finished Goods Inventory, and Cost of Goods Sold accounts. For example, assume that at year end the products the West Company worked on during the year were located as follows: 30 percent in Work in Process Inventory, 20 percent in Finished Goods Inventory, and 50 percent sold. In such a case the following entry would be made:

Factory Overhead Applied	6,650	
Cost of Goods Sold (50% × $290)	145	
Work in Process Inventory (30% × $290)	87	
Finished Goods Inventory (20% × $290)	58	
Factory Overhead Control		6,940
To close out overhead accounts and to		
account for underapplied factory		
overhead		

The breakdown of the $290 into the three accounts could be based on the number of units worked on during the period, the direct labor hours incurred and attached to units in the three accounts, or the dollar balances in the three accounts. The Review Problem at the end of this chapter provides more guidance in accounting procedures for underapplied or overapplied overhead.

Product Costing and Inventory Valuation

OBJECTIVE 5
Explain the relationship between product costing and inventory valuation

One of the main goals of a cost accounting system is to supply management with information about production costs. This information is useful in many ways. It assists those making internal decisions. It helps the accountant control costs. And through inventory valuation it forms the link between financial accounting and management accounting.

All manufacturing costs incurred during a period must be accounted for in the year-end financial statements. However, not all of these costs will appear on the income statement. Only those costs assigned to units sold will be reported on the income statement. Costs assigned to units sold have "expired." They were used up in producing revenue. Costs assigned to unsold units (ending inventory) are "unexpired," or unused, costs. They are classified as assets and included in either the Work in Process Inventory or the Finished Goods Inventory on the balance sheet. Product unit cost information is needed to compute end-of-period balances in the Work in Process Inventory and the Finished Goods Inventory as well as to compute the cost of goods sold.

The Job Order Cost Accounting System

OBJECTIVE 6
Describe cost flow in a job order cost accounting system

As shown, a job order cost system is designed to gather manufacturing costs for a specific order or batch of products and to aid in determining product unit costs. Price-setting decisions, production scheduling, and other management tasks depend on information from a company's cost accounting system. For these reasons it is necessary to maintain a system that gives timely, correct data about product costs. In Chapter 2 the three main cost elements—materials, labor, and factory overhead—were discussed. Here, these costs are accounted for in a job order cost system.

Incurrence of Materials, Labor, and Factory Overhead Costs

A basic part of a job order cost system is the set of procedures and journal entries used when the company incurs materials, labor, and factory overhead costs. To help control these costs, businesses use various documents for each transaction. The effective use of these procedures and documents promotes accounting accuracy. Such use also makes for a smooth, efficient flow of cost information through the accounting record system. Note that all inventory balances in a job order cost system are kept on a perpetual basis.

Materials. Careful use of materials improves a company's overall efficiency. It conserves production resources and can bring about large cost savings. At the same time, good records ensure accountability and cut down waste. Controlling the physical materials and keeping good records enhance profits.

To help record and control materials costs, accountants rely heavily on a connected series of cost documents. These documents include the purchase request, purchase order, receiving report, inventory records, and materials requisition. Each of these documents was discussed in Chapter 2 and is an important link in accounting for materials costs. Direct materials costs are traced to specific jobs or products. Costs of indirect materials and supplies are charged to factory overhead.

Labor. Labor is one production resource that cannot be stored and used later. So it is important to link labor costs to each job or product. Labor timecards and job cards are used to record labor costs as they are incurred. Indirect labor costs are routed through the Factory Overhead Control account.

Factory Overhead. All indirect manufacturing costs are classified as factory overhead. Unlike materials and direct labor, overhead costs do not call for special documents. Vendors' bills support most payments. Factory depreciation expenses and prepaid expenses are charged to the Factory Overhead Control account through journal entries. Overhead costs may be accounted for in separate accounts, but that is not done in a job order cost system. As shown earlier, factory overhead costs are all debited to a Factory Overhead Control account.

A control account, you will recall, sums up several similar account balances to reduce accounting detail. A separate subsidiary account is also kept for each type of factory overhead cost. These separate accounts make up a subsidiary ledger to the Factory Overhead Control account.

Factory overhead costs, by nature, cannot be traced directly to jobs or products. For this reason an estimate of factory overhead costs is applied to products by means of the predetermined overhead rate. This process was discussed earlier, and it will be illustrated later in this chapter (see Exhibit 3-2) on pages 94–95.

The Work in Process Inventory Account

Job order costing focuses on the flow of costs through the Work in Process Inventory account. All manufacturing costs incurred and charged to production are routed through the Work in Process Inventory. Figure 3-1 shows cost flow in a job order cost system. Materials costs are debited to Work in Process Inventory. But indirect materials and supplies are debited to the Factory Overhead Control account. All labor costs traceable to specific jobs are debited to Work in Process Inventory, but indirect labor costs are charged against the Factory Overhead Control account balance. By using a predetermined overhead rate, overhead costs are applied to specific jobs by debiting Work in Process Inventory and crediting Factory Overhead Applied.

Figure 3-1. Job Order Cost Flow

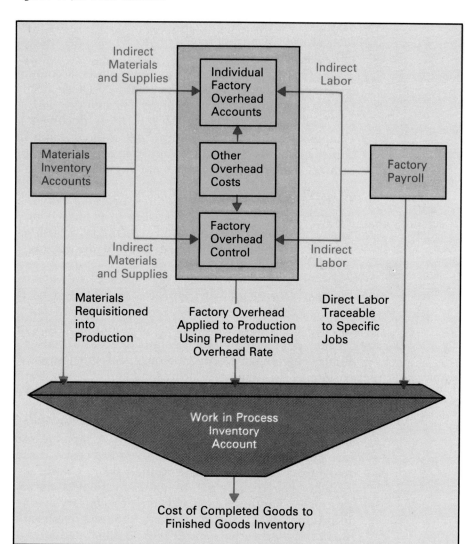

Attaching costs of direct materials, direct labor, and factory overhead to specific jobs and products is not an automatic process. Even though all manufacturing costs are debited to Work in Process Inventory, a separate accounting procedure is necessary for linking those costs to specific jobs. For this purpose a subsidiary ledger made up of **job order cost cards** is used. There is one job order cost card for each job being worked on, and all costs for that job are recorded on it. As costs are debited to Work in Process Inventory, the costs must also be reclassified by job and added to their job order cost cards.

A typical job order cost card is shown in Figure 3-2. Each card has space for materials, direct labor, and factory overhead costs. There is also space to write the job order number, product specifications, name

Figure 3-2. Job Order Cost Card

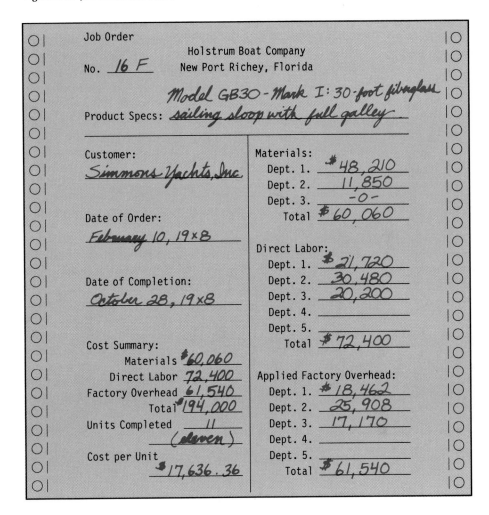

of customer, date of order, projected completion date, and summary cost data. As each department incurs materials and labor costs, the job order cost cards are updated. Factory overhead, as applied, is also posted to the job order cost cards. Job order cost cards for incomplete jobs make up the subsidiary ledger for the Work in Process Inventory Control account. To ensure that the ending balance in the Work in Process Inventory Control account is right, compare it with the total costs shown on the job order cost cards.

Accounting for Finished Goods

Once a job has been completed, all costs assigned to that job order are moved to Finished Goods Inventory. This is done in the accounting records by debiting the Finished Goods Inventory account and crediting the Work in Process Inventory account. When this entry is made, the job order cost card should be removed from the subsidiary ledger file. It is then used to help update the finished goods inventory records.

When goods are shipped, the order for them is recorded as a sale. Accounts Receivable is debited and Sales is credited for the entire selling price. But the cost of the goods shipped must also be accounted for. The proper procedure is to debit Cost of Goods Sold and to credit Finished Goods Inventory for the *cost* of the goods shipped.

To learn the mechanics of operating the system just described, you really need to go through an analysis of transactions and related journal entries. While studying the journal entry analysis that follows, review the preceding paragraphs. Try to keep in mind the cost flow concept shown in Figure 3-1.

Journal Entry Analysis

OBJECTIVE 7
Journalize transactions in a job order cost accounting system

Because a job order cost system emphasizes cost flow, you must understand journal entries that record various costs as they are incurred. You also must know the entries that transfer costs from one account to another. In fact, these entries along with job order cost cards and other subsidiary ledgers for materials and finished goods inventories are a major part of the job order cost system. As each area in the analysis of the Holstrum Boat Company is covered, the related transaction will be described first. The journal entry needed to record the transaction will follow. Each section will end with a discussion of the unique features of the transaction or the accounts being used. Exhibit 3-2 shows the entire job order cost flow through the general ledger, including supporting subsidiary ledgers. As each entry is discussed, trace its number and related debits or credits as shown in Exhibit 3-2 on pages 94–95.

Materials Purchased. In recording direct materials purchases, note the differences between journal entries used in the perpetual inventory approach and those used for periodic inventories. For example, Holstrum Boat Company purchased the following materials: Material 5X for $28,600 and Material 14Q for $17,000. Materials purchases were recorded at cost in the Materials Inventory Control account.

Entry 1:   Materials Inventory Control   45,600
          Accounts Payable (or Cash)   45,600
             To record purchase of $28,600
             of Material 5X and $17,000 of
             Material 14Q

This procedure differs in several ways from the recording of purchases discussed in your financial accounting course. First, the debit is to an inventory account instead of a purchases account because the inventory system is perpetual. All costs of materials flow through the inventory account. Second, there is a difference in the entry above because of the use of a **control** or **controlling account**. The term *control* means the account is an accumulation of several account balances. Some companies have hundreds of items in inventory. To keep a separate account for each item in the general ledger would make the ledger crowded and hard to work with. A control account is used for each area in which several similar items are being accounted for, and only one cumulative total appears in the general ledger. Each control account is supported by a subsidiary ledger that holds all individual account balances. When entry 1 is posted to the general ledger, the accounts in the materials ledger are also updated (see Exhibit 3-2).

Purchase of Supplies. The following transaction and entry are for the purchase of supplies for production. The company purchased $4,100 in operating supplies for the manufacturing process.

Entry 2:	Materials Inventory Control	4,100	
	Accounts Payable (or Cash)		4,100
	To record the purchase of operating supplies		

The procedures used to account for the purchase of supplies are much like those used to record direct materials purchases. Supplies Inventory in the example is assumed to be one subsidiary account, and is part of the total Materials Inventory Control account. If the supplies inventory is large, a separate general ledger account may be used. Regardless of which method is selected, the accountant should be able to give reasons to support the approach taken and should follow this approach consistently.

Requisitioning of Materials and Supplies. When a properly prepared materials requisition form is received, the following direct materials and supplies are issued from inventory to production: Material 5X for $62,000, Material 14Q for $32,000, and operating supplies for $4,800.

Entry 3:	Work in Process Inventory Control	94,000	
	Factory Overhead Control	4,800	
	Materials Inventory Control		98,800
	To record issuance of $62,000 of Material 5X, $32,000 of Material 14Q, and $4,800 of operating supplies into production		

The entry above shows that $94,000 of direct materials and $4,800 of indirect materials were issued. The debit to the Work in Process Inventory Control account records the cost of direct materials issued to production. Such costs are directly traceable to specific job orders. As the direct materials costs are charged to work in process, amounts for individual jobs are entered on the job order cost cards. As shown in Exhibit 3-2, $51,900 in materials were used on Job 16F, and materials costing $42,100 were used on Job 23H. Indirect materials costs (supplies) are debited to the Factory Overhead Control account.

Exhibit 3-2. The Job Order Cost System—Holstrum Boat Company

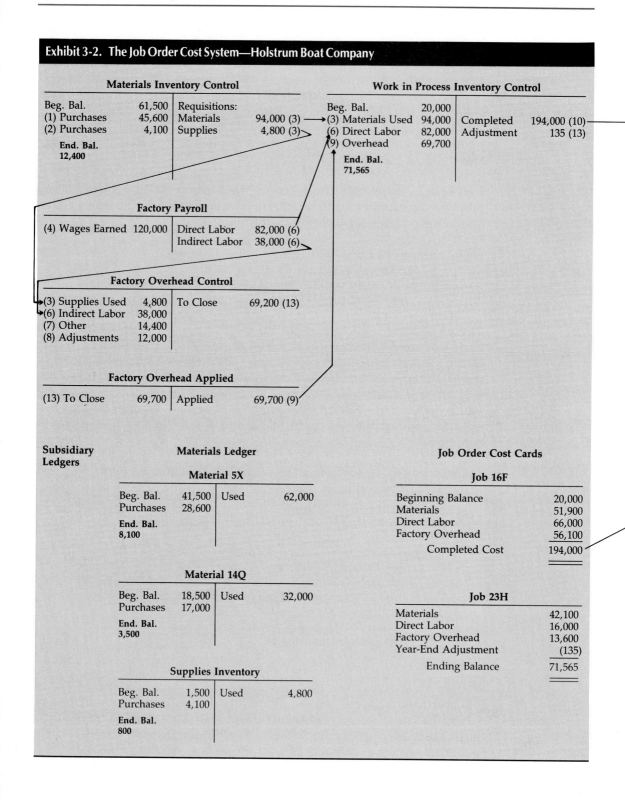

Materials Inventory Control

Beg. Bal.	61,500	Requisitions:	
(1) Purchases	45,600	Materials	94,000 (3)
(2) Purchases	4,100	Supplies	4,800 (3)
End. Bal.			
12,400			

Work in Process Inventory Control

Beg. Bal.	20,000		
(3) Materials Used	94,000	Completed	194,000 (10)
(6) Direct Labor	82,000	Adjustment	135 (13)
(9) Overhead	69,700		
End. Bal.			
71,565			

Factory Payroll

(4) Wages Earned	120,000	Direct Labor	82,000 (6)
		Indirect Labor	38,000 (6)

Factory Overhead Control

(3) Supplies Used	4,800	To Close	69,200 (13)
(6) Indirect Labor	38,000		
(7) Other	14,400		
(8) Adjustments	12,000		

Factory Overhead Applied

(13) To Close	69,700	Applied	69,700 (9)

Subsidiary Ledgers

Materials Ledger

Material 5X

Beg. Bal.	41,500	Used	62,000
Purchases	28,600		
End. Bal.			
8,100			

Material 14Q

Beg. Bal.	18,500	Used	32,000
Purchases	17,000		
End. Bal.			
3,500			

Supplies Inventory

Beg. Bal.	1,500	Used	4,800
Purchases	4,100		
End. Bal.			
800			

Job Order Cost Cards

Job 16F

Beginning Balance	20,000
Materials	51,900
Direct Labor	66,000
Factory Overhead	56,100
Completed Cost	194,000

Job 23H

Materials	42,100
Direct Labor	16,000
Factory Overhead	13,600
Year-End Adjustment	(135)
Ending Balance	71,565

Exhibit 3-2. (*continued*)

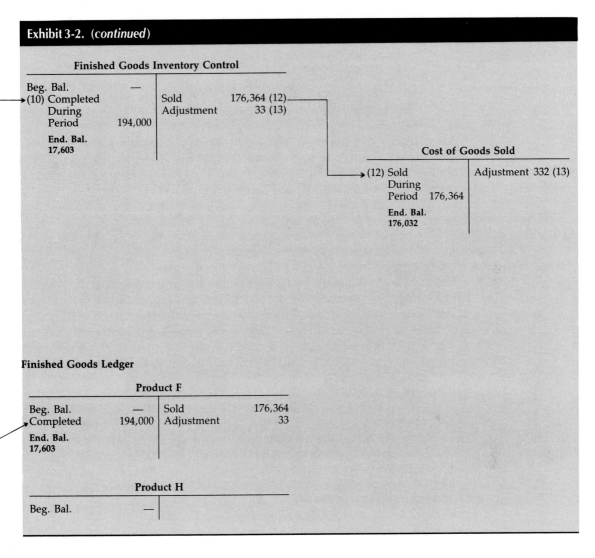

Finished Goods Inventory Control

Beg. Bal.	—	Sold	176,364 (12)
(10) Completed During Period	194,000	Adjustment	33 (13)
End. Bal. 17,603			

Cost of Goods Sold

| (12) Sold During Period | 176,364 | Adjustment 332 (13) |
| End. Bal. 176,032 | | |

Finished Goods Ledger

Product F

Beg. Bal.	—	Sold	176,364
Completed	194,000	Adjustment	33
End. Bal. 17,603			

Product H

| Beg. Bal. | — |

Labor Costs. Recording labor costs for a manufacturing company takes three journal entries. Journal entries to record payroll for a merchandising company were discussed in the financial accounting course. Recording payroll for a manufacturing company is more complex, but the same basic payroll documents and transactions are used. In accounting for factory labor costs, however, some new account titles are needed. Costs are assigned to specific products and jobs.

The first labor cost entry records the total payroll liability of the company. Although only $107,640 in net earnings are to be paid to employees, the gross direct and indirect labor costs will be used for product and job costing. In the transaction described in entry 4, payroll liability for the period was recorded as follows: gross direct labor wages, $82,000; gross indirect labor wages, $38,000; gross administrative salaries, $36,000; FICA (social security) taxes withheld, $9,360; federal income taxes withheld, $39,000. Entry 4 is shown on the following page.

Entry 4:   Factory Payroll   120,000
          Administrative Salaries Expense   36,000
             FICA Tax Payable   9,360
             Employees' Federal Income Tax Payable   39,000
             Wages and Salaries Payable   107,640
                To record payroll liability
                for the period

A follow-up entry is now needed to account properly for labor costs. The next entry, entry 5, will record the payment of the payroll liability established in entry 4. In this transaction, payroll checks for the period were prepared and given to the employees.

Entry 5:   Wages and Salaries Payable   107,640
          Cash   107,640
             To record payment of payroll

The total payroll dollars for factory personnel first debited to the Factory Payroll account must now be moved to the production accounts. Gross direct labor costs are debited to Work in Process Inventory Control, and total indirect wages (including factory supervisors' salaries) are debited to Factory Overhead Control. Factory Payroll is credited to show that the total amount has been distributed to the production accounts.

Entry 6:   Work in Process Inventory Control   82,000
          Factory Overhead Control   38,000
             Factory Payroll   120,000
                To record the distribution of
                factory payroll to production
                accounts

In addition, direct labor costs are recorded by job on job order cost cards. The distribution of $66,000 to Job 16F and $16,000 to Job 23H is shown in Exhibit 3-2.

Other Factory Overhead Costs. As factory overhead costs other than indirect materials and indirect labor charges are incurred, the sum of these costs is charged (debited) to the Factory Overhead Control account. Each cost is identified in the explanation of the journal entry. In the example, factory overhead costs were paid as follows: electricity, $3,100; maintenance and repair, $8,400; insurance, $1,300; and property taxes, $1,600.

Entry 7:   Factory Overhead Control   14,400
          Cash   14,400
             To record incurrence of the
             following overhead costs:
             electricity, $3,100; maintenance
             and repair, $8,400; insurance
             expense, $1,300; and property
             taxes, $1,600

From the information in the journal entry explanation, individual subsidiary ledger accounts are updated. Because of the amount of information already included in Exhibit 3-2, the subsidiary ledger for the Factory Overhead Control account is not shown. However, the subsidiary ledger would include an account for each type of factory overhead cost. The costs would be accounted for in much the same way as those described for the materials ledger and the job order cost cards.

The next transaction is an adjusting entry needed to record depreciation on factory equipment for the period.

Entry 8:   Factory Overhead Control   12,000
             Accumulated Depreciation, Equipment   12,000
               To record depreciation on
               factory equipment for the
               period

This entry is out of order, since adjusting entries are usually prepared after all transactions for the period have been recorded. But it is introduced at this point because depreciation of factory equipment is a part of total factory overhead costs. The actual depreciation expense account will be part of the overhead subsidiary ledger.

Factory Overhead Applied. Factory overhead is applied by using a predetermined overhead rate and an allocation base (direct labor hours, direct labor dollars, machine hours, or units of output). In this transaction factory overhead costs were applied to production by using a rate of 85 percent of direct labor dollars.

Entry 9:   Work in Process Inventory Control   69,700
             Factory Overhead Applied   69,700
               To apply factory overhead
               costs to production

The amount of overhead charged to production is found by multiplying the overhead rate by the units of the applicable overhead allocation base. In the example 85 percent was multiplied by the direct labor dollars ($82,000), which came to $69,700 ($82,000 × .85). This amount was debited to the Work in Process Inventory Control account. Because the overhead application is related to direct labor dollars, the job order cost cards may be updated by the same procedure. Job 16F is assigned $56,100 in overhead costs ($66,000 × .85). Job 23H receives a charge of $13,600 ($16,000 × .85). These amounts have been posted to the job order cost cards in Exhibit 3-2.

Accounting for Completed Units. As various job orders are completed, their costs are moved to the Finished Goods Inventory Control account. In this case, goods costing $194,000 for Job 16F were completed and transferred to Finished Goods Inventory (see the job order cost card, Exhibit 3-2).

Entry 10:   Finished Goods Inventory Control   194,000
                  Work in Process Inventory Control   194,000
                  To record transfer of completed
                  goods for Job 16F from Work
                  in Process Inventory to
                  Finished Goods Inventory

When a job is completed, its job order cost card is pulled from the Work in Process subsidiary ledger. The card is then used to help update the Finished Goods ledger. Specifically, costs recorded on the job order cost card are used to compute unit costs and to determine the amount of the transfer entry (see Exhibit 3-2).

Accounting for Units Sold. The final phase of manufacturing cost flow is to transfer costs from the Finished Goods Inventory Control account to the Cost of Goods Sold account. At this point ten sailing sloops from Job 16F were shipped to the customer. The selling price for the goods shipped was $260,000. The cost to manufacture these products totaled $176,364.

Entry 11:   Accounts Receivable   260,000
                  Sales   260,000
                        To record sale of portion of Job 16F

Entry 12:   Cost of Goods Sold   176,364
                  Finished Goods Inventory Control   176,364
                  To record the transfer of the
                  cost of shipped goods for
                  Job 16F from Finished Goods
                  Inventory to Cost of Goods Sold

Both the entry to record the sale and the entry to establish the cost of the goods sold are shown here. Entry 12 is made at the same time the sale is recorded. When the costs of the products sold are transferred out of the Finished Goods Inventory Control account, the Finished Goods ledger (subsidiary ledger) should be updated, as shown in Exhibit 3-2.

Underapplied or Overapplied Overhead Disposition. At the end of an accounting period, the Factory Overhead Control account and the Factory Overhead Applied account are totaled. Then an entry to close these accounts and dispose of any underapplied or overapplied overhead is made.

Entry 13:   Factory Overhead Applied   69,700
                  Work in Process Inventory Control   135
                  Finished Goods Inventory Control   33
                  Cost of Goods Sold   332
                  Factory Overhead Control   69,200
                        To close out factory overhead
                        account balances and to dispose
                        of the overapplied balance

In this transaction factory overhead was overapplied by $500. So, as the Factory Overhead Control and Factory Overhead Applied accounts were closed, the $500 difference was distributed among Work in Process Inventory Control, Finished Goods Inventory Control, and Cost of Goods Sold. These changes were made based on each account's balance before the adjustment.

The following T accounts summarize the overhead account balances before entry 13. Numbers in parentheses refer to earlier journal entries.

Factory Overhead Control		Factory Overhead Applied	
(3)	4,800	(9)	69,700
(6)	38,000		
(7)	14,400		
(8)	12,000		
	69,200		69,700

Overhead has been overapplied by $500 ($69,700 − $69,200). This amount can be either credited to the Cost of Goods Sold account or distributed among the Work in Process Inventory Control, Finished Goods Inventory Control, and Cost of Goods Sold accounts. Since it is assumed the amount is significant, it is distributed among the three accounts on the basis of their ending balances (see Exhibit 3-2). The following table shows how the distribution amounts were computed:

Account	Ending Balance	Percentage of Each to Total	×	Amount to Be Allocated	=	Allocation of Overapplied Overhead
Work in Process Inventory Control	$ 71,700	27.0		$500		$135
Finished Goods Inventory Control	17,636	6.6		500		33
Cost of Goods Sold	176,364	66.4		500		332
Totals	$265,700	100.0				$500

After entry 13 has been posted to the general ledger, the accounts will look like those in Exhibit 3-2. In addition, all subsidiary ledgers affected by the overhead adjustment must be updated. In the example the entire $135 adjustment to Work in Process was credited to Job 23H. Because Job 16F had been completed, its share of the adjustment was assigned to the Finished Goods Inventory and the Cost of Goods Sold accounts.

Computing Product Unit Costs

OBJECTIVE 8
Compute product unit cost for a specific job order

The process of computing product unit cost is fairly simple in a job order costing system. All costs of materials, direct labor, and factory overhead for each job are recorded on a job order cost card as the job progresses to completion. When the job is finished, all costs on the job order cost card are totaled. The unit cost is then computed by dividing total manufacturing costs for the job by the number of good units produced. Job 16F was completed in the journal entry analysis just finished. The cost data for this job are shown on the job order cost card in Figure 3-2. Eleven sailing sloops were produced at a total cost of $194,000, which worked out to a cost of $17,636.36 per sloop before adjustments. Note in Exhibit 3-2 that only ten of the sloops were actually shipped during the year. One still remains in Finished Goods Inventory Control at the adjusted cost.

Fully and Partly Completed Products

In a job order costing system, as shown, manufacturing costs are accumulated, classified, and reclassified several times. As products near completion, all manufacturing costs for their production are linked to them. These costs then follow the products first to Finished Goods Inventory Control and then to Cost of Goods Sold. Exhibit 3-2 illustrates the accounting procedures and cost flows of units worked on during the period. Dollar amounts in that exhibit came from posting the journal entries just discussed.

At period end some costs remain in the Work in Process Inventory Control and the Finished Goods Inventory Control accounts. The ending balance of $71,565 in Work in Process Inventory Control is from costs attached to partly completed units in Job 23H. These costs are traceable to the specific job order cost cards for partly completed jobs in the subsidiary ledger. Finished Goods Inventory Control also has an ending balance. Of all units completed during the period, one sloop from Job 16F, costing $17,603 (after the adjustment), has not been sold or shipped. Its cost now appears as the ending balance in Finished Goods Inventory Control.

Chapter Review

Review of Learning Objectives

1. **Identify the differences between job order costing and process costing.**
   Both job order costing and process costing are basic, traditional approaches to product cost accounting. However, they have different characteristics. A job order costing system is used for unique or special-order products. In such a system, materials, direct labor, and factory overhead costs are assigned to specific job orders or batches of products. In determining unit costs, the total manufacturing cost assigned to each job order is divided by the number of good units produced for that order. A process costing system is used by companies that produce many similar products or have a continuous production flow. These companies find it more economical to account for product-related costs for a period of time (a week or month) than to assign them to specific products or job orders. Unit costs in a process costing system are found by dividing total manufacturing costs for a department or work center during a time period by the number of good units produced.

2. Describe the concept of absorption costing.

   Absorption costing is an approach to product costing that assigns a representative portion of *all* manufacturing costs to individual products. The costs of direct materials, direct labor, variable factory overhead, and fixed factory overhead are all assigned to products.

3. Compute a predetermined overhead rate, and use this rate to apply overhead costs to production.

   A predetermined overhead rate is computed by dividing total estimated overhead costs for a period by the total activity basis expected for that period. Factory overhead costs are applied to a job order by multiplying the predetermined overhead rate by the amount of the activity base (such as machine hours) used for the job order.

4. Dispose of underapplied or overapplied overhead.

   If there is any difference between the balances in the Factory Overhead Control and Factory Overhead Applied accounts at year end, there are two ways to dispose of the difference. If the difference is small, it should be assigned to the Cost of Goods Sold account. Often, however, the amount of the adjustment is large or the costs of the products worked on during the period are spread among the Work in Process Inventory, Finished Goods Inventory, and Cost of Goods Sold accounts. In such cases the difference should be assigned proportionately to these three accounts.

5. Explain the relationship between product costing and inventory valuation.

   Product costing techniques are necessary to attach costs to job orders or units of product worked on during a given time period. At period end when financial statements are prepared, these product costs are used in costing the Work in Process and Finished Goods Inventories.

6. Describe cost flow in a job order cost accounting system.

   A job order cost accounting system generally follows the concept of absorption costing. It also uses the perpetual approach to inventory maintenance and valuation. Within these limits, materials and supplies costs are first debited to the Materials Inventory Control account. Labor costs are debited to the Factory Payroll account. And the various factory overhead costs are debited to the Factory Overhead Control account. As the products are being manufactured, costs of direct materials and direct labor are transferred to the Work in Process Inventory Control account. Factory overhead costs are applied and charged to the Work in Process Inventory Control account by using a predetermined overhead rate. These overhead cost charges are credited to the Factory Overhead Applied account. When products or jobs are completed, the costs assigned to them are transferred to the Finished Goods Inventory Control account. These same costs are transferred to the Cost of Goods Sold account when the products are sold and shipped.

7. Journalize transactions in a job order cost accounting system.

   Mastery of a job order costing system requires that the user be able to prepare journal entries for each of the following transactions: (a) purchase of materials; (b) purchase of operating supplies; (c) requisition of materials and supplies into production; (d) recording of payroll liability; (e) payment of payroll to employees; (f) distribution of factory payroll to production accounts; (g) cash payment of overhead costs; (h) recording of noncash overhead costs, such as depreciation of factory and equipment; (i) application of factory overhead costs to production; (j) transfer of costs of completed jobs from the Work in Process Inventory Control account to the Finished Goods Inventory Control account;

(k) sale of products and transfer of related costs from the Finished Goods Inventory Control account to the Cost of Goods Sold account; and (l) disposition of underapplied or overapplied factory overhead.

8. Compute product unit cost for a specific job order.
    Product costs in a job order costing system are computed by first totaling all manufacturing costs accumulated on a particular job order cost card. This amount is then divided by the number of good units produced for that job to find the unit cost for the order. Unit cost information is entered onto the job order cost card and used for inventory valuation purposes.

Review of Concepts and Terminology

The following important concepts were introduced in this chapter:

(L.O. 1)   **Job order cost accounting system:** A product costing system used in making one-of-a-kind or special-order products.

(L.O. 1)   **Process cost accounting system:** A product cost accounting system used by companies that make many similar products or that have a continuous production flow.

(L.O. 2)   **Absorption costing:** An approach to product costing that assigns all types of manufacturing costs to individual products.

(L.O. 3)   **Predetermined overhead rate:** An overhead cost factor used to assign factory overhead costs to specific products or jobs.

(L.O. 7)   **Control or controlling account:** An account in the general ledger that summarizes the total balance of a group of related accounts in a subsidiary ledger.

Other important terms introduced in this chapter are:

job order (p. 80)
job order cost cards (p. 90)
underapplied or overapplied factory overhead (p. 84)

Review Problem
Journal Entry Analysis: Job Order Costing System

The Neilsson Manufacturing Company produces "uniframe" desk and chair assemblies and study carrels for libraries. The firm uses a job order cost system and a current factory overhead application rate of 220 percent of direct labor dollars. The following transactions and events occurred during September 19xx:

Sept.   4   Direct materials costing $9,540 and purchased on account were received.
        7   The production department requisitioned $2,700 of materials and $650 of operating supplies.
        14 Gross factory payroll of $16,000 was paid to factory personnel. Of this amount $11,500 represents direct labor, and the remaining amount is indirect labor. (Prepare only the entry to distribute factory payroll to production accounts.)
        14 Factory overhead costs were applied to production.
        16 Supplies costing $3,500 and direct materials costing $17,000 were received. Both were ordered on 9/11/xx and purchased on account.

Sept. 20 $9,000 of direct materials and $1,750 of supplies were requisitioned into production.

26 The following overhead costs were paid: heat, light, and power, $1,400; repairs by outside firm, $1,600; property taxes, $2,700.

28 Gross factory payroll of $15,600 was earned by factory personnel. Of this amount indirect wages and supervisors' salaries totaled $6,400. Prepare only the entry to distribute factory payroll to production accounts.

28 Factory overhead costs were applied to production.

29 Completed units costing $67,500 were transferred to Finished Goods Inventory.

30 Depreciation of plant and equipment for September was $24,000. During the same period $1,200 in prepaid fire insurance expired.

30 Library carrel units costing $32,750 were shipped to a customer for a total selling price of $53,710.

Required

1. Record journal entries for all the above transactions and events.
2. Assume that: (a) the beginning balance in Materials Inventory Control was $4,700; (b) the beginning balance in Work in Process Inventory Control was $6,200; and (c) the beginning balance in Finished Goods Inventory Control was $9,000. Compute the ending balances in these inventory accounts.
3. Determine the amount of underapplied or overapplied overhead.
4. If 131 carrels were included in the order sold and shipped on September 30, compute the cost and selling price per carrel shipped.

Answer to Review Problem

1. Journal entries:

Sept. 4	Materials Inventory Control	9,540	
	Accounts Payable		9,540
	To record purchase of direct materials on account		
7	Work in Process Inventory Control	2,700	
	Factory Overhead Control	650	
	Materials Inventory Control		3,350

	To record requisition of direct
	      materials and supplies into
	      production		

14	Work in Process Inventory Control	11,500	
	Factory Overhead Control	4,500	
	Factory Payroll		16,000
	To distribute payroll to production accounts		
14	Work in Process Inventory Control	25,300	
	Factory Overhead Applied		25,300
	To apply factory overhead costs to production ($11,500 × 220%)		

Sept. 16	Materials Inventory Control		20,500	
	Accounts Payable			20,500
	To record purchase of $3,500 of operating supplies and $17,000 of direct materials			
20	Work in Process Inventory Control		9,000	
	Factory Overhead Control		1,750	
	Materials Inventory Control			10,750
	To record requisition of direct materials and supplies into production			
26	Factory Overhead Control		5,700	
	Cash			5,700
	To record payment of the following overhead costs: heat, light, and power, $1,400; outside repairs, $1,600; and property taxes, $2,700			
28	Work in Process Inventory Control		9,200	
	Factory Overhead Control		6,400	
	Factory Payroll			15,600
	To distribute payroll to production accounts			
28	Work in Process Inventory Control		20,240	
	Factory Overhead Applied			20,240
	To apply factory overhead costs to production ($9,200 × 220%)			
29	Finished Goods Inventory Control		67,500	
	Work in Process Inventory Control			67,500
	To transfer costs of completed goods to Finished Goods Inventory			
30	Factory Overhead Control		25,200	
	Accumulated Depreciation, Plant and Equipment			24,000
	Prepaid Insurance			1,200
	To charge Factory Overhead Control for expired asset costs			
30	Accounts Receivable		53,710	
	Sales			53,710
	To record sales for September			
30	Cost of Goods Sold		32,750	
	Finished Goods Inventory Control			32,750
	To record transfer of costs from Finished Goods Inventory to Cost of Goods Sold			

2. Ending balances of inventory accounts:

Materials Inventory Control

Beg. Bal.	4,700	9/7	3,350
9/4	9,540	9/20	10,750
9/16	20,500		
	34,740		**14,100**
End. Bal.	**20,640**		

Work in Process Inventory Control

Beg. Bal.	6,200	9/29	67,500
9/7	2,700		
9/14	11,500		
9/14	25,300		
9/20	9,000		
9/28	9,200		
9/28	20,240		
	84,140		**67,500**
End. Bal.	**16,640**		

Finished Goods Inventory Control

Beg. Bal.	9,000	9/30	32,750
9/29	67,500		
	76,500		**32,750**
End. Bal.	**43,750**		

3. Underapplied or overapplied overhead:

Factory Overhead Control

9/7	650		
9/14	4,500		
9/20	1,750		
9/26	5,700		
9/28	6,400		
9/30	25,200		
End. Bal.	**44,200**		

Factory Overhead Applied

		9/14	25,300
		9/28	20,240
		End. Bal.	**45,540**

Factory overhead is overapplied by $1,340 ($45,540 − $44,200).

4. Cost and selling price per unit:

Cost per unit: $32,750 ÷ 131 = $250 per unit
Selling price per unit: $53,710 ÷ 131 = $410 per unit

Chapter Assignments

Questions

1. What is the common goal of a job order cost accounting system and a process cost accounting system?
2. Explain the concept of absorption costing.
3. What is the connection between manufacturing cost flow and the perpetual inventory method?
4. Describe the steps used to arrive at a predetermined overhead rate based on machine hours.
5. What are the factors for success in applying overhead to products and job orders?
6. What is meant by underapplied or overapplied overhead?
7. Describe two ways to adjust for underapplied or overapplied overhead.
8. "Some costs of direct materials, direct labor, and factory overhead used during a period will be reported in the company's income statement. Others will be reported in the company's balance sheet." Discuss the accuracy of this statement.
9. What are the differences between a job order cost system and a process cost system? (Focus on the characteristics of each system.)
10. In what way is timely purchasing a do-or-die function?
11. How does materials usage influence the efficiency of operations?
12. "Purchased labor resource services cannot be stored." Discuss this statement.
13. Discuss the role of the Work in Process Inventory account in a job order cost system.
14. What is the purpose of a job order cost card? Identify the types of information recorded on such a card.
15. Define the terms *control account* and *subsidiary ledger*. How are they related?
16. Management accounting is often overshadowed by financial accounting, since it is better publicized. Describe the importance of a product costing system to (a) the preparation of financial statements and (b) profitability.

Classroom Exercises

Exercise 3-1.
Cost System:
Industry Linkage
(L.O. 1)

Which of the following types of manufactured products would normally be produced using a job order costing system? Which would be produced using a process costing system? (a) paint; (b) automobiles; (c) 747 jet aircraft; (d) bricks; (e) large milling machines; (f) liquid detergent; (g) aluminum compressed-gas cylinders of standard size and capacity; (h) aluminum compressed-gas cylinders with a special fiber-glass overwrap for a Mount Everest expedition; (i) nails from wire; (j) television sets; (k) printed wedding invitations; (l) a limited edition of lithographs; (m) pet flea collars; (n) high-speed lathes with special-order threaded drills; (o) breakfast cereal; and (p) an original evening gown.

Exercise 3-2.
Concept of
Absorption Costing
(L.O. 2)

Using the absorption costing concept, determine a product's unit cost from the following costs incurred during March: (a) $3,500 in Liability Insurance, Factory; (b) $2,900 in Rent Expense, Sales Office; (c) $4,100 in Depreciation Expense, Factory Equipment; (d) $20,650 in Materials Used; (e) $3,480 in Indirect Labor, Factory; (f) $1,080 in Factory Supplies; (g) $1,510 in Heat, Light, and Power,

Factory; (h) $2,600 in Fire Insurance, Factory; (i) $4,250 in Depreciation Expense, Sales Equipment; (j) $3,850 in Rent Expense, Factory; (k) $28,420 in Direct Labor; (l) $3,100 in Manager's Salary, Factory; (m) $5,800 in President's Salary; (n) $8,250 in Sales Commissions; (o) $2,975 in Advertising Expenses. The Inspection Department reported that 150,800 good units were produced during March.

Exercise 3-3.
Overhead
Application Rate
(L.O. 3)

Gustafson Compumatics specializes in the analysis and reporting of complex inventory costing projects. Materials costs are minimal, consisting entirely of operating supplies such as data processing cards, inventory sheets, and other recording tools. Labor is the highest single expense item, and it totaled $645,250 for 72,400 hours of work in 19x7. Factory overhead costs for 19x7 were $825,450, and this amount was applied to specific jobs on the basis of labor hours worked.

In 19x8 the company anticipates a 30 percent increase in overhead costs. Labor costs will increase by as much as $130,000, and the number of hours worked during 19x8 is expected to increase 20 percent.

1. Determine the total amount of factory overhead anticipated by the company in 19x8.
2. Compute the predetermined overhead rate for 19x8. (Round your answer to the nearest penny.)
3. During April 19x8 the following jobs were completed and the related hours worked: Job 16A4, 2,490 hours; Job 21C2, 5,220 hours; and Job 17H3, 4,270 hours. Prepare the journal entry required to apply overhead costs to operations for April.

Exercise 3-4.
Predetermined
Overhead Rate
Computation
(L.O. 3)

The overhead costs used by Gerald Industries, Inc., to compute its predetermined overhead rate for 19x8 were as follows:

Indirect Materials and Supplies	$ 66,200
Repairs and Maintenance	28,900
Outside Service Contracts	27,300
Indirect Labor	79,100
Factory Supervision	52,900
Depreciation, Machinery	85,000
Factory Insurance	38,200
Property Taxes	7,500
Heat, Light, and Power	11,700
Miscellaneous Factory Overhead	6,045
	$402,845

A total of 45,600 direct labor hours were used as the 19x8 allocation base.

In 19x9 all overhead costs except depreciation, property taxes, and miscellaneous factory overhead are expected to increase by 10 percent. Depreciation should increase by 15 percent, and a 20 percent increase in property taxes and miscellaneous factory overhead is expected. Plant capacity in terms of direct labor hours used will increase by 3,850 hours in 19x9.

1. Compute the 19x8 predetermined overhead rate.
2. Compute the predetermined overhead rate for 19x9.

Exercise 3-5.
Disposition of
Overapplied
Overhead
(Extension of
Exercise 3-3)
(L.O.4)

By the end of 19x8, Gustafson Compumatics had compiled a total of 81,340 hours worked. The overhead incurred during the year was $999,850.

1. Using the predetermined overhead rate computed in Exercise 3-3, determine the total amount of overhead applied to operations during 19x8.
2. Compute the amount of overapplied overhead for the year.
3. Prepare the journal entry to close out the overhead accounts and to dispose of the overapplied overhead amount for 19x8. Assume that the amount is insignificant.

Exercise 3-6.
Disposition of
Underapplied
Overhead
(L.O.4)

The Hendel Manufacturing Company ended the year with a total of $26,200 in underapplied overhead. Because management thinks this amount is significant, this unfavorable difference should be distributed among the three appropriate accounts in proportion to their ending balances. The ending account balances are Materials Inventory Control, $214,740; Work in Process Inventory Control, $312,500; Finished Goods Inventory Control, $250,000; Cost of Goods Sold, $687,500; Factory Overhead Control, $215,400; and Factory Overhead Applied, $189,200.

Using good form, close out the factory overhead accounts, and dispose of the underapplied overhead. Show your work in journal entry form. Separately, give supporting computations.

Exercise 3-7.
Job Order Cost
Flow
(L.O.6)

The three manufacturing cost elements—direct materials, direct labor, and factory overhead—flow through a job order cost system in a structured, orderly fashion. Specific general ledger accounts, subsidiary ledgers, and source documents are used to verify and record cost information. In paragraph and diagram form, describe cost flow in a job order cost accounting system.

Exercise 3-8.
Unit Cost
Computation
(L.O.8)

Webster Corporation manufactures a line of women's apparel known the world over as Robertson Fashions. During February the corporation worked on three special orders, A-16, A-20, and B-14. Cost and production data for each order are as follows:

	Job A-16	Job A-20	Job B-14
Direct materials:			
Fabric Q	$ 6,840	$10,980	$14,660
Fabric Z	10,400	8,200	12,440
Fabric YB	4,260	5,920	8,900
Direct labor:			
Seamstress labor	12,900	18,400	26,200
Layout labor	7,450	9,425	12,210
Packaging labor	2,950	3,875	5,090
Factory overhead:			
90% of direct labor dollars	?	?	?
Number of units produced	600	675	1,582

1. Compute the total cost associated with each job, and indicate subtotals for each cost category in your analysis.
2. Compute each job's unit cost. (Round to the nearest penny.)

Exercise 3-9.
Work in Process
Inventory Account:
Journal Entry
Analysis
(L.O.7)

On July 1 there was a $29,073 beginning balance in the Work in Process Inventory account of the Glaser Specialty Company. Production activity for July was as follows: (a) Materials costing $138,820, along with $17,402 of operating supplies, were requisitioned for production. (b) Total factory payroll for July was $184,239, of which $43,989 were payments for indirect labor. (Assume that payroll has been recorded but not distributed to production accounts.) (c) Factory overhead was applied at a rate of 80 percent of direct labor costs.

1. Prepare journal entries to record the materials, labor, and overhead costs for July.
2. Compute the ending balance in the Work in Process Inventory Control account. Assume that a transfer of $381,480 to the Finished Goods Inventory Control account occurred during the period.

Interpreting Accounting Information

Internal
Management
Information: Dion
Company and
Wilton
Corporation
(L.O.3,5)

Both Dion Company and Wilton Corporation use predetermined overhead rates for product costing, inventory pricing, and sales quotations. The two businesses are about the same size, and they compete in the corrugated-box industry. Dion Company's management believes that since the predetermined overhead rate is an estimated measure, the controller's department should spend little effort developing the rate. The company computes the rate once a year based on a trend analysis of last year's costs. It does not monitor the accuracy of the rate.

Wilton Corporation takes a more sophisticated approach. One person in the controller's office is assigned the responsibility of developing predetermined overhead rates on a monthly basis. All cost inputs are checked out carefully to ensure that the estimates are realistic. Accuracy checks are a routine procedure during each month's closing analysis. Foreseeing normal business changes is part of the overhead rate analyst's regular performance evaluation by her supervisor.

1. Describe the advantages and disadvantages of each company's approach to overhead rate determination.
2. Which company has taken the most cost-effective approach in developing predetermined overhead rates? Defend your answer.
3. Is an accurate overhead rate most important for product costing, inventory valuation, or sales quotations? Why?

Problem Set A

Problem 3A-1.
Application of
Factory Overhead
(L.O.3,4)

Hosseini Laser Products, Inc., uses a predetermined overhead rate in its production, assembly, and testing departments. One rate is used for the entire company, and it is applied based on direct labor hours. The current year's rate was determined by analyzing data from the previous two years and projecting the current year's information, adjusted to reflect expected changes. Mr. Roubi is about to compute the rate for 19x8, and the following data were compiled to assist him in this project:

	19x6	19x7
Direct labor hours	32,500	36,250
Factory overhead costs:		
Indirect materials	$ 32,500	$ 42,250
Indirect labor	26,200	31,440
Factory supervision costs	46,800	51,480
Factory utilities	7,400	8,880
Labor-related costs	18,100	19,910
Depreciation, factory	9,700	10,670
Depreciation, machinery	15,700	18,840
Factory property taxes	2,200	2,640
Factory insurance	1,900	2,280
Miscellaneous factory expenses	3,400	3,740
Total overhead	$163,900	$192,130

In 19x8 the percentage increase of each factory overhead cost item is expected to be the same as its 19x6–19x7 increase. Direct labor hours are anticipated to be 39,650 hours during 19x8.

Required

1. Compute the overhead rate for 19x8. (Round answer to three decimal places.)
2. During 19x8 Hosseini Laser Products, Inc., produced the following jobs with related direct labor hours:

Job	Actual Direct Labor Hours
B142	7,240
B164	4,960
B175	7,800
B201	10,280
B218	11,310
B304	1,460

Determine the amount of factory overhead applied to each job in 19x8. What was the total overhead applied during the year?
3. Prepare the journal entry needed to close the overhead accounts and to dispose of the underapplied or overapplied overhead. Actual factory overhead for 19x8 was $247,840. Assume that the difference between actual and applied overhead costs is considered insignificant.

Problem 3A-2.
Job Order Cost
Flow
(L.O. 6, 8)

Alice James is chief financial officer for Meridian Industries, makers of special-order printers for home personal computers. Her records for February 19x8 reveal the information shown on the following page:

Beginning Inventory balances:

Materials Inventory Control	$42,450
Work in Process Inventory Control	26,900
Finished Goods Inventory Control	31,200

Materials purchased and received:

February 6	$ 6,200
February 12	7,110
February 24	5,890

Direct labor costs:

February 14	$14,750
February 28	15,230

Materials requisitioned into production:

February 4	$ 8,080
February 13	4,940
February 25	9,600

Job order cost cards for jobs in process on February 28:

Job No.	Materials	Direct Labor	Factory Overhead
H310	$2,220	$1,860	$2,232
H414	3,080	2,410	2,892
H730	2,180	1,940	2,328
H916	4,290	2,870	3,444

The predetermined overhead for the month was 120 percent of direct labor dollars. Sales for February totaled $153,360, which represents an 80 percent markup over cost of production.

Required

1. Using T accounts, reconstruct the transactions for February.
2. Compute the cost of units completed during the month.
3. What was the total cost of units sold during February?
4. Determine the ending inventory balances.
5. During the first week of March, Jobs H310 and H414 were completed. No additional materials costs were incurred, but Job H310 needed $920 more in direct labor and Job H414 required additional direct labor of $1,240. Job H310 was composed of 40 units, and Job H414 contained 55 units. Compute each job's unit cost.

Problem 3A-3.
Job Order Costing:
Unknown Quantity
Analysis
(L.O. 6)

Baggett Enterprises makes an assortment of computer support equipment. Mr. Ruggle, the new controller for the organization, can find only partial information from the past two months, which is shown on the following page. The current year's predetermined overhead rate is 80 percent of direct labor dollars.

	May	June
Materials Inventory Control, Beginning	$ 46,240	(e)
Work in Process Inventory Control, Beginning	66,480	(f)
Finished Goods Inventory Control, Beginning	54,260	(g)
Materials Purchased	(a)	$ 96,120
Materials Requisitioned	82,220	(h)
Direct Labor Costs	(b)	71,250
Factory Overhead Applied	52,400	(i)
Cost of Units Completed	(c)	221,400
Cost of Units Sold	209,050	(j)
Materials Inventory Control, Ending	48,810	51,950
Work in Process Inventory Control, Ending	(d)	(k)
Finished Goods Inventory Control, Ending	56,940	61,180

Required

Using the information given, compute the unknown values. Show all your work.

Problem 3A-4.
Job Order Costing:
Journal Entry
Analysis and
T Accounts
(L.O.7)

Vagge, the finest name in parking attendant apparel, has been in business for more than thirty years. Its colorful and stylish uniforms are special ordered by exclusive hotels and country clubs around the world. During April 19x9 Vagge Industries, Inc., performed the transactions described below. Factory overhead was applied at a rate of 90 percent of direct labor cost.

April 1 Materials costing $39,400 were purchased on account.

    3 Materials costing $16,850 were requisitioned into production.

    4 Operating supplies costing $12,830 were purchased for cash.

    8 The company issued checks for the following factory overhead costs: utilities, $1,310; factory insurance, $1,825; repairs charges, $2,640.

    10 The cutting department manager requisitioned $18,510 of materials and $6,480 of operating supplies into production.

    15 Payroll was distributed to the employees. Gross wages and salaries were: direct labor, $72,900; indirect labor, $41,610; factory supervision, $22,900; and sales commissions, $32,980.

    15 Overhead was applied to production.

    22 Overhead expenses were paid: utilities, $1,270; factory maintenance, $1,380; and factory rent, $4,250.

    23 The receiving department recorded purchases and receipts of $21,940 of materials and $8,260 of operating supplies.

    27 Production requisitions for $18,870 of materials and $6,640 of operating supplies were recorded.

    30 The following gross wages and salaries were paid to employees: direct labor, $74,220; indirect labor, $39,290; factory supervision, $24,520; and sales commissions, $36,200.

    30 Factory overhead was applied to production.

April 30   Units completed during the month were transferred to Finished Goods Inventory Control; total cost was $298,400.

30   Sales on account of $398,240 were shipped to customers. Their cost was $264,200.

30   Adjusting entries for the following were recorded:

Depreciation, factory equipment	$1,680
Factory property taxes	1,130

Required

1. Record the journal entries for all April transactions and events. For the payroll entries, concern yourself only with the distribution of factory payroll to the production accounts.
2. Post the entries prepared in part 1 to T accounts, and determine the partial accounts balances.
3. Compute the amount of underapplied or overapplied overhead for April.

Problem 3A-5.
Job Order Costing:
Comprehensive
Journal Entry
Analysis
(L.O.7)

Merriman Information Systems Company is a division of Hilbrich International, Inc. The company designs unique management information systems and produces specialty computer equipment for use on heavy road-construction machinery and underwater search equipment. A job order cost accounting system is used, and the current year's predetermined overhead rate is 80 percent of direct labor dollars.

The Materials Inventory Control account had a balance of $286,750 at the beginning of business on March 1, 19x8. Materials Inventory Subsidiary records revealed the following breakdown: sheet metal, $64,820; casings, $46,110; computer components, $164,880; and supplies inventory, $10,940. There were three jobs in process on March 1, 19x8, and job order cost cards showed the following amounts: Job P-284, $96,250; Job E-302, $61,810; and Job G-325, $22,250. The Work in Process Inventory Control account balance at March 1 was $180,310. All Finished Goods Inventory items had been sold and shipped in February, and no balance existed in the account at the beginning of March. In addition, the Factory Payroll, Factory Overhead Control, and Factory Overhead Applied accounts had no balances carried forward from February because these accounts are closed at the end of each month.

The following transactions occurred during March:

March 1   Received recent purchases along with invoices: sheet metal, $26,440, and casings, $14,980.

2   Requisitioned $2,710 in operating supplies into production.

4   Paid factory overhead costs: electricity, $1,240; water, $290; heat, $1,450; and repairs and maintenance, $620.

5   Received new purchases along with invoices: computer components $42,810; casings, $12,550; and operating supplies, $3,070.

7   Requisitioned materials into production:

Job E-302: sheet metal, $6,480, and computer components, $12,270.

Job G-325: casings, $4,760, and computer components, $16,960.

Job G-410: sheet metal, $12,420; casings, $5,130; and computer components, $3,230.

March   9   Requisitioned operating supplies costing $1,840 into production.

14   Recorded and distributed semimonthly payroll liability to the production accounts: total direct labor, $57,020 (Job P-284, $13,940; Job E-302, $16,720; Job G-325, $20,110; and Job G-410, $6,250); indirect labor wages, $36,190; administrative salaries, $54,200; FICA taxes withheld, $10,320; and federal income taxes withheld, $26,534.

14   Applied factory overhead costs to production.

16   Received purchases of materials along with invoices: sheet metal, $14,520; casings, $13,960; computer components, $26,280; and operating supplies, $3,110.

18   Requisitioned materials into production:
Job E-302: computer components, $12,890.
Job G-325: casings, $14,780, and computer components, $20,520.
Job G-410: sheet metal, $11,460; casings, $11,220; and computer components, $14,610.
Job Y-160: sheet metal, $7,810; casings, $8,730; and computer components, $3,230.

20   Requisitioned operating supplies into production, $4,620.

23   Paid factory overhead expenses: property taxes, $2,470; unemployment compensation taxes, factory, $460; repairs, $1,680; contractual, indirect labor, $2,170; and rent, $1,110.

28   Recorded semimonthly payroll liability and distributed it to the production accounts: total direct labor, $63,080 (Job P-284, $6,210; Job E-302, $9,760; Job G-325, $22,560; Job G-410, $18,940; and Job Y-160, $5,610); indirect labor, $38,770; administrative salaries, $56,540; FICA taxes withheld, $11,090; and federal income taxes withheld, $28,510.

28   Applied factory overhead costs to production.

29   Completed and transferred Jobs P-284 and E-302 to Finished Goods Inventory control.

30   Recorded depreciation on equipment, $1,090.

31   Sold and shipped Job P-284 to customer; selling price, $267,940.

31   Closed out Factory Overhead Control and Factory Overhead Applied accounts and distributed the difference to the Cost of Goods Sold account.

Required

1. Prepare journal entries for all of the preceding transactions and events.
2. Prepare T accounts for all of the general ledger and subsidiary ledger accounts relevant to the job order costing system. Enter the beginning balances when applicable, and post the journal entries prepared in part 1 to these accounts.
3. Check the accuracy of ending inventory control account balances by reconciling them with the totals of their respective subsidiary ledger accounts.

Problem Set B

Problem 3B-1.
Application of
Factory Overhead
(L.O. 3, 4)

Crowley Cosmetics Company applies factory overhead costs on the basis of direct labor dollars. The current predetermined overhead rate is computed by using data from the two prior years, in this case 19x7 and 19x8, adjusted to reflect expectations for the current year, 19x9. Using the information that follows, the controller prepared the overhead rate analysis for 19x9.

	19x7	19x8
Direct labor dollars	$57,500	$ 69,000
Factory overhead costs:		
Indirect labor	$23,100	$ 30,030
Employee fringe benefits	19,000	21,850
Manufacturing supervision	14,800	16,280
Utilities	9,350	13,090
Factory insurance	10,000	13,500
Janitorial services	9,000	11,250
Depreciation, factory and machinery	7,750	9,300
Miscellaneous manufacturing expenses	4,750	5,225
Total overhead	$97,750	$120,525

For the year 19x9 each item of factory overhead costs is expected to increase by the same percentage as it did from 19x7 to 19x8. Direct labor expense is expected to total $82,800 for the year 19x9.

Required

1. Compute the overhead rate for 19x9. Round answer to nearest whole percent.
2. The company actually surpassed its sales and operating expectations. Jobs completed during 19x9 and the related direct labor dollars were as follows: Job 2214, $14,000; Job 2215, $16,000; Job 2216, $11,000; Job 2217, $18,000; Job 2218, $22,000; and Job 2219, $9,000. The total was $90,000. Determine the amount of factory overhead to be applied to each job and to total production during 19x9.
3. Prepare the journal entry needed to close the overhead accounts and to dispose of the underapplied or overapplied overhead. Assume that $160,245 in factory overhead was incurred in 19x9. Also assume that the difference between actual and applied overhead costs is considered insignificant.

Problem 3B-2.
Job Order Cost
Flow
(L.O. 6, 8)

September 1 inventory balances of Granger House, manufacturers of high-quality children's clothing, were as follows:

Materials Inventory Control	$41,360
Work in Process Inventory Control	25,112
Finished Goods Inventory Control	27,120

Job order cost cards for jobs in process as of September 30, 19x7, revealed the following:

Job No.	Materials	Direct Labor	Factory Overhead
24A	$1,496	$1,390	$1,529
24B	1,392	1,480	1,628
24C	1,784	1,960	2,156
24D	1,408	1,760	1,936

Materials purchased and received in September:

September 4	$23,120
September 16	18,600
September 22	21,920

Direct labor costs for September:

September 15 payroll	$33,680
September 29 payroll	35,960

Predetermined overhead rate: 110 percent of direct labor dollars

Materials requisitioned into production during September:

September 6	$27,240
September 23	28,960

Finished goods with a 75 percent markup over cost were sold during September for $350,000.

Required

1. Using T accounts, reconstruct the transactions for September.
2. Compute the cost of units completed during the period.
3. What was the total cost of units sold during September?
4. Determine the ending inventory balances.
5. During the first week of October, Jobs 24A and 24C were completed. No additional materials costs were incurred, but Job 24A required $960 more in direct labor, and Job 24C needed additional direct labor of $1,610. Job 24A was composed of 1,200 pairs of trousers, and Job 24C's customer ordered 950 shirts. Compute each job's unit cost.

Problem 3B-3.
Job Order Costing:
Unknown Quantity
Analysis
(L.O. 6)

Partial operating data for the Duckworth Picture Company for March and April are given below. Management has decided on an overhead rate of 140 percent of direct labor dollars for the current year.

	March	April
Beginning Materials Inventory Control	(a)	(e)
Beginning Work in Process Inventory Control	$ 99,505	(f)
Beginning Finished Goods Inventory Control	89,764	$ 77,660
Materials Requisitioned	58,025	(g)
Materials Purchased	57,090	60,116
Direct Labor Costs	48,760	54,540
Factory Overhead Applied	(b)	(h)
Cost of Units Completed	(c)	229,861
Cost of Goods Sold	165,805	(i)
Ending Materials Inventory Control	43,014	38,628
Ending Work in Process Inventory Control	(d)	(j)
Ending Finished Goods Inventory Control	77,660	40,515

Required

Using the data provided, compute the amount of each lettered unknown. Show your computations.

Problem 3B-4.
Job Order Costing:
Journal Entry
Analysis and
T Accounts
(L.O. 7)

Schoenthal Manufacturing, Inc., produces electric golf carts. These carts are special-order items, so a job order cost accounting system is needed. Factory overhead is applied at the rate of 80 percent of direct labor cost. Below is a listing of events and transactions for January.

Jan. 1 Materials costing $196,400 were purchased on account.

2 $38,500 in operating supplies were purchased on account.

4 Production personnel requisitioned materials costing $184,200 and operating supplies costing $32,100 into production.

10 The following overhead costs were paid: utilities, $4,400; factory rent, $3,500; and maintenance charges, $2,800.

15 Payroll was distributed to employees. Gross wages and salaries were as follows: direct labor, $138,000; indirect labor, $52,620; sales commissions, $32,400; and administrative salaries, $38,000.

15 Overhead was applied to production.

19 Operating supplies costing $37,550 and materials listed at $210,450 were purchased on account.

21 Materials costing $202,750 and operating supplies costing $39,400 were requisitioned into production.

26 Production completed during the month was transferred to Finished Goods Inventory Control. Total costs assigned to these jobs were $473,590.

31 The following gross wages and salaries were paid to employees: direct labor, $152,000; indirect labor, $56,240; sales commissions, $31,200; and administrative salaries, $38,000.

31 Overhead was applied to production.

31 Products costing $404,520 were shipped to customers during the month. Total selling price of these goods was $536,800, and the sales should be recorded at month end.

31 The following overhead costs (adjusting entries) should be recorded: prepaid insurance expired, $4,900; property taxes (payable at year end), $4,200; and depreciation, machinery, $53,500.

Required

1. Record the journal entries for all January transactions and events. For the payroll entries concern yourself only with the distribution of factory payroll to the production accounts.
2. Post the entries prepared in part 1 to T accounts, and determine the partial account balances.
3. Compute the amount of underapplied or overapplied factory overhead on January 31.

Problem 3B-5.
Job Order Costing:
Comprehensive
Journal Entry
Analysis
(L.O.7)

The Benz Manufacturing Company maintains a job order cost accounting system. The company uses an overhead application rate of 130 percent of direct labor costs.

Accounting records on August 1 showed that the Materials Inventory Control account balance was $93,390 and the materials subsidiary ledger balances were $41,800 for mixing fluid, $38,610 for MX powder, and $12,980 for supplies inventory. The Work in Process Inventory Control account balance was $85,060, and the subsidiary ledger job order cost card balances were $61,910 for Job 16-A; $19,730 for Job 18-A; and $3,420 for Job 20-A. The Finished Goods Inventory Control account balance was $67,850, and the finished goods subsidiary ledger balances were: none for Product 16; $29,240 for Product 18; and $38,610 for Product 20.

The Factory Payroll, Factory Overhead Control, and Factory Overhead Applied accounts have no balances carried forward from July because these accounts are closed at the end of each month. The following transactions and events occurred during August:

Aug. 1 Operating supplies totaling $8,740 were requisitioned into production.

4 $55,650 in mixing fluid and $36,720 in MX powder were purchased and received on account.

6 The following factory overhead costs were paid in cash: factory rent, $2,850; heat, light, and power, $1,290; repairs and maintenance, $5,240; and outside contractual services, $6,525.

9 The following semimonthly payroll liability was recorded: gross direct labor wages, $40,250 (Job 16-A, $26,640; Job 18-A, $7,800; and Job 20-A, $5,810); gross indirect labor wages, $19,420; gross administrative salaries, $9,250; FICA taxes withheld, $4,535; federal income taxes withheld, $16,320.

9 Factory payroll was distributed to the production accounts.

9 Factory overhead costs were applied to production.

12 $14,120 in operating supplies were purchased and received on account.

13 $35,280 in mixing fluid and $19,960 in MX powder were requisitioned into production for Job 18-A.

14 Payroll checks for the liability recorded on August 9 were prepared and distributed to the employees.

15 Property taxes of $4,100 were paid and chargeable to factory overhead.

18 Job 16-A was completed and transferred to Finished Goods Inventory.

20 $21,890 in mixing fluid and $16,770 in MX powder were requisitioned into production for Job 20-A.

23 The following semimonthly payroll liability was recorded: gross direct wages, $31,220 (Job 18-A, $19,410; Job 20-A, $11,810); gross indirect labor wages, $18,140; gross administrative salaries, $8,250; FICA taxes payable, $3,460; and federal income taxes withheld, $14,980.

23 Factory payroll was distributed to production accounts.

23 Factory overhead costs were applied to production.

26 A major portion of Job 16-A was sold and shipped to a customer. Four thousand liters were shipped at a cost of $23 per liter. This shipment sold for $139,840.

28 Payroll checks for the liability recorded on August 23 were prepared and distributed to the employees.

Aug. 30   Depreciation on machinery of $14,940 for the month was recorded.

30   The Factory Overhead Control and the Factory Overhead Applied accounts were closed out, and the difference was distributed to the Cost of Goods Sold account.

Required

1. Prepare journal entries for all the preceding transactions and events.
2. Prepare T accounts for all general ledger and subsidiary ledger accounts relevant to the job order costing system.   Enter the beginning balances when applicable, and post the journal entries prepared in part **1** to these accounts.
3. Check the accuracy of ending inventory control account balances by comparing them with the totals on the subsidiary ledger accounts.

Management Decision Case

Fornstrom Manufacturing Company *(L.O. 5, 6, 8)*   Fornstrom Manufacturing Company is a small, family-owned business that makes specialty plastic products.   Since it started three years ago, the company has grown quickly and now employs ten production people.   Because of its size, the company uses a job order cost accounting system designed around a periodic inventory method.   Work sheets and special analyses are used to account for manufacturing costs and inventory valuations.

Two months ago the company's accountant quit.   You have now been called in to assist management.   The following information has been given to you:

Beginning inventory balances (1/1/x7):

Materials	$20,420
Work in Process (Job K-2)	69,100
Finished Goods (Job K-1)	81,700

Materials requisitioned into production during 19x7:

Job K-2	$19,000
Job K-4	38,800
Job K-6	58,000

Direct labor for the year:

Job K-2	$37,300
Job K-4	46,480
Job K-6	75,600

The company purchased materials only once during the year, and all jobs use the same material.   Purchases totaled $96,500.   For the current year the company has been using an overhead application rate of 125 percent of direct labor dollars. So far in 19x7, two jobs, K-2 and K-4, have been completed.   Jobs K-1 and K-2 have been shipped to customers.   Job K-1 was made up of 3,000 units.   Job K-2 contained 5,500 units.   Job K-4 has 4,800 units.

Required

1. Reconstruct the job order cost sheets for each job worked on during the period. What were the unit costs for jobs K-1, K-2, and K-4? Round answer to nearest cent.
2. From the information given and using T account analysis, compute the current balances in the three inventory accounts and the cost of goods sold.
3. The president has asked you to analyze the current job order cost accounting system. Should the system be changed? How? Why? Prepare an outline of your response to the president.

Product Costing:
The Process Cost System

A major goal in using any cost accounting system is to find product unit costs and to set ending values for Materials, Work in Process, and Finished Goods inventories. Continuous product flows (liquids) and long production runs of identical or standard products generally require a process cost accounting system. With this system, manufacturing costs are not traced to specific products or job orders. Instead, they are averaged over the units produced in each period of time.

Process costing depends on a three-schedule analysis: (1) the schedule of equivalent production; (2) the unit cost analysis schedule; and (3) the cost summary schedule. From the information in these three schedules, it is possible to tell what costs to attach to units completed and transferred out of the department. Then a journal entry is used to transfer these costs out of the Work in Process Inventory account. Those costs remaining in the Work in Process Inventory account belong to units still in process at period end.

This chapter will analyze the process cost accounting system and explain how to calculate product unit costs. It will also explain how to compute and verify the period-end balance for the Work in Process Inventory account and the costs assigned to units completed. These units will have been transferred either to the next department or to the Finished Goods Inventory account. After studying this chapter, you should be able to meet the learning objectives listed on the left.

In Chapter 3 we compared the characteristics of job order costing and process costing. You will remember that a process cost accounting system is used by companies in such environments as the paint, oil, fastener (screws and bolts), gas, and beverage industries, as well as companies employing a just-in-time (JIT) operating concept. These companies produce large amounts of similar products or have a continuous production flow. A process costing system has the following characteristics: (1) cost data are collected by department or work center, with little concern for specific job orders; (2) a weekly or monthly time period is emphasized rather than the time it takes to complete a specific order; and (3) the accounting system uses several Work in Process Inventory accounts—one for each department or work center in the manufacturing process. A complete discussion of the just-in-time approach to purchasing, product costing, inventory management, and production is included in Chapters 15 and 16.

Cost Flow Through
Work in Process Inventory Accounts

Accounting for the costs of materials, direct labor, and factory overhead does not differ much between job order costing and process costing. Under both systems costs must be recorded and eventually charged to production. Materials and supplies must be purchased and requisitioned into production. Direct labor wages must be paid to the employees and charged to production accounts. And costs of various types of factory overhead are assigned to production. Journal entries such as those described in Chapter 3 record these transactions and events. So as you can see, the flow of costs *into* the Work in Process Inventory account is very similar in the two product costing systems.

The major difference between job order cost accounting and process cost accounting is the way costs are assigned to products. In a job order cost system, costs are traced to specific jobs and products. In a process cost system, however, an averaging technique is used. For computing unit cost in the process cost system, all products worked on during a specific time period (a week or a month) are used as the output base. Total costs of materials, direct labor, and factory overhead accumulated in the Work in Process Inventory account (or accounts) are divided by the equivalent units worked on during the period. This procedure may seem clear enough, but technical aspects make it more difficult than it first appears. These aspects are discussed below.

Work in Process Inventory Accounts

OBJECTIVE 1

Explain the role of the Work in Process Inventory account(s) in a process cost accounting system

The Work in Process Inventory account is the focal point of process costing. Unlike the job order approach, a process cost system is not limited to one Work in Process Inventory account. In fact, process costing uses as many Work in Process Inventory accounts as there are departments or steps in the production process. The process shown in Figure 4-1 has two departments. Finished units of Department 1 become the direct materials input of Department 2. As shown in this figure, the three cost elements flow into the Work in Process Inventory account of Department 1. The total unit cost of each completed product from Department 1 moves to Department 2 along with the completed unit. In Department 2 the products from Department 1 are processed further. No more materials are needed in Department 2, but as shown in Figure 4-1, more labor is used and factory overhead is assigned, usually on the basis of machine hours, labor cost, or labor hours.

When the completed products are finished, they are transferred from Work in Process Inventory (Department 2) to Finished Goods Inventory. At that point each unit's cost amount is made up of five cost inputs. Three are from Department 1 and two from Department 2. A detailed breakdown, using hypothetical dollar amounts, is shown on the following page.

Figure 4-1. Cost Elements and Process Cost Accounts

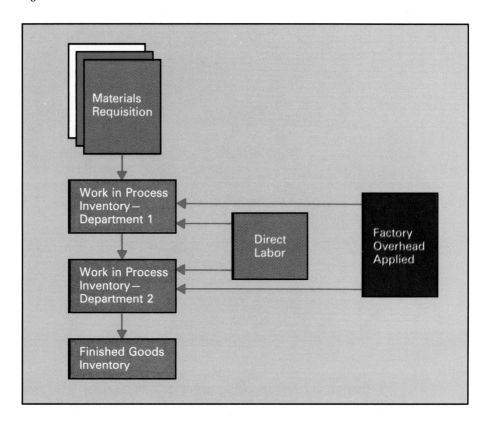

	Total Unit Cost	
Department 1		
Materials	$1.40	
Direct Labor	1.10	
Factory Overhead	.55	
Total, Department 1		$3.05
Department 2		
Direct Labor	$1.90	
Factory Overhead	2.09	
Total, Department 2		3.99
Total unit cost (to Finished Goods Inventory)		$7.04

Production Flow Combinations

There are hundreds of ways that product flows can combine with department or production processes. Two basic structures are illustrated in Figure 4-2. Example 1 shows a series of three processes or departments. The completed product of one department becomes the direct materials

Figure 4-2. Cost Flow for Process Costing

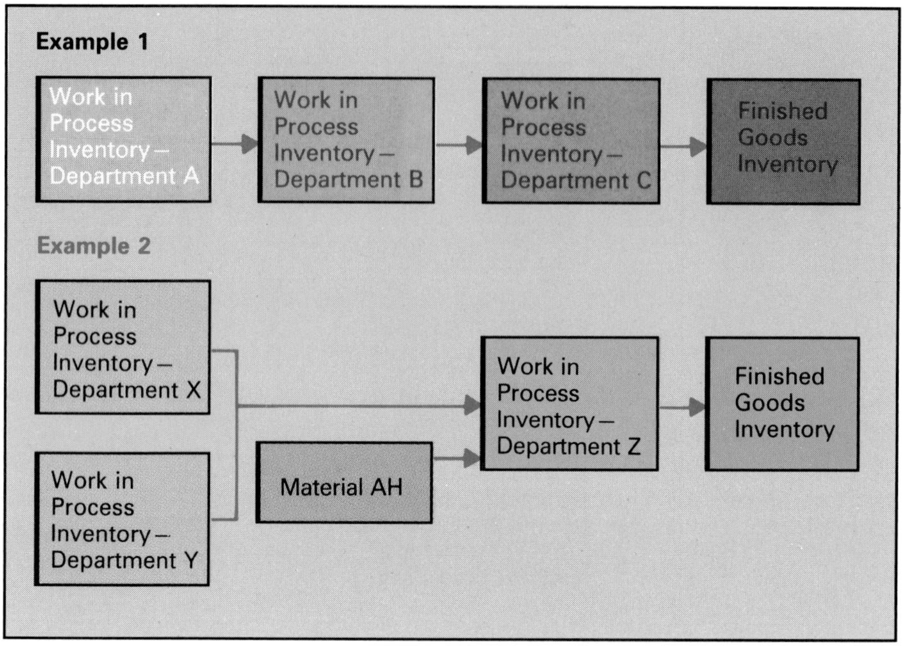

input of the next department. (Figure 4-1 also showed a series of departments.) The number of departments in a series can range from two to more than a dozen. The important point to remember is that product unit cost is the sum of the cost elements used in all departments.

OBJECTIVE 2
Describe product flow and cost flow through a process cost accounting system

Example 2 in Figure 4-2 shows a different type of production flow. Again, there are three departments. In this example, however, the product does not flow through all departments in a simple 1-2-3 order. Here, two separate products are developed, one in Department X and another in Department Y. Both products then go to Department Z, where they are joined with a third direct material input, Material AH. The unit cost transferred to Finished Goods Inventory when the products are completed includes cost elements from Departments X, Y, and Z. The possible combinations of departments or processes are limitless.

Note: The three-schedule cost analysis illustrated in this chapter must be prepared for *each* department for *each* time period. Thus, a company with three production departments and two monthly time periods must prepare six sets of the three-schedule analysis.

The Concept of Equivalent Production

A key component of a process cost accounting system is the computation of equivalent units of production for each accounting period. This computation is needed to arrive at product unit costs.

Remember that in process costing, an averaging approach is used. All manufacturing costs incurred by a department or production process are divided by the units produced during the period. No attempt is made to associate costs with particular job orders. There are, however, several important questions: How many units were produced? Do you count only those units completed during the period? What about partly completed units in the beginning Work in Process Inventory? Do you count units even if only part of the work needed to complete them was done during this period? What about products in ending Work in Process Inventory? Is it proper to focus only on those units started and completed during the period?

OBJECTIVE 3
Compute equivalent production for situations with and without units in the beginning Work in Process Inventory

The answers to all these questions are linked to the concept of equivalent production. **Equivalent production** (also called **equivalent units**) is a measure of units produced in a period of time. This measure is expressed in terms of fully completed or equivalent whole units produced. Partly completed units are restated in terms of equivalent whole units. The number of equivalent units produced must be found. It is equal to the sum of (1) total units started and completed during the period and (2) an amount for partly completed products. This amount is a restatement of these units in terms of equivalent whole units. A *percentage of completion* factor is used to calculate the number of equivalent whole units. Figure 4-3 illustrates the equivalent unit computation. Three automobiles were started and completed during February. In addition, one-half (.5) of Car A is completed in February, and three-quarters (.75) of Car E is completed. To find the total equivalent units for the month, the units started and completed (3.0) and the units partly completed (.5 and .75) are added

Figure 4-3. Equivalent Unit Computation

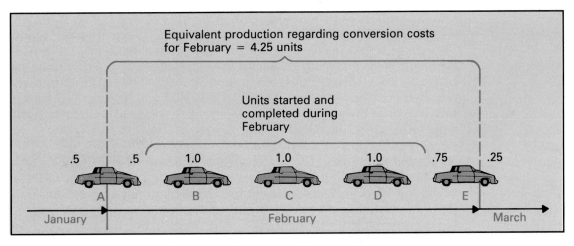

Facts: Conversion costs (those for direct labor and factory overhead) are incurred uniformly as each car moves through production. Equivalent production for February is 4.25 units as to conversion costs. But materials costs are all added to production at the beginning of the process. Since four cars entered production in February (cars B, C, D, and E), equivalent production for the month is 4.0 units as to materials costs.

together. Therefore, equivalent production for February for direct labor and factory overhead is 4.25 units.

Once you know the number of equivalent units produced, you can compute unit costs for materials and conversion costs for each department in the production process. **Conversion costs** are the combined total of direct labor and factory overhead costs incurred by a production department. The equations for computing unit cost amounts appear below. (Note the role of equivalent units.)

$$\text{Unit cost for materials} = \frac{\text{total materials costs}}{\text{equivalent units—materials}}$$

$$\text{Unit cost for conversion costs} = \frac{\text{total labor and factory overhead costs}}{\text{equivalent units—conversion costs}}$$

Computing equivalent units of production for materials usually differs from computing equivalent units of production for conversion costs. As shown in Figure 4-3, materials are usually all added in at the beginning of a process. Therefore, materials for Car A were added in January and do not influence equivalent units for materials in February. However, materials for Car E were *all* added to production in February. By adding 3.0 (units started and completed—Cars B, C, and D) and 1.0 (unit started but not completed—Car E) we get the equivalent units of production for materials for February (4.0 units).

The Average Costing Approach

Cost flow and accountability need not follow the same assumptions as those supporting the flow of products. Such is the case with the **average costing** approach to process cost accounting. Products flow in a first-in, first-out (FIFO) manner in a process costing environment. It is assumed that beginning inventory items are completed as new ones are brought into the production process. But following the average costing approach, we do not account for costs in the same manner as actual product flow. *The average process costing method is based on the assumption that the items in beginning Work in Process Inventory were started and completed during the current period.* Although a bit less accurate than the FIFO costing approach (an alternative approach to process costing that will be described later in this chapter), the average costing method is easier to understand and work with. It is illustrated below.

No Beginning Work in Process Inventory. To begin this detailed analysis for calculating equivalent production, assume that there are no units in beginning Work in Process Inventory. Thus, you need to consider only (1) units started and completed during the period and (2) units started but not completed. By definition, units started but not completed are the units in the ending Work in Process Inventory. Equivalent production is figured in parts as follows:

Part 1: Units started and completed = (number of units) × 100 percent

Part 2: Equivalent units in ending work in process inventory = (number of units) × (percentage of completion)

Exhibit 4-1. Equivalent Units: No Beginning Inventory

Danelid Clothing, Inc.
Schedule of Equivalent Production
For the Month Ended January 31, 19xx

Units—Stage of Completion	Units to Be Accounted For	Equivalent Units Materials Costs	Conversion Costs
Beginning inventory—units completed in this period	—	—	—
Units started and completed in this period: (47,500 − 6,200)	41,300	41,300	41,300
Ending inventory— units started but not completed in this period:	6,200		
Materials (100% complete)		6,200	
Conversion costs (60% complete)			3,720
Totals	47,500	47,500	45,020

The *sum* of these two amounts is the equivalent whole units completed during the period. The percentage of completion figures are supplied by engineers or supervisors in the production departments.

Earlier we noted an important point about computing unit cost. Direct labor and factory overhead costs are usually lumped together and called conversion costs. The reason is that both costs are usually incurred uniformly throughout the production process. Combining them is convenient. Materials costs are generally not incurred uniformly throughout the process. They are normally incurred either at the beginning of the process (materials input) or at the end of it (packing materials). Because of this difference, the equivalent unit amount for materials will not be the same as that for conversion costs. Separate computations are necessary.

For example, assume that the records of Danelid Clothing, Inc., for January 19xx show the following information: (a) 47,500 units were started during the period; (b) 6,200 units were partly complete at period end; (c) units in ending Work in Process Inventory were 60 percent complete; (d) materials were added at the *beginning* of the process; (e) conversion costs were incurred *uniformly* throughout the process; and (f) no units were lost or spoiled during the month.

In the **schedule of equivalent production**, equivalent production is computed for the period for both materials and conversion costs. This schedule is shown for Danelid Clothing in Exhibit 4-1. Because there were no units in beginning Work in Process Inventory, dashes are entered in that row. As you can see, 41,300 units were started and completed during the period (47,500 units started less 6,200 units not completed).

All 41,300 received 100 percent of the materials, labor, and overhead effort needed to complete them. Therefore, 41,300 equivalent units are recorded in both the Materials Costs and Conversion Costs columns.

Accounting for equivalent units in ending inventory is a bit more complicated. These 6,200 units received all materials inputs because materials were added to each product as it entered the production process. Therefore, in the materials column 6,200 equivalent units are entered. However, as you know, conversion costs are added uniformly as the products move through the process. The 6,200 units in ending inventory are only 60 percent complete. So the number of equivalent whole units can be calculated by multiplying the number of actual units by the percentage completed. In Exhibit 4-1 the amount of equivalent units for conversion costs of ending inventory is 6,200 units × 60% completion = 3,720 equivalent units. As a result of these computations for January, we know there are 47,500 equivalent units for materials costs and 45,020 equivalent units for conversion costs.

With Beginning Work in Process Inventory. A situation with no beginning Work in Process Inventory is almost never found in industry. By definition, process costing techniques are used in industries in which production flows continuously or in which there are long runs of identical products. In these cases, there is always something in process at month end. So there are always units in beginning Work in Process Inventory in the next period. Now turn to the following situation, which expands on the example used above.

During February 19xx, unit production information for Danelid Clothing, Inc., was as follows: (a) 6,200 units were in beginning Work in Process Inventory; (b) beginning inventory items were 60 percent completed; (c) 57,500 units were started during the period; (d) 5,000 units were in ending Work in Process Inventory; and (e) ending inventory was 45 percent completed as to conversion costs (all materials have been added).

The presence of beginning inventories makes it a little more difficult to compute equivalent units. Exhibit 4-2 illustrates the computation of equivalent units using the *average costing approach* when beginning inventory items must be accounted for. Remember, in average costing we treat all units in beginning Work in Process Inventory as if they were started and completed in the current period. With the inclusion of beginning inventories, equivalent production is calculated in three parts as follows:

Part 1: Equivalent units in beginning inventory = number of units × 100 percent

Part 2: Units started and completed = number of units × 100 percent

Part 3: Equivalent units in ending inventory:

> Materials costs = number of units × percentage of completion
> Conversion costs = number of units × percentage of completion

Exhibit 4-2. Equivalent Units: With Beginning Inventory

Danelid Clothing, Inc.
Schedule of Equivalent Production
For the Month Ended February 29, 19xx

Units—Stage of Completion	Units to Be Accounted For	Equivalent Units	
		Materials Costs	Conversion Costs
Beginning inventory—units completed in this period	6,200	6,200	6,200
Units started and completed in this period	52,500	52,500	52,500
Ending inventory— units started but not completed in this period:	5,000		
Materials (100% complete)		5,000	
Conversion costs (45% complete)			2,250
Totals	63,700	63,700	60,950

February operations of Danelid Clothing, Inc., involve both beginning and ending balances in Work in Process Inventory. As shown in Exhibit 4-2, the 6,200 units in beginning inventory are extended at their full amount to the materials costs and conversion costs columns of the schedule. This treatment is the same as that given to the 52,500 units started and completed during February (57,500 units started minus 5,000 unfinished units). Units started and completed receive the full amount of materials costs and conversion costs. Ending inventory is 100 percent complete as to materials (5,000 units). It is 45 percent complete as to conversion costs (5,000 × 45% = 2,250). The end result is that February produced 63,700 equivalent units that had materials costs added and 60,950 equivalent units that used conversion costs. (Note that these illustrations cover only two of the hundreds of possible process costing situations that could arise with varying percentages of completion.)

FIFO Costing Approach

Figure 4-3 on page 125 illustrated the *FIFO product flow* normally associated with process cost accounting. Industries that produce liquid products or engage in long production runs of identical products use the process costing method. With such a production flow, the first unit to enter the production process during a period is the first to be completed. Therefore, the FIFO product flow is part of the process cost accounting system.

FIFO cost flow is an assumption underlying the FIFO method of determining product unit cost. This method assigns costs to products based on FIFO product flow and the work performed in a given time period. It is a second method used for product costing in a process cost accounting system. The first method, the average costing approach, has already been discussed. Although a bit more accurate, the FIFO approach is a more complex method and will be left for a more advanced course in cost accounting. The FIFO approach is mentioned only to make you aware of an alternative method to the one disclosed in this chapter.

Cost Analysis Schedules

OBJECTIVE 4
Compute product unit cost for a specific time period (unit cost analysis schedule)

So far, accounting for *units* of productive output has been emphasized. In the schedule of equivalent production, the total units to be accounted for were determined. Then equivalent units for materials costs and conversion costs were computed. Once the unit information is sorted out and equivalent unit figures have been computed, the dollar information can be considered. Now manufacturing costs, cost per equivalent unit, and inventory costing are brought into the analysis.

Unit Cost Analysis Schedule

The **unit cost analysis schedule** is the second of the three schedules used in process costing. This schedule does two things: (1) All costs charged to the Work in Process Inventory account of a particular department or production process are added together. (2) Costs per equivalent unit for materials and conversion costs are computed. A unit cost analysis schedule is shown in Exhibit 4-3.

Unit costs are arrived at in two steps. The first step in the schedule is to summarize all costs for the period. These costs are made up of costs

Exhibit 4-3. Unit Cost Determination: No Beginning Inventories

Danelid Clothing, Inc.
Unit Cost Analysis Schedule
For the Month Ended January 31, 19xx

| | Total Costs | | | | Equivalent Unit Costs | | |
	Costs from Beginning Inventory	Costs from Current Period	Total Costs to Be Accounted For	÷	Equivalent Units	=	Cost per Equivalent Unit
Materials	—	$154,375	$154,375		47,500		$3.25
Conversion costs	—	258,865	258,865		45,020		5.75
Totals	—	$413,240	$413,240				$9.00

of materials and conversion costs incurred in the current period plus the costs included in the beginning Work in Process Inventory. (The Total Costs to Be Accounted For later serves as a figure for checking the third schedule—the cost summary schedule.)

The second step in the unit cost analysis is to divide the costs by the number of equivalent units. Total costs for materials are divided by the equivalent units for materials. In the same way, total conversion costs are divided by the equivalent units for conversion costs. When you use the average cost flow assumption, units and costs in beginning inventory are included in figuring the period's costs per equivalent unit.

Cost Summary Schedule

OBJECTIVE 5
Prepare a cost summary schedule that assigns costs to units completed and transferred out of the department during the period, and find the ending Work in Process Inventory balance

The final phase of the process costing analysis is to distribute the total costs accumulated during the period among all the units of output. Some costs may stay in ending Work in Process Inventory. Others must go with the units completed and transferred out of the department. Costs are assigned by means of the **cost summary schedule**. Information in this schedule comes from both the schedule of equivalent production and the unit cost analysis schedule.

It is fairly easy to compute the total costs to be transferred out of the department. Suppose that 16,500 units were completed during the period and moved to Finished Goods Inventory. Cost per equivalent unit was found to be $3.30. Therefore, $54,450 (16,500 × $3.30) is transferred out of Work in Process Inventory by making a journal entry. All costs remaining in Work in Process Inventory after costs of completed units have been transferred out represent the cost of ending units in process.

To complete the analysis, add together the total cost of units transferred and the costs belonging to ending Work in Process Inventory. Then compare the total with the total costs to be accounted for in the unit cost analysis schedule. If the two totals are not equal, there has been an arithmetic error (normally due to rounding).

Illustrative Analysis

To fully explain the form and use of the cost schedules, the Danelid Clothing, Inc., example will be expanded. Besides the equivalent unit information discussed earlier, the company has the following cost data:

January 19xx	
Beginning Work in Process Inventory	—
Cost of materials used	$154,375
Conversion costs for the month	258,865
February 19xx	
Cost of materials used	$190,060
Conversion costs for the month	319,930

From these data the equivalent unit costs, total costs transferred to Finished Goods Inventory, and the ending balance in Work in Process Inventory for January and February 19xx will be computed.

January. The unit cost analysis schedule for January is shown in Exhibit 4-3. Total costs to be accounted for are $413,240. Of this amount, costs for materials are $154,375, and conversion costs are $258,865. When these costs are divided by the equivalent unit amounts (computed in Exhibit 4-1), you get costs per equivalent unit of $3.25 for materials ($154,375 ÷ 47,500) and $5.75 for conversion costs ($258,865 ÷ 45,020). Total unit cost for the period is $9.00. The per unit cost amounts are used in the cost summary schedule shown in Exhibit 4-4 to compute costs transferred to Finished Goods Inventory and the costs assigned to ending Work in Process Inventory.

In Danelid's cost summary schedule for January, shown in Exhibit 4-4, no units were in process at the beginning of January, so no costs are entered for beginning inventory. (Even though there was no beginning inventory for January, the headings are included so the form can be used for any process costing situation.) Units transferred to Finished Goods Inventory in January are made up entirely of units started and completed,

Exhibit 4-4. Ending Inventory Computation: No Beginning Inventories

Danelid Clothing, Inc.
Cost Summary Schedule
For the Month Ended January 31, 19xx

	Costs of Goods Transferred to Finished Goods Inventory	Costs in Ending Work in Process Inventory
Beginning inventory		
None	—	
Units started and completed:*		
41,300 units × $9.00 per unit	$371,700	
Ending inventory:*		
Materials: 6,200 units × $3.25		$ 20,150
Conversion costs:		
3,720 units × $5.75		21,390
Totals	$371,700	$ 41,540
Check on computations:		
Costs to Finished Goods Inventory		$371,700
Costs in ending Work in Process Inventory		41,540
Total costs accounted for (unit cost analysis schedule)		$413,240

*Note: Unit figures come from the schedule of equivalent production for January (Exhibit 4-1).

since there were no units in beginning inventory. These 41,300 units cost $9.00 each to produce (total cost per equivalent unit). So $371,700 must be transferred to Finished Goods Inventory.

During January $413,240 was debited to Work in Process Inventory. Of that amount, $371,700 was transferred to Finished Goods Inventory. The difference of $41,540 remaining in the account is the ending Work in Process Inventory balance. This amount is verified in Exhibit 4-4. Using the ending inventory amounts from the schedule of equivalent production in Exhibit 4-1 and the costs per equivalent unit from the cost analysis schedule in Exhibit 4-3, we make the following computations:

Materials costs: 6,200 equivalent units × $3.25 per unit	$20,150
Conversion costs: 3,720 equivalent units × $5.75 per unit	21,390
Ending Work in Process Inventory balance	$41,540

The check of computations at the bottom of Exhibit 4-4 ensures that all the arithmetic is right. Total costs computed in Exhibit 4-3 have been accounted for.

February. The cost analysis for February is a bit more difficult because units and costs in beginning Work in Process Inventory must be considered. February operating results are analyzed in Exhibits 4-5 and 4-6. Total costs to be accounted for in February are $551,530. Included in this amount is the beginning inventory balance of $41,540 (see Exhibit 4-4) plus current costs from February of $190,060 and $319,930 for materials and conversion costs, respectively. These costs are then added to the materials and conversion costs carried over from January in the Work in Process Inventory account. The total costs to be accounted for are then divided by the equivalent unit figures computed in Exhibit 4-2. February's $8.90 cost per equivalent unit includes $3.30 per unit for materials and $5.60 per unit for conversion costs.

Exhibit 4-5. Unit Cost Determination: With Beginning Inventories

Danelid Clothing, Inc.
Unit Cost Analysis Schedule
For the Month Ended February 29, 19xx

	Total Costs				Equivalent Unit Costs	
	Costs from Beginning Inventory	Costs from Current Period	Total Costs to Be Accounted For	÷	Equivalent Units	=	Cost per Equivalent Unit
Materials	$20,150	$190,060	$210,210		63,700		$3.30
Conversion costs	21,390	319,930	341,320		60,950		5.60
Totals	$41,540	$509,990	$551,530				$8.90

Exhibit 4-6. Ending Inventory Computation: With Beginning Inventories

Danelid Clothing, Inc.
Cost Summary Schedule
For the Month Ended February 29, 19xx

	Cost of Goods Transferred to Finished Goods Inventory	Costs in Ending Work in Process Inventory
Beginning inventory:*		
6,200 units × $8.90 per unit	$ 55,180	
Units started and completed:*		
52,500 units × $8.90 per unit	467,250	
Ending inventory:*		
Materials: 5,000 units × $3.30		$ 16,500
Conversion costs:		
2,250 units × $5.60		12,600
Totals	$522,430	$ 29,100
Check on computations:		
Costs to Finished Goods Inventory		$522,430
Costs in ending Work in Process		
Inventory		29,100
Total costs to be accounted for		
(unit cost analysis schedule)		$551,530

*Note: Unit figures come from schedule of equivalent production (Exhibit 4-2).

    The February cost analysis is finished by preparing the cost summary schedule (Exhibit 4-6). Costs transferred to Finished Goods Inventory total $522,430. This amount includes costs of $55,180 for the 6,200 units in beginning inventory and costs of $467,250 for the 52,500 units started and completed during February.

    The ending Work in Process Inventory balance of $29,100 is made up of $16,500 in materials costs and $12,600 in conversion costs. At the bottom of the cost summary schedule, a check ensures that no arithmetic errors were made.

Journal Entry Analysis

Although schedules for (1) equivalent production, (2) unit cost analysis, and (3) cost summary have been emphasized, none of these schedules offers a direct way to transfer costs in the accounting records. All three schedules deal mostly with the Work in Process Inventory account. The goal of doing a process costing analysis is to compute dollar totals for goods completed and transferred to Finished Goods Inventory and for partly completed products staying in the Work in Process Inventory account. However, the three schedules alone do not cause costs to flow through accounts in the general ledger. They only give the information needed for journal entries. It is the journal entries that actually move costs from one account to another.

The final step in a process costing analysis, then, is a journal entry to transfer costs of completed products out of Work in Process Inventory. Remember that all entries analyzed in Chapter 3 are also necessary in a process costing system. Only one entry is highlighted here, however, because it is directly involved with the transfer of costs of completed goods. To transfer the costs of units completed, you debit Finished Goods Inventory (or the Work in Process Inventory of a subsequent department) and credit Work in Process Inventory. The amount of the cost transfer was calculated in the cost summary schedule.

In the example of Danelid Clothing, Inc., the following entries would be made at the end of each time period:

Jan. 31	Finished Goods Inventory	371,700	
	Work in Process Inventory		371,700
	To transfer cost of units completed in January to Finished Goods Inventory		

Feb. 29	Finished Goods Inventory	522,430	
	Work in Process Inventory		522,430
	To transfer cost of units completed in February to Finished Goods Inventory		

Once the entries are posted, the Work in Process Inventory account would appear as follows on February 29, 19xx:

Work in Process Inventory

Balance	—	Transferred to Finished	
Jan. materials	154,375	Goods in Jan.	371,700
Jan. conversion costs	258,865		
Balance 1/31/xx	**41,540**		
Feb. materials	190,060	Transferred to Finished	
Feb. conversion costs	319,930	Goods in Feb.	522,430
Balance 2/29/xx	**29,100***		

*This amount is confirmed by the cost summary schedule in Exhibit 4-6.

In the analysis of Danelid Clothing, Inc., it is assumed that the company had only *one* production department, and the example centered on two consecutive monthly accounting periods. Because only one production department was used, only one Work in Process Inventory account was needed. The following example deals with *two* production departments in a series. The product passes from the first to the second department and then to Finished Goods Inventory. This production flow is similar to that illustrated in Figure 4-1. When the production process requires two departments, the accounting system must maintain two Work in Process Inventory accounts, one for each department. This situation calls for more work, but the computations are the same. The key point is to treat *each* department and related Work in Process Inventory account in a separate analysis. The three schedules must be prepared for *each* department. Departments should be analyzed in the same order in which they appear in the series.

Illustrative Problem: Two Production Departments

Zarycki Manufacturing Company produces a liquid chemical for converting salt water into fresh water. The production process involves the Mixing Department and the Cooling Department. Every unit produced must be processed by both departments. Cooling is the final operation.

In the Mixing Department a basic chemical powder, Material BP, is added to salt water, heated to 88° Celsius, and mixed for two hours. Assume that no evaporation occurs and that Material BP is added at the beginning of the process. Conversion costs are incurred uniformly throughout the process. Operating data for the Mixing Department for April 19xx are as follows:

Beginning Work in Process Inventory	
Units (30% complete)	1,450 liters
Costs: Materials	$ 13,050
Conversion costs	1,760
Ending Work in Process Inventory	
All units 60% complete	
April operations	
Units started	55,600 liters
Costs: Materials used	$488,990
Conversion costs	278,990
Units completed and transferred to the Cooling Department	54,800 liters

Required

1. Using good form, prepare: (a) a schedule of equivalent production; (b) a unit cost analysis schedule; and (c) a cost summary schedule.
2. From information in the cost summary schedule, prepare the proper journal entry for transferring costs of completed units for April out of the Mixing Department.

Solution

1. Before doing the three schedules and preparing the journal entry, you should make a special analysis of the units (liters) worked on during April. To complete the schedule of equivalent production, you must first find the number of units started and completed and the number of units in ending Work in Process Inventory. These amounts were not given above, but they can easily be computed, as shown below.

Units started and completed:

	Units completed and transferred (given)	54,800 liters
Less:	Units in beginning inventory (given)	1,450 liters
Equals:	Units started and completed	53,350 liters

Units in ending inventory:

	Units started during April (given)	55,600 liters
Less:	Units started and completed (above)	53,350 liters
Equals:	Units in ending inventory	2,250 liters

Once you know the number of units started and completed and the number of units in ending Work in Process Inventory, you can prepare the three schedules in the cost analysis (shown on this and the following page).

Zarycki Manufacturing Company
Mixing Department
Process Cost Analysis
For the Month Ended April 30, 19xx

1a. Schedule of Equivalent Production

Units—Stage of Completion	Units to Be Accounted For	Equivalent Units	
		Materials Costs	Conversion Costs
Beginning inventory	1,450	1,450	1,450
Units started and completed in this period	53,350	53,350	53,350
Ending inventory—units started but not completed in this period:	2,250		
Materials (100% complete)		2,250	
Conversion costs (60% complete)			1,350 (60% of 2,250)
Totals	57,050	57,050	56,150

1b. Unit Cost Analysis Schedule

	Total Costs			Equivalent Unit Costs		
	Costs from Beginning Inventory	Costs from Current Period	Total Costs to Be Accounted For	÷	Equivalent Units	=	Cost per Equivalent Unit
Materials	$13,050	$488,990	$502,040		57,050		$ 8.80
Conversion costs	1,760	278,990	280,750		56,150		5.00
Totals	$14,810	$767,980	$782,790				$13.80

1c. Cost Summary Schedule

	Cost of Goods Transferred to Cooling Department	Costs in Ending Work in Process Inventory
Beginning inventory:		
1,450 units × $13.80 per unit	$ 20,010	
Units started and completed:		
53,350 units × $13.80 per unit	736,230	
Ending inventory		
Materials: 2,250 units × $8.80		$19,800
Conversion costs:		
1,350 units × $5.00		6,750
Totals	$756,240	$26,550
Check on computations:		
Costs to Cooling Department	$756,240	
Costs in ending Work in Process Inventory	26,550	
Total costs accounted for (unit cost analysis schedule)	$782,790	

2. The costs of completed units for April are now ready to be transferred from the Mixing Department to the Cooling Department. The required journal entry would be as follows:

Work in Process—Cooling Department	756,240	
Work in Process—Mixing Department		756,240
To transfer cost of units completed in April from Mixing Department to Cooling Department		

Note that the $756,240 is being transferred from one Work in Process Inventory account to another. The $756,240 attached to the units transferred into the Cooling Department during April would be accounted for in the same way as materials used in the Mixing Department. All other procedures and schedules illustrated in the Mixing Department example would be used again for the Cooling Department. See the special problem at the end of this chapter for the accounting treatment of the Cooling Department.

Chapter Review

Review of Learning Objectives

1. **Explain the role of the Work in Process Inventory account(s) in a process cost accounting system.**
   The Work in Process Inventory account is the heart of the process cost accounting system. Each production department or operating unit has its own Work in Process Inventory account. All costs charged to that department flow into this inventory account. Special analysis, using three schedules, is needed at period end to determine the costs flowing out of the account. All special analyses in process cost accounting are related to costs in the Work in Process Inventory account.

2. **Describe product flow and cost flow through a process cost accounting system.**
   Products in a process costing environment are liquids or long production runs of identical products. Therefore, products flow in a FIFO fashion (first in, first out). Once a product is started into production, it flows on to completion. Manufacturing costs are handled differently than in a job order costing system. Current costs of materials, direct labor, and factory overhead are added to costs in beginning inventory when computing unit costs. The unit costs are then assigned either to completed units or to units in ending Work in Process Inventory.

3. **Compute equivalent production for situations with and without units in the beginning Work in Process Inventory.**
   The number of equivalent units is found with the aid of a schedule of equivalent production. Units worked on during the period are classified as being: (a) in beginning inventory (started last period and completed this period); (b) started and completed this period; or (c) started this period and still in process at period end. Percentage of completion data are used to compute equivalent units separately for materials and conversion costs.

4. **Compute product unit cost for a specific time period (unit cost analysis schedule).**
   Unit costs are found with the aid of a unit cost analysis schedule. Materials costs for units in beginning inventory and costs for the current period are added together. The same is done for conversion costs. Next, the total cost of materials is divided by the equivalent unit amount for materials. The same procedure is followed for conversion costs. Then, unit cost for materials and unit cost for conversion costs are added to reach total unit cost.

5. Prepare a cost summary schedule that assigns costs to units completed and transferred out of the department during the period, and find the ending Work in Process Inventory balance.

The first part of the cost summary schedule helps you to compute costs assigned to units completed and transferred out during the period. This part is done in two steps: (a) Units in beginning inventory are assigned a full share of production costs. (b) Units started and completed during the current period are also assigned a full share of production costs. The total of these two calculations represents costs attached to units completed and transferred out during the period. The second part of the cost summary schedule assigns costs to units still in process at period end. Unit costs for materials and conversion costs are multiplied by their respective equivalent units. The total of these two dollar amounts represents the ending Work in Process Inventory balance for the period.

6. Make the journal entry(ies) needed to transfer costs of completed units out of the Work in Process Inventory account.

The first part of the cost summary schedule is completed (the part that assigns costs to units completed and transferred out during the period). Then, a journal entry should be prepared to transfer these costs out of the Work in Process Inventory account. A credit is made to the inventory account for the amount being transferred. The debit can be either to Finished Goods Inventory or to another Work in Process Inventory account, depending on the network of production departments in the process.

Review of Concepts and Terminology

The following important concepts were introduced in this chapter:

(L.O.3) **Equivalent production or equivalent units:**   A measure of units produced in a period of time, expressed in terms of fully completed or equivalent whole units produced.

(L.O.3) **Conversion costs:**   The combined total of direct labor and factory overhead costs incurred by a production department.

(L.O.3) **Average costing:**   A process costing method under which unit costs are computed based on the assumption that the items in beginning Work in Process Inventory were started and completed during the current period.

Other important terms introduced in this chapter are:

cost summary schedule (p. 131)
schedule of equivalent production (p. 127)
unit cost analysis schedule (p. 130)

Extended Illustrative Problem: Costs Transferred In

This problem reviews the three-schedule analysis used in process costing. It also introduces two new situations common in process costing.

1. **Transferred-in costs.** Accounting for the second in a series of Work in Process Inventory accounts is much like accounting for the first department's costs.

The only difference is that instead of accounting for current materials costs, you are dealing with *costs transferred in* during the period. All procedures used to account for costs transferred in are exactly the same as those used for materials costs and units. *When accounting for costs and units transferred in, treat them as you would materials added at the beginning of the process.*

2. **Rounding of numerical answers.** Unlike the problems discussed so far in this chapter, most real-world unit costs do not work out to even-numbered dollars and cents. The concept of rounding helps deal with this problem. Remember these three simple rules: (a) Round off all unit cost computations to three decimal places. (b) Round off cost summary data to the nearest dollar. (c) On the cost summary schedule, any difference caused by rounding should be added to or subtracted from the amount being transferred out of the department before the journal entry is prepared.

The purpose of this review problem is to illustrate the accounting approach for the second in a series of production departments and to show how to use cost rounding. We will go on with the example of the Zarycki Manufacturing Company's Cooling Department. Operating data for the Cooling Department for April 19xx are shown below. No new materials are added in this department. Only conversion costs are added in the cooling process.

Beginning Work in Process Inventory
Units (40% complete)		2,100 liters
Costs:	Transferred-in	$ 29,200
	Conversion costs	2,654

Ending Work in Process Inventory
All units 60% complete

April operations
Units transferred-in		54,800 liters
Costs:	Transferred-in	$756,240
	Conversion costs	172,130
Units completed and transferred to Finished Goods Inventory		54,450 liters

Required

1. Using good form, prepare: (a) a schedule of equivalent production; (b) a unit cost analysis schedule; and (c) a cost summary schedule.
2. From the cost summary schedule, prepare the journal entry to transfer costs of completed units for April to Finished Goods Inventory.

Answer to Extended Illustrative Problem

1. Before doing the three-schedule analysis, you should first analyze the unit information, just as before.

Units started and completed:
	Units completed and transferred (given)	54,450 liters
Less:	Units in beginning inventory (given)	2,100 liters
Equals:	Units started and completed	52,350 liters

Zarycki Manufacturing Company
Cooling Department
Process Cost Analysis
For the Month Ended April 30, 19xx

1a. Schedule of Equivalent Production

Units—Stage of Completion	Units to Be Accounted For	Equivalent Units Transferred In	Equivalent Units Conversion Costs
Beginning inventory—units completed in this period	2,100	2,100	2,100
Units started and completed in this period	52,350	52,350	52,350
Ending inventory—units started but not completed in this period:	2,450		
Transferred-in costs (100% complete)		2,450	
Conversion costs (60% complete)			1,470
Totals	56,900	56,900	55,920

1b. Unit Cost Analysis Schedule

	Total Costs Costs from Beginning Inventory	Total Costs Costs from Current Period	Total Costs Total Costs to Be Accounted For	÷	Equivalent Unit Costs Equivalent Units	=	Equivalent Unit Costs Cost per Equivalent Unit
Transferred-in costs	$29,200	$756,240	$785,440		56,900		$13.804*
Conversion costs	2,654	172,130	174,784		55,920		3.126*
Totals	$31,854	$928,370	$960,224				$16.930

1c. Cost Summary Schedule

	Cost of Goods Transferred to Finished Goods Inventory	Costs in Ending Work in Process Inventory
Beginning inventory:		
2,100 units × $16.930 per unit	$ 35,553†	
Units started and completed:		
52,350 units × $16.930 per unit	886,286†	
Ending inventory:		
Transferred-in costs: 2,450 units × $13.804		$33,820†
Conversion costs: 1,470 units × $3.126		4,595†
Totals	$921,839	$38,415
Check on computations:		
Costs to Finished Goods Inventory	$921,839	
Costs in ending Work in Process Inventory	38,415	
Error caused by rounding—subtract from costs transferred to Finished Goods Inventory	(30)	
Total costs to be accounted for (unit cost analysis schedule)	$960,224	

*Answer is rounded to three decimal places.   †Answer is affected by using rounded unit cost amounts.

Units in ending Work in Process Inventory:

	Units transferred in during April (given)	54,800 liters
Less:	Units started and completed (above)	52,350 liters
Equals:	Units in ending inventory	2,450 liters

With this unit information you can then prepare the three schedules shown on the preceding page.

2. The costs of completed units for April are now ready to be transferred from the Cooling Department to Finished Goods Inventory. The proper journal entry is:

Finished Goods Inventory ($921,839 − $30)	921,809	
Work in Process—Cooling Department		921,809
To record the transfer of cost of completed		
units in April from the Cooling Department to		
Finished Goods Inventory		

Chapter Assignments

Questions

1. What types of production are suited to a process cost accounting system?
2. "For job order costing, *one* Work in Process Inventory account is used. However, in process costing there are often *several* Work in Process Inventory accounts in use." Explain.
3. Define *equivalent units*.
4. Why do actual unit data need to be changed to equivalent unit data for product costing purposes in a process costing system?
5. Define *conversion costs*. Why is this concept used in process costing computations?
6. What are the three schedules used in process costing analysis?
7. Why is it easier to compute equivalent production without units in beginning inventory?
8. What are the purposes of the unit cost analysis schedule?
9. What two important dollar amounts come from the cost summary schedule? How do they relate to the year-end financial statements?
10. Describe how to check the accuracy of results in a cost summary schedule.
11. What is the significance of the journal entry used to transfer costs of completed products out of the Work in Process Inventory account?
12. What is a transferred-in cost? Where does it come from? Why is it handled like materials added at the beginning of the process?

Classroom Exercises

**Exercise 4-1.
Process Cost Flow
Diagram
(L.O.2)**

Berg Paint Company uses a process costing system to analyze the costs incurred in making paint. Production of Quality Brand starts in the Blending Department, where materials SM and HA are added to a water base. The solution is heated to 70° Celsius and then transferred to the Mixing Department, where it is mixed for one hour. Then the paint goes to the Settling/Canning Department, where it is cooled and put into 4-liter cans. Direct labor and factory overhead charges are incurred uniformly throughout each part of the process.

In diagram form, show product flow for Quality Brand paint.

Exercise 4-2.
Work in Process
Inventory
Accounts: Total
Unit Costs
(L.O.4)

Scientists at Brooks Laboratories, Inc., have just perfected a liquid substance called D.K. Rid, which dissolves tooth decay without the dentist needing to use the infamous drill. The substance, which is generated from a complex process using five departments, is very costly. Cost and equivalent unit data for the latest week are as follows (units are in ounces):

	Materials Costs		Conversion Costs	
Dept.	Dollars	Equivalent Units	Dollars	Equivalent Units
A	$25,000	4,000	$34,113	4,110
B	23,423	3,970	26,130	4,020
C	48,204	4,120	20,972	4,280
D	—	—	22,086	4,090
E	—	—	15,171	3,890

From the data above, compute (a) the unit cost for each department and (b) the total unit cost of producing an ounce of D.K. Rid.

Exercise 4-3.
Equivalent Units:
No Beginning
Inventories
(L.O.3)

Slumpstone bricks are produced by the Strefeler Stone Company. Although it has been operating for only twelve months, the company already enjoys a good reputation for quality bricks. During its first year, materials for 460,500 bricks were put into production, and 456,900 bricks were completed and transferred to Finished Goods Inventory. The remaining bricks were still in process at year end, 65 percent completed. In their process costing system, all materials are added at the beginning of the process. Conversion costs are incurred uniformly throughout the production process.

From the information provided, prepare a schedule of equivalent production for the year. Use the average costing approach.

Exercise 4-4.
Equivalent Units:
Beginning
Inventories
(L.O.3)

Harwood Enterprises makes Sweetwater Shampoo for professional hair stylists. On January 1, 19x7, 18,400 liters of shampoo were in process, 70 percent complete as to conversion costs and 100 percent complete as to materials. During the year, 212,500 liters of materials were put into production. Data for Work in Process Inventory on December 31, 19x7, were as follows: shampoo, 7,500 liters; stage of completion, 60 percent of conversion costs and 100 percent of materials.

From this information, prepare a schedule of equivalent production for the year. Use the average costing approach.

Exercise 4-5.
Equivalent Units:
Beginning
Inventories
(L.O.3)

The Lucas Company, a major producer of liquid vitamins, uses a process cost accounting system. During January, 65,000 gallons of Material CIA and 20,000 gallons of Material CMA were put into production. Beginning Work in Process Inventory was 27,500 gallons of product, 80 percent complete as to labor and overhead. Ending Work in Process Inventory was made up of 18,000 gallons,

25 percent complete as to conversion costs. All materials were added at the beginning of the process.

From the above information, prepare a schedule of equivalent production for January 19xx. Use the average costing approach.

Exercise 4-6.
Unit Cost
Determination
(L.O.4)

Guide Kitchenwares, Inc., manufactures heavy-duty cookware. Production has just been completed for July. Beginning Work in Process Inventory cost was made up of (a) materials, $20,200 and (b) conversion costs, $26,800. Costs of materials used in July were $128,057. Conversion costs for the month were $152,858. During July, 45,190 units were started and completed. A schedule of equivalent production for July has already been prepared. It shows 54,910 equivalent units as to conversion costs and 55,450 equivalent units as to materials.

With this information, prepare a unit cost analysis schedule for July 19xx. Use the average costing approach.

Exercise 4-7.
Cost Transfer:
Journal Entry
Required
(L.O.3,6)

The following cost summary schedule was prepared for the La Cava Paste Company for the year ended July 31, 19xx.

1. From the information given, prepare the journal entry for July 31, 19xx.
2. Draw up the company's schedule of equivalent production. Assume that materials are added at the beginning of the process.

La Cava Paste Company
Cost Summary Schedule
For the Year Ended July 31, 19xx

	Cost of Goods Transferred to Finished Goods Inventory	Costs in Ending Work in Process Inventory
Beginning inventory:		
9,140 units × $2.60	$ 23,764	
Units started and completed:		
74,960 units × $2.60	194,896	
Ending inventory:		
Materials: 8,400 units × $1.40		$11,760
Conversion costs: 4,200		
units × $1.20		5,040
Totals	$218,660	$16,800

Exercise 4-8.
Cost Summary
Schedule
(L.O.5)

The Nelson Danish Bakery, which produces its world famous "Kringle" coffee bread, uses a process cost system for internal record-keeping purposes. Production for August was as follows: (a) Beginning inventory was 14,900 units; costs attached from the preceding period were materials at $7,400 and conversion costs at $6,700. (b) Units started and completed totaled 124,100 Kringles during the month. (c) Ending Work in Process Inventory was: materials, 9,000 units, 100 percent complete as to materials and 80 percent complete as to conversion costs. (d) Unit costs per equivalent unit have been computed for August: Materials, 50¢; Conversion costs, 65¢.

Using the information given, compute the cost of goods transferred to Finished Goods Inventory, the cost of ending Work in Process Inventory, and the total costs to be accounted for. Use the average costing approach.

Interpreting Accounting Information

Internal Management Information: Tennant Tire Corporation *(L.O.4)*

Tennant Tire Corporation makes several lines of automobile and truck tires. The company operates in a competitive marketplace, so it relies heavily on cost data from its process cost accounting system. It uses this information to set prices for its most competitive tires. The company's "Blue Radial" line has lost some of its market share during each of the past four years. Management believes price breaks allowed by the three competitors are the major reason for the decline in sales.

The company controller, Linda Sugarman, has been asked to review the product costing information that supports price decisions on the Blue Radial line. In preparing her report, she collected the following data related to 19x8, the last full year of operations.

	Units	Dollars
Equivalent units: Materials costs	88,540	
Conversion costs	86,590	
Manufacturing costs: Materials		$1,981,050.00
Direct labor		770,410.00
Factory overhead applied		1,540,820.00
Unit cost data: Materials		23.50
Conversion costs		27.00
Work in Process Inventory:		
Beginning (30% complete)	4,240	
Ending (50% complete)	6,900	

There were 80,400 units started and completed during 19x8. The costs attached to the year's beginning Work in Process Inventory were materials costs, $99,640, and conversion costs, $26,700.

Sugarman found that little spoilage had occurred. The proper cost allowance for spoilage was included in the predetermined overhead rate of $2.00 per direct labor dollar. Examination of direct labor cost, however, revealed that $173,180 was charged twice to the production account, the second time in error.

So far in 19x9 Blue Radial has been selling for $91 per tire. This price was based on the 19x8 unit cost data plus 50 percent to cover operating costs and 20 percent of the sum of these two cost factors for profit. During 19x9 the three competitors' prices have been about $85 per tire.

In the company's process costing system, all materials are added at the beginning of the process, and conversion costs are incurred uniformly throughout.

Required

1. Point out how such a cost-charging error could affect the company.
2. Prepare a revised unit cost analysis schedule for 19x8. Use the average costing approach.

3. What should have been the minimum selling price per tire in 19x9?
4. Suggest to the controller ways of preventing such errors in the future.

Problem Set A

Problem 4A-1.
Process Costing:
No Beginning
Inventories
(L.O. 3, 4, 5, 6)

Winter Industries specializes in making "Slik," a high-moisture, low-alkaline wax used to protect and preserve skis. Production of a new, improved brand of Slik began January 1, 19xx. For this new product, Materials A14 and C9 are introduced at the beginning of the production process along with a wax-based product. During January, 260 pounds of A14, 820 pounds of C9, and 5,600 pounds of wax base were used at a cost of $10,400, $8,460, and $11,200, respectively. Direct labor of $12,976 and factory overhead costs of $25,952 were incurred uniformly throughout the month. By January 31, 19xx, 6,200 pounds of Slik had been completed and transferred to Finished Goods Inventory. Much of the already finished product had been shipped to customers. Since no spoilage occurred, the pounds not yet finished stayed in production, on the average 60 percent completed.

Required

1. Using proper form, prepare: (a) a schedule of equivalent production; (b) a unit cost analysis schedule; and (c) a cost summary schedule for Winter Industries for January.
2. From the cost summary schedule, prepare the journal entry to transfer costs of completed units for January to Finished Goods Inventory.

Problem 4A-2.
Process Costing:
With Beginning
Inventories
(L.O. 3, 4, 5, 6)

Many of the products made by Baucom Plastics Company are standard replacement parts for telephones and involve long production runs. One of these parts, a wire clip, is produced continuously. During April materials for 50,500 units of wire clips were put into production (1 unit contains 1,000 clips). Total cost of materials used during April was $2,273,000. Direct labor costs for the month totaled $1,135,000. Factory overhead is applied to production using a rate of 150% of direct labor costs. Beginning Work in Process Inventory contained 3,200 units, 100 percent complete as to materials and 50 percent complete as to conversion costs. Costs attached to the units in beginning inventory totaled $232,000, including $143,500 in materials costs. There were 2,500 units in ending Work in Process Inventory; all materials have been added, and the units are 80 percent complete as to conversion costs.

Required

1. Using good form, and assuming an average costing approach and no loss due to spoilage, prepare: (a) a schedule of equivalent production; (b) a unit cost analysis schedule; and (c) a cost summary schedule.
2. From the cost summary schedule, prepare a journal entry to transfer costs of units completed in April to Finished Goods Inventory.

Problem 4A-3.
Process Costing:
With Beginning
Inventories
(L.O. 3, 4, 5, 6)

Lasciandro Liquid Extracts Company produces a line of fruit extracts for use in producing such homemade products as wines (grapes), jams and jellies, pies, and meat sauces. Fruits are introduced into the production process in pounds, and the product unit emerges in quarts. (Note: 1 pound of input equals 1 quart of output.) On June 1, 19x9, there were 6,250 units in process; all materials had been added, and the units were 90 percent completed as to conversion costs. There were $12,810 in materials costs and $7,319 in conversion costs attached to the beginning Work in Process Inventory. During June, 50,300 pounds of fruit were added: apples, 20,500 pounds, costing $36,900; grapes, 18,600 pounds, costing $40,920; and bananas, 11,200 pounds, costing $28,125. Direct labor for the month of June totaled $12,662, and overhead costs were applied at the rate of 400 percent of direct labor dollars. On June 30, 7,400 units of work remained in process; all materials had been added, and 70 percent of conversion costs had been incurred.

Required

1. Using good form and an average costing approach, prepare the following schedules for June: (a) a schedule of equivalent production; (b) a unit cost analysis schedule; and (c) a cost summary schedule.
2. From the cost summary schedule, prepare a journal entry to transfer the costs of completed units to Finished Goods Inventory.

**Problem 4A-4.
Process Costing:
One Process/Two
Time Periods
(L.O.3,4,5,6)**

Cassagio Laboratories produces liquid detergents that leave no soap film. All elements are biodegradable. The production process has been automated so that the product can now be produced in one operation instead of separately going through heating, mixing, and cooling. All materials are added at the beginning of the process, and conversion costs are incurred uniformly throughout the process. Operating data for July and August are shown below.

	July	August
Beginning Work in Process Inventory		
Units (pounds)	4,650	?
Costs: Materials costs	$ 4,750	?
Conversion costs	1,580	?
Production during the period		
Units started (pounds)	63,000	65,600
Current period costs:		
Materials costs	$64,253	$68,346
Conversion costs	$54,367	$54,867
Ending Work in Process Inventory		
Units (pounds)	6,100	7,200

Beginning Work in Process Inventory was 40 percent complete as to conversion costs, and point of completion information for ending work in process inventories was: July, 70 percent; August, 60 percent. Assume that loss from spoilage and evaporation was negligible.

Required

1. Using good form and an average costing approach, prepare the following schedules for July: (a) a schedule of equivalent production; (b) a unit cost analysis schedule; and (c) a cost summary schedule.
2. From the cost summary schedule, prepare a journal entry to transfer costs of completed units in July to Finished Goods Inventory.
3. Repeat **1** and **2** for August.

Problem 4A-5.
Process Costing:
With Beginning
Inventories/Two
Departments
(L.O. 3, 4, 5, 6)

David Ganz Enterprises produces dozens of products linked to the housing construction industry. Its most successful product is called "Sta-Soft" plaster, a mixture that is easy to apply and is used to finish off wall surfaces after dry-wall sheets have been positioned. Its unique quality is that the substance never hardens until it comes into contact with the dry wall. Sta-Soft is produced using three processes: blending, conditioning, and canning. All materials are introduced at the beginning of the blending operation, except for the can, which is added at the end in the final canning operation. Direct labor and factory overhead costs are applied to the products uniformly throughout each process. Production and cost information for September 19x8 is summarized below.

Blending Department. Beginning Work in Process Inventory contained 11,460 pounds of Sta-Soft, 60 percent complete as to conversion costs. There was $38,900 assigned to these units, $28,600 of which was for materials costs. During September, 121,140 pounds of materials were put into production, costing $302,900. Direct labor for the month was $88,210, and an equal amount of factory overhead costs was charged to the work in process. Ending Work in Process Inventory was made up of 16,240 pounds, 50 percent complete as to conversion costs.

Conditioning Department. During September, 116,360 pounds of Sta-Soft were received from the Blending Department. Beginning Work in Process Inventory consisted of 5,250 pounds, costing $30,250 ($21,000 was transferred-in costs). Direct labor costs incurred during September totaled $115,625, and factory overhead costs applied were $138,751. Ending Work in Process Inventory contained 4,450 pounds, 60 percent complete as to conversion costs.

Assume there was no measurable loss due to spoilage or waste in the month.

Required

1. Using proper form and an average costing approach, prepare the following schedules for the Blending Department for September: (a) a schedule of equivalent production; (b) a unit cost analysis schedule; and (c) a cost summary schedule.
2. From the cost summary schedule, prepare the journal entry needed to transfer costs of completed units for September from the Blending Department to the Conditioning Department.
3. Prepare the same schedules for the Conditioning Department that were requested in **1.**
4. Prepare the journal entry needed to transfer costs of completed units from the Conditioning Department to the Canning Department.

Problem Set B

Problem 4B-1.
Process Costing:
No Beginning
Inventories
(L.O. 3, 4, 5, 6)

The Solinko Chewing Gum Company, which produces several flavors of bubble gum, began production of a new kumquat-flavored gum on June 1, 19xx. Two basic materials, gum base and kumquat-flavored sweetener, are blended at the beginning of the process. Direct labor and factory overhead costs are incurred uniformly throughout the blending process. During June, 270,000 kilograms of gum base and 540,000 kilograms of kumquat-flavored sweetener were used at costs of $324,000 and $162,000 respectively. Direct labor charges were $720,620, and factory overhead costs applied during June were $368,020. The ending Work in Process Inventory was 43,200 kilograms. All materials have been added to these units, and 25 percent of the conversion costs have been assigned.

Required

1. Using proper form, prepare: (a) a schedule of equivalent production; (b) a unit cost analysis schedule; and (c) a cost summary schedule for the Blending Department for June.
2. From the cost summary schedule, prepare the journal entry to transfer costs of completed units for June from the Blending Department to the Forming and Packing Department.

Problem 4B-2.
Process Costing:
With Beginning
Inventories
(L.O. 3, 4, 5, 6)

O'Hara Food Products, Inc., makes high-vitamin, calorie-packed wafers used by professional sports teams to supply quick energy to players. Production of these thin white wafers is through a continuous product flow process. The company, which uses a process costing system based on the average costing approach, recently purchased several automated machines so that the wafers could be produced in a single department. The materials are all added at the beginning of the process. The costs for the machine operator's labor and production-related overhead are incurred uniformly throughout the process.

In February a total of 115,600 liters of materials was put into production; cost of the materials was $294,780. Two liters of materials are used to produce one unit of output (one unit = 144 wafers). Labor costs for February were $60,530. Factory overhead was $181,590. Beginning Work in Process Inventory on February 1 was 28,000 units. The units were 100 percent complete as to materials and 40 percent as to conversion costs. The total cost of beginning inventory was $126,420, with $64,220 assigned to the cost of materials. The ending Work in Process Inventory of 24,000 units is fully complete as to materials, but only 30 percent complete as to conversion costs.

Required

1. Using good form and assuming no loss due to spoilage, prepare: (a) a schedule of equivalent production; (b) a unit cost analysis schedule, rounding off unit cost computations to *four* decimal places; and (c) a cost summary schedule.
2. From the cost summary schedule, prepare a journal entry to transfer costs of completed units in February to Finished Goods Inventory.

Problem 4B-3.
Process Costing:
With Beginning
Inventories
(L.O. 3, 4, 5, 6)

Ezckannagha Bottling Company makes and sells several types of soft drinks. Materials (sugar syrup and artificial flavoring) are added at the beginning of production in the Mixing Department. Direct labor and factory overhead costs are applied to products throughout the process. The following information is for the Citrus Punch product for August. Beginning Work in Process Inventory (60 percent complete) was 4,800 liters. Ending inventory (50 percent complete) was 7,200 liters. Production data showed 180,000 liters started. A total of 177,600 liters was completed and transferred to the Bottling Department. Beginning inventory data showed $1,200 for materials and $1,152 for conversion costs. Current period costs were $45,000 for materials and $71,328 for conversion costs.

Required

1. Using good form and an average costing approach, prepare the following schedules for the Mixing Department for August: (a) a schedule of equivalent production; (b) a unit cost analysis schedule; and (c) a cost summary schedule.
2. From the cost summary schedule, prepare a journal entry to transfer costs of completed units to the Bottling Department.

Problem 4B-4.
Process Costing:
One Process/Two
Time Periods
(L.O. 3, 4, 5, 6)

The Kockentiedt Natural Products Company, which owns thousands of beehives, produces organic honey for sale to health food stores. No materials other than the honey from the hives are used. The production operation is a simple one in which the impure honey is added at the beginning of the process. A series of filterings follows, leading to a pure finished product. Production data for April and May are shown below.

	April	May
Beginning Work in Process Inventory		
Units (liters)	14,200	?
Costs: Materials	$ 17,600	?
Conversion costs	$ 23,860	?
Production during the period		
Units started (liters)	388,000	410,000
Current period costs: Materials	$ 481,128	$ 491,008
Conversion costs	$1,046,748	$1,137,304
Ending Work in Process Inventory		
Units (liters)	24,800	33,800

For the incomplete inventory figures, assume that all materials have already been added. Beginning inventory for April was 60 percent complete as to conversion costs, and ending inventory was 20 percent complete. Ending inventory for May was 30 percent complete as to conversion costs. Costs of labor and factory overhead are incurred uniformly throughout the filtering process. Assume that there was no loss from spoilage or evaporation.

Required

1. Using good form and an average costing approach, prepare the following schedules for April: (a) a schedule of equivalent production; (b) a unit cost analysis schedule; and (c) a cost summary schedule.
2. From the cost summary schedule, prepare a journal entry to transfer costs of completed units in April to Finished Goods Inventory.
3. Repeat 1 and 2 for May.

Problem 4B-5.
Process Costing:
With Beginning
Inventories/Two
Departments
(L.O. 3, 4, 5, 6)

Canned fruits and vegetables are the main products of Culley/Grove Foods, Inc. When canned peaches are being prepared, all basic materials go in at the beginning of the Mixing Department's process. When mixed, the solution goes to the Cooking Department. There it is heated to 100° Celsius and left to simmer for twenty minutes. When cooled, the mixture goes to the Canning Department for final processing. Throughout these operations direct labor and factory overhead costs are incurred uniformly. No materials are added in the Cooking Department.

Cost data and other information for January are shown below.

Production Cost Data	Materials	Conversion Costs
Mixing Department		
Beginning Inventory	$ 28,800	$ 4,800
Current Period Costs	432,000	182,400

Production Cost Data	Transferred-in Costs	Conversion Costs
Cooking Department		
Beginning Inventory	$ 63,000	$ 13,320
Current Period Costs	?	671,040

Work in Process Inventories	
Beginning Inventories:	
Mixing Department (40% complete)	12,000 liters
Cooking Department (20% complete)	18,000 liters
Ending Inventories:	
Mixing Department (70% complete)	16,000 liters
Cooking Department (80% complete)	20,000 liters

Unit Production Data	Mixing Department	Cooking Department
Units started during January	180,000 liters	176,000 liters
Units transferred out during January	176,000 liters	174,000 liters

Assume that no spoilage or evaporation loss occurred during January. (Before completing this problem, refer to the Extended Illustrative Problem on pages 140–143.)

Required

1. Using proper form and an average costing approach, prepare the following schedules for the Mixing Department for January: (a) a schedule of equivalent production; (b) a unit cost analysis schedule; and (c) a cost summary schedule.
2. From the cost summary schedule, prepare the journal entry to transfer costs of completed units for January from the Mixing to the Cooking Department.
3. Prepare the following three schedules for the Cooking Department: (a) a schedule of equivalent production; (b) a unit cost analysis schedule; and (c) a cost summary schedule.
4. Prepare the journal entry to transfer costs of completed units in January from the Cooking Department to the Canning Department.

Management Decision Case

CT&H Cola, Inc.
(L.O. 3, 4)

For the past four years, three companies have dominated the soft drink industry, controlling 85 percent of market share. CT&H Cola, Inc., ranks second nationally in soft drink sales with gross revenues last year of $27,450,000. Management wants to introduce a new low-calorie drink called Slimit Cola.

Soft drinks at CT&H are completely processed in a single department. All materials are added at the beginning of the process. Fluids are bottled at the end of the process into bottles costing one cent each. Direct labor and factory overhead costs are applied uniformly throughout the process.

Corporate controller Robert Buttery believes that costs for the new cola will be similar to those for the company's Cola Plus drink. Last year the data on the following page related to Cola Plus:

	Units	Costs
Work in Process Inventory		
January 1, 19x8[1]	12,840	
Materials Costs		$ 10,280
Conversion Costs		3,876
December 31, 19x8[2]	17,800	
Materials Costs		14,240
Conversion Costs		7,476
Units Started During the Year	918,760	
Costs for 19x8		
Liquid Materials Added		735,000
Direct Labor		344,925
Factory Overhead Applied		206,955
Bottles		219,312

[1] 50% complete   [2] 70% complete   Note: Each unit is a 24-bottle case.

Variable operating and selling costs are $1.10 per unit. Fixed operating and selling costs are assigned to products at the rate of $.50 per unit. The two major competitors have already introduced a diet cola into the marketplace. Company A's product sells for $4.00 per unit; Company B's, for $3.95.

All costs in 19x9 are expected to increase by 10 percent over 19x8 costs. The company tries to earn a profit of at least 12 percent over cost.

Required

1. What factors should be considered in setting a selling price for Slimit Cola?
2. Using the average costing approach, compute (a) the total production cost per unit and (b) the total cost per unit of Cola Plus for 19x8.
3. What is the expected total cost per unit of Slimit Cola for 19x9?
4. Recommend a unit price range for selling Slimit Cola and give your reason(s).

PART THREE

Management Planning and Control

Parts One and Two introduced you to the field of management accounting, focusing on the development of useful cost information for product costing and management reporting purposes. Emphasis was on the first of three aspects of management accounting: management's need for product or service costing information.

In Part Three we analyze the second aspect of the field of management accounting, management's need for data used for operations planning and control. Special concepts and techniques are used for cost planning and control. When integrated with an existing accounting system, these concepts and techniques are used to develop reports that facilitate budgetary control activities.

Chapter 5 introduces the topics of cost behavior and cost allocation, knowledge of which is essential to understanding managerial planning and control and decision analysis of management.

Chapter 6 continues the study of cost behavior by concentrating on the relationships between costs, operating activity (volume), and profit. Emphasis is on the effects of a change in one variable on the other two areas.

Chapter 7 explains the responsibility accounting system and introduces the principles of performance evaluation. The evaluations of managers of a cost/expense center, a profit center, and an investment center are illustrated.

Chapter 8 uses the cost planning tools described in Chapters 5, 6, and 7 to implement the planning function of the budgetary control process. Emphasis is on budgeting principles and preparation, including the preparation of a cash budget.

Chapters 9 and 10 conclude your study of the budgetary control process. In Chapter 9, the standard costing system is introduced, and materials and labor variances are analyzed. Chapter 10 continues your study of standard costing by analyzing the overhead variances and accounting for their disposition. Evaluating employee performance using variances is discussed.

1. *Explain the concept of cost behavior as it relates to total costs and costs per unit.*
2. *Identify specific types of variable costs and compute changes in variable costs caused by changes in operating activity.*
3. *Identify specific types of fixed costs and describe the impact of changes in the level of operating activity on fixed costs.*
4. *Differentiate a semivariable cost from a mixed cost and apply methods used to separate their variable and fixed cost components.*
5. *Define cost allocation and describe the role of cost objectives in the cost allocation process.*
6. *Identify specific uses of cost allocation in corporate accounting and reporting practices.*
7. *Assign costs of supporting service functions to operating departments.*
8. *Allocate common costs to joint products.*

CHAPTER 5

Cost Behavior and Allocation

Cost planning and control activities are vital to the ongoing life of any type of organization, whether it is a profit-oriented or a not-for-profit enterprise. Effective cost planning results in a strong and continuous flow of operations, and cost control leads to target attainment, whether the target is overall profit or completion of a project. An integrated cost planning and control system is usually referred to as a budgetary control system. To help achieve good cost planning and control, such a system relies on a set of management accounting techniques, including cost-volume-profit analysis, responsibility accounting applications, standard cost accounting systems, and direct costing procedures. All of these techniques are supported by basic cost behavior and cost allocation concepts and practices. The study of cost behavior centers on the way costs react to changes in operating variables such as total productive output, total sales, and total machine hours used. Cost allocation techniques are used not only to assign incurred costs to products or services but also to plan future activities. This chapter explains cost behavior patterns and explores and applies cost allocation techniques. After studying this chapter, you should be able to meet the learning objectives listed on the left.

Cost Behavior Patterns

Before estimating a future cost or preparing a budget, a manager must know the basic behavior patterns of costs. We define cost behavior as the ways costs respond to changes in activity or volume. To understand cost behavior, we need to look at the basic characteristics and the accounting classifications of costs. Some costs are entirely variable in relation to volume or operating activity, whereas other costs remain fixed as volume changes. Within these two polar extremes are costs that exhibit characteristics of both fixed and variable costs. Complex cost behavior patterns must be separated into variable and fixed cost components before more sophisticated cost planning techniques can be applied. Knowledge of cost behavior is useful for predicting future costs as well as analyzing past cost performance.

The meaning of cost behavior depends on whether total costs are being analyzed or cost per unit is being computed. Variable costs vary in total; as activity or volume increases, total costs increase in direct proportion. But variable costs per unit remain constant if there are no price changes in goods and services

OBJECTIVE 1
Explain the concept of cost behavior as it relates to total costs and costs per unit

consumed. Fixed costs, on the other hand, react in an opposite fashion. In total, fixed costs remain constant as volume increases. But on a per unit basis, fixed costs decrease as volume increases. Fixed costs are spread over productive output. Since a fixed cost is constant in total, the more that is produced, the less fixed cost is assigned per unit. We discuss these principles further as we discuss variable and fixed costs in more detail. But it is important that you begin thinking about this phenomenon now. *Variable costs vary in total as volume changes but are constant per unit; fixed costs are fixed in total but vary per unit as volume changes.*

Although we now focus on cost behavior as it relates to production, you should realize that some costs are *not* measured according to production volume. Sales commissions, for example, depend on the number of units sold, or total sales revenue, not on production measures. Also, service businesses experience cost behavior patterns in much the same manner as do manufacturing enterprises. As we discuss examples for a manufacturing company, remember that the same concept applies to a department store or a bank.

Variable Cost Behavior

OBJECTIVE 2
Identify specific types of variable costs and compute changes in variable costs caused by changes in operating activity

Nature of Variable Costs. Total costs that change in direct proportion to changes in productive output (or any other volume measure) are called **variable costs.** To see how variable costs work, consider an automobile maker. Each new car has four tires, and each tire costs $48. Thus the total cost of tires (four tires per automobile) is $192 for one automobile, $384 for two, $576 for three, $768 for four, $960 for five, $1,920 for ten, and $19,200 for one hundred. In the production of automobiles, the total cost of tires is a variable cost. On a per unit basis, however, a variable cost remains constant. In this case, the cost of tires per automobile is $192 ($48 × 4) whether one or one hundred cars are produced. True, the cost of tires varies depending on the number purchased, and purchase discounts are available for purchases of large quantities. But once the purchase has been made, the cost per tire has been established.

In discussing variable costs, we assume that there is a linear relationship between cost and volume. Figure 5-1 shows this relationship. In this example, each unit of output requires $2.50 of labor cost. Total labor costs grow in direct proportion to the increase in units of output: For 2 units, total labor cost is $5, and for 6 units, the company incurs $15 of labor costs.

Operating Capacity: Definition and Cost Influence. Operating capacity plays an important part in our study of cost behavior. **Operating capacity** is the upper limit of a company's productive output capability given existing resources. Any increase in activity or volume over operating capacity requires additional expenditures for building, machinery, personnel, and operating expenses. Existing cost behavior patterns may change when additional operating capacity is added. In our discussion of cost behavior patterns, we assume that operating capacity is a constant and all activity is within current operating capacity limits.

Figure 5-1. A Common Cost Behavior Pattern: Variable Cost

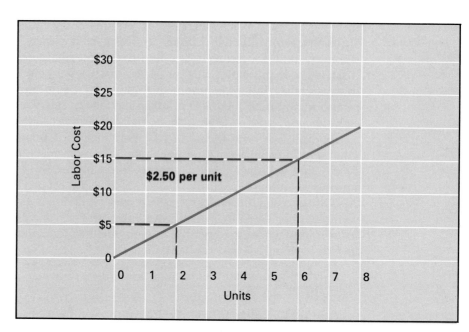

Operating activity or volume can be expressed several different ways, including total units produced, total units sold, total machine hours, and total labor hours. The general guide for selecting an activity or volume base is to relate costs to their most logical or causal factor. For example, machinery setup costs should be considered variable in relation to the number of machinery setup operations needed for a particular job or function. Using this approach, machinery setup costs can be budgeted and controlled more effectively. Each cost with variable behavior characteristics should be related to an appropriate measure of production or sales volume. Thus operating costs could be related to machine hours used or total units produced. Sales commissions can usually be related to total dollar sales on a percentage basis.

There are two reasons for being careful when selecting an activity measure for variable costs. First, each variable cost should be related to an activity base that permits cost planning and control. Second, the management accountant must combine (aggregate) many different variable costs associated with the same activity base so the costs can be analyzed in some reasonable fashion. Such aggregation also permits prediction of future costs for budgeting purposes.

Examples of Variable Cost Behavior. Table 5-1 identifies specific examples of variable costs. A manufacturing company experiences variable costs such as direct materials costs, hourly direct labor costs, operating supplies, hourly indirect labor costs, and small tools costs. A department store incurs such variable costs as cost of merchandise, sales commissions,

Table 5-1. Examples of Variable, Semivariable, and Fixed Costs

Costs	Manufacturing Company	Department Store	Bank
Variable	Direct materials Direct labor (hourly) Operating supplies Indirect labor (hourly) Small tools cost	Cost of merchandise Sales commissions Shelf stockers (hourly)	Computer equipment leasing (based on usage) Computer operators (hourly) Operating supplies Data storage disks
Semivariable	Electrical power Telephone	Electrical power Telephone	Electrical power Telephone Gas heating expense

Fixed	Labor (salaried)
	Depreciation of machinery
	Insurance premiums
	Property taxes
	Supervisory expense
		Buyers (salaried)
		Depreciation
		Insurance premiums
		Property taxes
		Supervisory expense
			Depreciation, furniture and fixtures
			Rent, buildings
			Insurance premiums
			Salaries:
			    Programmers
			    Systems designers
			    Bank administration

and hourly wages of shelf stockers. A bank incurs variable costs such as leasing expense of computer equipment (based on usage), operating supplies, hourly computer operator wages, and the cost of data storage disks. All of these examples, whether they are incurred by a manufacturing company or a service-oriented business, are variable based on either productive output or total sales.

To this point we have viewed a variable cost as the one depicted in Figure 5-1. This traditional definition of a variable cost contemplates a linear behavior pattern, such as that for the tires of the automobile discussed earlier. But many costs vary with operating activity in a nonlinear fashion. Figure 5-2 illustrates nonlinear variable costs. Figure 5-2 (*a*) illustrates the behavior of power costs when unit cost of power consumption declines as usage increases. Example (*b*) shows the behavior pattern of computer cost when each additional hour of usage costs more than the previous hour. Example (*c*) depicts a situation where first there is increasing efficiency of labor cost followed by a decreasing stage of efficiency. These three nonlinear costs are variable in nature, but they are different from the straight-line variable cost pattern in Figure 5-1.

Nonlinear costs can be variable in relation to volume or activity and should be considered variable costs. The concept of relevant range is useful for many nonlinear cost functions. **Relevant range** is the range

Figure 5-2. More Variable Cost Behavior Patterns

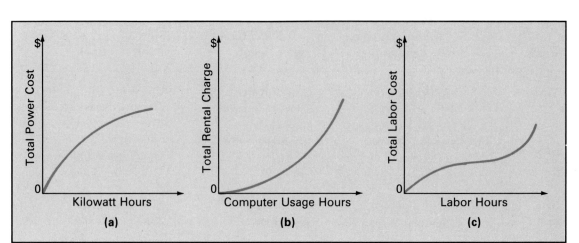

of activity in which a company expects to operate. Within this range, many nonlinear costs can be estimated using the straight-line linear approximation approach Figure 5-3 illustrates. By using linear approximation, variability within the relevant range can be estimated, and this cost can then be treated as part of the other variable costs. A linear approximation is not a precise measure, but it does permit inclusion of nonlinear variable costs in cost behavior analysis. The objective of cost behavior studies is to permit cost estimation and budgeting. Knowledge that a particular cost is nonlinear at some low-activity level is hardly useful if the firm will not operate at that level.

Figure 5-3. The Relevant Range and Linear Approximation

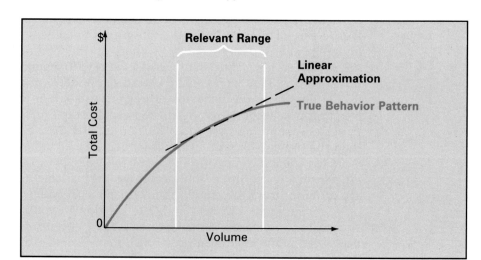

Fixed Cost Behavior

OBJECTIVE 3
Identify specific types of fixed costs and describe the impact of changes in the level of operating activity on fixed costs

Nature of Fixed Costs. Fixed costs behave entirely different than variable costs. **Total fixed costs** remain constant within a relevant range of activity or volume. As we stated, a relevant range of activity is the range in which actual operations are likely to occur. Annual straight-line depreciation of $400,000 and annual property taxes of $19,400 are examples of fixed costs. Reference to a particular time period is essential to the concept of a fixed cost because, according to economic theory, all costs tend to be variable in the long run. This long-run viewpoint means that a fixed cost can be increased or decreased within whatever time period is required to increase or decrease plant capacity, machinery, labor requirements, and other production factors associated with fixed costs. Thus a cost is fixed only within a limited time period. For planning purposes, management usually considers an annual time period, and fixed costs are expected to be fixed within this period.

Supervisory salaries are a good example of a fixed cost. Assume that a local manufacturing company needs one supervisor for an eight-hour work shift. Production can range from 0 to 500,000 units per month per shift. The supervisor's salary is $3,000 per month, and the relevant range is from 0 to 500,000 units. The cost behavior analysis is as follows:

Units of Output	Total Supervisory Salaries per Month
100,000	$3,000
200,000	3,000
300,000	3,000
400,000	3,000
500,000	3,000
600,000	6,000

As noted, a maximum of 500,000 units can be produced per shift, so any output above 500,000 units calls for another work shift and another supervisor.

A fixed cost remains constant in total, but the unit fixed cost changes as volume increases or decreases. *Unit fixed costs vary inversely with activity or volume.* On a per unit basis, fixed costs go down as volume goes up. This is true as long as you produce within the relevant range of activity. In our example, supervisory costs per unit would change as follows:

Volume of Activity	Cost per Unit
100,000 units	$3,000/100,000 = $.03
200,000 units	$3,000/200,000 = $.015
300,000 units	$3,000/300,000 = $.01
400,000 units	$3,000/400,000 = $.0075
500,000 units	$3,000/500,000 = $.006
600,000 units	$6,000/600,000 = $.01

The per unit cost increased at the 600,000-unit level because this activity level was not within the relevant range and another supervisor had to be hired.

Total fixed costs stay the same for all levels of activity within the relevant range. Figure 5-4 is a graphic view of this fixed overhead cost. Fixed supervisory costs of $3,000 are needed for the first 500,000 units of production. Fixed supervisory costs hold steady at $3,000 for any level of output within the relevant range, but output above 500,000 units calls for another supervisor, and the cost level jumps to $6,000.

Examples of Fixed Costs. Refer again to Table 5-1 for examples of fixed costs. The manufacturing company, the department store, and the bank all incur depreciation costs and fixed annual insurance premiums. In addition, all salaried personnel have fixed earnings for a particular time period. The manufacturing company and the department store own their buildings and must pay annual property taxes. The bank, on the other hand, pays an annual fixed rental charge for use of its building.

Committed Versus Discretionary Fixed Costs. Fixed costs are classified as either committed costs or discretionary costs. **Committed** costs are costs of capacity that include depreciation of fixed assets, insurance, property taxes, rental charges, and supervisory salaries. These costs must be incurred if a company continues to use its existing capacities to produce or create and sell its product or service. **Discretionary costs,** such as advertising, product/service development, basic research, and

Figure 5-4. A Common Cost Behavior Pattern: Fixed Cost

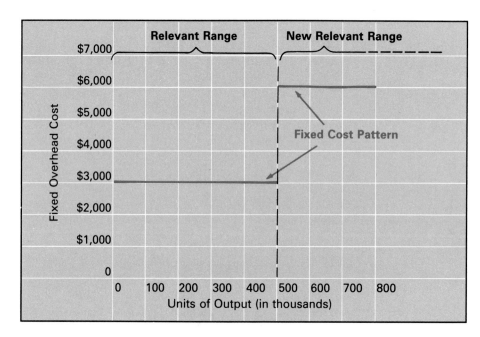

employee training, are incurred because of policy decisions by management. Discretionary costs are subject to periodic review and are more likely to change during a time period than committed costs. For instance, fixed costs incurred during a depressed operating time period (recession or labor strike) could be substantially different from the fixed costs incurred during normal operating activity levels.

Step-Variable Costs. Step-cost functions, as shown in Figure 5-5, are called **step-variable costs**. Is the cost fixed or variable? The answer depends on the activity range under consideration. Over wide activity ranges, the step cost varies or changes in relation to changes in operating activity. Within a narrow range of planned activity, however, the step cost most likely will remain constant, and it should be budgeted as a fixed cost. The important point is not whether the cost is called fixed or variable but how the cost will behave over the relevant range of activity. The ability to estimate and predict the cost of supervision is the objective, regardless of the label attached to the behavior pattern. For practical purposes, supervisory salaries are considered fixed costs within the activity range that is relevant to future operations.

Semivariable and Mixed Costs

OBJECTIVE 4
Differentiate a semivariable cost from a mixed cost and apply methods used to separate their variable and fixed cost components

Some costs cannot be classified as either variable or fixed. A **semivariable cost** has both variable cost and fixed cost components. Part of the cost is fixed per time period, and part changes with volume or usage, such as telephone expense. Monthly telephone charges are made up of a service charge plus extra charges for extra telephones and long-distance calls. The service charge and the cost of the additional telephones are fixed costs, but the long-distance charges are variable because they depend on monthly use.

Figure 5-5. Step-Variable Costs

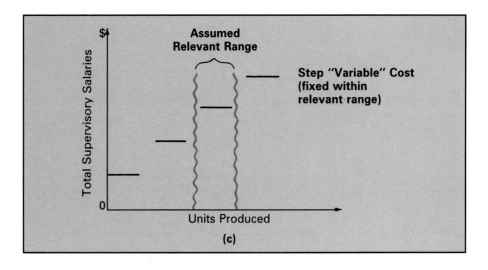

Mixed costs are also made up of variable and fixed costs. **Mixed costs** result when both variable and fixed costs are charged to the same general ledger account. The Repairs and Maintenance account is a good example of an account balance made up of mixed costs. Labor charges to this account may vary in proportion to the amount of repairs done. However, only one repair and maintenance worker may be employed on a full-time basis (a fixed cost if salaried), and extra help is hired only when needed (a variable cost). Depreciation costs for repair and maintenance machinery are also fixed costs, but costs of repair supplies depend on use. *For purposes of cost planning and control, semivariable and mixed costs must be divided into their respective variable and fixed cost parts.* They can then be grouped with other variable and fixed costs for analysis.

Examples of Semivariable Costs. Many costs demonstrate both variable and fixed behavior characteristics. As Table 5-1 reveals, utility costs often fall in this category. Electrical power costs, gas heating expense, and telephone charges normally have a fixed base amount, with additional amounts based on usage. Figure 5-6 illustrates three different types of semivariable cost patterns. Figure 5-6 (*a*) depicts the normal factory power cost. The monthly bill begins with a fixed charge for the service and increases as kilowatt hours are consumed. Example (*b*) shows a special contractual rent-labor incentive agreement. Factory rent has a fixed basis for the year but is reduced as labor hours are paid down to a minimum annual guaranteed rental charge. Example (*c*) also depicts a special contractual arrangement: The cost of annual equipment mainte-nance by an outside company is variable per maintenance hour worked up to a maximum per time period. After the maximum is reached, additional maintenance is done at no cost. There are many other types

Figure 5-6. Semivariable Cost Examples

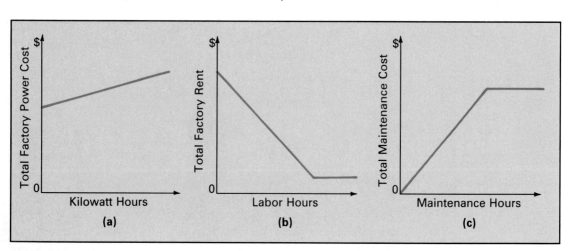

of semivariable cost patterns, but these examples will serve for further study of cost behavior patterns.

Cost Separation Methods. When there is doubt about the behavior pattern of a particular cost, it helps to prepare a scatter diagram of cost amounts and related volume measures for past time periods. In particular, this approach should be used for costs that are thought to have a semivariable behavior pattern. The scatter diagram in Figure 5-7 is a chart containing plotted points that help determine whether there is a linear relationship between the cost item and the related activity measure. If a linear relationship appears reasonable, a cost line can be fit to the data by either visual means or statistical analysis. Two of the most common statistical approaches are the high-low method and the least squares method.

Figure 5-7. Scatter Diagram of Machine Hours and Repairs and Maintenance Costs

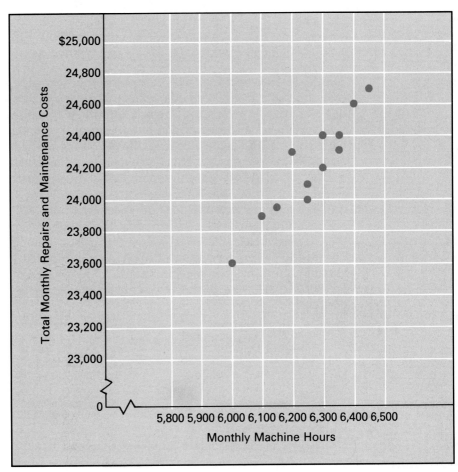

To help understand these cost separation methods, assume that the de Hoyos Corporation's Winter Park Division incurred the following machine hours and repairs and maintenance costs during last year:

Month	Machine Hours	Repairs and Maintenance Cost
January	6,250	$ 24,000
February	6,300	24,200
March	6,350	24,350
April	6,400	24,600
May	6,300	24,400
June	6,200	24,300
July	6,100	23,900
August	6,000	23,600
September	6,150	23,950
October	6,250	24,100
November	6,350	24,400
December	6,450	24,700
Totals	75,100	$290,500

The High-Low Method. The easiest approach to separating the variable costs from the fixed costs in a semivariable or a mixed cost analysis is to use the **high-low method**, which identifies the linear relationship of semivariable cost observations by simply analyzing the paired data for high volume and related cost and low volume and related cost. In our example, the Winter Park Division experienced high machine hour activity in December and low machine hour activity in August. As the following calculations show, the first step is to determine the difference between the high and low amounts for both machine hours and the related repairs and maintenance costs. By dividing the change in machine hours into the change in cost, the variable cost rate per machine hour is computed. The fixed cost for any month can then be computed by multiplying the variable rate times the machine hours and subtracting the amount from the total cost. The difference is an estimate of the fixed cost for the period.

Volume	Month	Cost	Activity Level
High	December	$24,700	6,450 machine hours
Low	August	23,600	6,000 machine hours
Difference		$ 1,100	450 machine hours

Variable rate per machine hour

$1,100/450$ machine hours $= \$2.4444$ per machine hour

Fixed cost per month

December: $24,700 − (6,450 × $2.4444) = $ 8,933.33

August: $23,600 − (6,000 × $2.4444) = $ 8,933.33

Breakdown of total costs for the year
  Variable cost: 75,100 × $2.4444 = $183,574.44
  Fixed costs: $290,500 − (75,100 × $2.4444) =   106,925.56
                                                         $290,500.00

The linear relationship of the data for the Winter Park Division as determined by the high-low method is:

Total cost per month = $8,933.33 + $2.4444 per machine hour

The Least Squares Method. In the **least squares method**, simple linear regression analysis is used to fit a straight line to paired observations of an independent variable (volume or activity) and a dependent variable (repairs and maintenance costs). This line-fitting procedure is called the least squares method because the statistical computations result in a cost line for which the squared differences between each observation and the cost line are a minimum sum.[1] The scatter diagram in Figure 5-7 plots each pair of cost and machine hour observations from the Winter Park Division example. The remaining task is to fit a line to the plotted data. Using regression analysis, information needed to construct the cost line is provided by solving Equations (1) and (2):

$$a = \frac{\Sigma Y}{N} - \frac{b(\Sigma X)}{N} \tag{1}$$

$$b = \frac{N\Sigma XY - \Sigma X\Sigma Y}{N\Sigma X^2 - (\Sigma X)^2} \tag{2}$$

where X = values of independent variable, volume or activity
        Y = values of dependent variable, cost
        a = value of Y where cost line intersects vertical axis
        b = slope of line (variable cost rate)
        N = number of paired observations for X and Y in analysis
        Σ = summation sign

Thus regression analysis provides numerical values for elements a and b such that the cost curve is a straight line of the general form $Y = a + bX$. Solving the equations requires the data computations shown on the following page:

---

1. A description of the least squares criterion and derivation of the equations for elements a and b can be found in most elementary statistics textbooks.

Month	Machine Hours (X)	Repairs and Maintenance Cost (Y)	XY	X²
January	6,250	$ 24,000	150,000,000	39,062,500
February	6,300	24,200	152,460,000	39,690,000
March	6,350	24,350	154,622,500	40,322,500
April	6,400	24,600	157,440,000	40,960,000
May	6,300	24,400	153,720,000	39,690,000
June	6,200	24,300	150,660,000	38,440,000
July	6,100	23,900	145,790,000	37,210,000
August	6,000	23,600	141,600,000	36,000,000
September	6,150	23,950	147,292,500	37,822,500
October	6,250	24,100	150,625,000	39,062,500
November	6,350	24,400	154,940,000	40,322,500
December	6,450	24,700	159,315,000	41,602,500
Totals	75,100	$290,500	1,818,465,000	470,185,000

To solve the two equations for a and b, we perform the following:

$$b = \frac{N\Sigma XY - \Sigma X \Sigma Y}{N\Sigma X^2 - (\Sigma X)^2} = \frac{12(1,818,465,000) - [(75,100)(290,500)]}{12(470,185,000) - [(75,100)(75,100)]}$$

$$= \frac{5,030,000}{2,210,000}$$

$$= \$2.276 \text{ per machine hour}$$

$$a = \frac{\Sigma Y}{N} - \frac{b(\Sigma X)}{N} = \frac{290,500}{12} - \frac{(2.276)(75,100)}{12}$$

$$= \$9,964.25$$

The complete regression equation in general form ($y = a + bx$) for monthly repairs and maintenance cost is:

$$Y = \underline{\$9,964.25 + \$2.276 \text{ per machine hour}}$$

Approximate monthly fixed costs are $9,964.25, and the variable cost per machine hour is $2.276 for this mixed cost.

Note that the equation and resulting cost line or curve for monthly repairs and maintenance costs differ with the method of analysis used.

For the high-low method:

Repairs and maintenance cost = $8,933.33 + $2.4444 per machine hour

For the least squares method:

Repairs and maintenance cost = $9,964.25 + $2.276 per machine hour

In the Winter Park Division case, there is a significant difference between the two analyses. Most statistical methods have certain limitations, and their solutions should be reviewed with the concept of reasonableness in mind. In many cases, the high-low method will be a close approximation of the least squares line, but because all observations were used in the regression analysis and only two in the high-low method, the least squares method should yield more accurate results.

Cost Allocation

OBJECTIVE 5
Define cost allocation and describe the role of cost objectives in the cost allocation process

Cost allocation, or assignment, is important to every part of management accounting, including the determination of unit costs for products and services. Some operating costs (direct costs) can be easily traced and assigned to products or services, but other costs (indirect costs) must be assigned by using some form of allocation method. The need for cost allocation goes beyond just identifying product or service costs. Every report a company's accountants prepare requires some form of cost allocation. Depreciation expense on a building, for example, is often allocated to the departments housed in that building. Depreciation expense is originally established by allocating an investment's total cost to various time periods. Even the president's salary is allocated to the various divisions of a company.

In accounting for operating costs, each cost must be assigned to products, services, departments, or jobs before accounting reports can be prepared. Without proper cost allocation techniques, management accountants cannot do their work. Management accountants have three major tasks in preparing internal accounting documents: (1) they must find product or service unit costs; (2) they must work out cost budgets and cost controls for management; and (3) they must prepare reports to aid and support management decisions. Each task requires proper cost allocation procedures.

Several terms are unique to the concept of cost allocation and thus are discussed further. For instance, the terms *cost allocation* and *cost assignment* are often used interchangeably, although *cost allocation* is the more popular of the two. For our purposes **cost allocation** is the process of assigning a specific cost to a specific cost objective.[2] Understanding such terms as *cost center, cost objective, direct cost,* and *indirect cost* is also vital to the study of cost allocation.

A **cost center** is any organizational segment or area of activity for which there is a reason to accumulate costs. Cost centers include the company

2. Cost Accounting Standard 402, promulgated by the Cost Accounting Standards Board in 1972, defined the term *allocate* as follows: "To assign an item of cost, or group of items of cost, to one or more cost objectives. This term includes both direct assignment of cost and the reassignment of a share from an indirect cost pool."

as a whole, corporate divisions, specific operating plants, departments, and even specific machines or work areas. Once a cost center has been selected, methods can be worked out to assign costs accurately to that cost center. Most accounting reports of a cost center can be prepared only after all the proper cost allocation procedures have been carried out.

A cost objective is the destination of an assigned cost.[3] If the purpose of a certain cost analysis is to evaluate the operating performance of a division or department, the cost objective would be that department or division (cost center). But if product costing is the reason for accumulating costs, a specific product, order, or an entire contract could be the cost objective. The important point is that cost classification and cost allocation results differ, depending on the cost objective being analyzed.

Now, we can expand the definitions of direct and indirect costs used earlier in relation to product costing. A direct cost is any cost that can be conveniently and economically traced to a *specific cost objective*. Direct materials costs and direct labor costs are normally thought of as direct costs. However, costs considered direct will vary with individual cost objectives. In general, the number of costs classified as direct increases with the size of the cost objective. If the cost objective is a large division of a company, then electricity, maintenance, and special tooling costs of the division may be classified as direct costs. An indirect cost is any cost that cannot be conveniently or economically traced and assigned to a specific cost objective. In an actual situation, any production cost not classified as a direct cost is an indirect cost.

Allocation of Manufacturing Costs

All manufacturing costs can be traced or assigned to a company's divisions, departments, or units of productive output. Direct costs, such as the cost of direct materials, can be assigned to specific products, departments, or jobs. Many manufacturing costs, however, are indirect costs incurred for the benefit of more than one product or department. These costs should be allocated to the departments and products that benefit from the costs. For example, electricity cost is incurred for the benefit of all departments or divisions of a company. This cost must be allocated to all work done during a week or a month. Assigning it all to one department would not give a true picture of events. This benefit theory and the methods used to distribute costs are basic to cost allocation.

Figure 5-8 shows the cost allocation process. All three cost elements are included: materials, labor, and factory overhead. The costs of lumber and the cabinetmaker's wages are direct costs of the product. Factory overhead costs include depreciation of the table saw, cleanup and janitorial services, and nails. All factory overhead costs are indirect costs of the product and must be assigned by an allocation method. In this example,

3. Cost Accounting Standard 402, promulgated by the Cost Accounting Standards Board in 1972, defined the term *cost objective* as follows: "A function, organizational subdivision, contract or other work unit for which cost data are desired and for which provision is made to accumulate and measure the cost of processes, products, jobs, capitalized projects, etc."

Figure 5-8. Cabinet Making: Assigning Manufacturing Costs to the Product

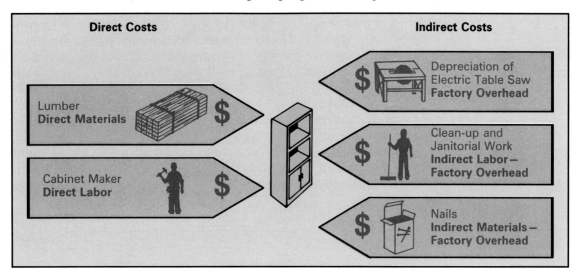

the cost objective is the product. Various cost classifications and cost allocation methods are used depending on the specific cost objective being analyzed.

To summarize, allocation of production costs calls for assigning direct and indirect manufacturing costs to specific cost objectives. A cost may be a direct cost to a large cost objective (a large division) but an indirect cost to a smaller cost objective (a product). In each case, all manufacturing costs are assigned to the specific cost objectives being analyzed as either direct or indirect costs.

The Role of Cost Allocation in Corporate Reporting

OBJECTIVE 6
Identify specific uses of cost allocation in corporate accounting and reporting practices

Accounting reports are prepared for all levels of management, from the president down to the department manager or supervisor. The president is responsible for all costs of the company. A department manager, on the other hand, is responsible only for costs connected to that one department. Reports must be prepared for all cost centers, including the company as a whole, each division, and all departments within each division. The same costs shown in departmental reports will appear again in divisional and corporate reports, but perhaps in summary form.

As focus shifts from one cost center or cost objective to another, so does the ease with which costs can be traced. Here is where cost allocation comes into the picture. The different types of accounting reports can be prepared only with the aid of cost allocation techniques. As costs are reclassified and assigned to smaller cost centers or cost objectives, they become more difficult to trace. More costs are accounted for as indirect when emphasis shifts from divisional to departmental reporting. When the size of the cost objective is reduced to focus on a single product, only direct materials and direct labor costs can be directly traced.   All other costs are classified as indirect and must be parceled out to the different products.   This distribution calls for special procedures.

Table 5-2 shows how three manufacturing costs are traced differently as cost objectives change.   Direct materials costs can be traced directly to any level of cost objective shown.   They are a direct cost at the divisional, departmental, and product levels.   All 40,000 pounds of sugar were issued to Division A, so they can be traced directly to that division.   Only half (20,000 pounds) of the division's sugar was used by Department XZ, so only that amount can be traced directly to that department.   At the product level, every unit of Product AB requires one-half pound of sugar. The cost of that one-half pound is a direct cost that can be traced to the product.   Depreciation of Factory Building G, which is used entirely by Division A, can be traced directly to Division A.   For any smaller cost

Table 5-2. Cost Classification and Traceability

| | Cost Objectives | | |
Costs	Division A	Department XZ	Product AB
Direct Materials	*Direct costs:* 40,000 pounds of sugar issued from inventory specifically for Division A.	*Direct cost:* 20,000 of the 40,000 pounds of sugar issued from inventory were used by Department XZ (can be directly traced).	*Direct cost:* Every unit of Product AB requires ½ pound of sugar.
Depreciation of Factory Building G	*Direct cost:* Factory Building G is used entirely by Division A. Therefore all depreciation expenses from usage of Factory Building G can be directly traced to Division A.	*Indirect cost:* Department XZ is one of four departments in Factory Building G. Depreciation of Factory Building G is allocated to the four departments according to square footage used by each department.	*Indirect cost:* Depreciation of Factory Building G is an indirect product cost. It is allocated to individual products as part of factory overhead charges applied to products using direct labor hours as a base.
Depreciation of Machine 201	*Direct cost:* Machine 201 is located in Department XZ and is used exclusively by Division A (can be directly traced).	*Direct cost:* Machine 201 is used only by Department XZ. Therefore its depreciation charges can be directly traced to Department XZ.	*Indirect cost:* Depreciation of Machine 201 cannot be directly traced to individual products it produces. Such depreciation charges are accounted for as part of factory overhead costs.

objectives, though, it becomes an indirect cost. Building depreciation expense must be shared by the various cost centers within the building. Such costs must be allocated to departmental or product cost objectives, using an allocation base, such as space occupied or direct labor hours. Depreciation costs of Machine 201 can be traced directly to either Division A or Department XZ. When Product AB is the cost objective, however, depreciation of machinery is considered an indirect manufacturing cost. It is accounted for as a factory overhead cost. Factory overhead costs are accumulated and then allocated to the products produced in Department XZ, as we saw in previous chapters. The principles of classifying and tracing costs discussed here play a part in the preparation of all internal accounting reports.

Assigning Costs of Supporting Service Functions

OBJECTIVE 7
Assign costs of supporting service functions to operating departments

Every company and manufacturing process depends on the aid of many supporting service functions or departments. A **supporting service function** is not directly involved in production, but it is an operating unit or department needed for the overall operation of the company. Examples include a repair and maintenance department, a production scheduling department, a central power department, an inspection department, and materials storage and handling.

Labor costs and various indirect operating costs are accumulated for each service function. The costs of these supporting departments are incurred for the purpose of producing a product, so the costs incurred by supporting service functions are product costs. They should be treated as indirect manufacturing costs and assigned to products through the Factory Overhead account. This type of cost allocation is a two-step process. First, the costs of the supporting service function are allocated to the departments or cost centers that benefited from the services. Second, the assigned costs are included in the production department's Factory Overhead account and allocated to the end product.

Allocating factory overhead costs to products was discussed in Chapter 3. Here we concentrate on assigning supporting service department costs to production departments. A service function must benefit other departments to justify its existence. It is on this concept of **benefit** that supporting service department costs are assigned to production departments. Benefit must be measured on some basis that shows how the service performed relates to the department receiving the service.

Table 5-3 gives examples of bases used to allocate costs of supporting service functions. Each base should be used when there is a benefit relationship between the service function and the production departments. Each service request may represent an equal amount of benefit or service to the receiving department, in which case the number of service requests can be the basis. Total benefit may be measured by the number of labor hours needed to complete the service, in which case labor hours can be the basis. Similar relationships justify the use of kilowatt hours or the number of materials requisitions as the allocation basis. The following problem will help you understand the process of assigning supporting service department costs.

Table 5-3. Cost Allocation Bases for Assigning Costs of Supporting Service Functions

Possible Allocation Basis	When to Use It
1. Number of service requests	Used when each service takes the same amount of time or when a record of service requests is maintained and no other basis is available
2. Labor hours	Used when service labor hours are recorded for each service performed; a very good basis when the different services take different amounts of time
3. Kilowatt hours used	Used to distribute the costs of a central power department maintained by the company
4. Number of materials requisitions	Used to allocate costs of a materials-storage area

Illustrative Problem:
Assigning Service Department Costs

Saleh Metal Products Company has six production departments. The company also has three supporting service departments, including the Repairs and Maintenance (R & M) Department. Costs of the R & M Department are assigned to the six production departments on the basis of the number of service requests each department makes.

The production departments made the following number of service requests during February: sixteen requests by the Cutting Department, twenty-one by the Extruding Department, eight by the Shaping Department, thirty-one by the Threading Department, twenty-four by the Polishing Department, and twenty-five by the Finishing Department.

Following are costs incurred and charged against the R & M Department during February:

Supplies and Parts	
Small Tools	$ 1,850
Lubricants and Supplies	940
Replacement Parts	2,100
Labor	
Repair and Maintenance	3,910
Supervision	1,600
Depreciation	
Equipment	1,290
Machinery	1,620
Other Operating Costs	2,440
Total Costs for February	$15,750

Required

1. Using the number of service requests, prepare a schedule allocating the R & M Department's operating costs for February to the six production departments.
2. Name and discuss another possible allocation basis for assigning the R & M Department's costs to the six production departments.

Solution

1. The goal of this part of the problem is to see what portion of February R & M costs should be assigned to each production department. The specific dollar amounts are found by using a ratio of the benefits each production department received to total benefits rendered by the R & M Department. Using the number of service requests as the cost allocation basis, we can approach this problem two ways:

   a. Find the average cost per request, and multiply this amount by each department's number of service requests:

   $$\frac{\text{Total cost}}{\text{Total service requests}} = \frac{\$15,750}{125} = \$126 \text{ per request}$$

   R & M Department cost allocation for February

To Cutting Department (16 × $126)	$ 2,016
To Extruding Department (21 × $126)	2,646
To Shaping Department (8 × $126)	1,008
To Threading Department (31 × $126)	3,906
To Polishing Department (24 × $126)	3,024
To Finishing Department (25 × $126)	3,150
Total Costs Allocated	$15,750

   b. The other approach is to take the ratio of each department's requests to the total number of requests and multiply by the total costs to be allocated. R & M Department cost allocation for February is:

To Cutting Department (16/125) ($15,750)	$ 2,016
To Extruding Department (21/125) ($15,750)	2,646
To Shaping Department (8/125) ($15,750)	1,008
To Threading Department (31/125) ($15,750)	3,906
To Polishing Department (24/125) ($15,750)	3,024
To Finishing Department (25/125) ($15,750)	3,150
Total Costs Allocated	$15,750

   The allocations are the same by method b as by method a, as they should be.

2. Labor hours used would be another possible allocation basis. Time records can be kept for each service call, and then costs can be allocated

by finding the average R & M Department cost per labor hour. This cost is then multiplied by the number of service labor hours each production department used.

Allocation of Joint Production Costs

OBJECTIVE 8
Allocate common costs to joint products

Joint, or common, costs present a special need for cost allocation. A **joint cost** (or common cost) relates to two or more products produced from a common input or raw material and can be assigned only by arbitrary cost allocation after the products become identifiable. Joint products cannot be identified as separate products during most of the production process. Only at a particular point in the manufacturing process, called the **split-off point,** do separate products evolve from a common processing unit. Joint products are often found in such industries as petroleum refining, wood processing, and meat packing. In all these industries, more than one end product arises from a single kind of input.

In the beef processing industry, the final cuts of meat (steaks, roasts, hamburger) do not appear until the end of the process. However, the cost of the steer, transportation costs, storage and hanging costs, and labor costs were incurred to get the side of beef ready for final butchering. How do we assign these joint costs to specific cuts of beef? This type of cost allocation is the objective of accounting for joint costs.

Figure 5-9 shows a joint production situation and the accounting problem of allocating joint costs. The joint costs of $420,000 can be assigned to Product AA and Product BB several ways. Here we outline the two most commonly used methods.

Physical Volume Method

One way to allocate joint production costs to specific products is the **physical volume method.** This approach uses a measure of physical volume (units, pounds, liters, or grams) as the basis for joint cost allocation. The following example shows how the physical volume method applies to the problem in Figure 5-9.

Assume that the Phillips Company makes two grades of paint from the same mixture of substances. During August, 75,000 liters of various ingredients were put into the production process. The final output for the month was 25,000 liters of Product AA and 50,000 liters of Product BB. Total joint production costs for August were $420,000, made up of $190,000 for direct materials, $145,000 for direct labor, and $85,000 for factory overhead. The joint products cannot be identified until the end of the production process. Product AA sells for $9 per liter; Product BB for $6 per liter.

Now, let us use the physical volume method of assigning joint costs. We select total liters as the allocation basis, and then we apply a ratio of the physical volume of each product to total physical volume, as shown on the following page:

Figure 5-9. Joint Product Cost Allocation

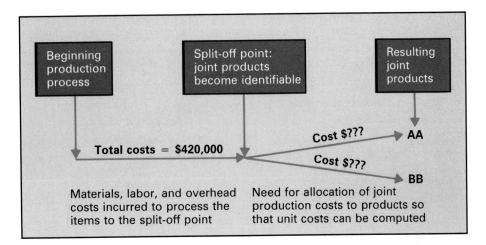

	Total Liters	Allocation Ratio	Joint Cost Allocation	
Product AA	25,000	$\frac{25,000}{75,000}$ or ⅓	$140,000	($420,000 × ⅓)
Product BB	50,000	$\frac{50,000}{75,000}$ or ⅔	280,000	($420,000 × ⅔)
Totals	75,000		$420,000	

Product AA generates $225,000 in revenues (25,000 liters at $9 per liter). Thus the gross margin for this product line will be $85,000. We compute this by subtracting $140,000 of assigned joint costs from the total revenues of $225,000. Product BB sells for a total of $300,000 (50,000 liters at $6 per liter) and will show only $20,000 in gross margin ($300,000 minus $280,000 of assigned joint costs).

The physical volume method is easy to use. However, it often seriously distorts net income because the physical volume of joint products may not be proportionate to each product's ability to generate revenue. In our example, Product BB's net income suffered because its high-volume content attracted two-thirds of the production costs even though its selling price was much less than Product AA.

Relative Sales Value Method

A different way to allocate joint production focuses on the relative sales value of the products. The **relative sales value method** allocates joint production costs to products in proportion to each product's ability to generate revenue. Extending the Phillips Company data, we can make the following analysis. (Costs are assigned to joint products on the basis of their relative sales value when they first become identifiable as specific products—that is, at the split-off point.)

	Liters Produced ×	Selling Price =	Sales Value at Split-Off Point	Allocation Ratio	Joint Cost Allocation
Product AA	25,000	$9	$225,000	$\frac{\$225,000}{\$525,000}$ or 3/7	$180,000 ($420,000 × 3/7)
Product BB	50,000	6	300,000	$\frac{\$300,000}{\$525,000}$ or 4/7	240,000 ($420,000 × 4/7)
Totals	75,000		$525,000		$420,000

Product AA has a relative sales value of $225,000 at the split-off point, and Product BB's relative sales value totals $300,000. The resulting cost allocation ratios are 3/7 and 4/7, respectively, for Products AA and BB. Applying these ratios to the total joint cost of $420,000, we assign $180,000 to Product AA and $240,000 to Product BB.

	Product AA		Product BB	
	Physical Volume Method	Relative Sales Value Method	Physical Volume Method	Relative Sales Value Method
Sales	$225,000	$225,000	$300,000	$300,000
Cost of goods sold	140,000	180,000	280,000	240,000
Gross margin	$ 85,000	$ 45,000	$ 20,000	$ 60,000
Gross margin as percentage of sales	37.8%	20%	6.7%	20%

If we compare the two joint cost allocation methods, we see a wide difference in gross margin for the two product lines.

The major advantage of the relative sales value method is that it allocates joint costs according to a product's ability to absorb the cost. For this reason equal gross margin percentages will always result when products are valued at the split-off point. Our example shows that under the relative sales value method, gross margin as a percentage of sales is 20 percent for both Products AA and BB.

As mentioned earlier, these approaches to assigning joint production costs are arbitrary. The reason for using arbitrary approaches is that it is difficult to determine just how the end products (cost objectives) specifically benefited from the incurred cost. These approaches—whether the physical volume method or the relative sales value method—should be used only when it is impossible to tell how the cost benefited the cost objective. Most cost assignment methods used for determining product unit costs are based on a beneficial relationship.

Chapter Review

Review of Learning Objectives

1. **Explain the concept of cost behavior as it relates to total costs and costs per unit.**
   Cost behavior is the way costs respond to changes in activity or volume. Some costs are entirely variable in relation to volume or operating activity, whereas other costs remain fixed as volume changes. The meaning of cost behavior depends on whether total costs are being analyzed or cost per unit is being computed. Variable costs vary in total as volume changes but are fixed per unit; fixed costs are fixed in total but vary per unit as volume changes.

2. **Identify specific types of variable costs and compute changes in variable costs caused by changes in operating activity.**
   Total costs that change in direct proportion to changes in productive output (or any other volume measure) are called variable costs. A manufacturing company experiences variable costs such as direct materials costs, hourly direct labor costs, and operating supplies; a department store incurs such variable costs as cost of merchandise sold, sales commissions, and hourly wages of shelf stockers; a bank incurs variable costs such as leasing expense of computer equipment (based on usage), hourly computer operator wages, and the cost of data storage disks.

3. **Identify specific types of fixed costs and describe the impact of changes in the level of operating activity on fixed costs.**
   Total fixed costs remain constant within a relevant range of activity or volume. Examples include depreciation costs, supervisory salaries, insurance premiums, rental charges, and property taxes. Fixed costs do vary in the long run but remain constant over short periods of time. They change only when activity exceeds the anticipated relevant range. Such a change usually necessitates the purchase of new equipment, new buildings, larger insurance premiums and property taxes, and additional supervisory personnel.

4. **Differentiate a semivariable cost from a mixed cost and apply methods used to separate their variable and fixed cost components.**
   A semivariable cost, such as the cost of electricity, has both variable cost and fixed cost components. Mixed costs result when both variable and fixed costs are charged to the same general ledger account. The balance in the Repairs and Maintenance account is an example of a mixed cost. To separate the variable cost from the fixed costs in these accounts, an accountant can apply

either the high-low method or the least squares method, which is based on regression analysis.

5. **Define cost allocation and describe the role of cost objectives in the cost allocation process.**
   Cost allocation is the process of assigning a specific cost to a specific cost objective. A cost objective is the destination of an assigned cost. The cost objective varies according to the focus of a particular report; it may range from an entire company or a division down to one particular product. Cost objectives are a target for the cost allocation process.

6. **Identify specific uses of cost allocation in corporate accounting and reporting practices.**
   Accounting reports are prepared for all levels of management, from the president down to the department manager or supervisor. Reports must be prepared for all cost centers, including the company as a whole, each division, and all departments within each division. To make these different reports possible, costs must be allocated in different ways. As the report focus (cost objective) decreases in size, more and more costs become indirect and subject to cost allocation procedures.

7. **Assign costs of supporting service functions to operating departments.**
   Costs incurred by supporting service departments must be accounted for as indirect operating costs. They are allocated to production or other operating departments on a benefit basis—a beneficial relationship of a cost to a cost objective. There are several allocation bases; each basis is suitable for a certain relationship between the service used and the department receiving the service.

8. **Allocate common costs to joint products.**
   Joint products evolve from a common processing unit. They cannot be identified as specific products until the split-off point in the process. All manufacturing costs incurred prior to the split-off point are shared by all the joint products. At the split-off point, costs are assigned to individual products by either the physical volume method or the relative sales value method.

Review of Concepts and Terminology

The following important concepts were introduced in this chapter:

(L.O.1) **Budgetary control:** An integrated cost planning and control system.

(L.O.1) **Cost behavior:** The way costs respond to changes in activity or volume.

(L.O.2) **Variable costs:** Total costs that change in direct proportion to changes in productive output (or any other volume measure).

(L.O.2) **Relevant range:** The range of activity in which a company expects to operate.

(L.O.3) **Fixed costs:** Total costs that remain constant within a relevant range of activity or volume.

(L.O.4) **Semivariable costs:** A cost that has both variable and fixed cost components.

(L.O.4) **Mixed costs:** Costs that result when both variable and fixed costs are charged to the same general ledger account.

(L.O.5) **Cost allocation:** The process of assigning a specific cost to a specific cost objective.

(L.O.7)   **Supporting service functions:**   A unit or department that is not directly involved in production but is an operating unit that the overall operation of the company needs.

(L.O.8)   **Joint cost:**   A cost that relates to two or more products produced from a common input or raw material and that can be assigned only by arbitrary cost allocation after the products become identifiable.   (Also a common cost.)

Other important terms introduced in this chapter are:

benefit (p. 173)
committed costs (p. 162)
cost center (p. 169)
cost objective (p. 170)
discretionary costs (p. 162)
high-low method (p. 166)
least squares method (p. 167)
nonlinear costs (p. 159)
operating capacity (p. 157)
physical volume method (p. 176)
relative sales value method (p. 177)
scatter diagram (p. 165)
split-off point (p. 176)
step-variable costs (p. 163)

Review Problem
Regression and High-Low Methods Demonstrated

Rosen & Fukuda Technetics, Inc., is in the process of creating a budget for 19xx. Most of the overhead costs can be classified easily as being either variable with a specific activity base or fixed for the time period under review.   However, the corporation's electricity cost is a semivariable cost, having both variable and fixed components.   The following data represent electricity cost incurred last year and related machine hour usage:

Month	Machine Hours	Electricity Cost
January	2,400	$ 10,800
February	2,240	10,000
March	2,680	11,800
April	3,000	11,380
May	3,200	12,200
June	3,480	11,420
July	3,820	13,200
August	4,200	13,480
September	4,100	13,200
October	3,740	12,040
November	3,820	12,200
December	3,860	12,800
Totals	40,540	$144,520

Required

1. Using the high-low method, compute the variable cost per machine hour and the fixed portion of the monthly utility cost.
2. Using regression analysis, compute the variable cost per machine hour and the fixed portion of the monthly utility cost.

Solution

1. High-low method

Volume	Month	Cost	Activity Level
High	August	$13,480	4,200 machine hours
Low	February	10,000	2,240 machine hours
Difference		$ 3,480	1,960 machine hours

Variable rate per machine hour
    $3,480/1,960 machine hours = $1.7755 per machine hour

Fixed cost per month
    August: $13,480 − (4,200 × $1.7755) = $ 6,022.86

    February: $10,000 − (2,240 × $1.7755) = $ 6,022.86

Breakdown of total costs for the year
    Variable cost: 40,540 × $1.7755 = $ 71,978.77
    Fixed costs: $144,520 − (40,540 × $1.7755) =   72,541.23
                                                    $144,520.00

2. Regression analysis

Month	Machine Hours (X)	Electricity Cost (Y)	XY	X²
January	2,400	$ 10,800	25,920,000	5,760,000
February	2,240	10,000	22,400,000	5,017,600
March	2,680	11,800	31,624,000	7,182,400
April	3,000	11,380	34,140,000	9,000,000
May	3,200	12,200	39,040,000	10,240,000
June	3,480	11,420	39,741,600	12,110,400
July	3,820	13,200	50,424,000	14,592,400
August	4,200	13,480	56,616,000	17,640,000
September	4,100	13,200	54,120,000	16,810,000
October	3,740	12,040	45,029,600	13,987,600
November	3,820	12,200	46,604,000	14,592,400
December	3,860	12,800	49,408,000	14,899,600
Totals (Σ)	40,540	$144,520	495,067,200	141,832,400

$$b = \frac{N\Sigma XY - \Sigma X\Sigma Y}{N\Sigma X^2 - (\Sigma X)^2} = \frac{12(495,067,200) - [(40,540)(144,520)]}{12(141,832,400) - [(40,540)(40,540)]}$$

$$= \frac{81,965,600}{58,497,200}$$

$$= \$1.401 \text{ per machine hour}$$

$$a = \frac{\Sigma Y}{N} - \frac{b(\Sigma X)}{N} = \frac{144,520}{12} - \frac{(1.401)(40,540)}{12}$$

$$= \$7,309.65$$

The cost equation in general form ($y = a + bx$) is

$$\$7,309.65 + \$1.401 \text{ per machine hour}$$

Chapter Assignments

Questions

1. Define cost behavior.
2. Why is knowledge of cost behavior useful to the management accountant?
3. What makes variable costs different from other costs?
4. Explain the statement, "Fixed costs remain constant in total but decrease per unit as output increases."
5. What does relevant range of activity mean?
6. Why is a telephone charge usually considered a semivariable cost?
7. What is a mixed cost? Give an example.
8. Distinguish a committed fixed cost from a discretionary fixed cost.
9. Describe the high-low cost separation method.
10. Identify the formulas used in the least squares cost separation method and state what each symbol means.
11. What is a cost objective? What is its role in management accounting?
12. State the definition of "allocate" developed by the Cost Accounting Standards Board.
13. "As the size of the cost center or cost objective decreases, the ability to trace cost and revenue becomes more limited." Is this statement true? Why?
14. What is a supporting service department? Give examples.
15. Explain the concept of "benefit" as it relates to the distribution of supporting service department costs.
16. What is a joint manufacturing cost?
17. Describe the physical volume method of allocating joint costs to products. List the advantages and disadvantages of the physical volume method.
18. Should joint costs be allocated to a product on the basis of the product's ability to generate revenue? Explain your answer.

Classroom Exercises

Exercise 5-1.
Concept of Cost
Behavior
(L.O.1)

Jim Ott has just inherited the Florida Keys Shrimp Company, which consists of an ice house/shrimp preparation building, a refrigerated van, and three shrimp boats. The company employs three four-person shrimp boat crews and five shrimp processing people. Offutt & Bain, a local accounting firm, has kept the financial records of the company for many years. In their last analysis of the company, Janet Offutt stated that the company's fixed cost base was satisfactory but the variable costs of operations were too high for the volume of business experienced in the past two years. As a result, the company has not been able to operate at a profit during that time period.

Mr. Ott is confused with the statement about the variable and fixed costs. Prepare a response to Mr. Ott from Ms. Offutt explaining the concept of cost behavior.

Exercise 5-2.
Variable Cost
Analysis
(L.O.2)

Quick Oil Change has been in business for six months. Each car serviced requires an average of 4.2 quarts of oil. The manager of Quick Oil Change pays 55¢ for each quart of oil. The manager has estimated the number of cars that will be serviced in the next six months. Use the estimates to compute the monthly oil cost and total oil costs that the manager of Quick Oil Change should incur in the next six months.

Month	Estimated Car Service	Oil Costs
March	240	?
April	288	?
May	360	?
June	480	?
July	600	?
August	720	?

Exercise 5-3.
Identification of
Variable and Fixed
Costs
(L.O.2)

From the following list of costs of productive output, indicate which are usually considered variable costs and which are fixed costs: (a) packing materials for stereo components, (b) real estate taxes, (c) gasoline for a delivery truck, (d) property insurance, (e) depreciation expense of buildings (straight-line method), (f) supplies, (g) indirect materials used, (h) bottles used in the sale of liquids, (i) license fees for company cars, (j) wiring used in radios, (k) machine helper's wages, (l) wood used in bookcases, (m) city operating license, (n) employer's share of Social Security payments, (o) machine operators' wages, and (p) cost of required outside inspection on each unit produced. Could any of these costs be considered a semivariable cost? Explain your answer.

Exercise 5-4.
Variable and Fixed
Costs
(L.O.2,3)

For each of the following types of costs, identify whether the cost is usually variable or fixed. Further identify the fixed costs as committed fixed costs or discretionary fixed costs.

Cost Type	Variable	Fixed	
		Committed	Discretionary
Supplies			
Freight costs			
Rent expense			
Telephone expense			
Direct labor			
Sales commissions			
Real estate taxes			
Fire insurance expense			
Manager's salary			
Advertising expense			
Research and development costs			
Depreciation expense			
Employee training costs			

**Exercise 5-5.
Semivariable Costs/
High-Low Method
(L.O.4)**

McMahan Electronics Company manufactures major appliances. The company just had its most successful year because of increased interest in its refrigerator line. While preparing the budget for next year, Mr. James, the company's controller, came across the following data related to utility costs:

Month	Power Costs	Volume in Machine Hours
July	$58,000	6,000
August	52,000	5,000
September	50,000	4,500
October	48,000	4,000
November	42,000	3,500
December	40,000	3,000

Using the high-low method, determine (1) the variable power cost per machine hour, (2) the monthly fixed power cost, and (3) the total variable power and fixed power costs for the six-month period.

**Exercise 5-6.
Cost Allocation
Basis
(L.O.6)**

A plan for cost assignment is vital to corporate reporting, product costing, and inventory valuation. Following are examples of costs and related cost objectives:

Cost	Cost Objective
Materials-handling costs	Product
Plant depreciation costs	Division
Repair and Maintenance Department costs	One of five production departments served
Corporate president's salary	Division

1. Which costs would be direct costs of the related cost objective? Which would be indirect costs?
2. For each indirect cost, choose a cost allocation basis that provides a logical relationship between the cost and the cost objective. Defend your answers.

Exercise 5-7.
Cost Allocation—
Direct Versus
Indirect
(L.O. 5, 6)

Classifying a cost as direct or indirect depends on the cost objective. Depreciation of a factory building is a direct cost when the plant is the cost objective, but when the cost objective is a product, the depreciation cost becomes indirect.
   Indicate for each cost objective listed in the following chart whether it is an indirect cost (I) or a direct cost (D). Be able to defend your answers.

	Cost Objective		
	Division	Department	Product
Direct labor			
Departmental supplies			
Division head's salary			
President's salary			
Department manager's salary			
Direct materials			
Fire insurance on specific machine			
Property taxes, division plant			
Department repairs and maintenance			

Exercise 5-8.
Service
Department Cost
Allocation
(L.O. 7)

Delta Fundraising, Inc., has six departments that must share the services of a single central computer. Management has decided that the best basis for cost allocation is the minutes of computer time each department uses. Usage per department for the month of June was as follows: 3,096 minutes for Department A, 4,128 minutes for Department B, 4,560 minutes for Department C, 2,064 minutes for Department D, 1,032 minutes for Department E, and 5,160 minutes for Department F. The total for all departments was 20,040 minutes. The total cost of operating the computer during the month was $14,028.
   Determine the computer expense to be assigned to each department for the one-month period.

Exercise 5-9.
Joint Cost
Allocation—
Relative Sales
Value Method
(L.O. 8)

In the processing of pulp for making paper, two distinct grades of wood pulp come out of a common crushing and mixing process. Ward Paper Products, Inc., produced 44,000 liters of pulp during January. Direct materials inputs cost the company $86,000. Labor and overhead costs for the month were $56,000 and $36,000, respectively. Output for the month was as follows:

Product	Quantity	Market Value at Split-Off Point
Grade A pulp	28,000 liters	$14.00 per liter
Grade B pulp	16,000 liters	$10.50 per liter

Using the relative sales value method, allocate common production costs to Grade A pulp and Grade B pulp.

Exercise 5-10.
Joint Cost
Allocation—
Physical Volume
Method
(L.O. 8)

Kennedy Company of Massachusetts produces molasses and refined sugar, joint products from juice extracted from sugar beets. The company will use the physical volume method to assign common costs to the products. The allocation base is liters. During February, Kennedy Company put 320,000 liters of sugar beet juice into production. The final products from this input were 48,000 liters of molasses and 272,000 liters of refined sugar. These joint product costs were incurred during February: $3,640 for materials, $9,240 for direct labor, and $11,520 for factory overhead. Thus total joint costs total $24,400.

Assuming no loss through evaporation, assign a portion of joint production costs to each product.

Interpreting Accounting Information

Rio Pinar Golf and
Tennis Club
(L.O. 4)

Officials of the Rio Pinar Golf and Tennis Club are putting together a budget for the year ending December 31, 19x9. Several problems have caused the budget to be delayed by more than four weeks. Ray Landry, club treasurer, indicated that the delay was caused by three expense items. These items were difficult to account for because they were called "semivariable or mixed costs," and he did not know how to break them down into their variable and fixed components for the budget. An accountant friend and golfing partner helped him identify the problem and told him to use either the high-low method or the least squares method to divide the costs into their variable and fixed parts.

The three cost categories are (a) Water Expense, (b) Electricity Expense, and (c) Repairs and Maintenance Expense. Information on last year's spending patterns and the measurement activity connected with each cost is as follows:

Month	Water Expense Amount	Gallons Used	Electricity Expense Amount	Kilowatt Hours	Repairs and Maintenance Amount	Labor Hours
January	$ 21,990	125,000	$ 7,500	210,000	$ 7,578	220
February	19,740	110,000	8,255	240,200	7,852	230
March	18,690	103,000	8,165	236,600	7,304	210
April	21,240	120,000	8,960	268,400	7,030	200
May	22,740	130,000	7,520	210,800	7,852	230
June	26,115	152,500	7,025	191,000	8,126	240
July	28,740	170,000	6,970	188,800	8,400	250
August	30,840	184,000	6,990	189,600	8,674	260
September	28,740	170,000	7,055	192,200	8,948	270
October	26,790	157,000	7,135	195,400	8,674	260
November	22,740	130,000	8,560	252,400	8,126	240
December	20,040	112,000	8,415	246,600	7,852	230
Totals	$288,405	1,663,500	$92,550	2,622,000	$96,416	2,840

Required

1. Using the high-low method, compute the variable cost rates used last year for each expense. What was the monthly fixed cost for water, electricity, and repairs and maintenance?
2. Compute the total variable cost and total fixed cost for each expense category for last year.
3. Compute the cost equation for Repairs and Maintenance using the least squares method.
4. Mr. Landry believes that for the coming year the variable water rate will go up $.05, the variable electricity rate will increase $.005, and the variable repairs rate will rise $1.20. Usage of all items and their fixed cost amounts will remain constant. Compute the projected total cost for each category.

Problem Set A

Problem 5A-1.
Cost Behavior and
Projection
(L.O.2,4)

Howard Anderson Painting Company, located in New Orleans, specializes in refurbishing exterior painted surfaces of homes and other buildings. In the humid south, exterior surfaces are hit hard with insect debris during the summer months. A special refurbishing technique called "pressure cleaning" is needed before the surface can be primed and repainted.

The pressure cleaning-resurfacing technique involves the following steps:

1. Trees and bushes near the building must be trimmed back and the ground cleared away for 2 feet from the structure. Unskilled labor is used for this function.
2. A pressure cleaning machine hooked to a water source and powered by a 12-horsepower motor is used to clean the entire exterior surface of the building. An average of 6 gallons of Debris-Luse are mixed with the water for each job. Skilled or specialized labor is used for this task, which generally takes about two hours.
3. Next, a coat of primer is applied to prepare the surface for the final coat of paint. Unskilled labor is often used for this task.
4. The final step is to apply a good oil-based exterior paint to the surface of the structure, including the trim. Specialized labor is required, and the task takes about ten hours.

Specialized or skilled labor accounted for twelve hours per job, and eight hours of unskilled, temporary labor was the norm per job. This special pressure cleaning and refurbishing process generated the following operation results during 19x8:

Number of structures refurbished	628
Specialized or skilled labor	$20.00 per hour
Unskilled, temporary labor	$8.00 per hour
Gallons of Debris-Luse used	3,768 gallons at $5.50 per gallon
Paint primer	7,536 gallons at $15.50 per gallon
Paint	12,560 gallons at $8.00 per gallon
Paint spraying equipment	$600.00 per month depreciation
Two leased vans	$800.00 per month total
Rent—storage building	$450.00 per month

Utility expenses:

Month	Expense	No. of Jobs	Hours Worked
January	$ 3,956.40	42	840
February	3,571.20	36	720
March	4,084.80	44	880
April	4,405.80	49	980
May	4,726.80	54	1,080
June	5,240.40	62	1,240
July	5,818.20	71	1,420
August	5,882.40	72	1,440
September	5,368.80	64	1,280
October	4,341.60	48	960
November	4,213.20	46	920
December	3,828.00	40	800
Totals	$55,437.60	628	12,560

Required

1. Classify the cost items as being variable, fixed, or semivariable costs.
2. Using the high-low method, separate semivariable costs into their variable and fixed components. Use total hours worked as a basis.
3. Project these same costs for next year assuming that the company completes 825 jobs.
4. Compute the average cost per job for next year.

Problem 5A-2.
Variable and Fixed
Costs
(L.O. 4)

José Ortiz, the branch manager of the Duplicate Financial Corporation, has been asked to project his 19x8 income. Most of the overhead costs of his branch can be classified as either variable or fixed costs. However, the branch's communication cost is a semivariable cost. The following data show last year's communication costs and the related loans to customers:

Month	Customer Loans	Communication Costs
January	800	$ 4,950
February	750	4,785
March	500	3,970
April	400	3,645
May	570	4,200
June	600	4,300
July	650	4,500
August	700	4,650
September	500	4,000
October	425	3,730
November	625	4,450
December	850	5,110
Totals	7,370	$52,290

Required

1. Use the data on the previous page to compute the variable cost per customer loan and the monthly fixed cost portion of the monthly communication costs using the high-low method.
2. Compute the variable cost per customer loan and the monthly fixed cost portion of the monthly communication costs using regression analysis.

Problem 5A-3.
Allocation
Process—
Cost Base
Relationship
(L.O. 6)

Following are five types of costs incurred by a typical manufacturing company. Each cost must be allocated to a cost objective.

Type of Cost	Cost Objective
1. Cost Accounting Department	Production departments
2. Engineering (service) Department	Products
3. Materials-handling function	Products
4. Cafeteria (service) function	Production departments
5. Production Scheduling Department	Production departments

A number of allocation bases can be used to assign these costs to their respective cost objectives, including (a) machine hours, (b) direct labor hours, (c) direct labor dollars, (d) engineering labor hours, (e) number of employees, (f) total labor hours, (g) units handled, (h) percentage of service costs, (i) number of service requests, and (j) direct charges.

Required

1. For each of the five types of costs, select the allocation base(s) that best expresses the beneficial relationship between the cost and the cost objective. State the reasons for your answers.
2. Some companies group all the costs listed into one factory overhead cost "pool" and allocate them to products, using just one allocation base, such as direct labor hours. What are the advantages and disadvantages of this approach?

Problem 5A-4.
Service
Department
Expense Allocation
(L.O. 7)

Tenants at the Two Flights Up Office Complex on Park Avenue enjoy the benefits of the pooled concept for supporting services. All operating costs are incurred centrally and allocated to the seven tenant businesses on the basis of usage. Word processing is one of these centralized services. For August the following costs were related to the word processing function: (a) operator labor, five people at $1,200 monthly salary each; (b) supplies, $820; (c) equipment depreciation, $1,250; (d) space rental, $2,000; (e) utility expenses, $550; and (f) overhead charge, $1,380. Thus total allocable costs for August were $12,000.

Usage of the word processing pool is recorded by hours of usage, which is also the basis for allocating the cost each month. During August tenant usage of the word processing service was as follows: (a) Hanna Catering Service, 64 hours; (b) Wooten Realtors, Inc., 142 hours; (c) High & Wide, Attorneys at Law, 211 hours; (d) Wilson Inventory Service, 85 hours; (e) Evers & Nagel, CPAs, 180 hours; (f) Boxwell Sporting Goods, 63 hours; and (g) Byrd Hair Styling Supplies Company, 55 hours.

Required

1. Assign the costs of the word processing function for August to each of the seven tenant businesses on the basis of hours used.
2. Explain other bases of allocation that could have been used to assign costs. Discuss the advantages and disadvantages of each allocation base.

Problem 5A-5.
Joint Cost
Allocation
(L.O. 8)

Crude oil must be processed before its joint products, gasoline, motor oil, and kerosene, can be produced. Paton Petroleum Products, Inc., a Chicago-based company, specializes in quality products. During April the company used 1,500,000 gallons of crude oil at $.20 per gallon, paid $225,000 in direct labor wages, and applied $180,000 of factory overhead to the crude oil processing department. Production during the period yielded 850,000 gallons of gasoline, 150,000 gallons of motor oil, and 400,000 gallons of kerosene. Evaporation caused the loss of 100,000 gallons. This amount of evaporation is normal, and its cost should be included in the costing of good units produced. Selling prices of the joint products are $.60 per gallon of gasoline, $.85 per quart of motor oil, and $.18 per gallon of kerosene. Assume that there were no beginning or ending Work in Process inventories and that everything produced was sold during the period. (*Note:* 4 quarts equal 1 gallon.)

Required

1. Using the physical volume method, allocate joint costs to the three joint products.
2. Using the relative sales value method, allocate joint costs to each of the three products.
3. Prepare a schedule that compares the gross margin at split-off point that results from the two methods of allocation for the three products. Compute gross margin both in total dollars and as a percentage of sales.
4. Gasoline could be processed further beyond the split-off point and become a top premium product. If the company incurred $153,500 in additional processing costs for gasoline in April, the selling price could be increased to $.80 per gallon. Under these circumstances, and assuming that joint cost is allocated using the relative sales value method, how much additional profit would be earned from the sale of gasoline? Should the company process the gasoline beyond split-off point?

Problem Set B

Problem 5B-1.
Cost Behavior and
Projection
(L.O. 2, 4)

Having opened for business on March 1, 19x7, Alluring Auto, Inc., specializes in revitalizing automobile exteriors. "Detailing" is the term used to describe this process. The objective is to detail an automobile to a point where it looks like it just rolled off the showroom floor. Area market research indicated that a full exterior detail should cost about $100. The company has just completed its first year of business and has requested their accountants to analyze the operating results. Management wants costs divided into their variable, fixed, and semi-variable components and would like them projected for the coming year. Anticipated volume for next year is 1,100 jobs.

The process used to detail a car's exterior is as follows:

1. The car's exterior is completely cleaned. One person is required for this operation, which usually takes ten minutes.

2. Trouble spots are given special attention after the general cleaning. Sections of the automobile body that have grease, tar, or other foreign substances are given an application of Tars-Off, a volatile chemical. One container is used for each car.
3. Once the cleaning has been done, the car's paint must be revitalized to restore the paint's original luster. A chemical compound called Buff Glow 7 is used to remove oxidants from the paint surface and restore the natural oils to the paint.
4. Waxing and buffing are the final steps to detailing the exterior of the car. Poly Wax is applied by hand, allowed to sit for ten minutes, and then buffed off. The employee then meticulously examines the entire surface to ensure that all wax and debris have been removed.

Temporary labor is hired as needed to handle daily work overloads at an average labor rate of $20 per hour. Each car takes two hours to detail. The following information has been made available from the first year of operations:

Number of automobiles detailed	840
Containers of Tars-Off consumed	840 at $3.50 per can
Pounds of Buff Glow 7 consumed	105 pounds at $32.00 per pound
Pounds of Poly Wax consumed	210 pounds at $8.00 per pound
Rent expense	$1,400.00 per month

Utility expenses:

Month	Expense	No. of Jobs
March 19x7	$ 800	40
April	850	50
May	900	65
June	1,000	85
July	1,600	105
August	1,800	110
September	1,300	90
October	850	65
November	900	75
December	925	60
January 19x8	890	50
February	880	45
Totals	$12,695	840

Required

1. Classify the costs as being variable, fixed, or semivariable costs.
2. Using the high-low method, separate the semivariable costs into their variable and fixed components. Use number of jobs as the basis.
3. Project these same costs for next year assuming the anticipated increase in activity and that fixed costs will remain constant.
4. Compute the unit cost per job for next year. Should the price be raised?

Problem 5B-2.
Variable and Fixed
Costs
(L.O. 4)

Kevin Jacobs is considering buying an automatic drape cleaning business. In his analysis, he has separated most of the operating costs into either variable or fixed categories. However, the electricity cost to operate the cleaning unit is a semivariable cost. Kevin needs to separate this cost into its variable and fixed components before total operating costs can be determined. Last year's cost of electricity and number of drapes cleaned were:

Month	Drapes Cleaned	Electricity Cost
January	2,500	$ 4,410
February	2,600	4,520
March	2,800	4,750
April	2,900	4,790
May	2,700	4,650
June	3,000	4,940
July	3,200	5,210
August	3,600	5,650
September	3,100	5,070
October	2,700	4,670
November	2,500	4,460
December	2,400	4,360
Totals	34,000	$57,480

Required

1. Use the information above to compute the variable cost per drape cleaned and the monthly fixed cost component of the electricity cost using the high-low method.
2. Compute the variable cost per drape cleaned and the monthly fixed cost component of the electricity cost using regression analysis.

Problem 5B-3.
Allocation Process:
Cost Base
Relationship
(L.O. 6)

Following are five types of costs for a typical manufacturing company. Each cost is allocated to a cost objective.

Type of Cost	Cost Objective
1. Cost of corporate computer center	Production departments
2. Depreciation of division factory buildings	Production departments
3. Tool and die making cost (service department)	Production departments
4. Materials-storage cost	Products
5. Repairs and Maintenance Department costs	Production departments

A number of allocation bases could be used to assign these manufacturing costs to their respective cost objectives. The allocation bases include (a) direct labor dollars, (b) direct labor hours, (c) machine hours, (d) facility or service usage hours, (e) direct materials costs, (f) square footage, and (g) number of service requests.

Required

1. For each of the five types of costs, select the allocation base that best expresses the beneficial relationship between the cost and the cost objective. State the reasons for your answers.
2. What would be wrong with including all these costs in one overhead cost pool and allocating them to production departments on the basis of direct labor dollars? What would be the advantage of such an approach?

**Problem 5B-4.
Service
Department
Expense Allocation
(L.O.7)**

Goldenrod Community Hospital has one respirator that the hospital's six departments must share. To judge efficiency and to aid in future budgeting, each department's operating income or loss is figured separately each month. Before these calculations can be made, expenses that are considered "common" expenses must be allocated to each department. Depreciation and maintenance expenses connected directly to the respirator are allocated to departments according to hours of usage.

The costs for upkeep of the respirator for July are as follows: (a) depreciation was $1,100 on the respirator and $240 on supplemental machinery; (b) labor costs were $6,000 for the operators and $1,800 for maintenance; and (c) materials costs were $3,200 for oxygen, $480 for small replacement parts, $960 for supplies, and $620 for other operating costs. Thus total costs for October were $14,400.

Respirator usage by department for July was as follows: 173.0 hours for the Oncology Department, 32.6 hours for the Orthopedics Department, 88.2 hours for the Nephrology Department, 73.8 hours for the Geriatrics Department, 37.4 hours for the Pediatrics Department, and 75.0 hours for the Maternity Department.

Required

1. Assign respirator costs for July to each of the six departments according to hourly usage.
2. Explain other bases of allocation that could be used to assign costs. Discuss the advantages and disadvantages of each allocation basis.

**Problem 5B-5.
Joint Cost
Allocation
(L.O. 8)**

The Thatcher Toppings Company makes three distinct grades of chocolate sauce. The initial ingredients for all three grades of chocolate sauce are first blended together. After this blending, other ingredients are added to produce the three grades. The Extra-Rich blend sells for $4.20 per liter; the Quality blend sells for $3.60 per liter; and the Regular blend sells for $3.00 per liter. In July, 372,000 liters of ingredients were put into production, with output as follows: 81,840 liters of Extra-Rich blend, 148,800 liters of Quality blend, and 141,360 liters of Regular blend. Joint costs for the period are made up of $301,200 for direct materials, $246,000 for direct labor, and $196,800 for factory overhead. Assume there were no beginning or ending inventories and no loss of input during production.

Required

1. Using the physical volume method, allocate joint costs to the three chocolate sauce blends.
2. Using the relative sales value method, allocate joint costs to the three blends.

3. Prepare a schedule that compares the gross profit at split-off point that results from the two allocation methods for the three products. Compute gross margin both in total dollars and as a percentage of sales.
4. Additional processing costs could be incurred after split-off point for a special ingredient for the Extra-Rich blend that would push up its selling price. If the company incurred $81,840 for this ingredient in this period, it is thought that the selling price could be increased to $6.00 per liter. Following these assumptions and assuming that joint costs are allocated using the relative sales value method, how much profit would be earned from Extra-Rich sales? Should the company add the extra ingredient?

Management Decision Case

Fullerton State Bank
(L.O.3)

California Bancorp is the parent corporation for two statewide banks, Fullerton State Bank and Long Beach State Bank. The Fullerton State Bank is the responsibility of its president, John Lawrence. Four senior vice presidents report to him and coordinate the activities of Marketing, Operations, Commercial Loans, and Investments. In addition, the Internal Audit Division reports directly to the Board of Directors. Within Operations there are five departments, as follows:

Departments	**Functions**
Controller's Department	General ledger maintenance
	Assistant controller
	Special cost and revenue analyses
Data Processing Department	Programming
	Systems design
	Data entry
	Computer operators
	Systems maintenance
Customer Service Department	Tellers
	New account representatives
	Customer concerns
Bookkeeping Department	Customer statement preparation
	Telephone and wire dollar transfers
	Service and vault charges
Proof Department	Proving of bulk deposits
	Internal check clearinghouse

The Customer Service Department is considered the primary department of this division, with the remaining four being support service departments.

According to the controller's department, fixed costs of the division are shared by all five departments and should therefore be grouped together in a fixed overhead cost pool and allocated based on total salary dollars. During 19xx the entire division expects to pay $1,200,000 in salaries. Projected costs to be charged to the fixed overhead cost pool include:

Depreciation, Furniture and Fixtures	$25,800
Telephone Charges	$640 per month plus $100 per month for long-distance calls

Property Taxes	$19,240
Electricity Expense	$820 per month plus $.001 per kilowatt hour of usage*
Rent, Buildings	$36,000
Insurance Expense	$11,960
Gas Heating Expense	$1,040 per month plus $.005 per cubic foot of gas consumption†
Equipment Leasing Expense	$165,000

Ms. Shu-Jen Chen, manager of the Data Processing Department, received the following performance report for the year ended December 31, 19xx.

The Fullerton State Bank
Operations Division
Data Processing Department
Performance Report
For the Year Ended December 31, 19xx

Amount Budgeted	Cost/Expense Item	Actual Amount	Over (Under) Budget
$ 96,000	Salaries, programmers	$ 95,060	$ (940)
96,000	Salaries, system designers	85,080	(10,920)
120,000	Salaries, computer operators	127,820	7,820
64,000	Salary, manager	64,960	960
25,620	Salaries, bank administration	37,520	11,900
165,000	Equipment leasing	172,880	7,880
30,000	Computer supplies	28,420	(1,580)
80,000	Software purchases	73,480	(6,520)
6,000	Data storage diskettes	6,560	560
4,920	Depreciation, furniture and fixtures	4,920	0
90,240	Fixed divisional overhead	111,876	21,636
27,000	Back-up data file maintenance	25,540	(1,460)
10,000	Bankwide overhead	10,500	500
4,000	Miscellaneous expenses	3,280	(720)
$818,780	Totals	$847,896	$29,116

*46,400,000 kilowatt hours are expected to be used.
†1,640,000 cubic feet of gas are expected to be consumed.

Required

1. Compute the fixed overhead cost rate for the Operations Division for 19xx.
2. During 19xx the departments incurred the following salary costs:

Controller's	$236,480
Data Processing	372,920
Customer Service	279,400
Bookkeeping	166,400
Proof	144,800

   Determine the fixed overhead costs that were allocated to each department during the year.
3. How good was Ms. Chen's performance for the year? Critique the performance report as part of your answer.

1. Explain how
   changes in cost,
   volume, or price
   affect the profit
   formula.
2. Compute the break-
   even point in units
   of output and in
   sales dollars.
3. Prepare a break-
   even graph and
   identify its
   components.
4. Define contribution
   margin and use the
   concept to
   determine a
   company's break-
   even point.
5. Apply contribution
   margin analysis to
   estimate levels of
   sales that will
   produce planned
   profits.
6. Prepare an analysis
   that shows the
   effects of changes in
   sales mix on the
   profits of a
   company.

CHAPTER 6

Cost-Volume-Profit Analysis

Knowledge of cost behavior is a key ingredient in the budgeting and planning activities of an enterprise. Distinguishing variable costs from fixed costs allows the management accountant to adjust anticipated profit contributions when future changes in sales and productive output are expected. Such knowledge also allows the accountant to analyze past performance and identify operating trouble spots.

In this chapter we take the study of cost behavior one step further. Cost behavior patterns underlie the relationship between cost, volume of output, and profit. These relationships are studied through **cost-volume-profit analysis** (commonly referred to as **C-V-P analysis**). A company may use C-V-P analysis as a planning tool when the sales volume is known and management needs to find out how much profit will result. Another way of planning is to begin with a target profit. Then, through C-V-P analysis, a company can decide the level of sales needed to reach that profit level. Our purpose here is to look at all aspects of cost-volume-profit relationships. After studying this chapter, you should be able to meet the learning objectives listed on the left.

What Is Cost-Volume-Profit Analysis?

Cost-volume-profit analysis is both a planning and a control tool. C-V-P analysis is used extensively in budgeting activities. For control purposes, C-V-P analysis is a way of measuring how well departments in a company are doing. At the end of a period, the company analyzes sales volume and related actual costs to find actual profit. Performance is measured by comparing actual costs with expected costs. These expected costs are computed by applying C-V-P analysis to actual sales volume. The result is a performance report on which management can base the control of operations. This process is explained further in Chapter 7.

Cost-volume-profit analysis includes a number of techniques and problem-solving procedures structured on knowledge of a company's cost behavior patterns. A basic application of C-V-P analysis is the computation of **break-even volume**, which is the sales volume at which total revenue equals total cost and profits are zero. C-V-P techniques express relationships among revenue, sales mix, cost, volume, and profits. These expressed relationships provide a general model of company financial activity that is useful for short-range planning, performance evaluation, and analysis of decision alternatives (discussed in Chapters 11 through 14).

Basic C-V-P Analysis

OBJECTIVE 1
Explain how changes in cost, volume, or price affect the profit formula

Cost-volume-profit relationships can be expressed and analyzed by formula or through the use of graphs. Suppose that a company sells its product for $20. Total annual fixed costs for production and distribution are expected to be $96,000. Variable costs for manufacturing and selling are $8 per unit.

Figure 6-1 graphically shows basic C-V-P relationships for this company. Lines for total sales and total costs are plotted by locating two points for each element and drawing a straight line through the two points. For sales, we used $0 of sales for 0 units and $200,000 of sales when 10,000 units were sold. The total cost line was plotted by first determining that

Figure 6-1. Cost-Volume-Profit Relationships

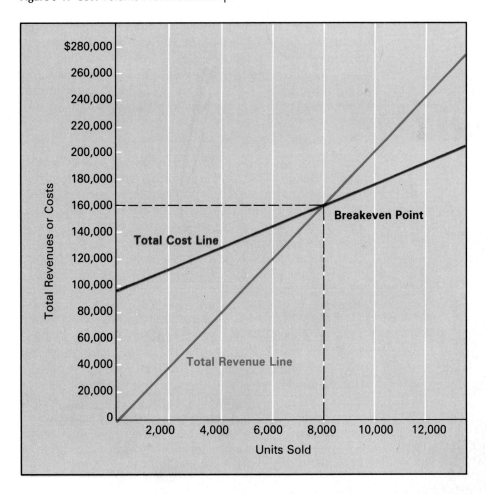

$96,000 of fixed costs would be incurred if 0 units were sold. At the 6,000-unit mark, $144,000 of costs would be incurred ($96,000 of fixed costs plus 6,000 × $8 or $48,000 of variable costs). Where the two lines intersect is known as the break-even point (total costs equal total revenue), which is discussed later in this chapter.

How Managers Use C-V-P Analysis

The graph in Figure 6-1 is a basic C-V-P model depicting the revenue, cost, volume, and profit elements of a company's operations. Similar analyses can be applied to multiproduct divisions or companies as long as a given sales mix of different products is assumed. The C-V-P model is useful because it gives a general overview of company financial operations. Also understand that the model is based on a set of fixed relationships. If unit prices, costs, operating efficiency, or other operating circumstances change, the model needs to be revised to fit the new C-V-P relationships.

Using income statements, graphic analysis, and algebraic computations, basic C-V-P analysis can be applied to measure the effects of management decision alternatives. These alternatives include possible changes in variable and fixed costs, expansion or contraction of sales volume, increases or decreases in selling prices, or other changes in operating methods or policies. Cost-volume-profit analysis is useful for problems of product pricing (Chapter 11), sales mix analysis, adding or deleting a product line, and accepting special orders (all analyzed in Chapter 12). In summary, there are many types of C-V-P applications, and all are used by managers to provide effective planning and control of operations.

Operating Capacity: Definition and Cost Influence

Operating capacity is an important part of cost-volume-profit relationships and budgetary control. Operating capacity is the upper limit on production output and related costs, so it is essential information when predictions are being made. Because variable costs increase or decrease in direct proportion to expected volume or output, it is important to know what the term *operating capacity* means. Theoretical, or ideal, capacity is the maximum productive output a department or company could reach for a given period if all machinery and equipment were operated at optimum speed without interruptions. Theoretical capacity is useful in thinking about maximum production levels. Although seemingly an unrealistic goal, this concept is becoming more popular as the just-in-time production philosophy is adopted by companies. (See Chapters 15 and 16.) Practical capacity is theoretical capacity reduced by normal and expected work stoppages. Production may be interrupted by machine downtime for retooling, repair and maintenance, or employee work breaks. These normal interruptions and the resulting lower output should be considered when measuring capacity.

A company seldom operates at either ideal or practical capacity. Excess capacity, which is extra machinery and equipment kept on hand on a standby basis, is part of practical and ideal capacity. Such extra equipment may be used when regular equipment is being repaired. Or during a slow season, a company may use only part of its equipment, or it may work just one or two shifts instead of around the clock. Because of these circumstances, normal capacity, rather than ideal or practical capacity, is often used for planning. **Normal capacity** is the average annual level of operating capacity needed to meet expected sales demands. This demand figure is adjusted for seasonal changes and business and economic cycles. Therefore normal capacity is a realistic measure of what *is likely* to be produced rather than what *can* be produced by an operating unit.

Break-Even Analysis

OBJECTIVE 2
Compute the break-even point in units of output and in sales dollars

Break-even analysis contains the basic elements of cost-volume-profit relationships. The **break-even point** is the point at which total revenue equals total costs incurred. Thus break-even is the point at which a company begins to earn a profit. When new ventures or product lines are being planned, the likelihood of success can be quickly measured by finding the project's break-even point. If, for instance, break-even is 50,000 units and the total market is only 25,000 units, the idea should be promptly abandoned. When finding a company's or a product's break-even point, only sales (S), variable costs (VC), and fixed costs (FC) are used. There is no net income (NI) to be concerned with when a company only breaks even. The objective of break-even analysis is to find the level of activity at which sales revenue equals the sum of all variable and fixed costs. Break-even data can be stated in break-even sales units or break-even sales dollars. The general equations for finding the break-even point are:

$$S = VC + FC \quad \text{or} \quad S - VC - FC = 0$$

The following example illustrates how the equation approach can be used to find break-even units and dollars. Reed Products, Inc., makes special wooden stands for portable compact disk players; the stands include a protective storage compartment for the disks. Variable costs are $25 per unit, and fixed costs average $20,000 per year. Each wooden stand sells for $45. Given this information, we can compute the break-even point for this product in sales units and dollars:

Break-even point in sales units (represented by x)

$$S = VC + FC$$

$$\$45x = \$25x + \$20,000$$

$$\$20x = \$20,000$$

$$x = 1,000 \text{ units}$$

Break-even point in sales dollars

$$\$45/\text{unit} \times 1,000 \text{ units} = \$45,000$$

OBJECTIVE 3
Prepare a break-even graph and identify its components

We can also make a rough estimate of the break-even point by using a graph. This method is less exact, but it does yield meaningful data. Figure 6-2 shows a break-even analysis for Reed Products, Inc. This standard break-even chart has five parts: (1) a horizontal axis in volume or units, (2) a vertical axis in dollars, (3) a horizontal line for the upper limit of fixed costs ($20,000), (4) a total cost line beginning at the point where the fixed cost line crosses the vertical axis and sloping upward to the right (the slope of the line depends on the variable costs per unit), and (5) a total revenue line beginning at the origin of the vertical and horizontal axes and sloping upward to the right (the slope depends on the selling price per unit). At the point where the total revenue line crosses the total cost line, revenues equal total costs. The break-even point, stated in either units or dollars of sales, is found by extending dotted lines from this point to the axes. As Figure 6-2 shows, Reed Products, Inc., will break even when 1,000 wooden stands have been made and sold for $45,000 in sales.

Figure 6-2. Graphic Break-Even Analysis: Reed Products, Inc.

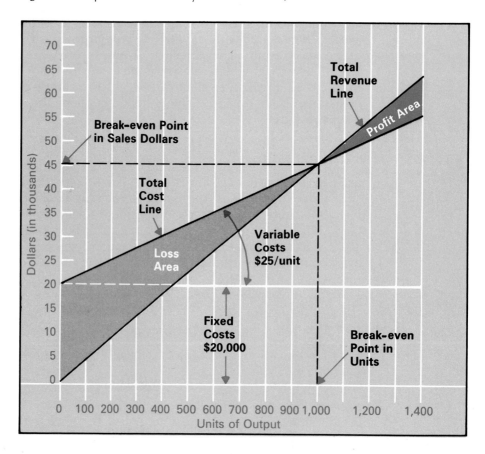

Contribution Margin Concept

OBJECTIVE 4
Define
contribution
margin and use
the concept to
determine a
company's break-
even point

Our analysis of cost-volume-profit relationships is not complete until we add the contribution margin concept. **Contribution margin** is the excess of revenues over *all* variable costs related to a particular sales volume. A product line's contribution margin represents its net contribution to paying off fixed costs and providing profits. Following is the net income (loss) computed for Reed Products, Inc., using the contribution approach:

Symbols		Units Produced and Sold		
		500	1,000	1,500
S	Sales revenue ($45 per unit)	$22,500	$45,000	$67,500
VC	Less variable costs ($25 per unit)	12,500	25,000	37,500
CM	Contribution margin	$10,000	$20,000	$30,000
FC	Less fixed costs	20,000	20,000	20,000
NI	Net income (loss)	($10,000)	—	$10,000

Adding contribution margin into C-V-P analysis changes the make-up of the equations as well as the format of the income statement as shown. The equation now becomes

$$(S - VC = CM) - FC = NI$$

Contribution margin (CM) is what remains after variable costs are subtracted from total sales. So the break-even point (BE) can be expressed as the point at which contribution margin (CM) minus total fixed costs (FC) equals zero. That is, break-even occurs when $CM - FC = 0$. In terms of units of product, the break-even point equation is changed as follows:

$$(CM/unit \times BE\ units) - FC = 0$$

At this point we need to develop an equation that isolates the expression *BE units*. The equation can be rearranged as follows:

1. Move FC the right side of the equation

$$CM/unit \times BE\ units = FC$$

2. Divide both sides of the equation by CM/unit

$$\frac{CM/unit \times BE\ units}{CM/unit} = \frac{FC}{CM/unit}$$

3. After canceling terms, the end result is

$$BE\ units = \frac{FC}{CM/unit}$$

To illustrate the use of this equation, we put in the data given earlier for Reed Products, Inc.:

$$\text{BE units} = \frac{\text{FC}}{\text{CM/unit}} = \frac{\$20,000}{\$45 - \$25} = \frac{\$20,000}{\$20} = 1,000 \text{ units}$$

Profit Planning

OBJECTIVE 5
Apply contribution margin analysis to estimate levels of sales that will produce planned profits

The primary goal of a business venture is not just to break even but also to make a profit. Break-even analysis adjusted for a profit factor can be used as a basis for estimating the profitability of a venture. In fact, such an approach is excellent for a "what if" analysis, where the accountant selects several different scenarios and computes the anticipated profit for each set of circumstances. For instance, what if the number of units to be sold is increased by 17,000 items? What effect will the increase have on anticipated profits? What if the increase in units sold is only 6,000? What if fixed costs were reduced by $14,500? What if the variable unit cost increases by $1.40? All these different scenarios will generate different amounts of profit or loss.

The break-even process can be easily extended to include profit planning. Assume that the president of Reed Products, Inc., Elaine Shirl, has set $10,000 in profit as the goal for the year. If all the previous data stay as they were in our earlier example, how many compact disk stands must Reed Products, Inc., make and sell to reach the target profit? The answer is computed ($x = $ number of units):

$$\text{S} = \text{VC} + \text{FC} + \text{NI}$$

$$\$45x = \$25x + \$20,000 + \$10,000$$

$$\$20x = \$30,000$$

$$x = 1,500 \text{ units}$$

To check the accuracy of this answer, put all known data into the equation for an income statement as follows:

$$\text{S} - \text{VC} - \text{FC} = \text{NI}$$

$$(1,500 \text{ units} \times \$45) - (1,500 \times \$25) - \$20,000 = \$10,000$$

$$\$67,500 - \$37,500 - \$20,000 = \$10,000$$

The contribution margin approach can also be used for profit planning. To put the contribution margin break-even equation into a profit planning mode, net income (NI) must be added to the numerator, as shown:

$$\text{Target unit sales} = \frac{\text{FC} + \text{NI}}{\text{CM/unit}}$$

By applying the equation to the data from the Reed Products, Inc., example, the number of units of sales needed to generate a $10,000 profit is computed as follows:

$$\text{Target unit sales} = \frac{\text{FC + NI}}{\text{CM/unit}} = \frac{\$20,000 + \$10,000}{\$20} = \frac{\$30,000}{\$20} = 1,500 \text{ units}$$

Once mastered, use of the contribution margin approach simplifies the determination of both the break-even point and a target net income.

Examples of Cost-Volume-Profit Applications

Cost-volume-profit analyses are used in almost every type of business venture. Once the financial information has been broken down into its selling price, volume, and variable and fixed cost components, manufacturing companies, banks, retail stores, and other service-related enterprises can all use C-V-P relationships for forecasting and operating control purposes.

To illustrate the use of cost-volume-profit analysis, we now look at the year-end planning activities of the Vingsbo Corporation. Stephan Olof, the company's controller, has asked several members of the Executive Council for their expectations of the business environment for the coming year. Each person was asked to write up his or her personal outlook, including changes in selling prices, product demand, variable production costs, variable selling costs, fixed production costs, and fixed selling and administration costs. Following is the current year's information in contribution margin format:

Vingsbo Corporation Contribution Income Statement For the Year Ending December 31, 19x8		
Total sales (66,000 units at $11.00 per unit)		$726,000
Less:		
Variable production costs (66,000 units at $4.40 per unit)	$290,400	
Variable selling costs (66,000 at $2.80 per unit)	184,800	
Total variable costs		475,200
Contribution margin		$250,800
Less fixed costs:		
Fixed production costs	$130,500	
Fixed selling and administrative costs	48,200	
Total fixed costs		178,700
Income before taxes		$ 72,100

A summary of the expectations of the members of the corporation's executive council is shown on the following page.

Vice President-Production:	Variable production costs will increase by 10 percent and fixed production costs will rise by 5 percent.
Vice President-Data Processing	All variable costs will increase by 10 percent and all fixed costs will go up by 5 percent.
Vice President-Finance	Unit demand will go up by 8 percent, all variable costs will increase by 20 percent, but all fixed costs will go down by 10 percent.
Vice President-Administration	Selling price should be increased by 5 percent to equal competition, variable production costs will increase by 5 percent, and variable selling costs will go up by 10 percent.
Vice President-Sales	Selling price will go up by 10 percent, unit demand will fall by 8 percent, variable selling costs will drop by 5 percent, and fixed selling costs will rise by 10 percent.
President	Selling price should be reduced by 6 percent, unit demand will rise by 10 percent, variable production costs will increase by 5 percent, and variable selling costs will go up by 10 percent.

In the following analysis, we assume that there were no changes in inventory levels and that each scenario is independent of the other projections.

Changes in Production Costs Only

The Vice President-Production believes that variable production costs will increase by 10 percent and fixed production costs will rise by 5 percent. With no other anticipated changes, what will be the projected profit for the coming year?

Solution

Total sales (66,000 units at $11.00 per unit)		$726,000
Less:		
Variable production costs (66,000 units at $4.84 per unit)	$319,440	
Variable selling costs (66,000 at $2.80 per unit)	184,800	
Total variable costs		504,240
Contribution margin		$221,760
Less fixed costs:		
Fixed production costs	$137,025	
Fixed selling and administrative costs	48,200	
Total fixed costs		185,225
Income before taxes		$ 36,535

As shown, if these changes do occur and no other adjustments to selling price or volume are made, the corporation's profit will decrease by $35,565 (from $72,100 to $36,535). Since both variable and fixed production costs are projected to increase, management may want to increase the selling price to offset the rise in costs. Increasing units produced and sold would also help offset the higher fixed costs. Since the Vice President-Production has commented on only production costs, the controller should try to augment this forecast.

Changes in All Cost Areas

All costs will change, according to the Vice President-Data Processing. She believes that all variable costs will go up by 10 percent and all fixed costs will rise by 5 percent. As in the previous scenario, no other changes are expected.

Solution

Total sales (66,000 units at $11.00 per unit)		$726,000
Less:		
Variable production costs		
(66,000 units at $4.84 per unit)	$319,440	
Variable selling costs		
(66,000 at $3.08 per unit)	203,280	
Total variable costs		522,720
Contribution margin		$203,280
Less fixed costs:		
Fixed production costs	$137,025	
Fixed selling and administrative costs	50,610	
Total fixed costs		187,635
Income before taxes		$ 15,645

The Vice President-Data Processing has taken the same approach as the production vice president. Both have concentrated only on projected costs. In this scenario, all costs are expected to increase. Profit suffers even more, being pushed down to $15,645 or decreased by $56,455 ($72,100 − $15,645). Again, the controller may want to adjust this projection to include changes in volume and selling price.

Changes in Demand and in All Cost Areas

Volume changes are anticipated by the Vice President-Finance as well as changes in all areas of cost. This person believes that unit demand will increase by 8 percent, all variable costs will go up by 20 percent, and all fixed costs will decrease by 10 percent.

Solution

Total sales (71,200 units at $11.00 per unit)		$783,200
Less:		
Variable production costs		
(71,200 units at $5.28 per unit)	$375,936	
Variable selling costs		
(71,200 at $3.36 per unit)	239,232	
Total variable costs		615,168
Contribution margin		$168,032
Less fixed costs:		
Fixed production costs	$117,450	
Fixed selling and administrative costs	43,380	
Total fixed costs		160,830
Income before taxes		$ 7,202

This projection is the most pessimistic of the six. The Vice President-Finance believes that not only are all variable costs going to increase but that volume will also increase. The $82,768 decrease in contribution margin far outweighs the positive aspects of lower fixed costs being spread over more units. If the Vice President-Finance is correct in his projections, something should be done to increase the selling price.

Changes in Selling Price and in Variable Costs

The Vice President-Administration thinks that the selling price needs to be increased by 5 percent to equal competition and that variable production costs will increase by 5 percent and variable selling costs will go up by 10 percent.

Solution

Total sales (66,000 units at $11.55 per unit)		$762,300
Less:		
Variable production costs		
(66,000 units at $4.62 per unit)	$304,920	
Variable selling costs		
(66,000 at $3.08 per unit)	203,280	
Total variable costs		508,200
Contribution margin		$254,100
Less fixed costs:		
Fixed production costs	$130,500	
Fixed selling and administrative costs	48,200	
Total fixed costs		178,700
Income before taxes		$ 75,400

In this scenario, profits will increase over those of the previous period because total contribution margin increased by $3,300. Although both variable production costs and variable selling costs are projected to increase, the increase in selling price more than offsets the rise in variable costs. Under this forecast, overall profits increase by $3,300, the amount of the increase in contribution margin.

Changes in Selling Price, Product Demand, and Selling Costs

According to the Vice President-Sales, the corporation should increase the selling price by 10 percent, which will cause demand to fall by 8 percent. In addition, variable selling costs will go down by 5 percent, and fixed selling costs will increase by 10 percent.

Solution

Total sales (60,720 units at $12.10 per unit)		$734,712
Less:		
Variable production costs (60,720 units at $4.40 per unit)	$267,168	
Variable selling costs (60,720 at $2.66 per unit)	161,515	
Total variable costs		428,683
Contribution margin		$306,029
Less fixed costs:		
Fixed production costs	$130,500	
Fixed selling and administrative costs	53,020	
Total fixed costs		183,520
Income before taxes		$122,509

The Vice President-Sales is the most optimistic person on the Executive Council. Overall, profits increased by $50,409. Although an increase in selling price caused demand to decrease, total revenue increased by $9,712. The increase in fixed selling costs was countered by an even larger decrease in variable selling costs.

Changes in Selling Price, Unit Demand, and All Variable Costs

The corporation's president sees the coming year a little differently than the other members of the Executive Council. He expects demand to rise by 10 percent if the selling price is dropped by 6 percent. In addition, he believes that variable production costs will increase by 5 percent and variable selling costs will rise by about 10 percent.

Solution

Total sales (72,600 units at $10.34 per unit)		$750,684
Less:		
Variable production costs		
(72,600 units at $4.62 per unit)	$335,412	
Variable selling costs		
(72,600 at $3.08 per unit)	223,608	
Total variable costs		559,020
Contribution margin		$191,664
Less fixed costs:		
Fixed production costs	$130,500	
Fixed selling and administrative costs	48,200	
Total fixed costs		178,700
Income before taxes		$ 12,964

The president is a bit pessimistic, even though total revenue is expected to top $750,000. He predicts a dip in the selling price, which should cause an increase in the number of units sold. The decrease in selling price coupled with increases in both variable production costs and variable selling costs caused the contribution margin to plunge $59,136. With no change predicted in the fixed cost areas, total profits also experienced a significant decline.

Comparative Summary

Exhibit 6-1 is a comparative summary of the six executives' predictions. The controller would probably use a document such as the one in Exhibit 6-1 as a basis for discussing predictions for the upcoming year. From the expectations of the six people and a general discussion of each viewpoint, the controller can merge all the projections and develop an expected environment from which he can develop the budget for 19x9.

Illustrative Problem: Profit Planning— Contribution Margin Approach

Producing college textbooks involves many complex steps, all of which add to the cost of published materials. Good paper and binding materials add much to a book's cost as well as its useful life. Golner Publishing Company is taking a careful look at a new manuscript on management information systems. Early estimates are that variable costs per book will be $6.80 and total fixed costs will be $60,000. The company plans to market the book wholesale at $12.80 per copy.

Required

1. Using the contribution margin approach, compute the number of copies the book must sell for the company to earn a profit of $30,000.

	VP Production	VP Data Processing	VP Finance	VP Administration	VP Sales	President
Exhibit 6-1. Comparative C-V-P Analysis						

Vingsbo Corporation
Summary of Projected Income Before Taxes
For the Year Ending December 31, 19x9

	VP Production	VP Data Processing	VP Finance	VP Administration	VP Sales	President
Total sales	$726,000	$726,000	$783,200	$762,300	$734,712	$750,684
Less:						
Variable production costs	$319,440	$319,440	$375,936	$304,920	$267,168	$335,412
Variable selling costs	184,800	203,280	239,232	203,280	161,515	223,608
Total variable costs	$504,240	$522,720	$615,168	$508,200	$428,683	$559,020
Contribution margin	$221,760	$203,280	$168,032	$254,100	$306,029	$191,664
Less:						
Fixed production costs	$137,025	$137,025	$117,450	$130,500	$130,500	$130,500
Fixed selling and administrative costs	48,200	50,610	43,380	48,200	53,020	48,200
Total fixed costs	$185,225	$187,635	$160,830	$178,700	$183,520	$178,700
Projected net income before taxes	$ 36,535	$ 15,645	$ 7,202	$ 75,400	$122,509	$ 12,964

2. Using the same approach and assuming that fixed costs are cut to $50,000, determine the number of copies that must be sold to earn a target profit of $61,000.
3. Given the original information and assuming that 21,000 copies of the book can be sold, find the selling price the company must set to earn a profit of $80,700.
4. The company's marketing director says the most optimistic sales estimate for the book would be 36,000 copies. Assume that the highest possible price the company can charge is $13.20 and that variable costs per unit cannot be reduced below $6.80. How much more can be spent on fixed advertising costs if the new target profit is $40,000?

Solution

1. Target units computed

$$\text{Unit sales} = (FC + NI) \div CM \text{ per unit}$$
$$= (\$60,000 + \$30,000) \div (\$12.80 - \$6.80)$$
$$= \$90,000 \div \$6$$
$$= 15,000 \text{ copies}$$

2. Units required for higher profit and lower cost computed

$$\text{Unit sales} = (FC + NI) \div CM \text{ per unit}$$
$$= (\$50,000 + \$61,000) \div (\$12.80 - \$6.80)$$
$$= \$111,000 \div \$6$$
$$= 18,500 \text{ copies}$$

3. Selling price determined

$$\text{Unit sales} = (FC + NI) \div CM \text{ per unit}$$
$$21,000 = (\$60,000 + \$80,700) \div (x - \$6.80)$$

Multiplying both sides of the equation by $(x - \$6.80)$, we get

$$21,000(x - \$6.80) = \$140,700$$
$$21,000x - \$142,800 = \$140,700$$
$$21,000x = \$283,500$$
$$x = \$13.50$$

4. Increased amount for advertising determined

$$\text{Unit sales} = (FC + NI) \div CM \text{ per unit}$$
$$36,000 = (x + \$40,000) \div (\$13.20 - \$6.80)$$
$$36,000 = (x + \$40,000) \div \$6.40$$

Multiplying both sides of the equation by $6.40, we get

$$\$6.40(36,000) = x + \$40,000$$
$$\$230,400 = x + \$40,000$$
$$x = \$230,400 - \$40,000$$
$$x = \$190,400$$

Total fixed costs allowed	$190,400
Less original fixed cost estimate	60,000
Additional dollars available for advertising	$130,400

Sales Mix and C-V-P

Thus far our discussion of the cost-volume-profit relationships has centered on situations where only one product was involved. The C-V-P elements of unit volume, unit selling price, variable unit cost, and total fixed cost were all discussed in terms of a one-product environment. But seldom in the real world does a company specialize in only one product; several product lines or variations of similar products are needed to spread the risk so that not "all the eggs are in one basket." When there is more than one product line, cost-volume-profit analysis is called sales mix analysis.

Sales Mix Analysis

OBJECTIVE 6
Prepare an analysis that shows the effects of changes in sales mix on the profits of a company

For companies with several product lines, **sales mix** refers to the relative proportions of different products that comprise total sales. For units with comparable physical measures, sales mix is the percentage of physical unit sales volume accounted for by each product. Sales mix can also be computed in sales dollars. Different products will often have different contribution margins. To the extent that product sales mix can change over time, knowing the effects of such a shift on total company contribution margin is a valuable management resource. Maximizing profit means that the company should try to shift sales mix toward those products with higher contribution margins. Interestingly, if sales mix shifts in this direction, the company could experience a situation where unit and even dollar sales volume decreases but overall profits increase. Therefore sales mix analysis is a valuable planning and control tool for management.

To illustrate C-V-P sales mix analysis, we analyze the case outlined in Exhibit 6-2. Three products are sold: G, R, and E. Product G earns a 25 percent contribution margin and accounts for 8 percent of the total sales dollars and 16.67 percent of the physical units sold. Product R generates a 50 percent contribution margin and represents 32 percent of total sales dollars and 33.33 percent of the total units sold. Product E earns a 30 percent contribution margin and represents 60 percent of total sales dollars and 50 percent of the total units sold.

Exhibit 6-3(*a*) shows the break-even analysis regarding sales dollars. First the average contribution margin percentage is computed (36 percent). Break-even sales dollars is then computed by dividing total fixed costs by the average CM percentage. If the sales mix percentages are applied to the break-even total, the total dollar sales needed from each product to break even are obtained. The proof is shown at the bottom of the analysis.

Exhibit 6-2. Sales Mix Analysis

Product	Unit Sales	Dollar Sales	Contribution Margin Dollars	CM %	Sales Mix Percentages Physical	Dollars
G	20,000	$ 80,000	$ 20,000	25%	16.67%	8.00%
R	40,000	320,000	160,000	50%	33.33%	32.00%
E	60,000	600,000	180,000	30%	50.00%	60.00%
	120,000	$1,000,000	$360,000		100.00%	100.00%
Less total fixed costs			144,000			
Income before taxes			$216,000			

Exhibit 6-3. Sales Mix Analysis—Break-Even Computations

(*a*) Analysis of Sales Dollars

1. Average contribution margin percentage $= \dfrac{\$360,000}{\$1,000,000} = \underline{\underline{36\%}}$

2.

Product	Dollar Sales	Sales Mix in Dollars
G	$ 80,000	8.00%
R	320,000	32.00%
E	600,000	60.00%
	$1,000,000	100.00%

3. $\dfrac{\text{Break-even in}}{\text{sales dollars}} = \dfrac{\text{total fixed costs}}{\text{average CM \%}} = \dfrac{\$144,000}{36\%} = \underline{\underline{\$400,000}}$

4. Distribution of break-even sales $= \$400,000$

(G = 8%)	$ 32,000
(R = 32%)	128,000
(E = 60%)	240,000
	$400,000

5. Proof of break-even point

Product	Break-Even Sales	CM Percentage	Total CM
G	$ 32,000	25%	$ 8,000
R	128,000	50%	64,000
E	240,000	30%	72,000
			$144,000
Less fixed costs			144,000
Profit			$ 0

A similar approach is taken to compute break-even unit sales. In Exhibit 6-3(*b*), break-even sales in units is determined. First, average CM per unit is computed. Dividing average contribution margin per unit into the total fixed costs generates the 48,000 unit break-even point. By multiplying this amount by the physical mix percentages, the total unit sales of each product required to break even is generated.

Exhibit 6-4 discloses two profit planning examples using the data from Exhibit 6-2. Example 1 assumes that there has been a 10,000-unit shift from product E to Product G. From only this one change, profit decreased $20,000. In Example 2, there has been a 5,000-unit shift from Product E

Exhibit 6-3. Sales Mix Analysis—Break-Even Computations (continued)

(b) Analysis of Unit Sales

1. Average contribution margin per unit $= \dfrac{\$360,000}{120,000} = \underline{\underline{\$3}}$

2.

Product	Unit Sales	Physical Mix
G	20,000	16.67%
R	40,000	33.33%
E	60,000	50.00%
	120,000	100.00%

3. $\dfrac{\text{Break-even in}}{\text{sales units}} = \dfrac{\text{total fixed costs}}{\text{average CM per unit}} = \dfrac{\$144,000}{\$3} = \underline{\underline{48,000 \text{ units}}}$

4. $\dfrac{\text{Distribution of}}{\text{break-even sales}} = \dfrac{48,000}{\text{units}}$

(G = 16.67%)	8,000
(R = 33.33%)	16,000
(E = 50.00%)	24,000
	48,000

5. Proof of break-even point

Product	Break-Even Unit Sales	CM per Unit	Total CM
G	8,000	$1	$ 8,000
R	16,000	$4	64,000
E	24,000	$3	72,000
			$144,000
Less fixed costs			144,000
Profit			$ 0

to Product R. No other changes have been made in the original data. The result is a $5,000 increase in the income before taxes. Many additional examples could be shown with changes in selling prices, variable costs, and fixed costs; each change would result in a change in income before taxes. Sales mix analysis has many uses in business and is a handy tool to have in your managerial background.

Assumptions Underlying C-V-P Analysis

Cost-volume-profit figures are useful only when certain assumptions hold true and certain conditions exist. If one or more of these assumptions

Exhibit 6-4. Sales Mix Analysis—Effects of Changes in Mix

Example 1

Product	Unit Sales	Dollar Sales	Contribution Margin Dollars	CM %	Sales Mix Percentages Physical	Dollars
G	30,000	$120,000	$ 30,000	25%	25.00%	12.77%
R	40,000	320,000	160,000	50%	33.33%	34.04%
E	50,000	500,000	150,000	30%	41.67%	53.19%
	120,000	$940,000	$340,000		100.00%	100.00%
Less total fixed costs			144,000			
Income before taxes			$196,000			

Example 2

Product	Unit Sales	Dollar Sales	Contribution Margin Dollars	CM %	Sales Mix Percentages Physical	Dollars
G	20,000	$ 80,000	$ 20,000	25%	16.67%	8.08%
R	45,000	360,000	180,000	50%	37.50%	36.36%
E	55,000	550,000	165,000	30%	45.83%	55.56%
	120,000	$990,000	$365,000		100.00%	100.00%
Less total fixed costs			144,000			
Income before taxes			$221,000			

and conditions are absent, the results of the analysis may be misleading. These assumptions and conditions are as follows:

1. Behavior of variable and fixed costs can be measured accurately.
2. Costs and revenues have a close linear approximation. For example, if costs rise, revenues will rise proportionately.
3. Efficiency and productivity will hold steady within the relevant range of activity.
4. Cost and price variables will also hold steady during the period being planned.
5. The product sales mix will not change during the planning period.
6. Production and sales volume will be about equal.

Chapter Review

Review of Learning Objectives

1. **Explain how changes in cost, volume, or price affect the profit formula.**
    The profit formula is sales (S) minus variable costs (VC) minus fixed costs (FC) equals net income (NI). If either variable costs or fixed costs changes, net income changes. If volume changes, then total sales changes, as does net income. A change in price will also change total sales, resulting in a change in net income.

2. **Compute the break-even point in units of output and in sales dollars.**
    The break-even point is the point at which total revenue equals total costs incurred. In formula form, break even occurs when S = VC + FC (sales equals variable costs plus fixed costs). In terms of contribution margin, the formula is

    $$\text{BE units} = \frac{FC}{CM/\text{unit}}$$

    Once the number of break-even units is known, it can be multiplied by the product's selling price to get the break-even point in dollars of sales.

3. **Prepare a break-even graph and identify its components.**
    The break-even graph is made up of a vertical axis (dollars) and a horizontal axis (volume). Three lines are plotted: the total revenue line runs from the intersection of the two axes upward to the right. The fixed cost line is horizontal from the point on the vertical axis representing total fixed cost. The total cost line begins at the intersection of the fixed cost line and the vertical axis and runs upward to the right. Two data points are needed before the total revenue and total cost lines can be plotted and drawn.

4. **Define contribution margin and use the concept to determine a company's break-even point.**
    Contribution margin is the excess of revenues over *all* variable costs related to a particular sales volume. A product line's contribution margin represents its net contribution to paying off fixed costs and providing profits. The break-even point in units can be computed by dividing total fixed costs by the contribution margin per unit.

5. **Apply contribution margin analysis to estimate levels of sales that will produce planned profits.**
    The addition of projected net income (NI) to the break-even equation makes it possible to plan levels of operation that yield target profits. The formula in terms of contribution margin is

    $$\text{Target unit sales} = \frac{FC + NI}{CM/\text{unit}}$$

6. **Prepare an analysis that shows the effects of changes in sales mix on the profits of a company.**
    Sales mix refers to the relative proportions of different products that comprise total sales. By computing product contribution margin, product percentage of total unit sales, and percentage of total sales dollars, the analyst can either perform break-even analysis or conduct profit planning activities by changing price, volume, variable cost, and/or fixed cost data.

Review of Concepts and Terminology

The following important concepts were introduced in this chapter:

(L.O. 1)   **Cost-volume-profit analysis:**   An analysis of the cost behavior patterns that underlie the relationship between cost, volume of output, and profit.   (Also C-V-P analysis.)

(L.O. 2)   **Break-even point:**   The point at which total revenue equals total cost incurred.

(L.O. 4)   **Contribution margin:**   The excess of revenues over all variable costs related to a particular sales volume.

(L.O. 6)   **Sales mix:**   The relative proportions of different products that comprise total sales for a company that has several product lines.

Other important terms introduced in this chapter are:

break-even volume (p. 198)
excess capacity (p. 200)
normal capacity (p. 201)
practical capacity (p. 200)
operating capacity (p. 200)
theoretical or ideal capacity (p. 200)

Review Problem
Break-Even/Profit Planning Analysis

TK Organs, Inc., is a major producer of large pipe organs. Model ERV is a two-manual organ with a large potential market. Following is a summary of data from 19x7 operations for Model ERV:

Variable Costs per Unit	
Direct Materials	$ 3,700
Direct Labor	5,200
Factory Overhead	2,600
Selling Expenses	2,500
Total Fixed Costs	
Factory Overhead	$390,000
Advertising	110,000
Administrative Expenses	136,000
Selling Price per Unit	29,900

Management is pondering alternate courses of action for 19x8. Each alternative should be treated as an independent action and not tied to the other alternatives.

Required

1. Compute the 19x7 break-even point in units.
2. Calculate the amount of net income generated if 45 ERV models were sold in 19x7.
3. For 19x8:
   a. Calculate the number of units that must be sold to generate a $190,800 profit. Assume that costs and selling price remain constant.

b. Calculate the net income if the company increases the number of units sold by 20 percent and cuts the selling price by $900 per unit.

c. Determine the number of units that must be sold to break even if advertising is increased by $47,700.

d. If variable costs are cut by 10 percent, find the number of units that must be sold to generate a profit of $315,500.

Answer to Review Problem

1. Break-even point in units for 19x7 computed

Variable costs per unit	$ 14,000
Contribution margin per unit:	
$29,900 − $14,000	15,900
Total fixed costs	$636,000

$$\text{Break-even point} = \frac{FC}{CM/unit} = \frac{\$636,000}{\$15,900} = 40 \text{ units}$$

2. Net income for 45 units calculated

Units sold	45
Units required to break even	40
Units over break even	5

19x7 net income = $15,900 per unit × 5 = $79,500

Contribution margin equals sales minus all variable costs. CM/unit equals the amount of sales dollars remaining, after variable costs have been subtracted, to cover fixed costs and provide a profit for the company. If all fixed costs have been absorbed by the time break even is reached, the whole contribution margin of each unit sold in excess of break even represents profit.

3. a. Number of units required to generate a given profit calculated

$$\text{Unit sales} = \frac{FC + NI}{CM/unit}$$

$$= \frac{\$636,000 + \$190,800}{\$15,900} = \frac{\$826,800}{\$15,900} = 52 \text{ units}$$

b. Net income under specified conditions calculated

Units to be sold = 40 × 120% = 48 units
New selling price = $29,000
Contribution margin = $29,000 − $14,000 = $15,000

$$\text{BE units} = \frac{\$636,000}{\$15,000} = 42.4 \text{ units}$$

Units to be sold in excess of break even

48 − 42.4 = 5.6 units

Projected net income

5.6 units × $15,000/unit = $84,000

c. Number of break-even units under specified conditions determined

$$\text{BE units} = \frac{\$636,000 + \$47,700}{\$15,900}$$

$$= \frac{\$683,700}{\$15,900} = \underline{\underline{43}} \text{ units}$$

d. Number of units required to generate a given profit determined

$$\text{Variable costs per unit} = \$14,000 \times .9 = \$12,600$$
$$\text{Contribution margin per unit} = \$29,900 - \$12,600 = \$17,300$$

$$\text{Unit sales} = \frac{\$636,000 + \$315,500}{\$17,300} = \frac{\$951,500}{\$17,300} = \underline{\underline{55}} \text{ units}$$

Chapter Assignments

Questions

1. Define cost-volume-profit analysis.
2. What is the relationship between cost-volume-profit analysis and the concept of cost behavior?
3. Discuss the uses of C-V-P analysis and its significance to management.
4. What is the difference between practical capacity and ideal capacity?
5. Why does a company seldom operate at either ideal or practical capacity?
6. What is normal capacity? Why is this expression of capacity more relevant and useful than either ideal or practical capacity?
7. Define break-even point. State why information about break even is useful to management.
8. Define contribution margin. How is this concept useful?
9. State the equation that determines target unit sales using the elements of fixed costs, net income, and contribution margin.
10. What conditions must be met for cost-volume-profit computations to be accurate?
11. Describe sales mix analysis.
12. How can sales mix analysis be used to compute the break-even point in sales dollars? Is there any difference in the determination of break-even unit sales?
13. Where is profit shown on a break-even graph? Describe the net loss area.
14. Discuss the statement, "The contribution approach is the foundation of C-V-P logic and related techniques."
15. Define excess capacity. How does excess capacity relate to the concept of normal capacity?

Classroom Exercises

Exercise 6-1.
Changes That
Affect Profit
(L.O. 1)

The members of the Eastgate Condominium Complex Association Board have just been approached by a developer and asked to consider permitting construction of forty additional condominium units on property adjacent to the existing eighty units. Since the street and utilities are already in place, the Board will not have to approve any new expenditures relating to this expansion. The Board president has asked the treasurer, Richard Spisak, to summarize the advantages of approving the expansion request. The president stated that someone had said that the variable maintenance costs per unit would decrease if the number of condominium units was increased.

Is this assumption correct? Defend your answer assuming that maintenance costs such as lawn care, pool maintenance, tennis court care, and street repair are the complex's primary maintenance costs.

Exercise 6-2.
Break-Even
Analysis
(L.O. 2, 3)

Ustinowich Manufacturing Company makes head covers for golf clubs. The company expects to make a profit next year. It anticipates fixed manufacturing costs to be $106,500, and fixed general and administrative expenses to be $102,030. Variable manufacturing and selling costs per set of head covers will be $3.65 and $1.75, respectively. Each set will sell for $11.40.

1. Compute the break-even point in sales units.
2. Compute the break-even point in sales dollars.
3. If the selling price were increased to $12.00 per unit and fixed general and administrative expenses were cut by $33,465, what would the new break-even point be in units?
4. Prepare a graph to illustrate the break-even point in **2**.

Exercise 6-3.
Break-Even
Analysis and
Pricing
(L.O. 2, 5)

Harrison Company has a plant capacity of 100,000 units per year, but the 19x6 budget indicates that only 60,000 units will be produced and sold. The entire 19x6 budget is as follows:

Sales revenues (60,000 units at $4)		$240,000
Less: Cost of goods produced (based on production of 60,000 units):		
Materials (variable)	$60,000	
Labor (variable)	30,000	
Variable manufacturing costs	45,000	
Fixed manufacturing costs	75,000	
Total cost of goods produced		210,000
Gross margin		$ 30,000
Less: Selling and administrative expenses:		
Selling (10% of sales)	$24,000	
Administrative (fixed)	36,000	
Total selling and administrative expenses		60,000
Net income (loss) from operations		$(30,000)

1. Given the budgeted selling price and cost data, how many units would Harrison have to produce and sell to break even?
2. Market research indicates that if Harrison were to drop its selling price to $3.80 per unit, it could sell 100,000 units in 19x6. Would you recommend the drop in price? Indicate the new profit or loss figure.

Exercise 6-4.
Graphical Analysis
(L.O.3)

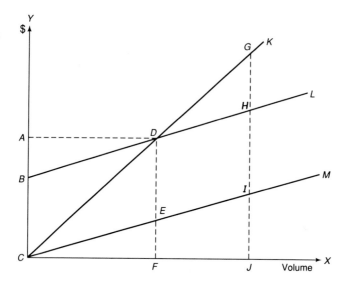

Identify the appropriate point, line segment, or area of the cost-volume-profit graph that corresponds with the following related questions:

1. The maximum possible operating loss is:
   a. *AB*   c. *BC*
   b. *DF*   d. *EF*
2. Break-even volume in sales dollars is:
   a. *CF*   c. *AD*
   b. *DE*   d. *AC*
3. At volume *CJ*, total contribution margin is:
   a. *IJ*   c. *HI*
   b. *GI*   d. *GH*
4. Profits are represented by area:
   a. *KDL*   c. *BDC*
   b. *KCM*   d. *MCX*
5. At volume *CJ*, total fixed costs are represented by:
   a. *IJ*   c. *HI*
   b. *HJ*   d. *GH*
6. If volume increases from *CF* to *CJ*, the change in total costs is:
   a. *HI–DE*   c. *GJ–DF*
   b. *IJ–EF*   d. *GI–DE*

Exercise 6-5.
Break-Even
Analysis and Profit
Planning
(L.O.2,4,5)

Nichole Corporation produces and distributes doorknobs. The present annual sales volume is 500,000 units, and the current selling price is $1.00 per unit. Variable expenses amount to $.60 per unit. Fixed expenses are $100,000 per year.

1. Consider each case separately.
   a. What is the present annual total profit?
   b. What is the present break-even point in dollars? In units?
2. Compute the profit for each of the following changes (consider each situation independently):
   a. A per unit increase of $.02 in variable expense

b. A 10 percent decrease in fixed expenses and a 10 percent increase in sales volume

c. A 20 percent increase in fixed expenses, a 20 percent decrease in selling price, a 10 percent decrease in variable expenses per unit, and a 30 percent increase in units sold

3. Compute the new break-even point *in units* for each of the following changes:

a. A 10 percent decrease in fixed expenses

b. A 10 percent increase in selling price and a $25,000 increase in fixed expenses

Exercise 6-6.
Profit Planning
(L.O. 4, 5)

Short-term automobile rentals are the specialty of Coffey Auto Loans, Inc. Average variable operating expenses have been $6.25 per day per automobile. The company owns thirty cars. Fixed operating costs for the next year are expected to be $75,050. Average daily rental revenue per automobile is expected to be $17.75. Management would like to earn $25,000 during the year.

1. Calculate the number of total daily rentals the company must have during the year to earn the target profit.

2. On the basis of your answer to **1**, determine the average number of days each automobile must be rented.

3. Find the total rental revenue for the year that is needed to earn the $25,000 profit.

4. What would the total rental revenue be if fixed operating costs could be lowered by $2,525 and target earnings increased to $35,000?

Exercise 6-7.
Contribution
Margin/Profit
Planning
(L.O. 4, 5)

Thom Systems, Ltd., makes undersea missiles for nuclear submarines. Management has just been offered a government contract that may result in a profit for the company. The contract purchase price is $30,000 per unit, but the number of units to be purchased has not been decided. The company's fixed costs are budgeted at $3,970,000. Variable costs are $18,500 per unit.

1. Compute the number of units at the stated contract price the company should agree to make to earn a target income of $5,000,000.

2. Using a lighter material, the variable unit cost can be reduced by $2,000, but that will cause total fixed overhead to increase by $7,500. How many units must now be produced to make $5,000,000 in profit?

3. Using the factors in **2**, how many additional units need to be produced to increase profit by $1,350,000?

Exercise 6-8.
Cost-Volume-Profit
Analysis and
Pricing
(L.O. 5)

The Columbia Furniture Company produces bridge tables and chairs for department and furniture stores. The current selling prices are $8 per chair and $16 per table. Based on these prices, the company is able to break even by selling 12,000 chairs and 3,000 tables. The estimated variable cost of each item is shown in the table on the next page. In addition, fixed costs were: Manufacturing, $37,500 and Selling and Administrative, $16,500. The company's competitors have recently reduced prices on similar items of equal quality to $7.50 for a chair and $15 for a table.

Assuming the same ratio of four chairs to one table, how many units of each would the company have to sell to meet competitors' prices and still make a profit of $51,000?

	Chairs	Tables
Variable costs		
Materials	$2.50	$ 7.50
Labor	1.00	2.00
Variable factory overhead	.50	2.50
Variable selling expenses	.40	.40
	$4.40	$12.40

Exercise 6-9.
Sales Mix Analysis
(L.O. 6)

Jo Lynn Mays is the owner of a hair design shop in Palm Springs, California. Her business activity is broken down into three primary areas: shampoo and set, permanents, and cut and blow dry. Following are operating results from the past six-month period:

	Number of Customers	Total Sales	Contribution Margin	
Type of Service			Dollars	CM %
Shampoo and set	1,300	$15,600	$ 7,020	45
Permanents	390	19,500	10,725	55
Cut and blow dry	910	13,650	5,460	40
	2,600	$48,750	$23,205	
Total fixed costs			12,100	
Income before taxes			$11,105	

Compute the break-even point in units based on the average contribution margin ratio for the given sales mix.

Interpreting Accounting Information

Trevor Corporation– Changes in Labor Cost
(L.O. 5)

The president of Trevor Corporation, which manufactures tape decks and sells them to producers of sound-reproduction systems, anticipates that manufacturing employees (variable labor) will get a 10 percent wage increase on January 1 of next year. No other changes in costs are expected. Overhead will not change as a result of the wage increase. The president has asked you to help develop the information that he needs to formulate a reasonable product strategy for next year.

You are satisfied by regression analysis that volume is the primary factor affecting costs and have separated the semivariable costs into their fixed and variable segments by the least squares criterion. You also observe that the beginning and ending inventories are never materially different. Following are current year data for your analysis:

Current selling price per unit	$80
Variable cost per unit:	
Material	$30
Labor	12
Overhead	6
	$48
Annual sales volume	5,000 units
Fixed costs	$51,000

Required

Provide the following information for the president using cost-volume-profit analysis:

1. What increase in the selling price is necessary to cover the 10 percent wage increase and still maintain the current contribution margin ratio of 40 percent?
2. How many tape decks must be sold to maintain the current net income if the sales price remains at $80 and the 10 percent wage increase goes into effect?

(AICPA adapted)

Problem Set A

Problem 6A-1.
Break-Even
Analysis
(L.O. 2)

Borman & Fess, a law firm in downtown San Francisco, is thinking of developing a legal clinic for middle- and low-income residents. Paraprofessional help will be employed, and a $16 per hour billing rate will be used. These paraprofessional employees will be law students who will work for $8 per hour. Other variable costs are anticipated to be $4.40 per hour, and annual fixed costs are expected to total $18,000.

Required

1. Compute the break-even point in billable hours.
2. Compute the break-even point in total billings.
3. Find the new break-even point in total billings if fixed costs go up by $2,340.
4. Using the original figures, compute the break-even point in total billings if the billing rate is decreased by $1 per hour, variable costs are decreased by $.40 per hour, and fixed costs are decreased by $3,600.

Problem 6A-2.
Break-Even
Analysis and Profit
Planning
(L.O. 2, 4, 5)

Selling citrus trees is the specialty of Orange County Nursery, Inc. The company grows its trees on a 200-acre farm outside Villa Park, California. The nursery is considering a new line of deciduous fruit trees, which will be sold only in 57-liter containers. Management expects that fixed costs will increase $61,200 per year because of the introduction of the new line of fruit trees. Variable costs are expected to be $28 per tree. Average selling price is anticipated to be $45 per tree.

Required

1. From this information, compute the number of trees that must be sold per year if the company is to break even on the new line of trees.

2. Determine the new break-even point in unit sales if the selling price were increased by 20 percent.
3. Assuming the original data, determine the break-even point in unit sales if fixed costs were reduced by $6,800.
4. Calculate the break-even point in unit sales if variable costs per tree were reduced to $25, assuming all other original data remained constant.
5. Compute the number of trees that must be sold to earn a profit of $14,200 assuming the original data.

Problem 6A-3.
Profit Planning—
Contribution
Margin Approach
(L.O. 4, 5)

Peck Financial Corporation is a subsidiary of Kramer Enterprises. Processing loan applications is the corporation's major task. Last year, Bob Singleton, manager of the Loan Department, established the policy of charging a fee for every loan processed, amounting to $150 per application. Next year's costs are projected as follows: (a) variable costs: loan consultant wages, $12.50 per hour (usually takes six hours to process a loan application); (b) supplies, $1.20 per application; and (c) other variable costs, $.30 per application. Fixed costs include depreciation of equipment, $7,500; building rental, $13,000; promotional costs, $11,500; and other fixed costs, $15,040.

Required

1. Using the contribution margin approach, compute the number of loan applications the company must process to (a) break even and (b) earn a profit of $14,700.
2. Continuing the same approach, compute the number of applications that must be processed to earn a target profit of $20,000, if promotional costs increase by $5,725.
3. Assuming the original information and the processing of 1,000 applications, compute the new loan application fee the company must use if the target profit is $41,460.
4. Mr. Singleton believes that processing 1,500 loan applications is the maximum his staff can handle. How much more can be spent on promotional costs if the highest fee tolerable to the customer is $200, if variable costs cannot be reduced, and if target net income for such an application load is $50,000?

Problem 6A-4.
Profit Planning
(L.O. 4, 5)

Baker Company, maker of quality handmade pipes, has experienced a steady growth in sales for the last five years. However, increased competition has led Ms. Baker, the company president, to believe that an aggressive advertising campaign will be necessary in 19x4 to maintain the company's present growth.

To prepare for the 19x4 advertising campaign, the company's accountants have prepared and presented Ms. Baker with the data in the table at the top of the next page, based on 19x3 operations.

Sales volume in 19x3 was 20,000 units at $25 per pipe. Target sales volume for 19x4 is $550,000, or 22,000 units. Assume a 34 percent tax rate.

Required

1. Compute the 19x3 after-tax net income.
2. Compute the break-even volume in units for 19x3.
3. Baker believes an additional selling expense of $11,250 for advertising in 19x4, with all other costs remaining constant, will be necessary to achieve the sales

Variable Cost (per Pipe)		Annual Fixed Costs	
Direct labor	$ 8.00	Manufacturing	$ 25,000
Direct materials	3.25	Selling	40,000
Variable overhead	2.50	Administrative	70,000
	$13.75		$135,000

target. Compute the after-tax net income for 19x4, assuming the target sales volume and expenditure for advertising occur as planned.

4. Compute the break-even volume in dollar sales for 19x4 assuming the additional $11,250 is spent for advertising.
5. If the additional $11,250 is spent for advertising in 19x4, what is the 19x4 dollar sales volume required to earn the 19x3 after-tax net income?
6. At a 19x4 sales level of 22,000 units, what is the maximum amount that can be spent on advertising if an after-tax profit of $60,000 is desired?

(ICMA adapted)

Problem 6A-5.
Sales Mix Analysis
(L.O. 6)

Eubanks Toy Company produces four dolls that are marketed under the trade names of Charlie, Bill, Carol, and Martha. Each doll is designed for a different age group, is handled by different types of retail establishments, and hence is priced differently in both retail and wholesale markets. Eubanks Company sells only to wholesale outlets. Despite these market differences, each doll is produced by similar operations using common plant facilities. During 19x0, Eubanks Company operated at 80 percent of maximum potential manufacturing volume with the following operating results:

Total 19x0 Operations		Product Name	Percentage of Total Dollar Sales	Contribution Margin Ratio
Sales	$2,000,000	Charlie	30	40%
Expenses	2,150,000	Bill	25	30%
Net income		Carol	35	50%
(loss)	$ (150,000)	Martha	10	60%

Required

1. With the 19x0 sales mix, determine the company's break-even point in dollar sales and as a percent of maximum capacity.
2. For 19x1, Eubanks Company has budgeted sales of $2,400,000. Fixed costs are budgeted at $1,160,000. What overall contribution margin ratio must be achieved to earn net income of $40,000 before taxes?

Problem Set B

Problem 6B-1.
Break-Even
Analysis
(L.O. 2, 3)

At the beginning of each year, the accounting department at Woolley Lighting, Ltd., must find the point at which projected sales revenue will equal total budgeted variable and fixed costs. The company makes custom-made, durable, low-voltage yard-lighting systems. Each system sells for an average of $738. Variable costs per unit are $410. Total fixed costs for the year are estimated to be $328,000.

Required

1. Compute the break-even point in sales units.
2. Compute the break-even point in sales dollars.
3. Find the new break-even point in sales units if fixed costs go up by $9,840.
4. Using the original figures, compute the break-even point in sales units if the selling price decreases to $730 per unit, fixed costs go up by $33,580, and variable costs decrease by $38 per unit.

Problem 6B-2.
Break-Even
Analysis and Profit
Planning
(L.O. 2, 4, 5)

In 19xx, Swad Enterprises is expecting to earn a profit of $86,500. The company manufactures ornamental concrete blocks. Each lot of one hundred blocks requires variable costs of $6.00 for raw materials, $3.50 for direct labor, $2.50 for manufacturing overhead, and $2.00 for selling costs. Total variable costs are thus $14.00 per lot. Fixed costs for 19xx are anticipated to be $381,500. Each hundred-block lot will sell for $40.

Required

1. Determine how many lots of ornamental block the company must sell to earn its target profit, and convert this amount to sales dollars.
2. Compute break-even sales in dollars.
3. Explain the dollar difference between break-even sales and dollar sales necessary to earn the target profit. Use contribution margin as part of your explanation.
4. Present a graphic analysis of the projected sales and profit figures.

Problem 6B-3.
Profit Planning—
Contribution
Margin Approach
(L.O. 4, 5)

Raoul Dean is president of the Baylor Plastics Division of Waco Industries. Management is considering a new product line that features a large bird posed in a running posture. Called "Chargin' Cardinal," this product is expected to have worldwide market appeal and become the mascot of many high school and university athletic teams. Expected variable unit costs are as follows: (a) direct materials, $8.90; (b) direct labor, $5.48; (c) production supplies, $.42; (d) selling costs, $3.80; and (e) other, $2.90. The following are annual fixed costs: depreciation, building and equipment, $26,000; advertising, $65,000; and other, $11,510. The company plans to sell the product for $55.

Required

1. Using the contribution margin approach, compute the number of products the company must sell in order to (a) break even and (b) earn a profit of $70,350.

2. Continuing with the same approach, compute the number of products that must be sold to earn a target profit of $140,230 if advertising costs rise by $40,000.
3. Assuming the original information and sales of 10,000 units, compute the new selling price the company must use to make $131,490 profit.
4. According to the vice president of marketing, Joyce Dean, the most optimistic annual sales estimate for the product would be 25,000 items. How much more can be spent on fixed advertising costs if the highest possible selling price the company can charge is $46.50, if variable costs cannot be reduced, and if target net income for 25,000 unit sales is $251,000?

Problem 6B-4.
Profit Planning
(L.O. 4, 5)

Wheeler Company has a maximum capacity of 200,000 units per year. Variable manufacturing costs are $12 per unit. Fixed factory overhead is $600,000 per year. Variable selling and administrative costs are $5 per unit, whereas fixed selling and administrative costs are $300,000 per year. Current sales price is $23 per unit.

Required

Consider each situation independently and show all computations in good form.

1. What is the break-even point in (a) units and (b) dollar sales?
2. How many units must be sold to earn a target net income of $240,000 per year?
3. Assume that the company's sales for the year just ended totaled 185,000 units. A strike at a major supplier has caused a material shortage, so that the current year's sales will reach only 160,000 units. Top management is planning to slash fixed costs so that the total for the current year will be $59,000 less than last year. Management also is thinking of either increasing the selling price or reducing variable costs or both to earn a target net income that will be the same dollar amount as last year's. The company already has sold 30,000 units this year at a sales price of $23 per unit with costs per unit unchanged. What contribution margin per unit is needed on the remaining 130,000 units to reach the target net income?

Problem 6B-5.
Sales-Mix Analysis
(L.O. 6)

De Hoyos Division produces and sells three broad product lines, A, B, and C. Individual products within each line are comparable, and the firm uses average selling prices and variable costs within each product line for budgeting purposes. Representative averages for the most recent year were:

Product	Sales Price	Variable Costs	Percentage of Total Dollar Sales
A	$30	$15	10
B	$20	$12	50
C	$40	$30	40

Estimated total fixed costs for the division are $700,000.

Required

1. Compute the division's annual break-even volume in sales dollars, showing required sales dollars for each product line and for the division in total. Fixed costs are common to all products and accordingly should not be allocated in the solution.
2. Assume that the average contribution margin ratio for the division as a whole is 40 percent. Determine the total dollar sales required to generate an after-tax profit of $250,000. Assume a 30 percent tax rate.

Management Decision Case

Candice Company
(L.O. 2)

Candice Company has decided to introduce a new product, which can be manufactured by either a capital intensive or a labor intensive method. The manufacturing method will not affect the quality of the product. Following are the estimated manufacturing costs by the two methods:

	Capital Intensive		Labor Intensive	
Raw materials		$5.00		$5.60
Direct labor	.5DLH at $12	6.00	.8DLH at $9	7.20
Variable overhead	.5DLH at $6	3.00	.8DLH at $6	4.80
Directly traceable incremental fixed manufacturing costs		$2,440,000		$1,320,000

Candice's market research department has recommended an introductory unit sales price of $30. The selling expenses are estimated to be $500,000 annually plus $2 for each unit sold regardless of manufacturing method.

Required

1. Calculate the estimated break-even point in annual unit sales of the new product if Candice Company uses the:
   a. capital intensive manufacturing method.
   b. labor intensive manufacturing method.
2. Determine the annual unit sales volume at which Candice Company would be indifferent between the two manufacturing methods.
3. Candice's management must decide which manufacturing method to employ. Explain the circumstances under which Candice should use each of the two manufacturing methods.
4. Identify the business factors that Candice must consider before selecting the capital intensive or labor intensive manufacturing method.

(ICMA adapted)

CHAPTER 7

Responsibility Accounting and Performance Evaluation

Whenever the term *management* is used, it is safe to assume that an organization is being discussed. An organization consists of many people doing different types of jobs. The term *management* is not used to describe the leadership of a husband and wife-operated grocery store down the street, even though the owners are also the managers. Whether a company needs levels of managers depends on its size. The bigger the organization, the more managers it needs to keep everything running smoothly. As a company grows, its functional operations and the responsibilities associated with those functions tend to become decentralized. Decentralization means that control of the company's operations is spread among several people. Decentralization requires a special approach to managing an enterprise.

In this chapter we discuss how accounting helps management control the operations of a decentralized company. One approach to this task is to use a process called responsibility accounting, which is the foundation on which plans and budgets are developed in a decentralized organization. A responsibility accounting system is also important in controlling actual operations.

After defining responsibility accounting and illustrating such a system, we focus on the costs and revenues a manager can control or take responsibility for. We then emphasize the responsibilities of various centers in a decentralized company: cost/expense centers, profit centers, and investment centers. The chapter concludes with a look at the performance evaluation process of a decentralized company, in particular, the behavioral and operational principles of performance evaluation.

After studying this chapter, you should be able to meet the learning objectives listed on the left.

Responsibility Accounting

Responsibility accounting is an information reporting system that (1) classifies financial data according to areas of responsibility in an organization and (2) reports managers' activities by including only revenue and cost categories that a particular manager can control. Also called activity accounting and profitability accounting, a responsibility accounting system personalizes accounting reports. Such a system emphasizes responsibility centers, which

OBJECTIVE 1
Define
responsibility
accounting and
describe a
responsibility
accounting
system

include (1) cost/expense centers, (2) revenue/profit centers, and (3) investment centers. By concentrating on these responsibility centers, a responsibility accounting system classifies and reports cost and revenue information according to responsibility areas assigned to managers or management positions.

Even though a company uses a responsibility accounting system, it still needs to collect normal cost and revenue data. To do so, a company must use normal recording methods and make normal debit and credit entries. A general ledger, special journals, and a defined chart of accounts are also used. Responsibility accounting focuses on the *reporting*—not the *recording*—of operating cost and revenue data. Once the financial data from daily operations have been recorded in the accounting system, specific costs and revenues can be reclassified and reported for specific areas of managerial responsibility.

Reporting operating costs requires special report formats and reporting techniques. The goal of the statement of cost of goods manufactured is to translate manufacturing cost data into information useful for inventory valuation, profit measurement, and external reporting. As discussed in Chapter 2, all costs of materials, direct labor, and factory overhead are used to compute the cost of goods manufactured. However, management needs more than the data included in the statement of cost of goods manufactured; it also needs information on many day-to-day activities. Budget preparation, revenue and cost analyses, cost control procedures, and managerial performance evaluation all call for a special system for classifying and reporting information. A responsibility accounting system and its network of reports satisfies this need.

Organizational Structure and Reporting

A responsibility accounting system is made up of several responsibility centers. There is a responsibility center for each area or level of managerial responsibility, and a report is generated for each center. The report for a responsibility center includes only those cost and revenue items the manager of that center can control. If a manager cannot influence a cost or revenue item, it is either not included in the manager's report or is segregated. Such segregation prevents the item from influencing the manager's performance evaluation. Cost and revenue controllability is discussed later in this chapter.

A look at a corporate organization chart and a series of related managerial reports shows how a responsibility accounting system works. Figure 7-1 shows a typical management hierarchy, with its three vice presidents reporting to the corporate president. The sales and finance areas have been condensed, however, to emphasize the manufacturing area. The production managers of Divisions A and B report to the vice president of manufacturing. In Division B, the managers of the Stamping Department, Painting Department, and Assembly Department report to the division's production manager.

In a responsibility accounting system, operating reports for each level of management are tailored to individual needs. Because a responsibility

Figure 7-1. Organization Chart Emphasizing the Manufacturing Area

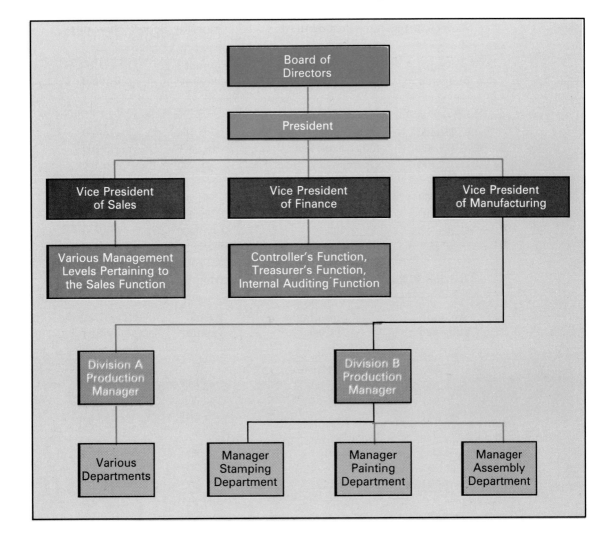

accounting system provides a report for every manager and lower-level managers report to higher-level managers, the same costs and revenues may appear in several reports. However, when lower-level operating data are included in reports to higher-level managers, the data are summarized.

Exhibit 7-1 illustrates how the responsibility reporting network is tied together. At the department level the report lists cost items under the manager's control and compares expected (or budgeted) costs with actual costs. This comparison is a measure of operating performance. The manager who receives the report on the Stamping Department should be particularly concerned with direct materials costs and maintenance salaries for they are significantly over budget. Also, the underutilization of small tools may signal problems with that department's productivity.

Exhibit 7-1. Reporting Within a Responsibility Accounting System

Manufacturing: Vice President   **Monthly Report: November**

Amount Budgeted	Controllable Cost	Actual Amount	Over (Under) Budget
	Central production		
$ 281,400	scheduling	$ 298,100	$16,700
179,600	Office expenses	192,800	13,200
19,800	Operating expenses	26,200	6,400
	Divisions		
339,500	A	348,900	9,400
426,200	B	399,400	(26,800)
$1,246,500	Totals	$1,265,400	$18,900

Division B: Production Manager   **Monthly Report: November**

Amount Budgeted	Controllable Cost	Actual Amount	Over (Under) Budget
	Division expenses		
$101,800	Salaries	$ 96,600	$ (5,200)
39,600	Utilities	39,900	300
25,600	Insurance	21,650	(3,950)
	Departments		
46,600	Stamping	48,450	1,850
69,900	Painting	64,700	(5,200)
142,700	Assembly	128,100	(14,600)
$426,200	Totals	$399,400	$(26,800)

Stamping Department: Manager   **Monthly Report: November**

Amount Budgeted	Controllable Cost	Actual Amount	Over (Under) Budget
$22,500	Direct materials	$23,900	$1,400
14,900	Factory labor	15,200	300
2,600	Small tools	1,400	(1,200)
5,100	Maintenance salaries	6,000	900
1,000	Supplies	1,200	200
500	Other costs	750	250
$46,600	Totals	$48,450	$1,850

The production manager of Division B is responsible for the three operating departments plus controllable divisionwide costs. The production manager's report includes a summary of results from the Stamping Department as well as from all other areas of responsibility. At the division level, the report does not present detailed data on each department; only department totals appear. As shown in Exhibit 7-1, the data are even more condensed in the vice president's report. Only corporate and summarized divisional data on costs controllable by the vice president are included. Note that the $1,200 for supplies, shown in the Stamping Department report, is part of the vice president's report. The cost is included in the $399,400. But like all costs reported at higher levels, specific identity has been lost.

Cost and Revenue Controllability

OBJECTIVE 2
Identify the cost and revenue classifications that are controllable by a particular manager

Management wants to incur the lowest possible costs while still producing a quality product or providing a useful service. Profit-oriented businesses want to maximize their profits. Not-for-profit organizations, such as government units or charitable associations, seek to accomplish a mission while operating within their appropriations or budgets. To achieve these goals, management must know the origin of a cost or revenue item and be able to identify the person who controls it.

A manager's **controllable** costs and revenues are those that result from his or her actions, influence, and decisions. If managers can regulate or influence a cost or revenue item, the item is controllable at that level of operation. Or if managers have the authority to acquire or supervise the use of a resource or service, they control its cost.

Determining controllability is the key to a successful responsibility accounting system. In theory it means that every dollar of a company's incurred costs or earned revenue is traceable to and controllable by at least one manager. However, identifying controllable costs at lower management levels is often difficult because these managers seldom have full authority to acquire or supervise the use of resources and services. For example, if resources are shared with another department, a manager has only partial control and influence over such costs. For this reason managers should help identify the costs for which they will be held accountable in their performance reviews. If cost and revenue items can be controlled by the person responsible for the area in which they originate, then it is possible to design an efficient, meaningful reporting system for measuring operating performance and for pinpointing trouble spots.

The activity of a responsibility center dictates the extent of the manager's responsibility. If a responsibility center only involves costs or expenditures, it is called a cost/expense center. On the other hand, if a manager is responsible for both revenues and costs, the department is called a profit center. Finally, if a manager is involved in decisions to invest in plant, equipment, and other capital resources and is also responsible for revenues and costs, the unit is called an investment center.

Cost/Expense Center

OBJECTIVE 3
Distinguish
between a
cost/expense
center, a profit
center, and an
investment
center

Any organizational unit, such as a department or division, whose manager is responsible only for costs incurred by that unit is known as a **cost center** or **expense center**. The manager of a cost or expense center has no direct influence over revenue generation or decisions to invest in capital equipment. Instead, he or she is charged with the responsibility of producing a quality product or service at a reasonable cost.

The two terms *cost center* and *expense center* are both used in this discussion because both are used in business. *Cost center* is the term used more often. However, it has two distinct meanings. When discussing the accumulation of cost data, the term often refers to the smallest segment for which costs are accumulated and analyzed. Thus if a machine were being analyzed and costs were collected for that analysis, the machine would be a cost center. When the term *cost center* is used in connection with responsibility centers and responsibility accounting, it means an organizational unit with a manager who is accountable for the unit's actions. To avoid confusion, expense center could be used to describe this type of responsibility center. But because that term is less widely used than *cost center*, this text refers to such organizational units as cost/expense centers.

What makes a cost controllable? Earlier we said a cost was controllable if the manager could influence its incurrence and amount. A manager cannot pick and choose the costs he or she can control. Those costs must be operating costs incurred by the cost/expense center. Such costs must also be variable depending on the center's activity. Fixed costs for supervising a cost/expense center should also be included in costs controllable by the manager. All other fixed costs, such as depreciation, insurance premiums, and property taxes, as well as the operating overhead allocated to the center cannot be controlled by the manager of a cost/expense center.

Cost/expense centers are unique in that their inputs (costs) are measurable in dollars, but their outputs (products or services) are not. Such organizational units must therefore add value to a product or service or support the business in another way. Cost/expense centers are not directly connected with the sale of a product or service. Consider the Teller Department and the Data Processing Department of a bank. Their roles in the continued successful operations of the bank are obvious. Tellers are critical to good customer relations and the orderly receipt and withdrawal of funds by customers. The Data Processing Department is responsible for accurately recording all funds received and expended by the bank. Yet neither department generates revenue. Hence both departments are considered cost/expense centers in the bank's responsibility accounting system. And respective managers are responsible only for the costs incurred to operate each department.

Profit Center

When the manager of an organizational unit is responsible for revenues, costs, and resulting profits, the responsibility center is known as a **profit** center. The term *revenue center* is sometimes used in practice. Nevertheless, a pure revenue center is one in which the department or business segment's manager is only responsible for revenue generation. The costs incurred to generate that revenue are not used to measure the manager's performance. Such a situation is quite uncommon. *Profit center* is the more common term used to describe a business unit in which the manager is responsible for generating revenues and incurring costs in such a way as to maximize profits.

Managers of profit centers are accountable for both the amount of revenues their departments generate and the costs incurred to reach that revenue level. A profit center is operated much like a separate mini-business since it shows a profit or loss for its actions during a particular period. Profit centers are useful in decentralized companies. From a control standpoint, it is much easier to monitor operations if the enterprise is broken up into minibusinesses (profit centers). Large, decentralized companies are difficult to manage because of the size and diversity of the products sold or services rendered. By operating within a responsibility accounting system, a company can place managers in charge of dozens of small profit centers. Each manager is then responsible for the expected profit from his or her operating unit.

Controllable costs for a profit center are determined much as they are for a cost/expense center. A cost is controllable only if the manager can decide if it should be incurred. Revenues of a profit center can also be controlled or influenced by the center's manager. Such revenues are used to determine a center's net income.

Large retail establishments provide a clear picture of how profit centers are used. Department stores, for example, usually have several departments, such as children's clothing, cosmetics, women's clothing, menswear, and jewelry. Each department sells directly to the public, with each manager being responsible for generating a profit from sales in his or her department.

Must an organizational unit be directly involved with selling a company's product or service to be a profit center? No. An artificial selling price can be created for a department's output even if the product or service is not in a finished or salable condition when leaving the department. This process is known as transfer pricing and is discussed in detail in Chapter 14. For purposes of this discussion, however, the analysis is limited to those business units involved in direct selling activities.

Investment Center

In an investment center the concept of a responsibility center is carried one step further. The manager must be responsible for the revenues, costs, and related profits of the department or business unit for it to qualify as an investment center. In addition, the manager must be evaluated on the effective use of assets employed to generate those profits. In other words, an **investment center** is a profit center whose manager can make significant decisions about the assets the center uses. On the surface there is little difference between a profit center and an investment center, but a closer look shows a very basic difference: Top management turns over the control of the center's assets to its manager. In a profit center, top management determines the quantity and quality of assets a department uses. If such assets are old or nonproductive, the manager can request improved equipment but cannot decide whether to replace or repair it.

Since the manager of an investment center has control over assets, he or she must be evaluated based on the effective use of those assets. Not only is the amount of profit earned important, so is the center's **return on investment**. *Return on investment* is computed as follows:

$$\text{Return on investment} = \frac{\text{net income}}{\substack{\text{dollar value of the assets} \\ \text{used in generating} \\ \text{that income}}}$$

The numerator, net income, can either be before or after taxes. In the examples here, before-tax net income is used to make the analysis simpler. But remember that after-tax net income is commonly used in practice. The denominator is usually the average cost of assets used to generate a center's profit. Although much has been written and debated about the methods of assigning value to the assets used, the most common approach is to use the historical cost of the assets and not reduce their value to book value. Such an approach tends to keep the denominator constant, and the results from year to year are more comparable. If book values are used, the denominator is decreased over the life of an asset. Thus one would expect the return on investment to increase.

To evaluate the performance of an investment center's manager, one must know the quantity and value of the assets under his or her control. One must also know the controllable costs and revenues for the period. Controllable costs and revenues are identified in the same manner as that discussed for a profit center. Because an investment center is similar to an autonomous business enterprise, the manager usually controls more costs, such as insurance premiums, depreciation of the center's assets, and property taxes traced to the center. The value of the assets used must be computed by someone familiar with the investment center. The manager should be able to verify this amount since he or she will be accountable for it at the end of the accounting period.

Later in this chapter we analyze three departments of Petosa Retail Centers, Inc. The focus is on evaluating the performance of each of the three managers. However, determining the type of responsibility center being evaluated has a direct bearing on deciding which cost and/or revenue items should be used in the evaluation process. In the Petosa case, the Maintenance Contract Department is accounted for as a cost/expense center, the Home Furnishings Department is treated as a profit center, and the Custom Draperies and Blinds Department is an investment center. But before the case can be discussed, we must study the process of performance evaluation.

Performance Evaluation

Performance evaluation is the application of financial measurement techniques so actual results can be compared with expectations and performance judged. This definition seems straightforward enough. An individual's performance is measured by comparing actual and budgeted results of operations. But the process is not so easy. Successful performance evaluation is the result of several factors, some involving company policies, others, human factors.

Performance evaluation is an important part of a company's budgetary control program. An effective budgetary control program includes policies and procedures for (1) preparing operational plans, (2) establishing responsibility for performance, (3) communicating operational plans to key personnel, (4) evaluating areas of responsibility, and (5) learning the causes of any variations between budgeted and actual results and making the needed corrections.

Operating policies alone will not give a company an effective performance evaluation system. The human aspect is critical to its success. People do the planning and perform the actions needed to generate a profit. They are also the evaluators and the evaluated.

Behavioral Principles of Performance Evaluation

OBJECTIVE 4
Identify and describe the behavioral principles of performance evaluation

Basic guidelines regarding people must be part of any effective cost and revenue control system. Behavioral considerations should include the following:

1. Managers should have input into the standards and goals set for their areas of responsibility.
2. Top management's support of the evaluation process should be evident.
3. Only *controllable* cost and revenue items with *significant* variances should be the focus of performance reports.
4. Opportunity for manager response should be part of the evaluation process.

All considerations assume that an effective reward system (compensation) for attaining set goals was previously established.

1. **Managers should have input into the standards and goals set for their areas of responsibility.** The manager responsible for an operating area must have direct input into the goal-setting process of his or her area. Having a desire to perform is a key factor in meeting goals and attaining targets. When a manager believes that an operating target is unrealistic, or that plans were developed without the participation of personnel from the department, the desire to reach those goals may not materialize. To prevent this negative reaction, top management should encourage participative goal setting. When departmental managers are involved in setting the targets against which they are to be evaluated, their incentive to perform is increased. They perceive

such goals as attainable, not a set of unrealistic targets set arbitrarily by top management.

2. **Top management's support of the evaluation process should be evident.** Top management must show its support by clearly communicating goals and plans, including each person's exact responsibilities, to all people involved. Failure to communicate plans to managers is a common cause of inefficient operating performance. Such communication accomplishes two important aspects of the budgetary control process. First, communication spells out in detail management's expectations of each manager. After discussing the plans with a superior, a manager knows the targets he or she should aim for and is more motivated to attain those targets. Second, the developing of an evaluation system and the communicating of that system to managers indicates that top management is deeply involved in the performance evaluation process and will support quests to meet set targets. Without the continued support of top management, a performance evaluation system fails to accomplish its objectives.

3. **Only controllable cost and revenue items with significant variances should be the focus of performance reports.** As discussed, performance reports should contain only those cost and revenue categories that a manager can influence or control. Holding someone responsible for costs outside his or her control causes negative feelings and decreases the effectiveness of the control process and the evaluation system. In addition, when there are many cost and revenue categories within a manager's domain, it is more effective to limit the items reported on the performance report to those with significant variations from budget. This process focuses attention on those areas needing immediate action, so the manager will not waste time evaluating insignificant differences.

4. **Opportunity for manager response should be a part of the evaluation process.** Managers should have a chance to give top management feedback on their performance. Top management should praise good performance and not take it for granted. Silence does not imply good performance; it means bad management. If performance is poor or substandard, the responsible person should have a chance to defend his or her actions. There may be a good reason for a variance, such as the cause being beyond the person's control. The key is to make the manager feel that he or she is an important part of the management team, not just someone on whom blame is placed when top management performs poorly.

Operational Principles of Performance Evaluation

Making a performance evaluation system operable requires that a set of operational principles be followed. Note that they are linked closely with the behavioral principles already discussed. The operational principles of performance evaluation are:

1. Provide accurate and suitable measures of performance.
2. Communicate expectations to appropriate managers and segment leaders to be evaluated.
3. Identify each manager's responsibilities.
4. Compare actual performance with a suitable base.
5. Prepare performance reports that highlight areas of concern.
6. Analyze important cause-and-effect relationships.

1. **Provide accurate and suitable measures of performance.** Expectations of a manager's performance must be realistic for budgetary control to be accomplished. Accurate and suitable measures of performance should include predetermined budgets and standards, performances of other people in comparable jobs, and past performances in the same job classification. A manager will be able to do an effective job if these performance measures are provided and if they represent attainable goals. Nonfinancial measures, such as machine hours or units of output, can be used to measure performance and may be as useful as dollar measures.

2. **Communicate expectations to appropriate managers and segment leaders to be evaluated.** When developing its performance evaluation process, a company should ensure that its system of communicating expectations to managers at all levels is well-defined. The communications system should be two-way: down through the organizational hierarchy and up from the lowest level of management to the board of directors. Each side must listen to the concerns and solutions of the other. Feedback is vital to the success of a performance evaluation system.

3. **Identify each manager's responsibilities.** Before expecting a person to do something, one should inform the person of what is expected. Identifying the specific responsibilities of each manager is part of the performance evaluation process. This step is usually accomplished when the company's responsibility accounting system is devised. One way to ensure that a performance evaluation process fails is to have managers held accountable for actions they thought were another's responsibility.

4. **Compare actual performance with a suitable base.** When evaluating performance, one must compare what actually happened with a measure of what was anticipated or expected. This measure may be a budget prepared before the current period began, the average performance on a particular task during the past three or four years, a standard cost (discussed in Chapters 9 and 10), or simply a rough estimate of expectations. Without some anticipated base, one has nothing to evaluate actual results against, and without that measurement ability, performance cannot be evaluated.

5. **Prepare performance reports that highlight areas of concern.** The preparation of performance reports is an important step in the performance evaluation process. The information in these reports should

specify a manager's responsibilities. These responsibilities may be limited to cost and revenue items that depart enough from anticipated targets to warrant analysis. If a manager's area of responsibility involves only fifteen or twenty cost and revenue items, then all controllable costs and revenues may be included. But if there are more than twenty items, only those needing analysis for being far over or under target should be included. Remember, only controllable cost and revenue items belong in a manager's performance report.

6. **Analyze important cause-and-effect relationships.** Isolating a variation between a budgeted amount and an actual cost is just the beginning of the performance evaluation process. Some people believe that once this variation has been determined, someone is guilty and should be reprimanded. But a performance report is more than a set of numbers compared with one another. One cost or revenue variation from budget may help cause a second reaction (domino effect). A performance report should reveal cause-and-effect factors and significant relationships. If, for instance, a furniture manufacturer purchases poor-quality lumber, labor costs might soar because the wood is difficult to work with. Such qualitative information can often explain differences between budgeted and actual dollars. Much of this information must come from the manager being evaluated.

Implementing a Performance Reporting System

You have now learned about the elements needed to develop a performance reporting system:

1. A performance reporting system is based on the concept of responsibility accounting. As mentioned, responsibility accounting is an information reporting system that classifies financial data according to specific areas of responsibility. If a detailed organization chart of the company is created, all managerial positions that will become part of the performance reporting system can be identified and areas of responsibility determined.
2. Adequate performance measures must be determined.
3. Specific duties and operating expectations must be identified and communicated to each manager.
4. A communications system must be established, and it must involve managers in determining their targets and goals for the period.
5. A reporting format must be devised, and it must contain only those cost and revenue items under a manager's control.
6. Once the budgeted and actual amounts have been measured and compared, the manager is expected to explain the significant differences on his or her report.
7. A manager and his or her superior must work out methods to correct problems.

8. A strong system of rewards and feedback is necessary for the performance evaluation process to succeed.

With these performance evaluation elements in mind, let us analyze the performance reporting techniques of Petosa Retail Centers, Inc.

Illustrative Case: Petosa Retail Centers, Inc.

Discussing performance evaluation according to behavioral principles and operational principles helps describe the process. But there is a large difference between discussing the concept and actually doing an evaluation. The Petosa Retail Centers, Inc., case analysis illustrates the process of performance evaluation in a decentralized company. Emphasis is on determining the costs and revenues a manager can control and on structuring and designing performance reports. This case analysis compares performance evaluation and reporting for a cost/expense center, a profit center, and an investment center.

Petosa Retail Centers, Inc., competes directly with Sears, Roebuck and J. C. Penney for customers who want a store with a full line of household goods and services. Petosa's stores, which are in all major metropolitan areas, are located near Sears' and Penney's stores. Store layouts closely resemble those of competitors. Because of its large size, the company operates as a decentralized organization. In all 117 stores, the departments are large and supervised by highly trained managers.

The following analysis concentrates on three supervisors and their performance reports. Bill Drown manages a service-oriented cost/expense center, Julia Mulligan supervises a profit center within a service business, and Nickolas Chrysochos supervises a production and service department that is treated as an investment center.

OBJECTIVE 6a
Prepare a performance evaluation report for a cost/expense center

Maintenance Contract Department. *Organization:* Bill Drown manages the Maintenance Contract Department at Petosa's Nashville, Tennessee, store. The company's Appliance and Gardening Departments sell maintenance contracts to customers who buy appliances and lawn and gardening equipment. These contracts guarantee that for a set annual contract price, all labor and parts needed to keep the item in operating order will be supplied by the Maintenance Contract Department of a Petosa store. The maintenance contracts are sold by the appliance and gardening equipment salespeople, not by people working for Bill Drown, so the Maintenance Contract Department and Mr. Drown do not have revenue responsibility.

Mr. Drown is responsible for thirty maintenance and repair people and a fleet of eighteen vans stocked with a full line of parts. Half the vans are involved in appliance repair activities; the other nine are used for lawn and garden equipment repairs. Twelve employees are support personnel involved in scheduling, purchasing, and stocking activities as well as assisting the eighteen full-time maintenance repair people who operate the vans. The department is housed in its own building, which has room for parts storage and two bays for repairing the vans.

Operating Results for March: Following are the costs identified with the Maintenance Contract Department for March 1989. The format is the original one Mr. Drown received. As you can see, the report lists all costs assigned to the Contract Maintenance Department and shows both budgeted and actual data. At the bottom of the report, performance is said to be $5,630 over budget. The report, however, provides little additional information. Although the columns are totaled, there is no information on the over- or underbudget spending in individual cost categories. Also, included in the listing of costs are several that Mr. Drown cannot control.

Petosa Retail Centers, Inc.
Maintenance Contract Department
Operating Report
For March 1989

Supervisor: B. Drown	Budgeted	Actual
Labor		
Appliance repair	$ 5,400	$ 5,940
Lawn and garden equipment repair	5,400	5,310
Support	6,000	6,240
Supervision	2,600	2,600
Labor-related benefits	3,600	3,920
Repair parts, appliances	12,500	10,800
Repair parts, lawn and garden equipment	16,400	17,250
Fuel, vans	2,250	2,520
Oil, tires, and repairs, vans	2,880	2,430
Depreciation, vans	2,400	3,000
Maintenance and upkeep, building	2,500	2,350
Property taxes, building	600	750
Depreciation, building	2,200	2,650
Insurance, building	450	510
Utilities, building	300	280
Local store overhead	2,100	4,070
Corporate general and administrative costs	6,290	8,880
Total costs	$73,870	$79,500

Performance: Operating costs were $5,630 over budget.

Petosa's national headquarters has recently installed a responsibility accounting system for all 117 stores. Mr. Drown was asked to help prepare a format for the responsibility accounting report for his department. Of the costs included in his regular monthly performance report,

Mr. Drown determined that the following costs were not under his control:

1. Fixed/allocated costs
   a. Depreciation, vans
   b. Property taxes, building
   c. Depreciation, building
   d. Insurance, building
2. Local store overhead
3. Corporate general and administrative costs

Using this information, the controller of the Nashville store put together a new report format.

Exhibit 7-2 is the revised performance report for the Maintenance Contract Department for March. Costs not controllable by Mr. Drown are summarized at the bottom. Those costs that Mr. Drown can influence are reported first. He can control and has responsibility for labor and labor-related costs, repair parts, van costs, and building costs.

Mr. Drown's performance during March was much better than that stated on the old performance report. Overall, his controllable costs were $190 under budget. Areas he needs to work on are labor costs, appliance repair ($540 over budget); repair parts, lawn and garden equipment ($850 over budget); and repair parts, appliances ($1,700 under budget). There may be a connection between the low cost of parts and the high cost of labor in the appliance repair area. Repair personnel people may be using too much time trying to fix existing parts rather than replacing them when making repairs. Such action could also lead to lower-quality repair service. Mr. Drown should take action in this area. Other than those areas mentioned, he seems to be doing a good job. Although the new report format still shows the department as $5,630 over budget, Mr. Drown is only accountable for the controllable costs of his unit.

OBJECTIVE 6b
Prepare a performance evaluation report for a profit center

Home Furnishings Department. *Organization:* Julia Mulligan is the supervisor of the Home Furnishings Department in Petosa's Irving, Texas, store. This location is convenient for customers living in both Dallas and Fort Worth, making the Irving store one of the largest Petosa stores in the country. Home furnishings include furniture, beddings, glassware, rugs, and carpeting. This department occupies 20 percent of the store's floor space allotted to sales. Storage space for inventory takes up almost 40 percent of the store's warehouse space.

Since Ms. Mulligan is responsible for both the purchase and sale of all goods listed as home furnishings, her department is considered a profit center. She employs thirty salespeople, four buyers, and twelve support people who work as sales-floor stockers, warehouse personnel, and delivery people. These three areas—sales, buying, and support—are operated as minidepartments, and each has a manager who reports to Ms. Mulligan.

Exhibit 7-2. Performance Reporting: Cost/Expense Center

Petosa Retail Centers, Inc.—Nashville, Tennessee
Maintenance Contract Department
Performance Report
For the Month Ended March 31, 1989

Supervisor: Bill Drown	Budgeted	Actual	Difference Over (Under) Budget
Costs Controllable by Supervisor			
Labor costs			
Maintenance repair personnel			
Appliance repair	$ 5,400	$ 5,940	$ 540
Lawn and garden equipment repair	5,400	5,310	(90)
Support personnel	6,000	6,240	240
Supervision	2,600	2,600	0
Labor-related benefits costs	3,600	3,920	320
Repair parts			
Appliances	12,500	10,800	(1,700)
Lawn and garden equipment	16,400	17,250	850
Van costs			
Fuel	2,250	2,520	270
Oil, tires, and repairs	2,880	2,430	(450)
Building costs			
Maintenance and upkeep	2,500	2,350	(150)
Utilities	300	280	(20)
Total controllable costs	$59,830	$59,640	$ (190)
Costs Uncontrollable by Supervisor			
Fixed/allocated costs			
Depreciation, vans	$ 2,400	$ 3,000	$ 600
Property taxes, building	600	750	150
Depreciation, building	2,200	2,650	450
Insurance, building	450	510	60
Local store overhead	2,100	4,070	1,970
Corporate general and administrative costs	6,290	8,880	2,590
Total uncontrollable costs	$14,040	$19,860	$5,820
Total costs	$73,870	$79,500	$5,630

Operating Results for March: The original performance report received by Ms. Mulligan for the Home Furnishings Department for March is shown on the next page. The report is divided into revenue and costs sections, and department income is shown. Budgeted and actual information is reported for each category. Ms. Mulligan's performance was judged to be $6,602 under the net income budgeted for the department.

Petosa Retail Centers, Inc.
Home Furnishings Department
Operating Report
For March 1989

Supervisor: J. Mulligan	Budgeted	Actual
Revenue		
Furniture sales	$187,500	$191,900
Carpeting sales	126,250	129,600
Other sales	98,500	106,200
Total revenue	$412,250	$427,700
Costs		
Cost of goods sold, furniture	$112,500	$111,302
Cost of goods sold, carpet	75,750	84,240
Cost of goods sold, other	68,950	63,720
Selling, commissions	16,490	17,108
Selling, supervision	1,200	1,250
Buying, salaries	5,600	5,000
Buying, supervision	1,200	1,200
Support, wages	8,400	8,160
Support, supervision	1,000	1,100
Department supervision	3,250	3,250
Employee benefits	7,428	7,610
Utilities, sales floor	4,200	4,450
Depreciation, sales floor	8,600	14,250
Utilities, warehouse	2,800	3,100
Depreciation, warehouse	4,700	5,900
Delivery costs	3,300	3,550
Local store overhead	13,450	15,120
Corporate general and administrative costs	26,980	37,540
Total costs	$365,798	$387,850
Department income	$ 46,452	$ 39,850

Performance: Department income was $6,602 under budget.

As with the Nashville, Tennessee, store, the Irving, Texas, store is shifting to the new responsibility accounting reporting system. With the cooperation of her store's controller, Ms. Mulligan identified the following items as being out of her control:

1. Depreciation, sales floor
2. Depreciation, warehouse
3. Local store overhead
4. Corporate general and administrative costs

With this input from Ms. Mulligan, the controller recast the performance report as shown in Exhibit 7-3.

As reflected in the new report, Ms. Mulligan produced department income in March that was $12,478 over budget. All cost categories were well within normal range. Selling commissions were $618 over budget, but that should be expected since sales were $15,450 over budget. Buying salaries were low, and the difference was probably caused by being one buyer short during the month.

What Exhibit 7-3 does not show, however, is the performance of the three minidepartment managers. For this purpose the sales, cost of goods sold, and gross margin from sales data are summarized:

	Budgeted	Actual	Difference Over (Under) Budget
Gross Margin from Sales			
Furniture sales	$ 75,000	$ 80,598	$ 5,598
Carpeting sales	50,500	45,360	(5,140)
Other sales	29,550	42,480	12,930
Totals	$155,050	$168,438	$13,388

This analysis is revealing. Even though the department's overall gross margin was $13,388, the carpeting minidepartment had a gross margin of $5,140 *under* budget for March. Looking further into the data, carpet sales were $3,350 over budget, but the cost of carpet sold was $8,490 *over* budget. Ms. Mulligan should request information from her carpeting manager about this situation. Either someone has been buying carpet at increased prices and/or of increased quality, or sales prices are too low. Of course, these reasons may be connected. In any event, Ms. Mulligan has a serious problem to deal with, even though overall department income is very favorable.

OBJECTIVE 6c

Prepare a performance evaluation report for an investment center

Custom Draperies and Blinds Department. *Organization:* Nickolas Chrysochos supervises the Custom Draperies and Blinds Department at the Petosa store in Seattle, Washington. He has three full-time salespeople working for him, and they are responsible for soliciting orders for custom-made draperies and window blinds. A major portion of this department's work involves making custom draperies for homes on special order. The salespeople visit customers' homes and take all measurements for each order.

Exhibit 7-3. Performance Reporting—Profit Center

Petosa Retail Centers, Inc.—Irving, Texas
Home Furnishings Department
Performance Report
For the Month Ended March 31, 1989

Supervisor: Julia Mulligan	Budgeted	Actual	Difference Over (Under) Budget
Costs Controllable by Supervisor			
Revenue from sales			
Furniture	$187,500	$191,900	$ 4,400
Carpet	126,250	129,600	3,350
Other	98,500	106,200	7,700
Total revenue	$412,250	$427,700	$15,450
Cost of goods sold			
Furniture	$112,500	$111,302	$ (1,198)
Carpet	75,750	84,240	8,490
Other	68,950	63,720	(5,230)
Total cost of goods sold	$257,200	$259,262	$ 2,062
Gross margin from sales	$155,050	$168,438	$13,388
Operating costs			
Selling			
Commissions	$ 16,490	$ 17,108	$ 618
Supervision	1,200	1,250	50
Buying			
Salaries	5,600	5,000	(600)
Supervision	1,200	1,200	0
Support			
Wages	8,400	8,160	(240)
Supervision	1,000	1,100	100
Department supervision	3,250	3,250	0
Employee benefits	7,428	7,610	182
Space costs			
Utilities, sales floor	4,200	4,450	250
Utilities, warehouse	2,800	3,100	300
Delivery costs	3,300	3,550	250
Total controllable costs	$ 54,868	$ 55,778	$ 910
Controllable department income	$100,182	$112,660	$12,478
Costs Uncontrollable by Supervisor			
Depreciation, sales floor	$ 8,600	$ 14,250	$ 5,650
Depreciation, warehouse	4,700	5,900	1,200
Local store overhead	13,450	15,120	1,670
Corporate general and administrative costs	26,980	37,540	10,560
Total uncontrollable costs	$ 53,730	$ 72,810	$19,080
Net department income	$ 46,452	$ 39,850	$ (6,602)

In addition to the sales staff, Mr. Chrysochos employs six drapery makers, five blinds makers, and four indirect labor personnel. The department uses a job order costing system for cost accumulation purposes. Seventy percent of the department's work is custom-made goods, and 30 percent of sales are ready-made draperies and blinds. Three salesclerks handle sales of ready-made goods.

The company considers the Custom Draperies and Blinds Department an investment center since Mr. Chrysochos is responsible for buying such capital assets as machinery and equipment to make the custom draperies and blinds. He is also responsible for three automobiles used for sales, 2,000 square feet of sales floor in the main building, and the drapery production shop located in its own building adjacent to the store.

Operating Results for March: Mr. Chrysochos' performance report for March, which follows the original format, is summarized in the operating report on page 251. Because the Custom Draperies and Blinds Department is an investment center, performance is judged by both the department's income and its return on investment. As shown, Mr. Chrysochos' overall performance was well below expectations. Department income was $3,881 *below* expectations for March. This situation meant that on the $1,559,600 investment base for the department, only a .5 percent return was realized. Target monthly return on investment was .75 percent.

As with the other stores, the Seattle, Washington, store changed to a responsibility accounting reporting system in March. After reviewing the cost and revenue categories with Mr. Chrysochos, the store's controller identified the following items as being out of the control of the department's supervisor:

1. Local store overhead
2. Corporate general and administrative costs

Using this information, the controller revised Mr. Chrysochos' performance report; it is shown in Exhibit 7-4 on page 252.

Unlike the reports for Mr. Drown and Ms. Mulligan, the new reporting format for the Custom Draperies and Blinds Department does not turn an unfavorable situation into a favorable one. Mr. Chrysochos has problems generating a favorable gross margin from sales. There are also two or three operating cost categories that he should be concerned about. A further look at gross margin revealed the following:

	Budgeted	Actual	Difference Over (Under) Budget
Gross Margin from Sales			
Custom draperies	$22,635	$18,810	$(3,825)
Custom blinds	11,850	13,895	2,045
Ready-mades	17,319	17,990	671
Totals	$51,804	$50,695	$(1,109)

Petosa Retail Centers, Inc.
Custom Draperies and Blinds Department
Operating Report
For March 1989

Supervisor: N. Chrysochos Investment base: $1,559,600	Budgeted	Actual
Revenue		
Custom drapery sales	$ 75,450	$ 79,410
Custom blinds sales	59,250	62,190
Ready-made sales	57,730	56,280
Total revenue	$192,430	$197,880
Costs		
Cost of goods sold		
Custom draperies, materials	$ 30,180	$ 33,480
Custom draperies, labor	15,090	19,100
Custom draperies, factory overhead	7,545	8,020
Custom blinds, materials	29,625	30,040
Custom blinds, labor	11,850	12,130
Custom blinds, factory overhead	5,925	6,125
Ready-made draperies and blinds	40,411	38,290
Selling commissions, custom-made	8,082	8,496
Selling commissions, ready-made	1,732	1,688
Automobile expenses, selling	4,620	3,750
Automobile depreciation, selling	8,160	8,430
Department supervision	2,700	2,700
Employee benefits	7,891	8,823
Utilities, sales floor	1,200	1,320
Depreciation, sales floor	1,610	1,750
Local store overhead	2,350	2,290
Corporate general and administrative costs	1,780	3,650
Total costs	$180,751	$190,082
Department income	$ 11,679	$ 7,798
Department rate of return	.75%	.50%

Performance: Department income was $3,881 under budget.
Department return on investment for March was .5%
(6% annualized), which is .25% under the anticipated
monthly return of .75%.

There is a definite problem in the production of custom draperies. Mr. Chrysochos should analyze all aspects of that area. Are cloth and other materials prices too high? Is too much labor employed for the volume of business? Do the salespeople need to revise retail price figures used

Exhibit 7-4. Performance Reporting: Investment Center

Petosa Retail Centers, Inc.—Seattle, Washington
Custom Draperies and Blinds Department
Performance Report
For the Month Ended March 31, 1989

Supervisor: Nickolas Chrysochos Investment base: $1,559,600	Budgeted	Actual	Difference Over (Under) Budget
Costs Controllable by Supervisor			
Revenue from sales			
Custom draperies	$ 75,450	$ 79,410	$3,960
Custom blinds	59,250	62,190	2,940
Ready-mades	57,730	56,280	(1,450)
Totals	$192,430	$197,880	$5,450
Cost of goods sold			
Custom draperies			
Materials	$ 30,180	$ 33,480	$3,300
Labor	15,090	19,100	4,010
Factory overhead	7,545	8,020	475
Subtotals	$ 52,815	$ 60,600	$7,785
Custom blinds			
Materials	$ 29,625	$ 30,040	$ 415
Labor	11,850	12,130	280
Factory overhead	5,925	6,125	200
Subtotals	$ 47,400	$ 48,295	$ 895
Ready-made draperies and blinds	$ 40,411	$ 38,290	($2,121)
Total cost of goods sold	$140,626	$147,185	$6,559
Gross margin from sales	$ 51,804	$ 50,695	($1,109)
Operating costs			
Sales commissions, custom-mades	$ 8,082	$ 8,496	$ 414
Sales commissions, ready-mades	1,732	1,688	(44)
Auto expenses	4,620	3,750	(870)
Auto depreciation	8,160	8,430	270
Department supervision	2,700	2,700	0
Employee benefits	7,891	8,823	932
Sales space costs			
Utilities, sales floor	1,200	1,320	120
Depreciation, sales floor	1,610	1,750	140
Total controllable costs	$ 35,995	$ 36,957	$ 962
Controllable departmental income	$ 15,809	$ 13,738	($2,071)
Controllable department rate of return	1.01%	0.88%	−0.13%
Costs Uncontrollable by Supervisor			
Local store overhead	$ 2,350	$ 2,290	($60)
Corporate general and administrative costs	1,780	3,650	1,870
Total uncontrollable costs	$ 4,130	$ 5,940	$1,810
Net departmental income	$ 11,679	$ 7,798	($3,881)

to develop customer quotes? There may be several possible causes for the poor performance. Other areas of concern include sales commissions for custom-made products and employee benefits. The high cost of benefits may be related to excess labor in the custom draperies area.

As shown, regardless of the result for each manager, the new reporting format has helped determine ways to improve performance. Responsibility accounting provides the tools necessary to establish a performance reporting system that highlights cost and revenue areas under the control of a manager.

Chapter Review

Review of Learning Objectives

1. **Define responsibility accounting and describe a responsibility accounting system.**
   Responsibility accounting is an information reporting system that (1) classifies financial data according to areas of responsibility in an organization and (2) reports managers' activities by including only revenue and cost categories that a particular manager can control. A responsibility accounting system personalizes accounting reports. It is composed of a series of reports, one for each person in a company's organization chart.

2. **Identify the cost and revenue classifications that are controllable by a particular manager.**
   A manager's controllable costs and revenues are those that result from his or her actions, influence, and decisions. If managers can regulate or influence a cost or revenue item, it is controllable at that level of operation. If managers have the authority to acquire or supervise the use of a resource or service, they control its cost.

3. **Distinguish between a cost/expense center, a profit center, and an investment center.**
   Any organizational unit, such as a department or division, whose manager is responsible only for costs incurred by that unit is known as a cost/expense center. Cost/expense centers are not directly connected with the sale of a product or service. When a unit manager is responsible for revenues, costs, and resulting profits, the responsibility center is known as a profit center. To qualify as an investment center, the organization must evaluate its managers on how effectively assets are used to generate profits.

4. **Identify and describe the behavioral principles of performance evaluation.**
   Behavioral principles of performance evaluation state that (1) managers should have input into the standards and goals set for their areas of responsibility; (2) top management's support of the evaluation process should be evident; (3) only controllable cost and revenue items with significant variances should be the focus of performance reports; and (4) managers should be given opportunities to respond to evaluations.

5. State the operational principles of performance evaluation and explain how they are interrelated.

   Operational principles of performance evaluation stipulate that management (1) provide accurate and suitable measures of performance; (2) communicate expectations to appropriate managers and segment leaders to be evaluated; (3) identify each manager's responsibilities; (4) compare actual performance with a suitable base; (5) prepare performance reports that highlight areas of concern; and (6) analyze important cause-and-effect relationships. These principles are all based on concern for the manager and his or her areas of responsibility.

6. Prepare a performance evaluation report for (a) a cost/expense center, (b) a profit center, and (c) an investment center.

   The key to preparing performance evaluation reports is to divide the report between those items a manager can and cannot control. A performance report for a cost/expense center contains only cost items, whereas a report for a profit and investment center contains both revenue and cost items. In addition, the report for an investment center provides information on the center's investment base and the rate of return on invested dollars.

Review of Concepts and Terminology

The following important concepts were introduced in this chapter:

(L.O. 1)   Responsibility accounting: An information reporting system that (1) classifies financial data according to areas of responsibility in an organization and (2) reports managers' activities by including only revenue and cost categories that a particular manager controls.   (Also activity accounting or profitability accounting.)

(L.O. 3)   Cost/expense center: Any organizational unit, such as a department or division, whose manager is responsible only for costs incurred by that unit.

(L.O. 3)   Profit center: An organizational unit whose manager is responsible for revenues, costs, and resulting profits.

(L.O. 3)   Investment center: A profit center whose manager can make significant decisions about the assets the center uses.

(L.O. 4, 5, 6)   Performance evaluation: The application of financial measurement techniques so actual results can be compared with expectations and performance judged.

Other important terms introduced in this chapter are:

controllability (p. 235)
decentralization (p. 231)
responsibility centers (p. 231)
return on investment (p. 238)

Review Problem
Allocation of and Responsibility for Overhead

Idaho Instruments Company is a high-tech firm engaged in the assembly of laser welders. The company is very employee oriented and has a complete workout room and indoor running track that any employee can use at any time, day or night. Included in the company's health facility is a special cafeteria serving only low-cholesterol, low-sodium foods. In 19x9 the cafeteria operated at a net loss of $178,950. Company policy is to allocate this excess cost to all responsibility centers since every employee has the opportunity to eat at the cafeteria. Management is considering three allocation bases—number of employees, meals purchased by employees, and total labor hours—from which to select the allocation base. Following are the data supporting each base under consideration:

Idaho Instruments Company
Allocation Analysis Data
For Year Ended December 31, 19x9

Responsibility Center	Number of Employees	Meals Purchased by Employees	Total Labor Hours
Materials-handling	9	655	50,400
Inventory storage	18	3,275	16,800
Electrical	63	10,480	100,800
Assembly	135	18,340	285,600
Engineering	54	9,170	134,400
Inspection	27	5,240	58,800
Accounting/Finance	9	2,620	33,600
Marketing/Sales	81	9,825	117,600
Purchasing/Shipping	18	1,965	8,400
Research/Design	36	3,930	33,600
Totals	450	65,500	840,000

Required

1. Allocate the net loss of the cafeteria to the ten responsibility centers, using as a basis (a) number of employees, (b) meals purchased by employees, and (c) total labor hours.
2. For purposes of traceability, which of the three allocation bases best associates the cafeteria's cost with the cost objective (responsibility centers)? Why?
3. For performance evaluation, which of the cafeteria loss distributions computed in part 1 leads to the most effective control of costs? Defend your answer.

Answer to Review Problem

1. Amount to be allocated: $178,950

    1a. Using number of employees basis:

Responsibility Center	Number of Employees	Percentage of Number of Employees	Amount Allocated to Each Department
Materials-handling	9	2.0	$ 3,579.00
Inventory storage	18	4.0	7,158.00
Electrical	63	14.0	25,053.00
Assembly	135	30.0	53,685.00
Engineering	54	12.0	21,474.00
Inspection	27	6.0	10,737.00
Accounting/Finance	9	2.0	3,579.00
Marketing/Sales	81	18.0	32,211.00
Purchasing/Shipping	18	4.0	7,158.00
Research/Design	36	8.0	14,316.00
Totals	450	100.0	$178,950.00

    1b. Using meals purchased by employees basis:

Responsibility Center	Meals Purchased by Employees	Percentage of Meals Purchased by Employees	Amount Allocated to Each Department
Materials-handling	655	1.0	$ 1,789.50
Inventory storage	3,275	5.0	8,947.50
Electrical	10,480	16.0	28,632.00
Assembly	18,340	28.0	50,106.00
Engineering	9,170	14.0	25,053.00
Inspection	5,240	8.0	14,316.00
Accounting/Finance	2,620	4.0	7,158.00
Marketing/Sales	9,825	15.0	26,842.50
Purchasing/Shipping	1,965	3.0	5,368.50
Research/Design	3,930	6.0	10,737.00
Totals	65,500	100.0	$178,950.00

1c. Using total labor hours as basis:

Responsibility Center	Total Labor Hours	Percentage of Total Labor Hours	Amount Allocated to Each Department
Materials-handling	50,400	6.0	$ 10,737.00
Inventory storage	16,800	2.0	3,579.00
Electrical	100,800	12.0	21,474.00
Assembly	285,600	34.0	60,843.00
Engineering	134,400	16.0	28,632.00
Inspection	58,800	7.0	12,526.50
Accounting/Finance	33,600	4.0	7,158.00
Marketing/Sales	117,600	14.0	25,053.00
Purchasing/Shipping	8,400	1.0	1,789.50
Research/Design	33,600	4.0	7,158.00
Totals	840,000	100.0	$178,950.00

2. For purposes of traceability. Of the three allocation bases, meals purchased by employees has to be the only basis with a direct connection between the loss and the cost objective. The loss is directly connected with the number of meals served. Therefore, number of meals served is the best allocation base to satisfy the test of traceability.
3. For purposes of performance evaluation. For performance evaluation, none of the three bases are applicable. Only *controllable* costs should be included in a manager's performance evaluation. None of the managers in the departments have any control over cafeteria costs.

Chapter Assignments

Questions

1. Define responsibility accounting.
2. Describe a responsibility accounting system.
3. What is a responsibility center?
4. How does a company's organizational structure affect its responsibility accounting system?
5. Discuss the statement, "In a responsibility accounting system, operating reports for each level of management are tailored to individual needs."
6. What role does controllability play in a responsibility accounting system?
7. Describe a cost/expense center. Give two examples.
8. What is a profit center?

9. How does a profit center differ from a revenue center?
10. Explain the statement, "A profit center is operated much like a separate minibusiness."
11. Describe an investment center.
12. Compare a cost/expense center, a profit center, and an investment center.
13. Describe how return on investment is computed.
14. What role does return on investment play in the evaluation of an investment center?
15. Define performance evaluation.
16. Identify the four behavioral principles of performance evaluation.
17. What does participative goal setting mean?
18. State the six operational principles of performance evaluation.
19. Explain the importance of a good communications system in performance evaluation.
20. Explain how a responsibility accounting system is linked to effective performance evaluation of managers.

Classroom Exercises

Exercise 7-1.
Responsibility
Accounting/
Organization Chart
(L.O. 1)

Pima Tennis and Golf Resort is in Apache, Arizona, at the foothills of the Painted Desert. Management has just hired your accounting firm to create and install a responsibility accounting system for reporting and performance evaluation purposes. Pima has two 18-hole golf courses, 24 lighted tennis courts, and a 450-room lodge.

The following managerial positions are to be included in your analysis:

Manager, golf course maintenance	President and chair of the board
Manager, customer relations	Manager, tennis court maintenance
Manager, collections, payables, and billings	Manager, room cleaning/customer services
Manager, building maintenance	Manager, tennis and golf activities
Vice president, accounting and finance	Vice president, building and grounds
Manager, resort reservations	Manager, cash management
Manager, resort grounds maintenance	Manager, discount convention sales
Vice president, resort occupancy	Manager, budgeting and reporting

Use these managerial positions to prepare an organization chart for use in developing a responsibility accounting system.

Exercise 7-2.
Controllable
Versus
Uncontrollable
Costs
(L.O. 2,3)

For each of the following costs, state whether it is controllable or uncontrollable for a supervisor of (1) a profit center and (2) an investment center:

Cost of goods purchased, Shoe Department
Electricity costs, allocated using an overhead application rate
Depreciation, store equipment
Insurance expense, fire insurance on equipment
Buyer's salary, Home Appliance Department
Advertising expense, Video & Sounds Department
President's salary, manufacturing company
Automobile and truck repair costs, Electrical Department

Contribution to local university, Garden Tools Department
Building repair costs, Reupholstering Department

Exercise 7-3.
Responsibility
Accounting/
Organizational
Structure
(L.O. 1, 2)

The Gregor Shewman Company uses the following job titles:

Sales manager   Internal auditor
Vice president, manufacturing   Supervisor, repairs and maintenance
President   Warehouse manager
Cashier   Marketing manager
Controller   Engineering research manager
Production supervisor   Personnel manager
Vice president, sales   Treasurer
Purchasing agent   Vice president, administration

1. Design an organization chart using these job titles.
2. For each job title, list some possible costs for which the person holding each position would be responsible.

Exercise 7-4.
Cost/Expense
Center:
Performance
Report
(L.O. 2, 6)

The Pima Tennis and Golf Resort, described in Exercise 7-1, has now been divided into responsibility centers. Mr. Ralph Beach is manager of golf course maintenance, which has been designated as a cost/expense center. During February the following costs, shown with their respective budgeted amounts, were incurred:

Pima Tennis and Golf Resort
Golf Course Maintenance
Operating Report
For February 19x0

Supervisor: R. Beach	Budgeted	Actual
Maintenance labor	$ 5,700	$ 6,200
Depreciation, equipment	3,000	3,300
Fuel and equipment repairs	2,450	2,200
Supervisors' salaries	2,500	2,500
Maintenance supplies	1,350	1,110
Sod and grass seed	3,100	3,340
Employee benefits	900	1,040
Resort overhead	5,000	5,790
Upkeep of storage sheds	400	240
Vandalism insurance	750	790
Depreciation, resort buildings	4,200	4,600
Small tools	400	260
Fertilizer and insect control powders	5,000	4,670
New trees and shrubberies	2,000	2,940
Water expense	2,600	2,180
Sprinkler system, parts and repairs	1,800	1,260
Totals	$41,150	$42,420

Prepare a performance report for Mr. Beach for February. Use a responsibility accounting format.

Exercise 7-5.
Identification of
Controllable Costs
(L.O.2)

Anderman Corporation produces computer equipment. Production has a three-tier management structure as follows:

Vice president, production

Plant superintendent

Production supervisors

Various production costs are accounted for each period. Examples include

Repair and maintenance costs   Superintendent's salary
Material handling costs   Materials usage costs
Direct labor   Storage, finished goods inventory
Supervisors' salaries   Property taxes, plant
Plant maintenance of grounds   Depreciation, plant
Depreciation, equipment

1. Identify each cost item as a variable or fixed cost.
2. Identify the manager responsible for each cost.

Exercise 7-6.
Performance
Report: Profit
Center
(L.O.2, 6)

Thomas Dry Goods, Ltd., is a worldwide merchandising concern with head-quarters in London, England. Thomas' store in Tempe, Arizona, is installing a responsibility accounting reporting system. Following is a summary of the Cosmetics Department's revenues and expenses for April:

Thomas Dry Goods, Ltd.
Cosmetics Department
Operating Report
For April 19x0

Supervisor: H. Rosalind	Budgeted	Actual
Sales, women's cosmetics	$54,600	$56,100
Sales, men's cosmetics	28,700	31,200
Total sales	$83,300	$87,300
Cost of goods sold, women's cosmetics	$38,000	$41,600
Cost of goods sold, men's cosmetics	15,700	17,740
Selling commissions	5,200	5,325
Buyer's salary	2,000	2,100
Supervisor's salary	2,400	2,400
Advertising expense	8,100	8,650
Depreciation, building	1,400	1,600
Depreciation, furniture and fixtures	800	950
Fire insurance expense	250	250
Travel expenses of buyer	1,640	2,110
Local store overhead charges	4,200	5,400
Total costs	$79,690	$88,125
Net income (loss) before taxes	$ 3,610	$ (825)

Assuming the Cosmetics Department is a profit center, prepare a performance report, in income statement format, for the department manager, Ms. Rosalind.

Exercise 7-7.
Evaluating
Performance:
Investment Center
(L.O. 6)

Operating results of the Boating Accessories Department of Robles Industries for January 19x1 is shown below.

Robles Industries
Performance Report
Boating Accessories Department
For the Month Ended January 31, 19x1

Supervisor: Aide Selbor Investment Base: $883,500	Budgeted	Actual	Difference Over (Under) Budget
Controllable by Supervisor			
Sales			
Boat motors	$ 52,400	$ 56,340	$3,940
Water-sports equipment	36,500	31,890	(4,610)
Boat-repair parts	18,200	16,430	(1,770)
Total sales	$107,100	$104,660	($2,440)
Cost of goods sold			
Boat motors	$ 36,680	$ 34,640	($2,040)
Water-sports equipment	21,900	19,220	(2,680)
Boat-repair parts	14,560	15,690	1,130
Total cost of goods sold	$ 73,140	$ 69,550	($3,590)
Gross margin from sales	$ 33,960	$ 35,110	$1,150
Less operating costs			
Heating and electricity	$ 1,460	$ 1,660	$ 200
Depreciation, building	1,980	2,240	260
Fire insurance, building	450	450	0
Employee fringe benefits	2,130	2,350	220
Supervisors' costs	4,600	4,850	250
Storewide overhead costs	2,880	3,260	380
Department overhead costs	1,920	1,430	(490)
Other operating costs	870	240	(630)
Total operating costs	$ 16,290	$ 16,480	$ 190
Controllable department income	$ 17,670	$ 18,630	$ 960
Controllable department return on investment	2.00%	2.11%	0.11%
Uncontrollable by Supervisor			
Depreciation, equipment	$ 3,800	$ 3,800	$ 0
Selling commissions	8,787	8,079	(708)
Repair labor	5,060	5,510	450
Total uncontrollable operating costs	$ 17,647	$ 17,389	($ 258)
Net department income before **taxes**	$ 23	$ 1,241	$1,218

Analyze this performance report. State your opinion of Ms. Selbor's performance. Was her performance report structured properly? As part of your analysis, prepare a gross margin report for the three sales categories.

Exercise 7-8.
Behavioral
Considerations
(L.O. 4)

An effective budget converts management's objectives and goals into data. A budget often serves as a blueprint of management's operating plans. A budget is frequently the basis of control. Management's performance can be evaluated by comparing actual results with budgeted results.

Thus creating the budget is essential to the success of an organization. Implementing the budget and getting to the ultimate goal require extensive use of human resources. How the people involved perceive their roles is important if the budget is to be used effectively as a management tool for planning, communicating, and controlling.

Discuss the behavioral implications of budgetary planning and control when a company's management uses

1. An imposed budgetary approach
2. A participative budgetary approach   (ICMA adapted)

Interpreting Accounting Information

Internal
Management
Information:
California Produce
Company
(L.O. 2, 6)

The Packing and Storage Department at California Produce Company is run by Elaine Waring. A responsibility accounting system was recently installed. A performance report is prepared monthly for each of the company's cost centers.

California Produce Company
Performance Report
Packing and Storage Department
For the Month Ended May 31, 19x9

Amount Budgeted	Cost Item	Actual Amount	Over (Under) Budget
$ 3,500	Packing materials	$ 3,600	$ 100
1,800	Packing supplies	1,700	(100)
8,240	Wages, packing	8,110	(130)
5,680	Wages, storage	5,820	140
4,500	Salaries, packing and storage	4,500	0
1,600	Salaries, vice president's staff	3,100	1,500
1,840	Depreciation, packing machinery	1,820	(20)
3,200	Depreciation, storage warehouse	3,200	0
1,250	Depreciation, companywide office building	2,500	1,250
870	Electric power, packing and storage	910	40
490	Electric power, main office	580	90
575	Heating, packing and storage	600	25
380	Heating, main office	420	40
780	Equipment rental, packing	750	(30)
410	Equipment rental, main office	450	40
290	Insurance expense, packing and storage	290	0
160	Insurance expense, total company	180	20
460	Equipment maintenance expense, packing and storage	440	(20)
220	Lift truck expense, packing and storage	200	(20)
250	Miscellaneous expense	260	10
$36,495	Totals	$39,430	$2,935

Look at Ms. Waring's performance report for May. Top management notices that the $2,935 is 8.04 percent over budget, far above the 4 percent tolerance agreed on. Amounts allocated to the Packing and Storage Department were figured by means of appropriate allocation bases.

Required

1. Using the concept of controllable costs, identify the costs that should not be in Ms. Waring's performance report.
2. Recast the performance report, using only those costs controllable by the department's supervisor.
3. How should Ms. Waring respond to top management?

Problem Set A

Problem 7A-1.
Allocation and
Responsibility of
Overhead
(L.O. 2, 6)

Eagle Manufacturing Company operates as a decentralized enterprise. There are seven responsibility centers in the factory area: molding, finishing, storage, receiving, shipping, scheduling, and inspection. During February, the Factory Overhead account was charged with $382,400 in indirect management-related expenses. Management wants these costs allocated to responsibility centers. It is considering three allocation bases: square footage, total costs incurred, and labor hours. The following information was provided to support the allocation analysis:

Department	Square Footage	Total Costs Incurred	Labor Hours
Molding	3,500	$ 435,060	640
Finishing	2,625	217,530	1,920
Storage	4,375	72,510	320
Receiving	1,750	145,020	1,280
Shipping	875	217,530	640
Scheduling	1,750	72,510	320
Inspection	2,625	290,040	1,280
Totals	17,500	$1,450,200	6,400

Required

1. Allocate the balance in the Factory Overhead account to the seven departments, using as a basis (a) square footage, (b) total costs incurred, and (c) labor hours.
2. For performance evaluation, which of the factory overhead distributions computed in **1** above leads to the most effective control of costs? Defend your answer.

Problem 7A-2.
Cost/Expense
Centers:
Performance
Evaluation
(L.O. 2, 6)

Burrows Brothers Specialty Company makes two types of road construction barricades. Department A produces brightly colored, cone-shaped support structures to identify detour areas. Department B specializes in colored crossbars, which are mounted onto vehicles to divert traffic from heavy construction areas. David Burrows manages Department A; Ron Burrows, Department B. Operating data for April are shown in the following chart. Each department is considered a cost/expense center because sales of each item are the Marketing Department's responsibility.

	Department A		Department B	
	Budgeted	Actual	Budgeted	Actual
Direct materials	$ 14,200	$ 16,100	$ 15,000	$ 14,100
Direct labor	34,100	35,400	41,000	40,200
Factory overhead				
Indirect labor	21,000	22,050	24,600	24,250
Supplies	3,400	3,520	6,400	6,650
Depreciation, building	2,100	2,350	2,700	2,800
Depreciation, equipment	3,600	3,900	3,700	4,200
Property taxes, factory	750	810	850	930
Electricity	1,340	1,360	1,410	1,400
Repairs, machinery	1,600	1,450	1,800	1,900
Insurance, building	900	1,020	950	1,100
Advertising expense	1,500	2,100	2,000	2,200
Packaging costs	6,400	6,600	7,100	6,940
Departmental supervision	5,900	6,100	5,900	6,240
General and administrative overhead	8,200	12,500	9,100	13,200
Interest expense				
Corporate loans	960	1,210	1,080	1,340
Total costs	$105,950	$116,470	$123,590	$127,450
Units of output	17,588	18,620	25,820	25,260

Required

1. Prepare a performance report for each of the two departments. Assume the company employs a responsibility accounting system.
2. Evaluate the performance of the two managers, using data provided in **1** above.

Problem 7A-3.
Profit Centers:
Performance
Evaluation
(L.O. 2, 6)

Label & Mori, a national men's clothing chain, has two stores in Honolulu, Hawaii. Wayne is the manager of the Manoa store; Joe, the Aloha store. The general ledger for the Hawaii branch revealed the data shown on the next page for April 1–June 30, 19x1.

Wayne and Joe are responsible for store revenues and specific store expenditures. They do not make decisions about store buildings or fixtures. Corporate expenses are allocated to the stores by the company's home office.

Salaries of $14,500 and $13,500 were budgeted for the Manoa and Aloha stores, respectively. Actual costs for salaries were $16,200 in Manoa and $12,900 in Aloha.

Selling commissions were 6 percent of total sales dollars in both stores for budgeted and actual sales as shown on the bottom of the next page.

Label & Mori
Operating Data
For April 1–June 30, 19x1

	Budgeted		Actual	
	Debit	Credit	Debit	Credit
Shoe sales				
Manoa store		$124,500		$122,100
Aloha store		110,900		114,750
Clothing sales				
Manoa store		296,000		286,900
Aloha store		245,000		256,200
Cost of goods sold, shoes				
Manoa store	$ 56,000		$ 55,940	
Aloha store	49,900		51,230	
Cost of goods sold, clothing				
Manoa store	262,800		259,790	
Aloha store	234,750		239,160	
Salaries and selling commissions	74,584		75,897	
Depreciation, store fixtures				
Manoa store	15,200		15,400	
Aloha store	12,400		12,400	
Depreciation, buildings				
Manoa store	8,100		8,300	
Aloha store	6,700		6,900	
Utility expense	9,340		9,540	
Advertising expense	13,000		15,790	
Miscellaneous selling expenses	4,660		4,679	
Insurance expense	2,400		2,600	
Corporate administrative salaries	12,500		14,600	
Interest expense, corporate loans	5,200		5,600	
Totals	$767,534	$776,400	$777,826	$779,950

	Budgeted	Actual
Manoa store	$25,230	$24,540
Aloha store	$21,354	$22,257

Utility expenses were:

	Budgeted	Actual
Manoa store	$5,240	$5,600
Aloha store	$4,100	$3,940

Advertising expense was:

	Budgeted	**Actual**
Manoa store	$7,400	$9,640
Aloha store	$5,600	$6,150

Miscellaneous selling expenses were:

	Budgeted	**Actual**
Manoa store	$2,520	$2,454
Aloha store	$2,140	$2,225

All insurance expense is assigned to the Manoa and Aloha stores on a 70 percent/30 percent basis, respectively.

All salaries and expenses for corporate administration are assigned to the Manoa and Aloha stores on a 60 percent/40 percent basis, respectively.

Required

1. Prepare a performance report for the quarter ended June 30, 19x1, using a responsibility accounting format for the Manoa store.
2. Prepare a performance report for the quarter ended June 30, 19x1, using a responsibility accounting format for the Aloha store.
3. Compare the performances of Wayne and Joe. As part of your report, prepare a gross margin analysis for each product line.

Problem 7A-4.
Performance
Evaluation:
Centralized Versus
Decentralized
Organization in an
Investment Center
(L.O. 2, 4, 5, 6)

Ferris Leather Processors, Inc., has twelve processing plants throughout the country. Its home office is Kansas City, Missouri. Organizationally, the corporation is operated in a centralized manner, with each plant targeting operations to the goals and budgets set by the home office. The targeted rate of return on investment is 12 percent before taxes for each plant.

Two plants being investigated for low operating results are in Michigan, one in Big Rapids, the other, just outside Mackinaw City. The plant in Big Rapids specializes in leather accessories and is managed by Dick Hanna. Leather clothing is the specialty of the Mackinaw City plant, which is managed by Dean Scheerens.

Leather goods are purchased centrally in raw finished form and shipped to each plant in bulk shipping cases. Each plant then cleans, shapes, and packages the goods for shipment to customers. Sales are made by salespeople connected with each plant, but advertising decisions and expenditures are made by the home office. All decisions on purchasing equipment and building space as well as truck fleet rental are made in Kansas City. Operating losses of other plants and general and administrative corporate expenses are allocated to each plant.

The performance report for the year ending May 31, 19x9, is shown on the next page.

Required

1. Identify the problems inherent in the organizational structure Ferris Leather Processors, Inc., uses. Also identify the behavorial and operational performance evaluation principles Ferris is not following.

Ferris Leather Processors, Inc.
Performance Report
For the Year Ended May 31, 19x9

	Leather Accessories Plant		Leather Clothing Plant	
	Budgeted	Actual	Budgeted	Actual
Sales				
Accessories	$1,400,000	$1,610,700	$ 0	$ 0
Clothing	0	0	2,750,000	3,242,000
Miscellaneous	250,000	239,400	350,000	410,290
Total sales	$1,650,000	$1,850,100	$3,100,000	$3,652,290
Cost of goods sold				
Accessories	$ 490,000	$ 669,400	$ 0	$ 0
Clothing	0	0	1,237,500	1,652,900
Miscellaneous	95,000	105,760	140,000	163,400
Cleaning and shaping labor	184,500	192,400	265,000	291,700
Outside contractual services	62,000	67,200	115,000	122,800
Corporate buyer's expenses	116,600	146,250	235,000	292,100
Special packaging costs	186,200	190,700	290,000	301,040
Depreciation expense, equipment	32,700	35,100	52,500	52,500
Depreciation expense, building	26,900	27,900	44,800	51,640
Utility expense	12,870	14,230	22,600	23,770
Telephone expense	3,200	3,470	5,400	5,880
Delivery trucks, fuel	4,250	4,510	7,500	7,390
Delivery trucks, repairs	3,900	4,110	5,800	5,410
Truck rental expense	10,400	10,400	20,800	20,800
Property taxes	17,500	19,100	31,200	33,810
Fire and liability insurance	2,400	2,600	3,900	3,950
Sales commissions	66,000	74,000	124,000	146,090
Other selling expenses	22,200	23,840	41,300	40,240
Advertising expense	49,300	67,400	84,200	102,720
Loss, Portland, Oregon, plant	16,100	17,900	16,100	17,900
Plantwide overhead	14,900	13,600	26,700	25,160
Corporate expense, general and administrative	42,500	51,400	81,600	97,270
Total expenses	$1,459,420	$1,741,270	$2,850,900	$3,458,470
Plant net income before taxes	$ 190,580	$ 108,830	$ 249,100	$ 193,820
Investment base	$1,588,160	$1,588,160	$2,075,830	$2,075,830
Plant return on investment	12.00%	6.85%	12.00%	9.34%

2. Recast the information given into a performance evaluation summary. Assume that Ferris' organizational structure is decentralized and that it uses a responsibility accounting reporting format. Also assume that everything except buyer's expenses and other corporate allocations is under the control of each manager.
3. Compute the rates of return for each plant, using the data generated in **2.**

Problem 7A-5.
Performance
Evaluation
(L.O. 2, 3, 6)

George Johnson was hired on July 1, 19x9, as assistant general manager of the Botel Division of Staple, Inc. Besides becoming acquainted with the division and the general manager's duties, Mr. Johnson was given specific responsibility for developing the 19x0 and 19x1 budgets. When he was hired, it was understood that he would be elevated to general manager of the division on January 1, 19x1,

Staple, Inc.
Comparative Profit Report ($000 Omitted)

	Actual			Budgeted	
Botel Division	**19x9**	**19x0**	**19x1**	**19x1**	**19x2**
Sales	$1,000	$1,500	$1,800	$2,000	$2,400
Less					
Divisional variable costs					
Materials and labor	$ 250	$ 375	$ 450	$ 500	$ 600
Repairs	50	75	50	100	120
Supplies	20	30	36	40	48
Less					
Division-managed costs					
Employee training	30	35	25	40	45
Maintenance	50	55	40	60	70
Less					
Division-committed costs					
Depreciation	120	160	160	200	200
Rent	80	100	110	140	140
Total	$ 600	$ 830	$ 871	$1,080	$1,223
Divisional net contribution	$ 400	$ 670	$ 929	$ 920	$1,177
Divisional investment					
Accounts receivable	$ 100	$ 150	$ 180	$ 200	$ 240
Inventory	200	300	270	400	480
Fixed assets	1,590	2,565	2,800	3,380	4,000
Less					
Accounts and wages payable	(150)	(225)	(350)	(300)	(360)
Net investment	$1,740	$2,790	$2,900	$3,680	$4,360
Contribution return on net investment	23%	24%	32%	25%	27%

when the current general manager retired. This was done. As general manager in 19x1, he was obviously responsible for the 19x2 budget.

Staple, Inc., is a multiproduct company that is highly decentralized. Each division is quite autonomous. The corporate staff approves operating budgets prepared by the divisions but seldom makes major changes in them. The corporate staff actively participates in decisions requiring capital investment for expansion or replacement and makes final decisions. Divisional management is responsible for implementing the capital investment program. The major method Staple, Inc., uses to measure divisional performance is contribution return on a division's net investments. The budgets on page 268 were approved by the corporation. (Revision of the 19x2 budget is considered unnecessary even though 19x1 actual departed from the 19x1 budgeted.)

Required

1. Identify Mr. Johnson's responsibilities under the management and measurement program described above.
2. Evaluate Mr. Johnson's performance in 19x1.
3. Recommend to the president any changes in the responsibilities assigned to managers or the measurement methods used to evaluate division managers.

(ICMA adapted)

Problem Set B

**Problem 7B-1.
Allocation and
Responsibility of
Overhead**

(L.O. 2, 6)

A division of Hal Reneau Enterprises makes special-order horse saddles for customers in the Southeast. Seven responsibility centers are used to manage the production operation: cutting, trimming, inspection, packing, storage/shipping, central receiving, and scheduling. Management has asked you to make a comparative analysis of the allocation methods that assign corporate overhead costs to these centers. The following data were developed for your use:

Department	Total Costs Incurred	Labor Hours	Labor Dollars
Cutting	$ 428,120	1,200	$ 16,800
Trimming	535,150	1,800	22,400
Inspection	214,060	2,400	11,200
Packing	107,030	1,800	16,800
Storage/Shipping	428,120	1,800	11,200
Central Receiving	321,090	1,800	22,400
Scheduling	107,030	1,200	11,200
	$2,140,600	12,000	$112,000

During July, $165,940 in corporate overhead were assigned to the Saddle Production Division for distribution to the responsibility centers.

Required

1. Allocate the balance of corporate overhead charges to the seven departments, using as a basis (a) total costs incurred, (b) labor hours, and (c) labor dollars.
2. For performance evaluation, which of the overhead distributions computed in 1 above most effectively controls costs? Defend your answer.

Problem 7B-2.
Cost/Expense
Center:
Performance
Evaluation
(L.O. 2, 6)

The City of Dalescotts has hired you as a consultant. Your job is to evaluate the performance of the city's Street Maintenance Department. Ms. Linda Mitchusson is the department's supervisor. To assist you in your analysis, similar costs for the Street Maintenance Department of the City of Fordrock have been assembled. These data for May are shown below:

	City of Dalescotts Street Maintenance Department		City of Fordrock Street Maintenance Department	
	Budgeted	Actual	Budgeted	Actual
Materials				
Concrete	$ 60,400	$ 58,100	$ 29,500	$ 34,600
Bedrock	52,900	48,990	22,000	24,280
Asphalt	294,800	281,420	146,100	159,200
Labor				
Heavy construction	116,740	118,410	62,400	64,100
Light construction	72,220	73,930	41,000	41,940
Overhead				
Helper labor	105,200	110,560	62,900	64,110
Equipment repairs	9,400	9,820	6,150	6,020
Vehicle repairs	4,210	4,470	2,050	2,000
Fuel expense	6,240	6,810	3,940	4,090
Depreciation, equipment	10,100	10,800	6,200	6,200
Depreciation, vehicles	17,000	19,450	11,000	13,200
Liability insurance	2,040	2,240	1,400	1,600
Operating supplies	3,210	3,620	1,800	1,890
Electricity expense	1,740	2,110	910	940
Construction-site housing	6,940	6,910	3,900	4,140
Supervision	9,280	9,280	6,100	6,310
City overhead charges	12,980	13,800	8,200	8,860
Mayor's election activities	4,200	4,400	2,600	3,600
City council charges	7,900	8,800	4,200	5,190
Total costs	$797,500	$793,920	$422,350	$452,270
Number of road repair requests honored	35	31	22	28

Required

1. Prepare a performance report for each of the two departments. Assume the two cities employ responsibility accounting systems.
2. Evaluate Ms. Mitchusson's performance, using data provided from **1** above.

Problem 7B-3.
Profit Centers:
Performance
Evaluation
(L.O. 2, 6)

Jim Peters and Larry Scott manage the E & W and PW branches of Recruiters Appliances, Inc. All goods sold by these stores fall into two groups: white goods and brown goods. White goods include refrigerators, freezers, washing machines, and clothes dryers; brown goods include televisions, radios, and stereos. The general ledger for Recruiters Appliances, Inc., for February revealed the following information:

Recruiters Appliances, Inc.
Operating Data
For February 19x1

	Budgeted		Actual	
	Debit	Credit	Debit	Credit
Sales, white goods				
E & W store		$125,400		$136,550
PW store		152,100		146,640
Sales, brown goods				
E & W store		86,200		97,240
PW store		120,700		116,120
Cost of goods sold, white goods				
E & W store	$ 68,970		$ 74,560	
PW store	83,655		81,650	
Cost of goods sold, brown goods				
E & W store	51,720		56,940	
PW store	72,420		70,880	
Salaries and selling commissions	56,552		58,595	
Utility expense	3,630		3,860	
Advertising expense	14,000		16,060	
Insurance expense	2,400		2,600	
Depreciation expense, fixtures				
E & W store	5,900		6,100	
PW store	8,200		9,980	
Rent expense	7,700		8,000	
Miscellaneous selling expenses	3,870		3,970	
Corporate administrative salaries	8,400		8,600	
Interest expense, corporate loans	2,500		2,900	
Totals	$389,917	$484,400	$404,695	$496,550

Peters and Scott are responsible for store profits based on each store's sales and expenditures, which are made and approved by each manager. None of the managers make decisions concerning fixture purchases, but all are responsible for store rent. Corporate expenses are allocated to each store from the corporation's home office.

Salaries of $8,200 and $9,600 were budgeted for the E & W and PW stores, respectively. Actual salaries were $8,450 for E & W and $10,410 for PW.
Selling commissions were as follows:

	Budgeted	Actual
E & W store	$16,928	$18,710
PW store	$21,824	$21,025

Utility expense was:

	Budgeted	Actual
E & W store	$1,640	$1,750
PW store	$1,990	$2,110

Advertising expense was:

	Budgeted	Actual
E & W store	$6,200	$6,450
PW store	$7,800	$9,610

Insurance expense was assigned to E & W and PW stores on a 35 percent/65 percent basis, respectively.

Rent expense was:

	Budgeted	Actual
E & W store	$3,200	$3,200
PW store	$4,500	$4,800

Miscellaneous selling expenses were:

	Budgeted	Actual
E & W store	$1,690	$1,870
PW store	$2,180	$2,100

Corporate administrative salaries and interest expense were assigned to E & W and PW stores on a 40 percent/60 percent basis, respectively.

Required

1. Prepare a monthly performance report, based on a responsibility accounting format, for the E & W store.
2. Prepare a monthly performance report, based on a responsibility accounting format, for the PW store.
3. For your report, compare Mr. Peters' and Mr. Scott's performances. Include a gross margin analysis of white goods and brown goods.

Problem 7B-4.
Investment Center
Performance
Evaluation:
Centralized Versus
Decentralized
Organization
(L.O. 2, 4, 5, 6)

Fritzemeyer Motors, Inc., is a retail automobile sales company with eight divisions in the Midwest. The company specializes in automobiles manufactured in Sweden and England. Organizationally, the company is operated in a centralized fashion. Each division patterns its budgets to the goals and targets set by the home office in Iowa City, Iowa. Top management has said that it expects a 14 percent rate of return on investment for the current quarter.

Two of the eight divisions have not been operating at the expected level. The troubled operations are in Akron, Ohio, and Peoria, Illinois. Akron is managed by Dick Metcalf; Peoria, by Mike Lane.

Fritzemeyer Motors, Inc.
Performance Report
For the Quarter Ended September 30, 19x8

	Akron, Ohio Division		Peoria, Illinois Division	
	Budgeted	Actual	Budgeted	Actual
Sales				
Swedish-made autos	$ 836,000	$ 914,440	$ 704,000	$ 802,390
English-made autos	736,000	702,960	552,000	562,610
Parts and repairs	125,500	136,130	98,600	101,840
Total sales	$1,697,500	$1,753,530	$1,354,600	$1,466,840
Cost of goods sold				
Swedish-made autos	$ 601,600	$ 690,440	$ 472,400	$ 561,230
English-made autos	504,800	491,960	353,600	363,740
Parts	37,650	47,560	29,580	34,660
Repair labor	43,925	49,880	34,510	37,230
Sales commissions, automobiles	141,480	145,566	113,040	129,675
Corporate buyer's expense	21,250	26,900	15,460	22,310
Utility expense	4,250	4,320	3,980	3,920
Demonstration automobile expense	2,750	3,810	3,250	3,140
Depreciation, demonstration automobiles	2,100	2,260	2,800	2,990
Depreciation, equipment	3,600	3,600	3,250	3,350
Depreciation, building	2,750	2,950	2,600	2,600
Telephone charges	1,440	1,520	1,350	1,390
Advertising expense	11,780	14,790	21,400	23,110
Promotion costs	8,550	9,920	10,640	9,750
Other selling expenses	2,340	2,440	2,280	2,280
Property taxes	920	970	880	910
Insurance, fire and liability	790	790	640	730
Divisional overhead	4,250	4,530	5,350	5,260
Loss, Lincoln, Nebraska, division	2,600	3,100	2,600	3,100
Corporate general and administrative expenses	7,250	7,750	6,150	6,320
Total expenses	$1,406,075	$1,515,056	$1,085,760	$1,217,695
Divisional net income before taxes	$ 291,425	$ 238,474	$ 268,840	$ 249,145
Investment base	$2,081,600	$2,081,600	$1,920,280	$1,920,280
Divisional return on investment	14.00%	11.46%	14.00%	12.97%

All automobiles are purchased by the home office and shipped to the divisions. Each division then cleans and otherwise prepares the cars for sale. Sales commissions are earned by local salespeople, but advertising and promotion costs are controlled by the home office. Central management makes all decisions concerning the purchase of equipment and buildings. Operating losses of other divisions as well as corporate general and administrative expenses are allocated to the divisions.

The performance report for the two divisions for the quarter ended September 30, 19x8 is on page 273.

Required

1. What problems are inherent in the organizational structure Fritzemeyer Motors, Inc., uses? In your discussion, include the behavioral and operational performance evaluation principles not being followed.
2. Recast the information given into a performance evaluation summary based on a decentralized organizational structure. Use a responsibility accounting reporting format. Assume that control is shifted to each manager for everything except buyer's expenses and other corporate allocations.
3. Compute the rates of return for each division, using the data from **2**.

**Problem 7B-5.
Responsibility
Accounting and
Budgets**
(L.O. 2,3,4,5)

Argon County Hospital is located in the county seat. Argon county is a well-known summer resort area. The county's population doubles during the vacation months of May through August, and hospital activity more than doubles. Although Argon is a relatively small hospital, its pleasant surroundings have attracted a well-trained and competent medical staff.

An administrator was hired a year ago to improve the hospital's business activities. Among the new ideas introduced was responsibility accounting. This program was announced in a memo accompanying quarterly cost reports supplied to department heads. Previously, cost data were presented to department heads infrequently. Excerpts from the announcement and the report the laundry supervisor received are on the next page.

The new administrator constructed the annual budget for 19x3. Quarterly budgets were computed as one-fourth of the annual budget. The administrator compiled the budget by analyzing costs from the prior three years. The analysis showed that all costs increased each year and that the increases were more rapid between the second and third years. The administrator considered establishing a budget according to an average of the prior three years' costs, hoping that installation of the system would reduce costs to this level. However, because of rapidly increasing prices, 19x2 costs, less 3 percent, were finally chosen for the 19x3 budget. The activity level measured by patient days and pounds of laundry processed was set at 19x2 volume, which was approximately equal to the volume in each of the past three years.

Required

1. Comment on the method used to construct the budget.
2. What information should be communicated by variations from budget?
3. Does the report effectively communicate the level of efficiency of this department? Give reasons for your answer.

(ICMA adapted)

Argon County Hospital
Performance Report: Laundry Department
For the Months July–September 19x3

	Budget	Actual	(Over) Under Budget	Percent (Over) Under Budget
Patient days	9,500	11,900	(2,400)	(25)
Pounds processed, laundry	125,000	156,000	(31,000)	(25)
Costs				
Laundry labor	$ 9,000	$12,500	($3,500)	(39)
Supplies	1,100	1,875	(775)	(70)
Water, water heating and softening	1,700	2,500	(800)	(47)
Maintenance	1,400	2,200	(800)	(57)
Supervisor's salary	3,150	3,750	(600)	(19)
Allocated administrative costs	4,000	5,000	(1,000)	(25)
Equipment depreciation	1,200	1,250	(50)	(4)
Totals	$21,550	$29,075	($7,525)	(35)

Administrator's comments:
Costs are significantly above budget for the quarter. Particular attention should be paid to labor, supplies, and maintenance. The hospital has adopted a responsibility accounting system. From now on you will receive quarterly reports, which will compare the costs of operating your department with budgeted costs. The reports will highlight differences (variations) so you can zero in on departures from budgeted costs. (This is called management by exception.) Responsibility accounting means you are accountable for keeping the costs in your department within budget. Variations from the budget will help you identify out-of-line costs. The size of the variation will indicate which costs are most important. Your first report accompanies this announcement.

Management Decision Case

Kelly Petroleum Company
(L.O.1,4,5,6)

Kelly Petroleum Company has a large oil and natural gas project in Oklahoma. The project has been organized into two production centers (Petroleum Production and Natural Gas Production) and one service center (Maintenance).

Don Pepper, maintenance center manager, has organized his maintenance workers into work crews that serve the two production centers. The crews perform preventive maintenance and repair equipment both in the field and in the central maintenance shop.

Pepper is responsible for scheduling all maintenance work in the field and at the central shop. Preventive maintenance is performed according to a set schedule established by Pepper and approved by production center managers.

Breakdowns are given immediate priority in scheduling, so downtime is minimized. Thus preventive maintenance must occasionally be postponed, but every attempt is made to reschedule it within three weeks.

Preventive maintenance is Pepper's responsibility. However, if a significant problem is discovered during the work, a production center supervisor authorizes and supervises the repair after checking with Pepper.

When there is a breakdown in the field, the production centers contact Pepper to initiate the repairs. The work is supervised by a production center supervisor. Machinery and equipment must sometimes be replaced while they are being repaired in the central shop. This procedure is followed only when the time to make a repair would significantly interrupt operations. Equipment replacement is recommended by the maintenance work crew supervisor and approved by a production center supervisor.

Routine preventive maintenance and breakdowns of automotive and mobile equipment used in the field are completed in the central shop. All repairs and maintenance activities in the central shop are under the direction of Pepper.

Maintenance Center Accounting Activities. Pepper has records identifying the work crews assigned to each job in the field, the number of hours spent on the job, and the parts and supplies used. In addition, records for the central shop (jobs, labor hours, and parts and supplies) have been maintained. However, this detailed maintenance information is not incorporated into Kelly's accounting system.

Pepper develops the annual budget for the maintenance center by (1) planning the preventive maintenance needed during the year, (2) estimating the number and seriousness of breakdowns, and (3) estimating shop activities. He then estimates the labor, parts, and supply costs and develops budget amounts by line item. Because the timing of the breakdowns is impossible to plan, Pepper divides the annual budget by 12 to derive monthly budgets.

All costs incurred by work crews in the field and in the central shop are accumulated monthly and are then allocated to the two production cost centers based on the field hours worked in each production center. This method of cost allocation has been used because of Pepper's recommendation that it was easy to implement and understand. Furthermore, he believed that a better allocation system was impossible to incorporate into monthly reports because of the wide range of salaries paid to maintenance workers and the fast turnover of materials and parts.

The November cost report for the Maintenance Center, provided by the Accounting Department, is shown on the next page.

Production Center Manager's Concerns. Both production center managers have been upset with the cost allocation method. Furthermore, they believe the report is virtually useless as a cost control device. Actual costs always seem to deviate from the monthly budget, and the proportion charged to each production center varies significantly from month to month. Maintenance costs have increased substantially since 1987, and production managers believe they have no way of judging whether such an increase is reasonable.

The two production managers, Pepper, and representatives of corporate accounting met to discuss these concerns. They concluded that a responsibility accounting system should be developed to replace the current system. In their opinion a responsibility accounting system would alleviate the production managers' concerns and accurately reflect activity in the Maintenance Center.

Oklahoma Project
Maintenance Center Cost Report
For the Month of November 1989
(in thousands of dollars)

	Budgeted	Actual	Petroleum Production	Natural Gas Production
Shop hours	2,000	1,800	—	—
Field hours	8,000	10,000	6,000	4,000
Labor, electrical	$ 25.0	$ 24.0	$ 14.4	$ 9.6
Labor, mechanical	30.0	35.0	21.0	14.0
Labor, instrumentation	18.0	22.5	13.5	9.0
Labor, automotive	3.5	2.8	1.7	1.1
Labor, heavy equipment	9.6	12.3	7.4	4.9
Labor, equipment operation	28.8	35.4	21.2	14.2
Labor, general	15.4	15.9	9.5	6.4
Parts	60.0	86.2	51.7	34.5
Supplies	15.3	12.2	7.3	4.9
Lubricants and fuels	3.4	3.0	1.8	1.2
Tools	2.5	3.2	1.9	1.3
Accounting and data processing	1.5	1.5	.9	.6
Totals	$213.0	$254.0	$152.3	$101.7

Required

1. Explain the purposes of a responsibility accounting system. Also, discuss how such a system could resolve the concern of production center managers.
2. Describe behavioral advantages generally attributed to responsibility accounting systems that management should expect if the system is effectively introduced into the maintenance center.
3. Describe a report format for the maintenance center based on an effective responsibility accounting system. Explain which, if any, of the maintenance center's costs should be charged to the two production centers.

(ICMA adapted)

CHAPTER 8

The Budgeting Process

The budgetary control process includes cost planning and cost control. In this chapter the focus is on cost planning. We outline the principles of budgeting, which deal with long-term and short-term goals, human responsibilities, housekeeping, and follow-up. Using these principles along with a number of cost accounting tools explained earlier in the book, we describe the preparation of period budgets, the master budget, and the cash budget. After studying this chapter, you should be able to meet the learning objectives listed on the left.

What Is a Budget and What Does It Look Like?

Someone who has never worked with a budget may consider such a document a cure-all for the financial problems of an enterprise because almost everyone uses the word *budget* in this context. Recall any discussion on television or in the newspapers regarding our federal budget. We have all heard about deficit spending by the U.S. government over the past four or five decades, and the cure for this deficit spending is to "balance the budget." This statement is misleading because the spending processes cannot be used to balance the budget. What politicians and news commentators are really saying is: To reduce or reverse the current deficit, one must ensure that the intake is greater than the payout. But there is only one way to balance a budget, and that is by preparing the document so the revenue side equals the expenditure side. That is all there is to it.

A budget is a financial document created before anticipated transactions occur and is often called a financial plan of action. The key to understanding the term budget is to realize that it is nothing more than a piece of paper on which financial data are printed. These data have been projected for a series of events that have yet to occur. It is a printed crystal ball view of a set of financial transactions.

Now that you have a feel for how a budget operates as a financial document, what does a budget look like? A budget can take on an infinite number of shapes and forms. The structure depends on what is being budgeted, the size of the organization preparing the budget, the degree to which the budgeting process is integrated into the financial structure of the enterprise, and the amount of training in the preparer's background. Unlike the

OBJECTIVE 1
Describe the structure and contents of a budget

formal income statement or the balance sheet, a budget does not have a standard form that the student of budgeting can memorize. A budget can be as simple as the projected sales and costs of a corner soft drink stand or as complicated as the financial projections of General Motors Corporation for the upcoming year.

A budget should contain enough information presented in an orderly manner so that its purpose is communicated to the reader or user. Too much information clouds the meaning and accuracy of the data. Too little information may result in overspending because the reader did not understand the spending limits suggested by the document. A budget need not contain both revenue and expense components, nor does it have to be balanced. A materials purchases budget, for example, contains only projected expenditures for materials for the period being analyzed. A budget can also be made up *entirely* of nondollar data, such as hours, units of product, or number of services.

When preparing a budget, make sure you include a clearly stated title or heading and the time period under consideration. Clearly label the budget's components, and list the unit and financial data in an orderly manner. The actual format of the budget is developed by the budget preparer. Of course, a company may have developed its own budget format for recurring budget instruments used on a regular basis. But if a new service or product needs budget information to support its value to the company, the document need not follow other budget structures and formats. The only underlying concept that must be followed is that the information contained in the budget should be as accurate as possible and meaningful to the recipient.

Exhibit 8-1 contains two simple budgets prepared for diverse purposes. They are for illustrative purposes only and should not be considered official guidelines for budget preparation when doing the chapter assignments. You should use your imagination and create your own budget formats. Example 1 is the revenues and expenditures budget of the Boosters Club for the homecoming football game of the State University Knights. Example 2 contains projections of hotel occupancy for the Down Home Resort. Note that in Example 2, the budget contains no dollar information and is not balanced.

Basic Principles of Budgeting

The preparation of an organization's budget is the single most important aspect of its success. First, it forces management to look ahead and try to see the future of the organization regarding both long- and short-term goals and events. Second, it requires that the entire management team, from the lowest-level supervisor to the chief executive officer, work together to make and carry out the yearly plans. Finally, by comparing the budget with actual results, it is possible to review performance at all levels of management. Table 8-1 summarizes the principles of effective budgeting. Each group of principles is explained further to show how closely connected the principles are to the whole budgeting process.

Exhibit 8-1. Examples of Budgets

Example 1

State University Knights
Boosters Club
Revenue and Expenditure Budget
Homecoming Activities—19x9

Budgeted revenues		
Football concession sales	$22,500	
Homecoming dance tickets		
1,200 at $20	24,000	
Parking fees	425	
Total budgeted revenues		$46,925
Budgeted expenditures		
Dance music group	$ 8,500	
Hall rental	2,000	
Refreshments	3,600	
Printing costs	1,450	
Concession purchases	12,200	
Clean-up costs	4,720	
Miscellaneous	800	
Total budgeted expenditures		33,270
Excess of revenues over expenditures		$13,655

Example 2

Down Home Resort
Room Occupancy Budget
For the Year Ending December 31, 19x7

	Projected Occupancy							
	Singles (50)		Doubles (80)		Minisuites (10)		Luxury Suites (6)	
Month	Rooms	%	Rooms	%	Rooms	%	Rooms	%
January	20	40.0	30	37.5	2	20.0	1	16.7
February	24	48.0	36	45.0	3	30.0	1	16.7
March	28	56.0	42	52.5	4	40.0	2	33.3
April	32	64.0	50	62.5	5	50.0	2	33.3
May	44	88.0	60	75.0	6	60.0	2	33.3
June	46	92.0	74	92.5	7	70.0	3	50.0
July	50	100.0	78	97.5	9	90.0	4	66.7
August	50	100.0	80	100.0	10	100.0	5	83.3
September	48	96.0	78	97.5	10	100.0	6	100.0
October	34	68.0	60	75.0	8	80.0	5	83.3
November	30	60.0	46	57.5	2	20.0	3	50.0
December	34	68.0	50	62.5	4	40.0	4	66.7

Table 8-1. Principles of Effective Budgeting

Group A: Long-Range Goals Principles

1. Develop long-range goals for the enterprise.
2. Convert the long-range goals into statements about long-range plans for product lines or services offered and associated profit plans in broad quantitative terms.

Group B: Short-Range Goals and Strategies Principles

3. Restate the long-range plan in terms of short-range plans for product lines or services available and a detailed profit plan.
4. Prepare a set of budget development plans and a specific timetable for the whole period.

Group C: Human Responsibilities and Interaction Principles

5. Identify the budget director and staff.
6. Identify all participants in budget development.
7. Practice participative budgeting.
8. Obtain the full support of top management, and communicate this support to budget participants.
9. Practice full communications during the entire budgeting process.

Group D: Budget Housekeeping Principles

10. Practice realism in the preparation of all budgets.
11. Require that all budget preparation deadlines be met.
12. Use flexible application procedures.

Group E: Follow-Up Principles

13. Maintain a continual budgeting process, and monitor the budget throughout the period.
14. Develop a system of periodic performance reports linked to assigned responsibilities.
15. Review problem areas to be studied before undergoing further planning.

Long-Range Goals Principles

OBJECTIVE 2
Identify the five groups of budgeting principles and explain the principles in each group

Annual operating plans cannot be made unless those responsible for preparing the budget know the direction in which top management expects the organization to go. Long-range goals must be set by top management. Statements about the expected quality of products or services and about growth rates and percentage-of-market targets are among the long-range goals. Economic and industry forecasts, employee-management relationships, and the structure and role of top management in leading the organization also influence these goals.

It is necessary to name those responsible for achieving the long-term goals and to set actual targets and expected timetables. For example, Kinlin Corporation has as one of its long-term goals the control of 15 percent of its product's market. At present the company holds only 4 percent of the market. The company's long-term goals may state that the vice president of marketing is to develop plans and strategies so the company controls 10 percent of the market in five years and increases its share to 15 percent by the end of ten years.

Once all the organization's goals have been developed, they should be brought together into a total long-range plan. This plan should state a broad range of targets and goals and direct management in trying to reach them. Specific statements about long-term goals, then, are the basis for preparing the annual budget.

Short-Range Goals and Strategies Principles

Using long-range goals, management must prepare yearly operating plans and targets. The short-range plan or budget involves every part of the enterprise and is much more detailed than long-range goals. The first order of business each year is to restate long-range goals as to what should be accomplished during the year. Statements must be made about sales targets by product or service line, profit expectations by division or product line, personnel needs and expected changes, and plans for introducing new products or services. Budget statements must also cover materials and supplies needed, forecasts of such overhead costs as electric power and expected costs of property taxes and insurance, and all capital expenditures, such as new buildings, machinery, and equipment. These short-range targets and goals are woven together to form the organization's operating budget for the year.

An important part of this process is the approach to collecting and processing the information that goes into the annual budget. Once management sets the short-range goals, the controller or budget director takes charge of preparing the budget. He or she designs a complete set of budget development plans and a timetable with deadlines for all levels and parts of the year's operating plan. Specific people must be named to carry out each part of the budget's development and their responsibilities, targets, and deadlines clearly described. The last step in the budget's development is to clearly communicate the plan to the participants. It may seem all too obvious that everyone should be fully aware of the need for and importance of budget development. But do not forget that each participant in the budgeting process has another job in the organization. The production supervisor, for instance, is most interested in what is happening on the production floor. Thinking about the next year's activities does not help meet the current month's production targets. The same can be said for the district sales managers, financial and cost accounting people, and the rest of the staff. It is the budget director's responsibility to organize the budget information, and a key part of that process is making sure each participant knows what he or she is expected to do and when information is due.

Human Responsibilities and Interaction Principles

Budgeting success or failure is largely determined by how well the human aspects of the process are handled. From top management down to the lowest-level supervisor in the organization, *all* appropriate people must take part actively and honestly if the process is to be successful. To get this kind of cooperation, each person must feel that he or she is an important link in the organizational chain.

Choosing a budget director (and staff if necessary) is important to an effective budgeting system. This person must be able to communicate well with people both above and below in the organization's hierarchy. Top management gives the budget targets and organizational goals to the budget director. This person in turn assigns those targets and goals to managers at various levels. The managers then try to put into operation the goals and targets assigned to them. Any problem areas managers find are communicated to the budget director who, after careful analysis, must pass the information on to top management. The targets and goals are then reassessed, restructured, and passed back to the budget director, and the process begins again. Since the budget director acts as an information-gathering center and clearing-house for the budgeting process, the success of the process depends on this person.

All participants in the budget development process should be identified and told early of their responsibilities in the program. The identification process begins with high-level managers. These people must then identify lower-level managers under their supervision who will actually prepare the data. At the lower levels the organization's main activities take place, whether they are production, sales, health care, or education. From these managers the information must flow through all supervisory levels up to top management. Each one of these people plays a part in developing the budget and putting it to work. It is the budget director's job to coordinate all the budgeting activities of the managers.

Participative budgeting means that all levels of supervisory and data input personnel take part in the budgeting process in a meaningful, active way. If every manager has significant input into the goals and expectations of his or her unit, personal motivation will be woven into the budgeting process. This sort of interaction and cooperation is what participative budgeting is all about.

Top management's role is also very important to the budgeting process. If top management simply dictates and sends down targets and goals for others to carry out, participative budgeting is not being practiced. Such dictated targets are often hard to attain and do not motivate lower-level managers to try to reach them. Similarly, if top management simply lets the budget director handle everything, other managers are likely to think that budgeting is a low priority and may not take it seriously. To have an effective budgeting program, top management must communicate its support and enthusiasm to all levels of management and let the managers take part in a meaningful way. If this happens, the principle of practicing full communication has also been followed.

Budget Housekeeping Principles

In terms of housekeeping, the budget process depends heavily on three things. First, participants must take a realistic approach. Second, all deadlines must be met. Third, the organization must use flexible application procedures.

Realism is a two-way street. Top management must first suggest realistic targets and goals. Then, each manager must provide realistic information and not place departmental goals ahead of the goals of the whole organization. Inflated expenditure plans or deflated sales targets in one or two cases may make life easier for a manager's unit. However, they can cause the entire budget to be inaccurate and hard to use as a guide and control mechanism for the organization as a whole.

The reason for having and meeting budget development deadlines is clear. Budget preparation depends on the timely cooperation of many people. If one or two people ignore a deadline for submitting information to their supervisor or the budget director, the budget will not be ready on time. Top management should communicate the importance of the budget development timetable to all participants and review timely budget data submission as part of each manager's performance evaluation.

Budgets are important guides to the actions of management. However, they should always be treated as guides, not as absolute truths. Remember that budgets are prepared almost a year in advance of the actual operating cycle. During that time, unexpected changes may take place. A manager cannot simply ignore these changes just because they were not a part of the original budget. Instead, a means of dealing with revenue and expenditure changes should be worked out as part of budget implementation. A procedure for notifying the budget director of a change and receiving approval for it takes care of the matter and does not upset the performance of the manager's operating unit.

Follow-Up Principles

Budget follow-up and data feedback are really part of the control aspect of budgetary control and are explained further in Chapters 9 and 10. The follow-up principles play an important role in budgeting. Since we are dealing with projections and estimates as the budget is being developed, it is important that the budget be checked continuously and corrected whenever necessary. If a budget is found to be in error, it makes more sense to correct the error than to work with a less accurate guide.

Organizational or departmental expectations can also be unrealistic. Such problems occur when performance reports are used to compare actual results with budgeted or planned operating results. These reports are the backbone of the responsibility accounting system presented in Chapter 7. The budgeting cycle is complete when problems are identified in the performance evaluation of the last budgeting cycle and are analyzed and restructured to become targets or goals of the next budgeting cycle.

The Need for Budgetary Control and Planning

OBJECTIVE 3
Define the concept of budgetary control

Planning and controlling costs and operations are keys to good management. The process of (1) developing plans for a company's expected operations and (2) controlling operations to help carry out those plans is known as **budgetary control**. In Chapters 5 and 6 you studied cost behavior patterns and cost-volume-profit analysis, which are two tools used in developing a company's annual budget and profit goals. Profit planning is important to all successful, profit-oriented companies as part of their budgeting program. In this chapter we deal mainly with the planning element.

A successful business does not reap the benefits of effective budgetary control by operating haphazardly day to day. The company must first set quantitative goals, define the roles of individuals, and set intermediate operating targets. Companies begin by making both long- and short-term operating plans.

First, they must prepare and maintain a long-term plan covering a five- or ten-year period. Such plans are general. They usually describe product-line changes, expansion of plant and facilities, machinery replacement, and changes in marketing strategies. Long-term plans are important because they provide broad goals to work toward through yearly operations.

Yearly operating plans do not automatically grow out of long-term plans. Even though long-term plans provide broad goals, they do not contain specific instructions on how to get the expected results through annual production and sales efforts. Given the five- or ten-year plan, management must translate long-term objectives into more specific goals for each year. Once the goals have been defined for the next accounting period, various levels of managers must work out details of the operations needed to meet them. This task centers on a one-year time period and stated targets.

Short-term or one-year plans are generally formulated in a set of period budgets (also known as detailed operating budgets). A **period budget** is a forecast of a year's operating results for a segment or function of a company. It is a quantitative expression of planned activities. Period budgets are prepared by the entire management team and require timely information and careful coordination. This process converts unit sales and production forecasts into revenue and cost estimates for each of the company's many operating segments. Everyone involved in budgeting should make these forecasts as accurate and realistic as possible.

Period budget preparation relies heavily on several management accounting tools already discussed. Knowledge of cost behavior patterns and use of cost-volume-profit analysis help management project departmental or product-line revenues and costs. Profit planning is possible only after all cost behavior patterns have been identified. Responsibility accounting, with its network of managerial responsibilities and information flows, provides a blueprint for the structure of the budget-data gathering process. These tools, together with the concepts of cost allocation and cost accumulation, provide the foundation for preparing an organization's budget.

The Master Budget

A **master budget** is a combined set of departmental or functional period budgets that have been consolidated into forecasted financial statements for the entire company. Each separate budget gives the projected costs

OBJECTIVE 4
*Identify the
components of a
master budget
and describe how
they relate to
each other*

and revenues for that part of the company. When combined, these budgets show all anticipated company transactions for a future accounting period. With this information, the anticipated results of the company's operations can be put together with the beginning general ledger balances to prepare forecasted statements of the company's net income and financial position for the time period.

Three steps lead to the completed master budget: (1) The period budgets are prepared; (2) the forecasted income statement is prepared; (3) the forecasted balance sheet is prepared. After describing each of these components, we explain how budgets are prepared.

Detailed Period Budgets

Period budgets are generally prepared for each departmental or functional cost and revenue producing segment of the company. These budgets consist of (1) sales budget (in units), (2) production budget (in units), (3) selling expense budget, (4) revenue budget, (5) materials usage budget, (6) materials purchase budget, (7) labor hour requirement budget, (8) labor dollar budget, (9) factory overhead budget, (10) general and administrative (G & A) expense budget, and (11) capital expenditures budget. Although these budgets are referred to by functional area, data are usually developed and transmitted to the budget director in departmental form and consolidated into the functional format described.

Sales Budget. The unit sales forecast is the starting point of the budgeting process and probably the most critical. The sales target is developed by top management with input from marketing and production. Since the entire cost portion of the budget is developed from this forecast, you can see how important it is to the master budget.

Production Budget. Once the sales target in units has been established, the units needed from production can be computed. Management must first determine if the Finished Goods Inventory level should remain the same or be increased or decreased. The unit sales forecast along with the desired changes in Finished Goods Inventory are then used to determine the unit production schedule.

Selling Expense Budget. Selling expenses, such as sales commissions and automobile expenses, may be variable. Other selling-related costs, such as advertising expenses and supervisory salaries, may be fixed. The selling expense budget is the responsibility of the sales department and can be prepared as soon as the sales budget has been completed.

Revenue Budget. The revenue budget is the result of decisions to establish the unit sales forecast and the unit selling prices. Forecasted unit sales are multiplied by selling prices to yield the expected revenue for the budget period.

Materials Usage and Purchase Budgets. The materials usage and purchase budgets can be prepared separately or as part of the same document.

Materials usage is determined by the production budget and the anticipated changes in Materials Inventory levels. This information will generate the units of materials to be purchased. Multiplying the number of units to be purchased by the estimated purchase price for those materials yields the materials purchase budget.

Labor Hour Requirement and Labor Dollar Budgets. As with the previous two budgets, the forecasted labor hours and labor dollars can be structured into two separate budgets or combined in one comprehensive schedule. Labor hours can be determined as soon as the unit production budget has been set. Labor hours needed per unit are multiplied by the anticipated units of production to compute labor hour requirements for the budget period. These labor hours, when multiplied by the various hourly labor rates, yield the labor dollar budget.

Factory Overhead Budget. The budget for factory overhead has two purposes: (1) to integrate overhead cost budgets developed by production and service department managers and (2) to compute factory overhead rates for the forthcoming accounting period after accumulating that information.

General and Administrative Expense Budget. In preparing a master budget, general and administrative expenses must be projected to provide information for the cash budgeting process. The G & A expense budget is also a means of controlling these costs. Most elements of this budget are fixed costs.

Capital Expenditures Budget. Determining capital facility needs and obtaining investment resources for such expenditures are complex areas of management accounting. Deciding what to buy or build and establishing the criteria for decisions regarding return on investment are topics covered in Chapter 13 and explored fully in an advanced management accounting course. For our purposes, information regarding capital facility investment decisions influences the cash budget, the interest expense and depreciation expense on the forecasted income statement, and the plant and equipment account balances on the forecasted balance sheet. Therefore, these decisions must be anticipated and integrated into the master budget.

Relationships Between the Period Budgets

Period budgets are closely related to each other. Following the sales unit forecast, the production budget can be prepared. The selling expense budget also depends on the sales forecast. Direct materials usage and resulting purchase requirements are related to the production forecast. The production budget also leads to labor and factory overhead budgets. In most cases, plans for general and administrative expenses and capital expenditures are made by top management. However, much of this information may be gathered at the departmental level and included in these period budgets. The key point to remember is that the whole budgeting process begins with the sales unit forecast. Figure 8-1 shows how these period budgets set the stage for determining the effects of planned operations on the company's financial position.

Forecasted Income Statement

Once the period budgets have been prepared, the controller or the budget director can begin to put all the information together. He or she prepares a cost of goods sold forecast from data in the direct materials, direct labor, and factory overhead budgets. Revenue information is figured from the unit sales budget. Using the expected revenue and cost of goods sold

Figure 8-1. Preparation of Master Budget

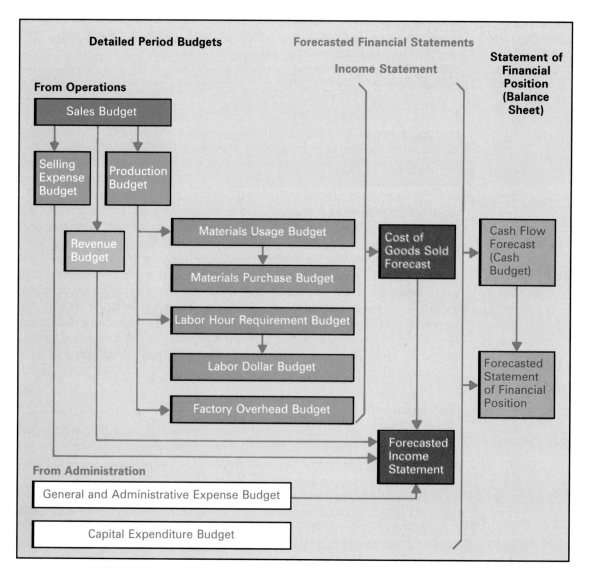

data and adding information from the selling expense and general and administrative expense budgets, the controller can prepare the forecasted income statement. This step is also shown in Figure 8-1.

Financial Position Forecast

The last step in the master budget process is to prepare a financial position forecast or projected balance sheet for the company, assuming that planned activities actually take place. As Figure 8-1 shows, all budget data are used in this process. The controller prepares a cash flow forecast, or cash budget, from all planned transactions requiring cash inflow or expenditure. (A more detailed explanation of cash budgeting follows later in this chapter.) In preparing the forecasted statement of financial position, the budget director must know the projected cash balance and must have determined the net income and amount of capital expenditures. All the expected transactions shown in the period budgets must be classified and posted to general ledger accounts. The projected financial statements are the end product of the budgeting process. At this point management must decide whether to accept the proposed master budget as well as the planned operating results or ask the budget director to change the plans and do parts of the budget over.

Budget Implementation

Budget implementation is the responsibility of the budget director. Two important factors determine the success of this process. First is proper communication of budget expectations and production and profit targets to key people in the company. All people involved in the operations of the business must know what is expected of them and receive directions on how to reach their goals. Second, and equally important, is support and encouragement by top management. No matter how sophisticated the budgeting process is, it will succeed only if middle- and lower-level managers can see that top management is truly interested in the final outcome and willing to reward people for meeting budget goals.

Illustrative Problem: Budget Preparation

OBJECTIVE 5
Prepare a period budget

Period budget preparation and the make-up of the master budget vary from one company to another, so it is impossible to cover all procedures found in actual practice. Our problem shows only one approach to preparing period budgets. However, by applying the tools of cost behavior, C-V-P analysis, and responsibility accounting to a particular case, one can prepare any kind of budget. There is also no standard format to use for budget preparation. The only guidelines are that the budget is clear and understandable and communicates information to the reader.

Downes Steelworks, Inc., manufactures cans from 4- × 8-foot sheets of steel of different thicknesses. The number of cans produced from each sheet of steel depends on the height and diameter of the cans. During 19xx the company expects the following sales and unit changes in inventory:

Can Size	Unit Sales	Unit Change in Finished Goods Inventory
6" × 3"	1,250,000	150,000 (increase)
8" × 4"	710,000	8,000 (decrease)

Direct materials requirements for these two products are as follows:

Can Size	Sheet Steel Type	Average Usable Cans per Sheet	Average Usable Lids per Sheet
6" × 3"	no. 16	90	500
8" × 4"	no. 22	45	270

Usage is the same over a twelve-month period. On the first day of each operating quarter, 25 percent of the year's direct materials requirements will be purchased, starting January 1. Assume no changes in the balances of the Materials Inventory and Work in Process Inventory accounts.

Required

Prepare a direct materials usage budget and a direct materials purchases budget for 19xx. Expected prices for the year are $11.00 per sheet for no. 16 and $13.40 per sheet for no. 22.

Solution

Before preparing the required budgets, you must first compute the total number of cans (including lids for tops and bottoms) to be produced per sheet of steel. The following relationships were supplied by the Engineering Department:

6" × 3" can: 450 cans (plus 900 lids) require 6.8 sheets of steel, so you can manufacture 66.176 cans and lids per sheet of steel

8" × 4" can: 135 cans (plus 270 lids) require 4 sheets of steel, so you can manufacture 33.75 cans and lids per sheet of steel

---

Downes Steelworks, Inc.
Materials Purchases Budget
For the Year Ended December 31, 19xx

Sheet Steel Type	Unit Cost/Sheet	Sheets to Be Purchased Quarterly*	Total Quarterly Purchase Cost	Annual Cost
No. 16	$11.00	5,289	$58,179	$232,716
No. 22	13.40	5,200	69,680	278,720
Total purchases budget				$511,436

---

*Purchases of one-fourth of annual usage on January 1, April 1, July 1, and October 1.

Downes Steelworks, Inc.
Materials Usage Budget
For the Year Ended December 31, 19xx

6″ × 3″ Can	Number of Cans
Expected sales	1,250,000
Plus increase in inventory	150,000
Total to be produced	1,400,000

No. 16 Sheets to be used

$$\frac{\text{Units to be produced}}{\text{Cans per sheet}} = \frac{1{,}400{,}000 \text{ cans}}{66.176 \text{ cans/sheet}} = 21{,}155.71 \text{ or } 21{,}156 \text{ sheets}$$

8″ × 4″ Can	
Expected sales	710,000
Less decrease in inventory	8,000
Total to be produced	702,000

No. 22 Sheets to be used

$$\frac{\text{Units to be produced}}{\text{Cans per sheet}} = \frac{702{,}000 \text{ cans}}{33.75 \text{ cans/sheet}} = 20{,}800 \text{ sheets}$$

Cash Budgeting

Cash flow is one of the most important aspects of a business's operating cycle. Within the master budget preparation cycle, the cash budget is developed after all period budgets are final and the forecasted income statement is complete. A **cash flow forecast**, or **cash budget**, is a projection of cash receipts and cash payments for a future period of time. It sums up the cash results of planned transactions in all phases of a master budget. Generally, it shows the company's projected ending cash balance and the cash position for each month of the year. This permits periods of high and low cash availability to be anticipated. Large cash balances mean funds of the company may not have been used to earn the best possible rate of return. Low cash reserves may mean that the company will be unable to make current payments on amounts it owes. To prevent either problem, careful cash planning is necessary.

The cash budget has two main parts: forecasted cash receipts and forecasted cash disbursements. Sales budgets, cash or credit sales data, and accounts receivable collection data are used to figure expected cash receipts for the period. Other sources of cash, such as the sale of stock, the sale of assets, or loans, also enter into cash receipts planning.

Expected cash disbursements are taken from period budgets. The person preparing the cash budget must know how direct materials, labor, and other goods and services will be purchased. That is, are they to be paid for with cash immediately or purchased on account with the cash payment delayed for a period of time? When dealing with accounts payable, it is important to know the company's payment policies. Besides its use in regular operating expenses, cash is also used for buying equipment and paying off loans and other long-term liabilities. All this information must be available before an accurate cash budget can be prepared.

Purposes and Nature

OBJECTIVE 6
State the purpose and make-up of a cash budget

The cash budget serves two purposes. First, it shows the ending cash balance, which is needed to complete the projected balance sheet (see Figure 8-1). Second, it highlights periods of excess cash reserves or cash shortages. The first purpose focuses on the role of the cash budget in the master budget preparation cycle. The second purpose reflects its use as a tool of cash management, which is important to any business. Without cash a business cannot function. By comparing projected cash receipts and cash payments, the budget director can advise financial executives of the months the company will need extra short-term financing because of cash shortages. Similarly, the budget director can point out times when excess cash will be available for short-term investments.

A cash budget combines information from several period budgets. All elements of cash flow, both cash inflows (cash receipts) and cash outflows (cash disbursements or payments) are brought together to show expected cash flows of the company. Exhibit 8-2 shows the cash budget of Neehon Shohkoo, Inc. To highlight the first quarter of the year, detailed cash inflows and outflows are shown for January, February, and March. The remaining nine months are lumped together in this annual cash forecast.

Now, let's explore the relationship of the cash budget in Exhibit 8-2 to the parts of the master budget in Figure 8-1. Somewhere in all business transactions, cash must come into the picture. Since the master budget is a summary of all expected transactions for a future time period, it must also be the key to all expected cash transactions. To prepare the cash budget, then, one must analyze the master budget in terms of cash inflows and outflows. Table 8-2 focuses on the relationships between the master budget and the cash budget and explains how the cash budget for Neehon Shohkoo, Inc., in Exhibit 8-2 is created. For the next year the company expects only cash receipts from sales. Note that 60 percent of all sales are for cash; 38 percent are credit sales collected in the following month. All the necessary cash inflow information comes from the sales and sales revenue budgets.

Information supporting cash disbursement forecasts comes from several sources. Cash used to purchase direct materials and operating supplies is determined by changing the materials purchase budget into a cash flow analysis. Materials are generally purchased on account. Every company should have a policy about payment on account as part of its cash

Exhibit 8-2. Typical Cash Budget

Neehon Shohkoo, Inc.
Cash Budget
For the Year Ending December 31, 19xx

	January	February	March	April–December	Totals
Cash receipts					
Sales—previous month (38%*)	$ 10,773	$ 7,182	$ 10,773	$ 14,364	$ 43,092
Sales—current month (60%*)	11,340	17,010	22,680	368,928	419,958
Total receipts	$ 22,113	$24,192	$ 33,453	$383,292	$463,050
Cash disbursements					
Direct materials	$ 7,146	$ 7,146	$ 7,622	$ 72,434	$ 94,348
Operating supplies	237	—	—	710	947
Direct labor	3,700	3,850	4,220	34,940	46,710
Factory overhead	3,440	3,480	3,750	32,580	43,250
Selling expenses	8,585	10,000	11,420	109,870	139,875
General and administrative expenses	4,500	4,500	4,500	40,500	54,000
Capital expenditures	4,200	—	7,920	14,780	26,900
Income taxes	—	—	22,640	†	22,640
Interest expense	6,000	—	—	8,920	14,920
Total disbursements	$ 37,808	$28,976	$ 62,072	$314,734	$443,590
Cash increase (decrease)	$(15,695)	$(4,784)	$(28,619)	$ 68,558	$ 19,460
Beginning cash balance	36,275	20,580	15,796	(12,823)	36,275
Ending cash balance	$ 20,580	$15,796	$(12,823)	$ 55,735	$ 55,735

*2% of sales result in uncollectible accounts.
†No payments. Estimated loss for the year.

management. If the company's policy is to pay everything within the discount period, cash flow would occur in 10 or 20 days if the terms of the purchase are 2/10, n/30 or 3/20, n/60. If, however, the company wants to hold its cash for the maximum time, cash payments would not be made for 30 or 60 days. In most cases, direct labor cash flow, for obvious reasons, is delayed very little. Information from the labor dollar budget is used to support the cash payments for both direct and indirect labor services. Cash payments for all factory overhead other than operating supplies and indirect labor are figured by using the factory overhead budget.

Cash requirements for selling expenses, general and administrative expenses, and capital expenditures are determined from their respective budgets. Again, the timing of the cash exchange is important. Selling expenditures, such as gasoline purchases and sales brochures, may be made on credit, and the actual payment may be postponed for thirty

Table 8-2. Master Budget and Cash Budget Interrelationships

Elements of the Cash Budget	Sources of the Information
Cash Receipts	
Cash sales	Sales budget (cash sales)
Cash collections of previous sales	Sales budget (credit sales) plus collection record—percent collected in first month, second month, etc.
Proceeds from sale of assets	Forecasted income statement
Loan proceeds	Previous month's information on cash budget
Cash Disbursements	
Direct materials	Materials purchase budget
Operating supplies	Factory overhead budget and materials purchase budget
Direct labor	Labor dollar budget
Factory overhead	Factory overhead budget
Selling expenses	Selling expense budget
General and administrative expenses	General and administrative expense budget
Capital expenditures	Capital expenditure budget
Income taxes	Estimated from previous year's income statement and current year's projections
Interest expense	Forecasted income statement
Loan payments	Loan record

Note: Other sources of cash receipts and possible cash disbursements exist. This analysis covers only the most common types of cash inflows and outflows.

days or more. The same may be true for large capital expenditures. When preparing a cash budget, one must concentrate on the time of actual cash flow, not the time of the original sale or purchase transaction.

The final two cash disbursements in Exhibit 8-2 are for income taxes and interest expense. Corporations usually make quarterly tax payments, which are applied against an estimate of the current year's tax liability. Any excess owed at year end is due on the fifteenth day of the third month following the close of the company's fiscal year. Interest expense payments may be made monthly, quarterly, semiannually, or annually, depending on the terms of the loan agreement. This information can be found in the organization's loan record.

Once the cash receipts and cash disbursements have been established, the cash increase or decrease for the period is computed. The resulting increase or decrease is added to the period's beginning cash balance to arrive at the projected cash balance at period end. In the case of Neehon

Shohkoo, Inc., the first three months will put a heavy drain on cash reserves, but positive cash flow will return during the last nine months of the year. The company seems to have a favorable cash position for the year except at the end of March. Depending on cash payment patterns, the company may need to take out a small loan to cover the cash shortage and protect itself in case a large unexpected payment becomes due. On the other hand, a $55,735 balance in cash at year end may be too much extra cash, so management may want to plan on investing this money in short-term securities.

Illustrative Problem: Worrell Information Processing Company

OBJECTIVE 7
Prepare a cash budget

Worrell Information Processing Company provides word processing services to its clients. Worrell uses state of the art computerized information processing equipment. It employs five keyboard operators who each average 120 hours of work a month. The following information was developed by the budget officer:

| | Actual—19x8 | | Forecast—19x9 | | |
	November	December	January	February	March
Client billings (sales)	$25,000	$35,000	$25,000	$20,000	$40,000
Selling expenses	4,500	5,000	4,000	4,000	5,000
General and administrative expenses	7,500	8,000	8,000	7,000	7,500
Operating supplies purchased	2,500	3,500	2,500	2,500	4,000
Factory overhead	3,200	3,500	3,000	2,500	3,500

The company has a bank loan of $12,000 at a 12 percent annual interest rate. Interest is paid monthly, and $2,000 of the principal is due on February 28, 19x9. No capital expenditures are anticipated for the first quarter of the coming year. Income taxes for calendar year 19x8 of $4,550 are due and payable on March 15, 19x9. The company's five employees earn $7.50 an hour, and all costs of payroll-related labor benefits are included in factory overhead.

For the revenue and cost items included in the chart just given, assume the following conditions:

Client billings	60% are cash sales collected during the current period
	30% are collected in the month following the sale
	10% are collected in the second month following the sale
Operating supplies	Paid in the month purchased

Selling expenses, general
  and administrative
  expenses & factory
  overhead   Paid in the month following the cost's incurrence

The beginning cash balance on January 1, 19x9, is expected to be $13,840.

Required

Prepare a monthly cash budget for the Worrell Information Processing Company for the three-month period ending March 31, 19x9.

Solution

The three-month cash budget for the Worrell Information Processing Company is in Exhibit 8-3. Details supporting the individual computations are shown below:

	January	February	March
Cash from client billings			
Current month = 60%	$15,000	$12,000	$24,000
Previous month = 30%	10,500	7,500	6,000
Month before last = 10%	2,500	3,500	2,500
Totals	$28,000	$23,000	$32,500
Operating supplies			
All paid in the month purchased	$ 2,500	$ 2,500	$ 4,000
Direct labor			
5 employees × 120 hours/month × $7.50/hour	$ 4,500	$ 4,500	$ 4,500
Factory overhead			
Paid in the following month	$ 3,500	$ 3,000	$ 2,500
Selling expenses			
Paid in the following month	$ 5,000	$ 4,000	$ 4,000
General and administrative expenses			
Paid in the following month	$ 8,000	$ 8,000	$ 7,000
Interest expense			
January and February = 1% of $12,000	$ 120	$ 120	
March = 1% of $10,000			$ 100
Loan payment	—	$ 2,000	—
Income tax payment	—	—	$ 4,550

The ending cash balances of $18,220, $17,100, and $22,950 for January, February, and March 19x9, respectively, appear to be comfortable but not too large for the company.

Exhibit 8-3. Example of a Period Budget

Worrell Information Processing Company
Monthly Cash Budget
For the Three-Month Period Ending March 31, 19x9

	January	February	March	Totals
Cash receipts				
Client billings	$28,000	$23,000	$32,500	$83,500
Cash disbursements				
Operating supplies	$ 2,500	$ 2,500	$ 4,000	$ 9,000
Direct labor	4,500	4,500	4,500	13,500
Factory overhead	3,500	3,000	2,500	9,000
Selling expenses	5,000	4,000	4,000	13,000
General and administrative expenses	8,000	8,000	7,000	23,000
Interest expense	120	120	100	340
Loan payment	—	2,000	—	2,000
Income tax payment	—	—	4,550	4,550
Total disbursements	$23,620	$24,120	$26,650	$74,390
Cash increase (decrease)	$ 4,380	$(1,120)	$ 5,850	$ 9,110
Beginning cash balance	13,840	18,220	17,100	13,840
Ending cash balance	$18,220	$17,100	$22,950	$22,950

Chapter Review

Review of Learning Objectives

1. **Describe the structure and contents of a budget.**
   There is no standard form or structure for a budget. A budget's structure depends on what is being budgeted, the size of the organization preparing the budget, the degree to which the budgeting process is integrated into the financial structure of the enterprise, and the amount of training the budget preparer has in his or her background. A budget should contain enough information in an orderly manner to communicate its purpose to the budget's reader or user. Too much information clouds the meaning and accuracy of the data. Too little information may result in overspending because the reader did not understand the spending limits suggested by the document.

2. **Identify the five groups of budgeting principles and explain the principles in each group.**
   The five groups of budgeting principles are (1) long-range goals principles, (2) short-range goals and strategies principles, (3) human responsibilities and

interaction principles, (4) budget housekeeping principles, and (5) follow-up principles. Every organization needs to set long-range goals and convert them into plans for product line or service offerings. Short-range goals and strategies must be restated in terms of the annual product line or service offerings and associated profit plans. The budget development plans and timetable must also be set up. The human side includes identifying a budget director, staff, and participants. These people must be informed of their duties and responsibilities. It is essential to practice participative budgeting, obtain the full support of top management, and ensure full and open communication among all participants. Being realistic, requiring that all deadlines be met, and using flexible application procedures are the house-keeping principles of budgeting. Finally, budget follow-up includes main-taining a continual budgeting process and using a system of periodic reports to measure performance of the operating segments. Problems are identified for analysis and inclusion into the next period's planning activities.

3. **Define the concept of budgetary control.**
   The budgetary control process consists of the cost planning and the cost control functions. Cost planning and control are key functions leading to effective management. Budgetary control is the total process of (1) developing plans for a company's expected operations and (2) controlling operations to help carry out those plans.

4. **Identify the components of a master budget and describe how they relate to each other.**
   A master budget is a combined set of departmental or functional period budgets that have been consolidated into forecasted financial statements for the entire company. First, the detailed operating or period budgets are prepared. These are the sales budget, production budget, selling expense budget, revenue budget, materials usage budget, materials purchases budget, labor hour requirements budget, direct labor dollars budget, factory overhead budget, general and administrative expense budget, and capital expenditures budget. The selling expense budget, revenue budget, and production budget are computed from the sales budget data. Materials usage, labor hour and dollars, and factory overhead budgets arise from the production budget. Materials purchases can be pinned down only after materials use is known. General and administrative expenses and proposed capital expenditures are determined by top management. Once these budgets have been prepared, a forecasted income statement, a forecasted cash flow statement (cash budget), and a forecasted balance sheet can be prepared, assuming that all planned activities actually occur.

5. **Prepare a period budget.**
   A period budget, also known as an operating budget, is the forecast of a year's operating results for a segment of a company. It is a quantitative expression of planned activities. For examples of period budgets, see the illustrative problem on pages 289 to 291. The period budgeting process converts unit sales and production forecasts into revenue and cost estimates for each of the company's many operating segments.

6. **State the purpose and make-up of a cash budget.**
   The cash budget's purposes are (1) to disclose the firm's projected ending cash balance and (2) to show the cash position for each month so that periods of excess cash or cash shortages can be planned for. Cash management is critical to the success of an organization, and the cash budget is a major tool used in that process. The cash budget begins with the projection of all

expected sources of cash (cash receipts). Next, all expected cash disbursements or payments are found by analyzing all other period budgets within the master budget. The difference between these two totals is the cash increase or decrease anticipated for the period. This total combined with the period's beginning cash balance yields the ending cash balance.

7. **Prepare a cash budget.**
   A cash budget or cash flow forecast is a projection of the cash receipts and payments for a future period of time. It summarizes the cash results of planned transactions in all parts of a master budget. For an example, see Exhibit 8-2.

Review of Concepts and Terminology

The following important concepts were introduced in this chapter:

(L.O. 1) **Budget:** A financial document created before anticipated transactions occur; it is often called a financial plan of action.

(L.O. 3) **Budgetary control:** The process of (1) developing plans for a company's expected operations and (2) controlling operations to help carry out those plans.

(L.O. 4) **Master budget:** A combined set of departmental or functional period budgets that have been consolidated into forecasted financial statements for the entire company.

(L.O. 6) **Cash budget or cash flow forecast:** A projection of cash receipts and cash payments for a future period of time.

Other important terms introduced in this chapter are:

participative budgeting (p. 283)
period budget (p. 285)

Review Problem

Hank Kindfish is president of Kindfish Economic Forecasting Services, Inc. On the next page is last year's forecasted income statement for the company. During 19x8, the following changes are anticipated:

1. Consulting fees and special forecasts revenues are expected to increase by 20 percent.
2. Economic information service costs are scheduled for a 30 percent increase in January 19x8.
3. Outside economists' fees and travel costs will rise 10 percent.
4. All salaries will be increased by 20 percent.
5. Rent, depreciation, and utility expenses are expected to stay the same throughout next year.
6. Supplies costs will decrease by 10 percent.
7. Brochure printing costs will rise by 40 percent.
8. Computer services costs will double because of expanded services.
9. Miscellaneous expenses should total $1,000 in 19x8.

Required

Prepare the forecasted income statement for 19x8.

Kindfish Economic Forecasting Services, Inc.
Forecasted Income Statement
For the Year Ending December 31, 19x7

Revenues		
Consulting fees	$246,500	
Special forecasts	137,800	
Total revenues		$384,300
Operating expenses		
Economic information service costs	$111,400	
Outside economists' fees	62,100	
Travel costs	12,800	
Salaries: staff	60,000	
executives	80,000	
Rent, building	6,400	
Depreciation, equipment	3,900	
Utilities	1,800	
Supplies	2,100	
Brochure printing	3,500	
Computer services	6,700	
Miscellaneous	900	
Total operating expenses		351,600
Income before taxes		$ 32,700
Federal income taxes (30%)		9,810
Net income after taxes		$ 22,890

Answer to Review Problem

Kindfish Economic Forecasting Services, Inc.
Forecasted Income Statement
For the Year Ending December 31, 19x8

Revenues		
Consulting fees ($246,500 × 1.2)	$295,800	
Special forecasts ($137,800 × 1.2)	165,360	
Total revenues		$461,160
Operating expenses		
Economic information service costs		
($111,400 × 1.3)	$144,820	
Outside economists' fees costs ($62,100 × 1.1)	68,310	
Travel costs ($12,800 × 1.1)	14,080	
Salaries: staff ($60,000 × 1.2)	72,000	
executives ($80,000 × 1.2)	96,000	
Rent, building	6,400	
Depreciation, equipment	3,900	
Utilities	1,800	
Supplies ($2,100 × .9)	1,890	
Brochure printing ($3,500 × 1.4)	4,900	
Computer services ($6,700 × 2)	13,400	
Miscellaneous	1,000	
Total operating expenses		428,500
Income before taxes		$ 32,660
Federal income taxes (30%)		9,798
Net income after taxes		$ 22,862

Chapter Assignments

Questions

1. "The structure of a budget varies with the task and its circumstances." Is this statement true? Defend your answer.
2. Describe the concept of budgetary control. Why is it important?
3. Distinguish between long-term plans and yearly operating plans.
4. What is a period budget?
5. How does responsibility accounting help in period budget preparation?
6. What is a master budget? What is its purpose?
7. Why is the preparation of a forecasted cash flow statement or cash budget so important to a company?
8. Name the three main phases of the budget preparation cycle.
9. Identify and discuss the interrelationship of detailed operating budgets.
10. What are the long-range goals principles of budgeting?
11. One of the budgeting principles we listed was "Restate the long-range plan in terms of short-range plans for product lines or services available and a detailed profit plan." What is the purpose of this principle?
12. Why is it necessary to identify all participants in budget development?
13. Describe participative budgeting.
14. State the budget housekeeping principles.
15. Why use a continuous budgeting process?
16. What is the connection between periodic performance reports and responsibility accounting?
17. In the budget preparation cycle, what steps must precede preparation of the cash budget?
18. How are the areas of sales and purchases on account handled when drawing up the cash budget?

Classroom Exercises

Exercise 8-1.
Budgeting
Principles
(L.O. 2)

Long-range goals principles and short-range goals and strategies principles are critical to a successful budgeting system. Assume that you work in the accounting department of a small wholesale warehousing business. The president has just returned from an industry association meeting where he attended a seminar on the values of a budgeting system. He wants to develop a budgeting system and has asked you to direct it.

State the points that you should communicate to the president about the initial development steps of the process. Concentrate on the two sets of principles mentioned above.

Exercise 8-2.
Budgetary Control
(L.O. 3)

You are a new employee of Sacks Laboratories, Inc., and have been assigned to the controller's department. This department employs twenty-five paraprofessionals (nondegreed people) who fill clerical and other repetitive skills positions. All are in need of supplemental knowledge in the budgetary control area.

The controller has asked you to team up with another accountant to prepare and present a four-hour seminar on budgetary control to these paraprofessional employees. Your particular assignment is to concentrate on the planning phase of budgetary control. Prepare an outline of the topics and ideas you would cover in this seminar.

Exercise 8-3.
Master Budget
Components
(L.O. 4)

Snorek Prototype Research, Inc., is in its sixth year of operation. Known for "accomplishing the impossible," the corporation has grown from a moonlighting operation in an engineer's garage to a company employing 120 professionals and 15 staff employees. High-tech prototype design is Snorek's main product.

Two years ago the financial vice president hired a controller who was instructed to install a complete budgeting system. To date the budgeting system consists of the following:

Sales Revenue Forecast
Cash Budget
Capital Expenditure Budget

The financial vice president has called you (the company's independent CPA) for advice and ideas regarding a complete budgeting system.

Prepare a response to your client, indicating what will be needed to put together an annual master budget.

Exercise 8-4.
Production Budget
Preparation
(L.O. 5)

The Holstrum Specialty Door Company's forecast of unit sales for 19x6 is as follows: (a) January, 40,000; (b) February, 50,000; (c) March, 60,000; (d) April, 70,000; (e) May, 60,000; (f) June, 50,000; (g) July, 40,000; (h) August, 50,000; (i) September, 60,000; (j) October, 70,000; (k) November, 80,000; and (l) December, 60,000.

The forecast of unit sales for January 19x7 is 50,000. Beginning Finished Goods Inventory on January 1, 19x6, contained 15,000 doors. Company policy states that minimum Finished Goods Inventory is 15,000 units and that the maximum is one-half of the following month's sales. Maximum productive capacity is 65,000 units per month.

Using this information, prepare a monthly production budget, stating the number of units to be produced. Note that the company wants a fairly constant productive output so a constant work force can be maintained. How many units will be in Finished Goods Inventory on December 31, 19x6?

Exercise 8-5.
Direct Materials
Purchases Budget
(Linked to Exercise 8-4)
(L.O. 5)

Refer to the data for the Holstrum Specialty Door Company in Exercise 8-4. Prepare a direct materials purchases budget for January, February, and March 19x6, assuming the following breakdown of parts needed:

Hinges	4 sets/door	$8.00/set
Door panels	4 panels/door	$17.00/panel
Other hardware	1 lock/door	$11.00/lock
	1 handle/door	$2.50/handle
	2 sets roller tracks/door	$22.00/set of two roller tracks
	8 rollers/door	$1.00/roller

All direct materials are purchased in the month before their use in production.

Exercise 8-6.
Factory Labor
Budget
(L.O. 5)

Sterling Metals Company manufactures three products in a single plant with four departments: Cutting, Grinding, Polishing, and Packing. The company has estimated costs for products T, M, and B and is currently analyzing direct labor hour requirements for the budget year 19xx. On the following page are the routing sequence and departmental data:

Unit of Product	Estimated Hours per Unit				Total Estimated Direct Labor Hours/Unit
	Cut	Grind	Polish	Pack	
T	.6	1.0	.4	.2	2.2
M	1.0	—	2.8	.6	4.4
B	1.6	3.0	—	.4	5.0
Hourly labor rate	$8	$6	$5	$4	
Annual DLH capacity	900,000	1,200,000	1,248,000	360,000	

The annual direct labor hour capacity for each department is based on a normal two-shift operation. Hours of labor exceeding capacity are provided by overtime labor at 150 percent of normal hourly rates. Budgeted unit production in 19xx for the products is 210,000 of T, 360,000 of M, and 300,000 of B.

Prepare a monthly direct labor hour requirements schedule for 19xx and the related direct labor cost budget. Assume that direct labor hour capacity is the same each month. Production should be close to constant each month.

Exercise 8-7.
Cash Budget
Preparation—
Revenues
(L.O.6,7)

Storevik Car Care, Inc., is an automobile maintenance and repair organization with outlets throughout the midwestern United States. Ms. Shanley, budget director for the home office, is assembling next quarter's operating cash budget. Sales are projected as follows:

	On Account	Cash
October	$742,000	$265,800
November	680,000	250,000
December	810,500	279,400

Past collection results for sales on account indicate the following pattern:

Month of sale	40%
1st month following sale	30%
2nd month following sale	28%
Uncollectible	2%

Sales on account during August and September were $846,000 and $595,000, respectively.

1. What is the purpose of preparing a cash budget?
2. Compute the amount of cash to be collected from sales during each month of the last quarter.

**Exercise 8-8.
Cash Budget
Preparation—
Expenditures
(L.O.7)**

Cabernet Corporation relies heavily on its cash budget to predict periods of high or low cash. The company considers proper cash management its primary short-range strategy for achieving higher profits. All materials and supplies are purchased on account with terms of either 2/10, n/30 or 2/30, n/60. Discounts are taken whenever possible, but payment is not made until the final day of the discount period. Purchases for the next quarter are expected to be as follows:

Date	Terms	Gross Amount	Date	Terms	Gross Amount
July 10	2/10, n/30	$ 6,400	Aug. 31	2/10, n/30	$ 6,800
July 16	2/30, n/60	8,200	Sept. 4	2/10, n/30	9,400
July 24	2/30, n/60	7,400	Sept. 9	2/10, n/30	8,100
Aug. 6	2/10, n/30	6,200	Sept. 18	2/10, n/30	7,500
Aug. 12	2/30, n/60	10,400	Sept. 20	2/10, n/30	10,400
Aug. 18	2/30, n/60	10,500	Sept. 24	2/30, n/60	9,400
Aug. 30	2/10, n/30	11,600	Sept. 29	2/10, n/30	4,900

Three purchases in June affected July cash flow: June 6, 2/30, n/60, $14,200; June 21, 2/30, n/60, $10,400; and June 24, 2/10, n/30, $6,400.

From the information given, compute total cash outflow for July, August, and September resulting from the purchases identified above.

Interpreting Accounting Information

**Internal
Management
Information:
Hedlund
Corporation
(L.O.1,2,4)**

Hedlund Corporation is a manufacturing company with annual sales of $25,000,000. The controller, Mr. Milton, appointed Ms. Maybelle as budget director. She created this budget formulation policy based on a calendar-year accounting period:

May 19x7   Meeting of corporate officers and budget director to discuss corporate plans for 19x8.

June 19x7   Meeting(s) of division managers, department heads, and budget director to communicate 19x8 corporate objectives. At this time relevant background data are distributed to all managers and a time schedule is established for development of 19x8 budget data.

July 19x7   Managers and department heads continue to develop budget data. Complete 19x8 monthly sales forecasts by product line and receive final sales estimates from sales vice president.

Aug. 19x7   Complete 19x8 monthly production activity and anticipated inventory level plans. Division managers and department heads should communicate preliminary budget figures to budget director for coordination and distribution to other operating areas.

Sept. 19x7   Development of preliminary 19x8 master budget. Revised budget data from all functional areas to be received. Budget director will coordinate staff activities, integrating manpower requirements, direct materials and supplies requirements, unit cost estimates, cash requirements, and profit estimates into 19x8 master budget.

Oct. 19x7   Meeting with corporate officers to discuss preliminary 19x8 master budget. Any corrections, additions, or deletions are to be communicated to budget director by corporate officers; all authorized changes are to be incorporated into the 19x8 master budget.

Nov. 19x7   Submit final draft of 19x8 master budget to corporate officers for approval. Publish approved budget and distribute to all corporate officers, division managers, and department heads.

Required

1. Comment on the proposed budget formulation policy.
2. What changes in the policy would you recommend?

Problem Set A

**Problem 8A-1.
Divisional Budget
Preparation
(L.O.5)**

Lester Twichell is budget director for Villa Park Spectaculars, Inc., a division of Diversified, Ltd., a multinational company based in California. Villa Park Spectaculars organizes and coordinates art shows and auctions throughout the world. Budgeted and actual costs and expenses for 19x7 are compared in the following schedule:

	19x7 Amounts	
Expense Item	**Budget**	**Actual**
Salary Expense, Staging	$ 130,000	$ 146,400
Salary Expense, Executive	390,000	423,600
Travel Costs	220,000	236,010
Auctioneer Services	170,000	124,910
Space Rental Costs	135,500	133,290
Printing Costs	76,000	81,250
Advertising Expense	94,500	101,640
Insurance, Merchandise	32,400	28,650
Insurance, Liability	22,000	23,550
Home Office Costs	104,600	99,940
Shipping Costs	22,500	26,280
Miscellaneous	12,500	11,914
Total Expenses	$1,410,000	$1,437,434
Net Receipts	$2,750,000	$2,984,600

For 19x8 the following fixed costs have been budgeted: executive salaries, $400,000; advertising expense, $95,000; merchandise insurance, $20,000; liability insurance, $34,000; for a total of $549,000. Additional information follows:

1. Net receipts are expected to be $2,900,000 in 19x8.
2. Staging salaries will increase 50% over 19x7 actual figures.
3. Travel costs are expected to be 11% of net receipts.
4. Auctioneer services will be billed at 9.5% of net receipts.
5. Space rental costs will go up 20% from 19x7 budgeted amounts.
6. Printing costs are expected to be $85,000 in 19x8.
7. Home office costs are budgeted for $125,000 in 19x8.
8. Shipping costs are expected to rise 20% over 19x7 budgeted amounts.
9. Miscellaneous expenses for 19x8 will be budgeted at $4,000.

Required

1. Prepare the division's budget for 19x8. Assume that only services are being sold and there is no cost of sales. (Net receipts equal gross margin.) Use a 30 percent federal income tax rate.
2. Should the budget director be worried about the trend of the company's operations? Be specific.

Problem 8A-2.
Factory Overhead
Expense Budget
(L.O. 5)

Stalcup Manufacturing Company has a home office and three operating divisions. The home office houses top management personnel, including all accounting functions. Following is a summary of the factory overhead costs incurred during 19x7:

Expense Categories	East Division	West Division	Central Division	Total	Expected Increase in 19x8
Indirect Labor	$ 34,500	$ 38,600	$ 40,200	$113,300	10%
Indirect Materials	14,800	15,200	16,000	46,000	20%
Supplies	13,900	13,900	14,000	41,800	10%
Utilities	16,200	17,400	17,100	50,700	10%
Computer Services	30,400	36,900	38,600	105,900	—
Insurance	13,400	13,500	13,600	40,500	10%
Repairs and Maintenance	15,600	16,000	15,400	47,000	20%
Miscellaneous	11,100	11,200	11,300	33,600	10%
Totals	$149,900	$162,700	$166,200	$478,800	

Expected percentage increases for 19x8 are shown for all categories except computer services. These services will increase by different amounts for each division: East Division, 25%; West Division, 30%; and Central Division, 40%. In 19x7 the home office was charged $52,500 for computer service costs. This amount is expected to rise by 25 percent in 19x8. During 19x8 the company will rent a new software package at an annual cost of $70,000.

Required

1. Find the total expected cost of computer services for 19x8 for the three divisions and the home office.
2. Assume the rental charge for the new software package is allocated to computer service users on the basis of their costs for normal computer use as a percentage of total computer service charges. Compute the allocation of the rental charges to the three divisions and the central office. (Use the 19x8 amounts computed in **1** above, and round to one percentage decimal place.)
3. Prepare the divisional factory overhead expense budget for Stalcup Manufacturing Company for 19x8.

Problem 8A-3.
Master Budget
(L.O. 4, 5)

Abramson Video Company, Inc., produces and markets two popular video games, "Grant Avenues" and "Thornton Adventures." The company's closing balance sheet account balances for 19x7 are as follows: (a) Cash, $17,450;

(b) Accounts Receivable, $21,900; (c) Materials Inventory, $18,510; (d) Work in Process Inventory, $28,680; (e) Finished Goods Inventory, $31,940; (f) Prepaid Expenses, $3,420; (g) Plant and Equipment, $262,800; (h) Accumulated Depreciation, Plant and Equipment, $52,560; (i) Other Assets, $9,480; (j) Accounts Payable, $76,640; (k) Mortgage Payable, $88,000; (l) Common Stock, $100,000; (m) Retained Earnings, $76,980.

Period budgets for the first quarter of 19x8 revealed the following: (a) materials purchases, $48,100; (b) materials usage, $50,240; (c) labor expense, $72,880; (d) factory overhead expense, $41,910; (e) selling expenses, $45,820; (f) general and administrative expenses, $60,230; (g) capital expenditures, $0; (h) ending cash balances by month: January—$34,610, February—$60,190, and March—$96,240; (i) Cost of Goods Manufactured, $163,990; and (j) Cost of Goods Sold, $165,440. Sales per month are projected to be $165,210 for January, $114,890 for February, and $132,860 for March. The accounts receivable balance will probably double during the quarter, and accounts payable will decrease by 25 percent. Mortgage payments for the quarter will total $6,000, of which $2,000 is interest expense. Prepaid expenses are expected to go up by $20,000, and other assets are projected to increase 50 percent over the budget period. Depreciation for plant and equipment (already included in the factory overhead budget) averages 10 percent per year. Federal income taxes are 30 percent of profits and payable in April.

Required

1. Prepare a forecasted income statement for the quarter ending March 31, 19x8.
2. Prepare a forecasted statement of financial position as of March 31, 19x8.

Problem 8A-4.
Basic Cash Budget
(L.O.7)

David Schuelke is president of United Nurseries of Idaho, Inc. This corporation has four locations in the state of Idaho and has been in business for six years. Each retail outlet offers its customers more than 200 varieties of plants and trees. Milly Cooper, the controller, has been asked to prepare a cash budget for the president for the Southern Division for the first quarter of 19x8. Projected data supporting the budget are summarized below. Collection history for the accounts receivable shows that 30 percent of all credit sales are collected in the month of sale, 60 percent in the month following the sale, and 8 percent in the second month following the sale. Two percent of credit sales are uncollectible. Purchases are all paid for in the month following the purchase. The cash balance as of December 31, 19x7, was $4,875.

Sales (60 percent on credit)

November 19x7	$80,000
December 19x7	90,000
January 19x8	40,000
February 19x8	70,000
March 19x8	30,000

Purchases

December 19x7	$28,400
January 19x8	49,350
February 19x8	21,720
March 19x8	32,400

Salaries and wages were $14,600 in January; $18,600 in February; and $12,600 in March. Monthly costs were (a) utilities, $1,110; (b) collection fees, $1,350; (c) rent, $2,850; (d) equipment depreciation, $3,720; (e) supplies, $3,240; (f) small tools, $570; and (g) miscellaneous, $850.

Required

1. Prepare a cash budget by month for the Southern Division for the first quarter of 19x8.
2. Should United Nurseries of Idaho, Inc., anticipate taking out a loan during the quarter? How much should be borrowed? When? (*Note:* Management maintains a $3,000 minimum cash balance at each of its four locations.)

**Problem 8A-5.
Cash Budget
Preparation:
Comprehensive
(L.O.7)**

Olson's Wellness Centers, Inc., operates three fully equipped personal health facilities in Minneapolis, Minnesota. In addition to the health facilities, the corporation maintains a complete medical center specializing in preventive medicine. Emphasis is on regular workouts and medical examinations. Care is taken to keep everything in good running order so members' personal fitness programs are not interrupted.

Budgeted Cash Receipts: First Quarter, 19x8

Membership dues

Memberships: Dec. 19x7, 970; Jan., 980; Feb., 1,010; and Mar., 1,025.

Dues: $80 per month, payable on the 10th day (80 percent collected on time; 20 percent collected one month late).

Special aerobics classes: Jan., $2,480; Feb., $3,210; and Mar., $4,680.

Suntan sessions: Jan., $1,240; Feb., $1,620; and Mar., $2,050.

High-protein food sales: Jan., $3,890; Feb., $4,130; and Mar., $5,280.

Medical examinations: Jan., $34,610; Feb., $39,840; and Mar., $43,610.

Budgeted Cash Disbursements: First Quarter, 19x8

Salaries/Wages

Corporate officers: $20,000/month

Medical doctors: 2 at $6,000/month

Nurses: 3 at $2,500/month

Clerical staff: 2 at $1,200/month

Aerobics instructors: 3 at $900/month

Clinic staff: 6 at $1,400/month

Maintenance staff: 3 at $1,000/month

Health food servers: 3 at $800/month

Purchases

Muscle-tone machines: Jan., $16,400; Feb., $12,800; and Mar., $0

Pool supplies: $420 per month

Health food: Jan., $2,290; Feb., $2,460; and Mar., $2,720

Medical supplies: Jan., $9,400; Feb., $10,250; and Mar., $11,640

Medical clothing: Jan., $6,410; Feb., $2,900; and Mar., $2,450

Medical equipment: Jan., $10,200; Feb., $2,400; and Mar., $4,900

Advertising: Jan., $1,250; Feb., $2,190; and Mar., $3,450

Utility expense: Jan., $6,450; Feb., $6,890; and Mar., $7,090

Insurance, fire: Jan., $2,470

          liability: Mar., $4,980

Property taxes: $4,760 due in Jan.

Federal income taxes: 19x7 taxes of $22,000 due in Mar., 19x8

Miscellaneous: Jan., $1,625; Feb., $1,800; and Mar., $2,150

The beginning cash balance for 19x8 is anticipated to be $20,840.

Required

Prepare a cash budget for Olson's Wellness Centers, Inc., for the first quarter of 19x8, using the following column headings:

| Item | January | February | March | Total |

Problem Set B

Problem 8B-1.
Budget Preparation
(L.O. 5)

The main product of Revell Enterprises, Inc., is a multipurpose hammer that carries a lifetime guarantee. The steps in the manufacturing process have been combined by using modern, automated equipment. Following is a list of cost and production information for the Revell hammer:

Direct materials

  Anodized steel: 2 kilograms per hammer at $.60 per kilogram

  Leather strapping for handle: ½ square meter per hammer at $4.80 per square meter

  (Packing materials are returned to the manufacturer and thus are not included as part of Cost of Goods Sold.)

Direct labor

  Forging operation: $10.50 per direct labor hour, 12 minutes per hammer

  Leather-wrapping operation: $10.00 per direct labor hour; 24 minutes per hammer

Factory overhead

  Forging operation: rate equals 70% of department's direct labor dollars

  Leather-wrapping operation: rate equals 50% of department's direct labor dollars

For the three months ended December 31, 19xx, management expects to produce 48,000 hammers in October, 42,000 hammers in November, and 40,000 hammers in December.

Required

1. For the three-month period ending December 31, 19xx, prepare monthly production cost information for manufacturing the Revell hammer. In your budget analysis, show a detailed breakdown of all costs involved and the computation methods used.
2. Prepare a quarterly production cost budget for the hammer. Show monthly cost data and combined totals for the quarter for each cost category.

Problem 8B-2.
General and
Administrative
Expense Budget
(L.O. 5)

Rogne Metal Products, Inc., has four divisions and a centralized management structure. The home office is located in Spencer, Iowa. Following are general and administrative expenses of the corporation for 19x8 and expected percentage increases for 19x9:

Expense Categories	19x8 Expenses	Expected Increase in 19x9
Administrative Salaries	$125,000	20%
Facility Depreciation	37,000	10%
Operating Supplies	24,500	20%
Insurance and Taxes	6,000	10%
Computer Services	200,000	40%
Clerical Salaries	55,000	15%
Miscellaneous	12,500	10%
Total	$460,000	

To determine divisional profitability, all general and administrative expenses except for computer services are allocated to divisions on a total labor dollar basis. Computer service costs are charged directly to divisions on the basis of percent of total usage charges. Computer charges and direct labor costs in 19x8 were as follows:

	Computer Charges	Direct Labor
Division A	$ 50,000	$150,000
Division B	44,000	100,000
Division C	36,000	125,000
Division D	30,000	125,000
Home Office	40,000	
Total	$200,000	

Required

1. Prepare the general and administrative expense budget for Rogne Metal Products, Inc., for 19x9.
2. Prepare a schedule of budgeted cost charges for computer service for each division and the home office. Assume that percentage of usage time and cost distribution in 19x9 will be the same as in 19x8.
3. Determine the amount of general and administrative expense to be allocated to each division in 19x9. Assume the same direct labor cost distribution percentages in 19x8. Do not include costs budgeted in part **2**.

Problem 8B-3.
Master Budget
(L.O. 4, 5)

The Bank of Seminole County has asked the president of Naruse Laser Products, Inc., for a forecasted income statement and balance sheet for the quarter ended June 30, 19x9. These documents will be used to support the company's request for a loan. A quarterly master budget is prepared on a routine basis by the company, so the president indicated that the requested documents would be forwarded to the bank in the near future.

To date (April 2) the following period budgets have been developed: Sales: April, $210,400; May, $154,220; and June, $155,980. Materials purchases for the period, $86,840; anticipated materials usage, $92,710; labor expenses, $81,460; projected factory overhead, $69,940; selling expenses for the quarter, $72,840; general and administrative expenses, $90,900; capital expenditures, $125,000 (to be spent on June 29); Cost of Goods Manufactured, $256,820; and Cost of Goods Sold, $262,910.

Balance sheet account balances at March 31, 19x9, were: Cash, $28,770; Accounts Receivable, $33,910; Materials Inventory, $41,620; Work in Process Inventory, $46,220; Finished Goods Inventory, $51,940; Prepaid Expenses, $9,200; Plant, Furniture, and Fixtures, $498,600; Accumulated Depreciation, Plant, Furniture, and Fixtures, $99,720; Patents, $89,680; Accounts Payable, $49,610; Notes Payable, $105,500; Common Stock, $250,000; and Retained Earnings, $295,110.

Monthly cash balances for the quarter are projected to be: April 30, $20,490; May 31, $5,610; and June 30, ($13,958). During the quarter accounts receivable are supposed to increase by 60 percent, patents will go up by $7,500, prepaid expenses will remain constant, accounts payable will go down by 20 percent, and the company will make a $5,000 payment on the note payable ($4,100 is principal reduction). The federal income tax rate is 30 percent, and the second quarter's tax is paid in July. Depreciation for the quarter will be $6,420, which is already included in the factory overhead budget.

Required

1. Prepare a forecasted income statement for the quarter ended June 30, 19x9.
2. Prepare a forecasted statement of financial position as of June 30, 19x9.

Problem 8B-4.
Basic Cash Budget
(L.O.7)

Produce World, Inc., is the creation of John Versackas, an immigrant from Lithuania. Versackas's dream was to develop the biggest produce store with the widest selection of fresh fruits and vegetables in the northern Illinois area. In three short years he accomplished his objective. Eighty percent of his business is conducted on credit with area retail enterprises, and 20 percent of the produce sold is to walk-in customers at his retail outlet on a cash-only basis. Collection experience shows that 20 percent of all credit sales are collected during the month of sale, 50 percent are received in the month following the sale, and 29 percent are collected in the second month after the sale. One percent of credit sales are uncollectible.

Mr. Versackas has asked you to prepare a cash budget for his business for the quarter ending September 30, 19x9. Operating data for the period are as follows: Total sales in May were $125,000; in June, $140,000. Anticipated sales include July, $115,000; August, $157,500; and September, $215,800. Purchases for the quarter are expected to be $67,400 in July; $92,850 in August; and $101,450 in September. All purchases are for cash. Other projected costs for the quarter include (a) salaries and wages of $39,740 in July, $42,400 in August, and $51,600 in September; (b) monthly costs of $3,080 for heat, light, and power; (c) $950 for bank collection fees; (d) $4,850 for rent; (e) $5,240 for supplies; (f) $2,410 for depreciation of equipment; (g) $1,570 for equipment repairs; and (h) $1,150 for miscellaneous expenses. The corporation's cash balance at June 30, 19x9, was $8,490.

Required

1. Prepare a cash budget by month for the quarter ending September 30, 19x9.
2. Should Produce World, Inc., anticipate taking out a bank loan during the quarter? How much should be borrowed? When? (*Note:* Management maintains a $5,000 minimum monthly cash balance.)

Problem 8B-5.
Cash Budget
Preparation:
Comprehensive
(L.O.7)

Texas Mountain Ski Resort, Inc., located in the Texas panhandle, has been in business for twenty-two years. Although the skiing season is difficult to predict, the company operates under the assumption that all of its revenues will be generated during the first three months of the calendar year. Routine maintenance and repair work is done during the remaining nine-month period. The following projections for 19x9 were developed by Lou Vlasho, company budget director:

Cash Receipts

Lift tickets: Jan., 14,800 people at $21; Feb., 12,400 people at $22; and Mar., 14,800 people at $23

Food sales: Jan., $72,000; Feb., $66,000; and Mar., $72,000

Skiing lessons: Jan., $258,000; Feb., $234,000; and Mar., $258,000

Equipment sales and rental: Jan., $992,000; Feb., $896,000; and Mar., $992,000

Liquor sales: Jan., $114,000; Feb., $102,000; and Mar., $118,000

Cash Disbursements

Salaries:

Ski area:

Lift operators: 10 people at $2,000 per month for January, February, and March (first quarter)

Instruction and equipment rental: 22 people at $2,200 per month for first quarter

Maintenance: $33,000 per month for first quarter and $94,000 for the rest of the year

Customer service: shuttle-bus drivers: 5 people at $1,200 per month for first quarter

Medical: 6 people at $4,400 per month for first quarter

Food service: 16 people at $1,000 per month for first quarter

Purchases:

Food: $20,000 per month for the first quarter

Ski equipment: purchases of $440,000 in both January and February plus a $600,000 purchase in December 19x9

Liquors: $40,000 in each month of the first quarter

Tickets and supplies: $50,000 in January, $40,000 in February, and $80,000 in December 19x9

Advertising: $30,000 in January, $20,000 in February, and $80,000 from April through the end of the year

Fire and liability insurance: January and June premium payments of $7,000

Medical facility costs: $5,000 per month during first quarter

Utilities: $3,000 per month for the first quarter and $1,000 per month for the rest of the year

Lift maintenance: $15,000 per month for the first quarter and $10,000 per month for the rest of the year

Property taxes: $280,000 due in June

Federal income taxes: 19x8 taxes of $564,000 due in March

The beginning cash balance for 19x9 is anticipated to be $10,000.

Required

Prepare a cash budget for Texas Mountain Ski Resort, Inc., for 19x9, using the following column headings:

Item	January	February	March	April–December	Total

Management Decision Case

P. C. Enterprises
(L.O.1,2,5)

During the past ten years, P. C. Enterprises has practiced participative budgeting all the way from the maintenance personnel to the president's staff. Gradually, however, the objectives of honesty and decisions made in the best interest of the company have given way at the divisional level to division-benefiting decisions and budgets biased in favor of divisional interests. Mr. Vrana, corporate controller, has asked Ms. Somer, budget director, to carefully analyze this year's divisional budgets before incorporating them into the company's master budget.

The Western Division was the first of six divisions to submit its 19x7 budget request to the corporate office. Its summary income statement and accompanying notes are on page 314.

Required

1. Recast the Western Division's Forecasted Income Statement into the following format (round percentages to two decimal places):

	Budget—12/31/x6		Budget—12/31/x7	
Account	Amount	Percent of Sales	Amount	Percent of Sales

2. Actual results for 19x6 revealed the following information about revenues and cost of goods sold:

	Amount	Percentage of Sales
Sales: Radios	$ 760,000	43.31
Appliances	560,000	31.91
Telephones	370,000	21.08
Miscellaneous	65,000	3.70
Total revenues	$1,755,000	100.00
Less Cost of Goods Sold	763,425	43.50
Gross margin	$ 991,575	56.50

On the basis of this information and your analysis in **1,** what should the budget director say to officials of the Western Division? Mention specific areas of the budget that need to be revised.

P. C. Enterprises
Western Division
Forecasted Income Statement
For the Years Ending December 31, 19x6 and 19x7

	Budget 12/31/x6	Budget 12/31/x7	Increase (Decrease)
Revenues			
Sales: radios	$ 840,000	$ 900,000	$ 60,000
appliances	690,000	750,000	60,000
telephones	265,000	300,000	35,000
miscellaneous	82,400	100,000	17,600
Total revenues	$1,877,400	$2,050,000	$172,600
Less cost of goods sold	750,960	717,500*	(33,460)
Gross margin	$1,126,440	$1,332,500	$206,060
Operating Expenses			
Wages: warehouse	$ 84,500	$ 92,250	$ 7,750
purchasing	67,800	74,000	6,200
delivery/shipping	59,400	64,780	5,380
maintenance	32,650	35,670	3,020
Salaries: supervisory	60,000	92,250	32,250
executive	120,000	164,000	44,000
Purchases, supplies	17,400	20,500	3,100
Merchandise moving equipment:			
maintenance	72,400	82,000	9,600
depreciation	62,000	71,750†	9,750
Building rent	96,000	102,500	6,500
Sales commissions	187,740	205,000	17,260
Insurance: fire	12,670	20,500	7,830
liability	18,200	20,500	2,300
Utilities	14,100	15,375	1,275
Taxes: property	16,600	18,450	1,850
payroll	26,520	41,000	14,480
Miscellaneous	4,610	10,250	5,640
Total operating expenses	$ 952,590	$1,130,775	$178,185
Net income before taxes	$ 173,850	$ 201,725	$ 27,875

*Less expensive merchandise will be purchased in 19x7 to boost profits.
†Depreciation is increased because of the need to buy additional equipment to handle increased sales.

CHAPTER 9

Introduction to Standard Cost Accounting

Standard cost accounting is a tool that management uses for cost planning and cost control. When a company uses standard costs, all costs affecting the three inventory accounts and the Cost of Goods Sold account are stated in terms of standard or predetermined costs rather than actual costs incurred. A standard cost system is used with a job order or process costing system and is not a full cost accounting system by itself. Together with cost behavior relationships and cost-volume-profit analyses, the incorporation of standard costs into a cost accounting system provides the foundation for the budgetary control process. Standard costs are useful for (1) evaluating the performance of workers and management, (2) preparing budgets and forecasts, and (3) determining appropriate selling prices.

Because standard cost accounting is so important and represents such a major change in costing concepts, this topic is covered in two chapters. In this chapter we look at the nature and purpose of standard costs, their make-up, their development, and their use in product costing. We also introduce variance analysis for direct materials and direct labor and their journal entry recording. In Chapter 10 we (1) continue to focus on variance analysis, this time in the overhead cost area, and (2) analyze variances as a basis for performance evaluation.

After studying this chapter you should be able to meet the learning objectives listed on the left.

Nature and Purpose of Standard Costs

Standard costs are realistically predetermined costs for direct materials, direct labor, and factory overhead. They are usually expressed as cost per unit of finished product. Predetermined overhead costs, which we discussed in Chapter 3, are different from standard costs. The concept of standard costing focuses on total unit cost, which includes all three manufacturing cost elements. It goes beyond factory overhead cost. In addition, a more detailed analysis is used when computing standard costs.

Predetermined overhead costing and standard costing do, however, share two important elements: both forecast dollar amounts to be used in product costing, and both depend on expected costs and quantities of budgeted items. But this is where the similarity ends. Standard costs depend on more than the simple projections of past costs that are used to develop predetermined overhead rates. They are based on engineering estimates, forecasted demand, worker input, time-and-motion studies, and direct materials types and quality. However, we should not play down the role of the predetermined overhead rate. It provides some of the same data as the standard overhead rate, and standard costing is both sophisticated and expensive. If a company cannot afford to add standard costing to its cost system, it should still continue to use predetermined overhead rates.

Standard costing is a total cost concept. As mentioned, it is made up of costs for direct materials, direct labor, and factory overhead. In a fully integrated standard cost system, all actual manufacturing cost data are replaced by standard (or predetermined) cost data. Accounts such as Direct Materials Inventory, Work in Process Inventory, Finished Goods Inventory, and Cost of Goods Sold are all stated in terms of standard costs. All debit and credit entries made to these accounts are in terms of standard costs, not actual costs. All inventory balances are figured by using standard unit costs. Separate records of actual costs are kept to compare standard costs (what should have been spent) with actual costs. The two types of cost are usually compared at the end of each accounting period, whether weekly, monthly, or quarterly. If there are large differences (variances), the management accountant looks for the cause of the differences. This process, known as variance analysis, is one of the most effective cost control tools. We discuss it later in this chapter and in Chapter 10.

Standard costs are introduced into a cost accounting system for several reasons. These costs are useful for preparing operating budgets. They make it easier to pinpoint production costs that need to be controlled. They help in setting realistic prices. And they basically simplify cost accounting procedures for inventories and product costing. Although expensive to set up and maintain, a standard cost accounting system can save a company much money by reducing waste and inefficiency.

Budgetary Control and Standard Costs

Budgetary control involves the successful planning of a company's operating activities and the control of operations to help attain those plans. In management accounting terms, the objectives of budgetary control are:

1. To help establish procedures for preparing a company's planned costs and revenues
2. To help coordinate and communicate these plans to all levels of management
3. To formulate a basis for effective cost control

Standard costs play a major role in budgetary control. Standard materials, labor, and factory overhead costs are useful in projecting anticipated costs. For example, assume that Arnold Company estimates that it will manufacture 35,000 type A products during the coming year. Each product requires 2.5 hours of labor (labor time standard) at a cost of $7.50 per hour (standard labor rate per hour). Planned labor costs for the year on this product would be

$$35,000 \text{ products} \times 2.5 \text{ hours} \times \$7.50 = \$656,250$$

This example involves estimates of the number of products, standard labor hours per product, and standard labor cost per hour. Such forecasted information facilitates planning by coordinating plans throughout the enterprise and by communicating information to managers responsible for production volume and factory labor. The estimate of 35,000 products gives the production superintendent an output goal for the year. Production personnel know that these 35,000 units should be produced by using an average of 2.5 labor hours on each unit with an average labor rate of $7.50 per hour.

Assume that at year end the Arnold Company has incurred actual labor costs of $662,350 to manufacture this product. In standard costing terms, a variance has been incurred:

$$\text{Actual cost} - \text{standard cost} = \text{variance}$$
or
$$\$662,350 - \$656,250 = \$6,100(\text{U})$$

A *variance* is the difference between actual results and related standard or budgeted results. In the example, actual costs exceeded standard costs, which resulted in an unfavorable variance. An unfavorable variance is designated by the letter U. If actual costs are less than standard costs, the variance is favorable and is noted by the letter F.

Variance analysis is used in the cost control phase of the budgetary control process. With the aid of standard costs, you can compute and analyze variances. Once the causes of a variance have been determined, corrective measures are implemented to prevent nonstandard performance in future periods.

What caused the Arnold Company to incur $6,100 more in labor costs than anticipated? From the information given, no single reason or cause can be isolated. The following list of possible causes indicates the types of factors that should be investigated to obtain an appropriate explanation:

1. The company produced more than 35,000 products during the year.
2. More than 2.5 labor hours were used per product.
3. The average labor rate exceeded the standard labor rate of $7.50.
4. The variance resulted from a combination of factors included in items 1, 2, and 3.

Standard cost variances measure the degree of nonstandard performance. Additional information must be obtained to identify the causes related to such performance. The Arnold Company example introduced you to cost control through the analysis of variances.

Behavioral Effects of Standard Costs

Managers in each area of the company's operations should view a standard cost as a target cost. The operating objective is to achieve the standard performance target in terms of materials usage and costs, labor time and costs, and overhead costs to produce a given volume of products or to provide a defined amount of service. Standard costs are carefully determined, but they are seldom precise since estimates are used in the computations. Meeting the standard performance target should be considered a reasonable measure of operating performance when evaluating managers. When actual costs are compared with related standards, variances should be expected. Large variances pinpoint operating efficiencies or inefficiencies. Remember, variances can be positive as well as negative.

If standard costs are to be accepted as targets or performance goals, the standards must be attainable and managers and employees must consider them reasonable. Standards that are unattainable will soon be recognized, and they will cease to inspire managers to operate efficiently. Therefore a successful standard cost system must include motivational considerations. All managers and employees should be advised of their specific areas of responsibility and should take part in developing related standards and budget targets. Basing standard costs on both motivational factors and efficient operating considerations will help management reach overall corporate objectives.

Types of Standard Costs

OBJECTIVE 2
Describe and differentiate among the three types of standard costs: ideal standards, basic standards, and currently attainable standards

Standard costs can be characterized as ideal standards, basic standards, or currently attainable standards. Each type of standard cost is useful, but ideal standards and basic standards require certain adjustments before they can be used to evaluate performance or assess the value of inventory.

Ideal Standards

Ideal standards, also called theoretical, or perfection, standards, are based on a maximum efficiency level with no breaks or work stoppages. These standards allow for minimum materials, labor time, and other cost constraints in producing a product or creating a service. Ideal standards are rarely attained because people and machines have periods of downtime. Standards based on this maximum efficiency approach are effective only when operating personnel are aware of this factor and are rewarded for performing at a percentage, say 85 or 90 percent, of standard.

For example, assume that Machine 1 can produce a maximum of 300 units per hour, which is the ideal standard. The supervisor tells Jackson, operator of the machine, that the target is to produce an average of 270 units per hour, even though the ideal standard is 300 units per hour. By adjusting ideal production standards downward, realistic operating goals can be communicated to employees to promote employee motivation. Ideal standards are based on theoretical capacity and result in minimum unit costs.

Figure 9-1(a) depicts an ideal standard cost for direct labor. The standard cost is set at such a low level that it can never be attained. To be useful, the standards must be adjusted. The cost standard must be increased to a reasonable level. Once the standard is adjusted, actual performance can be compared with the adjusted standard data for evaluation. In the figure, the actual labor cost varied above and below the adjusted standard amount, causing both unfavorable and favorable variances.

The concept of an ideal standard does provide a picture of a worker's or machine's maximum efficiency. However, ideal standards are difficult to understand and employ and therefore are seldom used in practice.

Basic Standards

Basic standards are projections that are seldom revised or updated to reflect current operating costs and price level changes. They remain the same after being computed for the first time. Basic standards are used primarily to measure trends in operating performance. Although useful, basic standards must be adjusted before they can be used to evaluate performance.

Figure 9-1(b) illustrates basic standards. The standard cost does not change over time. To be useful, the basic standard must be adjusted to reflect price level changes and improvements in operator and machine efficiency. Once the basic standard has been adjusted, actual cost can be plotted and compared with the expected cost. In Figure 9-1(b), actual cost is above adjusted standard cost for the first few time periods. Then,

Figure 9-1. Graphic Illustration of Ideal and Basic Standards

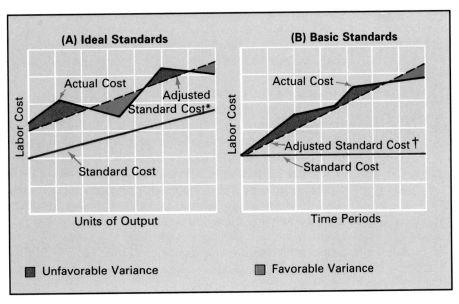

*Adjusted standard cost = standard cost × 1.5

†Adjusted standard increase above basic standard because of inflation and other factors

actual unit costs level off, and the adjusted standard is greater than the actual. The result is a favorable variance.

Like ideal standards, basic standards require adjustment before becoming useful targets. Because of this factor, basic standards tend to be confusing and lack motivational properties. They also have limited use in practice.

Currently Attainable Standards

Currently attainable standards are standard costs that are updated periodically to reflect changes in operating conditions and current price levels for direct materials, direct labor, and factory overhead costs. Unlike ideal standards, currently attainable standards measure reasonable performance under average operating conditions. Normal efficiency is assumed. Under these conditions, direct labor standards include allowances for recurring machine downtime and employee work stoppages. Direct materials standards are based on current market prices and include allowances for normal scrap and spoilage loss.

Currently attainable standards are acceptable for product costing, performance evaluation, planning, and employee motivation. Unless otherwise indicated, the remaining illustrations and problems in this text assume the use of currently attainable standards. Currently attainable standards should yield inventory valuations that closely approximate actual unit costs.

Development of Standard Costs

OBJECTIVE 3
Identify the six elements of a standard unit cost and describe the factors to consider in developing each element

A standard unit cost has six parts: (1) direct materials price standard, (2) direct materials quantity standard, (3) direct labor time standard, (4) direct labor rate standard, (5) standard variable factory overhead rate, and (6) standard fixed factory overhead rate. To develop a standard unit cost, we must identify and analyze each of these items.

Standard Direct Materials Cost. The standard direct materials cost is found by multiplying the standard price for direct materials by the standard quantity for direct materials. If the price standard for a certain item is $2.75 and a job calls for eight of these items, the standard direct materials cost for that job is $22.00 ($2.75 × 8).

The direct materials price standard is a careful estimate of the cost of a certain type of direct material in the next accounting period. Possible price changes, changes in quantities available, and new supplier sources must be considered when determining this standard; any of these factors could influence the price standard. A company's purchasing agent is responsible for developing price standards for all direct materials. The purchasing agent also follows through with actual purchases at the projected standard prices.

The standard use of direct materials is one of the most difficult standards to forecast. The direct materials quantity standard is an estimate of expected quantity use. It is influenced by product engineering specifications, quality of direct materials, age and productivity of machinery, and the quality and experience of the work force. Production managers are usually responsible for establishing and policing direct materials quantity standards. However, other people, such as engineers, the purchasing agent, and machine operators, can provide input into the development of these standards.

Standard Direct Labor Cost. The standard direct labor cost for a product, task, or job order is figured by multiplying the standard hours of direct labor by the standard wage for direct labor. Assume that a product takes 1.5 standard direct labor hours to produce and that the standard labor rate is $8.40 per hour. Even if the person actually making the product is paid only $7.90 per hour, $12.60 (1.5 × $8.40) of standard direct labor cost would be charged to the Work in Process Inventory account.

Current time-and-motion studies of workers and machines as well as past employee and machine performance are the basic inputs for a **direct labor time standard**. Such standards express the time it takes for each department, machine, or process to complete production on 1 unit or batch of output. In many cases, standard time per unit will be a small fraction of an hour. Meeting time standards is the department manager's or supervisor's responsibility. These standards should be revised whenever a machine is replaced or the quality of workers changes.

Labor rates are either set by labor contracts or defined by the company, so standard labor rates are fairly easy to develop. **Direct labor rate standards** are the hourly labor costs that are expected to prevail during the next accounting period for each function or job classification. Although rate ranges are established for each type of worker and rates vary within these ranges, an average standard rate is developed for each task. Problems in controlling costs arise when a highly paid worker performs a lower-level task. For instance, a machine operator making $9.25 per hour may actually perform the work of a setup person earning $4.50 per hour. Here, the actual cost for the work will be at variance with the standard direct labor rate.

Standard Factory Overhead Cost. Basically, a standard factory overhead cost is an estimate of variable and fixed overhead in the next accounting period. The variable overhead cost and the fixed overhead cost depend on standard rates computed in much the same way as the predetermined overhead rate discussed in Chapter 3. There are only two differences. First, the standard overhead rate is made up of two parts, the rate for variable costs and the rate for fixed costs. Second, more time and effort are put into calculating standard overhead rates.

The variable rate and the fixed rate are computed separately because different application bases are generally appropriate. The **standard variable overhead rate** is often computed on the basis of *expected* direct labor hours. (Other bases, such as machine hours, may be used if direct labor hours are not a good barometer of variable costs.) The formula is shown on the following page:

$$\text{Standard variable} \atop \text{overhead rate} = \frac{\text{total budgeted variable overhead costs}}{\text{expected number of standard} \atop \text{direct labor hours}}$$

The **standard fixed overhead rate,** on the other hand, is most often computed on the basis of normal operating capacity. This basis is expressed in the same terms as those used to compute the variable overhead rate.

$$\text{Standard fixed} \atop \text{overhead rate} = \frac{\text{total budgeted fixed overhead costs}}{\text{normal capacity in terms of standard} \atop \text{direct labor hours}}$$

By using normal capacity as the denominator, all fixed overhead costs should be applied to units produced by the time normal capacity is reached.

If actual output exceeds expectations and the standard hours allowed for good units produced is more than normal capacity, a favorable situation exists because more fixed overhead has been applied than was actually incurred. But if actual output does not meet expectations and is less than normal capacity, all expected fixed overhead costs have not been applied to units produced—an unfavorable condition. The difference (variance) between factory overhead incurred and factory overhead applied is discussed in greater detail in Chapter 10.

Updating and Maintaining Standards

Currently attainable standards will not remain so unless they are periodically reviewed and updated. Changing prices, new personnel, new machinery, changing quality of direct materials, and new labor contracts all tend to make currently attainable standards obsolete. Obsolete standards lead to unrealistic budgets, poor cost control, and unreasonable unit costs for inventory valuation.

To prevent standards from becoming obsolete, a company should install a program designed to update standards and maintain them at currently attainable levels. If labor rates are increased, labor rate standards should be adjusted immediately. If a new, more efficient piece of machinery is purchased to replace a relatively inefficient machine, labor time standards and material quantity standards should be updated. In addition to these obvious adjustments, a system for revising standard costs should require that every standard be analyzed for adequacy at least once a year. With this type of annual review system, a company will have standards that approximate currently attainable levels.

Using Standards for Product Costing

Using standard costs does away with the need to compute unit costs from actual cost data for every week or month or for each batch. Once standards are developed for direct materials, direct labor, and factory overhead, a total standard unit cost can be computed anytime.

Standard cost elements can be used to find the following: (1) cost of purchased direct materials entered into Materials Inventory, (2) cost of goods requisitioned out of Materials Inventory and into Work in Process Inventory, (3) cost of direct labor charged to Work in Process Inventory, (4) cost of factory overhead applied to Work in Process Inventory, (5) cost of goods completed and transferred to Finished Goods Inventory, and (6) cost of units sold and charged to the Cost of Goods Sold account. In other words, all transactions (entries) affecting the three inventory accounts and Cost of Goods Sold will be expressed in terms of standard costs, no matter what the actual costs incurred. The following illustrative problem shows how this concept works.

Illustrative Problem: Use of Standard Costs

OBJECTIVE 4
Compute a standard unit cost

McCall Industries, Inc., uses standard costs in its St. Louis, Missouri, division. Recently, the company changed the standards for its line of automatic pencils to agree with current costs for the year 19xx. New standards include the following: Direct materials price standards are $7.20 per square foot for casing material and $1.50 for each movement mechanism. Direct materials quantity standards are .125 square foot of casing material per pencil and one movement mechanism per pencil. Direct labor time standards are .01 hour per pencil for the Stamping Department and .05 hour per pencil for the Assembly Department. Direct labor rate standards are $6.00 per hour for the Stamping Department and $7.20 per hour for the Assembly Department. Standard factory overhead rates are $18.00 per direct labor hour for the standard variable overhead rate and $12.00 per direct labor hour for the standard fixed overhead rate.

Required

Compute the standard manufacturing cost of one automatic pencil.

Solution

Standard cost of one pencil is computed as follows:

Direct materials costs	
Casing ($7.20/sq ft × .125 sq ft)	$ .90
One movement mechanism	1.50
Direct labor costs	
Stamping Department (.01 hr/pencil × $6.00/hr)	.06
Assembly Department (.05 hr/pencil × $7.20/hr)	.36
Factory overhead	
Variable overhead (.06 hr/pencil × $18.00/hr)	1.08
Fixed overhead (.06 hr/pencil × $12.00/hr)	.72
Total standard cost per pencil	$4.62

Journal Entry Analysis

Recording standard costs is much like recording actual cost data. The only major difference is that any amount for direct materials, direct labor, or factory overhead entered into the Work in Process Inventory account is stated at standard cost. This means that the Work in Process Inventory account is stated entirely at standard cost. Any transfer of units to Finished Goods Inventory or to the Cost of Goods Sold account will automatically be at standard unit cost. When actual costs for direct materials, direct labor, and factory overhead are different from standard costs, the difference is recorded in a variance account. (We discuss such accounts in a later section.) In the following analysis, we assume that all costs incurred are at standard cost. Again, we use McCall Industries, Inc., as an example.

Transaction: Purchased 400 square feet of casing material at standard cost.

Entry:	Materials Inventory	2,880	
	Accounts Payable		2,880
	To record purchase of 400 sq ft of casing material at $7.20/sq ft		

(It does not matter if the actual purchase price is higher or lower than the standard price. The same $2,880 standard cost is still entered into the Materials Inventory account. See also the journal entry for purchases on page 331.)

Transaction: Requisitioned 60 square feet of casing material and 240 movement mechanisms into production.

Entry:	Work in Process Inventory	792	
	Materials Inventory		792
	To record requisition of 60 sq ft of casing material (at $7.20/sq ft) and 240 movement mechanisms (at $1.50 each) into production		

Transaction: At period end 300 pencils were completed and transferred to Finished Goods Inventory.

Entry:	Finished Goods Inventory	1,386	
	Work in Process Inventory		1,386
	To record the transfer of 300 completed units to Finished Goods Inventory (300 pencils × $4.62/pencil)		

This analysis shows only a few examples of the journal entries used in recording standard cost information. The examples given later in this chapter and in Chapter 10 are more realistic because they are joined with the analysis of variances. Our purpose here is just to show that when a standard cost accounting system is used, standard costs, rather than actual costs, flow through the production and inventory accounts.

Benefits and Drawbacks
of a Standard Costing System

The principal advantages of a standard costing system for pla.
control, and product costing are as follows:

1. The setting of standards requires a thorough analysis of all cost functions and often discloses inefficiencies.
2. Standard cost information is more useful than historical cost data for product costing and pricing.
3. Standard costs are the basis of an effective budgetary control system.
4. The speed with which regular operating data is recorded is increased.
5. Clearly defined lines of cost responsibility and authority are established by a standard costing system.
6. The setting of standards forces management to plan efficient operations.
7. Performance evaluation is enhanced through variance analysis.

There are also certain limitations regarding standard costing systems. The use of standard costing is not practical for every company because a standard cost system is expensive to develop. In addition, maintenance and updating requirements are costly. Before deciding to install a standard cost system, management should conduct some type of cost-benefit analysis. If the potential benefits exceed the costs, then standard costing should be introduced into the cost accounting system.

Variance Analysis:
Direct Materials and Direct Labor

Variance analysis is a cost control tool provided by standard cost accounting systems. Standard costs form the foundation for effective budgetary control. The development and use of standard costs facilitate the planning phase of budgetary control. However, budgetary control is successful only if management's effectiveness and operating efficiency can be analyzed. Such analyses involve cost control and are achieved by measuring and evaluating performance. **Variance analysis** is the process of computing the amount of and isolating the causes of differences between actual costs and standard costs.

As stated, a major objective of variance analysis is to measure management's effectiveness and operating efficiency. Comparisons of actual operating results with budgeted or planned operating activities are the foundation for performance evaluation. If actual operating costs deviate from anticipated costs, a cost variance is incurred. A variance indicates that management has failed to accomplish a stated objective. Variance analysis helps determine the reasons for unsatisfactory or superior operating results.

Variance analysis involves two phases: (1) computing individual variances and (2) determining the cause(s) of each variance. The remaining sections of this chapter concentrate on computing materials and labor variances. Overhead variance computations, analysis of causes, reporting of variances to managers, and accounting for the disposition of variances, which are covered in Chapter 10, conclude the study of standard cost variance analysis.

Direct Materials Variances

OBJECTIVE 5
Compute and evaluate direct materials and direct labor variances

To identify direct materials variances, we compare standard amounts for price and quantity with actual prices and quantities of materials used. Let us assume, for example, that Pearce Company makes leather chairs. Each chair should use 4 yards of leather (standard quantity), and the standard price of leather is $6.00 per yard. During August, 760 yards of leather, costing $5.90 per yard, were purchased and used to produce 180 chairs. The total direct materials cost variance is computed as follows:

Actual cost

      Actual quantity × actual price =
              760 yd at $5.90/yd = $4,484

Standard cost

    Standard quantity × standard price =
    (180 chairs × 4 yd/chair) at $6.00/yd =
            720 yd at $6.00/yd =   4,320
    Total direct materials cost variance $ 164(U)

Remember, the U following the dollar amount indicates an unfavorable situation. (A favorable situation would be indicated by an F.) The special problem facing Pearce Company is that part of this variance is caused by price differences and part is caused by direct materials usage. To find the area or people responsible for these variances, the total direct materials cost variance must be broken down into two parts: the direct materials price variance and the direct materials quantity variance.

The **direct materials price variance** is the difference between the actual price and the standard price, multiplied by the actual quantity purchased. For the Pearce Company it would be computed as follows:

Actual price $5.90
Less standard price   6.00
   Difference $ .10(F)

    Price variance = (actual price − standard price) × actual quantity
              = $.10(F) × 760 yards
              = $76(F)

The **direct materials quantity variance** is the difference between the actual quantity used and the standard quantity that should have been used, multiplied by the standard price:

Actual quantity	760 yd
Less standard quantity (180 × 4 yd/chair)	720 yd
Difference	40 yd(U)

Quantity variance = (actual quantity − standard quantity) × standard price
$$= 40 \text{ yd(U)} \times \$6/\text{yd}$$
$$\$240\text{(U)}$$

As a check of these answers, the sum of the price variance and the quantity variance should equal the total direct materials cost variance:

Price variance	$ 76(F)
Quantity variance	240(U)
Total direct materials cost variance	$164(U)

Sometimes it is easier to see cost relationships when shown in a diagram. Figure 9-2 illustrates the cost variance analysis described above. Materials are purchased at actual cost but entered into the Materials Inventory account at standard price. Therefore the materials price variance of $76(F) is determined before costs are entered into Materials Inventory. The materials quantity variance results from using too much or too little materials in making the product. Spoilage and waste occur, of which some may be unavoidable and, thus, anticipated when computing the standard quantity amount. A materials quantity variance occurs when the standard quantity is not used. If more quantity is used, as in the Pearce Company example, an unfavorable materials quantity variance results; here, $240(U). As shown, standard quantity times standard price is the amount entered into the Work in Process Inventory account.

Normally, the purchasing agent is responsible for price variances, and the production department supervisors are accountable for quantity variances. In cases such as this one, however, the less expensive materials may have been of such poor quality that higher scrap rates resulted. Each situation must be evaluated according to specific circumstances, not by general guidelines.

Direct Labor Variances

The approach to finding variances in direct labor costs parallels the approach to finding direct materials variances. Total direct labor variance is the difference between the actual labor cost and standard labor cost for the good units produced. Expanding the Pearce Company example, we find that each chair requires 2.4 standard labor hours, and the standard labor rate is $8.50 per hour. During August, 450 direct labor hours were used to make 180 chairs at an average pay rate of $9.20 per hour. The total direct labor cost variance is computed as shown on the following page:

Figure 9-2. Materials Variance Analysis

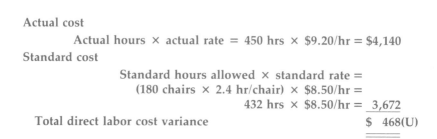

Using Data from the Pearce Company Illustration:

Actual Materials Cost	Costs Entered into Materials Inventory	Costs Entered into Work in Process Inventory
Actual Quantity at Actual Price	Actual Quantity at Standard Price	Standard Quantity at Standard Price
760 yds. @ $5.90/yd. $4,484	760 yds. @ $6.00/yd. $4,560	720 yds. @ $6.00/yd. $4,320

Price Variance	Quantity Variance
$76(F)	$240(U)

Total Materials Cost Variance
$164(U)

Actual cost

$$\text{Actual hours} \times \text{actual rate} = 450 \text{ hrs} \times \$9.20/\text{hr} = \$4,140$$

Standard cost

$$\text{Standard hours allowed} \times \text{standard rate} =$$
$$(180 \text{ chairs} \times 2.4 \text{ hr/chair}) \times \$8.50/\text{hr} =$$
$$432 \text{ hrs} \times \$8.50/\text{hr} = \underline{3,672}$$

Total direct labor cost variance $\$468(\text{U})$

Both the actual hours per chair and the actual labor rate varied from standard. For effective cost control, management must know how much of the total cost arose from varying labor rates and how much from varying labor hour usage. This information is found by computing the labor rate variance and the labor efficiency variance separately.

The **direct labor rate variance** is the difference between the actual labor rate and the standard labor rate, multiplied by the actual hours worked:

Actual rate	$9.20
Less standard rate	8.50
Difference	$ .70(U)

$$\text{Rate variance} = (\text{actual rate} - \text{standard rate}) \times \text{actual hours}$$
$$= .70(U) \times 450 \text{ hours}$$
$$= \$315(U)$$

The **direct labor efficiency variance** is the difference between actual hours worked and standard hours allowed for the good units produced, multiplied by the standard labor rate:

Actual hours worked	450 hrs
Less standard hours allowed (180 chairs × 2.4 hr/chair)	432 hrs
Difference	18 hrs(U)

$$\text{Efficiency variance} = (\text{actual hours} - \text{standard hours allowed}) \times \text{standard rate}$$
$$= 18 \text{ hrs}(U) \times \$8.50/\text{hr}$$
$$= \$153(U)$$

The following check shows that the variances were computed correctly:

Rate variance	$315(U)
Efficiency variance	153(U)
Total direct labor cost variance	$468(U)

Labor rate variances are generally the responsibility of the Personnel Department. A rate variance often occurs when a person is hired at an incorrect rate or performs the duties of a higher- or lower-paid employee. Labor efficiency variances can be traced to departmental supervisors. As with direct materials variances, an unfavorable labor efficiency variance can occur if an inexperienced, lower-paid person is assigned to a task requiring greater skill. Management should judge each situation only after looking at all circumstances.

The analysis in Figure 9-2 can be easily adjusted to fit the computations for labor variances. Figure 9-3 contains a summary of the direct labor variance analysis. Unlike materials variances, the labor rate and efficiency variances are usually computed and recorded at the same time. Thi approach is used because labor is not stored in an inventory ac before use, as are materials. The labor rate variance is the di

Figure 9-3. Direct Labor Variance Analysis

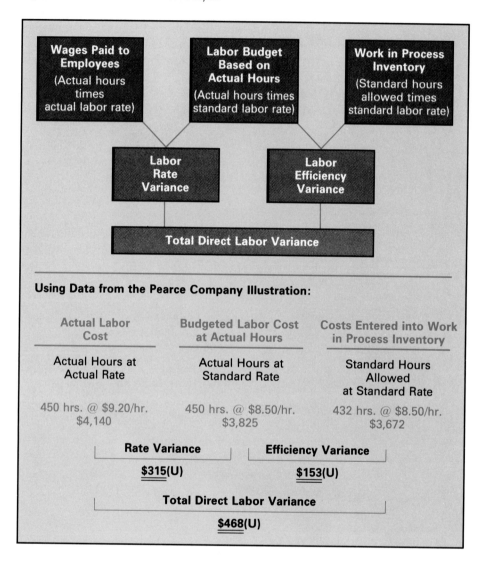

between wages paid to employees (actual direct labor expense) and the labor budget based on actual hours (direct labor expense if standard direct labor rates were paid). The difference between the labor budget based on actual hours and the labor cost entered into the Work in Process Inventory is the labor efficiency variance. Efficiency relates to the time taken to complete a task. Here, efficiency is measured as the difference between actual hours worked and standard hours allowed for the good units produced during the period. This difference is multiplied by the standard labor rate to compute the variance. Data from the Pearce Company were inserted into the lower portion of Figure 9-3 to illustrate this approach to labor variance analysis.

Variances in the Accounting Records

When variances from standard costs develop, special journal entries are needed. The few simple rules below will make this recording process easier to remember.

1. *All* inventory balances are recorded at standard cost, as stated earlier.
2. Separate accounts are created for each type of variance.
3. *Unfavorable* variances are *debited* to their accounts, and *favorable* variances are *credited*.

With these rules in mind, we will now record the direct materials and direct labor transactions of the Pearce Company described earlier.

Note that it is possible to operate a standard cost system without putting variances into the records with journal entries. Variances can be computed on work sheets, and actual costs can be run through accounts. This approach is less costly to operate. However, it loses the advantage of consistent pricing of products and inventories. It also makes it more difficult to record product cost flow.

Journal Entries for Direct Materials Transactions

There are two key points in these transactions: (1) The increase in Materials Inventory is recorded at the actual quantity purchased but priced at standard cost. (2) Accounts Payable is stated at the actual cost (actual quantity purchased × actual price paid per unit) to record the proper liability.

a. Direct Materials Purchase:

Materials Inventory (760 yds @ $6)	4,560	
Direct Materials Price Variance		76
Accounts Payable (actual cost)		4,484
To record purchase of direct materials and resulting variance		

b. Direct Materials Requisition:

Work in Process Inventory (720 yds @ $6)	4,320	
Direct Materials Quantity Variance	240	
Materials Inventory (760 yds @ $6)		4,560
To record usage of direct materials and resulting variance		

Note the important aspects of this entry: (1) Everything in the Work in Process Inventory is recorded at standard cost, which here means standard quantity × standard price. (2) Actual quantity at standard price must come out of Materials Inventory because that is how it was first recorded. Remember that quantities purchased may actually be used in smaller amounts. In our example, the entire amount of the purchase was used during the period.

Journal Entry for Direct Labor Transactions

Using the variance analysis data computed earlier, the journal entry to record this information is shown below:

Work in Process Inventory (432 hr @ $8.50/hr)	3,672	
Direct Labor Rate Variance	315	
Direct Labor Efficiency Variance	153	
Factory Payroll (450 hr @ $9.20/hr)		4,140
To charge labor cost to		
Work in Process and to identify		
the resulting variances		

When recording labor costs, the same rules hold true as for recording the requisition of materials: (1) Work in Process Inventory is charged with standard labor cost (standard hours allowed × standard labor rate). (2) Factory Payroll must be credited for the actual labor cost of the workers (actual hours worked × actual labor rate earned). The variances, if computed properly, will balance out the difference between these two amounts.

Graphical Approach to Variances

The beginning student does not always understand variance analysis using formulas and symbols. Often, a graphical approach provides a clearer picture of what a variance involves and the components necessary for its determination. As an example, the labor efficiency variance is derived from labor hour input-output comparisons, whereas labor rate comparisons lead to labor rate variances. Figure 9-4 is a graphic illustration of these variances. The vertical axis represents direct labor pay rates; the horizontal axis, direct labor hours. Total standard labor cost is shown by the large unshaded box and is computed by multiplying the standard direct labor rate (R_s) by the standard hours allowed (H_s). Actual labor cost is actual direct labor rate (R_a) multiplied by actual hours worked (H_a) and includes the shaded and unshaded parts of the diagram. As depicted in Figure 9-4:

$$\text{Rate variance} = (R_a - R_s) \times H_a$$
$$\text{Efficiency variance} = (H_a - H_s) \times R_s$$

Since actual labor costs exceed standard labor costs, the diagram illustrates the unfavorable labor rate and efficiency variances. If H_s were greater than H_a or R_s greater than R_a, favorable variances would result. The combined variance is really caused because both actual hours and actual rate exceeded standard. Since actual hours are used in computing the labor rate variance, this variance includes the combined variance shown in Figure 9-4.

Figure 9-4. Labor Variances—Graphic Illustration

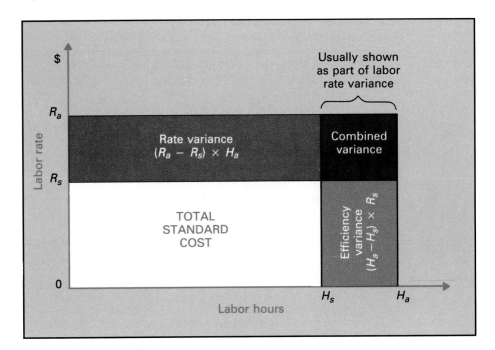

Chapter Review

Review of Learning Objectives

1. **Describe the nature and purpose of standard costs.**
   Standard costs are realistically predetermined costs for direct materials, direct labor, and factory overhead. They are usually expressed as cost per unit of finished product. They are introduced into a cost accounting system to help in the budgetary control process. Standard costs are used to evaluate performance and prepare operating budgets, to identify areas of the production process requiring cost control measures, to set realistic prices, and to simplify cost accounting procedures for inventories and product costing.

2. **Describe and differentiate among the three types of standard costs: ideal standards, basic standards, and currently attainable standards.**
   Ideal standards are perfection cost standards that allow for minimum direct materials, direct labor, and other cost constraints in the manufacturing of a product. Performance equivalent to ideal standard level is rarely accomplished. Basic standards are seldom revised or updated to reflect current operating costs and price level changes. They are left unchanged and are used primarily to measure trends in operating performance. Currently attainable standards are updated periodically to reflect changes in operating conditions and current price levels for direct materials, direct labor, and factory overhead costs.

3. Identify the six elements of a standard unit cost and describe the factors to consider in developing each element.

The six elements of a standard unit cost are (1) direct materials price standard, (2) direct materials quantity standard, (3) direct labor time standard, (4) direct labor rate standard, (5) standard variable factory overhead rate, and (6) standard fixed factory overhead rate. The direct materials price standard is found by carefully considering expected price increases, changes in quantities available, and possible new supplier sources. The direct materials quantity standard is an expression of forecasted, or expected, quantity usage. It is affected by product engineering specifications, quality of direct materials used, age and productivity of the machines being used, and the quality and experience of the machine operators and setup people. The direct labor time standard is based on current time-and-motion studies of workers and machines and past employee and machine performance. Labor union contracts and company personnel policies lead to direct labor rate standards. Standard variable and fixed factory overhead rates are found by taking total budgeted or forecasted variable and fixed factory overhead costs and dividing by an appropriate application base, such as standard direct labor hours or normal capacity.

4. Compute a standard unit cost.

A product's total standard unit cost is computed by adding the following costs: (1) direct materials cost (equals direct materials price standard × direct materials quantity standard), (2) direct labor cost (equals direct labor time standard × direct labor rate standard), and (3) factory overhead cost (equals standard variable and standard fixed factory overhead rates × standard direct labor hours per unit).

5. Compute and evaluate direct materials and direct labor variances.

Cost variances, or differences between actual and standard costs, can be computed for direct materials and direct labor. The direct materials price and quantity variances help explain differences between actual and standard direct materials costs. Direct labor cost differences are analyzed by identifying the direct labor rate variance and the direct labor efficiency variance. Each variance results from specific causes, and these causes help pinpoint reasons for the differences between actual and standard costs.

6. Prepare journal entries to record transactions involving direct materials and direct labor variances in a standard cost system.

Journal entries are used to integrate standard cost variance information into the accounting records. Unfavorable variances create debit balances, and favorable variances are credited. General ledger accounts are maintained for direct materials price variance, direct materials quantity variance, direct labor rate variance, and direct labor efficiency variance. The key point to remember in preparing journal entries to record transactions in a standard costing system is that all entries affecting Materials Inventory, Work in Process Inventory, Finished Goods Inventory, and Cost of Goods Sold accounts *must* be recorded at standard cost.

Review of Concepts and Terminology

The following important concepts were introduced in this chapter:

(L.O. 1) **Standard costs:** Realistically predetermined costs for direct materials, direct labor, and factory overhead.

(L.O.2) **Ideal standards:** Standards based on a maximum efficiency level with no allowances for breaks or other work stoppages. (Also called theoretical or perfection standards.)

(L.O.2) **Basic standards:** Projections that are seldom revised or updated to reflect current operating costs and price level changes.

(L.O.2) **Currently attainable standards:** Standard costs that are updated periodically to reflect changes in operating conditions and current price levels for direct materials, direct labor, and factory overhead costs.

(L.O.3) **Standard direct materials cost:** The standard price for direct materials multiplied by the standard quantity for direct materials.

(L.O.3) **Standard direct labor cost:** The standard hours of direct labor times the standard wage for direct labor.

(L.O.3) **Standard factory overhead cost:** An estimate of variable and fixed overhead in the next accounting period.

(L.O.5) **Variance analysis:** The process of computing the amount of and isolating the causes of differences between actual costs and standard costs.

Other important terms introduced in this chapter are:

direct labor rate standard (p. 321)
direct labor time standard (p. 321)
direct materials price standard (p. 320)
direct materials quantity standard (p. 321)
standard fixed overhead rate (p. 322)
standard variable overhead rate (p. 321)

Review Problem: Standard Process Costing System

The journal entry analysis described in this chapter centers on the use of standard costs in a job order costing system. Standard costs, however, are also applicable to a *process costing system.* Assume the following circumstances:

Bates, Inc., uses a standard process costing system in its East Texas plant, which manufactures a special chemical product. The standard cost per unit of finished product is

Direct materials (4 gal @ $2.50/gal)	$10.00
Direct labor (6 hr @ $4.00/hr)	24.00
Factory overhead (6 hr @ $5.00/hr)	30.00
Unit standard cost (4-gal container)	$64.00

All direct materials are introduced at the start of the process, and conversion costs are applied uniformly throughout the process. Assume an *average* cost flow approach. Also assume that any loss of materials is caused by normal evaporation or spoilage. During April 19x3 the Processing Department transferred 3,000 units to Finished Goods Inventory. Work in Process inventories at the beginning and end of April were 2,000 and 6,000 gallons, respectively. All partially processed units are considered 50 percent complete for conversion cost purposes. Actual production costs in beginning Work in Process Inventory and from usage in April were (a) direct materials, 18,100 gallons, costing $2.25 per gallon and (b) conversion costs of $192,500.

Required

1. Using the *average* process costing approach, prepare the following schedules for the month of April:
   a. Schedule of equivalent production.
   b. Unit cost analysis schedule.
   c. Cost summary schedule.
2. Prepare the journal entry to transfer costs of goods completed from Work in Process Inventory to Finished Goods Inventory.
3. Compute the materials price variance and the materials quantity variance for the period.

Answer to Review Problem

1a, b. The primary purpose of the Schedule of Equivalent Production is to provide data for computing unit cost in the Unit Cost Analysis Schedule. Since only standard costs are used in entries to the Work in Process Inventory account, unit cost will always be at standard. Therefore it is unnecessary to complete parts 1a and 1b of this problem.

1c. Before completing the Cost Summary Schedule, you should study the following analysis of units:

Units in beginning inventory (2,000 gal ÷ 4)	500
Units started	4,000*
Units to be accounted for	4,500
Units completed and transferred	3,000
Units in ending inventory (6,000 gal ÷ 4)	1,500
Units to be accounted for	4,500
Units started and completed: 4,000 − 1,500 =	2,500

*This amount is computed after you determine the number of units to be accounted for.

Bates, Inc. Cost Summary Schedule For the Month Ended April 30, 19x3		
	Cost of Goods Transferred to Finished Goods Inventory	Cost of Ending Work in Process Inventory
Beginning inventory		
500 units × $64/unit	$ 32,000	
Units started and completed		
2,500 units × $64/unit	160,000	
Ending inventory		
Materials		
1,500 units × $10/unit		$ 15,000
Conversion costs		
750 units × $54/unit		40,500
	$192,000	$ 55,500

(continued)

Computation check	
Cost to Finished Goods Inventory	$192,000
Cost to Ending Work in Process Inventory	55,500
Total standard costs to be accounted for	$247,500

2. The journal entry for April would be

Finished Goods Inventory	192,000	
Work in Process Inventory		192,000
To transfer costs of units		
completed in April from		
Work in Process Inventory to		
Finished Goods Inventory		

3. The materials price variance and the materials quantity variance for the period are computed as follows:

Actual cost of materials	
18,100 gal @ $2.25/gal =	$40,725
Standard cost of materials	
4,500 units $\times$ 4 gal $\times$ $2.50/gal =	45,000
Total materials cost variance	$ 4,275(F)
Materials price variance	
($2.25 $-$ $2.50) $\times$ 18,100 gal	
= $.25(F) $\times$ 18,100 gal =	$ 4,525(F)
Materials quantity variance	
(18,100 $-$ (4,500 $\times$ 4)) $\times$ $2.50/gal	
= 100(U) $\times$ $2.50/gal =	250(U)
Total materials cost variance	$ 4,275(F)

Chapter Assignments

Questions

1. Define the following terms and concepts:
   a. Standard costs
   b. Budgetary control
   c. Ideal standards
   d. Basic standards
   e. Currently attainable standards
   f. Direct materials price variance
   g. Direct materials quantity variance
   h. Direct labor rate variance
   i. Direct labor efficiency variance
2. Describe how standard costs are useful in the budgetary control process.

3. Identify and differentiate between the three types of standard costs.
4. What characteristics do predetermined overhead costing and standard costing share? How do these costing approaches differ?
5. Explain the statement, "Standard costing is a total cost concept in that standard unit costs are determined for direct materials, direct labor, and factory overhead."
6. Identify and describe the six standard cost elements used to compute total standard unit cost.
7. What factors could influence a direct materials price standard?
8. "Standard labor cost is a function of efficiency and unionization." Is this a true statement? Defend your answer.
9. What general ledger accounts are affected by installing a standard cost system?
10. Why is it important to update standard costs?
11. "In a standard costing system, all inventories are valued at standard cost." Is this statement true? For reporting purposes, when must standard costs be replaced by actual costs?
12. State and discuss three advantages of using a standard costing system.
13. What is the principal disadvantage of a standard costing system?
14. What motivational considerations are important when developing standard costs?
15. Compare and contrast the usefulness of ideal standards, basic standards, and currently attainable standards.
16. What is a variance?
17. What is the formula for computing a direct materials quantity variance?
18. How would you interpret an unfavorable direct materials price variance?

Classroom Exercises

Exercise 9-1.
Purpose of
Standard Costs
(L.O.1)

Ron Bawmann is a senior accountant for a large public accounting firm, Swanson & Oliver, CPAs. One of his duties is to counsel and advise clients regarding needed improvements or additions to their accounting systems. His newest client, Augustana Industries of Rock Island, Illinois, manufactures rubber gaskets for automobile engines. These products are homogeneous and produced in long production runs. The company, which uses a process cost accounting system, has been experiencing both labor and materials inefficiencies. Total cost increases have far exceeded the labor rate and materials price increases.

Augustana's president, an engineer, has asked Mr. Bawmann for advice. The president would like to know more about a standard cost accounting system and how it could possibly help control costs in her company.

Prepare a reply to the president.

Exercise 9-2.
Types of Standard
Costs
(L.O.2)

Accountants Torrington, Connor, and Leene are involved in a heavy discussion concerning the development of materials cost standards for their company's rock-music disk products.

Torrington: I think we should use maximum production data and minimum cost data to compute these standards. Our organization is operated at a very efficient level. Our standards should reflect this high level of productivity.

Connor: Listen, hip means being realistic. We must take a close look at what our productivity levels are and try to anticipate changes in our purchase prices when computing these standards.

Leene: You both are missing the boat. We already have a set of standards that have been used since my daddy worked for this company. They were useful then, and they are still useful now. They have been tested over the years, and the company has remained profitable during the entire period.

1. Identify the types of standards each accountant is advocating.
2. Discuss the advantages and disadvantages of each type of standard. Include behavioral considerations in your responses.

Exercise 9-3.
Keeping Standards Current
(L.O. 3)

Peters Paper Company recently installed a complete standard process cost accounting system. N. A. Always, controller of the Irvine Division, is concerned about keeping cost standards on a current basis. He is thinking about establishing a standard maintenance system and has asked U. R. Next, assistant controller, to take charge of the project and to outline the system.

List the suggested policies, procedures, and people that Ms. Next should include in her analysis.

Exercise 9-4.
Standard Unit Cost Computation
(L.O. 4)

Accountants and engineers of the Boyce Saw Company developed the following direct materials cost and usage standards and direct labor time and rate standards for producing a small chain saw, one of the company's main products. Direct materials required are a saw motor casing at $4.75, an operating chain at $3.50, a 3-horsepower motor at $19.90, and a chain housing at $6.25. Direct labor consists of .5 hour for a materials inspector at $7.50 per hour, .5 hour for an assembler at $9.00 per hour, and .25 hour for a product tester at $8.00 per hour. Factory overhead charges are figured at a variable rate of $10.00 per direct labor hour and at a fixed rate of $7.40 per direct labor hour.

Compute the total standard manufacturing cost of one chain saw.

Exercise 9-5.
Standard Unit Cost Computation
(L.O. 4)

Moustafa Aerodynamics, Inc., makes electronically equipped weather-detecting balloons for university meteorological departments. Recent effects of nationwide inflation have caused the company's management to recompute its standard costs.

New direct materials price standards are $620.00 per set for electronic components and $4.00 per square meter for heavy-duty canvas. Direct materials quantity standards include one set of electronic components per balloon and 95 square meters of heavy-duty canvas per balloon. Direct labor time standards are 14.5 hours per balloon for the Electronics Department and 12.0 hours per balloon for the Assembly Department. Direct labor rate standards are $9.00 an hour for the Electronics Department and $8.50 an hour for the Assembly Department. Standard factory overhead rates are $12.00 per direct labor hour for the standard variable overhead rate and $9.00 per direct labor hour for the standard fixed overhead rate.

Using the production standards provided, compute the standard manufacturing cost of one weather balloon.

Exercise 9-6.
Direct Materials Price and Quantity Variances
(L.O. 5)

The Marcos Elevator Company manufactures small hydroelectric elevators with a maximum capacity of ten passengers each. One of the direct materials the Production Department uses is heavy-duty carpet for the elevator floors. The direct materials quantity standard used for the month ended April 30, 19xx was 8 square yards per elevator. During April, the purchasing agent was able to purchase this carpet for $8 per square yard. Standard price for the period was $10. Eighty-two elevators were completed and sold during April, and the Production Department used 9.6 square yards of carpet per elevator.

Calculate the direct materials price variance and quantity variance for April 19xx.

Exercise 9-7.
Direct Labor Rate
and Efficiency
Variances
(L.O. 5)

Winter Park Foundry, Inc., produces castings used by other companies in the production of machinery. For the past two years the largest-selling product has been a casting for an eight-cylinder engine block. Standard direct labor hours per engine block are 1.8 hours. The labor contract requires that all direct labor employees be paid $9.50 an hour. During June, 16,500 engine blocks were produced. Actual direct labor hours and cost for June were 30,000 hours and $288,000, respectively.

1. Compute the direct labor rate variance for June for the engine block product line.
2. Using the same data, compute the direct labor efficiency variance for June for the engine block product line. [Check your answer. Assume that total direct labor variance is $5,850(U).]

Exercise 9-8.
Journal Entries—
Standard Costing
(L.O. 6)

Following are isolated transactions of the Cent Franc Corporation for August 19x8. The company uses a standard job order costing system.

August 6   Purchased direct materials
            Actual cost $13,450
            Standard cost   14,500
        9   Requisitioned a total of $7,500 in direct materials from inventory into production. An analysis of standard quantities required indicates that $400 worth of excess materials, which were spoiled, were included in the requisition.
       12   Paid factory wages and salaries and credited Factory Payroll account for $17,650. An analysis of factory wages disclosed that unfavorable labor variances of $400 were incurred, including a labor rate variance of $750(U).

Prepare journal entries to record these transactions.

Exercise 9-9.
Standard Cost
Journal Entries
(L.O. 6)

Bush-Hunt Battery Company produces batteries for automobiles, motorcycles, and mopeds. Transactions for direct materials and direct labor for March were as follows:

1. Purchased 1,000 type A battery casings for $6.50 each on account; standard cost, $7.00 per casing.
2. Purchased 5,000 type 4C lead battery plates for $2.40 each on account; standard cost, $2.25 per plate.
3. Requisitioned 32 type A battery casings and 128 type 4C lead plates into production. Order 647 called for 30 batteries, each using a standard quantity of four plates per casing.
4. Direct labor costs for Order 647 are shown on the next page:

Department H
Actual labor   26 hr @ $5/hr
Standard labor   24 hr @ $5/hr
Department J
Actual labor   10 hr @ $6.50/hr
Standard labor   12 hr @ $7.00/hr

Prepare journal entries for the four transactions.

Interpreting Accounting Information

Direct Materials Variances: Portsmouth Industries (L.O. 1, 3)

Portsmouth Industries produces a diverse line of paper products and uses a standard cost system for all inventories. Material 42H is a chemical dye used in several departments and in many products. The company has recently experienced a trend of unfavorable quantity variances for material 42H. The production vice president received a summary report of September's operations, which disclosed the following results:

Material 42H issued to production	438,000 lbs
Standard allowance for good production	412,000 lbs
Over standard	26,000 lbs
Current price (September 30, 19x5)	× $5.50
Unfavorable variance	$143,000

On inquiring, the vice president discovered that the purchase price of 42H has increased 8 percent since the beginning of the year. The standard allowances were derived by a clerical assistant who worked all day searching through completed production reports. The vice president could not readily determine the products or the departments that accounted for this quantity variance.

Required

Assume you are the production vice president. Write a memorandum to the company's controller that summarizes weaknesses in the standard cost system and recommends appropriate changes.

Problem Set A

Problem 9A-1. Standard Cost per Unit (L.O. 4)

The Columbia Products Company uses three production departments to produce Bold, a leading men's aftershave lotion. The product requires processing in the Blending, Cooling, and Bottling departments, in that order. The following data were used to establish standard overhead costs, materials, and labor for each 4-ounce unit of Bold:

Factory Overhead (plantwide rates)
Standard variable overhead rate $3.46/direct labor dollar
Standard fixed overhead rate $5.94/direct labor dollar

Direct Materials	Purchase Quantities and Prices	Normal Evaporation Loss
Sweet water	10,000 gallons @ $40.00/100 gallons	20%
Herbs and spices	1,500 pounds @ $180.00/100 pounds	
Bottles	1,000 bottles @ $.80/bottle	

Note: Average batch size is 1,000 gallons before evaporation, and 500 pounds of herbs and spices are added to each 1,000-gallon batch.

Labor	Blending	Cooling	Bottling
Standard time per batch in each department	7 hours	2 hours	12 hours
Number of direct labor workers required per batch	2	1	4
Standard wage rate per hour	$4.40	$4.25	$4.30

Required

Compute the standard production cost of

1. One batch of Bold
2. One 4-ounce bottle of Bold
   (*Note:* 1 gallon = 128 ounces.)

Problem 9A-2.
Development of Standards: Direct Materials
(L.O.3,4)

Lovett & Clayton, Ltd., assemble clock movements for grandfather clocks. Each movement has four components that have to be assembled: the clock facing, the clock hands, the time movement, and the spring assembly. For the current year, 19x7, the company used the following standard costs: facing, $14.60; hands, $16.90, time movement, $46.10; and spring assembly, $22.50.

Prices and sources of materials are expected to change in 19x8. Company A will supply 70 percent of the facings at $16.50 each, and the remaining 30 percent will be purchased from Company B at $17.90 each. The hands are produced for Lovett & Clayton by Albert Hardware, Inc., and will cost $19.75 per set in 19x8. Time movements will be purchased from three Swiss sources: Company Q, 20 percent of total need at $48.50 per movement; Company R, 30 percent at $49.50; and Company S, 50 percent at $51.90. Spring assemblies will be purchased from a French company and are expected to increase in cost by 30 percent.

Required

1. Determine the total standard materials cost per unit for 19x8.
2. If the company could guarantee the purchase of 2,500 sets of hands from Albert Hardware, Inc., the unit cost would be reduced by 10 percent. Find the resulting standard materials unit cost.

3. Substandard spring assemblies can be purchased at $25.50, but 15 percent of them will be unusable and nonreturnable. Compute the standard direct materials unit cost if the company follows this procedure, assuming the original facts of the case for the remaining data. The cost of the defective materials will be spread over good units produced.

**Problem 9A-3.
Developing and
Using Standard
Costs**
(L.O. 3, 4, 6)

Prefabricated, factory-built houses are the specialty of Young Homes, Inc., of Buffalo, New York. Although many models are produced and it is possible to special order a home, 60 percent of the company's business comes from the sale of the El Dorado home. The El Dorado is a three-bedroom, 2,200-square foot home, and the front entrance section is its real selling feature. Six basic materials are used to manufacture this section, and their 19x7 standard costs are as follows: (a) wood framing materials, $120; (b) the deluxe front door, $180; (c) door hardware, $60; (d) exterior siding, $210; (e) electrical materials, $80; and (f) interior finishing materials, $140. The three types of labor used for this section and their respective 19x7 standard costs are: (a) carpenter, 10 hours at $12 per hour; (b) door specialist, 4 hours at $15 per hour; and (c) electrician, 3 hours at $16 per hour. The company used 50 percent of direct labor dollars as an overhead rate for 19x7.

During 19x8 the following changes are anticipated:

Wood framing materials	increase by 20 percent
Deluxe front door	will need two suppliers; Supplier A, 40 percent of need @ $190 per door; Supplier B, 60 percent of need @ $200 per door
Door hardware	increase by 10 percent
Exterior siding	decrease by $10 per section
Electrical materials	increase by 20 percent
Interior finishing materials	remain the same
Carpenter wages	increase by $1 per hour
Door specialist wages	remain the same
Electrician wages	increase by 10 percent
Factory overhead rate	decrease to 40 percent of direct labor cost

Required

1. Compute the total standard direct materials cost per front entrance section for 19x7.
2. Using your answer from **1** and other information from the problem, compute the 19x8 standard manufacturing cost for the El Dorado's front entrance section.
3. From the information above, prepare journal entries for the following 19x8 transactions:

Jan. 6 Purchased 120 front doors from Supplier A for $22,800.
14 Requisitioned 60 sets of hardware into production to complete a job calling for 56 section units.
30 Transferred the 56 completed sections to Finished Goods Inventory.

Problem 9A-4.
Materials and
Labor Variances
(L.O. 5, 6)

Reggie Trophies Company produces a variety of athletic awards, most in the form of trophies or mounted replicas of athletes in action. Mr. Jackson, president of the company, is developing a standard cost accounting system. Trophies differ in size, and Reggie has six standard sizes. The deluxe trophy stands 3 feet above the base. Materials standards include 1 pound of metal and 3 ounces of plastic supported by a 6-ounce wooden base. Standard prices for 19x9 were $2.25 per pound of metal; $.20 per ounce of plastic; and $.50 per ounce of wood.

Direct labor is used in both the Molding and Trimming/Finishing Departments. Deluxe trophies require labor standards of .2 hours of direct labor in the Molding Department and .4 hours in the Trimming/Finishing Department. Standard labor rates for deluxe trophies include $8.50 per hour in Molding and $8.00 per hour in Trimming/Finishing.

During January 19x9, 14,400 deluxe trophies were made. The actual production data were as follows:

Materials
    Metal   15,840 pounds @ $2.20/pound
    Plastic   46,080 ounces @ $.25/ounce
    Wood   86,400 ounces @ $.60/ounce
Labor
    Molding   3,600 hours @ $8.60/hour
    Trimming/Finishing   5,040 hours @ $8.10/hour

Required

1. Compute the direct materials price and quantity variances for metal, plastic, and wood bases.
2. Compute the direct labor rate and efficiency variances for the Molding and the Trimming/Finishing Departments.
3. Prepare journal entries to record the transactions involving materials and labor for the period.

Problem 9A-5.
Standard Process
Costing
(L.O. 4, 5, 6)

Beauty Gloss is the primary paint product of Mary Jo Key Paints, Inc. The company produces its paint products in two departments, Mixing and Canning, and uses a standard process costing system. Three direct materials—water, material M, and material J—are added on a per batch basis at the beginning of the mixing process. Only gallon-size cans are added in the Canning Department at the end of the process. Labor costs are incurred uniformly throughout both departments.

Actual costs incurred for August
   Water: 2,400 gal @ $.022/gal $ 52.80
   Material M: 480 gal @ $4.90   2,352.00
   Material J: 120 gal @ $13.40   1,608.00
   Gallon cans: 3,100 @ $.85   2,635.00
   Direct labor, Mixing 730 hr @ $8.50/hr 6,205.00
   Direct labor, Canning 500 hr @ $6.60/hr 3,300.00
   Factory overhead, Mixing   8,850.00
   Factory overhead, Canning   7,690.00
     Total $32,692.80

Standard Cost Data per 25-Gallon Batch	Mixing Department	Canning Department
Direct materials: Water	20 gal @ $.02/gal	
Material M	4 gal @ $4.85/gal	
Material J	1 gal @ $13.20/gal	
Gallon cans		25 cans @ $.80/can
Direct labor	6 hr @ $8.50/hr	4 hr @ $6.50/hr
Factory overhead	$12/direct labor hr	$16/direct labor hr
Beginning inventories	Four batches, 40% complete	Six batches, 20% complete
Ending inventories	Two batches, 80% complete	Four batches, 60% complete
Batches started during August:	120 batches	?

Assume that nothing was lost because of spoilage or evaporation.

Required

1. Compute the number of batches started and completed in each department in August.
2. Compute the standard cost per batch of paint.
3. Using the *average* costing approach and process costing schedules when necessary, compute the costs attached to completed units and ending Work in Process Inventory in each department for August.
4. Prepare the appropriate journal entries to transfer the cost of completed work out of each department's Work in Process Inventory account.
5. Compute the materials price and quantity variances for materials M and J for August.

Problem Set B

**Problem 9B-1.
Standard Cost
Formulation
(L.O. 3, 4)**

Gorge Company developed material, labor, and overhead standards for its principal product, Quanto. Each unit of Quanto requires inputs of materials A and B plus work in the cutting and polishing operations. Standards per unit of Quanto were developed as follows:

Materials				Labor		
Type	Pounds	Price/lb		Operation	Hours	Rate
A	5	$4		Cut	3	$5
B	8	$2		Polish	2	$6

The standard overhead rate, including both variable and fixed costs, was established at $11.50 per direct labor hour.

Required

1. Prepare a summary of standard costs for 1 unit of Quanto.

2. If 8,000 good units of Quanto are produced during a period, what is the standard quantity allowed for material usage? What are the standard hours allowed for labor time?
3. Assume that 10,000 units of Quanto are produced during a period when the actual overhead incurred is $600,000. Determine the amount of under- or overapplied factory overhead.

Problem 9B-2.
Development of
Standards: Direct
Labor
(L.O. 3, 4)

A planned change in the employee labor rate structure has caused the Rollins Salt Company to develop a new standard direct labor cost for its product. Standard direct labor costs per 1,000 pounds of a new and healthy form of salt in 19x7 were (a) 1.5 hours in the Sodium Preparation Department at $10.40 per hour, (b) 1.8 hours in the Chloride Mixing Department at $11.00 per hour, and (c) 1.4 hours in the Cleaning and Packaging Department at $7.50 per hour. Labor rates are expected to increase in 19x8 by 10 percent in the Sodium Preparation Department, decrease by 10 percent in the Chloride Mixing Department, and decrease by 12 percent in the Cleaning and Packaging Department. New machinery in the Chloride Mixing Department will lower the direct labor time standard by 20 percent per 1,000 pounds of salt. All other time standards are expected to remain the same.

Required

1. Compute the standard direct labor cost per 1,000 pounds of salt in 19x8.
2. Management has a plan to improve productive output by 20 percent in the Sodium Preparation Department. If such results are achieved in 19x8, determine (a) the effect on the direct labor time standard and (b) the resulting total standard direct labor cost per 1,000 pounds of salt.
3. Unskilled labor can be hired to staff all departments in 19x8, with the result that all labor rates paid in 19x7 would be cut by 60 percent in the new year. Such a change in labor skill would cause the direct labor time standards to increase by 50 percent over their anticipated 19x8 levels using skilled labor. Compute the standard direct labor cost per 1,000 pounds of salt if this change occurs.

Problem 9B-3.
Developing and
Using Standard
Costs
(L.O. 3, 4, 6)

The Otani Supply Company makes swimming pool equipment and accessories. To make swimming pool umbrellas, waterproof canvas is first sent to the Cutting Department. In the Assembly Department the canvas is stretched over the umbrella's ribs on the center pole and opening mechanism; then the umbrella is mounted on a heavy base before being packed for shipment.

The company uses a standard cost accounting system. Direct labor standards for each pool umbrella for 19x9 are (a) direct labor of .2 hour charged to the Cutting Department at $8.00 per hour and (b) .8 hour charged to the Assembly Department at $9.50 per hour. Variable factory overhead is 150 percent, and fixed overhead is 130 percent of total direct labor dollars.

During 19x8 the company used the following direct materials standards: Waterproof canvas was $2.60 per square yard for 4 square yards per umbrella. The standard for a unit consisting of pole, ribs, and opening mechanism was $10.50 per unit. The base was $6.40 per unit.

Quantity standards are expected to remain the same during 19x9. However, the following price changes are likely: The cost of waterproof canvas will increase by 20 percent. The pole, ribs, and opening mechanism will be purchased from three vendors. Vendor A will provide 10 percent of the total supply at $10.60 per unit. Vendor B will provide 60 percent at $10.80. Vendor C will supply 30 percent at $11.00. The cost of each base will increase 20 percent.

Required

1. Compute the total standard direct materials cost per umbrella for 19x9.
2. Using your answer from **1** and information from the problem, compute the 19x9 standard manufacturing cost of one pool umbrella.
3. Using your answers from **1** and **2**, prepare journal entries for the following 19x9 transactions:

Jan. 20 Purchased 5,500 square yards of waterproof canvas at $3.20 per square yard on account.

Feb. 1 Requisitioned 625 pole, rib, and opening mechanism assemblies into production to complete a job calling for 600 umbrellas.

Mar. 15 Transferred 300 completed pool umbrellas to Finished Goods Inventory.

**Problem 9B-4.
Materials and
Labor Variances**
(L.O. 5, 6)

The Connecticut Fruit Packaging Company makes plastic berry baskets for food wholesalers. Each basket is made of .8 grams of liquid plastic and .6 grams of an additive, which provides the color and hardening agents. The standard prices are $.006 per gram of liquid plastic and $.008 per gram of additive.

There are three kinds of labor: molding, trimming, and packing. The labor time standard per 1,000-basket batch and the rate standards are molding, .6 hour per batch at an hourly rate of $10; trimming, .5 hour per batch at an hourly rate of $8; and packing, .4 hour at $5 per hour.

During 19xx, the company produced 450,000 berry baskets. Actual materials used were 367,000 grams of liquid plastic at a cost of $1,835 and 267,000 grams of additive at a cost of $2,403. Direct labor included 275 hours for molding, costing $2,695; 230 hours for trimming, costing $1,863; and 175 hours for packing, costing $910.

Required

1. Compute the direct materials price and quantity variances for both the liquid plastic and the additive. Show a check of your answers.
2. Compute the direct labor rate and efficiency variances for the molding, trimming, and packing processes. Show a check of your answers.
3. Prepare journal entries to record the transactions involving materials and labor for the period.

**Problem 9B-5.
Standard Process
Costing**
(L.O. 3, 4, 5)

Ruf-Jaw Cosmetics, Inc., produces Realwite, a brand of toothpaste sold primarily to smokers. One producing department is used, and costs are accumulated through a standard process costing system. All direct materials are added at the beginning of the process except packaging tubes, which are force filled at the end of the process. Labor and overhead costs are applied uniformly throughout the process. Cost reports for July 19x8 reveal the data shown on the following page:

Work in Process Inventory, July 1, 19x8
    400 lb, 40% completed
    Standard costs attached
        Materials $220.00
        Conversion costs   140.80
July 19x8 standard cost data
    Direct materials added
        Paste: 4,500 lbs at standard cost of $.50/lb
        Grit: 500 lbs at standard cost of $1.00/lb
        Tubes: 2-oz tubes used at standard cost of $.25/tube
    Direct labor
        One standard direct labor hour allowed for each
         5 lbs processed
        Standard labor rate = $2.10/standard direct labor hour
    Manufacturing overhead
        Standard variable overhead rate = $1.40/DLH
        Standard fixed overhead rate = $.90/DLH
Work in Process Inventory, July 31, 19x8
    900 lb, 60% completed

During the month no spoilage occurred. The company uses the *average* process costing method.

Required

1. Compute the number of tubes started and completed during July.
2. Compute the standard cost per tube of toothpaste.
3. Using process costing schedules when necessary, compute the costs attached to completed units and ending Work in Process Inventory at July 31, 19x8.
4. Prepare the appropriate journal entry to transfer the cost of completed units to Finished Goods Inventory. (*Note:* 16 ounces = 1 pound.)
5. Actual cost data for direct materials for July are:
    Paste: 4,600 lbs at $.52/lb
    Grit: 480 lbs at $.96/lb
    Tubes: No quantity variance existed, but the tubes used cost $.28 each
    Compute the materials price and quantity variances for the month.

Management Decision Case

Standard Costing and Employee Behavior: Mighty Mac Company
(L.O. 1, 2, 3)

Mighty Mac Company is expanding its Punch Press Department and wants to purchase three new punch presses from Equipment Manufacturers, Inc. Engineers at Equipment Manufacturers made mechanical studies, indicating that for Mighty Mac's intended use, the output rate for one press should be 1,000 pieces per hour. Mighty Mac has similar presses in operation. Production from these presses now averages 600 pieces per hour.

A study of the Mighty Mac experience shows that the average is derived from the individual outputs shown below:

Worker	Daily Output
A. Curley	750
B. Holdmeyer	750
C. Orme	600
D. Peach	500
E. Priest	550
F. Quade	450
Total	3,600
Average	600

Mighty Mac's management plans to institute a standard cost accounting system soon. Company engineers support a standard based on 1,000 pieces per hour. The Accounting Department wants 750 pieces per hour. The department supervisor suggests 600 pieces per hour.

Required

1. What argument is each proponent likely to offer to support his or her case?
2. Which alternative best reconciles the need for both cost control and better motivation to improve performance? Why?

(ICMA adapted)

LEARNING OBJECTIVES

1. Review the principles of performance evaluation.
2. Prepare a flexible budget.
3. Compute overhead variances using both the two-way and three-way analyses.
4. Prepare journal entries involving overhead variances.
5. Dispose of variance balances at period end.
6. Describe the concept of management by exception.
7. Evaluate employee performance using variances.

CHAPTER 10

Variance Analysis and Performance Reporting

Standard cost accounting is an important tool for measuring operating performance. Variance analysis helps identify areas with operating problems as well as efficient departments or work areas. Cost variances are usually associated with performance evaluation in the manufacturing environment. But as the review problem demonstrates, standard costing and variance analysis are equally important when promoting profitability and operating efficiency in service-oriented businesses as well as in selling and distributing products in a manufacturing company. Materials variances are unique to manufacturing activities, whereas labor variances and overhead variances may be computed for service enterprises as well as for manufacturing companies.

In this chapter the principles of performance evaluation are revisited. A study of the flexible budget leads into a discussion of the two-way and the three-way approaches to overhead variance analysis. Once variances have been computed, the chapter explains how they are entered into the accounting records through journal entries and how their balances are disposed of before final financial statements for the period are prepared. The chapter concludes with a discussion of the concept of management by exception and a look at performance reporting based on variance analysis. After studying this chapter, you should be able to meet the learning objectives listed on the left.

Principles of Performance Evaluation Revisited

The principles of performance evaluation were identified and discussed in Chapter 7. However, before continuing to discuss standard costing and related variance analyses, it is important to review the performance evaluation principles so they can be applied once variances have been determined. After all, variances are computed to help management attain optimal operating results. The actual variance numbers are useless until they are integrated into a performance report and evaluated. Determining the causes of variances is critical to moving toward optimal productivity and profitability.

Management's policies are intended to satisfy the overall objective of the enterprise—maximizing profitability for the profit-oriented company and successfully completing the mission of the not-for-profit organization. These company policies are important, but alone they will not effectively control operations. Performance must be accurately measured, comparatively analyzed and evaluated, and properly reported. Throughout the performance evaluation process, one must consider the behavior of the people involved, which is vital to successful performance. The human aspect is the most important part of trying to meet corporate goals. People do the planning, people perform the operations of the enterprise, people evaluate, and people are evaluated. The following performance evaluation principles were discussed in Chapter 7:

Behavioral Principles

1. **Managers should have input into the standards and goals set for their areas of responsibility.**
2. **Top management's support for the evaluation process should be evident.**
3. **Only controllable cost and revenue items with significant variances should be the focus of performance reports.**
4. **Opportunity for manager response should be a part of the evaluation process.**

Operational Principles

1. **Provide accurate and suitable measures of performance,** including (1) predetermined standards or budgets, (2) others' performance in comparable jobs, and (3) past performance. Nonfinancial measures, such as labor hours or units of output, may be used to measure performance and may be as useful as dollar measures.
2. **Communicate expectations to appropriate managers and segment leaders who will be evaluated.** Expectations should be clearly stated and contain relevant input from the manager being evaluated.
3. **Identify the responsibilities of each manager.** A manager assumes the obligation of being held accountable for a defined number of areas when he or she accepts a position.
4. **Compare actual performance to a suitable base.** Evaluating performance requires comparison because performance must be compared with some anticipated target or standard. Suitable measures of performance were mentioned above.
5. **Prepare performance reports that highlight areas of concern.** The information contained in a performance report should be specific about the manager's responsibilities, controllable by the manager, and represent a significant enough departure from the anticipated target to warrant analysis.
6. **Analyze important cause-and-effect relationships.** A performance report is more than a set of numbers to be compared against one another. One variation may help cause another (domino effect). A

performance report should reveal cause-and-effect factors and signifi-cant relationships. Nonquantitative information is often used to explain differences. Much of this information should come from the manager being evaluated.

In Chapter 7, performance evaluation and analysis was based on comparisons of actual data with budgeted data. Such comparisons make the analysis of current productivity against past or budgeted output possible. Still, pinpointing responsibility is often difficult. Standard costing helps solve this problem by enabling management to create a performance reporting system oriented toward specific managers and their areas of responsibility. This type of system is also based on cause-and-effect relationships, which help managers explain reasons for the variances.

The discussion of standard costing now continues with an analysis of overhead costs and computation of related variances. The chapter concludes with a look at performance analysis based on standard cost accounting and the materials, labor, and overhead variances generated by the system.

Cost Control Through Variance Analysis

The performance evaluation, which is an important part of cost control, should emphasize the comparison of what happened (actual results) with what was expected to happen (budgeted). Therefore this discussion continues to focus on the differences between (1) actual costs and budgeted costs and (2) actual costs and standard costs.

Cost variances are usually associated with performance evaluation in the manufacturing environment. But as the review problem and several problems in the assignment materials show, standard costs for evaluating service-oriented enterprises and such functions as selling in a manufac-turing company are equally important to profitability and operating efficiency.

Flexible Budgets

OBJECTIVE 2
Prepare a flexible budget

Budgets were emphasized in Chapter 8, which focused on the planning process. Why, then, you might ask, should the concept of flexible budgets be introduced as part of cost control rather than as a planning tool? This has been done because a flexible budget (also called a variable budget) is primarily a cost control tool to help evaluate performance. A flexible budget is a summary of expected costs for a range of activity levels; it is geared to changes in the level of productive output. The budgets discussed as part of the planning function are called static, or fixed, budgets because they describe just one level of expected sales and production activity. The master budget, including all the period budgets, is usually prepared for an expected or normal level of sales and productive output.

For budgeting or planning purposes, a set of static budgets based on a single level of output is good enough for management's needs. These budgets show management the desired picture of operating results and are also a target for managers to use in developing monthly and weekly operating plans. However, these budgets often prove inadequate for judging operating results. Exhibit 10-1 presents data for Arizona Industries, Inc. Actual costs exceed budgeted costs by $14,300, or 7.2 percent. Most managers consider such an overrun significant. But was there really a cost overrun? As explained in the notes to Exhibit 10-1, the budgeted amounts are based on expected output of 17,500 units, but actual output was 19,100 units.

Before analyzing the performance of the Tucson Division, you must change the budgeted data to reflect an output of 19,100 units. In this example, the static budget for 17,500 units is of no use in judging performance because you should expect more costs to be incurred in producing 19,100 units than in producing 17,500. The role of a flexible budget is to provide forecasted data that can be adjusted automatically for changes in the level of output. Exhibit 10-2 presents a flexible budget

Exhibit 10-1. Performance Analysis: Comparison of Actual and Budgeted Data

Arizona Industries, Inc.
Performance Report—Tucson Division
For the Year Ended December 31, 19xx

Cost Item	Budget*	Actual†	Difference Under (Over) Budget
Direct materials	$ 42,000	$ 46,000	$ (4,000)
Direct labor	68,250	75,000	(6,750)
Factory overhead			
Variable			
Indirect materials	10,500	11,500	(1,000)
Indirect labor	14,000	15,250	(1,250)
Utilities	7,000	7,600	(600)
Other	8,750	9,750	(1,000)
Fixed			
Supervisory salaries	19,000	18,500	500
Depreciation	15,000	15,000	—
Utilities	4,500	4,500	—
Other	10,900	11,100	(200)
Totals	$199,900	$214,200	$(14,300)

* Budget based on expected productive output of 17,500 units.
† Actual cost of producing 19,100 units.

Exhibit 10-2. Flexible Budget Preparation

Arizona Industries, Inc.
Flexible Budget Analysis—Tucson Division
For the Year Ended December 31, 19xx

Cost Item	Unit Levels of Activity			Variable Cost per Unit*
	15,000	17,500	20,000	
Direct materials	$ 36,000	$ 42,000	$ 48,000	$2.40
Direct labor	58,500	68,250	78,000	3.90
Variable factory overhead				
Indirect materials	9,000	10,500	12,000	.60
Indirect labor	12,000	14,000	16,000	.80
Utilities	6,000	7,000	8,000	.40
Other	7,500	8,750	10,000	.50
Total variable costs	$129,000	$150,500	$172,000	$8.60
Fixed factory overhead				
Supervisory salaries	$ 19,000	$ 19,000	$ 19,000	
Depreciation	15,000	15,000	15,000	
Utilities	4,500	4,500	4,500	
Other	10,900	10,900	10,900	
Total fixed costs	$ 49,400	$ 49,400	$ 49,400	
Total costs	$178,400	$199,900	$221,400	

Flexible budget formula:
(Variable cost per unit × number of units produced) + budgeted fixed costs
= ($8.60 × units produced) + $49,400

Note: Activity expressed in units was used as the basis for this analysis.   When units are used, direct material and direct labor costs are included in the analysis.   Flexible budgets are commonly restricted to overhead costs.   In such a situation, direct labor hours are used in place of units produced.
* Computed by dividing the dollar amount in any column by the respective activity level.

for Arizona Industries, Inc., with budgeted data for 15,000, 17,500, and 20,000 units of output.   The important part of this illustration is the flexible budget formula at the bottom.   This budget formula is an equation that can be used to determine the correct budgeted cost for any activity level.   It consists of a per unit amount for variable costs and a total amount for fixed costs.   In Exhibit 10-2, the $8.60 variable cost per unit is computed in the upper right column, and the $49,400 is found in the fixed cost section of the analysis.   Using this formula, you can draw up a budget for the Tucson Division for any level of output.

In Exhibit 10-1, budgeted data should have been adjusted for expected costs at the 19,100-unit level before such data could be compared with actual dollar amounts.   Exhibit 10-3 shows a performance report using

| Exhibit 10-3. Performance Analysis Using Flexible Budget Data |

Arizona Industries, Inc.
Performance Report—Tucson Division
For the Year Ended December 31, 19xx

Cost Item (Variable Unit Cost)	Budget Based on 19,100 Units Produced	Actual Costs at 19,100- Unit Level	Differences Under (Over) Budget
Direct materials ($2.40)	$ 45,840	$ 46,000	$(160)
Direct labor ($3.90)	74,490	75,000	(510)
Factory overhead			
Variable			
Indirect materials ($.60)	11,460	11,500	(40)
Indirect labor ($.80)	15,280	15,250	30
Utilities ($.40)	7,640	7,600	40
Other ($.50)	9,550	9,750	(200)
Fixed			
Supervisory salaries	19,000	18,500	500
Depreciation	15,000	15,000	—
Utilities	4,500	4,500	—
Other	10,900	11,100	(200)
Totals	$213,660	$214,200	$(540)

flexible budget data. Unit variable cost amounts have been multiplied by 19,100 units to arrive at total budgeted figures. Fixed overhead information has been carried over from the flexible budget developed in Exhibit 10-2. As the new performance report shows, costs exceeded budgeted amounts during the year by only $540, or two-tenths of 1 percent. Using the flexible budget concept, you can see that the performance of the Tucson Division is almost on target. Performance has now been measured and analyzed accurately.

Overhead Variance Analysis

Controlling overhead costs is more difficult than controlling direct materials and direct labor costs because responsibility for overhead costs is difficult to pin down. In addition, the analysis of factory (or service) overhead variances is more complex than analysis of materials and labor variances. These two factors explain why many students have problems coping with and adjusting to overhead variance analysis.

In this chapter the computing of overhead variances is viewed first from a conceptual level. Then the difference between overhead costs incurred and overhead costs applied, which is the total overhead variance, is broken down into a two-way variance analysis. To further help explain the overhead variances, in the third and final step the two-way approach is expanded into a three-way variance analysis. The goal, remember, is to explain to management through variance analysis why the company's cost targets were not met.

Conceptual View. The analysis of overhead variances is based on several ideas and concepts already discussed in this book. Figure 10-1 shows the underlying concepts of overhead variance analysis and their relationships to one another. The concept of operating capacity was discussed in Chapter 6. Although theoretical and practical capacity levels can be defined and computed, they are idealistic and nonrepresentative of the expected operating level of the enterprise. **Normal capacity**, which is the average annual level of operating capacity needed to meet expected sales demands, was selected as the most appropriate operating level on which to gauge expectations. Of course, this expectation level will

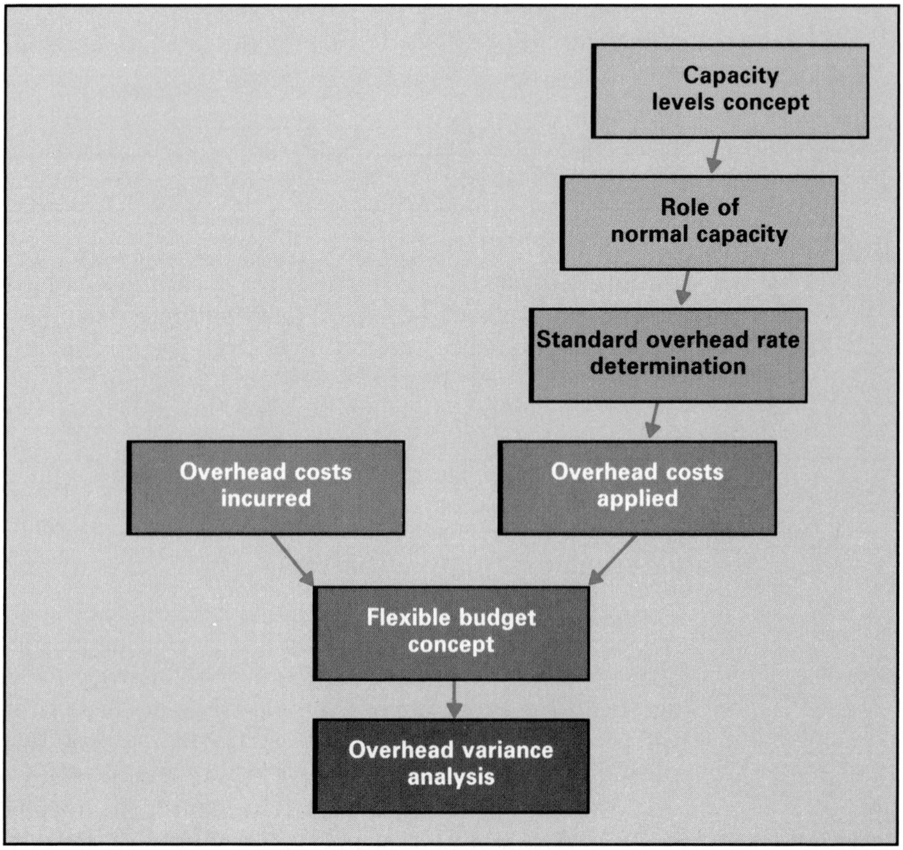

Figure 10-1. Conceptual Foundation: Overhead Variance Analysis

also be the basis for comparing actual operating results and analyzing performance.

Normal capacity plays a unique role in overhead variance analysis. As you should recall, when the standard overhead rates were computed in Chapter 9, the standard fixed overhead rate was computed by dividing the total budgeted fixed overhead costs by normal capacity in terms of standard direct labor hours. When analyzing variances of fixed overhead costs, you must again use the concept of normal capacity to help explain the variance.

Once variable and fixed standard overhead rates have been computed, overhead can be applied to units produced much as it was applied to Work in Process Inventory in Chapter 3. The over- or underapplied overhead, the difference between actual overhead costs incurred and overhead costs applied to units produced, now becomes the **total overhead variance**.

The next step, as Figure 10-1 shows, is to incorporate the flexible budget concept into the analysis. As explained earlier, performance cannot be properly analyzed unless actual costs incurred are compared with budgeted or standard costs that should have been incurred at the actual level of output. The tool available for this adjustment process is the **flexible budget** and the **flexible budget formula**. This formula is a key ingredient when computing overhead variances, as you will see later in this chapter.

In summary, the analysis of overhead variances depends on several fundamental concepts that should be familiar to you from previous discussions. If you have forgotten some of this information, you should review these topics before going on to the analysis of overhead variances.

OBJECTIVE 3a
Compute
overhead
variances using
the two-way
analysis

Two-Way Variance Analysis. Analyses of factory overhead variances vary in sophistication. One approach is to compute the total overhead variance and then divide this amount into two parts: (1) the controllable overhead variance and (2) the overhead volume variance. The controllable overhead variance is easily linked to areas of responsibility, so the term *controllable* is important. Return to the Pearce Company example begun in Chapter 9, and note that additional data are needed to continue the variance analysis into the overhead cost accounts. The flexible budget of overhead costs for the period revealed the following formula:

$5.75 per direct labor hour + $1,300 in monthly fixed overhead costs

Normal capacity was set at 400 direct labor hours per month. The company incurred $4,100 in actual overhead costs during August.

Before finding the overhead variances, you must calculate the total standard overhead rate, which has two parts. One part is the variable rate of $5.75 per direct labor hour; the other part is the standard fixed overhead rate. Divide budgeted fixed overhead ($1,300) by normal capacity, which works out to $3.25 per direct labor hour ($1,300/400 hours). Therefore the total standard overhead rate used to apply overhead was $9.00 per direct labor hour ($5.75 + $3.25). The total fixed overhead costs divided by normal capacity provides a rate that assigns all fixed overhead costs to products (or services) if total expected output is achieved. As you will recall from Chapter 9, the standard hours per chair are 2.4 direct labor hours. If 400 direct labor hours are normal for a month, then the output of chairs should be about 167 (400 hours/2.4 hours per chair). Given this information, you can now calculate the total overhead variance for the Pearce Company as follows:

Actual overhead costs incurred	$4,100
Standard overhead costs applied to good units produced	
$9.00/direct labor hour × (180 chairs × 2.4 hour/chair)	3,888
Total overhead variance	$ 212(U)

The controllable overhead variance is the difference between the actual overhead incurred and the factory overhead budgeted for the level of production reached. Thus the controllable variance for the Pearce Company for August would be as follows:

Actual overhead costs incurred		$4,100
Less budgeted factory overhead		
(flexible budget) for 180 chairs		
Variable overhead cost		
(180 chairs × 2.4 hour/chair)		
× $5.75/direct labor hour	$2,484	
Budgeted fixed overhead cost	1,300	
Total budgeted factory overhead		3,784
Controllable overhead variance		$ 316(U)

The overhead volume variance is the difference between the factory overhead budgeted for the level of production achieved and the overhead applied to production, using the standard overhead rate. Continuing with the Pearce Company example, you have

Budgeted factory overhead (see above)	$3,784
Less factory overhead applied	
(180 chairs × 2.4 hour/chair)	
× $9.00/direct labor hour	3,888
Overhead volume variance	$ 104(F)

By checking the computations, you will find that the two variances do equal the total overhead variance:

Controllable overhead variance	$316(U)
Overhead volume variance	104(F)
Total overhead variance	$212(U)

In this example, the company spent more than it should have, so the controllable variance is unfavorable.

Use of existing facilities and capacity is measured by the overhead volume variance. A volume variance will occur only if more or less capacity than normal is actually used. In the example, 400 direct labor hours is the measure of normal use of facilities. In producing 180 chairs, the company should have used 432 standard direct labor hours (standard hours allowed). Fixed overhead costs are applied on the basis of standard hours allowed. In the example, overhead would be applied on the basis of 432 hours, but the fixed overhead rate was computed by using 400 hours (normal capacity). Thus more fixed costs would be applied to products than were budgeted. Because the products can absorb no more than actual costs incurred, this level of production would tend to lower unit cost. When more than expected capacity is used, the result is a favorable overhead volume variance. When less than normal capacity is used, less than all fixed overhead costs will be applied to units produced. It is then necessary to add the amount of underapplied fixed overhead to the cost of the good units produced, thereby increasing their unit cost. This condition is unfavorable.

Figure 10-2 sums up the discussion of overhead variance analysis using the two-way overhead variance approach. All procedures shown are exactly the same as those explained above. To figure the controllable variance, subtract the budgeted overhead amount (using a flexible budget) for the level of output achieved from actual overhead costs incurred. A positive answer means an unfavorable variance because actual costs were greater than those budgeted. The controllable variance is favorable if the difference is negative. Subtracting total overhead applied from overhead budgeted at the level of output achieved produces the volume variance. As before, a positive answer means an unfavorable variance, and a negative answer means a favorable variance. The data from the Pearce Company example are shown in the lower part of Figure 10-2 on the next page. Carefully check the solution in the figure with the amount that was calculated earlier.

OBJECTIVE 3b
Compute overhead variances using the three-way analysis

Three-Way Variance Analysis. As the title indicates, the three-way approach to overhead variance analysis divides the total overhead variance into three parts instead of the two parts just studied. Remember, the purpose of variance analysis is to break down variations from budgeted information so that reasons for changes from planned operations can be determined. The three-way approach to overhead variance analysis breaks the controllable overhead variance into two parts and identifies an *overhead spending variance* and an *overhead efficiency variance*. The overhead volume variance is the third overhead variance, and it is computed as in the two-way variance analysis.

The **overhead spending variance** is the difference between the actual overhead costs incurred and the amount that should have been spent, based on actual hours worked or other productive input measures.

Figure 10-2. Two-Way Overhead Variance Analysis

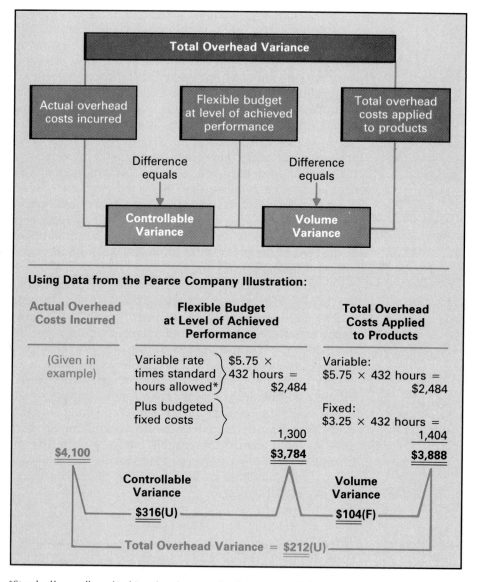

*Standard hours allowed (achieved performance level) is computed by multiplying good units produced by required standard time per unit. Here, the computation is as follows:

180 chairs produced × 2.4 hours per chair = 432 standard hours allowed

Therefore actual overhead costs incurred are compared with the costs of a flexible budget based on actual hours worked. When the Pearce Company example is expanded, the spending variance is computed as shown on the next page:

Actual overhead costs incurred		$4,100.00
Less budgeted factory overhead (flexible budget) for 450 hours worked		
Variable overhead cost		
450 hours × $5.75 per direct labor hour	$2,587.50	
Budgeted fixed overhead cost	1,300.00	
Total budgeted factory overhead		3,887.50
Overhead Spending Variance		$ 212.50(U)

Note that the total overhead spending variance can be broken down into its variable and fixed components. In the example, actual overhead incurred was given in total and details were not provided. If the actual variable and fixed cost components were given, however, you could easily generate a variable overhead spending variance and a fixed overhead spending variance. This further breakdown would give the supervisor additional information. If most of the spending variance involved fixed costs, much of the variance would be difficult for the manager to control. If, on the other hand, most of the spending variance were caused by noncompliance with variable cost targets, those responsible should be held accountable for the differences.

The **overhead efficiency variance** is linked directly with the labor efficiency variance. An efficiency variance occurs when actual hours worked differ from standard hours allowed for good units produced. The overhead efficiency variance is the difference between actual direct labor hours worked and standard labor hours allowed multiplied by the standard variable overhead rate. Computing the overhead efficiency variance involves comparing two flexible budgets, one based on actual hours worked and the other on standard hours allowed for good units produced. The overhead efficiency variance is computed as follows:

Budgeted factory overhead (flexible budget) for actual hours worked		
Variable overhead cost		
450 hours × $5.75 per direct labor hour	$2,587.50	
Budgeted fixed overhead cost	1,300.00	
Total budgeted overhead for actual hours worked		$3,887.50
Budgeted factory overhead (flexible budget) for standard hours allowed		
Variable overhead cost		
(180 chairs × 2.4 hours per chair) × $5.75 per direct labor hour	$2,484.00	
Budgeted fixed overhead cost	1,300.00	
Total budgeted overhead for standard hours allowed		3,784.00
Overhead efficiency variance		$ 103.50(U)

Note that by design the overhead efficiency variance is the difference between variable costs only. When two flexible budgets are compared, the fixed cost component is identical for each budget. The difference must come from the variable costs.

The overhead efficiency variance identifies the portion of the total overhead variance that occurs automatically when a labor efficiency variance develops. If the labor efficiency variance is unfavorable, the overhead efficiency variance will also be unfavorable. The person responsible for the labor efficiency variance is also responsible for the overhead efficiency variance.

As stated earlier, the **overhead volume variance** is computed as in the two-way approach. If you need to review its computation, refer to page 358 and Figure 10-3, which illustrates three-way overhead variance analysis.

In the upper portion of Figure 10-3, the total overhead variance is broken down into the three variances: (1) spending, (2) efficiency, and (3) volume variances. In addition, the cost totals compared to arrive at each variance are identified. Note that the only difference between Figures 10-2 and 10-3 is the introduction of the *flexible budget for effort expended*. Using this flexible budget, one can break down the controllable overhead variance into overhead spending variance and overhead efficiency variance.

In the bottom portion of Figure 10-3, the actual computation of the three variances is summarized. To check your answers to the three variances, perform the following calculation:

Overhead spending variance	$212.50(U)
Overhead efficiency variance	103.50(U)
Overhead volume variance	104.00(F)
Total overhead variance	$212.00(U)

Illustrative Problem: Variance Analysis

Broadt Manufacturing Company has a standard cost system and keeps all cost standards up to date. The company's main product is heating pipe, which is made in a single department. The standard variable costs for 1 unit of finished pipe are:

Direct materials (2 square meters @ $1.50)	$ 3.00
Direct labor (1.5 hours @ $7.00)	10.50
Variable overhead (1.5 hours @ $4.00)	6.00
Standard variable cost/unit	$19.50

Normal capacity is 18,000 direct labor hours, and budgeted fixed overhead costs for the year were $36,000. During the year, 12,200 units were produced and sold. Related transactions and actual cost data for the year were as follows: Direct materials consisted of 24,500 square meters purchased and used; unit purchase costs were $1.40 per square meter. Direct labor consisted of 18,200 direct labor hours worked at an average

Figure 10-3. Three-Way Overhead Variance Analysis

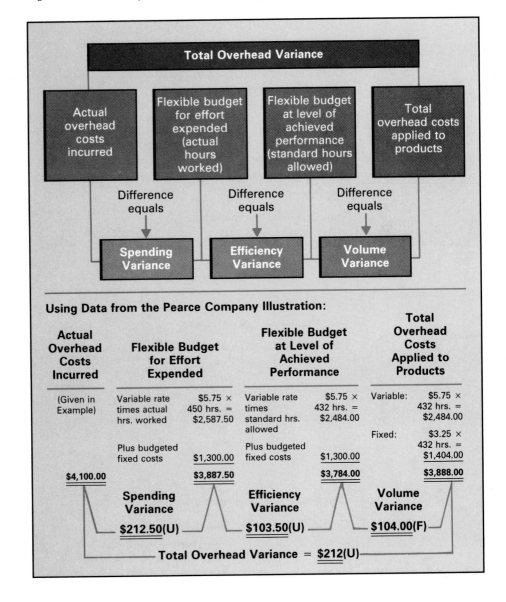

labor rate of $7.20 per hour. Factory overhead incurred consisted of variable overhead costs of $73,500 and fixed overhead costs of $36,000.

Required

Using the data above, compute the following:

1. Standard hours allowed
2. Standard fixed overhead rate
3. Direct materials price variance

4. Direct materials quantity variance
5. Direct labor rate variance
6. Direct labor efficiency variance
7. Overhead spending variance
8. Overhead efficiency variance
9. Controllable overhead variance
10. Overhead volume variance

Solution

1. Standard hours allowed = good units produced × standard direct labor hours per unit

$$12{,}200 \text{ units} \times 1.5 \text{ hours/unit} = 18{,}300 \text{ hours}$$

2. Standard fixed overhead rate = $\dfrac{\text{budgeted fixed overhead costs}}{\text{normal capacity}}$

$$= \frac{\$36{,}000}{18{,}000 \text{ hours}}$$

$$= \$2.00/\text{direct labor hour}$$

3. Direct materials price variance

Price difference: Actual price paid	$1.40/sq meter
Less standard price	1.50/sq meter
Difference	$ .10(F)

Direct materials price variance = (actual price − standard price) × actual quantity
= .10(F) × 24,500 sq meters
= $2,450(F)

4. Direct materials quantity variance

Quantity difference: Actual quantity used	24,500 sq meters
Less standard quantity (12,200 units × 2 sq meters)	24,400 sq meters
Difference	100(U)

Direct materials quantity variance = (actual quantity − standard quantity) × standard price
= 100(U) × $1.50/sq meter
= $150(U)

5. Direct labor rate variance

Rate difference: Actual labor rate	$7.20/hour
Less standard labor rate	7.00/hour
Difference	$ .20(U)

$$\text{Direct labor rate variance} = (\text{actual rate} - \text{standard rate}) \times \text{actual hours}$$
$$= .20(\text{U}) \times 18,200 \text{ hours}$$
$$= \$3,640(\text{U})$$

6. Direct labor efficiency variance

Difference in hours: Actual hours worked	18,200 hours
Less standard hours allowed	18,300 hours
Difference	100(F)

$$\text{Direct labor efficiency variance} = (\text{actual hours} - \text{standard hours allowed}) \times \text{standard rate}$$
$$= 100 \text{ hours}(\text{F}) \times \$7.00/\text{hour}$$
$$= \$700(\text{F})$$

7. Overhead spending variance

Overhead costs incurred		
Variable	$73,500	
Fixed	36,000	$109,500
Less flexible budget for effort expended		
Actual hours worked × variable overhead rate		
18,200 labor hours × $4/hour	$72,800	
Plus budgeted fixed costs	36,000	108,800
Overhead spending variance		$ 700(U)

8. Overhead efficiency variance

Flexible budget for effort expended (see computation in 7 above)		$108,800
Less flexible budget at level of achieved performance		
Standard hours allowed × variable overhead rate		
18,300 labor hours × $4/hour	$73,200	
Plus budgeted fixed costs	36,000	109,200
Overhead efficiency variance		$ 400(F)

9. Controllable overhead variance

Actual overhead costs incurred		$109,500
Less budgeted factory overhead for 18,300 hours		
Variable overhead cost		
18,300 hours at $4/hour	$73,200	
Budgeted fixed factory overhead	36,000	
Total budgeted factory overhead		109,200
Controllable overhead variance		$ 300(U)

Solution (continued):

10. Overhead volume variance

Total budgeted factory overhead (see computation in **9** above)		$109,200
Less factory overhead applied		
Variable: 18,300 hours at $4/hour	$73,200	
Fixed: 18,300 hours at $2/hour	36,600	
Total factory overhead applied		109,800
Overhead volume variance		$ 600(F)

Recording Overhead Variances

OBJECTIVE 4
Prepare journal entries involving overhead variances

In Chapter 9, variances associated with materials and labor costs were recorded. As you will recall, there are a few simple rules to follow when recording transactions involving variances: (1) record all inventory balances at standard cost; (2) create separate accounts for each type of variance; (3) *debit unfavorable* variances to their accounts, and (4) *credit favorable* variances.

Recording overhead variances differs in timing and technique from recording variances related to direct materials and direct labor. First, for a manufacturing company, factory overhead (the total of variable and fixed amounts) is charged to Work in Process Inventory at standard cost (direct labor hours allowed × standard variable and fixed overhead rates). The entry is identical to the one used in Chapter 3 to apply factory overhead to production except that here standard overhead rates are used. This same entry is used for both the two- and three-way approaches to overhead variance analysis. Second, the overhead variances are identified and recorded when the Factory Overhead Applied and Factory Overhead Control accounts are closed out at period end. These entries are illustrated using information from the Pearce Company example.

Journal Entry to Apply Factory Overhead to Production

Work in Process Inventory (432 standard hours allowed at $9/hour)	3,888	
Factory Overhead Applied		3,888
To apply factory overhead costs to Work in Process Inventory at standard cost		

Following this entry, there is a $4,100 debit balance in the Factory Overhead Control account and a $3,888 credit balance in the Factory Overhead Applied account.

Two-Way Analysis: Journal Entry to Record Variances

Factory Overhead Applied	3,888	
Controllable Overhead Variance	316	
Overhead Volume Variance		104
Factory Overhead Control		4,100
To close out Factory Overhead Control and Applied accounts and record the resulting variances		

Three-Way Analysis: Journal Entry to Record Variances

Factory Overhead Applied	3,888.00	
Overhead Spending Variance	212.50	
Overhead Efficiency Variance	103.50	
Overhead Volume Variance		104.00
Factory Overhead Control		4,100.00
To close out Factory Overhead Control and Applied accounts and record the resulting variances		

Once transactions involving direct materials, direct labor, factory overhead, and related variances have been recorded for the Pearce Company, the recording cycle must be completed. This is done by preparing entries to transfer completed units to finished goods inventory and units sold to cost of goods sold and by disposing of balances in the variance accounts at period end.

Journal Entry for Transfer of Completed Units to Finished Goods Inventory

There is now $11,880 in standard costs recorded in the Work in Process Inventory account. Assuming that these 180 chairs have been completed, the following entry would be made:

Finished Goods Inventory (180 chairs at $66/chair)	11,880	
Work in Process Inventory		11,880
To record transfer of completed units to finished goods inventory		

The standard unit cost of $66 was computed from information in Chapter 9 and this chapter as follows:

Direct materials:	
4 yards @ $6.00/yard	$24.00
Direct labor	
2.4 hours @ $8.50/hour	20.40
Factory overhead	
2.4 hours @ $9.00/hour	21.60
Total standard unit cost	$66.00

Because all costs went into the Work in Process Inventory account at standard cost, standard cost is also used when costs are transferred out of the account.

Journal Entry to Transfer Cost of Units Sold to Cost of Goods Sold Account

Assume that the 180 chairs completed were sold on account for $169 per chair and shipped to a customer.

Accounts Receivable (180 chairs at $169/chair)	30,420	
Sales		30,420
To record sale of 180 chairs		
Cost of Goods Sold	11,880	
Finished Goods Inventory		11,880
To record transfer of standard cost of units sold to Cost of Goods Sold account		

Journal Entry to Dispose of End-of-Period Variance Account Balances

OBJECTIVE 5
Dispose of variance balances at period end

The balances in the variance accounts at the end of the period are disposed of much as over- or underapplied overhead was earlier. Here, it is assumed that all units worked on were completed and sold, so a period-end journal entry is made to close all variances to Cost of Goods Sold. Remember, the balances of the variances related to direct materials and direct labor are brought forward from Chapter 9.

Cost of Goods Sold	844.00	
Direct Materials Price Variance	76.00	
Overhead Volume Variance	104.00	
Direct Materials Quantity Variance		240.00
Direct Labor Rate Variance		315.00
Direct Labor Efficiency Variance		153.00
Overhead Spending Variance[1]		212.50
Overhead Efficiency Variance[1]		103.50
To close all variance account balances to Cost of Goods Sold		

If balances still exist at period end in Materials Inventory, Work in Process Inventory, and Finished Goods Inventory and the variance amounts are significant, then the net amount of the variances ($844 here) should be divided among the inventory accounts and Cost of Goods Sold in proportion to their balances.

Note that part of the price variance will be allocated to the Materials Inventory. No other variance is connected with items in materials inventory. If the variances are significant, then items in materials inventory and products in work in process inventory, finished goods inventory,

---

1. This entry assumes the use of the three-way analysis of overhead variances. If the two-way analysis were used, the overhead spending variance and the overhead efficiency variance would be combined into the controllable overhead variance, and it would be credited for $316.

and cost of goods sold are either materially understated or overstated. Remember that for reporting purposes, inventory can only be stated at standard cost if its value corresponds to currently attainable prices. The existence of significant variances indicates that inventories are not stated at currently attainable prices and standard costs are not set at currently attainable cost levels. Therefore, by allocating variances back to all items in inventory and cost of goods sold, you are really restating the inventories at actual costs. They can then be used to prepare financial statements.

Performance Reporting and Cost Controllability

The budgetary control process requires that management formulate a basis for effective cost control. Standard cost variance analysis is a useful tool for achieving this objective. Once variances have been computed, managers responsible for the variances should be asked to give reasons for incurring them. In addition, management accounting personnel should try to determine other causes for each variance. This review process makes managers conscious of their cost responsibilities, permits timely standard cost revisions, and leads to effective cost control through a continuous evaluation process of past and future costs.

Responsibility for Variances

Responsibility for efficient or inefficient operating results passes from the company president down the corporate hierarchy to managers in charge of divisions and smaller segments of the company. Specific titles of individuals responsible for each type of standard cost variance differ between companies. The analysis in Table 10-1 indicates the managers generally held accountable for cost variances. When reviewing Table 10-1, remember that each company takes a unique approach to how it establishes a responsibility accounting system. Thus the titles and variance responsibilities shown may differ from the ones encountered in business. It is important to understand, however, that each variance can be traced to someone in the company who should answer for the difference between budgeted and actual results.

Causes of Variances

Operating performance can be evaluated by comparing actual results with either budgeted data or standard cost data. Budgeted data tend to be less precise than standard cost data, but both provide cost goals. In this section we focus on performance evaluation based on standard costs. The first step is to find out if a variance exists. Determining variances helps locate areas of operating efficiency or inefficiency so corrective steps can be taken. But the key to effectively controlling operations involves more than finding the variance amount. *Finding the reason(s) for the variance is essential.* Once the reason(s) is known, steps can be taken to correct the trouble spot.

Table 10-1. Responsibility for Standard Cost Variances

Variance	Personnel Responsible
Materials price variance	Purchasing agent or purchasing department manager
Materials quantity variance	Plant superintendent, departmental supervisors, machine operators, quality control department, and material handlers
Labor rate variance	Employment department manager, departmental supervisors, and plant superintendent
Labor efficiency variance	Plant superintendent, departmental supervisors, production scheduling department, quality control department, material handlers, and machine operators
Overhead spending variance	*Variable portion*—responsibility of individual supervisors, expected to keep actual expenses within budget *Fixed portion*—responsibility of top management
Overhead efficiency variance	Same personnel responsible for labor efficiency variance
Overhead volume variance	Top management and production schedulers

Source: Henry R. Anderson and Mitchell H. Raiborn, *Basic Cost Accounting Concepts* (Boston: Houghton Mifflin, 1977), p. 380. Reprinted by permission.

There are many possible causes for each standard cost variance. The list in Table 10-2 is not all-inclusive, but it does indicate reasons commonly used to explain why variances arise. Standard cost variances are reported to managers so they can identify causes of specific variances. Based on a functioning responsibility accounting system, the accounts associated with those variances are controllable by the managers. When reviewing the list, remember that some causes can result from events in the company not under the control of the manager being reviewed. Also remember that there are degrees of legitimacy, and only the supervisor's experience can help sort out sound reasons for inefficient operations.

Management by Exception: Using Standard Costs

OBJECTIVE 6
Describe the concept of management by exception

To facilitate performance evaluation, management needs a system for analyzing operations so areas functioning above or below expectations can be identified. Many companies are so large that it is virtually impossible to review all operating areas. Locating and analyzing only the areas of unusually good or bad performance is called **management by exception**. Variance analysis is the primary accounting tool that

---

Table 10-2. Possible Causes of Standard Cost Variances

Materials price variance
Recent purchase price changes not incorporated into the standard cost
Quantity purchase discount changes caused by changes in ordering policies
Substitute raw materials different from original material specifications
Freight cost changes

Materials quantity variance
Poor material handling
Inferior work by machine operator
Faulty equipment
Less expensive grade of raw material, causing excessive scrap
Inferior quality control inspection

Labor rate variance
Recent pay rate changes within industry
Employee hired at incorrect skill and experience level
Labor strike, causing utilization of unskilled help
Labor layoff, causing skilled labor to be retained to prevent resignations and
  job switching
Employee sickness and vacation time

Labor efficiency variance
Machine breakdown
Inferior raw materials
Poor supervision
Lack of timely material handling
Poor employee performance
Erratic production scheduling
Inferior engineering specifications
New, inexperienced employee

Overhead spending variance
Unexpected price changes
Excessive indirect labor usage
Excessive indirect material usage
Changes in employee overtime
Machine and personnel failures
Depreciation rate changes

Overhead efficiency variance
See labor efficiency variance

Overhead volume variance
Failure to utilize normal capacity
Lack of sales orders
Too much idle capacity
Inefficient or efficient utilization of existing capacity

Source: Henry R. Anderson and Mitchell H. Raiborn, *Basic Cost Accounting Concepts* (Boston: Houghton Mifflin, 1977), p. 381. Reprinted by permission.

management uses in exception reporting. Techniques are developed to isolate variances (differences) between standard and actual costs for direct materials, direct labor, and factory overhead. A variance must exceed, either favorably or unfavorably, a minimum amount or percentage difference before being considered an exception. The variance is then subjected to careful analysis to determine its cause. For example, assume management decides that performance within ±4 percent of budget or target is acceptable. When reviewing performance reports, a manager only analyzes cost areas in which differences exceed these limits. In Figure 10-4, only direct materials C and E are outside the 4 percent limit, and their purchasing practices will be analyzed. The standard or target unit costs mark the spots where the vertical bars should end. Actual unit costs are shown in parentheses under the letters identifying the materials.

Management by exception is a useful tool for controlling operations. Once the system is implemented, efforts are automatically directed toward major trouble spots. Management is freed from many details, enabling them to concentrate on more creative facets of the business.

Performance Reports Using Standard Costs

OBJECTIVE 7
Evaluate
employee
performance
using variances

As discussed in Chapter 7, performance reports should be tailored to areas of responsibility. The report should be accurate and clearly stated, and it should only contain cost or revenue items the manager receiving the report can control. In Exhibit 10-4, a performance report uses variance data from the Pearce Company example pertinent to the production

Figure 10-4. Management by Exception Technique

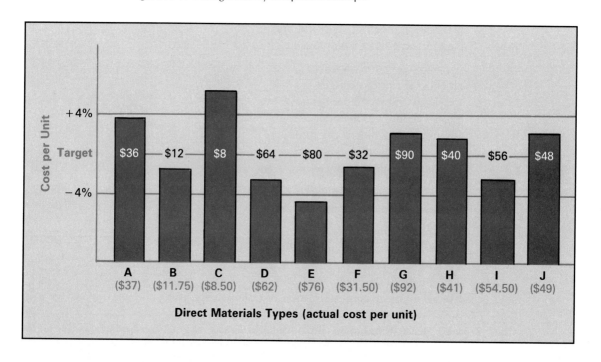

Exhibit 10-4. Performance Report Using Variance Analysis

Pearce Company
Production Department Performance Report—Cost Variance Analysis
For the Month Ended August 31, 19xx

400 hours: normal capacity (direct labor hours)
432 hours: capacity performance level achieved (standard hours allowed)
180 chairs: good units produced

	Cost		Variance	
Cost Analysis	**Budgeted**	**Actual**	**Amount**	**Type**
Direct materials used (leather)	$ 4,320	$ 4,560	$240.00(U)	Quantity variance
Direct labor usage	3,672	3,825	153.00(U)	Efficiency variance
Factory overhead	3,784	4,100	212.50(U)	Spending variance
			103.50(U)	Efficiency variance
Totals	$11,776	$12,485	$709.00(U)	

Reasons for Variances

Direct materials quantity variance: (1) inferior quality control inspection and (2) cheaper grade of direct materials caused excessive scrap

Direct labor efficiency variance: (1) inferior direct materials and (2) new, inexperienced employee

Overhead spending variance: (1) excessive indirect material usage, (2) changes in employee overtime, and (3) unexpected price changes

Overhead efficiency variance: reasons the same as those for direct labor efficiency variance

department supervisor. The production supervisor is responsible for (1) direct materials used and related direct materials quantity variance, (2) direct labor hours used and related direct labor and overhead efficiency variances, and (3) the cost areas used to compute the overhead spending variance. Dollar figures in Exhibit 10-4 are limited to these costs. It is important to leave enough space on the performance report for the manager to write in reasons for the variances.

The report in Exhibit 10-4 is simpler than most. Normally, such a report shows several items of direct materials, two or more direct labor classifications, and many items of overhead costs. In addition, companies do not all use the same format. In fact, as seen in Chapter 7, these differences can be significant. But the ingredients most important to any performance report are present in Exhibit 10-4. They are (1) appropriate title and identity of area or person being evaluated; (2) pertinent data supporting the computations; (3) a detailed breakdown of the cost and/or revenue items being analyzed, including the variance amounts; and (4) a specified place where the manager can respond about the variances. These elements should be included in all performance reports.

Chapter Review

Review of Learning Objectives

1. **Review the principles of performance evaluation.**
   Performance evaluation principles consist of both behavioral and operational principles. The behavioral principles are: (1) managers should have input into the standards set for their area of responsibility; (2) management support of the evaluation process should be evident; (3) only controllable cost and revenue items with significant variances should be included in the performance reports; and (4) opportunity for manager response should be part of the evaluation. Operational principles include (1) providing accurate and suitable measures of performance, (2) communicating with appropriate managers and segment leaders to be evaluated, (3) identifying the responsibilities of each manager, (4) comparing actual performance with a suitable base, (5) preparing performance reports that highlight areas of concern, and (6) analyzing important cause-and-effect relationships.

2. **Prepare a flexible budget.**
   A flexible budget summarizes anticipated costs prepared for various activity levels. It is geared toward changes in the level of productive output. Variable and fixed costs are given for several levels of capacity or output, with each column showing the total expected cost for an output level. Once prepared, the flexible budget is used to determine the flexible budget formula. This formula, which can be applied to any level of productive output, is a key tool in evaluating performance of individuals and departments.

3. **Compute overhead variances, using both the two-way and three-way analyses.**
   Cost variances for overhead costs can be computed using either the two-way or the three-way approach. Using two-way analysis, one can develop a controllable variance and a volume variance. The three-way approach to overhead variances refines the total overhead variance into a spending variance, an efficiency variance, and a volume variance. Comparing the two approaches, the three-way approach breaks the controllable variance of the two-way approach into a spending variance and an efficiency variance. The volume variance remains the same for both methods. Each variance results from specific causes, and these causes help pinpoint reasons for the differences between actual and standard costs.

4. **Prepare journal entries involving overhead variances.**
   The journal entries required to record overhead variances differ little from the set of entries illustrated for the job order costing system in Chapter 3. Actual overhead costs are still recorded in the overhead control account, and overhead costs applied using standard overhead rates are credited to the overhead applied account. The difference between the actual and applied overhead accounts represents the total overhead variance. When these two accounts are closed at period end, variances from standard cost can be assigned accounts in the general ledger and debited (unfavorable) or credited (favorable) to them. Only standard costs are charged to materials, work in process, and finished goods inventories. All differences between standard and actual costs are entered into the variance accounts.

5. Dispose of variance balances at period end.

At the close of an accounting period, balances in variance accounts are disposed of by either (1) closing them to Cost of Goods Sold if the balances are small or if most or all of the goods produced during the period were sold or (2) dividing the net variance balance among Work in Process Inventory, Finished Goods Inventory, and Cost of Goods Sold in proportion to their balances. The price variance, if significant, should be allocated separately because a portion should be assigned to Materials Inventory to convert that account balance into actual costs. Inventory balances can be stated at standard cost on period-end financial statements only when variance amounts are insignificant.

6. Describe the concept of management by exception.

Management by exception is a performance evaluation technique used to highlight significant variances from budgeted or planned operations and to analyze their causes. Variances within specific limits set by management are not analyzed. This technique is especially useful for companies trying to control a large number of cost centers or cost categories.

7. Evaluate employee performance using variances.

Introducing variances from standard costs into the performance report lends a degree of accuracy to the evaluation process. Variances tend to pinpoint efficient and inefficient operating areas more than comparisons between budgeted and actual data. The key factors in preparing a performance report based on standard costs and related variances are to (1) establish a responsibility accounting system and identify those responsible for each variance, (2) determine the causes for each variance, (3) establish a system of management by exception, and (4) develop a reporting format suited to the task. Following these basic rules will give the supervisor an effective tool for cost control and evaluation.

Review of Concepts and Terminology

The following important concepts were introduced in this chapter:

(L.O.2) **Flexible budget:** A summary of expected costs for a range of activity levels; it is geared to changes in the level of productive output.

(L.O.3) **Normal capacity:** Average annual level of operating capacity needed to meet expected sales demand; used to compute standard fixed overhead rate.

(L.O.3) **Total overhead variance:** The difference between actual overhead costs incurred and overhead costs applied to units produced.

(L.O.6) **Management by exception:** A management technique that locates and analyzes only the areas of unusually good or bad performance.

Other important terms introduced in this chapter are:

controllable overhead variance (p. 358)
flexible budget formula (p. 357)
overhead efficiency variance (p. 361)
overhead spending variance (p. 359)
overhead volume variance (p. 358)

Review Problem: Standard Costing in a Service Industry: Annuity Life Insurance Company

The Annuity Life Insurance Company (ALIC) markets several types of life insurance policies, but its permanent, twenty-year life annuity policy (P20A) is the company's most desired product. The P20A policy sells in $10,000 increments and features variable percentages of whole life insurance and single-payment annuity, depending on the potential policyholder's needs and age. There is an entire department devoted to developing and marketing the P20A policy. ALIC has determined that both the policy developer and policy salesperson contribute to creating each policy, so ALIC categorizes these people as direct labor for variance analysis, cost control, and performance evaluation purposes. For unit costing purposes, each $10,000 increment is considered 1 unit. Thus, a $90,000 policy comprises 9 units.

Standard unit cost information for the period is as follows:

Direct labor	
Policy developer	
3 hours at $12.00/hour	$ 36.00
Policy salesperson	
8.5 hours at $14.20/hour	120.70
Operating overhead	
Variable overhead	
11.5 hours at $26.00/hour	299.00
Fixed overhead	
11.5 hours at $18.00/hour	207.00
Standard unit cost	$662.70

Actual costs incurred during January for the 265 units sold were as follows:

Direct labor	
Policy developers	
848 hours at $12.50/hour	$10,600.00
Policy salespeople	
2,252.5 hours at $14.00/hour	31,535.00
Operating overhead	
Variable operating overhead	78,440.00
Fixed operating overhead	53,400.00

Normal monthly capacity was 260 units, and the budgeted fixed operating overhead for the month was $53,820.

Required

1. Compute the standard hours allowed in January for policy developers and policy salespeople.

2. What were the total actual costs incurred for January? What should have been the total standard costs for that period?
3. Compute the labor rate and efficiency variances for policy developers and policy salespeople.
4. Compute the overhead variances for January, using both the two-way and the three-way variance approaches.
5. Identify possible causes for each variance, and develop possible solutions.

Answer to Review Problem

1. Standard hours allowed = good units produced × standard hours per unit

   Policy developers
   Standard hours allowed = 265 × 3.00
   = 795 hours

   Policy salespeople
   Standard hours allowed = 265 × 8.50
   = 2,252.5 hours

2. Actual costs

Direct labor	
Policy developers	$ 10,600.00
Policy salespeople	31,535.00
Total direct labor cost	$ 42,135.00
Operating overhead	
Variable operating overhead	$ 78,440.00
Fixed operating overhead	53,400.00
Total operating overhead	$131,840.00
Total actual costs	$173,975.00

   Standard costs that should have been incurred for 265 units

Direct labor		
Policy developers	(795 × $12.00)	$ 9,540.00
Policy salespeople	(2,252.5 × $14.20)	31,985.50
Total direct labor cost		$ 41,525.50
Operating overhead		
Variable operating overhead	(265 × $299.00)	$ 79,235.00
Fixed operating overhead	(265 × $207.00)	54,855.00
Total operating overhead		$134,090.00
Total standard costs		$175,615.50

Total variance from standard cost	
($173,975.00 − $175,615.50)	$ 1,640.50(F)

3. Labor variances

Labor rate variances = (actual rate − standard rate)   × actual hours
    Policy developers =   ($12.50 − $12.00)   ×   848 hours
                = $424.00(U)

    Policy salespeople =   ($14.00 − $14.20)   × 2,252.5 hours
                = $450.50(F)

Efficiency variances = (actual hours − standard hours) × standard rate
    Policy developers =   (848.0 − 795.0)   × $12.00
                = $636.00(U)

    Policy salespeople =   (2,252.5 − 2,252.5)   × $14.20
                = $0.00

Check

Total actual labor cost	$ 42,135.00
Total standard labor cost	41,525.50
Total labor variance	$ 609.50(U)

Rate variances	
Developers	$ 424.00(U)
Salespeople	450.50(F)
Efficiency variances	
Developers	636.00(U)
Salespeople	0.00
Total labor variance	$ 609.50(U)

4(a). Overhead variances using the two-variance approach

Total overhead variance	
Actual overhead costs incurred	$131,840.00
Standard overhead costs applied to good units produced	
units produced × std hours/unit × total rate/hour	
265 × 11.50 × $44.00	134,090.00
Total overhead variance	$ 2,250.00(F)

Controllable overhead variance	
Actual overhead costs incurred	$131,840.00
Less budgeted factory overhead (flexible budget) for 265 units:	
Variable overhead cost	
units × hours/unit × rate/hour	
265 × 11.50 × $26.00	$ 79,235.00
Plus budgeted fixed overhead cost	53,820.00
Total budgeted factory overhead	$133,055.00
Controllable overhead variance	$ 1,215.00(F)

Overhead volume variance
Budgeted factory overhead $133,055.00
Less factory overhead applied:
units produced × std hours/unit × total rate/hour
265 × 11.50 × $44.00 134,090.00
Overhead volume variance $ 1,035.00(F)

Check of computations:
Controllable overhead variance $ 1,215.00(F)
Overhead volume variance 1,035.00(F)
Total overhead variance $ 2,250.00(F)

4(b). Overhead variances using the three-variance approach

Spending variance
Actual variable overhead cost $ 78,440.00
Budgeted variable overhead
(3,100.5 actual hours worked)
3,100.5 × $26.00/hour 80,613.00
Variable spending variance $ 2,173.00(F)
Actual fixed overhead cost $ 53,400.00
Budgeted fixed overhead cost 53,820.00
Fixed spending variance $ 420.00(F)
Spending variance $ 2,593.00(F)

Efficiency overhead variance:
Budgeted factory overhead (flexible budget
for actual hours worked)
Variable overhead cost
hours worked × rate paid
3,100.5 × $26.00 $ 80,613.00
Budgeted fixed overhead cost 53,820.00
Total budgeted overhead for actual
hours worked $134,433.00
Budgeted factory overhead (flexible budget
for standard hours allowed):
Variable overhead cost:
units × hour/unit × rate/hour
265 × 11.50 × $26.00 $ 79,235.00
Budgeted fixed overhead cost 53,820.00
Total budgeted overhead for standard
hours allowed $133,055.00
Overhead efficiency variance $ 1,378.00(U)

Overhead volume variance

Budgeted factory overhead (from above)	$133,055.00
Less factory overhead applied	
units produced × std hours/unit × total rate/hour	
265 × 11.50 × $44.00	134,090.00
Overhead volume variance	$ 1,035.00(F)

Check of computations	
Spending variance	$ 2,593.00(F)
Efficiency variance	1,378.00(U)
Overhead volume variance	1,035.00(F)
Total overhead variance	$ 2,250.00(F)

5. Although the total rate variance was favorable, a closer look shows that it is made up of a $424 unfavorable variance for policy developers and a $450 favorable variance for policy salespeople. There are several possible reasons for the unfavorable variance of $424. For instance, the industry's pay rate may have increased, forcing ALIC to increase the rate paid to policy developers. Or perhaps, needing more developers, ALIC hired those of greater skill and, thus, at a greater pay rate. A possible cause of the favorable labor rate variance could be a high turnover rate with new people being hired at a lower rate. An approach to the variance would be to determine if the actual rates were caused by a one-time situation, making them temporary, or by permanent changes in the labor market. If the change is permanent, the standard should be changed.

The unfavorable labor efficiency variance was caused entirely by policy developers, who took more time to complete 265 units than the standard allowed. This situation may have been caused by a high number of new, inexperienced employees. Also, the developers completed 5 more units than normal capacity. This may have resulted in longer than normal work days and a decrease in efficiency because of fatigue.

The total overhead variance was favorable. The three-way breakdown of the total variance showed favorable spending and volume variances and an unfavorable efficiency variance. This means that either someone did a good job controlling overhead costs and should be commended or the standards were set too low and should be adjusted. The overhead costs may have been less than expected because of an unexpected price change; a decrease in the amount of indirect labor used, such as less clerical staff; or a decrease in the utilities consumed. The cause of the favorable fixed overhead spending variance may have resulted from a lowering of the rent or a decrease in depreciation charges because some office equipment was sold.

The volume variance was actually favorable because 5 more units were sold than expected. This should again result in a reward for the person responsible and possibly an adjustment of normal capacity if it was set too low. Finally, the overhead efficiency variance was unfavorable for the same reason the labor efficiency variance was unfavorable.

Chapter Assignments

Questions

1. Define the following:
   a. Flexible budget
   b. Total overhead variance
   c. Controllable overhead variance
   d. Overhead spending variance
   e. Overhead efficiency variance
   f. Overhead volume variance
   g. Variance disposition
   h. Management by exception
2. What does the statement, "Performance is evaluated or measured by comparing what happened with what should have happened," mean? Relate your comments to the budgetary control process.
3. What is the purpose of a flexible budget?
4. What are the two parts of a flexible budget formula? How are they related?
5. Distinguish between the controllable overhead variance and the overhead volume variance.
6. How can a variance help management achieve effective control of operations?
7. If standard hours allowed are more than normal hours, will the period's overhead volume variance be favorable or unfavorable? Explain your answer.
8. Can an unfavorable direct materials quantity variance be caused, at least in part, by a favorable direct materials price variance? Explain.
9. Explain the statement, "Variance analysis is an integral part of standard cost accounting."
10. The two phases of standard cost variance analysis are (1) the initial computing of variances and (2) the identifying of underlying causes. Discuss the relationship between these two phases.
11. What three rules underlie the recording of standard cost variances?
12. What circumstances make a material quantity variance favorable?
13. Identify some possible causes of an unfavorable labor rate variance.
14. If the labor efficiency variance in the Pumping Department is unfavorable, would you also expect an unfavorable overhead efficiency variance in the department? Support your answer.
15. Discuss the relevance and importance of normal capacity and flexible budgets when determining overhead variances.
16. Identify and discuss the operating principles of performance evaluation.
17. Compare the two-way and three-way approaches to overhead variance analysis. Which is the better approach? Why?
18. How do you determine if an overhead efficiency variance is favorable or unfavorable?
19. Identify the supervisor(s) normally responsible for the material quantity variance.
20. Who is responsible for the overhead volume variance? How are these people held accountable for this variance?

Classroom Exercises

Exercise 10-1.
Performance
Evaluation
Principles
(L.O. 1)

Jill Langhorn was recently promoted to supervisor of the Water Conservation Department in the Mississippi Valley Bureau of Resources. Part of her duties as supervisor include managing a work force of fifty-two people. There are three assistant supervisors answering directly to Langhorn: Phil Hueidon, Brent Bergermust, and Barbara Terswal. All three have been with the department longer than Langhorn. All three have good records with the bureau, and each one is sensitive to his or her role in the department. Langhorn has never evaluated anyone before and has come to you, her immediate supervisor, for suggestions about preparing performance evaluations on these assistant supervisors.

Prepare a written response to Langhorn. Include an analysis of the principles of performance evaluation.

Exercise 10-2.
Flexible Budget
Preparation
(L.O. 2)

Fixed overhead costs for the Karolinski Kostume Company for 19xx are expected to be (a) depreciation, $84,000; (b) supervisor's salaries, $76,000; (c) property taxes and insurance, $24,000; and (d) other fixed overhead, $12,000. Total fixed overhead is therefore expected to be $196,000. Variable costs per unit are expected to be (a) direct materials, $5.00; (b) direct labor, $7.50; (c) operating supplies, $1.50; (d) indirect labor, $2.00; and (e) other variable overhead costs, $1.00.

Prepare a flexible budget for the following levels of production: 16,000 units, 18,000 units, and 20,000 units. What is the flexible budget formula for 19xx?

Exercise 10-3.
Factory Overhead
Variances: Two-
Way Approach
(L.O. 3a)

The Lowry Company produces handmade lobster pots, which are sold to distributors throughout New England. The company incurred $22,200 of actual overhead costs in May. Budgeted standard overhead costs were $8 of variable overhead costs per direct labor hour plus $2,500 in fixed overhead costs for May. Normal capacity was set at 2,000 direct labor hours per month. In May the company produced 800 lobster pots. The time standard is 3 direct labor hours per lobster pot.

Compute the controllable overhead variance, the overhead volume variance, and the total overhead variance for May.

Exercise 10-4.
Overhead Variance
Analysis: Three-
Way Approach
(L.O. 3b)

Budgeted fixed factory overhead for the Cahill Manufacturing Company is $29,565 per month. Variable overhead costs are budgeted at $2.60 per direct labor hour. Normal capacity for a given month is established at 8,100 direct labor hours. Actual operating data for November 19x9 were as follows:

Variable overhead costs	$21,240
Fixed overhead costs	29,840
Actual direct labor hours	8,310 hours
Standard hours allowed	8,120 hours

Compute the following amounts and label all answers carefully:

1. Total overhead applied
2. Over- or underapplied overhead
3. Overhead spending variance
4. Overhead efficiency variance
5. Overhead volume variance
6. Total overhead variance

Exercise 10-5.
Overhead Variance
Analysis: Three-
Way Approach
(L.O. 3b)

Chisarizk Industries uses a standard cost accounting system, which utilizes flexible budget procedures for planning and control purposes. The monthly flexible budget for overhead costs is $200,000 of fixed costs plus $4.80 per machine hour. Normal capacity of 100,000 machine hours is used to compute the standard fixed overhead rate.

During December 19x9, plant workers recorded 105,000 actual machine hours. The standard machine hours allowed for good production during December were only 98,500. Actual costs incurred during December were $541,000 of variable overhead and $204,500 of fixed overhead.

1. Compute the under- or overapplied overhead during December.
2. Prepare an analysis of the overhead spending variance, overhead efficiency variance, and overhead volume variance. Show all computations.

Exercise 10-6.
Journal Entries
and Overhead
Variances
(L.O. 3, 4)

John Espey is president of Cecil Appliance Repair Company, which employs more than seventy repair people when the normal operating schedule is met. During January 19x8, 11,200 standard hours allowed were produced by working 10,800 actual hours. The company's flexible budget for overhead costs is $3.40 per direct labor hour plus $22,300 in budgeted fixed costs. Actual costs for January were $36,800 of variable overhead and $23,050 of fixed overhead. Normal capacity is 11,150 direct labor hours per month.

1. Compute the overhead spending variance, the overhead efficiency variance, and the overhead volume variance for January.
2. Assuming actual overhead costs have been recorded, apply overhead to repair jobs worked on during the period.
3. Close the overhead applied and control accounts, and record overhead variances for the month.

Exercise 10-7.
Disposing of
Overhead Variance
Account Balances
(L.O. 5)

Long Island Company's controller, Myrna Fischman, is about to close the year's financial records. The following data related to overhead still appear in the accounting records:

Overhead spending variance	$ 1,660(U)
Overhead efficiency variance	2,720(F)
Overhead volume variance	200(F)
Work in process inventory	50,000
Finished goods inventory	75,000
Cost of goods sold	375,000

1. Prepare the journal entry to dispose of the variance balances. Assume that the total overhead variance is closed to Cost of Goods Sold.
2. Assuming the variance balances are significant, close the variance accounts for Work in Process Inventory, Finished Goods Inventory, and Cost of Goods Sold.

Exercise 10-8.
Management by
Exception
(L.O. 6)

Falcetta-Frank Instruments, Inc., produces scientific apparatus for food inspection. During the past five years, the corporation has grown from sales of $3,500,000 to sales exceeding $25,000,000. More than 500 types of materials are used in the production process, and labor skills of more than 80 specialists are utilized. The controller has been asked by the vice president of finance to develop an improved method of controlling costs. A standard cost accounting system was introduced two years ago, but the numerous variances identified by the system are not systematically analyzed for cause. Rapid growth, which has caused many of the variances, is also the reason the controller's department had no time to concentrate on the variances.

1. Describe the concept of management by exception.
2. Discuss how the controller of Falcetta-Frank Instruments, Inc., might use management by exception.

Exercise 10-9. Evaluating Performance Through Variances (L.O.3,7)

Evaluating the operating performance of the Morris Health Club is the responsibility of its controller, Charles Cheetham. The following information was available for March 19x8:

	Budget	Actual
Variable costs		
Operating labor	$ 5,760	$ 7,350
Utility costs	1,440	1,680
Repairs and maintenance	2,880	3,570
Fixed costs		
Depreciation, equipment	1,300	1,340
Rent expense	1,640	1,640
Other fixed costs	852	930
Totals	$13,872	$16,510

Normal operating hours call for six operators, working 160 hours each per month. During March, seven operators worked an average of 150 hours each.

With this limited information, compute as many variances as possible for labor and overhead, and prepare a performance report for the month.

Interpreting Accounting Information

Internal Management Information: Nassau Realtors (L.O.2,7)

Ms. Paluska, the managing partner of Nassau Realtors, Inc., received the performance report shown on page 385. The report showed that the company had experienced its biggest year in home resales since it began operating fifteen years ago. The report indicates that although fees were over budget by $244,800, all cost categories were also over budget, cutting the increase in net income to only $18,470.

During 19x7, company sales personnel marketed 186 homes, averaging $155,000 per unit. Budgeted data were based on 150 homes sold at an average market value of $165,000. Selling fees for all realty work are 6 percent of the selling price. Data supporting the budget figures were as follows:

Commissions: Salespersons: 25 percent of total fees
                Listing agents: 20 percent of total fees
                Listing companies: 25 percent of total fees
                 (Thirty-five percent of homes sold by Nassau
                 were listed by another company.)

Other variable expenses: Automobile expenses, $180 per sale
Advertising expenses, $420 per sale
Home repairs expenses, $230 per sale
Word processing expenses, $115 per sale

General overhead: 25 percent of total fees

Required

1. Recast the performance report, using a flexible budget based on the number of units sold.
2. Interpret the revised performance report for Paluska.

Nassau Realtors, Inc.
Performance Report
For the Year Ended December 31, 19x7

	Budget for the Year	Actual Fees and Costs	Variance Under (Over) Budget
Total Selling Fees	$1,485,000	$1,729,800	$(244,800)
Expenses			
Commissions			
Salespersons	$ 371,250	$ 432,450	$ (61,200)
Listing agents	297,000	345,960	(48,960)
Listing companies	129,938	151,358	(21,420)
Other variable expenses			
Automobile expenses	27,000	28,630	(1,630)
Advertising	63,000	72,940	(9,940)
Home repair expenses	34,500	43,110	(8,610)
Word processing expenses	17,250	19,880	(2,630)
General overhead expenses	371,250	443,190	(71,940)
Total expenses	$1,311,188	$1,537,518	$(226,330)
Net Income Before Taxes	$ 173,812	$ 192,282	$ (18,470)

Problem Set A

**Problem 10A-1.
Performance
Analysis/
Management by
Exception
*(L.O. 6, 7)***

Management at Alpha Motor Assembly, Inc., just introduced a management by exception component into its standard costing system. For the first few months, the purchase and use of materials will be emphasized. Variances are considered significant, and they need special analysis for cause, if they fall outside the following tolerances:

Price variance: ±5 percent of the item's total purchase price

Quantity variance: ±3 percent of the item's cost charged to Work in Process Inventory

During February the data shown below were generated.

	Quantities (Units)			Prices	
		Used			
Type of Material	Purchased	Actual	Standard	Actual	Standard
Motor A	14,200	13,700	13,500	$112	$110
Motor B	7,410	6,300	6,250	181	185
Motor C	4,820	4,605	4,600	212	200
Casing I	8,900	6,924	6,900	46	45
Casing II	20,000	17,992	17,450	38	44
Electrical components	26,400	24,492	24,350	22	20
Wood base R	15,400	13,020	12,840	82	88
Wood base Q	8,200	7,210	7,200	89	92
Metal base	4,800	4,460	4,310	125	120
Hardware components	25,600	24,380	24,350	26	29

Required

1. Prepare and complete a six-column analysis of these materials. Use the following column headings: Price Variance, Total Purchase Price, Percent of Variance, Quantity Variance, Cost of Materials Charged to Work in Process Inventory, and Percent of Variance.
2. Identify the variances that need to be analyzed for cause. Use the tolerances prescribed by management.
3. List three possible causes for each significant variance. Try identifying causes different from those in the book.

**Problem 10A-2.
Variance Review:
Missing
Information
(L.O. 3)**

Over- or underapplied overhead is the reason for analyzing overhead variances. These variances are interrelated. Felt Corporation and Temple Company have standard costing systems. Each firm uses the three-way approach to overhead variance analysis.

	Felt Corporation	Temple Company
Actual direct labor hours	17,100	_____
Standard hours allowed	17,500	8,800
Normal capacity in direct labor hours	_____	9,000
Total overhead rate per direct labor hour	_____	_____
Standard variable overhead rate	$ 2.50	$ 1.80
Actual variable and fixed overhead	_____	$43,850
Total overhead costs applied	_____	$44,000
Budgeted fixed overhead	$76,500	_____
Total overhead variance	_____	_____
Overhead spending variance	$ 700(F)	_____
Overhead efficiency variance	_____	$ 360(F)
Overhead volume variance	$ 2,250(F)	_____

Required

For each company, fill in the unknown amounts on the preceding page by analyzing the data for each organization. Capacities are expressed in direct labor hours. *Hint:* Use the structure of Figure 10-3 as a guide to your analysis.

Problem 10A-3.
Labor and
Overhead Variance
Analysis
(L.O.3,7)

Allied Discount Auto Repairs, Inc., is a high-volume business employing 125 mechanics in four locations. To charge discount rates, Allied is departmentalized. Standard costing is used for cost control purposes. The Overhaul/8 Department specializes in eight-cylinder engine overhauls. The following standards, which are in effect for the current period, cover the overhaul of an eight-cylinder engine:

Direct labor	
Senior mechanic	
6.5 hours @ $14.20/hour	$ 92.30
Junior mechanic	
12.4 hours @ $10.50/hour	130.20
Shop overhead	
Variable overhead	
18.9 hours @ $19.00/hour	359.10
Fixed overhead	
18.9 hours @ $8.00/hour	151.20
Standard cost per overhaul	$732.80

During September, the Overhaul/8 Department incurred the following costs:

Direct labor	
Senior mechanics	
1,057 hours @ $14/hour	$14,798
Junior mechanics:	
1,963 hours @ $11/hour	21,593
Shop overhead	
Variable shop overhead	54,100
Fixed shop overhead	22,200

Normal capacity for the Overhaul/8 Department per month is 140 jobs. During September, 151 complete overhauls were achieved. Budgeted fixed-shop overhead is $21,168 per month.

Required

1. Compute the standard hours allowed for September for senior mechanics and junior mechanics.
2. What was the total actual labor cost and overhead cost for September? What was the total standard cost (labor and overhead) charged to the Overhaul/8 Department for the month?
3. Compute the direct labor rate and efficiency variances for senior mechanics and junior mechanics.
4. Compute the shop overhead variances for September, using the two-variance and the three-variance approaches.

(continued)

5. Identify possible causes for each variance, and develop possible solutions to the causes.

Problem 10A-4.
Direct Materials,
Direct Labor, and
Factory Overhead
Variances
(L.O.3)

During 19x8, Navas Laboratories, Inc., researched and perfected a cure for the common cold. Called Cold-Gone, the series of five tablets sells for $9.50 per package. Standard costs for this product were developed in late 19x8 for use in 19x9. The costs per package were (a) chemical ingredients, 5 ounces at $.20/ounce; (b) materials for a safety package, $.80; (c) direct labor, .2 hours at $10.00/hour; (d) standard variable factory overhead, $2.00/direct labor hour; and (e) standard fixed factory overhead, $3.00/direct labor hour.

The first quarter of 19x9, the normal season for colds, saw demand for the new product rise above management's wildest expectations. During these three months, the company produced and sold 5 million packages of Cold-Gone. Production for the first week in April revealed the following: (a) 40,000 packages were produced; (b) 205,000 ounces of chemicals were used, costing $36,900; (c) materials for 40,400 packages were used, costing $34,340; (d) 8,140 direct labor hours cost $79,772; (e) total variable factory overhead cost, $15,650; and (f) total fixed factory overhead cost, $25,400. Budgeted fixed factory overhead for the period was $23,400.

Required

Compute (1) all direct materials price variances, (2) all direct materials quantity variances, (3) direct labor rate variance, (4) direct labor efficiency variance, (5) controllable overhead variance, and (6) overhead volume variance.

Problem 10A-5.
Comprehensive:
Standard Cost
Journal Entry
Analysis
(L.O.3,4,5)

Westchester Lamp Company manufactures several lines of home and business lights and lighting systems. Mahogany table lamps are one of the company's most popular product lines. Since mahogany is difficult to work with, special woodcarvers are employed. Deborah Goorbin, controller, has developed the following cost, quantity, and time standards for one mahogany table lamp for the current year:

Direct materials: wood, 10″ × 8″ × 18″ block of mahogany, $16.00; electrical fixture and cord, $6.50; and shade and mounting, $8.20

Direct labor: woodcarvers, 6 hours @ $12.50/hour, and assemblers and packers, 1.2 hours @ $8.00/hour

Factory overhead: variable rate, $2.60/direct labor hour, and fixed rate, $3.10/direct labor hour.

Mahogany table lamps sell for $350 each.

Selected transactions for August 19x8 are described as follows:

August 3 Purchased 700 blocks of mahogany for $11,060 on account.
        4 Requisitioned 60 blocks of wood into production for Order 16, calling for 50 lamps.
        5 Purchased 500 electrical fixture kits for $3,300 and 600 lamp shades and mountings for $4,950 on account.

August 7 Requisitioned 54 electrical fixture kits and 50 lamp shades and mountings into production for the same order of 50 lamps.

14 Semimonthly payroll was paid and included the following wages for Order 16: woodcarvers, 310 hours, $3,720, and assemblers and packers, 66 hours, $561. These labor efforts completed Order 16.

14 Factory overhead was applied to Order 16 units worked on during the payroll period.

16 Requisitioned 74 blocks of wood into production for Order 26, totaling 70 lamps.

19 Requisitioned 78 electrical fixture kits and 75 lamp shades and mountings into production for Order 26.

30 Labor for the previous half month was paid. Labor costs associated with Order 26 included: woodcarvers, 430 hours, $5,246, and assemblers and packers, 90 hours, $765.

30 Factory overhead was applied to work performed on Order 26 during the past two weeks.

30 Orders 16 and 26 were completed and transferred to Finished Goods Inventory.

31 Orders 16 and 26 were shipped to customers at the contracted price.

Beginning inventory information included: Materials Inventory Control, $31,410; Work in Process Inventory Control, $0; and Finished Goods Inventory Control, $14,600.

During August, actual factory overhead for these two orders was $2,100, variable, and $2,850, fixed. All actual overhead costs were recorded in the Factory Overhead Control account. Budgeted fixed factory overhead was $2,697 for August.

Required

1. Compute the standard cost for one mahogany table lamp.
2. Prepare the entries necessary to record the above transactions, and show calculations for each variance. For the direct labor entries, record only the distribution of direct labor to Work in Process Inventory Control.*
3. Analyze the factory overhead accounts, and compute the controllable and volume variances.
4. Prepare the entry to dispose of the overhead accounts and record the overhead variances.
5. Close all variance account balances to the Cost of Goods Sold account.

* Round answers to nearest dollar.

Problem Set B

Problem 10B-1.
Performance
Analysis/
Management by
Exception
(L.O. 6, 7)

Top management at the Jagat Jain Hotel in Niagara, New York, is interested in the effectiveness of the new management by exception program in their standard costing system. Past experience indicates that analyzing all variances is too cumbersome. In the new program, the only labor variances considered significant enough to need special analysis for cause are those falling outside the tolerances shown on the following page:

Rate variance:　　　±8 percent of the total standard labor cost for that category

Efficiency variance:　±10 percent of the total standard labor cost for that category

During March the following data were generated:

Labor Category	Labor Hours Actual	Labor Hours Standard	Labor Rates Actual	Labor Rates Standard
Bellhops	1,040	960	$ 5.80	$ 6.00
Cashiers	710	640	11.20	11.00
Registration clerks	1,570	1,440	9.40	9.00
Maids	5,240	4,800	4.80	4.50
Room service	1,390	1,280	5.00	5.50
Maintenance	1,080	960	6.40	7.00
Catering	3,390	3,200	7.70	7.50
Conference sales staff	910	800	11.20	10.00
Parking attendants	1,880	1,600	4.20	4.00

Required

1. Prepare and complete a five-column analysis using the following column headings: Standard Labor Cost, Rate Variance, Percent of Variance, Efficiency Variance, and Percent of Variance.
2. Identify the variances to be analyzed for cause. Use the tolerances prescribed by management.
3. List three possible causes for each significant variance. Try identifying some causes different from those in the book.

**Problem 10B-2.
Variance Review:
Missing
Information
(L.O. 3)**
Overhead variances are interrelated. The Meltzer Company and the Taylor Corporation both use standard costing systems. These systems depend on a standard overhead rate when overhead costs are applied to units produced.

	Meltzer Company	Taylor Corporation
Actual direct labor hours	7,500	4,200
Standard hours allowed	———	4,100
Normal capacity in direct labor hours	———	———
Total overhead rate per direct labor hour	$ 3.20	———
Standard variable overhead rate	$ 1.00	$ 4.00
Actual variable and fixed overhead	$26,200	———
Total overhead costs applied	$25,600	———
Budgeted fixed overhead	———	$24,000
Total overhead variance	———	$ 600(F)
Overhead spending variance	———	———
Overhead efficiency variance	———	$ 400(U)
Overhead volume variance	$ 440(F)	———
Controllable overhead variance	———	$ 8,200(U)

Fill in the unknown amounts on the preceding page by analyzing the data given for each company. Capacities are expressed in direct labor hours. *Hint:* Use Figure 10-3 as a guide.

Problem 10B-3.
Labor and
Overhead Variance
Analysis
(L.O.3,7)

Massasoit Secretarial Service operates a legal transcript department for their clients. Two people, a legal paraprofessional and a typist, are assigned to each case. Based on past history, a price is quoted for each job. This price is calculated on the basis of expected hours of work. A standard cost system is used for cost control purposes. The following standards are in effect for July for each case:

Labor
  Legal paraprofessional
    25 hours at $14.00/hour $ 350.00
  Typist
    40 hours at $9.50/hour   380.00
Overhead
  Variable overhead
    65 hours at $8.00/hour   520.00
  Fixed overhead
    65 hours at $5.40/hour   351.00
  Standard cost/case $ 1,601.00

During October, the Transcript Department incurred the following costs:

Labor
  Legal paraprofessional
    890 hours at $15/hour $13,350.00
  Typist
    1,360 hours at $9/hour   12,240.00
Overhead
  Variable overhead   18,550.00
  Fixed overhead   11,990.00

During July, work on 35 full (equivalent) cases was completed and billed. Normal capacity is thought to be 32 cases per month. Budgeted fixed overhead is $11,232.

Required

1. Compute the standard hours allowed for July for legal paraprofessionals and typists.
2. What were the total actual labor cost and actual overhead cost for July? How much labor cost should have been incurred? How much overhead cost was applied to the case accounts during July?
3. Compute the labor rate and efficiency variances for legal paraprofessionals and typists.

(continued)

4. Compute the overhead variances for July, using the two-variance and the three-variance approaches.
5. Identify possible causes for each variance, and develop possible solutions.

**Problem 10B-4.
Direct Materials,
Direct Labor, and
Factory Overhead
Variances**
(L.O. 3)

Monroe Shoe Company has a Sandal Division that produces a line of all-vinyl thongs. Each pair of thongs calls for .2 meter of vinyl material that costs $2.00 per meter. Standard direct labor hours and cost per pair of thongs are .2 hour and $1.25 (.2 hour × $6.25 per hour), respectively. The division's current standard variable overhead rate is $1.20 per direct labor hour, and the standard fixed overhead rate is $.70 per direct labor hour.

In August, the Sandal Division manufactured and sold 50,000 pairs of thongs. During the month, 9,980, meters of vinyl material were used, at a total cost of $20,958. The total actual overhead costs for August were $19,250. The total number of direct labor hours worked were 10,120, and August's factory payroll for direct labor was $60,720. Normal monthly capacity for the year was set at 48,000 pairs of thongs.

Required

Compute (1) direct materials price variance, (2) direct materials quantity variance, (3) direct labor rate variance, (4) direct labor efficiency variance, (5) controllable overhead variance, and (6) overhead volume variance. Show checks of your computations.

**Problem 10B-5.
Comprehensive:
Standard Cost
Journal Entry
Analysis**
(L.O. 3, 4, 5)

Plucinski Bottle Company makes wine bottles for many of the major wineries in California's Napa and Sonoma valleys as well as for wineries in the grape-growing regions around Cupertino and Santa Cruz, California. Ken Fredonia, controller of the company, installed these cost, quantity, and time standards for 19x8:

Direct materials: two 5-gallon pails of a special silicon dioxide and phosphorus pentoxide-based compound per 1 gross (144) of bottles; cost, $8 per pail

Direct labor: Forming Department—.2 hour per gross at $8.80 per direct labor hour; Finishing/Polishing Department—.1 hour per gross at $7.40 per direct labor hour

Factory overhead: variable—$2.20 per direct labor hour; fixed—$1.80 per direct labor hour

The direct materials are added at the beginning of the forming process. Much of the machinery is automated, and the compound is heated, mixed, and poured into molds in a short time. Once cooled, the new bottles move via conveyor belt to the Finishing/Polishing Department. Again, the process is highly automated. Machines scrape off excess material on the bottles and then polish all outside and inside surfaces. After polishing, the bottles are fed into large cartons for shipping to customers.

During March 19x8 the following selected transactions occurred:

March 2 Purchased 12,000 pails of compound at $7.80 per pail on account.
      3 Requisitioned 2,612 pails of compound into production for an order calling for 1,300 gross of wine bottles.

March   6   Requisitioned 5,880 pails of compound into production for an order of 2,900 gross of wine bottles.

12   Transferred 3,400 gross of bottles to finished goods inventory.

15   Requisitioned 4,630 pails of compound into production for an order calling for 2,300 gross of wine bottles.

16   For the two-week period ending March 14, actual labor costs included 860 direct labor hours in the Forming Department at $8.50 per hour and 410 direct labor hours in the Finishing/Polishing Department at $7.50 per hour. During the pay period, 4,200 gross of good bottles were produced.

16   Factory overhead was applied to units worked on during the previous two weeks.

18   Purchased 9,000 pails of compound at $8.10 per pail on account.

20   Requisitioned 6,960 pails of compound into production for an order of 3,500 gross of wine bottles.

28   Transferred 6,000 gross of bottles to finished goods inventory.

30   For the two-week period ending March 28, actual labor costs included 1,040 direct labor hours in the Forming Department at $9.00 per hour and 550 direct labor hours in the Finishing/Polishing Department at $7.50 per hour. During the pay period 5,300 gross of *good* bottles were produced.

30   Factory overhead was applied to units worked on during the two-week period.

31   During March, 9,800 gross of wine bottles were sold on account and shipped to customers. Selling price for these bottles was $36 per gross.

Actual factory overhead for February was $6,350 in variable and $5,300 in fixed overhead. These amounts were recorded in the Factory Overhead Control account. Budgeted fixed factory overhead was $5,000 for March. Beginning inventory information included: Materials Inventory, $21,360; Work in Process Inventory, $10,064; and Finished Goods Inventory, $17,760.

Required

1. Compute the standard cost per gross of wine bottles.
2. Prepare the entries necessary to record the above transactions, showing calculations for each variance. For the direct labor entries, record only the distribution of direct labor to Work in Process Inventory Control.
3. Analyze the factory overhead accounts, and compute the controllable and volume variances.
4. Prepare the entry to dispose of the overhead accounts, and record the overhead variances.
5. Close all variance account balances to the Cost of Goods Sold account.

Management Decision Case

Taube Aquatic Corporation
(L.O.3,6)

Taube Aquatic Corporation produces water sports gear, including safety cushions, water skis, towing lines, goggles, and snorkeling equipment. Much of the operation involves assembling parts purchased from outside vendors. However, all rubber parts are produced by the company in the Shaping Department. Face masks and goggles are assembled in the Face Wear Department, using purchased clear plastic lenses and fastener devices. Rubber mask casings and head straps are transferred in from the Shaping Department. Anthony Zazzara is in charge of the Shaping Department, and Jo Ann Wolfe supervises the Face Wear Department.

At the end of April 19x8, the Accounting Department developed the following performance reports for the two departments. When asked to comment on his performance, Zazzara stated, "Compared with the Face Wear Department, my performance is very good. Most of the $1,670(U) net variance arose because of two new, inexperienced workers, who increased the average labor hours for the department. Since overhead is applied based on direct labor hours, an unfavorable controllable variance was expected."

Ms. Wolfe was quite upset at Mr. Zazzara's comments. She said, "First of all, one of the variances is in error. The standard for direct labor usage should be $9,020 since 1,100 standard hours allowed were earned at an $8.20 standard labor rate. Also, the additional 100 standard hours allowed would cause the controllable variance to decrease by $420 because of the standard variable overhead rate of $4.20 per direct labor hour." She continued, "Now let's focus on the large unfavorable quantity and efficiency variances. All my production problems can be traced to the poor quality of mask casings coming from the Shaping Department. Poor quality of work meant dozens of spoiled mask assemblies, and my people had to work overtime to meet customer orders for the period. Had we had decent mask casings, we would have had an overall favorable performance for the period. Either the quality of the mask casings improves or I will ask to have them purchased from an outside vendor in the future."

Required

1. Recompute the variances and the performance report for the Face Wear Department. Assume Ms. Wolfe is correct.
2. Which supervisor's performance should be further analyzed? Why?
3. If you were vice president of production, what steps would you take to correct the situation? Develop a plan.

Taube Aquatic Corporation
Shaping Department
Performance Report—Cost Variance Analysis
For the Month Ended April 30, 19x8

Supervisor: A. Zazzara	Costs		Variance	
	Standard	Actual	Amount	Type
Direct materials used	$17,800	$18,000	$ 200(U)	Quantity variance
Direct labor usage	9,640	10,120	860(F)	Rate variance
			1,340(U)	Efficiency variance
Factory overhead	6,400	7,390	990(U)	Controllable variance
Totals	$33,840	$35,510	$1,670(U)	

Taube Aquatic Corporation
Face Wear Department
Performance Report—Cost Variance Analysis
For the Month Ended April 30, 19x8

Supervisor: J. Wolfe	Costs		Variance	
	Standard	Actual	Amount	Type
Direct materials used	$12,600	$16,450	$3,850(U)	Quantity variance
Direct labor usage	8,200	11,580	20(F)	Rate variance
			3,400(U)	Efficiency variance
Factory overhead	5,460	7,220	1,760(U)	Controllable variance
Totals	$26,260	$35,250	$8,990(U)	

Accounting for Management Decision Making

Providing information to support management decision making is the focal point of Part Four. Pricing decisions, government contract policies, short-run decision analyses, capital expenditure decision analyses, evaluation of decentralized operations, and transfer pricing policies are fundamental applications of management accounting concepts and techniques. Pricing decisions are based on cost analyses and external market factors. Government regulations underlie the pricing of federal government contracts. Short-run decisions require a knowledge of cost and revenue activities. Capital expenditure decisions are made following extensive analyses of future cost and revenue projections. Decentralized companies must apply evaluation methods to maintain control, including the use of transfer prices.

Chapter 11 exposes the difficulties of setting an accurate price for a good or a service. Both external and internal factors affect the price-setting process. Contracting with the federal government requires unique approaches to cost accumulation and contract pricing mandated by regulations and law.

Chapter 12 introduces the concepts of relevant decision information, variable costing, contribution margin reporting, and incremental decision analysis. Short-run decisions include make or buy, special order, scarce resource/sales mix, elimination of unprofitable segments, and sell or process further considerations.

Chapter 13 first looks at the steps in the capital expenditure decision process and then discusses the decision techniques of accounting rate of return, payback period, and net present value. The chapter ends with the concept of time value of money and income tax influences on the capital expenditure decision analysis.

Chapter 14 focuses on decentralized operating structures. Emphasis is on specific accounting methods, reporting techniques, and evaluation techniques. Transfer pricing is introduced because of its link to evaluation of corporate segments. Transfer prices are created and can be based on cost or competing prices.

LEARNING OBJECTIVES

1. Describe traditional economic pricing concepts.
2. Identify external and internal factors on which prices are based.
3. State the objectives managers use to establish prices of goods and services.
4. Create prices by applying the methods and tools of price determination.
5. Define Defense Acquisition Regulation (DAR) and state the purpose of these guidelines.
6. Describe the federal government procurement environment.
7. Identify and differentiate between the primary types of government contracts.
8. State the rules and conditions under which costs are judged unallowable for contract pricing purposes.
9. Apply the guidelines and procedures in Cost Accounting Standards 402 and 403.

CHAPTER 11

Pricing Decisions, Including Contract Pricing

Deciding on an appropriate price is one of a manager's most difficult day-to-day decisions. Such a decision affects the long-term life of any profit-oriented enterprise. To stay in business, a company's selling price must (1) be equal to or lower than the competition's price, (2) be acceptable to the customer, and (3) recover all costs incurred in bringing the product or service to a marketable condition. If a manager deviates from these three pricing rules, there must be a specific short-run objective; breaking these pricing rules for a long period will force a company into bankruptcy.

Doing business with the federal government involves a completely different approach to pricing goods and services. Roughly one-third of our economy involves dealings with the government, so it is important to know how to approach the pricing of government contracts. In a normal commercial business, the company developing a product or service assumes all the risk associated with a new venture, but in most large defense contracts the customer (the federal government) assumes the risk. These situations involve cost-plus contracts. The product is experimental, and the government has to assume the risk if a private company is to be attracted to the venture. Government purchases of normal goods and services often are linked to fixed price contracts in which the supplier or contractor assumes the risk of the transaction. A special set of Defense Acquisition Regulations, including specially designed cost accounting standards, are used as guidelines for cost assignment and contract pricing. After studying this chapter, you should be able to meet the learning objectives listed on the left.

The Pricing Decision

The process of establishing a correct price is more of an art than a science. There are many mechanical approaches to price setting, and each approach produces a price. But who knows if that price is the most correct? Six pricing methods may well produce six prices. The art of price setting stems from the ability to read the marketplace and anticipate customer reaction to a product and its price. Pricing methods do not give a manager the ability to react to the market. Much of market savvy is developed through years of experience in dealing with customers and products in an industry. Intuition also plays a major role in price setting.

So why study pricing methods? The methods discussed in the following pages illustrate the process of developing a specific price under defined circumstances or objectives. Some of the methods give the manager the minimum price he or she can charge and still make a profit. Other prices are based on the competition and market conditions. The concept of setting prices according to whatever the market will bear produces still another figure.

In making a final pricing decision, the manager must consider all these projected prices. The more data the manager has, the more he or she will be able to make a well-informed decision. But remember, pricing methods and approaches yield only decision data. The manager must still select the appropriate price and be evaluated on the consequences.

The Art of Setting a Price

Maison & Jardin is a gourmet restaurant in Altamonte Springs, Florida. Besides excellent food, the establishment boasts fine wines. Among its selections of California red wine is a 1982 Cabernet Sauvignon from Shafer Vineyards in Napa Valley, California. The restaurant's normal charge for a bottle of this wine is $18.50. However, for one or more reasons, this wine is being featured as the "special selection of the month" (perhaps there is an oversupply of the wine, the wine has matured and must be sold, or the vineyard is running a special promotion).

The restaurant is now charging the following prices for this wine:

	Price per Bottle
Purchased by the glass, $5.25 (4 glasses per bottle)	$21.00
Purchased by the bottle with your meal	16.75
Purchased by the bottle to take home	11.95
Purchased by the case to take home ($119.50 ÷ 12)	9.96

What is the correct price for a bottle of this wine?

The listed prices are all appropriate based on differing circumstances. The $18.50 price is based on the cost of the bottle, reputation of the vineyard, prices of wines of comparable quality, vintage (1982), mixture of varietal grapes, and alcohol level.

Once a bottle of quality red wine has been opened, the wine begins to oxidize, and it then spoils in two or three hours. Therefore, when wine is sold by the glass, the restaurant risks losing part of the bottle to spoilage. Thus $5.25 per glass seems appropriate under the circumstances.

To promote a specific product, many businesses run special sales. A restaurant is no different. This month Maison & Jardin's management decided to reduce the bottle's price by $1.75 to lure customers into trying this product with their meal.

Although the take-home feature is unusual, the pricing is appropriate. Part of the cost for a bottle of wine served with a meal is for the cost of serving it. The wine steward must fetch the bottle, bring a cooling device for white wine to the table, uncork the bottle, decant a bottle of older wine, present the wine for customer approval, and continue pouring the wine during the meal. In the example, the restaurant reduced the price of a take-home bottle $4.80. This means that the cost of serving a bottle of wine and the restaurant's profit margin on this labor is somewhere around $5.00 per bottle. And that price has been included in the price shown on the wine list.

Finally, consider the case price. On a per bottle basis, the case price is $1.99 less than purchasing a bottle to take home. This reduction is known as quantity discounting, a concept widely followed in the free enterprise system. As with the take-home bottle price, reduced handling costs support the use of quantity discount pricing.

Pricing is a fascinating topic to study and learn. It is the key to a successful business. Any entrepreneur is a student of pricing during his or her entire career. The ability to set the one perfect price will never be mastered for changes in circumstances will always justify a different price. Please keep this truth in mind as you begin this study of pricing decisions.

Traditional Economic Pricing Concepts

OBJECTIVE 1
Describe
traditional
economic pricing
concepts

The traditional approach to pricing is based on microeconomic theory. Pricing has a major role in the concepts underlying the theory of the firm. At the base of this concept, the firm is in business to maximize profits. Although each product has its own set of revenues and costs, microeconomic theory states that profit will be maximized when the difference between total revenues and total costs is the greatest. Recall the discussion of break-even analysis in Chapter 6. Figure 6-2 (page 202) illustrated a typical break-even chart. To the left of the break-even point of 1,000 units, the company will lose money since total costs exceed total revenues. To the right of the break-even point, profit will be realized since total revenues are greater than total costs. But where is the point at which profits are maximized, and what is the role of pricing in this discussion?

Total Revenue and Total Cost Curves. By looking at Figure 6-2, you see that the outlook for profits is a bit misleading. The profit area seems to increase significantly as more and more products are sold. Therefore, it seems that if the company could produce an infinite number of products, maximum profit would be realized. But this situation is untrue, and microeconomic theory tells you why.

Figure 11-1(*a*) shows the economist's view of the break-even chart. On the chart are two break-even points, between which is a large space labeled *profit*. Notice that the total revenue line is curved rather than straight. The theory is that as one markets a product, price reductions will be necessary to sell additional units because of competition and other factors. Total revenue will continue to increase, but the rate of increase will diminish as more units are sold. Therefore, the total revenue line curves toward the right.

Costs react in an opposite fashion. Over the assumed relevant range in Chapter 6, variable and fixed costs were fairly predictable, with fixed

Figure 11-1. Microeconomic Pricing Theory

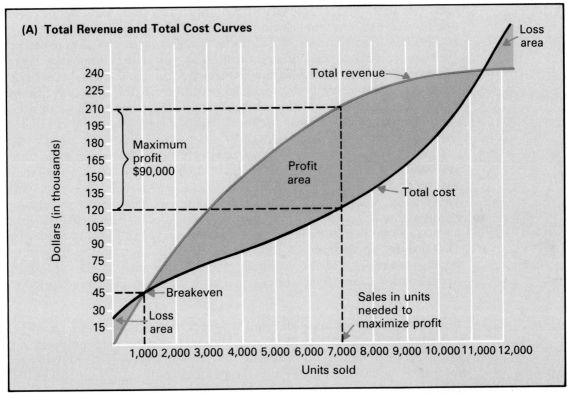

(A) Total Revenue and Total Cost Curves

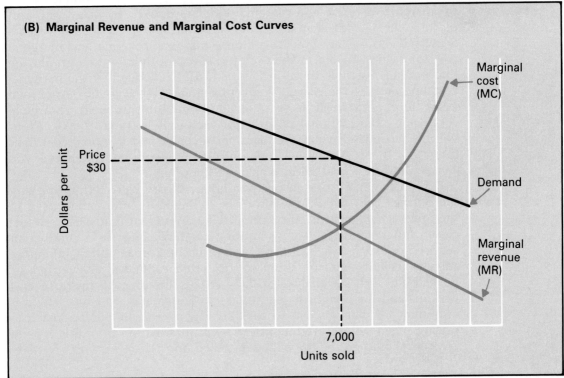

(B) Marginal Revenue and Marginal Cost Curves

costs remaining constant and variable costs being the same per unit. The result was a straight line for total costs. Following microeconomic theory, costs per unit will increase over time since fixed costs will change. As one moves into different relevant ranges, such fixed costs as supervision and depreciation increase. In addition, as the company pushes for more and more products from limited facilities, repair and maintenance costs increase. And as the push from management increases, total costs rise at an accelerating rate per unit. The result is that the total cost line in Figure 11-1(*a*) begins curving upward. The total revenue line and total cost lines then cross again. Beyond that crossing point, the company suffers a loss on additional sales.

Profits are maximized at the point at which the difference between total revenue and total cost is the greatest. In Figure 11-1(*a*), this point is assumed to be 7,000 units of sales. At that sales level, total revenue will be $210,000; total cost, $120,000; and profit, $90,000. In theory, if one additional unit is sold, profit per unit will drop because total cost is rising at a faster rate than total revenues. As you can see, if the company sells 11,000 units, total profits will be almost entirely eaten up by the rising costs. Therefore, in the example, 7,000 sales units is the optimum operating level, and the price charged at that level is the correct price.

Marginal Revenue and Marginal Cost Curves. Economists use the concepts of marginal revenue and marginal cost to help pinpoint an optimum price for a good or service. Marginal revenue is the change in total revenue caused by a 1-unit change in output. Marginal cost is the change in total cost caused by a 1-unit change in output. Graphic curves for marginal revenue and marginal cost are derived by measuring and plotting the rate of change in total revenue and total cost at various activity levels. Were you to compute marginal revenue and marginal cost for each unit sold in the example and plot them onto a graph, the lines would resemble those in Figure 11-1(*b*). Notice that the marginal cost line crosses the marginal revenue line at 7,000 units. After that point, total profits will decrease as additional units are sold. Marginal cost will exceed marginal revenue for each unit sold over 7,000. Profit will be maximized when the marginal revenue and marginal cost lines intersect. By projecting this point onto the product's demand curve, you can locate the optimal price, which is $30 per unit.

If all information used in microeconomic theory were certain, picking the optimal price would be fairly easy. But most information used in the previous analysis relied on projected amounts for unit sales, product costs, and revenues. Just computing total demand for a product or service from such data is difficult, and projecting repair and maintenance costs is usually done by using unsupported estimates. Nevertheless, developing such an analysis usually makes the analyst aware of cost patterns and the unanticipated influences of demand, which is why it is important for management to consider the microeconomic approach to pricing when setting product prices. But information from this type of analysis should not be the only data relied on.

Factors Influencing the Pricing Decision

OBJECTIVE 2
*Identify external
and internal
factors on which
prices are based*

Determining a price is an involved and difficult procedure. A manager must consider many factors when creating the best price for a product or service. Therefore, before exploring the methods used to compute a selling price, we analyze those influential factors, some of which are external to the company, some of which are internal.

External Factors. Each product or service has a targeted market that determines demand. Strong consideration should be given to this market before choosing a final price. Table 11-1 summarizes external factors to be considered in setting a price. Those factors include the following considerations:

1. What is total demand for the item?
2. Are there one or several competing products in the marketplace?
3. What prices are others already selling the item charging?
4. Do customers want the least expensive product, or are they more interested in quality than price?
5. Is the product so unique or new that the company is the only source in the marketplace?

Table 11-1. Factors to Consider When Setting a Price

External factors
Total demand for product or service
Number of competing products or services
Quality of competing products or services
Current prices of competing products or services
Customers' preferences for quality versus price
Sole source versus heavy competition
Seasonal demand or continual demand
Life of product or service

Internal factors
Cost of product or service
   Variable costs
   Full absorption costs
   Total costs
Price geared toward return on investment
Loss leader or main product
Quality of materials and labor inputs
Labor intensive or automated process
Markup percentage updated
Usage of scarce resources

All these questions should be answered by the person developing the price. If competition is keen and the quality is similar, market price will set the ceiling for any new entry into the market. If, however, a product is unique or new, a more flexible pricing environment exists. Customers' needs and desires are important for any new product. If quality is of primary importance, as is the case for top-of-the-line automobiles, then emphasis should be on using quality inputs; the price will be adjusted upward accordingly.

In summary: it is important to know the marketplace, including customers' needs and the competition, before determining a final price.

Internal Factors. Several internal factors also influence the price of a good or service, and these are also summarized in Table 11-1. Basic among these factors is an item's cost. What cost basis should be considered when determining price—variable costs, full absorption costs, or total costs? Should the price be based on a desired rate of return on assets? Is the product a loss leader, created to lure customers into considering additional, more expensive products? Where should one draw the line on the quality of materials and supplies? Is the product labor intensive, or can it be produced by using automated equipment? If markup percentages are used to establish prices, were they updated to reflect current operating conditions? Are the company's scarce resources being overtaxed by introducing an additional product or service, and does the price reflect this use of scarce resources?

As with external factors, each question should be answered before a manager establishes a price for a product or service. Underlying every pricing decision is the fact that all costs incurred must be recovered in the long run or the company will no longer be in business.

Pricing Policy Objectives

OBJECTIVE 3
State the objectives managers use to establish prices of goods and services

A company's long-run objectives should include a pricing policy. Such policies differentiate one company from another. For example, consider the pricing policies of Mercedes-Benz and Ford or Neiman-Marcus and K mart. All four companies are successful, but their pricing policies are quite different. Of primary importance in setting company objectives is identifying the market being served and meeting the needs of that market. Possible pricing policy objectives include

1. Identifying and adhering to short-run and long-run pricing strategies
2. Maximizing profits
3. Maintaining or gaining market share
4. Setting socially responsible prices
5. Maintaining stated rate of return on investment
6. Ensuring prices support trend of total sales increases

Pricing strategies depend on many factors and conditions. Companies producing standard items for a competitive marketplace will have different pricing strategies from firms making custom-designed items. In a competitive market, pricing can be reduced to gain market share by displacing sales of competing companies. Continuous upgrading of a product or service can help in this area. The company making custom-designed items can be more conservative in its pricing strategy.

Maximizing profits has always been considered the underlying objective of any pricing policy. Although still a dominant factor in price setting, profit maximization has been tempered in recent years by other more socially acceptable goals. Maintaining or gaining market share is closely related to pricing strategies. However, market share is important only if sales are profitable. To increase market share by reducing prices below cost can be disastrous unless this move is accompanied by other compensating objectives and goals.

Prices have a social effect, and companies are concerned about their public image. Recall the discussion about Mercedes-Benz, Ford, Neiman-Marcus, and K mart. Is there an individual image of each company in your mind? And are prices not a part of that image? Other social concerns, such as legal constraints and ethical considerations, also affect many companies' pricing policies.

Other pricing policy objectives include maintaining a minimum return on investment and concentrating on continuous sales growth. Return on investment involves markup percentages designed to provide a buffer between costs and prices. Such an objective is linked closely with the profit maximization objective. Maintaining a continuous sales growth is important for three reasons. First, it gives management a strong measure of performance for shareholders. Second, sales growth can be used to measure whether market share is increasing. Finally, such a policy gives managers yearly incentives and targets.

Pricing Methods

OBJECTIVE 4
Create prices by applying the methods and tools of price determination

There are as many pricing methods in business as there are people developing prices. And although managers may use one or two traditional approaches, at some point they must deviate from those approaches and use their experience.

Several pricing methods are available that the pricing manager can adopt. A good starting point is for a manager to develop a price based on the cost of producing a good or service. Here, four methods based on cost are discussed: (1) variable cost pricing, (2) gross margin pricing, (3) profit margin pricing, and (4) return on assets pricing. Remember that in a competitive environment, market prices and conditions also influence price. However, when prices do not cover a company's costs, the company will fail in the long run.

To illustrate the four methods of cost-base pricing, our example will use data on the Ron Jones Company. The Ron Jones Company assembles parts purchased from outside vendors into an Electric Car-Wax Buffer. Total costs and unit costs incurred in the previous accounting period to produce 14,750 wax buffers are shown on the following page:

	Total Costs	Unit Costs
Variable production costs		
Materials and parts	$ 88,500	$ 6.00
Direct labor	66,375	4.50
Variable factory overhead	44,250	3.00
Total variable production costs	$199,125	$13.50
Fixed factory overhead	$154,875	$10.50
Selling, general, & administrative expenses		
Selling expenses	$ 73,750	$ 5.00
General expenses	36,875	2.50
Administrative expenses	22,125	1.50
Total selling, general, & administrative expenses	$132,750	$ 9.00
Total costs and expenses	$486,750	$33.00

No changes in unit costs are expected this period. Desired profit for the period is $110,625. The company uses assets totaling $921,875 in producing the wax buffers. A 12 percent return on these assets is expected.

Variable Cost Pricing

One approach to cost-based pricing is to establish selling prices at a certain percentage above each item's variable production costs. This approach is called **variable cost pricing**. Basing a pricing decision on variable costs traceable to a product is useful if (1) the amount of assets attributable to each product in a company's line of products is similar and (2) the ratio of variable production costs to remaining operating costs is similar for each type of product. As in all cost-based methods for determining price, the method must attach a fair share of total costs to each product. In the case of variable cost pricing, the following two formulas are used:

$$\text{Markup percentage} = \frac{\text{desired profit} + \text{total fixed production costs} + \text{total selling, general, \& administrative expenses}}{\text{total variable production costs}}$$

Variable cost-based price = variable production costs per unit + (markup percentage × variable production costs per unit)

In the markup percentage formula, the numerator is composed of all costs, expenses, and targeted profit that must be recovered by the selling price over and above variable production costs. By adding desired profit, total fixed production costs, and total selling, general, and administrative costs in the numerator, the resulting markup factor forces these items to be considered in any decision on selling price. The denominator is the total variable production costs since this is the amount on which the markup factor is being based.

Once the markup percentage is computed, an item's selling price can be determined. The variable cost-based price formula illustrates this process. After calculating a product's variable production costs, one multiplies the markup percentage by the variable production costs per unit. The markup is then added to a unit's variable production costs to arrive at the selling price.

To examine this process, data from the Ron Jones Company are used. Following are the formulas and computations:

$$\text{Markup percentage} = \frac{\$110,625 + \$154,875 + \$132,750}{\$199,125}$$

$$= \frac{\$398,250}{\$199,125}$$

$$= 200.00\%$$

$$\text{Variable cost-based price} = \$13.50 + (\$13.50 \times 200\%)$$

$$= \$40.50$$

The numerator in the markup percentage formula contains the desired profit ($110,625); total fixed production costs ($154,875); and total selling, general, and administrative expenses ($132,750). This total amount ($398,250) is divided by total variable production costs ($199,125). The resulting markup percentage is 200 percent. To compute the variable cost-based price, one adds the markup of $27.00 ($13.50 × 200%) to the variable cost base of $13.50 per unit. The product should sell for $40.50 if all costs and expenses are to be covered and the desired profit realized.

Gross Margin Pricing

A second approach to determining a selling price based on costs is known as **gross margin pricing**. Gross margin is the difference between sales and total production costs of those sales. The markup percentage under the gross margin method is designed to include everything not included in gross margin in the computation of the selling price. The gross margin markup percentage is composed of selling, general, and administrative expenses and desired profit. Because an accounting system often provides management with unit production cost data, both variable and fixed, this method of determining selling price can be easily applied. Following are the formulas used:

$$\text{Markup percentage} = \frac{\text{desired profit} + \text{total selling, general, \& administrative expenses}}{\text{total production costs}}$$

$$\text{Gross margin-based price} = \text{total production costs per unit} + (\text{markup percentage} \times \text{total production costs per unit})$$

The numerator in the markup percentage formula contains desired profit plus total selling, general, and administrative expenses. As you can see, this numerator is divided by total production costs to arrive at the mark-up factor.

For the Ron Jones Company, the markup percentage and selling price are computed as shown:

$$\text{Markup percentage} = \frac{\$110,625 + \$132,750}{\$199,125 + \$154,875}$$

$$= \frac{\$243,375}{\$354,000}$$

$$= 68.75\%$$

$$\text{Gross margin-based price} = \$13.50 + \$10.50 + (\$24.00 \times 68.75\%)$$

$$= \$40.50$$

The numerator in the markup percentage formula is the sum of the desired profit ($110,625) and total selling, general, and administrative expenses ($132,750). The denominator contains all production costs, variable costs of $199,125, and fixed production costs of $154,875. Gross margin markup is 68.75 percent of total production costs, or $16.50 ($24 × 68.75%). Adding $16.50 to the total production cost base yields a selling price of $40.50.

As you can see, the same selling price was computed by using both the variable cost and gross margin approaches. Since the same base data were used in the computations, the answers should be the same. The only item that changed in the two methods was the base (variable production costs versus total production costs). The markup percentage compensated for this change, and the same selling price resulted. The remaining cost-based methods will also result in the same selling price, although the return on assets approach could have different results.

Profit Margin Pricing

When the profit margin approach is used, the markup percentage includes only the desired profit factor. For this method to be effective, all costs and expenses must be broken down into unit cost data. Since selling, general, and administrative costs tend to be more difficult to allocate to products or services than variable and fixed production costs, only arbitrary assignments can be used. However, arbitrary allocations can be mis-leading and may result in poor price setting. As long as market and competition factors are accounted for before establishing a final price, profit margin pricing can be used as a starting point in any price-setting decision analysis.

In the following markup percentage computation, all costs have shifted from the numerator to the denominator:

$$\text{Markup percentage} = \frac{\text{desired profit}}{\text{total costs and expenses}}$$

Profit margin-base price = total costs and expenses per unit +
(markup percentage × total costs and
expenses per unit)

As shown, only desired profit remains in the numerator. The denominator contains all production and operating costs related to the product or service being priced. In the profit margin pricing formula, total costs and expenses per unit are multiplied by the markup percentage to obtain the appropriate profit margin. The selling price is computed by adding profit margin to total unit costs.

Refer again to data on the Ron Jones Company. Notice that the following analysis computes the markup percentage and unit selling price by using the profit margin pricing approach:

$$\text{Markup percentage} = \frac{\$110,625}{\$199,125 + \$154,875 + \$132,750}$$

$$= \frac{\$110,625}{\$486,750}$$

$$= 22.73\%$$

$$\text{Profit margin-based price} = \$13.50 + \$10.50 + \$9.00 + (\$33.00 \times 22.73\%)$$

$$= \$40.50$$

Only the $110,625 in desired profit margin remains in the numerator, whereas the denominator increased to $486,750. The denominator represents total costs and expenses to be incurred. Markup percentage for this situation is 22.73 percent. The selling price is again $40.50. However, in this computation the markup percentage of 22.73 percent is applied to the total cost of $33.00 to obtain the profit margin of $7.50 per unit ($33.00 + $7.50 = $40.50).

Return on Assets Pricing

Return on assets pricing changes the objective of the price determination process. Earning a profit margin on total costs is replaced by earning a profit equal to a specified rate of return on assets employed in the operation. Since a business's primary objective should be earning a minimum desired rate of return, the return on assets pricing approach has a great appeal and support.

Assuming a company has a stated minimum desired rate of return, you can use the following formula to calculate return on assets-based price:

Return on assets-based price = total costs and expenses per unit +
(desired rate of return × total costs
of assets employed ÷ anticipated units
to be produced)

The return on assets-based price is computed by first dividing the cost of assets employed by projected units to be produced. This number is then multiplied by the rate of return to obtain desired earnings per unit. Desired earnings per unit plus total costs and expenses per unit yields unit selling price.

For the Ron Jones Company, one can compute the selling price per unit needed to earn a 12 percent return on the $921,875 asset base when estimated production is 14,750 units:

$$
\begin{aligned}
\text{Return on assets-based price} &= \$13.50 + \$10.50 + \$9.00 \\
&\quad + [12\% \times (\$921,875 \div 14,750)] \\
&= \$40.50
\end{aligned}
$$

The desired profit amount has been replaced by an overall company rate of return on assets. By dividing cost of assets employed by projected units of output and multiplying the result by the minimum desired rate of return, one obtains a unit profit factor of $7.50 [12% × ($921,875 ÷ 14,750)]. By adding this profit factor to total unit costs and expenses, one obtains a selling price of $40.50.

Summary of the Cost-Based Pricing Methods. The four cost-based pricing methods are summarized in Figure 11-2. All four methods— variable cost pricing, gross margin pricing, profit margin pricing, and return on assets pricing—will yield the same selling price if applied to the same data. Therefore companies select their methods based on their degree of trust in a cost base. The cost bases from which they can choose are (1) variable costs per unit, (2) total product costs per unit, or (3) total costs and expenses per unit. Often total product costs per unit are readily available, which makes gross margin pricing a good benchmark on which to compute selling prices. Return on assets pricing is also a good pricing method if the cost of the assets used on a product can be identified and a cost amount determined. If not, the method yields inaccurate results.

Pricing Services. Service-oriented businesses take a different approach to pricing their products. Although a service has no physical existence, it must still be priced and billed to the customer. Most service organizations use a form of time and materials pricing to arrive at the price of a service. Service companies, such as appliance repair shops, home-addition specialists, pool cleaners, and automobile repair businesses, arrive at prices by using two computations, one for labor and one for materials and parts. As with the cost-based approaches, a markup percentage is used to add the cost of overhead to the direct costs of labor, materials, and parts. If materials and parts are not a component of the service being performed, then only direct labor costs are used as a basis for developing price. For professionals, such as attorneys, accountants, and consultants, a factor representing all overhead costs is applied to the base labor costs to establish a price for the services.

Figure 11-2. Cost-Based Pricing Methods: Ron Jones Company

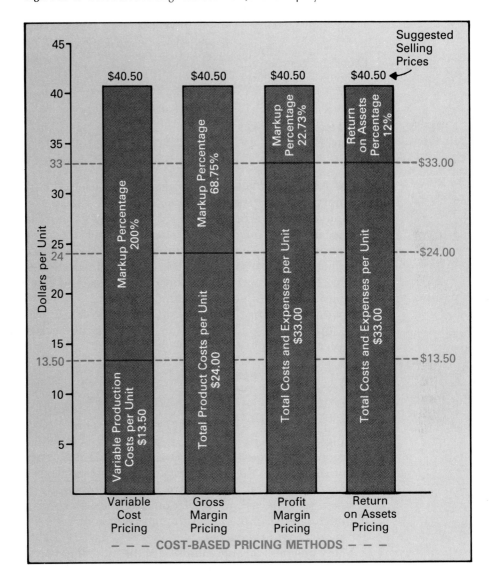

Ben's Auto Pampering just completed working on Mr. Crenshaw's 1983 Jaguar XJ6. Parts used to repair the vehicle cost $340. The company's 40 percent markup rate on parts covers parts-related overhead costs. Labor involved 9 hours of time from a Jaguar specialist whose wages are $15 per hour. The current overhead markup rate on labor is 80 percent. To see how much Mr. Crenshaw will be billed for these automobile repairs, review the computation shown on the following page:

Repair parts used	$340	
Overhead charges		
$340 × 40%	136	
Total parts charges		$476
Labor charges		
9 hours @ $15/hour	$135	
Overhead charges		
$135 × 80%	108	
Total labor charges		243
Total billing		$719

Final Notes on Pricing Methods. As emphasized earlier, pricing is an art, not a science. Although several methods can be used to mechanically compute the price of something, many factors external to the good or service influence price. Once the cost of a good or service is determined, the decision maker must account for such factors as competitors' prices, customers' expectations, and the cost of substitute goods and services. Pricing is a risky part of operating a business, and care must be taken to establish that all-important selling price.

Special-order pricing takes a different approach to price determination. This topic, along with other short-run operating decisions, is covered in Chapter 12.

Government Contract Pricing

Pricing government contracts is a specialized approach to the pricing decision. Care must be exercised to include only appropriate cost and profit elements in the pricing process because taxpayers' funds are being spent. The federal government procurement process is made up of a detailed set of laws and regulations designed to control the government contracting environment. Although most contract pricing is cost-based, there are other approaches.

Many business arrangements with the federal government, particularly defense contracts, require cost-based prices. These situations usually arise where the firm is a sole supplier of a good or a service, although they can also arise when the government requests a highly complex good or service. The federal government has established a set of rules and regulations relating to the procurement of goods and services and the accounting practices and standards to be followed. If a firm is to be awarded government business with contracts covered by such rules and regulations, it must understand the special features of the procurement process and the prescribed accounting provisions.

Two sets of procurement regulations underlie most of the contracting arrangements with the federal government. The **Defense Acquisition Regulation (DAR)** is applicable to all contracts with the Department of Defense. The Federal Procurement Regulation (FPR) is the primary

OBJECTIVE 5
*Define Defense
Acquisition
Regulation (DAR)
and state the
purpose of these
guidelines*

regulation governing the procurement activities of civilian agencies. Although these two documents are similar in certain respects, they do differ in many areas. For simplicity, we discuss only DAR and its procurement environment.

The Defense Acquisition Regulation is issued and updated periodically by the Department of Defense and contains the department's rules, regulations, policies, and procedures governing the procurement of supplies and services. Interwoven into DAR are the disciplines of contract administration, law, and accounting. More than twenty-five sections and several appendixes cover various broad subjects; Special Types and Methods of Procurement, Foreign Purchases, Contract Clauses, Patents, Data, and Copyrights, Taxes, and Government Property are just a few of the sections. All terms and conditions of a contract with any part of the Department of Defense or the National Aeronautics & Space Administration (NASA) must meet the conditions set forth in DAR.

The Federal Procurement Environment

OBJECTIVE 6
*Describe the
federal
government
procurement
environment*

Before dealing with several specifics of defense contract cost accounting, pricing, and the types of contracts used in government contracting, we need to review the elements of the procurement process. This section presents a view of the operating environment within which contract pricing is determined and cost accounting standards and principles are developed and applied. However, the following paragraphs are *not* a complete description of the government procurement process.[1]

The process begins with the determination of a government need for a service or supply item. In some respects, the government is not unlike a large corporation in its buying practices. Some items, usually of small unit dollar value, are purchased on the open market at catalogue or market prices. The remaining procurement needs are obtained through a process known as *formal advertising*, whereby a detailed government invitation is issued that spells out exactly what the government needs and the exact terms and conditions that will be applicable. Interested companies submit bids offering to meet all provisions, and the award is made to the lowest responsive bidder.

Much of the procurement money the government spends, however, is for costly, highly complex items, such as ships, planes, or guidance systems. Under these circumstances, the government must select a capable contractor and negotiate a price. In these cases, the negotiated price is heavily dependent on the contractor's estimated cost. In other cases, where the estimated costs are so uncertain that a price cannot be negotiated with any degree of confidence, the government will simply reimburse a contractor for his or her costs and pay a "fee" for the performance of the contract. At the completion of such cost-type contracts,

1. Many of the statements and ideas in this section are from Henry R. Anderson, "Why Cost Accounting Standards?" *D. R. Scott Memorial Lectures in Accountancy*, vol. 5, The University of Missouri, 1973.

and even under some types of fixed price contracts, the government and the contractor must reach a final agreement as to the total cost of performance. (The differences between various types of negotiated contracts are discussed in more detail in the following sections.) The process is now completed unless a dispute has arisen. If the contracting parties cannot resolve contract issues, the resultant disputes may be brought before the Armed Services Board of Contract Appeals (ASBCA), or, if desired, the contractor may appeal the ASBCA decision to the United States Courts of Claims.

Types of Defense Contracts

OBJECTIVE 7
Identify and differentiate between the primary types of government contracts

As stated, to the maximum extent practical, government procurements are required to be made by formal advertising. Following this procedure, contractors are asked to respond to the government's Invitation for Bids (IFB). Assuming several contractors respond and are in conformance with the specific requirements contained in the IFB, the bid selected, considering price and related factors, is the one most advantageous to the government. The contractor assumes all risks of the venture, and the government agrees to pay the contractor for the agreed-upon price when the contract obligations have been met and/or the goods have been delivered. This type of venture resembles a competitive market transaction in which, having surveyed the market place and being satisfied with the price and quality of the item, the consumer pays the supplier the stated price.

So why have government defense procurement activities not followed the advertised contract type of business agreement? Why in fiscal year 1982, for example, were over 80 percent of all defense procurement dollars spent through negotiated contract arrangements? Contracts are negotiated rather than advertised if, for some reason, the government agency is unable to advertise the requirement. DAR Regulations (DAR III, part 2) lists seventeen different circumstances prescribed by law under which negotiated contracts may be appropriate. These circumstances include, for example, procurements that involve security classifications; procurements that have insufficiently precise specifications or work statements to permit competition via the formally advertised route, including contracts for research and development; and procurements that have specific time requirements that will not permit the time delay involved with advertising. Because a large portion of defense procurements qualify under one or more of the stated circumstances, many defense contracts are negotiated.

Two basic types of negotiated contracts are used for defense procurement activities: firm fixed price and cost-type contracts. The firm fixed price contract, which provides for a price not subject to adjustment by reason of the contractor's cost experience, is the type of negotiated contract under which the contractor assumes full cost responsibility and is given a maximum profit incentive to control costs. However, the use of a firm fixed price contract may not always be appropriate. When the conditions of the contract do not contain reasonably definite performance and/or design specifications, other contract types may be employed. These contract types vary as to the degree and timing of responsibility the contractor assumes for the costs of performance and the amount and type of profit incentive offered the contractor to achieve or exceed specified standards or goals. The following types of negotiated contracts are used where the firm fixed price contract is inappropriate: (1) fixed price incentive contracts, (2) cost-plus–incentive fee contracts, and (3) cost-plus–fixed fee contracts. For a fixed price incentive contract (firm type) there is a negotiated target cost, target profit, price ceiling, and formula for establishing final price and profit figures. A cost-plus–incentive fee contract is a cost reimbursement type of contract with a flexible fee based on a formula utilizing the relationship between the total allowable cost and the initially projected or target cost. Under a cost-plus–fixed fee contract (CPFF), the contractor assumes little or no cost responsibility, risk, or motivation for effective and economic performance. The government simply reimburses the contractor for all reasonable costs incurred that are allowable under the terms of the contract plus a fixed fee encompassing the profit factor.

Government Contract Cost Accounting

Section XV of Defense Acquisition Regulation contains the cost principles and procedures that, along with existing cost accounting standards, are to be used in the cost determination process of defense contracts. In addition, the principles of DAR must be applied in the negotiation process for determination of contract prices. DAR cost principles contain a degree of flexibility. Using reasonableness as the guiding force, representatives of the government and the contractor participate in a tough but fair negotiation process for pricing, paying, and finally settling defense contracts.

Many of the cost accounting concepts and principles embodied in DAR XV are similar to those explained earlier in this text. However, there are major differences between government contract cost accounting and cost accounting used for commercial work.

Full Absorption Costing. Absorption costing, as referred to earlier, is an approach to product costing in which all manufacturing costs, including fixed manufacturing overhead costs, are assigned to units of output as product costs. Selling, general, and administrative costs are considered period costs and treated as costs of the accounting period, not costs of the product or final cost objective. However, for negotiated government contract cost accounting purposes, all "allowable" costs are assigned to the contract, including general and administrative expenses. Because of this unique characteristic, the term *full absorption costing* is applicable. The full absorption approach is used because, for price determination purposes, all allowable costs applicable to the contract must be assigned to that cost objective. The concept of "period cost" is, therefore, not applicable to government contract costing and pricing practices.

Direct and Indirect Costs. Paragraph 15-201.1 of DAR contains introductory remarks to the cost principles and includes the following statement:

The total cost of a contract is the sum of the allowable direct and indirect costs allocable to the contract, incurred or to be incurred, less any allocable credits.

This statement substantiates the theme of full absorption costing and includes four terms that form the basis for government contract costing and pricing: (1) **direct cost**, (2) **indirect cost**, (3) **allowable**, and (4) **allocable**. Each term has a unique meaning within the boundaries of the procurement process, and an understanding of the terms is essential to the development of cost accounting standards for contract costing usage.

For purposes of cost accounting standards, a direct cost is "any cost which is identified specifically with a particular final cost objective (i.e., a contract). Direct costs are not limited to items which are incorporated in the end product as material or labor."[2] Therefore, *any* cost of a contractor that is specifically incurred for and, in total, directly traceable to a particular contract, is a direct cost of that contract. The concept of a direct cost for defense contract costing purposes differs from the normal usage of the term, the latter usually encompassing only (1) the costs of raw materials that become an integral part of the finished goods and that are identifiable with specific physical units and (2) labor costs that are related to and unquestionably traceable to specific products.

The key to the identification of a direct cost, however, is its traceability, not the nature of a particular cost, such as materials, supplies, and labor. In actual commercial practice, manufacturing costs other than just direct materials and direct labor may be treated as direct costs for product costing purposes. Any differences between government and commercial practices in the direct cost area stem only from the inclusion or exclusion of general and administrative costs. Howard Wright summarized the direct cost issue when he stated:

The common belief that only materials and labor incorporated into an end product are direct costs is erroneous. The belief springs from a preoccupation with product cost accounting and a failure to recognize the essential relationship. The essential relationship is one of benefit, regardless of the nature of the goods or services used. Where only one cost objective benefits from the goods or services consumed, it alone should bear the expense. Thus, depreciation computed on the fixed assets of a single department is a direct expense of that department. However, if plant wide depreciation is computed, such depreciation can be direct only with respect to the plant. It is indirect with respect to plant departments, work centers, and products.[3]

An indirect cost is "Any cost not directly identified with a single final cost objective, but identified with two or more final cost objectives or

2. *Title 4, Code of Federal Regulations*, chapter III, subchapter G—Cost Accounting Standards, part 400—Definitions.
3. Howard W. Wright, *Accounting for Defense Contracts* (Englewood Cliffs: Prentice-Hall, 1962), p. 53.

with at least one intermediate cost objective."[4] The treatment of indirect costs of items produced for commercial markets generally includes only indirect materials, indirect labor, and other manufacturing overhead costs in the indirect cost category. In comparing the nature of indirect costs as between commercial product costing and government contract costing, each regards this type of cost as not being specifically associated with nor traceable to a specific product or final cost objective. The major difference, however, is that the commercial usage of the term usually limits indirect costs to only those associated with the manufacturing process, whereas for government contract costing purpose, the term includes all allowable indirect costs incurred in the performance of the business, including home office and segment general and administrative expenses.

OBJECTIVE 8
State the rules and conditions under which costs are judged unallowable for contract pricing purposes

Unallowable Costs. The question of cost allowability is of primary importance in the price determination process of government contracts. Unlike the normal approach to the pricing of commercially marketable goods and services, in which all costs incurred in the operation of a business plus a profit factor are used in determining an adequate selling price, the government disallows those costs that are (1) unreasonable in amount or (2) otherwise unallowable in accordance with existing government statutes or regulations of specific agencies. In addition, costs that are otherwise allowable must be allocable under the terms of the contract to be allowable to that contract. Unallowable costs may vary contract by contract and may be identified within a clause(s) of a contract or deemed unallowable during pre- and/or postcontract price negotiations. The second category of unallowable costs mentioned includes both costs deemed unallowable by statute for all government contracts or by individual agency regulations, wherein the question of allowability of certain costs is applicable to only contracts of a specific agency. Examples of costs normally associated with this category of unallowable costs include costs of entertainment, interest costs, advertising costs, and uncollectible accounts.

Cost Allocability. Within the government procurement environment, the following circular question regarding allowability versus allocability is often raised: Does a cost have to be allocable to be allowable or does it have to be allowable to be allocable? It is not within the scope of this section to debate this issue. Suffice it to say that a cost that is not unallowable may be considered for allocation to a government contract. DAR 15-201.4 defines allocability as follows:

A cost is allocable if it is assignable or chargeable to a particular cost objective, such as a contract, product, product line, process, or a class of customer or activity, in accordance with the relative benefits received or other equitable relationship. Subject to the foregoing, a cost is allocable to a Government contract

---

4. *Title 4, Code of Federal Regulations,* chapter III, subchapter G—Cost Accounting Standards, part 400—Definitions.

if it (i) is incurred specifically for the contract; (ii) benefits both the contractor and other work, or both Government work and other work, and can be distributed to them in reasonable proportion to the benefits received; or (iii) is necessary to the overall operation of the business, although a direct relationship to any particular cost objective cannot be shown.

The preceding was a brief description of the government procurement environment, including the procurement process, cost accounting terminology and concepts unique to procurement activities, and the type of contracts used in negotiated government procurements. Contract costing within the procurement process is governed by DAR, which incorporates all cost accounting standards. Other factors important to the understanding of the process include a working knowledge of contract administration, law, accounting, the contract negotiation process, DAR sources of disputes, and the different interpretations that are possible regarding contract cost principles.

Cost Accounting Standards

Cost Accounting Standards Board

The Cost Accounting Standards Board (CASB) was established by the Congress of the United States in August 1970 (Public Law 92-379). There had been significant cost overruns on major government contracts, and Congress decided to correct this situation by forming the CASB. The purpose of the CASB was to promulgate uniform and consistent cost accounting standards for all negotiated contracts in excess of $100,000. The standards apply to the cost accounting practices of private companies only with respect to their federal government contracts; for their commercial business, private companies are free to use any management accounting practices they wish.

The CASB was deemed to have completed its work in 1980, and Congress denied additional funding for the agency. However, the cost accounting standards promulgated by the CASB are still applicable and have the full force and effect of law. The *Federal Register* of December 1, 1980, reported that the General Accounting Office (GAO) "will be required to take an active role to determine whether the Standards, rules and regulations which the CASB has promulgated are applied properly by the procurement agencies." The GAO has assumed this role until such time as the Congress transfers the authority to amend the regulations to some other agency.

The CASB Standards

The Cost Accounting Standards Board promulgated nineteen standards and formally defined many of the terms included in the standards. These standards cover most of the topics considered trouble spots or areas in which cost disputes between the government and private contractors had occurred in the past. Table 11-2 summarizes the standards and their purposes. All the standards are intended to improve comparability and

Table 11-2. Summary of Purposes of Existing Cost Accounting Standards

Cost Accounting Standard	Purposes	Improve Comparability and Consistency of Cost-Accounting Practice	To Establish			To Improve		
			Specific Cost Measurements	General Cost-Accounting Practice(s)	Specific Cost-Accounting Practice(s)	Allocation to Time Periods	Allocation to Cost Objectives	Allocation to Final Cost Objectives
CAS 401	Consistency in Estimating, Accumulating, and Reporting Costs	X		X				
CAS 402	Consistency in Allocating Costs Incurred for the Same Purpose	X		X				
CAS 403	Allocation of Home Office Expenses to Segments	X	X		X		X	
CAS 404	Capitalization of Tangible Assets	X	X		X			
CAS 405	Accounting for Unallowable Costs	X		X			X	
CAS 406	Cost Accounting Period	X		X		X		
CAS 407	Use of Standard Costs for Direct Material and Direct Labor	X	X		X			
CAS 408	Accounting for Costs of Compensated Personal Absence	X	X		X		X	
CAS 409	Depreciation of Tangible Capital Assets	X	X		X	X	X	
CAS 410	Allocation of Business Unit General and Administrative Expenses to Final Cost Objectives	X	X		X			X
CAS 411	Accounting for Acquisition Costs of Material	X	X		X		X	
CAS 412	Composition and Measurement of Pension Cost	X	X		X	X		
CAS 413	Adjustment and Allocation of Pension Cost	X	X		X	X	X	
CAS 414	Cost of Money as an Element of the Cost of Facilities Capital	X	X		X			X
CAS 415	Accounting for the Cost of Deferred Compensation	X	X		X	X	X	
CAS 416	Accounting for Insurance Costs	X	X		X	X	X	
CAS 417	Cost of Money as an Element of the Cost of Capital Assets under Construction	X	X		X	X		
CAS 418	Allocation of Direct and Indirect Costs	X		X			X	
CAS 419	Withdrawn							
CAS 420	Accounting for Independent Research and Development Costs and Bid and Proposal Costs	X	X		X	X	X	

Source: Henry R. Anderson, "Federal Cost Accounting Standards and Principles," sec. 23, in *Accountants' Cost Handbook*, 3rd ed., ed. J. Bulloch (New York: Wiley, 1983), pp. 23-12, 23-13. Copyright © 1983 John Wiley & Sons, Inc. Reprinted by permission of John Wiley & Sons, Inc.

consistency in management accounting practices. Some of the standards are addressed to general cost accounting practices; others are designed to create and implement specific cost accounting practices. All the standards have an impact on contract pricing.

Usually specific cost measurement criteria are established if specific cost accounting practices are involved. In one way or another, most cost accounting standards are structured so as to improve cost allocation—to time periods, to all relevant cost objectives, or specifically to final cost objectives. The defined terms were accumulated in part 400 of subchapter G. The definitions included general terms such as "direct costs" and more specific terms such as "insurance administration expense." The definitions are an integral part of the standards and should not be overlooked.

Although the Cost Accounting Standards were developed for a specific purpose and affect only federal government contracts, their impact has also been felt in all aspects of contract pricing and commercial pricing. The federal government is the biggest "company" in the world; any of their regulated pricing practices are bound to influence private industry. Here we acquaint you with the field of contract costing and pricing; total coverage of the subject of contract pricing would form an entire book. We will look at only two of the standards. CAS 402 relates to general cost accounting practices, and CAS 403 is designed to influence a specific cost accounting practice.

OBJECTIVE 9a

Apply the guidelines and procedures in Cost Accounting Standard 402

CAS 402 Consistency in Allocating Costs Incurred for the Same Purpose. The primary goal of CAS 402 is to eliminate double counting, the charging of the same types of costs more than once to the same contract. This may sound very logical to you. In a cost-based contract price, it should be illegal to charge the same cost more than once. But accounting practices for large contractors may often overlook such double counting. As stated in CAS 402.40:

All costs incurred for the same purpose, in like circumstances, are either direct costs only or indirect costs only with respect to final cost objectives. No final cost objective shall have allocated to it as an indirect cost any cost, if other costs incurred for the same purpose, in like circumstances, have been incurred as a direct cost of that or any other final cost objective.

At first reading, this statement may seem to be double-talk. But let us examine the statement a bit further. Remember that we are referring to the pricing of a cost-based contract when the term final cost objective is used. The standard states that no type of cost that has been charged as a direct cost to a contract can also be included in an overhead pool and allocated to the same contract. "Type" of cost is important. Double counting a specific cost incurred for a contract is illegal, just as deducting the same expense twice on your income tax return is illegal. The standard is addressing types of costs that can be incurred as both a direct cost and an indirect cost.

The following example clarifies the intent of the standard. Assume that Contract 7249 is for a large jet aircraft and that the contract terms require that special fire-prevention personnel be employed to maintain around-the-clock surveillance of the project during construction. This cost is a direct cost to the contract because the cost can be traced directly to and is incurred specifically for a particular final cost objective. This same company has a regular fire-prevention crew on duty to protect all the company's aircraft assembly operations. Normally this regular fire-prevention cost is included in an overhead pool and allocated to all contracts and commercial jobs because it is incurred for all projects. CAS 402 states that if a cost is a direct cost to a contract (the special fire-prevention personnel), this same type of cost (the regular fire-prevention crew) cannot be charged to the contract. Therefore, before the overhead pool can be distributed to Contract 7249, the cost of the regular fire-prevention crew must be subtracted from the total being allocated; doing so prevents two different costs incurred for the same purpose from being charged to the same contract.

OBJECTIVE 9b
Apply the guidelines and procedures in Cost Accounting Standard 403

CAS 403 Allocation of Home Office Expenses to Segments. Cost Accounting Standard 403 establishes a hierarchy of allocation procedures for distributing costs to a company's segments that have been incurred and paid for by a central home office. A segment can be one of two or more divisions, production and/or service departments, plants, or other subdivisions reporting to a home office. The purpose of the standard is to minimize the home office costs that are allocated on a residual basis and to maximize the costs that are directly allocated or allocated through "logical and relatively homogeneous pools." Costs of a home office are often difficult to trace to specific contracts or final cost objectives.

The pricing of cost-based contracts is significantly influenced by how a company allocates its home office costs. If a company is engaged in only work for the federal government, the problem is not a serious one. In such a case, the method of allocation of home office costs to segments would not affect the total cost to the government. Eventually all costs of the contractor would be covered by a contract price. But most contractors have commercial business (sell their products and services in the private sector) as well as contracts with the federal government. It is within this environment that CAS 403 rules and procedures are critical to the pricing of government contracts. In many cases, prior to CAS 403 the contractor's objective was to find the allocation procedure that would distribute the most home office costs to government contracts. Since most contracts are cost-plus types, maximizing home office cost allocations to these contracts would do two things:

1. More costs would be reimbursed by the government.
2. The fixed fee or profit from the contract would be increased because it is usually a percentage of total cost of the contract.

Using CAS 403 guidelines helps alleviate this problem and ensure a fair and equitable distribution of home office costs to segments.

Because most of the costs being accounted for under CAS 403 are considered indirect costs to the contract (final cost objective), this standard creates the concept of "direct allocation" of an indirect cost. Home office costs that are traceable to specific segments must be accounted for in this manner. Costs that cannot be specifically traced to segments, but which can be included in logical and homogeneous cost pools, should be so accumulated and allocated. Cost allocation is a two-step process: (1) first the home office cost is allocated to an intermediate cost objective (the segment), and then (2) this same cost is allocated to a final cost objective of the segment (a contract). CAS 403 identifies several categories of activities whose costs would be appropriate for these allocation procedures:

1. Centralized service functions (data processing)
2. Staff management of certain specific activities of segments (personnel management)
3. Line management of particular segments or groups of segments
4. Central payments or accruals (pension expenses, state and local franchise and income taxes)
5. Independent research and development costs and bid and proposal costs

The remaining or residual costs are to be grouped and allocated to segments using an allocation technique that takes into account the number of employees, business volume, or net book value of assets.

Allocation heirarchy: CAS 403 creates the following cost allocation hierarchy:

1. Identification of expenses for direct allocation to segments to the maximum extent practical
2. Accumulation of significant nondirectly allocated expenses into logical and relatively homogeneous cost pools to be allocated on bases reflecting the relationship of the expenses to the segments concerned
3. Allocation of any remaining or residual home office expenses to all segments

Appropriate implementation of this standard will limit the amount of home office expenses classified as residual to the expenses of managing the organization as a whole.[5]

Examples of home office expense allocations: Corporate home offices incur numerous types of expenses paying for specific goods and services its various segments use. When allocating these costs to segments, the management accountant must first determine if a cost is directly traceable to and/or identifiable with a particular segment. If so, that cost must be assigned to that segment. If a cost is not directly traceable to a segment but was incurred for the benefit of one or more segments, then such costs must be distributed to the segments using a causal or beneficial basis. CAS 403 provides a comprehensive list of types of home office expenses and illustrative allocation bases, as shown in Table 11-3. If direct association and allocation is not possible, then these illustrative bases should be used to distribute home office expenses to segments.

Illustrative Problem: Cost Accounting Standard 403

Kinlin Industries, Inc., assembles and distributes high-tech monitors for space guidance systems. Ninety percent of its business is with the federal

---

5. *Title 4, Code of Federal Regulations,* chapter III, subchapter G—Cost Accounting Standards, part 403—Cost Accounting Standards Board.

Table 11-3. Cost Accounting Standard 403—Illustrative Allocation Bases

Home Office Expense or Function	Illustrative Allocation Bases
Centralized service functions	
1. Personnel administration	1. Number of personnel, labor hours, payroll, number of hires
2. Data processing services	2. Machine time, number of reports
3. Centralized purchasing and subcontracting	3. Number of purchase orders, value of purchases, number of items
4. Centralized warehousing	4. Square footage, value of material, volume
5. Company aircraft service	5. Actual or standard rate per hour, mile, passenger mile, or similar unit
6. Central telephone service	6. Usage costs, number of instruments
Staff management of specific activities	
1. Personnel management	1. Number of personnel, labor hours, payroll, number of hires
2. Manufacturing policies (quality control, industrial engineering, production, scheduling, tooling, inspection and testing, etc.).	2. Manufacturing cost input, manufacturing direct labor
3. Engineering policies	3. Total engineering costs, engineering direct labor, number of drawings
4. Material/purchasing policies	4. Number of purchase orders, value of purchases
5. Marketing policies	5. Sales, segment marketing costs
Central payments or accruals	
1. Pension expenses	1. Payroll or other factor on which total payment is based
2. Group insurance expenses	2. Payroll or other factor on which total payment is based
3. State and local income taxes and franchise taxes	3. Any base or method that results in an allocation that equals or approximates a segment's proportionate share of the tax imposed by the jurisdiction in which the segment does business, as measured by the same factors used to determine taxable income for that jurisdiction

Source: Title 4, Code of Federal Regulations, chapter III, subchapter G—Cost Accounting Standards, part 403—Cost Accounting Standards Board.

government. The company has ten divisions, and each division has at least one current contract with the government. All parts assembled by the divisions are purchased by the home office in Cleveland, Ohio, and stored in a central warehouse in that city. Parts are shipped to the divisions in bulk when needed. All costs of storing the parts are incurred by the home office and must be allocated to the divisions periodically. The corporation's controller has determined that three allocation bases could be used to assign these home office warehousing costs to the divisions: total square footage of storage space, total direct labor dollars of the divisions, or total cost of goods sold by the divisions. Following are the data supporting these allocation bases:

Kinlin Industries, Inc.
Proposed Allocation Bases and Supporting Data

Segment	Total Square Footage of Storage	Total Direct Labor Dollars	Total Cost of Goods Sold
New York division	62,400	$1,103,200	$1,995,000
Baltimore division	28,800	78,800	997,500
Atlanta division	38,400	157,600	1,140,000
Miami division	43,200	118,200	1,425,000
Los Angeles division	67,200	236,400	1,852,500
San Francisco division	96,000	275,800	2,707,500
Honolulu division	9,600	39,400	285,000
Seattle division	33,600	945,600	855,000
New Orleans division	86,400	275,800	2,422,500
Detroit division	14,400	709,200	570,000
Totals	480,000	$3,940,000	$14,250,000

During this past year, the company incurred a total of $5,460,000 of costs associated with storing parts and supplies. All these costs are to be allocated to the divisions for assignment to their government contracts and other commercial business. The company's auditor from the Defense Contract Audit Agency (DCAA) has asked to be informed of the allocation basis selected.

Required

1. Allocate the total central warehouse overhead to the ten divisions using each of the three bases identified.
2. Which of the overhead allocation bases would the DCAA auditor favor? Why?
3. Could total cost of goods sold be used as the allocation basis? If so, why?

Solution

Computations of allocation percentages:

Segment	Total Square Footage of Storage Amount	%	Total Direct Labor Dollars Amount	%	Total Cost of Goods Sold Amount	%
New York division	62,400	13	$1,103,200	28	$1,995,000	14
Baltimore division	28,800	6	78,800	2	997,500	7
Atlanta division	38,400	8	157,600	4	1,140,000	8
Miami division	43,200	9	118,200	3	1,425,000	10
Los Angeles division	67,200	14	236,400	6	1,852,500	13
San Francisco division	96,000	20	275,800	7	2,707,500	19
Honolulu division	9,600	2	39,400	1	285,000	2
Seattle division	33,600	7	945,600	24	855,000	6
New Orleans division	86,400	18	275,800	7	2,422,500	17
Detroit division	14,400	3	709,200	18	570,000	4
Totals	480,000	100	$3,940,000	100	$14,250,000	100

Part 1: Cost allocations using the three bases:

Segment	Total Warehouse Overhead Cost	Total Square Footage of Storage %	Amount	Total Direct Labor Dollars %	Amount	Total Cost of Goods Sold %	Amount
New York division	$5,460,000	13	$ 709,800	28	$1,528,800	14	$ 764,400
Baltimore division	5,460,000	6	327,600	2	109,200	7	382,200
Atlanta division	5,460,000	8	436,800	4	218,400	8	436,800
Miami division	5,460,000	9	491,400	3	163,800	10	546,000
Los Angeles division	5,460,000	14	764,400	6	327,600	13	709,800
San Francisco division	5,460,000	20	1,092,000	7	382,200	19	1,037,400
Honolulu division	5,460,000	2	109,200	1	54,600	2	109,200
Seattle division	5,460,000	7	382,200	24	1,310,400	6	327,600
New Orleans division	5,460,000	18	982,800	7	382,200	17	928,200
Detroit division	5,460,000	3	163,800	18	982,800	4	218,400
Totals		100	$5,460,000	100	$5,460,000	100	$5,460,000

Part 2: The DCAA auditor would require the total square footage of storage basis because it is one of the illustrative bases in Cost Accounting Standard 403.

Part 3: Yes, the total cost of goods sold basis could be used because the results approximate those from using the total square footage of storage basis.

Chapter Review

Review of Learning Objectives

1. **Describe traditional economic pricing concepts.**
   The traditional approach to pricing is based on microeconomic theory, which states that profits will be maximized at the point at which the difference between total revenue and total cost is greatest. Total revenue then tapers off, since as a product is marketed, price reductions are necessary to sell more units. Total cost increases when large quantities are produced because fixed costs change. To locate the point of maximum profit, marginal revenue and marginal cost must be computed and plotted. Profit is maximized at the point at which the marginal revenue and marginal cost curves intersect.

2. **Identify external and internal factors on which prices are based.**
   Many factors influence the process of determining a selling price. Factors external to a company include (1) total demand for the product or service, (2) number of competing products or services, (3) competitor's quality and price, (4) customer preference, (5) sole source versus heavy competition, (6) seasonal demand, and (7) life of product. Internal factors are (1) costs of producing the product or service, (2) purpose and quality of product, (3) type of process used—labor intensive versus automated, (4) markup percentage procedure, and (5) amount of scarce resources used.

3. **State the objectives managers use to establish prices of goods and services.**
   A company's long-run objectives should include statements on pricing policy. Possible pricing policy objectives include (1) adhering to short- and long-run pricing strategies, (2) maximizing profits, (3) maintaining or gaining market share, (4) ensuring prices are socially responsible, (5) maintaining a stated rate of return on investments, and (6) ensuring prices support a trend of total sales increases.

4. **Create prices by applying the methods and tools of price determination.**
   The pricing manager can adopt several pricing methods. However, experience in pricing a product often leads to adjustments in the formula used. Pricing methods include (1) variable cost pricing, (2) gross margin pricing, (3) profit margin pricing, and (4) return on assets pricing. Time and materials pricing is often used by service-oriented businesses.

5. **Define Defense Acquisition Regulation and state the purpose of these guidelines.**
   The Defense Acquisition Regulation (DAR) is a complete set of policies and procedures for contracting with the Department of Defense. The purpose of DAR is to bring together in one publication all prescribed policies, including

cost principles, that must be followed in contract pricing with the federal government's defense departments.

6. **Describe the federal government procurement environment.**
   Contracting with the federal government requires the contractor to follow specific regulations and laws when determining the contract's price. After a need has been established, a formal advertising process is initiated involving a detailed "invitation for bid." Interested parties have a certain time period within which to bid for the work. Usually the lowest bidder gets the job.

7. **Identify and differentiate between the primary types of government contracts.**
   There are two general categories of contracts: firm fixed price and cost type. The firm fixed price contract provides for a price that is not subject to adjustment by reason of the contractor's cost experience. Risk is on the side of the contractor, and the product or service is of a normal nature. Cost-type contracts reimburse the contractor for costs incurred plus a profit factor. Such contracts are used for experimental products, and the government assumes the risk.

8. **State the rules and conditions under which costs are judged unallowable for contract pricing purposes.**
   The government disallows those costs that are (1) unreasonable in amount or (2) otherwise unallowable in accordance with existing government statutes or regulations of specific agencies. Examples of costs normally associated with the second category include entertainment, interest, advertising, and uncollectible accounts.

9. **Apply the guidelines and procedures in Cost Accounting Standards 402 and 403.**
   Cost Accounting Standard (CAS) 402 covers consistency in allocating costs incurred for the same purpose. This standard is designed to prevent double counting. Often a contract calls for special services. If so, the cost of similar services provided under regular operating conditions and included in an overhead pool cannot be allocated to the contract. CAS 403 centers on the allocation of home office costs to company segments. Many of the costs of a company's divisions are paid centrally by the home office. CAS 403 prescribes methods that should be used when allocating these home office expenses to segments.

Review of Concepts and Terminology

The following important concepts were introduced in this chapter:

(L.O.4) **Variable cost pricing:** An approach to cost-based pricing that is linked to the variable production costs.

(L.O.4) **Gross margin pricing:** Cost-based pricing procedure centering on total production costs.

(L.O.4) **Profit margin pricing:** An approach to pricing in which the markup percentage includes only the desired profit factor, and total operating cost serves as the basis.

(L.O.4) **Return on assets pricing:** A pricing method in which the objective of price determination is earning a profit equal to a specific rate of return on assets employed in the operation.

(L.O.5)   Defense Acquisition Regulation (DAR):   Regulations that are applicable to all contracts with the Department of Defense.

Other important terms introduced in this chapter are:

allocable cost (p. 417)
direct cost (p. 416)
double counting (p. 420)
indirect cost (p. 416)
marginal cost (p. 402)
marginal revenue (p. 402)
time and materials pricing (p. 410)
unallowable cost (p. 417)

Review Problem:
Cost-Based Pricing

The Bengtson Toy Company makes a complete line of toy vehicles, including three types of trucks, a pickup, a dumpster, and a flatbed. These toy trucks are produced in assembly line fashion beginning with the Stamping operation and continuing through the Welding, Painting, and Detailing Departments. Following are projected costs of each toy truck and allocation percentages for fixed and common costs:

Cost Categories		Total Projected Costs	Toy Pickup Truck	Toy Dumpster Truck	Toy Flatbed Truck
Materials:	Metal	$137,000	$62,500	$29,000	$45,500
	Axles	5,250	2,500	1,000	1,750
	Wheels	9,250	3,750	2,000	3,500
	Paint	70,500	30,000	16,000	24,500
Labor:	Stamping	53,750	22,500	12,000	19,250
	Welding	94,000	42,500	20,000	31,500
	Painting	107,500	45,000	24,000	38,500
	Detailing	44,250	17,500	11,000	15,750
Indirect labor		173,000	77,500	36,000	59,500
Operating supplies		30,000	12,500	7,000	10,500
Variable production costs		90,500	40,000	19,000	31,500
Fixed production costs		120,000	45%	25%	30%
Distribution costs		105,000	40%	20%	40%
Variable marketing costs		123,000	55,000	26,000	42,000
Fixed marketing costs		85,400	40%	25%	35%
General and administrative costs		47,600	40%	25%	35%

Bengtson's policy is to earn a minimum of 30 percent over total cost on each type of toy produced. Expected sales for 19xx are: pickup, 50,000 units; dumpster, 20,000 units; and flatbed, 35,000 units. Assume no change in inventory levels.

Required

1. Compute the selling price for each toy truck using the gross margin pricing method.
2. Check your answers in 1 by computing the selling prices using the profit margin pricing method.
3. If the competition's selling price for a similar pickup truck is about $14.00 would this influence Bengtson's pricing decision? Give reasons defending your answer.

Answer to Review Problem

Before the various selling prices are computed, the cost analysis must be completed and restructured to supply the information needed for the pricing computations:

Cost Categories	Total Projected Costs	Toy Pickup Truck	Toy Dumpster Truck	Toy Flatbed Truck
Materials: Metal	$ 137,000	$ 62,500	$ 29,000	$ 45,500
Axles	5,250	2,500	1,000	1,750
Wheels	9,250	3,750	2,000	3,500
Paint	70,500	30,000	16,000	24,500
Labor: Stamping	53,750	22,500	12,000	19,250
Welding	94,000	42,500	20,000	31,500
Painting	107,500	45,000	24,000	38,500
Detailing	44,250	17,500	11,000	15,750
Indirect labor	173,000	77,500	36,000	59,500
Operating supplies	30,000	12,500	7,000	10,500
Variable production costs	90,500	40,000	19,000	31,500
Fixed production costs	120,000	54,000	30,000	36,000
Total production costs	$ 935,000	$410,250	$207,000	$317,750
Distribution costs	$ 105,000	$ 42,000	$ 21,000	$ 42,000
Variable marketing costs	123,000	55,000	26,000	42,000
Fixed marketing costs	85,400	34,160	21,350	29,890
General and administrative costs	47,600	19,040	11,900	16,660
Total selling, general, and administrative costs	$ 361,000	$150,200	$ 80,250	$130,550
Total Costs	$1,296,000	$560,450	$287,250	$448,300
Desired Profit	$ 388,800	$168,135	$ 86,175	$134,490

1. Pricing using the gross margin approach.
   Markup percentage formula:

$$\text{Markup percentage} = \frac{\text{desired profit} + \text{total selling, general, and administrative costs}}{\text{total production costs}}$$

Gross margin pricing formula:

Gross margin-based price = total production costs per unit + (markup percentage × total production costs)

Pickup truck:

$$\text{Markup percentage} = \frac{\$168{,}135 + \$150{,}200}{\$410{,}250} = 77.60\%$$

Gross margin-based price = (\$410,250/50,000) + (\$410,250/50,000) × 77.6% = \$14.57

Dumpster truck:

$$\text{Markup percentage} = \frac{\$86{,}175 + \$80{,}250}{\$207{,}000} = 80.40\%$$

Gross margin-based price = (\$207,000/20,000) + (\$207,000/20,000) × 80.4% = \$18.67

Flatbed truck:

$$\text{Markup percentage} = \frac{\$134{,}490 + \$130{,}550}{\$317{,}750} = 83.41\%$$

Gross margin-based price = (\$317,750/35,000) + (\$317,750/35,000) × 83.41% = \$16.65

2. Pricing using the profit margin approach.
   Markup percentage formula:

$$\text{Markup percentage} = \frac{\text{desired profit}}{\text{total costs and expenses}}$$

Profit margin pricing formula:

Profit margin-based price = total costs expenses per unit + (markup percentage × total costs and expenses)

Pickup truck:

$$\text{Markup percentage} = \frac{\$168{,}135}{\$560{,}450} = 30.00\%$$

Profit margin-based price = (\$560,450/50,000) + (\$560,450/50,000) × 30% = \$14.57

Dumpster truck:

$$\text{Markup percentage} = \frac{\$86{,}175}{\$287{,}250} = 30.00\%$$

$$\text{Profit margin-based price} = (\$287{,}250/20{,}000) + (\$287{,}250/20{,}000)$$
$$\times 30\% = \$18.67$$

Flatbed truck:

$$\text{Markup percentage} = \frac{\$134{,}490}{\$448{,}300} = 30.00\%$$

$$\text{Profit margin-based price} = (\$448{,}300/35{,}000) + (\$448{,}300/35{,}000)$$
$$\times 30\% = \$16.65$$

3. Competition's influence on price.
   If the competition's toy pickup truck was similar in quality as well as design and looks, then Bengtson's management would have to consider the $14. price range. At $14.57, they have a 30 percent profit factor built into their price. Break even is at $11.21 ($14.57/1.3). Therefore, they have the ability to reduce the price below the competition and still make a significant profit.

Chapter Assignments

Questions

1. List several considerations a decision maker must allow for when setting the price of a product or service.
2. Discuss the concept of making pricing decisions based on whatever the market will bear.
3. In the traditional economic pricing concept, what role does total revenue play in maximizing profit?
4. Why is profit maximized where marginal revenue equals marginal cost?
5. Identify five pricing policy objectives. Discuss each one briefly.
6. Do prices have a social effect? How or in what way?
7. List some external factors to consider when establishing an item's price.
8. List the internal factors one should use to gauge pricing decisions.
9. Describe the variable cost pricing method. Under what conditions will it yield useful data?
10. What is the gross profit pricing method? How is the markup percentage calculated under this method?
11. Differentiate the profit margin pricing method from the return on assets pricing method.
12. In pricing services, what does time and materials pricing mean?
13. What does DAR mean? How is DAR connected with contract pricing?
14. Differentiate between a firm fixed price contract and a cost-type contract.
15. What is an invitation for bid?
16. What does a CPFF contract mean?
17. Explain what full absorption costing is in relation to government contracting.
18. What is the difference between a cost objective and a *final* cost objective?
19. How can a cost be double counted in a contract price?
20. What is an unallowable cost? Give examples.

Classroom Exercises

Exercise 11-1.
Traditional
Economic Pricing
Theory
(L.O. 1)

McCome & Fritz are product designers. The firm has just completed a contract to develop a portable telephone. The telephone must be recharged only once a week and can be used up to 1 mile from the receiver. Initial fixed costs for this product are $4,000. The designers estimate the product will break even at the $5,000/100-unit mark. Total revenues will again equal total cost at the $25,000/ 900-unit point. Marginal cost is expected to equal marginal revenue when 550 units are sold.

1. Sketch total revenue and total cost curves for this product. Mark the vertical axis at each $5,000 increment, the horizontal axis at each 100-unit increment.
2. From your total revenue and total cost curves in **1**, estimate the unit selling price at which profits will be maximized.

Exercise 11-2.
External and
Internal Pricing
Factors
(L.O. 2)

Stanley Panin's Tire Outlet features more than a dozen brands of tires in many sizes. Two of the brands are Yerelle and Pokohama, both imported into the United States. The tire size, 205/70—VR15, is available in both brands. The following information was obtained:

	Yerelle	Pokohama
Selling prices		
Single tire, installed	$145	$124
Set of four tires, installed	520	460
Cost per tire	100	70

As shown, selling prices include installation costs. Each Yerelle tire costs $20 to mount and balance, each Pokohama tire, $15 to mount and balance.

1. Compute each brand's unit selling price for both a single tire and a set of four.
2. Was cost the major consideration in supporting these prices?
3. What other factors could have influenced these prices?

Exercise 11-3.
Pricing Policy
Objectives
(L.O. 3)

Lynda Lane, Ltd., is an international clothing company specializing in retailing medium-priced goods. Retail outlets are located throughout the United States, France, Germany, and Great Britain. Management is interested in creating an image of giving the customer the most quality for the dollar. Selling prices are developed to draw customers away from competitor's stores. First-of-the-month sales are a regular practice of all stores, and customers are accustomed to this practice. Company buyers are carefully trained to seek out quality goods at inexpensive prices. Sales are targeted to increase a minimum of 5 percent per year. All sales should yield a 15 percent return on assets. Sales personnel are expected to wear Lane's clothing while working, and all personnel can purchase clothing at 10 percent above cost. Cleanliness and an orderly appearance are required at all stores. Competitors' prices are checked daily.
Identify the pricing policy objectives of Lynda Lane, Ltd.

Exercise 11-4.
Price
Determination
(L.O.4)

Sopkiewicz Industries has just patented a new product called Toms, an automobile wax for lasting protection against the elements. Following is annual information developed by the company's controller for use in price determination meetings:

Variable production costs	$1,530,000
Fixed factory overhead	540,000
Selling expenses	360,000
General and administrative expenses	202,500
Desired profit	337,500

Annual demand for the product is expected to be 450,000 cans.

1. Compute the projected unit cost for one can of Toms.
2. Prepare formulas for computing the markup percentage and selling price for one can. Using the gross margin pricing method compute these amounts.
3. To check your answer to **2**, compute the selling price of one can of Toms using the profit margin pricing method.

Exercise 11-5.
Pricing a Service
(L.O.4)

Utah has just passed a law making it mandatory to have every head of cattle inspected at least once a year for a series of communicable diseases. Halbert Jensen Enterprises is considering entering this inspection business. After extensive studies, Jensen developed the following annual projections:

Direct service labor	$425,000
Variable service overhead costs	350,000
Fixed service overhead costs	237,500
Marketing expenses	162,500
General and administrative expenses	137,500
Minimum desired profit	125,000
Cost of assets employed	781,250

Jensen believes his company would inspect 125,000 head of cattle per year. On average the company now earns a 16 percent return on assets.

1. Compute the projected cost of inspecting each head of cattle.
2. Determine the price to charge for inspecting each head of cattle. Use the gross margin pricing method.
3. Using the return on assets method, compute the unit price to charge for this inspection service.

Exercise 11-6.
Time and Materials
Pricing
(L.O.4)

Nickie's Home Remodeling Service specializes in refurbishing older homes. Last week Nickie was asked to bid on a remodeling job for the town's mayor. Her list of materials and labor needed to complete the job is shown on the following page. The company uses an overhead markup percentage for both materials (60 percent) and labor (40 percent). These markups cover all operating costs of the business. In addition, Nickie expects to make at least a 25 percent profit on all jobs. Compute the price that Nickie should quote for the mayor's job.

Materials		Labor	
Lumber	$6,280	Carpenter	$2,160
Nails/bolts	260	Floor specialist	1,200
Paint	1,420	Painter	2,000
Glass	2,890	Supervisor	1,920
Doors	730	Helpers	1,680
Hardware	610		
Supplies	400		

Exercise 11-7.
Government
Contracting
Environment
(L.O. 5, 6)

Amelia Corporation recently acquired a rubber specialty company in northern Florida. Now the Florida Division, this new corporate segment produces ammunition casings for the federal government. All of the Florida Division's work is under government contract, and a new contract must be negotiated within the next two months. Being new to the government contracting game, the president has asked the controller to explain the following statements:

In the preparation of contract bids and proposals, the contractor's cost accounting practices used in accumulating and reporting actual costs for a contract shall be consistent with his practices used in estimating costs for the contract. The practices used in estimating and accumulating cost for a contract shall be consistent with those outlined in DAR Section XV, Contract Cost Principles and Procedures, with respect to (1) the classification of elements or functions of cost as direct or indirect, (2) the indirect cost pools to which each element or function is charged or proposed to be charged, and (3) the methods of allocating indirect costs to the contract.

Prepare a response to the president.

Exercise 11-8.
Types of
Government
Contracts
(L.O. 7)

Borden Gauett Construction, Inc., is a building contractor centered in the northeastern United States. The company has been approached by an official of the Department of Defense (DOD) because of the reputation for quality the firm earned during its first ten years of operation. The DOD is interested in having a special laser-oxinide testing facility constructed. Experimental materials are included in the specifications for the building. Mr. David Decker, president of the corporation, has expressed interest in the project but has never been involved in a contract with the federal government. He has been told that the company can enter into one of four types of contracts:

Firm fixed price contract

Fixed price incentive contract

Cost-plus–incentive fee contract

Cost-plus–fixed fee contract

You have been requested to (1) describe and differentiate between the four types of contracts identified and (2) make a recommendation to Mr. Decker as to the type of contract most appropriate for the project described. Defend your choice of contracts.

Exercise 11-9.
Unallowable Costs
(L.O. 8)

Martin Systems Corp. has been doing business with the federal government for almost ten years. During that time, the corporation has developed a good working relationship with the Defense Contract Audit Agency (DCAA). DCAA is responsible for the review and approval for payment of all negotiated government contracts. If a DCAA auditor disagrees with an accounting method used or a cost amount that has been allocated to a government contract, the parties to the contract attempt to settle the disagreement. If agreement cannot be reached, there is a formal legal process that must be followed to settle cost dispute cases.

Last week, the corporation's DCAA auditor informed the controller that several items of cost on contract 22188 had been found unallowable. These costs are identified in the following table. Why did the DCAA auditor determine that these costs were unallowable? Give specific reasons for each cost identified.

Unallowable Costs	Company's Budgeted Amount	Cost Charged to Contract	Unallowable Amount
Materials costs	$605,000	$987,400	$382,400
Travel and entertainment costs	52,600	65,420	46,520
Interest expense	27,500	27,500	27,500
Uncollectible accounts	12,200	12,740	12,740
Total			$469,160

Interpreting Accounting Information

Cost Accounting Standards and Contract Pricing: Callum Corporation
(L.O. 9)

Callum Corporation is a diversified manufacturing company with corporate headquarters in St. Louis. The three operating divisions are the Aerospace Division, the Ceramic Products Division, and the Glass Products Division.

Much of the manufacturing activity of the Aerospace Division is related to work performed for the National Aeronautics and Space Administration (NASA) under negotiated contracts. The contracts provide that cost shall be allocated to the contracts in accordance with the federal government's Cost Accounting Standards (as promulgated by the Cost Accounting Standards Board and administered by the General Accounting Office).

Callum Corporation headquarters provide general administrative support and computer services to each of the three operating divisions. The computer services are provided through a computer time-sharing arrangement, whereby the central processing unit (CPU) is located in St. Louis and the divisions have remote terminals connected to the CPU by telephone lines. The Cost Accounting Standards provide that the cost of general administration may be allocated to negotiated defense contracts. Further, the standards provide that, in situations in which computer services are provided by corporate headquarters, the actual costs (fixed and variable) of operating the computer department may be allocated to the defense division based on a reasonable measure of computer usage.

Another provision of the Cost Accounting Standards deals with the situation in which a defense division acquires noncommercial components from a sister division. The standards provide that when there is no established market price for the component, the component must be transferred to the defense division at cost without a markup for profit. This provision of the standards applies to Callum Corporation because the Aerospace Division purchases custom-designed ceramic components from the Ceramic Products Division. There is no established market price for these custom components.

The general managers of the three divisions are evaluated as profit center managers based on the before-tax profit of the division. Following are the November 1988 performance evaluation reports (in millions of dollars) for each division:

	Aerospace Division	Ceramic Products Division	Glass Products Division
Sales	$23.0	$15.0*	$55.0
Cost of goods sold	13.0	7.0	38.0
Gross profit	$10.0	$ 8.0	$17.0
Selling and administration:			
Division selling and administration	$ 5.0	$ 5.0	$ 8.0
Corporate-general administration	1.0	—	—
Corporate-computing	1.0	—	—
Total selling and administration	$ 7.0	$ 5.0	$ 8.0
Profit before taxes	$ 3.0	$ 3.0	$ 9.0

*Includes $3,000,000 of custom ceramic products sold to Aerospace Division at cost and the remainder ($12,000,000) sold to the Glass Products Division and outside customers at established market prices.

Required

1. Review the November performance evaluation reports for the three operating divisions of Callum Corporation.
   a. Identify specific instances where the federal government's Cost Accounting Standards have influenced Callum's divisional performance reporting.
   b. For each specific instance identified, discuss whether the use of accounting practices based on Cost Accounting Standards is desirable for internal reporting and performance evaluation.
2. Considering the accounting practices and reporting methods currently used by Callum Corporation, describe the suboptimal decision making that could result for the company as a whole if the demand for commercial (nondefense-related) ceramic products is equal to or greater than the productive capacity of the Ceramic Products Division.
3. Without a charge for computing services, the operating divisions may not make the most cost-effective use of the resources of the Computer Systems Department of Callum Corporation. Outline and discuss a method for charging the operating divisions for the use of computer services that would promote cost consciousness by the operating divisions and operating efficiency by the Computer Systems Department. (ICMA adapted)

Problem Set A

Problem 11A-1.
Cost-Based Pricing
(L.O. 2, 4)

Bodrero Coffee Company produces special types of blended coffee. Its products are used in exclusive restaurants throughout the world. Quality is the company's primary objective. A team of quality consultants is employed to continuously assess the quality of the purchased coffee beans and the blending procedures and ingredients used. The company's controller is in the process of determining prices for the coming year. Three blends are currently produced: Regular, Mint, and Choco blends. Expected profit on each blend is 20 percent above costs. Expected production for 19x8 is 120,000 pounds of Regular Blend, 50,000 pounds of Mint Blend, and 30,000 pounds of Choco Blend.

Following are total anticipated costs and percentages of total costs per blend for 19x8:

| | Percentage of Total Costs | | | Total |
| | Regular | Mint | Choco | Projected |
Cost Categories	Blend	Blend	Blend	Costs
Coffee beans	60	25	15	$770,000
Chocolate	0	10	90	45,000
Mint leaf	10	80	10	32,000
Labor				
Cleaning	60	25	15	148,000
Blending	40	30	30	372,000
Roasting	60	25	15	298,000
Indirect labor	60	25	15	110,000
Supplies	30	40	30	36,500
Other variable factory overhead	60	25	15	280,000
Fixed factory overhead	60	25	15	166,000
Variable selling expenses	40	30	30	96,500
Fixed selling expenses	40	30	30	42,000
General and administrative expenses	34	33	33	146,000

Required

1. Compute the selling price for each blend, using the gross margin pricing method.
2. Check your answers in **1** by computing selling prices using the profit margin pricing method.
3. If the competition's selling price for the Choco Blend averaged $24.50 per pound, should this influence the controller's pricing decision? Explain your answer.

Problem 11A-2.
Pricing Decision
(L.O.2,4)

Curtis Hawkins & Company is an assembly jobber specializing in home appliances. One division, Hart Operations, focuses most efforts on assembling a standard single-slice toaster. Projected costs on this product for 19x9 are as follows:

Cost Description	Budgeted Costs
Toaster casings	$1,344,000
Electrical components	1,860,000
Direct labor, electrical	2,520,000
Direct labor, assembly	1,128,000
Variable indirect assembly costs	780,000
Fixed indirect assembly costs	1,740,000
Variable selling expenses	1,032,000
Fixed selling expenses	504,000
General operating expenses	840,000
Administrative expenses	816,000

Estimated annual demand for the single-slice toaster is 1,200,000 per year. The budgeted amounts were geared to this demand. The company wants to make a $1,260,000 profit.

Competitors have just published their wholesale prices for the coming year; they range from $10.80 to $11.32 per toaster. The Curtis Hawkins toaster is known for its high quality, and it competes with products at the top end of the price range. Even with its high quality, however, every $.10 increase above the top competitor's price causes a drop in demand of 120,000 units below the original estimate. Assume all price changes are in $.10 increments.

Required

1. Compute the anticipated selling price. Use the gross margin pricing method.
2. Based on competitors' prices, what should the Curtis Hawkins Toaster sell for in 19x9? Defend your answer.
3. Would your pricing structure in **2** change if the company had only limited competition at its quality level? If so, in what direction? Why?

Problem 11A-3.
Time and Materials
Pricing
(L.O.4)

Thomason Construction Company specializes in additions to custom homes. Last week a potential customer called for a quote on a two-room addition to the family home. After visiting the site and taking all relevant measurements, Annette Thomason returned to the office to work on drawings for the addition. As part of the process of preparing a bid, a total breakdown of cost is required.

The company follows the time and materials pricing system and uses data from the previous six months to compute markup percentages for overhead. Separate rates are used for materials and supplies and for labor. During the past six months, $28,500 of materials and supplies-related overhead was incurred and $142,500 of materials and supplies was billed. Labor cost for the six-month period was $341,600. Labor-related overhead was $136,640. Add 20 percent to each markup percentage to cover desired profit. According to Thomason's design, the materials, supplies, and labor that are needed to complete the job are shown on the following page:

	Quantity	Unit Price
Materials		
	150 2″ × 4″ × 8′ cedar	$ 1.10
	50 2″ × 6″ × 8′ cedar	2.05
	14 2″ × 8″ × 8′ cedar	4.50
	25 4′ × 8′ sheets, ½″ plywood	10.40
	6 framed windows	80.00
	3 framed doors	110.00
	30 4′ × 8′ sheets, siding	14.00
Supplies		65.00

	Hours	Hourly Rate
Labor		
	120 Laborers/helpers	$ 9.50
	80 Semiskilled carpenters	11.00
	60 Carpenters	14.50

Required

1. Compute markup percentages for overhead and profit for both materials and supplies and labor.
2. Prepare a complete billing for this job. Include itemized amounts for each type of materials, supplies, and labor. Follow the time and material pricing approach and show total price for the job.

Problem 11A-4.
Cost Accounting
Standard 403
(L.O. 9)

The allocation of engineering overhead is a major concern for the Sunrise Technautics Corporation. The company specializes in providing engineering expertise for large project development that will complement any existing construction project design team. When seemingly insurmountable problems develop, Sunrise engineers are called in to help correct the problem. Forty percent of the corporation's revenue is from an on-going contract with the federal government. Although usually not for a specific construction project, the government expects immediate attention from Sunrise engineering personnel if a need arises. The entire amount of government contract revenue is from one contract that requires the immediate availability of the engineering personnel.

The problem of allocation arises when the engineering overhead of the home office is to be allocated to the ten divisions. Three allocation bases were proposed by the controller: total engineering costs, total square footage of engineering-related facilities, and total direct labor cost. Data supporting these allocation bases are on page 440. The corporation chose the total square footage basis because of the different sizes of the engineering facilities at the ten locations. DCAA auditors have rejected the basis. For 19x9, the total engineering overhead costs incurred by the home office for the benefit of the ten divisions amounted to $6,490,000.

Required

1. Allocate the total engineering overhead to the ten divisions using each of the three bases.

2. Which of the overhead allocation basis would the DCAA auditor favor? Why?
3. Could total direct labor costs be used as the allocation basis? If so, why?

Sunrise Technautics Corporation
Proposed Allocation Bases and Supporting Data

Segment	Total Engineering Costs	Total Square Footage	Total Direct Labor Costs
Boston division	$ 837,000	81,770	$ 572,000
Princeton division	232,500	31,450	143,000
Geneva division	372,000	25,160	228,800
Dallas division	465,000	12,580	257,400
Atlanta division	186,000	50,320	114,400
Flagstaff division	93,000	56,610	85,800
San Diego division	1,116,000	25,160	657,800
Palo Alto division	558,000	12,580	371,800
Reno division	279,000	6,290	171,600
Rock Island division	511,500	12,580	257,400
Totals	$4,650,000	314,500	$2,860,000

Problem 11A-5.
Contract Pricing/
CAS
(L.O. 8, 9)

Calderon Industries, Inc., has six divisions located throughout the United States. The Thomas Division, located in Blacksburg, Virginia, is about to enter into its first contract with the federal government. Contract A1A is a CPFF contract with a 20 percent fixed fee component. The Thomas Division is to develop special underwater testing equipment for the government. Company accountants have created the forecasted income statement shown on the following page for the division for the first quarter of this year.

When these contract amounts were communicated to the division's DCAA auditor, several items were found to be in error. Included in a special memorandum to corporate officials were the following changes:

1. Materials costs are unreasonable in amount. Reduce by 10 percent. Also affects materials-related costs, which are 60 percent of materials costs.
2. Entertainment costs of $6,420 have been charged to the contract.
3. Allocation of corporate aircraft costs from the home office to the division was done using the wrong basis. The amount should be 50 percent of the original amount. In addition, only 10 percent of the allocated amount should be assessed to the contract.
4. The contract calls for special secretarial support. The amount of procedural support charged to the contract contains $8,400 of secretarial support.
5. Interest expense has been charged to the contract.
6. Special equipment had to be purchased for the contract. No other equipment is necessary.

7. Advertising expenses have been charged to the contract.
8. Operating overhead is computed as 10 percent of all costs and expenses other than materials, materials-related overhead, direct labor, and fringe benefits costs.

Account	Contract A1A	All Other Business	Total Projected Operating Results
Revenues	$928,378	$4,199,100	$5,127,478
Costs			
Direct materials	$124,600	$ 842,450	$ 967,050
Materials-related overhead	74,760	505,470	580,230
Direct labor	102,300	645,100	747,400
Labor fringe benefits	71,610	451,570	523,180
Secretarial support	24,250	0	24,250
Operating supplies	18,430	71,180	89,610
Supervision expense	56,000	245,800	301,800
Travel and entertainment	16,470	38,750	55,220
Home office expenses			
Personnel costs	3,840	15,360	19,200
Corporate aircraft	8,700	26,100	34,800
Procedural support	12,460	29,980	42,440
Contract administration	24,660	86,800	111,460
Interest expense	17,450	65,420	82,870
Depreciation, building	31,400	98,700	130,100
Depreciation, equipment	16,400	37,560	53,960
Equipment expense	65,220	0	65,220
Utility expenses	7,980	22,100	30,080
Computer overhead	12,480	49,920	62,400
Advertising expenses	26,780	83,340	110,120
Other administrative costs	21,460	88,450	109,910
Operating overhead	36,398	95,946	132,344
Total expenses	$773,648	$3,499,996	$4,273,644
Projected income before taxes	$154,730	$ 699,104	$ 853,834

Required

1. Compute the new contract price.
2. What will be the division's revised total net income before taxes? (Remember that most divisional costs allocated to the contract in error must be absorbed by all other business.)

Problem Set B

Problem 11B-1.
Cost-Based Pricing
(L.O. 2, 4)

Jackson Publishing Company specializes in health-awareness books. Because the field of health awareness is very competitive, Anne Jackson, the company's president, maintains a strict policy about selecting books to publish. Jackson wants to publish only books whose projected earnings are 20 percent above total projected costs. Three titles were accepted for publication during 19x0; the authors were Krotec, Vawter, and Boyll. Following are projected costs for each book and allocation percentages for fixed and common costs:

Cost Categories	Total Projected Costs	Krotec Book	Vawter Book	Boyll Book
Labor				
Editing	$184,000	$55,200	$ 92,000	$36,800
Proofing	86,500	25,950	43,250	17,300
Development	94,400	28,320	47,200	18,880
Design	122,600	36,780	61,300	24,520
Royalty costs	120,000	36,000	60,000	24,000
Printing costs	248,600	74,580	124,300	49,720
Supplies	34,200	10,260	17,100	6,840
Variable production costs	142,000	42,600	71,000	28,400
Fixed production costs	168,000	35%	40%	25%
Distribution costs	194,000	30%	50%	20%
Variable marketing costs	124,600	37,380	62,300	24,920
Fixed marketing costs	69,400	35%	40%	25%
General and administrative costs	52,400	35%	40%	25%

Expected sales for 19x0 are as follows: Krotec, 25,000 copies; Vawter, 30,000 copies; and Boyll, 40,000 copies.

Required

1. Compute the selling price for each book. Use the gross margin pricing method.
2. Check your answers in **1** by computing selling prices under the profit margin pricing method.
3. If the competition's average selling price for a book on the same subject as Boyll's is $16, should this influence Jackson's pricing decision? State your reasons.

(*Hint:* In **1** and **2**, treat royalty costs as production costs.)

Problem 11B-2.
Pricing Decision
(L.O. 2, 4)

Jain & Gawel, Ltd., design and assemble handguns for police departments across the country. Only four other companies compete in this specialty market. The most popular police handgun is the Jain & Gawel .357-caliber magnum, Model

87, made of stainless steel. Jain & Gawel estimates there will be 47,000 requests for this model in 19x8.

Estimated costs related to this product for 19x8 are:

Description	Budgeted Costs
Gun casing	$ 573,400
Ammunition chamber	404,200
Trigger mechanism	1,151,500
Direct labor, assembly	991,700
Direct labor, finishing and testing	606,300
Variable indirect assembly costs	789,600
Fixed indirect assembly costs	338,400
Variable selling expenses	188,000
Fixed selling expenses	305,500
General operating expenses	183,300
Administrative expenses	126,900

This budget is based on the demand previously stated. The company wants to earn a $846,000 profit in 19x8.

Last week the four competitors released their wholesale prices for the next year:

Gunsmith A	$128.40
Gunsmith B	122.90
Gunsmith C	119.80
Gunsmith D	126.50

Jain & Gawel handguns are known for their high quality and compete with handguns at the top of the price range. Despite the high quality, however, every $5 price increase above the top competitor's price causes an 11,000-unit drop in demand from what was originally estimated. (Assume all price changes are in $5 increments.)

Required

1. Compute the anticipated selling price. Use the gross margin pricing method.
2. Based on competitors' prices, what should the Jain & Gawel handgun sell for in 19x8? Defend your answer.
3. Would your pricing structure in **2** change if the company had only limited competition at this quality level? If so, in what direction? Why?

Problem 11B-3.
Time and Materials
Pricing
(L.O. 4)

Cluff-Mack Maintenance, Inc., repairs heavy construction equipment and vehicles. Recently, the Ashton Construction Company had one of its giant Earthmovers overhauled and its tires replaced. Repair work for this size of vehicle usually takes one week to ten days. Extensive effort must be used to lift the vehicle enough to gain access to the engine. Parts are normally so large that a crane must be used to put them into place.

Cluff-Mack uses the time and materials pricing method for billing. A markup percentage is applied to the cost of parts and materials to cover materials-related overhead. A similar approach is used for labor-related overhead costs. During the previous year, the company incurred $779,040 in materials-related overhead costs and paid $486,900 for materials and parts. During that same time period, direct labor employees earned $347,200, and labor-related overhead of $520,800 was incurred. A factor of 20 percent is added to markup percentages to cover desired profit.

Here is a summary of the materials and parts used and the labor needed to repair the giant Earthmover:

Quantity	Unit Price
Materials and parts	
24 sparkplugs	$ 2.40
20 oil, quarts	3.90
12 hoses	11.60
1 water pump	964.00
30 coolant, quarts	6.50
18 clamps	5.90
1 distributor cap	128.40
1 carburetor	214.10
4 tires	1,020.00

Hours	Hourly Rate
Labor	
42 Mechanic	$18.20
54 Assistant mechanic	10.00

Required

1. Compute the markup percentages for overhead and profit for (a) materials and parts and (b) labor.
2. Prepare a complete billing for this job. Include itemized amounts for each type of material, part, and labor. Follow the time and materials pricing approach and show the total price for the job.

Problem 11B-4.
Cost Accounting
Standard 403
(L.O. 9)

Huston Air-Tech Corporation specializes in producing support equipment for jet aircraft. During the past ten years, the company has become heavily government contract-oriented. Last year, almost 60 percent of total sales revenue came from contracts with the federal government's Department of Defense. The home office in Minneapolis, Minnesota, supplies the company's ten production plants with several management support services. These services include personnel administration, central telephone service, centralized warehousing, and centralized data processing services. Before costs can be allocated to specific contracts, these centralized home office costs must be allocated from the home office to each plant. The costs can then be redistributed to the various government projects as well as the company's regular commercial business.

Three years ago, accounting management looked at three allocation bases for possible use in allocating centralized data processing services from the home office to the ten plants: (1) total computing time used, (2) total direct labor dollars, and (3) total sales revenue. Several of the members of the accounting management group wanted to use total direct labor dollars basis because most of the normal cost allocation is done using this basis. However, the company's contracting officer stated that the DCAA auditor would not let the company use total direct labor dollars because contract costing standards and principles would be violated. Following are the data supporting the three proposed bases. This year's total data processing overhead amounted to $9,420,000.

Huston Air-Tech Corporation
Proposed Allocation Bases and Supporting Data

Segment	Total Computing Time Used (hours)	Total Direct Labor Dollars	Total Sales Revenue
Colorado plant	816	$ 971,600	$ 3,672,000
Utah plant	612	694,000	2,448,000
Arizona plant	918	347,000	3,264,000
Texas plant	1,428	555,200	6,120,000
Illinois plant	1,530	485,800	6,528,000
California plant	2,040	624,600	7,752,000
Missouri plant	612	1,249,200	2,448,000
New York plant	714	1,388,000	2,856,000
Massachusetts plant	510	416,400	2,040,000
Georgia plant	1,020	208,200	3,672,000
Totals	10,200	$6,940,000	$40,800,000

Required

1. Allocate the total data processing overhead to the ten plants using each of the three bases.
2. Which of the overhead allocation bases would the DCAA auditor favor? Why?
3. Could total sales revenue be used as the allocation basis? Why?

Problem 11B-5.
Contract Pricing/
CAS
(L.O. 8, 9)

Federal Systems Company is just about to complete contract I95 with the Department of the Navy. A special building had to be rented and special police protection hired because of the highly classified nature of the contract. This is the company's first contract with the federal government; the company is a division of NAC Corporation. NAC has six divisions and its home office is in Rye, New York.

Federal Systems' accounting personnel have compiled initial costs and a projected total price for this CPFF contract. These amounts, along with all other company business are shown on the following page:

Account	Contract I95	All Other Business	Total Projected Operating Results
Revenues	$4,116,095	$12,435,600	$16,551,695
Costs			
Direct materials	$ 421,600	$ 1,142,450	$ 1,564,050
Materials-related overhead	210,800	571,225	782,025
Direct labor	1,255,500	4,665,100	5,920,600
Labor fringe benefits	502,200	1,866,040	2,368,240
Special police protection	42,250	0	42,250
Operating supplies	28,430	97,180	125,610
Supervision expense	176,000	475,800	651,800
Travel and entertainment	67,470	98,750	166,220
Home office expenses			
Personnel costs	9,840	29,520	39,360
Central warehousing	9,350	33,660	43,010
Secretarial support	31,460	56,980	88,440
Other project support	89,450	126,900	216,350
Interest expense	29,650	87,950	117,600
Depreciation, building	39,600	134,200	173,800
Depreciation, equipment	29,400	82,640	112,040
Special building rent	46,500	0	46,500
Utility expenses	11,230	43,100	54,330
Computer overhead	29,280	68,320	97,600
Advertising expense	32,700	84,550	117,250
Other administrative costs	32,960	104,450	137,410
Operating overhead	70,557	152,400	222,957
Total expenses	$3,166,227	$ 9,921,215	$13,087,442
Projected income before taxes	$ 949,868	$ 2,514,385	$ 3,464,253

After the division's DCAA auditor had a chance to review the information regarding the contract, several items were found to be in error. Included in a memorandum to corporate officials were the following changes:

1. Labor costs are unreasonable in amount. Reduce by 20 percent. Also affects labor fringe benefits, which are 40 percent of direct labor costs.
2. Entertainment costs of $41,600 have been charged to the contract.
3. Allocation of central warehousing costs from the home office to the division was done using the wrong basis. The amount should be 22 percent rather than 23 percent of the total of $187,000, with the amount allocated to the contract being reduced by 1 percent ($1,870).
4. The contract calls for special police protection. The amount of special project support charged to the contract contains $26,550 of regular police protection.

5. Interest expense has been charged to the contract.
6. A special building had to be rented for the contract. No other building facilities were necessary.
7. Advertising expenses have been charged to the contract.
8. Operating overhead is computed as 10 percent of all costs and expenses other than materials, materials-related overhead, direct labor, and fringe benefits costs.

Required

1. Compute the new contract price.
2. What will be the division's revised total net income before taxes? (Remember that most divisional costs allocated to the contract in error must be absorbed by all other business.)

Management Decision Case

Heitz Company
(L.O. 4)

The Heitz Company manufactures office equipment for retail stores. Tom Grant, Vice President of Marketing, has proposed that Heitz introduce two new products, an electric stapler and an electric pencil sharpener.

Grant has requested that the Profit Planning Department develop preliminary selling prices for the two new products for his review. Profit Planning is to follow the company's standard policy for developing potential selling prices. It is to use all data available on each product. Following are the data accumulated by Profit Planning on the two new products:

	Electric Stapler	Electric Pencil Sharpener
Estimated annual demand in units	12,000	10,000
Estimated unit manufacturing costs	$10.00	$12.00
Estimated unit selling and administrative expenses	$4.00	Not available
Assets employed in manufacturing	$180,000	Not available

Heitz plans to use an average of $2,400,000 in assets to support operations in the current year. The condensed pro forma operating income statement shown on the following page represents Heitz's planned costs and return on assets for the entire company for all products.

Required

1. Calculate a potential selling price for the
   a. electric stapler using return-on-assets pricing.
   b. electric pencil sharpener using gross margin pricing.
2. Could a selling price for the electric pencil sharpener be calculated using return-on-assets pricing? Explain your answer.
3. Which of the two pricing methods—return-on-asset pricing or gross margin pricing—is more appropriate for decision analysis? Explain your answer.

4. Discuss the additional steps Grant is likely to take after he receives the potential selling prices for the two new products (as calculated in **1**) to set an actual selling price for each of the two products.

Heitz Company	
Pro Forma Operating Income Statement	
For the Year Ended May 31, 19x5	
($000 omitted)	
Revenue	$4,800
Cost of goods sold, manufacturing costs	2,880
Gross profit	$1,920
Selling and administrative expenses	1,440
Operating profit	$ 480

(ICMA adapted)

Short-Run Decision Analysis

One of this book's main tenets is that the management accountant supplies management with three basic types of information: (1) product costing data for pricing and inventory valuation, (2) cost analyses for operational planning and control, and (3) special analyses to support management decision making. Product costing techniques and planning and control procedures were studied in earlier chapters. Decision making is the focus of Chapters 11, 12, 13, and 14.

Top management often depends on the management accountant for information to support its decision-making activities. Such information reveals important data about each alternate decision. To evaluate decision alternatives, the accountant uses special decision models, analyses, and reporting techniques. Decisions concerning long-term capital expenditures are the most complex, and they are studied in depth in the next chapter. This chapter emphasizes day-to-day operating decisions and information needed for implementation. After discussing the role of strategic planning, defining the term *relevant information*, and exploring management's decision cycle, this chapter discusses decision models. These models include variable costing procedures, contribution margin reporting, and the technique of incremental analysis. The remainder of the chapter focuses on specific types of decisions: (1) make-or-buy, (2) special-order, (3) scarce-resource/sales-mix, (4) unprofitable segment elimination, and (5) sell or process-further. After studying this chapter, you should be able to meet the learning objectives listed on the left.

Strategic Plans of Management

Strategic planning establishes an organization's basic objectives. This planning activity is critical to having a successful business because without strategic plans, management has no guidance or direction for its actions. Picture an airplane that has just taken off without a destination: The pilot is without direction and does not know where to go. Such is also true for a company without a strategic plan.

Management develops its strategic plan by creating company objectives, an organizational structure, and policies concerning growth and product or service lines. Identifying defined markets to which its products or services should be targeted is also a strategic matter, as are any other factors affecting the organization's structure.

Strategic planning is important to the topics covered in this chapter because it provides the framework for applying short-run period planning. All management decisions should be consistent with a company's strategic plans. For example, assume that management at Datalife Corporation, a supplier of quality computer equipment for the past twelve years, established a new objective: to enter the telecommunications field. Before making this change in its strategic plan, management had no guidelines when deciding about (1) purchasing a company specializing in telecommunications materials or (2) converting an existing product line from a low-profit computer memory chip to a special, potentially high-profit telecommunications memory chip. Without the new strategic plan, both decisions would have been negative because Datalife was not in the telecommunications business. With the change in its strategic plan, management will now consider these and other matters involving the telecommunications industry. As you study decision analyses, remember that before any positive decision is made, it should be consistent with the organization's strategic plan.

Relevant Information for Management

OBJECTIVE 1
Define and identify information relevant to decision making

The management decision process calls for comparing two or more possible solutions to a problem and deciding which one is the best. Supplying relevant information to management for each alternative is the responsibility of the management accountant. Members of top management should evaluate the possible solutions to a particular problem. To do so, they should not have to wade through pages and pages of data to find out how each alternative will affect the operations of the business. Many of the facts may be the same for each alternative. For instance, total sales may not be affected by a proposal to reduce labor costs by installing automatic machinery. If there are three possible courses of action (three machines to choose from) and total sales are the same in each case, the sales data would not influence the decision. In addition, the accountant often uses past data in preparing cost estimates of decision alternatives. However, it is the cost estimates that are relevant to the decision, not the historical data. **Relevant decision information** is future cost, revenue, or resource usage data, and it will be different for the various alternatives being evaluated. A decision must be made on the basis of the alternatives available. Information that is alike for those alternatives and costs or transactions that have already happened will not be helpful in picking out the best alternative. Relevant information is limited to future data that differ among the possible alternatives.

Management Decision Cycle

The decision-making process is an unstructured area of responsibility. Many decisions are unique and do not lend themselves to strict rules, steps, or timetables. However, certain events accompany each kind of

OBJECTIVE 2
Describe the steps in the management decision cycle

management decision analysis. Figure 12-1 shows the events that make up the management decision cycle. Following the discovery of a problem or resource need, the accountant should seek out all possible courses of action that are open to management and will solve the problem or meet the need. After identifying the alternatives, the accountant prepares a complete analysis for each action, showing its total cost, cost savings, or financial effects on business operations. Each type of decision calls for different information. When all the information has been gathered and organized in a meaningful way, management can decide the best course of action. After the decision has been carried out, the accountant should prepare a post-decision audit analysis to give management feedback about the results of the decision. If further action is needed, the decision cycle begins all over. If not, this particular decision process has been completed.

Accounting Tools and Reports for Decision Analysis

The accountant usually plays the role of data supplier in the management decision process. Certain accounting tools and reports are used for this purpose. Because management expects decision information to be accurate, timely, refined, and presented in a readable way, the accountant must be concerned not only with the information itself but with the reporting format as well.

Figure 12-1. The Management Decision Cycle

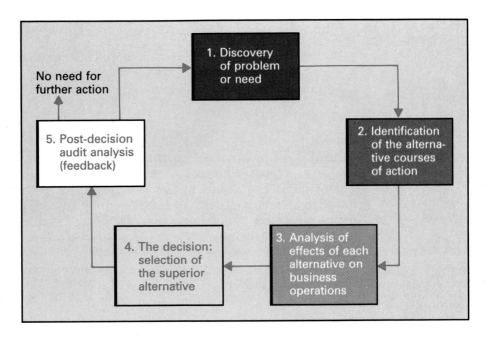

Variable costing, which is the basis for contribution margin reporting practices, and incremental analysis are the two most common decision support tools the accountant uses. Each technique helps identify information relevant to a decision, and each technique also gives the accountant a special decision-reporting format.

Decision Models in Management Accounting

When numerous alternatives are to be evaluated, the decision-making process becomes complex. In addition, many decisions are nonrecurring and cannot be resolved by relying on past experience. To facilitate a complex analysis, this chapter provides a guide to developing a decision model. A **decision model** is a symbolic or numerical representation of the variables and parameters affecting a decision. **Variables** are factors controlled by management. **Parameters** are uncontrollable factors and operating constraints and limitations. As an example, suppose you need to develop a decision model to evaluate new product lines. Your analysis would involve such parameters as customer demand, market growth, competitors' actions, and production capacity limitations. Variables in this decision model include product selling prices, production costs, and manufacturing methods. The key to developing such a model is to identify relevant variables and parameters and put the information together in an informative manner.

Figure 12-2 outlines the steps in the model-building process. Parameters affecting the decision are first defined, then possible alternatives are identified. In steps 3 and 4, appropriate cost and revenue information is developed and analyzed. After the irrelevant information has been eliminated, the relative benefits of each alternative are summarized and presented to management. Output of the decision model is a comparative analysis, using the measurement criterion selected for the particular decision problem. This analysis is a formal report to management, and it should include a

1. Brief description of the project or problem situation
2. Comparative financial analysis of each alternative
3. Summary of the relative advantages of each alternative

Variable Costing

Variable costing (also called direct costing) is an approach to product costing. However, variable costing is also the basis for developing an income statement using the contribution margin format. This income statement design is useful in decision-making activities. Unlike absorption costing, which assigns all manufacturing costs to products, **variable costing** uses only the variable manufacturing costs for product costing and inventory valuation. Direct materials costs, direct labor costs, and variable factory overhead costs are the only cost elements used to figure product costs. Fixed factory overhead costs are considered costs of the current accounting period.

Support for variable costing stems from the fact that a company has fixed operating costs whether it operates or not. For this reason, those

Figure 12-2. Steps in Developing a Decision Model

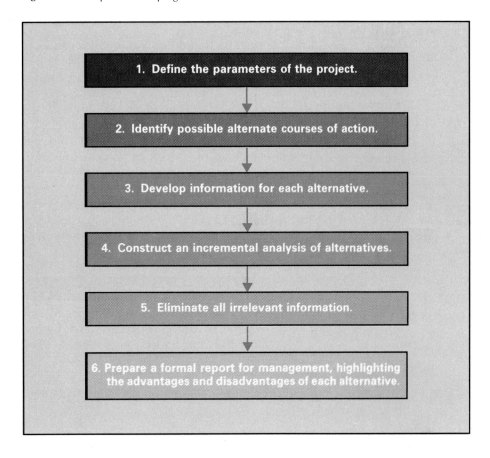

1. Define the parameters of the project.

2. Identify possible alternate courses of action.

3. Develop information for each alternative.

4. Construct an incremental analysis of alternatives.

5. Eliminate all irrelevant information.

6. Prepare a formal report for management, highlighting the advantages and disadvantages of each alternative.

who favor variable costing argue that such costs do not have a direct relationship to the product and should not be used to find the product's unit cost. Fixed manufacturing costs are linked more closely with time than with productive output. Opponents of variable costing say that without fixed manufacturing costs, production would stop. Therefore, such costs are an integral part of a product's cost.

Whatever side you are on, two points are certain. The first is that variable costing is *very* useful for internal management decision purposes. The second is that neither the Internal Revenue Service nor the public accounting profession accepts variable costing for external reporting purposes. They reject it because fixed costs are not included in inventory and cost of goods sold. Therefore this approach cannot be used for computing federal income taxes or for reporting the results of operations and financial position to stockholders and others outside the company.

Product Costing. For purposes of product costing, variable costing treats fixed manufacturing costs differently from production costs that vary with output. A point often overlooked is that fixed manufacturing costs

OBJECTIVE 3
Calculate unit
costs using
variable costing
procedures

are also left out of all inventories, which is why the value of inventories arrived at by variable costing is lower than the value of those computed by absorption costing.

The following example helps explain the differences between these two product costing approaches. McClure Industries, Inc., produces grills for outdoor cooking. During 19xx, the company put a new, disposable grill into production. A summary of 19xx cost and production data for the grill are: direct materials costs, $59,136; direct labor, $76,384; variable factory overhead, $44,352; and fixed factory overhead, $36,960. There were 24,640 units completed and 22,000 units sold during 19xx. There were no beginning or ending work in process inventories.

Using this data, we can find the unit cost as well as the ending inventory and cost of goods sold amounts for 19xx under a variable costing approach and under an absorption costing approach. This information is summarized in Exhibit 12-1. Unit production cost under variable costing is $7.30 per grill, whereas unit cost is $8.80 working with absorption costing.

Exhibit 12-1. Variable Costing Versus Absorption Costing

McClure Industries, Inc.
Unit Cost and Ending Inventory Values
For the Year Ended December 31, 19xx

	Variable Costing	Absorption Costing
Contribution Margin		
Unit Cost		
Direct materials ($59,136 ÷ 24,640 units)	$ 2.40	$ 2.40
Direct labor ($76,384 ÷ 24,640 units)	3.10	3.10
Variable factory overhead ($44,352 ÷ 24,640 units)	1.80	1.80
Fixed factory overhead ($36,960 ÷ 24,640 units)	—	1.50
Total unit cost	$ 7.30	$ 8.80
Ending Finished Goods Inventory		
2,640 units at $7.30	$ 19,272	
2,640 units at $8.80		$ 23,232
Cost of Goods Sold for 19xx		
22,000 units at $7.30	$160,600	
22,000 units at $8.80		$193,600
Plus fixed factory overhead	36,960	
Costs appearing on 19xx income statement	$197,560	$193,600
Total costs to be accounted for	$216,832	$216,832

Ending finished goods inventory balances are not the same because of the $1.50 difference in unit cost. Because fewer costs remain in inventory at year end with variable costing amounts, it is logical that greater costs will appear on the income statement. As shown in Exhibit 12-1, $197,560 of current manufacturing costs are considered costs of the period, to be subtracted from revenue in the variable costing income statement. Only $193,600 is shown as Cost of Goods Sold when absorption costing is used. The difference of $3,960 (2,640 units in inventory × $1.50 fixed costs per unit) is shown as part of inventory under absorption costing.

Contribution Margin Reporting Format

OBJECTIVE 4
Prepare an income statement using the contribution reporting format

Performance Analysis: The Income Statement. The use of variable costing leads to differences in financial reporting as well as in product costing. Putting together the concepts of contribution margin and variable costing results in an entirely new form of income statement. This new form emphasizes cost variability and segment or product-line contributions to income. Costs are no longer classified as either manufacturing or nonmanufacturing costs. Instead, attention is focused on separating variable costs from fixed costs.

Adding to the McClure Industries, Inc., example will help explain this point. Assume the following additional information for 19xx: selling price per grill is $24.50. Variable selling costs per grill are $4.80. Fixed selling expenses are $48,210, and fixed administrative expenses are $82,430. Net income under both variable costing and absorption costing procedures is compared in Exhibit 12-2. The contribution margin format is presented first. Note that the term *gross margin* is replaced by the term *contribution margin* and that only variable costs (including variable selling costs) are subtracted from sales to get the contribution margin. Contribution margin is the amount that each segment or product line is contributing to the company's fixed costs and profits. Net income calculated by using the conventional statement is shown in the lower part of Exhibit 12-2. Note that net income is different under the two methods. This difference, $3,960, is the same amount noted earlier. It is the part of fixed manufacturing overhead cost that is inventoried when absorption costing is used.

Contribution Reporting and Decisions. Variable costing and the contribution approach to income reporting are used a great deal in decision analysis, most commonly in deciding whether to continue a segment, division, or product line. Other uses are in the evaluation of new product lines and in sales-mix studies. Decisions about the contribution of sales territories also use the contribution approach to income reporting. These uses are explained later when we look at specific kinds of decisions.

Incremental Analysis

Incremental analysis, an approach often used in decision reporting, compares different alternatives by looking only at information differences. Only relevant information, decision data that differ between alternatives,

Exhibit 12-2. The Income Statement: Contribution Versus Conventional Formats

McClure Industries, Inc.
Disposable Grill Division
Income Statement
For the Year Ended December 31, 19xx

Contribution Format

Sales		$539,000
Variable Cost of Goods Sold		
Variable Cost of Goods Available		
for Sale	$179,872	
Less Ending Inventory	19,272*	
Variable Cost of Goods Sold	$160,600*	
Plus Variable Selling Costs		
(22,000 units at $4.80)	105,600	266,200
Contribution Margin		$272,800
Less Fixed Costs		
Fixed Manufacturing Costs	$ 36,960	
Fixed Selling Expenses	48,210	
Fixed Administrative Expenses	82,430	167,600
Net Income Before Taxes		$105,200

Conventional Format

Sales		$539,000
Cost of Goods Sold		
Cost of Goods Manufactured	$216,832*	
Less Ending Inventory	23,232*	193,600*
Gross Margin from Sales		$345,400
Selling Expenses		
Variable	$105,600	
Fixed	48,210	
Administrative Expenses	82,430	236,240
Net Income (before taxes)		$109,160

* Detailed computations are in Exhibit 12-1.

OBJECTIVE 5
*Develop decision
data using the
technique of
incremental
analysis*

are of concern. For decision purposes, only future data are included. By focusing on the differences between alternatives, incremental analysis helps highlight important points, makes the evaluation easier for the decision maker, and reduces the time needed to choose the best course of action.

For example, assume that the Eubanks Company is trying to decide which one of two machines, C or W, to buy. Management has been able to collect the following annual operating estimates on the two machines:

	Machine C	Machine W
Increase in revenue	$16,200	$19,800
Increase in annual operating costs		
Direct materials	2,800	2,800
Direct labor	4,200	6,100
Variable factory overhead	2,100	3,050
Fixed factory overhead (depreciation included)	5,000	5,000

The best method of comparing these two decision alternatives is to prepare an analysis that will show increases or decreases in revenues and costs relevant to the decision. Following is this analysis:

Eubanks Company
Incremental Decision Analysis

	Machine C	Machine W	Difference in Favor of Machine W
Increase in revenues	$16,200	$19,800	$3,600
Increase in operating costs			
Direct materials	$ 2,800	$ 2,800	—
Direct labor	4,200	6,100	$1,900
Variable factory overhead	2,100	3,050	950
Fixed factory overhead	5,000	5,000	—
Total operating costs	$14,100	$16,950	$2,850
Resulting increase in net income	$ 2,100	$ 2,850	$ 750

If you assume that the purchase price and useful life of the two machines are the same, the analysis shows that Machine W will generate $750 more in net income than Machine C. Thus the decision would be to purchase Machine W. Direct materials costs and fixed factory overhead costs need not be included in the analysis since they are similar for each alternative. These irrelevant costs are shown here only for purposes of explanation.

Special Reports

Qualitative as well as quantitative data are useful in decision making. When only quantitative data are being considered, most problems of choosing between alternatives can be solved by using either contribution reporting or incremental analysis. However, in some decisions there are many alternatives, each of which is the best one in certain circumstances.

One may be more profitable, but another may further diversify a company's product line. A third alternative may help prevent a huge layoff of personnel in some part of the country, thus bolstering the company's goodwill there. Even though many equally good qualitative decision alternatives may be available, management must choose only one course of action. In cases such as those described above, the accountant must use imagination and prepare the special decision report that demonstrates which alternative is best under the circumstances.

For most special decision reports, there is no one correct, set structure. These reports are created by skilled, experienced accountants to fit individual situations. Students of management accounting often have difficulty with decision analysis problems because there are infinite ways to develop these analyses. Students are used to referring to the text for examples of problem-solving techniques and simply inserting new numbers into a format to solve exercises and problems. Because this is a principles-level book, examples in the text may be used to solve most of the problems. But remember that as the accountant progresses in the field of management accounting, each adventure requires that he or she create a reporting format appropriate to the circumstances. Such challenges contribute to the dynamic nature of this discipline.

Operating Decisions of Management

Management depends on the accountant to supply relevant information for many kinds of decisions. Therefore, this chapter now turns to data relevant to the (1) make-or-buy decision, (2) special-order decision, (3) scarce-resource/sales-mix decision, (4) decision to eliminate an unprofitable segment, and (5) sell or process-further decision.

Make-or-Buy Decisions

OBJECTIVE 6a
Evaluate alternatives involving make-or-buy decisions

One common group of decision analyses centers on the many parts used in product assembly operations. Management is continually faced with the decision as to whether to make or buy some or all parts. The goal of the **make-or-buy decision** is to identify those cost and revenue elements relevant to this kind of decision. Following is the information to be considered:

To Make	To Buy
Need for expensive machinery	Purchase price of item
Other variable costs of making the item	Rent or net cash flow to be generated from vacated space in factory
Repair and maintenance expenses	Salvage value of machinery

The case of the Klock Electronics Company illustrates a make-or-buy decision. The firm has been purchasing a small transistor casing from an outside supplier for the past five years at a cost of $1.25 per casing. However, the supplier has just informed Klock Electronics that the price will be raised 20 percent, effective immediately. The company has idle machinery that could be used to produce the casings. Also, management has found that the costs of producing the casings would be $84 per 100 casings for direct materials, six minutes of labor per casing at $4 per direct labor hour, and variable factory overhead at $2 per direct labor hour. Fixed factory overhead would include $4,000 of depreciation per year and $6,000 of other fixed costs. Annual production and usage would be 20,000 casings. The space and machinery to be used would not be usable if the part were purchased. Should Klock Electronics Company make or buy the casings?

From the information given, the company should make the casings. Exhibit 12-3 presents an incremental cost analysis of the two decision alternatives. All costs connected with the decision are shown in the analysis. Because the machinery has already been purchased and neither the machinery nor the required factory space has any other use, the fixed factory overhead costs are the same for both alternatives, so they are not relevant to the decision. The costs of making the needed casings (leaving out the fixed overhead costs) are $28,800. The cost of buying 20,000 casings will be $30,000 at the increased purchase price. It is clear then that $1,200 will be saved if the casings are made within the company.

Exhibit 12-3. Incremental Analysis: Make-or-Buy Decision

Klock Electronics Company
Incremental Decision Analysis
Current Year—Annual Usage

	Make	Buy	Difference in Favor of Make
Raw materials (20,000 ÷ 100 × $84)	$16,800	—	$(16,800)
Direct labor (20,000 ÷ 10 × $4)	8,000	—	(8,000)
Variable factory overhead (20,000 ÷ 10 × $2)	4,000	—	(4,000)
Fixed factory overhead			
Depreciation*	4,000	4,000	—
Other*	6,000	6,000	—
To purchase completed casings 20,000 × $1.50	—	30,000	30,000
Totals	$28,800	$30,000	$ 1,200

* Irrelevant because these amounts are the same for both decision alternatives. Amounts have not been included in totals.

Using incremental analysis is a good approach to the make-or-buy decision. This approach allows the analyst to use all decision data available and quickly identify anything irrelevant to the final decision.

Special-Order Decisions

OBJECTIVE 6b
Evaluate
alternatives
involving special-
order decisions

Management is often faced with **special-order decisions**, that is, whether to accept special product orders. These orders are normally for large numbers of similar products to be sold at prices below those listed in advertisements. Because management did not expect such orders, the orders were not included in any annual cost or sales estimates. Generally, these orders are one-time events and should not be included in estimates of subsequent years' operations. (Because standard products are sold to the public at stated prices, legal advice on federal price discrimination laws should be obtained before accepting special orders.)

To illustrate special-order analysis, consider Landry Sporting Goods, Inc., which manufactures a complete line of sporting equipment. Kelliher Enterprises operates a large chain of discount stores and has approached the Landry company with a special order. The order calls for 30,000 deluxe baseballs to be shipped with bulk packaging of 500 baseballs per box. Kelliher is willing to pay $2.45 per baseball.

The Landry accounting department developed the following data: annual expected production, 400,000 baseballs; current year's production, 410,000 baseballs; maximum production capacity, 450,000 baseballs. Additional data are:

Unit cost data	
Direct materials	$ .60
Direct labor	.90
Factory overhead	
Variable	.50
Fixed ($100,000 ÷ 400,000)	.25
Packaging per unit	.30
Advertising ($60,000 ÷ 400,000)	.15
Other fixed selling and admin-	
istrative costs ($120,000 ÷ 400,000)	.30
Total	$ 3.00
Unit selling price	$ 4.00
Total estimated bulk packaging costs	
(30,000 baseballs: 500 per box)	$2,500

Should Landry Sporting Goods, Inc., accept the Kelliher offer?

A profitability analysis reveals that the special order from Kelliher Enterprises should be accepted. Exhibit 12-4 contains a comparative analysis based on the contribution reporting format. Net income before taxes is computed for the Baseball Division for operations both with and without the Kelliher order.

Exhibit 12-4. Contribution Reporting: Special Product Order

Landry Sporting Goods, Inc.
Comparative Decision Analysis
Special Product Order—Baseball Division

	Without Kelliher Order (410,000 products)	With Kelliher Order (440,000 products)
Sales	$1,640,000	$1,713,500
Less variable costs		
Direct materials	$ 246,000	$ 264,000
Direct labor	369,000	396,000
Variable factory overhead	205,000	220,000
Packaging costs	123,000	125,500
Total variable costs	$ 943,000	$1,005,500
Contribution margin	$ 697,000	$ 708,000
Less fixed costs		
Factory overhead	$ 100,000	$ 100,000
Advertising	60,000	60,000
Selling and administrative	120,000	120,000
Total fixed costs	$ 280,000	$ 280,000
Net income before taxes	$ 417,000	$ 428,000

The only costs affected by the order are for direct materials, direct labor, variable factory overhead, and packaging. Materials, labor, and overhead costs are shown for sales of 410,000 and 440,000 baseballs, respectively. Sales data were computed, using these same unit amounts. Packaging costs will increase, but only by the amount of the added bulk packaging costs. All other costs will remain the same. The net result of accepting the special order is an $11,000 increase in contribution margin (and net income before taxes). This amount can be verified by the following computations:

Net gain = [(unit selling price − unit variable mfg. costs) × units] − bulk pack costs
= [($2.45 − $2.00) 30,000] − $2,500
= $13,500 − $2,500 = $11,000

For special-order analysis, both the comparative contribution reporting approach and incremental analysis can be used. In the above case, contribution reporting was chosen because of the misleading fixed cost data in the problem. Contribution reporting highlights the effect of variable cost changes on contribution margin and net income.

Scarce-Resource/Sales-Mix Analysis

OBJECTIVE 6c
*Evaluate
alternatives
involving scarce-
resource/sales-
mix decisions*

Profit can be maximized only when the profitability of all product lines is known. Optimal use of scarce resources, such as labor hours or machine hours, is part of this maximizing process. The question is, Which product or products contribute most to company profitability in relation to the amount of capital assets or other scarce resources needed to produce the item(s)? To answer this question, the management accountant must first measure the contribution margin of each product. Next, he or she must determine a set of ratios of contribution margin to the required capital equipment or other scarce resource. This analysis identifies products or services yielding the most contribution margin per unit of scarce resource. Once this step has been completed, management should request a marketing study to establish the upper limits of demand for the most profitable products or services. If profitability per product or service can be computed and market demand exists, then management should shift its emphasis to the most profitable products or services.

Many decisions can be related to the approach described here. **Sales-mix analysis** means determining the most profitable combination of product sales when a company produces more than one product or offers more than one service. The contribution margin approach to decision analysis, as described above, can also be used for several other types of decisions. Closely connected with sales-mix analysis is the product-line profitability study designed to discover if any products are losing money for the company. Although the contribution margin approach is used, the objective is different. There is no longer interest in maximizing profits based on the use of scarce resources. Instead, interest centers on eliminating the unprofitable product line(s) or service(s). Identifying unprofitable corporate divisions or segments is another type of decision analysis relying on the contribution margin approach. Decisions to eliminate unprofitable products or services and unprofitable corporate segments are based on similar analyses of contribution margin. These types of decisions are discussed in the next section of this chapter.

An example of sales-mix analysis will aid understanding. The management of Christenson Enterprises is analyzing its sales mix. The company manufactures three products—C, A, and L—using the same production equipment for all three. Total productive capacity is being used. Following are the product line statistics:

	Product C	Product A	Product L
Current production and sales (units)	20,000	30,000	18,000
Machine hours per product	2	1	2.5
Selling price per unit	$24.00	$18.00	$32.00
Unit variable manufacturing costs	$12.50	$10.00	$18.75
Unit variable selling costs	$ 6.50	$ 5.00	$ 6.25

Should the company try selling more of one product and less of another?

Because total productive capacity is being used, the only way to expand production of one product is to reduce production of another product. Exhibit 12-5 shows the sales-mix analysis of Christenson Enterprises. Although contribution reporting is used here, contribution margin per product is not the important figure when deciding about shifts in sales mix. In the analysis, Product L has the highest contribution margin. However, all products use the same machinery and all machine hours are filled. Therefore machine hours become the scarce resource.

The analysis in Exhibit 12-5 goes one step beyond the computation of contribution margin per unit. Such a sales-mix decision should use two decision variables: (1) contribution margin per unit and (2) machine hours required per unit. For instance, Product C requires two machine hours to generate $5 of contribution margin. But Product A would generate $6 of contribution margin using the same two machine hours. For this reason, contribution margin is calculated per machine hour. Based on this information, management can readily see that it should produce and sell as much of Product A as possible. Next, it should push Product L. If any productive capacity remains, it should produce Product C.

Decisions to Eliminate Unprofitable Segments

OBJECTIVE 6d
Evaluate alternatives involving decisions to eliminate unprofitable segments

Whether to eliminate an unprofitable product, service, division, or other corporate segment is another type of operating decision management may face. The analysis prepared for this type of decision is an extension of the normal performance evaluation of the segment. As an overview, the analysis of unprofitable segments compares (1) operating results of the corporation with the segment in question included against (2) operating

Exhibit 12-5. Contribution Reporting: Sales-Mix Analysis

Christenson Enterprises
Sales-Mix Analysis
Contribution Reporting Format

	Product C	Product A	Product L
Sales price	$24.00	$18.00	$32.00
Variable costs			
Manufacturing	$12.50	$10.00	$18.75
Selling	6.50	5.00	6.25
Total	$19.00	$15.00	$25.00
Contribution margin (A)	$ 5.00	$ 3.00	$ 7.00
Machine hours required per unit (B)	2	1	2.5
Contribution margin per machine hour (A ÷ B)	$ 2.50	$ 3.00	$ 2.80

results for the same period that do not include data from that segment. The key to this analysis is to be able to isolate the segment, product, or service in question. Variable costs associated with a product or segment are easy to identify and account for. But each product or segment also has fixed costs associated with it. The fixed costs are commonly referred to as traceable fixed costs.

To analyze the financial consequences of eliminating a segment, one must concentrate on the incremental profit effect of the decision. The decision analysis consists of comparing contribution margin income statements for the company. One statement includes the segment under review, and the second excludes this information. The basic decision is a problem of choosing to keep the product, service, or segment or to eliminate it.

Assume management at Hugh Corporation wants to determine if Division B should be eliminated. Exhibit 12-6 provides basic cost and

Exhibit 12-6. Divisional Profit Summary and Decision Analysis

Hugh Corporation
Divisional Profit Summary and Decision Analysis

A. Income Statements	Divisions D and E	Division B	Total Company
Sales	$135,000	$15,000	$150,000
Less variable costs	52,500	7,500	60,000
Contribution margin	$ 82,500	$ 7,500	$ 90,000
Less traceable fixed costs	55,500	16,500	72,000
Divisional income	$ 27,000	($ 9,000)	$ 18,000
Less unallocated fixed costs			12,000
Income before taxes			$ 6,000

B. Incremental Decision Analysis	Company Profitability If It Elects To — Keep Division B	Company Profitability If It Elects To — Eliminate Division B	Benefit or (Cost) To Eliminate Division B	
Sales	$150,000	$135,000	($15,000)	sales decrease
Less variable costs	60,000	52,500	7,500	cost reduction
Contribution margin	$ 90,000	$ 82,500	($ 7,500)	CM decrease
Less total fixed costs	84,000	67,500	16,500	cost reduction
Income before taxes	$ 6,000	$ 15,000	$ 9,000	profit increase

revenue data and illustrates a format for evaluating alternate decisions. This analysis requires that an income statement be prepared for each alternative and that profits be compared. All traceable fixed costs of Division B are assumed to be avoidable. Avoidable costs are costs that will be eliminated if a particular product, service or corporate segment is discontinued. As the analysis in Exhibit 12-6 shows, the profits of Hugh Corporation will increase by $9,000 if Division B is eliminated.

Another way of looking at this decision is to concentrate on the third column in part B of Exhibit 12-6. Revenue and cost factors that are different under each alternative can be analyzed to explain the profit difference of $9,000. The incremental factors are analyzed in Exhibit 12-7. If all fixed costs traceable to Division B are avoidable, then the operating loss of $9,000 is also avoidable if the division is eliminated. The primary concept is to isolate avoidable costs, which may not always correspond with traceable costs. Avoidable costs are incremental costs since these amounts are incurred only if the division exists.

In trying to understand the significance of determining an accurate amount of avoidable costs, assume you discover that executives and supervisors in Division B will be reassigned to other divisions if Division B is eliminated. Included in the $16,500 of traceable fixed costs for Division B are salaries of $12,000 for these people. This assumption now changes the profit effect of eliminating Division B, as shown on the following page:

Exhibit 12-7. Incremental Revenue and Cost Analysis	
Hugh Corporation	
Incremental Revenue and Cost Analysis	
Advantage of Eliminating Division B	**Amount**
Increase in sales	None
Decrease in costs ($7,500 + $16,500)	$24,000
Total advantage	$24,000
Disadvantage of Eliminating Division B	**Amount**
Decrease in sales	$15,000
Increase in costs	None
Total disadvantage	$15,000
Incremental profit from eliminating Division B advantage less disadvantage	$ 9,000

Advantage of eliminating Division B	
Reduction of variable expenses	$ 7,500
Reduction of fixed expenses ($16,500 − $12,000)	4,500
Total benefits	$12,000

Disadvantage of eliminating Division B	
Reduction in sales	$15,000

Decrease in profit as a result of eliminating Division B (2 − 1)	$ 3,000

By following these revised assumptions, you compute that avoidable fixed costs for Division B are $4,500 (traceable fixed costs of $16,500 less the $12,000 cost of people to be reassigned to other divisions). Generally, it is unprofitable to eliminate any segment for which contribution margin exceeds avoidable fixed costs. This rule is actually a condensed version of the incremental profit analysis.

If you apply this rule to the Hugh Corporation example, the analysis would be as follows:

Division B

Contribution margin	$7,500
Less avoidable fixed costs	4,500
Profit contribution	$3,000

In such an analysis, corporate profits would actually decrease by $3,000 if Division B were eliminated. This conclusion is valid even though operating reports for Division B disclose a loss of $9,000.

As shown in Exhibit 12-6, the decision analysis used to decide about eliminating an unprofitable segment (product line, service, or division) requires two decision analysis tools: (1) contribution margin reporting and (2) incremental analysis. Contribution margin reporting helped identify traceable and avoidable fixed costs relevant to the decision, whereas incremental analysis assisted in comparing the operating results with and without the segment.

Sell or Process-Further Decisions

OBJECTIVE 6e
Evaluate alternatives involving sell or process-further decisions

The sell or process-further decision was briefly mentioned when analyzing the allocation of joint or common processing costs in Chapter 5. The choice between selling a product at the split-off point or processing it further is a short-run operating decision about joint products. The decision to process a joint product beyond split-off point requires an analysis of incremental revenues and costs of the two alternate courses of action. Additional processing adds value to a product and increases its selling price above the amount it may have been sold for at split-off. The decision to process further depends on whether the increase in total revenue exceeds additional costs for processing beyond split-off. *Joint costs incurred before split-off do not affect the decision.* These costs are incurred regardless of the point at which the products are sold. Thus they are irrelevant to the decision. Only future costs differing between alternatives are relevant to the decision.

Maximizing company profits is the objective of sell or process-further decisions. For example, assume that Buttery Gardening Supplies, Inc., produces various products to enhance plant growth. In one process three products emerge from the joint initial phase: Gro-Pow, Gro-Pow II, and Gro-Supreme. For each 20,000-pound batch of materials converted into products, $120,000 in joint production costs are incurred. At split-off, 50 percent of the output becomes Gro-Pow, 30 percent becomes Gro-Pow II, and 20 percent becomes Gro-Supreme. Each product is processed beyond split-off, and the following additional variable costs are incurred:

Product	Pounds	Additional Processing Costs
Gro-Pow	10,000	$24,000
Gro-Pow II	6,000	38,000
Gro-Supreme	4,000	33,500
Totals	20,000	$95,500

Christine & Hill, landscapers, has offered to purchase all joint products at split-off for the following prices per pound: Gro-Pow, $8; Gro-Pow II, $24; and Gro-Supreme, $40. To help decide whether to sell at split-off or process the products further, Buttery management requested an incremental analysis. This analysis is to compare increases in revenue and increases in processing costs for each alternative.

Exhibit 12-8 reveals the selling prices of the three products at split-off and if processed further. The exhibit also contains the incremental analysis. As illustrated, products Gro-Pow and Gro-Supreme should be processed further since each will cause a significant increase in overall company profit. If Gro-Pow II can be sold to Christine & Hill, the company will avoid a $2,000 loss from further processing. Note that the $120,000 joint processing costs are irrevelant to the decision since they will be incurred with either alternative.

Measuring incremental costs for additional processing beyond split-off can create problems. Additional costs of materials, labor, and variable overhead are incremental since these costs are caused by additional processing. However, supervisors' salaries, property taxes, insurance, and other fixed costs incurred regardless of the production decision are not incremental costs. Incremental processing costs should include only production costs if a product is processed beyond split-off. Fixed overhead costs common to other production activity must be excluded from a sell or process-further incremental analysis.

Exhibit 12-8.   Incremental Analysis—Sell or Process-Further Decision

Buttery Gardening Supplies, Inc.
Incremental Analysis—Sell or Process-Further Decision

Unit selling price data

Product	If Sold at Split-Off	If Sold After Additional Processing
Gro-Pow	$ 8	$12
Gro-Pow II	24	30
Gro-Supreme	40	50

Incremental analysis per 20,000-pound batch

Product	(1) Pounds	(2) Total Revenue if Sold at Split-Off	(3) Total Revenue if Sold After Processing Further	(4) Incremental Revenue (3) − (2)	(5) Incremental Costs	(6) Effect on Overall Profit (4) − (5)
Gro-Pow	10,000	$ 80,000	$120,000	$40,000	$24,000	$16,000
Gro-Pow II	6,000	144,000	180,000	36,000	38,000	(2,000)
Gro-Supreme	4,000	160,000	200,000	40,000	33,500	6,500

Chapter Review

Review of Learning Objectives

1. **Define and identify information relevant to decision making.**
   Any future cost, revenue, or resource usage data utilized in decision analyses that will be different for alternative courses of action are considered relevant decision information.   Recognition of relevant data comes from developing a comparative analysis of the decision alternatives.

2. Describe the steps in the management decision cycle.
   The decision cycle begins with discovery of a problem or resource need. Then various alternative courses of action to solve the problem or meet the need are identified. Next, a complete analysis to determine the effects of each alternative on business operations is prepared. With this supporting data, the decision maker chooses the best alternative. After the decision has been carried out, the accountant should do a post-audit to see if the decision was correct or if other needs have arisen.

3. Calculate unit costs using variable costing procedures.
   Variable costing uses only variable *manufacturing* costs for product costing and inventory valuation. Direct materials costs, direct labor costs, and variable factory overhead costs are the only elements used to compute product costs. Fixed factory overhead costs are considered costs of the current period and are not included in inventories.

4. Prepare an income statement using the contribution margin reporting format.
   Unlike the conventional form of income reporting that depends on the absorption costing concept, the contribution form is based on variable costing procedures. Variable costs of goods sold and variable selling expenses are subtracted from sales to arrive at contribution margin. All fixed costs, including those from manufacturing, selling, and administration, are subtracted from contribution margin to determine net income (before taxes).

5. Develop decision data using the technique of incremental analysis.
   Incremental analysis is a form of decision reporting in which various decision alternatives are identified and differences in information about them are examined. When all revenue and cost data are examined this way, data relevant to the decision are highlighted since they are the ones where differences exist. Revenue and cost items that are the same under the various alternatives are irrelevant to the decision.

6. Evaluate alternatives involving (a) make-or-buy decisions, (b) special-order decisions, (c) scarce-resource/sales-mix decisions, (d) decisions to eliminate unprofitable segments, and (e) sell or process-further decisions.
   Make-or-buy decision analysis helps management decide whether to buy a part used in product assembly or to make the part inside the company. This analysis centers on an incremental view of the costs of each alternative. Special-order decisions concern unused capacity and finding the lowest acceptable selling price of a product. Generally, fixed costs are irrelevant to the decision since these costs were covered by regular operations. Contribution margin is a key decision yardstick. Sales-mix analysis is used to find the most profitable combination of product sales when a company makes more than one product using a common scarce resource. A similar approach may be used for decisions about profitable sales territories, service lines, or corporate segments. Comparative analyses using the contribution reporting format are important in all these studies. The decision to eliminate unprofitable products, services, or company segments requires an incremental analysis. This analysis should compare operating results that include the questionable segment against operating results without the segment's traceable and avoidable revenues and costs. Both income statements are prepared by following the contribution margin reporting format. Sell or process-further decisions are also based on comparisons of incremental revenues and costs of the two alternatives. Joint processing costs are irrelevant to the decision since they are identical for either alternative.

Review of Concepts and Terminology

The following important concepts were introduced in this chapter:

(L.O.1)   Relevant decision information: Future cost, revenue, or resource usage data that will differ for the various alternatives being evaluated.

(L.O.3)   Variable costing: A costing method that uses only the variable manufacturing costs for product costing and inventory valuation.

(L.O.5)   Incremental analysis: An approach often used in decision reporting that compares different alternatives by looking only at information differences.

(L.O.6)   Make-or-buy decision: A decision analysis that identifies those cost and revenue elements relevant to deciding whether to make or buy some or all parts used in product assembly operations.

(L.O.6)   Special-order decisions: Whether to accept unexpected special product orders.

(L.O.6)   Sales-mix analysis: Determining the most profitable combination of product sales when a company produces more than one product or offers more than one service.

Other important terms introduced in this chapter are:

avoidable costs (p. 465)
decision model (p. 452)
parameters (p. 452)
traceable fixed costs (p. 464)
variables (p. 452)

Review Problem: Short-Run Operating Decision Analysis

In 1981, Frank Calacchi formed National Services, Inc., a company specializing in repair and maintenance services for the home and its surroundings. To date, National has six offices in major cities across the country. Fourteen services, ranging from plumbing repair to appliance repair to lawn care, are available to the home owner. During the past two years, the company's profitability has decreased, and Calacchi wants to determine which service lines are not meeting the company's profit targets. Once the unprofitable service lines are identified, he will either eliminate them or set higher prices. If higher prices are set, all variable and fixed operating, selling, and general administration costs will be covered by the price structure. The following data from the most recent year-end closing was available for the analysis. Four service lines are under serious review.

Required

1. Analyze the performance of the four services being reviewed.
2. Should Calacchi eliminate any of the service lines? Why?
3. Identify some possible causes for poor performance by the services.
4. What factors would lead you to raise the fee for a service rather than eliminate the service?

National Services, Inc.
Service Profit and Loss Summary
For the Year Ended December 31, 19x8

	Auto Repair Service	Boat Repair Service	Tile Floor Repair Service	Tree Trimming Service	Total Company Impact
Sales	$297,500	$114,300	$126,400	$97,600	$635,800
Less variable costs					
Direct labor	$119,000	$ 40,005	$ 44,240	$34,160	$237,405
Operating supplies	14,875	5,715	6,320	4,880	31,790
Small tools	11,900	4,572	5,056	7,808	29,336
Replacement parts	59,500	22,860	25,280	0	107,640
Truck expenses	0	11,430	12,640	14,640	38,710
Selling expenses	44,625	17,145	18,960	9,760	90,490
Other variable costs	5,950	2,286	2,528	1,952	12,716
Total	$255,850	$104,013	$115,024	$73,200	$548,087
Contribution margin	$ 41,650	$ 10,287	$ 11,376	$24,400	$ 87,713
Less traceable fixed costs	74,200	29,600	34,700	28,400	166,900
Service margin	($32,550)	($ 19,313)	($ 23,324)	($ 4,000)	($ 79,187)
Less nontraceable joint fixed costs					32,100
Net income before taxes					($111,287)
Avoidable fixed costs included in traceable fixed costs above	$ 35,800	$ 16,300	$ 24,100	$ 5,200	$ 81,400

Answer to Review Problem

1. When analyzing the performance of four service lines for possible elimination, you should concentrate on the revenues and costs to be eliminated if the service is eliminated. You should start your analysis with contribution margin because all sales and variable costs will be eliminated. By subtracting the avoidable fixed costs from contribution margin, you will find the profit or loss that will be eliminated if the service is eliminated. These calculations are shown on the following page.

	Auto Repair Service	Boat Repair Service	Tile Floor Repair Service	Tree Trimming Service	Total Company Impact
Contribution margin	$41,650	$10,287	$11,376	$24,400	$87,713
Less avoidable fixed costs	35,800	16,300	24,100	5,200	81,400
Profit (loss) lost if service is eliminated	$ 5,850	($ 6,013)	($12,724)	$19,200	$ 6,313

2. From the analysis in part 1, you can see that the company will improve by $18,737 ($6,013 + $12,724) if the Boat Repair Service and the Tile Floor Service are eliminated.
3. There are several possible causes for poor performance by the four services, including
   a. Low service fee being charged
   b. Inadequate advertising of the service
   c. High direct labor costs
   d. Other variable costs too high
   e. Poor management of fixed cost levels
   f. Excessive management costs
4. To judge the adequacy of the service fees being charged, you should first look at the contribution margin percentages. This additional bit of information will help support pricing decisions for the four services.

	Auto Repair Service	Boat Repair Service	Tile Floor Repair Service	Tree Trimming Service
Sales	$297,500	$114,300	126,400	$97,600
Contribution margin	$ 41,650	$ 10,287	$ 11,376	$24,400
Contribution margin percentage	14.00%	9.00%	9.00%	25.00%

As you can see, only 9 percent of the selling price is available for fixed costs and profit from the Boat Repair and Tile Floor Repair services. This is a thin margin with which to work. An increase in fees seems appropriate. Even fees for the Auto Repair Service may need to be increased.

Also, remember that there were large amounts of unavoidable and nontraceable fixed costs reported. These costs may need to be analyzed too. Although they may or may not be avoidable, these costs must be covered by fees if the company is to remain profitable.

Chapter Assignments

Questions

1. Define strategic planning.
2. "Strategic planning provides the basic framework for applying short-run period planning." Do you agree with this statement? If so, why?
3. What does the term *relevant decision information* mean? What are the two important characteristics of such information?
4. Describe and discuss the five steps of the management decision cycle.
5. Describe the concept of variable costing. How does variable costing differ from absorption costing?
6. Is variable costing widely used for financial reporting purposes? Defend your answer.
7. What is the connection between variable costing and the contribution margin approach to reporting?
8. Are variable costs always relevant? Defend your response.
9. Identify and discuss the steps required to build a decision model.
10. What are the objectives of incremental analysis? What types of decision analyses depend on the incremental approach?
11. Illustrate and discuss some qualitative inputs into decision analysis.
12. How does one determine which data are relevant to a make-or-buy decision?
13. Under what circumstances should profit contribution per machine hour be considered in a make-or-buy decision?
14. When pricing a special order, what justifies excluding fixed overhead costs from the analysis? Under what circumstances are fixed costs relevant to the pricing decision?
15. What questions must be answered in trying to make the most of product line profitability? Give examples of approaches to the solution of this question.
16. For sales-mix decisions, what criteria can be used to select products that will maximize net income?
17. Why is the term *avoidable cost* used in relation to alternatives to eliminating a segment?
18. Distinguish between the terms *avoidable cost* and *traceable cost.*
19. Why are joint processing costs irrelevant to the decision to sell a product at split-off or process it further?
20. Is incremental analysis important to the sell or process-further decision? If so, why?

Classroom Exercises

Exercise 12-1.
Relevant Data and
Incremental
Analysis
(L.O. 1, 5)

Mr. Richard, business manager for Bebee Industries, must select a new typewriter for his secretary. Rental of Model A, which is like the typewriter now being used, is $400 per year. Model B, a deluxe typewriter, rents for $600 per year, but it will require a new desk for the secretary. The annual desk rental charge is $200. The secretary's salary of $500 per month will not change. If Model B is rented, $80 in training costs will be incurred. Model B has greater capacity and is expected to save $550 per year in part-time secretarial wages. Upkeep and operating costs will not differ between the two models.

1. Identify the relevant data in this problem.
2. Prepare an incremental analysis to aid the business manager's decision.

Exercise 12-2.
Relevant Costs and
Revenues
(L.O. 1)

Old Dominion Enterprises manufactures various household metal products, such as window frames, light fixtures, and doorknobs. In 19x8 the company produced 20,000 square doorknobs but sold only 2,000 units at $10.00 each. The remaining units cannot be sold through normal channels. For inventory purposes, costs on December 31, 19x8, included the following data on unsold units:

Direct materials	$2.00
Direct labor	3.00
Variable overhead	.50
Fixed overhead	1.50
Cost per knob	$7.00

The 18,000 square knobs can be sold to a scrap dealer in another state for $3.50 each. A business license for this state will cost Old Dominion $400. Shipping expenses will average $.05 per knob.

1. Identify the relevant costs and revenues for the scrap-sale alternative.
2. Assume the square knobs can be reprocessed to produce round knobs, which normally have the same $7.00 unit cost components and sell for $8.00 each. Rework costs will be $4.50 per unit. Determine the most profitable alternative, reprocessing or selling as scrap.

Exercise 12-3.
Variable Costing:
Unit Cost
Computation
(L.O. 3)

Suny Corporation produces a full line of energy-tracking devices that can detect and track all forms of thermochemical energy-emitting space vehicles. The following cost data are provided: direct materials cost $985,000 for 4 units. Direct labor for assembly is 1,590 hours per unit at $11.50 per hour. Variable factory overhead is $28.00 per direct labor hour. Fixed factory overhead is $1,792,000 per month (based on an average production of 28 units per month). Packaging materials come to $27,200 for 4 units, and packaging labor is 20 hours per unit at $8.50 per hour. Advertising and marketing cost $196,750 per month, and other fixed selling and administrative costs are $287,680 per month.

1. From these cost data, find the unit production cost, using both variable costing and absorption costing methods.
2. Assume the current month's ending inventory is 15 units. Compute the inventory valuation under both variable and absorption costing methods.

Exercise 12-4.
Income Statement:
Contribution
Reporting Format
(L.O. 4)

The income statement in the conventional reporting format for Brosi Products, Inc., for the year ended December 31, 19x9, appeared as shown.
   Fixed manufacturing costs of $27,600 and $850 are included in Cost of Goods Available for Sale and Ending Inventory, respectively. Total fixed manufacturing costs for 19x9 were $26,540. There were no beginning or ending work in process inventories. All administrative expenses are considered fixed.
   Using this information, prepare an income statement for Brosi Products, Inc., for the year ended December 31, 19x9, based on the contribution reporting format.

Brosi Products, Inc. Income Statement For the Year Ended December 31, 19x9		
Sales		$396,400
Cost of goods sold		
Cost of goods available for sale	$225,290	
Less ending inventory	12,540	212,750
Gross margin from sales		$183,650
Less operating expenses		
Selling expenses		
Variable	$ 99,820	
Fixed	26,980	
Administrative expenses	37,410	164,210
Net income before taxes		$ 19,440

**Exercise 12-5.
Make-or-Buy
Decision
(L.O. 6a)**

One part for a radio assembly being produced by Mount Vernon Audio Systems, Inc., is being purchased for $155 per 100 parts. Management is studying the possibility of manufacturing these parts. Cost and production data are as follows: annual production (usage) is 60,000 units. Fixed costs (all of which remain unchanged whether the part is made or purchased) are $28,500. Variable costs are $.65 per unit for direct materials, $.45 per unit for direct labor, and $.40 per unit for manufacturing overhead.

Using incremental decision analysis, decide whether the company should make the part or continue to purchase it from an outside vendor.

**Exercise 12-6.
Special-Order
Decision
(L.O. 6b)**

Alvin, Kabot, & Hunter, Ltd., produces antique-looking lamp shades. Management has just received a request for a special-design order and must decide whether to accept it. The special order calls for 8,000 shades to be shipped in a total of 200 bulk pack cartons. Shipping costs of $60 per carton will replace normal packing and shipping costs. The purchasing company is offering to pay $24 per shade plus packing and shipping expenses.

The following information has been provided by the accounting department: Annual expected production is 250,000 shades, and the current year's production (before special order) is 260,000 shades. Maximum production capacity is 280,000 shades. Unit cost data include $6.20 for direct materials, $8.00 for direct labor, variable factory overhead of $5.80, and fixed factory overhead of $3.50 ($875,000/ 250,000). Normal packaging and shipping costs per unit come to $2.50, and advertising is $.36 per unit ($90,000/250,000). Other fixed administrative costs are $.88 per unit ($220,000/250,000). Thus total normal cost per unit is $27.24. Per unit selling price is set at $38.00. Total estimated bulk packaging costs ($60 per carton × 200 cartons) are $12,000.

Determine whether this special order should be accepted.

Exercise 12-7.
Scarce-Resource
Usage
(L.O. 6c)

Massasoit, Inc., manufactures two products, which require both machine proc-essing and labor operations. Although there is unlimited demand for both products, Massasoit could devote all its capacities to a single product. Unit prices, cost data, and processing requirements are:

	Product A	Product M
Unit selling price	$40	$110
Unit variable costs	$20	$ 45
Machine hours per unit	.4	1.4
Labor hours per unit	2	6

In 19x9 the company will be limited to 160,000 machine hours and 120,000 labor hours.

1. Compute the quantities of each product to be produced in 19x9.
2. Prepare an income statement for the product volume computed in **1**.

Exercise 12-8.
Elimination of
Unprofitable
Segment
(L.O. 6d)

Stockholm Glass, Inc., has three divisions: Atta, Nio, and Tio. The divisional income summaries for 19x8 revealed the following:

Stockholm Glass, Inc.
Divisional Profit Summary and Decision Analysis

	Atta Division	Nio Division	Tio Division	Total Company
Sales	$390,000	$433,000	$837,000	$1,660,000
Variable costs	247,000	335,000	472,000	1,054,000
Contribution margin	$143,000	$ 98,000	$365,000	$ 606,000
Less traceable fixed costs	166,000	114,000	175,000	455,000
Divisional income	($ 23,000)	($ 16,000)	$190,000	$ 151,000
Less unallocated fixed costs				82,000
Net income before taxes				$ 69,000

A detailed analysis of the traceable fixed costs revealed the following:

	Atta Division	Nio Division	Tio Division
Avoidable fixed costs	$154,000	$ 96,000	$139,000
Unavoidable fixed costs	12,000	18,000	36,000
Totals	$166,000	$114,000	$175,000

Based on the 19x8 income summaries, determine whether it would be profitable for the company to eliminate one or more of its segments. Identify which division(s) should be eliminated, and compute how much the resulting increase in total net income would be before taxes.

Exercise 12-9.
Sell or Process-
Further Decision
(L.O. 6e)

Bob Owens Marketeers, Inc., has developed a promotional program for a large shopping center in Hopewell, New Jersey. After investing $360,000 in the promotion campaign, the firm is ready to present its client with a (1) TV advertising program, (2) series of brochures for mass mailing, and (3) special rotating BIG SALE schedule for 10 of the 28 tenants in the shopping center. Following are the revenue from the original contract with the shopping center and an offer for an add-on contract, which extends the original contract terms:

	Contract Terms	
	Original Contract Terms	Extended Contract Including Add-On Terms
TV advertising program	$420,000	$480,000
Brochure package	110,000	130,000
Rotating BIG SALE schedule	70,000	90,000
Totals	$600,000	$700,000

Owens estimates that the following additional costs will be incurred by extending the contract:

	TV Program	Brochures	BIG SALE Schedule
Direct labor	$30,000	$ 9,000	$7,000
Variable overhead costs	22,000	14,000	6,000
Fixed overhead costs*	12,000	4,000	2,000

* 20% are unavoidable fixed costs applied to this contract.

1. Compute the costs that will be incurred for each part of the add-on portion of the contract.
2. Should Bob Owens Marketeers, Inc., accept the add-on contract or should they ask for a final settlement check based on the original contract only? Defend your answer.
3. If management of the shopping center indicated the terms of the add-on contract were negotiable, how should the Owens group respond?

Interpreting Accounting Information

Internal Management Information: Falcetta Can Opener Company, Special-Order Decision
(L.O. 6b)

Falcetta Can Opener Company is a subsidiary of Frank Appliances, Inc. The can opener Falcetta produces is in strong demand. Sales during the present year, 19x9, are expected to hit the 1,000,000 mark. Full plant capacity is 1,150,000 units, but the 1,000,000-unit mark was considered normal capacity for the current year. The following unit price and cost breakdown is applicable in 19x9:

	Per Unit
Sales price	$45.00
Less manufacturing costs	
Materials	$ 9.00
Direct labor	7.00
Overhead: variable	4.00
fixed	6.00
Total manufacturing costs	$26.00
Gross margin	$19.00
Less selling and administrative expenses	
Selling: variable	$ 2.50
fixed	2.00
Administrative, fixed	3.00
Packaging, variable*	1.50
Total selling and administrative expenses	$ 9.00
Net profit before taxes	$10.00

* Three types of packaging are available: deluxe, $1.50/unit; plain, $1.00/unit; bulk pack, $.50/unit.

During November, the company received three special-order requests from large chain-store companies. These orders are not part of the budgeted 1,000,000-unit sales for 19x9, but company officials think that sufficient capacity exists for one order to be accepted. Orders received and their terms are:

Order 1: 75,000 can openers @ $40.00/unit, deluxe packaging

Order 2: 90,000 can openers @ $36.00/unit, plain packaging

Order 3: 125,000 can openers @ $31.50/unit, bulk packaging

Since these orders were made directly to company officials, no variable selling costs will be incurred.

1. Analyze the profitability of each of the three special orders.
2. Which special order should be accepted?

Problem Set A

Problem 12A-1.
Variable Costing:
Contribution
Approach to
Income Statement
(L.O. 3, 4)

Interior designers often use the deluxe carpet products of McCoy Mills, Inc. The Thomas Blend is the company's top-of-the-line product. In March 19x8 McCoy produced 137,500 square yards and sold 124,900 square yards of Thomas Blend. Factory operating data for the year included (a) direct materials used, $1,203,125; (b) direct labor, .75 direct labor hours per square yard at $12 per hour; (c) variable factory overhead, $240,625; and (d) fixed factory overhead, $343,750. Other expenses included variable selling expenses, $149,880; fixed selling expenses, $155,000; and fixed general and administrative expenses, $242,500. Total sales revenue equaled $3,747,000. All production occurred in March, and there was no work in process at month end. Goods are usually shipped when completed, but at the end of March, 12,600 square yards still awaited shipment.

Required

1. Compute the unit cost and ending finished goods inventory value, using (a) variable costing procedures and (b) absorption costing procedures.
2. Prepare the year-end income statement for McCoy Mills, Inc., using the (a) contribution format based on variable costing data and (b) conventional format based on absorption costing data.

Problem 12A-2.
Make-or-Buy
Decision
(L.O. 6a)

The Dimon Furniture Company of Utica, New York, is famous for its lines of dining room furniture. One full department is engaged in the production of the Annette line, an elegant but affordable dining room set. To date the company has been manufacturing all pieces of the set, including the six chairs that go with each set.

Management has just received word that a company in Greenville, South Carolina, is willing to produce the chairs for Dimon Furniture Company at a total purchase price of $6,240,000 for the annual demand. Company records show that the following costs have been incurred producing the chairs: (a) wood materials, $1,250 for 100 chairs; (b) cloth materials, $650 for 100 chairs; (c) direct labor, 1.2 hours per chair at $12.00 per hour; (d) variable factory overhead, $6.00 per direct labor hour; and (e) fixed factory overhead: depreciation, $455,000; other, $309,400. Fixed factory overhead would continue whether or not the chairs are produced. Assume that idle facilities cannot be used for any other purpose and that annual usage is 156,000 chairs.

Required

1. Prepare an incremental decision analysis to determine whether the chairs should be made by the company or purchased from the outside supplier in Greenville.
2. Compute the unit cost to make one chair and to buy one chair.

Problem 12A-3.
Special-Order
Decision
(L.O. 6b)

On March 16, the Jean Harry Boat Division of Anderson Industries received a special-order request for 320, 10-foot aluminum row-type fishing boats. Operating on a fiscal year ending May 31, the division already had orders that would allow them to produce at budget levels for the period. However, extra capacity existed to produce the 320 additional boats.

Terms of the special order called for a selling price of $225 per boat, with the customer paying all shipping costs. No sales personnel were involved in soliciting this order.

The 10-foot fishing boat has the following cost estimates associated with it: (a) direct materials, aluminum, two $4' \times 8'$ sheets at $45 per sheet; (b) direct labor, 8 hours at $12 per hour; (c) variable factory overhead, $3.50 per direct labor hour; (d) fixed factory overhead, $5.50 per direct labor hour; (e) variable selling expenses, $36.50 per boat; and (f) variable shipping expenses, $27.25 per boat.

Required

1. Prepare an analysis for management of the Jean Harry Division to use in deciding whether to accept or reject the special order. What decision should be made?
2. What would be the lowest possible price the Jean Harry Division could charge per boat for this special order and still make a $3,000 profit on it?

Problem 12A-4.
Scarce-Resource/
Sales-Mix
Analysis
(L.O. 6c)

The vice president of finance for Arizona Machine Tool, Inc., is evaluating the profitability of the company's four product lines. During the current year the company will operate at full machine-hour capacity. The following production data have been compiled:

Product	Current Year's Production (Units)	Total Machine Hours Used
24F	60,000	150,000
37N	100,000	200,000
29T	40,000	40,000
40U	180,000	90,000

Sales and operating cost data are as follows:

	Product 24F	Product 37N	Product 29T	Product 40U
Selling price per unit	$40.00	$50.00	$60.00	$70.00
Unit variable manufacturing cost	16.00	34.00	42.00	58.00
Unit fixed manufacturing cost	8.00	6.00	5.00	4.00
Unit variable selling cost	4.00	4.00	9.00	6.50
Unit fixed administrative cost	6.00	4.00	6.00	3.50

Required

1. Compute the machine hours needed to produce one unit of each product type.
2. Determine the contribution margin of each product type.
3. Which product line(s) should the company's sales force push? Why?

**Problem 12A-5.
Analysis to
Eliminate an
Unprofitable
Product**
(L.O. 6d)

Seven years ago, Norton & Wilson Publishing Company produced its first book. Since then, the company has added four more books to its product list. Management is considering proposals for three more new books, but editorial capacity limits the company to producing seven books. Before deciding which of the proposed books to publish, management wants you to evaluate the performance of its present book list. Following are the revenue and cost data for the recent year (each book is identified by the author or authors):

Norton & Wilson Publishing Company
Product Profit and Loss Summary
For the Year Ended December 31, 19x6

	Marc & Bjorn	Polk & Lorenz	Wojeck & Williams	Harrison	Bornren	Company Totals
Sales	$813,800	$782,000	$634,200	$944,100	$707,000	$3,881,100
Less variable costs						
Materials and binding	$325,520	$312,800	$190,260	$283,230	$212,100	$1,323,910
Editorial services	81,380	78,200	63,420	47,205	70,700	340,905
Author royalties	130,208	125,120	101,472	151,056	113,120	620,976
Sales commissions	162,760	156,400	95,130	141,615	141,400	697,305
Other selling costs	40,682	54,740	31,708	28,334	70,700	226,164
Totals	$740,550	$727,260	$481,990	$651,440	$608,020	$3,209,260
Contribution margin	$ 73,250	$ 54,740	$152,210	$292,660	$ 98,980	$ 671,840
Less traceable fixed costs	87,250	91,240	79,610	100,460	72,680	431,240
Product margin	($ 14,000)	($ 36,500)	$ 72,600	$192,200	$ 26,300	$ 240,600
Less nontraceable joint fixed costs						82,400
Net income before taxes						$ 158,200
Avoidable fixed costs included in traceable fixed costs above	$ 31,200	$ 35,100	$ 29,400	$ 39,100	$ 28,800	$ 163,600

Projected data for the proposed new books are Book A, sales, $450,000, contribution margin, $45,000; Book B, sales, $725,000, contribution margin, $25,200; and Book C, sales, $913,200, contribution margin, $115,500.

Required

1. Analyze the performance of the five books being published.
2. Should the company eliminate any of its present products? If so, which one(s)?
3. List possible causes for the poor performance of the books you selected to eliminate.
4. Identify the new books you would use to replace those eliminated. Justify your answer.

Problem Set B

**Problem 12B-1.
Variable Costing:
Contribution
Approach to
Income Statement
(L.O. 3, 4)**

Roofing tile is the major product of the Maine/Orono Corporation. The company had a particularly good year in 19x9 producing 82,650 cases (units) of tile and selling 78,400 cases. Direct materials used cost $363,660; direct labor was $239,685; variable factory overhead was $247,950; fixed factory overhead was $165,300; variable selling expenses were $117,600; fixed selling expenses were $134,325; and fixed administrative expenses were $99,750. Selling price was $20 per case. There were no partially completed jobs in process at the beginning or the end of the year. Finished goods inventory had been used up at the end of the previous year, 19x8.

Required

1. Compute the unit cost and ending finished goods inventory value, using (a) variable costing procedures and (b) absorption costing procedures.
2. Prepare the year-end income statement for the Maine/Orono Corporation using the (a) contribution format based on variable costing data and (b) conventional format based on absorption costing data.

**Problem 12B-2.
Make-or-Buy
Decision
(L.O. 6a)**

The Goldey Beacom Refrigerator Company purchases and installs defrost clocks in its products. The clocks cost $232 per case, and each case contains twenty-four clocks. The supplier recently gave notice that effective in thirty days, the price will rise 50 percent. The company has idle equipment that could be used to produce similar defrost clocks with only a few changes in the equipment.

The following cost estimates have been prepared under the assumption that the company could make the product itself. Direct materials would cost $172.80 per twenty-four clocks. Direct labor required would be six minutes per clock at a labor rate of $18.00 per hour. Variable factory overhead would be $4.30 per clock. Fixed factory overhead, which would be incurred under either decision alternative, would be $96,400 a year for depreciation and $239,200 a year for other expenses. Production and usage are estimated to be 96,000 clocks a year. (Assume the idle equipment could not be used for any other purpose.)

Required

1. Prepare an incremental decision analysis to decide whether the defrost clocks should be made within the company or purchased from the outside supplier at the higher rate.
2. Compute the unit cost to make one clock and to buy one clock.

**Problem 12B-3.
Special-Order
Decision
(L.O. 6b)**

Hughson Resorts, Ltd., has approached NYC Technical Printers, Inc., with a special order to produce 300,000 two-page brochures. Most of NYC Technical's work consists of recurring short-run orders. Hughson Resorts is offering a one-time order, but NYC Technical does have the capacity to handle the order over a two-month period.

Hughson's management has stated that the company would be unwilling to pay more than $38 per 1,000 brochures. The following cost data were assembled by NYC Technical's controller for this decision analysis: direct materials (paper) would be $22.50 per 1,000 brochures. Direct labor costs would be $4.80 per 1,000 brochures. Direct materials (ink) would be $2.40 per 1,000 brochures. Variable production overhead would be $4.20 per 1,000 brochures. Machine maintenance (fixed cost) is $1.00 per direct labor dollar. Other fixed production overhead amounts to $2.40 per direct labor dollar. Variable packing costs would be $4.30 per 1,000 brochures. Also, the share of general and administrative expenses (fixed costs) to be allocated would be $5.25 per direct labor dollar.

Required

1. Prepare an analysis for NYC Technical's management to use in deciding whether to accept or reject Hughson Resorts' offer. What decision should be made?
2. What is the lowest possible price NYC Technical can charge per thousand and still make a $6,000 profit on the order?

Problem 12B-4.
Scarce-Resource/
Sales-Mix
Analysis
(L.O. 6c)

Management at Coppin Chemical Company is evaluating its product mix in an attempt to maximize profits. For the past two years, Coppin has produced five products, and all have a large market in which to expand market share. Marjorie Lyles, Coppin's controller, has gathered data from current operations and wants you to analyze it for her. Sales and operating data are as follows:

	Product AE42	Product BF53	Product CG64	Product DH75	Product EI86
Variable production costs	$ 51,000	$ 81,000	$101,920	$ 97,440	$156,800
Variable selling costs	10,200	5,400	12,480	20,160	26,880
Fixed production costs	20,400	21,600	29,120	18,480	22,400
Fixed administrative costs	3,400	5,400	6,240	10,080	8,960
Total sales	$102,000	$126,000	$166,400	$151,200	$224,000
Units produced and sold	85,000	45,000	26,000	14,000	32,000
Machine hours used*	17,000	18,000	20,800	16,800	22,400

* Coppin's scarce resource, machine hours, is operating at full capacity.

Required

1. Compute the machine hours needed to produce 1 unit of each product.
2. Determine the contribution margin per machine hour for each product.
3. Which product line(s) should be targeted for market share expansion? Why?

Problem 12B-5.
Analysis to
Eliminate an
Unprofitable
Segment
(L.O. 6d)

Don Baker Sporting Goods, Inc., is a nationwide distributor of sporting equipment. The home office is located in Winter Springs, Florida, and four branch distributorships are in Phenix City, Alabama; Rockford, Illinois; Temecula, California; and Helena, Montana. On the following page are the operating results for 19x8 (all amounts in the summary are in thousands of dollars):

Don Baker Sporting Goods, Inc.
Segment Profit and Loss Summary
For the Year Ended December 31, 19x8

	Phenix Branch	Rockford Branch	Temecula Branch	Helena Branch	Total Company
Sales	$6,008	$6,712	$6,473	$8,059	$27,252
Less variable costs					
Purchases	$3,471	$4,119	$3,970	$5,246	$16,806
Wages and salaries	694	702	687	841	2,924
Sales commissions	535	610	519	881	2,545
Selling expenses	96	102	79	127	404
Totals	$4,796	$5,533	$5,255	$7,095	$22,679
Contribution margin	$1,212	$1,179	$1,218	$ 964	$ 4,573
Less traceable fixed costs	972	1,099	808	1,059	3,938
Branch margin	$ 240	$ 80	$ 410	($ 95)	$ 635
Less nontraceable joint costs					325
Net income before taxes					$ 310

The corporate president, Mr. Shapiro, is upset with overall corporate operating results, particularly with results of the Helena branch. He has requested the controller to work up a complete profitability analysis of the four branch operations and to study the possibility of closing the Helena branch. The controller needed the following information before the analysis could be completed:

1. Shipping costs were 20 percent of the cost of goods purchased by the Helena branch.
2. Of the uncontrollable fixed costs traceable to the branch operations, the following were avoidable:

Phenix	$782,000	Temecula	$648,000
Rockford	$989,000	Helena	$849,000

3. An analysis of sales revealed

	Average Growth (%), Last Five Years	Growth (%), 19x8	Future Average Growth Rate (%)
Phenix	8	7	5
Rockford	7	5	6
Temecula	10	13	8
Helena	22	20	10

Required

1. Analyze the performance of each branch president. (*Hint:* Convert the segment profit and loss summary to a common-size statement.)

2. Should the corporation eliminate the Helena branch?
3. Are there other branches Shapiro should be concerned about? Why?
4. List possible causes for the corporation's poor performance.

Management Decision Case

**Metzger Company:
Sell or Process-
Further Decision
(L.O. 6e)**

Management at Metzger Company is considering a proposal to install a third production department within its factory building. With the company's present production setup, raw material is processed through Department I to produce materials A and B in equal proportions. Material A is then processed through Department II to yield product C. Material B is sold as-is at $20.25 per pound. Product C has a selling price of $100.00 per pound. Current per-pound standard costs used by Metzger Company are:

	Department I (Materials A & B)	Department II (Product C)	(Material B)
Prior department's cost	$ —	$53.03	$13.47
Direct materials	20.00	—	—
Direct labor	7.00	12.00	—
Variable overhead	3.00	5.00	—
Fixed overhead			
Traceable	2.25	2.25	—
Allocated (⅔, ⅓)	1.00	1.00	—
	$33.25	$73.28	$13.47

These standard costs were developed by using an estimated production volume of 200,000 pounds of raw material as the standard volume. The company assigns Department I costs to materials A and B in proportion to their net sales values at the point of separation. These values are computed by deducting subsequent standard production costs from sales prices. The $300,000 in common fixed overhead costs are allocated to the two producing departments on the basis of the space used by the departments.

The proposed Department III would be used to process material B into Product D. It is expected that any quantity of Product D can be sold for $30 per pound. Standard costs per pound under this proposal were developed by using 200,000 pounds of raw material as the standard volume. Those costs are as follows:

	Department I (Materials A & B)	Department II (Product C)	Department III (Product D)
Prior department's costs	$ —	$52.80	$13.20
Direct materials	20.00	—	—
Direct labor	7.00	12.00	5.50
Variable overhead	3.00	5.00	2.00
Fixed overhead			
Traceable	2.25	2.25	1.75
Allocated (½, ¼, ¼)	.75	.75	.75
	$33.00	$72.80	$23.20

Required

1. If (a) sales and production levels are expected to remain constant in the foreseeable future and (b) there are no foreseeable alternate uses for the factory space, should Metzger Company install Department III and produce Product D? Show calculations to support your answer.
2. Instead of constant sales and production levels, suppose that under the present production setup, $1,000,000 in additions to the factory building must be made every ten years to accommodate growth. Also suppose that proper maintenance gives these factory additions an infinite life and that all such maintenance costs are included in the standard costs set forth in the text. How would the analysis you performed in **1** be changed if installation of Department III shortened the interval at which the $1,000,000 in factory additions are made from ten years to six years? Be as specific as possible in your answer.

(ICMA adapted)

Capital Expenditure Decisions

LEARNING OBJECTIVES

1. Define and discuss the capital expenditure decision process.
2. Identify and describe steps in the capital expenditure decision cycle.
3. Describe the purpose of the minimum desired rate of return and explain the methods used to arrive at this rate.
4. Identify information relevant to the capital expenditure decision process.
5. Evaluate capital expenditure proposals using (a) the accounting rate-of-return method and (b) the payback period method.
6. Apply the concept of time value of money.
7. Evaluate capital expenditure proposals using the discounted cash flow—net present-value method.
8. Analyze capital expenditure decision alternatives that incorporate the effects of income taxes.
9. Rank proposals competing for limited capital expenditure funds.

CHAPTER 13

Capital expenditure decisions involve time periods that can span several years and capital asset purchases representing significant dollar amounts. The success or failure of capital expenditure decisions often makes the difference between operating at a profit or a loss. These long-term decisions require projections of revenues and expenses for many years. Whenever one deals with long-range predictions, much uncertainty is incorporated into the decision process. Therefore, the management accountant must consider all likely outcomes of proposed projects and use realistic rate-of-return forecasts when preparing decision support information for management.

This chapter first looks at the capital expenditure decision process, the steps in the decision cycle, and the meaning and computation of the minimum desired rate of return. After a lengthy review of information relevant to this decision process, the text analyzes three primary evaluation methods, including (1) accounting rate of return, (2) payback period, and (3) discounted cash flow—net present-value. In relation to the discounted cash-flow approach, the concept of time value of money is discussed. The capital expenditure evaluation methods are first analyzed by using before-tax amounts; they are then reanalyzed, using after-tax amounts. These analyses are done so you can see how income taxes affect these decisions. The chapter concludes with an approach to ranking various proposals competing for limited capital expenditure funds. After studying this chapter, you should be able to meet the learning objectives listed on the left.

The Capital Expenditure Decision Process

Among the most important types of decisions facing management are those about when and how much to spend on capital facilities for the company. These are called capital expenditure decisions. Under this heading are decisions about installing new equipment, replacing old equipment, expanding the production area by adding to a building, buying or building a new factory, or acquiring another company. All of these major spending decisions call for careful analysis by the accountant and generally involve comparative analysis of two or more alternatives.

Capital Budgeting: A Cooperative Venture

OBJECTIVE 1
Define and discuss the capital expenditure decision process

The capital expenditure decision-making process, often referred to as **capital budgeting,** consists of identifying the need for a facility, analyzing courses of action to meet that need, preparing reports for management, choosing the best alternative, and rationing capital expenditure funds among competing resource needs. This process calls for input from people in every part of the business organization. Finance people are expected to supply a target cost of capital or desired rate of return for the decision analysis and an estimate of how much money can be spent on any one project. Without this kind of information, a decision cannot be reached. Marketing people identify areas of the business that need plant and facility expansion through their predictions of future sales trends. Management people at all levels help identify facility needs and often prepare preliminary cost estimates of the desired facility. These same people help carry out capital expenditure decisions by trying to keep actual results within cost and revenue estimates.

The management accountant gathers and organizes the decision information into a workable, readable form. Generally, he or she applies one or more evaluation methods to the information gathered for each alternative. The most common capital expenditure proposal evaluation methods are (1) accounting rate-of-return method, (2) payback period method, and (3) discounted cash flow, or net present-value, method. Once these methods have been applied, management can make a choice based on the criteria used for the decision.

The Capital Expenditure Decision Cycle

OBJECTIVE 2
Identify and describe steps in the capital expenditure decision cycle

Capital expenditure decision analysis involves the evaluation of alternate proposals for large capital expenditures, including considerations for financing the projects. Referred to earlier as capital budgeting, capital expenditure decision analyses affect both short-term and long-term planning activities of management. Figure 13-1 illustrates the time span of the capital expenditure planning process. Most companies have developed a long-term plan, either a five- or ten-year projection of operations. Large capital expenditures should be an integral part of a long-term plan. Anticipated additions or changes to a product line, replacements of equipment, and acquisitions of other companies are examples of items to be included in long-term capital expenditure plans. In addition, capital expenditure needs may arise from changes in current operations and may not be part of the company's long-term plan.[1]

Chapter 8 discussed the master budget. Do you remember that one of the period budgets in the master budget is a capital expenditure budget? How does that capital expenditure budget fit into the planning process and the capital expenditure decision process? To understand this fit,

---

1. The comments in this section are summarized from Henry R. Anderson and Rickard P. Schwartz, ''The Capital Facility Decision,'' *Management Accounting* (National Association of Accountants, February, 1971). Used by permission of National Association of Accountants.

Figure 13-1. Time Span of Capital Expenditure Planning Process

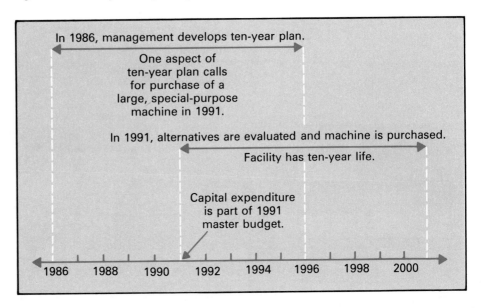

compare it with your current personal situation. You want to become a college graduate. This is your long-term plan. To succeed at this plan, you must take a specific number of courses over a defined time period, usually four or five years. Each of your semester schedules can be compared with the capital expenditure budget in a company's master budget. Long-term plans, such as your goal of a college degree, are not very specific; they are expressed in broad, goal-oriented terms.

As time passes, each annual budget must help accomplish long-term plans. Look again at Figure 13-1. In 1991, the company plans to purchase a large, special-purpose machine. When the ten-year plan was developed, only a broad statement about a plan to purchase the machine was included. There was nothing in the ten-year plan concerning the cost of the machine or the anticipated operating details and costs. The annual master budget for 1991 contains this detailed information. And it is in 1991 that the capital expenditure decision analysis will occur. So, even though capital expenditure decisions that will affect the company for many years are discussed and estimates of future revenues and expenditures are made, the analysis is for the current period. This point is often confusing and needs to be emphasized here so the remainder of the chapter can be studied in the proper perspective. When you have finished Chapter 13, you will have also completed the master budget structured in Chapter 8.

Evaluating capital expenditure proposals, deciding on proposals to be authorized, and implementing capital expenditures are long, involved procedures. Figure 13-2 depicts the capital expenditure, or capital facility, decision cycle. The management accountant's primary responsibilities

Figure 13-2. The Capital Facility Decision Cycle

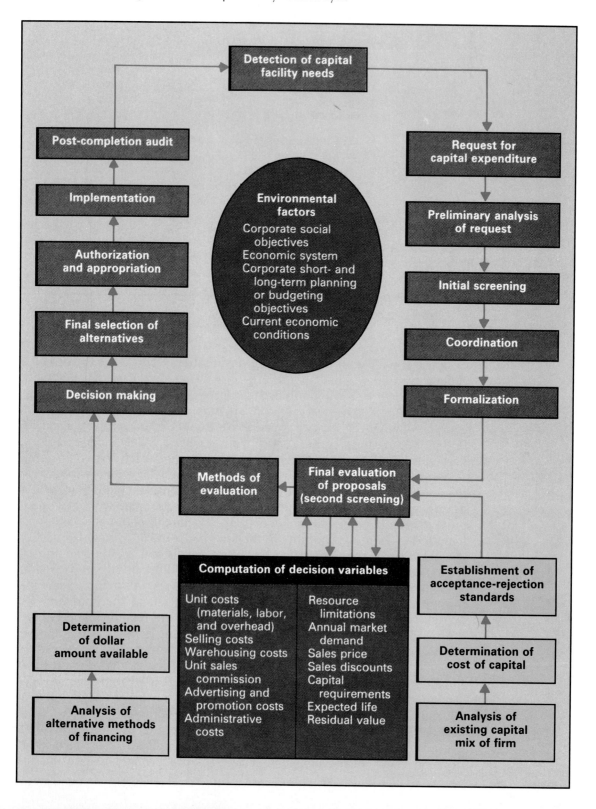

in the decision process center on three functions: (1) final evaluation of proposals, (2) methods of evaluation, and (3) post-completion audit. The first two functions use proposal evaluation methods described later in this chapter. But the management accountant also has related responsibilities in other areas of the decision process. Figure 13-2 places the various phases of capital expenditure planning in perspective. The following paragraphs discuss each phase of that process.

Environmental Factors. The capital expenditure, or capital facility, decision cycle occurs within a defined time period and under constraints imposed by economic policies, conditions, and objectives originating at corporate, industry, and/or national levels. Coordinating short- and long-term capital investment plans within this dynamic environment is management's responsibility, and it is vital to profitable operations.

Detection of Capital Facility Needs. Identifying the need for a new capital facility is the starting point of the decision process. Ideas for capital investment opportunities may originate from past sales experience, changes in sources and quality of raw materials, managerial suggestions, production bottlenecks caused by obsolete equipment, new production or distribution methods, or personnel complaints. Capital facility needs are also identified through proposals to

1. Add new products to the product line
2. Expand capacity in existing product lines
3. Reduce costs in production of existing products without altering operation levels

Request for Capital Expenditure. To facilitate control over capital expenditures, the appropriate manager prepares a formal request for a capital expenditure. The proposed request should include a complete description of the facility under review, reasons a new facility is needed, alternate means of satisfying the need, estimated costs and related cost savings for each alternative, and engineering specifications.

Preliminary Analysis of Requests. In a large company with a highly developed capital expenditure decision process, information contained in requests for a capital expenditure is often verified before initial screening of proposals. The management accountant plays a major role in this activity by helping to identify undesirable or nonqualifying proposals, computational errors, and deficiencies in request information.

Initial Screening. Initial screening processes are used by companies with several branch plants and a highly developed program for capital expenditures. The objective of initial screening is to ensure that the only proposals going forward for further review are those meeting company objectives and the minimum desired rate of return established by management.

Source for Figure 13-2: Henry R. Anderson and Rickard P. Schwartz, "The Capital Facility Decision," *Management Accounting* (National Association of Accountants, February 1971), p. 30.

Acceptance-Rejection Standards. When there are many requests for capital expenditures and limited funds for capital investment, one must establish some acceptance-rejection standard. Such a standard may be expressed as a minimum desired rate of return or as a minimum cash-flow payback period. As shown in Figure 13-2, acceptance-rejection standards are used in the screening processes to identify projects expected to yield inadequate or marginal returns. This step also identifies proposed projects with high demand and return expectations. Cost of capital information is often used to establish minimum desired rates of return on investment. Developing these rates is discussed in detail later in this chapter.

Coordination and Formalization. Before the final screening of proposed projects, alternate proposals must be coordinated and formalized for the decision maker. Coordination involves relating proposed projects to company objectives. Formalization is concerned with structuring the expenditure request to highlight its advantages and to summarize cost-benefit information for top management. Department or division managers often compete for limited capital expenditure funds. The more convincing a capital expenditure request is, the more likely it is to receive final authorization.

Final Evaluation of Proposals. Final evaluation of proposals involves verifying decision variables and applying capital expenditure proposal evaluation methods. The management accountant is primarily responsible for these procedures. The circular-flow diagram in Figure 13-2 lists several variables that may be relevant to a capital expenditure request. Generally, the variables in capital facility decisions are (1) project life, (2) estimated cash flow, and (3) investment cost. Each variable in a proposal should be checked for accuracy.

Methods of Evaluation. Techniques used for proposal evaluation include the accounting rate-of-return method, the payback period method, and the net present-value, or discounted cash flow, method. Using management's minimum acceptance-rejection standard as a cutoff point, the management accountant evaluates all proposals, using one or more evaluation methods. The approach selected should be used consistently to facilitate project comparison.

Final Selection of Alternatives. After passing through the final screening process, acceptable capital expenditure requests are given to management for final review. Before deciding which requests to implement, management must consider the funds available for capital expenditures. Requests that have made it through screening and evaluation are ranked in order of profitability or payback potential. The final capital expenditure budget is then prepared by allocating funds to the selected proposals.

Authorization, Appropriation, and Implementation. Positive action by the board of directors on the proposed capital expenditure budget represents formal authorization. Such authorization includes the appropriation of the funds to acquire, construct, and/or install capital facilities. The implementation period begins with authorization and ends when the facility is operational.

Post-Completion Audit. The decision process does not end when the facility is operational. The accountant should perform a post-completion audit for each project to evaluate the accuracy of forecasted results. Any weakness found in the decision process should be corrected to avoid the same problem in future decisions.

The post-completion audit is a difficult decision step. To isolate how a decision affects a company's overall operating results requires extensive analysis. Only when an entire new plant is constructed can one isolate and identify relevant information and measure a facility's performance. The main problems in the post-completion audit are that (1) long-term projects must be evaluated by concentrating on cash flows over the project's life, (2) a particular decision may influence the operations of existing facilities, and (3) profitability resulting from a decision may be difficult to isolate and identify.

In summary, the capital expenditure decision cycle is vital to managing a company. By making correct decisions about capital expenditures, management provides for the continued existence of the company. A series of incorrect decisions on capital expenditures could cause a company to fail. This topic by itself could fill several books. You will study various parts of the capital expenditure decision cycle in several other business courses. Each exposure will help you to fully appreciate the importance of the decision process. In the remaining parts of this chapter, we look at aspects of a decision that are the responsibility of the management accountant, including the development of a minimum desired rate of return on investment, proposal evaluation methods, and ranking of acceptable proposals. The topic of post-completion audit is a major responsibility of the management accountant. But as stated earlier, such a process is difficult, and its analysis will be left for a more advanced course in operational auditing.

Desired Rate of Return on Investment

Choosing the best capital expenditure alternative is not always the approach taken in the decision-making process. Most companies have a set minimum rate of return, below which the expenditure request is automatically refused. If none of the capital expenditure requests is expected to meet the minimum desired rate of return, all requests will be turned down.

OBJECTIVE 3
Describe the purpose of the minimum desired rate of return and explain the methods used to arrive at this rate

Why do companies use such a cutoff point? The idea is that if an expenditure request falls below the minimum rate of return, the funds can be used more profitably in another part of the company. Supporting poor-return proposals will lower the company's profitability later.

Deciding a company's minimum desired rate of return is not a simple task. Each measure that can be used to set a cutoff point has certain advantages. The most common measures used are (1) cost of capital, (2) corporate return on investment, (3) industry's average return on investment, and (4) bank interest rates. How to find the cost of capital is described in some detail, and then the use of other measures is briefly explained.

Cost of Capital Measures. Of all the measures for desired rates of return listed previously, cost of capital measures are the most widely used and discussed. The goal is to find the cost of financing the company's activities. However, to finance its activities, a company borrows funds and issues preferred and common stock. At the same time the company tries to operate at a profit. Each of these financing alternatives has a different cost rate. Furthermore, each company uses a different mix of these sources to finance current and future operations.

To set a desired cutoff rate of return, management can use cost of debt, cost of preferred stock, cost of equity capital, or cost of retained earnings. In many cases a company will average these cost results to establish an average cost of capital measure. Sophisticated methods are used to compute these financial return measures.[2] But the purpose here is simply to identify measures used, so we present only a brief description of each type of cost of financing.

Cost of debt is the ratio of loan charges to net proceeds of the loan. The effects of income taxes and the present value of interest charges must be taken into account, but the rate is essentially the ratio of costs to loan proceeds. Cost of preferred stock is the stated dividend rate of the individual stock issue. Tax effects are unimportant in this case because dividends, unlike interest charges, are a nondeductible expense. Cost of equity capital is the rate of return to the investor and is what makes stock valuable in the market. It is not just the dividend rate to the stockholder because management can raise or lower the dividend rate almost at will. This concept is very complex, but it has sound authoritative financial support.[3] Cost of retained earnings is the opportunity cost, or the dividends given up by the stockholder. Such a cost is linked closely with the cost of equity capital just described. The point is that a firm's cost of capital is hard to compute because it is a weighted average of the cost of various financing methods. However, this figure is the best estimate of a minimum desired rate of return.

Weighted average cost of capital is computed by first finding the cost rate for each source or class of capital-raising instrument. The second part of the computation is to figure the percentage of each source of capital to the company's total debt and equity financing. Weighted average cost of capital is the sum of the products of each financing source's percentage multiplied by its cost rate. For example, assume the Leventhal Company's financing structure is as shown on the following page:

---

2. See James C. Van Horne, "Cost of Capital of the Firm," *Financial Management and Policy,* 6th ed. (Englewood Cliffs, N.J.: Prentice-Hall, 1983), chap. 8, pp. 213–227.
3. Ibid.

Cost Rate (%)	Source of Capital	Amount	Capital Mix (Percentage of Each to Total)
10	Debt financing	$150,000	30
8	Preferred stock	50,000	10
12	Common stock	200,000	40
14	Retained earnings	100,000	20
	Totals	$500,000	100

Weighted average cost of capital of 11.4 percent would be computed the following way:

Source of Capital	Cost Rate	×	Ratio of Capital Mix	=	Portion of Weighted Average Cost of Capital
Debt financing	.10		.30		.030
Preferred stock	.08		.10		.008
Common stock	.12		.40		.048
Retained earnings	.14		.20		.028
Weighted average cost of capital					.114

Other Cutoff Measures. If cost of capital information is unavailable, management can use one of three less accurate but still useful amounts as the minimum desired rate of return. The first is average total corporate return on investment. The reasoning used to support such a measure is that any capital investment that produced a return lower than an amount earned historically by the company would negatively affect future operations. A second method is to use an industry's averages of the cost of capital. Most sizable industry associations supply such information. As a last resort a company might use the current bank lending rate. But because most companies are both debt and equity financed, this rate seldom reflects an accurate rate of return.

Capital Expenditure Evaluation Methods

Although many methods are used to evaluate capital expenditure proposals, the most common are (1) the accounting rate-of-return method, (2) the payback period method, and (3) the net present-value approach, which is the most common discounted cash flow method. These three methods are discussed in detail. However, before discussing evaluation methods, we first discuss types of information relevant to capital expenditure decision evaluations.

Information Relevant to
Capital Expenditure Decision Evaluations

OBJECTIVE 4
Identify
information
relevant to the
capital
expenditure
decision process

When evaluating capital expenditure alternatives, one must identify the types and compute the amounts of information relevant to capital expenditure proposals.

Cost Savings Versus Net Cash Flow. When evaluating a capital expenditure alternative, you must be interested in how the item will perform and how it will benefit the company. The accounting rate-of-return, payback period, and net present-value methods help in determining how a capital expenditure will increase an organization's profitability or liquidity. However, each evaluation method uses different information as a basis for analysis. Net income is used in computing the accounting rate of return. This amount is calculated in the normal fashion, and increases in net income resulting from the capital expenditure must be determined for each alternative.

Net cash inflow, the balance of increases in cash receipts over increases in cash payments resulting from the capital expenditure, is used in evaluating capital projects when either the payback period or net present-value method is employed. In some cases, equipment replacement decisions may involve several alternatives that do not increase current revenue. In these cases, cost savings resulting from each alternative may be used in evaluating the proposals. Both net cash flow and cost savings can be used as a basis for the evaluation, and you should not confuse one with the other. As long as decision alternatives are measured and evaluated consistently, the analysis will be beneficial to management in making its decisions.

Book Value of Assets. Book value is the undepreciated portion of the original cost of a fixed asset. When evaluating a decision to replace an asset, the book value of the old asset is irrelevant since it is a past, or historical, cost and will not be altered by the decision. Net proceeds from its sale or disposal are relevant because these proceeds affect cash flows. Also, such proceeds may be different for each alternative being considered to replace the asset. Gains or losses incurred in an exchange or sale of an old asset are relevant because of their tax consequences. The tax implications of capital expenditure decision evaluations are explained later in the chapter.

Disposal or Salvage Values. As explained above, sales proceeds from the disposal of an old asset represent current cash inflows and are relevant to evaluating capital expenditure decisions. Projected disposal or salvage values of alternative new replacement equipment are also relevant to the decision analysis. These values represent future cash inflows. And because the values usually differ between decision alternatives, they fit the definition of relevant decision information discussed in Chapter 12.

Remember, these salvage values will be received at the end of the asset's estimated life.

Depreciation Expense. All methods of evaluating capital expenditure proposals—except the accounting rate-of-return method—use cashflow information. Since depreciation is a **noncash expense**, it is irrelevant to decision analyses based on cash flow. However, because depreciation expense reduces net income and income tax expense, the tax-related cash savings is relevant to the evaluation process. The effect of tax savings on capital expenditure decisions is discussed later in this chapter.

Even Versus Uneven Cash Flows. As discussed above, future net cash inflows or cost savings are relevant to evaluations of capital expenditure proposals when the payback period or net present-value method is used. Projections of these cash flows may be the same for each year of the asset's life or vary from year to year. Unequal, or uneven, cash flows are common and must be analyzed yearly in the evaluation process. Equal, or even, cash flows require less detailed analysis. Evaluations for projects with even and uneven cash flows are illustrated and explained later in this chapter.

Accounting Rate-of-Return Method

OBJECTIVE 5a
Evaluate capital expenditure proposals using the accounting rate-of-return method

Among the methods used to measure estimated performance of a capital investment, the **accounting rate-of-return method** is a crude but easy approach. With this method one measures expected performance by using two variables: (1) estimated annual after-tax net income from the project and (2) average investment cost. The basic equation is as follows:

$$\text{Accounting rate of return} = \frac{\text{project's average annual after-tax net income}}{\text{average investment cost}}$$

To compute average annual after-tax net income, one uses the revenue and expense data prepared for evaluating the project. Average investment in the proposed capital facility is figured as follows:[4]

$$\text{Average investment} = \frac{\text{total investment} + \text{salvage value}}{2}$$

For example, assume the Cox-Erickson Company is interested in purchasing a new bottling machine. Only projects that promise to yield

---

4. The procedure of adding salvage value to the numerator may seem illogical. However, a fixed asset is never depreciated below its salvage value. Average investment is computed by determining the midpoint of the depreciable portion of the asset and adding back the salvage value. Another way of stating the above formula is

$$\text{Average investment} = \frac{\text{total investment} - \text{salvage value}}{2} + \text{salvage value}$$

Such a statement reduces to the formula used above.

more than a 16 percent return are acceptable to management. Estimates for the proposal include revenue increases of $17,900 a year and operating cost increases of $8,500 a year (including depreciation). The cost of the machine is $51,000. Its salvage value is $3,000. The company's income tax rate is 34 percent. Should the company invest in the machine? To answer the question, compute the accounting rate of return as follows:

$$\text{Accounting rate of return} = \frac{(\$17,900 - \$8,500) \times .66}{(\$51,000 + \$3,000) \div 2}$$

$$= \frac{\$6,204}{\$27,000} = 22.98\%$$

The projected rate of return is higher than the 16 percent minimum desired rate, so management should think seriously about making the investment.

Because this method is easy to understand and apply, it is widely used. However, it is important to know the disadvantages of the accounting rate-of-return method. First, the use of averages tends to equalize all information, leading to errors in annual income and investment data. Second, the method is unreliable if estimated annual net income differs from year to year. Finally, the time value of money is not considered in the computations. Thus future and present dollars are treated as equal.

Cash Flow and the Payback Period Method

OBJECTIVE 5b
Evaluate capital
expenditure pro-
posals using the
payback period
method

Instead of measuring the rate of return on investments, many managers would rather estimate the cash flow to be generated by a capital investment. In such cases the goal is to determine the minimum length of time it will take to get back the initial investment. If two investment alternatives are being studied, the choice will be the investment that pays back its initial amount in the shortest time. This period of time is known as the payback period, and the capital investment evaluation approach is called the **payback period method**.

You compute the payback period as follows:

$$\text{Payback period} = \frac{\text{cost of investment}}{\text{annual net cash inflow}}$$

To apply the payback period method to the proposed capital investment of the Cox-Erickson Company, you need further information. You need to determine the net cash flow. To do so, you find and eliminate the effects of all noncash revenue and expense items included in the analysis of net income. In this case it is assumed that the only noncash expense or revenue amount is machine depreciation. To calculate this amount, you must know the asset's life and the depreciation method. Suppose the Cox-Erickson Company uses the straight-line depreciation approach, and the new bottling machine will have a ten-year estimated service life. Using this information and the facts given earlier, the payback period is computed as shown on the next page:

$$\text{Annual depreciation} = \frac{\text{cost} - \text{salvage value}}{10 \text{ (years)}}$$

$$= \frac{\$51,000 - \$3,000}{10}$$

$$= \$4,800 \text{ per year}$$

$$\text{Payback period} = \frac{\text{cost of machine}}{\text{cash revenue} - \text{cash expenses} - \text{taxes}}$$

$$= \frac{\$51,000}{\$17,900 - (\$8,500 - \$4,800) - \$3,196}$$

$$= \frac{\$51,000}{\$11,004}$$

$$= 4.6347 \text{ years}$$

If the company's desired payback period is five years or less, the capital investment proposal would be approved.

Payback has the advantage of being easy to compute and understand, which is why it is widely used. However, the disadvantages of this approach far outweigh the advantages. First, the method does not measure profitability. Second, the present value of cash flows from different periods is not recognized. Finally, emphasis is on the time it takes to get out of the investment rather than on the long-run return on the investment.

Time Value of Money

OBJECTIVE 6
Apply the concept of time value of money

Today there are many opportunities to do something with investment capital besides buying fixed assets. Consequently, management expects an asset to yield a reasonable return during its useful life. Capital expenditure decision analysis calls for evaluating estimates for several future time periods. It is unrealistic for cash flows from different periods to have the same values when measured in current dollars, so treating all future income flows alike ignores the time value of money. Both the accounting rate-of-return and payback period evaluation methods have this disadvantage.

The time value of money implies that cash flows of equal dollar amounts separated by an interval of time have different values. The values differ because of the effect of compound interest. For example, assume that Greg Sundevil was awarded a $20,000 settlement in a lawsuit over automobile damages from an accident. The terms of the settlement dictate that the first payment of $10,000 is to be paid today, December 31, 1989. The second $10,000 installment is due on December 31, 1993. What is the value today (its present value) of the total settlement? Assume that Sundevil could earn 10 percent interest on his current funds. To compute the present value of the settlement, you must go to Table D-3 in Appendix D. There you will find the multiplier for 4 years at 10 percent, which is 0.683. The settlement's present value is computed as:

Present value of first payment on Dec. 31, 1989	$10,000
Present value of second payment to be received on Dec. 31, 1993:	
($10,000 × .683)	6,830
Present value of the total settlement	$16,830

If Sundevil had the choice of (1) accepting the $20,000 settlement as offered or (2) receiving $16,830 today as total compensation for the lawsuit, he would be indifferent.

As seen, the $10,000 to be received in four years is not worth $10,000 today. If funds can be invested to earn 10 percent interest, then each $1 to be received in four years is worth only $.683 today. To prove the indifference statement above, look at the value of the total settlement to Sundevil on December 31, 1993, for each choice. In this analysis, Table D-1 in Appendix D is used because this example deals with future values based on compounding of interest.

(1) Accepting the $20,000 settlement as offered
December 31, 1989 payment after earning four
years of interest income @ 10% annual rate

($10,000 × 1.464)	$14,640.00
December 31, 1993 payment	10,000.00
Total amount at December 31, 1993	$24,640.00

(2) Receiving $16,830 on 12/31/89 as total compensation
for the lawsuit December 31, 1989 payment after
earning four years of interest income @ 10% annual
rate

($16,830 × 1.464)	$24,639.12*

* Difference due to rounding.

The analysis above was based on single payments received either today or on a future date. Now, assume that Debbie Aztec was just told that she won the lottery. Her winnings are $1,000,000, to be paid in $50,000 amounts over the next 20 years. If she could choose to receive the value of the winnings today and earn 9 percent interest on her savings, how much should she settle for? Since a *series* of payments is being dealt with, you must use Table D-4 in Appendix D to locate the applicable multiplier of 9.129, which represents the discounting of twenty future payments back to the present assuming a 9 percent rate-of-return factor.

Present value of twenty annual future payments of
$50,000 commencing one year from now assuming a 9%
interest factor is used

($50,000 × 9.129)	$456,450

In other words, Aztec would be indifferent if given the choice of (1) receiving $1,000,000 in twenty future annual installments of $50,000 each or (2) receiving $456,450 today. To prove this point, determine the future value of the two alternatives by using data from Table D-2 in Appendix D. Such data are used because this example deals with a series of future payments and the compounding of interest on those payments.

(1) Receiving $1,000,000 in twenty future annual
    installments of $50,000 each
    ($50,000 × 51.16) $2,558,000.00

(2) Receiving $456,450 today, using Table D-1 be-
    cause you are dealing with a single payment
    ($456,450 × 5.604) $2,557,945.80*

*Difference due to rounding.

When dealing with the time value of money, use compounding to find the future value of an amount now held. To find the present value of an amount to be received, use discounting.

When determining future values, you should refer to Tables D-1 and D-2 in Appendix D. To determine present values of future amounts of money, use Tables D-3 and D-4 in Appendix D. Also, remember that Tables D-1 and D-3 deal with a single payment or amount, whereas Tables D-2 and D-4 are used for a *series* of *equal* annual amounts. There are additional exercises in Appendix C if you need more practice with the time value of money.

Discounted Cash Flow: Net Present-Value Method

OBJECTIVE 7
Evaluate capital expenditure proposals using the discounted cash flow—net present-value method

The concept of **discounted cash flow** helps overcome the disadvantages of the accounting rate-of-return and payback period methods in evaluating capital investment alternatives. By using the present-value tables in Appendix D, it is possible to discount future cash flows back to the present. This approach to capital investment analysis is called the **net present-value method**. Multipliers used to find the present value of a future cash flow are in the present-value tables. Which multipliers to use is computed by connecting the minimum desired rate of return and the life of the asset or length of time for which the amount is being discounted. Each element of cash inflow and cash outflow to be realized over the life of the asset is discounted back to the present. If the present value of all expected future net cash inflows is greater than the amount of the current investment, the expenditure meets the minimum desired rate of return, and the project should be carried out.[5]

The net present-value method is used in different ways, depending on whether annual cash flows are equal or unequal. If all annual cash flows (inflows less outflows) are equal, the discount factor to be used will come from Table D-4. This table gives multipliers for the present value of $1 received *each period* for a given number of time periods. One computation will cover the cash flows of all time periods involved. If, however,

5. This section is based on the concept of present value. Appendixes C and D explain this concept and provide tables of multipliers for computations.

expected cash inflows and outflows differ from one year to the next, each year's amount must be discounted back to the present. Discount factors used in this kind of analysis are in Table D-3. Multipliers in Table D-3 are used to find the present value of $1 to be received (or paid out) at the end of a given number of time periods.

The following example helps show the difference in the present-value analysis of expenditures with equal and unequal cash flows. Suppose the Bibb Metal Products Company is deciding which of two stamping machines to buy. The blue machine has equal expected annual net cash inflows, and the black machine has unequal annual amounts. Information on the two machines follows:

	Blue Machine	Black Machine
Purchase price: January 1, 19x4	$16,500	$16,500
Salvage	0	0
Expected life	5 years	5 years
Estimated net cash inflows		
19x4	$5,000	$6,000
19x5	$5,000	$5,500
19x6	$5,000	$5,000
19x7	$5,000	$4,500
19x8	$5,000	$4,000

The company's minimum desired rate of return is 16 percent. Which—if either—of the two alternatives should be chosen?

The evaluation process is shown in Exhibit 13-1. An analysis involving equal annual cash flows is easier to prepare. Present value of net cash inflows for the five-year period for the blue machine is found by multiplying $5,000 by 3.274. The multiplier, 3.274, is found in Table D-4 by using the 16 percent minimum desired rate of return and a five-year life for the blue machine. Present value of the total cash inflows from the blue machine is $16,370. Comparing this figure with the $16,500 purchase price results in a *negative* net present value of $130.

Analysis of the black machine alternative gives a different result. As shown in Exhibit 13-1, unequal net cash inflows cause more work. Multipliers for this part of the analysis are found by using the same 16 percent rate. But five multipliers, one for each year of the life of the asset, must be used. Table D-3 in Appendix D applies here since each annual amount must be individually discounted back to the present. For the black machine, the $16,851.50 present value of net cash inflows is more than the $16,500.00 purchase price of the machine. Thus there is a positive net present value of $351.50.

A positive net present-value figure means the return on the asset exceeds the 16 percent minimum desired rate of return. A negative figure means the rate of return is below the minimum cutoff point. In the Bibb Metal Products case, the right decision would be to purchase the black machine.

Exhibit 13-1. Net Present-Value Analysis: Equal Versus Unequal Cash Flows

Bibb Metal Products Company
Capital Expenditure Analysis
19x3

Blue Machine

Present value of cash inflows	$5,000 × 3.274 = $16,370.00
Less purchase price of machine	16,500.00
Negative net present value	($ 130.00)

Black Machine

Present value of cash inflows

19x4	($6,000 × .862)	$ 5,172.00
19x5	($5,500 × .743)	4,086.50
19x6	($5,000 × .641)	3,205.00
19x7	($4,500 × .552)	2,484.00
19x8	($4,000 × .476)	1,904.00
Total		$16,851.50
Less purchase price of machine		16,500.00
Positive net present value		$ 351.50

Incorporating time value of money into the evaluation of capital expenditure proposals is the major advantage of the net present-value method. This method also deals mainly with total cash flows from the investment over its useful life, so it brings total profitability into the analysis as well. The major disadvantage of the net present-value method is that many managers do not trust or understand the procedure. They prefer the payback period method or the accounting rate-of-return method because the computations are easier.

Income Taxes and Business Decisions

Tax Effects on Capital Expenditure Decisions

OBJECTIVE 8
Analyze capital expenditure decision alternatives that incorporate the effects of income taxes

Income taxes are an important cost of doing business, and they often have an important impact on business decisions. The aim of capital budgeting evaluation techniques, such as payback period and net present-value, is to measure and compare the relative benefits of proposed capital expenditures. These measurements focus on cash receipts and payments for a given project. For profit-oriented companies, income taxes are important in capital budgeting analyses because they affect the amount and timing of cash flows. For this reason capital expenditure evaluation analysis must take tax effects into account.

Corporate income tax rates range from 15 percent on low income to 34 percent on income of more than $335,000.

Taxable Income	Tax Rate
$0 to $50,000	15%
$50,000 to $75,000	$ 7,500 + 25% of amount over $50,000
$75,000 to $100,000	$ 13,750 + 34% of amount over $75,000
$100,000 to $335,000	$ 22,250 + 39% of amount over $100,000
Over $335,000	$110,000 + 34% of amount over $335,000

Because of different tax rates and changes from year to year, this text will show the effects of income taxes on cash flow by simply using a corporate tax rate of 34 percent on taxable income.

Now, suppose a project makes the following contribution to annual net income:

Cash revenues	$400,000
Cash expenses	(200,000)
Depreciation	(100,000)
Income before taxes	$100,000
Income taxes at 34%	(34,000)
Income after taxes	$ 66,000

Annual cash flow for this project can be determined by two different procedures:

1. Cash flow—receipts and disbursements

Revenues (cash inflow)	$400,000
Cash expenses (outflow)	(200,000)
Income taxes (outflow)	(34,000)
Net cash inflow	$166,000

2. Cash flow—income adjustment procedure

Income after taxes	$ 66,000
Add: noncash expenses (depreciation)	100,000
Less: noncash revenues	—
Net cash inflow	$166,000

In both computations the net cash inflow is $166,000, and the total effect of income taxes is to lower the net cash flow by $34,000.

Revenues and gains from the sale of equipment increase taxable income and tax payments. When dealing with cash inflows, you must distinguish between a gain on the sale of an asset and the proceeds received from the sale. *Gains* are the amount received over and above the book value of the asset, whereas *proceeds* include the whole sales price and represent the cash inflow. Gains are not cash-flow items, but they do raise tax payments. If equipment with a book value of $80,000 is sold for $180,000 in cash, the gain is $100,000. By assuming that this gain is taxable at the same rate of 34 percent,[6] you would analyze the cash flow as follows:

Proceeds from sale		$180,000
Gain on sale	$100,000	
Capital gains tax rate	× .34	
Cash outflow (tax increase)		(34,000)
Net cash inflow		$146,000

As cash flows from the receipt of revenues and proceeds from the sale of assets are reduced because of income taxes, so too are the amounts of potential expenses (cash outflows). Cash expenses lower net income and result in cash outflows only to the extent that they exceed related tax reductions. This generalization is true for both cash operating expenses and losses on the sale of fixed assets. The following examples show the cash-flow effects of increases in cash and noncash expenses and losses on the sale of equipment:

Cash expenses		
Increase in cash operating expenses	$100,000	
Less: tax reduction at 34%	(34,000)	
Net increase in cash outflow	$ 66,000	
Noncash expenses		
Annual depreciation expense	$200,000	
Corporate tax rate	× .34	
Tax reduction = cash savings	$ 68,000	
Loss on the sale of an asset		
Proceeds from sale		$150,000
Loss on sale	$100,000	
Corporate tax rate	× .34	
Reduction of taxes and cash outflow		34,000
Total cash inflow resulting from sale		$184,000

Depreciation expense is not a cash-flow item, but it does provide a cash benefit equal to the amount of the reduction in taxes. Losses on the sale of fixed assets are also not cash-flow items, but they provide a cash benefit by reducing the amount of taxes to be paid in cash. For illustrations of the above ideas, see the review problem for this chapter (page 509).

6. Capital gains will be taxable at the same rates as ordinary income from 1988 on.

Minimizing Taxes Through Planning

When operating a business, there are many ways to plan so tax liability is as low as possible. One of the most important is the timing of business transactions. For example, a corporation that is nearing $50,000 in taxable income for the year may want to put off an income-producing transaction until just after year-end to avoid the higher tax rate. Or it may speed up making certain expenditures for the same reason.

Another important way to reduce tax liability through operating decisions is by the timing of transactions involving depreciable business assets and land. For example, if possible, no such asset should be sold at a gain less than six months from date of purchase.

It is always good management to try to take advantage of provisions of the tax law that allow preferential treatment. For example, the tax law has often been used to encourage investment in areas thought to be important for national goals. Because these goals change over the years, the tax law has been used to promote everything from emergency war equipment to pollution-control devices. Special credits are also allowed for certain spending that lowers unemployment or encourages the hiring of such underemployed groups as the handicapped.

Ranking Capital Expenditure Proposals

OBJECTIVE 9
Rank proposals competing for limited capital expenditure funds

Generally, a company's requests for capital funds exceed the amount of dollars available for capital expenditures. Even after proposals have been evaluated and selected under minimum desired acceptance-rejection standards, there are normally too many to fund adequately. At that point the proposals must be ranked according to their rates of return or profitability. A second selection process is then imposed.

Assume that five acceptable proposals are competing for the same limited capital expenditure funds. Boston Enterprises has $4,500,000 to spend this year in capital improvements. It currently uses an 18 percent minimum desired rate of return. Following are the proposals under review:

Project	Rate of Return (%)	Capital Expenditure
A	32	$1,460,000
B	30	1,890,000
C	28	460,000
D	24	840,000
E	22	580,000
Total		$5,230,000

How would you go about selecting the capital expenditure proposals to be implemented for the year? Projects A, B, and C are obvious contenders, and their combined dollar needs total $3,810,000. There are $690,000 in capital funds remaining. Project D should be examined to see if it can be implemented for $150,000 less. If not, then Project E should be selected. The selection of projects A, B, C, and E means there will be $110,000 in uncommitted capital expenditure funds for the year.

Chapter Review

Review of Learning Objectives

1. **Define and discuss the capital expenditure decision process.**
   Capital expenditure decisions are concerned with when and how much to spend on a company's capital facilities. The capital expenditure decision-making process, often referred to as capital budgeting, consists of identifying the need for a facility, analyzing courses of action to meet that need, preparing reports for management, choosing the best alternative, and rationing capital expenditure funds among competing resource needs.

2. **Identify and describe steps in the capital expenditure decision cycle.**
   The capital expenditure decision cycle begins with detecting a facility's need. A proposal or request is then prepared and analyzed before being subjected to one or two screening processes, depending on the size of the business involved. Using various evaluation methods and a minimum desired rate of return, the proposal is determined to be either acceptable or unacceptable. If acceptable, the proposal is ranked with all other acceptable proposals. Total dollars available for capital investment are used to determine which of the ranked proposals to authorize and implement. The final step is a post-completion audit to determine the accuracy of the forecasted data used in the decision cycle and to find out if some of the projections need corrective action.

3. **Describe the purpose of the minimum desired rate of return and explain the methods used to arrive at this rate.**
   The minimum desired rate of return acts as a screening mechanism by eliminating capital expenditure requests with anticipated low returns from further consideration. By using such an approach to decision making, many unprofitable requests are turned away or discouraged without a great deal of wasted executive time. The most common measures used to compute minimum desired rates of return include (1) cost of capital, (2) corporate return on investment, (3) industry's average return on investment, and (4) federal and bank interest rates. The weighted average cost of capital and average return on investment are the most widely used measures.

4. **Identify information relevant to the capital expenditure decision process.**
   The definition of relevant information—that it be future data differing between two or more alternatives to a decision—is also applicable in the capital expenditure decision process. In addition, determining cost savings or net cash inflow from a project is important. Book values and depreciation expense of assets awaiting replacement are irrelevant. Net proceeds from the sale of an old asset and estimated salvage value of a new facility are relevant for they represent future cash flows. Gains and losses on the sale of old assets and

depreciation expense on replacement equipment are relevant to future cash flows only as they affect cash payments for income taxes.   Even versus uneven cash flows materially affect the decision analysis process.

5. **Evaluate capital expenditure proposals using (a) the accounting rate-of-return method and (b) the payback period method.**
   When using the accounting rate-of-return method to evaluate two or more capital expenditure proposals, the alternative that yields the highest ratio of net income after taxes to average cost of investment is chosen.   When using the payback period method to evaluate a capital expenditure proposal, emphasis is on the shortest time period needed to recoup the original amount of the investment in cash.

6. **Apply the concept of time value of money.**
   Time value of money implies that cash flows of equal dollar amounts at different times have different values because of the effect of compound interest. Of the evaluation methods discussed in this chapter, only the net present-value method is based on the concept of time value of money.

7. **Evaluate capital expenditure proposals using the discounted cash flow—net present-value method.**
   The discounted cash flow–net present-value method of evaluating capital expenditures depends very much on the time value of money.   Present values of future cash flows are studied to see if they are more than the current cost of the capital expenditure being evaluated.

8. **Analyze capital expenditure decision alternatives that incorporate the effects of income taxes.**
   Income taxes affect the results of all capital expenditure analyses.   Care must be taken to look at both sides of income tax effects.   Revenues and gains on the sale of assets increase taxes.   Increased expenditures, noncash expenditures, and losses from the sale of assets decrease taxes.   Tax-related inflows result from capital losses, increased expenses, and noncash expenditures, whereas tax-related cash outflows arise when a company has capital gains from the sale of fixed assets or from increased sales revenue.

9. **Rank proposals competing for limited capital expenditure funds.**
   When ranking capital expenditure proposals, acceptable projects are listed in their order of estimated rate of return.   They are then authorized in their order of ranking until all capital expenditure funds appropriated for the year have been taken.   If funds remain because the selection process was halted by a project too large to be funded, a smaller proposal, lower in priority, may be authorized.

Review of Concepts and Terminology

The following important concepts were introduced in this chapter:

(L.O. 1)   **Capital expenditure decisions:**   Management decisions about when and how much to spend on capital facilities for the company.

(L.O. 5)   **Accounting rate-of-return method:**   A method to measure estimated useful performance of a capital investment that has two variables: the project's average annual after-tax net income, and the average investment cost.

(L.O. 5)   **Payback period method:**   A capital investment decision method based on the minimum length of time it will take to get back the initial investment.

(L.O.7)   **Net present-value method:** Future cash flows are discounted to their present value to evaluate a capital investment option.

Other important terms introduced in this chapter are:

average cost of capital (p. 494)
book value (p. 496)
capital budgeting (p. 488)
cost of debt (p. 494)
cost of equity capital (p. 494)
cost of preferred stock (p. 494)
cost of retained earnings (p. 494)
discounted cash flow (p. 501)
noncash expense (p. 497)

Review Problem:
Tax Effects on a Capital Expenditure Decision

The Rudolph Construction Company specializes in developing large shopping centers. The company is considering the purchase of a new earth-moving machine and has gathered the following information:

Purchase price	$600,000
Salvage value	$100,000
Useful life	4 years
Effective tax rate*	34%
Depreciation method	Straight-line
Desired before-tax payback period	3 years
Desired after-tax payback period	4 years
Minimum before-tax rate of return	15%
Minimum after-tax rate of return	9%

The before-tax cash flow estimates are as follows:

Year	Revenues	Expenses	Net Cash Flow
1	$ 500,000	$260,000	$240,000
2	450,000	240,000	210,000
3	400,000	220,000	180,000
4	350,000	200,000	150,000
Totals	$1,700,000	$920,000	$780,000

Required

1. Using before-tax information, analyze the Rudolph Construction Company's investment in the new earth-moving machine. In your analysis use the (a)

---

*All company operations combined result in a 34 percent tax rate. Because of this, do not use specific tax rates in the tax schedule.

accounting rate-of-return method, (b) payback period method, and (c) not net present-value method.
2. Repeat **1** above, using after-tax information.

Answer to Review Problem

1. Before-tax calculations

The increase in net income is as follows:

Year	Before-Tax Net Cash Flow	Depreciation	Income Before Taxes
1	$240,000	$125,000	$115,000
2	210,000	125,000	85,000
3	180,000	125,000	55,000
4	150,000	125,000	25,000
Totals	$780,000	$500,000	$280,000

1a. (Before-tax) Accounting rate-of-return method

$$\text{Accounting rate of return} = \frac{\text{average annual net income}}{\text{average investment cost}}$$

$$= \frac{\$280,000 \div 4}{(\$600,000 + \$100,000) \div 2} = \frac{\$70,000}{\$350,000} = 20\%$$

1b. (Before-tax) Payback period method

Total cash investment		$600,000
Less cash-flow recovery		
Year 1	$240,000	
Year 2	210,000	
Year 3 (⅚ of $180,000)	150,000	(600,000)
Unrecovered investment		—

Payback period 2⅚ years, 2.833 years, or 2 years, 10 months

1c. (Before-tax) Net present-value method (multipliers are from Table D-3)

Year	Net Cash Flow	Present-Value Multiplier	Present Value
1	$240,000	.870	$208,800
2	210,000	.756	158,760
3	180,000	.658	118,440
4	150,000	.572	85,800
4	100,000 (salvage)	.572	57,200
Total present value			$629,000
Less cost of original investment			600,000
Positive net present value			$ 29,000

2. After-tax calculations

The increase in net income after taxes is:

Year	Before-Tax Net Cash Flow	Depreciation	Income Before Taxes	Taxes (34%)	Income After Taxes
1	$240,000	$125,000	$115,000	$39,100	$ 75,900
2	210,000	125,000	85,000	28,900	56,100
3	180,000	125,000	55,000	18,700	36,300
4	150,000	125,000	25,000	8,500	16,500
Totals	$780,000	$500,000	$280,000	$95,200	$184,800

The after-tax cash flow is as follows:

Year	Net Cash Flow Before Taxes	Taxes	Net Cash Flow After Taxes
1	$240,000	$39,100	$200,900
2	210,000	28,900	181,100
3	180,000	18,700	161,300
4	150,000	8,500	141,500
Totals	$780,000	$95,200	$684,800

2a. (After-tax) Accounting rate-of-return method

$$\text{Accounting rate of return} = \frac{\text{average annual after-tax net income}}{\text{average investment cost}}$$

$$= \frac{\$184,800 \div 4}{(\$600,000 + \$100,000) \div 2} = \frac{\$46,200}{\$350,000} = 13.2\%$$

2b. (After-tax) Payback period method

Total cash investment		$600,000
Less cash-flow recovery		
Year 1	$200,900	
Year 2	181,100	
Year 3	161,300	
Year 4 (.401 × $141,500)	56,700	(600,000)
Unrecovered investment		—

Payback period 3.401 years

2c. (After-tax) Net present-value method (multipliers are from Table D-3)

Year	Net Cash Inflow After Taxes	Present-Value Multiplier	Present Value
1	$200,900	.917	$184,225
2	181,100	.842	152,486
3	161,300	.772	124,524
4	141,500	.708	100,182
4	100,000 (salvage)	.708	70,800
Total present value			$632,217
Less cost of original investment			600,000
Positive net present value			$ 32,217

Rudolph Construction Company: Summary of Decision Analysis

	Before-Tax		After-Tax	
	Desired	Predicted	Desired	Predicted
Accounting rate of return	15%	20%	9%	13.2%
Payback period	3 years	2.833 years	4 years	3.401 years
Net present value	—	$29,000	—	$32,217

Based on the calculations in **1** and **2**, the Rudolph Company's proposed investment in the earth-moving machine meets all company criteria for such investments. Given these results, the company should invest in the machine.

Chapter Assignments

Questions

1. What is a capital expenditure? Give examples of types of capital expenditures.
2. Define capital budgeting.
3. Discuss the interrelationship of the following steps in the capital expenditure decision cycle:
   a. Determination of dollar amount available
   b. Final selection of alternatives
   c. Final evaluation of proposals
4. What are some difficulties encountered in trying to implement the post-completion audit step in the capital expenditure decision cycle?
5. Describe some approaches companies use in arriving at a minimum desired rate of return to use as its acceptance-rejection standard in capital expenditure decision making.
6. What is the importance of equal versus unequal cash flows in capital expenditure decisions? Are they relevant to the accounting rate-of-return method? The payback period method? The net present-value method?

7. What is a crude but easy method for evaluating capital expenditures? List the advantages and disadvantages of this method.
8. What is the formula used for determining payback period? Is this decision-measuring technique accurate? Defend your answer.
9. Distinguish between cost savings and net cash flow.
10. Discuss the statement, "To treat all future income flows alike ignores the time value of money."
11. Explain the relationship of compound interest to determination of present value.
12. What is the objective of using the concept of discounted cash flows?
13. "In using discounted cash-flow methods, the book value of an asset is irrelevant, whereas current and future salvage values are relevant." Is this statement valid? Defend your answer.
14. In evaluating equipment replacement decisions with net present-value measures, what justifies ignoring depreciation of the old equipment?
15. What is the role of cost of capital when using the net present-value method to evaluate capital expenditure proposals?
16. Why is it important to consider income taxes when evaluating a capital expenditure proposal?
17. Aljeannie Company has (a) net cash inflow from operations for 19x9 of $63,000, (b) noncash expenditures of $12,000, and (c) an asset sale that netted $54,000 in proceeds and involved a $20,000 capital gain. Using the 34 percent tax rate for normal income and capital gains, compute the company's tax liability.
18. When selecting capital expenditure proposals for implementation, final ranking of proposals may not follow the order in which they were presented. Why?

Classroom Exercises

Exercise 13-1.
Capital
Expenditure
Decision Cycle
(L.O. 2)

Newell Anthony was just promoted to supervisor of building maintenance for the Bob Carr Theatre complex in Grove City, Pennsylvania. The complex comprises seventeen buildings. Omni Entertainment, Inc., Anthony's employer, uses an integral system for evaluating capital expenditure requests from its twenty-two supervisors. Anthony has approached you, the corporate controller, for advice on preparing his first proposal. He would also like to become familiar with the entire decision cycle.

1. What advice would you give Anthony before he prepares his first capital expenditure request proposal?
2. Explain the capital expenditure decision cycle to Anthony.

Exercise 13-2.
Minimum Desired
Rate of Return
(L.O. 3)

The controller of Jessie Corporation wants to establish a minimum desired rate of return and would like to use a weighted average cost of capital. Current data about the corporation's financing structure are as follows: debt financing, 50 percent; preferred stock, 20 percent; common stock, 20 percent; and retained earnings, 10 percent. After-tax cost of debt is 8 percent. Dividend rates on the preferred and common stock issues are 6 and 10 percent, respectively. Cost of retained earnings is 12 percent.

Compute the weighted average cost of capital.

Exercise 13-3.
Analysis of
Relevant
Information
(L.O. 4)

Harold Randolph & Co., a scrap-metal company, supplies area steel companies with recycled materials. The company collects scrap metal, sorts and cleans the material, and compresses it into 1-ton blocks for easy handling. Increased demand for recycled metals has caused Mr. Randolph to consider purchasing an additional metal-compressing machine. He has narrowed the choice to 2 models. The company's management accountant has gathered the information related to each model:

	Model One	Model Two
Purchase price	$50,000	$ 60,000
Salvage value	6,000	10,000
Annual depreciation*	4,400	5,000
Resulting increases in annual sales	86,000	100,000
Annual operating costs		
Materials	30,000	35,000
Direct labor	20,000	20,000
Operating supplies	1,800	2,000
Indirect labor	12,000	18,000
Insurance and taxes	800	1,000
Plant rental	4,000	4,000
Electricity	500	560
Other overhead	2,500	2,840

* Computed using the straight-line method.

1. Identify the costs and revenues relevant to the decision.
2. Prepare an incremental cash-flow analysis for year 1.

Exercise 13-4.
Capital
Expenditure
Decision:
Accounting Rate-
of-Return Method
(L.O. 5a)

Castleberry Corporation manufactures metal hard hats for on-site construction workers. Recently, management tried to raise productivity to meet the growing demand from the real estate industry. The company is now thinking about a new computerized stamping machine. Management has decided that only projects yielding a 16 percent return before taxes will be accepted. The following projections for the proposal are given: the new machine will cost $255,000. Revenue will increase $85,600 per year. The salvage value of the new machine will be $35,000. Operating cost increases (including depreciation) will be $64,600 per year.

Using the accounting rate-of-return method, decide whether the company should invest in the machine. (Show all computations to support your decision, and ignore income tax effects.)

Exercise 13-5.
Capital
Expenditure
Decision: Payback
Period Method
(L.O. 5b)

Shively Sounds, Inc., a manufacturer of stereo speakers, wants to add a new injection molding machine. This machine can produce speaker parts the company now buys from outsiders. The machine has an estimated life of fourteen years and will cost $164,000. Gross cash revenue from the machine will be about $267,500 per year, and related cash expenses should total $186,000. Taxes on income are estimated to be $36,000 a year. The payback period as set by management should be four years or less.

On the basis of the data given, use the payback period method to determine whether the company should invest in this new machine. Show computations to support your answer.

Exercise 13-6.
Using the Present-
Value Tables
(L.O. 6)

For each of the following situations, identify the correct multiplier to use from the tables in Appendix D. Also, compute the appropriate present value.

1. Annual net cash inflow of $20,000 for five years, discounted at 16%
2. An amount of $35,000 to be received at the end of ten years, discounted at 12%
3. The amount of $22,000 to be received at the end of two years, and $16,000 to be received at the end of years four, five, and six, discounted at 10%
4. Annual net cash inflow of $32,500 for twelve years, discounted at 14%
5. The following five years of cash inflows, discounted at 10%:

Year 1	$35,000
Year 2	30,000
Year 3	40,000
Year 4	50,000
Year 5	60,000

6. The amount of $70,000 to be received at the beginning of year seven, discounted at 14%

Exercise 13-7.
Present-Value
Computations
(L.O. 6)

Three machines are being considered in a replacement decision. All have about the same purchase price and an estimated ten-year life. The company uses a 12 percent minimum desired rate of return as its acceptance-rejection standard. Following are the estimated net cash inflows for each machine:

Year	Machine A	Machine B	Machine C
1	$22,000	$10,000	$17,500
2	23,000	12,000	17,500
3	24,000	14,000	17,500
4	23,000	19,000	17,500
5	22,000	20,000	17,500
6	21,000	22,000	17,500
7	16,000	23,000	17,500
8	14,000	24,000	17,500
9	8,000	25,000	17,500
10	4,000	20,000	17,500
Salvage value	1,000	20,000	10,000

1. Compute the present value of future cash flows for each machine.
2. Which machine should the company purchase assuming they all involve the same capital expenditure?

Exercise 13-8.
Capital
Expenditure
Decision: Net
Present-Value
Method
(L.O. 7)

Esther Falkowitz and Associates wants to buy an automatic extruding machine. This piece of equipment would have a useful life of six years, would cost $75,000, and would increase annual after-tax net cash inflows by $19,260. Assume there is no salvage value at the end of six years. The company's minimum desired rate of return is 14 percent.

    Using the net present-value method, prepare an analysis to determine whether the company should purchase the machine.

Exercise 13-9.
Ranking Capital
Expenditure
Proposals
(L.O. 9)

Managers of the Santa Ana Furniture Company have all capital expenditure proposals for the year, and they are ready to make their final selections. The following proposals and related rate-of-return amounts were received during the period:

Project	Amount of Investment	Rate of Return (%)
AB	$ 450,000	19
CD	500,000	34
EF	654,000	12
GH	800,000	28
IJ	320,000	22
KL	240,000	18
MN	180,000	16
OP	400,000	26
QR	560,000	14
ST	1,200,000	23
UV	1,600,000	20

Assume the company's minimum desired rate of return is 15 percent and $5,000,000 are available for capital expenditures during the year.

1. List the acceptable capital expenditure proposals in order of profitability.
2. Which proposals will be selected for this year?

Interpreting Accounting Information

Internal
Management
Information:
Rancho California
Federal Bank
(L.O. 7)

Automatic round-the-clock tellers are becoming a common part of the banking industry. Several companies have developed these computerized money machines and are bombarding bank managers with salespeople and advertising brochures. Rancho California Federal Bank plans to install such a device and has decided on the S-JC machine. Ms. Chen, the controller, has prepared the following decision analysis. She has recommended purchase of the machine based on the positive net present value shown in the analysis on the next page.

    The S-JC machine has an estimated life of five years and an expected salvage value of $40,000. Its purchase price would be $440,000. Two existing teller machines, each having a book value of $35,000, would be sold for a total of $110,000 to a neighboring bank in Temecula. Annual operating cash inflow is expected to increase in the following manner:

Year 1	$ 65,000
Year 2	85,000
Year 3	95,000
Year 4	110,000
Year 5	75,000

The bank uses straight-line depreciation. The before-tax minimum desired rate of return is 16 percent, and a 10 percent rate is used for interpreting after-tax data. Assume a 34 percent tax rate for normal operations and capital gains items.

Rancho California Federal Bank
Capital Expenditure Decision Analysis
Before-Tax Net Present-Value Approach
March 2, 19x6

Year	Net Cash Inflow	Present-Value Multipliers	Present Value
1	$ 65,000	.909	$ 59,085
2	85,000	.826	70,210
3	95,000	.751	71,345
4	110,000	.683	75,130
5	75,000	.621	46,575
5 (salvage)	40,000	.621	24,840
Total present value			$347,185
Initial investment		$440,000	
Less proceeds from the sale of teller machines		110,000	
Net capital investment			330,000
Positive net present value			$ 17,185

Required

1. Analyze Chen's work. What changes need to be made in her capital expenditure decision analysis?
2. What would you recommend to bank management about the S-JC machine purchase?

Problem Set A

**Problem 13A-1.
Accounting Rate-
of-Return and
Payback Period
Methods**

(L.O. 5a, 5b)

St. Cloud Corporation wants to buy a new rubber-stamping machine. The machine will provide the company with a new product line, pressed-rubber food trays for kitchens. Two machines are being considered; on the following page are the data applicable to each machine:

	Lawrence Machine	Lange Machine
Estimated annual increase in revenue	$570,000	$600,000
Purchase price	300,000	340,000
Salvage value	30,000	34,000
Traceable annual costs		
Materials	216,420	165,200
Direct labor	130,500	184,600
Factory supervision	26,000	26,000
Indirect labor	62,480	82,750
Electrical power	7,200	7,200
Other factory overhead	42,800	33,550
Useful life in years	10	12

Depreciation is computed using the straight-line method net of salvage value. Assume a 34 percent income tax rate. The company's minimum desired after-tax rate of return is 16 percent, and the maximum allowable payback period is 5 years.

Required

1. From the information given, compute how the company's net income after taxes will change by each alternative.
2. For each machine compute the projected accounting rate of return.
3. Compute the payback period for each machine.
4. From the information generated in **2** and **3**, decide which machine should be purchased. Why?

Problem 13A-2.
Minimum Desired
Rate of Return
(L.O. 3)

Frank Marini, controller of the Akron Corporation, is developing his company's minimum desired rate of return for the year. This measure will be used as an acceptance-rejection standard in capital expenditure decision analyses during the coming year. As in the past, this rate will be based on the company's weighted average cost of capital. Capital mix and respective costs (after tax) for the previous twelve months were as follows:

	Percentage of Total Financing	Cost of Capital (%)
Debt financing	40	12
Preferred stock	10	14
Common stock	30	8
Retained earnings	20	12

The company will soon convert one-fourth of its debt financing into common stock. Changes in the cost of capital are anticipated only in debt financing, where the rate is expected to decrease to 10 percent.

Several capital expenditure proposals have been submitted for consideration for the current year. Those projects and their projected rates of return are as follows: Project A, 13 percent; Project B, 10 percent; Capital Equipment C, 12 percent; Project D, 9 percent; Capital Equipment E, 8 percent; and Project F, 14 percent.

Required

1. Compute the weighted average cost of capital for the previous year.
2. Using the anticipated adjustments to capital cost and mix, compute the weighted average cost of capital for the current year.
3. Identify the proposed capital expenditures that should be implemented on the basis of the minimum desired rate of return calculated in **2**.

**Problem 13A-3.
Capital
Expenditure
Decision: Net
Present-Value
Method**
(L.O. 7, 8)

The Twelfth of Leo is a famous restaurant in the New Orleans French Quarter. "Bouillabaisse Kathryn" is the specialty of the house. Management is considering buying a machine that would prepare all ingredients, mix them automatically, and cook the dish to the restaurant's rigid specifications. The machine will function for an estimated twelve years, and the purchase price, including installation, is $186,000. Estimated salvage value is $6,000. This labor-saving device is expected to increase cash flows by an average of $30,000 per year during its life. For purposes of capital expenditure decisions, the restaurant uses a 12 percent minimum desired rate of return.

Required

1. Using the net present-value method to evaluate this capital expenditure, determine whether the company should purchase the machine. Support your answer.
2. If management had decided on a minimum desired rate of return of 14 percent, should the machine be purchased? Show all computations to support your answers.
3. Assuming straight-line depreciation, a 34 percent tax rate, and an after-tax minimum desired rate of return of 7 percent, should the company purchase the machine? Show your computations.

**Problem 13A-4.
Capital
Expenditure
Decision:
Comprehensive**
(L.O. 5, 7, 8)

Quality work and timely output are the benchmarks on which Spoto Photo, Inc., was organized. Now a nationally franchised company, there are more than one hundred Spoto Photo outlets scattered throughout the eastern and midwestern states. Part of the franchise agreement promises a centralized photo-developing process with overnight delivery to the outlets.

Because of the tremendous increase in demand for the photo processing, Mr. Angelo, the corporation's president, is considering the purchase of a new, deluxe processing machine. At a cost of $380,000, the photo-processing machine will function for an estimated five years and should have a $40,000 salvage value at the end of that period. Angelo has specified that he expects all capital expenditures to produce a 20 percent before-tax minimum rate of return. The investment should be recouped in three years or less. All fixed assets are depreciated using the straight-line method. The forecasted increases in operating results because of the new machine are shown on the following page:

Cash Flow Estimates

	Cash Revenues	Cash Expenses
Year 1	$210,000	$ 90,000
Year 2	225,000	100,000
Year 3	240,000	110,000
Year 4	200,000	90,000
Year 5	160,000	60,000

Required

1. Ignoring income taxes, analyze the purchase of the machine and decide if the company should purchase it. Use the following evaluation approaches in your analysis: (a) the accounting rate-of-return method, (b) the payback period method, and (c) the net present-value method.
2. Rework **1**, assuming a 34 percent tax rate and after-tax guidelines of a 10 percent minimum desired rate of return and a four-year payback period. Does the decision change when after-tax information is used?

Problem 13A-5.
Even Versus
Uneven Cash Flows
(L.O.7,8)

Villa Park Entertainment, Ltd., operates a tour and sightseeing business in southern California. Their trademark is the use of trolley buses. Each vehicle has its own identity and is specially made for the company. Bentley, the name of the oldest bus, was purchased fifteen years ago and has five years of its estimated life remaining. The company paid $35,000 for Bentley, whose current market value is $20,000. Bentley is expected to generate an average annual net income of $22,000 before taxes for the remainder of its useful life.

Management wants to replace Bentley with a modern-looking vehicle called Keymo. Keymo has a purchase price of $120,000 and a useful life of twenty years. Net income before taxes is projected to be

Years	Annual Net Income
1–5	$45,000
6–10	50,000
11–20	60,000

Assume that (1) all cash flows occur at year-end, (2) the company uses a straight-line depreciation method, (3) the vehicles' salvage value equals 10 percent of their purchase price, (4) the minimum desired after-tax rate of return is 16 percent, and (5) the company is in the 34 percent income tax bracket.

Required

1. Compute the net present value of the future cash flows from Bentley.
2. What is the net present value of cash flows that would result if Keymo were purchased?
3. Should the company keep Bentley or purchase Keymo?

Problem Set B

The Senator Company is expanding its production facilities to include a new product line, a sporty automobile tire rim. Because of a new computerized machine, tire rims can be produced with little labor cost. The controller has advised management about two machines that could do the job. Following are the details about each machine:

	Benson Machine	Krause Machine
Estimated annual increase in revenue	$382,010	$379,250
Purchase price	390,000	410,000
Salvage value	39,000	41,000
Traceable annual costs		
Materials	175,400	160,800
Direct labor	21,200	36,900
Electrical power	4,980	4,980
Factory supervision	15,750	15,750
Factory supplies	25,150	23,750
Other factory overhead	31,320	40,250
Estimated useful life in years	8	12

The company uses the straight-line depreciation method and is in the 34 percent tax bracket. Their minimum desired after-tax rate of return is 16 percent. The maximum payback period is five years.

Required

1. From the information given, compute the change in the company's net income after taxes arising from each alternative.
2. For each machine compute the projected accounting rate of return.
3. Compute the payback period for each machine.
4. From the information generated in **2** and **3**, which machine should be purchased? Why?

Capital investment analysis is the main function of Marilyn Hunt, special assistant to the controller of UCF Manufacturing Company. During the previous twelve-month period, the company's capital mix and respective costs (after tax) were as follows:

	Percentage of Total Financing	Cost of Capital (%)
Debt financing	30	5
Preferred stock	20	8
Common stock	40	12
Retained earnings	10	12

Plans for the current year call for a 10 percent shift in total financing, from common stock financing to debt financing. Also, the after-tax cost of debt is expected to increase to 6 percent, although the cost of the other types of financing will remain the same.

Hunt has already analyzed several proposed capital expenditures. She expects the return on investment for each capital expenditure to be as follows: 7.5 percent on Project A, 8.5 percent on Equipment Item B, 15.0 percent on Product Line C, 6.9 percent on Project D, 9.0 percent on Product Line E, 11.9 percent on Equipment Item F, and 8.0 percent on Project G.

Required

1. Compute the weighted average cost of capital for the previous year.
2. Using the expected adjustments to cost and capital mix, compute the weighted average cost of capital for the current year.
3. Identify the proposed capital expenditures that should be implemented based on the minimum desired rate of return calculated in **2**.

**Problem 13B-3.
Capital
Expenditure
Decision: Net
Present-Value
Method
(L.O.7,8)**

Management at North Dallas Plastics has been looking at a proposal to purchase a new automated plastic injection-style molding machine. With the new machine the company would not have to buy small plastic parts to use in production. The estimated life of the machine is fifteen years. The purchase price, including all setup charges, is $185,000. Salvage value is estimated to be $5,000. The net addition to the company's cash inflow due to savings from making the plastic parts within the company is estimated to be $31,000 a year. Management has decided on a minimum desired before-tax rate of return of 14 percent.

Required

1. Using the net present-value method to evaluate this capital expenditure, determine whether the company should purchase the machine. Support your answer.
2. If management had decided on a minimum desired rate of return of 16 percent, should the machine be purchased? Show all computations to support your answers.
3. Assuming straight-line depreciation, a 34 percent tax rate, and an after-tax minimum desired rate of return of 8 percent, should the company purchase the machine? Show your computations.

**Problem 13B-4.
Capital
Expenditure
Decision:
Comprehensive
(L.O.5,7,8)**

The Duncan Manufacturing Company, based in Kissimmee, Florida, is one of the fastest-growing companies in its industry. According to Mr. James, the company's production vice president, keeping up with technological change is what makes the company a leader in the industry.

James thinks a new robotic machine introduced recently would fill an important need of the company. The machine has an expected useful life of four years, a purchase price of $125,000, and a salvage value of $20,000. The company controller's estimated operating results, using the new machine, are summarized in the chart on the next page. The company uses straight-line depreciation for all machinery. James uses a 12 percent minimum desired rate of return and a three-year payback period for capital expenditure evaluation purposes (before-tax decision guidelines).

Cash Flow Estimates

	Cash Revenues	Cash Expenses	Net Cash Inflow
Year 1	$195,000	$150,000	$45,000
Year 2	195,000	155,000	40,000
Year 3	195,000	160,000	35,000
Year 4	195,000	170,000	25,000

Required

1. Ignoring income taxes, analyze the purchase of the machine. Decide if the company should purchase it. Use the following evaluation approaches in your analysis: (a) the accounting rate-of-return method, (b) the payback period method, and (c) the net present-value method.
2. Rework **1**, assuming a 34 percent tax rate and after-tax guidelines of an 8 percent minimum desired rate of return and a 3.5-year payback period. Does the decision change when after-tax information is used?

Problem 13B-5.
Even Versus
Uneven Cash Flows
(L.O.7,8)

Pappas and Kollias, Inc., own and operate a group of apartment buildings. Management wants to sell one of its older four-family buildings and buy a new structure. The old building, which was purchased twenty-five years ago for $80,000, has a forty-year life. The current market value is $60,000. Annual net income before taxes on the old building is expected to average $15,000 for the remainder of its life.

The new building being considered will cost $450,000. It has a useful life of twenty-five years. Net income before taxes is expected to be as follows:

Years	Annual Net Income
1–10	$40,000
11–15	30,000
16–25	20,000

Assume that (1) all cash flows occur at year-end, (2) the company uses a straight-line depreciation method, (3) the buildings will have a salvage value equal to 10 percent of their purchase price, (4) the minimum desired rate of return is 14 percent, and (5) the company is in the 34 percent tax bracket.

Required

1. Compute the net present value of future cash flows from the old building.
2. What will be the net present value of cash flows if the new building is purchased?
3. Should the company keep the old building or purchase the new one?

Management Decision Case

McCall Hotel
Syndicate
(L.O.7,8)

The McCall Hotel Syndicate owns 4 resort hotels in southern Wisconsin and in Missouri. Because their St. Charles, Missouri, operation (hotel 3) has been booming over the past three years, management has decided to add a new wing, which will increase capacity by 30 percent.

A construction firm has bid on the proposed new wing. The building would have a twenty-year life with no salvage value. The company uses straight-line depreciation.

Deluxe accommodations are highlighted in this contractor's proposal. The new wing would cost $30,000,000 to construct, with the following estimates of cash flows:

	Increase in Cash Inflows from Room Rentals	Increase in Cash Operating Expenses
Years 1–7	$27,900,000	$20,400,000
Year 8	30,000,000	22,000,000
Year 9	32,100,000	23,600,000
Years 10–20	34,200,000	25,200,000

Capital investment projects must generate a 12 percent after-tax minimum desired rate of return to qualify for consideration. Assume a 34 percent tax rate.

Required

Evaluate the proposal from the contractor, using net present-value analysis. Make a recommendation to management.

LEARNING OBJECTIVES

1. *Identify the characteristics of a decentralized organization.*
2. *Describe the four-step performance evaluation process for decentralized operations.*
3. *Compute the performance margin and the segment margin for decentralized divisions.*
4. *Prepare a divisional performance report.*
5. *Apply return on investment measures to evaluate divisional performance.*
6. *Define and discuss transfer pricing.*
7. *Distinguish between a cost-based transfer price and a market-based transfer price.*
8. *Develop a transfer price.*
9. *Measure a manager's performance by using transfer prices.*

CHAPTER 14

Decentralized Operations and Transfer Pricing

Large, diversified organizations tend to decentralize managerial responsibility and authority so as to maximize output and profitability while still maintaining control of operations. Decentralized organizations also develop managers with strong leadership qualities who can progress up the managerial ladder because they have successfully guided a smaller segment of the company. But how do we evaluate the performance of these segment or division managers? In this chapter we look at the process of evaluating division management performance in decentralized companies. First introduced is an appropriate reporting format for performance evaluation that expands on the contribution margin approach and identifies two new guides: performance margin and segment margin. Next, an in-depth look at return on investment (ROI) differentiates ROI measures for operating management and financial management.

Transfer pricing is an integral part of many divisions' performance evaluation. Transfer pricing involves setting artificial prices on goods moving from one profit center to another within a company. Because such prices are used only for internal decisions and performance evaluation, they are unknown to the outside world. Rules different from those used to set external prices govern the development of transfer prices. Transfer prices force segments to compete for a company's resources and influence managers' behavior. Although not as critical to a company's future as external prices, transfer prices can influence operating efficiency and profitability. After studying this chapter, you should be able to meet the learning objectives listed on the left.

Decentralized Organizations

Any enterprise that has grown so big that one person alone can no longer adequately manage every aspect of the venture's activities is a candidate for decentralization. But size is not the only requirement for a decentralized classification. Many business enterprises, both profit and not-for-profit, break their activities into divisions or departments but still maintain control through a central home office or bureau; such enterprises are not considered decentralized. A **decentralized organization** or business has several operating segments; operating control of each segment's various activities is the responsibility of the segment's manager. In a decentralized organization, top management still maintains overall control and closely monitors each segment's activities and evaluates the segment's performance. But the segment managers usually have revenue and expense authority and make the decisions related to their area of responsibility.

OBJECTIVE 1
Identify the characteristics of a decentralized organization

The manager of a decentralized division or other segment normally makes decisions concerning the addition of a new product line, plant expansion, market development, product pricing, sales mix adjustments, and other financial or operating factors affecting the division. The primary element of a decentralized organization is that operating managers are free to make business decisions within the framework of the plans and policies established by top management of the entire company.

The characteristics of a decentralized organization can be summarized as follows:

1. The organization has more than one operating segment or division.
2. The manager of each division has autonomy regarding his or her operating segment.
3. Segment manager's decisions must be made within the constraints of the company's overall goals, objectives, plans, and policies.

Decentralization, then, refers to the location of decision-making authority within a diverse, multisegmented organization. A company is decentralized if divisional managers are given authority to direct their divisions as independent companies.

Manufacturing companies, merchandising establishments, and service organizations can operate as a decentralized enterprise. Decentralized segments can be cost/expense centers, profit centers, or investment centers. Responsibility accounting and reporting techniques are used to highlight the areas under the manager's control. Managers of both profit centers and investment centers have revenue and cost responsibilities, and their performance can be evaluated based on profitability. But a cost/expense center is a bit more difficult to evaluate because of the absence of revenue, so management often creates artificial prices, called transfer prices, to help evaluate the performance of such a center. Transfer pricing is discussed later in this chapter.

Evaluating the Performance of Decentralized Operations

OBJECTIVE 2
Describe the four-step performance evaluation process for decentralized operations

The management accountant is responsible for developing the internal reporting techniques for evaluating divisional performance. This task requires the cooperation of the management team, including production managers, engineers, marketing personnel, and financial management representatives. Top management's responsibility is to identify the segments to be evaluated and develop a set of goals and objectives that the management accountant can use for the evaluation process. The following four steps are critical to the development of an effective performance evaluation process for decentralized divisions:

1. Establish the company's segments.
2. Identify those revenues and costs traceable to and controllable by each segment's manager.
3. Communicate the performance indicators to be used for each segment.
4. Compare actual operating results with budgeted amounts.

Establish the Company's Segments. Establishing the segments to be evaluated is a basic function of management within a decentralized company. Sometimes the segments are obvious, such as plants in different states or countries organized as divisions. There may be other circumstances, such as a company having three plants making the same product lines in three different states. Should these plants be treated as three individual divisions or as one division? Management can take two very different approaches. Simple geographic separation is one approach to determining the segments of a decentralized company. For example, the country may be divided into ten regions, with the plants in each region treated as a division. The second approach is based on the premise that similar activities require similar resources and supervision. All similar product lines are grouped together within a division to help efficiently use the company's resources.

Once the divisional lines have been drawn, management must create the measures used to evaluate the performance of each division. Two sets of measures are needed, one for the division as a whole and one for the performance of individual managers. The division's measures should be long-term, evaluating its profitability and the merits of keeping the division as a continuing investment of the company. The second set of measures should be personal, measuring the aspects of business decisions that were controllable by the division's manager.

The need for both division and manager orientation in measuring performance is obvious if we consider the example of a talented, proven manager being assigned to an unprofitable division. The division's long-run potential is a performance evaluation problem of top management. Measuring the short-run financial improvement and the manager's performance is a distinctly different problem. Different measures of income and operating performance are necessary if both the division's and the manager's effectiveness are to be evaluated.

Identify Traceable and Controllable Revenues and Costs. Decentralized companies usually require a home base or home office where the activities of the various divisions are coordinated and corporatewide policy and long-range plans developed. In some cases, several layers of management are involved in the home office environment, and many companywide services may be offered to the divisions, such as a centralized computer service department. All the home office supervisory salaries and centralized service functions cost money. Are these costs to be charged to the divisions? If so, how is this process done? Do some divisions get a bigger share than others? Are these costs to be included in the division's and division manager's performance report?

The answers to these questions require the identification of those revenues and costs that are traceable to and controllable by the division and its manager. Allocating all central service costs is particularly necessary when you are being reimbursed through a government contract. But for performance evaluation, traceability and controllability are key factors in the allocation process. At the division level, everything traceable to the segment must be part of its financial analysis, including depreciation of division's assets, interest on the division's debt, and a portion of the home office's central services that are computed based on the amount of usage of the services. Those home office costs that do not have a direct relationship with the division should not be included in a division's performance evaluation. These companywide costs are relevant only when measuring companywide performance.

Let us return to the talented, experienced, and proven manager who is assigned to a previously unprofitable division. Should the manager be held responsible for the interest on the division's debt? Or the depreciation on unprofitable assets? Yes—if the manager has control of the asset. If the manager can replace unprofitable assets, then control exists. Old debts created by a previous manager are hardly controllable by the person who comes in to correct the unprofitable situation. Such interest expense is traceable to the division but is not controllable by the division's manager. When determining controllability and traceability, each revenue and cost item should be analyzed individually or as a part of a revenue or cost group.

Communicate a Segment's Performance Indicators. Operating performance can be expressed according to results achieved, costs incurred, effort expended, and/or resources employed. These performance indicators can be used individually, or they may be combined, such as the amount of cost incurred per unit of effort expended ($14 per machine hour). **Results achieved indicators** include total revenues, units produced, orders received, or any other aspect of output or accomplishment. **Costs incurred indicators** relate to (1) costs elements or groups reported on the income statement, such as total cost of operations or total variable costs, and (2) costs of capital expenditures, such as the purchase of a building or machine. **Effort expended indicators** consist of input factors such as machine hours, labor hours, new customers, service center hours, sales calls, and miles driven by salespeople. **Resources employed indicators** center on resource usage, including plant or supervisory personnel, machines, building occupancy, and other physical measures of capacity. These four groups of variables can be used to measure profitability, rate of return on assets, productivity, and operating efficiency for any segment of a decentralized company. Several performance measures may be developed for a division; the relative emphasis each receives is an important management decision.

Comparative Performance Reports. Usually divisional or individual manager performance is evaluated by comparing current performance of budgets, goals, standards, or trends with past performance. Performance evaluation reports should not only compare actual operating results with expected results, they should also provide a description of the differences and seek an explanation from either the manager or the division's management team.

One of the most significant problems involving divisional performance evaluation is **goal congruence,** the relative state of harmony between companywide goals and objectives and those of particular division managers. When managers know how their performance will be measured and evaluated, they will normally take those actions that maximize measured performance. When a manager's decisions benefit the division's performance but adversely affect total companywide performance, there is a lack of goal congruence.

The following example helps illustrate the lack of goal congruence. The Jogger Company is composed of six decentralized divisions. Corporate management emphasizes rate of return on assets employed as the primary performance indicator. Last year, the Eastern Division earned 20 percent on total assets. During the current year, Eastern Division's manager rejected a capital expenditure alternative that had an expected rate of return of 16 percent. Companywide rate of return on assets is normally about 12 percent. In this case, the negative decision of the Eastern Division benefits its performance, but total companywide performance would have been improved if the 16 percent project had been accepted. From this example, it is clear that goal congruence must be a key factor in establishing a system of performance evaluation for a decentralized company.

Contribution Approach
to Divisional Performance Evaluation

OBJECTIVE 3
Compute the performance margin and the segment margin for decentralized divisions

Contribution margin (total revenues minus total variable costs) measures the company's ability to cover fixed costs and earn a profit. This concept was introduced in Chapter 6 and expanded in Chapter 12 when we discussed various short-run decision analyses. Contribution margin can be broken down by operating segment, department, and even per product line so that management can evaluate operations. The contribution approach is also a useful technique in divisional performance evaluation of decentralized operations. Expanding the concept of contribution margin provides useful income measures for both divisional and manager performances.

The contribution approach for divisional performance evaluation is used to highlight dollar amounts that measure segment margin and performance margin. **Segment margin** expresses a division's overall profitability by identifying its contribution to unallocated fixed costs and the resulting company profit. **Performance margin** reflects the effects of divisional management decisions on divisional income. Segment margin is a measure of overall divisional profitability; performance margin narrows the analysis to only those cost and revenue items *controllable* by the division's manager.

To expand the concept of contribution margin to divisional performance analysis, let us look at the operating results of The Flexible Corporation for April 19xx. As Exhibit 14-1 shows, the company earned net income before taxes of $14,000. Information at the divisional level will give management data necessary to evaluate performance. Distributing the fixed costs to the divisions is very important to the evaluation procedure. Only *traceable* fixed costs should be charged to a division. Any fixed costs not traceable should be accounted for as common or joint fixed costs and treated as a cost of the company as a whole. As illustrated in Exhibit 14-1, of the total fixed costs of $96,000, $20,000 is traceable to Division H, $34,000 is traceable to Division J, $24,000 is traceable to Division L, and $18,000 is unallocable because it cannot be traced to any particular division.

Segment Margin Analysis. When preparing a divisional performance report under the contribution approach, only costs that are specifically traceable to a division are deducted from that division's revenue. The resulting segment margin, shown in Exhibit 14-2, indicates the contribution of each division to the unallocated common fixed costs and company profit. The segment margin, referred to earlier in Exhibit 12-6 as divisional income, is an appropriate income measure for evaluating the profit potential of each division. Notice in Exhibit 14-2 that the common or joint companywide fixed costs have not been allocated to the divisions. Although the divisions benefit from these common costs, the principal objective of the divisional performance report is to measure the division's ability to recover the traceable costs that result from their operations. Allocation is not desirable since joint fixed costs are controllable primarily at the corporate management level.

Exhibit 14-1. Contribution-Based Income Statement

The Flexible Corporation
April 19x9 Contribution-Based Income Statement

Total sales	$250,000	Fixed costs traceable to	
Variable costs/expenses	(140,000)	divisions without allocation	
Contribution margin	$110,000	Division H	$20,000
Fixed costs/expenses	(96,000)	Division J	34,000
Net income before taxes	$ 14,000	Division L	24,000
		Unallocated joint fixed costs	
		not traceable to divisions	18,000
		Total fixed costs/expenses	$96,000

Exhibit 14-2. Divisional Performance Report

The Flexible Corporation
April 19x9 Divisional Performance Report

	Division H	Division J	Division L	Totals
Sales	$60,000	$100,000	$90,000	$250,000
Variable costs/expenses	(30,000)	(70,000)	(40,000)	(140,000)
Contribution margin	$30,000	$ 30,000	$50,000	$110,000
Traceable fixed costs	(20,000)	(34,000)	(24,000)	(78,000)
Segment margin*	$10,000	$ (4,000)	$26,000	$ 32,000
Unallocated companywide fixed costs/expenses not traceable to divisions				(18,000)
Net income before taxes				$ 14,000

* Positive or negative contribution of each segment to the recovery of unallocated fixed costs and company profits.

Performance Margin. A further refinement to the contribution approach for divisions is to separate the traceable fixed costs of each division into those controllable and uncontrollable by the division manager. Certain costs, although traceable to a segment as big as a division, are incurred because top management in the home office decided to incur the expense. Examples include advertising costs, insurance costs, some building and equipment costs, and the division manager's own salary. All of these costs can be easily traced to a division but are not within the division manager's control. By separating controllable, traceable fixed costs from those not under the manager's control, performance measurement can be taken one step further. Whereas the segment margin measures the division's ability to contribute to the company's joint fixed costs and anticipated profit, performance margin relates directly to the manager's performance. Performance margin is a statement about how well the manager performed with the revenues and resources he or she controls.

In Exhibit 14-3, the traceable fixed costs of each division are broken down into those controllable by the manager and those considered uncontrollable. Of the $20,000 of fixed costs traceable to Division H, $11,200 is controllable by the division manager; the remaining $8,800 is uncontrollable. Division J's traceable and controllable fixed costs equals $19,100, and the amount applicable to Division L is $14,100.

OBJECTIVE 4
Prepare a divisional performance report

The April 19x9 performance report for The Flexible Corporation is recast in Exhibit 14-4 to show the computation of divisional performance and segment margins. This report format has several key features:

1. Performance can be viewed from three perspectives:
   a. *Divisional contribution margin.* What the division contributes to the absorption of fixed costs and profit

Exhibit 14-3. Traceability of Fixed Costs

The Flexible Corporation
Breakdown of Traceable Fixed Costs

	Controllable Costs	Uncontrollable Costs	Total Fixed Costs
Division H			
Depreciation, equipment	$ 1,500	$ 1,500	$ 3,000
Building rent	1,900		1,900
Divisional supervisory personnel	6,000	5,000	11,000
Advertising expenses		1,500	1,500
Computer center costs	1,800		1,800
Insurance expense		800	800
Total traceable fixed costs	$11,200	$ 8,800	$20,000
Division J			
Depreciation, equipment	$ 3,500	$ 4,200	$ 7,700
Building rent	2,800		2,800
Divisional supervisory personnel	9,200	6,000	15,200
Advertising expenses		1,900	1,900
Computer center costs	3,600		3,600
Insurance expense		2,800	2,800
Total traceable fixed costs	$19,100	$14,900	$34,000
Division L			
Depreciation, equipment	$ 1,800	$ 1,400	$ 3,200
Building rent	2,700		2,700
Divisional supervisory personnel	7,500	4,500	12,000
Advertising expenses		2,100	2,100
Computer center costs	2,100		2,100
Insurance expense		1,900	1,900
Total traceable fixed costs	$14,100	$ 9,900	$24,000
Total traceable corporate fixed costs			$78,000

    b. *Divisional performance margin.* How well the division manager utilized the resources under her or his control
    c. *Divisional segment margin.* The division's contribution to the joint companywide fixed costs and company profit
2. Divisional performance has been reduced to percentages of total sales, which makes performance comparisons easier and lets top management identify areas that may need attention.

    How are Divisions H, J, and L doing? From the standpoint of contribution margin, the company's average for April 19x9 was 44 percent of sales. Only Division J fell below this amount. Measuring manager

Exhibit 14-4. Performance Report with Performance Margin

The Flexible Corporation
April 19x9 Divisional Performance Report—Recast to Include Performance Margin

	Division H		Division J		Division L		Totals	
	Amount	% of Sales	Amount	% of Sales	Amount	% of Sales	Amount	% of Sales
Sales	$60,000	100.00	$100,000	100.00	$90,000	100.00	$250,000	100.00
Less variable costs/ expenses	30,000	50.00	70,000	70.00	40,000	44.44	140,000	56.00
Contribution Margin	$30,000	50.00	$ 30,000	30.00	$50,000	55.56	$110,000	44.00
Less traceable fixed costs controllable by manager	11,200	18.67	19,100	19.10	14,100	15.67	44,400	17.76
Performance Margin	$18,800	31.33	$ 10,900	10.90	$35,900	39.89	$ 65,600	26.24
Less traceable fixed costs controllable by top management, not division manager	8,800	14.67	14,900	14.90	9,900	11.00	33,600	13.44
Segment Margin	$10,000	16.67	($ 4,000)	−4.00	$26,000	28.89	$ 32,000	12.80
Less unallocated companywide fixed costs/expenses not traceable to divisions							18,000	7.20
Net income before taxes							$ 14,000	5.60

performance, the average performance margin was 26.24 percent. Both Divisions H and L are well above the average, with Division L hitting almost 40 percent. Division J's 10.9 percent is far out of line. At the segment margin level, the divisions averaged 12.8 percent. Again, only Division J fell below this amount. Although the manager of Division J has a larger percentage of uncontrollable fixed costs to contend with, the division's overall performance needs to be further analyzed.

One common method of further analyzing Division J is to compare budgeted and actual data using the same format as described in Exhibit 14-4. Exhibit 14-5 presents such a comparative performance analysis. As shown, Division J was supposed to have generated a $33,000 segment margin that was to be 27.5 percent of sales of $120,000. Instead, they lost $4,000 of segment margin. The comparative amounts reveal the reasons for Division J's poor performance. First, sales were $20,000

Exhibit 14-5. Comparative Performance Analysis

Division J—The Flexible Corporation
Comparative Performance Analysis

	Budgeted		Actual	
	Amount	% of Sales	Amount	% of Sales
Sales	$120,000	100.00	$100,000	100.00
Less variable costs/expenses	60,000	50.00	70,000	70.00
Contribution Margin	$ 60,000	50.00	$ 30,000	30.00
Less traceable fixed costs controllable by manager	19,000	15.83	19,100	19.10
Performance Margin	$ 41,000	34.17	$ 10,900	10.90
Less traceable fixed costs controllable by top management, not division manager	8,000	6.67	14,900	14.90
Segment Margin	$ 33,000	27.50	($ 4,000)	−4.00

under budget, which is a definite sign of poor performance. Second, variable cost and expenses amounted to 70 percent of sales rather than the 50 percent budgeted. Traceable fixed costs controllable by the manager were almost on target, even though the percentages differ. The third area of concern is the amount of traceable fixed costs controllable by top management, not the division manager. This figure increased from $8,000 budgeted to $14,900 actual. The overall assessment of Division J's poor performance is that the manager failed to meet the sales target and spent too much on variable cost items. However, part of the blame has to rest with top management, which overspent in the fixed cost area.

The Flexible Corporation's performance analysis demonstrates that several income measures can be developed to suit particular performance evaluation objectives. Similar analyses can be developed for companies using absorption costing procedures. Under such circumstances, performance margins and segment margins are derived by deducting the appropriate traceable costs from gross margin on sales. Since income measures under absorption costing are affected by production volume, the contribution margin approach is the more desirable because it distinguishes between fixed and variable cost behavior patterns.

The contribution approach to performance evaluation can be applied to segments such as divisions, sales territories, branch locations, product lines, or classes of customers. Extending the Flexible Corporation example, if Division H produces five separate products, then the contribution approach can be applied to each product line. Again, the guiding principle is that joint costs that benefit all products should not be allocated to the various product lines. As a general rule, as segments become smaller in scope, fewer fixed costs will be traceable to each segment.

Return on Investment
As a Performance Measure

OBJECTIVE 5

Apply return on investment measures to evaluate divisional performance

The rate of return earned on the assets a division or other company segment uses is a good measure of the segment's profitability.[1] For investment centers, return on investment is an important indicator because it takes into account both profits and the resources used to produce those profits. The basic **return on investment** (ROI) formula is the ratio of income to an investment base:

$$\text{ROI} = \frac{\text{income}}{\text{investment base}}$$

Of course, properly measuring the income and the investment base is critical to the value of this performance measure. Using this formula, both the income and investment base for a division must be defined and computed in accordance with specific company and/or division objectives.

Income Measurement Alternatives

Return on investment can be used to evaluate a business' financial management and operating management functions. **Financial management** is concerned with the acquisition of funds, capital structure, and debt-to-equity relationships. The appropriate ROI measure for evaluating financial management performance is net income *after* interest and taxes divided by stockholders' equity. **Operating management** is primarily concerned with the use of available resources to generate the largest income *before* interest and taxes that is consistent with a company's long-range policies and within social and environmental constraints. Evaluation of operating management must concentrate on the uses of resources and should not be affected by capital structure or the costs of obtaining capital funds.

The importance of using different ROI measures for financial and operating management is evident from the comparisons in Exhibit 14-6. We assume that a company has two separate divisions. Both divisions earned the same net operating income, but Division B, with long-term debt in its capital structure, has an interest expense deduction and lower income taxes. Based on ROI measures, which division is more profitable? The appropriate profit figure to compare is not clear because operating managements in both divisions were equally efficient and productive. That is, both divisions earned 30.19 percent ROI based on operating income and total assets.

From the stockholders' viewpoint, financial management was probably superior in Division B, which earned a 41.01 percent return on equity. The use of financial leverage in Division B enabled management to produce a higher return on stockholders' equity than the 10 percent return

---

1. Many of the ideas and concepts in this section were initially developed in *Basic Cost Accounting Concepts,* Henry R. Anderson and Mitchell H. Raiborn (Boston: Houghton Mifflin, 1977), pp. 580–585.

Exhibit 14-6. ROI Measures for Financial and Operating Management		
	Division A	**Division B**
Balance Sheet		
Current assets	$ 45,600	$ 45,600
Other assets	128,300	128,300
Total assets	$173,900	$173,900
Current liabilities	$ 13,900	$ 13,900
Long-term debt (10%)	0	90,000
Stockholders' equity	160,000	70,000
Total liabilities and capital	$173,900	$173,900
Income Statement		
Net income from operations	$ 52,500	$ 52,500
Less interest expense (10% of debt)	0	9,000
Income before taxes	$ 52,500	$ 43,500
Less income taxes (34%)	17,850	14,790
Net income	$ 34,650	$ 28,710
Return on Investment Measures		
1. Net income from operations/total assets	30.19%	30.19%
2. Net income/total assets	19.93%	16.51%
3. Net income/stockholders' equity	21.66%	41.01%

paid to the lenders of debt capital. However, if operating management is evaluated by comparing net income to total assets, then Division B's ROI is 16.51 percent. In comparison, Division A's ROI is 19.93 percent. Operating management performance in Division B suffers, but financial management appears excellent.

This brief analysis highlights some of the measurement problems in financial and managerial accounting. To resolve this apparent dilemma, the income measure for ROI computations must correspond with related performance evaluation objectives. Operating management should be evaluated by relating operating income to resources committed to operations. Interest expense and income taxes should be excluded from the operating income measure.

For investment centers, performance margin and segment margin can be used as income measures for two separate ROI computations. Return on investment as a measure of managerial performance should use performance margin and assets controllable by the division manager. To evaluate segment performance, ROI should be measured by relating segment margin to assets that are traceable to the division. By excluding interest and income taxes from the ROI analysis, operating management can be evaluated independently of the way the division managed its financial resources.

Investment Measurement Alternatives

The investment base used in ROI analyses must also conform to the objectives of each performance evaluation. Some measure of assets committed to operations must be developed to evaluate operating management. There are several variations in practice, but the best measure is total assets traceable to a particular segment. The total asset base must be reduced by excess and idle facilities, investments in securities and land, and current assets such as cash and receivables. The real issue is whether ROI should be measured in relation to total assets available or total assets employed. Judgment and individual preference must govern this choice. There is no single correct ROI measure, but once the investment base has been defined, it should be used consistently in ROI analysis. In some instances, several ROI measures can be developed for a particular division using a different asset base for each measure. The important point is to define what the ROI seeks to measure.

The assets included in the investment base should be stated at average total cost. Since additional investments and asset retirements may occur frequently, income for a period must be related to average assets employed during the same period. Averages can be developed from monthly or quarterly balance sheet data. Annual ROI analysis can use an average of beginning and ending asset balances for a year if there were no significant interim changes in total assets.

Another investment-base measurement problem is the treatment of fixed assets and accumulated depreciation. Should tangible fixed assets be included in the investment base at historical cost or at cost less accumulated depreciation (book value)? As Exhibit 14-7 shows, the alternatives give different results, depending on the assumptions involved. The better alternative is to include fixed assets at total cost without deducting accumulated depreciation.

The main reason for using total cost is to avoid the increasing ROI that occurs with the passage of time using book value. Note in Exhibit 14-7 on the next page that the ROI based on book value increases even though operating income is decreasing over the same period of time. The example in Exhibit 14-7 shows a slightly decreasing ROI when the measure is based on total fixed asset cost. The annual change in ROI occurs only because profits are declining each year. The logic of a constant dollar measure for particular fixed assets is sound and gives meaningful results. With fixed assets stated at total cost, ROI will increase or decrease in the same direction as operating income. As stated above, if book value of fixed assets is used, ROI increases each year simply because the ROI denominator is decreasing.

As an alternative to historical cost, some financial analysts prefer to value assets at current replacement cost. Replacement cost of assets reflects current conditions and is useful if divisions are being compared to determine where company funds could earn the best return. Since performance evaluation of operating management involves the comparison of ROI among divisions, assets in the investment base probably should be revalued for this purpose. Other analysts recommend restating

Exhibit 14-7. Effect of Valuation of Assets on ROI Measures

Information supporting example

   Fixed asset purchased in January 19x2 at a cost of $220,000

   Salvage value $20,000

   Asset has five-year life

   Assume straight-line depreciation over life

   Initial annual net operating income $30,000

   Net operating income decreases $2,000 annually because of decreased efficiency

   Assume no additional investments

End of Year	Valuation of Fixed Assets		Operating Income	Rate of Return Based On	
	Cost	Book Value		Cost (%)	Book Value (%)
19x2	$220,000	$180,000	$30,000	13.64	16.67
19x3	220,000	140,000	28,000	12.73	20.00
19x4	220,000	100,000	26,000	11.82	26.00
19x5	220,000	60,000	24,000	10.91	40.00
19x6	220,000	20,000	22,000	10.00	110.00

historical costs at current price levels by using appropriate index number adjustments. The use of price level adjustments to restate the historical cost of nonmonetary assets such as buildings, equipment, and land is useful. These adjustments partially compensate for the higher ROI some divisions otherwise would report on assets acquired several years ago at lower price levels.

Return on Investment Analysis

Return on investment is highly sensitive to the choice of income measure and investment-base valuation. As discussed, these measurement problems are solved partially by a clear definition of the objective for a particular ROI computation and the contents of the numerator and the denominator. Another technical factor about ROI is that the ratio is an aggregate measure of many interrelationships. The basic ROI equation of income divided by assets can be rewritten to show the many elements that influence the ultimate ROI number.

Two important factors are profit margin and asset turnover. Profit margin is the ratio of net income to sales; it represents the percentage of each sales dollar resulting in profits. Asset turnover is the ratio of sales to average assets and indicates the productivity of assets or the number of sales dollars generated by each dollar invested in assets. Return on investment is equal to profit margin times asset turnover:

$$ROI = \text{profit margin} \times \text{asset turnover}$$

or

$$ROI = \frac{income}{sales} \times \frac{sales}{assets} = \frac{income}{assets}$$

Profit margin and asset turnover are factors that explain changes in ROI for a single division or differences of ROI among divisions. Hence the formula ROI equals profit margin times asset turnover is useful for analyzing and interpreting the elements that make up the overall return on investment.

The data for two divisions, EF and GH, summarized in Table 14-1, help illustrate the dependency of ROI on profit margins and asset turnover. Division GH generated the larger net income, but Division EF shows a higher return on investment. Although company management is concerned with total income and earnings per share of common stock, they also are concerned with the relative profitability of invested capital. Division GH could improve its comparative standing by increasing profit margin or asset turnover. Actions to increase sales, reduce costs, or reduce the assets employed would produce positive increases in ROI.

The numerous interrelationships that affect the ROI measure are diagrammed in Figure 14-1. You can see that ROI is affected by pricing decisions, product sales mix, capital budgeting decisions for new facilities, product sales volume, operational efficiency, and other decisions having a financial dimension. In essence, a single ROI number is a composite index of many cause-and-effect relationships and interdependent financial elements.

Because of the many factors affecting return on investment, management should use this measure cautiously in evaluating performance. If ROI is overemphasized as a performance measure, division managers could react

---

Table 14-1. Comparison of ROI Calculations

	Division EF	Division GH
1. Total sales	$1,650,000	$2,840,000
2. Net income	180,000	210,000
3. Average total assets	940,000	1,250,000
4. Profit margin (2 ÷ 1)	10.91%	7.39%
5. Asset turnover (1 ÷ 3)	1.76 times	2.27 times
6. Return on investment (4 × 5)	19.15%	16.80%
7. Return on investment (2 ÷ 3)	19.15%	16.80%

Figure 14-1. The Du Pont Formula (named for the company that developed the concept). Interrelated Factors Affecting Return on Investment

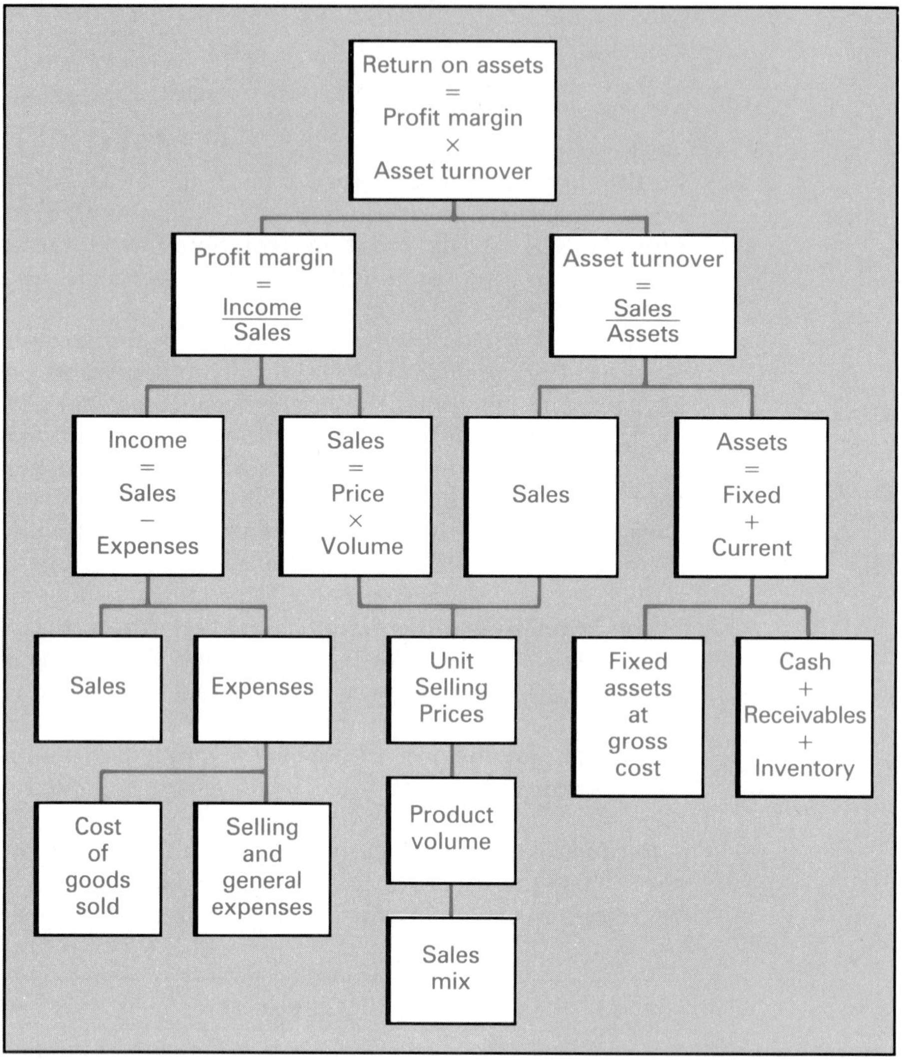

with business decisions that favor their personal ROI performance at the expense of companywide profits or long-run success of the divisions. A second strategy for performance evaluation systems is to develop several divisional performance indicators. Possible measures include performance margin, segment margin, one or more versions of return on investment, sales growth percentage, operating efficiency indices, share of product market, and other measures of the key variables in business activity. Return on investment for divisions should be shown as comparisons with budgeted goals and past ROI trends. Because of the technical problems in measuring ROI, changes in this ratio over time can be more revealing than any single number.

Transfer Pricing

In Chapter 7 the concept of responsibility centers was introduced. As you learned, cost/expense centers and profit centers are important to a decentralized organization because they help alleviate some of the difficulty of controlling diverse operations. Responsibility for a company's functions are placed with managers, and managers' performance is measured by comparing actual results with budgeted or projected results.

Profit measurement and return on investment are important gauges of performance in decentralized divisions. But at cost centers where only costs are involved, many people have difficulty measuring performance. This problem becomes more complicated when divisions within a company exchange goods or services and assume the role of customer or supplier to another division. As a result, transfer prices are used. A **transfer price** is the price at which goods are exchanged among a company's divisions. Such prices allow intracompany transactions to be measured and accounted for. These prices also affect the revenues and costs of the divisions involved. Furthermore, since a transfer price contains an estimated amount of profit, a manager's ability to meet a targeted profit can be measured. Although often called fictitious or created prices, company transfer prices as well as related policies are closely connected with performance evaluation.

Transfer Pricing Characteristics

The subject of transfer pricing is complex. Some people believe totally in the benefits of using transfer prices; others believe they should never be used because they are not real prices. To illustrate how transfer prices are used and to help explain the difficult operational and behavioral aspects of such prices, we analyze two situations requiring them. Figure 14-2 is a pictorial view of how products flow at the Creative Pulp Company. This company is composed of three divisions: the Pulp Division, the Cardboard Division, and the Box Division. Example 1 shows the Pulp Division transferring wood pulp to the Cardboard Division for use in making cardboard. The Cardboard Division also has the option of purchasing the pulp from an outside supplier. The cost of making the pulp, including materials, labor, variable overhead, and fixed overhead, is $12.90 per pound. By adding a 10 percent factor to cover miscellaneous and divisional overhead expenses as well as a small profit, the proposed transfer price amounts to $14.19 per pound. The outside supplier will sell the pulp to the company for $14.10 per pound. What should the manager of the Cardboard Division do?

Clearly, pressure is on the manager of the Pulp Division to lower the transfer price to an amount equal to or less than $14.10, the market price. If this action is taken, however, the $.09 per pound reduction will directly affect profits of the Pulp Division. In turn, that situation will affect the manager's performance. On the other hand, if the manager of the Cardboard Division agrees or is forced to pay the $14.19 price to benefit

Figure 14-2. Intracompany Transfer Pricing Examples—Creative Pulp Company

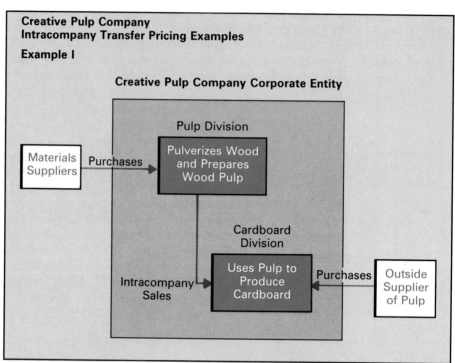

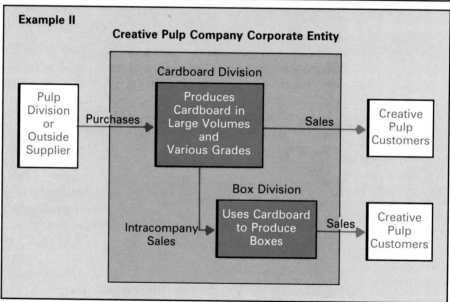

overall company operating results, that person's profit and performance will be negatively affected. Thus the question arises: Is either amount a fair price? Such a problem would not occur if costs were simply accumulated as the product travels through the production process. The Pulp Division could be treated as a cost center and the manager's performance evaluated on the basis of only budgeted and actual costs. But then the Pulp Division's return on investment could not be measured. These are the conflicting objectives of performance evaluation in a decentralized organization.

A second common situation is shown in Example 2 of Figure 14-2. Instead of an outside supplier's influencing an internal transfer price, the Cardboard Division has an outside customer. The manager of the Cardboard Division must decide whether to sell cardboard to the outside customer for $28.10 per pound or supply the Box Division at $27.90 per pound. (The $27.90 covers all costs plus a profit margin.)

Several possible problems must be considered here. Is the outside customer going to make boxes that compete with the company's Box Division? Should the Box Division pay a market value transfer price so the Cardboard Division's manager can be evaluated properly? What about the Box Division? Should that manager suffer because all profits were siphoned off by managers of the Pulp and Cardboard divisions?

These are but a few of the problems involved in using transfer prices. Perhaps you can now better understand why there are both proponents and opponents of this concept. From the example, it is easy to understand why transfer prices often cause internal bickering between managers. But measuring a manager's performance is still a major objective of decentralized companies. And the use of transfer prices is one important approach to that objective.

Transfer Pricing Methods

OBJECTIVE 7
Distinguish between a cost-based transfer price and a market-based transfer price

There are two primary approaches to developing a transfer price:

1. The price may be based on the cost of the item until its transfer to the next department or process.
2. A market value may be used if the item has an existing external market when transferred.

Both these pricing situations were present in our Creative Pulp Company example. There, the Pulp Division would be inclined to use the cost method since no apparent outside market exists for the pulp product. The only user of pulp is the Cardboard Division. However, the Box Division will probably have to pay a market-related price for the cardboard since the Cardboard Division can either sell its product outside or transfer it to the Box Division.

In a situation in which no external markets are involved, division managers in a decentralized company may agree on a *cost-plus transfer price* or a *negotiated transfer price*. A **cost-plus transfer price** is the sum of costs incurred by the producing division plus an agreed-on profit percentage. The weakness of cost-plus pricing is that cost recovery is guaranteed to the selling division, and guaranteed cost recovery fails to detect inefficient operating conditions as well as excessive cost incurrence.

A **negotiated transfer price**, on the other hand, is bargained for by the managers of the buying and selling divisions. From the cost-plus side, a transfer price may be based on an agreement to use a standard cost plus a profit percentage. This approach emphasizes cost control through the use of standard costs while still allowing the selling division to return a profit even though it is a cost center. A negotiated transfer price may also be based on a market price that was reduced in the bargaining process.

Market transfer prices are discussed but seldom used without being subjected to negotiations between managers. Using market prices may cause the selling division to ignore negotiation attempts from the buying division manager and sell directly to outside customers. If this causes an internal shortage of materials and forces the buying division to purchase materials from the outside, overall company profits may be lowered even when the selling division makes a profit. Such use of market prices works against a company's overall operating objectives. Therefore, when market prices are used to develop transfer prices, they are normally used only as a basis for negotiation.

Developing a Transfer Price

OBJECTIVE 8
Develop a
transfer price

Many of the normal pricing considerations introduced in Chapter 11 are also present in the development of a transfer price. The first step is to compute the unit cost of the item being transferred. Next, management must determine the appropriate profit markup. If the semifinished product (1) has an existing external market for the selling division to consider or (2) can be purchased in similar condition by the buying division from an outside source, then the market price must be included in the analysis used to develop a transfer price. The final step is to have the managers negotiate a compromise between the two prices.

Now, look again at the Creative Pulp Company example. The division manager's computations supporting the $14.19 cost-plus transfer price are shown in Exhibit 14-8.

This one-year budget is based on the expectation that the Cardboard Division will require 480,000 pounds of pulp. Unit costs are stated in the right column. Notice that allocated corporate overhead is not included in the computation of the transfer price. Only costs related to the Pulp Division are included. The profit markup percentage of 10 percent adds $1.29 to the final transfer price of $14.19.

At this point management could dictate that the $14.19 price be used. On the other hand, the manager of the Cardboard Division could bring the outside purchase price of $14.10 per pound to the attention of management. Usually, such situations end up being negotiated to determine the final transfer price. Each side has a position and strong arguments to support a price. And each manager's performance will be compromised by adopting the other's price.

In the example, both managers brought their concerns to the attention of top management. A unique settlement was reached. Since internal profits must be erased before financial statements are prepared, management allowed the Pulp Division to use the $14.19 price and the Cardboard Division the $14.10 price for purposes of performance evaluation. Obviously, the company did not want the Cardboard Division buying pulp from another company. At the same time, the Pulp Division had the

Exhibit 14-8. Transfer Price Computation		
Creative Pulp Company **Pulp Division—Transfer Price Computation**		
Cost Category	**Budgeted Costs**	**Cost per Unit**
Materials		
Wood	$1,584,000	$ 3.30
Scrap wood	336,000	0.70
Labor		
Shaving/cleaning	768,000	1.60
Pulverizing	1,152,000	2.40
Blending	912,000	1.90
Overhead		
Variable	936,000	1.95
Fixed	504,000	1.05
Subtotals	$6,192,000	$12.90
Costs allocated from corporate office	144,000	
Target profit, 10% of division's costs	619,200	1.29
Total costs and profit	$6,955,200	
Cost-plus transfer price		$14.19

right to a 10 percent profit. Such approaches are often used to maintain harmony within a corporation. In this case it allowed top management to measure the managers' performance while avoiding behavioral issues. After the period was over, all fictitious profits were canceled by using adjusting entries before preparing end-of-year financial statements. The final product, in this case the boxes, had a profit factor that took into account all operations of the business.

Measuring Performance by Using Transfer Prices

OBJECTIVE 9
Measure a manager's performance by using transfer prices

When transfer prices are used, performance reports on managers of cost centers will contain revenue and income figures used in the evaluation. The Pulp Division performance report in Exhibit 14-9 is a good example.

The Pulp Division supplied 500 more pounds of pulp than anticipated for the month. Sales were priced at $14.19 per pound. The variable costs per unit shown earlier were used to extend budgeted and actual amounts for materials, labor, and variable overhead. The result was that the manager of the Pulp Division earned a March profit of $43,350, which

Exhibit 14-9. Performance Report Using Transfer Prices			

Creative Pulp Company
Pulp Division—Performance Report
For March 19x0

	Budget (42,000 pounds)	Actual (42,500 pounds)	Difference Over/(Under) Budget
Costs Controllable by Supervisor			
Sales to Cardboard Division	$595,980	$603,075	$7,095
Cost of goods sold			
Materials			
Wood	$138,600	$140,250	$1,650
Scrap wood	29,400	29,750	350
Labor			
Shaving/cleaning	67,200	68,000	800
Pulverizing	100,800	102,000	1,200
Blending	79,800	80,750	950
Overhead			
Variable	81,900	82,875	975
Fixed	44,100	44,100	0
Total cost of goods sold	$541,800	$547,725	$5,925
Gross margin from sales	$ 54,180	$ 55,350	$1,170
Costs Uncontrollable by Supervisor			
Cost allocated from corporate office	$ 12,000	$ 12,000	$ 0
Division's income	$ 42,180	$ 43,350	$1,170

was $1,170 over budget. The transfer price made it possible for the division to be evaluated as if it were a profit center, even though the division does not sell to outside customers. Were the Pulp Division still accounted for as a cost center, the manager would have to explain costs being $5,925 over budget instead of divisional income's being over target.

(*Note:* Management may want the budget column restated at 42,500 pounds for evaluation purposes.)

Final Note on Transfer Prices

Problems in transfer price policy arise when buying divisions elect to purchase from outside suppliers. A selling division with adequate capacity to fulfill the buying division's demands should sell to that division at any price that recovers incremental costs. Incremental costs of intra-company sales include all variable costs of production and distribution plus any fixed costs directly traceable to intracompany sales. If a buying division can acquire products from outside suppliers at an annual cost that is less than the supplying division's incremental costs, then purchases should be made from the outside supplier because overall company profits will be enhanced. A thorough analysis of the supplying division's operations should also be conducted.

Chapter Review

Review of Learning Objectives

1. **Identify the characteristics of a decentralized organization.**
   The characteristics of a decentralized organization are: (1) the organization has more than one operating segment or division; (2) the manager of each division has autonomy regarding his or her operating segment; and (3) segment manager's decisions must be made within the constraints of the company's overall goals, objectives, plans, and policies.

2. **Describe the four-step performance evaluation process for decentralized operations.**
   The four steps critical to the development of an effective performance evaluation process for decentralized divisions are: (1) establish the company's segments; (2) identify those revenues and costs traceable to and controllable by each segment's manager; (3) communicate the performance indicators to be used for each segment; and (4) compare actual operating results with budgeted amounts.

3. **Compute the performance margin and the segment margin for decentralized divisions.**
   The contribution approach for divisional performance evaluation is used to highlight dollar amounts that measure performance margin and segment margin. Performance margin reflects the effects of divisional management decisions on divisional income. Segment margin expresses a division's overall profitability by identifying its contribution to unallocated fixed costs and the resulting company profit.

4. **Prepare a divisional performance report.**
   In a divisional performance report, total sales revenue is reduced by total variable costs and expenses to arrive at contribution margin. Subtracting all traceable fixed costs controllable by the division manager from contribution margin yields performance margin. Segment margin is computed by sub-tracting all traceable fixed costs uncontrollable by the division manager from performance margin. Costs that are not traceable to divisions are treated as common or joint companywide costs and not allocated to divisions for performance evaluation purposes.

5. **Apply return on investment measures to evaluate divisional performance.**
   Return on investment is computed by dividing net income by the appropriate investment base. Return on investment can be used to evaluate a business'

financial management and operating management functions. Financial management is concerned with the acquisition of funds, capital structure, and debt-to-equity relationships. The appropriate ROI measure for evaluating financial management performance is net income *after* interest and taxes divided by stockholders' equity. Operating management is primarily concerned with the use of available resources to generate the largest income *before* interest and taxes that is consistent with a company's long-range policies and within social and environmental constraints. Evaluation of operating management must concentrate on the uses of resources and should not be affected by capital structure or the costs of obtaining capital funds.

6. **Define and discuss transfer pricing.**
   A transfer price is the price at which goods are exchanged between a company's divisions. Since a transfer price contains an amount of estimated profit, a manager's ability to meet a profit target can be measured, even for a typical cost center. Although often called fictitious or created prices, company transfer prices and related policies are closely connected with performance evaluation.

7. **Distinguish between a cost-based transfer price and a market-based transfer price.**
   There are two primary approaches to developing transfer prices: (1) the price may be based on the cost of the item up to the point at which it is transferred to the next department or process or (2) a market value may be used if an item has an existing external market when transferred. A cost-plus transfer price is the sum of costs incurred by the producing division plus an agreed-on profit percentage. A market-based transfer price is geared to external market prices. In most cases a negotiated transfer price is used, that is, one that was bargained for between the managers of the selling and buying divisions.

8. **Develop a transfer price.**
   Many of the normal pricing considerations are also present in the development of a transfer price. The first step is to compute the unit cost of the item being transferred. Next, management must determine the appropriate profit markup. Then, those involved in the intracompany transfer must discuss any relevant market prices before negotiating a final transfer price.

9. **Measure a manager's performance by using transfer prices.**
   When transfer prices are used, performance reports on managers of cost centers must contain revenue and income figures used in the evaluation process. Actual performance reports on cost centers will look just like those used for profit centers. Evaluation procedures will also be similar in that the manager of the cost center will have to explain any differences between budgeted and actual revenues and income.

Review of Concepts and Terminology

The following important concepts were introduced in this chapter:

(L.O. 1)   **Decentralized organization**: A business having several operating segments; operating control of each segment's various activities is the responsibility of the segment's manager.

(L.O. 3)   **Segment margin**: A performance measure that expresses a division's overall profitability by identifying its contribution to unallocated fixed costs and the resulting company profit.

(L.O.3) **Performance margin:** A performance measure that reflects the effects of a divisional manager's decisions on divisional income.

(L.O.5) **Return on investment (ROI):** The ratio of an income measure to an investment base.

(L.O.6) **Transfer price:** The price at which goods are exchanged among a company's divisions.

Other important terms introduced in this chapter are:

asset turnover (p. 538)
costs incurred indicators (p. 528)
cost-plus transfer price (p. 543)
effort expended indicators (p. 528)
financial management (p. 535)
goal congruence (p. 529)
market transfer price (p. 544)
negotiated transfer price (p. 543)
operating management (p. 535)
profit margin (p. 538)
resources employed indicators (p. 528)
results achieved indicators (p. 528)

Review Problem: Performance and Segment Margins

Following is a partial trial balance of the Dictionary Division of Tageiher Publishing Company, Inc.:

Dictionary Division Tageiher Publishing Company, Inc. Partial Trial Balance		
	Debit	**Credit**
Sales		$4,268,000
Variable costs		
Paper materials	$320,100	
Materials-handling overhead	119,504	
Manuscript layout labor	102,432	
Direct labor	247,544	
Machine setup labor	136,576	
Machine maintenance	106,700	
Electrical power	51,216	
Supplies	64,020	
Packing materials and labor	59,752	
Variable selling costs	217,668	

(continued)

(continued)

Dictionary Division Tageiher Publishing Company, Inc. Partial Trial Balance	Debit	Credit
Fixed costs		
Machine depreciation*	$132,308	
Building depreciation†	140,844	
Home office general and administrative expenses‡	213,400	
Division manager's salary†	110,968	
Selling expenses		
Division*	183,524	
Home office‡	98,164	
Advertising		
Divisional*	230,472	
Companywide†	196,328	
Computer service fee*	145,112	
Division supervision salaries*	298,760	
Factory insurance		
Fire†	42,680	
Liability†	72,556	
Division administrative costs*	153,648	
Copyright write-off*	115,236	

* Traceable and controllable by division manager.
† Traceable to division but uncontrollable by manager.
‡ Not traceable and must be allocated to division.

Required

From the information given, prepare a divisional performance report that includes contribution margin, performance margin, and segment margin as well as the final profit margin.

Answer to Review Problem

The divisional performance report for the Dictionary Division of Tageiher Publishing Company, Inc., is shown on the following page.

Dictionary Division
Tageiher Publishing Company, Inc.
Divisional Performance Report

Sales		$4,268,000		100.00%
Less variable costs				
Paper and materials	$320,100		7.50%	
Materials-handling overhead	119,504		2.80%	
Manuscript layout labor	103,432		2.40%	
Direct labor	247,544		5.80%	
Machine setup labor	136,576		3.20%	
Machine maintenance	106,700		2.50%	
Electrical power	51,216		1.20%	
Supplies	64,020		1.50%	
Packing materials and labor	59,752		1.40%	
Variable selling costs	217,668	1,425,512	5.10%	33.40%
Contribution Margin		$2,842,488		66.60%
Less traceable fixed costs controllable by manager				
Machine depreciation	$132,308		3.10%	
Divisional selling expenses	183,524		4.30%	
Divisional advertising	230,472		5.40%	
Computer service fee	145,112		3.40%	
Division supervision salaries	298,760		7.00%	
Division administrative costs	153,648		3.60%	
Copyright write-off	115,236	1,259,060	2.70%	29.50%
Performance Margin		$1,583,428		37.10%
Less traceable fixed costs uncontrollable by manager				
Building depreciation	$140,844		3.30%	
Division manager's salary	110,968		2.60%	
Companywide advertising	196,328		4.60%	
Factory insurance				
Fire	42,680		1.00%	
Liability	72,556	251,812	1.70%	13.20%
Segment Margin		$1,331,616		23.90%
Less costs allocated to division by home office				
Home office general and administrative expenses	$213,400		5.00%	
Selling expenses from home office	98,164	311,564	2.30%	7.30%
Divisional Profit Margin		$1,020,052		16.60%

Chapter Assignments

Questions

1. Identify the characteristics of a decentralized organization.
2. Compare and contrast centralized and decentralized management styles.
3. State the four steps necessary for the development of an effective performance evaluation process for a decentralized division or segment.
4. What does the phrase "traceable and controllable costs and revenues" mean?
5. Give two examples of results achieved indicators of performance.
6. Differentiate between and give examples of effort expended indicators and resources employed indicators of performance.
7. Why is goal congruence especially critical when evaluating the performance of managers of decentralized divisions?
8. What is performance margin?
9. How does performance margin differ from segment margin?
10. Relate contribution margin to performance margin and segment margin.
11. Define return on investment.
12. What is the difference between measuring the performance of financial management versus operating management?
13. How does profit margin and asset turnover influence return on investment measures?
14. What is a transfer price?
15. Why are transfer prices associated with decentralized corporations?
16. Why is a transfer price often referred to as a fictitious or created price?
17. Describe the cost-plus approach to setting transfer prices.
18. How are market prices used to develop a transfer price?
19. Under what circumstances are market prices relevant to a transfer pricing decision?
20. Explain the statement, "Most transfer prices are negotiated prices."

Classroom Exercises

**Exercise 14-1.
Characteristics of
Decentralized
Organizations**
(L.O. 1)

Following are two independent scenarios describing company environments. For each scenario, state whether the company operates as a decentralized organization. Identify the reasons for your answers.

Scenario 1: Earnie Huband formed NAA Industries twenty-five years ago. Since then, the company has grown, and today there are fourteen divisions located in eight states and three foreign countries. Earnie is chairman of the board of directors. The company is run by a president, with the help of four vice presidents, six product line managers, and fourteen division managers. The research and development division operates adjacent to the main plant, located in Richmond, Virginia. All employee hiring is done at the division level, but the semimonthly payroll is prepared in the main plant and sent by overnight mail to the various divisions in the United States. Foreign employees are paid from the Stockholm, Sweden, division. Division managers are responsible to the operating vice presidents. Product-line decisions are made by the product line managers. Division managers are primarily responsible for cost control.

Scenario 2: Raubenstine Company operates using two divisions, one in Yonkers, New York, and one in Erie, Pennsylvania. The company's home office is in Philadelphia. The Yonkers Division is highly automated and employs only sixteen people. The Erie Division, on the other hand, is highly labor intensive and requires more than two hundred people to operate its four product lines. Product-line decisions are made at the division level but must meet company guidelines developed at the home office. The two division managers are evaluated on their overall profitability.

Exercise 14-2.
Evaluating a
Decentralized
Company
(L.O.2)

Bob White Enterprises has been organized as a decentralized company for the past twelve years. The company has twenty-six divisions and is structured so that division vice presidents are totally responsible for the revenues and costs of their operation. The home office provides centralized services that are allocated to the divisions based on usage. In addition, company officers and directors develop and implement the overall company strategic plans and policies.

During the past four months, several of the divisions have undergone a management revitalization program and have replaced or created several new middle-management positions. In total, more than one hundred new managers have accepted employment with the company. The division vice presidents are concerned that these new people do not fully understand how the company is organized and how the divisions are evaluated.

Using the four-step process that is the basis for the performance evaluation system for decentralized companies, prepare a memo to the new managers describing the company's structure and management philosophy.

Exercise 14-3.
Cost Traceability
(L.O.3)

Blanco Products, Inc., is a major supplier of quality home products and operates as a decentralized company with five divisions. The divisions are located in the Virginia, Washington, D.C., and Maryland areas. Each division functions as an autonomous segment under the structure created by top management. The profit performance report of the Alfonso Division for March 19x9 is shown on page 554.

Required

Identify those operating costs that are traceable to the Alfonso Division. Are all traceable costs controllable by the division manager?

Exercise 14-4.
Segment and
Performance
Margins
(L.O.3,4)

Using the information in the Blanco Products, Inc., performance report in Exercise 14-3 (shown on the following page), prepare a profit performance report using the contribution approach format. Within the report, identify the Alfonso Division's contribution margin, performance margin, and segment margin for March 19x9.

Blanco Products, Inc.
Profit Performance Report
For the Year Ended March 19x9

Sales revenues		$315,000
Operating costs		
Materials	$48,500	
Materials-handling overhead	23,200	
Direct labor	26,900	
Operating supplies	5,200	
Computer-assisted design labor	28,300	
Indirect labor	24,800	
Employee fringe benefits	9,600	
Heat, light, and power costs	6,100	
Depreciation, equipment	11,430	
Advertising expense		
Division products	17,260	
Home office related	14,180	
Division vice president salary	5,200	
Sales commissions	37,800	
Fixed selling costs of division	4,980	
Home office computer services		
Specific usage charges	8,190	
Allocated portion	5,680	
Company aircraft		
Specific usage charges	2,300	
Allocated portion	6,500	
Building rental—allocation from home office	8,490	
Interest expense—share of home office expense	11,320	
Companywide overhead (division's share)	7,840	
Total operating costs		313,770
Division profit before taxes		$ 1,230

Exercise 14-5.
Return on
Investment
Relationships
(L.O. 5)
Following are three independent cases with enough data presented so that return on investment can be computed as the product of asset turnover and profit margin. Assume the use of average total assets to compute asset turnover. Fill in all the missing values.

	Case 1	Case 2	Case 3
Sales revenue	$1,600,000	$1,200,000	?
Less variable costs	600,000	?	400,000
Contribution margin	$1,000,000	$ 800,000	$ 600,000
Less fixed costs	800,000	?	?
Net income	$ 200,000	$ 400,000	$ 400,000
Total assets, Jan. 1	$ 600,000	$3,600,000	?
Total assets, Dec. 31	$1,000,000	?	$2,400,000
Asset turnover	?	1/3	?
Profit margin	?	?	?
Return on investment	?	?	20.00%

Exercise 14-6.
Transfer Price
Comparison
(L.O. 6, 7)

David Koeppen and Gordon Pirrong are developing a transfer price for the first section of an automatic pool cleaning device. The housing is made in Department AA and then passed onto Department DG, wherein final assembly occurs. Unit costs for the housing are as follows:

Cost Categories	Unit Costs
Materials	$2.10
Direct labor	1.65
Variable factory overhead	1.15
Fixed factory overhead	0.80
Profit markup, 20% of cost	?

An outside supplier can supply the housing for $6.80 per unit.

1. Develop a cost-plus transfer price for the housing.
2. What should the transfer price be? Support your answer.

Exercise 14-7.
Developing a Cost-
Plus Transfer Price
(L.O. 8)

Management at Kaldenberg Industries has just decided to use a set of transfer prices for intracompany transfers between departments. Management's objective is to include return on assets in the performance evaluation of managers at its cost centers. Data from the Molding Department for the past six months are as follows:

Account	Total Costs	Expected Increases/Decreases
Raw plastic, ADG	$238,600	+10%
Raw plastic, XJS	398,700	-10%
Direct labor, Melting	145,300	—
Direct labor, Blending	167,200	—
Direct labor, Shaping	195,100	+ 5%
Variable factory overhead	92,300	+20%
Fixed factory overhead	125,900	—

During the six-month period, 52,500 plastic units were produced. The same number of units are expected to be completed during the next six-month period. The company uses a 15 percent profit markup percentage.

1. Compute estimated total costs for the Molding Department for the next six months.
2. Develop a cost-plus transfer price for the plastic unit.

Exercise 14-8.
Transfer Prices and
Performance
Evaluation
(L.O. 9)

The Jensen Fireplace Accessories Company uses transfer prices when evaluating division managers. Data from the Forging Department for April 19x9 are as follows:

	Budget	Actual
Steel ingots	$80,360	$ 80,780
Iron ingots	45,920	46,160
Brass ingots	183,680	184,640
Direct labor	235,340	236,570
Variable factory overhead	74,620	75,010
Fixed factory overhead	34,440	34,440
Corporate selling expenses	17,410	18,700
Corporate administrative expenses	18,200	19,100

A special alloy is prepared from iron, steel, and brass before the forging operation is begun.

The division's transfer price is $13.11 per unit. During April, the budget called for 57,400 units, and 57,700 units were actually produced and transferred.

Prepare a performance report for the Forging Division.

Interpreting Accounting Information

Transfer Price
Determination:
Orlando Industries,
Inc.
(L.O. 7, 8)

Two major operating divisions, the Cabinet Division and the Electronics Division, make up Orlando Industries, Inc. The company's major products are deluxe console television sets. The TV cabinets are manufactured by the Cabinet Division; the Electronics Division produces all electronic components and assembles the sets. The company uses a decentralized organizational structure.

The Cabinet Division not only supplies cabinets to the Electronics Division but also sells cabinets to other TV manufacturers. Based on a normal sales order of forty cabinets, the following unit cost breakdown for a deluxe television cabinet was developed:

Materials	$ 22.00
Direct labor	25.00
Variable factory overhead	14.00
Fixed factory overhead	16.00
Variable selling expenses	9.00
Fixed selling expenses	6.00
Fixed general and administrative expenses	8.00
Total unit cost	$100.00

The Cabinet Division's normal profit margin is 20 percent, and the regular selling price of a deluxe cabinet is $120. Divisional management recently decided that $120 will also be the transfer price used for all intracompany transactions.

Management at the Electronics Division is unhappy with that decision. They claim the Cabinet Division will show superior performance at the expense of the Electronics Division. Competition recently forced the company to lower prices. Because of a newly established transfer price for the cabinet, Electronics' portion of the profit margin on deluxe television sets was lowered to 18 percent. To counteract the new intracompany transfer price, management at the Electronics Division announced that effective immediately, all cabinets will be purchased from an outside supplier in lots of 200 cabinets at a unit price of $110 per cabinet.

The corporate president, J. J. Johnson, has called a meeting of both divisions to negotiate a fair intracompany transfer price. The following prices were listed as possible alternatives:

Current market price	$120 per cabinet
Current outside purchase price	
(This price is based on a large-quantity purchase discount. It will cause increased storage costs for the Electronics Division.)	$110 per cabinet
Total unit *manufacturing* costs plus a normal 20 percent profit margin	
$77.00 + $15.40	$92.40 per cabinet
Total unit costs, excluding variable selling expenses, plus a normal 20 percent profit margin	
$91.00 + $18.20	$109.20 per cabinet

Required

1. What price should be established for intracompany transactions? Defend your answer by showing the shortcomings of each alternative.
2. Were there an outside market for all units produced by the Cabinet Division at the $120 price would you change your answer to 1? Why?

Problem Set A

**Problem 14A-1.
Performance and
Segment Margins
(L.O.3,4)**

On the following page is a partial trial balance of the XJS Division of Lusignan Metalworks, Inc.

Required

From the information given, prepare a divisional performance report that includes contribution margin, performance margin, and segment margin as well as the final profit margin.

XJS Division Lusignan Metalworks, Inc. Partial Trial Balance		
	Debit	**Credit**
Sales		$1,346,000
Variable costs		
Materials	$107,680	
Materials-related overhead	33,650	
Direct labor	80,760	
Machine setup labor	40,380	
Machine maintenance	74,030	
Electrical power	10,768	
Supplies	21,536	
Packaging	59,224	
Variable selling costs	55,186	
Fixed costs		
Machine depreciation*	44,418	
Building depreciation†	39,034	
Factory insurance		
Fire†	18,844	
Liability†	25,574	
Advertising		
Divisional*	75,376	
Companywide†	64,608	
Computer service fee*	37,688	
Division supervision salaries*	91,528	
Home office general and administrative expenses‡	69,992	
Selling expenses		
Division*	55,186	
Home office‡	39,034	
Division manager's salary†	32,304	
Division administrative costs*	49,802	
Patent write-off*	34,996	

* Traceable and controllable by division manager.
† Traceable to division but uncontrollable by manager.
‡ Not traceable and must be allocated to division.

**Problem 14A-2.
Divisional
Performance
Measurement
(L.O. 3, 4)**

Utica Enterprises is located in upstate New York, just outside Syracuse. The company operates a mail-order business using three divisions, the Diamon Division, the Huta Division, and the Peek Division. The Diamon Division specializes in small home appliances, Huta Division sells clothing of all sizes, and Peek Division is known for its sports equipment. The home office is located adjacent to the Diamon plant but operates independently. All divisions are decentralized, and the division superintendents have profit and investment responsibilities. During 19xx, Utica Enterprises generated the following operating summary:

	Diamon Division	Huta Division	Peek Division	Company Totals
Sales revenue	$1,360,000	$1,845,000	$1,650,000	$4,855,000
Less variable costs	816,000	1,107,000	990,000	2,913,000
Contribution margin	$ 544,000	$ 738,000	$ 660,000	$1,942,000
Less fixed costs				
Factory overhead	$ 242,500	$ 337,500	$ 302,000	$ 882,000
Selling and administrative	194,700	267,600	264,400	726,700
	$ 437,200	$ 605,100	$ 566,400	$1,608,700
Net income before taxes	$ 106,800	$ 132,900	$ 93,600	$ 333,300
Profit margin	7.85%	7.20%	5.67%	6.87%

Top management asked the three divisional superintendents to prepare comments concerning their relatively poor showing for the year. The president pointed to the overall 6.87 percent profit margin as being far below the goal of a minimum 12 percent profit margin.

The three superintendents responded by stating that many of the costs being charged to their divisions are out of their control and should not be a part of their performance report. Each superintendent had divisional accountants prepare an analysis of the division's traceable and controllable costs, traceable but uncontrollable costs, and costs that are not traceable and are allocated by the home office to the divisions. Here is a summary of those findings:

	Diamon Division	Huta Division	Peek Division	Company Totals
Factory overhead				
Traceable and controllable	$ 96,300	$156,300	$124,900	$ 377,500
Traceable but uncontrollable	86,400	89,100	93,700	269,200
Not traceable	59,800	92,100	83,400	235,300
	$242,500	$337,500	$302,000	$ 882,000
Selling and administrative				
Traceable and controllable	$ 75,500	$ 97,600	$ 94,300	$ 267,400
Traceable but uncontrollable	69,800	92,500	88,200	250,500
Not traceable	49,400	77,500	81,900	208,800
	$194,700	$267,600	$264,400	$ 726,700
Total fixed cost	$437,200	$605,100	$566,400	$1,608,700

Required

1. Prepare a performance report for the period that identifies both the performance margin and the segment margin for each division as well as the overall profitability of the company.
2. From the information given, comment on the performance of each division superintendent.

Problem 14A-3.
Evaluating
Performance/
Return on
Investment
(L.O. 4, 5)

Following are the results of operations for the two divisions of the Patrick Robert Company:

	O'Shea Division	Muir Division	Company Totals
Total revenue	$2,134,000	$ 3,212,000	$ 5,346,000
Less variable costs			
Merchandise items	$ 768,240	$ 1,092,080	$ 1,860,320
Packaging materials	149,380	256,960	406,340
Packaging-related overhead	32,010	80,300	112,310
Packaging labor	74,690	144,540	219,230
Indirect labor	38,412	61,028	99,440
Sales commissions	192,060	353,320	545,380
Selling expenses	49,082	67,452	116,534
Total variable costs	$1,303,874	$ 2,055,680	$ 3,359,554
Contribution margin	$ 830,126	$ 1,156,320	$ 1,986,446
Less traceable fixed costs controllable by manager			
Equipment depreciation	$ 64,020	$ 83,512	$ 147,532
Divisional utility costs	25,608	51,392	77,000
Marketing development costs	40,546	70,664	111,210
Building depreciation	44,814	57,816	102,630
Divisional interest expense	89,628	115,632	205,260
Home office administration	34,144	54,604	88,748
Divisional administration costs	55,484	89,936	145,420
Totals	$ 354,244	$ 523,556	$ 877,800
Performance margin	$ 475,882	$ 632,764	$ 1,108,646
Less traceable fixed costs uncontrollable by manager			
Home office interest allocation	$ 76,824	$ 122,056	$ 198,880
Division manager's salary	42,680	77,088	119,768
Property insurance	17,072	38,544	55,616
Company product promotion	61,886	99,572	161,458
Totals	$ 198,462	$ 337,260	$ 535,722
Segment margin	$ 277,420	$ 295,504	$ 572,924
Total assets	$8,456,700	$10,672,300	$19,129,000
Total stockholders' equity	$2,564,200	$ 2,257,100	$ 4,821,300

The Patrick Robert Company is in the retail clothing business. Both divisions purchase clothing in bulk and repackage the items as individual garments. The O'Shea Division deals in women's and children's clothing; the Muir Division handles only men's clothing.

Since the two divisions used to be separate companies prior to their merger into the Patrick Robert Company, two classes of stock were created so that the original stockholders could remain associated with their respective companies. Divisional performance is evaluated using both performance and segment margin analysis and return on investment figures. Home office allocations should not be included in the divisional evaluation data.

Required

1. Recompute the performance margins and segment margins for the two divisions. Also convert the performance and segment margins into percentage of sales amounts for comparison purposes.
2. In preparation for return on investment analysis, compute the following amounts for each division:
   a. Net income from operations
   b. Net income before taxes
   c. Federal taxes for the period (at 34 percent)
   d. Net income after taxes (*Hint:* Allocated home office amounts should not be included in these totals.)
3. Compute the following return on investment measures:
   a. Net income from operations/total assets
   b. Net income/total assets
   c. Net income/stockholder's equity
4. Evaluate the performance of each division.

**Problem 14A-4.
Developing
Transfer Prices**
(L.O. 6, 8)

Seven years ago, Ed Browning formed The Browning Corporation and began producing sound equipment for home use. Because of the highly technical and competitive nature of the industry, Browning established the Research and Development Division, which is responsible for continually evaluating and updating critical electronic parts used in the corporation's products. The R & D staff has been very successful, contributing to the corporation's ranking as America's leader in the industry.

Two years ago, R & D took on the added responsibility of producing all microchip circuit boards for Browning's sound equipment. One of Browning's specialties is a sound dissemination board (SDB) used in videocassette recorders (VCRs). The SDB greatly enhances the sound quality of Browning's VCRs.

Demand for the SDB has increased significantly in the past year. As a result, R & D has increased its production and assembly labor force. Three outside customers want to purchase the SDB for their sound products. To date, R & D has been producing SDBs for internal use only.

The controller of the R & D Division wants to create a transfer price for the SDBs applicable to all intracompany transfers. The data on the following page show projections for the next six months:

Costs

Materials	
Boards	$ 253,050
Chips	1,229,100
Wire posts	325,350
Wire	144,600
Electronic glue	433,800
Labor	
Board preparation	759,150
Assembly	1,988,250
Testing	650,700
Supplies	90,375
Indirect labor	524,175
Other variable overhead costs	180,750
Fixed overhead, SDBs	397,650
Other fixed overhead, corporate	506,100
Variable selling expenses, SDBs	1,012,200
Fixed selling expenses, corporate	578,400
General corporate operating expenses	795,300
Corporate administrative expenses	614,550

A profit factor of at least 20 percent must be added to total unit cost for internal transfer purposes. Outside customers are willing to pay $36 for each SDB. Estimated demand over the next six months is 235,000 SDBs for internal use and 126,500 SDBs for external customers.

Required

1. Compute the cost of producing and distributing one SDB.
2. What transfer price should R & D use? What factors influenced your decision?

Problem 14A-5.
Transfer Prices and
Performance
Evaluation
(L.O. 9)

"That Culpepper Division is robbing us blind!" This statement by the director of the White Division was heard during the board of directors meeting at Arkansas Company. The company produces umbrellas in a two-step process. The Culpepper Division prepares the fabric tops and transfers them to the White Division. The White Division produces the ribs and handles, secures the tops, and packs all finished umbrellas for shipment.

Because of the director's concern, the company controller gathered the data shown on the next page on the past year. During the year, 400,000 regular umbrellas and 200,000 deluxe umbrellas were completed and transferred or shipped by the two divisions. Transfer prices used by the Culpepper Division were:

Regular	$2.20
Deluxe	3.60

The regular umbrella wholesales for $6.80; the deluxe model for $11.50. Selling, general operating, and company administrative costs are allocated to divisions by a preconceived formula.

Management has indicated the transfer price should include a 20 percent profit factor on total division costs.

	Culpepper Division	White Division	Company Totals
Sales			
Regular	$880,000	$2,720,000	$3,600,000
Deluxe	720,000	2,300,000	3,020,000
Materials			
Cloth	360,000	0	360,000
Aluminum	0	660,000	660,000
Closing mechanisms	0	1,560,000	1,560,000
Labor	480,000	540,000	1,020,000
Variable factory overhead	90,000	240,000	330,000
Fixed divisional overhead	150,000	210,000	360,000
Selling expenses	60,000	180,000	240,000
General operating expenses	72,000	192,000	264,000
Company administrative expenses	84,000	108,000	192,000

Required

1. Prepare a performance report on the Culpepper Division.
2. Prepare a performance report on the White Division.
3. Compute each division's rate of return on controllable and on total division costs.
4. Do you agree with the director's statement?
5. What procedures would you recommend to the board of directors?

Problem Set B

Problem 14B-1.
Performance and
Segment Margins
(L.O. 3, 4)

A partial balance of the Sedona Division of Red Mountain Goldsmiths, Inc. is shown on page 564.

Required

From the information given, prepare a divisional performance report that includes contribution margin, performance margin, and segment margin as well as the final profit margin.

Sedona Division
Red Mountain Goldsmiths, Inc.
Partial Trial Balance

	Debit	Credit
Sales		$2,615,000
Variable costs		
Materials	$470,700	
Materials-related overhead	39,225	
Machine setup labor	65,375	
Machine maintenance	196,125	
Direct labor	209,200	
Packaging	96,755	
Electrical power	26,150	
Supplies	54,915	
Variable selling costs	49,685	
Fixed costs		
Equipment depreciation*	65,375	
Building depreciation†	41,840	
Product promotion		
Divisional*	120,290	
Companywide†	99,370	
Insurance		
Property Damage†	36,610	
Liability†	49,685	
Marketing expenses		
Division*	81,065	
Home office‡	52,680	
Central computer service*	62,760	
Division management salaries*	151,670	
Home office general and administrative expenses‡	109,830	
Division manager's salary†	57,780	
Division administrative costs*	86,295	
Product development costs*	57,530	

* Traceable and controllable by division manager.
† Traceable to division but uncontrollable by manager.
‡ Not traceable and must be allocated to division.

Problem 14B-2.
Divisional
Performance
Measurement
(L.O.3,4)

Casboard Corporation was formed in 1970. Since then the company has flourished and now ranks as one of the world's premier financial services organizations. Now decentralized and operating with three divisions, the company's top management is disappointed with the past year's operating results:

	Abel Division	Rosen Division	Shapiro Division	Company Totals
Sales revenue	$750,000	$1,200,000	$980,000	$2,930,000
Less variable cost	525,000	840,000	686,000	2,051,000
Contribution margin	$225,000	$ 360,000	$294,000	$ 879,000
Less fixed costs				
Factory overhead	$115,000	$ 185,000	$145,000	$ 445,000
Selling and administrative	75,000	125,000	105,000	305,000
	$190,000	$ 310,000	$250,000	$ 750,000
Net income before taxes	$ 35,000	$ 50,000	$ 44,000	$ 129,000
Profit margin	4.67%	4.17%	4.49%	4.40%

The Abel Division specializes in cost allocation techniques and has gained a national reputation for creative but accurate approaches to allocation. The Rosen Division is centered in the tax consulting area and has been moderately successful. Investment advice is the main service provided by the Shapiro Division.

Home office management is disturbed by the overall 4.4 percent profit margin generated by the company and points out that the performance of the divisions is approximately equal, with no one division standing out as having had a good year. The division vice presidents, however, are unhappy with the company's performance measurement approach. They have had a special analysis prepared for each division showing the breakdown in fixed costs. Both fixed factory overhead and fixed selling and administrative costs have been reclassified as being traceable and controllable, traceable but uncontrollable, or not traceable to the division (allocated by the home office). The information is shown in the following summary:

	Abel Division	Rosen Division	Shapiro Division	Company Totals
Factory overhead				
Traceable and controllable	$ 55,000	$110,000	$ 90,000	$255,000
Traceable but uncontrollable	25,000	50,000	35,000	110,000
Not traceable	35,000	25,000	20,000	80,000
	$115,000	$185,000	$145,000	$445,000
Selling and administrative				
Traceable and controllable	$ 15,000	$ 80,000	$ 60,000	$155,000
Traceable but uncontrollable	40,000	17,500	20,000	77,500
Not traceable	20,000	27,500	25,000	72,500
	$ 75,000	$125,000	$105,000	$305,000
Total fixed cost	$190,000	$310,000	$250,000	$750,000

Required

1. Prepare a performance report for the period that identifies both the performance margin and the segment margin for each division as well as the overall profitability of the company.
2. From the information given, comment on the performance of each division vice president.

Problem 14B-3.
Evaluating
Performance/
Return on
Investment
(L.O. 4, 5)

Following are the operating data for the two divisions of the Christine Jojo Company:

	May Division	Carlson Division	Company Totals
Total revenue	$4,186,000	$2,989,000	$ 7,175,000
Less variable costs			
Materials and parts	$1,423,240	$1,225,490	$ 2,648,730
Assembly materials	334,880	221,186	556,066
Assembly-related overhead	163,254	83,692	246,946
Assembly labor	154,882	104,615	259,497
Indirect labor	58,604	38,857	97,461
Sales commissions	359,996	418,460	778,456
Selling expenses	104,650	71,736	176,386
Total variable costs	$2,599,506	$2,164,036	$ 4,763,542
Contribution margin	$1,586,494	$ 824,964	$ 2,411,458
Less traceable fixed costs controllable by manager			
Marketing development costs	$ 117,208	$ 62,769	$ 179,977
Divisional utility costs	54,418	41,846	96,264
Machinery depreciation	75,348	68,747	144,095
Building depreciation	96,278	50,813	147,091
Divisional interest expense	83,720	110,593	194,313
Divisional administration costs	71,162	47,824	118,986
Home office administration	87,906	80,703	168,609
Totals	$ 586,040	$ 463,295	$ 1,049,335
Performance margin	$1,000,454	$ 361,669	$ 1,362,123
Less traceable fixed costs uncontrollable by manager			
Division manager's salary	$ 79,534	$ 65,758	$ 145,292
Property insurance	46,046	44,835	90,881
Home office interest allocation	129,766	107,604	237,370
Company product promotion	133,952	86,681	220,633
Totals	$ 263,718	$ 194,285	$ 458,003
Segment margin	$ 736,736	$ 167,384	$ 904,120
Total assets	$9,187,400	$5,648,900	$14,836,300
Total stockholders' equity	$4,641,100	$1,394,900	$ 6,036,000

The company specializes in radio assemblies used in commercial aircraft. May Division assembles miniature radios; Carlson Division concentrates on high frequency models.

Both the May Division and the Carlson Division were originally separate companies that were merged into the Christine Jojo Company. Two classes of stock were created so that the original stockholders could remain associated with their initial investment. Divisional performance is evaluated using both performance and segment margin analysis and return on investment figures. Home office allocations should not be included in the divisional evaluation data.

Required

1. Recompute the performance margins and segment margins for the two divisions. Also convert the performance and segment margins into percentage of sales amounts for comparison purposes.
2. In preparation for return on investment analysis, compute the following amounts for each division:
   a. Net income from operations
   b. Net income before taxes
   c. Federal taxes for the period (at 34 percent)
   d. Net income after taxes (*Hint:* Allocated home office amounts should not be included in these totals.)
3. Compute the following return on investment measures:
   a. Net income from operations/total assets
   b. Net income/total assets
   c. Net income/stockholders' equity
4. Evaluate the performance of each division.

Problem 14B-4.
Developing
Transfer Prices
(L.O. 6, 8)

Beta Company has two divisions, Alpha and Psi. For several years Alpha Division has manufactured a special glass container, which it sells to the Psi Division at the prevailing market price of $20. Alpha produces the glass containers only for Psi and does not sell the product to outside customers. Annual production and sales volume is 20,000 containers. A unit cost analysis for Alpha showed the following:

Cost Categories	Costs per Container
Direct materials	$ 2.00
Direct labor, ½ hour	5.00
Variable factory overhead	4.00
Traceable fixed costs $40,000 ÷ 20,000	2.00
General and administrative overhead, $6 per hour	3.00
Variable shipping costs	1.00
Unit cost	$17.00

General and administrative overhead represents such allocated joint fixed costs of production as building depreciation, property taxes, fire insurance, and salaries of production executives. A normal profit allowance of 20 percent is used in determining transfer prices.

Required

1. What would be the appropriate transfer price for Alpha Division to use in billing its transactions with Psi Division?
2. If Alpha Division decided to sell some containers to outside customers, would your answer to **1** change? Defend your answer.

Problem 14B-5.
Transfer Prices and
Performance
Evaluation
(L.O. 9)

Edmonds Brick Company has two divisions involved in producing and selling bricks. The Mining Division produces clay, which is sold in 100-pound bags to the Production Division. All output of the Mining Division is shipped to the Production Division. These transfers are priced at the average unit cost of production and distribution. The Production Division sells each brick for $1. Each brick requires 1 pound of clay as raw material. Operating results for 19x7 for the two divisions were:

	Mining Division	Production Division
Total production costs	$ 700,000	$4,500,000
Selling, general, & administrative expenses	300,000	1,500,000
Total costs and expenses	$1,000,000	$6,000,000

In 19x7 the Mining Division produced and shipped 10 million pounds of clay, which were billed to the Production Division at $.10 per pound. The Production Division manufactured and sold 10 million bricks in 19x7. Other mines sell comparable clay material for $.30 per pound.

Required

1. Assume intracompany transfers are priced at average cost. Prepare an income statement for each division.
2. Assume intracompany transfers are billed at market price. Prepare an income statement for each division.

Management Decision Case

Clarkson Company
(L.O. 5)

Clarkson Company is a large multidivision firm with several plants in each division. A comprehensive budgeting system is used for planning operations and measuring performance. The annual budgeting process commences in August five months prior to the beginning of the fiscal year. At this time the division managers submit proposed budgets for sales, production and inventory levels, and expenses; capital expenditure requests also are formalized. These expense budgets include direct labor and all overhead items, which are separated into fixed and variable components. Direct materials are budgeted separately in developing the production and inventory schedules.

The expense budgets for each division are developed from its plants' results, as measured by the percent variation from an adjusted budget in the first six months of the current year and a target expense reduction percentage established by the corporation.

To determine plant percentages, the plant budget for the half-year period just completed is revised to recognize changes in operating procedures and costs outside the control of plant management (labor wage rate changes, product style changes, and so on). The difference between this revised budget and the actual expenses is the controllable variance, which is expressed as a percentage of the actual expenses. This percentage is added (if unfavorable) to the corporate target expense reduction percentage. A favorable plant variance percentage is subtracted from the corporate target. If a plant had a 2 percent unfavorable controllable variance and the corporate target reduction was 4 percent, the plant's budget for next year should reflect costs approximately 6 percent below this year's actual costs.

Next year's final budgets for the corporation, the divisions, and the plants are adopted after corporate analysis of the proposed budgets and a careful review with each division manager of the changes made by corporate management. Division profit budgets include allocated corporate costs, and plant profit budgets include allocated division and corporate costs.

Return on assets is used to measure the performance of divisions and plants. The asset base for a division consists of all assets assigned to the division, including its working capital, and an allocated share of corporate assets. For plants, the asset base includes the assets assigned to the plant plus an allocated portion of the division and corporate assets. Recommendations for promotions and salary increases for the executives of the divisions and plants are influenced by how well the actual return on assets compares with the budgeted return on assets.

The plant managers exercise control only over the cost portion of the plant profit budget because the divisions are responsible for sales. Only limited control over the plant assets is exercised at the plant level.

The manager of the Dexter Plant, a major plant in the Huron Division, carefully controls costs during the first six months so that any improvement appears after the target reduction of expenses is established. This is accomplished by careful planning and timing of discretionary expenditures.

During 19x3, Clarkson Company bought the property adjacent to the Dexter Plant. This expenditure was not included in the 19x3 capital expenditure budget. Corporate management decided to divert funds from a project at another plant since the property appeared to be a better long-term investment.

Also during 19x3 Clarkson Company experienced depressed sales. In an attempt to achieve budgeted profit, corporate management announced in August that all plants were to cut their annual expenses by 6 percent. To accomplish this expense reduction, the Dexter Plant manager reduced preventive maintenance and postponed needed major repairs. Employees who quit were not replaced unless absolutely necessary. Employee training was postponed whenever possible. Inventories of raw materials, supplies, and finished goods were reduced below normal levels.

Required

1. Evaluate Clarkson Company's budget procedures with respect to its effectiveness for planning and controlling operations.
2. Is Clarkson Company's use of return on assets to evaluate the performance of the Dexter Plant appropriate? Explain your answer.
3. Analyze and explain the Dexter Plant manager's behavior during 19x3.

(ICMA adapted)

PART FIVE

Recent Changes in Management Accounting: Automation and the Just-in-Time Philosophy

Although manufacturing processes have changed dramatically during the past decade, management accountants continue to use traditional procedures to account for these changes. However, because traditional accounting procedures for product costing, budgeting, measuring performance, and capital investing do not apply in the new manufacturing environment, a new set of management accounting practices and policies is slowly emerging. Computer-integrated manufacturing systems provide timely, accurate data that can be easily adapted to management accounting analysis.

Chapter 15 introduces computer-integrated manufacturing systems and compares them with the traditional systems. The just-in-time philosophy is then discussed, with its impact on management accounting highlighted. The chapter ends with a discussion of various changes in product costing.

Chapter 16 continues our look at the effects of computers and the just-in-time philosophy on management accounting. Additional attention is directed toward product costing, and changes in performance measurement and capital investment caused by the introduction of computer-integrated manufacturing systems are explained. A discussion of changes in recording and reporting concludes the chapter.

The Just-in-Time Philosophy

During the past twenty-five years, the manufacturing environment has been significantly changing. The *computer* is now an integral part of the manufacturing process. This change evolved slowly as isolated machines were equipped with automated devices. Today, many companies are installing computer-integrated manufacturing (CIM) systems in their factories. A CIM system is a fully integrated computer setup in which everything connected with the manufacturing system is performed automatically.

During the time manufacturing here was being computerized, the Japanese business community began to develop a production philosophy known as just-in-time (JIT). Its premise was that too much waste was occurring, too many company resources were tied up in inventories, and wasted time and resources were causing higher production costs. By combining the ideas and technologies of computer-integrated manufacturing and just-in-time concepts, companies are able to improve product quality and cut operating costs by large margins.

The impact of automation and the JIT philosophy on management accounting has been significant. Inventory management has been completely revamped. Product costing has been restructured. Cost planning and control has new guidelines and techniques. Performance evaluation benchmarks have shifted. The entire field of management accounting is changing. The topics we covered in Chapters 1 to 14 are still relevant because a significant majority of companies use semiautomated or functional production facilities. But more and more manufacturers are implementing automated and totally computer-integrated systems, and the JIT concept will eventually spill over into the service and merchandising industries as well.

This chapter introduces you to the concepts associated with just-in-time philosophy and computer-integrated manufacturing systems. Emphasis is on product costing and data recording in the new manufacturing environment. After studying this chapter, you should be able to meet the learning objectives listed on the left.

Computer-Integrated Manufacturing Systems

Computer-integrated manufacturing (CIM) is a production process in which all parts of the system are fully integrated through

OBJECTIVE 1
Describe a
computer-
integrated
manufacturing
system

computer technology. Let us peek into our crystal ball for a moment to see how CIM systems affect productivity. Nichole Marie has just received an order for 1,500 pool cabana awnings from the Porter Hotel chain. The order is entered into the computer at 9:00 A.M. on Monday; the following sequence of events ensues:

Monday   10:00 A.M. Order scheduled for production.

            10:10 A.M. Supplier's computer is contacted by manufacturer's
                        computer to order raw materials.

            12:30 P.M. Supplier ships raw materials.

            2:45 P.M.   Raw materials arrive.

            3:10 P.M.   Machines are set up according to specifications and
                        production begins.

            4:10 P.M.   Computer invoices for raw materials are electronically
                        received.

            5:00 P.M.   All machines required for the job are programmed to
                        run automatically throughout the night shift.

Tuesday   9:15 A.M.   Billings for raw materials are paid by electronic bank
                        transfers.

            11:00 A.M. Manufacturing and assembly of the 1,500 pool cabana
                        awnings are completed.

            1:00 P.M.   Goods have been packaged and shipped.

            1:15 P.M.   Porter Hotels is computer-billed for the order.

            2:30 P.M.   Payment from Porter Hotels is received by electronic
                        bank transfer.

Sound impossible? This scenario is far from impossible. Formerly, such an order took several weeks to fill; today, JIT work flow configurations are revolutionizing the business environment. Entire systems, including production, materials ordering, billing, payment, and accounting systems, are being reconfigured and linked by computers, eliminating 80 to 90 percent of the production time. Billing functions are performed automatically, and suppliers' computers can interact with manufacturers' computers to facilitate the materials ordering, billing, and payment processes. Verification procedures are also incorporated into the computer programs.

The Just-in-Time Philosophy Defined

The movement toward the just-in-time continuous work flow concept has been developing in Japan over the past decade. To improve productivity and gain a foothold in several world markets, companies began to look for ways to streamline their manufacturing processes. *Eliminating waste* in raw materials, labor, space, production time, record keeping, and working capital areas was the key ingredient to the firms' success.

Two independent approaches to eliminating waste in manufacturing companies have emerged: **automation** and an operating philosophy called just-in-time. Automation approached the problem of waste from a physical angle. Repetitive, mechanical operations lent themselves to automated processes, and automation greatly reduced the waste of scrap materials and defective units. Automation also significantly reduced processing time. Computer numerically-controlled (CNC) machines and computer-assisted machinery (CAM) injected new life into the production process.

The just-in-time (JIT) approach to production prompted a total revamping of both manufacturing facilities and the events that trigger the production process. **Just-in-time** is an overall operating philosophy of management in which all resources, including materials, personnel, and facilities, are used in a just-in-time manner. JIT is based on the objective of continuous flow and requires that each part of the entire production process work in concert. JIT also changed the role of the direct labor worker and significantly reduced waste of labor, space, and production time. JIT production also cut work-in-process and finished goods inventories by as much as 90 percent and has had a major impact in reducing the level of working capital tied up in inventories.

The most significant event during this period was the merging of these two manufacturing approaches. The synergism from the marriage of just-in-time and automation catapulted the Japanese manufacturing industry into world prominence. Waste was drastically reduced, product quality was enhanced and operations began to approach ideal capacity. Other manufacturers are now following the Japanese example. Over the next decade we will see continued movement toward this new manufacturing environment as more companies apply the JIT approach and install automated systems in order to compete in world markets.

Traditional Versus JIT Factory Layout

OBJECTIVE 2
Compare and contrast the traditional manufacturing system with the just-in-time approach to manufacturing

A critical change caused by applying the JIT philosophy focuses on the layout of machines and equipment on the factory floor. The key to an effective JIT environment is the elimination of all non-value added activities from the production and distribution processes. Breaking down the traditional manufacturing process, we find that the processing time of a product can be divided into five parts or time frames: actual processing (production) time, inspection time, move time, queue time, and storage time. A **non-value added activity** adds costs to the product but does not increase its market value. Traditional manufacturing and assembly operations have dozens of such activities incorporated into them. Of the five parts listed, the JIT environment tries to eliminate all but the actual production time because inspection time, move time, queue time, and storage time are activities that do not usually add value to the product.

The Traditional Manufacturing Environment

The most effective way to differentiate between the traditional and JIT environments is to analyze and compare product flow and plant layout. Figure 15-1 illustrates a traditional plant layout. Fasteners such as screws,

Figure 15-1. Overview of Traditional Plant Layout

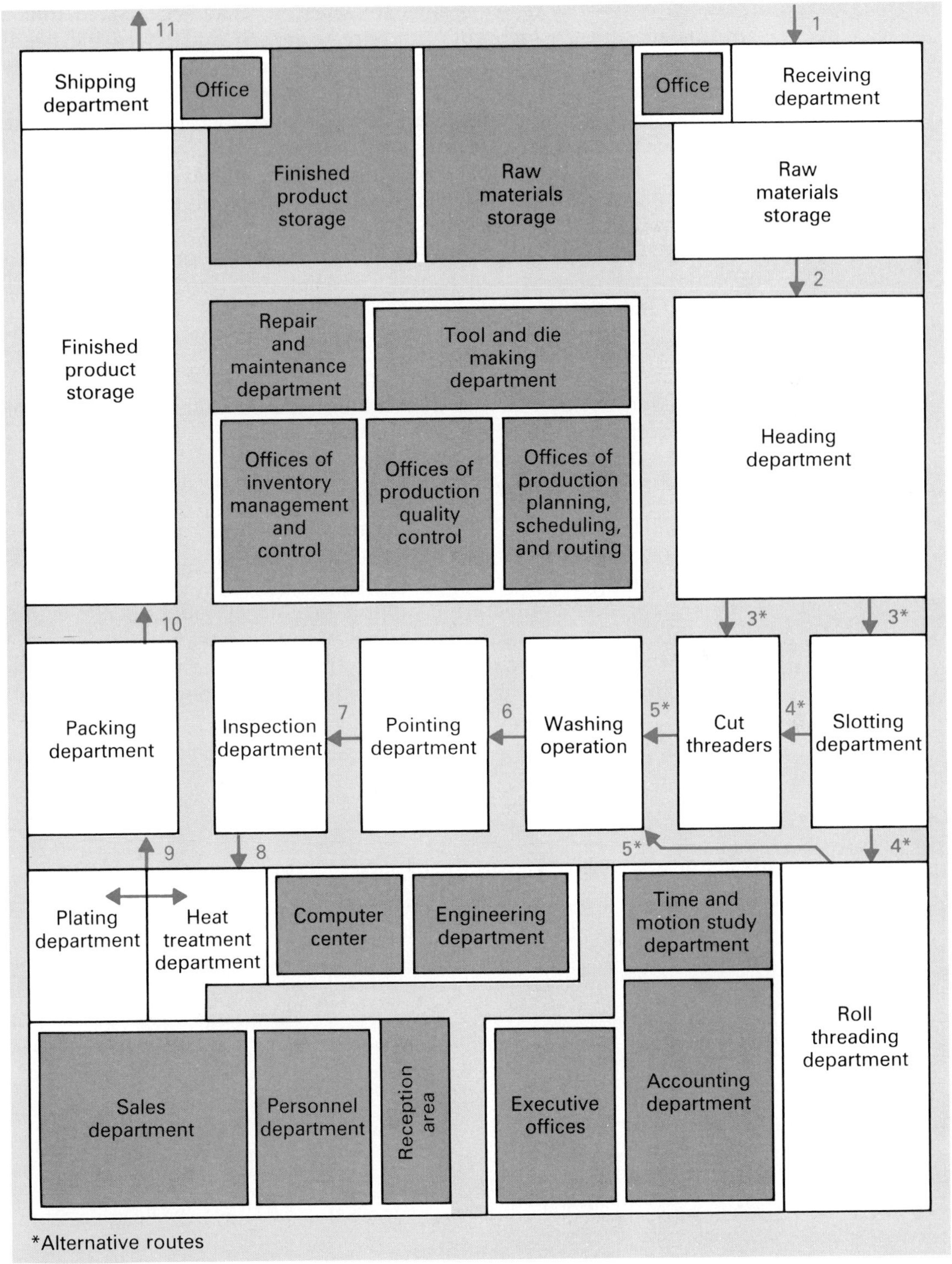

| Shipping department | Office | Finished product storage | Raw materials storage | Office | Receiving department |

Raw materials storage

| Finished product storage | Repair and maintenance department | Tool and die making department | Heading department |

| Offices of inventory management and control | Offices of production quality control | Offices of production planning, scheduling, and routing |

| Packing department | Inspection department | Pointing department | Washing operation | Cut threaders | Slotting department |

| Plating department | Heat treatment department | Computer center | Engineering department | Time and motion study department | Roll threading department |

| Sales department | Personnel department | Reception area | Executive offices | Accounting department |

*Alternative routes

bolts, shoe nails, and specialty items are produced in this plant. Figure 15-2 shows the operations needed to create a fastener. Raw materials arrive as coils of wire of various thicknesses. The wire is fed into a heading machine, which cuts the wire to length and forms the head. The headed blanks are then collected in large movable bins for temporary storage until transported to the next department. If the headed blank needs a slot (regular or Phillips head), it must be added. Then the products are again collected in movable bins. The next operation is threading the fastener, either by cutting away the excess metal or by rolling the headed blank between two dies to form the thread (similar to rolling a pencil between your hands).

At this point, the product looks like a screw or bolt, but additional operations are needed (see Figure 15-1) before it can be considered a finished product:

1. The product must be washed, to remove excess oils and foreign materials.
2. Inspection is necessary to determine if the product meets customer specifications.
3. Heat treatment and plating may be performed.
4. Special packaging may be required.

The products in process are stored and moved in large bins from one operation to the next. Finally, they are transported to the finished goods inventory storage area to await sale and shipment.

Two important manufacturing support areas are also identified in Figure 15-1. Product flow is designed so that production support services are located in the middle of the production process. The repair and maintenance, inventory management and control, production quality control,

Figure 15-2. Steps in the Production of a Fastener

THE BLANKING AND HEADING OPERATIONS

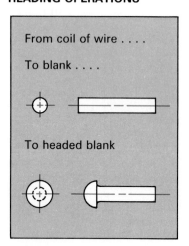

THE SLOTTING OPERATION

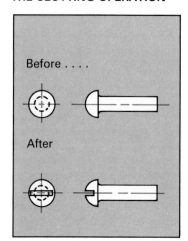

THE THREADING OPERATION

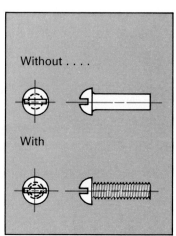

and production planning, scheduling, and routing functions are fairly self-explanatory. In addition, special tools and dies may be required to reshape the metal.

The lower part of Figure 15-1 shows other common support services. The accounting, time and motion study, engineering, computer services, sales, personnel, and executive activity functions all support either the production or distribution of the company's products.

Can you identify any non-value added activities in the layout in Figure 15-1? Several exist, but the most obvious are the raw materials and finished product storage areas and activities. The arrows represent product movements through the manufacturing process. The time taken to move the products between departments and the resulting queue time are also non-value added activities. Finally, the Inspection Department adds no value to the product, although it does contribute to the cost.

Many support functions are expensive to maintain and add cost to the product. When a company switches to a JIT environment, several of these functions are either reduced significantly or eliminated all together.

The JIT Production Environment

The JIT production philosophy completely revamps the manufacturing plant layout, operating techniques, and role of personnel. Machinery and equipment are moved into layouts that comprise small, autonomous production lines called "cells" or "islands." Each manufacturing cell or island has a complete set of machines that can produce a product from start to finish. Former direct labor employees are now in charge of each production cell. Machine operators are expected to run several different types of machines, help set up for a production run, and identify and repair machinery needing maintenance. Incentives encourage workers to spot areas of inefficiency.

Figure 15-3 depicts a hypothetical JIT plant layout. Instead of large departments containing dozens of similar machines (such as the Heading Department in Figure 15-1), small operating units start and complete a product with minimal time, movement, and storage. To compare the traditional manufacturing layout with that required for a JIT production process, we converted the plant layout of our fastener company in Figure 15-1 to satisfy the new JIT requirements.

In Subplant A (Figure 15-3), raw materials are received on a timely basis and placed in the materials storage area adjacent to the header scheduled to fill that order. Each one of the six work cells may include header, slotter, threader, and cleaning machines. Each cell is designed to work on different sizes and types of fasteners. Instead of work-in-process inventory sitting in travel bins as it moves from one department to the next, wire is fed into the header automatically. The blank is moved via a conveyor to subsequent operations. If order specifications call for additional processing, such as heat-treating and/or plating, the computerized routing system will move the products to those locations. Packaging is the final phase; then the goods are shipped to the customer. The fastener order is completed in a matter of hours, as compared to the days necessary when the order was moved and queued for each operation.

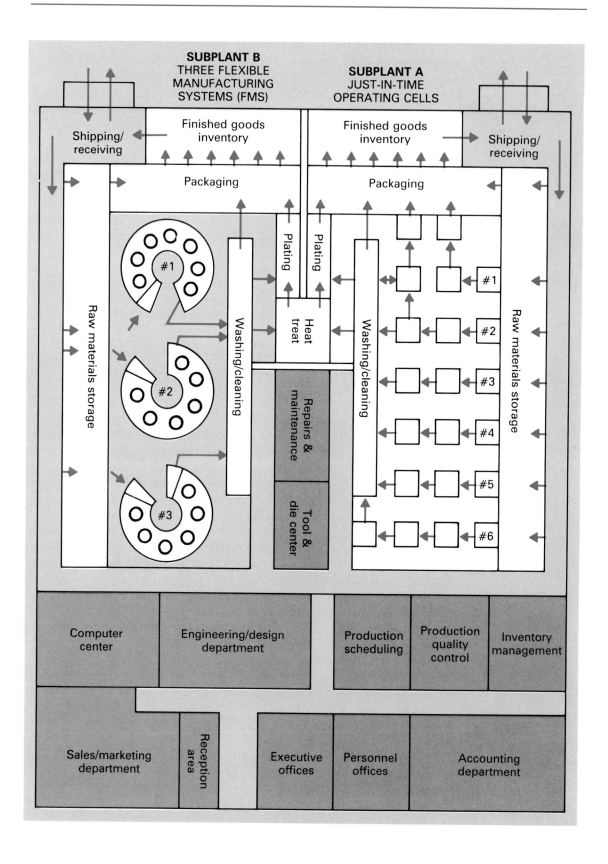

◀ **Figure 15-3.** Overview of Plant Layout—JIT Format

Subplant B in Figure 15-3 shows a flexible manufacturing system island or cell being used in a fastener manufacturing operation. A **flexible manufacturing system (FMS)** is an integrated set of computerized machines and systems designed to complete a series of operations automatically. An FMS often completes a product from beginning to end without the item being touched or moved by hand. Raw materials are fed in at one end of the FMS cell, and a finished product emerges at the other end.

Let us assume that Subplant B makes a special type of fastener called a "sems" screw. A locking washer is placed on the blank sems screw before the threading operation is performed. Once the threads are rolled on, the washer cannot be removed. The FMS island is used to produce all types and sizes of sems fasteners from start to finish. Each part of the FMS circular island represents a different operation, such as heading, slotting, lock washer fitting, threading, and pointing. All operations are computerized, and the manufacturing process is continuous. When the sems fasteners have been packaged, they are sent to the finished goods area to await shipment to the customer.

Several points are worth mentioning regarding the plant layouts in Figures 15-1 and 15-3. The support functions located in the front (lower part) of the drawings are similar, but the size of the Computer Center and the Engineering/Design Department has been enlarged in the JIT layout in Figure 15-3. Production Scheduling, Production Quality Control, and Inventory Management in the JIT environment have been reduced in size and moved to the managerial office area. These functions now need to be closer to the computer area than to the production process. Supporting services such as the Tool and Die Center and Repairs and Maintenance Department should remain close to the manufacturing operation. Heat-treating facilities are very expensive and products are still batch-processed, so both subplant layouts share the same heat-treating furnaces. The remaining parts of the factory in Figure 15-3 have been redesigned to satisfy the needs of the JIT production process.

JIT: Capital Intensive Versus Labor Intensive Manufacturing

Shifting the manufacturing process to a JIT approach increases the emphasis on the use of machine hours and reduces direct labor hour usage. The manufacturing process becomes capital intensive, with a heavy reliance on machinery. As the production process is automated, more capital is required. Of course, JIT practices can be followed without the process being completely computerized. Many companies have a partially computerized setup and use direct labor employees on independent computer numerically-controlled machines and other semiautomatic equipment. **Computer numerically-controlled machines (CNC)** are stand-alone pieces of equipment, including operating machines, computer-assisted design technology, and robots. The closer a CIM environment is approached, the wider the spread between machine hours and direct labor hours used in the production process. In business jargon, shifting to a JIT production process usually involves shifting from a labor intensive to a capital intensive process.

The characteristics of direct labor are changing as industry adopts more and more aspects of the JIT philosophy. In the new manufacturing environment, direct labor personnel no longer just "help shape" the product; workers are now responsible for many tasks that used to be indirect labor functions, including machine setup, machine maintenance, and product inspection. The new definition of a direct labor worker is a person who manages a JIT machine work cell. The indirect labor area has also changed: there is now heavy reliance on support labor to keep the manufacturing cells operating efficiently.

As the role of the direct labor employee changes, so do all of the management accounting procedures that depend on direct labor measures. This impact is significant. Direct labor has traditionally been the primary base for allocating factory overhead costs to products. Today, machine hours are replacing direct labor when overhead is assigned and product costs are established. Predetermined factory overhead rates used for pricing and budgeting can no longer use only direct labor as an application basis. Standard cost variance analysis must become more machine hour oriented to control manufacturing costs and labor-related variances are no longer relevant. Labor measures used in short-run decision analysis and capital budgeting techniques must be replaced with more relevant forecasting techniques. As you can see, the management accounting discipline is affected by the adoption of JIT techniques.

After we discuss the elements of the JIT philosophy, we focus on the impact of capital intensive processes on product costing. We explore the various approaches to automating the manufacturing process, and identify and analyze "cost drivers," the new name for cost allocation bases. We introduce the Raw-in-Process Inventory account. Finally, direct versus indirect cost classification and process costing practices are revisited because of their unique role in the JIT environment.

Elements Supporting the JIT Philosophy

OBJECTIVE 3
Identify the elements supporting a JIT operating environment

Just-in-time is usually referred to as a philosophy upon which an approach to accomplishing a task is based. Ideas supporting JIT include (1) simple is better; (2) emphasis on quality and continuous improvement; (3) maintaining inventories wastes resources and often hides bad work; (4) any activity or function that does not add value to the product should be eliminated; (5) goods are produced only when needed; and (6) workers should be multiskilled and participate in improving efficiency and product quality. This philosophy is contained in the following elements of the JIT approach to production:

1. Maintain minimum inventory levels.
2. Develop pull-through production planning and scheduling procedures.
3. Purchase materials and produce products as needed in smaller lot sizes.
4. Perform simple, inexpensive machine setups.
5. Develop a multiskilled work force.
6. Create a flexible manufacturing system.
7. Maintain high levels of product quality.
8. Enforce a system of effective preventive facility maintenance.
9. Encourage continuous work environment improvement.[1]

Maintain Minimum Inventory Levels

The JIT philosophy centers on the objective of maintaining minimum inventory levels. Raw materials and parts are purchased and received only when needed. This approach is in contrast to purchasing parts, materials, and supplies far in advance, to be stored until the Production Department needs them. Cost savings result from reducing the space needed for inventory storage, the amount of material handling, and the amount of inventory obsolescence. There is also less need for inventory control facilities, personnel, and record keeping. The amount of work-in-process inventory sitting around the plant waiting to be processed is significantly reduced. The amount of working capital tied up in inventories is also reduced. Computerization of the production process was the key feature that enabled the JIT operating concept of minimum inventory levels to become a reality.

Develop Pull-Through
Production Planning and Scheduling Procedures

The term **pull-through production** means that a customer order triggers the purchase of materials and the scheduling of production for the required products. This approach is in sharp contrast to the *push-through* method, whereby products were manufactured and stored in anticipation of customer orders. The pull-through approach is a fundamental characteristic of the JIT production concept and requires purchasing materials and parts as needed.

Purchase Materials and Produce
Products As Needed in Smaller Lot Sizes

Using the pull-through approach means that the sizes of production runs will be influenced by the size of customer orders. Thus low inventory levels will be maintained, but machines will have to be set up more frequently, resulting in more work stoppages. Long production runs, previously thought to be more cost effective, are no longer the rule in a JIT environment; products are not manufactured to be inventoried.

---

1. James B. Dilworth, *Production and Operations Management*, 3rd ed., New York: Random House, 1986, pp. 354–360.

Perform Quick, Inexpensive Machine Setups

One reason that traditional production processes relied on long production runs was to reduce the number of machine setups. Management felt that it was more practical to create large inventories rather than produce smaller lot sizes and cause frequent machine setups. This approach has been completely disproved during the past ten years. By placing machines in more efficient locations and scheduling similar products on common machine groupings, setup times can be minimized. In addition, more frequent setups provide experience for the workers. Suggestions for improvement from workers are encouraged, and ideas that result in reducing setup time are rewarded with bonuses.

Develop a Multiskilled Work Force

A key element of the JIT philosophy is that machines are grouped strategically into work centers and one worker may be required to operate several different types of machines simultaneously. Therefore, new operating skills must be learned. Many work centers are run by only one operator, who may, for example, have to participate in setting up machines and retooling.

Preventive maintenance of machines and equipment is an integral part of the JIT concept. Preventing machine breakdowns is considered more important and more cost effective than keeping the machine running continuously. Therefore, when machines are idle from a lack of work, the operator is expected to perform routine maintenance work on the equipment.

The multiskilled worker requirement has been very effective in the Japanese business environment. In the United States, labor union contracts often have a traditional focus on a single-skilled worker, which may cause problems as companies try to implement the JIT philosophy.

Create a Flexible Manufacturing System

In the traditional approach to factory layout, all similar machines are grouped together and functional departments or divisions are formed. Products needing work from several departments are routed through each department in proper sequence so that all the necessary operations are completed in order. This process can take several days or several weeks, depending on the size and complexity of the job.

A primary goal of the JIT production method is to cut the manufacturing time of processing for a product from days to hours or from weeks to days. In many cases, time can be reduced more than 80 percent by rearranging the machinery into flexible work cells or islands that perform all required operations efficiently and continuously. These cells are developed to handle jobs of similar shapes and/or sizes of products. Minimum setup changes are required to move from one job to the next. The more flexible the work cell, the more effective the operation is in accomplishing the goals of the JIT philosophy.

Maintain High Levels of Product Quality

High-quality products are a by-product of the JIT production approach. High quality is also required for JIT to work well. One of the non-value added functions in the traditional manufacturing process is inspection. Instead of treating inspection as a separate function, JIT incorporates inspection into the continuous production operation. Machine operators are responsible for inspecting the products as they pass through the process. An operator who detects a product flaw, then determines what caused the problem. The operator may even help the engineer or quality control person find a way to correct the process.

Enforce a System of
Effective Preventive Facility Maintenance

When a company's machinery is rearranged into flexible manufacturing units, each machine in the work cell or island becomes a critical, integral part of that cell. A machine breakdown causes the entire work cell to cease functioning. The product cannot be easily routed to another machine while the malfunctioning machine is repaired, so an effective preventive facility maintenance system is very important to the JIT environment. Machine operators are trained to perform minor repairs on machines as they detect problem areas. Machines are serviced regularly—much like an automobile—to help guarantee continued operation. The machine operator conducts routine maintenance during periods of machine downtime (caused by a lack of orders). Remember that in a JIT setting the work cell does not operate unless there is a customer order causing products to be pulled through the work cell. Machine operators take advantage of downtime to perform the maintenance procedures.

Encourage Continuous
Work Environment Improvement

The JIT environment fosters loyalty of company personnel. Workers feel more a part of the team because they are so involved in the production process. Machine operators must have skills to run several different types of machines, be able to detect defective products, suggest measures to correct the problem, and maintain the machinery within their work cell. In addition, each worker is urged to make suggestions for improving the manufacturing and assembly processes. Some Japanese companies have received more than 1 million employee suggestions and have implemented a high percentage of these suggestions. Workers are rewarded for successful suggestions that improve the process. Such an environment is healthy for both the worker and the company.

The JIT approach to production is more than just lowering inventory levels or cutting production time. As described, JIT is a philosophy dedicated to creating a product of the highest quality in the most efficient manner. Every action by machine operators, setup people, repair and maintenance personnel, and company management must be dedicated to satisfying this objective. Every person involved in the production of the product must strive to perform at theoretical or ideal capacity.

Product Costing in a JIT Environment

OBJECTIVE 4

Analyze the impact of a change from a labor intensive to a capital intensive production process on product costing concepts and techniques

The JIT production environment has caused a reassessment of product costing techniques. For the first time in more than forty years, established product costing doctrines are being challenged as outdated and inaccurate. Cost allocation approaches are at the root of the problem. What happened to cause such a change? Why would product costing techniques that have been used for more than four decades all of a sudden become obsolete? There are two answers to this question: (1) The JIT philosophy has changed many of the relationships and cost patterns associated with the traditional approach; (2) automation has caused direct labor hours to be replaced by machine hours.[2]

JIT's Influence on Product Costing

Product costing changes caused by the JIT philosophy can be linked to the concept of the operating cell or island. JIT is a never-ending war against waste and the elimination of non-value added aspects of the production process; product costing techniques are influenced by JIT's obsession to eliminate these non-value added parts. Simplification is also an objective of JIT. To better understand the JIT approach to product costing, we need to refer to the time elements of the traditional production process:

Processing time   The actual amount of time that a product is being worked on

Inspection time   The time spent either looking for product flaws or reworking defective units

Moving time   The time spent moving the products from one operation or department to another

Queue time   The time the products spend waiting to be worked on once they arrive at the next operation

Storage time   The time the product is either in materials storage, work-in-process inventory or in finished goods inventory waiting to be sold and shipped.

These five time classifications are important to product costing under JIT. As Table 15-1 shows, costs associated with actual processing time (product costs) are grouped as either materials costs or conversion costs and applied to products using the traditional process costing method. The costs associated with and traceable to the other four time classifications are not necessary to the production process and are either reduced or eliminated through cost control measures.

2. Source of ideas in this section are from Robert D. McIlhattan, "How Cost Management Systems Can Support the JIT Philosophy," *Management Accounting*, September 1987, pp. 20–26.

Table 15-1. Product Costing Under JIT

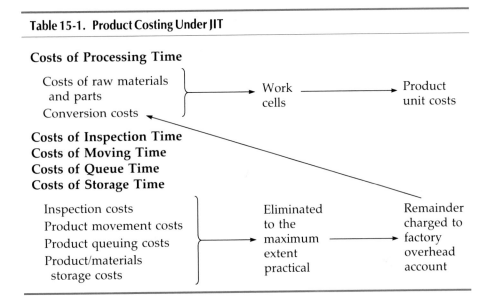

Costs of Processing Time

Costs of raw materials and parts
Conversion costs
→ Work cells → Product unit costs

Costs of Inspection Time
Costs of Moving Time
Costs of Queue Time
Costs of Storage Time

Inspection costs
Product movement costs
Product queuing costs
Product/materials storage costs
→ Eliminated to the maximum extent practical → Remainder charged to factory overhead account

Accounting for product costs under JIT is not an overly complicated procedure. A product cost is classified as either a materials cost or a conversion cost. Product costs are traced to work cells. The process costing method (described in Chapter 4) is then used to determine product unit cost. (Process costing in a JIT environment is described and illustrated later in this chapter.)

Costs associated with the other time units in the production process are accumulated and classified as inspection costs, moving costs, waiting or queue costs, and storage costs. These costs undergo special analyses to determine which are or will be eliminated by the JIT production process. Inspection costs are partially eliminated by adopting a JIT approach; the costs associated with work cell inspection are traceable to that cell. Costs associated with moving the work-in-process from department to department are eliminated under a JIT setting. Waiting or queue costs should also be reduced or eliminated following JIT procedures.

Storage costs are reduced significantly. If the JIT production process operates in an optimal fashion, raw materials and parts arrive just in time to be used in the production and/or assembly work cells. There are minimal costs associated with storing work in process because goods flow continuously through the work cell. Finished products are packaged and shipped immediately to customers, so there should be only minimal finished goods inventory storage costs. Thus a large percentage of the old costs of storage are eliminated under JIT. Costs not eliminated can be treated as factory overhead costs and charged to work cells as part of conversion costs.

New Cost Drivers

The term "cost driver" is very important to managerial accounting in a JIT setting. A **cost driver** is any activity that causes costs to be incurred. In a traditional production operation, emphasis is on cost control. Cost allocation procedures are used to assign costs to cost objectives on a causal or beneficial basis. The managerial accountant looked for these relationships when cost allocation was necessary.

In a JIT setting, the objective is to eliminate all unnecessary costs rather than just reducing them through control procedures. But before you can eliminate a cost or account for it properly, you must know what caused the cost—you must know what "drives" the cost. Once the cost driver has been determined, the indirect costs it causes can either be (1) treated as a legitimate product cost and allocated as part of the conversion costs or (2) eliminated by eliminating the need for the cost driver itself. Table 15-2 lists various cost drivers. Let us take one cost driver and develop a list of costs that it causes.

Number of Engineering Change Orders

Possible costs caused by an engineering change order include

    Additional engineering time and labor cost
    Utility and space costs associated with the extra work
    Machine setup time caused by the change order
    Product rework time in the work cell
    Other conversion costs of cell

These costs and possibly others are reduced if the number of engineering change orders are reduced. By focusing on cost drivers and the costs associated with each driver, management can get to the root of operating inefficiencies and reduce overall product cost. These cost reductions make price reductions possible, which helps increase sales and market share.

Standard Costs

A JIT environment enhances the role and use of standard costs. However, many of the common variances associated with a traditional standard

---

Table 15-2. Examples of Potential Cost Drivers

Number of labor transactions
Number of material moves
Number of parts received in a month
Number of products
Number of schedule changes
Number of vendors
Number of units reworked
Number of engineering change orders
Number of direct labor employees
Number of new parts added

Source: Robert D. McIlhattan, "How Cost Management Systems Can Support the JIT Philosophy," *Management Accounting,* September 1987, p. 22. Used by permission of National Association of Accountants.

costing system are no longer useful. But using standard costs for product costing and inventory valuation is very useful for JIT operations. Companies such as Harley Davidson and IBM retained their standard cost system when they adopted the JIT approach. Emphasis may be on only two cost elements (materials and conversion costs), but the use of standard costs still makes product costing easier. Now companies need only concentrate on maintaining two standard costs, materials cost and conversion cost, so the procedures for reporting, calculating, and updating standard costs are also simplified.

Variances based on direct labor data are not as useful in a JIT environment. In addition, product quality requires high quality inputs and little scrap or rework, so materials price and quantity variances should be minimal. Computerized data processing enables management to use actual cost data to evaluate performance, thereby replacing many of the standard costing contributions to pricing decisions and cost allocation procedures.

Direct Versus Indirect Costs

OBJECTIVE 6
Describe how the JIT philosophy and CIM affect the classification of direct and indirect costs

Product costs in a traditional manufacturing system are heavily weighted by variable costs and especially by direct labor costs. Because direct labor is such a dominant force in the traditional system, most factory overhead costs are allocated to the products based on direct labor hours or dollars. Direct labor is either the main cost component or the primary cause of overhead cost incurrence—direct labor is the main cost driver.

The use of flexible manufacturing systems and automated production cells has changed the nature of product costs and offers alternative approaches to the application of costs to products flowing through each operation. Here we analyze two specific areas: (1) the elimination of work orders and (2) the merging of direct labor with factory overhead costs and accounting for only conversion costs. Additional product costing issues under JIT are discussed in Chapter 16.

The work order is a primary document in a traditional manufacturing system. Labor time is accumulated as the order moves from one operation to the next. When the work order is completed, it is a record of all labor time required for that job. This labor time information makes it possible to determine the cost of direct labor and the application of factory overhead. By using JIT production cells and continuous production techniques, work orders are eliminated. Daily production schedules are maintained, and costs are assigned to the work completed during the day. Detailed reporting, such as completing documents like the work order, is not a part of the simplified JIT process.

In a JIT setting, costs have little correlation with direct labor time. Emphasis is on the time it takes to get a product through the entire process. Machine hours become more important than labor hours. Product velocity measures are used to apply conversion costs to products via process costing. In addition, theoretical capacity is used to establish conversion cost application rates. JIT means that the objective is no waste or downtime, or operating at theoretical capacity.

Sophisticated computer monitoring of the production cell allows many costs to be traced directly to the cells and the products being manufactured. As Table 15-3 shows, several costs that used to be treated as indirect costs and applied to products using a labor base are now treated as direct costs of a work cell. The JIT approach centers on the concept that if a cost cannot be traced directly to a work cell or product (caused by the actual shaping of the product), then it is suspect and should be analyzed to see if a non-value added function exists. If so, the cost should be eliminated.

Many of the costs in Table 15-3 are directly traceable to the JIT production cell. If standard costs are used, products are costed using predetermined rates for materials and conversion costs. The JIT philosophy requires that each cell manufacture identical or similar products to minimize setup time. Therefore, materials and conversion costs should be near uniform per product per cell. Costs such as material handling, utilities, operating supplies, and supervision can be traced directly to work cells as they are incurred. Depreciation is charged based on units of output rather than according to time, so depreciation can also be charged directly to work cells based on the number of units produced. Building occupancy costs, property and casualty insurance premiums, and property taxes remain as indirect costs and must be allocated to the production cells for inclusion in the conversion cost category.

The IBM Approach

As described in McIlhattan's article referred to earlier, IBM's switch to the JIT production concept has been very successful. The company's experience has allowed more than 75 percent of the production support costs to become directly traceable to products (this figure was 25 percent before JIT was instituted). At IBM, costs are classified into three groups and associated with products:

Table 15-3. Direct Versus Indirect Costs—Changes Caused by JIT

Traditional Environment		JIT Environment
Direct	Direct labor	Direct
Indirect	Repairs and maintenance	Direct
Indirect	Material handling	Direct
Indirect	Operating supplies	Direct
Indirect	Utility costs	Direct
Indirect	Supervision	Direct
Indirect	Depreciation	Direct
Indirect	Supporting service functions	Mostly direct
Indirect	Building occupancy	Indirect
Indirect	Insurance and taxes	Indirect

1. Production floor expenses are charged directly to products as they flow through manufacturing cells.
2. Nonoccupancy-related support costs, such as cost accounting and data processing, are "billed" directly to the products utilizing their services. The billing rates are negotiated between support function managers and product managers before services are rendered and are based on the amount of support given to a specific product.
3. Occupancy-related costs are still allocated to products.[3]

Direct charging of both production floor expenses and support costs provides product cost accuracy and increased knowledge about the importance of each cost to the manufacturing process.

The Raw-in-Process Inventory Account

OBJECTIVE 7
Record transactions involving the Raw-in-Process Inventory account

One of the most basic accounting changes caused by the JIT environment is the use of the **Raw-in-Process Inventory** account. This new inventory account replaces both the Materials Inventory and the Work-in-Process Inventory accounts. Because raw materials are ordered and received just in time for use, there is no need to debit them to a Materials Inventory account; they are debited directly to the Raw-in-Process Inventory account:

Raw-in-Process Inventory	50,000	
Accounts Payable		50,000
To record the purchase of raw materials		

In process costing situations, as goods were completed by one department and transferred to another department, the cumulative cost of the products had to be transferred from one work-in-process inventory account to another. This is also changed in the JIT environment. There is no need for numerous work-in-process inventory accounts because the products flow continuously through the flexible manufacturing cell. All conversion costs (direct labor and factory overhead costs) are debited to the single Raw-in-Process Inventory account. When the goods have been completed, the following entry is made:

Finished Goods Inventory	185,600	
Raw-in-Process Inventory		185,600
To record the transfer of completed products to Finished Goods Inventory		

If adjustments have to be made at the end of an accounting period because of over- or underapplied factory overhead, the debits or credits are made only to Raw-in-Process and Finished Goods Inventories. For example, assume that factory overhead was overapplied by $1,600 and that $100

---

3. Robert D. McIlhattan, "How Cost Management Systems Can Support the JIT Philosophy," *Management Accounting*, September 1987, p. 24.

should be taken back from goods in process and $500 from finished goods; the remaining $1,000 are in Cost of Goods Sold.   The entry would be:

Factory Overhead Applied	1,600	
Raw-in-Process Inventory		100
Finished Goods Inventory		500
Cost of Goods Sold		1,000
To adjust for overapplied factory overhead		

One last example helps clarify the Raw-in-Process Inventory account. Assume that $17,500 of raw materials were purchased and the accountant discovered that these goods were priced $1,500 over their standard cost. The following entry would be made to record the purchase:

Raw-in-Process Inventory	16,000	
Materials Price Variance	1,500	
Accounts Payable		17,500
To record the purchase of raw materials and		
the related price variance		

Using the Raw-in-Process Inventory account is an easy adjustment to make.   Remember that this new account is used in every situation in which either Materials Inventory or Work-in-Process Inventory was used in the past.

JIT and Process Costing

The process costing method can be easily adapted to compute product unit costs in a JIT manufacturing setting.   Every manufacturing cost is classified as being either a materials or materials-related cost or a conversion cost.   The following illustrative problem helps show how JIT product costs are developed and ties together several sections of the chapter.

Illustrative Problem: JIT/Process Costing

The Metro Company produces automobile steering wheels for all the major car producers in the United States.   Three FMS cells are used in the process: one cell produces leather steering wheels, a second concentrates on plastic models, and a third makes special wood-grained wheels. The day-shift operator of each cell prepares the equipment so that all machines can run automatically during the two night shifts.   Only indirect labor is needed during the night shifts.

During the week ended June 15, 19x9 the leather wheel JIT operating cell produced the following data:

Units:	
Beginning inventory	30
Units completed during week	4,600
Ending inventory (80 percent complete)	35

Hours worked:
   Direct labor— 40 hours
   Machine hours:
      Nine machines in cell
      FMS leather wheel cell ran
         110 hours during week

Costs in beginning Raw-in-Process Inventory:	
Materials costs	$1,080
Conversion costs	265

Direct costs incurred for leather wheel cell:	
Raw materials	$138,150
Direct labor (40 hours at $14 per hour)	560
Power costs	3,056
Cell machinery depreciation	2,420
Design costs	4,963
Indirect labor	11,970
Lubricants, supplies, and fasteners	7,242

Overhead rates used:
   Material handling overhead (included as part
      of materials cost in process costing analysis):
      20 percent of raw materials costs
   Factory overhead not traceable to cell:
      $37 per machine hour worked

Required

1. Compute the total materials costs and total conversion costs for the week.
2. Using good form and the average process costing approach, prepare
   a. Schedule of equivalent production
   b. Unit cost analysis schedule
   c. Cost summary schedule
3. From the cost summary schedule, prepare a journal entry to transfer costs of completed units to Finished Goods Inventory.

Solution

Before preparing the Cost of Production Report for the Metro Company, we will first categorize the costs of the period. Remember that two cost categories are used in a JIT system: materials cost and conversion costs. These same categories are also used in process costing.

Raw materials costs:	
In beginning inventory	$ 1,080
Used in production during the week	138,150
Material handling overhead for the week:	
$138,150 × 20%	27,630
Total materials costs	$166,860

Conversion costs:

In beginning inventory	$ 265
Charged to FMS cell during period:	
Directly traceable costs:	
Direct labor (40 hours at $14 per hour)	560
Power costs	3,056
Cell machinery depreciation	2,420
Design costs	4,963
Indirect labor	11,970
Lubricants, supplies, and fasteners	7,242
Indirect factory overhead:	
110 machine hr × 9 machines × $37/machine hr	36,630
Total conversion costs	$ 67,106

The Metro Company
Cost of Production Report
For the Week Ending June 15, 19x9

Schedule of Equivalent Production Completed

	Units to Be Accounted For	Equivalent Units	
Units—Stage of Completion		**Materials Costs**	**Conversion Costs**
Beginning inventory—units completed this period	30	30	30
Units started and completed this period	4,570	4,570	4,570
Ending inventory—units started but not completed	35		
(Materials—100% complete)		35	
(Conversion costs—80% complete)			28
Totals	4,635	4,635	4,628

Unit Cost Analysis Schedule Computed

	Total Cost Analysis			Equivalent Unit Costs	
	Costs from Beginning Inventory	**Costs from Current Period**	**Total Costs to Be Accounted For**	**Divided by Equivalent Units**	**Cost Per Equivalent Unit**
Materials costs	$1,080	$165,780	$166,860	4,635	$36.00
Conversion costs	265	66,841	67,106	4,628	14.50
Total	$1,345	$232,621	$233,966		$50.50

Cost Summary Schedule Computed

	Cost of Goods Transferred to Finished Goods Inventory	Cost of Ending Raw-in-Process Inventory
Beginning inventory		
30 units at $50.50 per unit	$ 1,515	
Units started and completed this period		
4,570 units at $50.50 per unit	230,785	
Ending inventory		
Materials:		
35 units at 100% at $36		$ 1,260
Conversion costs:		
35 units at 80% at $14.50		406
Totals	$232,300	$ 1,666
Computation check:		
Cost of goods transferred to Finished Goods Inventory		$232,300
Cost of ending Raw-in-Process Inventory		1,666
Error due to rounding		0
Total costs to be accounted for		$233,966

Journal entry prepared:

Finished Goods Inventory	232,300	
Raw-in-Process Inventory		232,300
To transfer cost of goods completed to Finished Goods Inventory		

Chapter Review

Review of Learning Objectives

1. **Describe a computer-integrated manufacturing system.**
   Computer-integrated manufacturing (CIM) refers to the production process in which all parts of the system are fully integrated through computer technology. Entirely automated systems, including production, materials ordering, billing, payment, and accounting systems, are linked by computers.

2. **Compare and contrast the traditional manufacturing system with the just-in-time approach to manufacturing.**
   The traditional manufacturing system is divided into five time frames: actual processing time, inspection time, move time, queue time, and storage time.

The JIT philosophy eliminates most or all of inspection time, move time, queue time, and storage time, resulting in significant reductions in product cycle time, a substantial cost savings to the company.

3. **Identify the elements supporting a JIT operating environment.**
   The elements supporting a JIT operating environment are (a) maintain minimum inventory levels, (b) develop pull-through production planning and scheduling procedures, (c) purchase materials and produce products as needed in smaller lot sizes, (d) perform simple, inexpensive machine setups, (e) develop a multiskilled work force, (f) create a flexible manufacturing system, (g) maintain high levels of product quality, (h) enforce a system of effective preventive facility maintenance, and (i) encourage continuous work environment improvement.

4. **Analyze the impact of a change from a labor intensive to a capital intensive production process on product costing concepts and techniques.**
   As the computer is integrated into the production process, more capital outlay is required. The more a CIM environment is approached, where every part of the process is linked via computer, the wider the spread between machine hours and labor hours used in the process. Manufacturing overhead allocation in a CIM system should be linked closely with measures of machine activity, not labor activity.

5. **Define and give examples of "cost drivers."**
   A cost driver is any activity that causes costs to be incurred. Before you can eliminate a cost or account for it properly, you must know what caused the cost—you must know what drives the cost. Once the cost driver has been determined, the indirect costs it is causing can either be (a) treated as a legitimate product cost and allocated as part of conversion costs or (b) eliminated by eliminating the need for the cost driver itself. Cost drivers include number of products, number of schedule changes, number of vendors, and number of units reworked.

6. **Describe how the JIT philosophy and CIM affect the classification of direct and indirect costs.**
   The application of the JIT philosophy and the use of CIM and flexible manufacturing systems and work cells has changed the nature of product costs. Computer facilities have made it possible for many costs that were indirect to be directly traceable to the cell. Costs such as electrical power, depreciation of machinery, indirect labor, operating supplies, and supervision can now be traced directly to the FMS work cell. Process costing techniques are then used to assign the costs to products.

7. **Record transactions involving the Raw-in-Process Inventory account.**
   The Raw-in-Process Inventory account has taken the place of both the Materials Inventory and the Work-in-Process Inventory accounts. Because raw materials are received as needed and the products flow continuously through the process, only one inventory account is needed in these areas.

8. **Use process costing procedures to compute JIT product costs.**
   Because manufacturing costs in a JIT/FMS environment are classified as materials costs and conversion costs, the process costing method can easily be adapted to compute product costs. There is usually very little beginning inventory in a JIT setting, so the stage of completion of goods in process can easily be determined. The unit cost analysis schedule is used for unit cost computations.

Review of Concepts and Terminology

The following important concepts were introduced in this chapter:

(L.O.1)   **Computer-integrated manufacturing (CIM) system:** A CIM system is a fully integrated computer setup in which everything connected with the manufacturing system is performed automatically.

(L.O.1)   **Just-in-time philosophy:** An overall operating philosophy of management in which all resources, including materials, personnel, and facilities, are used in a just-in-time manner.

(L.O.2)   **Non-value added activity:** An activity that adds cost to the product but does not increase its market value.

(L.O.2)   **Flexible manufacturing system (FMS):** An integrated set of computerized machines and systems designed to complete a series of operations automatically.

(L.O.5)   **Cost driver:** Any activity that causes costs to be incurred.

Other important terms introduced in this chapter are:

automation (p. 573)
computer numerically-controlled machines (CNC) (p. 579)
pull-through production (p. 581)
raw-in-process inventory (p. 589)

Review Problem
Unit Cost Analysis: A Comparison of Traditional and JIT/FMS Manufacturing Environments

Bennett & Hendricks Manufacturing Company has been in business for more than fifty years. At their last meeting, top management decided to implement a just-in-time/flexible manufacturing system for the DeKalb Division. DeKalb specializes in manufacturing deluxe home appliances. Their most popular item is a line of unique aluminum and oak barbeque grills. Various models are produced, but all are a standard shape and size. Currently, the company uses a traditional cost accounting system, and unit costs are determined by adding a manufacturing overhead factor to the unit's direct materials and direct labor amounts. Direct labor hours is the allocation base.

The controller has been asked to restructure the present manufacturing cost data so that the effect of the new system on product unit costs can be analyzed. Following are data for the past accounting period. Several changes will occur when the new system is installed. Several former indirect costs will be directly traceable to the JIT/FMS work cell. Also, separate allocations will be made for materials-related costs and engineering overhead. Indirect manufacturing costs will be allocated based on machine hours, materials storage and handling overhead will be allocated based on total dollars of materials and parts incurred, and engineering overhead will be allocated based on engineering hours. Process costing procedures will be used to compute unit costs.

	Traditional	JIT/Flexible
Costs directly traceable to product:		
Raw materials	$ 492,000	$ 492,000
Parts for assembly	1,456,000	1,456,000
Direct labor:		
Traditional: 3.8 hr at $16/hr per unit	4,864,000	
JIT/FMS: 0.6 hr at $20/hr per unit		960,000
Total costs traceable to product	$6,812,000	$2,908,000
Costs directly traceable to FMS cell:		
Electrical power		$ 60,000
Supervision		12,000
Depreciation, machinery		9,600
Setup labor		8,000
Other indirect labor		420,000
Repairs and maintenance		18,400
Operating supplies and lubricants		2,400
Total costs directly traceable to FMS cell		$ 530,400
Indirect manufacturing cost pool:		
Electrical power	$ 240,000	
Supervision	164,500	
Depreciation, machinery	53,400	
Inspection costs	299,000	
Product rework costs	966,000	
Engineering labor	184,000	
Power costs, engineering	55,200	
Depreciation, engineering equipment	69,000	
Engineering supervision	92,000	
Other engineering overhead	35,800	
Setup labor	46,000	
Other indirect labor	1,725,000	
Repairs and maintenance	114,100	
Operating supplies and lubricants	27,600	
Depreciation, building	128,800	$ 128,800
Property taxes	18,400	18,400
Fire insurance	9,200	9,200
Liability insurance	4,600	4,600
Building maintenance	13,000	13,000
Factory utilities	32,200	32,200
Factory employee cafeteria	101,200	101,200
Purchasing costs, materials, and parts	110,400	
Storage and handling, Work-in-Process inventory	736,000	
Materials/parts storage and handling	193,200	
Depreciation, materials moving trucks	41,400	
Total indirect manufacturing costs	$5,460,000	$ 307,400

	Traditional	JIT/Flexible
Engineering overhead cost pool:		
Engineering labor		$ 184,000
Power costs, engineering		55,200
Depreciation, engineering equipment		69,000
Engineering supervision		92,000
Other engineering overhead		35,800
Total engineering overhead costs		$ 436,000
Materials storage and handling overhead cost pool:		
Purchasing costs, materials and parts		$ 110,400
Materials/parts storage and handling		193,200
Depreciation, materials moving trucks		41,400
Total materials storage and handling overhead costs		$ 345,000

These data have been partially restructured in anticipation of the new system. Following is a summary of the other information that will be required for the analysis:

Total actual divisional direct labor hours for the period	2,100,000 DLHs
Total anticipated divisional machine hours for the period	1,060,000 MHs
Total anticipated divisional engineering hours for the period	27,250 Eng. Hrs.
Total anticipated divisional dollar value of materials and parts for the period	$15,000,000
Number of grills produced	80,000 grills
Anticipated machine hours for grill FMS	132,500 MHs
Anticipated engineering hours for grill FMS	3,400 Eng. Hrs.
Process costing information for grill FMS:	
Beginning inventory:	
Materials and parts	$5,460
Conversion costs	3,920
Equivalent units for period:	
Materials and parts	80,280 Equiv. Units
Conversion costs	80,200 Equiv. Units

Required

1. Under the traditional system,
   a. Compute the manufacturing overhead application rate.
   b. Compute the product unit cost for each grill.
2. Identify the cost categories that will likely be eliminated when the company adopts a JIT/FMS approach.

3. Compute the JIT/FMS application rates for the following:
   a. Indirect manufacturing costs
   b. Engineering overhead costs
   c. Materials storage and handling overhead costs
4. Identify the total materials costs and conversion costs for the period for the grill FMS cell.
5. Using the average process costing method, compute the grill unit cost under the new JIT/FMS setting.

Answer to Review Problem

1. Traditional system:
   a. Computation of manufacturing overhead application rate:

$5,460,000/2,100,000 direct labor hours	$ 2.60 per DLH

   b. Computation of product unit cost:

Raw materials cost	
$492,000/80,000 units	$ 6.15
Parts cost	
$1,456,000/80,000 units	18.20
Direct labor cost	
$4,864,000/80,000 units	60.80
Manufacturing overhead	
3.8 hr/unit × $2.60/DLH	9.88
Total unit cost	$95.03

2. The following cost categories are likely to be eliminated in a JIT/FMS setting:

Inspection costs	$ 299,000
Product rework costs	966,000
Storage and handling, Work-in-Process inventory	736,000
Total costs likely to be eliminated	$2,001,000

3. Computation of JIT/FMS overhead application rates:

   a. Indirect manufacturing costs

$307,400/1,060,000 machine hours	$ 0.29 per mh

   b. Engineering overhead costs

$436,000/27,250 engineering hours	$16.00 per eng. hr.

   c. Materials storage and handling overhead costs

$345,000/$15,000,000 materials and parts purchased	2.30 % of M&P cost

Molding machines	The Molding Department uses six molding machines. Each machine can be set up to make any keyboard casing sold by the company.
Trimming machines	In the Trimming Department, casings removed from the molds are trimmed of all excess materials left by the molding operation. Six trimming machines are used.
Packing machines	Packing machines wrap and individually box each completed computer keyboard casing. Each of the two packing machines can keep pace with three trimming machines.

Products are moved from the mixing operation to the molding machines in large 200-gallon drums, and the drums usually sit one to three days before being used. Sometimes the mixture must be remixed before it is usable by the Molding Department. From molding to trimming, the casings are stacked on wooden skids and moved by small lift trucks. The same moving procedure is used from trimming to the packing operation. Total production time can range from two weeks to three months, depending on the urgency of the order. B. J. Cook is not happy with this rate of output. Suggest a plan for B. J. Cook that will transform her manufacturing operation into a JIT production operation without new equipment having to be purchased.

Exercise 15-3.
Elements
Supporting JIT
(L.O. 3)

Barbara Wicks recently purchased Consolidated Metals Company from a family who owned the business seventy-two years. During that time, Consolidated reached world prominence as a producer of high-quality stainless steel cutting tools. However, about ten years ago the company let the quality begin to slip because competition kept driving down the price. Today the company has only a small share of the market, with total revenues only 12 percent of what they were at their peak.

Wicks has been told that it will take a complete revamping of the production facility and the adoption of a just-in-time operating philosophy to turn the company around. However, she is a bit hesitant to make any drastic moves with only this little knowledge of the proposed operating environment. She has heard two supporting comments about this approach: (1) The emphasis is on quality and continuous improvement, and (2) simple is better.

You have been asked to prepare a summary of the elements supporting the JIT production philosophy. Include a brief description of each element as part of your analysis.

Exercise 15-4.
Cost Driver
Determination
(L.O. 5)

Salesman Rick Vimmerstedt just stormed out of the office of controller Joe Umbriano. When asked what was wrong, Vimmerstedt stated that he had just been told to refuse any additional orders for goods that had to circumvent the existing three-week backlog period. Umbriano had just added $2,450 of additional scheduling costs to his recent order from Blaser Corp., and this charge turned a $2,200 profit into a $250 loss. Sales personnel earn commissions on the profitability of their orders.

Umbriano used the following analysis to back up his position regarding the Blaser order:

Costs associated with production schedule changes

Personnel overtime	$1,940
Extra computer time	1,260
Unanticipated supplies and utility costs	1,080
Communication with affected customers	620
Total costs of schedule changes	$4,900
50 percent traceable to Blaser order	$2,450

What is a cost driver? Does this case involve a cost driver? Should the cost of schedule changes be spread over all orders worked on or traced to specific orders? Do you agree with Umbriano's decision? Why or why not?

Exercise 15-5.
Costs and Their
Cost Drivers
(L.O. 5)

The following cost items are from the trial balance of the Elmore Corporation in Huntsville, Alabama. Company accountants are in the process of establishing an overhead allocation system for factory-related costs. To help guarantee accuracy, several cost pools based on separate activities are desired. The company has a fully automated flexible manufacturing system in operation. Budget costs for the period were:

Repairs and maintenance, plant building	$ 11,578
Engineering Department salaries	22,190
Raw materials	123,790
Depreciation, Tool and Die Department equipment	7,270
Depreciation, Engineering Department equipment	4,260
Marketing expenses	21,320
Depreciation, plant building	8,150
Tool and Die Department operating supplies	1,274
Insurance and taxes, plant building	3,520
Yard maintenance, plant building	1,250
Electrical costs, Tool and Die Department	2,310
Electrical costs, plant building	3,520
Tool and Die Department wages	19,740
Electrical costs, Engineering Department	1,980

Divide these costs into separate activity cost pools. Recommend an allocation base for each pool that will distribute the costs fairly and equitably. Alternative allocation bases include direct labor hours, tool and die orders, engineering change orders, machine hours, engineering hours, tool and die labor hours, direct labor dollars, and square footage.

Exercise 15-6.
Direct Versus
Indirect Costs
(L.O. 6)

The following cost categories are common types of costs in a manufacturing and assembly operation:

Raw materials:	Operating supplies
Sheet steel	Small tools
Iron castings	Depreciation, plant

Assembly parts: Depreciation, machinery
  Part 24RE6   Supervisory salaries
  Part 15RF8   Electrical power
Direct labor   Insurance and taxes, plant
Engineering labor   President's salary
Indirect labor   Employee benefits

Identify each type of cost as being either direct or indirect, assuming the cost was incurred in a

1. Traditional manufacturing setting
2. JIT flexible manufacturing system environment

State the reasons for any classification changes noted.

Exercise 15-7.
Raw-in-Process
Inventory
(L.O.7)

de Reyna Manufacturing Company installed a just-in-time flexible manufacturing system in its Shovel Division, and the system has been operating at near capacity for about eight months. Transactions related to the JIT/FMS are recorded when incurred. The following transactions took place last week:

Sept. 5   Wooden handles for jobs 12A, 14N, and 13F were ordered and received, $3,670.

Sept. 6   Sheet metal costing $5,630 received from vendor B.

Sept. 7   Work begun on job 14N.

Sept. 8   Job 12A completed and shipped to the customer; total cost, $13,600. [Company uses a 40 percent markup to establish selling price.]

Sept. 9   Spoiled goods with a net realizable value of $1,200 were moved to the shipping dock to be sold as scrap.

Using good journal entry form, record these transactions.

Interpreting Accounting Information

Creating a JIT/FMS
Environment:
Nease Corporation
(L.O.2,3,4)

Savannah, Georgia, is proud of the Nease Corporation because Marsha Nease's dream has become the town's primary employer. Fifteen years ago she teamed up with ten financial supporters and created a roller skate manufacturing company. Company design people soon turned the roller skate idea into a riding skateboard. Twelve years and more than 4 million skateboards later, Nease Corporation finds itself as the industry leader in both volume and quality.

To retain its market share, Nease Corporation has decided to completely automate the manufacturing process. Flexible manufacturing systems have been ordered for the Wheel Assembly and the Board Shaping Lines. Manual operations will be retained for the Board Decorating Line because some hand painting is involved. All operations will be converted to a just-in-time environment.

You have been called in as a consultant to Nease, who wants some idea of the impact of the new JIT/FMS approach on the company's product costing practices.

Required

1. Summarize the elements of a JIT environment.
2. What product costing changes should be anticipated when the new automated systems are installed?

3. What are some of the allocation bases that the company should employ? In what situations?
4. Are there any other accounting practices that will be affected? Why will they change?

Problem Set A

**Problem 15A-1.
Production Layout
Design
(L.O. 2)**

Bentley Automotive Products Company specializes in manufacturing chrome automobile parts, with front chrome grills being one of the company's most successful products. The following manufacturing operations and functions are part of the production of all types of automobile grills:

Assembly	Connecting devices are put on the completed grill.
Stamping	The grill shape is stamped out of a piece of sheet metal.
Plating	A chrome substance is adhered to a heat-treated product.
Receiving	The central receiving area receives sheet metal and assembly parts.
Welding	Connector pads are attached to a heat-treated product prior to plating.
Washing	Products are cleaned prior to being inspected for the first time.
Postassembly inspection	Products are inspected just prior to being packaged.
Raw materials storage	Sheet metal and assembly parts are stored prior to usage.
Drilling	Holes are drilled into the products before the connector pads can be welded.
Bending	Stamped grills are bent into shape.
Heat-treat	All products are heat-treated after passing the pre-assembly inspection point.
Sheet metal inspection	All sheet metal received is inspected.
Polishing	Plated grills are polished before being assembled.
Skid moving	All grills are moved on large wooden skids from operation to operation.
Shipping	Railroad cars are loaded for shipment to automobile-making companies.
Packing	Grills are packed in large wooden crates.
Preassembly inspection	All grills are inspected after the washing operation.

Required

1. Arrange these operations in the order they would be in a traditional manufacturing system.
2. Assume that a just-in-time approach is to be taken in redesigning this production process. Identify the
   a. Operations or process elements that would be eliminated
   b. Operations that would be automated
   c. Possible operations that could be combined into operating cell(s)
3. Would this company be considered a good candidate for the JIT/FMS environment? Defend your answer.

Problem 15A-2.
Cost Allocation in
an Automated
Process
(L.O. 4, 6)

William Epps created Augusta Music Company fifteen years ago. The company specializes in speaker systems for home stereos. Two different types of speakers are produced in the Sound Department. The Casings Department makes the speaker casings. Speakers and casings are assembled in the Assembly Department. The Sound and Casings Departments are operated autonomously. The Sound Department utilizes a modern flexible manufacturing system and has very little direct labor expense. Casings, on the other hand, is still mostly a functional operation, with many direct labor employees.

The two types of speakers the Sound Department manufactures are identified as models X20 and Y16, respectively. The X20 is completely made by FMS equipment, whereas model Y16 requires some manual detailing after it has completed the full FMS cycle.

Following is a summary of plantwide overhead costs for the month of March:

Indirect support labor	$34,190
Machine repairs and maintenance	3,650
Materials delivery trucker wages	2,820
Depreciation, materials delivery trucks	1,120
Depreciation, building	2,640
Depreciation, machinery	5,370
Electrical power	2,490
Machinery supplies and lubricants	1,370
Engineering salaries	11,880
Depreciation, engineering equipment	1,450
Operating supplies, engineering	950
Fuel, raw materials delivery	310
Purchasing Department costs	2,260
Fire insurance, building	420
Property taxes, plant	550
Total	$71,470

The following information was also made available:

	Sound Department				
	Model X20	Model Y16	Totals	Casings Department	Plantwide Totals
Direct labor hours	60	180	240	1,060	1,300
Machine hours	2,400	1,600	4,000	1,500	5,500
Engineering hours	30	120	150	300	450
Cost of raw materials used			$56,250	$28,125	$84,375
Floor square footage			7,500	15,000	22,500

Required

1. Allocate the plantwide overhead for the month to the Sound and Casings Departments using direct labor hours as a base.

2. Using direct labor hours, machine hours, cost of raw materials used, engineering hours, and floor square footage as cost drivers, separate the elements of the plantwide overhead cost pool into three or more different cost pools.
3. Using your answer to part **2** and the allocation bases mentioned, reallocate the plantwide overhead costs to the Sound and Casings Departments. Discuss the differences between the allocations of parts **1** and **3**.
4. What are the advantages and disadvantages of this approach versus the allocation of plantwide overhead costs to cost or profit centers?
5. Assume the overhead cost allocated to the Sound Department was $25,600. Allocate the $25,600 to the two products manufactured by the Sound Department based on (a) direct labor hours and (b) machine hours. Which allocation approach is better? Why?

Problem 15A-3.
Labor Versus
Capital Intensive
Operations
(L.O. 4)

Brad Christianson, controller for Karen Gears & Bearing Company is in the process of establishing new unit costing procedures. The company recently installed automated flexible manufacturing systems for its two successful gear bearing box products. The investment in machinery was nearly $30 million, and the new equipment reduced the number of direct labor workers from 160 to 35; the Regular model product line went down from 60 people to 15, and the Heavy-Duty line went down from 100 direct labor people to 20.

Under the traditional cost system used in 19x8, all factory overhead costs were pooled together and allocated to products based on direct labor hours. Each direct labor employee worked an average of 2,000 hours during 19x8. Christianson has decided to adjust the 19x8 data to reflect the new environment and to use the data to develop the new product costing procedures. The following adjustments need to be made:

1. Direct labor cost is to be recomputed based on 35 rather than 160 people.
2. Depreciation, machinery will increase from $34,000 to $1,450,000.
3. Indirect labor will increase $100,000.
4. Repairs and maintenance, lubricants and supplies, small tools expense, and electrical power will double.
5. Inspection wages, work-in-process handling, and storage space costs will all be eliminated by the new FMS processes.
6. Factory overhead costs will be apportioned or allocated as follows:

	Regular Gear Bearing Box	Heavy-Duty Gear Bearing Box
Engineering labor: based on engineering hours used	6,950	7,228
Raw materials handling: based on cost of raw materials used	$1,709,000	$950,000
Building occupancy costs and Depreciation, machinery: based on machine hours used	440,000	360,000
All other factory overhead costs are traceable to FMS cells	70%	30%
7. Units produced in 19x8	50,000	20,000

Karen Gears & Bearing Company
Operating Data
For Year Ended 19x8

	Regular Gear Bearing Box	Heavy-Duty Gear Bearing Box	Total 19x8 Operating Data
Raw materials:			
Rolled steel	$ 728,000	$ 378,400	$ 1,106,400
Bearings	981,000	571,600	1,552,600
Purchased parts	1,182,500	638,000	1,820,500
Direct labor (160 × 2,000 hr at $19/hr)	2,280,000	3,800,000	6,080,000
	$5,171,500	$5,388,000	$10,559,500
Engineering labor			425,340
Indirect support labor			396,720
Inspection wages			182,620
Supervisory salaries			392,450
Depreciation, machinery			34,000
Repairs and maintenance			37,890
Lubricants and supplies			12,750
Small tools expense			15,630
Electrical power			21,890
Raw materials handling:			
Lift truck drivers			55,200
Depreciation			7,210
Fuel and supplies			12,340
Work-in-process handling:			
Lift truck drivers			112,300
Depreciation			15,310
Fuel and supplies			25,730
Storage space costs			41,890
Building occupancy costs:			
Depreciation, building			35,800
Heat, light, and power			14,830
Property taxes and insurance			19,450
Maintenance and repairs			27,840
Total operating costs			$12,446,690

Required

1. Compute the factory overhead rate based on direct labor hours that were incurred in 19x8.
2. Using the traditional approach, compute the 19x8 unit costs for both the Regular and Heavy-Duty gear bearing boxes.

3. Assuming that both products were produced using a JIT/FMS, compute the overhead application rates for engineering labor; raw materials handling; depreciation, machinery; and building occupancy costs.
4. Compute the unit costs for both the Regular and Heavy-Duty gear bearing boxes under the new FMS setting.
5. Analyze the differences in the unit costs. What caused the differences?

Problem 15A-4.
JIT and Process
Costing
(L.O. 8)

The Forest Company is located in Durango, Colorado, and has been producing sink faucets for the past twelve years. The prices of the seven models of kitchen sink faucets range from $24 to $94. The Grand model is the highest-priced faucet, and its market share has been steadily declining during the past four years.

Bothered by the decline in market share, management recently purchased a JIT/FMS cell for the kitchen faucet line. Two day-shift operators are employed, and they prepare the equipment to run automatically during the two evening shifts. Only indirect support labor is needed during the night shifts. For the week ending July 30, 19x9, the Grand model was run and the following data were generated:

Units:

Beginning Raw-in-Process Inventory	45
Units completed during week	6,295
Ending Raw-in-Process Inventory (70 percent complete)	50

Hours worked:

Direct labor—80 hours

Machine hours:
  Fourteen machines in cell
  FMS cell ran
   116 hours during week

Costs in beginning inventory:

Materials costs	$ 2,410
Conversion costs	765

Direct costs incurred by faucet JIT/FMS cell:

Raw materials	$157,458
Direct labor (80 hours at $16 per hour)	1,280
Electricity costs	6,056
JIT cell machinery depreciation	3,890
Engineering design costs	7,934
Indirect labor	12,000
Lubricants, supplies, and fasteners	8,110

Overhead rates used:

Materials-handling overhead (included as part of raw materials cost in the process costing analysis):
  25 percent of raw materials costs
Factory overhead not traceable to cell:
  $42 per machine hour worked

Required

1. Compute the total materials cost and total conversion cost for the week.
2. Using good form and the average process costing approach, prepare a
   a. Schedule of equivalent production
   b. Unit cost analysis schedule
   c. Cost summary schedule
3. From the cost summary schedule, prepare a journal entry to transfer costs of completed units to Finished Goods Inventory.
4. Do you think the $94 price is too high for the Grand model? Why?

Problem 15A-5.
Traditional Versus
JIT/FMS Unit Cost
Analysis
(L.O. 2, 5, 6, 8)

Welch & Welch Products, Inc., produce fans for home and business use. The company was created in 1974 and has grown steadily over the years. Last year management decided to install the company's first flexible manufacturing system in the Ceiling Fan Department. The deluxe ceiling fan has become the company's most popular product. The fan's casing and wooden blades are manufactured by the company; the small motor and electrical parts are purchased from outside vendors and assembled by the company. Presently, the company uses a traditional cost accounting system, and unit costs are computed by adding a plantwide manufacturing overhead factor to the unit direct materials and direct labor costs. The overhead allocation basis has been direct labor hours.

You have been asked to restructure the present manufacturing cost data so that the influence of the new system on product unit costs can be analyzed. Following are data from the most recent accounting period. The new system will cause several changes. Many of the indirect costs will be directly traceable to the FMS work cell and do not have to be included in the regular overhead computation. Also, separate allocations will be made for materials-related overhead costs and engineering overhead. Remaining indirect manufacturing costs (building occupancy costs) will be allocated based on machine hours. Materials storage and handling overhead will be allocated based on total dollars of materials and parts incurred. Engineering overhead will be allocated based on engineering hours. Process costing procedures will be used to compute unit costs.

	Traditional Manufacturing System	JIT/Flexible Manufacturing System
Costs directly traceable to product:		
Raw materials	$ 539,280	$ 539,280
Parts for assembly	1,823,280	1,823,280
Direct labor:		
Traditional:		
4.2 hr at $14/hr per unit	3,774,960	
JIT/FMS:		
.8 hr at $18/hr per unit		924,480
Total costs traceable to product	$6,137,520	$3,287,040

	Traditional Manufacturing System	JIT/Flexible Manufacturing System
Costs directly traceable to FMS cell:		
Electrical power		$ 65,680
Supervision		24,630
Depreciation, machinery		19,704
Setup labor		197,040
Other indirect labor		361,240
Repairs and maintenance		57,470
Operating supplies and lubricants		29,556
Total costs directly traceable to FMS cell		$ 755,320
Plantwide indirect manufacturing cost pool:		
Product rework costs	$ 741,100	
Electrical power, factory	363,000	
Supervision, factory	246,800	
Depreciation, machinery	74,200	
Purchased motors, inspection costs	67,400	
Setup labor	231,120	
Other indirect labor	526,440	
Engineering labor	176,800	
Electrical costs, engineering	163,200	
Depreciation, engineering equipment	91,800	
Engineering supervision	104,720	
Other engineering overhead	53,040	
Operating supplies and lubricants	36,890	
Finished goods inspection costs	79,800	
Machinery repairs and maintenance	234,200	
Storage and handling, Work-in-Process Inventory	432,900	
Depreciation, building	154,700	$ 154,700
Property taxes	28,900	28,900
Fire insurance	11,320	11,320
Liability insurance	15,540	15,540
Building maintenance	43,500	43,500
Other factory utilities	21,900	21,900
Factory employee cafeteria	134,200	134,200
Purchasing costs, materials, and parts	96,700	
Materials/parts storage and handling	212,300	
Depreciation, materials moving trucks	68,700	
Total indirect manufacturing costs	$4,411,170	$ 410,060

	Traditional Manufacturing System	JIT/Flexible Manufacturing System
Engineering overhead cost pool:		
Engineering labor		$ 176,800
Power costs, engineering		163,200
Depreciation, engineering equipment		91,800
Engineering supervision		104,720
Other engineering overhead		53,040
Total engineering overhead costs		$ 589,560
Materials storage and handling overhead cost pool:		
Purchasing costs, materials and parts		$ 96,700
Materials/parts storage and handling		212,300
Depreciation, materials moving trucks		68,700
Total materials storage and handling overhead costs		$ 377,700

These data have been partially restructured in anticipation of the new system. Following is a summary of other information that will be required for the analysis:

Total plantwide direct labor hours:	
Actual for last period	1,956,000 DLHs
Anticipated for this period	782,400 DLHs
Total anticipated plantwide machine hours for the period	2,475,000 MHs
Total anticipated plantwide engineering hours for the period	25,340 Eng. Hrs.
Total anticipated plantwide dollar value of materials and parts for the period	$18,400,000
Number of fans produced	64,200 fans
Anticipated machine hours for fan FMS	131,360 MHs
Anticipated engineering hours for fan FMS	6,800 Eng. Hrs.
Process costing information for fan FMS:	
Beginning inventory:	
Materials and parts	$6,420
Conversion costs	4,960
Equivalent units for period:	
Materials and parts	64,320 Equiv. Units
Conversion costs	64,300 Equiv. Units

Required

1. Under the traditional system,
   a. Compute the plantwide manufacturing overhead application rate.
   b. Using traditional labor data, compute the product unit cost for each fan.

2. Identify the cost categories that will likely be eliminated when the company adopts a JIT/FMS approach.
3. Compute the JIT/FMS application rates for the following:
   a. Indirect manufacturing costs
   b. Engineering overhead costs
   c. Materials storage and handling overhead costs
4. Identify the total materials costs and conversion costs for the period for the fan FMS cell.
5. Using the average process costing method, compute the fan unit cost under the new JIT/FMS setting.

Problem Set B

Problem 15B-1.
Production Layout
Design
(L.O. 2)

Processing and canning vegetables and fruits is a major industry in many countries of the world. Pelican Food Products Company of Vero Beach, Florida, is one of the biggest food processors in the southeast. The following processing operations for black-eyed peas are common in this industry:

Cooking	Heating the peas to a proper temperature so that consumers only have to reheat and serve
Inspecting raw peas	Weeding out inedible peas
Canning	Automatically putting cooked peas into cans
Labeling	Placing labels on processed cans
Shelling	Taking shells off raw peas
Finished goods storage	Storing canned peas while they await shipment
Cleaning	Washing peas prior to processing
Receiving	Central receiving area for freshly picked peas
Packing	Placing labeled cans in boxes
Lid sealing	Sealing lids on cans to prevent spoilage or leakage
Shipping	Truck loading area: Cartons are shipped according to customer needs
Bin storage	Storing raw peas prior to processing
Can inspection	Isolating improperly sealed cans
Cooling	Reducing temperature of cooked peas to facilitate canning operation

Required

1. Arrange these operations in the order they would be in a traditional production system.
2. Assume that a just-in-time approach is to be taken in redesigning this production process. Identify the
   a. Operations or process elements that would be eliminated
   b. Operations that would be automated
   c. Possible operations that could be combined into operating cell(s)
3. Would this company be considered a good candidate for the JIT/flexible manufacturing system environment? Defend your answer.

Problem 15B-2.
Cost Allocation in
an Automated
Process
(L.O. 4, 6)

DeFoor Industries is a furniture manufacturing company in Birmingham, Alabama. The company's two departments, the Vulcan Department and the UAB Department, operate as autonomous segments. Vulcan makes wooden cabinet doors for home and business use; UAB specializes in wooden chairs and stools. The Vulcan Department was recently fully automated with the purchase of a flexible manufacturing system and is organized in a JIT fashion. Very little direct labor is used. The UAB Department, on the other hand, operates using a traditional production system. Significant direct labor and manual and semiautomatic machines are used.

The Vulcan Department makes two main products: a plain cabinet door and a fancy model. The plain door can be mass-produced by the FMS with only minimal direct labor. The fancy model goes through all the FMS operations used to produce the plain door and also requires some specialized labor.

Following is a summary of plantwide overhead costs for a recent month:

Property taxes	$ 1,250
Warehouse personnel wages	2,640
Warehouse machine depreciation	1,190
Accounting Department salaries	3,180
Personnel Department salaries	2,530
Lunchroom expenses	6,830
Insurance on building	640
Liability insurance	1,420
Employee benefits	1,730
Repairs and maintenance	1,750
Quality Control Department costs	2,190
Electrical power	1,960
Purchasing Department costs	1,830
Total	$29,140

The following information was also made available:

	Vulcan Department				
	Plain Model	Fancy Model	Totals	UAB Department	Plantwide Totals
Direct labor hours	50	150	200	800	1,000
Machine hours	1,200	800	2,000	400	2,400
Cost of raw materials used			$27,500	$13,750	$41,250
Size of dept. (square feet)			4,000	8,000	12,000

Required

1. Allocate the plantwide overhead for the month to the Vulcan and UAB Departments using direct labor hours as a base.
2. Using direct labor hours, machine hours, cost of raw materials used, and size of department as cost drivers, separate the elements of the plantwide overhead cost pool into four different cost pools.

3. Using your answer to part **2** and the four allocation bases mentioned, reallocate the plantwide overhead costs to the Vulcan and UAB Departments. Discuss the differences between the allocations of parts **1** and **3**.

4. What are the advantages and disadvantages of this approach versus the allocation of plantwide overhead costs to cost or profit centers?

5. Assume the overhead cost allocated to the Vulcan Department was $12,000. Allocate the $12,000 to the two products manufactured by the Vulcan Department based on (a) direct labor hours and (b) machine hours. Which allocation approach is better? Why?

Problem 15B-3.
Labor Versus
Capital Intensive
Operations
(L.O. 4)

Margie Weaver is the chief financial officer for the Daytona Beach Auto Engine Works. The company just purchased completely automated flexible manufacturing systems for their two engine block cover lines, and Weaver is in the process of developing new product costing procedures. The two FMS lines cost just under $35 million, and the new equipment reduced the need for direct labor personnel from 220 to just 42 people. The 6-cylinder engine block cover line went down from 100 direct labor workers to 24; the 8-cylinder line went down from 120 direct labor workers to only 18.

A traditional cost system was used in 19x9, and all factory overhead costs were pooled together and allocated to products based on direct labor hours. Each direct labor employee worked an average of 2,000 hours during 19x9. Weaver has decided to adjust the 19x9 data to reflect the new environment and to use the date to develop the new product costing procedures. The following adjustments need to be made:

1. Direct labor cost is to be recomputed based on 42 rather than 220 people.
2. Depreciation, machinery will increase from $46,500 to $1,620,000.
3. Indirect labor will increase $180,000.
4. Repairs and maintenance, lubricants and supplies, small tools expense, and electrical power will triple.
5. Inspection wages, work-in-process handling, and storage space costs will all be eliminated by the new FMS processes.
6. Factory overhead costs will be apportioned or allocated as follows:

	6-cylinder Engine Block Cover	8-cylinder Engine Block Cover
Engineering labor: based on engineering hours used	9,340	6,400
Raw materials handling: based on cost of raw materials used	$2,120,300	$1,682,340
Building occupancy costs and Depreciation, machinery: based on machine hours used	375,000	300,000
All other factory overhead costs are traceable to FMS cells	60%	40%

7. Units produced in 19x9 | 35,000 | 22,000 |

	6-cylinder Engine Block Cover	8-cylinder Engine Block Cover	Total 19x9 Operating Data
Daytona Beach Auto Engine Works			
Operating Data			
For Year Ended 19x9			
Raw materials:			
Iron castings	$1,199,100	$ 999,240	$ 2,198,340
Steel trim	921,200	683,100	1,604,300
Purchased parts	610,750	323,400	934,150
Direct labor (220 × 2,000 hr at $16/hr)	3,200,000	3,840,000	7,040,000
	$5,931,050	$5,845,740	$11,776,790
Raw materials handling:			
Lift truck drivers			64,890
Depreciation			9,240
Fuel and supplies			15,260
Work-in-process handling:			
Lift truck drivers			124,370
Depreciation			21,340
Fuel and supplies			32,910
Engineering labor			503,680
Indirect support labor			287,440
Inspection wages			176,390
Supervisory salaries			196,450
Depreciation, machinery			46,500
Repairs and maintenance			51,270
Lubricants and supplies			14,360
Small tools expense			16,290
Electrical power			19,880
Storage space costs			40,750
Building occupancy costs:			
Depreciation, building			31,600
Heat, light, and power			16,740
Property taxes and insurance			26,310
Maintenance and repairs			38,280
Total operating costs			$13,510,740

Required

1. Compute the factory overhead rate based on direct labor hours that were incurred in 19x9.
2. Using the traditional approach, compute the 19x9 unit costs for both the 6- and 8-cylinder engine block covers.
3. Assuming that both products were produced using a JIT/flexible manufacturing system, compute the overhead application rates for engineering labor; raw materials handling; depreciation, machinery; and building occupancy costs.
4. Compute the unit costs for both the 6- and 8-cylinder engine block covers under the new FMS setting.
5. Analyze the differences in the unit costs. What caused the differences?

**Problem 15B-4.
JIT and Process
Costing**
(L.O. 8)

Enzian Corporation has manufactured ladders for both home and business use for more than twenty-five years. Ten years ago the company introduced the all-aluminum models and the Enzian Ladder became a very popular brand. But recently several other brands of aluminum ladders were introduced into the marketplace. The Enzian models have suffered significant sales declines. Two major types of ladders are produced: collapsible stepladders and extension ladders. Three sizes of each type of ladder are produced. Extension ladders come in 8-, 10-, and 12-foot lengths and cost $80, $100, and $125, respectively. The 12-foot model is known as the Primo ladder.

To improve efficiency and reduce operating costs, the company purchased two JIT/flexible manufacturing systems last year, one for each type of ladder produced. Three direct labor workers run the extension ladder cell of machines, one worker for each of the three eight-hour shifts per day. Most of the operation is run automatically, and several indirect labor support people help with setups and maintenance work.

During the week ended August 12, 19x9, the extension ladder operating cell produced the following data pertaining to the manufacturing of the Primo extension ladder:

Units:

Beginning Raw-in-Process Inventory	60
Units completed during week	4,280
Ending Raw-in-Process Inventory (60 percent complete)	40

Hours worked:

Direct labor—120 hours

Machine hours:

Eleven machines in the cell

FMS cell ran
112 hours during week

Costs in beginning inventory:

Materials costs	$ 1,780
Conversion costs	1,450

Direct costs incurred by extension ladder JIT/FMS cell:

Raw materials	$96,994
Direct labor (120 hours at $19 per hour)	2,280
Electrical power costs	5,430
JIT cell machinery depreciation	2,780
Engineering design costs	8,570
Indirect labor	12,320
Lubricants, supplies, and fasteners	4,410

Overhead rates used:

Material handling overhead (included as part of raw materials cost in the process costing analysis):

30 percent of raw materials costs

Factory overhead not traceable to cell:

$53 per machine hour worked

Required

1. Compute the total materials cost and total conversion cost for the week.
2. Using good form and the average process costing approach, prepare a
   a. Schedule of equivalent production
   b. Unit cost analysis schedule
   c. Cost summary schedule
3. From the cost summary schedule, prepare a journal entry to transfer costs of completed units to Finished Goods Inventory.
4. Do you think the $125 price is too high for the Primo ladder? Why?

Problem 15B-5.
Traditional Versus
JIT/FMS Unit Cost
Analysis
(L.O. 2, 5, 6, 8)

Pearson Products Company specializes in producing quality home products. Currently they maintain production lines for twelve different types of items, including a world-famous line of fruit juice presses. The press is adjustable to various sizes of fruits, so one press fits all needs. Diane Pearson started the company in her garage eleven years ago, and the company has grown to a point where it is now among the largest in the industry. The fruit juice press is assembled from parts manufactured by the company and from parts purchased from outside vendors. Pearson just installed a flexible manufacturing system for the press line. Everything is automated, including materials handling between machine ports.

The company still uses traditional methods for product costing, even though the new FMS has been operating for several weeks. You have been contacted to restructure the present accounting system to compute a more realistic product unit cost under the FMS conditions. Following are data from the current accounting period. The new system will cause several changes. Several indirect costs will be traceable directly to the FMS work cell and will not be included in the regular overhead rate computation. In addition, separate allocation rates will be needed for materials-related overhead costs and engineering costs. Costs related to inspection, rework, and work-in-process handling will be eliminated. The remaining indirect manufacturing costs (building occupancy costs) will be allocated using a machine hours base. Materials storage and handling overhead will be allocated based on total dollars of materials and parts incurred. Engineering hours will be used as a basis for engineering overhead allocation. Process costing procedures will be used to compute unit costs.

	Traditional Manufacturing System	JIT/Flexible Manufacturing System
Costs directly traceable to product:		
Raw materials	$ 819,400	$ 819,400
Parts for assembly	482,000	482,000
Direct labor:		
Traditional:		
1.8 hr at $12/hr per unit	2,082,240	
JIT/FMS:		
.4 hr at $15/hr per unit		578,400
Total costs traceable to product	$3,383,640	$1,879,800

	Traditional Manufacturing System	JIT/Flexible Manufacturing System
Costs directly traceable to FMS cell:		
Setup labor		$ 115,680
Other indirect labor		212,080
Electrical power		38,560
Repairs and maintenance		33,740
Supervision salaries		43,380
Depreciation, machinery		79,048
Operating supplies and lubricants		17,352
Total costs directly traceable to FMS cell		$ 539,840
Companywide indirect manufacturing cost pool:		
Setup labor	$ 421,780	
Electrical power, factory	163,200	
Supervision, factory	210,670	
Purchased parts, inspection costs	78,230	
Product rework costs	142,500	
Depreciation, machinery	199,600	
Other indirect labor	391,990	
Purchasing costs, materials, and parts	148,200	
Materials/parts storage and handling	226,200	
Depreciation, materials moving trucks	31,200	
Engineering labor	360,000	
Electrical costs, engineering	28,800	
Depreciation, engineering equipment	32,400	
Engineering supervision	68,400	
Other engineering overhead	21,600	
Operating supplies and lubricants	38,450	
Finished goods inspection costs	89,760	
Machinery repairs and maintenance	174,560	
Storage and handling, Work-in-Process Inventory	234,190	
Depreciation, building	121,400	$ 121,400
Property taxes	24,360	24,360
Fire insurance	9,860	9,860
Liability insurance	8,540	8,540
Building maintenance	34,170	34,170
Other factory utilities	19,230	19,230
Factory employee cafeteria	165,290	165,290
Total indirect manufacturing costs	$3,444,580	$ 382,850

	Traditional Manufacturing System	JIT/Flexible Manufacturing System
Engineering overhead cost pool:		
Engineering labor		$ 360,000
Electrical costs, engineering		28,800
Depreciation, engineering equipment		32,400
Engineering supervision		68,400
Other engineering overhead		21,600
Total engineering overhead costs		$ 511,200
Materials storage and handling overhead cost pool:		
Purchasing costs, materials and parts		$ 148,200
Materials/parts storage and handling		226,200
Depreciation, materials moving trucks		31,200
Total materials storage and handling overhead costs		$ 405,600

These data have been partially restructured in anticipation of the new system. Following is a summary of other information that will be required for the analysis:

Total companywide direct labor hours:	
Actual for last period	1,216,600 DLHs
Anticipated for this period	714,000 DLHs
Total anticipated companywide machine hours for the period	1,850,400 MHs
Total anticipated companywide engineering hours for the period	18,000 Eng. Hrs.
Total anticipated companywide dollar value of materials and parts for the period	$7,800,000
Number of fruit juice presses produced	96,400 fans
Anticipated machine hours for press FMS	308,400 MHs
Anticipated engineering hours for press FMS	7,200 Eng. Hrs.
Process costing information for press FMS:	
Beginning inventory:	
Materials and parts	$ 4,040
Conversion costs	2,810
Equivalent units for period:	
Materials and parts	96,700 Equiv. Units
Conversion costs	96,600 Equiv. Units

Required

1. Under the traditional system,
   a. Compute the companywide manufacturing overhead application rate.
   b. Using traditional labor data, compute the product unit cost for each fruit juice press.

2. Identify the cost categories that will likely be eliminated when the company adopts a JIT/FMS approach.
3. Compute the JIT/FMS application rates for the following:
   a. Indirect manufacturing costs
   b. Engineering overhead costs
   c. Materials storage and handling overhead costs
4. Identify the total materials costs and conversion costs for the period for the press FMS cell.
5. Using the average process costing method, compute the unit cost of a fruit juice press under the new JIT/FMS setting.

Management Decision Case

Sheffield Iron Works
(L.O. 2, 5, 6)

The management of Sheffield Iron Works has decided to convert its present traditional manufacturing system in the Castings Department to a Just-In-Time setting. The following tasks have been accomplished:

1. An agreement was signed with a supplier for daily deliveries of iron ingots needed for the department's iron casting products. The department supervisor is responsible for ordering the ingots.
2. Responsibility for machine maintenance and for product inspection was shifted to the machine operators in the Castings Department.
3. Three CNC machines were purchased that are capable of melting the ingots, mixing specified alloys, and molding the castings ordered to specific shapes and sizes. In addition, an automated conveyor system was purchased for work in process movement between the new machines. The entire operation is now a flexible manufacturing system and is operated in a just-in-time manner.
4. New electrical power meters were installed in all departments of the plant so that each unit's power usage can be monitored and computed. Each machine's electrical power usage in the Castings Department can be identified.
5. Insurance rates on the plant machinery are broken down on a per machine hour usage basis.
6. Due to the streamlining of the Castings Department, its size was reduced by fifty percent.
7. The number of direct labor workers in the Castings Department is now 8 as compared to 26 before the FMS was installed.

Sheffield has a second department, the Small Tools Department, that specializes in making over twenty varieties of small iron and steel hand tools for business. The Small Tools Department still operates under the traditional methods and has only one automated machine. Thirty-six direct labor employees are needed to keep the department running. Since product movement is done manually, large bins of partially completed tools are everywhere. Individual machine power usage is not metered. Repair and maintenance of machines is done on an as-needed basis. Raw materials are ordered two months in advance so that there is never a "stock-out" situation.

The following facts relate to last month's operating activities:

	Castings Department	Small Tools Department	Totals
Direct labor hours	1,344	6,336	7,680
Machine hours:			
Castings department:			
Machine A	484		484
Machine B	440		440
Machine C	420		420
Small tools department:			
Semiautomatic machine		176	176
Non-programmed machinery		1,920	1,920
Engineering hours used	640	320	960
Computer time usage (hours)	300	25	325
Cost of raw materials used	$96,000	$120,000	$216,000
Square footage of department	3,000	9,000	12,000

Note: When using non-programmed machine hours for distribution purchases, they should count one-tenth as much as computer-driver machine hours.

Plantwide factory overhead costs:	
Property taxes, building	$ 2,400
Wages, warehouse	8,640
Depreciation, warehouse equipment	1,296
Depreciation, factory machines	5,992
Depreciation, engineering equipment	1,440
Raw materials handling costs	25,920
Indirect support labor	15,408
Computer center costs, factory	4,030
Salaries, engineering	8,160
Operating supplies, engineering	1,728
Salaries, accounting department	5,136
Salaries, personnel department	7,104
Cafeteria expenses	4,736
Insurance, building	600
Insurance, factory machinery	3,424
Employee benefits	3,552
Repairs and maintenance department	2,576
Quality control department	3,312
Electrical power, building	10,200
Electrical power, machines	5,136
Purchasing department expenses	3,240
Total	$124,030

Details for the Castings Department:

	Job 101	Job 105	Job 110	Totals
Direct labor hours	168	672	504	1,344
Machine hours:				
Machine A	220	132	132	484
Machine B	264	88	88	440
Machine C	84	210	126	420
Totals	568	430	346	1,344

Required

1. Compute the traditional plantwide factory overhead rate based on direct labor hours. Allocate the overhead costs to both departments and to the jobs in the Castings Department using this approach.
2. Recommend changes to the Sheffield management concerning the distribution of traditional indirect costs to both the departments. Identify the allocation basis to be used for each cost listed.
3. Distribute the costs to both departments and to the jobs in the Castings Department using the methods you recommended in part **2.** Use machine hours as the basis for the distribution of costs to Casting's jobs.
4. Highlight and explain the differences resulting from the two approaches.

LEARNING OBJECTIVES

1. State the three new areas of emphasis that accompany the JIT philosophy.
2. Identify the unique aspects of product costing in an automated manufacturing process.
3. Compute a product unit cost using data from a flexible manufacturing system.
4. Identify the types of financial and non-financial analyses used in a JIT environment to evaluate the performance of (a) product quality, (b) product delivery, (c) inventory control, (d) materials cost/scrap control, and (e) machine management and maintenance.
5. Define full cost profit margin and state the advantages of this measure of profitability.
6. Describe the special costs associated with capital expenditure decisions for automated machines and processes.
7. Identify the primary areas of management reporting in a JIT/FMS environment and give examples of reports needed.

JIT and Automation: Product Costs, Performance Measures, Capital Investments, and Reporting

In the new manufacturing environment introduced in Chapter 15, management accountants *must* assess the applicability of traditional internal accounting methods and procedures before using them with automated production systems. Many of the traditional approaches to product costing, performance measurement, and operating control need to be re-evaluated in the JIT environment. In this chapter we delve a bit deeper into the JIT philosophy. First we identify the three new areas of emphasis within the JIT environment that underlie the need for management accounting changes. Then we discuss specific changes recommended for product costing, performance measurement, capital expenditure decision analysis, and management reporting practices. Upon completion of this chapter, you should be able to meet the learning objectives listed on the left.

JIT and Automation Are Changing Management Accounting

The traditional discipline of management accounting is applicable in many different settings and can be applied within many different economic environments. But significant changes are underway in management accounting systems of companies that have adopted the JIT philosophy and are employing automated manufacturing processes. These changes stem from three new areas of accounting emphasis created by the move to JIT and automated production facilities: (1) a macro versus a micro approach to control of operations, (2) the increasing importance of nonfinancial data, and (3) using theoretical capacity to evaluate actual performance.

Macro Versus Micro Approach

The JIT management accountant approaches the control of operations by looking at the entire production process rather than small parts or segments of the process. Profit is maximized by

OBJECTIVE 1
State the three
new areas of
emphasis that
accompany the
JIT philosophy

supplying customers with a quality product on a timely basis at a reasonable price. With the more traditional approach, profits are thought to be increased by cutting labor time, buying large quantities of raw materials to take advantage of quantity discounts, or applying fixed overhead costs over an increased number of units of output. In a JIT setting, profitability is enhanced when the entire operation is running in a just-in-time fashion. Non-value added aspects such as storage time, inspection time, moving time, and waiting or queue time are the primary focus: If these wasted time periods are minimized or eliminated, profitability will increase.

Nonfinancial Data

A major part of the reporting and measurement aspects of the JIT operating environment involves nonfinancial considerations, which are linked closely with the macro approach to control of operations. Rather than being interested in labor efficiency or overhead volume variances, the management accountant must focus on time reduction, helping to determine (1) causes for excess storage time, (2) information sources that will reduce the need for separate inspection activities, (3) reporting methods that will help reduce the moving time associated with product flow through the process, and (4) causes for excessive waiting or queue time. All these analyses are nonfinancial in nature and require studies of time periods, distance factors or measures, and numbers of people involved.

The JIT environment also heavily emphasizes product distribution and customer satisfaction. Analyses leading to control in these areas require such reports as number and causes of customer complaints, average delivery time, and ability to meet promised delivery dates; all these analyses involve nonfinancial data.

Emphasis on Theoretical Capacity

Chapter 6 introduced the concept of normal capacity and Chapters 9 and 10 used normal capacity as a basis for developing standard costs and computing the related variances. Normal capacity is the average anticipated level of output for a period of time. To measure performance, actual productive output is compared with expected output based on normal capacity, and variances resulting from differences between these two amounts are reported.

One major objective of the JIT philosophy is to minimize nonproductive time in the total delivery cycle, which means that the company is expected to strive to operate at theoretical or ideal capacity. This goal may not be attained, but the philosophy is to always be working toward that ideal level. Machine operators, engineers, product designers, supervisors, salespeople, and management accountants are expected to continuously look for ways to cut non-value added time and related costs. The JIT environment exists when everyone involved in the operation of the company actively participates in a relentless effort of ongoing improvement.

Automation: Product Costing Issues

OBJECTIVE 2
Identify the unique aspects of product costing in an automated manufacturing process

Chapter 15 introduced and illustrated product costing procedures related to the just-in-time philosophy. In addition to JIT, automated manufacturing facilities have also influenced the computation of a product's cost. This section will take a deeper look at product costing in a **JIT/FMS environment**, an operating environment created by a flexible manufacturing system functioning within the just-in-time philosophy. The important thing to remember is that product costing methods must change as the manufacturing environment changes. And yet, many companies that have automated their production facilities try to use traditional methods to cost products produced on modern computer-aided machines and computer-integrated processes. In a 1987 study titled *Cost Accounting for Factory Automation* sponsored by the National Association of Accountants (NAA), researchers Robert E. Bennett, James A. Hendricks, David E. Keys, and Edward J. Rudnicki found that product costing problems and solutions differed with the degree of automation in the production process. These problems concern the allocation of factory overhead, the classification of costs as variable or fixed, and the changing nature of costs involving their direct versus indirect characteristics. The report was organized in order of the degree of computer integration:

1. **Computer numerically-controlled (CNC) machines** — Stand-alone machines that are computer controlled

2. **Computer-aided design/computer-aided manufacturing (CAD/CAM)** — Using computers in product design work, planning and controlling production, and linking CNC machines

3. **Flexible manufacturing systems (FMS)** — A computer-controlled production system comprised of several types of machines that perform a series of operations and/or assemble a number of parts in a flexible and automatic fashion

4. **Automated material handling system (AMHS)** — A necessary component of a computer-integrated manufacturing system in which the raw materials and partially completed product handling function is automatic, providing a continuous flow through the process

Computer Numerically-Controlled Machines

Automating the production process begins with the introduction of computer numerically-controlled (CNC) machines. Yet, even after introducing CNC machines into the process to reduce the dependency on labor and to increase efficiency, for product costing most companies continue to allocate factory overhead based on direct labor dollars or hours. This problem was a primary finding of the NAA research team's study of factory automation. They determined that there are five reasons why inaccurate factory overhead allocation exists in a CNC machine environment: (1) use of inappropriate allocation bases, (2) allocation of nonrelevant costs, (3) use of inappropriate activity levels, (4) use of plant or companywide overhead rates rather than departmental or FMS rates, and (5) misclassification of direct and indirect costs.

Inappropriate Allocation Base. Direct labor is not an appropriate allocation base in an automated production setting because there is very little connection between overhead costs incurred in a CNC machine environment and direct labor hours or cost—most of the overhead costs are associated with and caused by the operation of the machines. Machine hours differ from labor hours because of setup time, idle machine time, and the fact that one person can operate several machines simultaneously. Three machine time expressions can be used as a basis for factory overhead cost allocation: actual machine hours, **run time** (total machine hours less setup time), and **engineered time** (standard or predicted machine time for the product). Each expression of machine hours has advantages and disadvantages regarding cost and accuracy, but each is a far better factory overhead allocation base than direct labor hours or dollars.

Relevance of Costs Being Allocated. There is still an argument that allocating fixed factory overhead costs to products tends to introduce inaccuracy into the computation of product cost. These costs tend to be unrelated to the activity levels that are often used to assign costs to work cells or products. Building occupancy costs such as depreciation, building; insurance costs; and property taxes are included in this category. Even with improved cost traceability, these costs must still be considered indirect. Variable costing procedures are one answer to this concern, but to date few companies have adopted them.

Selection of Activity Levels. The selection of activity levels to be used for allocating factory overhead costs should be a primary concern for the management accountant because it is the activities within the factory that cause costs to be incurred. Therefore costs should be categorized by type of activity, and the activity itself should be used as a base for allocating those costs to the work cell or product. Approaching cost allocation from this direction will allow, for example, computer-related costs to be allocated using a computer-usage base.

Use of Work Cell or Departmental Versus Plantwide Rates. Fixed factory overhead can be more closely related to production if a company converts from a companywide or plantwide overhead rate to department or work cell overhead rates. The closer the factory overhead costs are brought to the product, the more accurate the resulting product cost. Many costs can be directly traced to a particular FMS, which further aids the product costing process.

Direct Versus Indirect Costs. With factory automation, the traditional approach to direct versus indirect costs is often reversed. CNC machine operators perform mostly backup or preparation tasks; very little of their time is spent actually shaping the product. Therefore much of what was called direct labor is now accounted for as indirect labor. Separating a worker's activities into direct and indirect labor may become very costly, so some companies are treating all labor on CNC machines as indirect. On the other hand, power costs are a good example of a former indirect cost now being treated as a direct cost. Special electrical power meters can be mounted on machines so that actual usage per job can be determined. Chapter 15 discussed several examples of the changing characteristics of direct and indirect production costs.

Computer-Aided Design/Computer-Aided Manufacturing

Most computer-aided design/computer-aided manufacturing (CAD/CAM) costs should be assigned to specific products. But the traditional methods used to accomplish this task do not usually yield accurate cost assignments. Many companies simply allocate these costs to overhead pools and then distribute them to products through the use of predetermined factory overhead rates. Yet many of these costs are traceable directly to specific orders; for instance, drafting/design costs incurred in connection with specifications for a particular order are traceable to and should be charged to that order. Because of sophisticated computer monitoring equipment, many CAD/CAM related costs can be easily traced to the order needing the design work. Routing these costs through plantwide overhead rates will seriously distort product costs.

Flexible Manufacturing System

Product costing within a flexible manufacturing system (FMS) further changes the characteristics of some common variable costs, fixed costs, and direct costs. The FMS island or cell itself becomes the cost center. The only variable costs of an FMS are direct materials, direct labor, and some indirect materials, tooling, and power costs.

Many fixed costs can be traced directly to FMS cost centers. Costs of machine depreciation, FMS computer depreciation, computer programmers and other computer backup people working only on FMS maintenance, product line supervision, and selected off-line inspection labor can be traced to specific FMS work cells. The work of setup personnel and machine operators who are trouble-shooters and move from one work cell to another can also be traced directly to specific FMS cost centers. The NAA researchers recommend that separate FMS factory overhead application rates be used because each FMS island is usually a self-contained operating unit.

Other fixed costs are not traceable and must be allocated to the FMS cost centers. CAD/CAM costs for total system maintenance are difficult to trace to specific FMS cells and must be allocated. Common computer center costs may be allocated to cost centers based on some expression of usage. In addition, building occupancy costs such as plant depreciation, building maintenance, taxes, and insurance are usually pooled and allocated.

But what base should be used to allocate these common occupancy costs to the FMS cells? Direct labor, hardly mentioned in this discussion, is of little use in trying to associate overhead costs with FMS cost centers. Table 16-1 reflects the views of the NAA research team regarding overhead allocation bases relevant to the FMS environment. Four bases are identified, one focusing on units of output and three focusing on time measures. Because by definition an FMS is *flexible*, units of output are not identical, so units of output is not the ideal base. Each of the three time measures has advantages and disadvantages. Remember that ease of use and operating at theoretical capacity are goals of the FMS environment. Engineered machine hours tend to approach these requirements. Although the product costing approach for an FMS differs from the traditional approach, the objective is the same: to compute an accurate unit cost for use in pricing decisions as well as for inventory valuation and cost of goods sold information.

Automated Material Handling System (AMHS)

An automated material handling system adds the final dimension to a fully integrated computerized production process. Early material handling systems required manual movement of materials and parts through

Table 16-1. Flexible Manufacturing Systems: Advantages and Disadvantages of Possible Overhead Allocation Bases

Overhead Allocation Base	Advantages	Disadvantages
Units of production	Simplicity; easy to use	Parts machined in the FMS often are not homogeneous and require different operations
Total time in FMS	Reflects productive capacity of entire FMS	Difficult to measure and record
Engineered machine hours	Reflects machine time that should be used; readily available	Does not represent actual machine time or total time used in FMS
Actual machine hours	Measures use of productive capacity of machine tools; can be recorded by machine computer or FMS central computer	Includes inefficiencies in operation of machine tools

Source: Robert E. Bennett, James A. Hendricks, David E. Keys, and Edward J. Rudnicki, *Cost Accounting for Factory Automation,* National Association of Accountants, 1987, p. 54. Used by permission of National Association of Accountants.

the manufacturing layout, and the paperwork needed to track the materials and product in process was also done manually. According to the *Cost Accounting for Factory Automation* study (page 59), today companies rely on automatic storage/retrieval systems (AS/RS) and AMHSs to move products within a computer-integrated manufacturing process. Hand-pushed carts, operator-directed forklifts, and manual conveyors are being replaced by power-rolled conveyors, shuttles, and raised track, towline, or computer-guided vehicles. Computer-controlled production scheduling and material handling trace and account for all product and parts movement, replacing the old punched card and off-line tracking systems.

Traditionally, material handling costs have been included in the factory overhead cost pool and allocated to products based on direct labor. In the new manufacturing environment, there is little relationship between the amount of labor cost incurred and the amount of material handling a process or FMS work cell needs. One present-day approach is to account for the material handling and purchasing functions as a separate cost center. Costs associated with these functions are grouped into a cost pool and allocated as part of the materials charged to production. Materials quantity, cost, or weight may be used as the allocation basis, depending on the relationship between the costs involved and the size and complexity of the products being produced.

Illustrative Problem: Product Costing in an Automated Environment

OBJECTIVE 3

Compute a product unit cost using data from a flexible manufacturing system

As you learned in Chapter 11, product pricing is heavily dependent on product costs. A 2 or 3 percent error in pricing a product may result in loss of customers and market share, so accurate product costs are very important to a company's overall profitability. In practice, although production processes have shifted from labor intensive to capital intensive operations, direct labor hours and dollars are still the most commonly used overhead allocation bases. Even as automation begins to dominate production lines, accountants continue to use these direct labor bases. Many existing allocation systems are at the point where there is little relationship between the factory overhead costs being incurred and the amount of direct labor being used. In addition, many of the indirect costs that used to be charged to overhead pools are now being traced directly to FMS operating cells.

This illustrative problem points out the significant difference in product cost that can arise when a company shifts from a direct labor dollar allocation basis to one centered on machine hours. Accounting for a separate materials storage and handling pool is also introduced. The company also changes from using companywide to flexible manufacturing system overhead rates.

Jagat Corporation's Warner Division produces three products: J12, K14, and L16. Four years ago the company completely revamped its manufacturing facilities and installed totally automated flexible manufacturing systems. Each product is produced in its own FMS cell, but the allocation of factory overhead continues to be based on direct labor dollars. The following information has been made available to you:

	Product J12	Product K14	Product L16
Unit information:			
Raw materials cost	$3	$4	$10
Direct labor hours	.5 hours	.8 hours	.2 hours
Direct labor cost per hour	$16	$16	$16
Machine hours	3.2 hours	4 hours	5 hours
Total annual unit sales	30,000	50,000	10,000
Total factory overhead	$1,680,000	$4,480,000	$1,568,000

Warner Division's policy is to set the selling price at 140 percent of the unit's production cost.

Required

1. Compute the division's plantwide factory overhead rate using total direct labor dollars as a basis.
2. Compute each product's total production cost and selling price using the application rate computed in part **1.**
3. Compute a new factory overhead application rate assuming that
   a. Material storage and handling overhead of 20 percent of the cost of raw materials is subtracted from the factory overhead cost totals.
   b. Machine hours is the overhead application basis.
   c. Product line overhead rates rather than a single plantwide rate are used.
4. Compute each product's total production cost and selling price using the application rates disclosed or computed in part **3.**
5. Compare product selling prices. Is there a problem?

Solution

1. Factory overhead rate based on direct labor dollars computed.

	Total Factory Overhead Cost	Total Direct Labor Cost
Product J12:		
Factory overhead cost	$1,680,000	
Direct labor cost:		
.5 hr × $16 × 30,000 units		$240,000
Product K14:		
Factory overhead cost	4,480,000	
Direct labor cost:		
.8 hr × $16 × 50,000 units		640,000
Product L16:		
Factory overhead cost	1,568,000	
Direct labor cost:		
.2 hr × $16 × 10,000 units		32,000
Totals	$7,728,000	$912,000

Factory overhead application rate:

$7,728,000/$912,000 = 847.37% of direct labor cost

2. Each product's unit cost and selling price based on plantwide overhead rate computed.

	Product J12	Product K14	Product L16
Unit cost information:			
Raw materials cost	$ 3.00	$ 4.00	$10.00
Direct labor cost:			
.5 hr at $16/hr	8.00		
.8 hr at $16/hr		12.80	
.2 hr at $16/hr			3.20
Factory overhead cost			
$8 × 8.4737	67.79		
$12.80 × 8.4737		108.46	
$3.20 × 8.4737			27.12
Total unit cost	$ 78.79	$125.26	$40.32
Unit selling price:			
J12: $78.79 × 140%	$110.31		
K14: $125.26 × 140%		$175.36	
L16: $40.32 × 140%			$56.45

3. Product line factory overhead rates based on machine hours computed.

	Net Factory Overhead Cost	Total Machine Hours Required
Product J12:		
Factory overhead cost	$1,680,000	
less: materials handling cost		
$3 × 30,000 units × 20%	18,000	
Net factory overhead cost	$1,662,000	
Machine hours required:		
3.2 hr × 30,000 units		96,000
Product K14:		
Factory overhead cost	$4,480,000	
less: materials handling cost		
$4 × 50,000 units × 20%	40,000	
Net factory overhead cost	$4,440,000	
Machine hours required:		
4 hr × 50,000 units		200,000
Product L16:		
Factory overhead cost	$1,568,000	
less: materials handling cost		
$10 × 10,000 units × 20%	20,000	
Net factory overhead cost	$1,548,000	
Machine hours required:		
5 hr × 10,000 units		50,000

	Net Factory Overhead Cost	Total Machine Hours Required

Product line FMS factory overhead application rates:
  Factory overhead rates per machine hour:

    J12: $1,662,100/96,000 MH = $17.3125/mh

    K14: $4,440,000/200,000 MH = $22.20/mh

    L16: $1,548,000/50,000 MH = $30.96/mh

4. Each product's unit cost and selling price based on product line overhead rates computed.

	Product J12	Product K14	Product L16
Unit cost information:			
Raw materials cost	$ 3.00	$ 4.00	$ 10.00
Materials handling overhead cost at 20%	0.60	0.80	2.00
Direct labor cost:			
.5 hr at $16/hr	8.00		
.8 hr at $16/hr		12.80	
.2 hr at $16/hr			3.20
Factory overhead cost:			
3.2 hr × $17.3125	55.40		
4 hr × $22.20		88.80	
5 hr × $30.96			154.80
Total unit cost	$67.00	$106.40	$170.00
Unit selling price:			
J12: $67.00 × 140%	$93.80		
K14: $106.40 × 140%		$148.96	
L16: $170.00 × 140%			$238.00

5. Selling prices compared and analyzed.

	Product J12	Product K14	Product L16
Selling prices using direct labor cost allocation basis and a plantwide rate	$110.31	$175.36	$ 56.45
Selling prices using machine hours basis and product line FMS rates	93.80	148.96	238.00
Differences	$ 16.51	$ 26.40	($181.55)

Conclusion: Products J12 and K14 are overpriced, and product L16 is way underpriced.

Performance Measures for Operating Control

As with product costing, many companies have installed an FMS or moved to a completely computer-integrated production system without changing their approaches to the monitoring and measurement of performance. One primary problem facing management regarding the adoption of JIT production procedures is relying on an obsolete management accounting system to measure operating performance. Traditional performance evaluation measures are used, but these measures are not designed to track the objectives of automated facilities and thus are not appropriate for the new manufacturing environment. For instance, measures that center on labor efficiency or factory overhead absorption rates do not fit with the objectives of JIT. Variance analysis based on direct labor hours will have very little to measure and evaluate. JIT/FMS emphasizes minimum labor usage and a rapid, automated production process. Because building inventory levels also contradicts the goals of JIT, lower overhead absorption rates is an antiquated performance measure.

In addition, the managerial accountant may not have kept up with or been closely associated with the production process and may have a difficult time identifying areas of weakness.[1] The new manufacturing environment has created a critical need for close cooperation between all parts of the management team. To be a contributing part of the team, the management accountant must get closer to the actual operations and become familiar with all aspects of the manufacturing process. The accountant, the engineer, and the production manager must work closely to ensure that the production process is being monitored fairly and accurately. Without a knowledge of the production facilities, the management accountant does not know what to measure or which cost drivers are appropriate under the circumstances.

Many nonfinancial measures have replaced traditional performance measures in a JIT/FMS setting. The primary control areas are product quality, product delivery, inventory control, material costs/scrap control, and machine management and maintenance. Although cost control is still important in these areas, emphasis is on the factors that make an FMS or a product line a successful part of a profitable operation. These factors "drive" or cause the costs to be incurred. The belief is that control of the business' nonfinancial performance aspects will ultimately maximize the financial return on operations.

Product Quality Performance

During the past two decades, the quality of American-made goods has slipped as manufacturers attempt to lower prices to meet world competition. During the same period, countries such as Japan have increased

---

1. Robert A. Howell and Stephen R. Soucy, "Operating Controls in the New Manufacturing Environment," *Management Accounting*, October 1987, p. 26.

OBJECTIVE 4a

Identify the types of financial and nonfinancial analyses used in a JIT environment to evaluate the performance of product quality

the quality of their goods while still lowering the price. Therefore the overall goal of American companies today is to produce a quality product at a price that will be competitive in world markets. But quality is not something that you can apply somewhere in the production process or assume will happen automatically. Inspection points can detect bad products, but having such a procedure does not ensure quality. Product quality starts with correct product design. The next steps are high-quality raw material inputs, quality processing and work, and proper handling and packaging to help guarantee that a product of high quality is shipped to the customer. We now discuss the controls used to measure performance in these areas.

Product Design Controls. Product quality is often undermined by poor design. In an automated production environment, computer-aided design (CAD) is an important feature. Detection of design flaws is built into the computer programs that support the engineering design function. The computer program automatically highlights improper or contradictory product design parts or manufacturing processes included by error so that corrective action can be taken before actual production begins. The managerial accountant is not involved in this process but should be aware of the existence of product design controls.

High-Quality Raw Material Input Controls. One of the most significant changes for a company converting to the JIT philosophy is its relationship with suppliers of raw materials and parts. Instead of dealing with dozens of suppliers to seek the lowest cost, JIT companies analyze their materials vendors to determine which are most reliable, have a record of timely deliveries, deal in quality goods, and have a competitive price. Once located, vendors with these characteristics become an integral part of the production team. A JIT company works closely with its vendors to ensure a continuing timely supply of quality raw material inputs. Vendors may even assist in the product design function to help ensure that the correct materials are used. Managerial accountants should conduct the necessary analyses to determine reliable vendors and continue such studies so that high-quality, minimum-priced materials are always available at short notice to arrive just in time.

In-Process Control Mechanisms. Automated machinery linked into an FMS can easily be programmed with in-process product control mechanisms. Product quality problems can be detected by computer-programmed control techniques and corrective action taken; no longer is it necessary to wait for a specified inspection point to detect a product flaw. In-process controls form a continuous inspection system that highlights trouble spots, helps significantly reduce the incidence of scrap, cuts overall machine rework time, and eliminates the non-value added product costs of the traditional inspection activities. Although the managerial accountant is not expected to develop and program these FMS product quality controls, the accountant should have knowledge of the control points and maintain records of the causes of manufacturing trouble spots.

Customer Acceptance Controls. The point of sale and shipment no longer marks the end of the managerial accountant's performance measurement duties. Within the JIT environment, customer follow-up is very important—emphasis is on customer satisfaction. Measures used to determine the degree of customer acceptance include (1) number and types of customer complaints, (2) analysis of field service costs, (3) warranty claim activity, and (4) product returns and allowances statistics. Several companies have developed their own customer satisfaction index from the measures just mentioned so that comparisons can be made between product lines and between different time periods.

Product Delivery Performance

OBJECTIVE 4b

Identify the types of financial and nonfinancial analyses used in a JIT environment to evaluate product delivery

Besides emphasizing product perfection and customer satisfaction, a JIT company is also interested in product delivery. The **delivery cycle** is the time period between acceptance of the order and final delivery of the product. It is important that the salesperson can promise accurate delivery schedules at the time the sales order is gained; the goal is for product delivery to be 100 percent on time and for the order to be filled 100 percent of the time. To meet this goal, the JIT company must establish and maintain consistency and reliability within the manufacturing process.

JIT companies place heavy importance on the delivery cycle. One company cut its delivery cycle from more than six months to less than five weeks; another company cut its four-week delivery cycle to less than five days. Such reductions in delivery time have a significant impact on income from operations. The delivery cycle is comprised of the **purchase order lead time** (the time it takes for raw materials and parts to be ordered and received so that production can begin), **production cycle time** (the time it takes for the production people to make the product available for shipment to the customer), and **delivery time** (the time period between product completion and customer receipt of the item).

The management accountant has several control measures to establish and maintain to help management minimize the delivery cycle. The accountant should maintain records and reports that are designed to monitor each product's purchase order lead time, production cycle time, delivery time, and total delivery cycle time. Trends should be highlighted, and the reports should be made available on a daily or weekly basis. Other measures designed to monitor the delivery cycle include an on-time delivery performance record and a daily or weekly report showing percentage of orders filled.

Inventory Control Performance

Within a JIT environment, the objective is to have *no inventory*. Therefore the management accountant must emphasize zero inventory balances and concentrate on measures that detect why inventory exists, not measures that lead to accurate inventory valuation. As pointed out in Chapter 15, storage is a non-value added activity and should be reduced or eliminated. Making this shift in accounting for and controlling of inventory cost has been very difficult for accounting personnel. For

OBJECTIVE 4c
*Identify the types
of financial and
nonfinancial
analyses used in a
JIT environment
to evaluate
inventory control*

decades, inventory has been one of the largest asset balances on the balance sheet, and accountants have been trained to very carefully verify inventory balances and compute the value of total inventory. JIT has made such concerns obsolete: Emphasis should be on reducing inventory.

Why have companies maintained inventories if they are so bad for business? Traditionally, inventory balances have been used as a buffer for unexpected work stoppages. Events such as unreliable raw material vendors, engineering change orders, equipment breakdown, and schedule changes all interfered with a continuous supply of salable goods. In addition, management wanted long production runs so that fixed costs could be spread over more products, thereby reducing product cost. Thus balances had to be kept on hand to guarantee continued customer satisfaction or continuous production flow. But what really happened was that the dollars saved by the long production runs were more than offset by the increased storage and obsolescence costs incurred.

The JIT/FMS environment utilizes only two inventory accounts, and both balances are kept at a minimum. As shown in Chapter 15, the old Materials Inventory and Work-in-Process Inventory accounts have been merged into the *Raw-in-Process Inventory* (RIP) account. All purchases of raw materials and parts are debited immediately to the RIP Inventory account. Because the goal is to eliminate storage as a cost, materials and parts are received only when needed. All costs of product conversion (labor and factory overhead) are also debited to the RIP Inventory account.

Inventory controls in the new manufacturing environment are designed to eliminate inventory balances and non-value added product costs. Old control measures such as the economic order quantity and reorder point computations are no longer as useful; now the concentration is on reducing the amount of space used to store raw materials, goods in process, and finished goods. Measures that detect possible product obsolescence are very important. Inventory turnover measures such as the ratio of inventory to total sales have become more important because the number of annual turnovers may double or triple with the adoption of JIT.

The inventory area remains critical to company profitability in a JIT environment. But there is heavy emphasis on nonfinancial measures to minimize the cost incurred in handling and storing inventory. The management accountant must develop measures that identify unreliable vendors because using fewer vendors who supply quality and timely raw material inputs is an objective of JIT. Another objective is to determine the amount of production time wasted because of engineering change orders and highlight the causes for management. The same approach must be applied to production schedule changes because time wasted here can be significant. As mentioned earlier, maintaining accurate records of required machine maintenance is an important JIT control measure. Cutting the downtime from machine breakdowns reduces the need for inventory. Every company's production process and inventory needs are different. Developing a set of inventory control measures must be tailored to a particular set of operating circumstances. Although most of these measures are nonfinancial, they are critical to gaining market share and remaining profitable.

Materials Cost/Scrap Control Performance

OBJECTIVE 4d
Identify types of financial and nonfinancial analyses used in a JIT environment to evaluate materials cost/ scrap control

In a traditional situation, controlling the cost of raw materials meant seeking the lowest possible price while maintaining some minimum level of quality. Responsibility for this transaction was given to the Purchasing Department. Performance was measured by analyzing the materials price variance, which is the difference between the standard price and the actual price of the goods purchased. Today, emphasis is on the quality of materials, timeliness of delivery, and reasonable price. Because materials cost is the largest single cost element in the new JIT/FMS environment, control in this area is extremely important.

Control of scrap also takes on a different slant in a JIT/FMS environment. The JIT objective is to incur no scrap in the production process, a significant difference from the traditional approach, which developed a normal scrap level or tolerance at or below which no corrective action was taken. The factory of the future sees scrap as a non-value added series of costs. Each defective product has already cost the company materials cost, labor cost, as well as materials handling and factory overhead costs. In the new manufacturing environment, specific records are kept regarding scrap, rework, and defective units. Machine operators are expected to detect flaws in the production process and are also asked to suggest possible corrective action on the spot. When a flaw is detected, the FMS cell should be stopped and a solution developed immediately. All personnel are working continuously to eradicate bad or defective output.

It is the management accountant's responsibility to develop a set of control measures for the scrap area. Although financial data on the cost of scrap are important and should be computed, nonfinancial measures should also be developed and maintained. Questions such as the following should be analyzed, answered, and reported:

1. Where was the scrap detected?
2. How often does a product flaw occur at each of these locations?
3. Was the flaw detected at the spot of machine or product failure, or were additional manufacturing costs wasted on the defective products? If so, why?
4. Who is responsible for feeding the information regarding scrap incurrence to the management accountant?
5. Who should the scrap control reports go to, and how often should they be prepared?

Machine Management and Maintenance Performance

One of the most challenging areas for the management accountant in the JIT setting is keeping records of machine maintenance and downtime. Automated equipment requires large capital expenditures. For a JIT company, the largest item on the balance sheet is often automated machinery and equipment. Each piece of equipment has a specific capability, above which continuous operation is threatened. The machine management and maintenance measures should have two objectives:

OBJECTIVE 4e
Identify the types of financial and nonfinancial analyses used in a JIT environment to evaluate machine management and maintenance

1. Evaluate performance in relation to each piece of equipment's capacity.
2. Evaluate performance of maintenance personnel to keep to a prescribed maintenance program.

Machines must operate within specified tolerances, or serious damage and downtime could result. Keeping track of proper machine operation is not easy, but electronic surveillance is possible because of the computer network connecting all of the machines in an JIT/FMS cell. These controls should be programmed into the system and tracked as a regular part of the operation. The accountant should help prepare the reporting format for this function and analyze and report the findings to appropriate production personnel.

Because automated equipment requires heavy investment and unanticipated machine downtime is not tolerated in a JIT/FMS environment, machine maintenance is critical. Minor maintenance tasks are part of the machine operator's duties. When the operating cell does not have an order to work on, the operator is expected to perform routine maintenance. A regular program of major maintenance should also be implemented. Timing can be flexible, based on work orders, but cannot be ignored. Detailed records on machine maintenance should be maintained, similar to the maintenance records required for commercial aircraft. If such maintenance is not performed, the responsible people will be held accountable for the resulting machine downtime. Table 16-2 is an example of a machine maintenance record.

Summary of Control Measures

Table 16-3 summarizes control measures in the new manufacturing environment. Quality performance is measured by tracking customer complaints, warranty claims, and vendor quality. Delivery performance is shown by on-time delivery, production backlog, lead time, cycle time, and waste time. Successful inventory performance is identified through turnover rates, space reduction, and automatic production cycle count accuracy. Materials cost/scrap control performance is measured by incoming materials inspection, materials as a percentage of total cost, actual scrap loss, and scrap as a percentage of total cost. Machine management and maintenance performance is revealed through machine maintenance records, availability/downtime experience, and equipment capacity/utilization information.

Full Cost Profit Margin

OBJECTIVE 5
Define full cost profit margin and state the advantages of this measure of profitability

The new manufacturing environment has yet another dimension that must be analyzed when dealing with performance measures. For years, management accountants have been touting the measurement qualities of **contribution margin**. This number concerns itself with only revenue and those costs that are variable in relation to the products being sold. Fixed costs are excluded from the analysis so that they will not cloud the measurement of the performance of a division or a product.

Table 16-2. Machine Maintenance Record as of April 30, 19x9—Milling Machine FMS

	January	February	March	April	May	June
Small mills						
Monthly						
Wash machine	×	×	×	×		
Replace oil	×	×	×	×		
Check bearing	×	×	×	×		
Stone sand ways	×	×	×	×		
Clean moving table	×	×	×	×		
Check cutter grip	×	×	×	×		
Quarterly						
Replace bearing	×			×		
Check wiring	×			×		
Check all motors	×			×		
Replace lights	×			×		
Check scrap removal system	×			×		
Check computer system	×			×		
Materials conveyor system						
Monthly						
Clean all belts	×	×	×	×		
Oil all parts	×	×	×	×		
Check all motors	×	×	×	×		
Clean electronic contact spots	×	×	×	×		
Quarterly						
Replace small motors	×			×		
Grease gears	×			×		
Check wiring	×			×		
Check computer system	×			×		

As a company moves in the direction of a computer-integrated manufacturing system, more and more direct labor hours are replaced by machine hours. When a complete JIT/CIM environment is attained, very little direct labor cost is being incurred. A major part of the traditional variable product cost has been replaced by costly machinery, a fixed cost, and as a result contribution margins also get larger and, more importantly, less meaningful.

Today, management accountants are turning to full cost profit margin to help measure the performance of a division or a product line. Full costing has always been an alternative for performance evaluation, but a stigma of inaccuracy was associated with the number because fixed costs had to be allocated to the product. Full cost profit margins are more appropriate in a capital intensive environment. A **full cost profit margin** is the difference between total revenue and total costs traceable to the

Table 16-3. Control Points in the New Manufacturing Environment

Quality Performance

Customer complaints

Customer surveys

Warranty claims

Vendor quality

Quality audits

Causes of cost of quality:

    Scrap and rework

    Returns and allowances

    Field service

    Warranty claims

    Lost business

Delivery Performance

On-time delivery

Setup time

Production backlog

Lead time (order to shipment)

Order fulfillment rate

Cycle time (materials receipt to product shipment)

Waste time (lead time less process time)

Inventory Performance

Turnover rates by product

Cycle count accuracy

Space reduction

Number of inventoried items

Turnover rates by location:

    Raw-in-process

    Finished goods

    Composite

Materials Cost/Scrap Control Performance

Actual scrap loss

Scrap by part, product, and operation

Scrap percentage of total cost

Quality—incoming materials inspection

Materials cost as a percentage of total cost

Machine Management and Maintenance Performance

Availability/downtime

Machine maintenance

Equipment capacity/utilization

Equipment experience

Source: Robert A. Howell and Stephen R. Soucy, "Operating Controls in the New Manufacturing Environment," *Management Accounting,* National Association of Accountants, October 1987, p. 31. Used by permission of National Association of Accountants.

work cell or product. As described in Chapter 15, the computer has enabled the accountant to more easily trace costs to FMS work cells. A CIM system can provide data that enable most costs to be treated as direct costs of these work cells. If direct traceability is not possible, new cost drivers have been established to more closely link indirect costs with cost objectives such as work cells or products. Only building occupancy costs remain as nontraceable costs to be allocated based on some causal allocation base such as machine hours or square footage occupied. Therefore full cost profit margin is a very meaningful figure for performance evaluation as well as for new product line decision analysis.

An example points out the differences between contribution margin and full cost profit margin as measures of performance. Exhibit 16-1 shows operating data for three product lines of the Merit Manufacturing Company. First, the cost data are summarized as they were before the FMS was installed. Next, the data have been reclassified to reflect the increased traceability aspects of a JIT/FMS environment. The bottom portion of the exhibit contains computations for contribution margins prior to FMS and for full cost profit margins following the installation of the new system.

The Merit Manufacturing Company example illustrates what is likely to happen with a switch from the contribution margin to the full cost profit margin approach to performance evaluation. Better methods of cost tracing and more direct cost elements provide a more complete picture of which product lines are most profitable. In our example, the most profitable product is 162 before the FMS was installed. Product 214 is the second most profitable, with Product 305 generating the lowest profit. The order of product profitability remains the same after FMS, but look at the percent of revenue for the contribution margins and the full cost profit margins: Costs have generally shifted from Products 162 and 305 to Product 214. This shift often occurs when more direct cost relationships are uncovered and better cost tracing is made possible. Under the traditional costing methods, Product 214 had an inflated profit structure that could have led to some bad decisions. With full cost profit margins, management receives more accurate decision support and price determination information.

Capital Expenditure Decision Changes[2]

OBJECTIVE 6
Describe the special costs associated with capital expenditure decisions for automated machines and processes

The capital expenditure decision analyses studied in Chapter 13 are still relevant in the new manufacturing environment. Changing to an automated process requires increased expenditures for capital equipment, so capital budgeting plays a very critical role in a computer-integrated manufacturing situation. Discounted cash flow methods such as the net present value approach are recommended when making decisions to implement a flexible manufacturing system or purchase a computer-aided machine. Payback period approaches are still used widely in industry but are not recommended.

---

2. Ideas for this section were developed from Robert A. Howell and Stephen R. Soucy, "Capital Investment in the New Manufacturing Environment," *Management Accounting,* National Association of Accountants, November 1987, pp. 26–32.

Exhibit 16-1. Contribution Margin Versus Full Cost Profit Margin

Merit Manufacturing Company
Product Performance Evaluation

	Product 162	Product 214	Product 305
Total revenue	$2,340,000	$2,400,000	$1,560,000
Before FMS installed:			
Variable costs:			
Direct materials	$ 450,000	$ 560,000	$ 270,000
Direct labor	660,000	600,000	420,000
Variable factory overhead	240,000	240,000	150,000
Variable selling expenses	90,000	80,000	60,000
Variable distribution costs	120,000	200,000	180,000
Total variable costs	$1,560,000	$1,680,000	$1,080,000
Allocated costs:			
Fixed factory overhead	$ 210,000	$ 360,000	$ 240,000
Fixed selling expenses	60,000	40,000	90,000
Fixed distribution costs	150,000	128,000	135,000
Total fixed costs	$ 420,000	$ 528,000	$ 465,000
After FMS installed:			
Traceable costs:			
Direct materials	$ 450,000	$ 560,000	$ 270,000
Materials-related overhead	72,000	88,000	54,000
Direct labor	90,000	128,000	84,000
Indirect labor	108,000	112,000	90,000
Setup labor	66,000	104,000	66,000
Electrical power	54,000	80,000	48,000
Supervision	96,000	120,000	96,000
Repairs and maintenance	78,000	96,000	78,000
Operating supplies/lubricants	36,000	56,000	42,000
Other traceable indirect costs	114,000	168,000	120,000
Traceable selling expenses	102,000	104,000	72,000
Traceable distribution costs	156,000	284,000	204,000
Total traceable costs	$1,422,000	$1,900,000	$1,224,000
Allocated costs:			
Nontraceable factory overhead	$ 126,000	$ 244,000	$ 132,000
Nontraceable selling and distribution costs	96,000	112,000	108,000
Total nontraceable costs	$ 222,000	$ 356,000	$ 240,000

	Product 162	Product 214	Product 305
Product Performance Measures			
Before FMS installed:			
Contribution margin:			
Total revenue	$2,340,000	$2,400,000	$1,560,000
Less variable costs	1,560,000	1,680,000	1,080,000
Contribution margin	$ 780,000	$ 720,000	$ 480,000
Less total fixed costs	420,000	528,000	465,000
Operating profit	$ 360,000	$ 192,000	$ 15,000
Contribution margin as a percent of revenue	33.33%	30.00%	30.77%
Operating profit as a percent of revenue	15.38%	8.00%	0.96%
After FMS installed:			
Full cost profit margin:			
Total revenues	$2,340,000	$2,400,000	$1,560,000
Less total traceable costs	1,422,000	1,900,000	1,224,000
Full cost profit margin	$ 918,000	$ 500,000	$ 336,000
Less total nontraceable costs	222,000	356,000	240,000
Operating profit	$ 696,000	$ 144,000	$ 96,000
Full cost profit margin as a percent of revenue	39.23%	20.83%	21.54%
Operating profit as a percent of revenue	29.74%	6.00%	6.15%

Four characteristics of JIT/FMS capital expenditures highlight why the net present value method of analysis is preferred. First, expenditures for automated equipment tend to be very expensive—$50 million is not an uncommon price for an FMS (some total CIM facilities have cost more than $100 million). Second, useful lives of automated equipment are longer and estimating future cash flows is more difficult. Third, the equipment is technically and operationally more complex, which makes estimating future operating costs more difficult. Benefits from the equipment tend to be more indirect and hidden. Intangible benefits such as increased customer satisfaction are hard to value but must be considered in the capital expenditure decision process.

The fourth characteristic is the increased amount of uncertainty present in capital expenditure decisions of automated equipment. With significantly larger capital outlays, increased useful lives, and more intangible benefits, a company must develop its own model or formula to predict future profitability. There are several hidden variables that make capital budgeting extremely difficult in a JIT/FMS environment. Even after costs have been classified as direct or indirect, uncertainty regarding product demand, product mix, market conditions, competition, and equipment obsolescence increase the risks associated with automation. Each factor must be part of the net present value computations. Special methods that integrate the sensitivity of these variables to the decision should be used (such approaches involve probability analysis and are topics for more advanced courses in management accounting).

Special Costs to Consider

Assume that you are going to replace four direct labor employees with a robotic machine. What kinds of costs should be part of this decision analysis? Three categories of costs should be analyzed:

1. Cost savings will result from reducing the amount of direct labor and the labor-related benefits of the four workers. Using the new equipment should reduce scrap and defective unit rework. Storage space and material handling costs will also be reduced because of reduced inventories.
2. New costs to consider include wages and related costs of workers who maintain and support the robotic machine, new direct costs such as electrical power and supervision that can be traced directly to the new machine, and costs associated with scheduling and product design.
3. New costs to be capitalized (in addition to the cost of the robotic machine) include engineering design work on the new system, computer programming and software development costs, and machine implementation costs.

Developing and analyzing these costs are new challenges for the management accountant and increase the accountant's responsibilities in the new manufacturing environment.

One additional area of uncertainty must be mentioned. Suppose the company is considering not to invest in automated equipment. What are the costs of not adopting automated manufacturing facilities? This is the most difficult question to address. Determining future cash flows is hard enough, but to estimate profits lost by not adopting the new methods is almost impossible. The effects of improved product quality and increased customer satisfaction are difficult to determine and value. Increased employee morale caused by feeling more a part of the team is another factor difficult to value. Dozens of other hidden and intangible benefits must be considered when making this type of decision. On the other hand, employee morale may increase because robots were denied in favor of human effort. The decision to automate or not to automate is an extremely difficult one. The continued existence of the company itself may be on the line.

Postcompletion Audit

As mentioned in Chapter 13, the postcompletion audit phase of the capital expenditure decision process is an important part of the analysis. But this task is seldom successfully performed because it is so difficult to isolate information connected with each decision. The reasons behind this failure to follow through on capital budget audits are amplified in the new manufacturing environment. The impact of a piece of automated equipment on the rest of the operation is uncertain. Costs of implementation may be classified many different ways and are difficult to accumulate. The longer time periods involved tend to extend the audit cycle period.

But some aspects of the new environment tend to make postcompletion audits easier to conduct. Costs associated with FMS cells or islands are mostly direct costs and easily traceable. Depreciation costs are linked to units of output rather than time, which also helps trace costs to the machines and processes being analyzed. Because of the significant costs of automated systems, postcompletion audits, no matter how difficult, should be attempted. The more information that is known about the benefits of the new system, the more informed will be the future decisions of the company's management.

Summary

Capital investments in a JIT/FMS environment have larger cash outlays, longer payback periods, more hidden benefits and costs, and increased levels of uncertainty associated with them. There must be more emphasis on developing the data that are used in net present value decision analysis. These conditions increase the importance of the roles of production managers, engineers, sales personnel, and management accountants in the decision process.

JIT/FMS Management Reporting Guidelines

OBJECTIVE 7
Identify the primary areas of management reporting in a JIT/FMS environment and give examples of reports needed

Reporting the results of operations to management is one of the management accountant's primary responsibilities. This role is amplified in the new manufacturing environment, but the accountant must be careful to identify reports prepared for the traditional manufacturing structure but still relevant for automated processes. Studies have shown that well over half the reports prepared for management each month have little relevance and are ignored by the recipients.

The management accountant faces a real challenge in the JIT/FMS management reporting areas. As with performance measurement and operations control, emphasis must shift from primarily financial operating reports to a wide range of both financial and nonfinancial data reports. But the need for a responsibility accounting and reporting structure is still present in the JIT/FMS environment for the nonfinancial as well as for the financial operating results of the period. Reporting emphasis must be directed at specific areas of interest, such as customer responsiveness, product line profitability, product contribution, operating effectiveness, and asset management.

Before we discuss JIT/FMS reporting, we must mention one unique aspect of the new manufacturing environment that affects preparation of reports. For decades, the management accountant has been the production managers' *only* source of information for running day-to-day operations. The accountant seldom visited the manufacturing site, and reports were in traditional form, highlighting comparisons between actual and budgeted financial data. Production people were seldom asked for input concerning the content or structure of a report.

Things have changed in today's environment. Production managers have their own personal computers out in the factory and know how to use them. If the management accountant will not supply needed information, these managers will develop their own reports. This factor should be an additional challenge to the accountant. Management accountants must become very familiar with the production operation and should prepare reports that those responsible for the product line or operating cell request. If the management accountant does not meet this challenge, the future need for an organization's entire internal accounting function is in jeopardy.

Customer Responsiveness Reporting

We pointed out that close contact with the level of customer satisfaction is a critical issue in the new manufacturing environment. Reports prepared for management should reflect this concern. The customer is interested in receiving a quality product on a timely basis. Price is a factor, but often the price is very competitive. Other factors such as customer service and follow-up can make the difference between retaining the customer or losing the sale.

Reporting should concentrate on tracking quality through the (1) number and types of customer complaints and (2) returns and allowances. Records of promised versus actual delivery dates can be important. Continuous records of backlogged orders and delayed delivery dates are critical to maintaining customer satisfaction. A report tracking shipments from the time they leave the plant until they arrive at the customer's facility is also a good measure of service performance. Any report that will enhance delivery and service should be prepared. All of these reports involve nonfinancial data.

Product Line Profitability Reporting

Reporting on product line profitability should concentrate on both the manufacturing and the selling and delivery costs. Minimizing the cost of operations does not guarantee product profitability. Selling and delivery costs could easily make a product line unprofitable if they are not continuously analyzed and controlled. In the manufacturing area, reports should focus on both materials and conversion costs. Materials cost is made up of purchase price and materials handling costs once the item has been received from the vendor. Non-value added costs in the materials handling area can be eliminated in part through effective tracking and reporting procedures. Conversion costs must be analyzed continuously using a combination of traditional methods and newly created reports for scrap control, operating cell yield, and the effective use of energy.

Selling and delivery costs must be monitored very closely to ensure that waste does not occur. Reports should be tailored by sales territory, product line, and mode of transportation. This information needs to be supplied to supervisory personnel on a timely basis.

Product Contribution Reporting

A product's contribution to the absorption of a company's untraceable fixed costs is still important in a JIT/FMS environment, but as pointed out in the section on full cost profit margin, product contribution can include traceable fixed costs in a CAD/CAM or an FMS work cell situation. Contribution margin is no longer the only measure of product contribution. If contribution margin is still requested, management accounting reports should also contain information regarding full cost profit margin so that managers have additional information upon which to base their decisions.

Operating Effectiveness Reporting

Reporting to enhance operating effectiveness concentrates on the non-value added areas of a traditional system. Reports that focus on product cycle times, including the process time, lead time, and waste time, are especially good for determining operating effectiveness. Reports that track causes of downtime and defective units should be prepared. Reports on inventory turnover and space utilization can lead to significant reductions in non-value added costs. Special studies on ways to decrease throughput (processing) time of a JIT and/or FMS cell should be prepared on request. Employee suggestions for operating improvement should be encouraged and the results reported to management. Most of the reports in this category are nonfinancial and yet all help reduce operating costs.

Asset Management Reporting

The final report preparation category centers on management of the company's fixed assets. Automation caused huge increases in capital asset expenditures. Special reporting is necessary to help manage this large resource. Machine maintenance must be recorded and tracked. Records of machine time availability or the lack thereof (downtime) is important information to production managers and scheduling personnel. Space utilization must be reported periodically. Equipment capacity and experience must be logged in continuously and reports generated. Again, most of these reports are nonfinancial but are critical to the successful operation of the manufacturing facilities. The management accountant is expected to provide these data.

Summary

Table 16-4 depicts the reporting network described above. Some reports are primarily financial in nature, whereas others contain only nonfinancial data. A few reporting areas have both financial and nonfinancial information. The important aspect of this analysis is that the management

Table 16-4. JIT Management Reporting Guidelines

Operations Reporting Areas	Nonfinancial	Financial
Customer responsiveness		
Number/types of customer complaints	×	
Returns and allowances by customer	×	×
Actual versus promised delivery	×	
Backlogged orders	×	
Product shipment tracking	×	
Product line profitability		
Materials purchasing	×	×
Materials handling costs		×
Conversion costs		×
Selling and delivery costs		×
Product contribution		
Full cost profit margins		×
Contribution margins		×
Operating effectiveness		
Product cycle times	×	
Product lead times	×	
Product waste times	×	
Scrap/defective units	×	
Machine yield rates	×	
Throughput time analyses	×	
Asset management		
Machine maintenance	×	
Machine availability/downtime	×	
Space utilization	×	
Equipment capacity/experience	×	

accountant's role and responsibilities have expanded in the new manufacturing environment. The accountant must become familiar with the manufacturing facilities to be able to supply management with relevant, timely data.

Chapter Review

Review of Learning Objectives

1. **State the three new areas of emphasis that accompany the JIT philosophy.**
   Management accounting is influenced by three new areas of emphasis connected with the JIT philosophy: taking a macro versus a micro approach to analyses, using large amounts of nonfinancial data in regular internal analyses, and using theoretical capacity as a prime benchmark for measuring performance.

2. **Identify the unique aspects of product costing in an automated manufacturing process.**
   With automation, machine hours replace direct labor hours or dollars and become the primary basis for overhead allocation. The use of several overhead cost pools and appropriate cost drivers is also encouraged. More costs are treated as direct costs because of their traceability to operating cells. Departmental or operating cell overhead rates are preferred over plantwide rates.

3. **Compute a product unit cost using data from a flexible manufacturing system.**
   Computing a product unit cost for an FMS cell consists of determining the unit cost of materials; material handling cost overhead; conversion costs per unit, including all traceable indirect costs and factory overhead allocations; and selling and distribution costs.

4. **Identify the types of financial and nonfinancial analyses used in a JIT environment to evaluate the performance of (a) product quality, (b) product delivery, (c) inventory control, (d) materials cost/scrap control, and (e) machine management and maintenance.**
   Product quality performance is measured by analyzing customer complaints, warranty claims, and causes of cost of quality. Customer surveys and quality audits are also used. Product delivery performance centers on tracking lead time, process time cycle time, setup time, production backlog, and on-time deliveries. Inventory control performance looks at turnover rates by product, space reduction for storage, and number of inventoried items. Materials cost/scrap control performance looks at actual scrap loss, scrap as a percentage of total cost, materials cost as a percentage of total cost, and quality of incoming goods. Machine management and maintenance performance considers each piece of equipment's performance in relation to its capacity and how maintenance personnel follow a prescribed maintenance program.

5. **Define full cost profit margin and state the advantages of this measure of profitability.**
   Full cost profit margin is the difference between total revenue and total costs traceable to the work cell or product. The measure is more meaningful than contribution margin because of the additional costs brought into the analysis. Profitability is measured more accurately using the full cost profit margin.

6. **Describe the special costs associated with capital expenditure decisions for automated machines and processes.**
   Capital budgeting in a JIT/FMS environment means more capital equipment needs at higher purchase prices. Labor and labor-related costs, scrap and rework costs, and storage space costs play a minor role in the analysis. Indirect labor for robot maintenance, electrical power, and supervision costs are traceable to the project under review. Cost of engineering design and computer programming and software development are part of the initial capital outlay.

7. **Identify the primary areas of management reporting in a JIT/FMS environment and give examples of reports needed.**
   The primary areas of management reporting in a JIT/FMS environment are (a) customer responsiveness reporting (number and types of customer complaints, backlogged orders, (b) product line profitability reporting (materials purchasing, materials handling costs), (c) product contribution reporting (full cost profit margins, contribution margins), (d) operating effectiveness reporting (product cycle times, product waste times) and (e) asset management reporting (machine maintenance, machine utilization/downtime).

Review of Concepts and Terminology

The following important concepts were introduced in this chapter:

(L.O.2) **JIT/FMS environment:** An operating environment created by a flexible manufacturing system functioning within the just-in-time philosophy.

(L.O.2) **Computer numerically-controlled (CNC) machines:** Stand-alone machines that are computer controlled.

(L.O.2) **Computer-aided design/computer-aided manufacturing (CAD/CAM):** Using computers in product design work, planning and controlling production, and linking CNC machines.

(L.O.2) **Automated material handling system (AMHS):** A necessary component of a computer-integrated manufacturing system in which the raw materials and partially completed product handling function is automatic, providing a continuous flow through the process.

(L.O.5) **Full cost profit margin:** The difference between total revenue and total costs traceable to the work cell or product.

Other important terms introduced in this chapter are:

run time (p. 626)
engineered time (p. 626)
purchase order lead time (p. 635)
production cycle time (p. 635)
delivery time (p. 635)

Review Problem
Analysis of Nonfinancial Data—C&L Products, Inc.

The Lazer Motor Division of C&L Products, Inc., has been in operation for six years. Three months ago a new flexible manufacturing system was installed in the small motors department. A just-in-time approach is followed for everything from ordering materials and parts to product shipment and delivery. The division's superintendent is very interested in the initial results of the venture. The following data have been collected for your analysis:

	Weeks							
	1	2	3	4	5	6	7	8
Warranty claims	2	4	1	1	0	5	7	11
Average setup time (hours)	0.3	0.25	0.25	0.3	0.25	0.2	0.2	0.15
Average lead time (hours)	2.4	2.3	2.2	2.3	2.35	2.4	2.4	2.5
Average cycle time (hours)	2.1	2.05	1.95	2	2	2.1	2.2	2.3
Average process time (hours)	1.9	1.9	1.85	1.8	1.9	1.95	1.95	1.9
Number of inventoried items	2,450	2,390	2,380	2,410	2,430	2,460	2,610	2,720
Customer complaints	12	12	10	8	9	7	6	4
Times inventory turnover	4.5	4.4	4.4	4.35	4.3	4.25	4.25	4.35
Production backlog (units)	9,210	9,350	9,370	9,420	9,410	8,730	8,310	7,950
Machine downtime (hours)	86.5	83.1	76.5	80.1	90.4	100.6	120.2	124.9

	Weeks							
	1	2	3	4	5	6	7	8
Parts scrapped	112	126	134	118	96	89	78	64
Equipment utilization rate (%)	98.2	98.6	98.9	98.5	98.1	97.3	96.6	95.7
On-time deliveries (%)	93.2	94.1	96.5	95.4	92.1	90.5	88.4	89.3
Machine maintenance time (hours)	34.6	32.2	28.5	22.1	18.5	12.6	19.7	26.4

Required

1. Analyze the performance of the Lazer Motor Division for the eight-week period, centering your analysis on the following areas of performance:
   a. Product quality
   b. Product delivery
   c. Inventory control
   d. Materials utilization/scrap control
   e. Machine management and maintenance
2. Summarize your findings in a report to the division's superintendent.

Answer to Review Problem

The data given were reorganized in the following manner, and two additional pieces of information, average waste time and estimated number of units sold, were calculated from the given information.

1. Analysis of performance

	Weeks								Weekly Average
	1	2	3	4	5	6	7	8	
Product quality performance									
Customer com-plaints	12	12	10	8	9	7	6	4	8.500 cmplt.
Warranty claims	2	4	1	1	0	5	7	11	3.875 claims
Product delivery performance									
On-time deliveries (%)	93.2	94.1	96.5	95.4	92.1	90.5	88.4	89.3	92.44 %
Average setup time (hours)	0.3	0.25	0.25	0.3	0.25	0.2	0.2	0.15	0.2375 hours
Average lead time (hours)	2.4	2.3	2.2	2.3	2.35	2.4	2.4	2.5	2.3563 hours
Average cycle time (hours)	2.1	2.05	1.95	2	2	2.1	2.2	2.3	2.0875 hours
Average process time (hours)	1.9	1.9	1.85	1.8	1.9	1.95	1.95	1.9	1.8938 hours
Production backlog (units)	9,210	9,350	9,370	9,420	9,410	8,730	8,310	7,950	8,969 units
Waste time (hours) (lead time less process time)	0.5	0.4	0.35	0.5	0.45	0.45	0.45	0.6	0.4625 hours

			Weeks						Weekly
	1	2	3	4	5	6	7	8	Average
Inventory control performance									
Number of inventoried items (units) (a)	2,450	2,390	2,380	2,410	2,430	2,460	2,610	2,720	2,481 units
Times inventory turnover (b)	4.5	4.4	4.4	4.35	4.3	4.25	4.25	4.35	4.35 times
Estimated number of units sold (a × b)	11,025	10,516	10,472	10,484	10,449	10,455	11,093	11,832	10,791 units
Materials cost/scrap control performance									
Parts scrapped (units)	112	126	134	118	96	89	78	64	102.13 units
Machine management and maintenance performance									
Machine downtime (hours)	86.5	83.1	76.5	80.1	90.4	100.6	120.2	124.9	95.29 hours
Equipment utilization rate (%)	98.2	98.6	98.9	98.5	98.1	97.3	96.6	95.7	97.74 %
Machine maintenance time (hours)	34.6	32.2	28.5	22.1	18.5	12.6	19.7	26.4	24.33 hours

2. Memorandum to division superintendent.

My analysis of the operating data for the Lazer Motor Division for the last eight weeks revealed the following:

Product quality performance:
Product quality seems to be improving, with the number of complaints decreasing rapidly. However, warranty claims rose significantly in the past three weeks, which may be a signal of quality problems ahead.

Product delivery performance:
Although the averages for the product delivery measures seem great when compared to our old standards, we are having trouble maintaining the averages established eight weeks ago. Waste time is increasing, which is contra to our goals. Backlogged orders are decreasing, which is a good sign from a JIT view but could spell problems in the future. On-time deliveries percentages are slipping. On the positive side, setup time seems to be under control. Emphasis needs to be placed on reducing lead time, cycle time, and process time.

Inventory control performance:
This area spells trouble. Inventory size is increasing, and the number of inventory turns is decreasing. The result is increased storage costs and decreased units sold.

Materials cost/scrap control performance:
The incidence of scrap has decreased significantly, which is very good. We had to increase cycle time to correct our manufacturing problems, which accounts for the increases in that area. With the scrap problem under control, processing and cycle time may improve in the future.

Machine management and maintenance performance:
Machine downtime is increasing, which is consistent with the scrap report. Also, the machine utilization rate is down. Machine maintenance has also tailed off but has increased in the past two weeks. Department managers should be made aware of these pending problem areas.

Overall, we can see good signs from the new equipment, but we need to stay on top of the pending problem areas mentioned above.

Chapter Assignments

Questions

1. Explain the statement, In a JIT environment, the accountant must take a macro approach to cost control and reporting.
2. Why is the analysis of nonfinancial data so important in a JIT environment?
3. Which level of capacity, normal or theoretical, is more important in analyzing a JIT/FMS operating cell? Why?
4. Contrast a computer numerically-controlled machine with a flexible manufacturing system.
5. "Direct labor is not an appropriate allocation base because there is very little connection between overhead costs incurred in an FMS and direct labor hours or cost." Is this statement true? Why?
6. Give three examples of costs treated as indirect costs in a traditional manufacturing environment but accounted for as direct costs in a JIT setting. Explain the reasons for the three changes.
7. An automatic storage/retrieval system (AS/RS) is the key reason for the decrease in the levels of work-in-process inventories in a JIT/FMS environment. Why?
8. Identify three types of nonfinancial analyses that are used to measure product quality performance. Describe the kind of data used in each analysis.
9. Why is there so much emphasis on customer satisfaction in a JIT environment? How is this attention linked to the profitability of a JIT approach?
10. Inventory controls in the new manufacturing environment are designed to eliminate inventory balances and non-value added product costs. Do you agree? Why is there emphasis on inventory elimination?
11. In a JIT/FMS environment, the formal inspection departments are eliminated but product quality controls are given high priority. How is this accomplished?
12. Why are accurate records of machine maintenance so critical to an FMS operation?
13. Define full cost profit margin and contrast it with contribution margin.
14. What three special cost areas should be carefully considered when making capital expenditure decisions in a JIT/FMS environment? Give examples of the areas.
15. What does customer responsiveness reporting mean? How does it differ from product line profitability reporting?
16. Identify and describe several of the reports needed to monitor an FMS's operating effectiveness.

Classroom Exercises

Exercise 16-1.
The Changing
Management
Accounting
Environment

(L.O. 1)

Bill Ross, president and CEO of Irving Products, Inc., has just called controller Kay Horstmann into his office. "Kay, I don't understand several parts of this request for a new management accounting system that you submitted yesterday. I thought that we already had a very modern, up-to-date system. Why this sudden request for a major change? Is your request in any way connected with our new flexible manufacturing system? If so, why does a new manufacturing system require a complete revamping of an accounting system? Can't existing accounting practices and procedures handle the new equipment?"

Prepare Kay Horstmann's reply to Bill Ross.

Exercise 16-2.
Product Costing
Changes Caused by
JIT and Automation

(L.O. 2)

Edberg Manufacturing Company produces high-tempered drill bits used by steel and aluminum products companies. The management accounting system uses standard costs. Cost control is accomplished by carefully computing and analyzing a series of price, rate, and efficiency variances. One factory overhead cost pool is used, and a plantwide overhead rate is the main aspect of the system. Direct labor hours is the base used to allocate factory overhead to products. Only raw materials and machinist labor are considered direct costs of the system.

Last week, the company installed its first FMS operating cell. The vice president of finance has asked the controller to identify specific changes to the management accounting system that are necessary because of the new flexible manufacturing system.

Prepare a summary of the information that should be included in the controller's response to the vice president of finance.

Exercise 16-3.
Product Costing in
a Flexible
Manufacturing
System

(L.O. 3)

Aust Enterprises, Inc., manufactures wooden serving trays using an FMS work cell. The wood is shaped and the tray assembled in one continuous operation. September's output totaled 42,300 units. Each unit requires two machine hours of effort. Materials handling cost is allocated to the product based on unit materials cost; engineering design costs are allocated based on units produced; and FMS overhead and building occupancy costs are allocated based on machine hours. Operating data for September are on the next page. Additional information is as follows:

Materials handling cost allocation rate per $ of materials:
$50,337/$148,050 = 34%

Engineering design cost allocation rate per unit:
$19,458/42,300 = $0.46

FMS overhead allocation rate per machine hour:
$87,984/84,600 = $1.04

Building occupancy allocation rate per machine hour:
$50,760/84,600 = $0.60

Materials:		
Wood	$97,290	
Hardware	50,760	$148,050
Materials handling:		
Labor	$22,208	
Equipment depreciation	7,403	
Electrical power	4,442	
Maintenance	16,286	50,337
Direct labor:		
Machinists		46,530
Engineering design:		
Labor	$ 9,729	
Electrical power	5,922	
Engineering overhead	3,807	19,458
FMS cell overhead:		
Indirect labor	$29,610	
Repairs and maintenance	20,304	
Supervision	16,920	
Equipment depreciation	6,768	
Operating supplies	4,230	
Electrical power	10,152	87,984
Building occupancy overhead		50,760
Total costs		$403,119

Compute the unit cost of one wooden serving tray. Identify the six elements of the computation as part of your answer.

Exercise 16-4.
Nonfinancial Data
Analysis
(L.O. 4)

Doarn & Company make racing bicycle products. Their Boyce model is considered top of the line within the industry. Three months ago the company purchased and installed a flexible manufacturing system for the Boyce line, with emphasis on improving quality as well as reducing production time. Management is very interested in cutting time in all phases of the delivery cycle.

Following are data the controller's office gathered for the past four-week period:

	Weeks			
	1	2	3	4
Average process time (hours)	23.6	23.4	22.8	22.2
Average setup time (hours)	2.4	2.3	2.2	2.1
Customer complaints	6	5	7	8
Delivery time (hours)	34.8	35.2	36.4	38.2
On-time deliveries (%)	98.1	97.7	97.2	96.3
Production backlog (units)	8,230	8,340	8,320	8,430
Production cycle time (hours)	28.5	27.9	27.2	26.4
Purchase order lead time (hours)	38.5	36.2	35.5	34.1
Warranty claims	2	3	3	2

Analyze the performance of the Boyce model line for the four-week period, centering your analysis on the following areas of performance:

1. Product quality
2. Product delivery

Exercise 16-5.
Full Cost Profit
Margin
(L.O. 5)

Mark Johnson Enterprises produces all-purpose sports vehicles. The company recently installed a flexible manufacturing system for its AJ-25 product line. The accounting system has been recast to reflect the new operating process. Following are monthly operating data for periods before and after the FMS installation:

	Product AJ-25
Average monthly revenue	$1,378,000
Total operating costs:	
For month before FMS installed:	
Direct materials	$ 330,720
Direct labor	454,740
Variable factory overhead	124,020
Variable selling expenses	41,340
Variable distribution costs	55,120
Fixed factory overhead	456,200
Fixed selling expenses	132,300
Fixed distribution costs	189,700
For month after FMS installed:	
Direct materials	$ 330,720
Materials-related overhead	48,230
Direct labor	62,010
Indirect labor	99,216
Setup labor	66,144
Electrical power	24,804
Supervision	35,828
Repairs and maintenance	46,852
Operating supplies/lubricants	11,024
Other traceable indirect costs	30,316
Traceable selling expenses	52,364
Traceable distribution costs	57,876
Nontraceable factory overhead	245,300
Nontraceable selling and distribution costs	178,200

Using the after FMS data, compute the full cost profit margin for product AJ-25. Also include full cost profit margin as a percent of revenue and operating profit as a percent of revenue as part of your answer.

**Exercise 16-6.
Reporting JIT Data**
(L.O. 7)

Customer responsiveness is a key area of concern for management, especially in a just-in-time environment. Bud Archer is chief executive officer of Tubac Machinery, Inc. The company adopted the JIT philosophy about five years ago. Since then, each segment of the company has been converted, and a complete computer-integrated manufacturing system now exists in all parts of the company's five plants. Processing of Tubac's products now averages less than four days once the materials have been placed into production.

Archer is worried about customer satisfaction and has asked his controller, Sue Bailey, for some advice and assistance. Bailey did a quick survey of customers to determine weak areas in customer relations. Here is a summary of four customer replies:

Customer A:
Customer for five years; waits an average of six weeks for delivery; located 1,200 miles from plant; returns an average of 3 percent of products; receives 90 percent on-time deliveries; never hears from salesperson after placing order; likes our quality or would go with competitor.

Customer B:
Customer for seven years; waits an average of five weeks for delivery; orders usually sit in backlog for at least three weeks; located fifty miles from plant; returns about 5 percent of products; receives 95 percent on-time deliveries; has great rapport with salesperson; salesperson is reason why this is a loyal customer.

Customer C:
Customer for twelve years; waits an average of seven weeks for delivery; located 1,500 miles from plant; returns about 4 percent of products; receives 92 percent on-time deliveries; salesperson is available but of little help in getting faster delivery cycle time; company is thinking about dealing with another source for their product needs.

Customer D:
Customer for fifteen years; very pleased with company's product; still waits almost five weeks for delivery; located 120 miles from plant; returns only 2 percent of goods received; rapport with salesperson very good; follow-up service of salesperson excellent; would like delivery cycle time reduced to equal that of competitors; usually deals with three-week backlog.

What types of reports would you recommend be included in the management reporting system? Defend the need for each report.

**Exercise 16-7.
Terminology
Review**
(L.O. 1, 2)

Test your knowledge of current management accounting terminology by reading the following memorandum:

Dear Client:

Incorporating MRP II into your JIT environment will enable your CIM system to operate with TQC. Now, a MIPS or a ZIPS approach is all right, but a FMS is possible only if your CAD/CAM systems and other CNC machines are linked as production cells or islands. An EDI allows for a MAN condition with PTP and enhances your MACS while identifying your FCPM.

We hope that these ideas meet with your approval, and we are ready to assist you in your move to maximize profit in a JIT fashion. Thank you.

Respectfully,

Identify all the acronyms used in the memo. Do you understand this memo? If not, review the new terminology discussed in Chapters 15 and 16.

Interpreting Accounting Information

The Need for an Automated System: Hamby Woodworks, Inc.
(L.O. 1, 7)

In 1968, Ernest Hamby began tinkering with woodworking machinery in his basement in Lafayette, Indiana. His first projects were small tables, such as end tables and coffee tables for homes. After five years of part-time effort, Hamby developed his hobby into a small company: Two employees were hired, material suppliers were located, a building was leased, and new machinery was acquired. Furniture and cabinetmaking became the specialties of Hamby Woodworks, Inc.

In 1978, a famous professional golfer asked Hamby to produce a custom set of cabinets for her new home. She was so impressed with the hand-crafted features of the final product that she asked Hamby if the company could make a personalized set of persimmon wood golf clubs. Intrigued by the challenge, Hamby ordered the special wood and began making the necessary tools and dies for the wood-shaping machinery. The wood arrived, and the machines were set up for this small, precision-oriented work order. Machine shaping was used in conjunction with special hand crafting to produce the set of four golf woods. Two weeks after first being used in professional-level play, the clubs helped the pro golfer win her first professional tournament. The Hamby Club had made a very successful debut.

Since that storybook beginning, the Hamby Club has gained worldwide recognition. Demand for the product is so great that the company built a special plant that makes only custom-crafted clubs. The clubs are machine shaped but vary according to the following constraints: female versus male, customer height, weight, and arm length. Ten basic sets of clubs are produced, five for females and five for males. Slight variations in machine setup provide the difference in the club weights and lengths.

In the past six months, several problems have developed at the golf club plant. Even though one computer numerically-controlled machine is used in the manufacturing process, the company's backlog is growing rapidly. Customers are complaining of slow delivery. Quality is declining because clubs are pushed through the production process and often shipped without proper inspection. Raw materials, work-in-process, and finished goods inventories are all over the plant, using up costly storage space and requiring thousands of dollars in invested working capital. Workers are complaining about the pressure to produce the backlogged orders. Machine breakdown is increasing. Production control reports are not useful because they are not timely and contain irrelevant information. Hamby's dream product has turned into a nightmare.

You have been hired by Hamby Woodworks, Inc., as a consultant to define the problem and suggest a possible solution to the current dilemma. Prepare a response to Hamby. Include in your analysis specific changes in the manufacturing process and the management reporting system. Defend each change suggested.

Problem Set A

Problem 16A-1. Product Costing in a Flexible Manufacturing System
(L.O. 2, 3)

Grego Company produces a complete line of bicycle seats in its Flagstaff plant. The four versions of model J17-21 are made on flexible manufacturing system #2. The four seats have different shapes but are identical regarding processing operations and production costs. During July, the following costs were incurred and traced to FMS #2:

Materials:

Leather	$23,520
Metal frame	38,220
Bolts	2,940

Materials handling:

Labor	7,350
Equipment depreciation	4,410
Electrical power	2,460
Maintenance	5,184

Direct labor:

Machinists	13,230

Engineering design:

Labor	4,116
Electrical power	1,176
Engineering overhead	7,644

FMS overhead:

Equipment depreciation	7,056
Indirect labor	30,870
Supervision	17,640
Operating supplies	4,410
Electrical power	10,584
Repairs and maintenance	21,168
Building occupancy overhead	52,920

July's output totaled 29,400 units. Each unit requires three machine hours of effort. Materials handling costs are allocated to the products based on unit materials cost; engineering design costs are allocated based on units produced; and FMS overhead is allocated based on machine hours.

Required

1. Compute the following:
   a. Materials handling cost allocation rate
   b. Engineering design cost allocation rate
   c. FMS overhead allocation rate
2. Compute the unit cost of one bicycle seat. Show details of your computation.

Problem 16A-2.
Machine Hours
Versus Labor Hours
(L.O. 2, 3)

Lou Weinstein has been in the manufacturing business for more than twenty years. Four months ago, Weinstein Products, Inc., made a major investment in automated machinery. The three new flexible manufacturing systems each have seven operating stations and produce chrome automobile bumpers in one operation. Each FMS specializes in one type of bumper; these products are identified as A-Bump, B-Bump and C-Bump, with A-Bump being the most complex and C-Bump the least difficult to make. After four months of operation, Weinstein began complaining to the controller about the ever-increasing factory overhead rate. Weinstein was under the impression that the new automated machinery was going to reduce product costs. A plantwide overhead rate is still being used, but the machinery installation consultant did suggest switching to individual FMS factory overhead rates, with materials handling costs being treated separately. These costs are currently included in the total factory overhead cost pool.

The following data are from the past month's records:

	A-Bump	B-Bump	C-Bump
Unit information:			
Raw materials cost	$96	$88	$82
Direct labor hours	1.2	1.5	0.8
Direct labor cost per hour	$20	$18	$16
Machine hours	4.2	3.1	3
Information totals:			
Unit sales during month	50,000	70,000	100,000
Total factory overhead	$2,950,000	$1,242,500	$1,431,000

Weinstein's policy has been to set selling prices at 160 percent of a product's production cost.

Required

1. Compute the company's plantwide factory overhead rate using total direct labor dollars as a basis.
2. Compute each product's total production costs and selling price using the application rate computed in part **1.**
3. Compute a new factory overhead application rate assuming:
   a. Materials storage and handling overhead equal to 5 percent of the cost of raw materials is subtracted from the factory overhead cost totals.
   b. Machine hours is the factory overhead allocation basis.
   c. Product line overhead rates are used rather than a plantwide rate.
4. Compute each product's total production cost and selling price using the allocation rates computed in part **3.**
5. Compare the old and new product selling prices and comment on your findings.

Problem 16A-3.
Full Cost Profit
Margin
(L.O. 5)

Nolan Molded Products Company produces three main products, identified as C2-24, K5-36, and R4-73. Two months ago, the company installed three fully automated flexible manufacturing systems for the product lines. The controller is anxious to see how the FMS machinery affects operating costs for the three products. Product K5-36 has been a low performer for the company and is being outpriced on the market. The line may have to be dropped.

Monthly operating data for before and after the FMS approach was adopted are shown on the next page.

Required

1. Recast the information given for the three products into an analysis that reveals total traceable and total nontraceable costs (a) before and (b) after the FMS was installed.
2. Describe and differentiate between full cost profit margin and contribution margin.

Nolan Molded Products Company
Product Performance Evaluation

	Assembly C2-24	Assembly K5-36	Assembly R4-73
Total revenue	$4,590,000	$5,180,000	$3,520,000
Total operating costs:			
Before FMS installed:			
Direct materials	$1,101,600	$1,346,800	$ 774,400
Direct labor	1,514,700	1,761,200	985,600
Variable factory overhead	413,100	259,000	158,400
Variable selling expenses	137,700	155,400	123,200
Variable distribution costs	183,600	310,800	193,600
Fixed factory overhead	456,200	654,200	432,600
Fixed selling expenses	132,300	103,290	196,700
Fixed distribution costs	189,700	304,520	291,800
After FMS installed:			
Direct materials	$1,101,600	$1,346,800	$ 774,400
Materials-related overhead	160,650	150,220	112,640
Direct labor	206,550	227,920	147,840
Indirect labor	330,480	331,520	260,480
Setup labor	220,320	217,560	154,880
Electrical power	82,620	93,240	56,320
Supervision	119,340	145,040	91,520
Repairs and maintenance	156,060	160,580	130,240
Operating supplies/lubricants	36,720	46,620	28,160
Other traceable indirect costs	100,980	108,780	84,480
Traceable selling expenses	174,420	170,940	133,760
Traceable distribution costs	192,780	202,020	154,880
Nontraceable factory overhead	245,300	323,100	241,100
Nontraceable selling and distribution costs	178,200	231,400	198,760

3. Using the before-FMS data, prepare an analysis that reveals contribution margin, operating profit, contribution margin as a percentage of revenue, and operating profit as a percentage of revenue.
4. Using the after-FMS data, prepare an analysis that reveals full cost profit margin, operating profit, full cost profit margin as a percentage of revenue, and operating profit as a percentage of revenue.
5. Should the company drop the K5-36 product line? Defend your answer.

Problem 16A-4.
Analysis of
Nonfinancial Data
(L.O. 4)

Henderson Electronics Company was formed in 1952. Over the years the company has become known for its high-quality electronics products and its dependability for on-time delivery. Six months ago management decided to install a flexible manufacturing system for its Electronic Components Department. With the new equipment, the entire component is produced by the FMS so the finished product is ready to be shipped when needed. Following are data the controller's staff gathered during the past eight-week period:

	Weeks							
	1	2	3	4	5	6	7	8
Average process time (hours)	11.9	12.1	11.6	11.8	12.2	12.8	13.2	14.6
Average setup time (hours)	1.5	1.6	1.6	1.8	1.7	1.4	1.2	1.2
Customer complaints	10	9	22	14	8	6	4	5
Delivery time (hours)	26.2	26.4	26.1	25.9	26.2	26.6	27.1	26.4
Equipment utilization rate (%)	97.2	97.1	97.3	98.2	98.4	97.2	97.4	96.3
Machine downtime (hours)	106.4	108.1	120.2	110.4	112.8	102.2	124.6	136.2
Machine maintenance time (hours)	66.8	68.7	74.6	76.2	78.8	68.6	82.4	90.2
Number of inventoried items	3,450	3,510	3,680	3,790	3,620	3,490	3,560	3,260
On-time deliveries (%)	97.2	97.5	97.6	98.2	98.4	96.4	94.8	92.6
Parts scrapped	243	268	279	245	256	280	290	314
Production backlog (units)	10,246	10,288	10,450	10,680	10,880	11,280	11,350	12,100
Production cycle time (hours)	16.5	16.4	16.3	16.1	16.3	17.6	19.8	21.8
Purchase order lead time (hours)	15.2	15.1	14.9	14.6	14.6	13.2	12.4	12.6
Times inventory turnover	2.1	2.3	2.2	2.4	2.2	2.1	2.1	1.9
Warranty claims	4	8	2	1	6	4	2	3

Required

1. Analyze the performance of the Electronic Components Department for the eight-week period, centering your analysis on performance in the following areas:
   a. Product quality
   b. Product delivery
   c. Inventory control
   d. Materials utilization/scrap control
   e. Machine management and maintenance
2. Summarize your findings in a report to the department's superintendent.

Problem 16A-5.
Capital
Expenditure
Decisions and
Automation
(L.O. 6)

Quality golf shoes are the specialty of Bartlett Sports Equipment Company. J. R. Bartlett founded the company in 1967, after seven years on the pro golf tour. Because of his extensive and unique background, Bartlett developed a style of golf shoe that was easy to mass produce and yet had the same qualities of the expensive hand-sewed models.

Demand for the Bartlett golf shoes has been increasing steadily, and the company management is now faced with a decision to either (1) purchase additional equipment similar to what has been used for the past ten to twelve years or (2) invest in a flexible manufacturing system for the golf shoe line. The controller developed the following information for use in deciding whether to invest in the FMS equipment:

Items to Consider in This Capital Expenditure Decision

One-time expenditures:

Six-phased FMS machine cell	$7,231,000
Machine installation costs	87,230
Automatic materials parts-moving equipment	1,892,700

Estimated annual operating costs/revenue changes:

Reduction in scrap costs	$ 43,560
Increased customer satisfaction	10%
Plant painting costs	52,300
Delivery time reduction	15%
Increased machine repairs and maintenance	29,800
Increased employee efficiency	35%
Increased market share	22%
Reduction in delivery costs	23,400
Reduction in direct labor and related benefits	98,420
Reduction in material handling costs	167,900
Reduction in storage costs	34,900
Increased indirect wages and related benefits	146,890
Increased electrical power	32,100
Management profit sharing costs	87,200
FMS computer programming costs	26,840
FMS computer software maintenance costs	45,600
Increased revenue	1,306,400

Current annual operating data:

Product sales revenue	$7,420,000
Processing costs	4,672,800
Delivery costs	989,200
Storage costs	732,100
Material handling costs	723,900

Estimated scrap value at end of life:

Six-phased FMS machine cell	$ 723,100
Automatic materials/parts-moving equipment	189,270

Required

1. Describe the four unique characteristics of FMS or CIM capital expenditure decisions.
2. From the costs listed above, identify those that are to be used in the FMS present value decision computation. Compute the net cash inflow from operations.
3. Assuming a twelve-year life and a 15% discount factor, compute the net present value of the FMS capital expenditure decision. Use total annual cash inflow from operations as the basis for your analysis. Should the capital expenditure be made?
4. What important costs and intangible data did you leave out of your decision analysis? Why?

Problem Set B

Problem 16B-1.
Product Costing in
a Flexible
Manufacturing
System
(L.O. 2, 3)

Slavin Apparel, Inc., specializes in manufacturing business suits for women. The company has three basic suit lines and can produce more than a dozen variations of each basic design. Last year, because of rising backlogs and declining quality, the company installed a flexible manufacturing system for all three suit lines. Operating results to date have been very good, but management would still like to improve its delivery cycle and reduce the cost per unit.

Following are the operating data for October:

Materials:	
Cloth material	$233,600
Lining material	94,900
Sewing supplies	29,200
Materials handling:	
Labor	4,380
Equipment depreciation	3,285
Electrical power	2,190
Maintenance	2,920
Direct labor:	
Machinists	80,300
Pattern design:	
Labor	22,806
Electrical power	5,475
Pattern design overhead	12,775
FMS overhead:	
Equipment depreciation	5,840
Indirect labor	26,280
Supervision	49,640
Operating supplies	13,140
Electrical power	8,760
Repairs and maintenance	7,300
Building occupancy overhead	67,160

October's output totaled 3,650 suits. Each suit requires four machine hours of effort. Materials handling cost is allocated to the product based on unit materials cost; pattern design costs are allocated based on units produced; and FMS overhead is allocated based on machine hours.

Required

1. Compute the following:
   a. Materials handling cost allocation rate
   b. Pattern design cost allocation rate
   c. FMS overhead allocation rate
2. Compute the unit cost of one business suit. Show details of your computation.

Problem 16B-2.
Machine Hours
Versus Labor Hours
(L.O. 2,3)

In 1977, Shelley Boyce and Aron Fleck formed S & A Industries, Inc. The company specializes in recreational furniture for all types of outdoor life. Portable tables are the company's best-selling product, and three models have become very popular products: the Mini, Max, and Deluxe models.

To keep up with the competition, the company purchased flexible manufacturing systems for these product lines about eight months ago. But since the purchase, factory overhead rates have been increasing, to the disappointment of Boyce and Fleck, who have asked the controller to prepare a comparative analysis of this situation.

The following data are from the past month's records:

	Mini	Max	Deluxe
Unit information:			
Raw materials cost	$21	$32	$46
Direct labor hours	2.2	2.8	3.4
Direct labor cost per hour	$16	$16	$16
Machine hours	3.4	3.2	3
Information totals:			
Unit sales during month	120,000	108,000	94,000
Total factory overhead	$2,904,000	$3,024,000	$2,876,400

The company's policy has been to set selling prices at 180 percent of a product's production cost.

Required

1. Compute the company's plantwide factory overhead rate using total direct labor dollars as a basis.
2. Compute each product's total production costs and selling price using the application rate computed in part **1.**
3. Compute a new factory overhead application rate assuming:
   a. Materials storage and handling overhead equal to 10 percent of the cost of raw materials is subtracted from the factory overhead cost totals.
   b. Machine hours is the factory overhead allocation basis.
   c. Product line overhead rates are used rather than a plantwide rate.
4. Compute each product's total production cost and selling price using the allocation rates computed in part **3.**
5. Compare the old and new product selling prices and comment on your findings.

Problem 16B-3.
Full Cost Profit
Margin
(L.O. 5)

Denise Martinez began producing scrap-iron art works seven years ago. Her business became so profitable that she converted to an assembly line approach two years ago. Concerned with continuously rising labor costs, Martinez recently agreed to purchase flexible manufacturing systems for her three largest selling products: the Meadow, Ridge, and Valley assemblies. Martinez is very concerned with the Valley assembly because of its recent poor profitability performance. Following are operating data from before and after the FMS installation:

Martinez Metal Products Company
Product Performance Evaluation

	Meadow Assembly	Ridge Assembly	Valley Assembly
Total revenue	$3,972,000	$6,731,000	$4,262,000
Total operating costs:			
Before FMS installed:			
Direct materials	$ 953,280	$1,750,060	$1,193,360
Direct labor	1,310,760	2,288,540	1,363,840
Variable factory overhead	357,480	336,550	230,148
Variable selling expenses	166,824	289,433	157,694
Variable distribution costs	158,880	403,860	242,934
Fixed factory overhead	461,100	647,700	515,600
Fixed selling expenses	146,100	153,400	166,700
Fixed distribution costs	191,600	299,600	249,800
After FMS installed:			
Direct materials	$ 953,280	$1,750,060	$1,193,360
Materials-related overhead	206,544	363,474	242,934
Direct labor	285,984	457,708	272,768
Indirect labor	278,040	430,784	315,388
Setup labor	190,656	282,702	187,528
Electrical power	71,496	121,158	68,192
Supervision	103,272	188,468	110,812
Repairs and maintenance	135,048	208,661	157,694
Operating supplies/lubricants	31,776	60,579	34,096
Other traceable indirect costs	87,384	141,351	102,288
Traceable selling expenses	150,936	222,123	161,956
Traceable distribution costs	166,824	262,509	183,266
Nontraceable factory overhead	276,300	341,300	253,400
Nontraceable selling and distribution costs	214,200	297,300	209,700

Required

1. Recast the information given for the three products into an analysis that reveals total traceable and total nontraceable costs (a) before and (b) after the FMS was installed.
2. Describe and differentiate between full cost profit margin and contribution margin.
3. Using the before-FMS data, prepare an analysis that reveals contribution margin, operating profit, contribution margin as a percentage of revenue, and operating profit as a percentage of revenue.

4. Using the after-FMS data, prepare an analysis that reveals full cost profit margin, operating profit, full cost profit margin as a percentage of revenue, and operating profit as a percentage of revenue.
5. Should the company drop the Valley assembly? Defend your answer.

Problem 16B-4.
Analysis of
Nonfinancial Data
(L.O. 4)

Heizenga Enterprises, Inc., manufactures several lines of small machinery. Before automated equipment was installed, the total delivery cycle for the Beki machine models averaged about three weeks. Last year management decided to purchase an FMS for the Beki line. The cost was $17,458,340 and included twelve separate work stations producing the four components needed to assemble a finished product. Each machine is linked to the next via an automated conveyor system. Assembly of the four parts, including the machine's entire electrical system, now takes only two hours. Following is a summary of operating data for the past eight weeks for the Beki line:

	Weeks							
	1	2	3	4	5	6	7	8
Average process time (hours)	8.2	8.2	8.1	8.4	8.6	8.2	7.8	7.6
Average setup time (hours)	1.2	1.2	1.1	0.9	0.9	0.8	1	0.9
Customer complaints	4	5	3	6	5	7	8	8
Delivery time (hours)	36.2	37.4	37.2	36.4	35.9	35.8	34.8	34.2
Equipment utilization rate (%)	99.1	99.2	99.4	99.1	98.8	98.6	98.8	98.8
Machine downtime (hours)	82.3	84.2	85.9	84.3	83.4	82.2	82.8	80.4
Machine maintenance time (hours)	52.4	54.8	51.5	48.4	49.2	47.8	46.8	44.9
Number of inventoried items	5,642	5,820	5,690	5,780	5,630	5,510	5,280	5,080
On-time deliveries (%)	92.4	92.5	93.2	94.2	94.4	94.1	95.8	94.6
Parts scrapped	98	96	102	104	100	98.2	98.6	100.6
Production backlog (units)	15,230	15,440	15,200	16,100	14,890	13,560	13,980	13,440
Production cycle time (hours)	12.2	12.6	11.9	11.8	12.2	11.6	11.2	10.6
Purchase order lead time (hours)	26.2	26.8	26.5	25.9	25.7	25.3	24.8	24.2
Times inventory turnover	3.2	3.4	3.4	3.6	3.8	3.8	4.2	4.4
Warranty claims	2	2	3	2	3	4	3	3

Required

1. Analyze the performance of the Beki machine line for the eight-week period, centering your analysis on performance in the following areas:
   a. Product quality
   b. Product delivery
   c. Inventory control
   d. Materials utilization/scrap control
   e. Machine management and maintenance
2. Summarize your findings in a report to the company management.

Problem 16B-5.
Capital
Expenditure
Decisions and
Automation
(L.O. 6)

Olson Manufacturing Company has been producing lawn sprinkler systems for more than fifteen years. Their Green-bug pop-up sprinkler head has the leading market share within the industry. The Green-bug sprinkler is reliable and a high-quality, long-lasting product. To date, the Green-bug has been made by a combination of semiautomatic machines and a hand-assembly operation. Management is considering purchasing a flexible manufacturing system that will produce and assemble the Green-bug sprinkler through an eight-phased operation. Product movement through the FMS will be accomplished by a computerized conveyor system. Because the present equipment is obsolete and worn out, replacement equipment will have to be purchased if the FMS idea is turned down.

To aid in the decision analysis, the chief financial officer developed the following information for use in deciding whether to invest in the FMS:

Items to Consider in This Capital Expenditure Decision

One-time expenditures:	
Eight-phased FMS machine cell	$8,029,000
Machine installation costs	204,500
Automatic materials/parts-moving equipment	1,651,500
Estimated annual operating costs/revenue changes:	
Reduction in scrap costs	$ 126,500
Increased customer satisfaction	12%
Regular plant maintenance costs	79,740
Delivery time reduction	18%
Increased machine repairs and maintenance	45,890
Increased employee efficiency	28%
Increased market share	26%
Reduction in delivery costs	41,560
Reduction in direct labor and related benefits	401,240
Reduction in material handling	237,500
Reduction in storage costs	102,200
Increased indirect wages and related benefits	298,400
Increased electrical power	76,340
Management pension costs	127,200
FMS computer programming costs	131,200
FMS computer software maintenance costs	97,340
Increased revenue	2,247,000
Current annual operating data:	
Product sales revenue	$9,564,300
Processing costs	6,231,800
Delivery costs	1,765,200
Storage costs	1,415,400
Material handling costs	942,600
Estimated scrap value at end of life:	
Eight-phased FMS machine cell	$1,204,350
Automatic materials/parts-moving equipment	247,725

Required

1. Describe the four unique characteristics of FMS or CIM capital expenditure decisions.
2. From the costs above, identify those that are to be used in the FMS present value decision computation. Compute the net cash inflow from operations.
3. Assuming a ten-year life and a 14% discount factor, compute the net present value of the FMS capital expenditure decision. Use total annual cash inflow from the Green-bug operation as the basis for your analysis. Should the capital expenditure be made?
4. What important costs and intangible data did you leave out of your decision analysis? Why?

Management Decision Case

Cooplan Saddle Company
(L.O. 2, 5, 6)

In 1848, Robert Cooper and Robin Kaplan joined forces and made their first horse saddle. Cooper had been a blacksmith for twenty years, and Kaplan was famous throughout Texas for his work with leather. In two short years, the partners were known for making the finest saddle in the entire Southwest. By 1861, the two saddle makers created the Cooplan Saddle Company just outside Dallas. The company has produced saddles continuously since 1861, and today it is world famous for its three types of riding saddles.

The company's current operating process involves two plants; the Dallas plant is responsible for producing the three types of handmade saddles, and the Fort Worth plant applies a special treatment to the leather saddles that provides a long-wearing, satin finish. The Dallas plant uses some machinery for cutting and trimming leather but is highly labor intensive. Fort Worth's operation, on the other hand, is highly automated, and the steam/oil maturing process is done using programmed machinery. The model A1 saddle is made for competitive equestrian riding, model A2 is a decorative western riding saddle, and model A3 is made for long-wear, hard-use cattle ranching work.

The following analysis shows the breakdown of machine hours and labor hours for the three saddles at the two plants:

	Model A1	Model A2	Model A3
Dallas Plant:			
Machine hours	0.2	0.4	0.6
Direct labor hours	3.0	2.0	1.0
Fort Worth Plant:			
Machine hours	2.0	3.0	6.0
Direct labor hours	0.4	0.2	0.1

Other operating data for the two plants:

	Model A1	Model A2	Model A3
Dallas Plant:			
Unit raw materials cost	$92.00	$154.00	$105.00
Hourly labor rate	20.00	20.00	20.00
Fort Worth Plant:			
Unit raw materials cost	12.00	16.00	8.00
Hourly labor rate	14.00	14.00	14.00

Projected overhead costs for next year:

	Dallas Plant	Fort Worth Plant	Totals
Electricity	$ 4,100	$ 9,620	$ 13,720
Water	3,740	2,830	6,570
Heating expense	5,820	3,690	9,510
Operating supplies	8,110	14,280	22,390
Depreciation, machinery	480	13,220	13,700
Depreciation, building	9,320	8,930	18,250
Insurance expense	4,540	5,640	10,180
Property taxes	1,980	3,120	5,100
Research and development*	14,670	480	15,150
Indirect labor	26,900	18,340	45,240
Spoilage	7,740	3,160	10,900
Supervision	44,000	26,000	70,000
Interest expense†	850	5,440	6,290
Miscellaneous costs	1,870	1,310	3,180
Totals	$134,120	$116,060	$250,180

* All research and development costs were incurred in the development of saddle model A4 (designed for military and law-enforcement use).
† Interest expense was allocated to the two plants by top management based on the age and book value of the buildings and equipment.

Expected machine and labor hours per plant:

	Machine Hours	Direct Labor Hours
Dallas Plant:		
Saddle A1 (500):		
(500 × .2 MH)	100	
(500 × 3 DLH)		1,500
Saddle A2 (1,000):		
(1,000 × .4 MH)	400	
(1,000 × 2 DLH)		2,000
Saddle A3 (4,000):		
(4,000 × .6 MH)	2,400	
(4,000 × 1 DLH)		4,000
Subtotals	2,900	7,500

	Machine Hours	Direct Labor Hours
Fort Worth Plant:		
Saddle A1 (500):		
(500 × 2 MH)	1,000	
(500 × .4 DLH)		200
Saddle A2 (1,000):		
(1,000 × 3 MH)	3,000	
(1,000 × .2 DLH)		200
Saddle A3 (4,000):		
(4,000 × 6 MH)	24,000	
(4,000 × .1 DLH)		400
Subtotals	28,000	800
Total projected hours	30,900	8,300

Required

1. Compute projected factory overhead rates based on the following assumptions:
   a. Companywide rates based on direct labor hours and machine hours
   b. Plantwide rates at the Dallas plant based on direct labor hours and on machine hours and at the Fort Worth plant based on direct labor hours and on machine hours
2. Compute product unit costs for the three saddles using
   a. Companywide direct labor hour overhead rate
   b. Companywide machine hour overhead rate
   c. Plantwide rates at the Dallas plant based on direct labor hour rate and at the Fort Worth plant based on machine hour rate
   d. Plantwide rates at the Dallas plant using machine hour rate and at the Fort Worth plant using direct labor hour rate
3. Which set of product costs are correct? Explain your answer.
4. Would your answer to part 3 change if interest expense were treated as a period cost?
5. Is research and development cost properly accounted for? How would you change the approach? Would your suggested change affect your recommendation in part 3? How? (Do not let FASB external reporting standards influence your answer—these reports are for internal use only.)

Special Reports and Analyses of Accounting Information

Because business organizations are so complex today, special reports are needed to present important information about their activities. In order to understand and evaluate financial statements, it is necessary to learn how to analyze them.

Part Six deals with these important special reports and with the analysis of financial statements.

Chapter 17 presents the statement of cash flows, which explains the major operating, financing, and investing activities of a business. The chapter presents this statement using both the direct approach and the indirect approach.

Chapter 18 explains the objectives and techniques of financial statement analysis from the standpoint of the financial analyst.

The Statement of Cash Flows

Earlier in this book you have used the balance sheet, the income statement, and the statement of stockholders' equity. In this chapter, you will learn to prepare a fourth major financial statement: the statement of cash flows. After studying this chapter, you should be able to meet the learning objectives listed on the left.

Each financial statement is useful in specific ways. The balance sheet shows, at a point in time, how management has invested a company's resources in assets, and how these assets are financed by liabilities and owners' equity. The income statement reports how much net income a company earned during the accounting period. The statement of stockholders' equity shows changes in the status of the ownership of a business during the accounting period including the cumulative income retained in the business.

These financial statements are useful and important, but there are important questions that they do not answer. For instance, did a company's operations generate enough cash to pay its dividends? If a company lost money during the year, did it still generate enough cash to pay its liabilities? What new financing and investing activities did the company engage in during the year? In what new assets did the company invest this year? If liabilities were reduced, how were they reduced? Or, if liabilities increased during the year, where were the proceeds invested? Did the company issue common stock during the year, and, if so, what was done with the proceeds?

Why can these questions not be answered by the income statement, balance sheet, or the statement of stockholders' equity? First, because the income statement is prepared on an accrual basis, the effect of operating activities on the cash or liquidity position of the business is not shown. Second, because the balance sheet is a static financial statement, the financing and investing activities that caused changes from one year to the next are not presented. Third, the statement of stockholders' equity discloses only transactions that affect stockholders' equity. To correlate this information, another major financial statement is necessary. Until recently, this need was met by the statement of changes in financial position. This statement, which could be prepared in two ways based on different definitions of funds, showed the sources of funds received by the business and the use of those funds in the business. Historically, the most common way of preparing the statement was to define funds as working capital (current assets minus current liabilities) and to show the

Figure 17-1. Use of Working Capital and Cash Flow Bases by 600 Large Companies

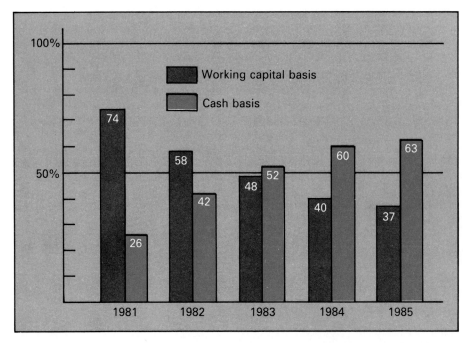

Source: American Institute of Certified Public Accountants, *Accounting Trends and Techniques* (New York, AICPA, 1987), p. 362.

sources and uses of working capital. Another way, which has rapidly become more popular, defines funds as cash and shows the sources and uses of cash. Figure 17-1 shows the change in popularity from 1981 to 1986 from the working capital approach to the cash approach. In 1988, it is estimated that 90 percent of the companies followed the cash approach. Because of the lack of a single definition of funds and the existence of various formats for the statement used, reporting practices by businesses have varied greatly.

To remedy the confusion and lack of comparability that results from these different approaches, the Financial Accounting Standards Board adopted in November 1987 a new statement called the statement of cash flows.[1] This statement is in accord with the FASB's long-held position that a primary objective of financial statements is providing information to investors and creditors on a business's cash flows.[2] This new statement replaces the statement of changes in financial position and is prepared

1. *Statement of Financial Accounting Standards No. 95,* "Statement of Cash Flows" (Stamford, Conn.: Financial Accounting Standards Board, 1987).
2. *Statement of Financial Accounting Concepts No. 1,* "Objectives of Financial Reporting for Business Enterprises" (Stamford, Conn.: Financial Accounting Standards Board, 1978), par. 37–39.

using a uniform format. The statement of cash flows is required every time a company prepares an income statement. The effective date of the requirement is for fiscal years ending after July 15, 1988.

Purposes, Uses and Components of the Statement of Cash Flows

OBJECTIVE 1
Define cash and
cash equivalents,
and describe the
statement of cash
flows

The **statement of cash flows** shows the effects on cash of the operating, investing, and financing activities of a company for an accounting period. It explains the net increase (or decrease) in cash during the accounting period. For purposes of preparing this statement, **cash** is defined to include both cash and cash equivalents. **Cash equivalents** are short-term, highly liquid investments including money market accounts, commercial paper, and U.S. Treasury bills. A company maintains cash equivalents as a vehicle for earning interest while it is temporarily not needed for operations. Suppose, for example, that a company has $1,000,000 that it will not need for thirty days. To earn a return on this sum, the company may place the cash in an account that earns interest (money market accounts); it may loan the cash to another corporation by purchasing that corporation's short-term note (commercial paper); or it might purchase a short-term obligation of the U.S. government (Treasury bill). In this context, short-term is defined as ninety days or less. Since cash and cash equivalents are considered the same, transfers between the cash account and cash equivalents are not treated as cash receipts or cash payments.

Cash equivalents should not be confused with short-term investments or marketable securities, which are not combined with the cash account on the statement of cash flows. Purchases of marketable securities are treated as cash outflows, and sales of marketable securities are treated as cash inflows, on the statement of cash flows. In this chapter, cash will be assumed to include both cash and cash equivalents.

Purposes of the Statement of Cash Flows

OBJECTIVE 2
State the princi-
pal purposes
and uses of the
statement of cash
flows

The primary purpose of the statement is to provide information about a company's cash receipts and cash payments during an accounting period. A secondary purpose is to provide information about a company's investing and financing activities during the accounting period. Some of the information on these activities may be inferred by examining the other financial statements, but it is on the statement of cash flows that all the transactions affecting cash are summarized.

Internal and External Uses of the Statement of Cash Flows

The statement of cash flows is useful internally to management and externally to investors and creditors. Management can use the statement of cash flows to assess the liquidity of the business, to determine dividend policy, and to evaluate the effects of major policy decisions involving investments and financing. In other words, management can use the statement of cash flows for such decisions as determining whether or not short-term financing is necessary to pay its current liabilities, to determine whether to raise or lower its dividends, and to plan its investing and financing needs.

Investors and creditors will find the statement useful in assessing the company's

1. Ability to generate positive future cash flows.
2. Ability to pay its liabilities.
3. Ability to pay dividends.
4. Need for additional financing.

In addition, the statement explains the differences between the net income on the income statement and the net cash flows generated from operations. It shows both cash and noncash effects of investing and financing activities during the accounting period.

Classification of Cash Flows

OBJECTIVE 3
Identify the principal components of the classifications of cash flows, and state the significance of noncash investing and financing transactions

The statement of cash flows classifies cash receipts and cash payments into the categories of operating, investing, and financing activities. The components of these activities are illustrated in Figure 17-2 and summarized below:

1. **Operating activities** include the cash effects of transactions and other events that enter into the determination of net income. Included in this category as cash inflows are cash receipts received from customers for goods and services, and interest and dividends received on loans and investments. Included as cash outflows are cash payments for wages, goods and services, interest, and taxes applied to employees, suppliers, government bodies, and others.

2. **Investing activities** include the acquiring and selling of long-term assets, the acquiring and selling of marketable securities other than cash equivalents, and the making and collecting of loans. Cash inflows include the cash received from selling long-term assets and marketable securities and from collecting loans. Cash outflows include the cash expended for purchases of long-term assets and marketable securities and the cash loaned to borrowers.

3. **Financing activities** include (1) obtaining or returning resources from or to owners and providing them with a return on their investment and (2) obtaining resources from creditors and repaying the amounts borrowed or otherwise settling the obligation. Cash inflows include the proceeds from issues of stocks and from short-term and long-term borrowing. Cash outflows include the repayments of loans and payments to owners, including cash dividends. Treasury stock transactions are also considered financing activities. Repayments of accounts payable or accrued liabilities are not considered repayments of loans under financing activities but are classified as cash outflows under operating activities.

Figure 17-2. Classification of Cash Inflows and Cash Outflows

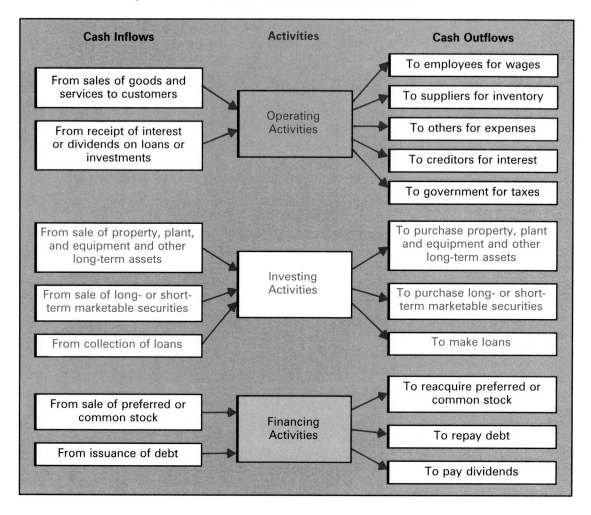

A company will occasionally engage in significant **noncash investing and financing transactions** such as the exchange of a long-term asset for a long-term liability or the settlement of a debt by issuing capital stock. For instance, a company might issue a long-term mortgage for the purchase of land and building, or it might convert long-term bonds into common stock. These transactions represent significant investing and financing activities, but they would not be reflected on the statement of cash flows because they do not involve either cash inflows or cash outflows. However, since one purpose of the statement of cash flows is to show investing and financing activities and since transactions like these will have future effects on cash flows, the FASB has determined that they should be disclosed in a separate schedule to the statement of cash flows. In this way, the reader of the statement will have a complete picture of the investing and financing activities.

Exhibit 17-1. Format for the Statement of Cash Flows

Company Name
Statement of Cash Flows
Period Covered

Cash Flows from Operating Activities
   (list of individual inflows and outflows)   xxx
   Net Cash Flows from Operating Activities   xxx

Cash Flows from Investing Activities
   (list of individual inflows and outflows)   xxx
   Net Cash Flows from Investing Activities   xxx

Cash Flows from Financing Activities
   (list of individual inflows and outflows)   xxx
   Net Cash Flows from Financing Activities   xxx

Net Increase (Decrease) in Cash   xx

Schedule of Noncash Investing and Financing Transactions

(List of individual transactions)   xxx

Format of the Statement of Cash Flows

The general format of the statement of cash flows, shown in Exhibit 17-1, is divided into three categories corresponding to the three activities discussed above. The cash flows from operating activities is followed by cash flows from investing activities and cash flows from financing activities. The individual inflows and outflows from investing and financing activities are shown separately in their respective categories. For instance, cash inflows from sale of property, plant, and equipment are shown separately from the cash outflows for the purchase of property, plant, and equipment. Similarly, cash inflows from borrowing are shown separately from cash outflows to retire loans. A list of noncash transactions appears in the schedule at the bottom of the statement.

Preparing the Statement of Cash Flows

To demonstrate the preparation of the statement of cash flows, an example will be worked step by step. The data for this example are presented in Exhibits 17-2 and 17-3 and consist of the balance sheets for December 31, 19x1 and 19x2 and the 19x2 income statement for Ryan Corporation with additional data about transactions affecting noncurrent accounts during 19x2. Since the changes in the balance sheet accounts will be used in analyzing the various accounts, these changes are entered in Exhibit

| Exhibit 17-2. | Balance Sheets with Changes in Accounts Indicated for Ryan Corporation | | | |

Ryan Corporation
Balance Sheets
December 31, 19x1 and 19x2

	19x2	19x1	Change	Increase or Decrease
Assets				
Current Assets				
Cash	$ 46,000	$ 15,000	$ 31,000	Increase
Accounts Receivable (net)	47,000	55,000	(8,000)	Decrease
Inventory	144,000	110,000	34,000	Increase
Prepaid Expenses	1,000	5,000	(4,000)	Decrease
Total Current Assets	$238,000	$185,000	$ 53,000	
Investments	$115,000	$127,000	$ (12,000)	Decrease
Plant Assets				
Plant Assets	$715,000	$505,000	$210,000	Increase
Accumulated Depreciation	(103,000)	(68,000)	(35,000)	Increase
Total Plant Assets	$612,000	$437,000	$175,000	
Total Assets	$965,000	$749,000	$216,000	
Liabilities				
Current Liabilities				
Accounts Payable	$ 50,000	$ 43,000	$ 7,000	Increase
Accrued Liabilities	12,000	9,000	3,000	Increase
Income Taxes Payable	3,000	5,000	(2,000)	Decrease
Total Current Liabilities	$ 65,000	$ 57,000	$ 8,000	
Long-term Liabilities				
Bonds Payable	$295,000	$245,000	$ 50,000	Increase
Total Liabilities	$360,000	$302,000	$ 58,000	
Stockholders' Equity				
Common Stock, $5 par value	$276,000	$200,000	$ 76,000	Increase
Paid-in Capital in Excess of Par Value	189,000	115,000	74,000	Increase
Retained Earnings	140,000	132,000	8,000	Increase
Total Stockholders' Equity	$605,000	$447,000	$158,000	
Total Liabilities and Stockholders' Equity	$965,000	$749,000	$216,000	

Exhibit 17-3. Income Statement and Other Information
          on Noncurrent Accounts for Ryan Corporation

Ryan Corporation
Income Statement
For the Year Ended December 31, 19x2

Sales		$698,000
Cost of Goods Sold		520,000
Gross Margin		$178,000
Operating Expenses (including Depreciation Expense of $37,000)		147,000
Operating Income		$ 31,000
Other Income (Expenses)		
Interest Expense	$(23,000)	
Interest Income	6,000	
Gain on Sale of Investments	12,000	
Loss on Sale of Plant Assets	(3,000)	(8,000)
Income Before Taxes		$ 23,000
Income Taxes		7,000
Net Income		$ 16,000

Other transactions affecting noncurrent accounts during 19x2:

1. Purchased investments in the amount of $78,000.
2. Sold investments for $102,000. These investments cost $90,000.
3. Purchased plant assets in the amount of $120,000.
4. Sold plant assets that cost $10,000 with accumulated depreciation of $2,000 for $5,000.
5. Issued $100,000 of bonds at face value in a noncash exchange for plant assets.
6. Repaid $50,000 of bonds at face value at maturity.
7. Issued 15,200 shares of $5 par value common stock for $150,000.
8. Paid cash dividends in the amount of $8,000.

17-2. For each individual account, an indication is made as to whether the change is an increase or decrease.

There are four steps in preparing the statement of cash flows:

1. Determining cash flows from operating activities.
2. Determining cash flows from investing activities.
3. Determining cash flows from financing activities.
4. Presenting the information obtained in the first three steps in the form of the statement of cash flows.

Determining Cash Flows from Operating Activities

The income statement indicates the success or failure of a business in earning an income from its operating activities, but it does not reflect the inflow and outflow of cash from operating activities. The reason for this is that the income statement is prepared on an accrual basis. Revenues are recorded even though the cash for them may not have been received, and expenses are incurred and recorded even though cash may not yet have been expended for them. As a result, to arrive at cash flows from operations, one must convert the figures on the income statement from an accrual basis to a cash basis by adjusting the earned revenues to cash received from sales and by adjusting incurred expenses to cash expended, as shown in Figure 17-3.

OBJECTIVE 4(a)
Determine cash flows from operating activities using the direct method

There are two methods of converting the income statement from an accrual basis to a cash basis: the direct method and the indirect method. The **direct method** is accomplished by adjusting each item in the income statement in turn from the accrual basis to the cash basis. The result is a statement that begins with cash receipts from sales, adds interest and dividends received, and then deducts cash payments for purchases, operating expenses, interest payments, and income taxes, to arrive at net cash flows from operating activities, as follows:

Cash Flows from Operating Activities
  Cash Receipts from
    Sales   xxx
    Interest and Dividends Received   xxx   xxx

  Cash Payments for
    Purchases   xxx
    Operating Expenses   xxx
    Interest Payments   xxx
    Income Taxes   xxx   xxx
  Net Cash Flows from Operating Activities   xxx

Figure 17-3. Relationship of Accrual and Cash Bases of Accounting

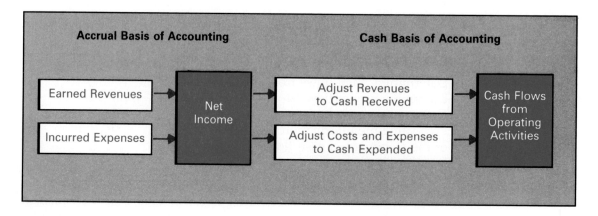

OBJECTIVE 4(b)
Determine cash flows from operating activities using the indirect method

The **indirect method,** on the other hand, does not adjust each item in the income statement individually but begins with net income and lists all the adjustments necessary to convert net income to cash flows from operations, as follows:

Cash Flows from Operating Activities
  Net Income   xxx
    Adjustments to Reconcile Net Income to
    Net Cash Provided by Operating Activities
    (list of individual items)   xxx   xxx
  Net Cash Flows from Operating Activities   xxx

Both approaches produce the same result, and the FASB accepts both methods. However, the FASB recommends that the direct method be used. In the paragraphs that follow, the direct method will be used to illustrate the conversion of the income statement for Ryan Corporation to a cash basis, and the process will be summarized using the indirect method.

Cash Receipts from Sales. Sales result in a positive cash flow for a company. Cash sales are direct increases in the cash flows of the company, but credit sales are not because they are recorded originally as accounts receivable. When they are collected, they become inflows of cash. One cannot, however, assume that credit sales are automatically inflows of cash, because the collections of accounts receivable in any one accounting period are not likely to equal credit sales. Receivables may prove to be uncollectible, sales from a prior period may be collected in the current period, or sales from the current period may be collected next period. For example, if accounts receivable increases from one accounting period to the next, cash receipts from sales will not be as great as sales. On the other hand, if accounts receivable decreases from one accounting period to the next, cash receipts from sales will exceed sales. The relationships among sales, changes in accounts receivable, and cash receipts from sales are reflected in the following transaction.

$$\begin{matrix} \textbf{Cash Receipts} \\ \textbf{from Sales} \end{matrix} = \textbf{Sales} \begin{cases} \textbf{+ Decrease in Accounts Receivable} \\ \text{or} \\ \textbf{− Increase in Accounts Receivable} \end{cases}$$

Refer to the balance sheets and income statement for Ryan Corporation in Exhibits 17-2 and 17-3. Note that sales are $698,000 and accounts receivable decreased by $8,000 in 19x2. Thus, cash received from sales is $706,000, calculated as follows:

$$\$706,000 = \$698,000 + \$8,000$$

Ryan Corporation collected $8,000 more from sales than it sold during the year. This relationship may be illustrated as follows:

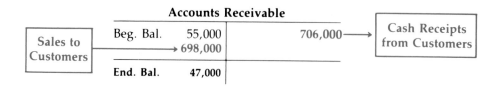

If Ryan Corporation had unearned revenues or advances from customers, an adjustment would be made for changes in these items as well.

Cash Receipts from Interest and Dividends Received. Although interest and dividends received are most closely associated with investment activity and are often called investment income, the FASB has decided to classify the cash received from these items as operating activities. To simplify the examples in this text, it is assumed that interest income equals interest received and that dividend income equals dividends received. Thus, from Exhibit 17-3, cash received from interest received for Ryan Corporation is assumed to equal $6,000, the amount of interest income.

Cash Payments for Purchases. Cost of goods sold from the income statement must be adjusted for changes in two balance sheet accounts to arrive at cash payments for purchases. First, cost of goods sold must be adjusted for changes in inventory to arrive at net purchases. Then, net purchases must be adjusted for the change in accounts payable to arrive at cash payments for purchases. If inventory has increased from one accounting period to another, net purchases will be more than cost of goods sold, and if inventory has decreased, net purchases will be less than cost of goods sold. Conversely, if accounts payable has increased, cash payments for purchases will be less than net purchases, and if accounts payable has decreased, cash payments for purchases will be more than net purchases. These relationships may be stated in equation form as follows:

$$\text{Cash Payments for Purchases} = \text{Cost of Goods Sold} \left\{ \begin{array}{c} + \text{ Increase in Inventory} \\ \text{or} \\ - \text{ Decrease in Inventory} \end{array} \right\} \left\{ \begin{array}{c} + \text{ Decrease in Accounts Payable} \\ \text{or} \\ - \text{ Increase in Accounts Payable} \end{array} \right.$$

From Exhibits 17-2 and 17-3, cost of goods sold is $520,000, inventory increased by $34,000, and accounts payable increased by $7,000. Thus, cash payments for purchases is $547,000, calculated as follows:

$$\$547,000 = \$520,000 + \$34,000 - \$7,000$$

In this example, Ryan Corporation purchased $34,000 more inventory than it sold, and it paid out $7,000 less in cash than it purchased. The net result is that cash payments for purchases exceeded cost of goods sold by $27,000 ($547,000 − $520,000). These relationships may be visualized as follows:

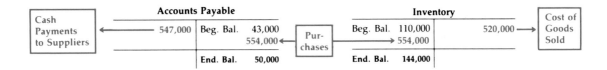

Cash Payments for Operating Expenses. Just as cost of goods sold does not represent the amount of cash paid for purchases during an accounting period, operating expenses does not match the amount of cash paid to employees, suppliers, and others for goods and services. Three adjustments must be made to operating expenses to arrive at the cash flows. The first adjustment is for changes in prepaid expenses such as prepaid insurance or prepaid rent. If prepaid assets increase during the accounting period, more cash will have been paid out than appears on the income statement in the form of expenses. If prepaid assets decrease, more expenses will appear on the income statement than cash spent.

The second adjustment is for changes in liabilities resulting from accrued expenses such as wages payable and payroll taxes payable. If accrued liabilities increase during the accounting period, operating expenses on the income statement will be more than the cash spent. And if accrued liabilities decrease, operating expenses will be less than the cash spent.

The third adjustment is made because certain expenses do not require a current outlay of cash, and so they must be subtracted from operating expenses to arrive at cash payments for operating expenses. The most common expenses in this category are depreciation expense, amortization expense, and depletion expense. The expenditures for plant assets, intangibles, and natural resources occur when they are purchased, and they are classified as an investing activity at that time. Depreciation expense, amortization expense, and depletion expense are simply allocations of the costs of those original purchases to the current accounting period and do not affect cash flows in the current period. For example, Ryan Corporation recorded 19x2 depreciation expense, as follows:

Depreciation Expense	37,000	
Accumulated Depreciation		37,000
To record depreciation on plant assets		

No cash payment is made in this transaction. Thus, to the extent that operating expenses include depreciation and similar items, an adjustment is needed to reduce operating expenses to the amount of cash expended. These three adjustments are summarized in the following equation.

$$
\begin{array}{l}
\text{Cash Payments} \\
\text{for Operating} \\
\text{Expenses}
\end{array}
=
\begin{array}{l}
\text{Operating} \\
\text{Expenses}
\end{array}
\left\{
\begin{array}{l}
+\ \text{Increase in} \\
\quad \text{Prepaid} \\
\quad \text{Expenses} \\
\quad\quad \text{or} \\
-\ \text{Decrease in} \\
\quad \text{Prepaid} \\
\quad \text{Expenses}
\end{array}
\right\}
\left\{
\begin{array}{l}
+\ \text{Decrease in} \\
\quad \text{Accrued} \\
\quad \text{Liabilities} \\
\quad\quad \text{or} \\
-\ \text{Increase in} \\
\quad \text{Accrued} \\
\quad \text{Liabilities}
\end{array}
\right\}
\left\{
\begin{array}{l}
-\ \text{Depreciation} \\
\quad \text{and Other Non-} \\
\quad \text{cash Expenses}
\end{array}
\right.
$$

From Exhibits 17-2 and 17-3, operating expenses (including depreciation of $37,000) were $147,000, prepaid expenses decreased by $4,000, and accrued liabilities increased by $3,000. As a result, the cash payments for operating expenses are $103,000, computed as follows:

$$\$103{,}000 = \$147{,}000 - \$4{,}000 - \$3{,}000 - \$37{,}000$$

If prepaid expenses and accrued liabilities that are not related to specific operating expenses exist, they are not to be used in these computations. An example of such a case is income taxes payable, which is the accrued liability related to income taxes expense. The cash payment for income taxes is discussed in a later section.

Cash Payments for Interest. The FASB classifies cash payments for interest as operating activities in spite of the fact that some authorities argue that they should be considered financing activities because of their association with loans incurred to finance the business. The FASB feels that interest expense is a cost of operating the business. We follow the FASB position in this text. Also, for the sake of simplicity, all examples in this text assume that interest payments are equal to interest expense on the income statement. Thus, from Exhibit 17-3, Ryan Corporation's interest payments are assumed to be $23,000 in 19x2.

Cash Payments for Income Taxes. The amount for income taxes expense that appears on the income statement rarely equals the amount of income taxes actually paid during the year. One reason for this difference is that the final payments for the income taxes in one year are not due until sometime in the following year. A second reason is that there may be differences between what is deducted from, or included in, income for accounting purposes and what is included or deducted for purposes of calculating income tax liability. The latter reason often results in a deferred income tax liability. Here, we deal only with the changes that result from increases or decreases in income taxes payable. To determine cash payments for income taxes, income taxes expense on the income statement is adjusted by the change in income taxes payable. If income taxes payable increased during the accounting period, the cash payments for taxes will be less than the expense on the income statement. If the income taxes payable decreased, the cash payments for taxes will be more than the income taxes on the income statement. In other words, the following equation is applicable.

$$\begin{matrix} \text{Cash Payments for} \\ \text{Income Taxes} \end{matrix} = \begin{matrix} \text{Income} \\ \text{Taxes} \end{matrix} \left\{ \begin{matrix} + \text{ Decrease in Income Taxes Payable} \\ \text{or} \\ - \text{ Increase in Income Taxes Payable} \end{matrix} \right.$$

From Exhibits 17-2 and 17-3, Ryan Corporation has income taxes on the income statement of $7,000 and a decrease of $2,000 in income taxes payable on the balance sheet. As a result, the cash payments for income taxes during 19x2 are $9,000, calculated as follows:

$$\$9{,}000 = \$7{,}000 + \$2{,}000$$

Other Income and Expenses. In computing cash flows from operations, some items classified on the income statement as other income and expenses are not considered operating items because they are more closely related to financing and investing activities than to operating activities. These items must be analyzed individually to determine their proper classification on the statement of cash flows. For instance, interest income and interest expense on Ryan Corporation's income statement have already been dealt with as operating activities. However, the effects on cash flows of gains and losses are considered with the item that gave rise to the gain or loss. The effects of gains or losses on the sale of assets are considered with investing activities, and the effects of gains or losses related to liabilities are considered with financing activities. Consequently, the effects of the gain on sale of investments and of the loss on sale of plant assets on Ryan Corporation's income statement are considered under cash flows from investing activities.

Schedule of Cash Flows from Operating Activities—Direct Method. It is now possible to prepare a schedule of cash flows from operations using the direct method and the calculations made in the preceding paragraphs. In Exhibit 17-4, Ryan Corporation has Cash Receipts from Sales and Interest Received of $712,000 and Cash Payments for Purchases, Operating Expenses, Interest Payments, and Income Taxes of $682,000, resulting in Net Cash Flows from Operating Activities of $30,000 in 19x2.

Schedule of Cash Flows from Operating Activities—Indirect Method. It is also possible to calculate net cash flows from operations using the indirect method, shown in Exhibit 17-5. Note that Net Cash Flows from Operating Activities is the same as it was under the direct method (Exhibit 17-4). Under the indirect method, the same adjustments for the changes in current assets and current liabilities are made as under the direct

---

Exhibit 17-4. Schedule of Cash Flows from Operating Activities—Direct Method

Ryan Corporation
Schedule of Cash Flows from Operating Activities
For the Year Ended December 31, 19x2

Cash Flows from Operating Activities		
Cash Receipts from		
Sales	$706,000	
Interest Received	6,000	$712,000
Cash Payments for		
Purchases	$547,000	
Operating Expenses	103,000	
Interest Payments	23,000	
Income Taxes	9,000	682,000
Net Cash Flows from Operating Activities		$ 30,000

Exhibit 17-5. Schedule of Cash Flows from Operating Activities—Indirect Method

Ryan Corporation
Schedule of Cash Flows from Operating Activities
For the Year Ended December 31, 19x2

Cash Flows from Operating Activities		
Net Income		$16,000
Adjustments to Reconcile Net Income to		
Net Cash Flows from Operating Activities		
Depreciation	$37,000	
Gain on Sale of Investments	(12,000)	
Loss on Sale of Plant Assets	3,000	
Decrease in Accounts Receivable	8,000	
Increase in Inventory	(34,000)	
Decrease in Prepaid Expenses	4,000	
Increase in Accounts Payable	7,000	
Increase in Accrued Liabilities	3,000	
Decrease in Income Taxes Payable	(2,000)	14,000
Net Cash Flows from Operating Activities		$30,000

method, except that they are all made as additions to or subtractions from net income instead of as adjustments to the individual income statement items.   For instance, under the direct method above, the decrease in Accounts Receivable was added to Sales to adjust sales from the accrual basis to the cash basis.   Since sales is included in the computation of net income, the same effect is achieved by adding the decrease in Accounts Receivable to Net Income.   The same logic applies to adjustments to Cost of Goods Sold, Operating Expenses, and Income Taxes, except that the signs will be opposite for these adjustments.   The following table summarizes these adjustments.

	Adjustments to Convert Net Income to Net Cash Flows from Operating Activities	
	Add to Net Income	Deduct from Net Income
Current Assets		
Accounts Receivable (net)	Decrease	Increase
Inventory	Decrease	Increase
Prepaid Expenses	Decrease	Increase
Current Liabilities		
Accounts Payable	Increase	Decrease
Accrued Liabilities	Increase	Decrease
Income Taxes Payable	Increase	Decrease

Net income must also be adjusted for expenses such as depreciation expense, amortization expense, depletion expense, and other income and expenses in accordance with the same logic as used in the preceding discussion. These items are to be added or deducted according to the following schedule:

	Adjustments to Convert Net Income to Net Cash Flows from Operating Activities
	Add to (Deduct from) Net Income
Depreciation Expense	Add
Amortization Expense	Add
Depletion Expense	Add
Losses	Add
Gains	Deduct

Note that these adjustments to net income are made for several reasons. Depreciation expense is added because it is a noncash expense that was deducted in the income statement to arrive at net income. Adjustments are made for gains and losses because of reasons that will become clear when investing and financing activities are discussed in the next section. The additions or deductions for the increases and decreases in current assets and current liabilities are included because each is necessary to adjust an income statement item from the accrual basis to the cash basis.

Determining Cash Flows from Investing Activities

OBJECTIVE 5(a)
Determine cash flows from investing activities

The second step in preparation of the statement of cash flows is determining cash flows from investing activities. The procedure followed in this step is to examine individually the accounts that involve cash receipts and cash payments from investing activities. The objective in each case is to explain the change in the account balance from one year to the next.

Investing activities center around the long-term assets on the balance sheet, but they also include transactions affecting short-term investments from the current asset section of the balance sheet and investment income from the income statement. From the balance sheet in Exhibit 17-2, Ryan Corporation has long-term assets of investments and plant assets, but it does not have short-term investments. From the income statement in Exhibit 17-3, it has investment income in the form of interest income and a gain on sale of investments. Also, from Exhibit 17-3, the following five items pertain to investing activities that took place during 19x2:

1. Purchased investments in the amount of $78,000.
2. Sold investments that cost $90,000 for $102,000, resulting in a gain of $12,000.
3. Purchased plant assets in the amount of $120,000.
4. Sold plant assets that cost $10,000 with accumulated depreciation of $2,000 for $5,000, resulting in a loss of $3,000.

5. Issued bonds at face value in the amount of $100,000 in a noncash exchange for plant assets.

The following paragraphs analyze the accounts related to investing activities for the purpose of determining their effects on cash flows.

Investments. The objective here is to explain the $12,000 decrease in investments (from Exhibit 17-2) by analyzing the increases and decreases in investments and determining the effects on the Cash account.   Purchases increase investments, and sales decrease investments.   Item **1** above shows purchases of $78,000 during 19x2.   This transaction is recorded as follows:

Investments	78,000	
Cash		78,000
To record purchase of investments		

The effect of this transaction is a $78,000 decrease in cash flows.
   Item **2** above shows a sale of investments at a gain.   It is recorded as follows:

Cash	102,000	
Investments		90,000
Gain on Sale of Investments		12,000
To record sale of investments for a gain		

The effect of this transaction is a $102,000 increase in cash flows.   Note that the gain on sale of investments is included in the $102,000.   This is the reason it was excluded earlier from the income statement in computing cash flows from operations.   If it had been left in that section, it would have been counted twice.
   The $12,000 decrease in the Investments account during 19x2 has now been explained, as may be seen in the following T account:

Investments			
Beg. Bal.	127,000	Sales	90,000
Purchases	78,000		
End. Bal.	115,000		

The cash flow effects from these transactions will be shown under cash flows from investing activities on the statement of cash flows as follows:

Purchase of Investments	$ (78,000)
Sale of Investments	102,000

Note that both purchases and sales are disclosed separately as cash outflows and cash inflows.   They are not netted against each other into a single figure.   This disclosure gives the reader of the statement a more complete view of this investing activity.

If Ryan Corporation had short-term investments or marketable securities, the analysis of cash flows would be the same as is presented in this
section for the Investments account.

Plant Assets. In the case of plant assets, it is necessary to explain the
changes in both the asset account and the related accumulated depreciation
account.   From Exhibit 17-2, Plant Assets increased by $210,000 and
Accumulated Depreciation increased by $35,000.   Purchases increase plant
assets, and sales decrease plant assets.   Accumulated Depreciation is
increased by the amount of depreciation expense and is decreased by the
removal of the accumulated depreciation associated with plant assets that
are sold.   There are three items listed in Exhibit 17-3 that affect plant
assets.   Item **3** indicates that Ryan Corporation purchased plant assets in
the amount of $120,000 during 19x2, as shown by this entry:

Plant Assets	120,000	
Cash		120,000
To record purchase of plant assets		

This transaction results in a cash outflow of $120,000.
      Item **4** states that Ryan Corporation sold plant assets for $5,000 that
had cost $10,000 and which had accumulated depreciation of $2,000.   The
entry to record this transaction is

Cash	5,000	
Accumulated Depreciation	2,000	
Loss on Sale of Plant Assets	3,000	
Plant Assets		10,000
To record sale of plant assets at a loss		

Note in this transaction that the positive cash flow is equal to the amount
of cash received, or $5,000.   The loss on sale of plant assets is considered
here rather than in the operating activities section, where it was deleted
from the income statement when computing cash flows from operating
activities.   The amount of loss or gain on the sale of an asset is determined
by the amount of cash received.
      The disclosure of the two preceding transactions in the investing
activities section of the statement of cash flows is as follows:

Purchase of Plant Assets	$(120,000)
Sale of Plant Assets	5,000

As with investment activities, cash outflows and cash inflows are not
netted but are presented separately to give full information to the statement
reader.
      Item **5** is a noncash exchange that affects two long-term accounts, Plant
Assets and Bonds Payable.   It is recorded as follows:

Plant Assets	100,000	
Bonds Payable		100,000
Issued bonds at face value for plant assets		

Although this transaction is not an inflow or outflow of cash, it is a significant transaction involving an investing activity (purchase of plant assets) and a financing activity (issue of bonds payable). Because one purpose of the statement of cash flows is to show important investing and financing activities, it is listed in a separate schedule accompanying the statement, as follows:

Schedule of Noncash Investing and Financing Transactions

Issue of Bonds Payable for Plant Assets $100,000

Using these transactions and the depreciation expense of $37,000 for plant assets, all the changes in the plant assets accounts are now accounted for, as shown in these T accounts:

Plant Assets

Beg. Bal.	505,000	Sale	10,000
Purchase	120,000		
Noncash Purchase	100,000		
End. Bal.	**715,000**		

Accumulated Depreciation

Sale	2,000	Beg. Bal.	68,000
		Dep. Exp.	37,000
		End. Bal.	**103,000**

If the balance sheet includes specific plant asset accounts such as Buildings and Equipment and their related accumulated depreciation accounts, and other long-term asset accounts such as intangibles or natural resources, the analyses would be the same.

The changes in all the asset accounts for Ryan Corporation are now explained, and the treatment of investment income has been presented. It is now possible to move to the financing activities.

Determining Cash Flows from Financing Activities

OBJECTIVE 5(b)
Determine cash flows from financing activities

The third step in preparation of the statement of cash flows is determining cash flows from financing activities. The procedure followed in this step is the same as that applied to the analysis of investing activities, including related gains and/or losses, except that the accounts to be analyzed are the long-term liability accounts and the stockholders' equity accounts. Also to be taken into account are cash dividends from the statement of stockholders' equity. From Exhibit 17-3, the following four items from 19x2 pertain to financing activities:

5. Issued $100,000 of bonds at face value in a noncash exchange for plant assets.
6. Repaid $50,000 of bonds at face value at maturity.
7. Issued 15,200 shares of $5 par value common stock for $150,000.
8. Paid cash dividends in the amount of $8,000.

Bonds Payable. From Exhibit 17-2, Bonds Payable increased by $50,000 and is affected by Items **5** and **6** above. Item **5** was analyzed previously under plant assets as it pertains to both plant assets and bonds payable. It is reported on the schedule of noncash investing and financing transactions, but it must be remembered here in preparing the T account for Bonds Payable. Item **6** results in a cash outflow, as can be seen in the following transaction:

Bonds Payable	50,000	
Cash		50,000
To record repayment of bonds at face value at maturity		

This cash outflow is shown in the financing activities section of the statement of cash flows as follows:

Repayment of Bonds $(50,000)

With knowledge of these transactions, the change in the Bonds Payable account is explained as follows:

Bonds Payable

Repayment	50,000	Beg. Bal.	245,000
		Noncash Issue	100,000
		End. Bal.	**295,000**

If Ryan Corporation had notes payable, either short-term or long-term, the same analysis would be used as presented here for Bonds Payable.

Common Stock. As with plant assets, related stockholders' equity accounts should be analyzed together. For example, Paid-in Capital in Excess of Par Value should be examined together with Common Stock. For Ryan Corporation, Common Stock increased by $76,000 and Paid-in Capital in Excess of Par Value increased by $74,000. These increases are explained by Item **7**, which states that Ryan Corporation issued 15,200 shares of stock for $150,000. The entry to record this cash inflow follows:

Cash	150,000	
Common Stock		76,000
Paid-in Capital in Excess of Par Value		74,000
Issue of 15,200 shares of $5 par value common stock		

This cash inflow is shown in the cash flows from financing activities section of the statement of cash flows as follows:

Issue of Common Stock $150,000

This transaction is all that is needed to explain the changes in these accounts during 19x2, as follows:

Common Stock

	Beg. Bal.	200,000
	Issue	76,000
	End. Bal.	276,000

Paid-in Capital in Excess of Par Value

	Beg. Bal.	115,000
	Issue	74,000
	End. Bal.	189,000

Retained Earnings. At this point in the analysis, there are several items already dealt with that affect Retained Earnings. For instance, in the case of Ryan Corporation, net income was used as part of the analysis of cash flows from operating activities. The only other item (Item 8) affecting the retained earnings of Ryan Corporation is cash dividends during 19x2 of $8,000, as reflected by the following entry:

Retained Earnings   8,000
  Cash   8,000
      To record cash dividend for 19x2

Ryan Corporation may have declared the dividend before paying it and debited the Dividends Declared account instead of Retained Earnings, but after paying the dividend and closing the Dividends Declared account to Retained Earnings, the effect is as shown. Cash dividends are displayed in the financing activities section of the statement of cash flows as follows:

Dividends Paid $(8,000)

The change in the Retained Earnings account is explained as follows:

Retained Earnings

Dividends	8,000	Beg. Bal.	132,000
		Net Income	16,000
		End. Bal.	140,000

Presenting the Information in the Form of the Statement of Cash Flows

OBJECTIVE 6
Prepare a statement of cash flows using the (a) direct and (b) indirect methods

At this point in the analysis, all income statement items have been analyzed, all balance sheet changes have been explained, and all additional information has been taken into account. The resulting information may now be assembled into a statement of cash flows for Ryan Corporation, as shown in Exhibit 17-6. The direct approach is used because the operating activities section contains the data from Exhibit 17-4, which shows the net cash flows from operating activities determined by the direct approach. The statement is just as easily prepared using the

---

Exhibit 17-6. Statement of Cash Flows—Direct Method

Ryan Corporation
Statement of Cash Flows
For the Year Ended December 31, 19x2

Cash Flows from Operating Activities		
Cash Receipts from		
Sales	$706,000	
Interest Received	6,000	$712,000
Cash Payments for		
Purchases	$547,000	
Operating Expenses	103,000	
Interest Payments	23,000	
Income Taxes	9,000	682,000
Net Cash Flows from Operating Activities		$ 30,000
Cash Flows from Investing Activities		
Purchase of Investments	$(78,000)	
Sale of Investments	102,000	
Purchase of Plant Assets	(120,000)	
Sale of Plant Assets	5,000	
Net Cash Flows Used by Investing Activities		(91,000)
Cash Flows from Financing Activities		
Repayment of Bonds	$(50,000)	
Issue of Common Stock	150,000	
Dividends Paid	(8,000)	
Net Cash Flows from Financing Activities		92,000
Net Increase (Decrease) in Cash		$ 31,000

Schedule of Noncash Investing and Financing Transactions

Issue of Bonds Payable for Plant Assets	$100,000

Exhibit 17-7. Statement of Cash Flows—Indirect Method

Ryan Corporation
Statement of Cash Flows
For the Year Ended December 31, 19x2

Cash Flows from Operating Activities		
Net Income		$ 16,000
Adjustments to Reconcile Net Income to Net Cash Flows from Operating Activities		
Depreciation	$ 37,000	
Gain on Sale of Investments	(12,000)	
Loss on Sale of Plant Assets	3,000	
Decrease in Accounts Receivable	8,000	
Increase in Inventory	(34,000)	
Decrease in Prepaid Expenses	4,000	
Increase in Accounts Payable	7,000	
Increase in Accrued Liabilities	3,000	
Decrease in Income Taxes Payable	(2,000)	14,000
Net Cash Flows from Operating Activities		$ 30,000
Cash Flows from Investing Activities		
Purchase of Investments	$(78,000)	
Sale of Investments	102,000	
Purchase of Plant Assets	(120,000)	
Sale of Plant Assets	5,000	
Net Cash Flows Used by Investing Activities		(91,000)
Cash Flows from Financing Activities		
Repayment of Bonds	$(50,000)	
Issue of Common Stock	150,000	
Dividends Paid	(8,000)	
Net Cash Flows from Financing Activities		92,000
Net Increase (Decrease) in Cash		$ 31,000

Schedule of Noncash Investing and Financing Transactions

Issue of Bonds Payable for Plant Assets	$100,000

indirect approach with the data in Exhibit 17-5; this approach is presented in Exhibit 17-7.   The only difference in these two statements is the approach used in the operating activities sections.   The Schedule of Noncash Investing and Financing Transactions is presented below each statement.

In *Statement No. 95*, the FASB states a preference for the direct method form of the statement of cash flows but allows companies to use the indirect method form if they wish.   When the direct method is used, a schedule explaining the difference between reported net income and cash flows from operating activities must be provided. An acceptable format for this schedule is the cash flows from operating activities section of the indirect method form as shown in Exhibit 17-5 or 17-7.

Interpretation of the Statement of Cash Flows

OBJECTIVE 7
Interpret the
statement of cash
flows

Now that the statement is prepared, it is important to know how to interpret and use it. What can one learn about Ryan Corporation and its management by reading its statement of cash flows?

Starting with the first section of the statement in Exhibit 17-6 or 17-7, note that Ryan Corporation generated net cash flows from operating activities of $30,000, which compares very favorably with the net income of $16,000. From Exhibit 17-7, the largest positive factor is the depreciation expense of $37,000. This is an expense that did not require a current cash outlay and is an important cause of the difference between net income and cash flows from operating activities.

The largest drain on cash in the operating activities section is the $34,000 increase in inventory. Management may want to explore ideas of reducing inventory during the next year, unless this increase was for increased sales activities next year. Other changes in current assets and current liabilities, except for the small decrease in income taxes payable, have positive effects on cash flows in this section.

Investors and creditors may want to compare net cash flows from operating activities to dividends paid in the financing activities section to determine if the company has adequate cash flows from operations to cover its payments to investors. Ryan Corporation is in good condition in this regard. Dividends paid are $8,000, compared to $30,000 in net cash flows from operating activities. The additional funds of $22,000 are available for other purposes and serve as a cushion for the payment of dividends.

Moving to the investing activities, it is apparent that the company is expanding because there is a net cash outflow of $91,000 in this section. The company has expanded by purchasing plant assets of $120,000. Various other investing activities have reduced the cash need to $91,000. This is not the whole story on the expansion of the business, however, because the schedule of noncash investing and financing transactions reveals that the company bought another $100,000 in plant assets by issuing bonds. In other words, total purchases of plant assets were $220,000. Part of this expansion was financed by issuing bonds in exchange for plant assets, and most of the rest was financed through other financing activities.

Net cash flows of $92,000 were provided by financing activities to offset most of the $91,000 net cash flows needed from the investing activities section. The company looked to its owners for this financing by issuing common stock for $150,000, while repaying $50,000 in bonds payable. Taking into account the noncash transaction, bonds payable increased by $50,000.

In summary, Ryan Corporation has paid for its expansion with a combination of cash flows from operating activities, net sales of investment assets, issuance of common stock, and a net increase in bonds payable.

Preparing the Work Sheet

OBJECTIVE 8

Prepare a work sheet for the statement of cash flows

Previous sections illustrated the preparation of the statement of cash flows for Ryan Corporation, a relatively simple company. To assist in preparation of the statement of cash flows in more complex companies, accountants have developed a work sheet approach. The work sheet approach is a special format that allows for the systematic analysis of all the changes in the balance sheet accounts to arrive at the statement of cash flows. In this section, this procedure is demonstrated by preparing the statement of cash flows for Ryan Corporation. The work sheet approach uses the indirect approach to determining cash flows from operating activities because this approach adjusts net income for the changes in each balance sheet account instead of adjusting each item individually in the income statement.

Procedures in Preparing the Work Sheet

The work sheet for Ryan Corporation is presented in Exhibit 17-8. The work sheet has four columns labeled as follows:

Column A: Description

Column B: Account balances at the end of the prior year (19x1)

Column C: Analysis of transactions for the current year

Column D: Account balances at the end of the current year (19x2)

The following steps are followed in the preparation of the work sheet. As you read each one, refer to Exhibit 17-8.

1. Enter the account names from the balance sheet (Exhibit 17-2 on page 680) in column A. Note that all accounts with debit balances are listed first, followed by all accounts with credit balances.
2. Enter the account balances for 19x1 in column B and the account balances for 19x2 in column D. In each column, total the debits and the credits. The total debits should equal the total credits in each column. This is a check on whether or not you transferred all the accounts from the balance sheet correctly.
3. Below the data entered in Step 2, insert the captions: Cash Flows from Operating Activities; Cash Flows from Investing Activities; and Cash Flows from Financing Activities, leaving several lines of space after each one. As you do the analysis, write the results in the appropriate categories.
4. Analyze the changes in each balance sheet account using information from both the income statement (see Exhibit 17-3) and from other appropriate transactions. The procedures for this analysis are in the following section. Enter the results in the debit and credit columns

Exhibit 17-8. Work Sheet for the Statement of Cash Flows

Ryan Corporation
Work Sheet for Statement of Cash Flows
For the Year Ended December 31, 19x2

Description	Account Balances 12/31/x1	Analysis of Transactions Debit		Analysis of Transactions Credit		Account Balances 12/31/x2
Debits						
Cash	15,000	(x)	31,000			46,000
Accounts Receivable (net)	55,000			(b)	8,000	47,000
Inventory	110,000	(c)	34,000			144,000
Prepaid Expenses	5,000			(d)	4,000	1,000
Investments	127,000	(h)	78,000	(i)	90,000	115,000
Plant Assets	505,000	(j)	120,000	(k)	10,000	715,000
		(l)	100,000			
Total Debits	817,000					1,068,000
Credits						
Accumulated Depreciation	68,000	(k)	2,000	(m)	37,000	103,000
Accounts Payable	43,000			(e)	7,000	50,000
Accrued Liabilities	9,000			(f)	3,000	12,000
Income Taxes Payable	5,000	(g)	2,000			3,000
Bonds Payable	245,000	(n)	50,000	(l)	100,000	295,000
Common Stock	200,000			(o)	76,000	276,000
Paid-in Capital	115,000			(o)	74,000	189,000
Retained Earnings	132,000	(p)	8,000	(a)	16,000	140,000
Total Credits	817,000		425,000		425,000	1,068,000
Cash Flows from Operating Activities						
Net Income		(a)	16,000			
Decrease in Accounts Receivable		(b)	8,000			
Increase in Inventory				(c)	34,000	
Decrease in Prepaid Expenses		(d)	4,000			
Increase in Accounts Payable		(e)	7,000			
Increase in Accrued Liabilities		(f)	3,000			
Decrease in Income Taxes Payable				(g)	2,000	
Gain on Sale of Investments				(i)	12,000	
Loss on Sale of Plant Assets		(k)	3,000			
Depreciation Expense		(m)	37,000			
Cash Flows from Investing Activities						
Purchase of Investments				(h)	78,000	
Sale of Investments		(i)	102,000			
Purchase of Plant Assets				(j)	120,000	
Sale of Plant Assets		(k)	5,000			
Cash Flows from Financing Activities						
Repayment of Bonds				(n)	50,000	
Issue of Common Stock		(o)	150,000			
Dividends Paid				(p)	8,000	
			335,000		304,000	
Net Increase in Cash				(x)	31,000	
			335,000		335,000	

(A) (B) (C) (D)

in column C.   Identify each item with a letter.   On the first line identify the change in cash with an (x).   In a complex situation, these letters will reference a list of explanations on another working paper.

5. When all the changes in the balance sheet accounts have been explained, add the debit and credit columns in both the top and bottom portions of column C.   The debit and credit columns in the top portion should equal each other.   They should not be equal in the bottom portion. If no errors have been made, the difference in the bottom portion should equal the increase or decrease in the cash account identified with an (x) on the first line of the work sheet.   Add this difference to the lesser of the two columns, and identify it as either an increase or decrease in cash.   Label the change with an (x) and compare it with the change in cash on the first line of the work sheet, also labeled (x). The amounts should be equal, as they are in Exhibit 17-8, where the net increase in cash is $31,000.

After completing the work sheet, the statement of cash flows may be prepared by using the information in the lower half of the work sheet, as shown previously in Exhibit 17-7.

Analyzing the Changes in Balance Sheet Accounts

The most important step in the preparation of the work sheet is the analysis of the changes in the balances of the balance sheet accounts. Although there are a number of transactions and reclassifications in this work sheet to analyze and record, the overall procedure is systematic and not so complicated.   These overall procedures are as follows:

1. Record net income.
2. Account for changes in current assets and current liabilities.
3. Account for changes in noncurrent accounts using the information about other transactions.
4. Reclassify any other income and expense items not already dealt with. In the following explanations, the identification letters refer to the corresponding transactions and reclassifications in the work sheet.

   a. *Net Income.* Net income results in an increase in Retained Earnings.   It is also the starting point under the indirect method for determining cash flows from operating activities.   Under this method, additions and deductions are made to net income to arrive at cash flows from operating activities.   Work sheet entry **a** is as follows:

      (a) Cash Flows from Operations: Net Income   16,000
              Retained Earnings   16,000

   b.–g. *Changes in Current Assets and Current Liabilities.* Entries **b** to **g** record the effects of the changes in current assets and current liabilities on cash flow.   In each case, there is a debit or credit to the current asset or current liability to account for the change during the year and a corresponding debit or credit in the operating activities section of the work sheet.   Recall that in the prior analysis, each item on the accrual-based income statement is adjusted for the change in the related current asset or current liability to arrive at the cash-based figure. The same reasoning applies in recording these changes in accounts as debits or credits in the operating activities section. For example, work sheet entry **b** records the decrease in Accounts Receivable as a credit (decrease) to Accounts Receivable and as a debit in the operating activities section because the decrease has a positive effect on cash flows, as follows:

(b) **Cash Flows from Operating Activities:**
　　　Decrease in Accounts Receivable　　　　　　　　8,000
　　　　　Accounts Receivable　　　　　　　　　　　　　　　　　　8,000

Work sheet entries **c–g** reflect the effects of the changes in the other current assets and current liabilities on cash flows from operating activities. As you study these entries below, note how the effects on cash flows of each entry are automatically determined by debits or credits that reflect the changes in the balance sheet accounts.

(c) **Inventory**　　　　　　　　　　　　　　　　　　　　　34,000
　　　Cash Flows from Operating Activities:
　　　Increase in Inventory　　　　　　　　　　　　　　　　34,000

(d) **Cash Flows from Operating Activities:**
　　　Decrease in Prepaid Expenses　　　　　　　　　4,000
　　　　　Prepaid Expenses　　　　　　　　　　　　　　　　　　4,000

(e) **Cash Flows from Operating Activities:**
　　　Increase in Accounts Payable　　　　　　　　　7,000
　　　　　Accounts Payable　　　　　　　　　　　　　　　　　　7,000

(f) **Cash Flows from Operating Activities:**
　　　Increase in Accrued Liabilities　　　　　　　　3,000
　　　　　Accrued Liabilities　　　　　　　　　　　　　　　　　3,000

(g) **Income Taxes Payable**　　　　　　　　　　　　　2,000
　　　Cash Flows from Operating Activities:
　　　Decrease in Income Taxes Payable　　　　　　　　2,000

h.–i. *Investments.* Among the other transactions affecting noncurrent accounts during 19x2 (see Exhibit 17-3), two items pertain to investments. One is the purchase of $78,000 and the other is the sale at $102,000. The purchase is recorded in the work sheet as a cash flow in the investing activities section, as follows:

(h) **Investments**　　　　　　　　　　　　　　　　　　78,000
　　　Cash Flows from Investing Activities:
　　　Purchase of Investments　　　　　　　　　　　　　78,000

Note that instead of crediting cash, a credit entry with the appropriate designation is made in the appropriate section in the lower half of the work sheet. The sale transaction is more complicated because it involves a gain that appears on the income statement and is included in net income. The work sheet entry accounts for this gain. The entry is as follows:

(i) Cash Flows from Investing Activities: Sale
of Investments   102,000
    Investments   90,000
    Cash Flows from Operating Activities:
    Gain on Sale of Investments   12,000

This entry records the cash inflow in the investing activities section, accounts for the remaining difference in the Investments account, and removes the gain on sale of investments from its inclusion in net income.

j.–m. **Plant Assets and Accumulated Depreciation.** There are four transactions in 19x2 that affect plant assets and the related accumulated depreciation. These are the purchase of plant assets, the sale of plant assets at a loss, the noncash exchange of plant assets for bonds, and depreciation expense for the year. Because these transactions can seem complicated, it is important to work through them systematically when preparing the work sheet. First, the purchase of plant assets for $120,000 is entered (entry **j**) in the same way the purchase of investments was entered in entry **h**. Second, the sale of plant assets is similar to the sale of investments, except that a loss is involved instead of a gain and accumulated depreciation is involved, as follows:

(k) Cash Flows from Investing Activities: Sale
of Plant Assets   5,000
    Cash Flows from Operating Activities: Loss
    on Sale of Plant Assets   3,000
    Accumulated Depreciation   2,000
        Plant Assets   10,000

The cash inflow from this transaction is $5,000. The rest of the entry is necessary to add the loss back into net income in the operating activities section of the statement, since it was deducted out to arrive at net income, and to record the effects on plant assets and accumulated depreciation.

The third transaction (entry **l**) is the noncash issue of bonds for the purchase of plant assets, as follows:

(l) Plant Assets   100,000
    Bonds Payable   100,000

Note that this transaction does not affect cash but needs to be recorded because the objective is to account for all the changes in the balance sheet accounts. It is listed in the schedule of noncash investing and financing transactions at the end of the statement of cash flows.

At this point the increase of $210,000 ($715,000 − $505,000) in plant assets has been explained by the two purchases less the sale ($120,000 + $100,000 − $10,000 = $210,000), but the change in

Accumulated Depreciation has not been completely explained. The depreciation expense for the year needs to be entered, as follows:

(m) **Cash Flows from Operating Activities:**
Depreciation Expense   37,000
    Accumulated Depreciation   37,000

The debit is to the operating activities section of the work sheet because, as explained earlier in the chapter, no current cash outflow is required for depreciation expense. The effect of this debit is to add the amount for depreciation expense back to net income. The $35,000 increase in Accumulated Depreciation has now been explained by the sale transaction and the depreciation expense $(-\$2,000 + \$37,000 = \$35,000)$.

n. ***Bonds Payable.*** Part of the change in Bonds Payable was explained in entry **l** when the noncash transaction, $100,000 issue of bonds for plant assets, was entered. All that remains is to enter the repayment of bonds, as follows:

(n) **Bonds Payable**   50,000
    Cash Flows from Financing Activities:
    Repayment of Bonds   50,000

o. ***Common Stock and Paid-in Capital in Excess of Par Value.*** Similarly, one transaction affects both of these accounts. It is an issue of 15,200 shares of $5 par value common stock for a total of $150,000. The work sheet entry is:

(o) **Cash Flows from Financing Activities:**
    Issue of Common Stock   150,000
        Common Stock   76,000
        Paid-in Capital in Excess of Par Value   74,000

p. ***Retained Earnings.*** Part of the change in Retained Earnings has already been recognized when net income was entered (entry **a**). The only remaining effect to be recognized is the effect of the $8,000 in cash dividends paid during the year, as follows:

(p) **Retained Earnings**   8,000
    Cash Flows from Financing Activities:
    Dividends Paid   8,000

x. The final step is to total the debit and credit columns in the top and bottom portions of the work sheet and enter the net change in cash at the bottom of the work sheet. The columns in the upper half equal $425,000. In the lower half, the debit column totals $335,000 and the credit column totals $304,000. The credit difference of $31,000 (entry **x**) equals the change in cash on the first line of the work sheet.

Chapter Review

Review of Learning Objectives

1. **Define cash and cash equivalents, and describe the statement of cash flows.**
   For purposes of preparing the statement of cash flows, cash is defined to include cash and cash equivalents. Cash equivalents are short-term (ninety days or less), highly liquid investments including money market accounts, commercial paper, and U.S. Treasury bills. The statement of cash flows explains the changes in cash and cash equivalents from one accounting period to the next by showing cash outflows and cash inflows from the operating, investing, and financing activities of a company for an accounting period.

2. **State the principal purposes and uses of the statement of cash flows.**
   The primary purpose of the statement of cash flows is to provide information about a company's cash receipts and cash payments during an accounting period. Its secondary purpose is to provide information about a company's operating, investing, and financing activities. It is useful to management as well as to investors and creditors in assessing the liquidity of a business, including the ability of the business to generate future cash flows and to pay its debts and dividends.

3. **Identify the principal components of the classifications of cash flows, and state the significance of noncash investing and financing transactions.**
   Cash flows are classified as operating activities, which include the cash effects of transactions and other events that enter into the determination of net income; investing activities, which include the acquiring and selling of long- and short-term marketable securities, property, plant, and equipment, and the making and collecting of loans excluding interest; and financing activities, which include obtaining and returning or repaying resources excluding interest to owners and creditors. Noncash investing and financing transactions are important exchanges of assets and/or liabilities that do not involve cash but nevertheless are of interest to investors and creditors in evaluating the financing and investing activities of the business.

4. **Determine cash flows from operating activities using the (a) direct and (b) indirect methods.**
   The direct method of determining cash flows from operating activities is accomplished by adjusting each item in the income statement from the accrual basis to the cash basis. The indirect method does not adjust each item in the income statement individually but begins with net income and lists all noncash effects to adjust net income to a cash flow basis.

5. **Determine cash flows from (a) investing activities and (b) financing activities.**
   Cash flows from investing activities are determined by identifying the cash flow effects of the transactions that affect each account relevant to investing activities. These accounts include all long-term assets and short-term marketable securities. The same procedure is followed for financing activities except that the accounts involved are short-term notes payable, long-term liabilities, and the owners' equity accounts. The effects of gains and losses from the income statement must also be considered with their related accounts. When the change in a balance sheet account from one accounting period to the next has been explained, all the cash flow effects should have been identified.

6. Prepare a statement of cash flows using the (a) direct method and (b) indirect method.

   The statement of cash flows has categories for cash flows from operating activities, investing activities, and financing activities. The section on cash flows from operating activities may be prepared using either the direct or indirect method. Significant noncash transactions are included in a schedule of noncash investing and financing transactions that accompanies the statement of cash flows.

7. Interpret the statement of cash flows.

   Interpretation of the statement of cash flows begins with the cash flows from operations to determine if it is positive and to assess the differences between net income and net cash flows from operating activities. It is usually informative to relate cash flows from operations to dividend payments in the financing section to see if the company is comfortably covering these important cash outflows. It is also useful to examine the investing activities to determine if the company is expanding, and if so, in what areas of business it is investing; and if not, in what areas it is contracting. Based on the analysis of the investing area, it is now possible to look to the financing section to evaluate how the company is financing the expansion, or if it is not expanding, how it is reducing its financing obligations. Finally, it is important to evaluate the impact of the noncash investing and financing transactions listed in the lower portion of the statement of cash flows.

8. Prepare a work sheet for the statement of cash flows.

   A work sheet is useful in preparing the statement of cash flows for complex companies. The basic procedures in the work sheet approach are to analyze the changes in the balance sheet accounts for the effects on cash flows in the top portion and to classify the effects according to the format of the statement of cash flows in the lower portion of the work sheet. When all the changes in the balance sheet accounts have been explained and entered on the work sheet, the change in the cash account will also be explained, and the information will be available to prepare the statement of cash flows. The work sheet lends itself to the indirect method of preparing the statement of cash flows.

Review of Concepts and Terminology

The following important concepts were introduced in this chapter:

(L.O.1) **Statement of cash flows:** A primary financial statement that shows the effect on cash flows of operating, investing, and financing activities for an accounting period.

(L.O.1) **Cash:** Cash and cash equivalents.

(L.O.1) **Cash equivalents:** Short-term (ninety days or less), highly liquid investments including money market accounts, commercial paper, and U.S. Treasury bills.

(L.O.3) **Noncash investing and financing transactions:** The exchange of a long-term asset for a long-term liability, the settlement of a debt by issuing capital stock, or other transactions involving only long-term assets, long-term liabilities, or stockholders' equity.

(L.O.4a) **Direct method:** The procedure of converting the income statement from an accrual basis to a cash basis by adjusting each item in the income statement in turn from the accrual basis to the cash basis.

(L.O.4b)   **Indirect method:**   The procedure of converting the income statement from an accrual basis to a cash basis by adjusting the net income amount by items not affecting cash flows, including depreciation, amortization, depletion, gains, losses, and changes in current assets and current liabilities.

Review Problem
The Statement of Cash Flows

The comparative balance sheets for the years 19x6 and 19x7 and the income statement of 19x7 for Northwest Corporation are shown below and on the next page.

Northwest Corporation
Balance Sheets
December 31, 19x7, and December 31, 19x6

	19x7	19x6	Change	Increase or Decrease
Assets				
Cash	$ 115,850	$ 121,850	$ (6,000)	Decrease
Accounts Receivable (net)	296,000	314,500	(18,500)	Decrease
Inventory	322,000	301,000	21,000	Increase
Prepaid Expenses	7,800	5,800	2,000	Increase
Long-term Investments	36,000	86,000	(50,000)	Decrease
Land	150,000	125,000	25,000	Increase
Building	462,000	462,000	—	—
Accumulated Depreciation, Building	(91,000)	(79,000)	(12,000)	Increase
Equipment	159,730	167,230	(7,500)	Decrease
Accumulated Depreciation, Equipment	(43,400)	(45,600)	2,200	Decrease
Intangible Assets	19,200	24,000	(4,800)	Decrease
Total Assets	$1,434,180	$1,482,780	$ (48,600)	
Liabilities and Stockholders' Equity				
Accounts Payable	$ 133,750	$ 233,750	$(100,000)	Decrease
Notes Payable (current)	75,700	145,700	(70,000)	Decrease
Accrued Liabilities	5,000	—	5,000	Increase
Income Taxes Payable	20,000	—	20,000	Increase
Bonds Payable	210,000	310,000	(100,000)	Decrease
Mortgage Payable	330,000	350,000	(20,000)	Decrease
Common Stock——$10 par value	360,000	300,000	60,000	Increase
Paid-in Capital in Excess of Par Value, Common	90,000	50,000	40,000	Increase
Retained Earnings	209,730	93,330	116,400	Increase
Total Liabilities and Stockholders' Equity	$1,434,180	$1,482,780	$ (48,600)	

Northwest Corporation
Income Statement
For the Year Ended December 31, 19x7

Sales		$1,650,000
Cost of Goods Sold		920,000
Gross Margin		$ 730,000
Operating Expenses (including Depreciation Expense of $12,000 on Buildings and $23,100 on Equipment and Amortization Expense of $4,800)		470,000
Operating Income		$ 260,000
Other Income (Expense)		
Interest Expense	$(55,000)	
Dividend Income	3,400	
Gain on Sale of Investment	12,500	
Loss on Disposal of Equipment	(2,300)	(41,400)
Income Before Taxes		$ 218,600
Income Taxes		52,200
Net Income		$ 166,400

The following additional information was taken from the company's records:

a. Long-term investments that cost $70,000 were sold at a gain of $12,500; additional long-term investments were made in the amount of $20,000.
b. Five acres of land were purchased for $25,000 for a parking lot.
c. Equipment that cost $37,500 with accumulated depreciation of $25,300 was sold at a loss of $2,300; new equipment in the amount of $30,000 was purchased.
d. Notes Payable in the amount of $100,000 were repaid; an additional $30,000 was borrowed by incurring notes payable.
e. Bonds Payable in the amount of $100,000 were converted into 6,000 shares of common stock.
f. Mortgage Payable was reduced by $20,000 during the year.
g. Cash dividends declared and paid were $50,000.

Required

1. Prepare a schedule of cash flows from operating activities using the (a) direct method and (b) indirect method.
2. Prepare a statement of cash flows using the direct method.

Answer to Review Problem

1. (a) Schedule of cash flows from operating activities—direct method prepared.

Northwest Corporation Schedule of Cash Flows from Operating Activities For the Year Ended December 31, 19x7		
Cash Flows from Operating Activities		
Cash Receipts from		
Sales	$1,668,500[1]	
Dividends Received	3,400	$1,671,900
Cash Payments for		
Purchases	$1,041,000[2]	
Operating Expenses	427,100[3]	
Interest Payments	55,000	
Income Taxes	32,200[4]	1,555,300
Net Cash Flows from Operating Activities		$ 116,600

[1] $1,650,000 + $18,500 = $1,668,500
[2] $920,000 + $21,000 + $100,000 = $1,041,000
[3] $470,000 + $2,000 − $5,000 − ($12,000 + $23,100 + $4,800) = $427,100
[4] $52,200 − $20,000 = $32,200

1. (b) Schedule of cash flows from operating activities—indirect method prepared.

Northwest Corporation Schedule of Cash Flows from Operating Activities For the Year Ended December 31, 19x7		
Net Income		$166,400
Adjustments to Reconcile Net Income to Net Cash Flows from Operating Activities		
Depreciation Expense, Buildings	$ 12,000	
Depreciation Expense, Equipment	23,100	
Amortization Expense, Intangible Assets	4,800	
Gain on Sales of Investments	(12,500)	
Loss on Disposal of Equipment	2,300	
Decrease in Accounts Receivable	18,500	
Increase in Inventory	(21,000)	
Increase in Prepaid Expenses	(20,000)	
Decrease in Accounts Payable	(100,000)	
Increase in Accrued Liabilities	5,000	
Increase in Income Taxes Payable	20,000	(49,800)
Net Cash Flows from Operating Activities		$116,600

2. Statement of cash flows—direct method prepared.

Northwest Corporation Statement of Cash Flows For the Year Ended December 31, 19x7		
Cash Flows from Operating Activities		
Cash Receipts from		
Sales	$1,668,500	
Dividends Received	3,400	$1,671,900
Cash Payments for		
Purchases	$1,041,000	
Operating Expenses	427,100	
Interest Payments	55,000	
Income Taxes	32,200	1,555,300
Net Cash Flows from Operating Activities		$ 116,600
Cash Flows from Investing Activities		
Sale of Long-term Investments	$ 82,500	
Purchase of Long-term Investments	(20,000)	
Purchase of Land	(25,000)	
Sales of Equipment	9,900	
Purchase of Equipment	(30,000)	
Net Cash Flows from Investing Activities		17,400
Cash Flows from Financing Activities		
Repayment of Notes Payable	$(100,000)	
Issuance of Notes Payable	30,000	
Reduction in Mortgage	(20,000)	
Dividends Paid	(50,000)	
Net Cash Flows Used by Financing Activities		(140,000)
Net Increase (Decrease) in Cash		$ (6,000)
Schedule of Noncash Investing and Financing Transactions		
Conversion of Bonds Payable into Common Stock		$100,000

(Note: When the direct method is used, a schedule explaining the difference between reported net income and cash flows from operating activities must be provided. An acceptable format for this schedule is the schedule of cash flows from operating activities under the indirect method shown in part 1b.)

Chapter Assignments

Questions

1. How has the practice in the reporting of changes in financial position and of investing and reporting activities changed during the 1980s?
2. What is the term *cash* in the statement of cash flows understood to mean and include?
3. In order to earn a return on cash on hand during 19x3, Sallas Corporation transferred $45,000 from its checking account to a money market account, purchased a $25,000 Treasury bill, and bought $35,000 in common stocks. How will each of these transactions affect the statement of cash flows?
4. What are the purposes of the statement of cash flows?
5. Why is the statement of cash flows needed when most of the information in it is available from comparative balance sheets and the income statement?
6. What are the three classifications of cash flows and some examples of each?
7. Why is it important to disclose certain noncash transactions? How should they be disclosed?
8. Cell-Borne Corporation has a net loss of $12,000 in 19x1 but has positive cash flows from operations of $9,000. What are some conditions that may have caused this situation?
9. What items on the income statement are not classified as operating activities? Why? Where are they classified?
10. Glen Corporation has other income and expenses: interest expense, $12,000; interest income, $3,000; dividend income, $5,000; and loss on retirement of bonds, $6,000. How do each of these items appear on or affect the statement of cash flows?
11. What are the essential differences between the direct method and the indirect method of determining cash flows from operations?
12. What are the effects of the following items on cash flows from operations: (a) an increase in accounts receivable, (b) a decrease in inventory, (c) an increase in accounts payable, (d) a decrease in wages payable, (e) depreciation expense, and (f) amortization of patents?
13. What is the proper treatment on the statement of cash flows of a transaction in which a building that cost $50,000 with accumulated depreciation of $32,000 is sold for a loss of $5,000?
14. What is the proper treatment on the statement of cash flows of (a) a transaction in which buildings and land are purchased by the issuance of a mortgage for $234,000 and (b) a conversion of $50,000 in bonds payable into 2,500 shares of $6 par value common stock?
15. Why is the work sheet approach considered to be more compatible with the indirect method as opposed to the direct method of determining cash flows from operations?
16. Assuming in each independent case that only one transaction occurred, what transactions would be likely to cause (1) a decrease in investments and (2) an increase in common stock? How would each case be treated on the work sheet for a statement of cash flows?
17. In interpreting the statement of cash flows, what are some comparisons that can be made with cash flows from operations? For what reasons would a company have a decrease in cash flows from investing activities?

Classroom Exercises

Exercise 17-1.
Classification of Cash Flow Transactions
(L.O. 3)

InterFirst Corporation engaged in the following transactions. Identify each as (1) an operating activity, (2) an investing activity, (3) a financing activity, (4) a noncash transaction, or (5) none of the above.

a. Declared and paid a cash dividend.
b. Purchased an investment.
c. Received cash from customers.
d. Paid interest.
e. Sold equipment at a loss.
f. Issued long-term bonds for plant assets.
g. Received dividends on securities held.

h. Issued common stock.
i. Declared and issued a stock dividend.
j. Repaid notes payable.
k. Paid wages to employees.
l. Purchased a 60-day Treasury bill.
m. Purchased land.

Exercise 17-2.
Computing Cash Flows from Operating Activities— Direct Method
(L.O. 4)

Rentral Corporation engaged in the following transactions in 19x2. Compute the various cash flows from operating activities as required.

a. During 19x2, Rentral Corporation had cash sales of $34,500 and sales on credit of $123,000. During the same year, accounts receivable decreased by $18,000. Determine the cash received from customers during 19x2.
b. During 19x2, Rentral Corporation had cost of goods sold of $119,000. During the same year, merchandise inventory increased by $12,500 and accounts payable decreased by $4,300. Determine the cash payments for purchases during 19x2.
c. During 19x2, Rentral Corporation had operating expenses of $45,000, including depreciation of $15,600. Also during 19x2, related prepaid expenses decreased by $3,100 and relevant accrued liabilities increased by $1,200. Determine cash payments to suppliers of goods and services during 19x2.
d. Income Taxes Expense for Rentral Corporation was $4,300 for 19x2, and Income Taxes Payable decreased by $230. Determine cash payment for income taxes during 19x2.

Exercise 17-3.
Computing Cash Flows from Operating Activities— Indirect Method
(L.O. 4)

During 19x1, Canton Corporation had net income of $34,000. Included on the income statement was Depreciation Expense of $2,300 and Amortization Expense of $300. During the year, accounts receivable increased by $3,400, inventories decreased by $1,900, prepaid assets decreased by $200, accounts payable increased by $5,000, and accrued liabilities decreased by $450. Determine cash flows from operating activities using the indirect method.

Exercise 17-4.
Computing Cash Flows from Operating Activities— Direct Method
(L.O. 4)

The income statement for the Cummings Corporation is presented on the following page.
Additional information: (a) All sales were on credit, and accounts receivable increased by $2,200 during the year. (b) All merchandise purchased was on credit. Inventories increased by $3,500, and accounts payable increased by $7,000 during the year. (c) Prepaid rent decreased by $700, salaries payable increased by $500. (d) Income taxes payable decreased by $300 during the year. Prepare a schedule of cash flows from operating activities using the direct method.

Cummings Corporation		
Income Statement		
For the Year Ended June 30, 19xx		
Sales		$60,000
Cost of Goods Sold		30,000
Gross Margin from Sales		$30,000
Other Expenses		
Salaries Expense	$16,000	
Rent Expense	8,400	
Depreciation Expense	1,000	25,400
Income Before Income Taxes		$ 4,600
Income Taxes		1,200
Net Income		$ 3,400

Exercise 17-5.
Calculating Cash Flows from Operating Activities— Indirect Method
(L.O. 4)

Using the data provided in Exercise 17-4, prepare a schedule of cash flows from operating activities for Cummings Corporation using the indirect method.

Exercise 17-6.
Calculating Cash Flows from Investing Activities— Investments
(L.O. 5)

The T account for the Investments account for Sader Company at the end of 19x3 is as follows:

Investments			
Beg. Bal.	38,500	Sales	42,000
Purchases	58,000		
End. Bal.	54,500		

In addition, the income statement shows a loss on the sale of investments of $6,500. Compute the amounts to be shown, and show how they are to appear as cash flows from investing activities on the statement of cash flows.

Exercise 17-7.
Calculating Cash Flows from Investing Activities— Plant Assets
(L.O. 5)

The T accounts for the Plant Assets and Accumulated Depreciation accounts for Sader Company at the end of 19x3 are as follows:

Plant Assets			
Beg. Bal.	65,000	Disposals	23,000
Purchases	33,600		
End. Bal.	75,600		

Accumulated Depreciation

Disposals	14,700	Beg. Bal.	34,500
		19x3 Depreciation	10,200
		End. Bal.	**30,000**

In addition, the income statement shows a gain on sale of plant assets of $4,400. Compute the amounts to be shown, and show how they are to appear as cash flows from investing activities on the statement of cash flows.

Exercise 17-8.
Calculating Cash Flows from Financing Activities
(L.O. 3, 5)

All transactions involving Notes Payable and related accounts engaged in by Sader Company during 19x3 are as follows:

Cash	12,000	
Notes Payable		12,000
Bank loan		
Patent	20,000	
Notes Payable		20,000
Purchase of patent by issuing note payable		
Notes Payable	5,000	
Interest Expense	500	
Cash		5,500
Repayment of note payable at maturity		

Determine the amounts and how these transactions are to be shown in the statement of cash flows for 19x3.

Exercise 17-9.
Preparing the Statement of Cash Flows
(L.O. 6)

Tsin Corporation's income statement for the year ended June 30, 19x2, and the comparative balance sheets for June 30, 19x1 and 19x2, appear below and on page 714.

Tsin Corporation
Income Statement
For the Year Ended June 30, 19x2

Sales	$234,000
Cost of Goods Sold	156,000
Gross Margin	78,000
Operating Expenses	45,000
Operating Income	33,000
Interest Expense	2,800
Income Before Income Taxes	30,200
Income Taxes	12,300
Net Income	$ 17,900

<table>
<tr><th colspan="3">Tsin Corporation
Balance Sheets
June 30, 19x1 and 19x2</th></tr>
<tr><th></th><th>19x2</th><th>19x1</th></tr>
</table>

	19x2	19x1
Assets		
Cash	$ 69,900	$ 12,500
Accounts Receivable (net)	21,000	26,000
Inventory	43,400	48,400
Prepaid Expenses	3,200	2,600
Furniture	55,000	60,000
Accumulated Depreciation, Furniture	(9,000)	(5,000)
Total Assets	$183,500	$144,500
Liabilities and Stockholders' Equity		
Accounts Payable	$ 13,000	$ 14,000
Income Taxes Payable	1,200	1,800
Notes Payable (long-term)	37,000	35,000
Common Stock—$5 par value	115,000	90,000
Retained Earnings	17,300	3,700
Total Liabilities and Stockholders' Equity	$183,500	$144,500

Additional information: (a) issued $22,000 note payable for purchase of furniture; (b) sold furniture that cost $27,000 with accumulated depreciation of $15,300 at carrying value; (c) recorded depreciation on the furniture during the year, $19,300; (d) repaid a note in the amount of $20,000; issued $25,000 of common stock at par value; (e) dividends declared and paid, $4,300.

Without using a work sheet, prepare a statement of cash flows for 19x2 using the direct method of determining cash flow.

Exercise 17-10.
Preparing a Work Sheet for the Statement of Cash Flows
(L.O. 8)

Using the information in Exercise 17-9, prepare a work sheet for the statement of cash flows for Tsin Corporation for 19x2. From the work sheet, prepare a statement of cash flows using the indirect method.

Interpreting Accounting Information

17-1.
National Communications, Inc.
(L.O. 6, 7)

The following statements of cash flows from the annual report of National Communications, Inc., a major television network broadcaster and publisher, were prepared before the new FASB requirements. Note, however, that it does not follow the format of the new statement.

National Communications, Inc.
Statements of Cash Flows
For the Years Ended January 31, 1988 and 1987
(in thousands)

	1988	1987
Cash provided		
Operations		
Net income	$ 267,693	$242,222
Depreciation	95,202	37,992
Amortization of intangible assets	63,403	19,712
Other noncash items, net	28,930	23,370
Total cash from operations	$ 455,228	$323,296
Capital expenditures for operations	(153,087)	(75,383)
Program licenses and rights, net	(2,732)	(1,734)
Available cash flow from operations	$ 299,409	$246,179
Issuance of Common Stock	517,500	—
Issuance of common stock warrants	97,197	—
Issuance of long-term debt	1,350,503	493,322
Long-term debt assumed on acquisitions	123,678	—
Disposition of operating properties, net of current taxes	625,677	7,229
Disposition of real estate	162,166	—
Other dispositions, net	29,495	3,114
	$3,205,625	$749,844
Cash applied		
Acquisition of television stations	$3,270,972	$ —
Common stock warrants purchased and redeemed	16,688	—
Acquisition of other operating properties	12,599	103,109
Reduction of long-term debt	367,521	7,874
Changes in other working capital items	86,645	2,322
Purchase of common stock for treasury	1,079	485
Dividends	3,210	2,594
	$3,758,714	$116,384
(Decrease) increase in cash and cash investments	(553,089)	$633,460
Cash and cash equivalents		
Beginning of period	687,413	53,953
End of period	$ 134,324	$687,413

Required

1. Recast the statements of cash flows using the indirect method for the statement of cash flows as shown in this chapter (ignore noncash transactions).
2. National Communications, Inc. places an emphasis on "available cash flow from operations." Evaluate this approach as compared to "net cash flows from operating activities" in the statement of cash flows.
3. Although net cash flow from operating activities increased from 1987 to 1988, cash and cash equivalents decreased significantly (from $687,413,000 to $134,324,000). What are the primary causes of this decline in cash and cash equivalents?

17-2.
Airborne Express*
(L.O.7)

Airborne Express is an air express transportation company, providing next-day morning delivery of small packages and documents throughout the United States. Airborne Express is one of three major participants, along with Federal Express and United Parcel Service, in the air express industry.

The letter to the stockholders from the 1986 annual report of Airborne Express, Inc. states, "Airborne Express enjoyed a very satisfying year in 1986, in that we made consistent progress toward accomplishing our major objectives: reducing average unit cost, enhancing our market position, and as a result improving earnings." It goes on to state, "We continue to operate in a highly volatile environment, in which many of our competitors faced with little or no growth scenarios engage in drastic price cutting practices in an effort to establish their niche in the industry."

Airborne's 1986 statement of changes in financial position is presented here in the format of the new statement of cash flows. (Note that although Airborne's statement of changes in financial position was prepared before the requirement for the new statement of cash flows, it is very similar in format to the new statement.)

Required

1. What are the primary causes of the difference between net earnings and net funds (cash) provided by operations in 1986?
2. Does Airborne Express generate enough net cash flows from operating activities to satisfy dividends and provide additional funds for expansion? Explain your answer.
3. Has Airborne Express been an expanding company over the last three years? If so, what are the primary means of financing the expansion?

---

* Excerpts from 1986 annual report used by permission of Airborne Express, P.O. Box 662, Seattle, Washington 98111. Copyright © 1986.

Airborne Freight Corporation and Subsidiaries
Consolidated Statements of Changes in Financial Position

Year Ended December 31	1986	1985	1984
	(in thousands)		
Cash, at January 1	$ 3,321	$ 1,222	$ 2,212
Funds Provided by Operations			
Net earnings	$ 13,215	$ 8,169	$ 10,829
Depreciation and amortization	26,270	19,100	15,889
Deferred taxes	4,297	2,747	5,333
Total Funds Provided by Operations	$ 43,782	$ 30,016	$ 32,051
Changes in working capital that provided (used) funds:			
Receivables	(2,353)	(13,748)	(5,913)
Inventories and prepaid expenses	(2,881)	(1,879)	(2,903)
Accounts payable	10,366	4,577	5,269
Accrued expenses, salaries, and taxes payable	(5,517)	8,872	696
Current portion of long-term debt	2,449	402	271
Net Funds Provided by Operations	$ 45,846	$ 28,240	$ 29,471
Dividends Paid	$ (3,512)	$ (3,494)	$ (3,461)
Investments			
Additions to property and equipment, net	$(75,862)	$(52,523)	$(31,853)
Additions to equipment under capital leases	(10,957)	—	—
Decrease (increase) in restricted construction funds	10,328	3,837	(13,674)
Increase in other assets	(1,548)	(1,704)	(791)
Funds Used For Investing Activities	$(78,039)	$(50,390)	$(46,318)
Financing			
Proceeds from issuance of subordinated debt	$ 50,000	$ —	$ —
Increase in long-term capital lease obligations	7,276	—	—
Increase (decrease) in long-term debt, net	(22,227)	27,277	18,704
Proceeds from issuance of common stock	467	466	614
Funds Provided by Financing Activities	$ 35,516	$ 27,743	$ 19,318
Increase (Decrease) In Cash	$ (189)	$ 2,099	$ (990)
Cash, at December 31	$ 3,132	$ 3,321	$ 1,222

See notes to consolidated financial statements.

Problem Set A

Problem 17A-1.
Classification of
Transactions
(L.O. 3)

Analyze the transactions presented in the following schedule, and place an X in the appropriate columns to indicate the classification of the transaction and its effect on cash flows using the direct method.

	Cash Flows Classification				Effect on Cash		
Transactions	Operating Activity	Investing Activity	Financing Activity	Noncash Transac-tions	Increase	Decrease	No Effect
a. Incurred a net loss.							
b. Declared and issued a stock dividend.							
c. Paid a cash dividend.							
d. Collected accounts receivable.							
e. Purchased inventory with cash.							
f. Retired long-term debt with cash.							
g. Sale of investment for a loss.							
h. Issued stock for equipment.							
i. Purchased a one-year insurance policy for cash.							
j. Purchased treasury stock with cash.							
k. Retired a fully depreciated truck (no gain or loss).							
l. Paid interest on note.							
m. Received dividend on investment.							
n. Sale of treasury stock.							
o. Paid income taxes.							
p. Transferred cash to money market account.							
q. Purchased land and building with a mortgage.							

Problem 17A-2.
Cash Flows from
Operating
Activities
(L.O. 4)

The income statement for Sandberg Clothing Store is shown below:

Sandberg Clothing Store		
Income Statement		
For the Year Ended June 30, 19xx		

Sales			$2,400,000
Cost of Goods Sold			
Beginning Inventory		$ 620,000	
Purchases (net)		1,520,000	
Goods Available for Sale		$2,140,000	
Ending Inventory		700,000	
Cost of Goods Sold			1,440,000
Gross Margin from Sales			$ 960,000
Operating Expenses			
Sales and Administrative Salaries			
Expense		$ 556,000	
Other Sales and Administrative Expenses		312,000	
Total Operating Expenses			868,000
Income Before Income Taxes			$ 92,000
Income Taxes			23,000
Net Income			$ 69,000

Additional information: (a) Other sales and administrative expenses include depreciation expense of $52,000 and amortization expense of $18,000. (b) At the end of the year, accrued liabilities for salaries were $12,000 less than the previous year, and prepaid expenses were $20,000 more than the previous year. (c) During the year, accounts receivable (net) increased by $144,000, accounts payable increased by $114,000, and income taxes payable decreased by $7,200.

Required

1. Prepare a schedule of cash flows from operating activities using the direct method.
2. Prepare a schedule of cash flows from operating activities using the indirect method.

Problem 17A-3.
Cash Flows from
Operating
Activities
(L.O. 4)

The income statement of Thompson Greeting Card Company is presented for 19x2. Relevant accounts from the balance sheet for December 31, 19x1 and 19x2, are as follows:

	19x1	19x2
Accounts Receivable (net)	$23,670	$18,530
Inventory	34,990	39,640
Prepaid Expenses	8,900	2,400
Accounts Payable	22,700	34,940
Accrued Liabilities	8,830	4,690
Income Taxes Payable	17,600	4,750

Thompson Greeting Card Company
Income Statement
For the Year Ended December 31, 19x2

Sales		$456,000
Cost of Goods Sold		286,700
Gross Margin from Sales		$169,300
Operating Expenses (including Depreciation Expense of $21,430)		87,400
Operating Income		$ 81,900
Other Income (Expenses)		
Interest Expense	$(8,400)	
Interest Income	4,300	
Loss on Sale of Investments	(5,800)	(9,900)
Income Before Income Taxes		$ 72,000
Income Taxes		18,500
Net Income		$ 53,500

Required

1. Prepare a schedule of cash flows from operating activities using the direct method.
2. Prepare a schedule of cash flows from operating activities using the indirect method.

Problem 17A-4.
The Statement of Cash Flows—Direct Method
(L.O. 6, 7)

Sanchez Corporation's income statement for June 30, 19x7 and its comparative balance sheets for June 30, 19x6 and 19x7 are as follows:

Sanchez Corporation
Income Statement
For the Year Ended June 30, 19x7

Sales		$1,040,900
Cost of Goods Sold		656,300
Gross Margin from Sales		$ 384,600
Operating Expenses (including Depreciation Expense of $60,000)		189,200
Income from Operations		$ 195,400
Other Income (Expenses)		
Loss on Disposal of Equipment	$ (4,000)	
Interest Expense	(37,600)	(41,600)
Income Before Income Taxes		$ 153,800
Income Taxes		34,200
Net Income		$ 119,600

Sanchez Corporation
Comparative Balance Sheets
June 30, 19x6 and 19x7

	19x7	19x6
Assets		
Cash	$167,000	$ 20,000
Accounts Receivable (net)	100,000	120,000
Finished Goods Inventory	180,000	220,000
Prepaid Expenses	600	1,000
Property, Plant, and Equipment	628,000	552,000
Accumulated Depreciation, Property, Plant, and Equipment	(183,000)	(140,000)
Total Assets	$892,600	$773,000
Liabilities and Stockholders' Equity		
Accounts Payable	$ 64,000	$ 42,000
Notes Payable (due in 90 days)	30,000	80,000
Income Taxes Payable	26,000	18,000
Mortgage Payable	360,000	280,000
Common Stock—$5 par value	200,000	200,000
Retained Earnings	212,600	153,000
Total Liabilities and Stockholders' Equity	$892,600	$773,000

Additional information about 19x7: (a) equipment assets that cost $24,000 with accumulated depreciation of $17,000 were sold at a loss of $4,000; (b) land and building were purchased in the amount of $100,000 through an increase of $100,000 in the mortgage payable; (c) a $20,000 payment was made on the mortgage; (d) the notes were repaid, but the company borrowed an additional $30,000 through the issuance of a new note payable; (e) a $60,000 cash dividend was declared and paid.

Required

1. Prepare a statement of cash flows using the direct method. Include a supporting schedule of noncash investing and financing transactions.
2. What are the primary reasons for Sanchez Corporation's large increase in cash from 19x6 to 19x7?

Problem 17A-5.
The Work Sheet
and the Statement
of Cash Flows—
Indirect Method
(L.O. 6, 8)

Use the information for Sanchez Corporation in Problem 17A-4.

Required

1. Prepare a work sheet for gathering information for the preparation of the statement of cash flows.

2. From the information on the work sheet, prepare a statement of cash flows using the indirect method. Include a supporting schedule of noncash investing and financing transactions.

Problem 17A-6.
The Work Sheet
and the Statement
of Cash Flows—
Indirect Method
(L.O. 6, 7, 8)

The comparative balance sheets for Sullivan Ceramics, Inc. for December 31, 19x2 and 19x3, are as follows:

Sullivan Ceramics, Inc.
Comparative Balance Sheets
December 31, 19x2 and 19x3

	19x3	19x2
Assets		
Cash	$ 138,800	$ 152,800
Accounts Receivable (net)	369,400	379,400
Inventory	480,000	400,000
Prepaid Expenses	7,400	13,400
Long-term Investments	220,000	220,000
Land	180,600	160,600
Building	600,000	460,000
Accumulated Depreciation, Building	(120,000)	(80,000)
Equipment	240,000	240,000
Accumulated Depreciation, Equipment	(58,000)	(28,000)
Intangible Assets	10,000	20,000
Total Assets	$2,068,200	$1,938,200
Liabilities and Stockholders' Equity		
Accounts Payable	$ 235,400	$ 330,400
Notes Payable (current)	20,000	80,000
Accrued Liabilities	5,400	10,400
Mortgage Payable	540,000	400,000
Bonds Payable	500,000	380,000
Common Stock	600,000	600,000
Paid-in Capital in Excess of Par Value	40,000	40,000
Retained Earnings	127,400	97,400
Total Liabilities and Stockholders' Equity	$2,068,200	$1,938,200

Additional information about Sullivan's operations during 19x3: (a) net income, $48,000; (b) building and equipment depreciation expense amounts were $40,000 and $30,000, respectively; (c) intangible assets were amortized in the amount of $10,000; (d) investments in the amount of $58,000 were purchased; (e) investments were sold for $75,000, on which a gain of $17,000 was made; (f) the company issued $120,000 in long-term bonds at face value; (g) a small warehouse building with the accompanying land was purchased through the issue of a $160,000 mortgage; (h) the company paid $20,000 to reduce mortgage payable during 19x7; (i) the company borrowed funds in the amount of $30,000 by issuing notes payable and repaid notes payable in the amount of $90,000; (j) cash dividends in the amount of $18,000 were declared and paid.

Required

1. Prepare a work sheet for the statement of cash flows for Sullivan Ceramics.
2. Prepare a statement of cash flows from the information on the work sheet using the indirect method. Include a supporting schedule of noncash investing and financing transactions.
3. Why did Sullivan Ceramics have a decrease in cash in a year when it had a net income of $48,000? Discuss and interpret.

Problem Set B

Problem 17B-1. Classification of Transactions (L.O.3)

Analyze the transactions in the following schedule, and place an X in the appropriate columns to indicate the classification of the transaction and its effect on cash flows using the direct method.

	Cash Flows Classification				Effect on Cash		
Transaction	**Operating Activity**	**Investing Activity**	**Financing Activity**	**Noncash Transactions**	**Increase**	**Decrease**	**No Effect**
a. Recorded net income.							
b. Declared and paid cash dividend.							
c. Issued stock for cash.							
d. Retired long-term debt by issuing stock.							
e. Paid accounts payable.							
f. Purchased inventory.							
g. Purchased a one-year insurance policy.							
h. Purchased a long-term investment with cash.							

(continued)

(continued)

| | Cash Flows Classification | | | | Effect on Cash | | |
	Operating Activity	Investing Activity	Financing Activity	Noncash Transac- tions	Increase	Decrease	No Effect
Transaction							
i. Sold marketable securities at a gain.							
j. Sold a machine for a loss.							
k. Retired fully depreciated equipment.							
l. Paid interest on debt.							
m. Purchased marketable securities.							
n. Received dividend income.							
o. Received cash on account.							
p. Converted bonds to common stock.							
q. Purchased short- term Treasury bill.							

Problem 17B-2.
Cash Flows from
Operating
Activities
(L.O. 4)

The income statement for Perelli Food Corporation is presented on page 725.

Additional information: (a) accounts receivable (net) increased by $18,000, and accounts payable decreased by $26,000 during the year; (b) salaries payable at the end of the year were $7,000 more than last year; (c) the expired amount of prepaid insurance for the year is $500 and equals the decrease in the Prepaid Insurance account; (d) income taxes payable decreased by $5,400 from last year.

Required

1. Prepare a schedule of cash flows from operating activities using the direct method.
2. Prepare a schedule of cash flows from operating activities using the indirect method.

Perelli Food Corporation
Income Statement
For the Year Ended December 31, 19xx

Sales		$520,000
Cost of Goods Sold		
Beginning Inventory	$220,000	
Purchases (net)	400,000	
Goods Available for Sale	$620,000	
Ending Inventory	250,000	
Cost of Goods Sold		370,000
Gross Margin from Sales		$150,000
Selling and Administrative Expenses		
Selling and Administrative Salaries Expense	50,000	
Other Selling and Administrative Expenses	11,500	
Depreciation Expense	18,000	
Amortization Expense (Intangible Assets)	1,500	81,000
Income Before Income Taxes		$ 69,000
Income Taxes		17,500
Net Income		$ 51,500

Problem 17B-3.
Cash Flows from
Operating
Activities
(L.O.4)

The income statement of Johnson Electronics, Inc. is presented below for 19x3.

Johnson Electronics, Inc.
Income Statement
For the Year Ended February 28, 19x3

Sales		$928,000
Cost of Goods Sold		643,500
Gross Margin from Sales		$284,500
Operating Expenses (including Depreciation Expense of $21,430)		176,900
Operating Income		$107,600
Other Income (Expenses)		
Interest Expense	$(27,800)	
Dividend Income	14,200	
Loss on Sale of Investments	(12,100)	(25,700)
Income Before Income Taxes		$ 81,900
Income Taxes		21,500
Net Income		$ 60,400

Relevant accounts from the balance sheets for February 28, 19x2 and 19x3, are as presented on page 726:

	19x2	19x3
Accounts Receivable (net)	$ 48,920	$65,490
Inventory	102,560	98,760
Prepaid Expenses	5,490	10,450
Accounts Payable	55,690	42,380
Accrued Liabilities	8,790	3,560
Income Taxes Payable	13,800	24,630

Required

1. Prepare a schedule of cash flows from operating activities using the direct method.
2. Prepare a schedule of cash flows from operating activities using the indirect method.

Problem 17B-4.
The Statement of Cash Flows—Direct Method
(L.O. 6, 7)

Glenview Corporation's comparative balance sheets for December 31, 19x1 and 19x2, and its 19x2 income statement are as follows:

Glenview Corporation
Comparative Balance Sheets
December 31, 19x1 and 19x2

	19x2	19x1
Assets		
Cash	$ 82,400	$ 25,000
Accounts Receivable (net)	82,600	100,000
Merchandise Inventory	175,000	225,000
Prepaid Rent	1,000	1,500
Furniture and Fixtures	74,000	72,000
Accumulated Depreciation, Furniture and Fixtures	(21,000)	(12,000)
Total Assets	$394,000	$411,500
Liabilities and Stockholders' Equity		
Accounts Payable	$ 71,700	$100,200
Notes Payable (long-term)	20,000	10,000
Bonds Payable	50,000	100,000
Income Taxes Payable	700	2,200
Common Stock—$10 par value	120,000	100,000
Paid-in Capital in Excess of Par Value	90,720	60,720
Retained Earnings	40,880	38,380
Total Liabilities and Stockholders' Equity	$394,000	$411,500

Glenview Corporation
Income Statement
For the Year Ended December 31, 19x2

Sales		$804,500
Cost of Goods Sold		563,900
Gross Margin from Sales		$240,600
Operating Expenses (including Depreciation Expense of $23,400)		224,700
Income from Operations		$ 15,900
Other Income (Expenses)		
Gain on Disposal of Furniture and Fixtures	$ 3,500	
Interest Expense	(11,600)	(8,100)
Income Before Income Taxes		$ 7,800
Income Taxes		2,300
Net Income		$ 5,500

Additional information about 19x2: (a) furniture and fixures that cost $17,800 with accumulated depreciation of $14,400 were sold at a gain of $3,500; (b) furniture and fixtures were purchased in the amount of $19,800; (c) a $10,000 note payable was paid, and $20,000 was borrowed on a new note; (d) bonds payable in the amount of $50,000 were converted into 2,000 shares of common stock; (e) $3,000 in cash dividends was declared and paid.

Required

1. Prepare a statement of cash flows using the direct method and a supporting schedule of noncash investing and financing transactions. (Do not use a work sheet.)
2. What are the primary reasons for Glenview Corporation's large increase in cash from 19x1 to 19x2 in spite of its low net income?

Problem 17B-5.
**The Work Sheet
and the Statement
of Cash Flows—
Indirect Method**
(L.O. 6, 8)

Use the information for Glenview Corporation in Problem 17B-4.

Required

1. Prepare a work sheet for gathering information for the preparation of the statement of cash flows.
2. From the information on the work sheet, prepare a statement of cash flows using the indirect method. Include a supporting schedule of noncash investing and financing transactions.

Problem 17B-6.
**The Work Sheet
and the Statement
of Cash Flows—
Indirect Method**
(L.O. 6, 7, 8)

The comparative balance sheets for Finnegan Fabrics, Inc., for December 31, 19x2 and 19x3, are shown on page 728. Additional information about Finnegan's operations during 19x3: (a) net loss, $28,000; (b) building and equipment depreciation expense amounts, $15,000 and $3,000, respectively; (c) equipment that cost $13,500, with accumulated depreciation of $12,500, sold for a gain of $5,300; (d) equipment purchases, $12,500; (e) patent amortization, $3,000; purchase of patent, $1,000; (f) funds borrowed by issuing notes payable, $25,000; notes payable repaid, $15,000; (g) land and building purchased for $162,000 by signing a mortgage for the total cost; (h) 3,000 shares of $10 par value common stock issued for a total of $50,000; (i) cash dividend, $9,000.

Finnegan Fabrics, Inc.
Comparative Balance Sheets
December 31, 19x2 and 19x3

	19x3	19x2
Assets		
Cash	$ 38,560	$ 27,360
Accounts Receivable (net)	102,430	75,430
Inventory	112,890	137,890
Prepaid Expenses	—	20,000
Land	25,000	—
Building	137,000	—
Accumulated Depreciation, Building	(15,000)	—
Equipment	33,000	34,000
Accumulated Depreciation, Equipment	(14,500)	(24,000)
Patents	4,000	6,000
Total Assets	$423,380	$276,680
Liabilities and Stockholders' Equity		
Accounts Payable	$ 10,750	$ 36,750
Notes Payable	10,000	—
Accrued Liabilities (current)	—	12,300
Mortgage Payable	162,000	—
Common Stock	180,000	150,000
Paid-in Capital in Excess of Par Value	57,200	37,200
Retained Earnings	3,430	40,430
Total Liabilities and Stockholders' Equity	$423,380	$276,680

Required

1. Prepare a work sheet for the statement of cash flows for Finnegan Fabrics.
2. Prepare a statement of cash flows from the information on the work sheet using the indirect method.
3. Why did Finnegan Fabrics have an increase in cash in a year when it had a net loss of $28,000? Discuss and interpret.

Management Decision Cases

17-1.
Dru's Exercise Shop
(L.O. 6, 7)

Dru Travalley opened a retail store that sells exercise equipment on January 1, 19x2. At the end of the year Dru prepared the following statement of cash flows for the company.

Dru's Exercise Shop		
Statement of Cash Flows		
For the Year Ended December 31, 19x2		
Sources of Cash		
From sale of capital stock	$600,000	
From sales of merchandise	550,000	
From sale of investments	50,000	
From depreciation	80,000	
From issuance of note for delivery truck	25,000	
From dividends on investments	5,000	
Total sources of cash		$1,310,000
Uses of cash		
For purchase of fixtures and equipment	$450,000	
For merchandise purchased for resale	400,000	
For operating expenses (including depreciation)	235,000	
For purchase of investments	60,000	
For purchase of delivery truck by issuance of note	25,000	
For purchase of treasury stock	27,000	
For interest on note	3,000	
Total uses of cash		1,200,000
Net increase in cash		$ 110,000

Dru is excited about the successful year she has had as shown by her statement of cash flows. She is happy that cash has increased by $110,000. However, based on your recent study of the new statement of cash flows, you see that this statement is incorrectly prepared and that what seems to be cash flow is not. You offer to help Dru in assessing her company's operations.

Required

1. Prepare a statement of cash flows in good form (use the direct method without a schedule reconciling net income to net cash flows from operating activities).
2. Write an assessment of the Exercise Shop's first year of operations.

17-2.
Adams Print
Gallery, Inc.
(L.O. 6, 7)

Bernadette Adams, president of Adams Print Gallery, Inc., is examining the income statement for 19x2, which has just been handed to her by her accountant, Jason Rosenberg, CPA.

Adams Print Gallery, Inc.
Income Statement
For the Year Ended December 31, 19x2

Sales	$432,000
Cost of Goods Sold	254,000
Gross Margin	178,000
Operating Expenses (including Depreciation Expense of $10,000)	102,000
Operating Income	76,000
Interest Expense	12,000
Income Before Taxes	64,000
Income Taxes	14,000
Net Income	$ 50,000

After looking at the statement, Ms. Adams said to Mr. Rosenberg, "Jason, the statement seems to be well done, but what I need to know is why I don't have enough cash to pay my bills this month. You show that I have earned $50,000 in 19x2, but I only have $2,000 in the bank. I know I bought a building on a mortgage and paid a cash dividend of $24,000, but what else is going on?" Mr. Rosenberg replied, "To answer your question, Bernadette, we have to look at comparative balance sheets and prepare another type of statement. Here, take a look at these balance sheets." The statements handed to Ms. Adams follow:

Adams Print Gallery, Inc.
Comparative Balance Sheets
December 31, 19x1 and 19x2

	19x2	19x1
Assets		
Cash	$ 2,000	$ 20,000
Accounts Receivable (net)	89,000	73,000
Inventory	120,000	90,000
Prepaid Expenses	5,000	7,000
Building	200,000	—
Accumulated Depreciation	(10,000)	—
Total Assets	$406,000	$190,000
Liabilities and Stockholders' Equity		
Accounts Payable	$ 37,000	$ 48,000
Income Taxes Payable	3,000	2,000
Mortgage Payable	200,000	—
Common Stock	100,000	100,000
Retained Earnings	66,000	40,000
Total Liabilities and Stockholders' Equity	$406,000	$190,000

Required

1. To what other type of statement is Mr. Rosenberg referring? From the information given, prepare the additional statement using the direct method, without a schedule reconciling net income to net cash flows from operating activities.
2. Explain why Ms. Adams has a cash problem in spite of profitable operations.

1. Describe and dis-
cuss the objectives
of financial
statement analysis.
2. Describe and dis-
cuss the standards
for financial
statement analysis.
3. State the sources of
information for
financial statement
analysis.
4. Identify the issues
related to the
evaluation of the
quality of a com-
pany's earnings.
5. Apply horizontal
analysis, trend
analysis, and vertical
analysis to financial
statements.
6. Apply ratio analysis
to financial state-
ments in the study of
an enterprise's
liquidity, profit-
ability, long-term
solvency, and
market tests.

CHAPTER 18

Financial Statement Analysis

This chapter presents a number of techniques intended to aid in decision making by highlighting important relationships in the financial statements. This process is called financial statement analysis. After studying this chapter, you should be able to meet the learning objectives listed on the left.

Effective decision making calls for the ability to sort out relevant information from a great many facts and to make adjustments for changing conditions. Very often, financial statements in a company's annual report run ten or more pages, including footnotes and other necessary disclosures. If these statements are to be useful in making decisions, decision makers must be able to find information that shows important relationships and helps them make comparisons from year to year and from company to company. The many techniques that together are called **financial statement analysis** accomplish this goal.

Objectives of Financial Statement Analysis

Users of financial statements fall into two broad categories: internal and external. Management is the main internal user. The tools of financial analysis are, of course, useful in management's operation of the business. However, because those who run the company have inside information on operations, other techniques are also available to them. Since those techniques are covered in managerial accounting courses, the main focus here is on the external use of financial analysis.

Creditors make loans in the form of trade accounts, notes, or bonds, on which they receive interest. They expect a loan to be repaid according to its terms. Investors buy capital stock, from which they hope to receive dividends and an increase in value. Both groups face risks. The creditor faces the risk that the debtor will fail to pay back the loan. The investor faces the risk that dividends will be reduced or not paid or that the market price of the stock will drop. In each case, the goal is to achieve a return that makes up for the risk taken. In general, the greater the risk taken, the greater the return required as compensation.

Any one loan or any one investment can turn out badly. As a result, most creditors and investors put their funds into a **portfolio**, or group of loans or investments. The portfolio allows them to average both the return and the risk. Nevertheless, the portfolio is made up of a number of loans or stocks on which individual

OBJECTIVE 1
*Describe and
discuss the
objectives of
financial state-
ment analysis*

decisions must be made. It is in making these individual decisions that financial statement analysis is most useful. Creditors and investors use financial statement analysis in two general ways. (1) They use it to judge past performance and current position. (2) They use it to judge future potential and the risk connected with the potential.

Assessment of Past Performance and Current Position

Past performance is often a good indicator of future performance. Therefore, an investor or creditor is interested in the trend of past sales, expenses, net income, cash flow, and return on investment. These trends offer a means for judging management's past performance and are a possible indicator of future performance. In addition, an analysis of current position will tell where the business stands today. For example, it will tell what assets the business owns and what liabilities must be paid. It will tell what the cash position is, how much debt the company has in relation to equity, and how reasonable the inventories and receivables are. Knowing a company's past performance and current position is often important in achieving the second general objective of financial analysis.

Assessment of Future Potential and Related Risk

The past and present information is useful only to the extent that it has bearing on future decisions. An investor judges the potential earning ability of a company because that ability will affect the value of the investment (market price of the company's stock) and the amount of dividends the company will pay. A creditor judges the potential debt-paying ability of the company. The potentials of some companies are easier to predict than others, and so there is less risk associated with them. The riskiness of the investment or loan depends on how easy it is to predict future profitability or liquidity. If an investor can predict with confidence that a company's earnings per share will be between $2.50 and $2.60 next year, the investment is less risky than if the earnings per share are expected to fall between $2.00 and $3.00. For example, the potential associated with an investment in an established and stable electric utility, or a loan to it, is relatively easy to predict on the basis of the company's past performance and current position. The potential associated with a small minicomputer manufacturer, on the other hand, may be much harder to predict. For this reason, the investment or loan to the electric utility is less risky than the investment or loan to the small computer company. Often, in return for taking the greater risk, the investor in the minicomputer company will demand a higher expected return (increase in market price plus dividends) than will the investor in the utility company. Also, a creditor of the minicomputer company will need a higher interest rate and possibly more assurance of repayment (a secured loan, for instance) than will a creditor of the utility company. The higher interest rate is payment to the creditor for assuming a higher risk.

Standards for Financial Statement Analysis

OBJECTIVE 2
Describe and discuss the standards for financial statement analysis

In using financial statement analysis, decision makers must judge whether the relationships they have found are favorable or unfavorable. Three standards of comparison often used are (1) rule-of-thumb measurements, (2) past performance of the company, and (3) industry norms.

Rule-of-Thumb Measures

Many financial analysts and lenders use "ideal" or rule-of-thumb measures for key financial ratios. For example, it has long been thought that a current ratio (current assets divided by current liabilities) of 2:1 is acceptable. The credit-rating firm of Dun & Bradstreet, in its *Key Business Ratios*, offers these guidelines:

Current debt to tangible net worth. Ordinarily, a business begins to pile up trouble when this relationship exceeds 80%.

Inventory to net working capital. Ordinarily, this relationship should not exceed 80%.

Although such measures may suggest areas that need further investigation, there is no proof they are best for a specific company. A company with a larger than 2:1 current ratio may have a poor credit policy (resulting in accounts receivable being too large), too much or out-of-date inventory, or poor cash management. Another company may have a less than 2:1 ratio resulting from excellent management in these three areas. Thus, rule-of-thumb measurements must be used with great care.

Past Performance of the Company

An improvement over the rule-of-thumb method is the comparison of financial measures or ratios of the same company over a period of time. This standard will at least give the analyst some basis for judging whether the measure or ratio is getting better or worse. It may also be helpful in showing possible future trends. However, since trends do reverse at times, such projections must be made with care. Another disadvantage is that the past may not be a good measure of adequacy. In other words, it may not be enough to meet present needs. For example, even if return on total investment improved from 3 percent last year to 4 percent this year, the 4 percent return may not be adequate.

Industry Norms

One way of making up for the limitations of using past performance as a standard is to use industry norms. This standard will tell how the company being analyzed compares with other companies in the same industry. For example, suppose that other companies in the same industry as the company in the paragraph above have an average rate of return on total investment of 8 percent. In such a case the 3 and 4 percent returns are probably not adequate. Industry norms can also be used to judge trends. Suppose that because of a downward turn in the economy, a company's profit margin dropped from 12 to 10 percent. A finding that other companies in the same industry had an average drop in profit margin from 12 to 4 percent would indicate that the company being analyzed did relatively well.

There are three limitations to using industry norms as standards. First, although two companies seem to be in the same industry, they may not be strictly comparable. Consider two companies said to be in the oil industry. The main business of one may be marketing oil products it buys from other producers through service stations. The other, an international company, may discover, produce, refine, and market its own oil products. The operations of these two different companies cannot be compared.

Second, most large companies today operate in more than one industry. Some of these **diversified companies**, or **conglomerates**, operate in many unrelated industries. The individual segments of a diversified company generally have different rates of profitability and degrees of risk. In using the consolidated financial statements of these companies for financial analysis, it is often impossible to use industry norms as standards. There are simply no other companies that are closely enough related. One partial solution to this problem is a requirement by the Financial Accounting Standards Board in *Statement No. 14*. This requirement states that diversified companies must report revenues, income from operations, and identifiable assets for each of their operating segments. Depending on specific criteria, segment information may be reported for operations in different industries, in foreign markets, or to major customers.[1] An example of reporting for industry segments is given in Exhibit 18-1, which comes from Eastman Kodak Company's annual report. It is interesting to compare the two reported segments, imaging and chemicals. Sales from the imaging segment have increased 28.2 percent from $8,531 million in 1985 to $10,941 million in 1987 whereas sales from the chemical segment increased only 10.7 percent over the same time period from $2,348 million to $2,600 million. The change in earnings from operations is even more dramatic. Imaging earnings from operations increased 356 percent from $378 million to $1,723 million, and chemical earnings increased 112 percent from $183 million to $388 million.

Third, companies in the same industry with similar operations may use different accounting procedures. That is, inventories may be valued by using different methods, or different depreciation methods may be used for assets that are alike. Even so, if little information is available about a company's prior performance, industry norms probably offer the best available standards for judging a company's current performance. They should be used with care.

---

1. *Statement of Financial Accounting Standards No. 14*, "Financial Reporting for Segments of a Business Enterprise" (Stamford, Conn.: Financial Accounting Standards Board, 1976).

Exhibit 18-1. Segment Information

(in millions)	1987	1986	1985
Sales, including intersegment sales*			
Imaging	$10,941	$ 9,408	$ 8,531
Chemicals	2,600	2,378	2,348
Intersegment sales			
Imaging	(6)	(12)	(12)
Chemicals	(230)	(224)	(236)
Sales to unaffiliated customers	$13,305	$11,550	$10,631
Earnings from operations			
Imaging	$ 1,723	$ 497	$ 378
Chemicals	388	227	183
Earnings from operations	$ 2,111	$ 724	$ 561
Interest and other income (charges)			
Imaging	27	(30)	(1)
Chemicals	(12)	18	14
Corporate	39	86	139
Interest expense	(181)	(200)	(183)
Earnings before income taxes	$ 1,984	$ 598	$ 530
Assets			
Imaging	$11,537	$10,309	$ 9,387
Chemicals	2,514	2,266	2,136
Corporate (cash and marketable securities)	620	501	734
Intersegment receivables	(220)	(174)	(115)
Total assets at year end	$14,451	$12,902	$12,142
Depreciation expense			
Imaging	$ 760	$ 767	$ 655
Chemicals	202	189	176
Total depreciation expense	$ 962	$ 956	$ 831
Capital expenditures			
Imaging	$ 1,258	$ 1,124	$ 1,244
Chemicals	394	314	251
Total capital expenditures	$ 1,652	$ 1,438	$ 1,495

* The products of each segment are manufactured and marketed in the U.S. and in other parts of the world. The imaging segment includes film, paper, equipment, and other related products. The chemical segment includes fibers, plastics, industrial and other chemicals. Sales between segments are made on a basis intended to reflect the market value of the products.

Sources of Information

OBJECTIVE 3
State the sources of information for financial state- ment analysis

The external analyst is often limited to publicly available information about a company. The major sources of information about publicly held corporations are published reports, SEC reports, business periodicals, and credit and investment advisory services.

Published Reports

The annual report of a publicly held corporation is an important source of financial information. The major parts of this annual report are (1) management's analysis of the past year's operations, (2) the financial statements, (3) the notes to the statements, including the principal accounting procedures used by the company, (4) the auditor's report, and (5) a summary of operations for a five- or ten-year period. Also, most publicly held companies publish interim financial statements each quarter. These reports present limited information in the form of condensed financial statements, which may be subject to a limited review or a full audit by the independent auditor. The interim statements are watched closely by the financial community for early signs of important changes in a company's earnings trend.[2]

SEC Reports

Publicly held corporations must file annual reports, quarterly reports, and current reports with the Securities and Exchange Commission (SEC). All such reports are available to the public at a small charge. The SEC calls for a standard form for the annual report (Form 10-K). This report is fuller than the published annual report. Form 10-K is, for this reason, a valuable source of information. It is available, free of charge, to stockholders of the company. The quarterly report (Form 10-Q) presents important facts about interim financial performance. The current report (Form 8-K) must be filed within fifteen days of the date of certain major events. It is often the first indicator of important changes that may affect the company's financial performance in the future.

Business Periodicals and
Credit and Investment Advisory Services

Financial analysts must keep up with current events in the financial world. Probably the best source of financial news is *The Wall Street Journal*, which is published daily and is the most complete financial newspaper in the United States. Some helpful magazines, published every week or every two weeks, are *Forbes, Barron's, Fortune,* and the

---

2. Accounting Principles Board, *Opinion No. 28,* "Interim Financial Reporting" (New York: American Institute of Certified Public Accountants, 1973); and *Statement of Financial Accounting Standards No. 3,* "Reporting Accounting Change in Interim Financial Statements" (Stamford, Conn.: Financial Accounting Standards Board, 1974).

Commercial and Financial Chronicle. For further details about the financial history of companies, the publications of such services as Moody's Investors Service and Standard & Poor's Industrial Surveys are useful. Data on industry norms, average ratios and relationships, and credit ratings are available from such agencies as Dun & Bradstreet Corporation. Dun & Bradstreet offers, among other useful services, an annual analysis using 14 ratios of 125 industry groups classified as retailing, wholesaling, manufacturing, and construction in its *Key Business Ratios.* Another important source of industry data is the *Annual Statement Studies,* published by Robert Morris Associates, which presents many facts and ratios for 223 different industries. Also, a number of private services are available to the analyst for a yearly fee.

Evaluating a Company's Quality of Earnings

OBJECTIVE 4
Identify the issues related to the evaluation of the quality of a company's earnings

It is clear from the preceding sections that the current and expected earnings of a company play an important role in the analysis of a company's prospects. In fact, a recent survey of 2,000 members of the Financial Analysis Federation indicated that the two most important economic indicators in evaluating common stocks were expected changes in earnings per share and expected return on equity.[3] Net income is an important component of both measures. Because of the importance of net income or the "bottom line" in measures of a company's prospects, interest in evaluating the quality of the net income figure, or the *quality of earnings,* has become an important topic. The quality of a company's earnings may be affected by (1) the accounting methods and estimates the company's management chooses and/or (2) the nature of nonoperating items in the income statement.

Choice of Accounting Methods and Estimates

There are two aspects to the choice of accounting methods that affect the quality of earnings. First, some accounting methods are by nature more conservative than others because they tend to produce a lower net income in the current period. Second, there is considerable latitude in the choice of the estimated useful life over which assets are written off or in the amount of estimated residual value. In general, an accounting method, an estimated useful life, and/or residual value that results in lower current earnings is considered to produce a better quality of earnings.

Various acceptable alternative methods are used in the application of the matching rule. These methods are based on allocation procedures, which in turn are based on certain assumptions. Here are some of these procedures:

3. Cited in *The Week in Review* (Deloitte, Haskins & Sells), February 28, 1985.

1. For estimating uncollectible accounts expense: percentage of net sales method and accounts receivable aging method.
2. For pricing the ending inventory: average cost method; first-in, first-out (FIFO); and last-in, first-out (LIFO).
3. For estimating depreciation expense: straight-line method, production method, sum-of-the-years'-digits method, and declining-balance method.
4. For estimating depletion expense: production (extraction) method.
5. For estimating amortization of intangibles: straight-line method.

All these procedures attempt to allocate the costs of assets to the periods in which those costs contribute to the production of revenue. They are based on a determination of the benefits to the current period (expenses) versus the benefits to future periods (assets). They are estimates, and the period or periods benefited cannot be demonstrated conclusively. They are also subjective, because in practice it is hard to justify one method of estimation over another. For this reason, it is important for the accountant as well as the financial statement user to understand the possible effects of different accounting procedures on net income and financial position. For example, suppose that two companies have similar operations but that one uses FIFO for inventory pricing and the straight-line (SL) method for computing depreciation, and the other company uses LIFO for inventory pricing and the sum-of-the-years'-digits (SYD) method for computing depreciation. The income statements of the two companies might appear as follows:

	FIFO and SL Company	LIFO and SYD Company
Sales	$500,000	$500,000
Goods Available for Sale	$300,000	$300,000
Less Ending Inventory	60,000	50,000
Cost of Goods Sold	$240,000	$250,000
Gross Margin	$260,000	$250,000
Less: Depreciation Expense	$ 40,000	$ 70,000
Other Expenses	170,000	170,000
Total Operating Expenses	$210,000	$240,000
Net Income	$ 50,000	$ 10,000

This fivefold difference in income stems only from the differences in inventory and depreciation methods. Differences in the estimated lives and residual values of the plant assets could cause an even greater difference. In practice, of course, differences in net income occur for many reasons, but the user must be aware of the differences that can occur as a result of the methods chosen by management.

The existence of these alternatives could cause problems in the interpretation of financial statements were it not for the conventions of full disclosure and consistency. Full disclosure requires that management explain the significant accounting policies used in preparing the financial statements in a note to the statements. Consistency requires that the same accounting procedure be followed from year to year. If a change in procedure is made, the nature of the change and its monetary effect must be explained in a note.

Nature of Nonoperating Earnings

The corporate income statement consists of several components. The top of the statement presents earnings from current ongoing operations called income from operations. The lower part of the statement can contain such nonoperating items as discontinued operations, extraordinary gains and losses, and effects of accounting changes. These items may drastically affect the bottom line, or net income, of the company. For example, Eastman Kodak Company (see Exhibit 18-3) had an unusual charge of $520 million in 1986 that related primarily to the discontinuing of its instant camera line and the loss of a patent suit with Polaroid. This loss had a detrimental effect on reported Net Earnings in 1986, and the loss of this business may adversely affect future years' earnings.

These nonoperating items should be taken into consideration when interpreting a company's earnings. For example, in 1983, U.S. Steel made an apparent turnaround by reporting first quarter earnings of $1.35 a share versus a deficit of $1.31 a year earlier. However, the "improved" earnings included a gain from sales of assets of $.45 per share and sale of tax benefits on newly acquired assets of $.40 per share, as well as other items totaling $.61 per share. These items total $1.46, an amount greater than the reported earnings for the year.[4] The opposite effect can also occur. For the first six months of 1984, Texas Instruments reported a loss of $112 million compared with a profit of $64.5 million the previous year. The loss was caused by write-offs of $58 million for nonoperating losses, $83 million for inventory, and $37 million for increased reserves for rebates, price protection for retailers, and returned inventory.[5] In reality this large write-off was a positive step on Texas Instruments' part because getting out of the low-profit home computer business meant TI's future cash flows would not be drained by the unprofitable home computer operations.

For practical reasons, the trends and ratios in the sections that follow use the net income component and other components as if they were comparable from year to year and from company to company. However, the astute analyst will always look beyond the ratios to the quality of the components in making interpretations.

---

4. Dan Dorfman, "Three Well-Known Stocks with Earnings of Dubious Quality," *Chicago Tribune* (June 28, 1984), p. 11.
5. "Loss at Texas Instruments Hits $119.2 Million," *The Wall Street Journal* (November 14, 1984).

Tools and Techniques of Financial Analysis

OBJECTIVE 5
Apply horizontal analysis, trend analysis, and vertical analysis to financial statements

Few numbers by themselves mean very much. It is their relationship to other numbers or their change from one period to another that is important. The tools of financial analysis are intended to show relationships and changes. Among the more widely used of these techniques are horizontal analysis, trend analysis, vertical analysis, and ratio analysis.

Horizontal Analysis

Generally accepted accounting principles call for presenting comparative financial statements that give the current year's and past year's financial information. A common starting point for studying such statements is horizontal analysis, which involves the computation of dollar amount changes and percentage changes from the previous to the current year. The percentage change must be figured to show how the size of the change relates to the size of the amounts involved. A change of $1 million in sales is not so drastic as a change of $1 million in net income, because sales is a larger amount than net income. Exhibits 18-2 and 18-3 (next two pages) present the comparative balance sheets and income statements, respectively, for Eastman Kodak Company, with the dollar and percentage changes shown. The percentage change is computed as follows:

$$\text{Percentage change} = 100\left(\frac{\text{amount of change}}{\text{previous year amount}}\right)$$

The base year in any set of data is always the first year being studied. For example, from 1986 to 1987, Kodak's current assets increased by $884 million, from $5,811 million to $6,695 million, or by 15.2 percent, computed as follows:

$$\text{Percentage increase} = 100\left(\frac{\$884 \text{ million}}{\$5,811 \text{ million}}\right) = 15.2\%$$

Care must be taken in the analysis of percentage change. For example, in analyzing the changes in the components of total assets in Exhibit 18-2, one might view the 20.4 percent increase in receivables as being less than the 153.8 percent increase in cash. In dollar amount, though, receivables increased by more than two times as much as cash did ($523 million versus $223 million). Dollar amounts and percentage increases must be considered together. On the liability and owners' equity side of the balance sheet, long-term bonds and Treasury Stock are up substantially (by 142.8 percent and 90.5 percent).

In the income statement (Exhibit 18-3), the most important changes from 1986 to 1987 show a 15.2 percent growth in sales compared to an 8.6 percent increase in costs and expenses. When the dollar amounts of these changes are combined, they result in a 69.7 percent increase in earnings from operations. In addition, net earnings were adversely affected by an unusual charge in 1986. Other income and expenses were almost unchanged. The provision for income taxes was up 259.8 percent,

Exhibit 18-2. Comparative Balance Sheet with Horizontal Analysis

Eastman Kodak Company
Consolidated Balance Sheets
December 27, 1987, and December 28, 1986

	(In millions)		Increase (Decrease)	
	1987	1986	Amount	Percentage
Assets				
Current Assets				
Cash	$ 368	$ 145	$ 223	153.8
Marketable securities	586	468	118	25.2
Receivables	3,086	2,563	523	20.4
Inventories	2,178	2,072	106	5.1
Prepaid expense and deferred charges	477	563	(86)	(15.3)
Total Current Assets	$ 6,695	$ 5,811	$ 884	15.2
Properties				
Land, buildings, machinery, and equipment less accumulated depreciation of $7,126 and $6,643	6,663	6,276	387	6.2
Long-term receivables and other noncurrent assets	1,093	815	278	34.1
Total Assets	$14,451	$12,902	$1,549	12.0
Liabilities				
Liabilities				
Current Liabilities				
Payables	$ 3,549	$ 3,440	$ 109	3.2
Taxes payable	380	209	171	81.8
Dividends payable	146	142	4	2.8
Total current liabilities	$ 4,075	$ 3,791	$ 284	7.5
Long-term Liabilities				
Long-term bonds	2,212	911	1,301	142.8
Other long-term liabilities	743	603	140	23.2
Deferred income tax liabilities	1,408	1,209	199	16.5
Total Liabilities	$ 8,438	$ 6,514	$1,924	29.5
Ownership				
Common stock (par value)	$ 933	$ 622	$ 311	50.0
Additional paid-in capital	—	314	(314)	(100.0)
Retained earnings	7,139	6,533	606	9.3
Treasury stock at cost	(2,059)	(1,081)	(978)	90.5
Total Ownership	6,013	6,388	(375)	(5.9)
Total Liabilities and Ownership	$14,451	$12,902	$1,549	12.0

| Exhibit 18-3. Comparative Income Statements with Horizontal Analysis |

Eastman Kodak Company
Consolidated Statements of Earnings
For Years Ended December 27, 1987, and December 28, 1986

	(In millions)		Increase (Decrease)	
	1987	1986	Amount	Percentage
Sales	$13,305	$11,550	$1,755	15.2
Costs and Expenses				
Cost of goods sold	8,004	7,613	391	5.1
Selling and administrative expenses	3,190	2,693	497	18.5
Total costs and expenses	11,194	10,306	888	8.6
Earnings from Operations	2,111	1,244	867	69.7
Unusual charges	—	(520)	520	100
Other income and expenses including interest expense of $181 and $200	(127)	(126)	(1)	(.8)
Earnings Before Income Taxes	1,984	598	1,386	231.8
Provision for income taxes	806	224	582	259.8
Net Earnings	$ 1,178	$ 374	804	215.0
Average number of common shares outstanding*	334.7	338.6	(3.9)	(1.2)
Net Earnings per Share*	$ 3.52	$ 1.10	2.42	220.0

* Per share data and average number of common shares outstanding for 1986 have been restated to reflect the 3-for-2 partial stock split in 1987.

reflecting the increase in earnings before income taxes. Overall net earnings were up 215.0 percent.

Trend Analysis

A variation of horizontal analysis is **trend analysis,** in which percentage changes are calculated for several successive years instead of between two years. Trend analysis is important because, with its long-run view, it may point to basic changes in the nature of the business. Besides comparative financial statements, most companies give out a summary of operations and data on other key indicators for five or more years. Selected items from Kodak's summary of operations together with trend analysis are presented in Exhibit 18-4. Trend analysis uses an **index number** to show changes in related items over a period of time. For index numbers, one year, the base year, is equal to 100 percent. Other years are measured in relation to that amount. For example, the 1987 index of 130.8 for sales was figured as follows:

$$\text{Index} = 100\left(\frac{\text{index year amount}}{\text{base year amount}}\right) = \left(\frac{\$13,305}{\$10,170}\right) = 130.8$$

Exhibit 18-4. Trend Analysis

Eastman Kodak Company
Summary of Operations
Selected Data
(Sales and Net Earnings in Millions)

	1987	1986	1985	1984	1983
Sales	$13,305	$11,550	$10,631	$10,600	$10,170
Net Earnings	1,178	374	332	923	565
Per Common Share*					
Earnings*	3.52	1.10	.97	2.54	1.52
Dividends*	1.71	1.63	1.62	1.60	1.58
Trend Analysis					
Sales	130.8	113.6	104.5	104.2	100.0
Net Earnings	208.5	66.2	58.8	163.4	100.0
Per Common Share					
Earnings	231.6	72.4	63.8	167.1	100.0
Dividends	108.2	103.2	102.5	101.3	100.0

* Per share data restated to reflect stock splits in 1985 and 1987.

An index number of 130.8 means that 1987 sales are 130.8 percent or 1.308 times 1983 sales. A study of the trend analysis in Exhibit 18-4 shows that after lagging sales growth during the first four years, net earnings caught up and surpassed sales in 1987 by 208.5 to 130.8. This improvement in earnings relative to sales is dramatically shown when graphed as in Figure 18-1. Earnings per common share increased more rapidly than net earnings (231.6 in 1987 versus 208.5), while dividends per share increased by a modest amount each year (108.2 in 1987). Apparently, the company felt it was important to keep up a small but steady increase in dividends in spite of the increase in net earnings from 1983 to 1987.

Vertical Analysis

Vertical analysis uses percentages to show the relationship of the different parts to the total in a single statement. Vertical analysis sets a total figure in the statement equal to 100 percent and computes the percentage of each component of that figure. (This figure would be total assets or total liabilities and stockholders' equity in the case of the balance sheet, and revenues or sales in the case of the income statement.) The resulting statement of percentages is called a common-size statement. Common-size balance sheets and income statements for Kodak are shown graphically in piechart form in Figures 18-2 and 18-3, and in financial statement form in Exhibits 18-5 and 18-6 (pages 744–745 and 746).

Figure 18-1. Trend Analysis for Eastman Kodak Company

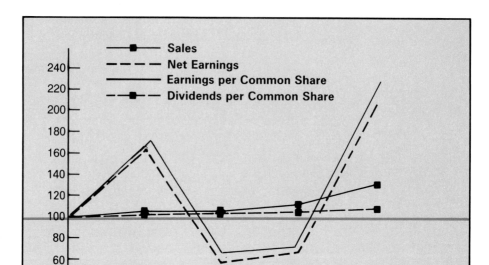

Figure 18-2. Common-size Balance Sheet Presented Graphically

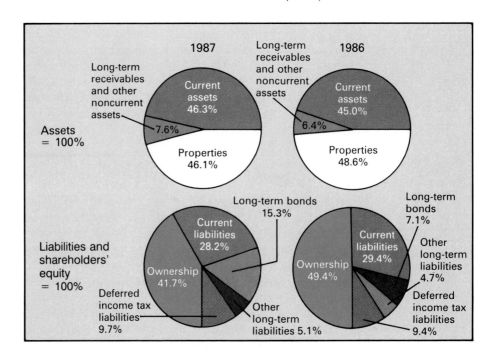

Generally, current assets and current liabilities are given only in total, because ratios are used to analyze their components very carefully. Vertical analysis is useful for comparing the importance of certain components in the operation of the business. It is also useful for pointing out important changes in the components from one year to the next when comparative common-size statements are presented. For Kodak, the composition of assets in Exhibit 18-5 changed from one year to the next. Slightly fewer assets were in properties (46.1 percent versus 48.6 percent) and more in current assets (46.3 percent versus 45.0 percent) in 1987 as opposed to 1986. However, more assets were in long-term receivables and other noncurrent assets. Also, the part of total liabilities made up of current liabilities decreased from 29.4 percent to 28.2 percent. However, long-term bonds increased from 7.1 percent to 15.3 percent.

Exhibit 18-5. Common-size Balance Sheets

Eastman Kodak Company
Common-size Balance Sheets
December 27, 1987, and December 28, 1986

	1987	1986
Assets		
Current Assets	46.3%	45.0%
Properties (less Accumulated Depreciation)	46.1	48.6
Long-term Receivables and Other Noncurrent Assets	7.6	6.4
Total Assets	100.0%	100.0%
Liabilities		
Current Liabilities	28.2%	29.4%
Long-term Bonds	15.3	7.1
Other Long-term Liabilities	5.1	4.7
Deferred Income Tax Liabilities	9.7	9.4
Total Liabilities	58.3%	50.6%
Ownership		
Common Stock	6.5%	4.8%
Additional Paid-in Capital	—	2.4
Retained Earnings	49.4	50.6
Treasury Stock at Cost	(14.2)	(8.4)
Total Ownership	41.7%	49.4%
Total Liabilities and Ownership	100.0%	100.0%

Results are rounded in some cases to equal 100%

Figure 18-3. Common-size Income Statement Presented Graphically

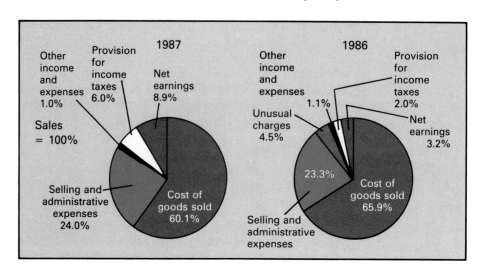

Exhibit 18-6. Common-size Income Statements

Eastman Kodak Company
Common-size Statements of Earnings
For Years Ended December 27, 1987, and December 28, 1986

	1987	1986
Sales	100.0%	100.0%
Costs and Expenses		
Cost of Goods Sold	60.1	65.9
Selling and Administrative Expenses	24.0	23.3
Total Costs and Expenses	84.1%	89.2%
Earnings from Operations	15.9%	10.8%
Unusual Charges	—	(4.5)
Other Income and Expenses	(1.0)	(1.1)
Earnings Before Income Taxes	14.9%	5.2%
Provision for Income Taxes	6.0	2.0
Net Earnings	8.9%	3.2%

This latter change contributed to a much higher percentage of the company financed by total liabilities in 1987 than in 1986 (58.3 percent versus 50.6 percent). The common-size statements of earnings (Exhibit 18-6) show the importance of the decrease in costs and expenses from 89.2 to 84.1 percent of sales. This decrease was the major cause of the increase in earnings from operations from 10.8 to 15.9 percent of sales. Unusual charges were 4.5 percent of 1986 sales, further decreasing earnings before income taxes in that year. The unfavorable change in income taxes is shown by the increase in the provision for income taxes from 2.0 percent to 6.0 percent of sales.

Common-size statements are often used to make comparisons between companies. They allow an analyst to compare the operating and financing characteristics of two companies of different sizes in the same industry. For example, the analyst may want to compare Kodak to other companies in terms of the percentage of total assets financed by debt or the percentage of general administrative and selling expenses to sales and revenues. Common-size statements would show these relationships.

Ratio Analysis

Ratio analysis is an important way to state meaningful relationships between components of financial statements. To be most useful, a ratio must also include a study of the underlying data. Ratios are guides or short cuts that are useful in evaluating the financial position and operations of a company and in comparing them to previous years or to other companies. The primary purpose of ratios is to point out areas for further investigation. They should be used in connection with a general understanding of the company and its environment.

Ratios may be stated in several ways. For example, the ratio of net income of $100,000 to sales of $1,000,000 may be stated as (1) net income is 1/10 or 10 percent of sales; (2) the ratio of sales to net income is 10 to 1 (10:1) or 10 times net income, or (3) for every dollar of sales, the company has an average net income of 10 cents.

Survey of Commonly Used Ratios

OBJECTIVE 6
Apply ratio analysis to financial statements in the study of an enterprise's liquidity, profitability, long-term solvency, and market tests

In the following sections, ratio analysis is applied to four objectives: the evaluation of (1) liquidity, (2) profitability, (3) long-term solvency, and (4) market strength. We expand the evaluation to bring in ratios related to these objectives and to introduce the ratios related to the objectives. Data for the analyses come from the financial statements of Kodak presented in Exhibits 18-2 and 18-3. Other data are presented as needed.

Evaluating Liquidity

The aim of liquidity is for a company to have enough funds on hand to pay bills when they are due and to meet unexpected needs for cash. The ratios that relate to this goal all have to do with working capital or some part of it, because it is out of working capital that debts are paid as they mature. Some common ratios connected with evaluating liquidity are the current ratio, the quick ratio, receivable turnover, and inventory turnover.

Current Ratio. The current ratio expresses the relationship of current assets to current liabilities. It is widely used as a broad indicator of a company's liquidity and short-term debt-paying ability. The ratio for Kodak for 1987 and 1986 is figured as follows:

Current Ratio	1987	1986
$\dfrac{\text{Current assets}}{\text{Current liabilities}}$	$\dfrac{\$6,695}{\$4,075} = 1.64$	$\dfrac{\$5,811}{\$3,791} = 1.53$

The current ratio for Eastman Kodak Company shows a small improvement from 1986 to 1987.

Quick Ratio. One of the current ratio's faults is that it does not take into account the make-up of current assets. They may appear to be large enough, but they may not have the proper balance. Clearly, a dollar of cash or even accounts receivable is more readily available to meet obligations than is a dollar of most kinds of inventory. The quick ratio is designed to overcome this problem by measuring short-term liquidity. That is, it measures the relationship of the more liquid current assets (cash, marketable securities or short-term investments, and receivables) to current liabilities. This ratio for Kodak for 1987 and 1986 is figured as follows:

Quick Ratio	1987	1986
$\dfrac{\text{Cash + marketable securities + receivables}}{\text{Current liabilities}}$	$\dfrac{\$368 + \$586 + \$3,086}{\$4,075}$	$\dfrac{\$145 + \$468 + \$2,563}{\$3,791}$
	$= \dfrac{\$4,040}{\$4,075} = 0.99$	$= \dfrac{\$3,176}{\$3,791} = 0.84$

This ratio also shows an improvement from 1986 to 1987.

Receivable Turnover. The ability of a company to collect for credit sales in a timely way affects the company's liquidity. The receivable turnover ratio measures the relative size of a company's accounts receivable and the success of its credit and collection policies. This ratio shows how many times, on average, the receivables were turned into cash during the period. Turnover ratios usually consist of one balance sheet account and one income statement account. The receivable turnover is computed by dividing net sales by average accounts receivable. Theoretically, the numerator should be net credit sales, but the amount of net credit sales is rarely made available in public reports. So we will use total net sales. Further, in this ratio and others where an average is required, we will take the beginning and ending balances and divide by 2. If we had internal financial data, it would be better to use monthly balances to find the average, because the balances of receivables, inventories, and other accounts can vary widely during the year. In fact, many companies choose a fiscal year that begins and ends at a low period of the business cycle when inventories and receivables may be at the lowest levels of the year. Using a 1985 accounts receivable ending balance of $2,346 million, Kodak's receivable turnover is computed as follows:

Receivable Turnover	1987	1986
$\dfrac{\text{Net sales}}{\substack{\text{Average accounts} \\ \text{receivable}}}$	$\dfrac{\$13,305}{(\$3,086 + \$2,563)/2}$	$\dfrac{\$11,550}{(\$2,563 + \$2,346)/2}$
	$= \dfrac{\$13,305}{\$2,824.5} = \begin{array}{c}4.71 \\ \text{times}\end{array}$	$= \dfrac{\$11,550}{\$2,454.5} = \begin{array}{c}4.71 \\ \text{times}\end{array}$

When the previous year's balance is not available for computing the average, it is common practice to use the ending balance for the current year.

Within reasonable ranges, the higher the turnover ratio the better. With a higher turnover the company is turning receivables into cash at a faster pace. The speed at which receivables are turned over depends on the company's credit terms. Since a company's credit terms are usually stated in days, such as 2/10, n/30, it is helpful to convert the receivable turnover to *average days' sales uncollected*. This conversion is made by dividing the length of the accounting period (usually 365 days) by the receivable turnover (as computed above) as follows:

Average Days' Sales Uncollected	1987	1986
$\dfrac{\text{Days in year}}{\text{Receivable turnover}}$	$\dfrac{365 \text{ days}}{4.71} = 77.5 \text{ days}$	$\dfrac{365 \text{ days}}{4.71} = 77.5 \text{ days}$

In the case of Kodak, both the receivable turnover and the average days' sales uncollected were unchanged from 1986 to 1987. The average accounts receivable was turned over about 4.7 times both years. This means Kodak had to wait on average about 77.5 days to receive payment for credit sales.

Inventory Turnover. Inventory is two steps removed from cash (sale and collection). The *inventory turnover* ratio measures the relative size of inventory. The proportion of assets tied up in inventory, of course, affects the amount of cash available to pay maturing debts. Inventory should be maintained at the best level to support production and sales. In general, however, a smaller, faster-moving inventory means that the company has less cash tied up in inventory. It also means that there is less chance for the inventory to become spoiled or out of date. A build-up in inventory may mean that a recession or some other factor is preventing sales from keeping pace with purchasing and production. Using a 1985 ending inventory balance of $1,940 million, inventory turnover for 1987 and 1986 at Eastman Kodak Company is computed as follows on page 750:

Inventory Turnover	1987	1986
$\dfrac{\text{Cost of goods sold}}{\text{Average inventory}}$	$\dfrac{\$8,004}{(\$2,178 + \$2,072)/2}$	$\dfrac{\$7,613}{(\$2,072 + \$1,940)/2}$
	$= \dfrac{\$8,004}{\$2,125} = \begin{matrix} 3.77 \\ \text{times} \end{matrix}$	$= \dfrac{\$7,613}{\$2,006} = \begin{matrix} 3.80 \\ \text{times} \end{matrix}$

Consistent with receivable turnover, there was little change in inventory turnover from 1986 to 1987.

Evaluating Profitability

A company's long-run survival depends on its being able to earn a satisfactory income. Investors become and remain stockholders for only one reason. They believe that the dividends and capital gains they will receive will be greater than the returns on other investments of about the same risk. An evaluation of a company's past earning power may give the investor a better basis for decision making. A company's ability to earn an income usually affects its liquidity position. For this reason, evaluating profitability is important to both investors and creditors. In judging the profitability of Kodak, five ratios will be presented: profit margin, asset turnover, return on assets, return on equity, and earnings per share.

Profit Margin. The **profit margin** ratio measures the amount of net income produced by each revenue dollar. It is computed for Kodak as follows:

Profit Margin[6]	1987	1986
$\dfrac{\text{Net income}}{\text{Net sales}}$	$\dfrac{\$1,178}{\$13,305} = 8.9\%$	$\dfrac{\$374}{\$11,550} = 3.2\%$

The ratio confirms what was clear from the common-size income statement (Exhibit 18-6): that the profit margin improved from 1986 (3.2 percent) to 1987 (8.9 percent). The analysis of the common-size income statement showed that this increase was due to a decrease in costs and expenses as a percentage of total sales as well as to unusual charges that reduced net income in 1986.

Asset Turnover. **Asset turnover** is a measure of how efficiently assets are used to produce sales. It shows how many dollars in sales are produced by each dollar invested in assets. In other words, it tells how many times in the period assets were "turned over" in sales. The higher the asset turnover, the more concentrated is the use of assets. Using the data for Kodak from Exhibits 18-2 and 18-3 and 1985 total assets of $12,142 million, the asset turnovers for 1987 and 1986 are as follows:

6. In comparing companies in an industry, some analysts use net income before income taxes as the numerator to eliminate the effect of differing tax rates among the individual firms.

Asset Turnover	1987	1986
$\dfrac{\text{Net sales}}{\text{Average total assets}}$	$\dfrac{\$13,305}{(\$14,451 + \$12,902)/2}$	$\dfrac{\$11,550}{(\$12,902 + \$12,142)/2}$
	$= \dfrac{\$13,305}{\$13,676.50} = \dfrac{.97}{\text{times}}$	$= \dfrac{\$11,550}{\$12,522} = \dfrac{.92}{\text{times}}$

Compared to other industries, Kodak needs a large investment in assets for each dollar of sales. A retailer may have an asset turnover of between 4.0 and 6.0. In the case of Kodak, however, the turnover was only .92 in 1986 and .97 in 1987. This fact means that Kodak makes sales of a little less than one dollar for each dollar of assets. Yet, the small increase is significant because of the company's large amount of sales and assets. In 1987, each dollar invested produced almost a dollar in sales.

Return on Assets. The best overall measure of the earning power or profitability of a company is **return on assets,** which measures the amount earned on each dollar of assets invested. The return on assets for 1987 and 1986 for Kodak is as follows:

Return on Assets[7]	1987	1986
$\dfrac{\text{Net income}}{\text{Average total assets}}$	$\dfrac{\$1,178}{\$13,676.50} = 8.6\%$	$\dfrac{\$374}{\$12,522} = 3.0\%$

Kodak's return on assets increased from 3.0 percent in 1986 to 8.6 percent in 1987, a favorable change.

One reason why return on assets is a good measure of profitability is that it combines the effects of profit margin and asset turnover. The 1987 and 1986 results for Kodak can be analyzed as follows:

	Profit Margin		Asset Turnover		Return on Assets
Ratios:	$\dfrac{\text{net income}}{\text{net sales}}$	$\times$	$\dfrac{\text{net sales}}{\text{average total assets}}$	$=$	$\dfrac{\text{net income}}{\text{average total assets}}$
1987	8.9%	$\times$	.97	$=$	8.6%
1986	3.2%	$\times$	.92	$=$	3.0%*

* Rounded

From this analysis, it is clear that the increase in return on assets in 1987 can be attributed mainly to the increase in profit margin.

Return on Equity. An important measure of profitability from the stockholders' standpoint is **return on equity.** This ratio measures how much was earned for each dollar invested by owners. For Kodak, this ratio for 1987 and 1986 is figured as follows on page 752 (1985 owners' equity equaled $6,562 million):

7. Some authorities would add interest expense to net income in the numerator because they view interest expense as a cost of acquiring capital, not a cost of operations.

Return on Equity	1987	1986
$\dfrac{\text{Net income}}{\text{Average stockholders' equity}}$	$\dfrac{\$1,178}{(\$6,013 + \$6,388)/2}$	$\dfrac{\$374}{(\$6,388 + \$6,562)/2}$
	$= \dfrac{\$1,178}{\$6,200.5} = 19.0\%$	$= \dfrac{\$374}{\$6,475} = 5.8\%$

As might be expected from the analysis of other profitability ratios above, this ratio also went up from 1986 to 1987.

A natural question is, Why is there a difference between return on assets and return on equity? The answer lies in the company's use of **leverage,** or debt financing. A company that has interest-bearing debt is said to be leveraged. If the company earns more with its borrowed funds than it must pay in interest for those funds, then the difference is available to increase the return on equity. Leverage may work against the company as well. Thus, an unfavorable situation occurs when the return on assets is less than the rate of interest paid on borrowed funds. Because of Kodak's leverage, the increase in return on assets from 1986 to 1987 of 3.0 to 8.6 percent resulted in a larger increase in return on equity of 5.8 to 19.0 percent for the same two years. (The debt to equity ratio is presented later in this chapter.)

Earnings per Share. One of the most widely quoted measures of profitability is earnings per share of common stock. Exhibit 18-3 shows that the net earnings per share for Kodak improved from $1.10 to $3.52, reflecting the increase in net earnings from 1986 to 1987. These disclosures must be made in financial statements.

Evaluating Long-term Solvency

Long-term solvency has to do with a company's ability to survive over many years. The aim of long-term solvency analysis is to point out early if a company is on the road to bankruptcy. Studies have shown that accounting ratios can show as much as five years in advance that a company may fail.[8] Declining profitability and liquidity ratios are key signs of possible business failure. Two other ratios that analysts often consider as indicators of long-term solvency are the debt to equity ratio and the interest coverage ratio.

Debt to Equity Ratio. The existence of increasing amounts of debt in a company's capital structure is thought to be risky. The company has a legal obligation to make interest payments on time and to pay the principal at the maturity date. And this obligation holds no matter what the level of the company's earnings is. If the payments are not made, the company

8. William H. Beaver, "Alternative Accounting Measures as Indicators of Failure," *Accounting Review* (January 1968); and Edward Altman, "Financial Ratios, Discriminant Analysis and the Prediction of Corporate Bankruptcy," *Journal of Finance* (September 1968).

may be forced into bankruptcy. In contrast, dividends and other distributions to equity holders are made only when the board of directors declares them. The debt to equity ratio shows the relationship of the company's assets provided by creditors to the amount provided by stockholders; it measures the extent to which the company is leveraged. The larger the debt to equity ratio, the more fixed obligations the company has and so the riskier the situation. It is computed as follows:

Debt to Equity Ratio	1987	1986
$\dfrac{\text{Total liabilities}}{\text{Stockholders' equity}}$	$\dfrac{\$8,438}{\$6,013} = 1.40$	$\dfrac{\$6,514}{\$6,388} = 1.02$

From 1986 to 1987, the debt to equity ratio for Kodak went up from 1.02 to 1.40. This finding agrees with the analysis of the common-size balance sheet (Exhibit 18-5), which shows that the total debt of the company increased as a percentage of total assets in 1987. Also, note the adverse effect the increase in treasury stock (see Exhibit 18-2) has on the debt to equity ratio.

Interest Coverage Ratio. One question that usually arises at this point is, If debt is bad, why have any? The answer is that, as with many ratios, it is a matter of balance. In spite of its riskiness, debt is a flexible means of financing certain business operations. Also, because it usually carries a fixed interest charge, it limits the cost of financing and presents a situation where leverage can be used to advantage. Thus, if the company is able to earn a return on the assets greater than the cost of the interest, the company makes an overall profit.[9] However, the company runs the risk of not earning a return on assets equal to the interest cost of financing those assets, thereby incurring an overall loss. One measure of the degree of protection creditors have from a default on interest payments is the interest coverage ratio, computed as follows:

Interest Coverage Ratio	1987	1986
$\dfrac{\text{Net income before}}{\text{taxes + interest expense}}$ $\dfrac{}{\text{Interest expense}}$	$\dfrac{\$1,984 + \$181}{\$181}$	$\dfrac{\$598 + \$200}{\$200}$
	$= 11.96$ times	$= 3.99$ times

Interest coverage improved in 1987; the interest payments are protected by a ratio of 11.96 times, versus only 3.99 in 1986.

Market Test Ratios

The market price of a company's shares of stock is of interest to the analyst because it represents what investors as a whole think of a company at a point in time. Market price is the price at which people are willing

---

9. In addition, there are advantages to being a debtor in periods of inflation because the debt, which is fixed in dollar amount, may be repaid with cheaper dollars.

to buy and sell the stock. It provides information about how investors view the potential return and risk connected with owning the company's stock. This information cannot be obtained simply by considering the market price of the stock by itself. Companies have different numbers of outstanding shares and different amounts of underlying earnings and dividends. Thus, the market price must be related to the earnings per share, dividends per share, and prices of other companies' shares to get the necessary information. This analysis is done through the price/earnings ratio, the dividends yield, and market risk.

Price/Earnings Ratio. The price/earnings (P/E) ratio measures the ratio of the current market price of the stock to the earnings per share. Assuming a current market price of $60 and using the 1987 earnings per share for Kodak of $3.52 from Exhibit 18-4, we can compute the price/earnings ratio as follows:

$$\frac{\text{Market price per share}}{\text{Earnings per share}} = \frac{\$60}{\$3.52} = 17.0 \text{ times}$$

This ratio changes from day to day and from quarter to quarter as market price and earnings change. It tells how much the investing public as a whole is willing to pay for $1 of Kodak's earnings per share. At this time, Kodak's P/E ratio is 17.0 times the underlying earnings for that share of stock. This is a high ratio due to the company's improved performance in 1987 and investors' expectations that the company's earnings will continue to increase.

This ratio is very useful and widely applied because it allows companies to be compared. When a company's P/E ratio is higher than the P/E ratios for other companies, it *usually* means that investors feel that the company's earnings are going to grow at a faster rate than those of the other companies. On the other hand, a lower P/E ratio *usually* means a more negative assessment by investors. To compare two well-known companies, the market was less favorable toward General Motors (7.0 times earnings per share) than it was toward IBM (14.0 times earnings per share) in 1988.

Dividends Yield. The dividends yield is a measure of the current return to an investor in the stock. It is found by dividing the current annual dividend by the current market price of the stock. Assuming the same $60 per share and using the 1987 dividends of $1.71 per share for Kodak from Exhibit 18-4, we can compute the dividends yield as follows:

$$\frac{\text{Dividends per share}}{\text{Market price per share}} = \frac{\$1.71}{\$60} = 2.9\%$$

Thus, an investor who owns Kodak stock at $60 had a return from dividends in 1987 of 2.9 percent. The dividends yield is only one part of the investor's total return from investing in Kodak. The investor must add to or subtract from the dividends yield the percentage change (either up or down) in the market value of the stock.

Market Risk. It was pointed out earlier that besides assessing the potential return from an investment, the investor must also judge the risk associated with the investment. Many factors may be brought into assessing risk— the nature of the business, the quality of the business, the track record of the company, and so forth. One measure of risk that has gained increased attention among analysts in recent years is market risk. **Market risk** is the volatility of (or changes up and down in) the price of a stock in relation to the volatility of the prices of other stocks. The computation of market risk is complex, because it requires computers and sophisticated statistical techniques such as regression analysis. The idea, however, is simple. Consider the following data about the changes in the prices of the stocks of Company A and Company B and the average change in price of all stocks in the market:

Average Percentage Change in Price of All Stock	Percentage Change in Price of Company A's Stock	Percentage Change in Price of Company B's Stock
+10	+15	+5
-10	-15	-5

In this example, when the average price of all stocks went up by 10 percent, Company A's price increased 15 percent and Company B's increased only 5 percent. When the average price of all stocks went down by 10 percent, Company A's price decreased 15 percent and Company B's decreased only 5 percent. Thus, relative to all stocks, Company A's stock is more volatile than Company B's stock. If the prices of stocks go down, the risk of loss is greater in the case of Company A than in the case of Company B. If the market goes up, however, the potential for gain is greater in the case of Company A than in the case of Company B.

Market risk can be approximated by dividing the percentage change in price of a particular stock by the average percentage change in the price of all stocks, as follows:

$$\text{Company A} \quad \frac{\text{specific change}}{\text{average change}} = \frac{15}{10} = 1.5$$

$$\text{Company B} \quad \frac{\text{specific change}}{\text{average change}} = \frac{5}{10} = .5$$

These measures mean that an investor can generally expect the value of an investment in Company A to increase or decrease 1.5 times as much as the average increase or decrease in the price of all stocks. An investment in Company B can be expected to increase or decrease only .5 times as much as the price of all stocks.

Analysts call this measure of market risk **beta** (β), after the mathematical symbol used in the formula for calculating the relationships of the stock prices. The actual betas used by analysts are based on several years of data and are continually updated. These calculations require the use of computers and are usually obtained from investment services.

The market risk or beta for U.S. Steel in a recent year was 1.01. This means that, other things being equal, a person who invests in the stock of U.S. Steel can expect its volatility or risk to be about the same as the stock market as a whole (which has a beta of 1.0). This makes sense when one considers that U.S. Steel is a mature company and the largest steel producer, with output closely related to the ups and downs in the economy as a whole.

If the investor's objective is to assume less risk than that of the market as a whole, other companies in the steel industry can be considered. The second largest steel company is Bethlehem Steel, but it can be eliminated because its beta of 1.25 makes it riskier than U.S. Steel. National Steel, the third largest steel processor, has been more stable over the years than its competitors, with a beta of only .75. It is a less risky stock in that there is less potential for loss in a "down" market, but there is also less potential for gain in an "up" market. The beta for National Steel is very low and compares favorably with that of a major utility such as American Telephone and Telegraph, which has a beta of .65.

Typically, growth stocks and speculative stocks are riskier than stocks in the market as a whole. Tandy Corporation (Radio Shack), a good example of a growth company, has had a beta of 1.45. It has rewarded investors' patience over the years but has been much more volatile and thus riskier than the average stock with a beta of 1.00.

Investment decisions are not made on the basis of market risk alone, of course. First, other risk factors such as those indicated by the other ratios and analyses discussed in this chapter as well as by the industry, national, and world economic outlooks must be considered. Second, the expected return must be considered. Further, most investors try to own a portfolio of stocks whose average beta corresponds to the degree of risk they are willing to assume in relation to the average expected return of their portfolio.

Chapter Review

Review of Learning Objectives

1. **Describe and discuss the objectives of financial statement analysis.**
   Creditors and investors use financial statement analysis to judge the past performance and current position of a company. In this way they also judge its future potential and the risk associated with this potential. Creditors use the information gained from analysis to help them make loans that will be repaid with interest. Investors use the information to help them make investments that provide a return that is worth the risk.

2. **Describe and discuss the standards for financial statement analysis.**
   Three commonly used standards for financial statement analysis are rule-of-thumb measures, past performance of the company, and industry norms.

Rule-of-thumb measures are weak because of the lack of evidence that they can be applied widely. The past performance of a company can offer a guideline for measuring improvement but is not helpful in judging performance relative to other companies. Although the use of industry norms overcomes this last problem, its disadvantage is that firms are not always comparable, even in the same industry.

3. State the sources of information for financial statement analysis.
   The major sources of information about publicly held corporations are published reports such as annual reports and interim financial statements, SEC reports, business periodicals, and credit and investment advisory services.

4. Identify the issues related to the evaluation of the quality of a company's earnings.
   Current and prospective net income is an important component in many ratios used to evaluate a company. The user should recognize that the quality of reported net income can be influenced by the choices made by the company's management. First, management has control over accounting methods and estimates used in computing net income. Second, discontinued operations, extraordinary gains or losses, or accounting changes may affect net income positively or negatively.

5. Apply horizontal analysis, trend analysis, and vertical analysis to financial statements.
   Horizontal analysis involves the computation of dollar amount changes and percentage changes from year to year. Trend analysis is an extension of horizontal analysis in that percentage changes are calculated for several years. The changes are usually computed by setting a base year equal to 100 and calculating the measures for subsequent years as a percentage of that base year. Vertical analysis uses percentages to show the relationship of the component parts to the total in a single statement. The resulting statements in percentages are called common-size statements.

6. Apply ratio analysis to financial statements in the study of an enterprise's liquidity, profitability, long-term solvency, and market tests.
   The following table summarizes the basic information on ratio analysis.

Ratio	Components	Use or Meaning
Liquidity Ratios		
Current ratio	$\dfrac{\text{current assets}}{\text{current liabilities}}$	Measure of short-term debt-paying ability
Quick ratio	$\dfrac{\text{cash + marketable securities + receivables}}{\text{current liabilities}}$	Measure of short-term liquidity
Receivable turnover	$\dfrac{\text{net sales}}{\text{average accounts receivable}}$	Measure of relative size of accounts receivable balance and effectiveness of credit policies

(continued)

(continued)

Ratio	Components	Use or Meaning
Liquidity Ratios		
Average days' sales uncollected	$\dfrac{\text{days in year}}{\text{receivable turnover}}$	Measure of time it takes to collect an average receivable
Inventory turnover	$\dfrac{\text{cost of goods sold}}{\text{average inventory}}$	Measure of relative size of inventory
Profitability Ratios		
Profit margin	$\dfrac{\text{net income}}{\text{net sales}}$	Net income produced by each dollar of sales
Asset turnover	$\dfrac{\text{net sales}}{\text{average total assets}}$	Net measure of how efficiently assets are used to produce sales
Return on assets	$\dfrac{\text{net income}}{\text{average total assets}}$	Overall measure of earning power or profitability of all assets employed in the business
Return on equity	$\dfrac{\text{net income}}{\text{average stockholders' equity}}$	Profitability of stockholders' investment
Earnings per share	$\dfrac{\text{net income}}{\text{weighted average of outstanding shares}}$	Means of placing earnings on a common basis for comparisons
Long-term Solvency Ratios		
Debt to equity	$\dfrac{\text{total liabilities}}{\text{stockholders' equity}}$	Measure of relationship of debt financing to equity financing
Interest coverage	$\dfrac{\text{net income before taxes + interest expense}}{\text{interest expense}}$	Measure of protection of creditors from a default on interest payments
Market Test Ratios		
Price/earnings (P/E)	$\dfrac{\text{market price per share}}{\text{earnings per share}}$	Measure of amount the market will pay for a dollar of earnings
Dividends yield	$\dfrac{\text{dividends per share}}{\text{market price per share}}$	Measure of current return to investor
Market risk	$\dfrac{\text{specific change in market price}}{\text{average change in market price}}$	Measure of volatility of the market price of a stock in relation to that of other stocks

Review of Concepts and Terminology

The following important concepts were introduced in this chapter:

(L.O.1) **Financial statement analysis:** A collective term for the techniques used to show important relationships in financial statements.

(L.O.3) **Interim financial statements:** Financial statements issued for a period of less than one year, usually monthly or quarterly.

(L.O.5) **Horizontal analysis:** A technique for analyzing financial statements that involves the computation of dollar amount changes and percentage changes from the previous to the current year.

(L.O.5) **Trend analysis:** A type of horizontal analysis in which percentage changes are calculated for several successive years instead of two years.

(L.O.5) **Vertical analysis:** A technique for analyzing financial statements that uses percentages to show the relationship of the different parts to the total in a single statement.

(L.O.5) **Common-size statement:** A financial statement in which the components are stated in terms of percentages.

(L.O.5) **Ratio analysis:** A technique for analyzing financial statements in which meaningful relationships are shown between components of financial statements. (For a summary of ratios see the Review of Learning Objective Number 6, pages 757–758.)

(L.O.6) **Leverage:** Debt financing. The amount of debt financing in relation to equity financing is measured by the debt to equity ratio.

Other important terms introduced in this chapter are:

base year (p. 740)
beta (p. 755)
diversified companies (conglomerates) (p. 734)
index number (p. 742)
portfolio (p. 731)

Review Problem
Comparative Analysis of Two Companies

Maggie Washington is considering an investment in one of two fast-food restaurant chains because she believes the trend toward eating out more often will continue. Her choices have been narrowed to Quik Burger and Big Steak, whose balance sheets and income statements are shown on page 760. In addition to information in the financials, dividends paid were $500,000 for Quik Burger and $600,000 for Big Steak. The market prices of the stock were $30 and $20, respectively. And the betas were 1.00 and 1.15. Information pertaining to prior years is not readily available to Maggie. Assume that all notes payable are current liabilities and that all bonds payable are long-term liabilities.

Required

Conduct a comprehensive ratio analysis of each company and compare the results. This analysis should be done in the following steps:

1. Prepare an analysis of liquidity.
2. Prepare an analysis of profitability.
3. Prepare an analysis of long-term solvency.
4. Prepare an analysis of market tests.
5. Compare the analysis of the two companies by inserting the ratio calculations from the preceding four steps in a table with the following columns: Ratio Name, Quik Burger, Big Steak, and Company with More Favorable Ratio. Indicate in the last column the company that apparently had the more favorable ratio in each case. (If ratios are within .1 of each other, consider the difference indeterminate.)
6. In what ways would having prior years' information aid this analysis?

Balance Sheets (in thousands)		
	Quik Burger	Big Steak
Assets		
Cash	$ 2,000	$ 4,500
Accounts Receivable (net)	2,000	6,500
Inventory	2,000	5,000
Property, Plant, and Equipment (net)	20,000	35,000
Other Assets	4,000	5,000
Total Assets	$30,000	$56,000
Liabilities and Stockholders' Equity		
Accounts Payable	$ 2,500	$ 3,000
Notes Payable	1,500	4,000
Bonds Payable	10,000	30,000
Common Stock ($1 par value)	1,000	3,000
Paid-in Capital in Excess of Par Value, Common	9,000	9,000
Retained Earnings	6,000	7,000
Total Liabilities and Stockholders' Equity	$30,000	$56,000

Income Statements (in thousands)		
	Quik Burger	Big Steak
Sales	$53,000	$86,000
Cost of Goods Sold (including restaurant operating expense)	37,000	61,000
Gross Margin from Sales	$16,000	$25,000
General Operating Expenses		
Selling Expenses	7,000	10,000
Administrative Expenses	4,000	5,000
Interest Expense	1,400	3,200
Income Taxes Expense	1,800	3,400
Total Operating Expenses	$14,200	$21,600
Net Income	$ 1,800	$ 3,400

Answer to Review Problem

Ratio Name	Quik Burger	Big Steak

1. Liquidity analysis

a. Current ratio

$$\frac{\$2,000 + \$2,000 + \$2,000}{\$2,500 + \$1,500}$$

$$= \frac{\$6,000}{\$4,000} = 1.5$$

$$\frac{\$4,500 + \$6,500 + \$5,000}{\$3,000 + \$4,000}$$

$$= \frac{\$16,000}{\$7,000} = 2.3$$

b. Quick ratio

$$\frac{\$2,000 + \$2,000}{\$2,500 + \$1,500}$$

$$= \frac{\$4,000}{\$4,000} = 1.0$$

$$\frac{\$4,500 + \$6,500}{\$3,000 + \$4,000}$$

$$= \frac{\$11,000}{\$7,000} = 1.6$$

c. Receivable turnover

$$\frac{\$53,000}{\$2,000} = 26.5 \text{ times}$$

$$\frac{\$86,000}{\$6,500} = 13.2 \text{ times}$$

d. Average days' sales uncollected

$$\frac{365}{26.5} = 13.8 \text{ days}$$

$$\frac{365}{13.2} = 27.7 \text{ days}$$

e. Inventory turnover

$$\frac{\$37,000}{\$2,000} = 18.5 \text{ times}$$

$$\frac{\$61,000}{\$5,000} = 12.2 \text{ times}$$

2. Profitability analysis

a. Profit margin

$$\frac{\$1,800}{\$53,000} = 3.4\%$$

$$\frac{\$3,400}{\$86,000} = 4.0\%$$

b. Asset turnover

$$\frac{\$53,000}{\$30,000} = 1.8 \text{ times}$$

$$\frac{\$86,000}{\$56,000} = 1.5 \text{ times}$$

c. Return on assets

$$\frac{\$1,800}{\$30,000} = 6.0\%$$

$$\frac{\$3,400}{\$56,000} = 6.1\%$$

d. Return on equity

$$\frac{\$1,800}{\$1,000 + \$9,000 + \$6,000}$$

$$= \frac{\$1,800}{\$16,000} = 11.3\%$$

$$\frac{\$3,400}{\$3,000 + \$9,000 + \$7,000}$$

$$= \frac{\$3,400}{\$19,000} = 17.9\%$$

e. Earnings per share

$$\frac{\$1,800,000}{1,000,000 \text{ shares}} = \$1.80$$

$$\frac{\$3,400,000}{3,000,000 \text{ shares}} = \$1.13$$

3. Long-term solvency

a. Debt to equity

$$\frac{\$2,500 + \$1,500 + \$10,000}{\$1,000 + \$9,000 + \$6,000}$$

$$= \frac{\$14,000}{\$16,000} = .9$$

$$\frac{\$3,000 + \$4,000 + \$30,000}{\$3,000 + \$9,000 + \$7,000}$$

$$= \frac{\$37,000}{\$19,000} = 1.9$$

b. Interest coverage

$$\frac{\$1,800 + \$1,800 + \$1,400}{\$1,400}$$

$$= \frac{\$5,000}{\$1,400} = 3.6 \text{ times}$$

$$\frac{\$3,400 + \$3,400 + \$3,200}{\$3,200}$$

$$= \frac{\$10,000}{\$3,200} = 3.1 \text{ times}$$

4. Market test analysis

a. Price/earnings ratio $\dfrac{\$30}{\$1.80} = 16.7 \text{ times}$ $\dfrac{\$20}{\$1.13} = 17.7 \text{ times}$

b. Dividends yield $\dfrac{\$500{,}000 \div 1{,}000{,}000}{\$30} = 1.7\%$ $\dfrac{\$600{,}000 \div 3{,}000{,}000}{\$20} = 1.0\%$

c. Market risk   1.00   1.15

5. Comparative analysis

Ratio Name	Quik Burger	Big Steak	Company with More Favorable Ratio*
1. Liquidity analysis			
a. Current ratio	1.5	2.3	Big Steak
b. Quick ratio	1.0	1.6	Big Steak
c. Receivable turnover	26.5 times	13.2 times	Quik Burger
d. Average days' sales uncollected	13.8 days	27.7 days	Quik Burger
e. Inventory turnover	18.5 times	12.2 times	Quik Burger
2. Profitability analysis			
a. Profit margin	3.4%	4.0%	Big Steak
b. Asset turnover	1.8 times	1.5 times	Quik Burger
c. Return on assets	6.0%	6.1%	Indeterminate
d. Return on equity	11.3%	17.9%	Big Steak
e. Earnings per share	$1.80	$1.13	Noncomparable†
3. Long-term solvency			
a. Debt to equity	.9	1.9	Quik Burger
b. Interest coverage	3.6 times	3.1 times	Quik Burger
4. Market test analysis			
a. Price/earnings ratio	16.7 times	17.7 times	Big Steak
b. Dividends yield	1.7%	1.0%	Quik Burger
c. Market risk	1.00	1.15	Quik Burger is less risky

* This analysis indicates the company with the apparently more favorable or unfavorable ratio. Class discussion may focus on conditions under which different conclusions may be drawn.
† Earnings per share is noncomparable because of the considerable difference in the number of common stockholders of the two firms. If information for prior years were available, it would be helpful in determining the earnings trend of each company.

6. Usefulness of prior years' information

The availability of prior years' information would be helpful in two ways. First, turnover and return ratios could be based on average amounts. Second, a trend analysis could be performed for each company.

Chapter Assignments

Questions

1. What differences and similarities exist in the objectives of investors and creditors in using financial statement analysis?
2. What role does risk play in making loan and investment decisions?
3. What standards are commonly used to evaluate financial statements, and what are their relative merits?
4. Where can an investor look to find information about a company in which he or she is thinking of investing?
5. What is the basis of the following statement: "Accounting income is a useless measurement because it is based on so many arbitrary decisions"? Is it true?
6. Why would an investor want to do both horizontal and trend analyses of a company's financial statements?
7. What is the difference between horizontal and vertical analysis?
8. What does the following sentence mean: "Based on 1967 equaling 100, net income increased from 240 in 1983 to 260 in 1984"?
9. What is the purpose of ratio analysis?
10. Why would a financial analyst compare the ratios of Steelco, a steel company, to the ratios of other companies in the steel industry? What might cause such a comparison to be invalid?
11. In a period of high interest rates, why are receivable and inventory turnovers especially important?
12. The following statements were made on page 35 of the November 6, 1978, issue of *Fortune* magazine: "Supermarket executives are beginning to look back with some nostalgia on the days when the standard profit margin was 1 percent of sales. Last year the industry overall margin came to a thin 0.72 percent." How could a supermarket earn a satisfactory return on assets with such a small profit margin?
13. Circo Company has a return on assets of 12 percent and a debt to equity ratio of .5. Would you expect return on equity to be more or less than 12 percent?
14. Under what circumstances would a current ratio of 3:1 be good? Under what circumstances would it be bad?
15. Company A and Company B both have net incomes of $1,000,000. Is it possible to say that these companies are equally successful? Why or why not?
16. The market price of Company J's stock is the same as Company Q's stock. How might one determine whether investors are equally confident about the future of these companies?
17. Why is it riskier to own a stock whose market price is more changeable than the market price of other stocks? Why may it be beneficial to own such a stock?
18. "By almost any standard, Chicago-based Helene Curtis rates as one of America's worst-managed personal care companies. In recent years its return on equity has hovered between 10% and 13%, well below the industry average of 18% to 19%. Net profit margins of 2% to 3% are half that of competitors. . . . As a result, while leading names like Revlon and Avon are trading at three and four times book value, Curtis' trades at less than

two-thirds book value."[10] Considering that many companies are happy with a return on equity (owners' investment) of 10% and 13%, why is this analysis so critical of Curtis' performance? Assuming that Curtis could double its profit margin, what other information would you need to project the resulting return on owners' investment? Why does the writer feel that it is obvious that Revlon's and Avon's stocks are trading for more than Curtis'?

Classroom Exercises

Exercise 18-1.
Effect of Alternative Accounting Methods
(L.O. 4)

At the end of its first year of operations, a company could calculate its ending merchandise inventory according to three different methods, as follows: FIFO, $62,500; weighted average, $60,000; LIFO, $58,000.   If the weighted-average method is used, the net income for the year would be $28,000.

1. Determine the net income if the FIFO method is used.
2. Determine the net income if the LIFO method is used.
3. Which method is most conservative?
4. Will the consistency convention be violated if the LIFO method is chosen?
5. Does the full-disclosure convention require that the inventory method selected by management be disclosed in the financial statements?

Exercise 18-2.
Effect of Alternative Accounting Methods
(L.O. 4)

Jeans F' All and Jeans 'R' Us are very similar companies in size and operations. Jeans F' All uses FIFO and straight-line depreciation methods, and Jeans 'R' Us uses LIFO and accelerated depreciation methods.   Prices have been rising during the past several years.   Each company has paid its taxes in full for the current year, and each uses the same method for income taxes as it does for financial reporting.   Identify which company will report the greater amount for each of the following ratios:

a. current ratio
b. inventory turnover
c. profit margin
d. return on assets

If you cannot tell which is greater, explain why.

Exercise 18-3.
Trend Analysis
(L.O. 5)

Prepare a trend analysis of the following data using 19x1 as a base year, and tell whether the situation shown by the trends is favorable or unfavorable.   (Round your answers to one decimal point.)

	19x5	19x4	19x3	19x2	19x1
Sales	$12,760	$11,990	$12,100	$11,440	$11,000
Cost of Goods Sold	8,610	7,700	7,770	7,350	7,000
General and Administrative Expenses	2,640	2,592	2,544	2,448	2,400
Operating Income	1,510	1,698	1,786	1,642	1,600

10. *Forbes* (November 13, 1978), p. 154.

Exercise 18-4.
Vertical Analysis
(L.O. 5)

Express the comparative income statements below as common-size statements, and comment on the changes from 19x1 to 19x2. (Round computations to one decimal point.)

Kravitz Company
Comparative Income Statements
For the Years Ended December 31, 19x2 and 19x1

	19x2	19x1
Sales	$212,000	$184,000
Cost of Goods Sold	127,200	119,600
Gross Margin from Sales	$ 84,800	$ 64,400
Selling Expenses	$ 53,000	$ 36,800
General Expenses	25,440	18,400
Total Operating Expenses	$ 78,440	$ 55,200
Net Operating Income	$ 6,360	$ 9,200

Exercise 18-5.
Horizontal Analysis
(L.O. 5)

Compute amount and percentage changes for the balance sheet below, and comment on the changes from 19x1 to 19x2. (Round the percentage changes to one decimal point.)

Kravitz Company
Comparative Balance Sheets
December 31, 19x2 and 19x1

	19x2	19x1
Assets		
Current Assets	$ 18,600	$ 12,800
Property, Plant, and Equipment (net)	109,464	97,200
Total Assets	$128,064	$110,000
Liabilities and Stockholders' Equity		
Current Liabilities	$ 11,200	$ 3,200
Long-term Liabilities	35,000	40,000
Stockholders' Equity	81,864	66,800
Total Liabilities and Stockholders' Equity	$128,064	$110,000

Exercise 18-6.
Liquidity Analysis
(L.O. 6)

Partial comparative balance sheet and income statement information for Harmon Company appear below.

	19x2	19x1
Cash	$ 3,400	$ 2,600
Marketable Securities	1,800	4,300
Accounts Receivable (net)	11,200	8,900
Inventory	13,600	12,400
Total Current Assets	$30,000	$28,200
Current Liabilities	$10,000	$ 7,050
Sales	$80,640	$55,180
Cost of Goods Sold	54,400	50,840
Gross Margin from Sales	$26,240	$ 4,340

In addition, the year-end balances of accounts receivable and inventories were $8,100 and $12,800, respectively, in 19x0. Compute the current ratio, quick ratio, receivable turnover, average days' sales uncollected, and inventory turnover for each year. Comment on the change in liquidity position from 19x1 to 19x2. (Round computations to one decimal point.)

Exercise 18-7.
Turnover Analysis
(L.O. 6)

McEnroe's Men's Shop has been in business for four years. Because the company has recently had a cash flow problem, management wonders whether there is a problem with receivables or inventories. Here are selected figures from the company's financial statements (in thousands):

	19x1	19x2	19x3	19x4
Net Sales	80	96	112	144
Cost of Goods Sold	48	60	72	90
Accounts Receivable (net)	12	16	20	24
Merchandise Inventory	10	16	22	28

Compute receivable turnover and inventory turnover for each of the four years, and comment on the results relative to the cash flow problem that McEnroe's Men's Shop has been experiencing.

Exercise 18-8.
Profitability
Analysis
(L.O. 6)

At year end, Ortiz Company had total assets of $320,000 in 19x0, $340,000 in 19x1, and $380,000 in 19x2 and a debt to equity ratio of .67 in all three years. In 19x1, the company made a net income of $38,556 on revenues of $612,000. In 19x2, the company made a net income of $49,476 on revenues of $798,000. Compute the profit margin, asset turnover, return on assets, and return on equity for 19x1 and 19x2. Comment on the apparent cause of the increase in profitability or decrease in profitability. (Round the percentages and other ratios to one decimal point.)

Exercise 18-9.
Long-term
Solvency and
Market Test Ratios
(L.O. 6)

An investor is considering investments in the long-term bonds and common stock of Companies S and T. Both companies operate in the same industry, but Company S has a beta of 1.0 and Company T has a beta of 1.2. In addition, both companies pay a dividend per share of $2, and the yield of both companies' long-term bonds is 10 percent. Other data for the two companies are as follows:

	Company S	Company T
Total Assets	$1,200,000	$540,000
Total Liabilities	540,000	297,000
Net Income Before Taxes	144,000	64,800
Interest Expense	48,600	26,730
Earnings per Share	1.60	2.50
Market Price on Common Stock	20	23¾

Compute debt to equity ratios, interest coverage ratios, price/earnings (P/E) ratios, and dividend yield ratios, and comment on the results. (Round computations to one decimal point.)

Exercise 18-10.
Preparation of
Statements from
Ratios and
Incomplete Data
(L.O. 6)

Presented below and on page 768 are the balance sheet and income statement of Schlegel Corporation with most of the amounts missing.

Schlegel Corporation
Balance Sheet
December 31, 19x1
(in thousands of dollars)

Assets

Cash	$?	
Accounts Receivable (net)	?	
Inventories	?	
Total Current Assets		$?
Property, Plant, and Equipment (net)		2,700
Total Assets		$?

Liabilities and Stockholders' Equity

Current Liabilities	$?	
Bond Payable, 9% interest	?	
Total Liabilities		$?
Common Stock—$10 par value	$1,500	
Paid-in Capital in Excess of Par Value, Common	1,300	
Retained Earnings	2,000	
Total Stockholders' Equity		4,800
Total Liabilities and Stockholders' Equity		$?

Schlegel Corporation
Income Statement
For the Year Ended December 31, 19x1
(in thousands of dollars)

Sales		$9,000
Cost of Goods Sold		?
Gross Margin from Sales		$?
Operating Expenses		
Selling Expenses	$?	
Administrative Expenses	117	
Interest Expense	81	
Income Taxes Expense	310	
Total Operating Expenses		?
Net Income		$?

Additional information: (a) the only interest expense is on long-term debt; (b) the debt to equity ratio is .5; (c) the current ratio is 3:1, and the quick ratio is 2:1; (d) the receivable turnover is 4.5, and the inventory turnover is 4.0; (e) the return on assets is 10 percent; (f) all ratios are based on the current year's information.

Complete the financial statements using the information presented. Show supporting computations.

Interpreting Accounting Information

18-1.
Walt Disney
Productions
(L.O.4)

Walt Disney Productions is, of course, a famous entertainment company that produces films and operates theme parks, among other things. The company is also well-known as a profitable and well-managed business. On November 15, 1984, *The Wall Street Journal* ran the following article by Michael Cieply, under the title "Disney Reports Fiscal 4th-Period Loss After Taking $166 Million Write-Down."

Walt Disney Productions reported a $64 million net loss for its fiscal fourth quarter ended Sept. 30, after writing down a record $166 million in movies and other properties.

In the year-earlier quarter, Disney had net income of $24.5 million, or 70 cents a share. Fourth-quarter revenue this year rose 28% to $463.2 million from $363 million.

In the fiscal year, the entertainment company's earnings rose 5% to $97.8 million, or $2.73 a share, from $93.2 million, or $2.70 a share, a year earlier. Revenue rose 27% to $1.66 billion from $1.31 billion.

The company said it wrote down $112 million in motion picture and television properties. The write-down involves productions that already have been released as well as ones still under development, but Disney declined to identify the productions or projects involved.

"This just reflects the judgment of new management about the ultimate value of projects we had under way," said Michael Bagnall, Disney's executive vice president for finance. . . ."

The company also said it charged off $40 million to reflect the "abandonment" of a number of planned projects at its various theme parks. An additional $14 million was charged off as a reserve to cover possible legal obligations resulting from the company's fight to ward off a pair of successive takeover attempts last summer, Mr. Bagnall said.

Disney said its full-year net included a $76 million gain from a change in its method of accounting for investment tax credits. The change was made retroactive to the fiscal first quarter ended Dec. 31, and will boost that quarter's reported net to $85 million, from $9 million.

Mr. Bagnall said the $76 million credit stemmed largely from construction of Disney's Epcot Center theme park in Florida. By switching to flow-through from deferral accounting, the company was able to take the entire credit immediately instead of amortizing it over 18 years, as originally planned, Mr. Bagnall said. Flow-through accounting is usual in the entertainment industry.[11]

Required

1. What two categories of issues does the user of financial statements want to consider when evaluating the quality of a company's reported earnings? Does Disney have one or both types of items in fiscal 1984?
2. Compare the fourth period earnings or losses for 1983 and 1984 and full fiscal 1983 and 1984 earnings or losses before and after adjusting for the item or items described in **1**. Which comparisons do you believe give the best picture of Disney's performance?

18-2.
Ford Motor
Company I*
(L.O. 6)

Standard & Poor's Corporation (S & P) offers a wide range of financial information services to investors. One of its services is rating the quality of bond issues of U.S. corporations. Its top bond rating is AAA, followed by AA, A, BBB, BB, B, and so forth. The lowest rating of C is reserved for companies that are in or near bankruptcy. *Business Week* reported on February 2, 1981, that S & P had downgraded the bond rating for Ford Motor Company, a leading U.S. automobile maker, from AAA to AA. The cause of the downgrading was a deterioration of Ford's financial strength as indicated by certain ratios considered important by S & P. These ratios, S & P's guidelines, and Ford's performance are summarized in the following table:

Ratio	S & P Guideline for AAA Rating	Ford's Performance		
		1978	1979	1980
Interest Coverage	15 times	15.3 times	6.5 times	Loss
Pretax Return on Assets	15% to 20%	13.4%	6.6%	Loss
Debt to Equity	50%	34%	37.8%	63.4%
Cash Flow as a Percentage of Total Debt*	100%	152.6%	118.5%	91%
Short-term Debt as a Percentage of Total Debt	25%	43.1%	48.3%	52.5%

* Cash flow includes net income plus noncash charges to earnings.

11. "Disney Reports Fiscal 4th-Period Loss After Taking $166 Million Write–Down," *The Wall Street Journal* (November 15, 1984). Reprinted by permission of *The Wall Street Journal*, © Dow Jones & Company, Inc. 1984. All Rights Reserved.

* Excerpts from the 1978, 1979, and 1980 annual reports used by permission of Ford Motor Company. Copyright © 1978, 1979, and 1980.

Required

1. Identify the objective (profitability, liquidity, long-term solvency) measured by each of the S & P ratios. Why is each ratio important to the rating of Ford's long-term bonds?
2. In the *Business Week* article, several actions were suggested for Ford to take to regain its previous status. Tell which of the ratios each of the following actions would improve: (a) "cutting operating costs"; (b) "scrapping at least part of its massive spending plans over the next several years"; (c) "eliminate cash dividends to stockholders"; (d) "sale of profitable nonautomobile-related operations such as its steelmaker, aerospace company, and electronic concerns."

18-3.
Ford Motor
Company II*
(L.O. 6)

Part A: By 1983 S & P had dropped the rating on Ford's bond issues to BBB. Selected data for the years ended December 31, 1982 and 1983, from Ford Motor Company's 1983 annual report appear below (in millions):

	1982	1983
Balance Sheet Data		
Short-term Debt	$10,424.0	$10,315.9
Long-term Debt	2,353.3	2,712.9
Stockholders' Equity	6,077.5	7,545.3
Total Assets	21,961.7	23,868.9
Income Statement Data		
Income (Loss) Before Income Taxes	(407.9)	2,166.3
Interest Expense	745.5	567.2
Statement of Changes in Financial Position		
Net Cash Flows from Operating Activities	2,632.0	5,001.5

Required

1. Compute for 1982 and 1983 the same ratios that were used by S & P in Interpreting Financial Information 18-2.
2. If you were S & P, would you raise the rating on Ford's long-term bonds in 1984? Why or why not?

Part B: By the end of 1986, Ford's financial situation had improved enough to warrant an A rating from Standard & Poor's. Selected data for the years ended December 31, 1985 and 1986, from Ford Motor Company's 1987 annual report appear at the top of page 771 (in millions):

Required

1. Compute for 1985 and 1986 the same ratios that were used by Standard & Poor's in Interpreting Financial Information 18-2.
2. Do you agree that Ford's performance has improved enough since 1983 (see Part A) to warrant an increase to an A rating?

* Excerpts from the 1983 and 1987 annual reports used by permission of Ford Motor Company. Copyright © 1983 and 1987.

	1985	1986
Balance Sheet Data		
Short-term Debt	$12,777.4	$15,625.6
Long-term Debt	2,157.2	2,137.1
Stockholders' Equity	12,268.6	14,859.5
Total Assets	31,603.6	37,993.0
Income Statement Data		
Income (Loss) Before Income Taxes	4,076.9	5,552.2
Interest Expense	446.6	482.9
Statement of Changes in Financial Position		
Net Cash Flows from Operating Activities	5,371.6	7,624.4

Total assets in 1984 were $27,485.6

18-4.
IBM
(L.O.4)

On Tuesday, January 19, 1988, International Business Machines Corporation, the world's largest computer manufacturer, reported greatly increased earnings for the fourth quarter of 1987. In spite of this reported gain in earnings, the price of IBM's stock declined by $6 per share on the New York Stock Exchange to $111.75. In sympathy with this move, most other technology stocks also declined.

Fourth quarter net earnings rose from $1.39 billion, or $2.28 a share, to $2.08 billion, or $3.47 a share, an increase of 49.6 percent and 52.2 percent over the year-earlier period. Management declared that these results demonstrate the effectiveness of IBM's efforts to become more competitive, and that, in spite of the economic uncertainties of 1988, the company was planning for growth.

The stock price declined, however, apparently because the huge increase in income was the result of nonrecurring gains. Investment analysts pointed out that IBM's high earnings stemmed primarily from elements such as a lower tax rate. Despite most analyst's expectations of a tax rate between 40 and 42 percent, IBM's rate was down from last year's 45.3 percent to a low 36.4 percent.

In addition, analysts were disappointed in the revenue growth. Revenues within the United States were down, and much of the growth in revenues came through favorable currency translations, increases that may not be repeated. In fact, some estimates of the fourth-quarter earnings attributed $.50 per share to currency translations and another $.25 to tax rate changes.

Other factors contributing to the rise in earnings were one-time transactions such as the sale of Intel Corporation stock and bond redemptions, which, along with a corporate stock buyback program, reduced the amount of stock outstanding in the fourth quarter by 7.4 million shares.

Required

1. The analysts are concerned about the quality of IBM's earnings. Identify four quality of earnings issues reported in the case and the analysts' concern about each.
2. In percentage terms, what is the impact of the currency changes on fourth quarter earnings?
3. Comment on management's assessment of IBM's performance. Do you agree with management?

Problem Set A

Problem 18A-1.
Analyzing the
Effects of
Transactions
on Ratios
(L.O. 6)

Sabo Corporation engaged in the transactions listed in the first column of the following table. Opposite each transaction is a ratio and space to indicate the effect of each transaction on the ratio.

			Effect	
Transaction	**Ratio**	**Increase**	**Decrease**	**None**
a. Sold merchandise on account.	Current ratio			
b. Sold merchandise on account.	Inventory turnover			
c. Collected on accounts receivable.	Quick ratio			
d. Wrote off an uncollectible account.	Receivable turnover			
e. Paid on accounts payable.	Current ratio			
f. Declared a cash dividend.	Return on equity			
g. Incurred advertising expense.	Profit margin			
h. Issued stock dividend.	Debt to equity			
i. Issued bond payable.	Asset turnover			
j. Accrued interest expense.	Current ratio			
k. Paid previously declared cash dividend.	Dividends yield			
l. Purchased treasury stock.	Return on assets			

Required

Place an X in the appropriate column, showing whether the transaction increased, decreased, or had no effect on the indicated ratio.

Problem 18A-2.
Horizontal and
Vertical Analysis
(L.O. 5)

The condensed comparative income statements and comparative balance sheets of Kuo Corporation follow. All figures are given in thousands of dollars.

Required

(Round percentages to one decimal point.)

1. Prepare schedules showing amount and percentage changes from 19x1 to 19x2 for the corporate income statements and balance sheets.
2. Prepare common-size income statements and balance sheets for 19x1 and 19x2.
3. Comment on the results found in **1** and **2** by identifying favorable and unfavorable changes in components and composition.

Kuo Corporation
Comparative Income Statements
For the Years Ended 19x2 and 19x1

	19x2	19x1
Sales	$1,625,600	$1,573,200
Cost of Goods Sold	1,044,400	1,004,200
Gross Margin from Sales	$ 581,200	$ 569,000
Operating Expenses		
Sales Expenses	238,400	259,000
Administrative Expenses	223,600	211,600
Interest Expense	32,800	19,600
Income Taxes Expense	31,200	28,400
Total Operating Expenses	$ 526,000	$ 518,600
Net Income	$ 55,200	$ 50,400

Kuo Corporation
Comparative Balance Sheets
For the Years Ended 19x2 and 19x1

	19x2	19x1
Assets		
Cash	$ 40,600	$ 20,400
Accounts Receivable (net)	117,800	114,600
Inventory	287,400	297,400
Property, Plant, and Equipment (net)	375,000	360,000
Total Assets	$820,800	$792,400
Liabilities and Stockholders' Equity		
Accounts Payable	$133,800	$238,600
Notes Payable	100,000	200,000
Bonds Payable	200,000	—
Common Stock—$5 par value	200,000	200,000
Retained Earnings	187,000	153,800
Total Liabilities and Stockholders' Equity	$820,800	$792,400

Problem 18A-3.
Ratio Analysis
(L.O. 6)

Additional data for Kuo Corporation in 19x1 and 19x2 appear below. This information should be used along with the data in Problem 18A-2.

	19x2	19x1
Dividends Paid	$22,000,000	$17,200,000
Number of Common Shares	40,000,000	40,000,000
Market Price per Share	$9.00	$15.00
Beta	1.40	1.25

Balances of selected accounts (in thousands) at the end of 19x0 are Accounts Receivable (net), $103,400; Inventory, $273,600; Total Assets, $732,800; and Stockholders' Equity, $320,600. All of Kuo's notes payable are current liabilities; all the bonds payable are long-term liabilities.

Required

(Round percentages and ratios to one decimal point, and consider changes of .1 or less to be indeterminate.)

1. Conduct a liquidity analysis by calculating for each year the: (a) current ratio, (b) quick ratio, (c) receivable turnover, (d) average days' sales uncollected, and (e) inventory turnover. Indicate whether each ratio had a favorable (F) or unfavorable (U) change from 19x1 to 19x2.
2. Conduct a profitability analysis by calculating for each year the: (a) profit margin, (b) asset turnover, (c) return on assets, (d) return on equity, and (e) earnings per share. Indicate whether each ratio had a favorable (F) or unfavorable (U) change from 19x1 to 19x2.
3. Conduct a long-term solvency analysis by calculating for each year the: (a) debt to equity ratio and (b) interest coverage ratio. Indicate whether each ratio had a favorable (F) or unfavorable (U) change from 19x1 to 19x2.
4. Conduct a market test analysis by calculating for each year the: (a) price/earnings ratio, (b) dividends yield, and (c) market risk. Note the market beta measures, and indicate whether each ratio had a favorable (F) or unfavorable (U) change from 19x1 to 19x2.

Problem 18A-4.
Effect of Alternative Accounting Methods
(L.O. 4, 6)

Burnett Company began operations this year. At the beginning of the year, the company purchased plant assets of $330,000, with an estimated useful life of ten years and no salvage value.

During the year, the company had sales of $600,000, salary expense of $100,000, and other expenses of $40,000, excluding depreciation. In addition, the company purchased inventory as follows:

January 15	400 units at $200	$ 80,000
March 20	200 units at $204	40,800
June 15	800 units at $208	166,400
September 18	600 units at $206	123,600
December 9	300 units at $210	63,000
Total	2,300 units	$473,800

At the end of the year, a physical inventory disclosed 500 units still on hand. The managers of Burnett Company know they have a choice of accounting methods but are unsure how the methods will affect net income. They have heard of FIFO and LIFO for inventory methods and straight-line and sum-of-the-years'-digits for depreciation methods.

Required

1. Prepare two income statements for Burnett Company: one using FIFO basis and straight-line method; the other using LIFO basis and sum-of-the-years'-digits method.
2. Prepare a schedule to account for the difference in the two net income figures obtained in **1.**
3. What effect does the choice of accounting methods have on Burnett's inventory turnover? What conclusions can you draw?
4. What effect does the choice of accounting methods have on Burnett's return on assets? Use year-end balances to compute ratios. Assume that the only other asset in addition to plant assets and inventory is cash of $40,000. Is your evaluation of Burnett's profitability affected by the choice of accounting methods?

Problem 18A-5.
Comprehensive
Ratio Analysis of
Two Companies
(L.O. 6)

Felipe Cardenas is considering an investment in the common stock of a chain of retail department stores. He has narrowed his choice to two retail companies, Bing Corporation and Sadecki Corporation, whose balance sheets and income statements are presented below.

	Bing Corporation	Sadecki Corporation
Assets		
Cash	$ 80,000	$ 192,400
Marketable Securities (at cost)	203,400	84,600
Accounts Receivable (net)	552,800	985,400
Inventory	629,800	1,253,400
Prepaid Expenses	54,400	114,000
Property, Plant, and Equipment (net)	2,913,600	6,552,000
Intangibles and Other Assets	553,200	144,800
Total Assets	$4,987,200	$9,326,600
Liabilities and Stockholders' Equity		
Accounts Payable	$ 344,000	$ 572,600
Notes Payable	150,000	400,000
Accrued Liabilities	50,200	73,400
Bonds Payable	2,000,000	2,000,000
Common Stock—$10 par value	1,000,000	600,000
Paid-in Capital in Excess of Par Value, Common	609,800	3,568,600
Retained Earnings	833,200	2,112,000
Total Liabilities and Stockholders' Equity	$4,987,200	$9,326,600

	Bing Corporation	Sadecki Corporation
Sales	$12,560,000	$25,210,000
Cost of Goods Sold	6,142,000	14,834,000
Gross Margin from Sales	$ 6,418,000	$10,376,000
Operating Expenses		
Sales Expense	$ 4,822,600	$ 7,108,200
Administrative Expense	986,000	2,434,000
Interest Expense	194,000	228,000
Income Taxes Expense	200,000	300,000
Total Operating Expenses	$ 6,202,600	$10,070,200
Net Income	$ 215,400	$ 305,800

During the year, Bing Corporation paid a total of $50,000 in dividends. The market price per share of its stock is currently $30. In comparison, Sadecki Corporation paid a total of $114,000 in dividends during the year, and the current market price of its stock is $38 per share. An investment service indicated that the beta associated with Bing's stock is 1.20 and that associated with Sadecki's stock is .95. Information for prior years is not readily available. Assume that all notes payable are current liabilities and all bonds payable are long-term liabilities.

Required

Conduct a comprehensive ratio analysis of each company, using the available information, and compare the results. (Round percentages and ratios to one decimal point, and consider changes of .1 or less to be indeterminate.) This analysis should be done in the following steps:

1. Prepare an analysis of liquidity by calculating for each company the: (a) current ratio, (b) quick ratio, (c) receivable turnover, (d) average days' sales uncollected, and (e) inventory turnover.
2. Prepare an analysis of profitability by calculating for each company the: (a) profit margin, (b) asset turnover, (c) return on assets, (d) return on equity, and (e) earnings per share.
3. Prepare an analysis of long-term solvency by calculating for each company the: (a) debt to equity ratio and (b) interest coverage ratio.
4. Prepare an analysis of market tests by calculating for each company the: (a) price/earnings ratio, (b) dividends yield, and (c) market risk.
5. Compare the two companies by inserting the ratio calculations from 1 through 4 in a table with the following column heads: Ratio Name, Bing Corporation, Sadecki Corporation, and Company with More Favorable Ratio. Indicate in the right-hand column which company had the more favorable ratio in each instance.
6. In what ways could the analysis be improved if prior years' information were available?

Problem Set B

**Problem 18B-1.
Analyzing the
Effects of
Transactions
on Ratios
(L.O. 6)**

Brock Corporation engaged in the transactions listed in the first column of the table below. Opposite each transaction is a ratio and spaces to mark the effect of each transaction on the ratio.

			Effect		
Transaction	Ratio		Increase	Decrease	None
a. Issued common stock for cash.	Asset turnover				
b. Declared cash dividend.	Current ratio				
c. Sold treasury stock.	Return on equity				
d. Borrowed cash by issuing a note payable.	Debt to equity				
e. Paid salary expense.	Inventory turnover				
f. Purchased merchandise for cash.	Current ratio				
g. Sold equipment for cash.	Receivable turnover				
h. Sold merchandise on account.	Quick ratio				
i. Paid current portion of long-term debt.	Return on assets				
j. Gave a sales discount.	Profit margin				
k. Purchased marketable securities for cash.	Quick ratio				
l. Declared a 5% stock dividend.	Current ratio				

Required

Place an X in the appropriate column to show whether the transaction increased, decreased, or had no effect on the indicated ratio.

**Problem 18B-2.
Horizontal and
Vertical Analysis
(L.O. 5)**

The condensed comparative statements of Jamali Corporation appear as shown on page 778.

Required

(Round all ratios and percentages to one decimal point.)

1. Prepare schedules showing amount and percentage changes from 19x1 to 19x2 for the comparative income statements and balance sheets.
2. Prepare common-size income statements and balance sheets for 19x1 and 19x2.
3. Comment on the results found in **1** and **2** by identifying favorable and unfavorable changes in components and composition.

Jamali Corporation
Comparative Income Statements
For the Years Ended December 31, 19x2 and 19x1

	19x2	19x1
Sales	$791,200	$742,600
Cost of Goods Sold	454,100	396,200
Gross Margin from Sales	$337,100	$346,400
Operating Expenses		
Selling Expenses	130,100	104,600
Administrative Expenses	140,300	115,500
Interest Expense	25,000	20,000
Income Taxes Expense	14,000	35,000
Total Operating Expenses	$309,400	$275,100
Net Income	$ 27,700	$ 71,300

Jamali Corporation
Comparative Balance Sheets
December 31, 19x2 and 19x1

	19x2	19x1
Assets		
Cash	$ 31,100	$ 27,200
Accounts Receivable (net)	72,500	42,700
Inventory	122,600	107,800
Property, Plant, and Equipment	577,700	507,500
Total Assets	$803,900	$685,200
Liabilities and Stockholders' Equity		
Accounts Payable	$104,700	$ 72,300
Notes Payable	50,000	50,000
Bonds Payable	200,000	110,000
Common Stock—$10 par value	300,000	300,000
Retained Earnings	149,200	152,900
Total Liabilities and Stockholders' Equity	$803,900	$685,200

Problem 18B-3.
Ratio Analysis
(L.O. 6)

Additional data for Jamali Corporation in 19x1 and 19x2 appear below. These data should be used in conjunction with the data in Problem 18B-2.

	19x2	19x1
Dividends Paid	$31,400	$35,000
Number of Common Shares	30,000	30,000
Market Price per Share	40	60
Beta	1.00	.90

Balances of selected accounts for 19x0 are Accounts Receivable (net), $52,700; Inventory, $99,400; Total Assets, $647,800; and Stockholders' Equity, $376,600. All of Jamali's notes payable are current liabilities; all the bonds payable are long-term liabilities.

Required

(Note: Round all answers to one decimal point, and consider changes of .1 or less to be indeterminate.)

1. Prepare a liquidity analysis by calculating for 19x1 and 19x2 the (a) current ratio, (b) quick ratio, (c) receivable turnover, (d) average days' sales uncollected, and (e) inventory turnover. Indicate whether each ratio improved or not from 19x1 to 19x2 by using an F for favorable or U for unfavorable.
2. Prepare a profitability analysis by calculating for each year the (a) profit margin, (b) asset turnover, (c) return on assets, (d) return on equity, and (e) earnings per share. Indicate whether each ratio had a favorable (F) or unfavorable (U) change from 19x1 to 19x2.
3. Prepare a long-term solvency analysis by calculating for each year the (a) debt to equity ratio and (b) interest coverage ratio. Indicate whether each ratio had a favorable (F) or unfavorable (U) change from 19x1 to 19x2.
4. Conduct a market test analysis by calculating for each year the (a) price/ earnings ratio, (b) dividends yield, and (c) market risk. Note the market risk measure, and indicate whether each ratio had a favorable (F) or unfavorable (U) change from 19x1 to 19x2.

Problem 18B-4.
Effect of
Alternative
Accounting
Methods
(L.O. 4, 6)

Owen Company began operations by purchasing $200,000 in equipment that has an estimated useful life of nine years and an estimated residual value of $20,000. During the year, the company purchased inventory as follows:

January	2,000 units at $25	$ 50,000
March	4,000 units at $24	96,000
May	1,000 units at $27	27,000
July	5,000 units at $27	135,000
September	6,000 units at $28	168,000
November	2,000 units at $29	58,000
December	3,000 units at $28	84,000
Totals	23,000 units	$618,000

The company sold 19,000 units for a total of $880,000 and incurred salary expenses of $170,000 and expenses other than depreciation of $120,000.

Owen's management is anxious to present its income statement most fairly in its first year of operation and realizes that there are alternative accounting methods available for accounting for inventory and equipment. Management wants to determine the effect of various alternatives on this year's income. Two sets of alternatives are required.

Required

1. Prepare two income statements for Owen Company: one using FIFO basis for inventory and straight-line method for depreciation; the other using LIFO basis for inventory and sum-of-the-years'-digits method for depreciation.
2. Prepare a schedule accounting for the difference in the two net income figures obtained in **1**.
3. What effect does the choice of accounting methods have on Owen's inventory turnover? What conclusion can you draw?
4. What effect does the choice of accounting methods have on Owen's return on assets? Use year-end balances to compute ratios, assuming that the only other asset in addition to plant assets and inventory is cash of $30,000. Is your evaluation of Owen's profitability affected by the choice of accounting methods?

Problem 18B-5.
Comprehensive
Ratio Analysis of
Two Companies
(L.O. 6)

Geraldine Ming has decided to invest some of her savings in common stock. She feels that the chemical industry has good growth prospects and has narrowed her choice to two companies in that industry. As a final step in making the choice, she decided to make a comprehensive ratio analysis of two companies, Berland and Schmidt. Income statement and balance sheet data for the two companies appear below and at the top of page 781.

	Berland	**Schmidt**
Sales	$9,486,200	$27,287,300
Cost of Goods Sold	5,812,200	$18,372,400
Gross Margin from Sales	$3,674,000	$ 8,914,900
Operating Expenses		
Selling Expense	1,194,000	1,955,700
Administrative Expense	1,217,400	4,126,000
Interest Expense	270,000	1,360,000
Income Taxes Expense	450,000	600,000
Total Operating Expenses	$3,131,400	$ 8,041,700
Net Income	$ 542,600	$ 873,200

	Berland	**Schmidt**
Assets		
Cash	$ 126,100	$ 514,300
Marketable Securities (at cost)	117,500	1,200,000
Accounts Receivable (net)	456,700	2,600,000
Inventories	1,880,000	4,956,000
Prepaid Expenses	72,600	156,600
Property, Plant, and Equipment (net)	5,342,200	19,356,000
Intangibles and Other Assets	217,000	580,000
Total Assets	$8,212,100	$29,362,900
Liabilities and Stockholders' Equity		
Accounts Payable	$ 517,400	$ 2,342,000
Notes Payable	1,000,000	2,000,000
Income Taxes Payable	85,200	117,900
Bonds Payable	2,000,000	15,000,000
Common Stock—$1 par value	350,000	1,000,000
Paid-in Capital in Excess of Par Value, Common	1,747,300	5,433,300
Retained Earnings	2,512,200	3,469,700
Total Liabilities and Stockholders' Equity	$8,212,100	$29,362,900

During the year, Berland paid a total of $140,000 in dividends, and the current market price per share of its stock is $20. Schmidt paid a total of $600,000 in dividends during the year, and the current market price per share of its stock is $9. An investment service reports that the beta associated with Berland's stock is 1.05 and that associated with Schmidt's is .8. Information pertaining to prior years is not readily available. Assume that all notes payable are current liabilities and that all bonds payable are long-term liabilities.

Required

Conduct a comprehensive ratio analysis of each company using the current end-of-year data. Compare the results. (Round all ratios and percentages to one decimal point.) This analysis should be done in the following steps:

1. Prepare an analysis of liquidity by calculating for each company the (a) current ratio, (b) quick ratio, (c) receivable turnover, (d) average days' sales uncollected, and (e) inventory turnover.
2. Prepare an analysis of profitability by calculating for each company the (a) profit margin, (b) asset turnover, (c) return on assets, (d) return on equity, and (e) earnings per share.
3. Prepare an analysis of long-term solvency by calculating for each company the (a) debt to equity ratio and (b) interest coverage ratio.

4. Prepare an analysis of market tests by calculating for each company the (a) price/earnings ratio, (b) dividends yield, and (c) market risk.
5. Compare the two companies by inserting the ratio calculations from **1** through **4** in a table with the following column heads: Ratio Name, Berland, Schmidt, and Company with More Favorable Ratio. Indicate in the right-hand column which company had the more favorable ratio in each case.
6. In what ways could the analysis be improved if prior years' information were available?

Management Decision Cases

18-1.
Medtrix
Corporation
(L.O. 4)

Ashley Medlow retired at the beginning of 19x1 as president and principal stockholder in Medtrix Corporation, a successful producer of medical software for microcomputers. As an incentive to the new management, Ashley supported the board of directors' new executive compensation plan, which provides cash bonuses to key executives for the years in which the company's earnings per share exceed the current dividends per share of $2.00, plus a $.20 per share increase in dividends for each future year. Thus, for management to receive the bonuses, the company must earn per share income of $2.00 the first year, $2.20 the second, $2.40 the third, and so forth. Since Ashley owns 500,000 of the 1,000,000 common shares outstanding, the dividend income will provide for his retirement years. He is also protected against inflation by the regular increase in dividends.

Earnings and dividends per share for the first three years of operation under the new management were as follows:

	19x3	19x2	19x1
Earnings per share	$2.50	$2.50	$2.50
Dividends per share	2.40	2.20	2.00

During this time management earned bonuses totaling more than $1,000,000 under the compensation plan. Ashley, who had taken no active part on the board of directors, began to worry about the unchanging level of earnings and decided to study the company's annual report more carefully. The notes to the annual report revealed the following information:

a. Management changed from using the LIFO inventory method to the FIFO method in 19x1. The effect of this change was to decrease cost of goods sold by $200,000 in 19x1, $300,000 in 19x2, and $400,000 in 19x3.
b. Management changed from using the double-declining-balance accelerated depreciation method to the straight-line method in 19x2. The effect of this was to decrease depreciation by $400,000 in 19x2 and by $500,000 in 19x3.
c. In 19x3, management increased the estimated useful life of intangible assets from five to ten years. The effect of this change was to decrease amortization expense by $100,000 in 19x3.

Required

1. Compute earnings per share for each year according to the accounting methods in use at the beginning of 19x1.
2. Have the executives earned their bonuses? What serious effect has the compensation package apparently had on the net assets of Medtrix? How could Ashley have protected himself from what has happened?

18-2.
Great Lakes
Seafood
Restaurant, Inc.
(L.O. 2, 5)

Sam Slaski is the owner of Great Lakes Seafood Restaurant, Inc., which operates a 100-seat seafood restaurant in a suburb of a large midwestern city. Teresa Kelly, Sam's CPA, is going over with Sam the recently prepared income statement for last year.

Income Statements
For the Year Ended December 31, 19x7

	Great Lakes Seafood Restaurant, Inc.		Profitable Restaurants in the U.S.— Average Dollars per Seat
Sales			
Food		$272,100	$3,935
Beverage		98,400	1,457
Total Sales		$370,500	$5,392
Cost of Goods Sold			
Food	$112,400		$1,608
Beverage	29,300		377
Total Cost of Goods Sold		141,700	1,985
Gross Margin from Sales		$228,800	$3,407
Operating Expenses			
Wages and Salaries Expense	$116,500		$1,410
Employee Benefits Expense	19,900		237
Direct Operating Expenses	30,700		290
Music and Entertainment Expenses	3,800		40
Advertising and Promotion Expenses	8,300		97
Utilities Expenses	11,900		128
Administrative and General Expenses	22,800		278
Repairs and Maintenance Expenses	6,200		89
Rent, Property Taxes, and Insurance Expenses	22,800		249
Depreciation Expense	12,900		117
Interest Expense	5,100		53
Total Operating Expenses		260,900	2,988
Net Income (Loss) Before Other Items		$(32,100)	$ 419
Other Income and Expenses			
Other Income	$ 2,400		$ 43
Less Other Expenses	1,200		16
Net Other Income		1,200	27
Net Income (Loss) Before Taxes		$(30,900)	$ 446

Sam is disturbed to see that the restaurant had a net loss for the year. "I honestly don't know what to do," Sam comments. "I think I run an efficient operation, and people say I have a good restaurant. Do you think I should try to cut costs or try to get more business?" Teresa replies, "Maybe it would be helpful to compare your restaurant with other successful restaurants. I will try to see if any industry data are available."

One week later Teresa returns with the "Restaurant Industry Operations Report," published by the National Restaurant Association in cooperation with the international accounting firm of Laventhol & Horwath. "Sam, let's see how your restaurant compares. On page 23 is an income statement for restaurants in the United States that showed a profit last year. The amounts are on a per seat basis, so we can make a direct comparison with your restaurant." Data from the national survey (slightly rearranged) are shown in comparative form with Sam's income statement on page 783.

Required

1. Prepare comparative income statements on a per seat basis and common-size income statements for Great Lakes Seafood Restaurant, Inc., and the average profitable restaurant.
2. Identify and comment on the areas where Great Lakes is significantly different from the national average.
3. On the basis of your analysis, what would you say is Great Lakes' major problem? How would the items identified in **2** be affected if this problem were solved?

1. *Describe the basic concepts related to government and not-for-profit accounting.*
2. *Identify and describe the types of funds used in government accounting.*
3. *Apply the modified accrual basis of accounting used by state and local government units.*
4. *Describe the reporting systems used in government accounting.*
5. *Identify the various types of not-for-profit organizations and their accounting methods.*
6. *Describe the unique aspects of the budgeting process in government and not-for-profit organizations.*
7. *Apply and interpret the basic techniques used by government and not-for-profit organizations to control costs of operations.*

APPENDIX A

Accounting for Government and Not-for-Profit Organizations

Federal, state, and local governments and not-for-profit organizations account for a significant share of all spending within the United States. Courses in introductory accounting, however, have devoted relatively little time to discussing the accounting, planning and control, and reporting issues unique to these organizations. This appendix is a brief introduction to accounting for several types of government and not-for-profit groups, including state and local governments, colleges and universities, hospitals, and voluntary professional, health, and welfare organizations.

After reviewing the financial accounting aspects of government and not-for-profit organizations, we look at the management accounting techniques these groups use. Budgeting has a special meaning for both government and not-for-profit entities because control of spending is critical to the success of these organizations. After studying this appendix, you should be able to meet the learning objectives listed on the left.

Government Versus Business Accounting

Businesses in the United States are organized to produce profits for their owners or shareholders. This fact requires that the accounting system provide shareholders, creditors, and other interested parties with information that will help them evaluate the firm's success in making a profit. The rules and practices of business accounting are referred to as generally accepted accounting principles (GAAP). Historically, government GAAP have been the responsibility of the National Council on Governmental Accounting (NCGA). Recently, however, the Financial Accounting Federation established the Governmental Accounting Standards Board (GASB). Although the GASB will not have the power to dictate accounting practice for government units, its responsibilities will parallel those of the FASB in that it will define good accounting practices for government units. As a result, most observers believe that the GASB will be increasingly active in all aspects of government accounting.

State and local governments have different objectives from those of businesses, and thus they traditionally have had different GAAP. Government units chiefly provide services to citizens, with expenditures for these services limited to the amounts legally available. Government units need not be profitable in the business sense; however, they do need to limit their spending to the funds made available for specific purposes. The primary objective of government GAAP is, therefore, not profit measurement but the measurement of changes in the funds available for government activities. To help satisfy this objective,

OBJECTIVE 1
*Describe the
basic concepts
related to
government and
not-for-profit
accounting*
government GAAP have several unique accounting features, the most important of which are the use of funds to account for various activities and the use of modified accrual accounting. A **fund** is defined as a fiscal and accounting entity. **Modified accrual accounting** attempts to provide an accurate measure of increases and decreases in resources available (especially in cash) to fulfill government obligations.

The operations of state and local governments are recorded in a variety of funds, each of which is designated for a specific purpose. This means that each fund simultaneously shows (1) the financial position and results of operations during the period and (2) compliance with legal requirements of the state or local government. State and local governments rely on the following types of funds:

OBJECTIVE 2
*Identify and
describe the
types of funds
used in
government
accounting*
General fund   To account for all financial resources not accounted for in any other fund. This fund accounts for most of the current operating activities of the government unit (administration, police, fire, health, and sanitation, for example).

Special revenue funds   To account for revenues legally restricted to specific purposes.

Capital projects funds   To account for the acquisition and construction of major capital projects.

Debt service fund   To account for resources accumulated to pay the interest and principal of general obligation long-term debt.

Special assessment funds   To account for the financing of public improvements or services that benefit primarily the owners of special properties.

Enterprise funds   To account for activities that are financed and operated in a manner similar to private business activities. These funds are most appropriate for activities that charge the public for goods or services, such as municipal golf courses or utilities.

Internal service funds   To account for the financing of goods or services provided by one department or agency of a government unit to another department or agency of the same government unit.

Trust and agency funds   To account for assets held by a government unit acting as a trustee or agent for individuals, private organizations, or other funds.

The first five funds are called **government funds**. The enterprise and internal service funds are **proprietary funds**. Trust and agency funds are **fiduciary funds**. A political unit may properly have only one general fund. There is no limit, however, on the number of other funds used. There is also no requirement that a state or local government have all these funds; individual needs govern the type and number of funds used.

In addition to the above funds, state and local governments use two unique kinds of **account groups** to record certain fixed assets and long-term liabilities.

General fixed assets account group   To account for all long-term assets of a government unit, except long-term assets related to specific proprietary or trust funds. This account group does not record depreciation.

General long-term debt group   To account for all long-term liabilities of a government unit, except for long-term liabilities related to specific proprietary or trust funds. This account group records the principal amounts of long-term debt as well as the amounts available in the debt service fund to retire the debt.

Long-term assets and long-term liabilities related to proprietary and trust funds are accounted for in essentially the same manner as in business accounting.

Modified Accrual Accounting

Government funds, as well as certain types of trust funds, use the modified accrual method of accounting. Proprietary funds, as well as certain types of trust funds, use the familiar full accrual accounting common to business organizations. This section concentrates on the less familiar modified accrual basis of accounting.

Modified accrual accounting has several features that distinguish it from accrual accounting used in business. The measurement and recognition of revenues and expenditures, the incorporation of the budget into the formal accounting system, and the use of encumbrances to account for purchase commitments are each described briefly.

In government accounting, revenues are defined as increases in fund resources from sources other than interfund transactions or proceeds of long-term debt. They are recognized in the accounts when "measurable and available." In most cases these conditions are met when cash is received. Expenditures are defined as decreases in fund resources caused by transactions other than interfund transfers. These concepts of revenues and expenditures result in some unusual situations, as the following examples illustrate:

OBJECTIVE 3
Apply the modified accrual basis of accounting used by state and local government units

1. Assume that a city sells a used police car for $2,500 cash. This transaction would be recorded in the general fund as follows:

Cash	2,500	
Revenues		2,500
Sale of used police car		

2. When a city purchases a new police car for $12,000 cash, the transaction would be recorded in the general fund as follows:

Expenditures	12,000	
Cash		12,000
Purchase of new police car		

The transactions are recorded this way because they satisfy the definitions of revenues and expenditures.

To further illustrate the contrast between government and business-type accrual accounting, we can examine the way in which a business would record the above transactions:

1. Assume that a firm sells a used car for $2,500 cash and that the car has a carrying value of $2,000 (cost of $7,500 less accumulated depreciation of $5,500):

Cash	2,500	
Accumulated Depreciation, Car	5,500	
Car		7,500
Gain on disposal		500
Sale of used car		

Unlike government accounting, accrual accounting recognizes revenues only to the extent that cash received exceeds carrying value.

2. If a firm purchases a new car for $12,000 cash, the transaction would be recorded as follows:

Car	12,000	
Cash		12,000
Purchase of new car		

The car would be shown as an asset on the firm's balance sheet. No expense would be recorded until depreciation is recognized in subsequent years. Business accounting focuses on the matching of revenues and expenses to compute net income or loss for the period. Government accounting, in contrast, concentrates on inflows and outflows of fund resources.

Another unique feature of government accounting is the formal incorporation of the budget into the accounts of the particular fund. This approach is required for the general and the special revenue funds and is optional for the other government funds. The general fund, for example, would record its budget as follows:

Estimated Revenues	1,000,000	
Appropriations		950,000
Fund Balance		50,000
To record budget for fiscal year		

This example assumes that the government unit expects revenues to exceed legally mandated expenditures (or appropriations). The use of budgetary accounts enables the government unit to have a continuous check or control on whether actual revenues and expenditures correspond to original estimates. In addition, the various funds' financial statements will show both the budgeted and actual amounts of major revenue and expenditure categories. At the end of the accounting period, the budget entry would be reversed since its control function is no longer needed. A new budget would then be recorded in the subsequent period to control revenues and expenditures in that period. Businesses also use budgets, but they do not integrate those budgets formally into the regular accounting system.

A third unique feature of government accounting is the use of encumbrance accounting. Since governments cannot legally spend more than the amounts appropriated for specific purposes, it is necessary to keep track of anticipated, as well as actual, expenditures. Whenever a significant lapse of time is expected between a commitment to spend and the actual expenditure, government GAAP require the use of encumbrance accounting.

For example, a city orders $10,000 of supplies on July 1, but does not expect to receive the supplies until September 1. The bill received on September 1 amounts to $10,200. The general fund would record this transaction as follows:

July 1	Encumbrances	10,000	
	Reserve for encumbrances		10,000
	Order of supplies		

Sept. 1	Reserve for encumbrances	10,000	
	Encumbrances		10,000
	Reserve encumbrance upon receipt of bill for supplies		
1	Expenditures	10,200	
	Cash (or Vouchers Payable)		10,200
	Payment for supplies		

The purpose of an encumbrance system is to ensure that the government unit does not exceed its spending authority. This is accomplished by recording both actual expenditures and anticipated expenditures under the current period's appropriations. In addition to normal expenditures, the Reserve for Encumbrances account represents that portion of the fund balance already committed to future expenditures. Regardless of the original estimated encumbrance amounts, on September 1, the encumbrance is eliminated by reversing the original entry of July 1, and expenditures is debited for the actual amount spent.

Financial Reporting System

OBJECTIVE 4
Describe the reporting systems used in government accounting

The accounting system we described is designed to produce periodic financial statements. The financial statements recommended by the NCGA include the following:

Combined Balance Sheet This statement is prepared for all fund types and account groups. Each fund type and account group lists major categories of assets, liabilities, and either fund balances or owners' equity accounts.

Combined Statement of Revenues, Expenditures, and Changes in Fund Balances— All Government Funds This statement is prepared for all government fund types. Since only government funds are reported in this statement, all revenues and expenditures would be measured according to the principles of modified accrual accounting.

Combined Statement of Revenues, Expenditures, and Changes in Fund Balances— Budget and Actual—General and Special Revenue Funds This statement presents budget and actual amounts for general and special revenue fund types. The statement includes the budgetary data described earlier and directly compares actual revenues and expenditures to budgeted revenues and expenditures. It indicates, for each type of revenue and expenditure, the amount by which actual amounts differ from budgeted amounts.

Combined Statement of Revenues, Expenses, and Changes in Retained Earnings (or Equity) This statement is prepared for all proprietary fund types. It is prepared on the full accrual basis and resembles the financial statements prepared by businesses.

Combined Statement of Changes in Financial Position This statement is prepared for all proprietary fund types. This statement also resembles that prepared by businesses.

Not-for-Profit Organizations

OBJECTIVE 5
*Identify the
various types of
not-for-profit
organizations
and their
accounting
methods*

This section is a very brief view of accounting for certain types of not-for-profit organizations. Colleges and universities, hospitals, and voluntary professional, health, and welfare organizations, among others, share characteristics of both government and business entities. Like government, they are not intended to make a profit; however, they lack the taxing ability of a government. Because the lack of taxing ability requires that the revenues of not-for-profit organizations must at least equal expenses over the long run, these organizations rely on accrual accounting for most of their activities. These organizations also use funds to account for different types of resources and activities. The use of funds is necessary because of the legal restrictions imposed on many of the resources available to these groups.

Colleges and Universities

Colleges and universities, with a few exceptions, use full accrual accounting. One exception is that depreciation need not be recorded on fixed assets. Another exception is that revenues from restricted sources can be recognized only when expenditures are made for the purposes specified by the revenue source. Several types of funds are employed:

Current unrestricted fund   Accounts for general operating activities.

Current restricted fund   Accounts for funds available for a specific purpose, as designated by groups or individuals outside the school.

Loan funds   Account for funds available for loans to students, faculty, and staff.

Endowment funds   Account for gifts or bequests, the principal of which usually cannot be spent.

Annuity and life income funds   Similar to Endowment Funds, except that the donor receives some form of financial support from the school.

Plant funds   Account for funds available for acquisition and replacement of plant assets, as well as retirement of debt. These funds also account for all plant assets of the school, except any that may be part of an Endowment Fund.

Agency funds   Similar to those state and local governments use.

Financial statements used by colleges and universities include the following: (a) statement of current revenues, expenditures, and other changes; (b) combined balance sheet; and (c) statement of changes in fund balances.

Hospitals

Accounting for not-for-profit hospitals closely resembles the accrual accounting methods businesses use. Funds used include the following:

Unrestricted fund   Accounts for the hospital's normal operating activities. This is the only fund that records revenues and expenses. It accounts for all assets and liabilities not included in other funds, including plant assets and long-term debt.

Specific purpose fund   Similar to that colleges and universities use; to account for funds available for stated purposes (example: plant replacement and expansion fund).

Endowment funds Similar to those colleges and universities use (example: annuity and life income funds).

Not-for-profit hospitals prepare a statement of revenues and expenses for the unrestricted fund as well as a statement of changes in financial position. They also prepare balance sheets and statements of changes in fund balances for all funds.

An important aspect of hospital accounting is the classification of revenues and expenses. Revenues must be separated by *source,* including patient service and other operating and nonoperating revenues. Expenses must be classified by *function,* including nursing services, other professional services, administrative services, and so forth. Unlike other organizations described in this appendix, hospitals recognize depreciation on plant assets.

Voluntary Professional, Health, and Welfare Organizations

Voluntary professional, health, and welfare organizations encompass many diverse groups, such as the American Institute of Certified Public Accountants, the Sierra Club, the American Cancer Society, and the National Rifle Association. Although accounting practices vary considerably, these organizations usually follow the full accrual basis of accounting. They use funds such as those colleges and universities employ, as follows: current unrestricted fund; current restricted fund; land, building, and equipment fund; endowment funds; custodial (similar to agency) funds; and loan and annuity funds.

Two financial statements are prepared: (a) statement of support, revenue, and expenses, and changes in fund balances; and (b) balance sheets. These organizations must strictly classify revenues and expenses. Revenues must be separated into public support revenues, for which the donor expects nothing in return, and revenues from charges for goods and services. Expenses must be separated by *program* (those activities for which the organization has been established) and by *supporting services* (overhead). These classifications are useful in evaluating the relative efficiency of the groups' activities.

Summary

Government and not-for-profit accounting, as we have seen, shares some of the characteristics of business accounting but has its own unique features. Primary among such features is the use of funds to organize transactions. Table A-1 summarizes the types of funds various organizations use and reviews important details of their accounting systems.

Budgeting in Not-for-Profit Organizations

OBJECTIVE 6
Describe the unique aspects of the budgeting process in government and not-for-profit organizations

As pointed out earlier, the major difference between not-for-profit and profit organizations is the overall goal of each group. On the one hand, some enterprises must make a profit to exist, so making a profit must be their major objective. On the other hand, the not-for-profit organization is meant to serve some function or purpose other than making a profit. This purpose can be served, however, only if the organization carefully controls its funds and their use. For this reason, organizations that are not profit oriented depend heavily on budgeting to maintain control over their funds and to help carry out their goals.

Table A-1. Overview of Government and Not-for-Profit Accounting

	Type of Organization			
	Government Units	Colleges and Universities	Hospitals	Voluntary Professional, Health, and Welfare
Funds and Account Groups	General	Current unrestricted	Unrestricted	Curent unrestricted
	Special revenue	Current restricted	Specific purpose	Current restricted
	Capital projects		Plant replacement and expansion	
	Debt service			
	Special assessment			
	Enterprise			
	Internal service			
	Trust and agency	Loan		
		Endowment	Endowment	Endowment
		Annuity and life income	Annuity and life income	
		Agency		Custodian
	General long-term assets	Plant		Plant
	General long-term debt			
Special Characteristics	1. Only one general fund	1. Revenues recognized in restricted funds only as specified expenditures made	1. Depreciation may be computed on a replacement cost basis	1. Revenues segregated between voluntary contributions charges for goods or services
	2. Proprietary funds (enterprise, internal service) use full accrual accounting	2. Depreciation not recorded as an expense	2. Only unrestricted fund shows revenues and expenses	2. Expenses segregated by program services and by supporting (overhead) services
	3. Number of funds used depends on needs and complexity of government unit			

(Continued on next page)

Table A-1 (continued)

	Type of Organization			
				Voluntary Professional, Health, and Welfare
	Government Units	Colleges and Universities	Hospitals	
	Basis of Accounting			
	Modified Accrual	Accrual	Accrual	Accrual
Financial Statements	Combined balance sheet—all fund types and account groups	Combined balance sheet	Balance sheet	Balance sheet
	Combined statement of revenues, expenditures and changes in fund balances—all government fund types	Statement of current funds, revenues, expenditures, and other changes	Statement of revenues and expenses	Statement of support, revenue and expenses and changes in fund balances
	Combined statement of revenues, expenditures and changes in fund balances—budget and actual—general and special revenue fund types	Statement of changes in fund balances	Statement of changes in fund balances	Statement of functional expenses
	Combined statement of revenues, expenses, and changes in retained earnings—all proprietary fund types			
	Combined statement of changes in financial position—all proprietary fund types		Statement of changes in financial position	

Budgeting is a major project for large government organizations at the federal, state, and municipal levels. Public officials are charged with the safety and wise use of the public's money. Careful preparation of the annual budget plays an important role in this process. Officials of organizations such as professional groups, civic organizations, clubs, charitable organizations, and student fraternities and sororities face the same concerns.

Except for the profit element, the budgeting principles illustrated in Figure 8-1 (page 288) also apply to not-for-profit and government organizations. These entities must have long-term objectives as well as short-term goals and operating strategies. Human responsibilities and interaction principles are as much a part of the budgeting process in the public sector as they are in the private sector. Budget housekeeping rules apply as well as the follow-up principles. In other words, making a profit is not the only reason for participating in the budgeting function.

However, government units and other not-for-profit organizations need budgeting data on anticipated changes in fund balances rather than amounts of profit or loss. Such organizations rely heavily on cash budgeting techniques since their budgets are related to expected fund changes. The budgeted amount of each cost or expense item or grouping is the maximum expenditure approved for the period. Any changes in such an amount must have official approval.

Figure A-1 describes the budgeting procedure the government of the United States uses. Preparing the country's annual budget is an enormous undertaking that involves hundreds of people and agencies. The steps of the process in

Figure A-1. Congressional Budget Process Timetable

Suggested Deadlines	Action to Be Completed
On or before:	
November 10	President submits current services budget
Fifteenth day after Congress meets [Jan. 15]	President submits budget
March 15	Committees and joint committees submit reports to Budget Committees
April 1	Congressional Budget Office submits report to Budget Committees
April 15	Budget Committees report first concurrent resolution on the budget to their houses
May 15	Committees report bills and resolutions authorizing new budget authority
May 15	Congress completes action on first concurrent resolution on the budget
7th day after Labor Day	Congress completes action on bills and resolutions providing new budget authority and new spending authority
September 15	Congress completes action on second required concurrent resolution on the budget
September 25	Congress completes action on reconciliation bill or resolution, or both, implementing second required concurrent resolution
October 1	Fiscal year begins

Source: Title III, U.S. Code Congressional and Administrative News, §300, 93rd Cong., 2d Sess., 1974, p. 336.

Figure A-1 take almost a whole year. Note that the process begins with the president submitting a complete budget proposal to Congress for study and approval. Thousands of hours have already been spent putting together this proposal. This early stage adds several more months to the U.S. budgeting process.

Congress and the president control the country's purse strings through budgeting. Emphasis is on trying to cut down overspending and waste and prevent misuse of the taxpayers' money. Not-for-profit organizations generally operate with a board of directors having the same sort of responsibilities as the U.S. Congress or state legislature.

To present a more detailed picture of the budgeting process of a not-for-profit organization, we turn to Beta Alpha Psi, the national accounting fraternity for honor students. Beta Alpha Psi was founded to recognize honor students in accounting and to expose them to professional issues while they are still in school. Its size makes its budgeting procedures much easier to analyze than those of the federal government.

Beta Alpha Psi's budget for the year ending April 30, 1988, and related actual expenditures are shown in Figure A-2. The budget is prepared by the director of administration during the spring. The director first gets input from the other five directors and the national president. Past expenditure patterns and expected future events are used as the basis for projecting each revenue and expense item. An early draft of the budget is sent to board members before the organization's spring meeting. Then certain items are questioned at the meeting, and the revised budget is submitted for the board's approval about the first of June.

Actual results will of course be different from the budgeted figures. To control cost overruns, the board of directors should set up a policy that calls for board approval before any increases are funded. A small overrun does not call for such action. Only the significant increases must be controlled.

Expenditure Control— Government and Not-for-Profit Organizations

OBJECTIVE 7
Apply and interpret the basic techniques used by government and not-for-profit organizations to control costs of operations

The way to approach effective cost control in government and not-for-profit organizations is through the budgeting process. These organizations rely heavily on expected revenues for the coming period, and their budgets are linked closely with this figure. For government organizations such as the federal government, a state university, or a municipal government unit, revenues would be the funds *appropriated* for that period of time. Sometimes dollars can be shifted from one operating fund to another during the period, but the total appropriation sets the upper limit on spending. A not-for-profit organization such as a charitable group or a professional organization (the National Association of Accountants, for example) depends on the forecast of charitable contributions or membership dues for its spending limit.

Expenditure budgets for government and not-for-profit enterprises are usually developed independently of the revenue projection for the period. Once both budgets are completed, the budgeted expenditures normally need to be trimmed to match the spending limit set in the revenue forecast. Budgets approved by the legislature, city council, board of trustees, or board of directors then become the standard against which all expenditures are judged.

Figure A-2. Typical Not-for-Profit Budget

National Council of Beta Alpha Psi (The National Accounting Fraternity) Statements of Revenue, Expenditures, and Changes in Fund Balance For the Year Ended April 30, 1988		
	Actual	**Budget**
Revenue and support		
Initiation fees	$197,650	$204,000
Associates program contributions	115,000	120,000
Chapter fees	35,000	33,000
Superior chapter awards contributions	50,000	50,000
Outstanding faculty vice president awards contributions	6,000	6,000
Charter fees	9,500	6,000
Membership insignia royalties	2,148	—
Interest	19,985	12,000
Miscellaneous	22,363	9,000
Total revenue and support	$457,646	$440,000
Expenses by activity:		
General and administrative	$ 88,844	$ 85,000
National council:		
Annual banquet and student, mid-year and spring meetings	86,604	90,000
Faculty vice president and student expense reimbursements	35,255	40,000
Chapter installations and visitations	4,720	8,000
Local chapter:		
Membership certificates	14,500	20,000
Banners and miscellaneous	1,752	2,000
Special projects:		
Faculty vice president awards	6,000	6,000
Regional meetings	54,393	59,000
Student seminar	18,427	20,000
Publications	20,267	20,000
Superior chapter awards	50,000	50,000
Honorarium	1,000	1,000
Total expenses	$379,762	$401,000
Excess of revenue and support over expenses	$ 77,884	$ 39,000
Fund balance, beginning of year	225,592	225,592
Fund balance, end of year	$303,476	$264,592

Government Organizations

For government organizations, an appropriation means that expenditures have been formally approved and dollars have been set aside for specific purposes. When those dollars are gone, expenditures must cease. Therefore, administrative control over the use of these funds becomes extremely important. Each government unit has at least two main uses for its funds: (1) to carry out its mission and (2) to cover its day-to-day operations.

Funds to cover operating costs such as salaries, supplies, and equipment are distributed to each operating department or unit as part of the budgeting process. Each manager must then account for the specific uses of funds within his or her unit and is held responsible for any deviation from the budget. Since revenues are limited, any increase in cost over budgeted amounts must be formally requested and approved by the organization's governing body.

Expenditures used to carry out the intended mission of government organization are controlled in a different manner. Let's compare cost control techniques for two types of government units: the Department of Defense and a municipal street department. Both these units contract with outside, profit-oriented companies for specific projects such as building a new jet fighter or paving a street. The contract itself is the cost control mechanism many government organizations use.

If at all possible, a firm fixed price contract should be obtained. With this kind of contract, the government unit establishes an upper expenditure limit, above which the contractor must absorb all costs and still complete the project. All costs and profit are included in the firm fixed price. Most of the projects of a municipal street department will be under firm fixed price contracts, but the Department of Defense can make only limited use of this kind of contract. Why? Because it is easy to forecast costs for paving a street, as it is for building one hundred more tanks. But what about designing and building a new jet fighter or a nuclear submarine? Imagine the amount of uncertainty involved in projecting costs for such projects. Because of this uncertainty, profit-oriented companies will not take on such a project under a firm fixed price contract. For these situations, a cost plus fixed or variable fee contract is used. Such a contract shifts the risks from the contractor to the government unit. These risks and uncertainties often cause cost overruns that become targets of the news media. Without such contracts, however, no profit-oriented company would accept risky projects, and the Department of Defense would have to build its own factories for new defense projects. The government to date has been unwilling to compete with the private sector in this way. Since the Department of Defense must, as must the municipal street department, operate within set spending limits, any cost overrun that cannot be absorbed by other units within the department must come before Congress for approval. Such a procedure—submitting excess costs to a governing body for approval—is another type of cost control for government organizations.

Not-for-Profit Organizations

Many of the cost control procedures not-for-profit enterprises use have already been discussed in general terms. We now show how these procedures might be used in a church. The United Church has a budget committee charged with developing the church's operating budget each year. The Board of Deacons of the church then approves the budget after making adjustments for events unforeseen by the budget committee. Last year, the board approved a budget with the following items: Building Repairs, $6,500; Utility Costs, $3,450; and New Hymnals, $1,200. A hot water heater explosion, increased utility rates, and an unexpected new edition of the hymnal caused all three cost categories to be questioned during the year. Since donations and member offerings were not expected to increase much even with these unusual needs, the board had to decide how to keep costs within the set limits and still keep the church operating.

Building repairs after the explosion amounted to $10,000, $6,000 of which was covered by insurance. The $4,000 difference brought the total building repairs for the year to $7,200. Utility bills shot up 15 percent, and actual utility bills totaled $3,970. New hymnals for the church would cost $4,500. The board, after discussing these events, decided that the building repairs and payment of utility bills were necessary for the continued operation of the church. Therefore, the purchase of new hymnals was put off until the following year. The current year's appropriation of $1,200 for hymnals was diverted to Building Repairs ($700) and Utility Costs ($500) to help cover the increases. It took formal approval of the Board of Deacons to make these cost overrun payments. Cost control takes many forms in not-for-profit organizations, but all are connected with the budget and the approval/review process of the governing body.

Questions

1. How do the objectives of government accounting differ from the objectives of business accounting?
2. What is the purpose of a *fund,* as that term is used in government accounting?
3. Contrast the measurement of *revenues* and *expenditures* in government accounting with the measurement of *revenues* and *expenses* in business accounting.
4. What is a *proprietary fund* in government accounting? Why do such funds use accrual accounting?
5. What is the purpose of budgetary accounts in government accounting?
6. What are the major characteristics of *modified accrual accounting* as used in government accounting?
7. What are the purpose and meaning of recording *encumbrances*?
8. In what ways does accounting for colleges and universities resemble business accounting? How does it differ from business accounting?
9. Describe how revenues and expenses are classified in hospital accounting.
10. Describe and contrast the two types of revenues recognized in the accounts of voluntary professional, health, and welfare organizations.
11. Do not-for-profit organizations require budgets just as profit-oriented enterprises do? Explain your answer.
12. How do budgets help control costs for government and not-for-profit organizations?
13. "Contracts with outside contractors is a common means of cost control for government organizations." Explain this statement.
14. In not-for-profit organizations, how are potential cost overruns handled? Why is this action necessary?

Exercises

**Exercise A-1.
Basic Concepts
and Funds
(L.O.3,5)**

Select the most appropriate answer for the following multiple-choice questions:

1. The fund that accounts for the day-to-day operating activities of a local government is the
   a. enterprise fund.
   b. general fund.
   c. operating fund.
   d. special revenue fund.
2. Accrual accounting is recommended for which of the following funds?
   a. Debt service fund
   b. General fund
   c. Internal service fund
   d. Fiduciary fund
3. A debt service fund of a municipality is an example of what type of fund?
   a. Internal service fund
   b. Government fund
   c. Proprietary fund
   d. Fiduciary fund
4. What basis of accounting would a not-for-profit hospital use?
   a. Cash basis for all funds
   b. Modified accrual basis for all funds
   c. Accrual basis for all funds
   d. Accrual basis for some funds and modified accrual basis for other funds
5. Which of the following types of organizations are *required* to record depreciation expense on property, plant, and equipment?
   a. State and local governments
   b. Colleges and universities
   c. Hospitals
   d. All the above

**Exercise A-2.
Recording the
Budget in the
General Fund
(L.O.4)**

The Village of Glencoe has adopted the following budget items for 19x4:

Estimated Revenues	$10,000,000
Appropriations	9,800,000

a. Prepare the journal entry to record the budget in the general fund for Glencoe on January 1, 19x4.
b. What entry, if any, would be required at the end of Glencoe's accounting year, December 31, 19x4?

**Exercise A-3.
Budgeting for
Not-for-Profit
Organizations
(L.O.6)**

The Board of Directors of the Apple County Animal Shelter has been discussing budget strategy for several months. Recently, Ms. Jonathan was appointed budget director. She is now putting together the cash expenditure budget for 19x6. Following is a listing of 19x5 expenditures:

Salaries and wages	$ 80,900
Employee benefits expense	25,430
Truck expenses	6,540
Medical lab expenses	26,400
Medical supplies expense	12,600
Repairs and maintenance expense	7,260
Heating costs	2,800
Electricity expense	3,400
Water charges	200
Insect control costs	260
Building rent expense	3,500
Animal food costs	4,200
Miscellaneous expenses	620
Total	$174,110

During 19x6, salaries, wages, and related employee benefits are expected to rise by 10 percent. Medical lab and supplies expenses will go up 20 percent next year. All other expenses should be 5 percent higher in 19x6.

Prepare the cash expenditure budget for the Apple County Animal Shelter for 19x6.

Interpreting Accounting Information

Not-for-Profit Organization: The National Association of Accountants
(L.O. 7)

The National Association of Accountants (NAA), originally called the National Association of Cost Accountants, was created to assist in the development of the management accounting profession. Its primary purpose is continued education of its members, even though its more than 300 local chapters engage in some activities that are not strictly educational. The NAA publishes many items, including *Management Accounting,* a monthly professional magazine. Through its sister organization, the Institute of Certified Management Accountants (ICMA), the organization promotes and administers the Certified Management Accountants (CMA) examination and program.

The NAA operates through an executive committee of 33 members and a large board of directors. Included on the executive committee are the national president, the chairperson of the association, twelve national vice presidents, the treasurer, the past president, eleven chairpersons of standing committees, and six appointed members. The annual budget is developed by several people and committees during the year, and then it is pulled together by the Finance Committee and presented to the Board of Directors for approval at the June meeting. Following is the Association's Budget and Statement of Revenues and Expenses and Changes in Fund Balance for 1987–1988. After studying it carefully, respond to the following questions:

1. What concerns should the NAA have about revenues?
2. What expenses should be questioned and analyzed for the next budget cycle?
3. What overall thoughts do you have about the financial direction of the association?

National Association of Accountants Statement of Revenues and Expenses and Changes in Fund Balance—Current Operating Fund For the Year Ended June 30, 1988		
	Budget	**Actual**
Revenues		
Membership dues	$ 6,887,000	$ 6,822,000
Professional education program	572,000	1,117,000
Advertising and sales of publications	1,681,000	1,374,000
Controllers council/business and tax planning board	442,000	449,000
Annual conference	591,000	570,000
Research fund contributions applied	34,000	10,000
Academic relations symposia	20,000	—
Interest and dividends on investments	335,000	296,000
Gain on security sales	150,000	237,000
Miscellaneous	43,000	40,000
Total revenue	$10,755,000	$10,915,000
Expenses		
Payments to chapters	$ 1,160,000	$ 1,121,000
Professional educational program	606,000	872,000
Technical information and library	151,000	148,000
Technical publications	2,048,000	2,052,000
Controllers council/business and tax planning board	432,000	376,000
Annual conference	461,000	562,000
Research fund expenditures	306,000	282,000
Management accounting practices	193,000	192,000
Academic relations	165,000	132,000
Marketing and membership	548,000	533,000
Chapter operations	530,000	533,000
Public relations and promotion	126,000	124,000
Accounting, information services, general office, and food services	1,733,000	2,017,000
Occupancy costs	769,000	741,000
Administration	1,030,000	882,000
Meetings planning	246,000	283,000
International department	98,000	84,000
Long-range strategy	—	19,000
Total expenses	$10,602,000	$10,953,000
Excess (deficiency) of revenues over expenses	$ 153,000	$ (38,000)
Fund balance, beginning of year	1,486,000	1,486,000
Capital additions		
Building fund contributions	—	20,000
Transfers		
Video education program	25,000	25,000
Long-range strategy	—	19,000
Reimbursement of funds advanced	—	(20,000)
Fund balance, end of year	$ 1,664,000	$ 1,492,000

Problems

**Problem A-1.
Journal Entries for
the General Fund
(L.O. 4)**

The following transactions occurred in North Shore City during 19x1. Record the journal entries necessary to account for these transactions in North Shore's general fund.

19x1

a. Jan. 1   The budget was adopted. Estimated revenues are $4,000,000; appropriations are $4,100,000.

b. Feb. 11 Supplies with an estimated cost of $22,000 were ordered.

c. Mar. 1   Property taxes totaling $3,500,000 were levied. North Shore City expects 2 percent of this amount to be uncollectible.

d. Apr. 10 The supplies ordered on February 11 were received. The actual bill for these supplies amounted to $21,750.

e. June 1   Property tax collections totaled $3,450,000. The rest were classified as delinquent.

f. Aug. 10 Equipment costing $11,300 was purchased for cash.

g. Dec. 31 Actual revenues for 19x1 totaled $4,050,000. Actual expenditures totaled $3,975,000.

**Problem A-2.
Budget
Preparation—
Not-for-Profit
Organization
(L.O. 3, 6)**

Hayward College is a small liberal arts school with an enrollment of about 2,500 students. The college was founded in 1860 by a missionary and his wife and has become well known over the years. Graduates of the school have been very successful and include senators, corporate presidents, military leaders, famous academic and research personnel, and even two state governors.

The college's development program has been in operation for fifty years and is now under the direction of Dr. Jay Tontz. During the past twelve years, the college's endowment has grown from $15,500,000 to an expected $165,450,000 at the close of operation on December 31, 19x6. The breakdown of that amount is as follows (information in parentheses shows how each part of the endowment is invested and its current yield):

Unrestricted

Corporate "silver plate" program	
(12% money market fund)	$ 23,400,000
Alumni open donation account	
(10% corporate bonds)	14,900,000
Alumni/college beneficiary insurance proceeds	
(14% certificate of deposit)	46,850,000
Friends of the College fund	
(12% money market fund)	7,280,000
Total unrestricted	$ 92,430,000

Restricted

Endowed professorships:	
Science—6 at $1,000,000	$ 6,000,000
Business—3 at $1,000,000	3,000,000
Religion—1 at $800,000	800,000
History—1 at $600,000	600,000
(10% corporate bonds and preferred stock)	

Alumni student scholarship fund (12% certificate of deposit)	4,900,000
Building maintenance program (14% second mortgage loans)	16,850,000
Capital facility expansion fund (12% government securities)	40,870,000
Total restricted	$ 73,020,000
Total college endowment	$165,450,000

After careful analysis, Dr. Tontz anticipates the following additions to the endowment next year:

Corporate "silver plate" program	$ 640,000
Alumni open donation	110,000
Alumni/college beneficiary insurance proceeds	1,500,000
Friends of the College	410,000
Endowed professorships:	
One in science	1,000,000
One in social science	400,000
Alumni student scholarship fund	550,000
Building maintenance program	310,000
Capital facility expansion fund	2,500,000

Note: The endowed professorship in science and the addition to the capital facility expansion fund will be received in January. Assume that the other endowment additions earn half the normal interest for the year.

Required

1. Prepare the complete projected college endowment budget as of December 31, 19x7.
2. Compute the projected interest income for the year from each part of the endowment.
3. The interest income from the unrestricted part of the endowment must first be used to cover expenses of $2,460,000 for the development program operation. Explain what kinds of uses the college could make of the remaining funds. Give at least four examples.

Quantitative Tools for Analysis

Management accountants rely on several quantitative tools to fulfill their day-to-day duties and responsibilities. Some of these tools were explained within the text such as (1) the high-low method and simple linear regression analysis for use in determining the mix of variable and fixed costs in a semivariable cost and (2) the net present value computation used in capital expenditure decision analysis. This appendix introduces additional quantitative tools used by the management accountant to help management maximize profits or minimize costs. In the inventory management area, we discuss methods of computing the economic order quantity, reorder point, and safety stock considerations. Linear programming is introduced at a very simple level. This quantitative tool is useful when limited resources constrain profit potential. Linear programming can become very complex in real world situations, and only a computer can solve such a series of equations in a reasonable amount of time. When you have completed this appendix, you should be able to meet the learning objectives listed on the left.

Inventory Planning and Control

Inventory planning and control are critical to the success of a company. The keys to success are the identification and maintenance of an optimum inventory level. An optimum inventory level allows a manager to minimize the costs of carrying inventory while avoiding production interruptions due to stockouts.

Relevant costs for inventory planning and control are the costs of ordering and carrying inventories as shown below.

Inventory Ordering Costs	Inventory Carrying Costs
Placing a purchase order	Storage costs
Transportation	Insurance
Receiving and storing	Property taxes
	Obsolescence
	Interest on investments in inventory

These costs offset each other. For example, carrying costs will increase if your order size increases, but your ordering cost will decline. For a manager to minimize the cost of inventory, these costs must be balanced. To balance these costs, a manager must determine how much to order and when to order.

Economic Order Quantity

OBJECTIVE 1
Compute the
economic order
quantity (EOQ)
for inventory
using a table and
formula approach

The **economic order quantity** (EOQ) is the amount of inventory to order that minimizes the ordering and carrying costs. There are several ways to compute the EOQ. We will use a table and a formula approach for this computation.

To illustrate the use of the table method, assume the Hawk Bus Manufacturer buys tires from a supplier at $200 a tire. The annual need for tires is 10,000. The inventory carrying costs are $1.00 per tire and the cost of placing an order is $15.00.

Exhibit B-1 shows the table of the relevant costs for various order sizes of tires. The EOQ is identified by the column with the lowest cost. Exhibit B-1 shows the lowest cost to be at the 500 unit level. You may find a lower EOQ by testing order sizes between 400–500 units and 500–750 units. However, the cost difference would be immaterial and not worth the effort. The same information is shown graphically in Exhibit B-2. You can see the annual inventory costs are minimized where annual carrying cost equals annual purchase order cost. This intersection represents the economic order quantity.

The economic order quantity can be computed using a formula. Using calculus, the formula is shown below:

$$E = \sqrt{\frac{2QP}{AC}}$$

E = Economic Order Quantity in units
Q = Annual inventory used in units
P = Cost of placing an order
AC = Annual Carrying cost of one unit of inventory

If we use the data from our table, the economic order quantity is computed as follows:

$$E = \sqrt{\frac{2(10,000)(\$15)}{\$1.00}}$$

$$E = \sqrt{\frac{\$300,000}{\$1.00}}$$

$$E = \sqrt{300,000}$$

$$E = 548$$

As you can see, the formula approach is more accurate than the table approach. However, the difference in the accuracy is not material.

Reorder Point and Safety Stock

OBJECTIVE 2
Determine the
reorder point for
inventory when
usage is known

A manager may know how much inventory to order but must also know when to order. The **reorder point** is the number of items remaining in inventory that will be used before an order can be placed and stock replenished. To identify the reorder point, a manager must know the economic order quantity, lead time, and the average usage of inventory during the lead time. The lead time is the time interval between placing an order and receiving delivery of the order. The usage rate may be known with certainty or it may fluctuate from day to day.

Exhibit B-1. Relevant Costs for Various Order Sizes

Symbols	Description	Order Sizes							
O	Order size in units	250	400	500	750	1,000	2,000	5,000	10,000
O/2	Average inventory in units	125	200	250	375	500	1,000	2,500	5,000
Q/O	Number of purchase orders	40	25	20	13.3	10	5	2	1
AC(O/2)	Annual carrying cost at $1.00/unit	$125	$200	$250	$375	$500	$1,000	$2,500	$5,000
P(Q/O)	Annual purchase order cost at $15 per order	$600	$375	$300	$200	$150	$ 75	$ 30	$ 15
TC	Total annual cost	$725	$575	$550	$575	$650	$1,075	$2,530	$5,015

O = Order size in units; Q = Annual inventory used in units; AC = Annual cost of carrying one unit in inventory; P = Cost of placing a purchase order; TC = Total annual costs

Exhibit B-2. Graphic Approach to Economic Order Size

The reorder point is straightforward when the usage rate is known with certainty. The reorder point can be determined as follows:

$$\text{Reorder point} = \text{Lead time} \times \text{Usage rate}$$

If the Hawk Bus Manufacturer uses 200 tires per week and the lead time for the tires is 2 weeks, the reorder point is:

$$\text{Reorder point} = 2 \text{ weeks} \times 200 \text{ tires per week}$$
$$\text{Reorder point} = 400 \text{ tires}$$

This means the manager would reorder 548 tires (the economic order quantity) when the inventory level drops to 400 units. This computation is shown graphically in Exhibit B-3.

OBJECTIVE 3
Compute safety stock for inventory when usage is unknown

Most companies cannot determine their usage of inventory with certainty. Usage tends to vary from day to day, week to week or month to month. These variances could be caused by a change in demand for their products, a delay in processing their purchase order, or shipping delays. When a company has these problems, they need to provide for **safety stock**, a cushion to prevent stockouts. Safety stock is computed by subtracting average usage from the maximum usage during the lead time. For example, assume Hawk Bus Manufacturer's usage of tires is not known with certainty. The maximum usage per week is 240 tires and on the average they use 200 tires. The safety stock for the company is:

$$\frac{\text{Safety}}{\text{Stock}} = \frac{\text{Maximum}}{\text{Usage}} - \frac{\text{Average}}{\text{Usage}} \times \frac{\text{Lead}}{\text{Time}}$$

$$\text{Safety Stock} = (240 - 200) \times 2$$
$$\text{Safety Stock} = 40 \times 2$$
$$\text{Safety Stock} = 80 \text{ tires}$$

Exhibit B-3. Reorder Point Under Conditions of Certainty

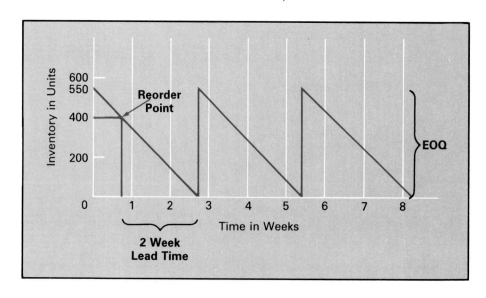

Exhibit B-4. Reorder Point Under Varying Conditions

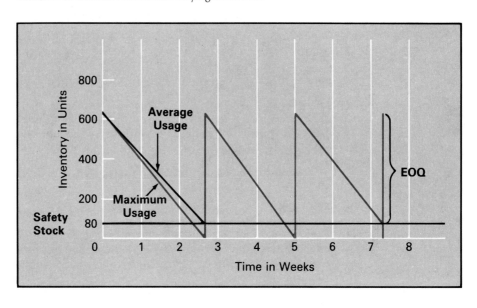

The reorder point is computed by adding the safety stock to the average usage during the lead time as shown below:

Reorder Point = (Average usage × Lead time) + Safety Stock
Reorder Point = (200 × 2) + 80
Reorder Point = 400 + 80
Reorder Point = 480 tires

This computation is shown graphically in Exhibit B-4.

Linear Programming

OBJECTIVE 4
Develop objective function and constraint equations for solving linear programing problems

Linear programming is a mathematical tool that can be used by managers to help them make key decisions about the allocation of limited resources or demand for their products. The objective of the allocation is to maximize the profits or minimize the costs of the company. The limited resources could be a shortage of materials used in the production of the company's product or limited machine hours to meet the market demand for the company's product. In linear programming, the limiting item is called a constraint.

The use of linear programming requires a manager to express his business problem in algebraic equations. The equations required include the manager's objective function (that which is to be maximized or minimized) and the constraints of the situation. The objective function equation sets the goal the manager is trying to attain. The constraint equations are the limitations which the manager must manage. Examples include limited materials, labor, machine hours or product demand.

To illustrate linear programming, assume the following facts about the Mainline Company:

They produce two products, A and B.

The contribution margin of A is $6 per unit and $8 per unit for B.

Mainline has 28 hours of machine time available each period to produce A and B.

One unit of A can be produced in 4 machine hours and one unit of B in 7 machine hours.

Raw material T is used in producing both A and B. Four quarts of T are used to produce a unit of A, and two quarts to produce a unit of B. The current inventory of T is 16 quarts.

The sales manager believes that a maximum of 2 units of B can be sold each period.

Company management's goal is to maximize their contribution margin.

The challenge for Mainline's management is to find the combination of A and B to produce and sell that will maximize their contribution margin.

    The first step to solving the problem is to determine management's objective function and express it in an algebraic equation. We said earlier, the objective function equation was the goal a manager is trying to attain. In our example, Mainline's management wants to maximize its contribution margin. The total contribution margin for Mainline can be expressed by the following objective function equation:

$$M = \$6A + \$8B \qquad (1)$$

Where:

M = the total contribution margin when the optimum number of units of A and B are produced and sold each period

$6 = Contribution margin for each unit of A

A = Optimum units of A that must be produced and sold to maximize the contribution margin.

$8 = Contribution margin for each unit of B

B = Optimum units of B that must be produced and sold to maximize the contribution margin.

    Our second step is to determine the constraint equations for the Mainline Company. Remember the constraint equations are the limitations which Mainline's management must manage. The constraints for Mainline are 28 hours of machine time, 16 quarts of T, and only 2 units of B can be sold each period.

    Product A can be produced in 4 hours of machine time and Product B in 7 hours of machine time. The machine hour constraint can be expressed as follows:

$$4A + 7B \leq 28 \qquad (2)$$

This equation indicates that the total production of A and B together cannot exceed 28 machine hours but could require less than the 28 machine hours.

    Since it takes 4 quarts of T to produce one unit of A and 2 quarts to produce a unit of B, we can express this constraint in the following equation:

$$4A + 2B \leq 16 \qquad (3)$$

The final constraint of market demand for product B is expressed as:

$$B \leqslant 2 \tag{4}$$

OBJECTIVE 5
Prepare a graphic solution for a linear programming problem

The third step is to plot the constraint equations on a graph. Start with equation (2) and assume only product A and no product B will be produced. This results in the following:

$$
\begin{aligned}
4A + 7B &\leqslant 28 \\
4A + 7(0) &\leqslant 28 \\
4A &\leqslant 28 \\
A &= 7
\end{aligned}
\tag{2}
$$

Now assume that only product B and no product A will be produced. This results in the following:

$$
\begin{aligned}
4A + 7B &\leqslant 28 \\
4(0) + 7B &\leqslant 28 \\
7B &\leqslant 28 \\
B &= 4
\end{aligned}
\tag{2}
$$

Plot the machine time constraint on a graph as (A = 7, B = 0) and (A = 0, B = 4) and connect the two points as shown on Exhibit B-5.

Apply the same steps to equations (3) and (4) and plot on a graph as shown below and on Exhibit B-5.

$$
\begin{aligned}
4A + 2B &\leqslant 16 \\
4A + 2(0) &\leqslant 16 \\
4A &\leqslant 16 \\
A &= 4
\end{aligned}
\tag{3}
$$

$$
\begin{aligned}
4A + 2B &\leqslant 16 \\
4(0) + 2B &\leqslant 16 \\
2B &\leqslant 16 \\
B &= 8
\end{aligned}
\tag{3}
$$

$$
\begin{aligned}
B &\leqslant 2 \\
B &= 2
\end{aligned}
\tag{4}
$$

Once all the constraint equations are plotted on a graph on lines drawn connecting the various sets of points, a feasible solution area will be identified. This area is shaded on Exhibit B-5 and falls beneath all the constraint lines. All points within this area are possible production combinations of products A and B. However, one point in this area represents the optimal production mix of A and B, which will maximize the objective function equation or contribution margin for the Mainline Company.

Our final step is to find the point within the feasible solution area that maximizes the objective function equation. This point will always fall on one of the corner points of the feasible solution. In our example, the corner points are:

1. (A = 0, B = 0)
2. (A = 0, B = 2)
3. (A = 3, B = 2)
4. (A = 4, B = 0)

We determine the optimum production of A and B by computing the contribution margin at each of these corner points. This computation is made by using the objective function equation (1) as shown on the following page:

Exhibit B-5. Linear Programming Graphic Solution

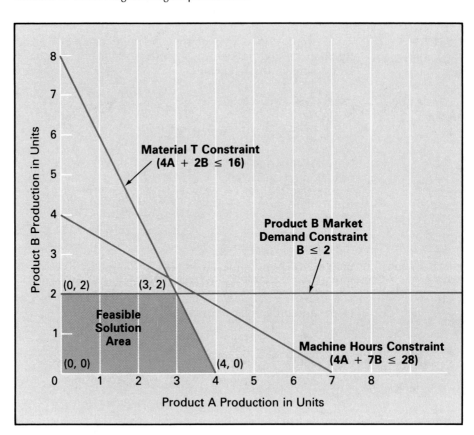

$$M = \$6A + 8B \qquad (1)$$

1. $M = \$6(0) + \$8(0)$
   $M = 0$

2. $M = \$6(0) + \$8(2)$
   $M = 16$

3. $M = \$6(3) + \$8(2)$
   $M = 18 + 16$
   $M = 34$

4. $M = \$6(4) + \$8(0)$
   $M = 24$

The Mainline Company should produce and sell 3 units of A and 2 units of B during any period. This level of production and sales will maximize the company's contribution margin. They cannot gain a higher contribution margin with any other combination of A and B due to the constraints under which the company must operate.

Our example is very simple. Linear programming problems can become very complex when there are more than two variables. These conditions are solved by the simplex method of linear programming, a method that is covered in an advanced course in management accounting.

Questions

1. Why does a manager seek an optimum inventory level?
2. Define inventory ordering and carrying costs.
3. What is the economic order quantity?
4. What is the reorder point?
5. Identify safety stock.
6. When would a manager use linear programming?
7. What is the purpose of an objective function equation in the application of linear programming?
8. Explain the feasible solution area of a linear programming graphic application.

Exercises

Exercise B-1.
Economic Order
Quantity
(L.O.1)

Outcall produces pay telephones. They purchase a special telecommunication unit for the phone from an out-of-state supplier. Outcall uses 7,000 telecommunication units each year at a unit price of $30. The cost of carrying these units in inventory is $.20. Placing a purchase order for these units costs $8.00. Use the formula approach to determine the economic order quantity for the units.

Exercise B-2.
Reorder Point
(L.O.2)

Green Chips Corporation produces potato chips and other salty snacks. They use 2,000 tons of raw potatoes weekly in producing their chips. The lead time for potatoes is 3 weeks. What is the reorder point in tons of potatoes?

Exercise B-3.
Reorder point with
Safety Stock
(L.O.3)

Assume the same data in Exercise B-2. Due to a change in demand for potato chips, Green Chips Corporation's use of potatoes has changed. Their average use of potatoes remains at 2,000 tons per week. However, for several weeks they have used 2,200 tons of potatoes. Compute the reorder point with safety stock under these new conditions.

Exercise B-4.
Linear
Programming
(L.O.4)

The Holman Company produces two products, M and N. The contribution margins for M and N are $10 and $7, respectively. What is the objective function equation if the company wants to maximize the contribution margin from these two products?

Exercise B-5.
Linear
Programming
Constraints
(L.O.4)

The Holman Company (see Exercise B-4) has several constraints associated with the production and sale of their products M and N. The labor available each period to produce the products is 200 hours. It takes 10 hours and 12 hours to produce M and N, respectively. Products M and N contain a common material called Telon. Product M contains 10 pounds and product N requires 5 pounds of Telon. The inventory of Telon is 150 pounds. Holman's marketing vice president says that only 15 units of N can be sold during the period. The president asks you to help make a decision on how many units of M and N to produce this period. Use linear programming and remember that each constraint must be expressed algebraically. What are the equations for each constraint?

Problems

Johnson Manufacturing produces a heavy duty drilling unit. They also purchase a high quality motor for each drilling unit. The company produces 5,000 drilling units a year. The cost of the motor for each unit is $2,500. Other inventory cost data are:

Annual inventory carrying cost per unit—$120

Cost of placing a purchase order—$9.00

Required

1. Determine the economic order quantity for the motors using the table approach. Use order quantities of 20, 22, 24, 26, 28, and 30 as headings in your table.
2. Determine the economic order quantity for the motors using the formula approach.

The Trident Corporation manufactures and sells two products, hand-held televisions and radios. Trident's management wants to maximize the contribution margin from these two products. However, there are several limiting factors associated with the manufacturing of them. The company has 90 hours of production time each period available to make the products. It takes 4 hours to make a television and 2 hours for a radio. Each product includes an electronic component C526. Each television uses two C526 components and each radio requires one. There are only 180 of the C526 components in stock. The marketing department believes they can only sell 20 televisions this period. The contribution margin for each television is $8 and $4 for each radio.

Required

Determine the optimum mix of televisions and radios Trident Corporation should produce to maximize its contribution margin for the period.

The Use of Future Value and Present Value in Accounting

1. *Distinguish simple interest from compound interest.*
2. *Use compound interest tables to compute (a) the future value of a single invested sum at compound interest, and (b) the future value of an ordinary annuity.*
3. *Use present value tables to compute (a) the present value of a single sum due in the future, and (b) the present value of an ordinary annuity.*
4. *Apply the concept of present value to some simple accounting situations.*

Interest is an important cost to the debtor and an important revenue to the creditor. Because interest is a cost associated with time, and "time is money," it is also an important consideration in any business decision. For example, an individual who holds $100 for one year without putting that $100 in a savings account has forgone the interest that could have been earned. Thus there is a cost associated with holding this money equal to the interest that could have been earned. Similarly, a business person who accepts a noninterest-bearing note instead of cash for the sale of merchandise is forgoing the interest that could have been earned on that money. These examples illustrate the point that the timing of the receipt and payment of cash must be considered in making business decisions. After studying this appendix, you should be able to meet the learning objectives listed on the left.

Simple Interest and Compound Interest

Interest is the cost associated with the use of money for a specific period of time. Simple interest is the interest cost, for one or more periods, if we assume that the amount on which the interest is computed stays the same from period to period. Compound interest is the interest cost, for two or more periods, if we assume that after each period the interest of that period is added to the amount on which interest is computed in future periods. In other words, compound interest is interest earned on a principal sum that is increased at the end of each period by the interest of that period.

Example: Simple Interest. Joe Sanchez accepts an 8 percent, $30,000 note due in 90 days. How much will he receive in total at that time? Remember the formula for calculating simple interest, which was presented in Chapter 8, on notes receivable:

$$\text{interest} = \text{principal} \times \text{rate} \times \text{time}$$
$$\text{interest} = \$30,000 \times 8/100 \times 90/360$$
$$\text{interest} = \$600$$

The total that Sanchez will receive is computed as follows:

$$\text{total} = \text{principal} + \text{interest}$$
$$\text{total} = \$30,000 + \$600$$
$$\text{total} = \$30,600$$

OBJECTIVE 1
Distinguish
simple interest
from compound
interest

Example: Compound Interest. Ann Clary deposits $5,000 in a savings account that pays 6 percent interest. She expects to leave the principal and accumulated interest in the account for three years. How much in total will be in her account at the end of three years? Assume that the interest is paid at the end of the year and is added to the principal at that time and that this total in turn earns interest. The amount at the end of three years can be figured as follows:

(1) Year	(2) Principal Amount at Beginning of Year	(3) Annual Amount of Interest (col. 2 × .06)	(4) Accumulated Amount at End of Year (col. 2 + col. 3)
1	$5,000.00	$300.00	$5,300.00
2	5,300.00	318.00	5,618.00
3	5,618.00	337.08	5,955.08

At the end of three years, Clary will have $5,955.08 in her savings account. Note that the annual amount of interest increases each year by the interest rate times the interest of the previous year. For example, between year 1 and year 2, the interest increased by $18 ($318 − $300), which exactly equals .06 times $300.

Future Value of a Single Sum Invested at Compound Interest

OBJECTIVE 2a
Use compound
interest tables to
compute the
future value of a
single invested
sum at
compound
interest

Another way to ask the question in the example of compound interest above is, What is the future value of a single sum ($5,000) at compound interest (6 percent) for three years? **Future value** is the amount an investment will be worth at a future date if invested at compound interest. A businessperson often wants to know future value, but the method of finding future value above takes too much time. Imagine how long the calculation would take if the example were ten years, not three. Fortunately, there are tables that make problems involving compound interest much quicker to solve. Table C-1, showing the future value of $1 after a given number of time periods, is an example. It is actually part of a larger table, D-1, in Appendix D. Suppose we want to solve the problem of Clary's savings account above. We simply look down the 6 percent column in Table C-1 until we reach period 3 and find the factor 1.191. This factor when multiplied by $1 gives the future value of that $1 at compound interest of 6 percent for three periods (years in this case). Thus we solve the problem:

$$\text{principal} \times \text{factor} = \text{future value}$$
$$\$5,000 \quad \times \ 1.191 \ = \quad \$5,955$$

Except for a rounding error of $.08, the answer is exactly the same. Another example will illustrate this simple technique again.

Example: Future Value of a Single Invested Sum at Compound Interest. Ed Bates invests $3,000, which he believes will return 5 percent interest compounded over a five-year period. How much will Bates have at the end of five years? From Table C-1, the factor for period 5 of the 5 percent column is 1.276. Therefore, we calculate as follows:

Table C-1. Future Value of $1 After a Given Number of Time Periods

Periods	1%	2%	3%	4%	5%	6%	7%	8%	9%	10%	12%	14%	15%
1	1.010	1.020	1.030	1.040	1.050	1.060	1.070	1.080	1.090	1.100	1.120	1.140	1.150
2	1.020	1.040	1.061	1.082	1.103	1.124	1.145	1.166	1.188	1.210	1.254	1.300	1.323
3	1.030	1.061	1.093	1.125	1.158	1.191	1.225	1.260	1.295	1.331	1.405	1.482	1.521
4	1.041	1.082	1.126	1.170	1.216	1.262	1.311	1.360	1.412	1.464	1.574	1.689	1.749
5	1.051	1.104	1.159	1.217	1.276	1.338	1.403	1.469	1.539	1.611	1.762	1.925	2.011
6	1.062	1.126	1.194	1.265	1.340	1.419	1.501	1.587	1.677	1.772	1.974	2.195	2.313
7	1.072	1.149	1.230	1.316	1.407	1.504	1.606	1.714	1.828	1.949	2.211	2.502	2.660
8	1.083	1.172	1.267	1.369	1.477	1.594	1.718	1.851	1.993	2.144	2.476	2.853	3.059
9	1.094	1.195	1.305	1.423	1.551	1.689	1.838	1.999	2.172	2.358	2.773	3.252	3.518
10	1.105	1.219	1.344	1.480	1.629	1.791	1.967	2.159	2.367	2.594	3.106	3.707	4.046

Source: Henry R. Anderson and Mitchell H. Raiborn, *Basic Cost Accounting Concepts* (Boston: Houghton Mifflin, 1977), excerpt from Table 1, p. 552. Reprinted by permission.

$$\text{principal} \times \text{factor} = \text{future value}$$
$$\$3,000 \quad \times 1.276 = \quad \$3,828$$

Bates will have $3,828 at the end of five years.

Future Value of an Ordinary Annuity

OBJECTIVE 2b
Use compound interest tables to compute the future value of an ordinary annuity

Another common problem involves an **ordinary annuity,** which is a series of equal payments made at the end of equal intervals of time, with compound interest on these payments.

Example: Future Value of an Ordinary Annuity. Assume that Ben Katz deposits $200 at the end of each of the next three years in a savings account that pays 5 percent interest.   How much money will he have in his account at the end of the next three years? One way of computing the amount is shown in the following table:

(1) Year	(2) Beginning Balance	(3) Interest Earned (5% × col. 2)	(4) Periodic Payment	(5) Accumulated at End of Period (col. 2 + col. 3 + col. 4)
1	$ —	$ —	$200	$200.00
2	200.00	10.00	200	410.00
3	410.00	20.50	200	630.50

Katz would have $630.50 in his account at the end of three years, made up of $600 in periodic payments and $30.50 in interest.

Table C-2. Future Value of $1 Paid in Each Period for a Given Number of Time Periods

Periods	1%	2%	3%	4%	5%	6%	7%	8%	9%	10%	12%	14%	15%
1	1.000	1.000	1.000	1.000	1.000	1.000	1.000	1.000	1.000	1.000	1.000	1.000	1.000
2	2.010	2.020	2.030	2.040	2.050	2.060	2.070	2.080	2.090	2.100	2.120	2.140	2.150
3	3.030	3.060	3.091	3.122	3.153	3.184	3.215	3.246	2.278	3.310	3.374	3.440	3.473
4	4.060	4.122	4.184	4.246	4.310	4.375	4.440	4.506	4.573	4.641	4.779	4.921	4.993
5	5.101	5.204	5.309	5.416	5.526	5.637	5.751	5.867	5.985	6.105	6.353	6.610	6.742
6	6.152	6.308	6.468	6.633	6.802	6.975	7.153	7.336	7.523	7.716	8.115	8.536	8.754
7	7.214	7.434	7.662	7.898	8.142	8.394	8.654	8.923	9.200	9.487	10.09	10.73	11.07
8	8.286	8.583	8.892	9.214	9.549	9.897	10.26	10.64	11.03	11.44	12.30	13.23	13.73
9	9.369	9.755	10.16	10.58	11.03	11.49	11.98	12.49	13.02	13.58	14.78	16.09	16.79
10	10.46	10.95	11.46	12.01	12.58	13.18	13.82	14.49	15.19	15.94	17.55	19.34	20.30

Source: Henry R. Anderson and Mitchell H. Raiborn, *Basic Cost Accounting Concepts* (Boston: Houghton Mifflin, 1977), excerpt from Table 2, p. 553. Reprinted by permission.

This calculation can also be simplified by using Table C-2. We look down the 5 percent column until we reach period 3 and find the factor 3.153. This factor when multiplied by $1 gives the future value of a series of three $1 payments (years in this case) at compound interest of 5 percent. Thus we solve the problem:

$$\text{periodic payment} \times \text{factor} = \text{future value}$$
$$\$200 \qquad \times \ 3.153 \ = \quad \$630.60$$

Except for a rounding error of $0.10, this result is the same as the one above.

Present Value

OBJECTIVE 3a
Use present value tables to compute the present value of a single sum due in the future

Suppose that you had the choice of receiving $100 today or one year from today. Without even thinking about it, you would choose to receive the $100 today. Why? You know that if you have the $100 today, you can put it in a savings account to earn interest and will have more than $100 a year from today. Therefore, we can say that an amount to be received in the future (future value) is not worth as much today as an amount to be received today (present value) because of the cost associated with the passage of time. In fact, present value and future value are closely related. **Present value** is the amount that must be invested now at a given rate of interest to produce a given future value.

Example: Present Value. Sue Dapper needs $1,000 one year from now. How much should she invest today to achieve that goal if the interest rate is 5 percent? From earlier examples, the following equation may be established:

$$\text{present value} \times (1.0 + \text{interest rate}) = \text{future value}$$
$$\text{present value} \times \qquad 1.05 \qquad\quad = \$1,000$$
$$\text{present value} \qquad\qquad\qquad\qquad\quad = \$1,000 \div 1.05$$
$$\text{present value} \qquad\qquad\qquad\qquad\quad = \$952.38$$

Thus to achieve a future value of $1,000, a present value of $952.38 must be invested. Interest of 5 percent on $952.38 for one year equals $47.62, and these two amounts added together equal $1,000.

Present Value of a Single Sum Due in the Future

When more than one time period is involved, the calculation of present value is more complicated. Consider the following example.

Example: Present Value of a Single Sum in the Future. Don Riley wants to be sure of having $4,000 at the end of three years. How much must he invest today in a 5 percent savings account to achieve this goal? Adapting the equation, we compute the present value of $4,000 at compound interest of 5 percent for three years in the future.

Year	Amount at End of Year	Divide by		Present Value at Beginning of Year
3	$4,000.00	÷	1.05 =	$3,809.52
2	3,809.52	÷	1.05 =	3,628.12
1	3,628.12	÷	1.05 =	3,455.35

Riley must invest a present value of $3,455.35 to achieve a future value of $4,000 in three years.

This calculation is again made much easier by using the appropriate table. In Table C-3, we look down the 5 percent column until we reach period 3 and find the factor 0.864. This factor when multiplied by $1 gives the present value of that $1 to be received three years from now at 5 percent interest. Thus we solve the problem:

$$\text{future value} \times \text{factor} = \text{present value}$$
$$\$4,000 \quad \times 0.864 = \quad \$3,456$$

Except for a rounding error of $0.65, this result is the same as the one above.

Table C-3. Present Value of $1 to Be Received at the End of a Given Number of Time Periods

Periods	1%	2%	3%	4%	5%	6%	7%	8%	9%	10%
1	0.990	0.980	0.971	0.962	0.952	0.943	0.935	0.926	0.917	0.909
2	0.980	0.961	0.943	0.925	0.907	0.890	0.873	0.857	0.842	0.826
3	0.971	0.942	0.915	0.889	0.864	0.840	0.816	0.794	0.772	0.751
4	0.961	0.924	0.888	0.855	0.823	0.792	0.763	0.735	0.708	0.683
5	0.951	0.906	0.883	0.822	0.784	0.747	0.713	0.681	0.650	0.621
6	0.942	0.888	0.837	0.790	0.746	0.705	0.666	0.630	0.596	0.564
7	0.933	0.871	0.813	0.760	0.711	0.665	0.623	0.583	0.547	0.513
8	0.923	0.853	0.789	0.731	0.677	0.627	0.582	0.540	0.502	0.467
9	0.914	0.837	0.766	0.703	0.645	0.592	0.544	0.500	0.460	0.424
10	0.905	0.820	0.744	0.676	0.614	0.558	0.508	0.463	0.422	0.386

Source: Henry R. Anderson and Mitchell H. Raiborn, *Basic Cost Accounting Concepts* (Boston: Houghton Mifflin, 1977), excerpt from Table 3, p. 554. Reprinted by permission.

Present Value of an Ordinary Annuity

OBJECTIVE 3b
Use present value
tables to
compute the
present value of
an ordinary
annuity

It is often necessary to find the present value of a series of receipts or payments. When we calculate the present value of equal amounts equally spaced over a period of time, we are computing the present value of an ordinary annuity.

Example: Present Value of an Ordinary Annuity. Assume that Kathy Foster has sold a piece of property and is to receive $15,000 in three equal annual payments of $5,000, beginning one year from today. What is the present value of this sale, assuming a current interest rate of 5 percent? This present value may be computed by calculating a separate present value for each of the three payments (using Table C-3) and summing the results, as shown below.

Future Receipts (Annuity)			Present Value Factor at 5 percent (from Table A-3)		Present Value
Year 1	Year 2	Year 3			
$5,000			× 0.952	=	$ 4,760
	$5,000		× 0.907	=	4,535
		$5,000	× 0.864	=	4,320
Total Present Value					$13,615

The present value of this sale is $13,615. Thus there is an implied interest cost (given the 5 percent rate) of $1,385 associated with the payment plan that allows the purchaser to pay in three installments.

We can make this calculation by using Table C-4. We look down the 5 percent column until we reach period 3 and find factor 2.723. This factor when multiplied by $1 gives the present value of a series of three $1 payments (spaced one year apart) at compound interest of 5 percent. Thus we solve the problem:

$$\text{periodic payment} \times \text{factor} = \text{present value}$$
$$\$5,000 \times 2.723 = \$13,615$$

This result is the same as the one computed above.

Time Periods

In all the examples above and in most other cases, the compounding period is one year, and the interest rate is stated on an annual basis. However, in each of the four tables the left-hand column refers, not to years, but to periods. This wording is used because there are compounding periods of less than one year. Savings accounts that record interest quarterly and bonds that pay interest semiannually are cases in point. To use the tables in such cases, it is necessary to (1) divide the annual interest rate by the number of periods in the year, and (2) multiply the number of periods in one year by the number of years.

Example: Time Periods. Assume that a $6,000 note is to be paid in two years and carries an annual interest rate of 8 percent. Compute the maturity (future) value of the note, assuming that the compounding period is semiannual. Before

Table C-4. Present Value of $1 Received Each Period for a Given Number of Time Periods

Periods	1%	2%	3%	4%	5%	6%	7%	8%	9%	10%
1	0.990	0.980	0.971	0.962	0.952	0.943	0.935	0.926	0.917	0.909
2	1.970	1.942	1.913	1.886	1.859	1.833	1.808	1.783	1.759	1.736
3	2.941	2.884	2.829	2.775	2.723	2.673	2.624	2.577	2.531	2.487
4	3.902	3.808	3.717	3.630	3.546	3.465	3.387	3.312	3.240	3.170
5	4.853	4.713	4.580	4.452	4.329	4.212	4.100	3.993	3.890	3.791
6	5.795	5.601	5.417	5.242	5.076	4.917	4.767	4.623	4.486	4.355
7	6.728	6.472	6.230	6.002	5.786	5.582	5.389	5.206	5.033	4.868
8	7.652	7.325	7.020	6.733	6.463	6.210	5.971	5.747	5.535	5.335
9	8.566	8.162	7.786	7.435	7.108	6.802	6.515	6.247	5.995	5.759
10	9.471	8.983	8.530	8.111	7.722	7.360	7.024	6.710	6.418	6.145

Source: Henry R. Anderson and Mitchell H. Raiborn, *Basic Cost Accounting Concepts* (Boston: Houghton Mifflin, 1977), excerpt from Table 4, p. 556. Reprinted by permission.

using the table, it is necessary to compute the interest rate that applies to the compounding period and the number of periods. First, the interest rate to use is 4 percent (8% annual rate ÷ 2 periods per year). Second, the number of compounding periods is 4 (2 periods per year × 2 years). From Table C-1, therefore, the maturity value of the note may be computed as follows:

$$\text{principal} \times \text{factor} = \text{future value}$$
$$\$6,000 \times 1.170 = \$7,020$$

The note will be worth $7,020 in two years.

This procedure for determining the interest rate and the number of periods when the compounding period is less than one year may be used with all the tables.

Applications of Present Value to Accounting

The concept of present value is used widely in accounting. Here, the purpose is to show its usefulness in some simple applications. In-depth study of present value is left up to more advanced courses.

Imputing Interest on Noninterest-Bearing Notes

OBJECTIVE 4
Apply the concept of present value to some simple accounting situations

Clearly there is no such thing as an interest-free debt, regardless of whether the interest rate is explicitly stated. The Accounting Principles Board has declared that when a long-term note does not explicitly state an interest rate (or if the interest rate is unreasonably low), a rate based on the normal interest cost of the company in question should be assigned, or imputed.[1] The next example applies this principle.

1. Accounting Principles Board, *Opinion No. 21,* "Interest on Receivables and Payables" (New York: American Institute of Certified Public Accountants, June 1, 1982), par. 13.

Example: Imputing Interest on Noninterest-Bearing Notes. On January 1, 19x8, Gato purchases merchandise from Haines by making an $8,000 noninterest-bearing note due in two years. Gato can borrow money from the bank at 9 percent interest. Gato pays the note in full after two years. Prepare journal entries to record these transactions.

Note that the $8,000 note represents partly a payment for merchandise and partly a payment of interest for two years. In recording the purchase and sale, it is necessary to use Table C-3 to determine the present value of the note. The calculation follows.

$$\text{future value} \times \text{present value factor (9\%, 2 years)} = \text{present value}$$
$$\$8,000 \quad \times \quad 0.842 \quad = \quad \$6,736$$

The imputed interest cost is $1,264 ($8,000 − $6,736). The entries necessary to record the purchase in the Gato records and the sale in the Haines records are shown below.

Gato Journal			Haines Journal		
Purchases	6,736		Notes Receivable	8,000	
Discount on Notes			Discount on		
Payable[2]	1,264		Notes Receivable		1,264
Notes Payable		8,000	Sales		6,736

On December 31, 19x8, the adjustments to recognize the interest expenses and interest income will be:

Gato Journal			Haines Journal		
Interest Expense	606.24		Discount on Notes		
Discount on			Receivable	606.24	
Notes Payable		606.24	Interest Income		606.24

The interest is found by multiplying the original purchase by the interest for one year ($6,736 × .09 = $606.24). When payment is made on December 31, 19x9, the following entries will be made in the respective journals:

Gato Journal			Haines Journal		
Interest			Discount		
Expense	657.76		on Notes		
Notes Payable	8,000.00		Receivable	657.76	
Discount on			Cash	8,000.00	
Notes Payable		657.76	Interest		
Cash		8,000.00	Income		657.76
			Notes		
			Receivable		8,000.00

The interest entries represent the remaining interest to be expensed or realized ($1,264 − $606.24 = $657.76). This amount approximates (because of rounding

2. Under APB, *Opinion No. 21,* notes payable and receivable are to be shown net of any discount or premium. This example shows the face value of the notes and the discount separately for purposes of instructional clarity.

errors in the table) the interest for one year on the purchases plus last year's interest [($6,736 + $606.24) × .09 = $660.80].

Valuing an Asset

An asset is recorded because it will provide future benefits to the company that owns it. This future benefit is the basis for the definition of an asset. Usually, the purchase price of the asset represents the present value of these future benefits. It is possible to evaluate a proposed purchase price of an asset by comparing that price with the present value of the asset to the company.

Example: Valuing an Asset. Sam Hurst is thinking of buying a new labor-saving machine that will reduce his annual labor cost by $700 per year. The machine will last eight years. The interest rate that Hurst assumes for making managerial decisions is 10 percent. What is the maximum amount (present value) that Hurst should pay for the machine?

The present value of the machine to Hurst is equal to the present value of an ordinary annuity of $700 per year for eight years at compound interest of 10 percent. From Table C-4, we compute the value as follows:

periodic savings × factor = present value
$700   × 5.335 = $3,734.50

Hurst should not pay more than $3,734.50 for the new machine.

Other Accounting Applications

There are many other applications of present value to accounting. Some examples are its application to bond valuation, finding the amount of mortgage payments, and accounting for leases. Others are the recording of pension obligations; the determination of premium and discount on debt; accounting for depreciation of plant, property, and equipment; analysis of the purchase price of a business; evaluation of capital expenditure decisions; and generally any problem where time is a factor.

Exercises

Tables D-1 to D-4 in Appendix D may be used to solve these exercises.

Exercise C-1.
Future Value
Calculations
(L.O.2)

Naber receives a one-year note that carries a 12 percent annual interest rate on $1,500 for the sale of a used car.

Compute the maturity value under each of the following assumptions: (1) The interest is simple interest. (2) The interest is compounded semiannually. (3) The interest is compounded quarterly. (4) The interest is compounded monthly.

Exercise C-2.
Future Value
Calculations
(L.O.2)

Find the future value of (1) a single payment of $10,000 at 7 percent for ten years, (2) ten annual payments of $1,000 at 7 percent, (3) a single payment of $3,000 at 9 percent for seven years, and (4) seven annual payments of $3,000 at 9 percent.

Exercise C-3.
Present Value
Calculations
(L.O.3)

Find the present value of (1) a single payment of $12,000 at 6 percent for twelve years, (2) twelve annual payments of $1,000 at 6 percent, (3) a single payment of $2,500 at 9 percent for five years, and (4) five annual payments of $2,500 at 9 percent.

Exercise C-4.
Future Value
Calculations
(L.O.2)

Assume that $20,000 is invested today. Compute the amount that would accumulate at the end of seven years when the interest is (1) 8 percent annual interest compounded annually, (2) 8 percent annual interest compounded semi-annually, and (3) 8 percent annual interest compounded quarterly.

Exercise C-5.
Future Value
Calculations
(L.O.2)

Calculate the accumulation of periodic payments of $500 for four years, assuming (1) 10 percent annual interest compounded annually, (2) 10 percent annual interest compounded semiannually, (3) 4 percent annual interest compounded annually, and (4) 16 percent annual interest compounded quarterly.

Exercise C-6.
Future Value
Applications
(L.O.2)

a. Two parents have $10,000 to invest for their child's college tuition, which they estimate will cost $20,000 when the child enters college twelve years from now.
　　Calculate the approximate rate of annual interest that the investment must earn to reach the $20,000 goal in twelve years. (Hint: Make a calculation; then use Table D-1.)
b. Bill Roister is saving to purchase a summer home that will cost about $32,000. He has $20,000 now, on which he can earn 7 percent annual interest.
　　Calculate the approximate length of time he will have to wait to purchase the summer home. (Hint: Make a calculation; then use Table D-1.)

Exercise C-7.
Working Backward
from a Future Value
(L.O.2)

May Marquez has a debt of $45,000 due in four years. She wants to save money to pay it off by making annual deposits in an investment account that earns 8 percent annual interest.
　　Calculate the amount she must deposit each year to reach her goal. (Hint: Use Table D-2; then make a calculation.)

Exercise C-8.
Present Value of a
Lump-Sum
Contract
(L.O.3)

A contract calls for a lump-sum payment of $30,000. Find the present value of the contract, assuming that (1) the payment is due in five years, and the current interest rate is 9 percent; (2) the payment is due in ten years, and the current interest rate is 9 percent; (3) the payment is due in five years, and the current interest rate is 5 percent; and (4) the payment is due in ten years, and the current interest rate is 5 percent.

Exercise C-9.
Present Value of an
Annuity Contract
(L.O.3)

A contract calls for annual payments of $600. Find the present value of the contract, assuming that (1) the number of payments is seven, and the current interest rate is 6 percent; (2) the number of payments is fourteen, and the current interest rate is 6 percent; (3) the number of payments is seven, and the current interest rate is 8 percent; and (4) the number of payments is fourteen, and the current interest rate is 8 percent.

Exercise C-10.
Noninterest-
Bearing Note
(L.O. 4)

On January 1, 19x8, Olson purchases a machine from Carter by signing a two-year, noninterest-bearing $16,000 note. Olson currently pays 12 percent interest to borrow money at the bank.

Prepare journal entries in Olson's and Carter's records to (1) record the purchase and the note, (2) adjust the accounts after one year, and (3) record payment of the note after two years (on December 31, 19x9).

Exercise C-11.
Valuing an Asset for
the Purpose of
Making a
Purchasing
Decision
(L.O. 4)

Kubo owns a service station and has the opportunity to purchase a car wash machine for $15,000. After carefully studying projected costs and revenues, Kubo estimates that the car wash will produce a net cash flow of $2,600 annually and will last for eight years. Kubo feels that an interest rate of 14 percent is adequate for his business.

Calculate the present value of the machine to Kubo. Does the purchase appear to be a correct business decision?

Exercise C-12.
Determining
an Advance
Payment
(L.O. 3)

Ellen Saber is contemplating paying five years' rent in advance. Her annual rent is $4,800. Calculate the single sum that would have to be paid now for the advance rent, if we assume compound interest of 8 percent.

APPENDIX D

Future Value and Present Value Tables

Table D-1 provides the multipliers necessary to find the future value of a *single* cash deposit made at the *beginning* of year 1. Three factors must be known before the future value can be figured: (1) time period in years, (2) stated annual rate of interest to be earned, and (3) dollar amount invested or deposited.

Example. Find the future value of $5,000 deposited now that will earn 9 percent interest compounded annually for five years. From Table D-1, the necessary multiplier for five years at 9 percent is 1.539, and the answer is:

$$\$5,000(1.539) = \underline{\underline{\$7,695}}$$

Situations requiring the use of Table D-2 are similar to those requiring Table D-1 except that Table D-2 is used to find the future value of a *series* of *equal* annual deposits.

Example. What will be the future value at the end of thirty years if $1,000 is deposited each year on January 1, assuming 12 percent interest compounded annually? The required multiplier from Table D-2 is 241.3, and the answer is:

$$\$1,000(241.3) = \underline{\underline{\$241,300}}$$

Table D-3 is used to find the value today of a *single* amount of cash to be received sometime in the future. To use Table D-3, you must first know: (1) time period in years until funds will be received, (2) annual rate of interest, and (3) dollar amount to be received at end of time period.

Example. What is the present value of $30,000 to be received twenty-five years from now, assuming a 14 percent interest rate? From Table D-3, the required multiplier is 0.038, and the answer is:

$$\$30,000(0.038) = \underline{\underline{\$1,140}}$$

Table D-1. Future Value of $1 After a Given Number of Time Periods

Periods	1%	2%	3%	4%	5%	6%	7%	8%	9%	10%	12%	14%	15%
1	1.010	1.020	0.030	1.040	1.050	1.060	1.070	1.080	1.090	1.100	1.120	1.140	1.150
2	1.020	1.040	1.061	1.082	1.103	1.124	1.145	1.166	1.188	1.210	1.254	1.300	1.323
3	1.030	1.061	1.093	1.125	1.158	1.191	1.225	1.260	1.295	1.331	1.405	1.482	1.521
4	1.041	1.082	1.126	1.170	1.216	1.262	1.311	1.360	1.412	1.464	1.574	1.689	1.749
5	1.051	1.104	1.159	1.217	1.276	1.338	1.403	1.469	1.539	1.611	1.762	1.925	2.011
6	1.062	1.126	1.194	1.265	1.340	1.419	1.501	1.587	1.677	1.772	1.974	2.195	2.313
7	1.072	1.149	1.230	1.316	1.407	1.504	1.606	1.714	1.828	1.949	2.211	2.502	2.660
8	1.083	1.172	1.267	1.369	1.477	1.594	1.718	1.851	1.993	2.144	2.476	2.853	3.059
9	1.094	1.195	1.305	1.423	1.551	1.689	1.838	1.999	2.172	2.358	2.773	3.252	3.518
10	1.105	1.219	1.344	1.480	1.629	1.791	1.967	2.159	2.367	2.594	3.106	3.707	4.046
11	1.116	1.243	1.384	1.539	1.710	1.898	2.105	2.332	2.580	2.853	3.479	4.226	4.652
12	1.127	1.268	1.426	1.601	1.796	2.012	2.252	2.518	2.813	3.138	3.896	4.818	5.350
13	1.138	1.294	1.469	1.665	1.886	2.133	2.410	2.720	3.066	3.452	4.363	5.492	6.153
14	1.149	1.319	1.513	1.732	1.980	2.261	2.579	2.937	3.342	3.798	4.887	6.261	7.076
15	1.161	1.346	1.558	1.801	2.079	2.397	2.759	3.172	3.642	4.177	5.474	7.138	8.137
16	1.173	1.373	1.605	1.873	2.183	2.540	2.952	3.426	3.970	4.595	6.130	8.137	9.358
17	1.184	1.400	1.653	1.948	2.292	2.693	3.159	3.700	4.328	5.054	6.866	9.276	10.76
18	1.196	1.428	1.702	2.026	2.407	2.854	3.380	3.996	4.717	5.560	7.690	10.58	12.38
19	1.208	1.457	1.754	2.107	2.527	3.026	3.617	4.316	5.142	6.116	8.613	12.06	14.23
20	1.220	1.486	1.806	2.191	2.653	3.207	3.870	4.661	5.604	6.728	9.646	13.74	16.37
21	1.232	1.516	1.860	2.279	2.786	3.400	4.141	5.034	6.109	7.400	10.80	15.67	18.82
22	1.245	1.546	1.916	2.370	2.925	3.604	4.430	5.437	6.659	8.140	12.10	17.86	21.64
23	1.257	1.577	1.974	2.465	3.072	3.820	4.741	5.871	7.258	8.954	13.55	20.36	24.89
24	1.270	1.608	2.033	2.563	3.225	4.049	5.072	6.341	7.911	9.850	15.18	23.21	28.63
25	1.282	1.641	2.094	2.666	3.386	4.292	5.427	6.848	8.623	10.83	17.00	26.46	32.92
26	1.295	1.673	2.157	2.772	3.556	4.549	5.807	7.396	9.399	11.92	19.04	30.17	37.86
27	1.308	1.707	2.221	2.883	3.733	4.822	6.214	7.988	10.25	13.11	21.32	34.39	43.54
28	1.321	1.741	2.288	2.999	3.920	5.112	6.649	8.627	11.17	14.42	23.88	39.20	50.07
29	1.335	1.776	2.357	3.119	4.116	5.418	7.114	9.317	12.17	15.86	26.75	44.69	57.58
30	1.348	1.811	2.427	3.243	4.322	5.743	7.612	10.06	13.27	17.45	29.96	50.95	66.21
40	1.489	2.208	3.262	4.801	7.040	10.29	14.97	21.72	31.41	45.26	93.05	188.9	267.9
50	1.645	2.692	4.384	7.107	11.47	18.42	29.46	46.90	74.36	117.4	289.0	700.2	1,084

Source: All tables in Appendix D are from Henry R. Anderson and Mitchell H. Raiborn, *Basic Cost Accounting Concepts* (Boston: Houghton Mifflin, 1977), pp. 552–557. Reprinted by permission.

Table D-2. Future Value of $1 Paid in Each Period for a Given Number of Time Periods

Periods	1%	2%	3%	4%	5%	6%	7%	8%	9%	10%	12%	14%	15%
1	1.000	1.000	1.000	1.000	1.000	1.000	1.000	1.000	1.000	1.000	1.000	1.000	1.000
2	2.010	2.020	2.030	2.040	2.050	2.060	2.070	2.080	2.090	2.100	2.120	2.140	2.150
3	3.030	3.060	3.091	3.122	3.153	3.184	3.215	3.246	3.278	3.310	3.374	3.440	3.473
4	4.060	4.122	4.184	4.246	4.310	4.375	4.440	4.506	4.573	4.641	4.779	4.921	4.993
5	5.101	5.204	5.309	5.416	5.526	5.637	5.751	5.867	5.985	6.105	6.353	6.610	6.742
6	6.152	6.308	6.468	6.633	6.802	6.975	7.153	7.336	7.523	7.716	8.115	8.536	8.754
7	7.214	7.434	7.662	7.898	8.142	8.394	8.654	8.923	9.200	9.487	10.09	10.73	11.07
8	8.286	8.583	8.892	9.214	9.549	9.897	10.26	10.64	11.03	11.44	12.30	13.23	13.73
9	9.369	9.755	10.16	10.58	11.03	11.49	11.98	12.49	13.02	13.58	14.78	16.09	16.79
10	10.46	10.95	11.46	12.01	12.58	13.18	13.82	14.49	15.19	15.94	17.55	19.34	20.30
11	11.57	12.17	12.81	13.49	14.21	14.97	15.78	16.65	17.56	18.53	20.65	23.04	24.35
12	12.68	13.41	14.19	15.03	15.92	16.87	17.89	18.98	20.14	21.38	24.13	27.27	29.00
13	13.81	14.68	15.62	16.63	17.71	18.88	20.14	21.50	22.95	24.52	28.03	32.09	34.35
14	14.95	15.97	17.09	18.29	19.60	21.02	22.55	24.21	26.02	27.98	32.39	37.58	40.50
15	16.10	17.29	18.60	20.02	21.58	23.28	25.13	27.15	29.36	31.77	37.28	43.84	47.58
16	17.26	18.64	20.16	21.82	23.66	25.67	27.89	30.32	33.00	35.95	42.75	50.98	55.72
17	18.43	20.01	21.76	23.70	25.84	28.21	30.84	33.75	36.97	40.54	48.88	59.12	65.08
18	19.61	21.41	23.41	25.65	28.13	30.91	34.00	37.45	41.30	45.60	55.75	68.39	75.84
19	20.81	22.84	25.12	27.67	30.54	33.76	37.38	41.45	46.02	51.16	63.44	78.97	88.21
20	22.02	24.30	26.87	29.78	33.07	36.79	41.00	45.76	51.16	57.28	72.05	91.02	102.4
21	23.24	25.78	28.68	31.97	35.72	39.99	44.87	50.42	56.76	64.00	81.70	104.8	118.8
22	24.47	27.30	30.54	34.25	38.51	43.39	49.01	55.46	62.87	71.40	92.50	120.4	137.6
23	25.72	28.85	32.45	36.62	41.43	47.00	53.44	60.89	69.53	79.54	104.6	138.3	159.3
24	26.97	30.42	34.43	39.08	44.50	50.82	58.18	66.76	76.79	88.50	118.2	158.7	184.2
25	28.24	32.03	36.46	41.65	47.73	54.86	63.25	73.11	84.70	98.35	133.3	181.9	212.8
26	29.53	33.67	38.55	44.31	51.11	59.16	68.68	79.95	93.32	109.2	150.3	208.3	245.7
27	30.82	35.34	40.71	47.08	54.67	63.71	74.48	87.35	102.7	121.1	169.4	238.5	283.6
28	32.13	37.05	42.93	49.97	58.40	68.53	80.70	95.34	113.0	134.2	190.7	272.9	327.1
29	33.45	38.79	45.22	52.97	62.32	73.64	87.35	104.0	124.1	148.6	214.6	312.1	377.2
30	34.78	40.57	47.58	56.08	66.44	79.06	94.46	113.3	136.3	164.5	241.3	356.8	434.7
40	48.89	60.40	75.40	95.03	120.8	154.8	199.6	259.1	337.9	442.6	767.1	1,342	1,779
50	64.46	84.58	112.8	152.7	209.3	290.3	406.5	573.8	815.1	1,164	2,400	4,995	7,218

Table D-3. Present Value of $1 to Be Received at the End of a Given Number of Time Periods

Periods	1%	2%	3%	4%	5%	6%	7%	8%	9%	10%	12%
1	0.990	0.980	0.971	0.962	0.952	0.943	0.935	0.926	0.917	0.909	0.893
2	0.980	0.961	0.943	0.925	0.907	0.890	0.873	0.857	0.842	0.826	0.797
3	0.971	0.942	0.915	0.889	0.864	0.840	0.816	0.794	0.772	0.751	0.712
4	0.961	0.924	0.888	0.855	0.823	0.792	0.763	0.735	0.708	0.683	0.636
5	0.951	0.906	0.863	0.822	0.784	0.747	0.713	0.681	0.650	0.621	0.567
6	0.942	0.888	0.837	0.790	0.746	0.705	0.666	0.630	0.596	0.564	0.507
7	0.933	0.871	0.813	0.760	0.711	0.665	0.623	0.583	0.547	0.513	0.452
8	0.923	0.853	0.789	0.731	0.677	0.627	0.582	0.540	0.502	0.467	0.404
9	0.914	0.837	0.766	0.703	0.645	0.592	0.544	0.500	0.460	0.424	0.361
10	0.905	0.820	0.744	0.676	0.614	0.558	0.508	0.463	0.422	0.386	0.322
11	0.896	0.804	0.722	0.650	0.585	0.527	0.475	0.429	0.388	0.350	0.287
12	0.887	0.788	0.701	0.625	0.557	0.497	0.444	0.397	0.356	0.319	0.257
13	0.879	0.773	0.681	0.601	0.530	0.469	0.415	0.368	0.326	0.290	0.229
14	0.870	0.758	0.661	0.577	0.505	0.442	0.388	0.340	0.299	0.263	0.205
15	0.861	0.743	0.642	0.555	0.481	0.417	0.362	0.315	0.275	0.239	0.183
16	0.853	0.728	0.623	0.534	0.458	0.394	0.339	0.292	0.252	0.218	0.163
17	0.844	0.714	0.605	0.513	0.436	0.371	0.317	0.270	0.231	0.198	0.146
18	0.836	0.700	0.587	0.494	0.416	0.350	0.296	0.250	0.212	0.180	0.130
19	0.828	0.686	0.570	0.475	0.396	0.331	0.277	0.232	0.194	0.164	0.116
20	0.820	0.673	0.554	0.456	0.377	0.312	0.258	0.215	0.178	0.149	0.104
21	0.811	0.660	0.538	0.439	0.359	0.294	0.242	0.199	0.164	0.135	0.093
22	0.803	0.647	0.522	0.422	0.342	0.278	0.226	0.184	0.150	0.123	0.083
23	0.795	0.634	0.507	0.406	0.326	0.262	0.211	0.170	0.138	0.112	0.074
24	0.788	0.622	0.492	0.390	0.310	0.247	0.197	0.158	0.126	0.102	0.066
25	0.780	0.610	0.478	0.375	0.295	0.233	0.184	0.146	0.116	0.092	0.059
26	0.772	0.598	0.464	0.361	0.281	0.220	0.172	0.135	0.106	0.084	0.053
27	0.764	0.586	0.450	0.347	0.268	0.207	0.161	0.125	0.098	0.076	0.047
28	0.757	0.574	0.437	0.333	0.255	0.196	0.150	0.116	0.090	0.069	0.042
29	0.749	0.563	0.424	0.321	0.243	0.185	0.141	0.107	0.082	0.063	0.037
30	0.742	0.552	0.412	0.308	0.231	0.174	0.131	0.099	0.075	0.057	0.033
40	0.672	0.453	0.307	0.208	0.142	0.097	0.067	0.046	0.032	0.022	0.011
50	0.608	0.372	0.228	0.141	0.087	0.054	0.034	0.021	0.013	0.009	0.003

Table D-3. (*continued*)

14%	15%	16%	18%	20%	25%	30%	35%	40%	45%	50%	Periods
0.877	0.870	0.862	0.847	0.833	0.800	0.769	0.741	0.714	0.690	0.667	1
0.769	0.756	0.743	0.718	0.694	0.640	0.592	0.549	0.510	0.476	0.444	2
0.675	0.658	0.641	0.609	0.579	0.512	0.455	0.406	0.364	0.328	0.296	3
0.592	0.572	0.552	0.516	0.482	0.410	0.350	0.301	0.260	0.226	0.198	4
0.519	0.497	0.476	0.437	0.402	0.320	0.269	0.223	0.186	0.156	0.132	5
0.456	0.432	0.410	0.370	0.335	0.262	0.207	0.165	0.133	0.108	0.088	6
0.400	0.376	0.354	0.314	0.279	0.210	0.159	0.122	0.095	0.074	0.059	7
0.351	0.327	0.305	0.266	0.233	0.168	0.123	0.091	0.068	0.051	0.039	8
0.300	0.284	0.263	0.225	0.194	0.134	0.094	0.067	0.048	0.035	0.026	9
0.270	0.247	0.227	0.191	0.162	0.107	0.073	0.050	0.035	0.024	0.017	10
0.237	0.215	0.195	0.162	0.135	0.086	0.056	0.037	0.025	0.017	0.012	11
0.208	0.187	0.168	0.137	0.112	0.069	0.043	0.027	0.018	0.012	0.008	12
0.182	0.163	0.145	0.116	0.093	0.055	0.033	0.020	0.013	0.008	0.005	13
0.160	0.141	0.125	0.099	0.078	0.044	0.025	0.015	0.009	0.006	0.003	14
0.140	0.123	0.108	0.084	0.065	0.035	0.020	0.011	0.006	0.004	0.002	15
0.123	0.107	0.093	0.071	0.054	0.028	0.015	0.008	0.005	0.003	0.002	16
0.108	0.093	0.080	0.060	0.045	0.023	0.012	0.006	0.003	0.002	0.001	17
0.095	0.081	0.069	0.051	0.038	0.018	0.009	0.005	0.002	0.001	0.001	18
0.083	0.070	0.060	0.043	0.031	0.014	0.007	0.003	0.002	0.001		19
0.073	0.061	0.051	0.037	0.026	0.012	0.005	0.002	0.001	0.001		20
0.064	0.053	0.044	0.031	0.022	0.009	0.004	0.002	0.001			21
0.056	0.046	0.038	0.026	0.018	0.007	0.003	0.001	0.001			22
0.049	0.040	0.033	0.022	0.015	0.006	0.002	0.001				23
0.043	0.035	0.028	0.019	0.013	0.005	0.002	0.001				24
0.038	0.030	0.024	0.016	0.010	0.004	0.001	0.001				25
0.033	0.026	0.021	0.014	0.009	0.003	0.001					26
0.029	0.023	0.018	0.011	0.007	0.002	0.001					27
0.026	0.020	0.016	0.010	0.006	0.002	0.001					28
0.022	0.017	0.014	0.008	0.005	0.002						29
0.020	0.015	0.012	0.007	0.004	0.001						30
0.005	0.004	0.003	0.001	0.001							40
0.001	0.001	0.001									50

Table D-4. Present Value of $1 Received Each Period for a Given Number of Time Periods

Periods	1%	2%	3%	4%	5%	6%	7%	8%	9%	10%	12%
1	0.990	0.980	0.971	0.962	0.952	0.943	0.935	0.926	0.917	0.909	0.893
2	1.970	1.942	1.913	1.886	1.859	1.833	1.808	1.783	1.759	1.736	1.690
3	2.941	2.884	2.829	2.775	2.723	2.673	2.624	2.577	2.531	2.487	2.402
4	3.902	3.808	3.717	3.630	3.546	3.465	3.387	3.312	3.240	3.170	3.037
5	4.853	4.713	4.580	4.452	4.329	4.212	4.100	3.993	3.890	3.791	3.605
6	5.795	5.601	5.417	5.242	5.076	4.917	4.767	4.623	4.486	4.355	4.111
7	6.728	6.472	6.230	6.002	5.786	5.582	5.389	5.206	5.033	4.868	4.564
8	7.652	7.325	7.020	6.733	6.463	6.210	5.971	5.747	5.535	5.335	4.968
9	8.566	8.162	7.786	7.435	7.108	6.802	6.515	6.247	5.995	5.759	5.328
10	9.471	8.983	8.530	8.111	7.722	7.360	7.024	6.710	6.418	6.145	5.650
11	10.368	9.787	9.253	8.760	8.306	7.887	7.499	7.139	6.805	6.495	5.938
12	11.255	10.575	9.954	9.385	8.863	8.384	7.943	7.536	7.161	6.814	6.194
13	12.134	11.348	10.635	9.986	9.394	8.853	8.358	7.904	7.487	7.103	6.424
14	13.004	12.106	11.296	10.563	9.899	9.295	8.745	8.244	7.786	7.367	6.628
15	13.865	12.849	11.938	11.118	10.380	9.712	9.108	8.559	8.061	7.606	6.811
16	14.718	13.578	12.561	11.652	10.838	10.106	9.447	8.851	8.313	7.824	6.974
17	15.562	14.292	13.166	12.166	11.274	10.477	9.763	9.122	8.544	8.022	7.102
18	16.398	14.992	13.754	12.659	11.690	10.828	10.059	9.372	8.756	8.201	7.250
19	17.226	15.678	14.324	13.134	12.085	11.158	10.336	9.604	8.950	8.365	7.366
20	18.046	16.351	14.878	13.590	12.462	11.470	10.594	9.818	9.129	8.514	7.469
21	18.857	17.011	15.415	14.029	12.821	11.764	10.836	10.017	9.292	8.649	7.562
22	19.660	17.658	15.937	14.451	13.163	12.042	11.061	10.201	9.442	8.772	7.645
23	20.456	18.292	16.444	14.857	13.489	12.303	11.272	10.371	9.580	8.883	7.718
24	21.243	18.914	16.936	15.247	13.799	12.550	11.469	10.529	9.707	8.985	7.784
25	22.023	19.523	17.413	15.622	14.094	12.783	11.654	10.675	9.823	9.077	7.843
26	22.795	20.121	17.877	15.983	14.375	13.003	11.826	10.810	9.929	9.161	7.896
27	23.560	20.707	18.327	16.330	14.643	13.211	11.987	10.935	10.027	9.237	7.943
28	24.316	21.281	18.764	16.663	14.898	13.406	12.137	11.051	10.116	9.307	7.984
29	25.066	21.844	19.189	16.984	15.141	13.591	12.278	11.158	10.198	9.370	8.022
30	25.808	22.396	19.600	17.292	15.373	13.765	12.409	11.258	10.274	9.427	8.055
40	32.835	27.355	23.115	19.793	17.159	15.046	13.332	11.925	10.757	9.779	8.244
50	39.196	31.424	25.730	21.482	18.256	15.762	13.801	12.234	10.962	9.915	8.305

Table D-4. (*continued*)

14%	15%	16%	18%	20%	25%	30%	35%	40%	45%	50%	Periods
0.877	0.870	0.862	0.847	0.833	0.800	0.769	0.741	0.714	0.690	0.667	1
1.647	1.626	1.605	1.566	1.528	1.440	1.361	1.289	1.224	1.165	1.111	2
2.322	2.283	2.246	2.174	2.106	1.952	1.816	1.696	1.589	1.493	1.407	3
2.914	2.855	2.798	2.690	2.589	2.362	2.166	1.997	1.849	1.720	1.605	4
3.433	3.352	3.274	3.127	2.991	2.689	2.436	2.220	2.035	1.876	1.737	5
3.889	3.784	3.685	3.498	3.326	2.951	2.643	2.385	2.168	1.983	1.824	6
4.288	4.160	4.039	3.812	3.605	3.161	2.802	2.508	2.263	2.057	1.883	8
4.639	4.487	4.344	4.078	3.837	3.329	2.925	2.598	2.331	2.109	1.922	8
4.946	4.772	4.607	4.303	4.031	3.463	3.019	2.665	2.379	2.144	1.948	9
5.216	5.019	4.833	4.494	4.192	3.571	3.092	2.715	2.414	2.168	1.965	10
5.453	5.234	5.029	4.656	4.327	3.656	3.147	2.752	2.438	2.185	1.977	11
5.660	5.421	5.197	4.793	4.439	3.725	3.190	2.779	2.456	2.197	1.985	12
5.842	5.583	5.342	4.910	4.533	3.780	3.223	2.799	2.469	2.204	1.990	13
6.002	5.724	5.468	5.008	4.611	3.824	3.249	2.814	2.478	2.210	1.993	14
6.142	5.847	5.575	5.092	4.675	3.859	3.268	2.825	2.484	2.214	1.995	15
6.265	5.954	5.669	5.162	4.730	3.887	3.283	2.834	2.489	2.216	1.997	16
6.373	6.047	5.749	5.222	4.775	3.910	3.295	2.840	2.492	2.218	1.998	17
6.467	6.128	5.818	5.273	4.812	3.928	3.304	2.844	2.494	2.219	1.999	18
6.550	6.198	5.877	5.316	4.844	3.942	3.311	2.848	2.496	2.220	1.999	19
6.623	6.259	5.929	5.353	4.870	3.954	3.316	2.850	2.497	2.221	1.999	20
6.687	6.312	5.973	5.384	4.891	3.963	3.320	2.852	2.498	2.221	2.000	21
6.743	6.359	6.011	5.410	4.909	3.970	3.323	2.853	2.498	2.222	2.000	22
6.792	6.399	6.044	5.432	4.925	3.976	3.325	2.854	2.499	2.222	2.000	23
6.835	6.434	6.073	5.451	4.937	3.981	3.327	2.855	2.499	2.222	2.000	24
6.873	6.464	6.097	5.467	4.948	3.985	3.329	2.856	2.499	2.222	2.000	25
6.906	6.491	6.118	5.480	4.956	3.988	3.330	2.856	2.500	2.222	2.000	26
6.935	6.514	6.136	5.492	4.964	3.990	3.331	2.856	2.500	2.222	2.000	27
6.961	6.534	6.152	5.502	4.970	3.992	3.331	2.857	2.500	2.222	2.000	28
6.983	6.551	6.166	5.510	4.975	3.994	3.332	2.857	2.500	2.222	2.000	29
7.003	6.566	6.177	5.517	4.979	3.995	3.332	2.857	2.500	2.222	2.000	30
7.105	6.642	6.234	5.548	4.997	3.999	3.333	2.857	2.500	2.222	2.000	40
7.133	6.661	6.246	5.554	4.999	4.000	3.333	2.857	2.500	2.222	2.000	50

Table D-4 is used to find the present value of a *series* of *equal* annual cash flows.

Example. Arthur Howard won a contest on January 1, 1985, in which the prize was $30,000, payable in fifteen annual installments of $2,000 every December 31, beginning in 1985. Assuming a 9 percent interest rate, what is the present value of Mr. Howard's prize on January 1, 1985? From Table D-4, the required multiplier is 8.061, and the answer is:

$$\$2,000(8.061) = \underline{\underline{\$16,122}}$$

Table D-4 applies to *ordinary annuities*, in which the first cash flow occurs one time period beyond the date for which present value is to be computed. An *annuity due* is a series of equal cash flows for N time periods, but the first payment occurs immediately. The present value of the first payment equals the face value of the cash flow; Table D-4 then is used to measure the present value of $N - 1$ remaining cash flows.

Example. Find the present value on January 1, 1985, of twenty lease payments; each payment of $10,000 is due on January 1, beginning in 1985. Assume an interest rate of 8 percent:

$$\text{present value} = \text{immediate payment} + \begin{cases} \text{present value of 19} \\ \text{subsequent payments of 8\%} \end{cases}$$

$$= \$10,000 + [10,000(9.604)]$$

$$= \underline{\underline{\$106,040}}$$

1. Define exchange
rate and state its
significance.
2. Record transactions
that are affected by
changes in foreign
exchange rates.

APPENDIX E

International Accounting

Money is the basic unit by which accountants measure business transactions and present financial information. Chapter 1 noted that accountants generally assume that the monetary unit, the dollar in the United States, is a stable measuring unit. Most of the accounting methods presented so far have adhered to this assumption. This appendix is devoted to an important case where the stability of the monetary unit is not assumed, that is, the changing rates at which the dollar can be exchanged for foreign currencies, or international accounting. After studying this appendix, you should be able to meet the learning objectives listed on the left.

As businesses grow, it is natural for them to look for new sources of supply and new markets in other countries. Today, it is common for businesses, called multinational or transnational corporations, to operate in more than one country, and many of them operate throughout the world.[1] Table E-1 shows the extent of foreign business for a few multinational corporations. IBM, for example, has operations in eighty countries and receives about half of its sales and income from outside the United States. Nestlé, the giant Swiss chocolate and food products company, operates in fifteen countries and receives 98 percent of its sales from outside Switzerland. The economies of such industrial countries as the United States, Japan, Great Britain, West Germany, and France have given rise to large worldwide corporations. In addition, sophisticated investors no longer restrict their investment activities to their domestic securities markets. Many Americans invest in foreign securities markets, and non-Americans invest heavily in the stock market in the United States.

Such transactions have two major effects on accounting. First, most sales or purchases of goods and services in other countries involve different currencies. Thus, one currency needs to be translated into another, using exchange rates. An exchange rate is the value of one currency in terms of another. For example, an English person purchasing goods from a U.S. company and paying in U.S. dollars must exchange British pounds for U.S. dollars before making payment. In effect, the currencies are goods that can be bought and sold. Table E-2 illustrates the exchange rates of several currencies in terms of dollars. It shows the exchange rate for British pounds as $1.49 per pound on a particular date. Like the price of any good or service, these prices change daily according to supply and demand for the currencies. For example, less than three years earlier the exchange rate for British pounds was $2.00, and last year it was $1.20. Accounting for these price changes in recording foreign transactions is the subject of the next section.

1. At the time this appendix was written, exchange rates were fluctuating rapidly. Thus, the examples, exercises, and problems in this book use exchange rates in the general range for the countries involved.

Table E-1. Extent of Foreign Business for Selected Companies

Company	Country	Total Revenue (Millions)	Foreign Revenue as % of Total
Exxon	U.S.A.	$86,673	68.1
Mitsubishi	Japan	70,520	64.0
General Motors	U.S.A.	96,372	16.8
British Petroleum	Britain	53,131	81.0
International Business Machines (IBM)	U.S.A.	50,056	43.0
Volkswagenwerk	Germany	17,935	51.5
Bank America	U.S.A.	13,390	38.4
Nestlé	Switzerland	17,184	98.1
Procter & Gamble	U.S.A.	13,552	26.7
Xerox	U.S.A.	11,736	27.2

Source: Forbes, July 28, 1986, pp. 176, 183, and 207–208. Used by permission.

Accounting for Transactions in Foreign Currencies

OBJECTIVE 2
Record transactions that are affected by changes in foreign exchange rates

Among the first activities of an expanding company in the international market are the buying and selling of goods and services. For example, a maker of precision tools may try to expand by selling its product to foreign customers. Or it might try to lower its product cost by buying a less expensive part from a source in another country. Up to this point in the text, all transactions were recorded in dollars, and it was assumed that the dollar is a uniform measure in the same way that inches and centimeters are. In the international marketplace, a transaction may take place in Japanese yen, British pounds, or some other currency. The values of these currencies rise and fall daily in relation to the dollar.

Foreign Sales. When a domestic company sells merchandise abroad, it may bill either in its own country's currency or in the foreign currency. If the billing and the subsequent payment are both in the domestic currency, no accounting problem arises. For example, assume that the precision toolmaker sells $150,000 worth of tools to a British company and bills the British company in dollars. The entry to record the sale and payment is very familiar:

Date of sale:

Accounts Receivable, British company	150,000	
Sales		150,000

Date of payment

Cash	150,000	
Accounts Receivable, British company		150,000

However, if the U.S. company bills the British company in British pounds and accepts payment in pounds, the U.S. company may incur an exchange gain or loss. An exchange gain or loss will occur if the exchange rate of dollars to pounds changes between the date of sale and the date of payment. For example, assume that the sale of $150,000 above was billed as £100,000, reflecting an exchange rate of 1.50 (that is, $1.50 per pound) on the sale date. Now assume that by the date of payment, the exchange rate had fallen to 1.45. The entries to record the transactions are shown below.

Date of sale:

Accounts Receivable, British company	150,000	
Sales		150,000
£100,000 × $1.50 = $150,000		

Date of payment:

Cash	145,000	
Exchange Gain or Loss	5,000	
Accounts Receivable, British company		150,000
£100,000 × $1.45 = $145,000		

The U.S. company has incurred an exchange loss of $5,000 because it agreed to accept a fixed number of British pounds in payment, and before the payment was made, the value of each pound went down in value. Had the value of the pound in relation to the dollar increased in value, the U.S. company would have made an exchange gain.

Foreign Purchases. Purchases are the opposite of sales. So the same logic applies to them except that the relation of exchange gains and losses to the changes in exchange rates is reversed. For example, assume that the above maker of precision tools purchases $15,000 of a certain part from a Japanese supplier. If the purchase and subsequent payment are made in U.S. dollars, no accounting problem arises.

Date of purchase:

Purchases	15,000	
Accounts Payable, Japanese company		15,000

Date of payment:

Accounts Payable, Japanese company	15,000	
Cash		15,000

Table E-2. Partial Listing of Foreign Exchange Rates

Country	Prices in $ U.S.	Country	Prices in $ U.S.
Britain (pound)	1.49	Japan (yen)	.0065
Canada (dollar)	.72	Mexico (peso)	.003
France (franc)	.14	West Germany (mark)	.45
Italy (lira)	.0006		

Source: The Wall Street Journal (June 6, 1986). Used by permission.

However, the Japanese company may bill the U.S. company in yen and be paid in yen. If so, the U.S. company will incur an exchange gain or loss if the exchange rate changes between the dates of purchase and payment. For example, assume that the transaction above is in yen and the exchange rates of the dates of purchase and payment are $.0060 and $.0055 per yen, respectively. The entries follow.

Date of purchase:

Purchases	15,000	
Accounts Payable, Japanese company		15,000
Y2,500,000 × $.006 = $15,000		

Date of payment:

Accounts Payable, Japanese company	15,000	
Exchange Gain or Loss		1,250
Cash		13,750
Y2,500,000 × $.0055 = $13,750		

In this case, the U.S. company received an exchange gain of $1,250 because it had agreed to pay a fixed Y2,500,000 and, between the dates of purchase and payment, the exchange value of the yen in relation to the dollar decreased.

Realized Versus Unrealized Exchange Gain or Loss. The preceding illustration dealt with completed transactions (in the sense that payment was completed), and the exchange gain or loss was recognized on the date of payment in each case. If financial statements are prepared between the sale or purchase and the subsequent receipt or payment, there will be unrealized gains or losses if the exchange rates have changed. The Financial Accounting Standards Board, in its *Statement No. 52,* requires that exchange gains and losses "shall be included in determining net income for the period in which the exchange rate changes,"[2] including interim (quarterly) periods and whether or not the transaction is complete.

This ruling has caused much debate. Critics charge that it gives too much influence to temporary exchange rate changes, leading to random changes in earnings that hide long-run trends. Others feel the use of current exchange rates on the balance sheet date to value receivables and payables is a major step toward economic reality (current values).

To show these effects, we will assume the following facts about the preceding case, in which a U.S. company buys parts from a Japanese supplier:

	Date	Exchange Rate ($ per Yen)
Date of purchase	Dec. 1	.0060
Balance sheet date	Dec. 31	.0051
Date of payment	Feb. 1	.0055

The only difference is that the transaction has not been completed by the balance sheet date and the exchange rate was $.0051 per yen on that date. The facts and entries can be shown as follows.

---

2. *Statement of Financial Accounting Standards No. 52,* "Foreign Currency Translation" (Stamford, Conn.: Financial Accounting Standards Board, 1981), par. 15.

	Dec. 1	Dec. 31	Feb. 1
Purchase recorded in U.S. dollars (billed as Y2,500,000)	$15,000	$15,000	$15,000
Dollars to be paid to equal Y2,500,000	15,000	12,750	13,750
Unrealized gain (or loss)	—	$ 2,250	
Realized gain (or loss)			$ 1,250

Dec. 1	Purchases	15,000	
	Accounts Payable, Japanese company		15,000
Dec. 31	Accounts Payable, Japanese company	2,250	
	Exchange Gain or Loss		2,250
Feb. 1	Accounts Payable, Japanese company	12,750	
	Exchange Gain or Loss	1,000	
	Cash		13,750

In this case, the original sale was billed in yen by the Japanese company. Following the rules of *Statement No. 52,* an exchange gain of $2,250 is recorded on December 31, and an exchange loss of $1,000 is recorded on February 1. Even though the net effect of these large up-and-down changes is the net exchange gain of $1,250 over the whole transaction, the effect on each year may be important.

Questions

1. What does it mean to say that the exchange rate of a French franc in terms of the U.S. dollar is .15? If a bottle of French perfume costs 200 francs, how much will it cost in dollars?
2. If an American firm does business with a German firm and all their transactions take place in German marks, which firm may incur an exchange gain or loss and why?

Exercises

Exercise E-1. Recording International Transactions: Fluctuating Exchange Rate (L.O. 2)

U.S. Corporation purchased a special-purpose machine from German Corporation on credit for 30,000 DM (marks). At the date of purchase, the exchange rate was $.39 per mark. On the date of payment, which was made in marks, the value of the mark had increased to $.41.

Prepare journal entries to record the purchase and payment in the U.S. Corporation's accounting records.

Exercise E-2. Recording International Transactions (L.O. 2)

U.S. Corporation made a sale on account to British Company on November 15 in the amount of £200,000. Payment was to be made in British pounds on February 15. U.S. Corporation's fiscal year is the same as the calendar year. The British pound was worth $1.20 on November 15, $1.08 on December 31, and $1.28 on February 15.

Prepare journal entries on U.S. Corporation's books to record the sale, year-end adjustment, and collection.

Problems

Shore Company, whose year end is June 30, engaged in the following international transactions:

May 15   Purchased goods from a Japanese firm for $110,000; terms n/10 in U.S. dollars (yen = $.0040).

17   Sold goods to a German company for $140,000; terms n/30 in marks (mark = $.35).

21   Purchased goods from a Mexican company for $120,000; terms n/30 in pesos (peso = $.004).

25   Paid for the goods purchased on May 15 (yen = $.0045).

31   Sold goods to an Italian firm for $200,000; terms n/60 in lira (lira = $.0005).

June 5   Sold goods to a British firm for $56,000; terms n/10 in U.S. dollars (pound = $1.30).

7   Purchased goods from a Japanese firm for $162,000; terms n/30 in yen (yen = $.0045).

15   Received payment for the sale made on June 5 (pound = $1.40).

16   Received payment for the sale made on May 17 (mark = $.40).

17   Purchased goods from a French firm for $66,000; terms n/30 in U.S. dollars (franc = $.11).

20   Paid for the goods purchased on May 21 (peso = $.003).

22   Sold goods to a British firm for $84,000; terms n/30 in pounds (pound = $1.40).

30   Made year-end adjustment for incomplete foreign exchange transactions (franc = $.12; peso = $.003; mark = $.40; lira = $.0003; pound = $1.30; yen = $.0050).

July 7   Paid for the goods purchased on June 7 (yen = $.0045).

19   Paid for the goods purchased on June 17 (franc = $.10).

22   Received payment for the goods sold on June 22 (pound = $1.20).

30   Received payment for the goods sold on May 31 (lira = $.0004).

Required

Prepare general journal entries for the above transactions.

Hiu Import/Export Company, whose year end is December 31, engaged in the following transactions (exchange rates in parentheses):

Oct. 14   Sold goods to a Mexican firm for $20,000; terms n/30 in U.S. dollars (peso = $.004).

26   Purchased goods from a Japanese firm for $40,000; terms n/20 in yen (yen = $.0040).

Nov. 4   Sold goods to a British firm for $39,000; terms n/30 in pounds (pound = $1.30).

14   Received payment in full for October 14 sale (peso = $.003).

15   Paid for the goods purchased on October 26 (yen = $.0044).

23   Purchased goods from an Italian firm for $28,000; terms n/10 in U.S. dollars (lira = $.0005).

30   Purchased goods from a Japanese firm for $35,200; terms n/60 in yen (yen = $.0044).

Dec. 2 Paid for the goods purchased on November 23 (lira = $.0004).
   3 Received payment in full for goods sold on November 4 (pound = $1.20).
   8 Sold goods to a French firm for $66,000; terms n/30 in francs (franc = $.11).
   17 Purchased goods from a Mexican firm for $37,000; terms n/30 in U.S. dollars (peso = $.004).
   18 Sold goods to a German firm for $90,000; terms n/30 in marks (mark = $.30).
   31 Made year-end adjusting entries for incomplete foreign exchange transactions (franc = $.09; peso = $.003; pound = $1.10; mark = $.35; lira = $.0004; yen = $.0050).
Jan. 7 Received payment for goods sold on December 8 (franc = $.10).
   16 Paid for goods purchased on December 17 (peso = $.002).
   17 Received payment for goods sold on December 18 (mark = $.40).
   28 Paid for goods purchased on November 30 (yen = $.0045).

Required

Prepare general journal entries for the above transactions.

Glossary

Note: The number in parentheses after each definition refers to the chapter where the term is first defined.

Absorption costing: An approach to product costing that assigns a representative portion of *all* manufacturing costs to individual products. (3)

Accounting rate of return: A method used to measure the estimated performance of a capital investment that yields an accounting rate of return computed by dividing the project's average after-tax net income by the average cost of the investment over its estimated life. (13)

Activity accounting: See Responsibility accounting

Allocation base: The base used in reapportioning costs that best measures the causal or beneficial relationship involved. (6)

Applied factory overhead: The amount of overhead costs charged to specific jobs using predetermined overhead rates. (3)

Asset turnover: The ratio of sales to average assets; indicates the productivity of assets or the number of sales dollars generated by each dollar invested in assets. (14)

Automated material handling system (AMHS): A necessary component of a computer-integrated manufacturing system in which the raw materials and partially completed product handling function is automatic, providing a continuous flow through the process. (16)

Average cost of capital: A minimum desired rate of return on capital expenditures computed by finding the average of the cost of debt, cost of preferred stock, cost of equity capital, and cost of retained earnings. (13)

Average days' sales uncollectible: A ratio that measures how many days it takes before the average receivable is collected. (18)

Avoidable costs: Costs that will be eliminated if a particular product, service, or corporate segment is discontinued. (12)

Base year: The first year to be considered in any set of data. (18)

Basic standards: Standards that are seldom revised or updated to reflect current operating costs and price level changes. (9)

Batch processing: A type of computer system design in which separate computer jobs such as purchasing, inventory control, payroll, production scheduling, and so forth are processed individually but in a carefully coordinated way. (15)

Book value: Total cost of an asset less accumulated depreciation, depletion, or amortization. (12)

Break-even point: That point in financial analysis at which total revenue equals total cost incurred and at which the company begins to generate a profit. (6)

Break-even volume: The sales volume at which total revenue equals total costs and profits are zero. (6)

Budgetary control: The total process of developing plans for a company's anticipated operations and controlling operations to aid in accomplishing those plans. (8)

Budgetary control system: An integrated cost planning and control system. (5)

Capital budgeting: The combined process of identifying a facility need, analyzing alternative courses of action to satisfy that need, preparing the reports for management, selecting the best alternative, and rationing available capital expenditure funds among competing resource needs. (13)

Capital expenditure: An expenditure for the purchase or expansion of plant assets. (13)

Capital expenditure decision: The decision to determine when and how much money to spend on capital facilities for the company. (13)

Cash budget: A forecast of cash receipts and disbursements for a future time period. (8)

Cash equivalents: Short-term, highly liquid investments, including money market accounts, commercial paper, and U.S. treasury bills. (17)

Cash flow forecast: A forecast or budget that shows the firm's projected ending cash balance and the cash position for each month of the year so that periods of high or low cash availability can be anticipated; also called a cash budget. (8)

Cash flow statement: A financial statement that shows a company's sources and uses of cash during an accounting period. (17)

Certified management accountant (CMA): Management accountants who have met stringent requirements and passed the three-day CMA examination. (1)

Committed costs: Costs of capacity. Examples include depreciation of fixed assets, insurance, property taxes, rental charges, and supervisory salaries. (5)

Common-size statement: A statement in which all components of the statement are shown as a percentage of a total in the statement; results from applying vertical analysis. (18)

Computer-aided design/computer-aided manufacturing (CAD/CAM): Using computers in product design work, planning and controlling production, and linking CNC machines. (16)

Computer-integrated manufacturing (CIM) system: A fully integrated computer setup in which everything connected with the manufacturing system is performed automatically. (15)

Computer numerically-controlled (CNC) machines: Stand-alone pieces of equipment, including operating machines, computer-assisted design technology, and robots. (15)

Conglomerate: A company that operates in more than one industry; a diversified company. (18)

Continuous production flow: A system in which products completed by one department, function, or operation are transferred immediately to a subsequent operation for additional processing; all departments, functions, or operations are simultaneously engaged in production activity. (15)

Contribution margin: The excess of revenues over all variable costs related to a particular product, process, segment, or sales volume. (6)

Controllable costs and revenues: Those costs and revenues that result from a particular manager's actions and decisions and over which he or she has full control. (7)

Controllable overhead variance: The difference between actual overhead costs incurred and factory overhead budgeted for the level of production achieved. (10)

Control (or controlling) account: An account in the general ledger that summarizes the total balance of a group of related accounts in a subsidiary ledger. (3)

Conversion costs: The combined total of direct labor and factory overhead costs incurred by a production department, FMS work cell, or other work center. (4, 15)

Cost Accounting Standards Board (CASB): A federal agency created by Congress in 1970 to promulgate uniform and consistent cost accounting standards for all negotiated contracts in excess of $100,000. (11)

Cost allocation (assignment): The process of allocating or assigning a specific cost or pool of costs to a specific cost objective or cost objectives. (5)

Cost behavior: The ways that costs respond to changes in activity or volume. (5)

Cost-benefit principle: A principle of systems design that holds that the value or benefit from a system and its information output must be equal to or greater than its cost. (14)

Cost center: Any organizational segment or area of activity for which there is a reason to accumulate costs. (5)

Cost/expense center: An organizational unit with a manager who is responsible for its actions and costs. (7)

Cost driver: Any activity that causes costs to be incurred. (15)

Cost objective: The destination of an assigned cost. (5)

Cost of debt: The ratio of loan charges to net proceeds of the loan. After-tax considerations and present value of interest charges should be acknowledged in the computation. (13)

Cost of equity capital: The rate of return to the investor that maintains the stock's value in the marketplace. (13)

Cost of goods manufactured: A term used in the statement of cost of goods manufactured that represents the total manufacturing costs attached to units of product completed during an accounting period. (2)

Cost of preferred stock: The stated dividend rate of the individual stock issue. (13)

Cost of retained earnings: The opportunity cost or dividends forgone by the stockholder. (13)

Cost-plus transfer price: The sum of costs incurred by the producing division plus an agreed-on profit percentage. (14)

Cost summary schedule: A process costing schedule in which total manufacturing costs accumulated during the period are distributed to units completed and transferred out of the department and to the units in ending Work-in-Process Inventory. (4)

Cost-volume-profit (C-V-P) analysis: An analysis based on the relationships among operating cost, sales volume, revenue, and the target net income; used as a planning device to predict one of the factors when the others are known. (6)

Costs incurred indicators: Segment performance indicators that relate to (1) cost elements or groups reported on the income statement, such as total cost of operations or total variable costs, and (2) costs of capital expenditures, such as the purchase of a building or machine. (14)

Current ratio: A measure of liquidity; current assets divided by current liabilities. (18)

Currently attainable standards: Standard costs that are updated periodically to reflect changes in operating conditions and current price levels for direct materials, direct labor, and factory overhead costs. (9)

Decentralization: A system of management in which operating managers are free to make business decisions within their own departments, as long as the decisions fit into the framework of strategic policies established by top management for the entire company. (14)

Decentralized organization: A business or organization that has several operating segments; operating control of each segment's various activities is the responsibility of the segment manager. (14)

Decision model: A symbolic or numerical representation of the variables and parameters affecting a decision. (12)

Defense Acquisition Regulation (DAR): A set of procurement regulations that underlie most of the contracting arrangements with the federal government's Department of Defense. (11)

Delivery cycle: The time period between acceptance of the order and final delivery of the product. (16)

Delivery time: The time period between product completion and customer receipt of the product. (16)

Direct cost: A manufacturing cost that is traceable to a specific product or cost objective. (2)

Direct labor: All labor costs for specific work performed on products that are conveniently and economically traceable to end products. (2)

Direct labor efficiency variance: The difference between actual hours worked and standard hours allowed for the good units produced, multiplied by the standard labor rate. (9)

Direct labor rate standards: The hourly labor cost per function or job classification that is expected to exist during the next accounting period. (9)

Direct labor rate variance: The difference between the actual labor rate paid and the standard labor rate, multiplied by the actual hours worked. (9)

Direct labor time standard: An hourly expression of the time it takes for each department, machine, or process to complete production on one unit or one batch of output; based on current time and motion studies of workers and machines and past employee/machine performances. (9)

Direct materials: Materials that become an integral part of the finished product and are conveniently and economically traceable to specific units of productive output. (2)

Direct materials price standard: A carefully derived estimate or projected amount of what a particular type of material will cost when purchased during the next accounting period. (9)

Direct materials price variance: The difference between the actual price paid for materials and the standard price, multiplied by the actual quantity purchased. (9)

Direct materials quantity standard: An expression of forecasted or expected quantity usage that is influenced by product engineering specifications, quality of materials used, productivity of the machines being used, and the quality and experience of the machine operators and set-up people. (9)

Direct materials quantity variance: The difference between the actual quantity of materials used and the standard quantity that should have been used, multiplied by the standard price. (9)

Direct method: Method of preparing the statement of cash flows by adjusting each item in the income statement in turn from the accrual basis to the cash basis. The result is a statement that begins with cash receipts from sales and then deducts cash payments for purchases, operating expenses, and income taxes, to arrive at net cash flows from operating activities. (17)

Discounted cash flow: The process of discounting future cash flows back to the present using an anticipated discount rate. (13)

Discretionary costs: Costs incurred because of policy decisions of management. Examples include advertising, product/service development, basic research, and employee training. (5)

Dividends yield: A ratio that measures the current return to an investor in a stock of a corporation. (18)

Double counting: The charging of the same types of costs more than once to the same contract. (11)

Early extinguishment of debt: The extraordinary gain that occurs when a company purchases its bonds on the open market and retires them, rather than waiting to pay them off at face value. (18)

Effort expended indicators: Segment performance indicators that consist of input factors such as machine hours, labor hours, new customers, service center hours, sales calls, and miles driven by salespeople. (14)

Engineered time: Standard or predicted machine time for the product. (16)

Equivalent units: A measure of productive output of units for a period of time, expressed in terms of fully completed or equivalent whole units produced; partially completed units are restated in terms of equivalent whole units; also called equivalent production. (4, 15)

Excess capacity: Machinery and equipment purchased in excess of needs so that extra capacity is available on a stand-by basis during peak usage periods or when other machinery is down for repair. (6)

Factory overhead: A diverse collection of production-related costs that are not practically or economically traceable to end products and must be assigned by some allocation method; also called manufacturing overhead. (2)

Favorable standard cost variance: A variance occurring when actual costs are less than stan-

dard costs. (9, 10)

Financial management: The acquisition and use of funds, capital structure, and debt-to-equity relationships; the return on investment (ROI) measurement of performance is net income *after* interest and taxes divided by stockholders' equity. (14)

Financial statement analysis: The collective term used for the techniques that show significant relationships in financial statements and that facilitate comparisons from period to period and among companies. (18)

Finished goods inventory: An inventory account unique to the manufacturing or production area to which the costs assigned to all completed products are transferred. The balance at period-end represents all manufacturing costs assigned to goods completed but not sold as of that date. (2)

Fixed cost: A cost that remains constant in total within a relevant range of volume or activity. (5)

Fixed manufacturing costs: Production-related costs that remain relatively constant in amount during the accounting period and vary little in relation to increases or decreases in production. (2)

Flexible budget: A summary of anticipated costs prepared for a range of different activity levels and geared to changes in the level of productive output. (9, 10)

Flexible manufacturing system (FMS): An integrated set of computerized machines and systems designed to complete a series of operations automatically. (15)

Full absorption costing: A contract costing approach in which all allowable costs, including general and administrative expenses, are assigned to the contract. (11)

Full cost profit margin: The difference between total revenue and total costs traceable to the work cell or product. (16)

Goal congruence: The relative state of harmony between companywide goals and objectives and those of particular division managers. (14)

Gross margin pricing: An approach to price determination in which the projected price equals total production cost per unit plus the total production cost per unit times a markup percentage. The markup percentage is computed by dividing total selling, general, and administrative expenses plus the desired profit by total production cost. (11)

Gross payroll: A measure of the total wages or salary earned by an employee before any deductions are subtracted. This amount is also used to determine total manufacturing labor costs. (2)

High-low method: A mathematical method used to measure cost behavior by analyzing paired data for the high point and the low point of paired cost and volume (activity) observations. (5)

Horizontal analysis: The computation of dollar amount changes and percentage changes from year to year. (18)

Ideal capacity: See Theoretical capacity. (6)

Ideal standards: Perfection standards that allow minimum materials, labor time, and cost constraints for manufacturing a particular product or creating a service. (9)

Idle capacity: Facilities to be used only during peak production periods or during downtime of similar equipment. (2)

Incremental analysis: A decision analysis format that highlights only relevant decision information or the differences between costs and revenues under two or more alternative courses of action. (12)

Index number: A number constructed by setting a base year equal to 100 percent and calculating other years in relation to the base year. (18)

Indirect cost: A manufacturing cost that is not traceable to a specific product or cost objective and must be assigned using some allocation method. (2)

Indirect labor: Labor costs for production-related activities that cannot be associated with, or are not conveniently or economically traceable to end products and must be assigned using some allocation method. (2)

Indirect materials: Less significant materials and other production supplies that cannot be conveniently or economically assigned to specific products and must be assigned using some allocation method. (2)

Indirect method: Method for preparing the statement of cash flows by beginning with the net income and listing all the adjustments necessary to convert net income to cash flows from operating activities. (17)

Interest coverage ratio: A ratio that measures the protection of creditors from a default on interest payments. (18)

Interim financial statements: Financial statements prepared on a condensed basis for an accounting period of less than one year. (18)

Inventory turnover: A ratio that measures the relative size of inventory. (18)

Investment center: An organizational unit with a manager who is responsible for its actions, including costs, revenues, and resulting profit. In addition, the manager must be evaluated on the effective use of assets employed to generate those profits. (7)

Job card: A labor card supplementing the time card, on which each employee's time on a specific job is recorded; used to support an employee's daily time recorded on the time card and assign labor costs to specific jobs or batches of products. (2)

Job order: A customer order for a specific number of specially designed, made-to-order products. (3)

Job order cost accounting system: A product costing system used in the manufacturing of unique or special-order products in which direct materials, direct labor, and manufacturing overhead costs are assigned to specific job orders or batches of products. (3)

Job order cost card: A document maintained for each job or work order in process, upon which all costs of that job are recorded and accumulated as the job order is being worked on. These cards make up the subsidiary ledger of the Work-in-Process Inventory Control account. (3)

Joint cost: A cost that collectively applies or relates to several products or cost objectives and can be assigned to those cost objectives only by means of arbitrary cost allocation techniques; also called common cost. (5)

JIT/FMS environment: An operating environment created by a flexible manufacturing system functioning within the just-in-time operating philosophy. (16)

Just-in-time philosophy: An overall operating philosophy of management in which all resources, including materials, personnel, and facilities are used in a just-in-time manner. (15)

Least squares method: A mathematical method based on simple linear regression used to fit a straight line to paired observations of an independent variable (volume or activity) and a dependent variable (repairs and maintenance costs). (5)

Leverage: The use of debt financing. (18)

Linear regression analysis: A statistical method for fitting a straight line to paired observations of an independent variable and a dependent variable. (6)

Make-or-buy decision: A decision commonly faced by management as to whether to make the item, product, or component or to purchase it from an outside source. (12)

Management accounting: A segment of the field of accounting that consists of specific information gathering and reporting concepts and accounting procedures that, when applied to a company's financial and production data, will satisfy internal management's needs for product costing information, data used for planning and control of operations, and special reports and analyses used to support management's decisions. (1)

Management by exception: A review process whereby management locates and analyzes only the areas of unusually good or bad performance. (10)

Manufacturing cost flow: The defined or structured flow of direct materials, direct labor, and manufacturing overhead costs from their incurrence through the inventory accounts and finally to the Cost of Goods Sold account. (2)

Marginal cost: The change in total cost caused by a one-unit change in output. (11)

Marginal revenue: The change in total revenue caused by a one-unit change in output. (11)

Master budget: An integrated set of departmental or functional period budgets that have been consolidated into forecasted financial statements for the entire company. (8)

Materials inventory: An inventory account made up of the balances of materials and supplies on hand at a given time; also called *stores* and *materials inventory control account*. (2)

Materials price standard: A predetermined cost reflecting the current market price per unit of raw materials and parts used in the production process. (9)

Materials price variance: The difference between actual price paid for materials and standard price multiplied by the actual quantity purchased. (9)

Materials quantity standard: A predetermined measure that expresses expected normal usage of raw materials per unit of finished product. (9)

Materials quantity variance: The difference between actual quantity of materials used and standard quantity of materials allowed multiplied by standard price per unit. (9)

Materials requisition: A document that must be completed and approved before raw materials are issued to production. This form is essential to the control of raw materials and contains such information as the types and quantities of raw materials and supplies needed and the supervisor's approval signature. (2)

Mixed cost: A cost category that results when both variable and fixed costs are charged to the same general ledger account. The Repairs and Maintenance account is an example of a mixed cost account. (5)

Negotiated transfer price: A transfer price that is negotiated by the managers of the buying and selling divisions. (14)

Net payroll: The amount paid to the employee (cash or check) after all payroll deductions have been subtracted from gross wages. (2)

Net present value: The difference between future net cash inflows of a project discounted at the minimum acceptable return on investment and the estimated cost of the project. (13)

Noncash expense: An expense—such as depreciation—that reduces net income and income tax expense, but for which there is no cash outflow in the period in which the expense is recognized. (13,17)

Non-value added activity: An activity that adds cost to the product but does not increase its market value. (15)

Normal capacity: The average annual level of operating capacity that is required to satisfy anticipated sales demand, adjusted to reflect seasonal business factors and operating cycles. (6, 10)

Operating capacity: The upper limit of a company's productive output capability given existing resources. (5)

Operating management: The use of available resources to generate the largest income *before* interest and taxes that is consistent with a company's long-range policies and within social and environmental constraints. (14)

Overapplied (or underapplied) factory overhead: The difference resulting when the amount of factory overhead costs applied to products during the accounting period is more (or less) than the actual amount of factory overhead costs incurred during that period. (3)

Overhead allocation: The systematic assignment of manufacturing overhead costs to batches of products or other cost objectives. (6)

Overhead budget variance: The difference between actual overhead costs incurred and a flexible budget amount for overhead costs based on standard hours allowed. (10)

Overhead efficiency variance: The difference between actual direct labor hours worked and standard labor hours allowed, multiplied by the standard variable overhead rate. (10)

Overhead spending variance: The difference between the actual overhead costs incurred and the amount that should have been spent, based on actual hours worked or other productive input measures. (10)

Overhead volume variance: The difference between the factory overhead budgeted for the level of production achieved and the overhead applied to production using the standard overhead rate. (10)

Parameters: Uncontrollable factors and operating constraints and limitations in a management decision model. (12)

Participative budgeting: All levels of supervisory and data input personnel take part in the budgeting process in a meaningful, active way. (8)

Payback method: A method used to evaluate a capital expenditure proposal that focuses on the cash flow of the project and determines the payback period or time required to recoup the original investment through cash flow from the item or project. (13)

Performance evaluation: The application of financial management techniques so that actual results can be compared with expectations and performance judged. (7)

Performance margin: A performance measure that reflects the effects of divisional management decisions on divisional income; computed by subtracting all traceable fixed costs controllable by the division manager from the division's contribution margin. (14)

Period budget: A forecast of annual operating results for a segment or functional area of a company that represents a quantitative expression of planned activities. (8)

Period costs (expenses): Expired costs of an accounting period that represent dollars attached to resources used or consumed during the period; any cost or expense item on an income statement. (2)

Periodic inventory method: A method of accounting for inventory under which the cost of goods sold is determined by adding the net cost of purchases to beginning inventory and subtracting the ending inventory. (2)

Perpetual inventory method: A method of accounting for inventory under which the purchases and usage (or sales) of individual items of inventory are recorded continuously, therefore allowing cost of goods sold to be determined without taking a physical inventory. (2)

Physical volume method: An approach to the problem of allocating joint production costs to specific products that is based on or uses some measure of physical volume (units, pounds, liters, grams, etc.) as the basis for joint cost allocation. (5)

Practical capacity: Theoretical capacity reduced by normal and anticipated work stoppages. (6)

Predetermined overhead rate: An overhead cost factor that is used to assign factory (manufacturing) overhead costs (all indirect manufacturing costs) to specific units, jobs, or cost objectives. (3)

Present value method: A discounted cash flow approach to measure the estimated performance of a capital investment. The value of all future cash flows discounted back to the present (present value) must equal or exceed the initial investment if a positive decision is to be made. (13)

Price/earnings (P/E) ratio: A ratio that measures the relationship of the current market price of a stock to the earnings per share. (18)

Price index: A series of numbers, one for each period, that represents an average price for a group of goods or services, relative to the average price of the same group of goods and services at a beginning date. (18)

Process cost accounting system: A product costing system used by companies that produce a large number of similar products or have a continuous production flow where manufacturing costs are accumulated by departments, processes, or FMS work cells rather than by batches of products. (3, 4)

Product cost: Costs identified as being either direct materials, direct labor, or factory overhead, traceable or assignable to products; they become part of a product's unit manufacturing cost and are in inventories at period end. (2)

Production cycle time: The time it takes for the production people to make a product available for shipment to the customer. (16)

Profit center: An organizational unit with a manager who is responsible for its actions, including costs, revenues, and resulting profit. (7)

Profit margin: A measure of profitability; the percentage of each sales dollar that results in net income; net income divided by sales. (18)

Profit margin pricing: An approach to price determination in which the projected price equals total costs per unit plus the total costs per unit times a markup percentage. The markup percentage is computed by dividing the desired profit by total costs and expenses.

Pull-through production (PTP): The customer order triggers the purchase of materials and the scheduling of production for the required products. (15)

Purchase order: A document prepared by the accounting department authorizing a supplier to ship specified goods or provide specified services. (2)

Purchase order lead time: The time it takes for raw materials and parts to be ordered and received so that production can begin. (16)

Purchase requisition (request): A document used to begin the raw materials purchasing function that originates in the production department and identifies the items to be purchased, states the quantities required, and must be approved by a qualified manager or supervisor. (2)

Qualitative characteristics: Criteria for judging the information accountants provide to decision makers; the primary criteria are relevance and reliability. (13)

Quick ratio: A ratio that measures the relationship of the more liquid current assets (cash, marketable securities, and accounts receivable) to current liabilities. (18)

Ratio analysis: A means of stating a meaningful relationship between two numbers. (18)

Raw-in-process (RIP) inventory: An inventory account in the new manufacturing environment that replaces both the Materials Inventory and the Work-in-Process Inventory accounts. (15)

Receivable turnover: A ratio that measures the relative size of accounts receivable. (18)

Receiving report: A document prepared when ordered goods are received, the data on which are matched with the descriptions and quantities listed on the purchase order to verify that the goods ordered were actually received. (2)

Relative sales value method: An approach to the problem of allocating joint production costs to specific products that is based on or uses the product's revenue-producing ability (sales value) as the basis for joint cost allocation. (5)

Relevant decision information: Future cost, revenue, or resource usage data used in decision analysis that differ among the decision's alternative courses of action. (12)

Relevant range: A range of productive activity that represents the potential volume levels within which actual operations are likely to occur. (5)

Resources employed indicators: Segment performance indicators that center on resource usage, including plant and supervisory personnel, machines, building occupancy, and other physical measures of capacity. (14)

Responsibility accounting system: An accounting system that personalizes accounting reports by classifying and reporting cost and revenue information according to defined responsibility areas of specific managers or management positions; also called *activity accounting* or *profitability accounting*. (7)

Responsibility center: An organizational unit identified in a responsibility accounting system whose manager is responsible for its actions; examples include a cost/expense center, a profit center, and an investment center. (7)

Results achieved indicators: Segment performance indicators such as total revenues, units produced, orders received, or any other aspect of output or accomplishment. (14)

Return on asset pricing: An approach to price determination in which a profit factor is added to the total costs and expenses per unit to arrive at the objective price. The profit factor is computed by multiplying the desired rate of return by the total cost of assets employed and dividing this product by anticipated units to be produced. (11)

Return on assets: A measure of profitability that shows how efficiently a company is using all of its assets; net income divided by total assets. (18)

Return on equity: A measure of profitability related to the amount earned by a business in relation to the owners' investment in the business; net income divided by stockholders' equity. (18)

Return on investment: A performance indicator for divisions that relates properly measured operating income to average assets employed during the period. (7, 14)

Run time: Total machine hours in an FMS cell less setup time. (16)

Sales mix: The relative proportions of different products that comprise total sales. (6)

Sales mix analysis: An analysis to determine the most profitable combination of product sales when a company produces more than one product. (6, 12)

Scatter diagram: A chart containing plotted points that help determine whether there is a linear relationship between the cost item and the related activity measure. (5)

Schedule of equivalent production: A process costing schedule in which equivalent production is computed for the period for both materials and conversion costs. (4, 15)

Segment margin: A performance measure that expresses a division's overall profitability by identifying its contribution to unallocated fixed costs and the resulting company profit; computed by subtracting all traceable fixed costs controllable by top management (not the division manager) from performance margin. (14)

Semivariable cost: A cost that possesses both variable and fixed cost behavior characteristics in that part of the cost is fixed and part varies with the volume of output. (5)

Source documents: Written evidence supporting and detailing transactions. (2)

Special order decision: A type of decision faced by management in which a customer wishes to purchase a large number of similar or identical products at prices below those listed in brochures or advertisements. If capacity exists to produce the order while not disturbing the regular production process, the company can consider the order; also called special product order decision. (12)

Split-off point: A particular point in a manufacturing process where a joint product splits or divides and two or more separate products emerge. (5)

Standard costs: Realistically predetermined costs for direct materials, direct labor, and factory overhead that are usually expressed as a cost per unit of finished product. (9)

Standard direct labor cost: A standard cost computed by multiplying the direct labor time standard by the direct labor rate standard. (9)

Standard direct materials cost: A standard cost computed by multiplying the direct materials price standard by the direct materials quantity standard. (9)

Standard factory overhead cost: A standard cost computed by multiplying the standard variable overhead rate and the standard fixed overhead rate by the appropriate application base. (9)

Standard fixed overhead rate: An overhead application rate computed by dividing the total budgeted fixed overhead costs by the normal capacity for the period. (9)

Standard variable overhead rate: An overhead application rate computed by dividing the total budgeted variable overhead costs by the application base being used by the company. (9)

Statement of cash flows: Shows the effects on cash of the operating, investing, and financing activities of a company for an accounting period. This statement will explain the causes of the net increase or decrease in cash during the accounting period. (17)

Statement of cost of goods manufactured: A formal statement summarizing the flow of all manufacturing costs incurred during a period; yields the dollar amount of costs of products completed and transferred to Finished Goods Inventory during the period. (2)

Step-variable cost: A cost that remains constant in a small relevant range but varies in subsequent ranges. (5)

Supporting service function: An operating unit or department not directly involved in production but needed for the overall operation of the company. (5)

System design: A phase of system installation the purpose of which is to formulate the new system or changes in the existing system. (15)

System implementation: A phase of system installation the purpose of which is to put in operating order a new system or changes in an existing system. (15)

Theoretical capacity: The maximum productive output of a department or a company if all machinery and equipment were operated at optimum speed without any interruptions in production for a given time period; also called *ideal capacity*. (6)

Timecard: A basic time record document of an employee upon which either the supervisor or a time clock records the daily starting and finishing times of a person. (2)

Time and materials pricing: An approach to price determination for a service-oriented business in which actual parts and labor costs are used as the basis for computing the projected price. In addition to actual materials and labor costs, a factor that includes overhead costs and profit is multiplied by the actual materials and labor costs to include overhead and profit in the final price. (11)

Time value of money: The concept that cash flows of equal dollar amounts that are separated by a time interval will have different present values because of the effect of compound interest. (13)

Total manufacturing costs: A term used in the statement of cost of goods manufactured that represents the total direct materials used, direct labor, and factory overhead costs incurred and charged to production during an accounting period. (2)

Total overhead variance: The difference between actual overhead costs incurred and overhead costs applied to good units produced. (10)

Traceable fixed costs: Fixed costs that are directly identified with a segment's operations and are assignable to a product or segment without proration or allocation. (12)

Transfer price: The price at which goods and services are exchanged among company divisions. (14)

Transferred-in cost: Costs transferred from a previous department or process in a process costing system. When accounting for costs and units transferred-in, treat them as you would materials added at the beginning of the process. (4)

Unallowable cost: A cost of a contract that is not reimbursable because the cost is either unreasonable in amount or otherwise unallowable in accordance with existing government statutes or regulations of specific agencies. (11)

Underapplied factory overhead: See Overapplied factory overhead

Unfavorable standard cost variance: A variance occurring when actual costs are greater than standard costs. (9, 10)

Unit cost: The amount of manufacturing costs incurred in the completion or production of one unit of product; usually computed by dividing total production costs for a job or period of time by the respective number of units produced. (3)

Unit cost analysis schedule: A process costing statement used to (1) accumulate all costs charged to the Work-in-Process Inventory account of each department or production process, and (2) compute cost per equivalent unit for materials and conversion costs. (4)

Variable cost: A cost that changes in total in direct proportion to productive output or any other volume measure. (5)

Variable costing: An approach to product costing in which only variable manufacturing costs are assigned to products for product costing and inventory valuation purposes; also called *direct costing*. (12)

Variable cost pricing: An approach to price determination in which the projected price equals the variable costs per unit plus the variable costs per unit times a markup percentage. The markup percentage is computed by dividing the sum of the desired profit, total fixed production costs, and total selling, general, and administrative expenses by total variable production costs. (11)

Variable manufacturing costs: Types of manufacturing costs that increase or decrease in direct proportion to the number of units produced. (2)

Variables: Factors controlled by management in a management decision model. (12)

Variance analysis: The process of computing the amount of, and isolating the causes of, differences between actual costs and standard costs. (9)

Vertical analysis: The calculation of percentages to show the relationship of the component parts of a financial statement to the total in the statement. (18)

Work-in-process inventory: An inventory account unique to the manufacturing or assembly areas to which all manufacturing costs incurred and assigned to products are charged. The balance at period-end represents all costs assigned to goods partially completed at that particular time. (2)

INDEX

Note: Boldface indicates a key term and the page where it is defined.